BASIC STANDARD DEDUCTION AMOUNTS

Filing Status	Standard Deduction Amount	
	1997	1998
Single	$4,150	$4,250
Married, filing jointly	6,900	7,100
Surviving spouse	6,900	7,100
Head of household	6,050	6,250
Married, filing separately	3,450	3,550

AMOUNT OF EACH ADDITIONAL STANDARD DEDUCTION

Filing Status	1997	1998
Single	$1,000	$1,050
Married, filing jointly	800	850
Surviving spouse	800	850
Head of household	1,000	1,050
Married, filing separately	800	850

PERSONAL AND DEPENDENCY EXEMPTION

1997	1998
$2,650	$2,700

INCOME TAX RATES—CORPORATIONS

Taxable Income	Tax Rate
Not over $50,000	15%
Over $50,000 but not over $75,000	25%
Over $75,000 but not over $100,000	34%
Over $100,000 but not over $335,000	39%*
Over $335,000 but not over $10,000,000	34%
Over $10,000,000 but not over $15,000,000	35%
Over $15,000,000 but not over $18,333,333	38%**
Over $18,333,333	35%

*Five percent of this rate represents a phase-out of the benefits of the lower tax rates on the first $75,000 of taxable income.

**Three percent of this rate represents a phase-out of the benefits of the lower tax rate (34% rather than 35%) on the first $10 million of taxable income.

An Introduction to Business Entities

1999 Edition

General Editors

Eugene Willis, Ph.D., C.P.A. **Jon S. Davis,** Ph.D., C.P.A.

Contributing Authors

Eugene Willis
Ph.D., C.P.A.
University of Illinois at Urbana

William A. Raabe
Ph.D., C.P.A.
Samford University

Howard S. Engle
B.S., M.S., C.P.A.
Arthur Andersen & Co.

Jon S. Davis
Ph.D., C.P.A.
University of Illinois at Urbana

Richard L. Kaplan
J.D., C.P.A.
University of Illinois College of Law

Authors for West's Federal Taxation Series

James H. Boyd
Ph.D., C.P.A.
Arizona State University

Mary Sue Gately
Ph.D., C.P.A.
Texas Tech University

Boyd C. Randall
J.D., Ph.D.
Brigham Young University

D. Larry Crumbley
Ph.D., C.P.A.
Louisiana State University

William H. Hoffman, Jr.
J.D., Ph.D., C.P.A.
University of Houston

W. Eugene Seago
J.D., Ph.D., C.P.A.
Virginia Polytechnic Institute and State University

Steven C. Dilley
J.D., Ph.D., C.P.A.
Michigan State University

David M. Maloney
Ph.D., C.P.A.
University of Virginia

James E. Smith
Ph.D., C.P.A.
College of William and Mary

WEST/SOUTH-WESTERN College Publishing

An International Thomson Publishing Company

Accounting Team Director: Richard Lindgren
Acquisitions Editor: Alex von Rosenberg
Developmental Editor: Esther Craig
Production Editor: Rebecca Glaab
Copyediting: Patricia A. Lewis
Production House: Peggy Williams with Texterity
Index: Catalyst Communication Arts
Cover Design: Matulionis Design
Internal Design: LightSource Images
Marketing Manager: Maureen L. Riopelle

TurboTax is a registered trademark of Intuit Inc.
Thomson World Class Learning is a trademark used herein under license.

Copyright © 1999
By West/South-Western College Publishing
Cincinnati, Ohio

ALL RIGHTS RESERVED
The text of this publication, or any part thereof, may not be reproduced or transmitted in any form or by any means, electronic or mechanical, including photocopying, recording, storage in an information retrieval system, or otherwise, without the prior written permission of the publisher.

ISBN: 0–538–88589–0

1 2 3 4 5 6 7 8 9 C 5 6 5 4 3 2 1 0 9 8

Printed in the United States of America

Library of Congress Cataloging-in-Publication Data

ISSN 1093-5134

1999 ANNUAL EDITION

I(T)P®
WEST/South-Western College Publishing
An International Thomson Publishing Company

PREFACE

West's *Federal Taxation: An Introduction to Business Entities* is characterized by the same qualities of accuracy, readability, and pedagogical design that have made the WFT series the most popular tax texts on the market, with sales surpassing one million copies.

An Introduction to Business Entities is designed for those who wish to emphasize business taxation, rather than individual taxation, in the introductory tax course. Part I—An Introduction to Taxation covers the various types of taxes in the U.S. system, conceptual underpinnings of the Federal income tax system, a tax planning framework, and tax research methodology. These topics are applicable to all approaches to educating tax students. Tax planning concepts and tax research methodology are used as unifying themes throughout the text. Coverage of these topics in Part I provides the skills for solving tax planning and research problems contained in each of the remaining chapters in the text.

Part II—Provisions Applicable to All Taxpayers focuses on income, deductions, losses, and property transactions. While most of the topics covered in Part II are relevant to both individuals and businesses, the emphasis is on the taxation of business entities. Individuals may be shareholders, partners, or proprietors in business entities, particularly in small businesses. Because of this, limited coverage of provisions relevant only to individuals is included when necessary to explain the tax impact of transactions on business owners.

Part III—Introduction to Entities deals with the formation and operation of regular corporations, S corporations, partnerships, limited liability entities, and individual proprietorships. Because the foundation for the study of taxation has been provided in Parts I and II, there is opportunity for flexibility in covering Part III. Those who wish to restrict coverage only to business entities can skip individual tax topics, covered in Chapters 15 and 16. Instructors who prefer to address individual tax provisions and proprietorships first may cover Chapters 15 and 16, then change the focus to business entities for the remainder of the course.

RIA ONPOINT SYSTEM 4 STUDENT VERSION CD-ROM

As a result of a partnership with RIA and West/South-Western College Publishing, the RIA OnPoint tax research system is now available for student use. The student version of RIA OnPoint System 4 offers a full-featured edition of this extensive and respected tax database. The CD-ROM provides detailed analysis and coherent explanation of the tax law by RIA's in-house experts, primary source materials, practice aids, and more!

RIA OnPoint lets you access a complete and fully integrated tax law database with accuracy, precision, and ease. The student version of this database includes:

- The Federal Tax Coordinator and United States Tax Reporter.
- In-depth analysis, expert commentary, and practical guidance for income, estate and gift tax, excise tax, and employment tax.
- The Internal Revenue Code, including a complete legislative history since 1954.
- Treasury Regulations, including proposed regulations.
- Congressional committee reports.
- Revenue Rulings, Procedures, and Notices from 1954 to present.
- The full text of current year American Federal Tax Report cases and over 600 watershed court cases, specially selected to integrate with the West Federal Taxation series.
- Over 230 of the most frequently requested IRS publications.
- A multimedia tutorial to help students learn how to use the CD-ROM and a multimedia tutorial on tax ethics and practice.

This item can be shrinkwrapped with the text and used by students to conduct computerized tax research.

PEDAGOGICAL FEATURES

The pedagogy of this textbook is designed to assist the student in the learning process and to address the recommendations of the Accounting Education Change Commission (AECC) and the AICPA Model Tax Curriculum. A list of special features follows.

- *Learning Objectives*. Each chapter begins with student learning objectives for the chapter. These behavioral objectives provide the students with guidance in learning the essential concepts and principles.
- *Chapter Outline*. The learning objectives are followed by a topical outline of the material in the chapter. Page references appear in the outline to provide the student with ready access to each topic.
- *Margin Notes*. Each of the learning objectives appears in the margin when the text introduces related material.
- *Readability of the text* is enhanced with bold print to identify key terms when they are introduced. In addition, the text uses frequent examples and Concept Summaries to help students understand and synthesize important concepts.
- *Tax in the News*. Tax in the News items appear in each chapter as a boxed feature to enliven the text discussion. These items are drawn from today's business and popular press and present current issues that are relevant to the chapter material.
- *Planning Considerations*. Once knowledge of the tax law has been acquired, it needs to be used. Because we recognize the importance of applying tax rules in a business context, each chapter features planning considerations illustrating the application of tax laws in a business environment.
- *Key Terms*. Before the Problem Materials in each chapter is a list of key terms to assist student learning. When the key term is introduced in the chapter, it appears in bold print. The list of key terms includes page references to the chapter coverage. In addition, each key term is defined in the Glossary (Appendix C).
- *Communication Assignments*. In recognition of the importance of communication in tax and accounting practice, specially-marked items in the Problem Materials include a written communication component. Selected Problems, Cumulative Problems, and Research Problems are identified as communication assignments with a "scroll" icon. These problems ask the student to

- *Issue Identification Questions.* These questions, identified by a "light bulb" icon, are unstructured and open-ended. There is not enough information given in the problem to enable the student to develop a definitive answer. However, students are given sufficient information to identify the important tax questions. These problems are designed to help students develop critical thinking skills.

- *Decision-Making Problems.* The Problem Materials include decision-making problems that are designed to enhance the student's analytical skills. These problems are defined with a "balance" icon.

- *Ethical Problems.* Ethical problems, identified by a "magnifying glass" icon, introduce thought-provoking ethical issues related to the chapter topics. In response to the recommendations of the AECC, they also demonstrate that many issues do not have a single correct answer. The ethical problems were selected to provoke discussion and provide opportunities for debate based on the student's value system rather than to provide a defensible answer.

- *Tax Research Problems.* Tax Research problems require extensive tax research skills and sometimes require students to deal with complex questions with no clear answer in the law. These problems can also be resolved with the use of RIA OnPoint or another tax research service.

prepare a tax client letter, a memorandum for the tax files, or other oral or written communications. To aid the student in preparation of these assignments, Chapter 2 includes an illustration of a client letter and memo.

SUPPLEMENTS

The 1999 instructional package includes a variety of supplements for instructor and student use. These supplements are listed below.

- The *Instructor's Guide with Lecture Notes* contains outlines that can be used as lecture notes as well as teaching aids and information not contained in the text. The lecture notes are also available on disk and as *PowerPoint* slides.
- A *Solutions Manual* that has been carefully checked to ensure accuracy. A matrix is included indicating topic coverage for each problem. The solutions are also referenced to pages in the text. The *Solutions Manual* is also available on disk.
- A *Test Bank* with a comprehensive set of examination questions and solutions, with answers referenced to pages in the text. The questions are arranged in accordance with the material in the chapter. To assist the professor in selecting questions for an examination, all questions are labeled by topical coverage.
- *ITP World Class Test*™, test generation software for IBM PCs and compatibles.
- An enhanced, full-featured version of *RIA OnPoint System 4*. RIA OnPoint includes a wide range of statutory and administrative law, together with extensive editorial materials from RIA. With this special edition, selected federal court decisions and online tutorials are also included.
- Limited free use to qualified adopters of *WESTLAW*, a computer-assisted tax and legal research service that provides access to hundreds of valuable information sources.
- *PowerPoint* slides of the teaching notes found in the Instructor's Guide are also available.
- *Teaching Transparency Acetates* contain the key slides from the PowerPoint version of the Instructor's Guide for instructors who may wish to use traditional transparencies.

- *WFT Individual Practice Sets* prepared by Mark Nixon, Bentley College and *WFT Corporation, S Corporation, and Partnership Practice Sets*, prepared by Donald Trippeer, Lehigh University. They are designed to cover most of the common forms that would be used by a tax practitioner for the average client.
- *West's Internal Revenue Code of 1986 and Treasury Regulations: Annotated and Selected*, 1999 Edition by James E. Smith, College of William and Mary. This resource, available for student purchase, provides the opportunity for the student to be exposed to the Code and the Regulations in a single-volume book that also contains useful annotations.
- The WFT WEB SITE puts the most current information and supplements in the user's hands as soon as it is available. Adopters can log onto the web site (swcollege.com or wft.swcollege.com) and gain access to key information and supplements before they are available in print. The web site also includes extra problem material and quizzes, topical news items, the latest news of West's Federal Tax supplements and publications, and more.

TAX PREPARATION SOFTWARE

The following tax software product is available to be used with the 1999 edition.

- *TurboTax®* for Windows 97.01 by Intuit is a commercial tax preparation package. It enables students to prepare over 80 forms, schedules, and worksheets and automatically performs all mathematical calculations. *TurboTax* also assists students with tax planning and allows them to forecast tax liabilities under alternative planning scenarios. The *TurboTax* package, available for student purchase, includes software bound with a workbook containing exercises and problems.

To enable students to take advantage of this software product, the text contains several tax return problems. Problems that lend themselves to computerized solutions are identified by a computer symbol to the left of the problem number.

TAX FORMS COVERAGE

Although it is not our purpose to approach the presentation and discussion of taxation from the standpoint of preparation of tax forms, some orientation to forms is necessary. Because 1998 forms will not be available until later in the year, most tax return problems in the 1999 edition are written for the 1997 tax year. The 1997 problems can be solved manually or with tax return preparation software (e.g., *TurboTax*).

For the reader's convenience, Appendix B contains a full reproduction of many of the 1997 tax forms frequently encountered in practice. This textbook is published in the spring, long before tax forms for the year of publication are available from the government. Because we believe that students should be exposed to the most current tax forms, several new return problems (with solutions) and 1998 tax forms will be provided to adopters. This supplement will arrive after the beginning of 1999.

TAX LAW UPDATES

In the WFT series, we follow a policy of annually revising the text material to reflect changes in the Federal tax law. Errors and other shortcomings are also corrected annually. However, in the event of *significant* tax law changes, we will provide a timely, complete, and easy-to-use supplement.

ACKNOWLEDGMENTS

As is the case with any literary undertaking, we welcome user comments. Such comments will not be taken lightly and, we hope, will lead to improvements in later editions of *West's Federal Taxation: An Introduction to Business Entities*.

We are most appreciative of the many suggestions that we have received while preparing the text, many of which have been incorporated in this edition. We would also like to thank Donald Trippeer, Montana State University, who has painstakingly assembled the Test Bank, Solutions Manual, Instructor's Guide, and PowerPoint Slides. In addition, we would like to thank Chad Munz of Arthur Andersen for his help on this edition.

Finally, this textbook would not have been possible without the support of Alex von Rosenberg, Esther Craig, and Maureen Riopelle at South-Western College Publishing and the editorial assistance of Peggy Williams and Pat Lewis. Their editorial and development assistance is greatly appreciated.

Eugene Willis
Jon S. Davis

April 1, 1998

About the Editors

Eugene Willis is the Arthur Andersen Alumni Professor of Accountancy at the University of Illinois at Urbana-Champaign. He joined the Illinois faculty in 1975 after receiving his Ph.D. from the University of Cincinnati. He serves as Head of the department. His articles have appeared in leading academic and professional journals, including the *Accounting Review, Journal of the American Taxation Association, The Journal of Accountancy*, and *The Journal of Taxation*. Professor Willis is co-director of the National Tax Education Program, a continuing education program co-sponsored by the American Institute of CPAs and the University of Illinois.

Jon Davis is an associate professor at the University of Illinois at Urbana-Champaign. He received his Ph.D. degree from the University of Arizona. He has taught for the University of Colorado at Boulder (1990–1994), the University of Illinois (1987–1990 and 1994 to present), the AICPA National Tax Education Program, and several Big 6 Public Accounting Firm programs in tax. Professor Davis is currently Ph.D. Program Director for the Illinois Department of Accountancy. He has participated in a variety of conferences and workshops, and he has been the recipient of major research grants from the KPMG Peat Marwick Foundation and other organizations. His articles appear in The *Accounting Review, Journal of Accounting Research, Contemporary Accounting Research, Journal of the American Taxation Association* and *Journal of Accounting Literature*. Professor Davis is a member of several professional organizations including the AICPA, the American Accounting Association, and the American Taxation Association.

Contents in Brief

Preface iii

CHAPTER 1	Introduction to Taxation	1–1
CHAPTER 2	Working with the Tax Law	2–1
CHAPTER 3	Gross Income	3–1
CHAPTER 4	Business Deductions	4–1
CHAPTER 5	Losses and Loss Limitations	5–1
CHAPTER 6	Accounting Periods and Methods	6–1
CHAPTER 7	Property Transactions: Basis, Gain and Loss, and Nontaxable Exchanges	7–1
CHAPTER 8	Property Transactions: Capital Gains and Losses, Section 1231, and Recapture Provisions	8–1
CHAPTER 9	Corporations: Organization, Capital Structure, and Operating Rules	9–1
CHAPTER 10	Corporations: Earnings & Profits and Dividend Distributions	10–1
CHAPTER 11	Partnerships and Limited Liability Entities	11–1
CHAPTER 12	S Corporations	12–1
CHAPTER 13	Business Tax Credits and Corporate Alternative Minimum Tax	13–1
CHAPTER 14	Comparative Forms of Doing Business	14–1
CHAPTER 15	Introduction to the Taxation of Individuals	15–1
CHAPTER 16	Individuals as Employees and Proprietors	16–1

Contents

Preface   iii

CHAPTER 1
Introduction to Taxation   1–1

The Structure of Taxes   1–2
Tax Rates   1–3
Tax Bases   1–3

Types of Taxes   1–4
Types of Transaction Taxes   1–4
Taxes on the Production and Sale of Goods   1–4
Employment Taxes   1–6
Death Taxes   1–8
Gift Taxes   1–9
Property Taxes   1–10
Tax in the News: Does Bill Gates Have a Fancy Pad, or What?   1–11
Taxes on Privileges and Rights   1–12
Income Taxes   1–13
Tax in the News: Visitors Beware! The City and State You Visit May Not Be All That Friendly   1–17

An Introduction to the Income Taxation of Business Entities   1–17
Proprietorships   1–17
Corporations   1–18
Partnerships   1–18
S Corporations   1–19
Limited Liability Companies and Limited Liability Partnerships   1–19
Relationships between Individuals and Entities   1–19

Tax Planning Fundamentals   1–20
Overview of Tax Planning   1–20
The Goal of Tax Planning   1–20
Determining the Tax Burden   1–21
Tax Minimization Strategies   1–23

Summary   1–26

Understanding the Federal Tax Law   1–26
Revenue Needs   1–27
Economic Considerations   1–27
Social Considerations   1–28
Equity Considerations   1–29
Political Considerations   1–31
Influence of the Internal Revenue Service   1–33
Influence of the Courts   1–34
Summary   1–35

Problem Materials   1–36

CHAPTER 2
Working with the Tax Law   2–1

Tax Sources   2–2
Tax in the News: Small is Beautiful?   2–3
Statutory Sources of the Tax Law   2–3
Administrative Sources of the Tax Law   2–7
Judicial Sources of the Tax Law   2–12

Working with the Tax Law—Tax Research   2–20
Identifying the Problem   2–20
Refining the Problem   2–20
Locating the Appropriate Tax Law Sources   2–21
Assessing Tax Law Sources   2–23
Tax in the News: Internal Revenue Code: Interpretation Pitfalls   2–24
Arriving at the Solution or at Alternative Solutions   2–27
Communicating Tax Research   2–27
Follow-Up Procedures   2–28
Computer-Assisted Tax Research   2–28

Problem Materials   2–33

CHAPTER 3
Gross Income — 3–1

The Tax Formula — 3–2
Components of the Tax Formula — 3–2

Gross Income—What Is It? — 3–4
Economic and Accounting Concepts of Income — 3–4
Comparison of the Accounting and Tax Concepts of Income — 3–5
Tax in the News: IRS Calls Foul on NBA Referees — 3–6
Form of Receipt — 3–6

Year of Inclusion — 3–7
Taxable Year — 3–7
Accounting Methods — 3–7
Planning Considerations: Cash Receipts Method — 3–9
Tax in the News: A Fender-Bender with the IRS — 3–10
Exceptions Applicable to Cash Basis Taxpayers — 3–10
Tax in the News: Original Issue Discount Rules May Dampen Enthusiasm for Inflation-Adjusted Bonds — 3–12
Exceptions Applicable to Accrual Basis Taxpayers — 3–13
Planning Considerations: Prepaid Income — 3–14

Income Sources — 3–14
Personal Services — 3–14
Income From Property — 3–15
Income Received by an Agent — 3–17

Specific Rules Related to Income — 3–17
Imputed Interest on Loans for Money — 3–18
Tax Benefit Rule — 3–21
Interest on Certain State and Local Government Obligations — 3–22
Planning Considerations: Municipal Bonds — 3–22
Improvements on Leased Property — 3–23
Life Insurance Proceeds — 3–23
Planning Considerations: Life Insurance — 3–25
Income from Discharge of Indebtedness — 3–25
Tax in the News: When Public Housing and Tax Policies Collide — 3–26
Gains and Losses from Property Transactions — 3–28

Problem Materials — 3–31

CHAPTER 4
Business Deductions — 4–1

Overview of Business Deductions — 4–2
Ordinary and Necessary Requirement — 4–2
Tax in the News: Paying Retainers to Keep Lawyers from Rivals — 4–3
Reasonableness Requirement — 4–3
Planning Considerations: Unreasonable Compensation — 4–4

Timing of Expense Recognition — 4–5
Cash Method Requirements — 4–5
Planning Considerations: Time Value of Tax Deductions — 4–6
Accrual Method Requirements — 4–6

Disallowance Possibilities — 4–7
Public Policy Limitations — 4–7
Political Contributions and Lobbying Activities — 4–9
Excessive Executive Compensation — 4–10
Disallowance of Deductions for Capital Expenditures — 4–10
Investigation of a Business — 4–11
Transactions between Related Parties — 4–12
Lack of Adequate Substantiation — 4–14
Expenses and Interest Related to Tax-Exempt Income — 4–14

Charitable Contributions — 4–15
Property Contributions — 4–16
Limitations Imposed on Charitable Contribution Deductions — 4–17

Research and Experimental Expenditures — 4–18
Expense Method — 4–18
Deferral and Amortization Method — 4–19

Other Expense Rules — 4–19
Interest Expense — 4–20
Taxes — 4–20

Cost Recovery Allowances — 4–21
Overview — 4–21
Modified Accelerated Cost Recovery System (MACRS) — 4–22
Eligible Property under MACRS — 4–22
Tax in the News: Who Gets the Refund? — 4–23
Cost Recovery for Personal Property — 4–24
Cost Recovery for Real Estate — 4–26
The MACRS Straight-Line Election — 4–27
Election to Expense Assets under § 179 — 4–28
Tax in the News: A Ferrari as Medical Equipment — 4–29

Business and Personal Use of Automobiles and Other Listed Property	4–29
Alternative Depreciation System (ADS)	4–32

Amortization 4–33

Planning Considerations: Structuring the Sale of a Business — *4–33*

Depletion 4–34

Intangible Drilling and Development Costs (IDC)	4–34
Depletion Methods	4–35
Tax in the News: Percentage Depletion	*4–36*
Planning Considerations: Switching Depletion Methods	*4–37*

Cost Recovery Tables 4–38

Problem Materials 4–43

CHAPTER 5
Losses and Loss Limitations 5–1

Bad Debts 5–2

Specific Charge-Off Method	5–3
Business versus Nonbusiness Bad Debts	5–3
Tax in the News: A Bank or a Savings and Loan? Loss of Bad Debt Reserve Influences Decision	*5–4*
Loans between Related Parties	5–4

Worthless Securities 5–5

Small Business Stock	5–6
Planning Considerations: Maximizing the Benefits of § 1244	*5–6*

Casualty and Theft Losses 5–7

Definition of Casualty	5–7
Definition of Theft	5–8
Planning Considerations: Documentation of Related-Taxpayer Loans, Casualty Losses, and Theft Losses	*5–8*
When to Deduct Casualty Losses	5–9
Measuring the Amount of Loss	5–9
Tax in the News: Filing Relief for Disaster Area Victims	*5–10*
Casualty and Theft Losses of Individuals	5–11

Net Operating Losses 5–12

Introduction	5–12
Carryback and Carryover Periods	5–14
Tax in the News: NOLs of a Biotech Company: The Valuable Asset	*5–15*

The Tax Shelter Problem 5–15

Tax in the News: The Impact of Recent Tax Legislation on Investment Choices — *5–17*

At-Risk Limitations 5–17

Passive Loss Limits 5–18

Classification and Impact of Passive Income and Loss	5–18
Tax in the News: Knowledge of Tax Laws is a Key to Real Estate Success	*5–20*
Taxpayers Subject to the Passive Loss Rules	5–23
Activity Defined	5–24
Material Participation	5–25
Rental Activities	5–30
Interaction of At-Risk and Passive Activity Limits	5–33
Special Rules for Real Estate	5–33
Tax in the News: Shelter for College Students May Be Tax Shelter for Parents	*5–35*
Disposition of Passive Activities	5–36
Planning Considerations: Utilizing Passive Losses	*5–36*

Problem Materials 5–38

CHAPTER 6
Accounting Periods and Methods 6–1

Accounting Periods 6–2

In General	6–2
Specific Provisions for Partnerships, S Corporations, and Personal Service Corporations	6–3
Making the Election	6–6
Changes in the Accounting Period	6–7
Taxable Periods of Less Than One Year	6–7
Mitigation of the Annual Accounting Period Concept	6–8

Change of Accounting Methods 6–9

Tax in the News: IRS Fails to Impose Accrual Method-And Pays for Trying	*6–10*
Correction of an Error	6–10
Change from an Incorrect Method	6–11
Net Adjustments Due to Change in Accounting Method	6–11

Installment Method 6–12

In General	6–12
Planning Considerations: The Installment Method	*6–14*
Contingent Sales Prices	6–15

Imputed Interest	6–16
Related-Party Sales	6–17
Disposition of Installment Obligations	6–19
Planning Considerations: Terminating the Installment Method	*6–20*
Interest on Deferred Taxes	6–20
Electing Out of the Installment Method	6–20

Long–Term Contracts — 6–21

Tax in the News: IRS Says the Cash Method Does Not Clearly Reflect the Income of Small Contractors — *6–23*

Completed Contract Method	6–24
Percentage of Completion Method	6–24

Inventories — 6–26

Determining Inventory Cost	6–27
The LIFO Election	6–30
Planning Considerations: LIFO Inventory	*6–31*

Problem Materials — 6–32

CHAPTER 7
Property Transactions: Basis, Gain and Loss, and Nontaxable Exchanges — 7–1

Determination of Gain or Loss — 7–3

Realized Gain or Loss	7–3
Recognized Gain or Loss	7–6
Nonrecognition of Gain or Loss	7–6
Recovery of Capital Doctrine	7–7

Basis Considerations — 7–8

Determination of Cost Basis	7–8
Gift Basis	7–10
Planning Considerations: Gift Planning	*7–11*
Property Acquired from a Decedent	7–13
Planning Considerations: Property from a Decedent	*7–14*
Disallowed Losses	7–15
Planning Considerations: Avoiding Wash Sales	*7–16*
Conversion of Property from Personal Use to Business or Income-Producing Use	7–16
Summary of Basis Adjustments	7–18

General Concept of a Nontaxable Exchange — 7–18

Like-Kind Exchanges—§ 1031 — 7–21

Planning Considerations: Like-Kind Exchanges	*7–21*
Like-Kind Property	7–22
Tax in the News: My Land for Your Jail	*7–23*
Tax in the News: Are the Cleveland Indians Still the Cleveland Indians?	*7–24*
Exchange Requirement	7–24
Boot	7–24
Basis and Holding Period of Property Received	7–25

Involuntary Conversions—§ 1033 — 7–28

Planning Considerations: Recognizing Involuntary Conversion Gains	*7–29*
Involuntary Conversion Defined	7–29
Tax in the News: A Sound Investment—Not	*7–30*
Replacement Property	7–30
Time Limitation on Replacement	7–31
Reporting Considerations	7–32

Other Nonrecognition Provisions — 7–32

Transfer of Assets to Business Entity—§§ 351 and 721	7–32
Exchange of Stock for Property—§ 1032	7–32
Certain Exchanges of Insurance Policies—§ 1035	7–33
Exchange of Stock for Stock of the Same Corporation—§ 1036	7–33
Certain Reacquisitions of Real Property—§ 1038	7–33
Rollovers into Specialized Small Business Investment Companies—§ 1044	7–33
Sale of a Principal Residence—§ 121	7–34
Transfers of Property between Spouses or Incident to Divorce—§ 1041	7–34

Problem Materials — 7–35

CHAPTER 8
Property Transactions: Capital Gains and Losses, Section 1231, and Recapture Provisions — 8–1

General Considerations — 8–2

Rationale for Separate Reporting of Capital Gains and Losses	8–2
General Scheme of Taxation	8–3

Capital Assets — 8–3

Definition of a Capital Asset	8–3
Tax in the News: An Artist's Dilemma	*8–5*
Statutory Expansions	8–6

Sale or Exchange — 8–7

Worthless Securities and § 1244 Stock	8–7

Retirement of Corporate Obligations	8–8	Death	8–40
Options	8–8	Charitable Transfers	8–41
Patents	8–10	Certain Nontaxable Transactions	8–41
Franchises, Trademarks, and Trade Names	8–11	Like-Kind Exchanges (§ 1031) and Involuntary Conversions (§ 1033)	8–41
Lease Cancellation Payments	8–12		

Holding Period — 8–13

Special Holding Period Rules — 8–13
Short Sales — 8–15

Tax Treatment of Capital Gains and Losses of Noncorporate Taxpayers — 8–15

Capital Gains — 8–15
Planning Considerations: Timing Capital Gains — *8–16*
Planning Considerations: Gifts of Appreciated Securities — *8–17*
Tax in the News: Should You Invest in Stocks or Stock Funds? — *8–18*
Capital Losses — 8–18
Planning Considerations: Matching Gains with Losses — *8–22*
Small Business Stock — 8–23

Tax Treatment of Capital Gains and Losses of Corporate Taxpayers — 8–24

Section 1231 Assets — 8–24

Relationship to Capital Assets — 8–24
Rationale for Favorable Tax Treatment — 8–25
Property Included — 8–26
Property Excluded — 8–26
Nonpersonal-Use Capital Assets — 8–26
General Procedure for § 1231 Computation — 8–27

Section 1245 Recapture — 8–29

Section 1245 Property — 8–32
Observations on § 1245 — 8–33
Planning Considerations: Depreciation Recapture and § 179 — *8–33*

Section 1250 Recapture — 8–34

Computing Recapture on Nonresidential Real Property — 8–34
Computing Recapture on Residential Rental Housing — 8–35
Section 1250 Recapture Situations — 8–36
Additional Recapture for Corporations — 8–36
Unrecaptured § 1250 Gains — 8–39

Exceptions to §§ 1245 and 1250 — 8–40

Gifts — 8–40
Death — 8–40
Charitable Transfers — 8–41
Certain Nontaxable Transactions — 8–41
Like-Kind Exchanges (§ 1031) and Involuntary Conversions (§ 1033) — 8–41

Special Recapture Provisions — 8–42

Sale of Depreciable Property between Certain Related Parties — 8–42
Installment Sales — 8–42
Intangible Drilling Costs — 8–42

Reporting Procedures — 8–43

Problem Materials — 8–43

CHAPTER 9
Corporations: Organization, Capital Structure, and Operating Rules — 9–1

An Introduction to Corporate Tax — 9–2

Comparison of Corporations and Other Forms of Doing Business — 9–3
Nontax Considerations — 9–4
Entity Classification Prior to 1997 — 9–5
Entity Classification After 1996 — 9–6
Planning Considerations: Consolidated Groups May Utilize New Regulations — *9–8*

Organization of and Transfers to Controlled Corporations — 9–8

In General — 9–8
Transfer of Property — 9–10
Tax in the News: Making the Most Out of Stock Options — *9–11*
Stock — 9–11
Control of the Corporation — 9–11
Planning Considerations: Utilizing § 351 — *9–12*
Assumption of Liabilities—§ 357 — 9–15
Planning Considerations: Avoiding § 351 — *9–17*
Basis Determination and Other Issues — 9–18
Recapture Considerations — 9–20
Planning Considerations: Other Considerations When Incorporating a Business — *9–20*

Capital Structure of a Corporation — 9–21

Capital Contributions — 9–21
Debt in the Capital Structure — 9–22

Corporate Operations — 9–24

Deductions Available Only to Corporations — 9–24

Planning Considerations: Organizational Expenditures	*9–27*
Determining the Corporate Income Tax Liability	9–27
Tax Liability of Related Corporations	9–28
Controlled Groups	9–29
Procedural Matters	**9–32**
Filing Requirements for Corporations	9–32
Estimated Tax Payments	9–33
Reconciliation of Taxable Income and Financial Net Income	9–34
Form 1120 Illustrated	9–35
Tax in the News: Software Issues Affect Taxpayers	*9–37*
Consolidated Returns	9–38
Summary	9–38
Problem Materials	**9–43**

CHAPTER 10
Corporations: Earnings & Profits and Dividend Distributions — 10–1

Taxable Dividends—In General	**10–2**
Tax in the News: Chrysler Keeps Promise by Boosting Dividend and Stock Buyback Payouts	*10–3*
Earnings and Profits (E & P)—§ 312	**10–3**
Computation of E & P	10–3
Summary of E & P Adjustments	10–6
Current versus Accumulated E & P	10–6
Allocating E & P to Distributions	10–7
Planning Considerations: Corporate Distributions	*10–9*
Property Dividends	**10–11**
Property Dividends—Effect on the Shareholder	10–11
Tax in the News: Stock Buybacks Continue to Grow	*10–12*
Property Dividends—Effect on the Corporation	10–12
Constructive Dividends	**10–14**
Types of Constructive Dividends	10–14
Tax in the News: When is Compensation Unreasonable?	*10–16*
Tax Treatment of Constructive Dividends	10–16
Planning Considerations: Constructive Dividends	*10–17*
Stock Dividends and Stock Rights	**10–18**
Stock Dividends—§ 305	10–18
Stock Rights	10–20
Restrictions on Corporate Accumulations	**10–21**
Problem Materials	**10–22**

CHAPTER 11
Partnerships and Limited Liability Entities — 11–1

Overview of Partnership Taxation	**11–2**
Forms of Doing Business—Federal Tax Consequences	11–3
What is a Partnership?	11–3
Tax in the News: Partnerships in the Movies	*11–4*
Partnership Taxation and Reporting	11–5
Partner's Ownership Interest in a Partnership	11–7
Conceptual Basis for Partnership Taxation	11–8
Anti-Abuse Provisions	11–9
Formation of a Partnership: Tax Effects	**11–9**
Gain or Loss on Contributions to the Partnership	11–9
Exceptions to § 721	11–10
Tax Issues Related to Contributed Property	11–12
Inside and Outside Bases	11–14
Tax Accounting Elections	11–15
Initial Costs of a Partnership	11–15
Operations of the Partnership	**11–17**
Reporting Operating Results	11–17
Planning Considerations: Drafting the Partnership Agreement	*11–19*
Partnership Allocations	11–20
Basis of a Partnership Interest	11–22
Loss Limitations	11–28
Planning Considerations: Formation and Operation of a Partnership	*11–31*
Transactions between Partner and Partnership	**11–32**
Guaranteed Payments	11–32
Other Transactions between a Partner and a Partnership	11–33
Partners as Employees	11–34
Planning Considerations: Transactions between Partners and Partnerships	*11–35*

Limited Liability Entities	**11–36**
Limited Liability Companies	11–36
Tax in the News: Partnerships Around the World—and Beyond	*11–38*
Limited Liability Partnerships	11–39
Summary	11–39
Problem Materials	**11–40**

CHAPTER 12
S Corporations — 12–1

Introduction	**12–2**
An Overview of S Corporations	12–2
When to Elect S Corporation Status	12–4
Qualifying for S Corporation Status	**12–5**
Definition of a Small Business Corporation	12–5
Making the Election	12–7
Shareholder Consents	12–8
Planning Considerations: Making a Proper Election	*12–9*
Loss of the Election	12–9
Planning Considerations: Preserving the S Election	*12–11*
Operational Rules	**12–12**
Computation of Taxable Income	12–12
Allocation of Income and Loss	12–14
Planning Considerations: Salary Structure	*12–15*
Tax Treatment of Distributions to Shareholders	12–16
Planning Considerations: The Accumulated Adjustments Account	*12–20*
Tax Treatment of Property Distributions by the Corporation	12–20
Shareholder's Basis	12–21
Planning Considerations: Working with Suspended Losses	*12–24*
Treatment of Losses	12–24
Planning Considerations: Loss Considerations	*12–27*
Tax on Pre-Election Built-in Gain	12–28
Planning Considerations: Managing the Built-in Gains Tax	*12–31*
Passive Investment Income Penalty Tax	12–32
Other Operational Rules	12–32
Summary	**12–33**
Problem Materials	**12–34**

CHAPTER 13
Business Tax Credits and Corporate Alternative Minimum Tax — 13–1

Tax Policy and Tax Credits	**13–2**
Tax in the News: A Credit That Went Up in Smoke	*13–3*
Specific Business–Related Tax Credit Provisions	**13–3**
General Business Credit	13–3
Tax Credit for Rehabilitation Expenditures	13–5
Business Energy Credits	13–6
Work Opportunity Tax Credit	13–7
Welfare-to-Work Credit	13–8
Research Activities Credit	13–8
Low-Income Housing Credit	13–10
Disabled Access Credit	13–11
Foreign Tax Credit	13–11
Corporate Alternative Minimum Tax	**13–13**
The AMT Formula	13–14
Tax in the News: The AMT May Harm the U.S. Steel Industry	*13–16*
Tax Preferences	13–16
AMT Adjustments	13–17
Tax in the News: Municipal Bonds and the AMT	*13–18*
Planning Considerations: Avoiding Preferences and Adjustments	*13–22*
Adjusted Current Earnings (ACE)	13–23
Computing Alternative Minimum Taxable Income	13–25
Planning Considerations: Optimum Use of the AMT and Regular Corporate Income Tax Rate Difference	*13–27*
Exemption	13–27
Planning Considerations: Controlling the Timing of Preferences and Adjustments	*13–27*
Minimum Tax Credit	13–28
Other Aspects of the AMT	13–28
Planning Considerations: The Subchapter S Option	*13–28*
The Individual Alternative Minimum Tax	**13–28**
Tax in the News: The AMT and Inflation	*13–29*
Problem Materials	**13–30**

CHAPTER 14
Comparative Forms of Doing Business — 14–1

Tax in the News: Should You Check That Box?   14–3

Forms of Doing Business   14–3
Principal Forms   14–3
Limited Liability Companies   14–4
Tax in the News: Big 6 Partnerships Reorganize as LLPs   14–5

Nontax Factors   14–5
Capital Formation   14–5
Limited Liability   14–6
Other Factors   14–7

Single Versus Double Taxation   14–7
Overall Impact on Entity and Owners   14–7
Alternative Minimum Tax   14–8
Planning Considerations: Planning for the AMT   14–9
State Taxation   14–9
Tax in the News: Who Pays Corporate AMT?   14–10

Minimizing Double Taxation   14–10
Making Deductible Distributions   14–10
Not Making Distributions   14–11
Return of Capital Distributions   14–12
Electing S Corporation Status   14–12

Conduit versus Entity Treatment   14–13
Effect on Recognition at Time of Contribution to the Entity   14–14
Effect on Basis of Ownership Interest   14–14
Effect on Results of Operations   14–15
Effect on Recognition at Time of Distribution   14–16
Effect on Passive Activity Losses   14–17
Effect of At-Risk Rules   14–17
Tax in the News: Is Gold at Risk?   14–18
Effect of Special Allocations   14–18

Disposition of a Business or an Ownership Interest   14–19
Sole Proprietorships   14–19
Partnerships and Limited Liability Entities   14–20
C Corporations   14–21
Planning Considerations: Selling Stock or Assets   14–21
S Corporations   14–22

Overall Comparison of Forms of Doing Business   14–22
Planning Considerations: Choosing a Business Form: Case Study   14–23

Problem Materials   14–30

CHAPTER 15
Introduction to the Taxation of Individuals   15–1

The Individual Tax Formula   15–2
Components of the Tax Formula   15–3
Application of the Tax Formula   15–7
Individuals Not Eligible for the Standard Deduction   15–8
Special Limitations for Individuals Who Can Be Claimed as Dependents   15–8

Personal and Dependency Exemptions   15–9
Personal Exemptions   15–9
Dependency Exemptions   15–10
Planning Considerations: Multiple Support Agreements and the Medical Expense Deduction   15–12
Planning Considerations: Problems with a Joint Return   15–14
Phase-Out of Exemptions   15–14

Tax Determination   15–15
Tax Table Method   15–15
Tax Rate Schedule Method   15–16
Planning Considerations: Shifting Income and Deductions across Time   15–17
Computation of Net Taxes Payable or Refund Due   15–17
Unearned Income of Children under Age 14 Taxed at Parents' Rate   15–18
Planning Considerations: Income of Minor Children   15–20

Filing Considerations   15–20
Filing Requirements   15–21
Tax in the News: Is Allowing the Use of Plastic to Pay Taxes a Good Idea?   15–23
Filing Status   15–23

Overview of Income Provisions Applicable to Individuals   15–26

Specific Inclusions Applicable to Individuals   15–26
Alimony and Separate Maintenance Payments   15–26
Prizes and Awards   15–28
Unemployment Compensation   15–29
Social Security Benefits   15–29

Specific Exclusions Applicable to Individuals   15–29
Gifts and Inheritances   15–29

Scholarships	15–30
Damages	15–31
Workers' Compensation	15–32
Accident and Health Insurance Benefits	15–33
Educational Savings Bonds	15–33

Itemized Deductions — 15–34

Medical Expenses	15–35
Tax in the News: Average Itemized Deductions	*15–37*
Taxes	15–38
Tax in the News: Working to Pay Taxes	*15–40*
Planning Considerations: Timing the Payment of Deductible Taxes	*15–40*
Interest	15–40
Charitable Contributions	15–44
Miscellaneous Itemized Deductions Subject to Two Percent Floor	15–49
Other Miscellaneous Deductions	15–50
Overall Limitation on Certain Itemized Deductions	15–50
Tax in the News: Few Taxpayers Are Affected by the Three Percent Floor	*15–52*
Planning Considerations: Effective Utilization of Itemized Deductions	*15–52*

Individual Tax Credits — 15–52

Adoption Expenses Credit	15–52
Child Tax Credit	15–53
Credit for Child and Dependent Care Expenses	15–54
Education Tax Credits	15–55
Tax Credit for Elderly or Disabled Taxpayers	15–57
Tax in the News: Paying for College— Understanding the Tax Law May Be Half the Battle	*15–58*
Earned Income Credit	15–59

Problem Materials — 15–61

CHAPTER 16
Individuals as Employees and Proprietors — 16–1

Employee Versus Self–Employed — 16–2

Factors Considered in Classification	16–3
Tax in the News: Are Golf Clubs in Trouble with the IRS?	*16–4*
Planning Considerations: Self-Employed Individuals	*16–4*

Exclusions Available to Employees — 16–5

Advantages of Qualified Fringe Benefits	16–5
Employer-Sponsored Accident and Health Plans	16–5
Medical Reimbursement Plans	16–6
Long-Term Care Benefits	16–7
Meals and Lodging Furnished for the Convenience of the Employer	16–7
Tax in the News: The IRS Finds Compensatory Reason for Providing Employee Meals	*16–9*
Group Term Life Insurance	16–9
Qualified Tuition Reduction Plans	16–10
Other Specific Employee Fringe Benefits	16–11
Cafeteria Plans	16–12
Flexible Spending Plans	16–12
General Classes of Excluded Benefits	16–13
Taxable Fringe Benefits	16–17

Employee Expenses — 16–19

Transportation Expenses	16–19
Travel Expenses	16–21
Planning Considerations: Transportation and Travel Expenses	*16–25*
Moving Expenses	16–25
Planning Considerations: Moving Expenses	*16–27*
Education Expenses	16–27
Planning Considerations: Education Expenses	*16–29*
Entertainment Expenses	16–30
Planning Considerations: Entertainment Expenses	*16–31*
Other Employee Expenses	16–33
Classification of Employee Expenses	16–35
Tax in the News: NBA Referees May Pay a Price for Not Reporting Income	*16–36*
Planning Considerations: Unreimbursed Employee Business Expenses	*16–38*
Contributions to Individual Retirement Accounts	16–39

Individuals as Proprietors — 16–41

The Proprietorship as a Business Entity	16–41
Income of a Proprietorship	16–42
Deductions Related to a Proprietorship	16–42
Retirement Plans for Self-Employed Individuals	16–44
Planning Considerations: Important Dates Related to IRAs and Keogh Plans	*16–45*
Planning Considerations: Factors Affecting Retirement Plan Choices	*16–46*
Accounting Periods and Methods	16–46

Estimated Payments	16–46	**Tax Forms**	**B–1**
Hobby Losses	**16–48**	**Glossary of Tax Terms**	**C–1**
General Rules	16–48		
Presumptive Rule of § 183	16–49	**Table of Code Sections Cited**	**D–1**
Determining the Amount of the Deduction	16–49	**Table of Regulations Cited**	**D–8**
Problem Materials	**16–51**	**Table of Revenue Procedures and Revenue Rulings Cited**	**D–11**

Appendixes

		Table of Cases Cited	**E–1**
Tax Rate Schedules and Tables	**A–1**	**Index**	**I–1**

CHAPTER 1

Introduction to Taxation

LEARNING OBJECTIVES

After completing Chapter 1, you should be able to:

1. Understand the components of a tax.

2. Identify the various taxes affecting business enterprises.

3. Understand some of the history of the Federal income tax.

4. Recall the basic tax formula for individuals and taxable business entities.

5. Understand the relationship between business entities and their owners.

6. Recognize tax planning opportunities and apply a simplified model of tax planning.

7. Recognize the economic, social, equity, and political considerations that underlie the tax law.

8. Describe the role played by the IRS and the courts in the evolution of the Federal tax system.

OUTLINE

The Structure of Taxes, 1–2
Tax Rates, 1–3
Tax Bases, 1–3
Types of Taxes, 1–4
Types of Transaction Taxes, 1–4
Taxes on the Production and Sale of Goods, 1–4
Employment Taxes, 1–6
Death Taxes, 1–8
Gift Taxes, 1–9
Property Taxes, 1–10
Taxes on Privileges and Rights, 1–12
Income Taxes, 1–13

An Introduction to the Income Taxation of Business Entities, 1–17
Proprietorships, 1–17
Corporations, 1–18
Partnerships, 1–18
S Corporations, 1–19
Limited Liability Companies and Limited Liability Partnerships, 1–19
Relationships between Individuals and Entities, 1–19
Tax Planning Fundamentals, 1–20
Overview of Tax Planning, 1–20
The Goal of Tax Planning, 1–20

Determining the Tax Burden, 1–21
Tax Minimization Strategies, 1–23
Summary, 1–26
Understanding the Federal Tax Law, 1–26
Revenue Needs, 1–27
Economic Considerations, 1–27
Social Considerations, 1–28
Equity Considerations, 1–29
Political Considerations, 1–31
Influence of the Internal Revenue Service, 1–33
Influence of the Courts, 1–34
Summary, 1–35

Taxes have a pervasive impact on our lives. They affect every individual in the United States from birth to death, and even beyond death (through taxation of the individual's estate). Taxes likewise affect every business from formation of the business entity to its operations, distribution of profits to owners, and ultimate disposition or liquidation.

Despite the wide-ranging impact of taxes, most introductory textbooks adopt a narrow view; they overemphasize the laws applying to individual taxpayers and ignore much of the tax law relevant to business. That approach fails to address business students' need to understand the role of taxes in *business* decisions, and it fails to provide the broad knowledge base necessary to succeed in today's business environment. This textbook adopts a more balanced approach; it introduces the tax laws that apply to all business entities and surveys the tax rules specific to each entity. It also recognizes that both tax and nontax considerations are important in business planning and therefore presents the tax laws within the context of the business transactions to which they relate.

The primary objective of this chapter is to provide a background for studying the Federal income tax. To accomplish this objective, the chapter begins by describing the common structure of taxes and briefly surveying the kinds of taxes in use today. Next, the chapter provides an overview of how business entities are taxed. Then, some fundamentals of tax planning are introduced. Finally, some of the factors that have influenced the development of the various tax laws are described.

THE STRUCTURE OF TAXES

1 LEARNING OBJECTIVE
Understand the components of a tax.

Most taxes have two components: a tax rate and a base (such as income, wages, or sales price). Tax liability is computed by multiplying these two components. Taxes vary by the structure of their rates and by the base subject to tax.

TAX RATES

Tax rates can be either progressive, proportional, or regressive. A tax rate is *progressive* if it increases as the tax base increases. The Federal income tax and the Federal estate and **gift taxes** are progressive. For example, the Federal income tax rates for corporations range from 15 to 39 percent for taxable incomes from $1 to $100,000. These rates increase with increases in taxable income.

Refer to the corporate Tax Rate Schedule inside the front cover of this textbook. If Abel Corporation has taxable income of $5,000 in 1998, its income tax is $750 and its average tax rate is 15% ($750/$5,000, or the ratio of tax liability to the tax base). If, however, Abel's taxable income is $200,000, its tax will be $61,250 [$22,250 + 0.39 ($200,000 − $100,000)], and its average tax rate is 30.63% ($61,250/$200,000). The tax is progressive because the average tax rate increases with increases in the tax base (income). ▼

A tax is *proportional* if the rate of tax is constant, regardless of the size of the tax base. State retail **sales taxes** are proportional, as is the Federal Medicare tax on salaries and wages. Proportional tax rates also underlie the various "flat tax" proposals recently in the news.[1]

Bob purchases an automobile for $6,000. If the sales tax on automobiles is 7% in Bob's state, he will pay a $420 tax. Alternatively, if Bob pays $20,000 for a car, his sales tax will be $1,400 (still 7% of the sales price). Because the average tax rate does not change with the tax base (sales price), the sales tax is proportional. ▼

Finally, *regressive* tax rates decrease as the tax base increases. Federal **employment taxes**, such as FICA and FUTA, are regressive. When the tax base and the taxpayer's ability to pay are positively correlated (i.e., when they move in the same direction), many tax pundits view regressive tax rates as unfair. This is because the tax burden decreases as a *percentage* of the taxpayer's ability to pay.

The combined FICA and Medicare tax rate levied on the wages of employees is 7.65% up to a maximum of $68,400 and 1.45% on all wages over $68,400. Sarah earns a salary of $30,000 in 1998. She will pay FICA taxes of $2,295, with an average tax rate of 7.65%. Alternatively, if Sarah earns $100,000, she will pay $5,690.80 [(0.0765 × $68,400) + 0.0145 ($100,000 − $68,400)], with an average tax rate of 5.7%. The FICA tax is regressive since the average tax rate decreases as the tax base increases. ▼

Under all three tax rate structures, the *amount* of taxes due increases as the tax base increases. The structure of tax rates only affects the *rate* of increase (i.e., progressive taxes increase at an increasing rate, proportional taxes increase at a constant rate, and regressive taxes increase at a decreasing rate).

TAX BASES

Most taxes are levied on one of four kinds of tax bases:

- Transactions (including sales or purchases of goods and services and transfers of wealth).
- Property or wealth (including ownership of specific kinds of property).

---

[1] Flat tax proposals call for a new tax with one low, proportional rate (between 15% and 20%). Such a tax would have a very broad base, taxing almost all forms of income with few deductions. To avoid taxing the poor, large personal exemptions would be provided (e.g., $30,000 for a family of four).

- Privileges and rights (including the ability to do business as a corporation, the right to work in a certain profession, and the ability to move goods between countries).
- Income.

Because the Federal income tax usually has the most significant influence on business decisions, it is the principal focus of this textbook. Other taxes can play an important role, however, so it is important to have at least some familiarity with them. The next section introduces many of the taxes imposed on individuals and businesses in the United States.

TYPES OF TAXES

TYPES OF TRANSACTION TAXES

LEARNING OBJECTIVE 2
Identify the various taxes affecting business enterprises.

After taxes on income, the various transaction taxes usually play the most widespread role in business (and personal) contexts. In many countries, transaction taxes are even more important than income taxes. There are three types of transaction taxes: sales and certain **excise taxes**, employment taxes, and taxes on the transfer of wealth.

TAXES ON THE PRODUCTION AND SALE OF GOODS

Sales tax and some excise taxes are imposed on the production, sale, or consumption of commodities or the use of services. Excise taxes and general sales taxes differ by the breadth of their bases. An excise tax base is limited to a specific kind of good or service while a general sales tax is broad based (e.g., it might be levied on all retail sales). All levels of government impose excise taxes while state and local governments make heavy use of the general sales tax.

Federal Excise Taxes. Together with customs duties, excise taxes served as the principal source of revenue for the United States during its first 150 years of existence. Since World War II, the role of excise taxes in the Federal government's fund-raising efforts has steadily declined, falling from about 30 to 40 percent of revenues just prior to the war to 4 percent in 1997. During this time, the Federal government came to rely upon income and employment taxes as its principal sources of funds.

Despite the decreasing contribution of excise taxes to the Federal coffers, they continue to have a significant impact on specific industries. Currently, trucks, trailers, tires, liquor, tobacco, firearms, sporting equipment, luxury automobiles, air travel, and telephone service are all subject to Federal excise taxes. In the past, the sale and manufacture of a variety of other goods, including furs, jewelry, boats, and theater tickets, have been taxed. Excise taxes extend beyond sales transactions. They are also levied on privileges and rights, as discussed below.

The bases used for Federal excise taxes are as diverse as the goods that are taxed. Fuels are taxed by the gallon, vaccines by the dose, telephone service and air travel by the price paid for the service, sport fishing equipment and bows and arrows by the sales price of the good, water travel by the passenger, coal by the ton extracted or by the sales price, insurance by the premiums paid, and the gas guzzler tax by the mileage rating on the automobile produced. Some of these taxes are levied on producers, some on resellers, and some on consumers. In almost every circumstance, the tax rate structure is proportional.

With the exception of Federal excise taxes on alcohol, tobacco, and firearms, Federal excise taxes are due at least quarterly, when the Federal excise tax return (Form 720) is filed.

State Excise Taxes. Many states levy excise taxes on the same items taxed by the Federal government. For example, most states have excise taxes on gasoline, liquor, and tobacco. However, the tax on specific goods can vary dramatically between states. Compare Alaska's $1.00 tax on each pack of cigarettes to Virginia's $0.025 tax. These differences at the state level provide ample incentive for smuggling between states and for state-line enterprises specializing in taxed goods.[2]

Other goods and services subject to state and local excise taxes include admission to amusement facilities, hotel occupancy, rental of other facilities, and sales of playing cards, oleomargarine products, and prepared foods. Also, most states impose a tax on transfers of property that require recording of documents (such as real estate sales and sales of stock and securities).

General Sales Tax. The broad-based general sales tax is a major source of revenue for most state and local governments. It is used in all but five states (Alaska, Delaware, Montana, New Hampshire, and Oregon). While specific rules vary from state to state, the sales tax typically has a proportional tax rate and includes retail sales of tangible personal property (and occasionally personal services) in the base. Some states exempt medicine and food from the base, and sometimes tax rates vary with the good being sold (e.g., the sales tax rate for automobiles may differ from the normal rate). The sales tax is collected by the retailer and then paid to the state government.

Local general sales taxes, over and above those levied by the state, are common. It is not unusual to find taxpayers living in the same state who pay different general sales taxes due to the location of their residence.

EXAMPLE 4   Pete and Sam both live in a state that has a general sales tax of 3%. Sam, however, resides in a city that imposes an additional general sales tax of 2%. Even though Pete and Sam live in the same state, one is subject to a rate of 3%, while the other pays a tax of 5%. ▼

Use Taxes. One obvious approach to avoiding state and local sales taxes is to purchase goods in a state that has little or no sales tax and then transport the goods back to one's home state. **Use taxes** exist to prevent this tax planning ploy. The use tax is a value-based tax, usually imposed at the same rate as the sales tax, on the use, consumption, or storage of tangible property. Every state that imposes a general sales tax levied on the consumer also has a use tax. Alaska, Delaware, Montana, New Hampshire, and Oregon have neither tax.

EXAMPLE 5   Susan resides in a jurisdiction that imposes a 5% general sales tax but lives near a state that has no sales or use tax. Susan purchases an automobile for $10,000 from a dealer located in the neighboring tax-free state. Though Susan will pay no sales tax to the dealer when

---

[2]Excise taxes are sometimes referred to as "sin" taxes (because goods such as liquor and tobacco are subject to the tax). Although it is commonly believed that these taxes are imposed for the purpose of discouraging consumption, evidence frequently fails to show that sin taxes have a significant impact on consumption. Usually, the impact of excise taxes depends on the price elasticity of demand for the good. Since demand for cigarettes and gasoline tends to be relatively inelastic (insensitive to price), the increase in price caused by excise taxes has little impact on consumption.

she purchases her car, she will be assessed a use tax when she returns to her home state and licenses the automobile. ▼

The use tax is difficult to enforce for many purchases and is therefore often avoided. In some cases, for example, it may be worthwhile to make purchases through an out-of-state mail-order business. In spite of shipping costs, the avoidance of the local sales tax that otherwise might be incurred often makes the price of such products as computer components cheaper. Some states are taking steps to curtail this loss of revenue. For an item such as an automobile (refer to Example 5), the use tax probably will be collected when the purchaser registers the vehicle in his or her home state.

Value Added Tax. The **value added tax (VAT)** is a sales tax levied at each stage of production on value added by the producer. VAT is in widespread use in many countries around the world (most notably in the European Community and in Canada). The tax typically serves as a major source of revenue for governments that use it. Some proposals to reduce the Federal government's reliance on income tax have focused on VAT as an alternative tax system.

EXAMPLE 6

Farmer Brown sells wheat to a flour mill for $100. If the wheat cost $65 for Brown to produce and if the VAT rate is 10%, then Brown will owe a VAT of $3.50 [0.10 ($100 − $65)]. If the mill sells the flour for $200 to a baker and if it cost the mill $120 to make the flour (including the cost of Brown's wheat), then it will pay a VAT of $8 [0.10 ($200 − $120)]. If the baker sells the bread he makes from the flour for $400 and if it cost the baker $280 to make the bread, then he will pay a VAT of $12 [0.10 ($400 − $280)]. The consumer who buys the bread will not pay any VAT directly. It is likely, however, that some or all of the total VAT paid of $23.50 ($3.50 + $8 + $12) will be paid by the consumer in the form of higher prices for the bread. ▼

Example 6 introduces a concept known as **implicit tax** (implicit taxes are also addressed in Example 26). While the VAT is directly imposed on producers, a large portion of the tax is indirectly paid by consumers in the form of higher prices. These higher prices are a form of implicit tax borne by consumers.[3]

EMPLOYMENT TAXES

Both Federal and state governments tax the salaries and wages paid to employees. On the Federal side, employment taxes represent a major source of funds. For example, the **FICA tax** accounts for 33 percent of revenues in the 1998 Federal budget, second only to the income tax in its contribution.

The Federal government imposes two kinds of employment tax. The Federal Insurance Contributions Act (FICA) imposes a tax on self-employed individuals, employees, and employers. The proceeds of the tax are used to finance Social Security and Medicare payments. The Federal Unemployment Tax Act (FUTA) imposes a tax on employers. The **FUTA tax** provides funds to state unemployment benefit programs. Most state employment taxes are similar to the FUTA tax, with proceeds used to finance state unemployment benefit payments.

---

[3] In the area of economics dealing with taxation (public finance), the issue of who ultimately pays a tax is known as *tax incidence*.

FICA Taxes. The FICA tax has two components: old age, survivors and disability insurance payments (commonly referred to as Social Security) and Medicare health insurance payments. The Social Security tax rate is 6.2 percent for 1997 and 1998, and the Medicare tax rate is 1.45 percent for these years. The maximum base for Social Security tax is $65,400 for 1997 and $68,400 for 1998. There is no ceiling on the base amount for the Medicare tax. The employer must withhold the FICA tax from an employee's wages and must also pay a matching tax.

Payments are usually made through weekly or monthly deposits to a Federal depository. Employers must also file Form 941, Employer's Quarterly Federal Tax Return, by the end of the first month following each quarter of the calendar year (e.g., by July 31 for the quarter ending on June 30) and pay any remaining amount of employment taxes due for the previous quarter. Failure to pay can result in large and sometimes ruinous penalties.

EXAMPLE 7

Janet receives $90,000 in salary in 1998. She pays FICA taxes of $5,545.80 [7.65% × $68,400 + 1.45%($90,000 − $68,400)]. Her employer is required to pay a matching FICA tax of $5,545.80. Janet's share of FICA taxes is withheld from her salary by her employer and deposited on a regular basis together with the employer's share of FICA. ▼

If an employee has two or more employers during any year, FICA tax withheld from salary may exceed the amount due. When this occurs, the employee will receive a refundable credit[4] against Federal income taxes equal to the excess FICA tax paid.

EXAMPLE 8

Miguel worked in two jobs in 1998. In his first job, he earned $55,000 in wages, and $4,207.50 in FICA was withheld. In his second job, his salary was $60,000, and $4,590 in FICA was withheld. Total FICA withheld for Miguel by employers during the year amounted to $8,797.50. Since Miguel's salary and wages in 1998 amounted to $115,000, he should have paid $5,908.30 [7.65% × $68,400 + 1.45%($115,000 − $68,400)]. Hence, he overpaid FICA by $2,889.20 ($8,797.50 − $5,908.30). This amount will be available as a reduction in Miguel's Federal income tax liability for 1998 or as a refund when Miguel files his Form 1040, Federal Individual Income Tax Return. ▼

Finally, FICA tax is not assessed on all wages paid. For example, wages paid to children under the age of 18 who are employed in a parent's trade or business are exempt from the tax.

Self-Employment Tax. Self-employed individuals also pay FICA in the form of a self-employment (SE) tax (determined on Schedule SE, filed with Form 1040, U.S. Individual Income Tax Return). Self-employed individuals are required to pay both the employer and the employee portion of the FICA tax. Therefore, the SE tax rate is 15.3 percent (2 × 7.65%) on income up to $68,400 and 2.9 percent (2 × 1.45%) on all additional income. Self-employed individuals are allowed to deduct half of the SE tax—the amount normally deductible by an employer as a business expense. The self-employment tax is covered in more detail in Chapter 16.

---

[4]For tax purposes, it is always crucial to appreciate the difference between a deduction and a credit. A credit is a dollar-for-dollar reduction of tax liability. A deduction, however, reduces taxable income so that any benefit is limited by the taxpayer's marginal tax rate. An estate subject to a 50% tax rate, for example, would need $2 of deductions to prevent $1 of tax liability from developing; that is, if taxable income is reduced by $2, the tax is reduced by $1 ($2 × 50%). In contrast, $1 of credit completely offsets $1 of tax liability.

Unemployment Taxes. In 1998, FUTA applies at a rate of 6.2 percent on the first $7,000 of covered wages paid during the year to each employee. As with FICA, this represents a regressive rate structure. The Federal government allows a credit for unemployment tax paid (or allowed under a merit rating system)[5] to the state. The credit cannot exceed 5.4 percent of the covered wages. Thus, the amount required to be paid to the IRS could be as low as 0.8 percent (6.2% − 5.4%).

FUTA and state unemployment taxes differ from FICA in that the tax is imposed only on the employer. A few states, however, levy a special tax on employees to provide either disability benefits or supplemental unemployment compensation, or both.

Employers must file Form 940, Employer's Annual Federal Employment Tax Return, to determine the amount of Federal unemployment taxes due in a given year. The return is due on or before January 31 of the following year. Employers may also be required to make more frequent payments of the tax (estimated payments) if their FUTA liability is sufficiently large. Most states also require unemployment tax returns to be filed with quarterly estimated payments.

DEATH TAXES

A **death tax** is a tax on the transfer of property upon the death of the owner. If the death tax is imposed on the transferor at death, it is classified as an **estate tax**. If it taxes the recipient of the property, it is termed an **inheritance tax**. As is typical of other types of transaction taxes, the value of the property transferred provides the base for determining the amount of the death tax.

The Federal government imposes only an estate tax. State governments, however, levy inheritance taxes, estate taxes, or both.

EXAMPLE 9

At the time of her death, Wilma lived in a state that imposes an inheritance tax but not an estate tax. Mary, one of Wilma's heirs, lives in the same state. Wilma's estate is subject to the Federal estate tax, and Mary is subject to the state inheritance tax. ▼

The Federal Estate Tax. The Revenue Act of 1916 incorporated the estate tax into the tax law. Never designed to generate a large amount of revenue, the tax was originally intended to prevent large concentrations of wealth from being kept within a family for many generations. Whether this objective has been accomplished is debatable, because estate taxes can be substantially reduced (or deferred for decades) through careful planning.

Determination of the estate tax base begins with the gross estate, which includes property the decedent owned at the time of death. It also includes life insurance proceeds when paid to the estate or when paid to a beneficiary other than the estate if the deceased-insured had any ownership rights in the policy. All property included in the gross estate is valued at fair market value as of the date of death or at a special alternate valuation date, six months after death.

Deductions from the gross estate in arriving at the taxable estate include funeral and administration expenses, certain taxes, debts of the decedent, **casualty losses**[6] incurred during the administration of the estate, transfers to charitable organizations, and, in some cases, an unlimited marital deduction. The marital

---

[5]States follow a policy of reducing unemployment tax on employers with stable employment. Thus, an employer with no employee turnover might face state unemployment tax rates as low as 0.1% or, in some cases, zero. This *merit rating system* explicitly accounts for the savings generated by steady employment.

[6]For a definition of casualty losses, see the Glossary of Tax Terms in Appendix C.

deduction is available for amounts actually passing to a surviving spouse (a widow or widower).

Once the taxable estate has been determined and certain taxable gifts have been added to it, progressive estate tax rates ranging from 18 to 55 percent are applied to determine a tentative tax liability. The tentative liability is reduced by a variety of credits to arrive at the amount due. Although many credits are available, probably the most significant is the *unified transfer tax credit*. This credit eliminates estate tax liability for most individuals. For 1998, the amount of the credit is $202,050. Based on the estate tax rates, the credit covers a tax base of $625,000.[7]

Ildiko made no taxable gifts before her death in 1998. If Ildiko's taxable estate amounts to $625,000 or less, no Federal estate tax is due because of the application of the unified transfer tax credit. Under the tax law, the tentative estate tax on a taxable estate of $625,000 is $202,050, exactly equal to the maximum unified transfer tax credit allowed. ▼

State Death Taxes. As noted earlier, states usually levy an inheritance tax, an estate tax, or both. The two forms of death taxes differ according to whether the tax is imposed on the heirs or on the estate.

Characteristically, an inheritance tax divides the heirs into classes based on their relationship to the decedent. The more closely related the heir, the lower the rates imposed and the greater the exemption allowed. Some states completely exempt amounts passing to a surviving spouse from taxation.

GIFT TAXES

Like death taxes, the gift tax is an excise tax levied on the right to transfer property. In this case, however, the tax is imposed on transfers made during the owner's life rather than at death. A gift tax applies only to transfers that are not supported by full and adequate consideration (i.e., gifts).

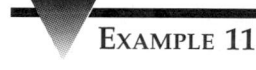

Carl sells property worth $20,000 to his daughter for $1,000. Although property worth $20,000 has been transferred, only $19,000 represents a gift, since this is the portion not supported by full and adequate consideration. ▼

The Federal Gift Tax. First enacted in 1932, the Federal gift tax was intended to complement the estate tax. Prior to the enactment of the gift tax, it was possible to avoid the estate tax entirely by distributing one's assets through lifetime gifts.

The gift tax base is equal to the sum of all taxable gifts made *during one's lifetime*. Gifts are valued at the date of transfer. To compute the tax due in a year, the tax rate schedule is applied to the sum of all lifetime taxable gifts. The resulting tax is then reduced by gift taxes paid in prior years.

In 1995, Waqar gave $700,000 of taxable gifts to his son. The gift tax paid in 1995 (before application of any credits) was $229,800. In 1998, Waqar will give an additional $100,000 in taxable gifts to his son. The tax base in 1998 will be $800,000 of lifetime gifts, and the tax will be $267,800. However, the actual gift tax due in 1998 (before credits) will be $38,000 ($267,800 − $229,800 tax paid on prior-year gifts). ▼

---

[7]The unified transfer tax credit is scheduled to increase annually until 2006. In 2006, the credit will equal $345,800, covering a taxable estate of $1 million.

Under current law, the Federal gift tax and the Federal estate tax are *unified*. The transfer of assets by a decedent at death is effectively treated as a final gift under the tax law. Thus, the $202,050 unified transfer tax credit available under the estate tax is also available to reduce the tax liability generated by lifetime gifts. If the credit is exhausted during one's lifetime, it will not be available to reduce estate tax liability. In addition, the same tax rate schedule applies to both lifetime gifts and the estate tax.

EXAMPLE 13

Before his death, Gyung gives $1 million of taxable gifts. Because the unified transfer tax credit was used during his life to offset the tax due on some of these gifts, no credit is left to reduce Gyung's estate tax liability. ▼

Annual taxable gifts are determined by reducing the fair market value of gifts given by an annual exclusion of $10,000 per donee.[8] A married couple can elect *gift splitting*, which enables them to transfer twice the annual exclusion ($20,000 in 1998) per donee per year.

EXAMPLE 14

On December 31, 1997, Vera (a widow) gives $10,000 to each of her four married children, their spouses, and her eight grandchildren. On January 3, 1998, she repeats the same procedure. Due to the annual exclusion, Vera has *not* made a taxable gift, although she transferred $160,000 [$10,000 × 16 (the number of donees)] in 1997 and $160,000 [$10,000 × 16 (the number of donees)] in 1998 for a total of $320,000 ($160,000 + $160,000). If Vera were married, she could have given twice as much ($640,000) by electing gift splitting with her husband. ▼

State Gift Taxes. The states currently imposing a gift tax are Connecticut, Delaware, Louisiana, New York, North Carolina, and Tennessee. Most of the laws provide for lifetime exemptions and annual exclusions. Like the Federal gift tax, the state taxes are cumulative in effect. But unlike the Federal version, the amount of tax depends on the relationship between the donor and the donee. As with state inheritance taxes, larger exemptions and lower rates apply when the donor and donee are closely related to each other.

PROPERTY TAXES

A property tax can be a tax on the ownership of property or a tax on wealth, depending on the base used. Any measurable characteristic of the property being taxed can be used as a base (e.g., weight, size, number, or value). Most property taxes in the United States are taxes on wealth since they use value as a base. These value-based property taxes are known as **ad valorem taxes**. Individual taxpayers are generally allowed to deduct nonbusiness ad valorem property taxes for income tax purposes. In addition, all property taxes related to business activities are deductible against income. Property taxes are generally administered by state and local governments where they serve as a significant source of revenue.

In addition to the difference between property taxes based on value and those based on other characteristics, a further distinction can be drawn between taxes on real estate and taxes on personal property. The specifics of these two kinds of property taxes are discussed in detail below.

---

[8]The $10,000 annual exclusion is indexed for inflation annually, beginning in 1999.

TAX IN THE NEWS

DOES BILL GATES HAVE A FANCY PAD, OR WHAT?

For property tax purposes, Bill Gates's new house has an assessed value of approximately $53 million, the cost of its construction. With this assessment, Gates pays annual ad valorem taxes of $600,000. Gates considered disputing the use of construction cost as the measure of value. He feels that, because the house is unique, it would be difficult to sell. Consequently, he thinks the assessed value should be discounted for lack of marketability.

Incidentally, the residence is situated on a five-acre wooded lakefront tract near Seattle. The main manor has 40,000 square feet (with a separate 1,700-square-foot guest house), a 60-foot pool, a sauna, two spas, a 20-seat theater, a reception hall for 100 people, an arcade, a boat dock for water skiing, and a library.

Real Property Taxes. Property taxes on **realty** are exclusively within the province of the states and their local political subdivisions (e.g., cities, counties, school districts). They represent a major source of revenue for local governments, but their importance at the state level has waned over the past few years. Some states, for example, have imposed freezes on the upper revaluations of residential housing.

How realty is defined can have an important bearing on which assets are subject to tax. This is especially true in jurisdictions that do not impose ad valorem taxes on **personalty**. Although the definition is primarily a question of state property law, realty generally includes real estate and any capital improvements that are classified as fixtures. A fixture is something so permanently attached to the real estate that its removal will cause irreparable damage. A built-in bookcase might well be a fixture, whereas a movable bookcase would not be a fixture. Certain items such as electrical wiring and plumbing change from personalty to realty when installed in a building.

The following are some of the characteristics of ad valorem taxes on realty:

- Property owned by the Federal government is exempt from tax. Similar immunity usually is extended to property owned by state and local governments and by certain charitable organizations.
- Some states provide for lower valuations on property dedicated to agricultural use or other special uses (e.g., wildlife sanctuaries).
- Some states partially exempt the homestead portion of property from taxation. Modern homestead laws normally protect some or all of a personal residence (including a farm or ranch) from the actions of creditors pursuing claims against the owner.
- Lower taxes may apply to a residence owned by an elderly taxpayer (e.g., age 65 and older).
- When non-income-producing property (e.g., a personal residence) is converted to income-producing property (e.g., a rental house), typically the appraised value (the tax base) increases.
- Some jurisdictions extend immunity from tax for a specified period of time (a tax holiday) to new or relocated businesses.

Ad Valorem Taxes on Personalty. Personalty can be defined as all assets that are not realty. It may be helpful to distinguish between the classification of an asset (realty or personalty) and the use to which it is put. Both realty and personalty can be either business-use or personal-use property. Examples include a residence (personal-use realty), an office building (business-use realty), surgical instruments (business-use personalty), and regular clothing (personal-use personalty).[9]

Personalty can also be classified as tangible property or intangible property. For property tax purposes, intangible personalty includes stocks, bonds, and various other securities (e.g., bank shares).

The following generalizations may be made concerning the property taxes on personalty:

- Particularly with personalty devoted to personal use (e.g., jewelry, household furnishings), taxpayer compliance ranges from poor to zero. Some jurisdictions do not even attempt to enforce the tax on these items. For automobiles devoted to personal use, many jurisdictions have converted from value as the tax base to a tax based on the weight of the vehicle. Some jurisdictions also consider the vehicle's age (e.g., automobiles six years or older are not subject to the ad valorem tax because they are presumed to have little value).
- For personalty devoted to business use (e.g., inventories, trucks, machinery, equipment), taxpayer compliance and enforcement procedures are notably better.
- Which jurisdiction possesses the authority to tax movable personalty (e.g., railroad cars) always has been and continues to be a troublesome issue.
- Some jurisdictions impose an ad valorem property tax on intangibles.

TAXES ON PRIVILEGES AND RIGHTS

Taxes on privileges and rights are usually considered excise taxes. A few of the most important of these taxes are reviewed here.

Federal Customs Duties. Customs duties or tariffs can be characterized as a tax on the right to move goods across national borders. These taxes, together with selective excise taxes, provided most of the revenues needed by the Federal government during the nineteenth century. For example, tariffs and excise taxes alone paid off the national debt in 1835 and enabled the U.S. Treasury to pay a surplus of $28 million to the states. Today, however, customs duties account for only 1 percent of revenues in the Federal budget.

In recent years, tariffs have served the nation more as an instrument for carrying out protectionist policies than as a means of generating revenue. Thus, a particular U.S. industry might be saved from economic disaster, so the argument goes, by placing customs duties on the importation of foreign goods that can be sold at lower prices. Protectionists contend that the tariff therefore neutralizes the competitive edge held by the producer of the foreign goods.[10]

---

[9] The distinction, important for property tax and Federal income tax purposes, often becomes confused when personalty is referred to as "personal" property to distinguish it from "real" property. This designation does not give a complete picture of what is involved. The description "personal" residence is clearer, since a residence can be identified as being realty. What is meant, in this case, is realty that is personal-use property.

[10] The North American Free Trade Agreement (NAFTA), enacted in 1993, substantially reduced the tariffs on trade between Canada, Mexico, and the United States. The General Agreement on Tariffs and Trade (GATT) legislation enacted in 1994 also reduced tariffs on selected commodities among 124 countries.

Protectionist policies seem more appropriate for less-developed countries whose industrial capacity has not yet matured. In a world where a developed country should have everything to gain by encouraging international free trade, such policies may be of dubious value since tariffs often lead to retaliatory action on the part of the nation or nations affected.

Franchise Taxes and Occupational Taxes. A **franchise tax** is a tax on the privilege of doing business in a state or local jurisdiction. Typically, the tax is imposed by states on corporations. The tax base varies from state to state. While some states use a measure of corporate net income as part of the base, most states base the tax on the capitalization of the corporation (with or without certain long-term debt).

Closely akin to the franchise tax are **occupational taxes** applicable to various trades or businesses, such as a liquor store license, a taxicab permit, or a fee to practice a profession such as law, medicine, or accounting. Most of these are not significant revenue producers and fall more into the category of licenses than taxes. The revenue derived is used to defray the cost incurred by the jurisdiction to regulate the business or profession for the public good.

Severance Taxes. Severance taxes are based on the extraction of natural resources (e.g., oil, gas, iron ore, and coal). They are an important source of revenue for many states.

INCOME TAXES

Income taxes are levied by the Federal government, most states, and some local governments. In recent years, the trend in the United States has been to place greater reliance on this method of taxation while other countries are relying more heavily on transactions taxes such as the VAT.

Income taxes are generally imposed on individuals, corporations, and certain fiduciaries (estates and trusts). Most jurisdictions attempt to assure the collection of income taxes by requiring certain pay-as-you-go procedures (e.g., withholding requirements for employees and estimated tax prepayments for other taxpayers).

3 LEARNING OBJECTIVE
Understand some of the history of the Federal income tax.

A Brief History. The first income tax in America was introduced by English colonists in Massachusetts Bay Colony in 1634. However, it was not until the increased revenue needs brought on by the Civil War that the U.S. government introduced an income tax (from 1861 to 1872). At its peak in 1866, the first U.S. income tax raised $376 million, or 25 percent of Federal revenue collections for the year (in contrast, the Federal income tax accounted for about 52 percent of Federal revenues in the 1998 Federal budget). The Civil War tax was levied only on the wealthy with graduated rates from 1 to 10 percent. The Confederate States of America also employed an income tax to help finance their war effort.

After the Civil War, the income tax was repealed, and the Federal government returned to a reliance on tariffs and excise taxes. Following an economic depression in 1893, the Democratic Party reinstated the individual income tax in an attempt to address a deficit in the Treasury. The tax used a proportional 2 percent rate on incomes over $4,000. The tax was very controversial and was found unconstitutional in *Pollock v. Farmer's Loan and Trust Co.*[11] The tax was attacked on the grounds that

---

[11] 3 AFTR 2602, 157 U.S. 429 (USSC, 1895).

it was a *direct* tax that required apportionment.[12] This failed to meet a requirement of the U.S. Constitution, which stated:

> ... No Capitation, or other direct, Tax shall be laid, unless in Proportion to the Census or Enumeration herein before directed to be taken.

Thus, any direct tax imposed by Congress was required to be apportioned among the states on the basis of their relative populations. Consequently, each state would need to have a different Federal income tax rate for its citizens because the size of each state's population differed.

In 1909, a coalition of liberal Republicans and midwestern Populists sought relief from the ever-increasing burden of tariffs by imposing a tax on inheritances and income. President Taft successfully redirected this movement toward the enactment of a 4 percent corporate income tax. The constitutionality of this tax was challenged unsuccessfully in *Flint v. Stone Tracy Co.*[13] In this instance, the Supreme Court held the tax to be indirect and said it was essentially an excise tax on the right to do business as a corporation.

At this point, politicians, sensing that tariffs affected consumers (voters) more than an income tax on the wealthy, began to move toward individual income taxes. Finally, on February 25, 1913, the Sixteenth Amendment was passed. It provided that:

> The Congress shall have the power to lay and collect taxes on incomes from whatever source derived, without apportionment among the several States, and without regard to any census or enumeration.

Promptly after passage of the amendment, on October 3, 1913, Congress passed the first individual income tax and made it retroactive to March 1, 1913. In its original form, the income tax of 1913 had a 1 percent tax rate on incomes in excess of $3,000 ($4,000 for married couples) plus a 6 percent surtax on very high incomes over $500,000. In 1913, the average personal income was $621; only 2 percent of the U.S. population paid income tax from 1913 to 1915, and 90 percent of Federal revenues were still collected from tariffs and excise taxes.

In 1916, as the United States became involved in World War I, all this began to change. Maximum income tax rates were raised to 15 percent. In 1917, they were raised again to 67 percent; in 1918, they were increased to 77 percent. Exemptions were reduced to $1,000 ($2,000 for married couples). At its peak, the income tax provided 60 percent of Federal revenues during World War I. These high rates remained in effect after the war to speed debt reduction. Despite the rapid increase in rates, the income tax remained steeply progressive, with the top 1 percent of taxpayers paying 70 percent of the tax bill. By 1925, as the Federal debt was eliminated, maximum individual tax rates were dropped to 25 percent.

It took a second world war for the income tax to have an impact on the average citizen. In 1939, less than 6 percent of the U.S. population paid any income tax. By 1945, over 74 percent paid income tax. In the interim, Congress introduced a pay-as-you-go system by enacting the Current Tax Payment Act of 1943, which required withholding of Federal income taxes from salaries.

---

[12] In an earlier case, *Springer v. U.S.*, 102 U.S. 586 (USSC, 1880), the constitutionality of the Civil War era income tax was challenged on the same grounds. In *Springer*, the Supreme Court held that the income tax was indirect (and that only head taxes and real estate taxes were direct). When addressing *Pollock*, the Supreme Court distinguished the two cases, saying that *Pollock* focused on taxation of income generated from real estate; the Court then held that a tax on income from real estate was equivalent to a direct tax on real estate.

[13] 3 AFTR 2834, 220 U.S. 107 (USSC, 1911).

CHAPTER 1 Introduction to Taxation

▼ **FIGURE 1–1**
Basic Formula for Federal Income Tax

Income (broadly conceived)	$xxx,xxx
Less: Exclusions (income that is not subject to tax)	(xx,xxx)
Gross income	$xxx,xxx
Less: Deductions	(xx,xxx)
Taxable income	$xxx,xxx
Federal income tax (see Tax Rate Schedule inside front cover of text)	$ xx,xxx
Less: Tax credits (including Federal income tax withheld and other prepayments of Federal income taxes)	(x,xxx)
Tax owed (or refund)	$ xxx

The Federal government never looked back. Since 1945, the scope of the income tax and its complexity have continued to increase, and the income tax remains every person's tax.

4 LEARNING OBJECTIVE
Recall the basic tax formula for individuals and taxable business entities.

The Structure of the Federal Income Tax. Although some variations exist, the basic Federal income tax formula is similar for all taxable entities. This formula is shown in Figure 1–1.

The income tax is based on the assumption that all income is subject to tax and that no deductions are allowed unless specifically provided for in the law. Some types of income are specifically excluded on the basis of various economic, social, equity, and political considerations. Examples include gifts, inheritance, life insurance proceeds received by reason of death, and interest income from state and local bonds. All entities are allowed to deduct business expenses from gross income, but a number of limitations and exceptions are applied. A variety of credits against the tax are also allowed, again on the basis of economic, social, equity or political goals of Congress.

Income tax rates for all entities are progressive. The corporate rates range from 15 percent on the lowest level of taxable income to 35 percent on the highest level. Individual rates range from 15 percent to 39.6 percent. Estates and trusts are also subject to taxation, with rates ranging from 15 percent to 39.6 percent. Partnerships, qualifying small business corporations, and some limited liability companies are not taxable entities, but must file information returns. A more detailed introduction to the income tax treatment of various business entities is presented in the next section.

In the case of individuals, deductions are separated into two categories—deductions *for* adjusted gross income (AGI) and deductions *from* AGI. Generally, deductions *for* AGI are related to business activities, while deductions *from* AGI are often personal in nature (e.g., medical expenses, mortgage interest and taxes on a personal residence, charitable contributions, and personal casualty losses) or related to investment activities. Deductions *from* AGI are also known as *itemized deductions*. Individuals also may elect to take a *standard deduction* (a specified amount based on filing status) rather than itemizing actual deductions. In addition, reductions in taxable income through personal and dependency exemptions are allowed.[14]

---

[14]Personal and dependency exemptions are fixed reductions in taxable income allowed for each taxpayer on a return and for each of the taxpayer's dependents. This amount is equal to $2,700 for each exemption in 1998 and is indexed for inflation.

▼ FIGURE 1-2
Federal Income Tax Formula for Individuals

Income (broadly conceived)	$xx,xxx
Less: Exclusions (income that is not subject to tax)	(x,xxx)
Gross income (income that is subject to tax)	$xx,xxx
Less: Certain business, investment, and personal deductions (usually referred to as deductions *for* adjusted gross income)	(x,xxx)
Adjusted gross income	$xx,xxx
Less: The greater of certain personal and employee deductions (usually referred to as *itemized deductions*) or The standard deduction (including any *additional* standard deduction)	(x,xxx)
Less: Personal and dependency exemptions	(x,xxx)
Taxable income	$xx,xxx
Federal income tax (see Tax Rate Schedules inside front cover of text)	$ x,xxx
Less: Tax credits (including Federal income tax withheld and other prepayments of Federal income taxes)	(xxx)
Tax owed (or refund)	$ xxx

An overview of the individual income tax formula is provided in Figure 1–2. Details of the individual formula are covered in Chapter 15.

State Income Taxes. Most states (except Alaska, Florida, Nevada, South Dakota, Texas, Washington, and Wyoming) impose an income tax on individuals. Tennessee taxes only income from stocks and bonds, and New Hampshire taxes only dividend and interest income. Most states also impose either a corporate income tax or a franchise tax based in part on corporate income. The following additional points can be made about state income taxes:

- State income tax usually relies on Federal income tax laws to some degree—the states use Federal taxable income as a base, with a few adjustments (e.g., a few allow a deduction for Federal income taxes paid and sometimes an exclusion on interest income earned on Federal securities).
- For individual income tax purposes, a few states impose a flat rate on Federal AGI.
- Several states piggyback directly on the Federal income tax system by using the Federal income tax liability as a base.
- Most states also require withholding of state income tax from salaries and wages and estimated payments by corporations and self-employed individuals.
- Most states have their own set of rates, exemptions, and credits.
- Many states also allow a credit for taxes paid to other states.

Local Income Taxes. Cities imposing an income tax include, but are not limited to, Baltimore, Cincinnati, Cleveland, Detroit, Kansas City (Mo.), New York, Philadelphia, and St. Louis. City income taxes usually apply to anyone who earns income in a city. They are not limited to local residents.

CHAPTER 1 Introduction to Taxation   1–17

> ### TAX IN THE NEWS
>
> ### VISITORS BEWARE! THE CITY AND STATE YOU VISIT MAY NOT BE ALL THAT FRIENDLY
>
> Even if you are not a resident, you may be subject to local and state income taxes if you earn money in that jurisdiction. Besides the nonresident who commutes (e.g., a taxpayer who lives in Connecticut but works full-time in New York City), taxpayers who perform services on an itinerant basis may be vulnerable. For example, the Dallas Cowboys are subject to the city of Philadelphia income tax every time they are hosted by the Eagles. This must be particularly distressing to Troy Aikman, who lives in a city (Dallas) and a state (Texas) that do not have an income tax.
>
> Although these situations are often publicized as the "jock tax," other persons besides professional athletes get hit. Particularly susceptible are entertainers, doctors, lawyers, lecturers, and anyone who generates large fees and has a high profile. Ordinary professionals are not targeted because the amount of taxes involved would not justify the collection effort.
>
> Is it any wonder that Las Vegas, which has no city or state income tax, is such a popular place to perform highly paid services (e.g., entertainment, prize fighting)?

AN INTRODUCTION TO THE INCOME TAXATION OF BUSINESS ENTITIES

PROPRIETORSHIPS

5 LEARNING OBJECTIVE
Understand the relationship between business entities and their owners.

The simplest form of business entity is a **proprietorship**, which is not a separate taxable entity. Instead, the proprietor reports the net profit of the business on his or her own individual tax return.

Individuals who own proprietorships often have specific tax goals with regard to their financial interactions with the business. Because a proprietorship is, by definition, owned by an individual, the individual has great flexibility in structuring the entity's transactions in a way that will minimize his or her income tax (or, in some cases, the income tax of the family unit).

EXAMPLE 15
Susan, a single individual, is the sole proprietor of Quality Fabrics, a retail store in which she works full-time. The business is her only source of income. Susan's taxable income in 1998 is $106,550, and her Federal income tax is $27,893 ($13,896.50 + 31% of the amount over $61,400). Thus, her *marginal tax rate* (the rate she pays on the highest *layer* of taxable income) is 31%. ▼

EXAMPLE 16
Assume the same facts as in the previous example, except that Susan pays her nondependent 19-year-old son a $10,000 salary to work part-time at Quality Fabrics. This will reduce her 1998 taxable income by $10,000 and will reduce her tax bill by $3,100 ($10,000 deduction × 31% marginal tax rate). Her son will have $3,050 in taxable income (after the standard deduction and personal exemption) and will be taxed at a 15% rate, which results in Federal income tax of $457.50. In summary, Susan (the individual taxpayer) is able to operate the business entity (Quality Fabrics) in a way that will save the family unit $2,642.50 in Federal income tax ($3,100 saved by Susan − $457.50 paid by her son). ▼

Examples 15 and 16 reflect the fact that a proprietorship itself is not a taxpaying entity. The owner of the proprietorship must report the income and deductions of the business on a Schedule C (Profit or Loss from Business) and must report the net profit (or loss) of the proprietorship on his or her Form 1040 (U.S. Individual Income Tax Return). Specific issues related to the taxation of sole proprietorships are covered in detail in Chapter 16.

CORPORATIONS

Some corporations pay tax on corporate taxable income while others pay no tax at the corporate level. Corporations that are separate taxable entities are referred to as **C corporations**, because they are governed by Subchapter C of the Internal Revenue Code. Corporations that meet certain requirements and pay no tax at the corporate level are referred to as **S corporations**, because they are governed by Subchapter S of the Code. S corporations are discussed briefly later in this chapter and will be covered in detail in Chapter 12. C corporations will be covered in Chapters 9 and 10.

A C corporation is required to file a tax return (Form 1120) and is subject to the Federal income tax. The shareholders must then pay income tax on the dividends they receive when the corporation distributes its profits. Thus, the profits of the corporation are subject to double taxation, first at the corporate level and then at the shareholder level.

EXAMPLE 17 Joseph is single, has no dependents, and does not itemize deductions. He is the president and sole shareholder of Falcon Corporation. Falcon's taxable income for 1998 is $100,000, and its tax liability is $22,250. If Joseph has the corporation pay all of its after-tax income to him as a dividend, he will receive $77,750, have taxable income of $70,800 (after the standard deduction and personal exemption), and will pay Federal income tax of $16,810.50 ($13,896.50 + 31% of the amount over $61,400). The combined Federal income tax paid by Joseph and the corporation will be $39,060.50. ▼

EXAMPLE 18 Assume the same facts as in the previous example, except that Joseph has the corporation pay him a salary of $100,000, which is deductible by the corporation. Thus, the corporation will have zero taxable income and zero tax liability. Joseph will have taxable income of $93,050, and his Federal income tax will be $23,708 ($13,896.50 + 31% of the amount over $61,400). Thus Joseph can save $15,352.50 in combined Federal income tax ($39,060.50 − $23,708) by having the corporation pay him a salary instead of a dividend. ▼

PARTNERSHIPS

A partnership is not a separate taxable entity. The partnership is required to file a tax return (Form 1065), on which it summarizes the financial results of the business. Each partner then reports his or her share of the net income or loss and other special items that were reported on the partnership return.

EXAMPLE 19 Cameron and Connor form a partnership in which they are equal partners. The partnership reports a $100,000 net profit on its tax return, but is not subject to the Federal income tax. Cameron and Connor each report $50,000 net income from the partnership on their separate individual income tax returns. ▼

S CORPORATIONS

An S corporation is like a C corporation with regard to nontax factors. Shareholders have limited liability, shares are freely transferable, there is a centralized management (vested in the board of directors), and there is continuity of life (i.e., the corporation continues to exist after the withdrawal or death of a shareholder). With regard to tax factors, however, an S corporation is more like a partnership. The S corporation is not subject to the Federal *income* tax. Like a partnership, it does file a tax return (Form 1120S), but the shareholders report their share of net income or loss and other special items on their own returns.

EXAMPLE 20

Kay and Dawn form a corporation and elect to have it treated as an S corporation. Kay owns 60% of the stock of the corporation, and Dawn owns 40%. The S corporation reports a $100,000 net profit on its tax return, but is not subject to the income tax. Kay will report $60,000 net income from the S corporation on her individual income tax return, and Dawn will report $40,000 on her return. ▼

An S corporation can be very attractive as a form of business entity because it combines the many *nontax advantages* offered by the corporate form with some of the tax advantages offered by the partnership form. The S corporation, limited liability company, and partnership forms of organization, which are referred to as *flow-through* entities, avoid the double taxation problem associated with the C corporation.

LIMITED LIABILITY COMPANIES AND LIMITED LIABILITY PARTNERSHIPS

Limited liability companies (LLCs) and limited liability partnerships (LLPs) have grown rapidly in popularity over the last few years. These organizations exist under state laws, and the specific rules vary somewhat from state to state. Both forms have limited liability and some (but not all) of the other nontax features of corporations. Additionally, both forms may be treated as partnerships for tax purposes. LLCs and LLPs are examined in detail in Chapter 11, with partnerships.

RELATIONSHIPS BETWEEN INDIVIDUALS AND ENTITIES

Many of the provisions in the tax law deal with the relationships between owners and the business entities they own. The following are some of the major interactions between owners and business entities:

- Owners put assets into a business when they establish a business entity (e.g., a proprietorship, partnership, or corporation).
- Owners take assets out of the business during its existence in the form of salary, dividends, withdrawals, redemptions of stock, etc.
- Through their entities, owner-employees set up retirement plans for themselves, including IRAs, Keogh plans, and qualified pension plans.
- Owners dispose of all or part of a business entity.

Every major transaction that occurs between an owner and a business entity has important tax ramifications. The following are a few of the many tax issues that arise:

- How to avoid taxation at both the owner level and the entity level (i.e., the multiple taxation problem).
- How to get assets into the business with the least adverse tax consequences.
- How to get assets out of the business with the least adverse tax consequences.

- How to dispose of the business entity with the least adverse tax consequences.

When addressing these (and other) tax issues, a common set of tax planning tools can be applied. These tax planning fundamentals are introduced in the next section.

TAX PLANNING FUNDAMENTALS

OVERVIEW OF TAX PLANNING

6 LEARNING OBJECTIVE
Recognize tax planning opportunities and apply a simplified model of tax planning.

Taxpayers generally attempt to minimize their tax liabilities, and it is perfectly acceptable to do so by using legal means.[15] It is a long-standing principle that taxpayers have no obligation to pay more than their fair share of taxes. The now-classic words of Judge Learned Hand in *Commissioner v. Newman* reflect the true values a taxpayer should have:

> Over and over again courts have said that there is nothing sinister in so arranging one's affairs as to keep taxes as low as possible. Everybody does so, rich or poor; and all do right, for nobody owes any public duty to pay more than the law demands; taxes are enforced exactions, not voluntary contributions. To demand more in the name of morals is mere cant.[16]

Minimizing taxes legally is referred to as **tax avoidance**. On the other hand, some taxpayers attempt to *evade* income taxes illegally. There is a major distinction between tax avoidance and **tax evasion**. Though eliminating or reducing taxes is also a goal of tax evasion, the term *evasion* implies the use of subterfuge and fraud as a means to this end. Tax avoidance is legal, while tax evasion subjects the taxpayer to numerous civil and criminal penalties, including prison sentences.

Clients expect tax practitioners to provide advice to help them minimize their tax costs. This part of the tax practitioner's practice is referred to as *tax planning*. In order to structure a sound tax minimization plan, a practitioner must have a thorough knowledge of the tax law. Tax planning skill is based on a knowledge of tax saving provisions in the tax law, as well as provisions that contain pitfalls for the unwary. Thorough study of the remainder of this text will provide the knowledge required to recognize opportunities and avoid pitfalls.

THE GOAL OF TAX PLANNING

The goal of tax planning is to design a transaction so as to minimize its tax costs, while meeting the other nontax objectives of the client. Two key notions are implicit in this goal. First, proper minimization of a transaction's tax costs refers to the overall tax costs to *all* parties to a transaction. This notion is known as **equilibrium tax planning**.

EXAMPLE 21

Green, Inc., is in the process of designing a compensation plan for its CEO, Ms. Merbaum. The corporation expects to face a 35% tax rate for the foreseeable future, while Merbaum has a 31% tax rate in 1998. If Green pays a bonus of $45,000 to Merbaum in 1998, then she will retain $31,050 after taxes [$45,000 − (0.31 × $45,000)]. Since the bonus will be deductible currently, Green will have an after-tax cost of $29,250 [$45,000 − (0.35 × $45,000)]. Merbaum

---

[15] Many of the ideas in this section were introduced in the literature by Myron Scholes and Mark Wolfson in *Taxes and Business Strategy: A Global Planning Approach* (Prentice Hall, 1992).

[16] 47–1 USTC ¶9175, 35 AFTR 857, 159 F.2d 848 (CA–2, 1947)

has expressed interest in receiving deferred compensation, since she will be retiring in 2000 with a 28% marginal tax rate in that year. Green has elected to pay all the bonus currently, reasoning that a deduction for the bonus now is more beneficial to the company than a deduction in two years (due to the time value of money). ▼

In Example 21, Green, Inc., failed to consider the tax consequences to the other party in the transaction and, instead, focused on minimizing its own tax liability. Compare this result to the following example, where the parties employ equilibrium tax planning.

▼ EXAMPLE 22

Using the same facts as in Example 21, Green, Inc., decides to compensate Merbaum with a deferred compensation plan. Assume a discount rate of 10% for Green and Merbaum. If Green pays $53,250 to Merbaum in two years, its after-tax cost at that time will be $34,612.50 [$53,250 − (0.35 × $53,250)]. The present value of this cost is $28,605, or $645 *less* in cost than paying $45,000 currently ($29,250 after-tax cost). Merbaum will also benefit from receiving the deferred compensation. Her after-tax income in two years, assuming a 28% tax rate, will be $38,340. The present value of this after-tax income is $31,686, or $636 *more* in compensation than under the bonus plan in Example 21. Hence, by considering the tax consequences to both Merbaum and Green, the positions of both parties are improved. ▼

A second key goal of tax planning is adequate consideration of all nontax aspects of the transaction.

▼ EXAMPLE 23

Orange, Inc., is a franchise in the Pacific Northwest. It would like to expand to other areas of the United States and is considering the acquisition of Tangerine, Inc., which is based in Chicago. There are a number of ways to structure the acquisition of Tangerine. Aside from tax consequences, a variety of other business issues should play a role in the structuring of the transaction. When designing the acquisition, the companies and their shareholders would carefully consider the type of consideration to be paid for Tangerine, the impact of minority or dissenting shareholders, and the importance of contingent liabilities and nonassignable contracts. For example, the existence of large contingent liabilities might lead Orange to prefer an asset purchase (thereby avoiding the liabilities), while valuable nonassignable contracts in Tangerine could cause Orange to prefer a stock purchase (to retain the contracts). ▼

Selecting a specific form of transaction solely for the sake of tax minimization often leads to poor business decisions. Effective tax planning requires careful consideration of the nontax issues involved in addition to tax consequences.

DETERMINING THE TAX BURDEN

To engage in effective tax planning, one must be able to identify the relevant tax rate that will be applied to a transaction. There are three kinds of tax rates. A taxpayer's *marginal* tax rate (or tax bracket) is the rate that would be paid on an additional dollar of income earned. Referring to the corporate income tax rate schedule inside the front cover of this textbook, a corporation's marginal tax rate on its first dollar of income is 15 percent. Similarly, the marginal tax rate faced by a corporation with $100,000 of income is 39 percent.[17] The *average* tax rate is the ratio of taxes paid to the tax base. Thus, a corporation with $100,000 of taxable income in 1997 will have an average tax rate of 22.25 percent

---

[17]Note that corporate tax rates are steeply progressive over the first $100,000 in taxable income. Congress adopted this approach to aid small businesses.

($22,250 in tax divided by $100,000 in taxable income). A third kind of tax rate, the *effective* rate, has been defined as either (1) the ratio of taxes paid to financial net income before tax or (2) the sum of currently payable and deferred tax expense divided by net income before tax. Of these approaches to determining a taxpayer's rate, the marginal rate is most appropriate for tax planning purposes.

EXAMPLE 24

Azure Corporation has taxable income of $80,000 in 1998. Azure also has $10,000 of tax-free interest income from municipal bonds. Using the corporate tax rate schedule inside the front cover of this textbook, one can determine that the company's tax liability is $15,450. If Azure were to earn an additional dollar in taxable income, it would pay $0.34 in tax. Thus, the company's marginal tax rate is 34%. Azure's average tax rate is the ratio of taxes paid to taxable income or 19.3% ($15,450/$80,000). Finally, the company has an effective rate of tax of 17.2% ($15,450/$90,000), the ratio of taxes paid to financial net income before tax (here, the sum of taxable income and tax-free income). ▼

The actual tax paid may not always be apparent. For example, the amount of taxes paid should include both current taxes and the present value of future taxes generated by a transaction.

EXAMPLE 25

Magenta Corporation is a publishing company that specializes in electronic media. It is a new corporation that was formed on January 1, 1998. During the year it generated a net operating loss (NOL) of $300,000. The NOL can be carried forward to offset future years' taxable income and thereby reduce Magenta's future tax liabilities. Magenta expects to earn $100,000 of income each year over the next four years. The NOL should completely offset the company's taxable income for the first three of these years.[18]

At the beginning of 1999, Magenta must decide whether to invest in a project that will earn an additional $40,000 of taxable income during 1999 or a project that will generate $36,000 tax-free. The company's president reasons that, since the company has an NOL carryforward, the applicable tax rate is 0%, so the taxable project should be chosen.

The president's reasoning is incorrect, because an additional $40,000 of income now will result in $40,000 of taxable income in 2001 (since there will be $40,000 less NOL available in that year). This is illustrated as follows:

	1999	2000	2001	2002
Alternative 1 (tax-free investment)				
Pre-NOL taxable income	$ 100,000	$ 100,000	$ 100,000	$100,000
NOL carryforward (from 1998)	(300,000)	(200,000)	(100,000)	–0–
Taxable income	$ –0–	$ –0–	$ –0–	$100,000
Alternative 2 (taxable investment)				
Pre-NOL taxable income	$ 140,000	$ 100,000	$ 100,000	$100,000
NOL carryforward (from 1998)	(300,000)	(160,000)	(60,000)	–0–
Taxable income	$ –0–	$ –0–	$ 40,000	$100,000

The tax on the $40,000 project will equal the discounted value of the tax due in 2001. Assuming a 10% discount rate and a 15% corporate tax rate, the present value of taxes paid in three years is $4,508, and the discounted tax rate is 11.3%. Thus, the after-tax

---

[18] For simplification purposes, this example ignores the effect of an alternative income tax system known as the alternative minimum tax, which normally would generate some tax liability in an NOL carryover year.

CHAPTER 1 Introduction to Taxation

proceeds on the taxable project will be $35,492, or $508 *less* than the earnings on the tax-free project. ▼

Finally, the amount of tax paid should include both *explicit* taxes (paid directly to the government) and *implicit* taxes (paid through higher prices or lower returns on tax-favored investments).

EXAMPLE 26

Ellen, an individual taxpayer with a 15% marginal tax rate, has inherited $100,000 that she wants to invest in bonds. She has the option of investing in taxable corporate bonds that yield 9% or tax-free municipal bonds that yield 6%. Assume that the bonds are identical, except for their tax status.

Ellen's tax rate on the corporate bonds is explicit at 15%. The tax rate on the municipal bonds is implicit, evidenced by the lower return on the bonds. Since the bonds are identical, if the municipal bonds were taxable, they would yield a 9% pre-tax rate. Their after-tax rate is 6% because they are tax-free. Hence, the implicit tax rate on the municipal bonds equals 33%, or the tax rate that would generate a 6% after-tax return on a 9% bond [9% − (0.33 × 9%)].

Since Ellen is in a 15% tax bracket, she should invest in the taxable bond because she would face a higher marginal tax rate (a 33% implicit rate) if she invested in the municipal bond. Stated another way, Ellen's after-tax return on the taxable bond is greater than the 6% return available on the tax-free bond. ▼

In investment decisions, taxpayers minimize their tax burden by selecting the investment that has the lowest marginal tax rate. If Ellen had been in a 39.6 percent tax bracket, the explicit marginal rate on the taxable bonds would have been 39.6 percent, so she would have been better off selecting the municipal bonds (which have a 33 percent implicit marginal rate).

TAX MINIMIZATION STRATEGIES

Changing the Character of Income and Expense. One approach to minimizing tax costs is to change the character of income and expenses from tax-disfavored to tax-favored categories. For individual taxpayers, the tax treatment of long-term capital gains versus ordinary income provides one example. Long-term capital gains are subject to a top tax rate of 20 percent, while ordinary income is subject to a top tax rate of 39.6 percent for individuals.

EXAMPLE 27

Betty, who is in the 39.6% marginal income tax bracket, has held Elk Corporation stock for 11 months. Betty paid $10,000 for the stock, which is now worth $30,000. She wants to sell the stock to buy a new sailboat. If she sells the stock now, she will have a short-term capital gain of $20,000 ($30,000 selling price − $10,000 cost). Short-term capital gains are taxed as ordinary income, so Betty will pay tax of $7,920 ($20,000 ordinary income × 39.6%). If her holding period for the stock is *more than 18 months*, however, she will have a long-term capital gain and will pay tax of $4,000 ($20,000 long-term capital gain × 20%). Thus, Betty can save $3,920 ($7,920 − $4,000) in income tax if she holds the stock for seven more months before selling it. ▼

Similarly, dividends paid by one corporation to another receive preferential treatment through a dividend received deduction, as illustrated in the following example.

EXAMPLE 28

Pelican Corporation, which has a 35% marginal tax rate, is considering two potential investments for $200,000 using working capital that it will not need until its next busy season begins six months from now. Pelican is considering investing in corporate stock or corporate bonds. The stock investment will yield $8,000 of dividends during the six-month holding period, and the bond investment will yield $10,000 of interest. Both dividends and interest are includible in gross income. However, a corporation that owns less than 20% of the stock of another corporation is allowed a *dividends received deduction* equal to 70% of the amount earned.[19] Pelican's after-tax income with both investments is computed as follows:

	Stock	Bond
Income	$8,000	$10,000
− Dividends received deduction	5,600	−0−
= Taxable income	$2,400	$10,000
Income tax at 35%	$ 840	$ 3,500
Income	$8,000	$10,000
− Income tax	840	3,500
= After-tax income	$7,160	$ 6,500

In this situation, Pelican can generate greater pre-tax income by investing in the corporate bond, but will increase after-tax income by $660 ($7,160 − $6,500) by investing in the stock. Therefore, the stock investment leads to the best financial outcome (assuming risk is equal between the two alternatives). ▼

Many other situations present an opportunity for changing or choosing the character of income or deductions available to a taxpayer. For example, whether income is *earned* (salary, wages, commissions, etc.) or *unearned* (interest or dividends) can make a difference in computing taxable income. Also, whether a loss is an *active loss* or a *passive loss* can make a difference. These issues will be discussed in subsequent chapters.

Shifting Tax Liability across Time. Taxpayers are required to file annual tax returns. The IRS requires that both income and expenses be reported in the proper year. If not for this requirement, taxpayers could freely shift income and expenses from year to year and take advantage of tax rate differentials or could defer tax liabilities indefinitely.

EXAMPLE 29

Otter Company, a calendar year, cash basis proprietorship, mails payroll checks to its employees on the last day of each month. On December 31, 1998, Otter mailed a $2,000 payroll check to Kayna, an employee who is on the cash basis. The tax law regards payment as having been made when the check was mailed so Otter is allowed to deduct the salary payment in 1998. On the other hand, Kayna is not required to report the income until 1999, the year she received the payment. Otter would not have the option of deducting the payment in 1999, nor would Kayna have the option of reporting the income in 1998. ▼

Although rules limit the shifting of income and deductions across time periods, some opportunities still exist. Generally, time-shifting strategies call for income to be deferred or shifted from high-tax to low-tax years and deductions and credits to be accelerated or shifted from low-tax to high-tax years. The

---

[19] The dividends received deduction is discussed in greater detail in Chapter 9.

following examples illustrate the implementation of selected time-shifting strategies.

EXAMPLE 30

Egret Corporation is in the 34% bracket in 1998, but expects to be in the 25% bracket in 1999. The corporation, which is negotiating a $10,000 service contract with a client, decides to wait until 1999 to sign the contract and perform the services. The client is indifferent as to when the contract is completed. Thus, Egret saves $900 in income tax by deferring the service contract income to 1999, when it will be taxed at the 25% rate instead of the current 34% rate. This illustrates the use of the *income deferral strategy* to reduce taxes. ▼

EXAMPLE 31

Flamingo Corporation, a calendar year taxpayer, is in the 34% bracket in 1998, but expects to be in the 25% bracket in 1999. The corporation plans to make a $20,000 charitable contribution to State University in March 1999. Flamingo's tax adviser points out that the deduction will save $6,800 in income tax if made in 1998, but will save only $5,000 if made in 1999. The president of the corporation responds that the corporation will not have the funds to make the contribution until 1999. The tax adviser informs the president that there is a tax provision that will allow the corporation to deduct the charitable contribution in 1998 if the board of directors authorizes the contribution in 1998 and payment is made before March 15, 1999. Thus, Flamingo saves $1,800 in income tax [$20,000 deduction × (34% − 25%)] by *accelerating the deduction* into 1998, when the tax rate is 9% higher. ▼

The decision about whether to defer income from a low-tax to a high-tax year (or accelerate deductions or credits from a high-tax to a low-tax year) should rest on the trade-off between taxes saved and the time value of money. This is illustrated in the following example.

EXAMPLE 32

Refer to the facts in Example 30. If Egret faces a 15% cost of capital, then the choice for the company is between $6,600 after taxes in 1998 ($10,000 − $3,400 in taxes) versus the *present value* of $7,500 after taxes in 1999, or $6,521. With a 15% discount rate, Egret would be better off signing the contract and performing the services in 1998. ▼

Shifting Tax Liability between Entities.
Shifting income and deductions between entities can be a very effective tool in plans to minimize tax liability. Examples 16 and 18 earlier in the chapter illustrate the effective use of this approach.

The tax law introduces numerous restrictions that limit the number of entity-shifting possibilities available to taxpayers. For example, the law provides that income from property or services cannot be assigned. Thus, the son in Example 16 had to work for his wages; income from the sole proprietorship could not be shifted to him otherwise. Similarly, to shift income from property from one taxpayer to another, the property must also be transferred.

EXAMPLE 33

Jack and Jill, both age 24, are married and are graduate students at State University. Their income places them in the 15% income tax bracket, and they are struggling to make ends meet. Jill's parents, the Harts, are quite wealthy, and their high income places them in the 39.6% marginal income tax bracket. To help Jack and Jill meet their financial obligations, the Harts give them stock in the family corporation. The stock pays $5,000 per year in dividends. In addition, they give Jack and Jill bond coupons that are subsequently redeemed for interest of $3,600 during the year. The dividend income will be taxable to Jack and Jill, because the stock that generates the dividend income is owned by them. On the other hand, the interest income will be taxable to the Harts because they gave only the interest coupons (i.e., the right to receive income) and retained ownership of the bonds. Observe that shifting the dividend income to Jack and Jill saves the family unit $1,230 [$5,000 × (39.6% − 15%)]. ▼

Shifting Tax Liability across Jurisdictions. The state or country where income is earned (or where a deduction is incurred) can have a large impact on an entity's overall tax liability. Hence, shifting income from high-tax jurisdictions to low-tax jurisdictions or shifting deductions from low-tax jurisdictions to high-tax jurisdictions is an important tax planning strategy.

EXAMPLE 34

Gold International owns a sales subsidiary in Texas and a manufacturing subsidiary in Ireland (which imposes a 10% tax rate on income). The Irish subsidiary makes drill presses and sells them to the Texas subsidiary for $4,000,000, which then modifies them and offers them for sale to businesses in the United States for $8,400,000. The cost of manufacturing and modifying each drill press is $3,000,000. Of the $5,400,000 of profit earned, $1,000,000 is attributable to the Irish corporation (which is subject to a 10% tax rate), and $4,400,000 is attributable to the U.S. corporation (which is subject to a 34% tax rate). Gold will have a total tax liability of $1,596,000 [($1,000,000 × 10%) + ($4,400,000 × 34%)]. ▼

EXAMPLE 35

Assume the same facts as in the previous example, except $5,000,000 of the profit is attributable to the Irish corporation and $400,000 is attributable to the U.S. corporation. In this case, Gold's total tax liability will be $636,000 [($5,000,000 × 10%) + ($400,000 × 34%)]. Thus, by altering the amount of work done in each of the two subsidiaries and the amount of income generated by each, Gold's tax liability changed by $960,000 ($1,596,000 − $636,000). ▼

SUMMARY

Effective tax planning considers both the tax and the nontax aspects of a transaction. In addition, the tax consequences of a transaction on all parties should be explicitly considered. When evaluating tax consequences, the tax adviser should consider not only current explicit tax costs, but also implicit and future taxes that may arise as a result of a transaction. Tax minimization strategies include shifting income and deductions across time, between entities, and across jurisdictions in ways that reduce the tax cost of a transaction. Taxes can also be minimized by changing the character of income and deductions from tax-disfavored to tax-favored varieties.

UNDERSTANDING THE FEDERAL TAX LAW

7 LEARNING OBJECTIVE
Recognize the economic, social, equity, and political considerations that underlie the tax law.

The Federal tax law is a mosaic of statutory laws, administrative pronouncements, and court decisions. Anyone who has attempted to work with these provisions would have to admit to their complexity. For the person who has to trudge through a mass of rules to find the solution to a tax problem, it may be of some consolation to know that the law's complexity can generally be explained. Whether sound or not, there are reasons for the formulation of every rule. Knowing these reasons, therefore, is an important step toward understanding the Federal tax law.

The Federal tax law has as its major objective the raising of revenue. Other considerations also explain certain portions of the law. Economic, social, equity, and political factors play significant roles. In addition to these factors, the IRS and the courts have marked impacts on the evolution of Federal tax law. These matters are treated in the remainder of the chapter; wherever appropriate, the discussion is referenced to subjects covered later in the text.

REVENUE NEEDS

The foundation of the income tax system is the raising of revenue to cover the cost of government operations. Ideally, annual outlays should not exceed anticipated revenues, thereby leading to a balanced budget with no resulting deficit. Many states have achieved this objective by passing laws or constitutional amendments precluding deficit spending. Unfortunately, the Federal government has no such prohibition, and annual deficits have become an increasing concern for many. Recent legislation (enacted in 1997) was passed in an attempt to alleviate this problem.

In addition to making revenue neutral changes in the tax law, Congress uses several other approaches to reduce net revenue loss. When tax reductions are involved, the full impact of the legislation can be phased in over a period of years. Or, as an alternative, the tax reduction can be limited to a period of years. When the period expires, Congress can then renew or not renew the provision in light of budget considerations.[20]

ECONOMIC CONSIDERATIONS

Using the tax system in an effort to accomplish economic objectives has become increasingly popular in recent years. Generally, proponents of this approach use tax legislation to promote measures designed to help control the economy or encourage certain economic activities and businesses.

Encouragement of Certain Activities. Without passing judgment on the wisdom of any such choices, it is quite clear that the tax law does encourage certain types of economic activity or segments of the economy. For example, the favorable treatment allowed research and development expenditures can be explained by the desire to foster technological progress. Under the tax law, such expenditures can be either deducted in the year incurred or capitalized and amortized over a period of 60 months or more. In terms of the timing of the tax savings, these options usually are preferable to capitalizing the cost with a write-off over the estimated useful life of the asset created. If the asset developed has an indefinite useful life, no write-off would be available without the two options allowed by the tax law.

Similarly, Congress has used depreciation deductions as a means of encouraging investment in business capital. Theoretically, shorter asset lives and accelerated methods should encourage additional investment in depreciable property acquired for business use. Conversely, longer asset lives and the required use of the straight-line method of depreciation dampen the tax incentive for capital outlays.

Is it desirable to encourage the conservation of energy resources? Considering the world energy situation and our own reliance on foreign oil, the answer to this question has to be yes. The concern over energy usage was a prime consideration in the enactment of legislation to make various tax savings for energy conservation expenditures available to taxpayers.

Is preserving the environment a desirable objective? Ecological considerations explain why the tax law permits a 60-month amortization period for costs incurred in the installation of pollution control facilities.

---

[20]An example of a gradual phase-in is the increase in the unified transfer tax credit (discussed earlier in this chapter), which does not become fully implemented at $1 million until the year 2006. An example of a temporary tax reduction is the exclusion from gross income of employer-provided educational assistance benefits (see Chapter 16), which are scheduled to expire during the year 2000.

Is it wise to stimulate U.S. exports of goods and services? Considering the pressing and continuing problem of a deficit in the U.S. balance of payments, the answer should be clear. Along this line, Congress has created Foreign Sales Corporations (FSCs), which are designed to encourage domestic exports of goods. The FSC provisions exempt from tax a percentage of profits from export sales. Also in an international setting, Congress has deemed it advisable to establish incentives for U.S. citizens who accept employment overseas. Such persons receive generous tax breaks through special treatment of their foreign-source income and certain housing costs.

Is saving desirable for the economy? Saving leads to capital formation and thereby makes funds available to finance home construction and industrial expansion. The tax law encourages saving by according preferential treatment to private retirement plans. Not only are contributions to Keogh (H.R. 10) plans and certain Individual Retirement Accounts (IRAs) deductible, but income on the contributions is not taxed until withdrawn. As noted below, the encouragement of private-sector pension plans can also be justified under social considerations.

Encouragement of Certain Industries. No one can question the proposition that a sound agricultural base is necessary for a well-balanced national economy. Undoubtedly, this explains why farmers are accorded special treatment under the Federal tax system. Among the benefits available to farmers are the election to expense rather than capitalize certain soil and water conservation expenditures and fertilizers and the election to defer the recognition of gain on the receipt of crop insurance proceeds.

Encouragement of Small Business. At least in the United States, a consensus exists that what is good for small business is good for the economy as a whole. Whether valid or not, this assumption has led to a definite bias in the tax law favoring small business.

In the corporate tax area, several provisions can be explained by the desire to benefit small business. The S corporation provisions permit the shareholders of a small business corporation to make a special election that generally will avoid the imposition of the corporate income tax.[21] Furthermore, such an election enables the corporation to pass through its operating losses to its shareholders. Small businesses are also permitted to expense a portion of fixed assets placed in service each year.

SOCIAL CONSIDERATIONS

Some provisions of the Federal tax law, particularly those dealing with the income tax of individuals, can be explained by social considerations. Some notable examples and their rationales include the following:

- Certain benefits provided to employees through accident and health plans financed by employers are nontaxable to employees. Encouraging such plans is considered socially desirable since they provide medical benefits in the event of an employee's illness or injury.
- Premiums paid by an employer for up to $50,000 of group term insurance covering the life of the employee are nontaxable to the employee. These arrangements can be justified on social grounds in that the insurance provides funds for the family unit to help it adjust to the loss of wages caused by the employee's death.

---

[21] Known as the S election, it is discussed in Chapter 12.

- A contribution made by an employer to a qualified pension or profit sharing plan for an employee receives special treatment. The contribution and any income it generates are not taxed to the employee until the funds are distributed. Such an arrangement also benefits the employer by allowing a tax deduction when the contribution is made to the qualified plan. Private retirement plans are encouraged to supplement the subsistence income level the employee would otherwise have under the Social Security system.[22]
- A deduction is allowed for contributions to qualified charitable organizations.[23] The deduction attempts to shift some of the financial and administrative burden of socially desirable programs from the public (government) to the private (citizens) sector.
- Various tax credits, deductions, and exclusions that are designed to encourage taxpayers to obtain additional education are allowed.[24]
- A tax credit is allowed for amounts spent to furnish care for certain minor or disabled dependents to enable the taxpayer to seek or maintain gainful employment.[25] Who could deny the social desirability of encouraging taxpayers to provide care for their children while they work?
- A tax deduction is not allowed for certain expenditures deemed to be contrary to public policy. This disallowance extends to such items as fines, penalties, illegal kickbacks, bribes to government officials, and gambling losses in excess of gains. Social considerations dictate that the tax law should not encourage these activities by permitting a deduction.

Many other examples could be cited, but the conclusion would be unchanged. Social considerations explain a significant part of the structure of the Federal tax law.

EQUITY CONSIDERATIONS

The concept of equity is relative. Reasonable persons can, and often do, disagree about what is fair or unfair. In the tax area, moreover, equity is most often tied to a particular taxpayer's personal situation. To illustrate, compare the tax positions of those who rent their personal residences with those who own their homes. Renters may not take a Federal income tax deduction for the rent they pay. For homeowners, however, a large portion of the house payments they make may qualify for the Federal interest and property tax deductions. Although renters may have difficulty understanding this difference in tax treatment, the encouragement of home ownership can be justified on both economic and social grounds.

In many other parts of the law, however, equity concerns are evident. The concept of equity appears in tax provisions that alleviate the effect of multiple taxation and postpone the recognition of gain when the taxpayer lacks the ability or **wherewithal to pay** the tax. Provisions that mitigate the effect of the application of the annual accounting period concept and help taxpayers cope with the eroding results of inflation also reflect equity considerations.

Alleviating the Effect of Multiple Taxation.
The income earned by a taxpayer may be subject to taxes imposed by different taxing authorities. If, for example, the taxpayer is a resident of New York City, income might be subject to Federal, state of New York, and city of New York income taxes. To compensate for this

---

[22]The same rationale explains the availability of similar arrangements for self-employed persons (the H.R. 10, or Keogh, plan).

[23]The charitable contribution deduction is discussed in Chapters 9 and 15.

[24]These provisions can also be justified by economic considerations. No one can take issue with the conclusion that a better educated workforce carries a positive economic impact.

[25]See Chapter 15.

apparent inequity, the Federal tax law allows a taxpayer to claim a deduction for state and local income taxes. The deduction does not, however, neutralize the effect of multiple taxation, since the benefit derived depends on the taxpayer's Federal income tax rate. Only a tax credit, rather than a deduction, would completely eliminate the effects of multiple taxation on the same income.

Equity considerations can also explain the Federal tax treatment of certain income from foreign sources. Since double taxation results when the same income is subject to both foreign and U.S. income taxes, the tax law permits the taxpayer to choose between a credit and a deduction for the foreign taxes paid.

The Wherewithal to Pay Concept.
The wherewithal to pay concept recognizes the inequity of taxing a transaction when the taxpayer lacks the means to pay the tax. It is particularly suited to situations in which the taxpayer's economic position has not changed significantly as a result of the transaction.

The wherewithal to pay concept underlies a provision in the tax law dealing with the treatment of gain resulting from an involuntary conversion. An involuntary conversion occurs when property is destroyed by casualty or taken by a public authority through condemnation. If gain results from the conversion, it need not be recognized if the taxpayer replaces the property within a specified period of time. The replacement property must be similar or related in service or use to that involuntarily converted (see Chapter 7).

EXAMPLE 36   Ron, a rancher, has some pasture land that is condemned by the state for use as a game preserve. The condemned pasture land cost Ron $120,000, but the state pays him $150,000 (its fair market value). Shortly thereafter, Ron buys more pasture land for $150,000. ▼

In Example 36, Ron has realized gain of $30,000 [$150,000 (condemnation award) − $120,000 (cost of land)]. It would be inequitable to require Ron to pay a tax on this gain for two reasons. First, without disposing of the property acquired (the new land), Ron would be hard-pressed to pay the tax. Second, his economic position has not changed.

A warning is in order regarding the application of the wherewithal to pay concept. If the taxpayer's economic position changes in any way, tax consequences may result.

EXAMPLE 37   Assume the same facts as in Example 36, except that Ron reinvests only $140,000 of the award in new pasture land. Now, Ron has a taxable gain of $10,000. Instead of ending up with only replacement property, Ron now has $10,000 in cash. ▼

Mitigating the Effect of the Annual Accounting Period Concept.
For purposes of effective administration of the tax law, all taxpayers must report to and settle with the Federal government at periodic intervals. Otherwise, taxpayers would remain uncertain as to their tax liabilities, and the government would have difficulty judging revenues and budgeting expenditures. The period selected for final settlement of most tax liabilities is one year. At the close of each year, therefore, a taxpayer's position becomes complete for that particular year. Referred to as the annual accounting period concept, its effect is to divide each taxpayer's life, for tax purposes, into equal annual intervals.

The application of the annual accounting period concept can lead to dissimilar tax treatment for taxpayers who are, from a long-range standpoint, in the same economic position.

EXAMPLE 38

José and Alicia, both sole proprietors, have experienced the following results during the past three years:

	Profit (or Loss)	
Year	José	Alicia
1996	$50,000	$150,000
1997	60,000	60,000
1998	60,000	(40,000)

Although José and Alicia have the same profit of $170,000 over the period from 1996 through 1998, the annual accounting period concept places Alicia at a disadvantage for tax purposes. However, the net operating loss deduction generated in 1998 offers Alicia some relief by allowing her to carry back some or all of her 1998 loss to the earlier profitable years (in this case, 1996). Thus, with a net operating loss carryback, Alicia is in a position to obtain a refund for some of the taxes she paid on the $150,000 profit reported for 1996. ▼

The same reasoning used to support the deduction of net operating losses can explain the special treatment the tax law accords to excess capital losses and excess charitable contributions.[26] Carryback and carryover procedures help mitigate the effect of limiting a loss or a deduction in the accounting period in which it was incurred. With such procedures, a taxpayer may be able to salvage a loss or a deduction that might otherwise be wasted.

The installment method of recognizing gain on the sale of property allows a taxpayer to spread tax consequences over the payout period.[27] The harsh effect of taxing all the gain in the year of sale is thereby avoided. The installment method can also be explained by the wherewithal to pay concept since recognition of gain is tied to the collection of the installment notes received from the sale of the property. Tax consequences, then, tend to correspond to the seller's ability to pay the tax.

Coping with Inflation. Because of the progressive nature of the income tax, a wage adjustment to compensate for inflation can push the recipient into a higher income tax bracket without increasing real income. Known as bracket creep, this phenomenon's overall impact is an erosion of purchasing power. Congress recognized this problem and began to adjust various income tax components, such as marginal tax brackets, standard deduction amounts, and personal and dependency exemptions, through an indexation procedure. Indexation is based upon the rise in the consumer price index over the prior year.

POLITICAL CONSIDERATIONS

A large segment of the Federal tax law is made up of statutory provisions. Since these statutes are enacted by Congress, is it any surprise that political considerations influence tax law? For purposes of discussion, the effect of political considerations on the tax law is divided into the following topics: special interest legislation, political expediency, and state and local government influences.

---

[26] The tax treatment of these items is discussed in Chapters 4, 7, and 15.
[27] Under the installment method, each payment received by the seller represents both a recovery of capital (the nontaxable portion) and profit from the sale (the taxable portion). The tax rules governing the installment method are discussed in Chapter 6.

Special Interest Legislation. There is no doubt that certain provisions of the tax law can largely be explained by the political influence some groups have had on Congress. For example, is there any other realistic reason that prepaid subscription and dues income is not taxed until earned, while prepaid rents are taxed to the landlord in the year received?

A recent example of special interest legislation was a provision attached to the House of Representatives version of the Taxpayer Relief Act of 1997. The provision would have exempted "bakery drivers" from being classified as employees. Since the drivers would have become self-employed independent contractors, the baking companies would no longer have needed to cover them under Social Security, Medicare, and FUTA. The representative who originated the provision is from Nebraska and represents the district that is the home of Pepperidge Farm and Interstate Bakeries (maker of Wonder bread).

Special interest legislation is not necessarily to be condemned if it can be justified on economic, social, or some other utilitarian grounds. At any rate, it is an inevitable product of our political system.

Political Expediency. Various tax reform proposals rise and fall in favor with the shifting moods of the American public. That Congress is sensitive to popular feeling is an accepted fact. Therefore, certain provisions of the tax law can be explained by the political climate at the time they were enacted.

Measures that deter more affluent taxpayers from obtaining so-called preferential tax treatment have always had popular appeal and, consequently, the support of Congress. Provisions such as the alternative minimum tax, the imputed interest rules, and the limitation on the deductibility of interest on investment indebtedness can be explained on this basis.

Other changes explained at least partially by political expediency include the increase in the personal and dependency exemptions and the increase in the amount of the earned income credit. One of the expressed objectives of legislation enacted in 1993 was to increase taxes levied on wealthy individuals by instituting new 36 and 39.6 percent rates on higher-income individuals.

State and Local Government Influences. Political considerations have played a major role in the nontaxability of interest received on state and local obligations. In view of the furor that has been raised by state and local political figures every time any modification of this tax provision has been proposed, one might well regard it as next to sacred.

Somewhat less apparent has been the influence state law has had in shaping our present Federal tax law. One example of this effect is the evolution of Federal tax law in response to states with community property systems. The nine states with community property systems are Louisiana, Texas, New Mexico, Arizona, California, Washington, Idaho, Nevada, and Wisconsin. The rest of the states are classified as common law jurisdictions. The difference between common law and community property systems centers around the property rights possessed by married persons. In a common law system, each spouse owns whatever he or she earns. Under a community property system, one-half of the earnings of each spouse is considered owned by the other spouse.

EXAMPLE 39

Al and Fran are husband and wife, and their only income is the $60,000 annual salary Al receives. If they live in New Jersey (a common law state), the $60,000 salary belongs to Al. If, however, they live in Arizona (a community property state), the $60,000 is divided equally, in terms of ownership, between Al and Fran. ▼

CHAPTER 1 Introduction to Taxation

At one time, the tax position of the residents of community property states was so advantageous that many common law states actually adopted community property systems. Needless to say, the political pressure placed on Congress to correct the disparity in tax treatment was considerable. To a large extent this was accomplished in the Revenue Act of 1948, which extended many of the community property tax advantages to residents of common law jurisdictions.

The major advantage extended was the provision allowing married taxpayers to file joint returns and compute the tax liability as if the income had been earned one-half by each spouse. This result is automatic in a community property state, since half of the income earned by one spouse belongs to the other spouse. The income-splitting benefits of a joint return are now incorporated as part of the tax rates applicable to married taxpayers (see Chapter 15).

INFLUENCE OF THE INTERNAL REVENUE SERVICE

8 LEARNING OBJECTIVE
Describe the role played by the IRS and the courts in the evolution of the Federal tax system.

The influence of the IRS is apparent in many areas beyond its role in issuing the administrative pronouncements that make up a considerable portion of our tax law. In its capacity as the protector of the national revenue, the IRS has been instrumental in securing the passage of much legislation designed to curtail the most flagrant tax avoidance practices (to close tax loopholes). In its capacity as the administrator of the tax law, the IRS has also sought and obtained legislation to make its job easier (to attain administrative feasibility).

The IRS as Protector of the Revenue. Innumerable examples can be given of provisions in the tax law that stem from the direct influence of the IRS. Usually, such provisions are intended to prevent a loophole from being used to avoid the tax consequences intended by Congress. Working within the letter of existing law, ingenious taxpayers and their advisers devise techniques that accomplish indirectly what cannot be accomplished directly. As a consequence, legislation is enacted to close the loopholes that taxpayers have located and exploited. Some tax law can be explained in this fashion and is discussed in the chapters to follow.

In addition, the IRS has secured from Congress legislation of a more general nature that enables it to make adjustments based on the substance, rather than the formal construction, of what a taxpayer has done. One such provision permits the IRS to make adjustments to a taxpayer's method of accounting when the method used by the taxpayer does not clearly reflect income.

EXAMPLE 40
Tina owns a cash basis pharmacy. All drugs and other items acquired for resale (e.g., cosmetics) are charged to the purchases account and written off (expensed) for tax purposes in the year of acquisition. As this procedure does not clearly reflect income, it would be appropriate for the IRS to require that Tina establish and maintain an ending inventory account. ▼

Administrative Feasibility. Some of the tax law is justified on the grounds that it simplifies the task of the IRS in collecting the revenue and administering the law. With regard to collecting the revenue, the IRS long ago realized the importance of placing taxpayers on a pay-as-you-go basis. Elaborate withholding procedures apply to wages, while the tax on other types of income may be paid at periodic intervals throughout the year. The IRS has been instrumental in convincing the courts that accrual basis taxpayers should pay taxes on prepaid income in the year received and not when earned. The approach may be contrary to generally accepted accounting principles, but it is consistent with the wherewithal to pay concept.

Of considerable aid to the IRS in collecting revenue are the numerous provisions that impose interest and penalties on taxpayers for noncompliance with the tax law. Provisions such as the penalties for failure to pay a tax or to file a return that is due, the negligence penalty for intentional disregard of rules and regulations, and various penalties for civil and criminal fraud serve as deterrents to taxpayer noncompliance.

One of the keys to an effective administration of our tax system is the audit process conducted by the IRS. To carry out this function, the IRS is aided by provisions that reduce the chance of taxpayer error or manipulation and therefore reduce the audit effort that is necessary. An increase in the amount of the standard deduction, for example, reduces the number of individual taxpayers who will choose the alternative of itemizing their personal deductions.[28] With fewer deductions to check, the audit function is simplified.[29]

INFLUENCE OF THE COURTS

In addition to interpreting statutory provisions and the administrative pronouncements issued by the IRS, the Federal courts have influenced tax law in two other respects.[30] First, the courts have formulated certain judicial concepts that serve as guides in the application of various tax provisions. Second, certain key decisions have led to changes in the Internal Revenue Code.

Judicial Concepts Relating to Tax.
A leading tax concept developed by the courts deals with the interpretation of statutory tax provisions that operate to benefit taxpayers. The courts have established the rule that these relief provisions are to be narrowly construed against taxpayers if there is any doubt about their application.

EXAMPLE 41

When a taxpayer has a gain on an involuntary conversion, the gain is not subject to Federal income tax if the proceeds from the conversion are reinvested in qualified replacement property. The tax law specifies a period of time in which the reinvestment must take place. The courts have held that the nontaxability of gain is a relief provision to be narrowly construed. Thus, failure to meet the replacement period requirements, even if beyond the control of the taxpayer, will cause the gain to be taxed.[31]

Also important in this area is the *arm's length concept*. Particularly in dealings between related parties, transactions may be tested by looking to whether the taxpayers acted in an arm's length manner. The question to be asked is: Would unrelated parties have handled the transaction in the same way?

EXAMPLE 42

Rex, the sole shareholder of Silver Corporation, leases property to the corporation for a yearly rent of $6,000. To test whether the corporation should be allowed a rent deduction for this amount, the IRS and the courts will apply the arm's length concept. Would Silver Corporation have paid $6,000 a year in rent if it had leased the same property from an unrelated party (rather than from Rex)? Suppose it is determined that an unrelated third party would have paid an annual rent for the property of only $5,000. Under these circumstances, Silver Corporation will be allowed a deduction of only $5,000.

---

[28]For a detailed discussion of the standard deduction, see Chapter 15.

[29]The same justification was given by the IRS when it proposed to Congress the $100 limitation on personal casualty and theft losses. Imposition of the limitation eliminated many casualty and theft loss deductions and, as a consequence, saved the IRS considerable audit time. Later legislation, in addition to retaining the $100 feature, limits deductible losses to those in excess of 10% of a taxpayer's adjusted gross income. See Chapter 5.

[30]A great deal of case law is devoted to ascertaining congressional intent. The courts, in effect, ask: What did Congress have in mind when it enacted a particular tax provision?

[31]These rules are discussed further in Chapter 7.

The other $1,000 it paid for the use of the property represents a nondeductible dividend. Accordingly, Rex will be treated as having received rent income of $5,000 and dividend income of $1,000. ▼

Judicial Influence on Statutory Provisions. Some court decisions have been of such consequence that Congress has incorporated them into statutory tax law. For example, many years ago the courts found that stock dividends distributed to the shareholders of a corporation were not taxable as income. This result was largely accepted by Congress, and a provision in the tax statutes now covers the issue.

On occasion, however, Congress has reacted negatively to judicial interpretations of the tax law.

▼
EXAMPLE 43

Nora leases unimproved real estate to Wade for 40 years. At a cost of $200,000, Wade erects a building on the land. The building is worth $100,000 when the lease terminates and Nora takes possession of the property. Does Nora have any income either when the improvements are made or when the lease terminates? In a landmark decision, a court held that Nora must recognize income of $100,000 upon the termination of the lease. ▼

Congress felt that the result reached in Example 43 was inequitable in that it was not consistent with the wherewithal to pay concept. Consequently, the tax law was amended to provide that a landlord does not recognize any income either when the improvements are made (unless made in lieu of rent) or when the lease terminates.

SUMMARY

In addition to its necessary revenue-raising objective, the Federal tax law has developed in response to several other factors:

- *Economic considerations*. The emphasis here is on tax provisions that help regulate the economy and encourage certain activities and types of businesses.
- *Social considerations*. Some tax provisions are designed to encourage (or discourage) socially desirable (or undesirable) practices.
- *Equity considerations*. Of principal concern in this area are tax provisions that alleviate the effect of multiple taxation, recognize the wherewithal to pay concept, mitigate the effect of the annual accounting period concept, and recognize the eroding effect of inflation.
- *Political considerations*. Of significance in this regard are tax provisions that represent special interest legislation, reflect political expediency, and reflect the effect of state and local law.
- *Influence of the IRS*. Many tax provisions are intended to aid the IRS in the collection of revenue and the administration of the tax law.
- *Influence of the courts*. Court decisions have established a body of judicial concepts relating to tax law and have, on occasion, led Congress to enact statutory provisions to either clarify or negate their effect.

These factors explain the rationale underlying many tax provisions and thereby help in understanding how the tax law developed to its present state. Another important step involves learning to work with the tax law, which is the subject of Chapter 2.

KEY TERMS

Ad valorem tax, 1–10
C corporation, 1–18
Casualty loss, 1–8
Death tax, 1–8
Employment tax, 1–3
Equilibrium tax planning, 1–20
Estate tax, 1–8
Excise tax, 1–4
FICA tax, 1–6
Franchise tax, 1–13
FUTA tax, 1–6
Gift tax, 1–3
Implicit tax, 1–6
Inheritance tax, 1–8
Occupational tax, 1–13
Personalty, 1–11
Proprietorship, 1–17
Realty, 1–11
S corporation, 1–18
Sales tax, 1–3
Tax avoidance, 1–20
Tax evasion, 1–20
Use tax, 1–5
Value added tax (VAT), 1–6
Wherewithal to pay, 1–29

PROBLEM MATERIALS

1. Aqua Corporation believes that it will have a better distribution location for its product if it relocates the corporation to another state. What considerations (both tax and nontax) should Aqua Corporation weigh before making a decision on whether to make the move?

2. Before passage of the Sixteenth Amendment to the U.S. Constitution, there was no income tax in the United States. Please comment.

3. Did the passage of the Sixteenth Amendment to the U.S. Constitution have any effect on the income tax imposed on corporations? Explain.

4. Jim, a resident of Washington (which imposes a general sales tax), goes to Oregon (which does not impose a general sales tax) to purchase his automobile. Will Jim successfully avoid the Washington sales tax? Explain.

5. Explain the difference between an inheritance tax and an estate tax.

6. In 1998, Horace makes a taxable gift of $250,000 upon which he pays a Federal gift tax of $70,800. In 1999, Horace makes another taxable gift of $250,000. Will the 1999 taxable gift result in the same gift tax as the 1998 gift? Why or why not?

7. How much property can Herman, a widower, give to his four married children, their spouses, and eight grandchildren over a period of 10 years without making a taxable gift?

8. When married persons elect to split a gift, what tax advantages do they enjoy?

9. The Toth family lives in a residence that they have owned for several years. They purchased the residence from St. Matthew's Catholic Church, which had used the house as a rectory for its priest. To the Toths' surprise, since they purchased the residence, they have not received any ad valorem property tax bills from either the city or the county. Is there a plausible explanation for this? Explain. What, if anything, should the Toths do about the property tax matter?

10. When Gull Company constructs a climate-controlled warehouse, it is very careful to keep as many of the components as portable as possible. Thus, the sprinkler system is detachable, window units provide air conditioning and heating, and the interior walls can be removed. What is Gull trying to accomplish?

11. John, a nationally known vocalist, lives in Nevada. John's agent has been trying to convince him to go on tour to increase his record sales. John, however, refuses to perform anywhere but in Las Vegas clubs. What might explain John's attitude?

12. Is the Medicare component of FICA a proportional or a progressive tax? Explain.

13. Dan, the owner and operator of a construction company that builds outdoor swimming pools, releases most of his construction personnel during the winter months. Should this hurt Dan's FUTA situation? Why or why not?

14. Compare FICA and FUTA in connection with each of the following:
    a. Incidence of taxation.
    b. Justification for taxation.
    c. Rates and base involved.

15. What is a "flat tax"? What is its major advantage?

16. Indicate the major differences between the Federal income tax applicable to individuals and the Federal income tax applicable to corporations.

17. Jill is a single individual. In 1998, she has total income of $150,000, credits of $20,000, exclusions of $30,000, deductions for AGI of $50,000, itemized deductions of $20,000 (assume no AGI limitations are applicable), a standard deduction of $4,150, a personal exemption equal to $2,650, and estimated payments of $3,000.
    a. What is her tax due?
    b. If Jill were a corporation instead of an individual, and if all of her deductions were business related, what would be the tax due?

18. Cory and Cynthia have decided to go into business together. They will operate a sandwich delivery business. They expect to have a loss in the first and second years of the business and subsequently expect to make a substantial profit. Both are also concerned about potential liability if a customer ever gets sick. They have called your office and asked for advice about whether they should run their business as a partnership or as a corporation. Write a letter to Cynthia Clay, at 1206 Seventh Avenue, Fort Worth, TX 76101, describing the alternative forms of business that they can select. In your letter, explain what form or forms of business you recommend and why.

19. Ashley runs a small business in Boulder, Colorado, that makes snow skis. She expects the business to grow substantially over the next three years. Because she is concerned about product liability and is planning to take the company public in the year 2000, she is currently considering incorporating the business. Financial data are as follows:

	1998	1999	2000
Sales revenue	$150,000	$320,000	$600,000
Tax-free interest income	5,000	8,000	15,000
Deductible cash expenses	30,000	58,000	95,000
Tax depreciation	25,000	20,000	40,000

    Ashley expects her marginal tax rate to be 39.6% over the next three years before any profits from the business are considered. Her cost of capital is 10%.
    a. Compute the present value of the future cash flows for 1998 to 2000, assuming Ashley incorporates the business and pays all after-tax income as dividends.
    b. Compute the present value of the future cash flows for 1998 to 2000, assuming Ashley continues to operate the business as a sole proprietorship.
    c. Should Ashley incorporate the business this year? Why or why not?

20. Sienna, Inc., faces a marginal tax rate of 25%, an average tax rate of 17.5%, and an effective marginal tax rate of 16.8%. Sienna is considering investing in Kiowa County bonds, which currently pay a 5% return (equivalent taxable bonds are paying an 8% return).
    a. What is the implicit tax rate on the Kiowa County bonds?
    b. Are the Kiowa County bonds a good investment for Sienna? Why or why not?

21. Chartreuse, Inc., has a net operating loss carryforward of $100,000. If Chartreuse continues its business with no changes, it will have $50,000 of taxable income (before

the NOL) in both 1998 and 1999. If Chartreuse decides to invest in a new product line instead, it expects to have taxable income of $70,000 in 1998 and $50,000 in 1999. What marginal tax rate does the new product line face in 1998?

22. Mauve Supplies, Inc., reports total income of $120,000 in 1998. The corporation's taxable income is $105,000. What are Mauve's marginal, average, and effective tax rates?

23. How does the tax law foster technological progress?

24. Discuss the probable justification for the following provisions of the tax law:
    a. The election permitting certain corporations to avoid the corporate income tax.
    b. A provision that excludes from gross income certain benefits furnished to employees through accident and health plans financed by employers.
    c. Nontaxable treatment for an employee for premiums paid by an employer for group term insurance covering the life of the employee.

25. The tax law encourages private retirement plans and contributions to charitable organizations. In terms of nonrevenue objectives, what is the common justification for these special tax treatments?

26. What purpose is served by allowing individuals to deduct home mortgage interest and property taxes?

27. In what manner does the tax law mitigate the effect of the annual accounting period concept for a net operating loss?

28. How does the tax law cope with the impact of inflation?

CHAPTER 2

WORKING WITH THE TAX LAW

LEARNING OBJECTIVES

After completing Chapter 2, you should be able to:

1. Understand the statutory, administrative, and judicial sources of the tax law and the purpose of each source.

2. Locate and work with the tax law and understand the tax research process.

3. Communicate the results of the tax research process in a client letter and a tax file memorandum.

4. Have an awareness of computer-assisted tax research.

OUTLINE

Tax Sources, 2–2

Statutory Sources of the Tax Law, 2–3

Administrative Sources of the Tax Law, 2–7

Judicial Sources of the Tax Law, 2–12

Working with the Tax Law—Tax Research, 2–20

Identifying the Problem, 2–20

Refining the Problem, 2–20

Locating the Appropriate Tax Law Sources, 2–21

Assessing Tax Law Sources, 2–23

Arriving at the Solution or at Alternative Solutions, 2–27

Communicating Tax Research, 2–27

Follow-up Procedures, 2–28

Computer-Assisted Tax Research, 2–28

TAX SOURCES

1 LEARNING OBJECTIVE
Understand the statutory, administrative, and judicial sources of the tax law and the purpose of each source.

Understanding taxation requires a mastery of the sources of the *rules of tax law*. These sources include not only legislative provisions in the form of the Internal Revenue Code, but also congressional Committee Reports, Treasury Department Regulations, other Treasury Department pronouncements, and court decisions. Thus, the *primary sources* of tax information include pronouncements from all three branches of government: legislative, executive, and judicial.

In addition to being able to locate and interpret the sources of the tax law, a tax professional must understand the relative weight of authority within these sources. The tax law is of little significance, however, until it is applied to a set of facts and circumstances. This chapter, therefore, both introduces the statutory, administrative, and judicial sources of the tax law *and* explains how the law is applied to individual and business transactions. It also explains how to apply research techniques effectively.

Tax research is necessary because the application of the law to a specific situation is often not clear. As complicated as the Internal Revenue Code is, it cannot clearly address every conceivable situation. Accordingly, the tax professional must search other sources (such as administrative rulings and judicial decisions) to determine the most likely tax treatment of a transaction.

Often, this search process will yield widely differing results for similar fact patterns. One of the goals of tax research is to discover which facts and which legal rules are most relevant in determining the ultimate tax consequences. Working with such knowledge, a tax professional can then advise the client about the tax consequences of several possible courses of action. Tax research, in other words, is of critical importance not only in properly characterizing completed events but also in planning proposed transactions.

As noted in Chapter 1, the tax tail should never wag the economic dog; that is, the importance of tax considerations should not be overstated. A client's objective is to maximize after-tax returns, and nontax factors (together with the tax consequences to other parties in the transaction) must also be considered. To take the simplest case, a taxpayer subject to a high tax rate on a planned transaction is still better off than the taxpayer who forgoes all economic opportunities completely. Tax planning seeks to minimize the tax consequences of a transaction, to be sure, but not at the cost of the client's general and economic well-being.

> ## TAX IN THE NEWS
>
> ### SMALL IS BEAUTIFUL?
>
> In income tax history, 1913 was an important year. In that year, the Sixteenth Amendment to the Constitution was ratified. It stated:
>
>> The Congress shall have power to tax and collect taxes on incomes, from whatever source derived, without apportionment among the several States, and without regard to any census or enumeration.
>
> The first income tax legislation that definitely was constitutional was passed that same year.
>
> Since 1913, Congress has enacted hundreds of tax bills. The *Internal Revenue Code* is now more than 2,200 pages in length. Of course, this seems short when compared to a tax service such as CCH's *Standard Federal Tax Reporter* or RIA's *United States Tax Reporter*, which fill up library shelves. As an example of how the size and complexity of the income tax have changed, consider that when CCH's first tax guide was published in 1913, it was only 400 pages long.

STATUTORY SOURCES OF THE TAX LAW

Origin of the Internal Revenue Code. Before 1939, the statutory provisions relating to taxation were contained in the individual revenue acts enacted by Congress. The inconvenience and confusion that resulted from dealing with many separate acts led Congress to codify all of the Federal tax laws. Known as the Internal Revenue Code of 1939, this codification arranged all Federal tax provisions in a logical sequence and placed them in a separate part of the Federal statutes. A further rearrangement took place in 1954 and resulted in the Internal Revenue Code of 1954, which continued in effect until it was replaced by the Internal Revenue Code of 1986.

The following observations help clarify the codification procedure:

- Neither the 1939, the 1954, nor the 1986 Code changed all of the tax law existing on the date of enactment. Much of the 1939 Code, for example, was incorporated into the 1954 Code. The same can be said for the transition from the 1954 to the 1986 Code.[1] This point is important in assessing judicial and administrative decisions interpreting provisions under prior codes. For example, a decision interpreting § 703 of the Internal Revenue Code of 1954 has continuing validity since this provision carried over unchanged to the Internal Revenue Code of 1986.
- Statutory amendments to the tax law are integrated into the existing Code. Thus, subsequent tax legislation, such as the Taxpayer Relief Act of 1997, has become part of the Internal Revenue Code of 1986. In view of the frequency with which tax legislation has been enacted in recent years, it appears that the tax law will continue to be amended frequently.

The Legislative Process. Federal tax legislation generally originates in the House of Representatives, where it is first considered by the House Ways and Means Committee. Tax bills can originate in the Senate if they are attached as riders to other legislative proposals. If acceptable to the committee, the proposed bill is

---

[1] Aside from changes due to a large tax act, the organization of the Internal Revenue Code of 1986 is not substantively different from the organization of the 1954 Code. In contrast, the numbering scheme of sections in the 1939 Code differs from that used in the 1954 Code.

referred to the entire House of Representatives for approval or disapproval. Approved bills are sent to the Senate, where they initially are considered by the Senate Finance Committee.

The next step is referral from the Senate Finance Committee to the entire Senate. Assuming no disagreement between the House and Senate, passage by the Senate means referral to the President for approval or veto. If the bill is approved or if the President's veto is overridden, the bill becomes law and part of the Internal Revenue Code of 1986.

When the Senate version of the bill differs from that passed by the House, the Conference Committee, which includes members of both the House Ways and Means Committee and the Senate Finance Committee, is called upon to resolve the differences. House and Senate versions of major tax bills frequently differ. One reason bills are often changed in the Senate is that each senator has considerable latitude to make amendments when the Senate as a whole is voting on a bill referred to it by the Senate Finance Committee. In contrast, the entire House of Representatives either accepts or rejects what is proposed by the House Ways and Means Committee, and changes from the floor are rare. The deliberations of the Conference Committee usually produce a compromise between the two versions, which is then voted on by both the House and the Senate. If both bodies accept the revised bill, it is referred to the President for approval or veto. The typical legislative process dealing with tax bills is summarized in Figure 2–1.

Referrals from the House Ways and Means Committee, the Senate Finance Committee, and the Conference Committee are usually accompanied by *Committee Reports*. These Committee Reports often explain the provisions of the proposed legislation and are therefore a valuable source for ascertaining the *intent of Congress*. What Congress had in mind when it considered and enacted tax legislation is the key to interpreting legislation. Since Regulations interpreting new legislation normally are not issued immediately after a statute is enacted, taxpayers and the courts look to Committee Reports to determine congressional intent.

The role of the Conference Committee indicates the importance of compromise in the legislative process. As an example of the practical effect of the compromise process, consider what happened to a provision allowing the amortization of certain intangible assets in the Revenue Reconciliation Act of 1993 (see Figure 2–2).

Arrangement of the Code. The Internal Revenue Code of 1986 is found in Title 26 of the U.S. Code. In working with the Code, it helps to understand the format. Note the following partial table of contents:

Subtitle A. Income Taxes
    Chapter 1. Normal Taxes and Surtaxes
        Subchapter A. Determination of Tax Liability
            Part I. Tax on Individuals
                Sections 1–5
            Part II. Tax on Corporations
                Sections 11–12

* * *

In referring to a provision of the Code, the key is usually the Section number. In citing Section 2(a) (dealing with the status of a surviving spouse), for example, it is unnecessary to include Subtitle A, Chapter 1, Subchapter A, Part I. Merely mentioning Section 2(a) will suffice, since the Section numbers run consecutively and do not begin again with each new Subtitle, Chapter, Subchapter, or Part. Not all Code Section numbers are used, however. Note that Part I ends with Section 5

CHAPTER 2 Working with the Tax Law

▼ **FIGURE 2-1**
Legislative Process for Tax Bills

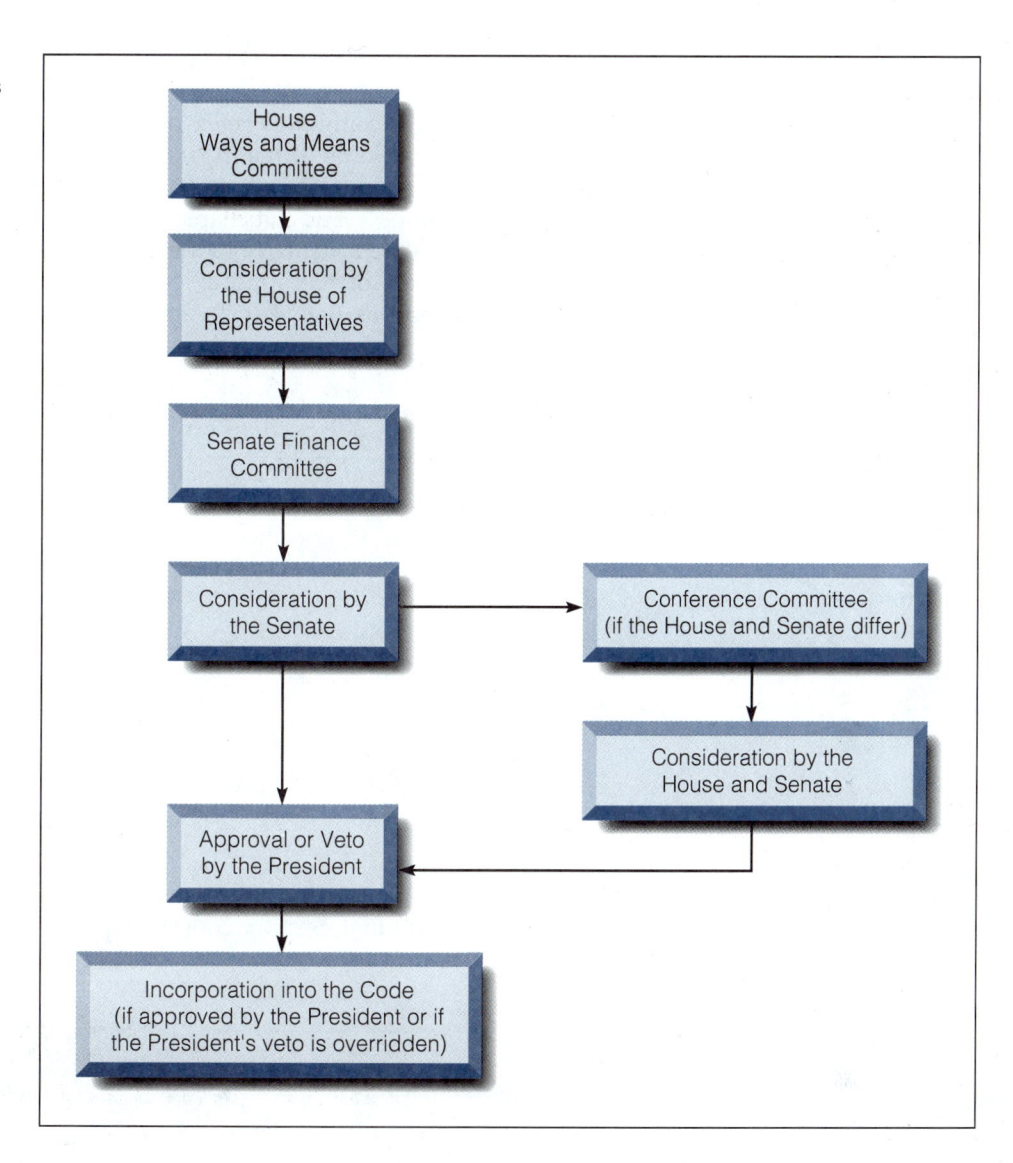

- House Ways and Means Committee
- ↓
- Consideration by the House of Representatives
- ↓
- Senate Finance Committee
- ↓
- Consideration by the Senate → Conference Committee (if the House and Senate differ)
- ↓ ↓
- Approval or Veto by the President ← Consideration by the House and Senate
- ↓
- Incorporation into the Code (if approved by the President or if the President's veto is overridden)

▼ **FIGURE 2-2**
Example of Compromise in the Conference Committee

- **House Version**: Amortization of goodwill and other intangible assets over 14 years
- **Senate Version**: Amortization of only 75% of goodwill and other intangible assets over 14 years
- **Conference Committee Result**: Straight-line amortization of goodwill and other intangible assets over 15 years

and Part II starts with Section 11 (at present there are no Sections 6, 7, 8, 9, and 10).[2]

Tax practitioners commonly refer to a specific area of income tax law by Subchapter designation. Some of the more common Subchapter designations include Subchapter C ("Corporate Distributions and Adjustments"), Subchapter K ("Partners and Partnerships"), and Subchapter S ("Tax Treatment of S Corporations and Their Shareholders"). Particularly in the last situation, it is much more convenient to describe the effect of the applicable Code provisions (Sections 1361–1379) as "Subchapter S" than as the "Tax Treatment of S Corporations and Their Shareholders."

Citing the Code. Code Sections are often broken down into subparts.[3] Section 2(a)(1)(A) serves as an example.

§ 2 (a) (1) (A)
- Abbreviation for "Section"
- Section number
- Subsection designation[4]
- Paragraph designation
- Subparagraph designation

Broken down by content, Section 2(a)(1)(A) appears as follows:

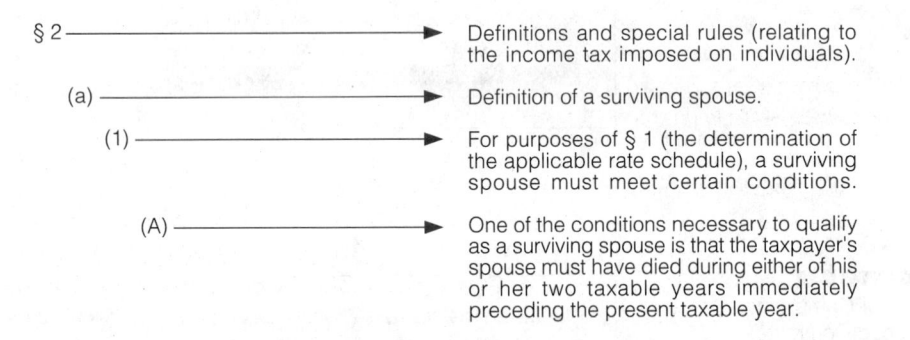

§ 2 → Definitions and special rules (relating to the income tax imposed on individuals).

(a) → Definition of a surviving spouse.

(1) → For purposes of § 1 (the determination of the applicable rate schedule), a surviving spouse must meet certain conditions.

(A) → One of the conditions necessary to qualify as a surviving spouse is that the taxpayer's spouse must have died during either of his or her two taxable years immediately preceding the present taxable year.

Throughout the text, references to the Code Sections are in the form given above. The symbols "§" and "§§" are used in place of "Section" and "Sections." Unless otherwise stated, all Code references are to the Internal Revenue Code of 1986. The following table summarizes the format used in the text:

---

[2] When the Code was drafted, Section numbers were intentionally omitted so that later changes could be incorporated into the Code without disrupting its organization. When Congress does not leave enough space, subsequent Code Sections are given A, B, C, etc., designations. A good example is the treatment of Sections 280A through 280H.

[3] Some Code Sections do not have subparts. See, for example, Sections 211 and 241.

[4] Some Code Sections omit the subsection designation and use, instead, the paragraph designation as the first subpart. See, for example, Sections 212(1) and 1221(1).

Complete Reference	Text Reference
Section 2(a)(1)(A) of the Internal Revenue Code of 1986	§ 2(a)(1)(A)
Sections 1 and 2 of the Internal Revenue Code of 1986	§§ 1 and 2
Section 2 of the Internal Revenue Code of 1954	§ 2 of the internal revenue Code of 1954
Section 12(d) of the Internal Revenue Code of 1939[5]	§ 12(d) of the internal Revenue Code of 1939

Effect of Treaties. The United States signs certain tax treaties (sometimes called tax conventions) with foreign countries to render mutual assistance in tax enforcement and to avoid double taxation. These treaties affect transactions involving U.S. persons and entities operating or investing in a foreign country, as well as persons and entities of a foreign country operating or investing in the United States. Although these bilateral agreements are not codified in any one source, they are published in various Internal Revenue Service publications as well as in privately published tax services.

Neither a tax law nor a tax treaty automatically takes precedence. When there is a direct conflict, the most recent item will take precedence. With certain exceptions, a taxpayer must disclose on the tax return any position where a treaty overrides a tax law.[6] There is a $1,000 per *failure to disclose* penalty for individuals and a $10,000 per failure to disclose penalty for corporations.[7]

ADMINISTRATIVE SOURCES OF THE TAX LAW

The administrative sources of the Federal tax law can be grouped as follows: Treasury Department Regulations, Revenue Rulings and Revenue Procedures, and various other administrative pronouncements (see Exhibit 2–1). All are issued by either the U.S. Treasury Department or the IRS.

Treasury Department Regulations. Regulations are issued by the U.S. Treasury Department under authority granted by Congress.[8] Usually interpretive by nature, they provide taxpayers with considerable guidance on the meaning and application of the Code and often include examples. Regulations carry considerable authority as the official interpretation of tax statutes. They are an important factor to consider in complying with the tax law.

Treasury Regulations are arranged in the same sequence as the Code. A number is added at the beginning, however, to indicate the type of tax or other matter to which they relate. For example, the prefix 1 designates the Regulations under the income tax law. Thus, the Regulations under Code § 2 would be cited as Reg. § 1.2, with subparts added for further identification. The numbering pattern of these subparts often has no correlation with the Code subsections. The prefix 20 designates estate tax Regulations, 25 covers gift tax Regulations, 31 relates to employment taxes, and 301 refers to procedure and administration. This list is not all-inclusive. Reg. § 1.351–1(a)(2) serves as an example of a citation:

---

[5]Section 12(d) of the Internal Revenue Code of 1939 is the predecessor to § 2 of the Internal Revenue Codes of 1954 and 1986.
[6]§ 7852(d).
[7]Reg. §§ 301.6114–1 and 301.6712–1.
[8]§ 7805.

▼ EXHIBIT 2–1
Administrative Sources

Source	Location	Authority†
Regulations	*Federal Register** *Internal Revenue Bulletin* *Cumulative Bulletin*	Force and effect of law. May be cited as a precedent.
Temporary Regulations	*Federal Register** *Internal Revenue Bulletin* *Cumulative Bulletin*	May be cited as a precedent.
Proposed Regulations	*Federal Register** *Internal Revenue Bulletin* *Cumulative Bulletin*	Preview of final Regulations. Not precedent.
Revenue Rulings Revenue Procedures Action on Decision	*Internal Revenue Bulletin*** *Cumulative Bulletin*	Do not have the force and effect of law. Not precedent.
General Counsel Memoranda Technical Advice Memoranda	Tax Analysts' *Tax Notes*; RIA's *Internal Memoranda of the IRS*; CCH's *IRS Position Reporter*	May not be cited as a precedent.
Letter Rulings	Research Institute of America and Commerce Clearing House loose-leaf services**	Applicable only to taxpayer addressed. Not precedent.

*Final, Temporary, and Proposed Regulations are published in soft-cover form and on CD-ROM by several publishers (including *RIA OnPoint*).

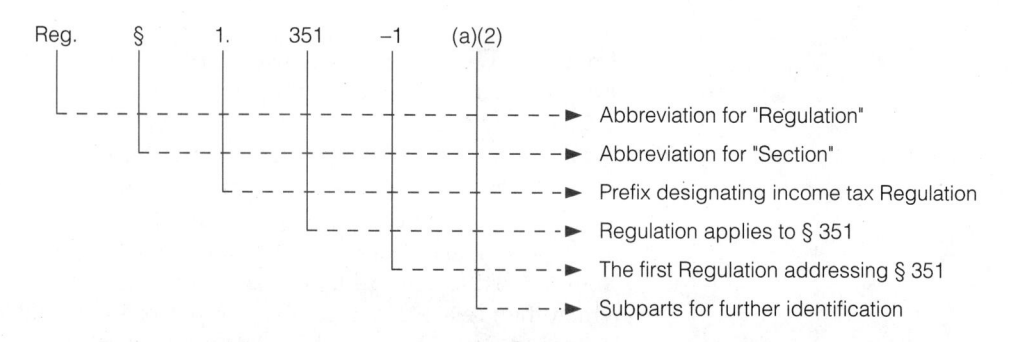

**Revenue Rulings, Revenue Procedures, and letter rulings are also published on CD-ROM by several publishers (including *RIA OnPoint*).

†Each of these sources may be substantial authority for purposes of the accuracy-related penalty in § 6662. notice 90–20, 1990–1 C.B. 328.

```
Reg.    §    1.    351    -1    (a)(2)
  |     |    |      |     |      |
  |     |    |      |     |      └──▶ Subparts for further identification
  |     |    |      |     └─────────▶ The first Regulation addressing § 351
  |     |    |      └───────────────▶ Regulation applies to § 351
  |     |    └──────────────────────▶ Prefix designating income tax Regulation
  |     └───────────────────────────▶ Abbreviation for "Section"
  └─────────────────────────────────▶ Abbreviation for "Regulation"
```

New Regulations and changes in existing Regulations are usually issued in proposed form before they are finalized. The interval between the proposal of a Regulation and its finalization permits taxpayers and other interested parties to comment on the propriety of the proposal. These comments are usually provided in writing, but oral comments can be offered at hearings held by the IRS on the Regulations in question pursuant to a public notice. This practice of notice-and-comment is a major distinction between Regulations and other forms of Treasury guidance such as Revenue Rulings, Revenue Procedures, and the like.

Proposed Regulations under Code § 2, for example, are cited as Prop.Reg. § 1.2. The Tax Court indicates that Proposed Regulations carry little weight—no more than a position advanced in a written brief prepared by a litigating party before the Tax Court.⁹

Sometimes the Treasury Department issues **Temporary Regulations** relating to matters where immediate guidance is important. These Regulations are issued without the comment period required for Proposed Regulations. Temporary Regulations have the same authoritative value as final Regulations and may be cited as precedents. Since 1989, Temporary Regulations must also be issued as Proposed Regulations and automatically expire within three years after the date of their issuance.¹⁰

Proposed, Temporary, and **Final Regulations** are published in the *Federal Register*, the *Internal Revenue Bulletin*, and major tax services.

Regulations may also be classified as *legislative, interpretive,* or *procedural*. This classification scheme is discussed later in the chapter.

Revenue Rulings and Revenue Procedures. **Revenue Rulings** are official pronouncements of the National Office of the IRS.¹¹ Like Regulations, they are designed to provide interpretation of the tax law. However, they do not carry the same legal force and effect as Regulations and usually deal with more restricted problems. In addition, Regulations are approved by the Secretary of the Treasury, whereas Revenue Rulings generally are not. Both Revenue Rulings and Revenue Procedures serve an important function in providing *guidance* to IRS personnel and taxpayers in handling routine tax matters. Revenue Rulings and Revenue Procedures generally apply retroactively and may be revoked or modified by subsequent rulings or procedures, Regulations, legislation, or court decisions.

Revenue Rulings typically provide one or more examples of how the IRS would apply a law to specific fact situations. Revenue Rulings may arise from technical advice to District Offices of the IRS, court decisions, suggestions from tax practitioner groups, and various tax publications. A Revenue Ruling may also arise from a specific taxpayer's request for a letter ruling. If the IRS believes that a taxpayer's request for a letter ruling deserves official publication due to its widespread impact, the letter ruling will be converted into a Revenue Ruling and issued for the information and guidance of taxpayers, tax practitioners, and IRS personnel. Names, identifying descriptions, and money amounts are changed to conceal the identity of the requesting taxpayer.

Revenue Procedures are issued in the same manner as Revenue Rulings, but deal with the internal management practices and procedures of the IRS. Familiarity with these procedures increases taxpayer compliance and helps make the administration of the tax laws more efficient. The failure of a taxpayer to follow a Revenue Procedure can result in unnecessary delay or, in a discretionary situation, can cause the IRS to decline to act on behalf of the taxpayer. Some recent Revenue Procedures:

- Announced deduction limits for cars placed in service during the year.
- Specified the procedures for requesting consent to changes in accounting methods.
- Provided a safe harbor that may be used to determine a majority of interest for a limited partnership.

Revenue Rulings and Revenue Procedures are published weekly by the U.S. Government in the *Internal Revenue Bulletin* (I.R.B.). Semiannually, the *Bulletins* for

---

⁹*F. W. Woolworth Co.*, 54 T.C. 1233 (1970); *Harris M. Miller*, 70 T.C. 448 (1978); and *James O. Tomerlin Trust*, 87 T.C. 876 (1986).

¹⁰§ 7805(e).
¹¹§ 7805(a).

a six-month period are gathered together, reorganized by Code Section classification, and published in a bound volume called the *Cumulative Bulletin* (C.B.).[12]

The proper form for citing Rulings and Procedures depends on whether the item has been published in the *Cumulative Bulletin* or is available only in I.R.B. form. Consider, for example, the following transition:

Temporary Citation { Rev.Rul. 96–48, I.R.B. No. 40, 4.
Explanation: Revenue Ruling Number 48, appearing on page 4 of the 40th weekly issue of the *Internal Revenue Bulletin* for 1996.

Permanent Citation { Rev.Rul. 96–48, 1996–2 C.B. 31.
Explanation: Revenue Ruling Number 48, appearing on page 31 of Volume 2 of the *Cumulative Bulletin* for 1996.

Since the second volume of the 1996 *Cumulative Bulletin* was not published until late in 1997, the I.R.B. citation had to be used until that time. After the publication of the *Cumulative Bulletin*, the C.B. citation is proper. The basic portion of both citations (Rev.Rul. 96–48) indicates that this was the 48th Revenue Ruling issued by the IRS during 1996. Revenue Procedures are cited in the same manner, except that "Rev.Proc." is substituted for "Rev.Rul."

Letter Rulings. Letter rulings are issued for a fee upon a taxpayer's request and describe how the IRS will treat a *proposed* transaction for tax purposes. Letter rulings can be useful to taxpayers who wish to be certain of how a transaction will be taxed before proceeding with it. Letter rulings allow taxpayers to avoid unexpected tax costs. The procedure for requesting a ruling can be quite cumbersome, although it sometimes is the most effective way to carry out tax planning. The IRS limits the issuance of individual rulings to restricted, pre-announced areas of taxation and generally will not rule on situations that are fact-intensive. Thus, a ruling may not be obtained on many of the problems that are particularly troublesome to taxpayers.[13]

Although letter rulings once were private and not available to the public, the law now requires the IRS to make such rulings available for public inspection after identifying details are deleted.[14] Published digests of private letter rulings can be found in RIA's *Private Letter Rulings*, BNA *Daily Tax Reports*, and Tax Analysts' *Tax Notes*. *IRS Letter Rulings Reports* (published by Commerce Clearing House) contain both digests and full texts of all letter rulings. *Letter Ruling Review* (published by Tax Analysts), a monthly publication, selects and discusses the most important of the approximately 300 letter rulings issued each month. In addition, computerized databases of letter rulings are also available through several private publishers.

Letter rulings are issued multidigit file numbers, which indicate the year and week of issuance as well as the number of the ruling during that week. Consider, for example, Ltr.Rul. 9749005, which deals with an election by a corporation to be treated as an S corporation:

---

[12]Usually, only two volumes of the *Cumulative Bulletin* are published each year. However, when Congress has enacted major tax legislation, additional volumes may be published containing the congressional Committee Reports supporting the Revenue Act. See, for example, the two extra volumes for 1984 dealing with the Deficit Reduction Act of 1984. The 1984–3 *Cumulative Bulletin*, Volume 1, contains the text of the law itself; 1984–3, Volume 2, contains the Committee Reports. Thus, there are a total of four volumes of the *Cumulative Bulletin* for 1984: 1984–1; 1984–2; 1984–3, Volume 1; and 1984–3, Volume 2.

[13]The first *Internal Revenue Bulletin* issued each year contains a list of areas in which the IRS will not issue advance rulings. This list may be modified throughout the year. See, for example, Rev.Proc. 98–3, 1998–1 I.R.B. 100.

[14]§ 6110.

97	49	005
Year 1997	49th week of issuance	Fifth ruling issued during the 49th week

Other Administrative Pronouncements. *Treasury Decisions* (TDs) are issued by the Treasury Department to promulgate new Regulations, amend or otherwise change existing Regulations, or announce the position of the Government on selected court decisions. Like Revenue Rulings and Revenue Procedures, TDs are published initially in the *Internal Revenue Bulletin* and subsequently transferred to the *Cumulative Bulletin.*

The IRS publishes other administrative communications in the *Internal Revenue Bulletin,* such as Announcements, Notices, LRs (Proposed Regulations), Termination of Exempt Organization Status, Practitioner Disciplinary Actions, and Prohibited Transaction Exemptions.

Like letter rulings, **determination letters** are issued at the request of taxpayers and provide guidance on the application of the tax law. They differ from letter rulings in that the issuing source is the District Director rather than the National Office of the IRS. Also, determination letters usually involve *completed* (as opposed to proposed) transactions. Determination letters are not published and are made known only to the party making the request.

EXAMPLE 1 The shareholders of Red Corporation and Green Corporation want assurance that the consolidation of their corporations into Blue Corporation will be a nontaxable reorganization. The proper approach would be to ask the National Office of the IRS to issue a letter ruling concerning the income tax effect of the proposed transaction. ▼

EXAMPLE 2 Chris operates a barber shop in which he employs eight barbers. To comply with the rules governing income tax and payroll tax withholdings, Chris wants to know whether the barbers working for him are employees or independent contractors. The proper procedure would be to request a determination letter on their status from the appropriate District Director. ▼

The National Office of the IRS releases **Technical Advice Memoranda (TAMs)** weekly. TAMs resemble letter rulings in that they give the IRS's determination of an issue. Letter rulings, however, are responses to requests by taxpayers, whereas TAMs are issued by the National Office of the IRS in response to questions raised by IRS field personnel during audits. TAMs deal with completed rather than proposed transactions and are often requested for questions relating to exempt organizations and employee plans.

The law now requires that several internal memoranda that constitute the working law of the IRS be released. TAMs, together with General Counsel Memoranda (GCMs), are not officially published, and the IRS indicates that they may not be cited as precedents by taxpayers.[15] However, these working documents do explain the IRS's position on various issues.

---

[15]These are unofficially published by the sources listed in Exhibit 2–1. Internal memoranda after 1984 may be substantial authority for purposes of the § 6662 accuracy-related penalty. Notice 90–20, 1990–1 C.B. 328.

▼ **FIGURE 2-3**
Federal Judicial System

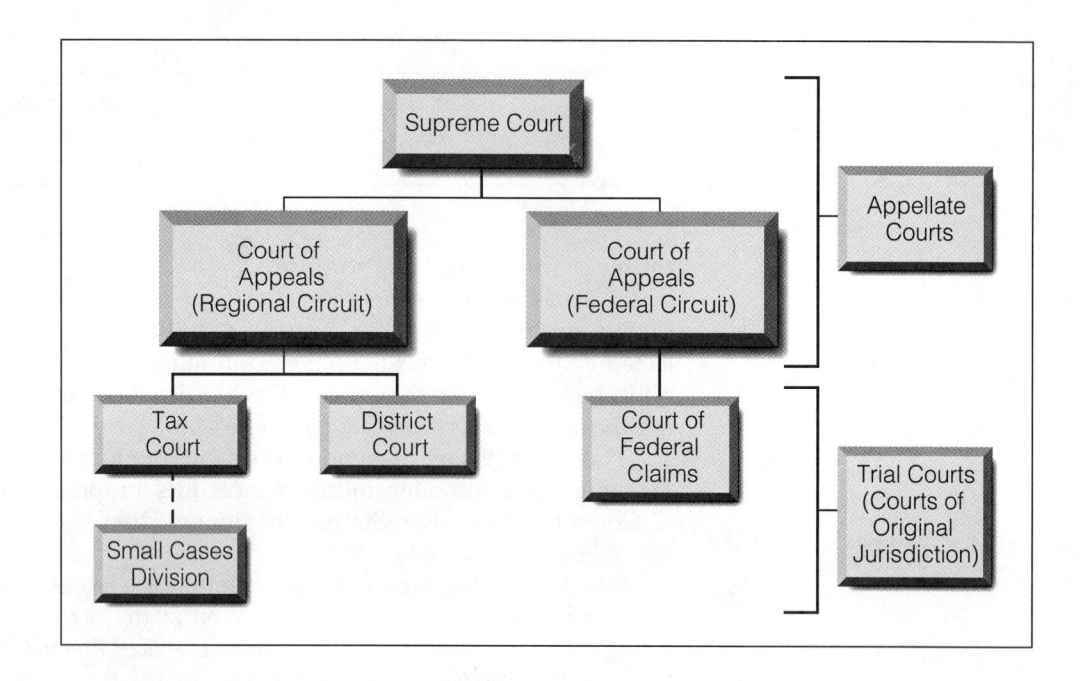

JUDICIAL SOURCES OF THE TAX LAW

The Judicial Process in General. After a taxpayer has exhausted some or all of the remedies available within the IRS (no satisfactory settlement has been reached at the agent level or at the Appeals Division level), the dispute can be taken to the Federal courts. The dispute is first considered by a **court of original jurisdiction** (known as a trial court), with any appeal (either by the taxpayer or the IRS) taken to the appropriate appellate court. In most situations, the taxpayer has a choice of four trial courts: a **District Court,** the **Court of Federal Claims,** the **Tax Court,** or the **Small Cases Division** of the Tax Court. The court system for Federal tax litigation is illustrated in Figure 2–3.

The broken line between the Tax Court and the Small Cases Division indicates that there is no appeal from the Small Cases Division. Decisions from the Small Cases Division are not published and have no precedential value. They may not be relied upon by other taxpayers or even by the taxpayer in question in subsequent years. The jurisdiction of the Small Cases Division is limited to cases involving amounts of $10,000 or less.

Trial Courts. The differences among the various trial courts (courts of original jurisdiction) can be summarized as follows:

- *Number of courts.* There is only one Court of Federal Claims and only one Tax Court, but there are many District Courts. The taxpayer does not select the District Court that will hear the dispute but must sue in the one that has jurisdiction where the taxpayer resides.
- *Number of judges.* Each District Court has only 1 judge, the Court of Federal Claims has 16 judges, and the Tax Court has 19 regular judges. The entire Tax Court, however, will review a case (the case is sent to court conference) only when important or novel tax issues are involved. Most cases will be heard and decided by 1 of the 19 judges.
- *Location.* The Court of Federal Claims meets most often in Washington, D.C., while a District Court meets at a prescribed seat for the particular district. Each state has at least one District Court, and many of the populous states

have more than one. Choosing the District Court usually minimizes the inconvenience and expense of traveling for the taxpayer and his or her counsel. The Tax Court is officially based in Washington, D.C., but the various judges travel to different parts of the country and hear cases at predetermined locations and dates. This procedure eases the distance problem for the taxpayer, but it can mean a delay before the case comes to trial and is decided.

- *Jurisdiction of the Court of Federal Claims.* The Court of Federal Claims has jurisdiction over any claim against the United States that is based upon the Constitution, any Act of Congress, or any Regulation of an executive department. Thus, the Court of Federal Claims hears nontax litigation as well as tax cases.
- *Jurisdiction of the Tax Court and District Courts.* The Tax Court hears only tax cases and is the most popular forum. The District Courts hear a wide variety of nontax cases, including drug crimes and other Federal violations, as well as tax cases. For this reason, some people suggest that the Tax Court has more expertise in tax matters.
- *Jury trial.* The only court in which a taxpayer can obtain a jury trial is a District Court. Juries can decide only questions of fact and not questions of law. Therefore, taxpayers who choose the District Court route often do not request a jury trial. If a jury trial is not elected, the judge will decide all issues. Note that a District Court decision is controlling only in the district in which the court has jurisdiction.
- *Payment of deficiency.* Before the Court of Federal Claims or a District Court can have jurisdiction, the taxpayer must pay the tax deficiency assessed by the IRS and then sue for a refund. If the taxpayer wins (assuming no successful appeal by the Government), the tax paid plus appropriate interest will be recovered. Jurisdiction in the Tax Court, however, is usually obtained without first paying the assessed tax deficiency. In the event the taxpayer loses in the Tax Court (and no appeal is taken or an appeal is unsuccessful), the deficiency must be paid with accrued interest. With the elimination of the deduction for personal (consumer) interest, the Tax Court route of delaying payment of the deficiency can become expensive. For example, to earn 11 percent after tax, a taxpayer with a 39.6 percent marginal tax rate will have to earn 18.2 percent. By paying the tax, a taxpayer limits interest and penalties on the underpayment.
- *Appeals.* Appeals from a District Court or a Tax Court decision go to the Court of Appeals for the circuit in which the taxpayer resides. Appeals from the Court of Federal Claims go to the Federal Circuit Court of Appeals.
- *Bankruptcy.* When a taxpayer files a bankruptcy petition, the IRS, like other creditors, is prevented from taking action against the taxpayer. Sometimes a bankruptcy court may settle a tax claim.

For a summary of the Federal trial courts, see Concept Summary 2–1.

Appellate Courts. The losing party can appeal a trial court decision to a **Circuit Court of Appeals.** The 11 geographical circuits, the circuit for the District of Columbia, and the Federal Circuit[16] are shown in Figure 2–4.

If the Government loses at the trial court level (District Court, Tax Court, or Court of Federal Claims), it need not (and frequently does not) appeal. The fact

---

[16]The Federal Circuit Court of Appeals was created, effective October 1, 1982, by P.L. 97–164 (April 2, 1982) to hear decisions appealed from the Claims Court (now the Court of Federal Claims).

Concept Summary 2-1

Federal Judicial System: Trial Courts

Issue	Tax Court	District Court	Court of Federal Claims
Number of judges per court	19*	1	16
Payment of deficiency before trial	No	Yes	Yes
Jury trial available	No	Yes	No
Types of disputes	Tax cases only	Mostly criminal and civil issues	Claims against the United States
Jurisdiction	Nationwide	Location of taxpayer	Nationwide
Appeal route	Court of Appeals	Court of Appeals	Federal Circuit Court of Appeals

*There are also 14 special trial judges and 9 senior judges.

that an appeal is not made, however, does not indicate that the IRS agrees with the result and will not litigate similar issues in the future. The IRS may decide not to appeal for a number of reasons. First, its current litigation load may be heavy. As a consequence, the IRS may decide that available personnel should be assigned to other, more important cases. Second, the IRS may not appeal for strategic reasons. For example, the taxpayer may be in a sympathetic position, or the facts may be particularly strong in his or her favor. In that event, the IRS may wait for a weaker case to test the legal issues involved. Third, if the appeal is from a District Court or the Tax Court, the Court of Appeals of jurisdiction could have some bearing on whether the IRS decides to pursue an appeal. Based on past experience and precedent, the IRS may conclude that the chance for success on a particular issue might be more promising in another Court of Appeals. If so, the IRS will wait for a similar case to arise in a different jurisdiction.

The Federal Circuit at the appellate level provides a taxpayer with an alternative forum to the Court of Appeals of his or her home circuit. If that Court of Appeals has issued an adverse decision, the taxpayer may prefer the Court of Federal Claims route since any appeal will be to the Federal Circuit Court of Appeals.

District Courts, the Tax Court, and the Court of Federal Claims must abide by the **precedents** set by the Court of Appeals of their jurisdiction. A particular Court of Appeals need not follow the decisions of another Court of Appeals. All courts, however, must follow decisions of the **Supreme Court.**

This pattern of appellate precedents raises an issue for the Tax Court. Because the Tax Court is a national court, it decides cases from all parts of the country. Appeals from its decisions, however, go to all of the Courts of Appeals except the Federal Circuit Court of Appeals. Accordingly, identical Tax Court cases might be appealed to different circuits with different results. As a result of the *Golsen*[17] case, the Tax Court will not follow its own precedents in a subsequent case if the Court of Appeals with jurisdiction over the taxpayer in question has previously reversed the Tax Court on the specific issue at hand.

---

[17]*Jack E. Golsen*, 54 T.C. 742 (1970).

CHAPTER 2 Working with the Tax Law

▼ **FIGURE 2–4**
The Circuit Courts of Appeals

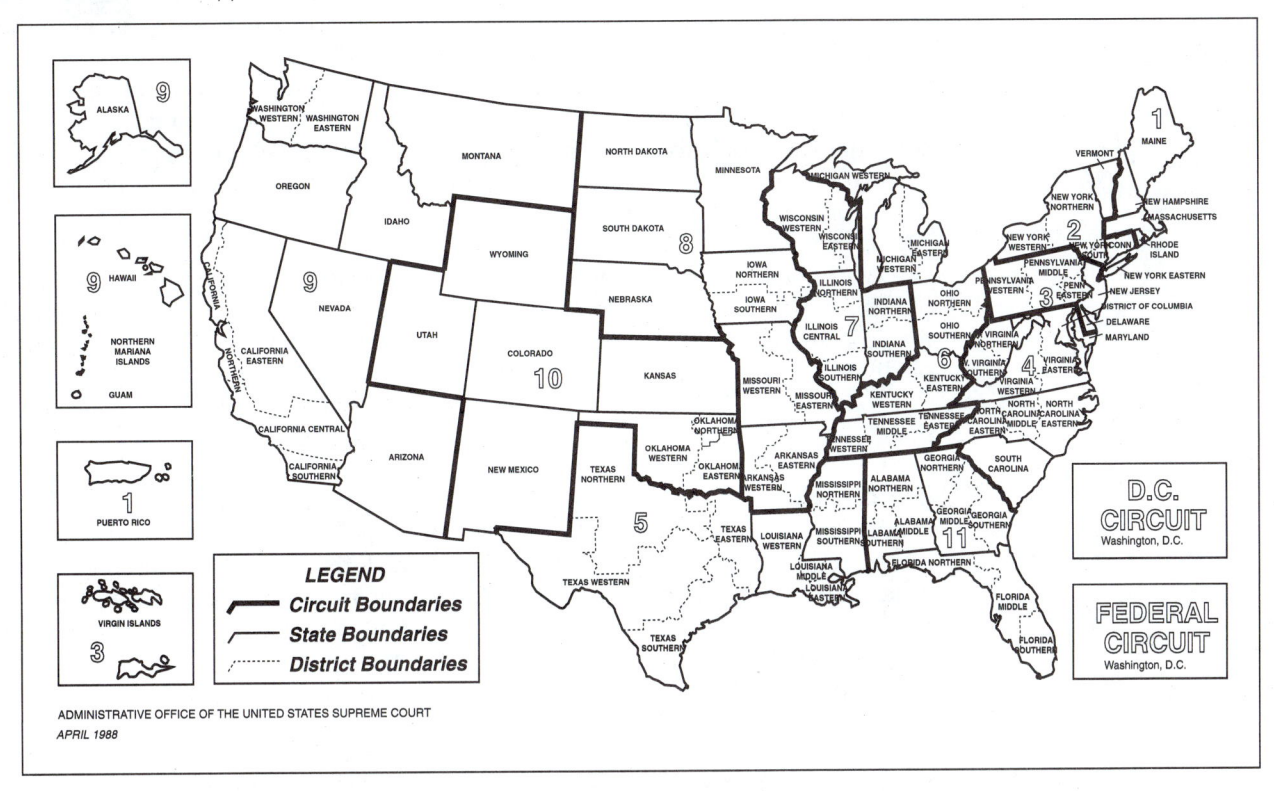

[Map of the United States showing the Circuit Courts of Appeals boundaries, with circuits numbered 1 through 11, plus the D.C. Circuit and Federal Circuit in Washington, D.C. Legend indicates Circuit Boundaries, State Boundaries, and District Boundaries. Source: Administrative Office of the United States Supreme Court, April 1988.]

EXAMPLE 3

Emily lives in Texas and sues in the Tax Court on Issue A. The Fifth Circuit Court of Appeals is the appellate court with jurisdiction. The Fifth Circuit Court of Appeals has already decided, in a case involving similar facts but a different taxpayer, that Issue A should be resolved against the Government. Although the Tax Court feels that the Fifth Circuit Court of Appeals is wrong, under its *Golsen* policy it will render judgment for Emily. Shortly thereafter, in a comparable case, Rashad, a resident of New York, sues in the Tax Court on Issue A. Assume that the Second Circuit Court of Appeals, the appellate court with jurisdiction in New York, has never expressed itself on Issue A. Presuming the Tax Court has not reconsidered its position on Issue A, it will decide against Rashad. Thus, it is entirely possible for two taxpayers suing in the same court to end up with opposite results merely because they live in different parts of the country. ▼

Appeal to the Supreme Court is not automatic. It must be applied for via a **Writ of Certiorari.** If the Court agrees to hear the case, it will grant the Writ (*Cert. Granted*). Most often, it will decline to hear the case (*Cert. Denied*). In fact, the Supreme Court rarely hears tax cases. The Court usually grants certiorari to resolve a conflict among the Courts of Appeals (e.g., two or more appellate courts have opposing positions on a particular issue) or where the tax issue is extremely important. The granting of a *Writ of Certiorari* indicates that at least four members of the Supreme Court believe that the issue is of sufficient importance to be heard by the full Court.

The *role* of appellate courts is limited to a review of the record of trial compiled by the trial courts. Thus, the appellate process usually involves a determination of whether the trial court applied the proper law in arriving at its decision, rather than a consideration of the trial court's factual findings.

An appeal can have any of a number of possible outcomes. The appellate court may approve (affirm) or disapprove (reverse) the lower court's finding, or it may send the case back for further consideration (remand). When many issues are involved, a mixed result is not unusual. Thus, the lower court may be affirmed (*aff'd.*) on Issue A and reversed (*rev'd.*) on Issue B, while Issue C is remanded (*rem'd.*) for additional fact finding.

When more than one judge is involved in the decision-making process, disagreements are not uncommon. In addition to the majority view, one or more judges may concur (agree with the result reached but not with some or all of the reasoning) or dissent (disagree with the result). In any one case, the majority view controls. But concurring and dissenting views can influence other courts or, at some subsequent date when the composition of the court has changed, even the same court.

Judicial Citations—General. Having briefly described the judicial process, it is appropriate to consider the more practical problem of the relationship of case law to tax research. As previously noted, court decisions are an important source of tax law. The ability to locate a case and to cite it is therefore a must in working with the tax law. Judicial citations usually follow a standard pattern: case name, volume number, reporter series, page or paragraph number, court (where necessary), and the year of decision. Specific citation formats for each court are presented in the following sections.

Judicial Citations—The Tax Court. A good starting point is the Tax Court. The Tax Court issues two types of decisions: Regular and Memorandum. The Chief Judge decides whether the opinion is issued as a Regular or Memorandum decision. The distinction between the two involves both substance and form. In terms of substance, *Memorandum* decisions deal with situations necessitating only the application of already established principles of law. *Regular* decisions involve novel issues not previously resolved by the Court. In actual practice, however, this distinction is not always so clear. Be that as it may, both Regular and Memorandum decisions represent the position of the Tax Court and, as such, can be relied upon.

Regular and Memorandum decisions issued by the Tax Court also differ in form. Memorandum decisions are not officially published while Regular decisions are published by the U.S. Government in a series called *Tax Court of the United States Reports* (T.C.). Each volume of these *Reports* covers a six-month period (January 1 through June 30 and July 1 through December 31) and is given a succeeding volume number. But there is usually a time lag between the date a decision is rendered and the date it appears in official form. A temporary citation may be necessary to help the researcher locate a recent Regular decision. Consider, for example, the temporary and permanent citations for *Sprint Corporation and Subsidiaries*, a decision filed on April 30, 1997:

Temporary Citation { *Sprint Corporation and Subsidiaries*, 108 T.C. ___, No. 4 (1997).
Explanation: Page number left blank because not yet known.

Permanent Citation { *Sprint Corporation and Subsidiaries*, 108 T.C. 384 (1997).
Explanation: Page 384 of Vol. 108 of *Tax Court of the United States Reports*.

Both citations tell us that the case will ultimately appear in Volume 108 of the *Tax Court of the United States Reports*. Until this volume becomes available to the general public, however, the page number must be left blank. Instead, the temporary citation identifies the case as being the 4th Regular decision issued by the Tax Court since Volume 107 ended. With this information, the decision can easily be located in either of the special Tax Court services published by Commerce Clearing House and Research Institute of America (formerly by Prentice-Hall). Once Volume 108 is released, the permanent citation can be substituted and the number of the case dropped.

Before 1943, the Tax Court was called the Board of Tax Appeals, and its decisions were published as the *United States Board of Tax Appeals Reports* (B.T.A.). These 47 volumes cover the period from 1924 to 1942. For example, the citation *Karl Pauli*, 11 B.T.A. 784 (1928) refers to the 11th volume of the *Board of Tax Appeals Reports*, page 784, issued in 1928.

If the IRS loses a decision, it may indicate whether it agrees or disagrees with the results reached by the court by publishing an **acquiescence** ("A" or "Acq.") or **nonacquiescence** ("NA" or "Nonacq."), respectively. Until 1991, acquiescences and nonacquiescences were published only for certain Regular decisions of the Tax Court, but the IRS has expanded its acquiescence program to include other tax cases where guidance is helpful. The acquiescence or nonacquiescence is published in the *Internal Revenue Bulletin* and the *Cumulative Bulletin* as an *Action on Decision*. The IRS can retroactively revoke an acquiescence.

Curiously, the IRS can issue a nonacquiescence even though it chooses *not* to appeal the case. In this manner, the government indicates that it disagrees with the result reached, despite its decision not to seek review of the matter in an appellate court.

Although Memorandum decisions are not published by the U.S. Government, they are published by Commerce Clearing House (CCH) and Research Institute of America (RIA [formerly by Prentice-Hall]).[18] Consider, for example, the three different ways that *Jack D. Carr* can be cited:

Jack D. Carr, T.C.Memo. 1985–19.
The 19th Memorandum decision issued by the Tax Court in 1985.

Jack D. Carr, 49 TCM 507.
Page 507 of Vol. 49 of the CCH *Tax Court Memorandum Decisions*.

Jack D. Carr, RIA T.C.Mem.Dec. ¶85,019.
Paragraph 85,019 of the RIA *T.C. Memorandum Decisions*.

Note that the third citation contains the same information as the first. Thus, ¶85,019 indicates the following information about the case: year 1985, 19th T.C. Memo. decision.[19] Although the RIA citation does not include a specific volume number, the paragraph citation (85,019) indicates that the decision can be found in the 1985 volume of the RIA Memorandum Decision service.

Judicial Citations—The District Courts, Court of Federal Claims, and Courts of Appeals.

District Court, Court of Federal Claims, and Court of Appeals decisions dealing with Federal tax matters are reported in both the CCH *U.S. Tax Cases* (USTC) and the RIA *American Federal Tax Reports* (AFTR) series.

District Court decisions, dealing with *both* tax and nontax issues, are also published by West Publishing Company in its *Federal Supplement* series. A District Court case can be cited in three different forms as the following examples illustrate:

---

[18]Prentice-Hall Information Services is now owned by Research Institute of America. Although recent volumes contain the RIA imprint, many of the older volumes continue to have the P-H imprint.

[19]In this text, this Memorandum decision of the Tax Court would be cited as *Jack D. Carr*, 49 TCM 507, T.C.Memo. 1985–19.

Simons-Eastern Co. v. U.S., 73–1 USTC ¶9279 (D.Ct.Ga., 1972).

Explanation: Reported in the first volume of the *U.S. Tax Cases* (USTC) published by Commerce Clearing House for calendar year 1973 (73–1) and located at paragraph 9279 (¶9279).

Simons-Eastern Co. v. U.S., 31 AFTR2d 73–640 (D.Ct.Ga., 1972).

Explanation: Reported in the 31st volume of the second series of the *American Federal Tax Reports* (AFTR2d) published by RIA, beginning on page 640. The "73" preceding the page number indicates the year the case was published but is a designation used only in recent decisions.

Simons-Eastern Co. v. U.S., 354 F.Supp. 1003 (D.Ct.Ga., 1972).

Explanation: Reported in the 354th volume of the *Federal Supplement* series (F.Supp.) published by West Publishing Company, beginning on page 1003.

In all of the preceding citations, note that the name of the case is the same (Simons-Eastern Co. being the taxpayer), as are the references to the District Court of Georgia (D.Ct.Ga.) and the year the decision was rendered (1972).[20]

Decisions of the Court of Federal Claims[21] and the Courts of Appeals are published in the USTCs, AFTRs, and a West Publishing Company reporter called the *Federal Second* series (F.2d). Volume 999, published in 1993, is the last volume of the *Federal Second* series. It is followed by the *Federal Third* series (F.3d). Beginning with October 1982, decisions of the Court of Federal Claims are published in another West Publishing Company reporter entitled the *Claims Court Reporter* (abbreviated as Cls.Ct.). Beginning with Volume 27 on October 30, 1992, the name of the reporter changed to the *Federal Claims Reporter* (abbreviated as Fed.Cl.). The following examples illustrate the different forms:

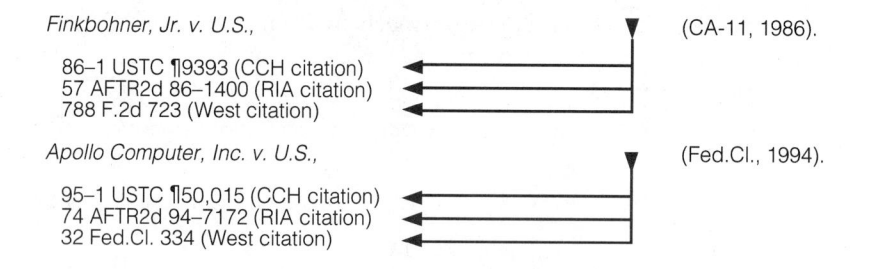

Finkbohner, Jr. v. U.S., (CA-11, 1986).
86–1 USTC ¶9393 (CCH citation)
57 AFTR2d 86–1400 (RIA citation)
788 F.2d 723 (West citation)

Apollo Computer, Inc. v. U.S., (Fed.Cl., 1994).
95–1 USTC ¶50,015 (CCH citation)
74 AFTR2d 94–7172 (RIA citation)
32 Fed.Cl. 334 (West citation)

Note that *Finkbohner, Jr.* is a decision rendered by the Eleventh Circuit Court of Appeals in 1986 (CA–11, 1986), while *Apollo Computer, Inc.* was issued by the Court of Federal Claims in 1994 (Fed.Cl., 1994). If *Apollo Computer, Inc.* had been issued by the Court of Claims prior to 1982, it would have been located in the *Federal Second* series instead of the *Claims Court Reporter* or *Federal Claims Reporter*.

Judicial Citations—The Supreme Court. Like all other Federal tax decisions (except those rendered by the Tax Court), Supreme Court decisions dealing with Federal tax matters are published by Commerce Clearing House in the USTCs and by RIA (formerly by Prentice-Hall) in the AFTRs. The U.S. Government Printing Office publishes all Supreme Court decisions in the *United States Supreme Court Reports* (U.S.), as do West Publishing Company in its *Supreme Court Reporter* (S.Ct.)

---

[20] In this text, the case would be cited in the following form: *Simons-Eastern Co. v. U.S.,* 73–1 USTC ¶9279, 31 AFTR2d 73–640, 354 F.Supp. 1003 (D.Ct.Ga., 1972).

[21] Before October 29, 1992, the Court of Federal Claims was called the Claims Court. Before October 1, 1982, the Court of Federal Claims was called the Court of Claims.

Concept Summary 2-2

Judicial Sources

Court	Location	Authority
Supreme Court	S.Ct. Series (West) U.S. Series (U.S. Gov't.) L.Ed. (Lawyer's Co-op.) AFTR (RIA) USTC (CCH)	Highest authority
Courts of Appeal	Federal 3d (West) AFTR (RIA) USTC (CCH)	Next highest appellate court
Tax Court (Regular decisions)	U.S. Gov't. Printing Office. RIA/CCH separate services	Highest trial court*
Tax Court (Memorandum decisions)	RIA T.C.Memo. (RIA) TCM (CCH)	Less authority than Regular T.C. decision
Court of Federal Claims**	Federal Claims Reporter (West) AFTR (RIA) USTC (CCH)	Authority similar to Tax Court
District Courts	F.Supp. Series (West) AFTR (RIA) USTC (CCH)	Lowest trial court
Small Cases Division of Tax Court	Not published	No precedential value

*Theoretically, the Tax Court, Court of Federal Claims, and District Courts have the same level of authority. But some people believe that since the Tax Court hears and decides only tax cases on a national level, its decisions may be more authoritative than a Court of Federal Claims or District Court decision.
**Before October 29, 1992, the Claims Court.

and the Lawyer's Co-operative Publishing Company in its *United States Reports, Lawyer's Edition* (L.Ed.). The following illustrates the different ways the same decision can be cited:

U.S. v. The Donruss Co., (USSC, 1969).
    69–1 USTC ¶9167 (CCH citation)
    23 AFTR2d 69–418 (RIA citation)
    89 S.Ct. 501 (West citation)
    393 U.S. 297 (U.S. Government Printing Office citation)
    21 L.Ed.2d 495 (Lawyer's Co-operative Publishing Co. citation)

The parenthetical reference (USSC, 1969) identifies the decision as having been rendered by the U.S. Supreme Court in 1969. In this text, the citations of Supreme Court decisions are limited to the CCH (USTC), RIA (AFTR), and West (S.Ct.) versions. See Concept Summary 2–2.

Working with the Tax Law—Tax Research

LEARNING OBJECTIVE 2
Locate and work with the tax law and understand the tax research process.

Tax research is undertaken to determine the best available solution to a situation that has tax consequences. In the case of a completed transaction, the objective of the research is to determine the tax result of what has already taken place. For example, is the expenditure incurred by the taxpayer deductible or not deductible for tax purposes? When dealing with proposed transactions, tax research is concerned with the determination of possible alternative tax consequences to facilitate effective tax planning.

Tax research involves the following procedures:

- Identifying and refining the problem.
- Locating the appropriate tax law sources.
- Assessing the tax law sources.
- Arriving at the solution or at alternative solutions while giving due consideration to nontax factors.
- Effectively communicating the solution to the taxpayer or the taxpayer's representative.
- Following up on the solution (where appropriate) in light of new developments.

This process is depicted schematically in Figure 2–5. The broken lines indicate steps of particular interest when tax research is directed toward proposed, rather than completed, transactions.

IDENTIFYING THE PROBLEM

Problem identification starts with a compilation of the relevant facts involved. In this regard, *all* of the facts that may have a bearing on the problem must be gathered, as any omission could modify the solution reached. To illustrate, consider what appears to be a very simple problem.

EXAMPLE 4

In reviewing their tax and financial situation, Fred and Megan, a married couple, notice that Fred's investment in Airways Co. stock has declined from its purchase price of $8,000 to a current market value of $5,500. Megan wants to sell this stock now and claim the $2,500 loss ($5,500 value − $8,000 cost) as a deduction this year. Fred, however, believes that Airways Co. will yet prosper and does not want to part with its stock. Their daughter suggests that they sell the Airways Co. stock to Maple, Inc., a corporation owned equally by Fred and Megan. That way, they can claim the deduction this year while still holding the stock through their corporation. Will this suggestion work? ▼

REFINING THE PROBLEM

Fred and Megan in Example 4 face three choices: (1) sell the Airways stock through their regular investment broker and get a deduction in the current year (Megan's plan); (2) continue to hold the Airways stock (Fred's plan); and (3) sell the Airways stock to a corporation owned 50–50 by Fred and Megan (their daughter's suggestion). The tax consequences of plans (1) and (2) are clear, but the question that Fred and Megan want to resolve is whether plan (3) will work as anticipated. Refining the problem further, can shareholders deduct a loss from the sale of an asset to a corporation that they control? Section 267(a)(1) indicates that losses from the sale of property between persons specified in § 267(b) are not deductible. This subsection lists 12 different relationships, including, in § 267(b)(2): "an individual

FIGURE 2–5
Tax Research Process

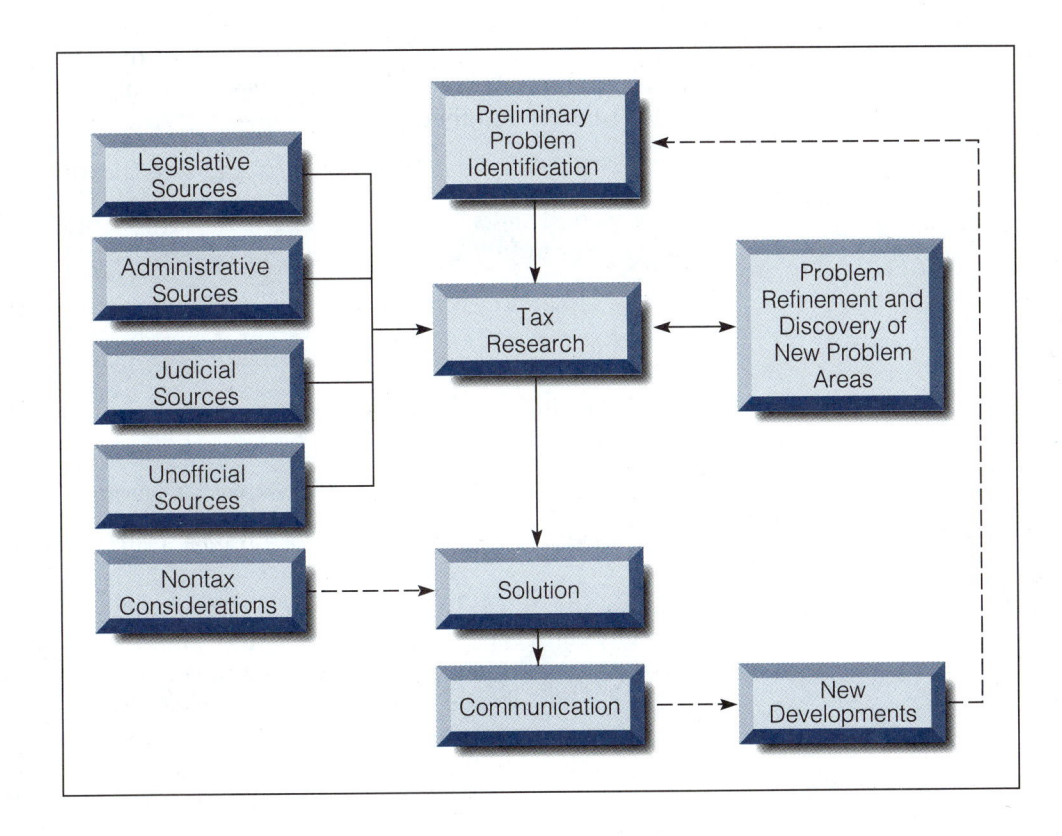

and a corporation more than 50 percent in value of the outstanding stock of which is owned, directly or indirectly, by or for such individual." Thus, if Fred and Megan each own 50 percent of Maple, Inc., neither owns *more than* 50 percent, as § 267(b) requires. Accordingly, the loss disallowance rule would not apply to Fred, and their daughter's suggestion would appear to be sound.

The language of the statute, however, indicates that any stock owned *directly or indirectly* by an individual is counted toward the 50 percent test. Might Megan's stock be considered owned "indirectly" by Fred? Further research is necessary. Section 267(c) contains rules for determining "constructive ownership of stock," or when stock owned by one person will be attributed to someone else. One of the rules in this subsection declares that an individual is considered to own any stock that is owned by that person's *family*, and family is defined in § 267(c)(4) as including a person's spouse, among others. Therefore, Megan's stock will be attributed to Fred, so that Fred is treated as owning all of the stock of Maple, Inc. As a result, § 267(a) would indeed apply, and no loss would be deductible if Fred sells his Airways Co. stock to Maple, Inc. In short, the daughter's suggestion will not work.

LOCATING THE APPROPRIATE TAX LAW SOURCES

Once the problem is clearly defined, what is the next step? While it is a matter of individual judgment, most tax research begins with the index volume of a paper-based tax service or a keyword search of an on-line or CD-ROM tax service (see the subsequent discussion of Computer-Assisted Tax Research). If the problem is not complex, the researcher may bypass the tax service and turn directly to the Internal Revenue Code and the Treasury Regulations. For the beginner, the latter procedure saves time and will solve many of the more basic problems. If the researcher does not have a personal copy of the Code or Regulations, resorting to the appropriate volume(s) of a tax service or a CD-ROM is necessary.[22] The major tax services and their publishers are:

Standard Federal Tax Reporter, Commerce Clearing House.

United States Tax Reporter, Research Institute of America (entitled *Federal Taxes* prior to July 1992).

Federal Tax Coordinator 2d, Research Institute of America.[23]

Tax Management Portfolios, Bureau of National Affairs.

Rabkin and Johnson, *Federal Income, Gift and Estate Taxation*, Matthew Bender, Inc.

CCH's Federal Tax Service, Commerce Clearing House.

Mertens Law of Federal Income Taxation, Callaghan and Co.

Working with Tax Services. In this text, it is not feasible to explain the use of any particular tax service—this ability can be obtained only by practice. However, several important observations about the use of tax services cannot be overemphasized. First, always check for current developments. The main text of any service is revised too infrequently to permit reliance on that portion as the *latest* word on any subject. Where current developments can be found depends on which service is being used. Commerce Clearing House's *Standard Federal Tax Reporter* contains a special volume devoted to current matters. Both RIA's *United States Tax Reporter* and *Federal Tax Coordinator 2d* integrate the new developments into the body of the service throughout the year. Second, when dealing with a tax service synopsis of a Treasury Department pronouncement or a judicial decision, there is no substitute for the original source. Do not base a conclusion solely on a tax service's commentary. If the Code Section, Regulation, or case is vital to the research, read it. This is not to say that the synopsis contained in the tax service is wrong—it might just be incomplete.

Tax Periodicals. The various tax periodicals are another source of information. The easiest way to locate a journal article on a particular tax problem is through CCH's *Federal Tax Articles*. This six-volume service includes a subject index, a Code Section number index, and an author's index. In addition, RIA's tax service has a topical "Index to Tax Articles" section that is organized using the RIA paragraph index system. Also, beginning in 1992, *The Accounting & Tax Index* is available in three quarterly issues plus a cumulative year-end volume covering all four quarters. The original *Accountant's Index* started in 1921 and ended in 1991.

The following are some of the more useful tax periodicals:

The Journal of Taxation
Warren, Gorham and Lamont
31 St. James Avenue
Boston, MA 02116

Tax Law Review
Warren, Gorham and Lamont
31 St. James Avenue
Boston, MA 02116

---

[22] Several of the major tax services publish paperback editions of the Code and Treasury Regulations that can be purchased at modest prices. These editions are usually revised twice each year. For an annotated and abridged version of the Code and Regulations that is published annually, see James E. Smith, *West's Internal Revenue Code of 1986 and Treasury Regulations: Annotated and Selected* (St. Paul, Minn.: West Publishing Company, 1998). The complete Code and Regulations are also available in *RIA OnPoint*.

[23] Both the *United States Tax Reporter* and *Federal Tax Coordinator 2d* are included in *RIA OnPoint*.

Trusts and Estates
6151 Powers Ferry Road, NW
Atlanta, GA 30339

Oil, Gas and Energy Quarterly
Matthew Bender & Co.
2 Park Avenue
New York, NY 10016

The International Tax Journal
Panel Publishers
14 Plaza Road
Greenvale, NY 11548

TAXES—The Tax Magazine
Commerce Clearing House, Inc.
2700 Lake Cook Road
Riverwood, IL 60015

National Tax Journal
5310 East Main Street
Columbus, OH 43213

The Tax Adviser
AICPA
1211 Avenue of the Americas
New York, NY 10036

The Practical Accountant
11 Penn Plaza
New York, NY 10001

Estate Planning
Warren, Gorham and Lamont
31 St. James Avenue
Boston, MA 02116

Taxation for Accountants
Warren, Gorham and Lamont
31 St. James Avenue
Boston, MA 02116

The Tax Executive
1001 Pennsylvania Avenue, NW
Suite 320
Washington, D.C. 20004

Journal of Corporate Taxation
Warren, Gorham and Lamont
31 St. James Avenue
Boston, MA 02116

Journal of Taxation for Individuals
Warren, Gorham and Lamont
31 St. James Avenue
Boston, MA 02116

The Tax Lawyer
American Bar Association
750 N. Lake Shore Drive
Chicago, IL 60611

Journal of the American Taxation Association
American Accounting Association
5717 Bessie Drive
Sarasota, FL 34233

Tax Notes
6830 Fairfax Drive
Arlington, VA 22213

ASSESSING TAX LAW SOURCES

Once a source has been located, the next step is to assess it in light of the problem at hand. Proper assessment involves careful interpretation of the tax law and consideration of its relevance and significance.

Interpreting the Internal Revenue Code. The language of the Code is often difficult to comprehend fully. Contrary to many people's suspicions, the Code is not written deliberately to confuse. Nevertheless, it often has that effect. The Code is intended to apply to over 260 million taxpayers, most of whom are willing to exploit any linguistic imprecision to their benefit—to find a "loophole," in popular parlance. Moreover, many of the Code's provisions are limitations or restrictions involving two or more variables. Expressing such concepts algebraically would be more direct; using words to accomplish this task instead is often quite cumbersome. Among the worst such attempts is § 341(e) relating to so-called collapsible corporations, which includes one sentence that has more than 450 words.

Nevertheless, the Code is the governing law, the only source of tax law (other than treaties) that has received the actual approval of Congress and the President.

> ### TAX IN THE NEWS
>
> ### INTERNAL REVENUE CODE: INTERPRETATION PITFALLS
>
> One author has noted 10 common pitfalls in interpreting the Code:
>
> 1. Determine the limitations and exceptions to a provision. Do not permit the language of the Code Section to carry greater or lesser weight than was intended.
> 2. Just because a Section fails to mention an item does not necessarily mean that the item is excluded.
> 3. Read definitional clauses carefully.
> 4. Do not overlook small words such as *and* and *or*. There is a world of difference between these two words.
> 5. Read the Code Section completely; do not jump to conclusions.
> 6. Watch out for cross-referenced and related provisions, since many Sections of the Code are interrelated.
> 7. At times Congress is not careful when reconciling new Code provisions with existing Sections. Conflicts among Sections, therefore, do arise.
> 8. Be alert for hidden definitions; terms in a particular Code Section may be defined in the same Section or in a separate Section.
> 9. Some answers may not be found in the Code; therefore, a researcher may have to consult the Regulations and/or judicial decisions.
> 10. Take careful note of measuring words such as *less than 50 percent, more than 50 percent,* and *at least 80 percent*.
>
> SOURCE: Adapted by permission from Henry G. Wong, "Ten Common Pitfalls in Reading the Internal Revenue Code," *Journal of Business Strategy*, July–August 1972, pp. 30–33. Reprinted with permission by Faulkner & Gray, Inc., 11 Penn Plaza, New York, NY 10001.

Accordingly, it is usually the first source to be consulted, and often it is the only source needed.

Assessing the Significance of a Treasury Regulation. Treasury Regulations are the official interpretation of the Code and are entitled to great deference. Occasionally, however, a court will invalidate a Regulation or a portion thereof on the grounds that the Regulation is contrary to the intent of Congress. Usually, courts do not question the validity of Regulations because of the belief that "the first administrative interpretation of a provision as it appears in a new act often expresses the general understanding of the times or the actual understanding of those who played an important part when the statute was drafted."[24]

Keep in mind the following observations when assessing the significance of a Regulation:

- IRS agents *must* give the Code and the Regulations issued thereunder equal weight when dealing with taxpayers and their representatives.

---

[24]*Augustus v. Comm.*, 41–1 USTC ¶9255, 26 AFTR 612, 118 F.2d 38 (CA–6, 1941).

- Proposed Regulations provide a preview of future final Regulations, but they are not binding on the IRS or taxpayers.
- In a challenge, the burden of proof is on the taxpayer to show that a Regulation varies from the language of the statute and has no support in the Committee Reports.
- If the taxpayer loses such a challenge, the negligence penalty may be imposed.[25] This accuracy-related penalty applies to any failure to make a reasonable attempt to comply with the tax law and to any disregard of rules and Regulations.[26]
- Final Regulations can be classified as procedural, interpretive, or legislative. **Procedural Regulations** neither establish tax laws nor attempt to explain tax laws. Procedural Regulations are *housekeeping* instructions, indicating information that taxpayers should provide the IRS, as well as information about the internal management and conduct of the IRS itself.
- **Interpretive Regulations** rephrase and elaborate what Congress stated in the Committee Reports that were issued when the tax legislation was enacted. Such Regulations are *hard and solid* and almost impossible to overturn unless they do not clearly reflect the intent of Congress.
- In some Code Sections, Congress has given the *Secretary or his delegate* the specific authority to prescribe Regulations to carry out the details of administration or to otherwise create rules not included in the Code. Under such circumstances, Congress is effectively delegating its legislative powers to the Treasury Department. Regulations issued pursuant to this type of authority possess the force and effect of law and are often called **Legislative Regulations** (e.g., see § 385(a)).

Assessing the Significance of Other Administrative Sources of the Tax Law. Revenue Rulings issued by the IRS carry much less weight than Treasury Department Regulations. Revenue Rulings are important, however, in that they reflect the position of the IRS on tax matters. In any dispute with the IRS on the interpretation of tax law, taxpayers should expect agents to follow the results reached in applicable Revenue Rulings. It is not unusual, however, for courts to overturn Revenue Rulings as incorrect applications of the law to the facts presented.

Actions on Decisions further tell the taxpayer the IRS's reaction to certain court decisions. Recall that the IRS follows a practice of either acquiescing (agreeing) or nonacquiescing (not agreeing) with selected judicial decisions. A nonacquiescence does not mean that a particular court decision is of no value, but it does indicate that the IRS may choose to litigate the issue involved.

Assessing the Significance of Judicial Sources of the Tax Law. The judicial process as it relates to the formulation of tax law has been described. How much reliance can be placed on a particular decision depends upon the following factors:

- The level of the court. A decision rendered by a trial court (e.g., a District Court) carries less weight than one issued by an appellate court (e.g., the Fifth Circuit Court of Appeals). Unless Congress changes the Code, decisions by the U.S. Supreme Court represent the last word on any tax issue.
- The legal residence of the taxpayer. If, for example, a taxpayer lives in Texas, a decision of the Fifth Circuit Court of Appeals means more than one rendered by the Second Circuit Court of Appeals. This is the case because

---

[25] §§ 6662(a) and (b)(1). [26] § 6662(c).

any appeal from a District Court or the Tax Court would be to the Fifth Circuit Court of Appeals and not to the Second Circuit Court of Appeals.[27]
- A Tax Court Regular decision carries more weight than a Memorandum decision because the Tax Court does not consider Memorandum decisions to have precedential value.[28] Furthermore, a Tax Court *reviewed* decision carries even more weight, because *all* of the Tax Court judges participate in a reviewed decision.
- A Court of Appeals decision where certiorari that has been requested and denied by the Supreme Court carries slightly more weight than a Court of Appeals decision that was not appealed. A Court of Appeals decision heard *en banc* (all the judges participate) carries more weight than a normal Court of Appeals case.
- A decision that is supported by cases from other courts carries more weight than a decision that is not supported by other cases.
- The weight of a decision can also be affected by its status on appeal. For example, was the decision affirmed or overruled?

In connection with the last two factors, a citator is helpful to tax research.[29] A citator lists subsequent published opinions that refer to the case being assessed. Reviewing these references enables the tax researcher to determine whether the decision in question has been reversed, affirmed, followed by other courts, or distinguished in some way. If one plans to rely on a judicial decision to any significant degree, "running" the case through a citator is imperative.

Understanding Judicial Opinions. Reading judicial opinions can be more productive if certain conventions of usage are understood. In tax cases, the taxpayer is usually the person initiating the court action and accordingly is labeled the *plaintiff*. The government generally is the party against whom the case is being brought and accordingly is called the *defendant*. Some courts, including the Tax Court, apply the terms *petitioner* and *respondent* to the plaintiff and defendant, respectively, particularly when the case is an appellate proceeding. Appellate courts often use the terms *appellant* and *appellee* instead.

It is also important to distinguish between a court's final determination, or *holding*, and passing comments made in the course of its opinion. These latter remarks, examples, and analogies, often collectively termed *dicta*, are not part of the court's conclusion and do not have precedential value. Nevertheless, they often facilitate one's understanding of the court's reasoning and can enable a tax adviser to better predict how the court might resolve some future tax case.

Assessing the Significance of Other Sources. *Primary sources* of tax law include the Constitution, legislative history materials (e.g., Committee Reports), statutes, treaties, Treasury Regulations, IRS pronouncements, and judicial decisions. In general, the IRS regards only primary sources as substantial authority. However, reference to *secondary materials* such as legal periodicals, treatises, legal opinions, General Counsel Memoranda, and written determinations may be useful. In general, secondary sources are not authority.

Although the statement that the IRS regards only primary sources as substantial authority is generally true, there is one exception. In Notice 90–20,[30] the IRS expanded the list of substantial authority *for purposes of* the accuracy-related penalty

---

[27]Before October 1, 1982, an appeal from the then-named Court of Claims (the other trial court) was directly to the Supreme Court.
[28]*Severino R. Nico, Jr.*, 67 T.C. 647 (1977).
[29]The major citators are published by Commerce Clearing House, RIA, and Shepard's Citations, Inc.
[30]1990–1 C.B. 328; see also Reg. § 1.6661–3(b)(2).

in § 6662 to include a number of secondary materials (e.g., letter rulings and General Counsel Memoranda). "Authority" does not include conclusions reached in treatises, legal periodicals, and opinions rendered by tax professionals.

A letter ruling or determination letter can be relied upon *only* by the taxpayer to whom it is issued, except as noted above with respect to the accuracy-related penalty.

Upon the completion of major tax legislation, the staff of the Joint Committee on Taxation (in consultation with the staffs of the House Ways and Means and Senate Finance Committees) often will prepare a General Explanation of the Act, commonly known as the Bluebook because of the color of its cover. The IRS will not accept this detailed explanation as having legal effect. The Bluebook does, however, provide valuable guidance to tax advisers and taxpayers until Regulations are issued. Some letter rulings and General Counsel Memoranda of the IRS cite Bluebook explanations.

ARRIVING AT THE SOLUTION OR AT ALTERNATIVE SOLUTIONS

Example 4 raises the question of whether taxpayers would be denied a loss deduction from the sale of stock to a corporation that they own. The solution depends, in part, on the relationship of the corporation's shareholders to each other. Since Fred and Megan are married to each other, § 267(c)(2) attributes Megan's stock to Fred in applying the "more than 50 percent" test of § 267(c)(2). Accordingly, Fred and Maple, Inc., are considered related parties under § 267(a), and a sale between them does not provide a deductible loss. If Fred and Megan were not related to each other, the constructive stock ownership rules would not apply, and a loss could be deducted on a sale by Fred to Maple, Inc.

If Maple, Inc., were a *partnership* instead of a corporation, § 267 would not apply, per Regulation § 1.267(b)–1(b)(1). That Regulation, however, references a different Code Section, namely § 707, which produces the same result: no deduction of the loss from a sale between a "more than 50 percent" partner and the partnership. This additional research prevents Fred and Megan from erroneously selling their Airways stock to a partnership in hopes of obtaining a loss deduction from the sale. Accordingly, Fred must sell the Airways stock to an unrelated party in order to deduct the loss.

Since Fred still wants to own Airways Co. stock, he might consider purchasing new Airways Co. stock to replace the stock he sells. Additional research reveals that for the loss on the sale to be deductible, § 1091 requires that 30 days elapse between the purchase of the new stock and the sale of the old stock. This section applies to purchases and sales of *substantially identical stock or securities*. As a result, to deduct the loss on the Airways stock, Fred must either wait at least 30 days after selling this stock to buy new Airways stock or acquire stock in a different company at any time. This new company can even be in the same general business as Airways Co.[31]

COMMUNICATING TAX RESEARCH

3 LEARNING OBJECTIVE
Communicate the results of the tax research process in a client letter and a tax file memorandum.

Once the problem has been researched adequately, a memorandum, letter, or speech setting forth the result may need to be prepared. The form the communication takes could depend on a number of considerations. For example, does an employer or instructor recommend a particular procedure or format for tax research memos? Is the memo to be given directly to the client or will it first go to the preparer's

---

[31]Rev.Rul. 59–44, 1959–1 C.B. 205.

employer? If the communication is a speech, who is the audience? How long should one speak?[32] Whatever form it takes, a good research communication should contain the following elements:

- A clear statement of the issue.
- In more complex situations, a short review of the fact pattern that raises the issue.
- A review of the pertinent tax law sources (e.g., Code, Regulations, Revenue Rulings, judicial authority).
- Any assumptions made in arriving at the solution.
- The solution recommended and the logic or reasoning supporting it.
- The references consulted in the research process.

Illustrations of the memo for the tax file and the client letter associated with Example 4 appear in Figures 2–6 and 2–7.

FOLLOW-UP PROCEDURES

Because tax research may involve a proposed (as opposed to a completed) transaction, a change in the tax law (either legislative, administrative, or judicial) could alter the original conclusion. Additional research may be necessary to test the solution in light of current developments (refer to the broken lines at the right in Figure 2–5).

COMPUTER-ASSISTED TAX RESEARCH

4 LEARNING OBJECTIVE
Have an awareness of computer-assisted tax research.

Computer-based tax research tools hold a prominent position in tax practice. Electronic tax resources allow the tax library to better reflect the tax law's dynamic and daily changes. Nevertheless, using a computer to locate tax law sources cannot substitute for developing and maintaining a thorough knowledge of the tax law or for careful analysis when addressing tax research issues.

Accessing tax documents electronically offers several important advantages over a paper-based approach:

- Materials generally are available to the practitioner faster through an electronic system.
- Some tax documents, such as slip opinions of trial-level court cases and interviews with policymakers, are available *only* through electronic means.
- Commercial subscriptions to electronic tax services sometimes provide, at little or no cost, additional tax law sources to which the researcher would not have access through stand-alone purchases of traditional material. For example, the full text of private letter rulings is costly to acquire in a paper-based format, but electronic publishers may bundle the rulings with other materials for a reasonable cost.

Strict cost comparisons of paper and electronic tax research materials are difficult to make, especially when the practitioner uses computers that are already in place and employed elsewhere in the practice. Over time, however, the convenience, cost, and reliability of electronic research tools clearly make them the dominant means of finding and analyzing tax law.

---

[32]See W. A. Raabe and G. E. Whittenburg, "Talking Tax: How to Make a Tax Presentation," *The Tax Adviser*, March 1997, pp. 179–182.

CHAPTER 2 Working with the Tax Law 2–29

FIGURE 2–6
Tax File Memorandum

> August 26, 1998
>
> **TAX FILE MEMORANDUM**
>
> FROM: John J. Jones
>
> SUBJECT: Fred and Megan Taxpayer
> Engagement: Issues
>
> Today I talked to Fred Taxpayer with respect to his August 14, 1998 letter requesting tax assistance. He wishes to know if he can sell his stock in Airways Co. to Maple, Inc., and deduct the $2,500 loss on his Airways stock.
>
> FACTS: Maple, Inc., is owned 50% by Fred and 50% by Megan. Fred wants to continue holding Airways Co. stock in anticipation of a rebound in its value, and that is why he has asked about a proposed sale of this stock to Maple, Inc.
>
> ISSUE: Can shareholders deduct a loss on the sale of an asset to a corporation all of whose stock they own?
>
> ANALYSIS: Section 267(a) provides that no loss will be deductible on a sale or exchange between certain related parties. One of these relationships involves a corporation and a shareholder who owns "more than 50 percent" of that corporation's stock [see § 267(b)(2)]. Although Fred owns only 50% of Maple, Inc., his wife, Megan, owns the other 50%. The constructive ownership rule of § 267(c)(2) attributes stock held by family members, and a spouse is part of a taxpayer's family for this purpose, according to § 267(c)(4). Consequently, Megan's stock will be attributed to Fred, who is then treated as owning 100% of Maple, Inc. The related-party disallowance rule would then apply to the loss from Fred's selling his Airways Co. stock to Maple, Inc. Accordingly, Fred must sell this stock to an unrelated party to make his loss deductible.
>
> Since Fred really wants to retain an investment in Airways Co., he can purchase replacement stock either before or after he sells his original Airways stock. Section 1091(a), however, requires that at least 30 days elapse between the purchase and the sale, or the sale and the purchase, as the case may be. Moreover, for this purpose, an option to buy the stock is treated as equivalent to the stock itself. As a result, Fred must wait at least 30 days between transactions and cannot utilize stock options in the interim to minimize his stock market exposure.
>
> A final alternative might be to replace the Airways Co. stock with securities of a comparable company in the same industry. Although no two companies are exactly alike, there may be another company whose management philosophy, marketing strategy, and financial data are sufficiently similar to Airways Co. to provide an equivalent return on investment. Under this alternative, Fred could acquire the new company's shares immediately without waiting the 30 days mandated by § 1091(a). Despite the two companies' investment similarity, they would not be treated as "substantially identical" for this purpose [see Rev.Rul. 59–44, 1959–1 C.B. 205].
>
> CONCLUSION: Fred should *not* sell his Airways Co. stock to Maple, Inc. Instead, he should sell this stock via his regular broker and either acquire new Airways stock 30 days before or after the date of sale, or acquire stock of a similar company whenever he chooses.

Using Electronic Tax Services. Usually, tax professionals use one of the following strategies when performing computer-based tax research:

- *Search* various databases using keywords that are likely to be found in the underlying documents, as written by Congress, the judiciary, or administrative sources.
- *Link* to tax documents for which all or part of the proper citation is known.
- *Browse* the tax databases, examining various tables of contents and indexes in a traditional manner or using cross-references in the documents to jump from one tax law source to another.

FIGURE 2–7
Client Letter

>Willis, Davis, Raabe, Kaplan, and Engle, CPAs
>5101 Madison Road
>Cincinnati, OH 45227
>
>August 30, 1998
>
>Mr. and Ms. Fred Taxpayer
>111 Boulevard
>Williamsburg, Virginia 23185
>
>Dear Mr. and Ms. Taxpayer:
>
>This letter is in response to your request for us to review your family's financial and tax situation. Our conclusions are based upon the facts as outlined in your August 14th letter. Any change in the facts may affect our conclusions.
>
>Mr. Taxpayer owns stock in Airways Co. that has declined in value, but he would like to retain this stock in anticipation of a rebound in its worth. You have proposed a sale of this stock at its current market value to Maple, Inc., a corporation owned 50–50 by Mr. and Mrs. Taxpayer. Such a sale, however, would not permit the loss to be deducted.
>
>A better approach would be to sell the Airways Co. stock before year-end and repurchase this stock through your regular stockbroker. Please understand that the loss will not be deductible unless at least 30 days elapse between the sale and the repurchase of the stock. You can either sell the old stock first and then buy the new stock, or buy the new stock first and then sell the old stock. However, it is essential that 30 days elapse between the sale and purchase transactions. Using options during this 30-day period is ineffective and will prevent the loss from being deducted in the current taxable year.
>
>If the 30-day requirement is unacceptable, you might consider replacing the Airways stock with securities of some other company, perhaps even a company in the same general business as Airways Co. Your regular stockbroker should be able to suggest appropriate possibilities. In that situation, your loss on Airways Co. stock can be deducted without regard to when you buy the new stock.
>
>Should you need more information or need to clarify our conclusions, do not hesitate to contact me.
>
>Sincerely yours,
>
>John J. Jones, CPA
>Partner

Virtually all of the major commercial tax publishers and some of the primary sources of the law itself, such as the Supreme Court and some of the Courts of Appeals, provide tax material in a variety of electronic formats, including CD-ROM services and on-line services.

CD-ROM Services. The CD-ROM has been a medium for tax data for about a decade. CCH, RIA, WESTLAW and others offer vast tax libraries to the practitioner, often in conjunction with a subscription to traditional paper-based resources and accompanied by newsletters, training seminars, and ongoing technical support.

At its best, a CD-ROM tax library provides the archival data that make up a permanent, core library of tax documents. For about $200 a year, a CD-ROM is updated quarterly, providing more comprehensive tax resources than the researcher is ever likely to need. The CD-ROM is comparable in scope to a paper-based library of a decade ago costing perhaps $20,000 to establish and $5,000 per year in perpetuity to maintain. If the library is contained on a small number of disks, it also can offer portability through use on laptop computers. Exhibit 2–2 summarizes the most popular of the CD-ROM tax services on the market today.

▼ EXHIBIT 2–2
CD-ROM Tax Services

CD-ROM Service	Description
CCH ACCESS	Includes the CCH tax service, primary sources including treatises, and other subscription materials. Ten to twenty disks.
RIA OnPoint	Includes primary sources, the *Federal Tax Coordinator*, and the *United States Tax Reporter*. The citator has elaborate document-linking features. Major tax treatises and other subscription materials also are provided. One to ten disks.
WESTLAW	Code, Regulations, *Cumulative Bulletins,* cases, citator, and editorial material are included. Twelve disks.
Kleinrock's	A single disk with all tax statutory, administrative, and judicial law. Another disk provides tax forms and instructions for Federal and state jurisdictions.

On-Line Services. On-line research systems allow practitioners to obtain virtually instantaneous use of tax law sources by accessing databases via a modem connection or via the Internet. On-line services generally employ price-per-search cost structures, which can average close to $200 per hour, significantly higher than the cost of CD services. Thus, unless a practitioner can pass along related costs to clients or others, on-line searching generally is limited to the most important issues and to the researchers with the most experience and training in search techniques.

Perhaps the best combination of electronic tax resources is to conduct day-to-day work on a CD system, so that the budget for the related work is known in advance, and augment the CD search with on-line access where it is judged to be critical. Exhibit 2–3 lists the most commonly used commercial on-line tax services.

The Internet. The Internet provides a wealth of tax information in several popular forms, sometimes at no direct cost to the researcher. Using web browser software and a modem, the tax professional can access information provided around the world that can aid the research process.

▼ EXHIBIT 2–3
On-Line Tax Services

On-Line Service	Description
LEXIS/NEXIS	Includes Federal and state statutory, administrative, and judicial material. Extensive libraries of newspapers, magazines, patent records, and medical and economic databases, both U.S. and foreign-based.
RIA Checkpoint	Includes the RIA tax service, major tax treatises, Federal and state statutes, administrative documents, and court opinions. Extensive citator access, editorial material, and practitioner aids.
CCH ACCESS	Includes the CCH tax service, primary sources including treatises, and other subscription materials. Tax and economic news sources, extensive editorial material, and practitioner support tools.
WESTLAW	Federal and state statutes, administrative documents, and court opinions. Extensive citator access, editorial material, and gateways to third-party publications. Extensive government document databases.

▼ EXHIBIT 2-4
Tax-Related Web Sites

Web Site	WWW Address at Press Date	Description
Internal Revenue Service	http://www.irs.ustreas.gov/prod/	News releases, downloadable forms and instructions, tables, and E-mail.
Court opinions	http://www.law.emory.edu/FEDCTS/	Allows the researcher to link to the site of the jurisdiction (other than the Tax Court) that is the subject of the query.
Discussion groups moderated by Tax Analysts	http://www.tax.org/notes/	Policy-oriented discussions of tax laws and proposals to change the law, links to student tax clinics, excerpts from the *Tax Notes* newsletter, and a tax calendar.
Tax Sites Directory	http://www.taxsites.com	References and links to tax sites on the Internet, including state and Federal tax sites, academic and professional pages, tax forms and software.
Tax laws on-line	http://www.access.gpo.gov/nara.cfr	Treasury Regulations.
	http://www.fourmilab.ch/ustax/ustax.html	Internal Revenue Code.
Tax World	http://omer.actg.uic.edu/home	References and links to tax sites on the Internet, including property tax and international tax links.
Commercial tax publishers	For instance, **http://www.riatax.com** and **http://cch.com**	Information about products and services available by subscription, and newsletter excerpts.
Large accounting firms and professional organizations	For instance, the AICPA's page is at **http://www.aicpa.org.** and an Ernst & Young LLP Tax Services page is at **http://www.taxcast.com**	Tax planning newsletters, descriptions of services offered and career opportunities, and exchange of data with clients and subscribers.
South-Western College Publishing	http://www.swcollege.com/tax/tax.html	Informational updates, newsletters, support materials for subscribers and adopters, and continuing education.

Caution: Addresses change frequently.

- *The World Wide Web (WWW)* provides access to a number of sites maintained by accounting and consulting firms, publishers, tax academics and libraries, and governmental bodies. The best sites offer links to other sites and direct contact to the site providers. Exhibit 2-4 lists some of the Web sites that may be most useful to tax researchers and their Internet addresses as of press date.
- *Newsgroups* provide a means by which information related to the tax law can be exchanged among taxpayers, tax professionals, and others who subscribe to the group's services. Newsgroup members can read the exchanges among other members and offer replies and suggestions to inquiries as desired. Discussions address the interpretation and application of existing law, analysis of proposals and new pronouncements, and reviews of tax software.

CHAPTER 2 Working with the Tax Law 2–33

While tax information on the Internet is plentiful, freely accessed information should never be relied upon without referring to other, more reliable sources. Always remember that anyone can set up a Web site and quality control is often lacking.

In many situations, solutions to research problems will benefit from, or require, the use of various electronic tax research tools. A competent tax professional must become familiar and proficient with these tools and be able to use them to meet the expectations of clients and the necessities of work in the modern world.[33]

KEY TERMS

Acquiescence, 2–17
Circuit Court of Appeals, 2–13
Court of Federal Claims, 2–12
Court of original jurisdiction, 2–12
Determination letters, 2–11
District Court, 2–12
Final Regulations, 2–9
Interpretive Regulations, 2–25

Legislative Regulations, 2–25
Letter rulings, 2–10
Nonacquiescence, 2–17
Precedents, 2–14
Procedural Regulations, 2–25
Proposed Regulations, 2–8
Revenue Procedures, 2–9

Revenue Rulings, 2–9
Small Cases Division, 2–12
Supreme Court, 2–14
Tax Court, 2–12
Technical Advice Memoranda (TAMs), 2–11
Temporary Regulations, 2–9
Writ of Certiorari, 2–15

PROBLEM MATERIALS

1. Judicial decisions interpreting a provision of the Internal Revenue Code of 1939 or 1954 are no longer of any value in view of the enactment of the Internal Revenue Code of 1986. Assess the validity of this statement.

2. Paul Jacobs operates a small international firm named Teal, Inc. A new treaty between the United States and Ukraine conflicts with a Section of the Internal Revenue Code. Paul asks you for advice. If he follows the treaty position, does he need to disclose this on his tax return? If he is required to disclose, are there any penalties for failure to disclose? Prepare a letter in which you respond to Paul. Teal's address is 100 International Drive, Tampa, FL 33620.

3. Distinguish between legislative, interpretive, and procedural Regulations.

4. Distinguish between the following:
    a. Treasury Regulations and Revenue Rulings.
    b. Revenue Rulings and Revenue Procedures.
    c. Revenue Rulings and letter rulings.
    d. Letter rulings and determination letters.

5. Rank the following items from the highest authority to the lowest in the Federal tax law system:

---

[33]For a more detailed discussion of the use of electronic tax research in the modern tax practice, see W. A. Raabe, G. E. Whittenburg, and J. C. Bost, *West's Federal Tax Research*. 4th ed (St. Paul, Minn.: West Publishing Co., 1997).

a. Interpretive Regulation.
b. Legislative Regulation.
c. Letter ruling.
d. Revenue Procedure.
e. Internal Revenue Code.
f. Proposed Regulation.

6. Interpret each of the following citations:
    a. Rev.Rul. 65–235, 1965-2 C.B. 88.
    b. Rev.Proc. 87–56, 1987–2 C.B. 674.
    c. Ltr.Rul. 9046036.

7. Which of the following would be considered advantages of the Small Cases Division of the Tax Court?
    a. Appeal to the Tax Court is possible.
    b. A hearing of a deficiency of $12,000 is considered on a timely basis.
    c. Taxpayer can handle the litigation without using a lawyer or certified public accountant.
    d. Taxpayer can use Small Cases Division decisions for precedential value.
    e. The actual hearing is conducted informally.
    f. Travel time will probably be reduced.

8. List an advantage and a disadvantage of using the Tax Court as the trial court for Federal tax litigation.

9. Sam Brown is considering litigating a tax deficiency of approximately $317,000 in the court system. He asks you to provide him with a short description of his alternatives indicating the advantages and disadvantages of each. Prepare your response to Sam in the form of a letter. His address is 200 Mesa Drive, Tucson, AZ 85714.

10. List an advantage and a disadvantage of using a District Court as the trial court for Federal tax litigation.

11. A taxpayer lives in Michigan. In a controversy with the IRS, the taxpayer loses at the trial court level. Describe the appeal procedure for each of the following trial courts:
    a. Small Cases Division of the Tax Court.
    b. Tax Court.
    c. District Court.
    d. Court of Federal Claims.

12. Suppose the U.S. Government loses a tax case in the District Court of South Carolina and does not appeal the result. What does the failure to appeal signify?

13. For the Tax Court, District Court, and the Court of Federal Claims, indicate the following:
    a. Number of regular judges per court.
    b. Availability of a jury trial.
    c. Whether the deficiency must be paid before the trial.

14. In which of the following states could a taxpayer appeal the decision of a District Court to the Ninth Circuit Court of Appeals?
    a. Alaska.
    b. Arkansas.
    c. New York.
    d. South Carolina.
    e. Utah.

15. What is the Supreme Court's policy on hearing tax cases?

16. In assessing the validity of a prior court decision, discuss the significance of the following on the taxpayer's issue:
    a. The decision was rendered by the District Court of Wyoming. Taxpayer lives in Wyoming.
    b. The decision was rendered by the Court of Federal Claims. Taxpayer lives in Wyoming.

c. The decision was rendered by the Second Circuit Court of Appeals. Taxpayer lives in California.
d. The decision was rendered by the Supreme Court.
e. The decision was rendered by the Tax Court. The IRS has acquiesced in the result.
f. Same as (e), except that the IRS has nonacquiesced in the result.

17. What is the difference between a Regular and a Memorandum decision of the Tax Court?

18. Interpret each of the following citations:
    a. 54 T.C. 1514 (1970).
    b. 408 F.2d 117 (CA–2, 1969).
    c. 69–1 USTC ¶9319 (CA–2, 1969).
    d. 23 AFTR2d 69–1090 (CA–2, 1969).
    e. 293 F.Supp. 1129 (D.Ct.Miss., 1967).
    f. 67–1 USTC ¶9253 (D.Ct.Miss., 1967).
    g. 19 AFTR2d 647 (D.Ct.Miss., 1967).
    h. 56 S.Ct. 289 (USSC, 1935).
    i. 36–1 USTC ¶9020 (USSC, 1935).
    j. 16 AFTR 1274 (USSC, 1935).
    k. 422 F.2d 1336 (Ct.Cls., 1970).

19. Explain the following abbreviations:
    a. CA–2   i. USTC
    b. Fed.Cl.   j. AFTR
    c. *aff'd.*   k. F.3d
    d. *rev'd.*   l. F.Supp.
    e. *rem'd.*   m. USSC
    f. *Cert. denied*   n. S.Ct.
    g. *acq.*   o. D.Ct.
    h. B.T.A.

20. Give the Commerce Clearing House citation for each of the following courts:
    a. Small Cases Division of the Tax Court.
    b. District Court.
    c. Supreme Court.
    d. Court of Federal Claims.
    e. Tax Court Memorandum decision.

21. Where can you locate a published decision of the Court of Federal Claims?

22. Which of the following items can probably be found in the *Cumulative Bulletin*?
    a. Revenue Ruling.
    b. Small Cases Division of the Tax Court decision.
    c. Letter ruling.
    d. Revenue Procedure.
    e. Proposed Regulation.
    f. District Court decision.
    g. Senate Finance Committee Report.
    h. Acquiescences to Tax Court decisions.
    i. Tax Court Memorandum decision.

23. As part of her coursework for a Masters of Tax degree, Ann is required to prepare a 30-page term paper about limited liability partnerships. Identify some relevant research steps Ann may take.

24. Constance is developing an outline for younger associates to follow when researching tax issues in her office. Identify the relevant alternatives available to a tax researcher.

25. Tom has just been audited by the IRS and, as a result, has been assessed a substantial deficiency (which he has not yet paid) in additional income taxes. In preparing his defense, Tom advances the following possibilities:
    a. Although a resident of Kentucky, Tom plans to sue in a District Court in Oregon that appears to be more favorably inclined toward taxpayers.

b. If (a) is not possible, Tom plans to take his case to a Kentucky state court where an uncle is the presiding judge.
c. Since Tom has found a B.T.A. decision that seems to help his case, he plans to rely on it under alternative (a) or (b).
d. If he loses at the trial court level, Tom plans to appeal to either the Court of Federal Claims or the Second Circuit Court of Appeals because he has relatives in both Washington, D.C., and New York. Staying with these relatives could save Tom lodging expense while his appeal is being heard by the court selected.
e. Even if he does not win at the trial court or appeals court level, Tom feels certain of success on an appeal to the Supreme Court.

Evaluate Tom's notions concerning the judicial process as it applies to Federal income tax controversies.

26. Using the legend provided, classify each of the following statements (more than one answer per statement may be appropriate):

Legend

D = Applies to the District Court
T = Applies to the Tax Court
C = Applies to the Court of Federal Claims
A = Applies to the Court of Appeals
U = Applies to the Supreme Court
N = Applies to none of the above

a. Decides only Federal tax matters.
b. Decisions are reported in the F.3d Series.
c. Decisions are reported in the USTCs.
d. Decisions are reported in the AFTRs.
e. Appeal is by *Writ of Certiorari*.
f. Court meets most often in Washington, D.C.
g. Offers the choice of a jury trial.
h. Is a trial court.
i. Is an appellate court.
j. Allows appeal to the Federal Circuit Court of Appeals and bypasses the taxpayer's particular Circuit Court of Appeals.
k. Has a Small Cases Division.
l. Is the only trial court where the taxpayer does not have to first pay the tax assessed by the IRS.

27. Using the legend provided, classify each of the following citations as to the type of court:

Legend

D = Applies to the District Court
T = Applies to the Tax Court
C = Applies to the Court of Federal Claims
A = Applies to the Court of Appeals
U = Applies to the Supreme Court
N = Applies to none of the above

a. 241 F.2d 197 (CA–4, 1957).
b. 90 T.C. 1 (1988).

c. 54 S.Ct. 8 (USSC, 1933).
d. 3 B.T.A. 1042 (1926).
e. T.C.Memo. 1954–141.
f. 597 F.2d 760 (Ct.Cls., 1979).
g. Ltr. Rul. 9414051.
h. 354 F.Supp. 1003 (D.Ct.Ga., 1972).
i. Rev.Rul. 74–164.

28. Using the legend provided, classify each of the following citations as to publisher:

Legend

RIA = Research Institute of America
CCH = Commerce Clearing House
W = West Publishing Company
U.S. = U.S. Government
O = Others

a. 83–2 USTC ¶9600.
b. 52 AFTR2d 83–5954.
c. 49 T.C. 645 (1968).
d. 39 TCM 32 (1979).
e. 416 U.S. 938.
f. RIA T.C.Memo. ¶80,582.
g. 89 S.Ct. 501.
h. 2 Cl.Ct. 600.
i. 415 F.2d 488.
j. 592 F.Supp. 18.
k. Rev.Proc. 77–37, 1977–2 C.B. 568.
l. 21 L.Ed.2d 495.

29. An accountant friend of yours tells you that he "almost never" does any tax research, because he feels that "research usually reveals that some tax planning idea has already been thought up and shot down." Besides, he points out, most tax returns are never audited by the IRS. Can a tax adviser who is dedicated to reducing his client's tax liability justify the effort to engage in tax research? Do professional ethics *demand* such efforts? Which approach would a client probably prefer?

30. Another friend of yours, who is a philosophy major, has overheard the conversation described in the previous problem and declares that all tax research is "immoral." She says that tax research enables people with substantial assets to shift the burden of financing public expenditures to those who "get up every morning, go to work, play by the rules, and pay their bills." How do you respond?

31. Some politicians have suggested that the United States should replace the Federal income tax with a national sales tax or other consumption-based levy that would be collected at the point of purchase. Such a system, its advocates say, would make tax planning unnecessary and render tax research skills obsolete. How would you respond to a client that has asked you for your evaluation of this proposal?

32. In the tax publications matrix that follows, place an X if a court decision can be found in the publication. There may be more than one X in a row for a particular court.

Court	U.S. Govt. Printing Office	West Publishing Company				Research Institute of America			Commerce Clearing House	
		Federal Supp.	Federal 3d	Federal Claims Reporter	S.Ct.	B.T.A. Memo.	T.C. Memo.	AFTR	T.C. Memo.	USTC
Supreme Court										
Court of Appeals										
Court of Federal Claims										
District Court										
Tax Court (Regular decisions)										
Tax Court (Memo decisions)										
Board of Tax Appeal										
BTA Memo										

RESEARCH PROBLEMS

Note: The RIA OnPoint System 4 Student Version CD-ROM *available with this text can be used in preparing solutions to the Research Problems. Alternatively, tax research materials contained in a standard tax library can be used.*

33. Your client is planning to change its method of depreciation for assets in situations not covered by Rev.Proc. 96–31. Your research has suggested that a private letter ruling might be advisable. Please determine whether the IRS would be willing to issue such a ruling and how it might be obtained.

34. Determine what is covered in the following subchapters in Chapter 1, Subtitle A of the Internal Revenue Code of 1986:
    a. B.
    b. D.
    c. F.
    d. K.
    e. P.

35. Locate the following Internal Revenue Code citations and give a brief description of each:
    a. § 708(a).
    b. § 1371(a)(1).
    c. § 2503(a).

36. Locate the following Regulations and give a brief description of each:
    a. Reg. § 1.170A–4A(b)(2)(ii)(C).
    b. Reg. § 1.672(b)–1.
    c. Reg. § 20.2031–7(f).

37. Find Rev.Rul. 78–325, 1978–2 C.B. 124 and give a brief description of it.

38. Find *Francis Levien*, 103 T.C. 120 (1994), and answer these questions:
    a. Who was the petitioner (plaintiff)?
    b. Who was the respondent (defendant)?
    c. What was the court's holding with respect to issue one?
    d. Was this a reviewed decision?
    e. How many judges agreed with the majority opinion?
    f. Who wrote a concurring opinion?
    g. Was this decision entered under Rule 155?

39. Complete the following citations:
    a. *Foxman v. Comm.*, 352 F.2d 466 (CA–3, _____).
    b. Rev.Rul. 79-_____, 1979–1 C.B. 144.
    c. *Clark v. Comm.*, 489 U.S. _____ (1989).
    d. Rev.Proc. 92–89, 1992–2 C.B. _____.
    e. *U.S. v. Catto*, 223 F.Supp. 663 (W.D. Tex., _____).
    f. *Korn Industries, Inc., v. U.S.*, 532 F.2d _____ (Ct.Cl., 1976).
    g. *Miller v. Comm.*, 45 B.T.A. _____ (1941).

CHAPTER 3

GROSS INCOME

LEARNING OBJECTIVES

After completing Chapter 3, you should be able to:

1. Explain the concepts of gross income and realization and distinguish between the economic, accounting, and tax concepts of gross income.

2. Understand when the cash, accrual, and hybrid methods of accounting are used and how they are applied.

3. Identify who should pay the tax on a particular item of income in various situations.

4. Understand that statutory authority is required to exclude an item from gross income.

5. Apply the Internal Revenue Code provisions on loans made at below-market interest rates.

6. Determine the extent to which receipts can be excluded under the tax benefit rule.

7. Understand the Internal Revenue Code provision that excludes interest on state and local government obligations from gross income.

8. Understand the Internal Revenue Code provision that excludes leasehold improvements from gross income.

9. Determine the extent to which life insurance proceeds are excluded from gross income.

10. Describe the circumstances under which income must be reported from the discharge of indebtedness.

OUTLINE

The Tax Formula, 3–2
Components of the Tax Formula, 3–2

Gross Income—What Is It?, 3–4
Economic and Accounting Concepts of Income, 3–4
Comparison of the Accounting and Tax Concepts of Income, 3–5
Form of Receipt, 3–6

Year of Inclusion, 3–7
Taxable Year, 3–7
Accounting Methods, 3–7
Exceptions Applicable to Cash Basis Taxpayers, 3–10
Exceptions Applicable to Accrual Basis Taxpayers, 3–13

Income Sources, 3–14
Personal Services, 3–14
Income from Property, 3–15
Income Received by an Agent, 3–17

Specific Rules Related to Income, 3–17
Imputed Interest on Loans for Money, 3–18
Tax Benefit Rule, 3–21
Interest on Certain State and Local Government Obligations, 3–22
Improvements on Leased Property, 3–23
Life Insurance Proceeds, 3–23
Income from Discharge of Indebtedness, 3–25
Gains and Losses from Property Transactions, 3–28

This chapter begins with an overview of the tax formula. Next, the determination of gross income is examined. Questions that are addressed include the following:

- What: What is income?
- When: In which tax period is the income recognized?
- Who: Who is taxed on the income?

THE TAX FORMULA

The basic income tax formula is introduced in Chapter 1 and summarized in Figure 1–1 on page 1–15. This chapter, together with Chapters 4 through 8, examines the elements of this formula in detail. However, before embarking on a detailed study of the income tax, a brief introduction of each component of the tax formula is provided below as an overview.

COMPONENTS OF THE TAX FORMULA

Income (Broadly Conceived). This includes all of the taxpayer's income, both taxable and nontaxable. Although it is essentially equivalent to gross receipts, it does not include a return of capital or borrowed funds.

Exclusions. For various reasons, Congress has chosen to exclude certain types of income from the income tax base. The principal income exclusions that apply to all entities (e.g., life insurance proceeds received by reason of death of the insured and state and local bond interest) are discussed later in this chapter, while exclusions that are unique to individuals are addressed in Chapters 15 and 16.

Gross Income. Section 61 of Internal Revenue Code provides the following definition of **gross income**:

> Except as otherwise provided in this subtitle, gross income means all income from whatever source derived.

This language is derived from the language of the Sixteenth Amendment to the Constitution. The "except as otherwise provided" phrase refers to exclusions.

Supreme Court decisions have made it clear that *all* sources of income are subject to tax unless Congress specifically excludes the type of income received:

> The starting point in all cases dealing with the question of the scope of what is included in "gross income" begins with the basic premise that the purpose of Congress was to use the full measure of its taxing power.[1]

While it is clear that income is to be broadly construed, the statutory law fails to provide a satisfactory definition of the term and lists only a small set of items that are specifically included in income, including

- Compensation for services,
- Business income,
- Gains from sales and other disposition of property,
- Interest,
- Dividends,
- Rents and royalties,
- Certain income arising from discharge of indebtedness, and
- Income from partnerships.

General rules related to the determination of gross income are addressed in the present chapter, while special accounting rules (needed to accurately determine when income is taxed) are discussed in Chapter 6. Rules for determining the gain from disposition of property are addressed in Chapters 7 and 8.

Deductions. Generally, all ordinary and necessary trade or business expenses are deductible by taxpaying entities. Such expenses include the cost of goods, salaries, wages, operating expenses (such as rent and utilities), research and development expenditures, interest, taxes, depreciation, amortization, and depletion. Rules related to business expenses are addressed in Chapter 4, while special rules pertaining to losses are addressed in Chapter 5.

As noted in Chapter 1, individuals have two categories of deductions—deductions *for* AGI and deductions *from* AGI. In addition, individuals are unique among taxpaying entities in that they are permitted to deduct a variety of personal expenses (i.e., expenses unrelated to business or investment) and they are allowed a standard deduction and personal dependency exemptions. These issues are discussed at length in Chapters 15 and 16.

Determining the Tax. Taxable income is determined by subtracting deductions (after any applicable limitations) from gross income. The tax rates (located inside the front cover of the textbook) are then applied to determine the tax. Finally, tax prepayments (such as Federal income tax withholding on salaries and estimated tax payments) and a wide variety of credits are subtracted from the tax to determine the amount due to the Federal government.

General issues related to tax determination are addressed in Chapter 13, including a discussion of business tax credits and the alternative minimum tax (a special alternative tax applicable in some cases). Tax credits available only to individuals are discussed in Chapter 15.

---

[1] *James v. U.S.*, 61–1 USTC ¶9449, 7 AFTR2d 1361, 81 S.Ct. 1052 (USSC, 1961)

GROSS INCOME—WHAT IS IT?

ECONOMIC AND ACCOUNTING CONCEPTS OF INCOME

LEARNING OBJECTIVE 1
Explain the concepts of gross income and realization and distinguish between the economic, accounting, and tax concepts of gross income.

As noted above, Congress failed to provide a clear definition of income when drafting the statutory law. Instead, it was left to the judicial and administrative branches of government to thrash out the meaning of income. As the income tax law developed, two competing models of income were considered by these agencies: economic income and accounting income.

The term **income** is used in the Code but is defined very broadly. Early in the history of our tax laws, the courts were required to interpret "the commonly understood meaning of the term which must have been in the minds of the people when they adopted the Sixteenth Amendment to the Constitution."[2]

Economists measure income (**economic income**) by determining the change (increase or decrease) in the fair market value of the entity's net assets from the beginning to the end of the year. This focus on change in *net worth* as a measure of income (or loss) requires no disposition of assets. For *individual* taxpayers, an additional adjustment is necessary to reflect personal consumption of goods and services (e.g., food, the rental value of owner-occupied housing, etc.).[3]

EXAMPLE 1

Helen's economic income for 1998 is calculated as follows:

Fair market value of Helen's assets on December 31, 1998	$220,000	
Less liabilities on December 31, 1998	(40,000)	
Net worth on December 31, 1998		$ 180,000
Fair market value of Helen's assets on January 1, 1998	$200,000	
Less liabilities on January 1, 1998	(80,000)	
Net worth on January 1, 1998		(120,000)
Increase in net worth		$ 60,000
Consumption		
Food, clothing, and other personal expenditures	25,000	
Imputed rental value of the home Helen owns and occupies	12,000	
Total consumption		37,000
Economic income		$ 97,000

The tax law relies to some extent on net worth as a measure of income.[4] Potentially, anything that increases net worth is income, and anything that decreases net worth is deductible (if permitted by statute). Thus, *windfall income* such as buried treasure found in one's backyard is taxable under the theory that net worth has been increased.[5] Likewise, a lender does *not* recognize gross income on receipt of loan principal repayments. The lender's investment simply changes from a loan receivable to cash, so net worth does not change.

---

[2] *Merchants Loan and Trust Co. v. Smietanka*, 1 USTC ¶42, 3 AFTR 3102, 41 S.Ct. 386 (USSC, 1921).

[3] See Henry C. Simons, *Personal Income Taxation* (Chicago: University of Chicago Press, 1933), Chapters 2–3.

[4] *Comm. v. Glenshaw Glass Co.*, 55–1 USTC ¶9308, 47 AFTR 162, 348 U.S. 426 (USSC, 1955).

[5] *Cesarini v. U.S.*, 69–1 USTC ¶9270, 23 AFTR2d 69–997, 296 F.Supp. 3 (D.Ct. Oh., 1969), aff'd 70–2 USTC ¶9509, 26 AFTR2d 70–5107, 428 F.2d 812 (CA–6, 1970); Rev.Rul. 61, 1953–1 CB 17.

Because strict application of a tax based on economic income would require taxpayers to determine the value of their assets annually, compliance would be burdensome. Controversies between taxpayers and the IRS would inevitably arise under an economic approach to income determination because of the subjective nature of valuation in many circumstances. In addition, using market values to determine income for tax purposes could result in liquidity problems. That is, a taxpayer's assets could increase in value but not be easily converted into the cash needed to pay the resulting tax (e.g., increases in the value of commercial real estate). Thus, the IRS, Congress, and the courts have rejected broad application of the economic income concept as impractical.

Accountants use an alternative definition of income that relies on the realization principle.[6] According to this principle, income (**accounting income**) is not recognized until it is realized. For realization to occur, (1) an exchange of goods or services must take place between the accounting entity and some independent, external party, and (2) the goods or services received by the accounting entity must be capable of being objectively valued. Thus, an increase in market value of assets before a sale or other disposition is *not* sufficient to warrant recognition of accounting income. In addition, the imputed savings that arise when an entity creates assets for its own use (e.g., feed grown by a farmer for his livestock) are not included in accounting income because no exchange has occurred.

The Supreme Court expressed an inclination toward the accounting concept of income when it adopted the realization requirement in *Eisner v. Macomber*:

> Income may be defined as the gain derived from capital, from labor, or from both combined, provided it is understood to include profit gained through a sale or conversion of capital assets. . . . Here we have the essential matter: not a gain accruing to capital; not a *growth* or *increment* of value in investment; but a gain, a profit, something of exchangeable value, *proceeding from* the property, *severed from* the capital however invested or employed, and *coming in*, being *"derived"*—that is, *received* or *drawn by* the recipient for his separate use, benefit and disposal—*that is*, income derived from the property.[7]

Thus, the realization requirement underlying accounting income is a central concept in tax law and is generally a prerequisite for increases in net worth to be recognized as gross income.

COMPARISON OF THE ACCOUNTING AND TAX CONCEPTS OF INCOME

Although income tax rules frequently parallel financial accounting measurement concepts, differences do exist. Of major significance, for example, is the fact that unearned (prepaid) income received by an accrual basis taxpayer often is taxed in the year of receipt. For financial accounting purposes, such prepayments are not treated as income until earned.[8] Because of this and other differences, many corporations report financial accounting income that is substantially different from the amounts reported for tax purposes (see Chapter 9, Reconciliation of Taxable Income and Accounting Income).

The Supreme Court provided an explanation for some of the variations between accounting and taxable income in a decision involving inventory and bad debt adjustments:

---

[6] See the American Accounting Association Committee Report on the "Realization Concept," *The Accounting Review* (April 1965): 312–322.

[7] 1 USTC ¶32, 3 AFTR 3020, 40 S.Ct. 189 (USSC, 1920).

[8] Similar differences exist in the deduction area.

TAX IN THE NEWS

IRS CALLS FOUL ON NBA REFEREES

Four NBA referees were called for "tax fouls" and ejected from the game for not reporting income. The rules of the game follow:

- Through a travel agent, the referees purchased first-class airline tickets to cities where they were officiating.
- The referees turned the tickets in to the travel agent in exchange for coach tickets and cash.
- The NBA reimbursed the referees for first-class tickets.
- The referees chose not to include the cash differential received in their gross income.

The IRS filed criminal charges against the four referees (i.e., filing false Federal income tax returns). Three of the four pled guilty.

The primary goal of financial accounting is to provide useful information to management, shareholders, creditors, and others properly interested; the major responsibility of the accountant is to protect these parties from being misled. The primary goal of the income tax system, in contrast, is the equitable collection of revenue.... Consistently with its goals and responsibilities, financial accounting has as its foundation the principle of conservatism, with its corollary that "possible errors in measurement [should] be in the direction of understatement rather than overstatement of net income and net assets." In view of the Treasury's markedly different goals and responsibilities, understatement of income is not destined to be its guiding light....

Financial accounting, in short, is hospitable to estimates, probabilities, and reasonable certainties; the tax law, with its mandate to preserve the revenue, can give no quarter to uncertainty.[9]

FORM OF RECEIPT

Gross income is not limited to cash received. "It includes income realized in any form, whether in money, property, or services. Income may be realized [and recognized], therefore, in the form of services, meals, accommodations, stock or other property, as well as in cash."[10]

EXAMPLE 2 Ostrich Corporation allows Cameron, an employee, to use a company car for his vacation. Cameron realizes income equal to the rental value of the car for the time and mileage. ▼

EXAMPLE 3 Plover, Inc., owes $10,000 on a mortgage. The creditor accepts $8,000 in full satisfaction of the debt. Plover realizes income of $2,000 from retiring the debt.[11] ▼

---

[9]*Thor Power Tool Co. v. Comm.*, 79–1 USTC ¶9139, 43 AFTR2d 79–362, 99 S.Ct. 773 (USSC, 1979).
[10]Reg. § 1.61–1(a).
[11]Reg. § 1.61–12. See *U.S. v. Kirby Lumber Co.*, 2 USTC ¶814, 10 AFTR 458, 52 S.Ct. 4 (USSC, 1931). Note that exceptions to this general rule will be discussed later in this chapter under Income from Discharge of Indebtedness.

EXAMPLE 4

Donna is a CPA specializing in individual tax return preparation. Her neighbor, Jill, is a dentist. Each year, Donna prepares Jill's tax return in exchange for two dental checkups. Jill and Donna each have gross income equal to the fair market value of the services they provide. ▼

YEAR OF INCLUSION

TAXABLE YEAR

The annual accounting period or **taxable year** is a basic component of our tax system. Generally, an entity must use the *calendar year* to report its income. However, a *fiscal year* (a period of 12 months ending on the last day of any month other than December) can be elected if the taxpayer maintains adequate books and records. This fiscal year option generally is not available to partnerships, S corporations, and personal service corporations, as discussed in Chapter 6.

Determining the particular year in which the income will be taxed is important for determining the tax consequences of the income. This is true for the following reasons:

- With a progressive tax rate system, a taxpayer's marginal tax rate can change from year to year.
- Congress may change the tax rates.
- The relevant rates may change because of a change in the entity's status (e.g., a proprietorship may incorporate).
- Several provisions in the code depend on the taxpayer's income for the year (e.g., the charitable contribution deduction).

ACCOUNTING METHODS

LEARNING OBJECTIVE 2
Understand when the cash, accrual, and hybrid methods of accounting are used and how they are applied.

The year in which an item of income is subject to tax often depends upon the **accounting method** the taxpayer employs. The three primary methods of accounting are (1) the cash receipts and disbursements method, (2) the accrual method, and (3) the hybrid method. Most individuals use the cash receipts and disbursements method of accounting, whereas most corporations use the accrual method. Because the Regulations require the accrual method for determining purchases and sales when inventory is an income-producing factor,[12] some businesses employ a hybrid method that is a combination of the cash and accrual methods.

In addition to these overall accounting methods, a taxpayer may choose to spread the gain from an installment sale of property over the collection period by using the *installment method* of income recognition. Contractors may either spread profits from contracts over the period in which the work is done (the percentage of completion method) or defer all profit until the year in which the project is completed (the completed contract method, which can be used only in limited circumstances).[13]

The IRS has the power to prescribe the accounting method to be used by the taxpayer. Section 446(b) grants the IRS broad powers to determine if the accounting method used clearly reflects income:

---

[12] Reg. § 1.446–1(c)(2)(i). Other circumstances in which the accrual method must be used are presented later in this chapter.

[13] §§ 453 and 460. Limitations on the use of the installment method and the completed contract method are addressed in Chapter 6.

Exceptions—If no method of accounting has been regularly used by the taxpayer, or *if the method used does not clearly reflect income, the computation of taxable income shall be made under such method as, in the opinion of the Secretary. . .does clearly reflect income.*

A change in the method of accounting requires the consent of the IRS.[14]

Cash Receipts Method.
Under the **cash receipts method,** property or services received are included in the taxpayer's gross income in the year of actual or constructive receipt by the taxpayer or agent, regardless of whether the income was earned in that year.[15] The income received need not be reduced to cash in the same year. All that is necessary for income recognition is that property or services received have a fair market value—a cash equivalent.[16] Thus, a cash basis taxpayer that receives a note in payment for services has income in the year of receipt equal to the fair market value of the note. However, a creditor's mere promise to pay (e.g., an account receivable), with no supporting note, is not usually considered to have a fair market value.[17] Thus, the cash basis taxpayer defers income recognition until the account receivable is collected.

EXAMPLE 5

Finch & Thrush, a CPA firm, uses the cash receipts method of accounting. In 1998, the firm performs an audit for Orange Corporation and bills the client for $5,000, which is collected in 1999. In 1998, the firm also performs an audit for Blue Corporation. Because of Blue's precarious financial position, Finch & Thrush requires Blue to issue an $8,000 secured negotiable note in payment of the fee. The note has a fair market value of $6,000. The firm collects $8,000 on the note in 1999. Finch & Thrush has the following gross income for the two years:

	1998	1999
Fair market value of note received from Blue	$6,000	
Cash received		
From Orange on account receivable		$ 5,000
From Blue on note receivable		8,000
Less: Recovery of capital	–0–	(6,000)
Total gross income	$6,000	$ 7,000

Generally, a check received is considered a cash equivalent. Thus, a cash basis taxpayer must recognize the income when the check is received. This is true even if the taxpayer receives the check after banking hours.[18]

As noted previously, use of the cash method is prohibited when inventories are material to the business (instead, the accrual method is required). In addition, certain taxpayers are not permitted to use the cash method of accounting regardless of whether inventories are material. Specifically, the accrual basis must be used to report the income earned by (1) corporations (other than S corporations), (2)

---

[14]§ 446(e). See Chapter 6 for a detailed discussion of changes in accounting method.

[15]*Julia A. Strauss,* 2 B.T.A. 598 (1925). The doctrine of constructive receipt holds that, if income is unqualifiedly available although not physically in the taxpayer's possession, it is subject to the income tax. An example is accrued interest on a savings account. Under the doctrine of constructive receipt, the interest is taxed to a depositor in the year available, rather than the year actually withdrawn. The fact that the depositor uses the cash basis of accounting for tax purposes is irrelevant. See Reg. § 1.451–2.

[16]Reg. §§ 1.446–1(a)(3) and (c)(1)(i).

[17]*Bedell v. Comm.,* 1 USTC ¶359, 7 AFTR 8469, 30 F.2d 622 (CA–2, 1929).

[18]*Charles F. Kahler,* 18 T.C. 31 (1952).

partnerships with a corporate partner, and (3) tax shelters.[19] This accrual basis requirement has three exceptions:[20]

- A farming business.
- A qualified personal service corporation (e.g., a corporation performing services in health, law, engineering, architecture, accounting, actuarial science, performing arts, or consulting).
- Any entity that is not a tax shelter whose average annual gross receipts for the most recent three-year period are $5 million or less.

Thus, a corporation with average gross receipts of less than $5 million may be permitted to use the cash method of accounting, provided that inventory is not a material income-producing factor.

Planning Considerations

Cash Receipts Method

The timing of income from services can often be controlled through the cash method of accounting. Although taxpayers are somewhat constrained by the constructive receipt doctrine (discussed later in this chapter), seldom will customers and clients offer to pay before they are asked. The usual lag between billings and collections (e.g., December's billings collected in January) will result in a deferral of some income until the last year of operations. For example, before rendering services, a corporate officer approaching retirement may contract with the corporation to defer a portion of her compensation to the lower tax bracket retirement years.

Accrual Method. Under the **accrual method,** an item is generally included in gross income for the year in which it is earned, regardless of when the income is collected. The income is earned when (1) all the events have occurred that fix the right to receive the income and (2) the amount to be received can be determined with reasonable accuracy.[21]

Generally, the taxpayer's rights to the income accrue when title to property passes to the buyer or the services are performed for the customer or client.[22] If the rights to the income have accrued but are subject to a potential refund claim (e.g., under a product warranty), the income is reported in the year of sale, and a deduction is allowed in subsequent years when actual claims accrue.[23]

Where the taxpayer's rights to the income are being contested (e.g., when a contractor fails to meet specifications), the year in which the income is subject to tax depends upon whether payment has been received. If payment has not been received, no income is recognized until the claim is settled. Only then is the right to the income established.[24] If the payment is received before the dispute is settled, however, the court-made **claim of right doctrine** requires the taxpayer to recognize the income in the year of receipt.[25]

---

[19] § 448(a). For this purpose, the hybrid method of accounting is considered the same as the cash method.
[20] § 448(b).
[21] Reg. § 1.451–1(a).
[22] *Lucas v. North Texas Lumber Co.*, 2 USTC ¶484, 8 AFTR 10276, 50 S.Ct. 184 (USSC, 1930).
[23] *Brown v. Helvering*, 4 USTC ¶1222, 13 AFTR 851, 54 S.Ct. 356 (USSC, 1933).
[24] *Burnet v. Sanford and Brooks*, 2 USTC ¶636, 9 AFTR 603, 51 S.Ct. 150 (USSC, 1931).
[25] *North American Oil Consolidated Co. v. Burnet*, 3 USTC ¶943, 11 AFTR 16, 52 S.Ct. 613 (USSC, 1932).

TAX IN THE NEWS

A FENDER-BENDER WITH THE IRS

Should used-car dealers be required to include in their gross income amounts they may never receive? They say no—doing so will drive them out of business. The IRS says yes—it is the law.

Creditors such as Credit Acceptance and National Auto Credit provide financing on used-car sales to buyers with poor credit ratings. This enables used-car dealers to sell more cars. But there is a catch. When a sale is financed through such a lender, the used-car dealer receives as little as half of the proceeds right away. To reduce their risk, the lenders turn over the rest of the money to the dealer only after they have collected it from the buyer. If the buyer defaults, the used-car dealer may not receive any of the remaining balance.

Dealers complain that having to record all the income at the time of the sale is driving them out of business. The amount involved is huge. For example, at the end of 1997, Credit Acceptance owed $469 million to nearly 5,400 dealers. The National Independent Automobile Dealers Association, which represents used-car dealers, is lobbying Congress for relief.

SOURCE: Adapted from Michael Selz, "Used-Car Dealers Face Fender-Benders with the IRS," *Wall Street Journal*, February 25, 1997, p. B2.

EXAMPLE 6

Tangerine Construction, Inc., completes construction of a building in 1998 and presents a bill to the customer. The customer refuses to pay the bill and claims that Tangerine has not met specifications. A settlement with the customer is not reached until 1999. No income accrues to Tangerine until 1999. Alternatively, if the customer pays for the work and then files suit for damages, Tangerine cannot defer the income, and it is taxable in 1998. ▼

The measure of accrual basis income is generally the amount the taxpayer has a right to receive. Unlike the cash basis, the fair market value of the customer's obligation is irrelevant in measuring accrual basis income.

EXAMPLE 7

Assume the same facts as in Example 5, except that Finch & Thrush uses the accrual basis of accounting. The firm must recognize $13,000 ($8,000 + $5,000) income in 1998, the year its rights to the income accrue. ▼

Hybrid Method. The Regulations require that the accrual method be used for determining sales and cost of goods sold. To simplify record keeping, some taxpayers account for inventory using the accrual method and use the cash method for all other income and expense items. This approach, called the **hybrid method,** is used primarily by small businesses when inventory is an income-producing factor.

EXCEPTIONS APPLICABLE TO CASH BASIS TAXPAYERS

Constructive Receipt. Income that has not actually been received by the taxpayer is taxed as though it had been received—the income is constructively received—under the following conditions:

- The amount is made readily available to the taxpayer.

- The taxpayer's actual receipt is not subject to substantial limitations or restrictions.[26]

The rationale for the **constructive receipt** doctrine is that if the income is available, the taxpayer should not be allowed to postpone income recognition. For instance, a taxpayer is not permitted to defer income for December services by refusing to accept payment until January. However, determining whether the income is *readily available* and whether *substantial limitations or restrictions exist* often requires a judgment call. The following are some examples of the application of the constructive receipt doctrine.

EXAMPLE 8
Rob, a doctor, operates his own business as a sole proprietorship. Rob is also a member of a barter club. In 1998, Rob provided medical care for other club members and earned 1,000 points. Each point entitles him to $1 in goods and services sold by other members of the club; the points can be used at any time. In 1999, Rob exchanged his points for a new color TV. Rob must recognize $1,000 income in 1998 when the 1,000 points were credited to his account.[27] ▼

EXAMPLE 9
On December 31, an employer issued a bonus check to an employee but asked her to hold it for a few days until the company could make deposits to cover the check. The income was not constructively received on December 31 since the issuer did not have sufficient funds in its account to pay the debt.[28] ▼

EXAMPLE 10
Mauve, Inc., an S corporation, owned interest coupons that matured on December 31. The coupons could be converted to cash at any bank at maturity. Thus, the income was constructively received on December 31, even though Mauve failed to cash in the coupons until the following year.[29] ▼

EXAMPLE 11
Flamingo Company mails dividend checks on December 31, 1998. The checks will not be received by the shareholders until January. The shareholders do not realize income until 1999.[30] ▼

The constructive receipt doctrine does not reach income that the taxpayer is not yet entitled to receive even though the taxpayer could have contracted to receive the income at an earlier date.

EXAMPLE 12
Murphy offered to pay Peach Corporation (a cash basis taxpayer) $100,000 for land in December 1998. Peach Corporation refused but offered to sell the land to Murphy on January 1, 1999, when the corporation would be in a lower tax bracket. If Murphy accepts Peach's offer, the gain is taxed to Peach in 1999 when the sale is completed.[31] ▼

Original Issue Discount. Lenders frequently make loans that require a payment at maturity of more than the amount of the original loan. The difference between the amount due at maturity and the amount of the original loan is actually interest but is referred to as **original issue discount.** Under the general rules of tax accounting, a cash basis lender would not report the original issue discount as interest income until the year the amount is collected, although an accrual basis borrower would deduct the interest as it is earned. However, the Code puts the lender and borrower on parity by requiring that the original issue discount be

---

[26] Reg. § 1.451–2(a).
[27] Rev.Rul. 80–52, 1980–1 C.B. 100.
[28] *L. M. Fischer*, 14 T.C. 792 (1950).
[29] Reg. § 1.451–2(b).
[30] Reg. § 1.451–2(b).
[31] *Cowden v. Comm.*, 61–1 USTC ¶9382, 7 AFTR2d 1160, 289 F.2d 20 (CA–5, 1961).

> **TAX IN THE NEWS**
>
> **ORIGINAL ISSUE DISCOUNT RULES MAY DAMPEN ENTHUSIASM FOR INFLATION-ADJUSTED BONDS**
>
> The U.S. Treasury Department is now issuing inflation-adjusted bonds. The bonds are aimed at small investors looking for a hedge against inflation. The interest paid each year and the principal are adjusted to reflect the effects of inflation. These bonds present some unique tax accounting issues. In particular, while the interest payment is clearly income, how should the annual adjustment to principal be taxed?
>
> In Temporary Regulation § 1.1275–7T, the Treasury Department concluded that the taxpayer is required to treat the adjustment to principal as original issue discount amortized during the year. For example, if a bond is issued for $1,000 when the inflation index is 100, and the index at the end of the first year is 102, the bondholder is entitled to $1,020 at maturity assuming no further changes in price level. The investor is required to include $20 in gross income for the increase in principal that will not be received until maturity. Thus, inflation adjustments can create gross income before any cash has been received.

reported when it is earned, regardless of the taxpayer's accounting method.[32] The *interest earned* is calculated by the effective interest rate method.

EXAMPLE 13

On January 1, 1998, Blue and White, a cash basis partnership, pays $82,645 for a 24-month certificate of deposit. The certificate is priced to yield 10% (the effective interest rate) with interest compounded annually. No interest is paid until maturity, when Blue and White receives $100,000. Thus, the partnership's gross income from the certificate is $17,355 ($100,000 − $82,645). Blue and White calculates income earned each year as follows:

1998: (0.10 × $82,645) =	$ 8,264
1999: [0.10($82,645 + $8,264)] =	9,091
	$17,355

The original issue discount rules do not apply to U.S. savings bonds or to obligations with a maturity date of one year or less from the date of issue.[33]

Amounts Received under an Obligation to Repay. The receipt of funds with an obligation to repay that amount in the future is the essence of borrowing. The taxpayer's assets and liabilities increase by the same amount, so no income is realized when the borrowed funds are received. Because amounts paid to the taxpayer by mistake and customer deposits are often classified as borrowed funds, receipt of the funds is not a taxable event.

EXAMPLE 14

A landlord receives a damage deposit from a tenant. The landlord does not recognize income until the deposit is forfeited because the landlord has an obligation to repay the deposit if no damage occurs.[34] However, if the deposit is in fact a prepayment of rent, it is taxed in the year of receipt. ▼

---

[32] §§ 1272(a)(3) and 1273(a).
[33] § 1272(a)(2).

[34] *John Mantell*, 17 T.C. 1143 (1952).

EXCEPTIONS APPLICABLE TO ACCRUAL BASIS TAXPAYERS

Prepaid Income. For financial reporting purposes, advance payments received from customers are reflected as prepaid income and as a liability of the seller. For tax purposes, however, the prepaid income often is taxed in the year of receipt.

EXAMPLE 15

In December 1998, a company pays its January 1999 rent of $1,000. The accrual basis landlord must include the $1,000 in 1998 income for tax purposes, although the unearned rent income is reported as a liability on the landlord's balance sheet for December 31, 1998. ▼

Taxpayers have repeatedly argued that deferral of income until it is actually earned properly matches revenues and expenses. Moreover, a proper matching of income with the expenses of earning that income is necessary to clearly reflect income, as required by the Code. The IRS responds that § 446(b) grants it broad powers to determine whether an accounting method clearly reflects income. The IRS further argues that generally accepted financial accounting principles should not dictate tax accounting for prepaid income because of the practical problems of collecting Federal revenues. Collection of the tax is simplest in the year the taxpayer receives the cash from the customer or client.

Over 40 years of litigation, the IRS has been only partially successful in the courts. In cases involving prepaid income from services to be performed at the demand of customers (e.g., dance lessons to be taken at any time in a 24-month period), the IRS's position has been upheld.[35] In such cases, the taxpayer's argument that deferral of the income was necessary to match the income with expenses was not persuasive because the taxpayer did not know precisely when each customer would demand services and, thus, when the expenses would be incurred. However, taxpayers have had some success in the courts when the services were performed on a fixed schedule (e.g., a baseball team's season-ticket sales).[36] In some cases involving the sale of goods, taxpayers have successfully argued that the prepayments were mere deposits or in the nature of loans.[37]

Against this background of mixed results in the courts, congressional intervention, and taxpayers' strong resentment of the IRS's position, in 1971 the IRS modified its prepaid income rules, as explained in the following paragraphs.

Deferral of Advance Payments for Goods. Generally, an accrual basis taxpayer can elect to defer recognition of income from advance payments for goods if the method of accounting for the sale is the same for tax and financial reporting purposes.[38]

EXAMPLE 16

Brown Company ships goods only after payment for the goods has been received. In December 1998, Brown receives $10,000 for goods that are not shipped until January 1999. Brown can elect to report the income in 1999 for tax purposes, assuming the company reports the income in 1999 for financial reporting purposes. ▼

---

[35]*American Automobile Association v. U.S.*, 61–2 USTC ¶9517, 7 AFTR2d 1618, 81 S.Ct. 1727 (USSC, 1961); *Schlude v. Comm.*, 63–1 USTC ¶9284, 11 AFTR2d 751, 83 S.Ct. 601 (USSC, 1963).

[36]*Artnell Company v. Comm.*, 68–2 USTC ¶9593, 22 AFTR2d 5590, 400 F.2d 981 (CA–7, 1968). See also *Boise Cascade Corp. v. U.S.*, 76–1 USTC ¶9203, 37 AFTR2d 76–696, 530 F.2d 1367 (Ct.Cls., 1976).

[37]*Veenstra & DeHavaan Coal Co.*, 11 T.C. 964 (1948); *Consolidated-Hammer Dry Plate & Film Co. v. Comm.*, 63–1 USTC ¶9494, 11 AFTR2d 1518, 317 F.2d 829 (CA–7, 1963); *Comm. v. Indianapolis Power & Light Co.*, 90–1 USTC ¶50,007, 65 AFTR2d 90–394, 110 S.Ct. 589 (USSC, 1990).

[38]Reg. § 1.451–5(b). See Reg. § 1.451–5(c) for exceptions to this deferral opportunity. The financial accounting conformity requirement is not applicable to contractors who use the completed contract method.

Deferral of Advance Payments for Services. Revenue Procedure 71–21[39] permits an accrual basis taxpayer to defer recognition of income for advance payments for services to be performed by the end of the tax year following the year of receipt. No deferral is allowed if the taxpayer might be required, under the agreement, to perform any services after the tax year following the year of receipt of the advance payment.

EXAMPLE 17

Canary Corporation, an accrual basis taxpayer, sells its services under 12-month, 18-month, and 24-month contracts. The corporation provides services to each customer every month. In April 1998, Canary sold the following customer contracts:

Length of Contract	Total Proceeds
12 months	$6,000
18 months	3,600
24 months	2,400

Fifteen hundred dollars of the $6,000 may be deferred ($3/12 \times \$6,000$), and $1,800 of the $3,600 may be deferred ($9/18 \times \$3,600$) because those amounts will not be earned until 1999. However, the entire $2,400 received on the 24-month contract is taxable in the year of receipt (1998), since a part of the income will still be unearned by the end of the tax year following the year of receipt (part will be earned in 2000). ▼

Revenue Procedure 71–21 does not apply to prepaid rent or prepaid interest. These items are always taxed in the year of receipt.

PLANNING CONSIDERATIONS

Prepaid Income

The accrual basis taxpayer who receives advance payment from customers should structure the transactions using the rules discussed above to avoid having to pay tax on income before the time the income is actually earned. In addition, both cash and accrual basis taxpayers can sometimes defer income by stipulating that the payments are deposits rather than prepaid income. For example, a landlord might consider requiring an equivalent damage deposit rather than prepayment of the last month's rent under a lease.

INCOME SOURCES

PERSONAL SERVICES

3 LEARNING OBJECTIVE
Identify who should pay the tax on a particular item of income in various situations.

It is a well-established principle of taxation that income from personal services must be included in the gross income of the person who performs the services. This principle was first established in a Supreme Court decision, *Lucas v. Earl*[40] Mr. Earl entered into a binding agreement with his wife under which Mrs. Earl was to receive one-half of Mr. Earl's salary. Justice Holmes used the celebrated **fruit and tree metaphor** to explain that the fruit (income) must be attributed to the tree

---

[39] 1971–2 C.B. 549.

[40] 2 USTC ¶496, 8 AFTR 10287, 50 S.Ct. 241 (USSC, 1930).

from which it came (Mr. Earl's services). A mere **assignment of income** does not shift the liability for the tax.

Services of an Employee. Services performed by an employee for the employer's customers are considered performed by the employer. Thus, the employer is taxed on the income from the services provided to the customer, and the employee is taxed on any compensation received from the employer.[41]

EXAMPLE 18

Dr. Shontelle incorporates her medical practice and enters into a contract to work for the corporation for a salary. All patients contract to receive their services from the corporation, and those services are provided through the corporation's employee, Dr. Shontelle. The corporation must include the patients' fees in its gross income. Dr. Shontelle must include her salary in her gross income. The corporation is allowed a deduction for a reasonable salary paid to Dr. Shontelle. ▼

INCOME FROM PROPERTY

Income earned from property (interest, dividends, rent) must be included in the gross income of the owner of the property. If a shareholder clips interest coupons from bonds shortly before the interest payment date and transfers the coupons to his solely owned corporation, the interest will still be taxed to the shareholder. Similarly, a parent who assigns rents from rental property to a child will be taxed on the rent, since the parent retains ownership of the property.[42]

Often income-producing property is transferred after income from the property has accrued but before the income is recognized under the transferor's method of accounting. The IRS and the courts have developed rules to allocate the income between the transferor and the transferee. These allocation rules are addressed below.

Interest. According to the IRS, interest accrues daily. Therefore, the interest for the period that includes the date of the transfer is allocated between the transferor and the transferee based on the number of days during the period that each owned the property.

EXAMPLE 19

Floyd, a cash basis taxpayer, gives his son, Seth, bonds with a face amount of $10,000 and an 8% stated annual interest rate. The gift is made on January 31, 1998, and the interest is paid on December 31, 1998. Floyd must recognize $68 in interest income (8% × $10,000 × $31/365$). Seth recognizes $732 in interest income ($800 − $68). ▼

When the transferor must recognize the income from the property depends upon the method of accounting and the manner in which the property was transferred. In the case of a gift of income-producing property, the donor's share of the accrued income must be recognized at the time it would have been recognized had the donor continued to own the property.[43] If the transfer is a sale, however, the transferor must recognize the accrued income at the time of the sale. This results because the accrued interest will be included in the sales proceeds.

---

[41]*Sargent v. Comm.*, 91–1 USTC ¶50,168, 67 AFTR2d 91–718, 929 F.2d 1252 (CA–8, 1991).

[42]*Galt v. Comm.*, 54–2 USTC ¶9457, 46 AFTR 633, 216 F.2d 41 (CA–7, 1954); *Helvering v. Horst*, 40–2 USTC ¶9787, 24 AFTR 1058, 61 S.Ct. 144 (USSC, 1940).

[43]Rev.Rul. 72–312, 1972–1 C.B. 22.

EXAMPLE 20

Assume the same facts as in the preceding example, except that the interest payable on December 31 is not actually or constructively received by the bondholders until January 3, 1999. As a cash basis taxpayer, Floyd generally does not recognize interest income until it is received. If Floyd continues to own the bonds, the interest will be included in his gross income in 1999, the year it is received. Therefore, Floyd must include the $68 accrued income in his gross income as of January 3, 1999.

Further assume that Floyd sells identical bonds on the date of the gift. The bonds sell for $9,900, including accrued interest. On January 31, 1998, Floyd must recognize the accrued interest of $68 on the bonds sold. Thus, the selling price of the bonds is $9,832 ($9,900 − $68). ▼

Dividends. A corporation is taxed on its earnings, and the shareholders are taxed on the dividends paid to them from the corporation's after-tax earnings. The dividend can take the form of an actual dividend or a constructive dividend (e.g., shareholder use of corporate assets).

Unlike interest, dividends do not accrue on a daily basis because the declaration of a dividend is at the discretion of the corporation's board of directors. Generally, dividends are taxed to the person who is entitled to receive them—the shareholder of record as of the corporation's record date.[44] Thus, if a taxpayer sells stock after a dividend has been declared but before the record date, the dividend generally will be taxed to the purchaser.

If a donor makes a gift of stock to someone (e.g., a family member) after the declaration date but before the record date, the Tax Court has held that the donor does not shift the dividend income to the donee. The *fruit* has sufficiently ripened as of the declaration date to tax the dividend income to the donor of the stock.[45] In a similar set of facts, the Fifth Court of Appeals concluded that the dividend income should be included in the gross income of the donee (the owner at the record date). In this case, the taxpayer gave stock to a qualified charity (a charitable contribution) after the declaration date and before the record date.[46]

EXAMPLE 21

On June 20, the board of directors of Black Corporation declares a $10 per share dividend. The dividend is payable on June 30, to shareholders of record on June 25. As of June 20, Kathleen owns 200 shares of Black Corporation's stock. On June 21, Kathleen sells 100 of the shares to Jon for their fair market value and gives 100 of the shares to Andrew (her son). Assume both Jon and Andrew are shareholders of record as of June 25. Jon (the purchaser) is taxed on $1,000 since he is entitled to receive the dividend. However, Kathleen (the donor) is taxed on the $1,000 received by Andrew (the donee) because the gift was made after the declaration date of the dividend. ▼

The following payments are frequently referred to as dividends but are not considered dividends for tax purposes:

- Dividends received on deposits with savings and loan associations, credit unions, and banks are actually interest (a contractual rate paid for the use of money).
- Patronage dividends paid by cooperatives (e.g., a farm cooperative) are rebates made to users and are considered reductions in the cost of items purchased from the association. The rebates are usually made after year-end

---

[44]Reg. § 1.61–9(c). The record date is the cutoff for determining the shareholders who are entitled to receive the dividend.

[45]*M. G. Anton*, 34 T.C. 842 (1960).

[46]*Caruth Corporation v. U.S.*, 89–1 USTC ¶9172, 63 AFTR2d 89–716, 865 F.2d 644 (CA-5, 1989).

(after the cooperative has determined whether it has met its expenses) and are apportioned among the members on the basis of their purchases.
- Mutual insurance companies pay dividends on unmatured life insurance policies that are considered nontaxable rebates of premiums.
- Shareholders in mutual investment funds are allowed to report as capital gains their proportionate share of the funds' gains that are realized and distributed. The capital gain and ordinary income portions are reported on the Form 1099 that funds supply to shareholders each year.
- When a corporation issues a simple stock dividend (e.g., common stock issued to common shareholders), the shareholder has merely received additional shares that represent the same total investment. Thus, the shareholder does not recognize income. See Chapter 10 for a more detailed discussion of stock dividends.

INCOME RECEIVED BY AN AGENT

Income received by the taxpayer's agent is considered to be received by the taxpayer. A cash basis principal must recognize the income at the time it is received by the agent.[47]

EXAMPLE 22

Longhorn, Inc., a cash basis corporation, delivers cattle to the auction barn in late December. The auctioneer, acting as the corporation's agent, sells the cattle and collects the proceeds in December. The auctioneer does not pay Longhorn until the following January. The corporation must include the sales proceeds in its gross income in the year the auctioneer received the funds. ▼

SPECIFIC RULES RELATED TO INCOME

LEARNING OBJECTIVE 4
Understand that statutory authority is required to exclude an item from gross income.

The all-inclusive principles of gross income determination (discussed in the previous sections) as applied by the IRS and the courts have, on occasion, been expanded or modified by Congress through legislation. This legislation generally provides more specific rules for determining gross income from certain sources. Most of these special rules appear in §§ 71–90 of the Code.

In addition to provisions describing how specific sources of gross income are to be taxed, several specific rules *exclude* items from gross income. Authority for excluding specific items is provided in §§ 101–150 and in various other provisions in the Code. Each exclusion has its own legislative history and reason for enactment. Many statutory exclusions are unique to *individual taxpayers* (e.g., gifts and inheritances [§ 102], scholarships [§ 117], and a variety of fringe benefits paid to *employees*). These exclusions are discussed in Chapters 15 and 16. Other exclusions are broader and apply to all entities. These exclusions include interest on state and local bonds (§ 103), life insurance proceeds received by reason of death of the insured (§ 101), the fair market value of leasehold improvements received by the lessor when a lease is terminated (§ 109),[48] and income from discharge of indebtedness (§ 108). Some of the broadly applied statutory rules describing inclusions and exclusions are discussed below.

---

[47]Rev.Rul. 79–379, 1979–2 C.B. 204.
[48]If the tenant made the improvements in lieu of rent, the value of the improvements is not eligible for exclusion.

IMPUTED INTEREST ON LOANS FOR MONEY

LEARNING OBJECTIVE 5
Apply the Internal Revenue Code provisions on loans made at below-market interest rates.

As discussed earlier in the chapter, generally no income is recognized unless it is realized. Realization occurs when the taxpayer performs services or sells goods and thus becomes entitled to a payment from the other party. It follows that no income is realized if the goods or services are provided at no charge. Under this interpretation of the realization requirement, before 1984, interest-free loans were used to shift income between taxpayers.

EXAMPLE 23

Brown Corporation is in the 35% tax bracket and has $200,000 in a money market account earning 10% interest. Jack is the sole shareholder of Brown. He is in the 15% tax bracket and has no investment income. In view of the difference in tax rates, Jack believes that it would be better for him to receive and pay tax on the earnings from Brown's $200,000 investment. Jack does not wish to receive the $200,000 from Brown as a dividend because that would trigger a tax.

Before 1984, Jack could achieve his goals as follows. He could take the money market account from Brown Corporation in exchange for a $200,000 non-interest-bearing note, payable on Brown's demand. As a result, Jack would receive the $20,000 earnings on the money market account, and the combined taxes of Brown Corporation and Jack would be decreased by $4,000.

Decrease in Brown's tax—(0.10 × $200,000) × 0.35 =	($7,000)
Increase in Jack's tax—(0.10 × $200,000) × 0.15 =	3,000
Overall decrease in tax liability	$4,000

Under the 1984 amendments to the Code, Brown Corporation in the preceding example is deemed to have received an interest payment from Jack even though no interest was actually paid.[49] This payment of imputed interest is taxable to Brown Corporation. Jack may be able to deduct the imaginary interest payment on his return as investment interest if he itemizes deductions (see Chapter 15). To complete the fictitious series of transactions, Brown Corporation is deemed to return the interest to Jack in the form of a taxable dividend.

Imputed interest is calculated using rates the Federal government pays on new borrowings and is compounded semiannually. The Federal rates are adjusted monthly and are published by the IRS.[50] There are three Federal rates: short-term (not over three years and including demand loans), mid-term (over three years but not over nine years), and long-term (over nine years).

EXAMPLE 24

Assume the Federal rate applicable to the loan in the preceding example is 7% through June 30 and 8% from July 1 through December 31. Brown Corporation made the loan on January 1, and the loan is still outstanding on December 31. Brown must recognize interest income of $15,280, and Jack has interest expense of $15,280. Brown is deemed to have paid a $15,280 dividend to Jack.

Interest Calculations	
January 1 to June 30—(0.07 × $200,000) (½ year)	$ 7,000
July 1 to December 31—[0.08($200,000 + $7,000)] (½ year)	8,280
	$15,280

---

[49] § 7872(a)(1).

[50] §§ 7872(b)(2) and (f)(2).

Concept Summary 3–1

Effect of Certain Below-Market Loans on the Lender and Borrower

Type of Loan		Lender	Borrower
Gift	Step 1	Interest income	Interest expense
	Step 2	Gift made*	Gift received
Compensation related	Step 1	Interest income	Interest expense
	Step 2	Compensation expense	Compensation income
Corporation to shareholder	Step 1	Interest income	Interest expense
	Step 2	Dividend paid	Dividend income

*The gift may be subject to the gift tax (refer to Chapter 1).

If interest is charged on the loan but is less than the Federal rate, the imputed interest is the difference between the amount that would have been charged at the Federal rate and the amount actually charged.

EXAMPLE 25

Assume the same facts as in Example 24, except that Brown Corporation charged 6% interest, compounded annually.

Interest at the Federal rate	$ 15,280
Less interest charged (0.06 × $200,000)	(12,000)
Imputed interest	$ 3,280

The imputed interest rules apply to the following types of below-market loans:[51]

1. Gift loans (made out of love, affection, or generosity).
2. Compensation-related loans (employer loans to employees).
3. Corporation-shareholder loans (a corporation's loans to its shareholders, as in Example 23).
4. Tax avoidance loans and other loans that significantly affect the borrower's or lender's Federal tax liability (discussed in the following paragraphs).

The effects of the first three types of loans on the borrower and lender are summarized in Concept Summary 3–1.

Tax Avoidance and Other Below-Market Loans. In addition to the three specific types of loans that are subject to the imputed interest rules, the Code includes a catchall provision for *tax avoidance loans* and other arrangements that have a significant effect on the tax liability of the borrower or lender. The Conference Report provides the following example of an arrangement that might be subject to the imputed interest rules.[52]

EXAMPLE 26

Annual dues for the Good Health Club are $400. In lieu of paying dues, a member can make a $4,000 deposit, refundable at the end of one year. The club can earn $400 interest on the deposit. ▼

---

[51] § 7872(c).

[52] H. Rep. No. 98–861, 98th Cong., 2d Sess., 1984, p. 1023.

If interest were not imputed, an individual with $4,000 could, in effect, earn tax-exempt income on the deposit. That is, rather than invest the $4,000, earn $400 in interest, pay tax on the interest, and then pay $400 in dues, the individual could avoid tax on the interest by making the deposit. Thus, income and expenses are imputed as follows: interest income and nondeductible health club fees for the club member; income from fees and interest expense for the club.

Many commercially motivated transactions could be swept into this other below-market loans category. However, the temporary Regulations have carved out a frequently encountered exception for customer prepayments. If the prepayments are included in the recipient's income under the recipient's method of accounting, the payments are not considered loans and thus are not subject to the imputed interest rules.[53]

EXAMPLE 27

Landlord, a cash basis taxpayer, charges tenants a damage deposit equal to one month's rent on residential apartments. When the tenant enters into the lease, the landlord also collects rent for the last month of the lease. ▼

The prepaid rent for the last month of the lease is taxed in the year received and thus is not considered a loan. The security deposit is not taxed when received and is therefore a candidate for imputed interest. However, neither the landlord nor the tenant derives any apparent tax benefit, so the security deposit should not be subject to the imputed interest provisions. But if making the deposit would reduce the rent paid by the tenant, the tenant could derive a tax benefit, much the same as the club member in Example 26.

Exceptions and Limitations. No interest is imputed on total outstanding *compensation-related loans* or *corporation-shareholder loans* of $10,000 or less unless the purpose of the loan is tax avoidance.[54] This vague tax avoidance standard exposes practically all compensation-related and corporation-shareholder loans to possible imputed interest problems. Nevertheless, the $10,000 exception should apply when an employee's borrowing was necessitated by personal needs (e.g., to meet unexpected expenses) rather than tax considerations. Similarly, no interest is imputed on outstanding *gift loans* of $10,000 or less between individuals, unless the loan proceeds are used to purchase income-producing property.[55] This exemption eliminates from these complex provisions immaterial amounts that do not result in apparent shifts of income. If the proceeds of gift loans between individuals are used to purchase income-producing property, the limitations discussed in the next paragraph apply instead.

On loans of $100,000 or less between individuals, the imputed interest cannot exceed the borrower's net investment income for the year (gross income from all investments less the related expenses).[56] Through the gift loan provision, the imputed interest rules are designed to prevent high-income individuals from shifting income to relatives in a lower marginal bracket. This shifting of investment income is considered to occur only to the extent that the borrower has investment income. Thus, the income imputed to the lender is limited to the borrower's net investment income. As a further limitation or exemption, if the borrower's net investment income for the year does not exceed $1,000, no interest is imputed on loans of $100,000 or less. However, these limitations for loans of $100,000 or less do not apply if a principal purpose of a loan is tax avoidance. In such a case, interest is imputed, and the imputed interest is not limited to the borrower's net investment

---

[53]Prop.Reg. § 1.7872–2(b)(1)(i).
[54]§ 7872(c)(3).
[55]§ 7872(c)(2).
[56]§ 7872(d).

Concept Summary 3-2

Exceptions to the Imputed Interest Rules for Below-Market Loans

Exception	Eligible Loans	Ineligible Loans and Limitations
De minimis—aggregate loans of $10,000 or less	Gift loans	Proceeds used to purchase income-producing assets.
	Employer-employee	Principal purpose is tax avoidance.
	Corporation-shareholder	Principal purpose is tax avoidance.
Aggregate loans of $100,000 or less	Between individuals	Principal purpose is tax avoidance. For all other loans, interest is imputed to the extent of the borrower's net investment income, if it exceeds $1,000.

income.[57] These exceptions to the imputed interest rules are summarized in Concept Summary 3–2.

TAX BENEFIT RULE

6 LEARNING OBJECTIVE
Determine the extent to which receipts can be excluded under the tax benefit rule.

Generally, if a taxpayer obtains a deduction for an item in one year and in a later year recovers all or a portion of the prior deduction, the recovery is included in gross income in the year received.[58]

EXAMPLE 28

A business deducted as a loss a $1,000 receivable from a customer when it appeared the amount would never be collected. The following year, the customer paid $800 on the receivable. The business must report the $800 as income in the year it is received. ▼

However, the § 111 **tax benefit rule** limits income recognition when a deduction does not yield a tax benefit in the year it is taken. If the taxpayer in Example 28 has no tax liability in the year of the deduction, the $800 receipt will be excluded from income in the year of the recovery.

EXAMPLE 29

Before deducting a $1,000 loss from an uncollectible business receivable, Tulip Company had taxable income of $200. The business bad debt deduction yields only a $200 tax benefit (assuming no loss carryback is made). That is, taxable income is reduced by only $200 (to zero) as a result of the bad debt deduction. Therefore, if the customer makes a payment on the previously deducted receivable in the following year, only the first $200 is a taxable recovery of a prior deduction. Any additional amount collected is nontaxable because only $200 of the loss yielded a reduction in taxable income (i.e., a tax benefit). ▼

---

[57]*Deficit Reduction Tax Bill of 1984: Explanation of the Senate Finance Committee* (April 2, 1984), p. 484.

[58]§ 111(a).

INTEREST ON CERTAIN STATE AND LOCAL GOVERNMENT OBLIGATIONS

LEARNING OBJECTIVE 7
Understand the Internal Revenue Code provision that excludes interest on state and local government obligations from gross income.

At the time the Sixteenth Amendment was ratified by the states, there was some question as to whether the Federal government possessed the constitutional authority to tax interest on state and local government obligations. Taxing such interest was thought to violate the doctrine of intergovernmental immunity because the tax would impair the ability of state and local governments to finance their operations.[59] Thus, interest on state and local government obligations was specifically exempted from Federal income taxation.[60] However, the Supreme Court has concluded that there is no constitutional prohibition against levying a nondiscriminatory Federal income tax on state and local government obligations.[61] Nevertheless, currently the statutory exclusion still exists.

Obviously, the interest exclusion reduces the cost of borrowing for state and local governments. A taxpayer with a 36 percent marginal tax rate requires only a 5.12 percent yield on a tax-exempt bond to obtain the same after-tax income as a taxable bond paying 8 percent interest [5.12% ÷ (1 − 0.36) = 8%].

The lower cost for the state and local governments is more than offset by the revenue loss of the Federal government. Also, tax-exempt interest is considered to be a substantial loophole for the very wealthy. For these reasons, bills have been introduced in Congress calling for Federal government subsidies to state and local governments that voluntarily choose to issue taxable bonds. Under the proposals, the tax-exempt status of existing bonds would not be eliminated.

The current exempt status applies solely to state and local government bonds. Thus, income received from the accrual of interest on a condemnation award or an overpayment of state tax is fully taxable.[62] Nor does the exemption apply to gains on the sale of tax-exempt securities.

EXAMPLE 30
Macaw Corporation purchases State of Virginia bonds for $10,000 on July 1, 1998. The bonds pay $400 interest each June 30 and December 31. On March 31, 1999, Macaw sells the bonds for $10,500 plus $200 of accrued interest. Macaw must recognize a $500 taxable gain ($10,500 − $10,000), but the $200 accrued interest is exempt from taxation. ▼

State and local governments have developed sophisticated financial schemes to attract new industry. For example, local municipalities have issued bonds to finance construction of plants to be leased to private enterprise. Because the financing could be arranged with low-interest municipal obligations, the plants could be leased at lower cost than other facilities the private business could obtain. However, Congress has placed limitations on the use of tax-exempt securities to finance private business.[63]

PLANNING CONSIDERATIONS

Municipal Bonds

Tax-exempt state and local bonds are almost irresistible investments for taxpayers with high marginal tax rates. To realize the maximum benefit from the exemption, the investor can purchase zero coupon bonds, which pay interest only at maturity.

---

[59] *Pollock v. Farmer's Loan & Trust Co.*, 3 AFTR 2602, 15 S.Ct. 912 (USSC, 1895).
[60] § 103(a).
[61] *South Carolina v. Baker III*, 88–1 USTC ¶9284, 61 AFTR2d 88–995, 108 S.Ct. 1355 (USSC, 1988).
[62] *Kieselbach v. Comm.*, 43–1 USTC ¶9220, 30 AFTR 370, 63 S.Ct. 303 (USSC, 1943); *U.S. Trust Co. of New York v. Anderson*, 3 USTC ¶1125, 12 AFTR 836, 65 F.2d 575 (CA–2, 1933).
[63] See § 103(b).

The advantage of the zero coupon feature is that the investor can earn tax-exempt interest on the accumulated principal and interest. If the investor purchases a bond that pays interest each year, the interest received may be such a small amount that an additional tax-exempt investment cannot be made. In addition, reinvesting the interest may entail transaction costs (broker's fees). The zero coupon feature avoids these problems. Note, however, that municipal bond interest may increase the base of the alternative minimum tax, as discussed in Chapter 13. For companies that face an alternative minimum tax, zero coupon bonds may not be a desirable option.

IMPROVEMENTS ON LEASED PROPERTY

8 LEARNING OBJECTIVE
Understand the Internal Revenue Code provision that excludes leasehold improvements from gross income.

When a real property lease expires, the landlord regains control of both the real property and any improvements to the property (e.g., buildings and landscaping) made by the tenant during the term of the lease. In 1940, the Supreme Court held that the fair market value of improvements made by a tenant to the landlord's property should be included in the landlord's gross income upon termination of the lease.[64] Congress effectively reversed this decision by enacting § 109, which defers tax on the value of improvements until the property is sold. More specifically, any improvements made to the leased property are excluded from the landlord's income unless the improvement is made to the property in lieu of rent.

EXAMPLE 31

Mahogany Corporation leases office space to Zink and Silver, Attorneys-at-Law. When the law firm took possession of the office space, it added wall partitions, an in-wall computer network, and a variety of other improvements to the space. The improvements were not made in lieu of rent payments to Mahogany. When the lease expires and Mahogany regains possession of the space, the improvements will be excluded from Mahogany's income. ▼

LIFE INSURANCE PROCEEDS

9 LEARNING OBJECTIVE
Determine the extent to which life insurance proceeds are excluded from gross income.

General Rule. **Life insurance proceeds** paid to the beneficiary because of the death of the insured are exempt from income tax.[65] Congress chose to exempt life insurance proceeds for the following reasons:

- For family members, life insurance proceeds serve much the same purpose as a nontaxable inheritance.
- In a business context (as well as in a family situation), life insurance proceeds replace an economic loss suffered by the beneficiary.

Thus, Congress concluded that, in general, making life insurance proceeds exempt from income tax was a good policy.

EXAMPLE 32

Sparrow Corporation purchased an insurance policy on the life of its CEO and named itself as the beneficiary. Sparrow paid $24,000 in premiums. When the company's CEO died, Sparrow collected the insurance proceeds of $60,000. The $60,000 is exempt from Federal income tax. ▼

---

[64]*Helvering v. Bruun*, 40–1 USTC ¶9337, 24 AFTR 652, 60 S.Ct. 631 (USSC, 1940).

[65]*Estate of D. R. Daly*, 3 B.T.A. 1042 (1926).

Exceptions to Exclusion Treatment. The income tax exclusion applies only when the insurance proceeds are received because of the death of the insured. If the owner cancels the policy and receives the cash surrender value, he or she must recognize gain to the extent of the excess of the amount received over the cost of the policy.[66]

Another exception to exclusion treatment applies if the policy is transferred after the insurance company issues it. If the policy is transferred for valuable consideration, the insurance proceeds are includible in the gross income of the transferee to the extent the proceeds received exceed the amount paid for the policy by the transferee plus any subsequent premiums paid.[67]

EXAMPLE 33

Platinum Corporation pays premiums of $5,000 for an insurance policy with a face amount of $12,000 on the life of Beth, an officer of the corporation. Subsequently, Platinum sells the policy to Beth's husband for $6,000. On Beth's death, her husband receives the proceeds of $12,000. The amount that Beth's husband can exclude from gross income is limited to $6,000 plus any premiums he paid subsequent to the transfer. ▼

The Code, however, provides four exceptions to the rule illustrated in the preceding example. These exceptions permit exclusion treatment for transfers to the following:

1. A partner of the insured.
2. A partnership in which the insured is a partner.
3. A corporation in which the insured is an officer or shareholder.
4. A transferee whose basis in the policy is determined by reference to the transferor's basis (see Chapters 7, 9, and 11).

The first three exceptions facilitate the use of insurance contracts to fund **buy-sell agreements.** The fourth exception applies to policies that were transferred pursuant to a tax-free exchange or were received by gift.[68]

EXAMPLE 34

Rick and Sam are equal partners who have a buy-sell agreement that allows either partner to purchase the interest of a deceased partner for $50,000. Neither partner has sufficient cash to actually buy the other partner's interest, but each has a life insurance policy on his own life in the amount of $50,000. Rick and Sam could exchange their policies (usually at little or no taxable gain), and upon the death of either partner, the surviving partner could collect tax-free insurance proceeds. The proceeds could then be used to purchase the decedent's interest in the partnership. ▼

Investment earnings arising from the reinvestment of life insurance proceeds are generally subject to income tax. For example, the beneficiary may elect to collect the insurance proceeds in installments that include taxable interest income.

---

[66]*Landfield Finance Co. v. U.S.*, 69–2 USTC ¶9680, 24 AFTR2d 69–5744, 418 F.2d 172 (CA–7, 1969).

[67]Chronically or terminally ill taxpayers can exclude gain on surrender or transfer of life insurance policies for valuable consideration under certain circumstances. See § 101(g).

[68]See the discussion of gifts and tax-free exchanges in Chapter 7.

PLANNING CONSIDERATIONS

Life Insurance

Life insurance is a tax-favored investment. The annual increase in the cash surrender value of the policy is not taxable because it is subject to substantial restrictions (no income has been actually or constructively received). By borrowing on the policy's cash surrender value, the owner can actually receive the policy's increase in value in cash without recognizing income.

INCOME FROM DISCHARGE OF INDEBTEDNESS

LEARNING OBJECTIVE 10
Describe the circumstances under which income must be reported from the discharge of indebtedness.

Income is generated when appreciated property is used to pay a debt or when the creditor cancels debt. If appreciated property is used to pay a debt, the transaction is treated as a sale of the appreciated property followed by payment of the debt.[69] Foreclosure by a creditor is also treated as a sale or exchange of the property.[70]

EXAMPLE 35

Juan owed the State Bank $100,000 on an unsecured note. Juan satisfied the note by transferring to the bank common stock with a basis of $60,000 and a fair market value of $100,000. Juan must recognize $40,000 gain on the transfer. Juan also owed the bank $50,000 on a note secured by land. When Juan's basis in the land was $20,000 and the land's fair market value was $50,000, the bank foreclosed on the loan and took title to the land. Juan must recognize a $30,000 gain on the foreclosure. ▼

A creditor may cancel debt to assure the vitality of the debtor. In such cases, the debtor's net worth is increased by the amount of debt forgiven.

EXAMPLE 36

Brown Corporation is unable to meet the mortgage payments on its factory building. Both the corporation and the mortgage holder are aware of the depressed market for industrial property in the area. Foreclosure would only result in the creditor's obtaining unsellable property. To improve Brown's financial position and thus improve its chances of obtaining from other lenders the additional credit necessary for survival, the creditor agrees to forgive all amounts past due and to reduce the principal amount of the mortgage. Brown's net worth is increased by the amount of past due debt that was forgiven *plus* the reduction in the mortgage balance. ▼

Generally, the debtor will recognize *taxable income* equal to the amount of debt canceled.[71] The following two examples illustrate additional circumstances where taxable income results from cancellation of indebtedness.

EXAMPLE 37

A corporation issues bonds with a face value of $500,000. Subsequently, the corporation repurchases the bonds in the market for $150,000. It has effectively canceled its $500,000 debt with a $150,000 payment, so it recognizes $350,000 in gross income.[72] ▼

EXAMPLE 38

In 1993, Turquoise Corporation borrowed $60,000 from National Bank to purchase a warehouse. Turquoise agreed to make monthly principal and interest payments for 15 years. The interest rate on the note was 7%. In 1998, when the balance on the note had been reduced

---

[69] Reg. § 1.1001–2(a).
[70] *Estate of Delman v. Comm.*, 73 T.C. 15 (1979).
[71] § 61(a)(12).
[72] See *U.S. v. Kirby Lumber Co.*, 2 USTC ¶814, 10 AFTR 458, 52 S.Ct. 4 (USSC, 1931).

TAX IN THE NEWS

WHEN PUBLIC HOUSING AND TAX POLICIES COLLIDE

Recently, the Department of Housing and Urban Development wanted to reduce the rent subsidy payments to landlords. However, many of the housing projects eligible for the payments were subject to large mortgages. The reduced subsidy payments would cause the project owners to default on their mortgages, which were guaranteed by the Federal government. Since the government did not want to be a landlord, the House Banking Subcommittee was considering proposals to restructure the debt by reducing principal.

In testimony before the House Banking Subcommittee on September 17, 1997, Kenneth Kies, chief of staff of the Joint Committee on Taxation, explained how efforts to rescue government-subsidized housing might be thwarted by the tax laws. Mr. Kies explained that altering the mortgages could create income from discharge of indebtedness to the landlord. This income would be taxable in the year the debt was restructured.

---

through monthly payments to $48,000, the bank offered to accept $45,000 in full settlement of the note. The bank made the offer because interest rates had increased to 11%. Turquoise accepted the bank's offer. As a result, Turquoise must recognize $3,000 ($48,000 − $45,000) income.[73] ▼

Though discharge of indebtedness generally produces taxable income, in the following cases, the reduction in debt is excluded from gross income:[74]

1. Creditors' gifts.
2. Discharges under Federal bankruptcy law.
3. Discharges that occur when the debtor is insolvent.
4. Discharge of the farm debt of a solvent taxpayer.
5. Discharge of **qualified real property business indebtedness.**
6. A seller's cancellation of a buyer's indebtedness.
7. A shareholder's cancellation of a corporation's indebtedness.
8. Forgiveness of loans to students.

Creditors' Gifts. If the creditor reduces the debt as an act of *love, affection or generosity*, the debtor has simply received a nontaxable gift (situation 1). Such motivations generally arise only on loans between friends or family members. Rarely will a gift be found to have occurred in a business context. A businessperson may settle a debt for less than the amount due, but as a matter of business expediency (e.g., high collection costs or disputes as to contract terms) rather than generosity.[75]

Insolvency and Bankruptcy. Cancellation of indebtedness income is excluded when the debtor is insolvent (i.e., the debtor's liabilities exceed the fair market value of the assets) or when the cancellation of debt results from a bankruptcy proceeding (situations 2 and 3). The insolvency exclusion is limited to the amount

---

[73]Rev.Rul. 82–202, 1982–1 C.B. 35.
[74]§§ 108 and 1017.

[75]*Comm. v. Jacobson*, 49–1 USTC ¶9133, 37 AFTR 516, 69 S.Ct. 358 (USSC, 1949).

of insolvency. The tax law permits this exclusion to avoid imposing undue hardship on the debtor (under the notion of wherewithal to pay discussed in Chapter 1).

The law imposes a cost for the insolvency and bankruptcy exclusion. More specifically, the debtor must decrease certain tax benefits (capital loss carryforwards, net operating loss carryforwards, some tax credits, and suspended passive losses)[76] by the amount of income excluded. In addition, if the amount of excluded income exceeds these tax benefits, the debtor must then reduce the basis in assets.[77] Thus, excluded cancellation of indebtedness income either accelerates recognition of future income (by reducing tax benefit carryforwards) or is deferred until the debtor's assets are sold (or depreciated).

EXAMPLE 39

Before any debt cancellation, Maroon Corporation has assets with a fair market value of $500,000 and liabilities of $600,000. A creditor agrees to cancel $125,000 of liabilities. Maroon will be permitted to exclude $100,000 of the debt cancellation income (the amount of insolvency) and will be taxed on $25,000. Maroon must also reduce any tax benefits and the basis of its assets by $100,000 (the excluded income). ▼

Qualified Real Property Indebtedness. Taxpayers (other than C corporations) can elect to exclude income from cancellation of indebtedness if the canceled debt is secured by real property used in a trade or business (situation 5). In addition, debt incurred after 1992 must also be used to acquire or improve real property in a trade or business to qualify for the exclusion.[78] The amount of exclusion is limited to the lesser of (1) the excess of the debt over the fair market value of the real property or (2) the adjusted basis of all depreciable real property held. In addition, the basis of all depreciable real property held by the debtor must be reduced by the amount excluded.

EXAMPLE 40

Blue, Inc., owns a warehouse worth $5 million, with a $3 million basis. The warehouse is subject to a $7 million mortgage that was incurred in connection with the acquisition of the warehouse. In lieu of foreclosure, the lender decides that it will reduce the mortgage to $4.5 million. Blue may elect to exclude $2 million from gross income ($7 million − $5 million). If Blue makes the election, it must reduce the aggregate basis of its depreciable realty by $2 million. ▼

EXAMPLE 41

Assume the same facts as in the preceding example, except that the basis of the warehouse is $1 million. If the warehouse is the only piece of depreciable realty that Blue owns, only $1 million of the debt cancellation income may be excluded. ▼

Seller Cancellation. When a seller of property cancels debt previously incurred by a buyer in a purchase transaction, the cancellation generally is not treated as income to the buyer (situation 6). Instead, the reduction in debt is considered to be a reduction in the purchase price of the asset. Consequently, the basis of the asset is reduced in the hands of the buyer.[79]

EXAMPLE 42

Snipe, Inc., purchases a truck from Sparrow Autos for $10,000 in cash and a $25,000 note payable. Two days after the purchase, Sparrow announces a sale on the same model truck, with a sales price of $28,000. Snipe contacts Sparrow and asks to be given the sales price on the truck. Sparrow complies by canceling $7,000 of the note payable. The $7,000 is excluded from Snipe's income, and the basis of the truck to Snipe is $28,000. ▼

---

[76]See Chapter 5 for a discussion of net operating loss carryforwards and suspended passive losses. Chapter 8 discusses capital loss carryforwards. Chapter 13 discusses tax credits.

[77]§ 108(b).
[78]§ 108(a)(1)(D).
[79]§ 108(e)(5).

Shareholder Cancellation. If a shareholder cancels the corporation's indebtedness to him or her (situation 7) and receives nothing in return, the cancellation usually is considered a contribution of capital to the corporation. Thus, the corporation recognizes no income. Instead, its paid-in capital is increased, and its liabilities are decreased by the same amount.[80] Alternatively, if the corporation transfers stock in exchange for discharge of its indebtedness to a shareholder, the corporation may recognize income, and the shareholder may recognize gain or loss.

EXAMPLE 43

Red Corporation owes Connor $10,000. Connor is a shareholder of Red. If Connor cancels the debt in exchange for $9,000 of Red's stock, Red will have income of $1,000. If Connor's basis for the Red Corporation debt is $9,500, Connor will have a bad debt of $500 (see Chapter 5 for a discussion of the bad debt deduction).[81] ▼

Student Loans. Many states make loans to students on the condition that the loan will be forgiven if the student practices a profession in the state upon completing his or her studies. The amount of the loan that is forgiven (situation 8) is excluded from gross income.[82]

GAINS AND LOSSES FROM PROPERTY TRANSACTIONS

In General. Gains and losses from property transactions are discussed in detail in Chapters 7 and 8. Because of their importance in the tax system, however, they are introduced briefly at this point.

When property is sold or otherwise disposed of, gain or loss may result. Such gain or loss has an effect on the gross income of the party making the sale or other disposition when the gain or loss is realized and recognized for tax purposes. The concept of realized gain or loss is expressed as follows:

$$\begin{array}{c} \text{Amount realized} \\ \text{from the sale} \end{array} - \begin{array}{c} \text{Adjusted basis of} \\ \text{the property} \end{array} = \begin{array}{c} \text{Realized gain} \\ \text{(or loss)} \end{array}$$

The amount realized is the selling price of the property less any costs of disposition (e.g., brokerage commissions) incurred by the seller. Adjusted basis of the property is determined as follows:

	Cost (or other original basis) at date of acquisition[83]
Add:	Capital additions
Subtract:	Depreciation (if appropriate) and other capital recoveries (see Chapter 4)
Equals:	Adjusted basis at date of sale or other disposition

Without realized gain or loss, generally, there can be no recognized (taxable) gain or loss. All realized gains are recognized unless some specific part of the tax law provides otherwise (see Chapter 7 for a discussion of nonrecognition provisions). Realized losses may or may not be recognized (deductible) for tax purposes, depending on the circumstances involved. For example, losses realized from the disposition of personal-use property (property held by individuals and not used for business or investment purposes) are not recognized.

---

[80] § 108(e)(6).
[81] The bad debt might not be deductible if the exchange of stock for debt was part of a corporate recapitalization under § 368(a)(1)(E).
[82] § 108(f).

[83] Cost usually means purchase price plus expenses related to the acquisition of the property and incurred by the purchaser (e.g., brokerage commissions). For the basis of property acquired by gift or inheritance and other basis rules, see Chapter 7.

EXAMPLE 44

During the current year, Ted sells his sailboat (adjusted basis of $4,000) for $5,500. Ted also sells one of his personal automobiles (adjusted basis of $8,000) for $5,000. Ted's realized gain of $1,500 from the sale of the sailboat is recognized. The $3,000 realized loss on the sale of the automobile, however, is not recognized. Thus, the gain is taxable, but the loss is not deductible. ▼

Once it has been determined that the disposition of property results in a recognized gain or loss, the next step is to classify the gain or loss as capital or ordinary. Although ordinary gain is fully taxable and ordinary loss is fully deductible, the same is not true for capital gains and capital losses.

Capital Gains and Losses. Gains and losses from the disposition of capital assets receive special tax treatment. Capital assets are defined in the Code as any property held by the taxpayer *other than* property listed in § 1221. The list in § 1221 includes, among other things, inventory, accounts receivable, and depreciable property or real estate used in a business. The sale or exchange of assets in these categories usually results in ordinary income or loss treatment (see Chapter 8). The sale of any other asset generally creates a capital gain or loss.

EXAMPLE 45

Cardinal, Inc., owns a pizza parlor. During the current year, Cardinal sells an automobile. The automobile, which had been used as a pizza delivery car for three years, was sold at a loss of $1,000. Because this automobile was a depreciable asset used in its business, Cardinal has an ordinary loss of $1,000, rather than a capital loss. Cardinal also sold securities held for investment during the current year. The securities were sold for a gain of $800. The securities are capital assets. Therefore, Cardinal has a capital gain of $800. ▼

Individuals and corporations are taxed differently on capital gains and losses. Individuals' net capital gains are subject to the following maximum tax rates:

	Maximum Rate
Short-term gains (assets held for 12 months or less)	39.6%
Mid-term gains (assets held for more than 12 and not more than 18 months)	28%
Long-term gains (assets held for more than 18 months)	20%

Alternative rates apply to individuals with low marginal rates. The net capital losses of individuals can be used to offset up to $3,000 of ordinary income each year. Any remaining capital loss is carried forward indefinitely until exhausted. In contrast, the net capital gains of corporations are taxed at the same rate as other corporate income, and corporations may deduct capital losses only to the extent of capital gains. Capital losses of corporations in excess of capital gains may not be deducted against ordinary income. A corporation's unused capital losses can be carried back three years and then carried forward five years to offset capital gains in those years.

EXAMPLE 46

Tina has a short-term capital loss of $5,000 during 1999 and no capital gains. She can deduct $3,000 of this amount as an ordinary loss. The remaining $2,000 loss is carried over to 2000 and will continue to be carried forward until it is fully deducted.

If Tina were a corporation, none of the capital loss would be deductible in 1999. All $5,000 would be carried back and offset against capital gains in 1996, 1997, and 1998 (generating an immediate tax refund). Any unused capital loss would be carried forward and offset against capital gains in 2000 to 2004. ▼

To ascertain the appropriate tax treatment of capital gains and losses, a complex netting process must be applied. First, capital gains and losses must be classified as short term, mid-term, or long term, based on the holding periods noted above.[84] Capital gains and losses are then netted *within* each category. In particular, short-term capital losses (STCL) are offset against short-term capital gains (STCG), resulting in either a net short-term capital loss (NSTCL) or a net short-term capital gain (NSTCG). Similarly, mid-term capital losses (MTCL) are offset against mid-term capital gains (MTCG), and long-term capital losses (LTCL) are offset against long-term capital gains (LTCG), resulting in either a net gain or net loss in each category (i.e., either a NMTCG or a NMTCL, and either a NLTCG or a NLTCL). After netting within category, the categories are netted against each other, with losses in the highest-taxed category always being netted first against gains in the category carrying the highest tax rate.

EXAMPLE 47

In 1999, Colin has a 31% marginal tax rate and has the following capital transactions for the year:

Penguin Corporation stock (held for 7 months)	$ 1,000
Owl Corporation stock (held for 9 months)	(3,000)
Flamingo Corporation bonds (held for 14 months)	2,000
Land (held for 3 years)	4,000

The Penguin Corporation gain of $1,000 is offset by the Owl Corporation loss of $3,000. The resulting NSTCL of $2,000 then completely offsets the Flamingo bond mid-term gain of $2,000. The end result is a NLTCG of $4,000 from the sale of land that will be taxed at a rate of 20%. Note that the gain from sale of the Flamingo bonds would have been taxed at a higher 28% rate had it not been offset by the NSTCL. ▼

KEY TERMS

Accounting income, 3–5

Accounting method, 3–7

Accrual method, 3–9

Assignment of income, 3–15

Buy-sell agreements, 3–24

Cash receipts method, 3–8

Claim of right doctrine, 3–9

Constructive receipt, 3–11

Economic income, 3–4

Fruit and tree metaphor, 3–14

Gross income, 3–2

Hybrid method, 3–9

Income, 3–4

Life insurance proceeds, 3–23

Original issue discount, 3–11

Qualified real property business indebtedness, 3–26

Tax benefit rule, 3–21

Taxable year, 3–7

---

[84]Certain assets, such as collectibles (e.g., art, antiques, stamps, etc.) and some real estate, receive special treatment.

CHAPTER 3 Gross Income

PROBLEM MATERIALS

1. Jack, a cash basis taxpayer, operated Donna's farm under an arrangement whereby Jack would receive one-half of the grain crop, less the cost of seed and fertilizer. The seed and fertilizer cost $10,000, which was paid during the year. In September, Jack harvested the crop. A portion of the grain was sold for $30,000 cash in September, and Jack received $12,000 as his share of the $30,000 in October. Also in October, more of the grain was sold for $40,000. The grain was delivered to the purchaser in October, but payment was not to be received until January of the following year. Jack also used a portion of the grain for his personal use. The cost of the personal-use grain was $1,400, but it could have been sold for $3,000. In February of the following year, Jack collected the balance Donna owed to him. Identify the relevant tax issues for Jack.

2. Compute the taxpayer's (1) economic income and (2) gross income for tax purposes from the following events:
   a. The taxpayer sold stock for $10,000. The stock cost $6,000 in 1994. The fair market value of the stock at the beginning of the year was $9,000.
   b. The taxpayer used her controlled corporation's automobile for her vacation. The rental value of the automobile for the vacation period was $800.
   c. The taxpayer raised vegetables in her garden. The fair market value of the vegetables was $900, and the cost of raising them was $100. She ate some of the vegetables and gave the remainder to neighbors.
   d. The local government changed the zoning ordinances so that some of the taxpayer's residential property was reclassified as commercial. Because of the change, the fair market value of the taxpayer's property increased by $10,000.
   e. During the year, the taxpayer borrowed $50,000 for two years at 9% interest. By the end of the year, interest rates had increased to 12%, and the lender accepted $49,000 in full satisfaction of the debt.

3. The roof of your corporation's office building recently suffered some damage as the result of a storm. You, the president of the corporation, are negotiating with a carpenter who has quoted two prices for the repair work: $600 if you pay in cash ("folding money") and $700 if you pay by check. The carpenter observes that the IRS can more readily discover his receipt of a check. Thus, he hints that he will report the receipt of the check (but not the cash). The carpenter has a full-time job and will do the work after hours and on the weekend. He comments that he should be allowed to keep all he earns after regular working hours. Evaluate what you should do.

4. Samantha, a cash basis taxpayer, received the following from her employer during 1998:

   - Salary of $80,000.
   - Bonus of $12,000. In 1999, the company determined that the bonus had been incorrectly computed and required Samantha to repay $5,000.
   - Use of a company car for her vacation. Rental value for the period would have been $800. Samantha paid for the gas.
   - $6,000 advance for travel expenses. Samantha had spent only $4,500 at the end of the year.

   Determine the effects of these items on Samantha's gross income.

5. Which of the following investments of $10,000 each will yield the greater after-tax value, assuming the taxpayer is in the 40% tax bracket (combined Federal and state) for ordinary income and 26% for qualifying capital gains in all years and the investments will be liquidated at the end of five years?
   a. Land that will increase in value by 10% each year.
   b. A taxable bond yielding 10% before tax. The interest can be reinvested at 10% before tax.

   Prepare a brief speech for your tax class in which you explain why the future value of the land will exceed the future value of the taxable bond. Given: Compound amount of $1 and compound value of annuity payments at the end of five years:

Interest Rate	$1 Compounded for Five Years	$1 Annuity Compounded for Five Years
6%	$1.33	$5.64
10%	1.61	6.10

6. Determine the taxpayer's income for tax purposes in each of the following cases:
   a. Zelda borrowed $30,000 from the First National Bank. The bank required her to deliver collateral for the loan in the form of stocks with a value of $30,000 and a cost of $10,000.
   b. Zelda owned a lot on Sycamore Street that measured 100 feet by 100 feet. The cost of the lot to her is $10,000. The city condemned a 10-foot strip of the land so that it could widen the street. Zelda received a $2,000 condemnation award.
   c. Zelda owned land zoned for residential use only. The land cost $5,000 and had a market value of $7,000. Zelda spent $500 and several hundred hours petitioning the county supervisors to change the zoning to A–1 commercial. When the county approved the zoning change, the value of the property immediately increased to $20,000.

7. Al is an attorney who conducts his practice as a sole proprietor. During the year, he received cash of $100,000 for legal services. At the beginning of the year, he had receivables from clients of $45,000. At the end of the year, his receivables totaled $40,000. Compute Al's gross income from the practice for the year:
   a. Using the cash basis of accounting.
   b. Using the accrual basis of accounting.

8. Robin Company began operating a grocery store during the year. Robin's only books and records are based on cash receipts and disbursements, but the company president has asked you to compute the company's gross profit from the business for tax purposes.

Sale of merchandise	$350,000
Purchases of merchandise	220,000

   You determine that as of the end of the year Robin has accounts payable for merchandise of $15,000 and accounts receivable from customers totaling $6,000. The cost of merchandise on hand at the end of the year was $9,000. Compute Robin's accrual method gross profit for the year.

9. Your client is a new partnership, Aspen Associates, which is an engineering consulting firm. Generally, Aspen bills clients for services at the end of each month. Client billings are about $50,000 each month. On average, it takes 45 days to collect the receivables. Aspen's expenses are primarily for salary and rent. Salaries are paid on the last day of each month, and rent is paid on the first day of each month. The partnership has a line of credit with a bank, which requires monthly financial statements. These must be prepared using the accrual method. Aspen's managing partner, Amanda Sims, has suggested that the firm should also use the accrual method for tax purposes and thus reduce accounting fees by $500. Write a letter to your client explaining why you believe it would be worthwhile for Aspen to file its tax return on the cash basis even though its financial statements are prepared on the accrual basis. Aspen's address is 100 James Tower, Denver, CO 80208.

10. Color Paint Shop, Inc. (459 Ellis Avenue, Harrisburg, PA 17111), is an accrual basis taxpayer that paints automobiles. During 1998, the company painted Samuel's car and was to receive a $1,000 payment from his insurance company. Samuel was not satisfied with the work, however, and the insurance company refused to pay. In December 1998, Color and Samuel agreed that Color would receive $600 for the work, subject to final approval by the insurance company. In the past, Color had come to terms with customers only to have the insurance company negotiate an even smaller amount. In May 1999, the insurance company reviewed the claim and paid the $600 to Color. An IRS agent thinks that Color should report $1,000 of income in 1998 and deduct a $400 loss in 1999.

Prepare a memo to Susan Apple, a tax partner for whom you are working, with the recommended treatment for the disputed income.

11. Dance, Inc., is a dance studio that sells dance lessons for cash, on open account, and for notes receivable. The company also collects interest on bonds held as an investment. The company's cash receipts for the year totaled $219,000:

Cash sales	$ 70,000
Collections on accounts receivable	120,000
Collections on notes receivable	20,000
Interest on bonds	9,000
	$219,000

The balances in accounts receivable, notes receivable, and accrued interest on bonds at the beginning and end of the year were as follows:

	1–1	12–31
Accounts receivable	$24,000	$24,000
Notes receivable	9,000	13,000
Accrued interest on bonds	2,500	4,000
	$35,500	$41,000

The fair market value of the notes is equal to 60% of their face amount. There were no bad debts for the year, and all notes were for services performed during the year. Compute the corporation's gross income:
   a. Using the cash basis of accounting.
   b. Using the accrual basis of accounting.
   c. Using a hybrid method—accrual basis for lessons and cash basis for interest income.

12. Determine the effect of the following on a cash basis taxpayer's gross income for 1998:
   a. Received his paycheck for $3,000 from his employer on December 31, 1998. He deposited the paycheck on January 2, 1999.
   b. Received a bonus of $5,000 from his employer on January 10, 1999. The bonus was for the outstanding performance of his division during 1998.
   c. Received a dividend check from IBM on November 28, 1998. He mailed the check back to IBM in December requesting that additional IBM stock be issued to him under IBM's dividend reinvestment plan.

13. Pelican, Inc., an accrual basis taxpayer, sells and installs consumer appliances. Determine the effects of each of the following transactions on the company's 1998 gross income:
   a. In December 1998, Pelican received a $1,200 advance payment from a customer. The payment was for an appliance that Pelican specially ordered from the manufacturer. The appliance had not arrived at the end of 1998.
   b. At the end of 1998, Pelican installed an appliance and collected the full price of $750 for the item. However, the customer claimed the appliance was defective and asked for a refund. Pelican conceded that the appliance was defective but claimed that the customer should collect from the manufacturer. The dispute was not settled in 1998. In early 1999, it was determined that the appliance had not been installed properly and Pelican was required to refund the full sales price.
   c. Pelican sold an appliance for $1,200 (plus a market rate of interest) and received the customer's note for that amount. However, because of the customer's poor credit rating, the value of the note was only $700.

14. Quail & Associates is a cash basis partnership. In 1998, Quail's partners negotiated with a client for services to be performed in 1999. Quail's client offered to pay $20,000 each month—a total of $240,000 for the year. Quail's partners countered that they would accept $20,000 each month for the first nine months of the year and the remaining $60,000 in January 2000. The client accepted Quail's terms in 1999 and 2000.

a. Did Quail actually or constructively receive $240,000 in 1999?
b. What could explain Quail's willingness to spread the payments over a longer period of time?

15. The Heron Apartments requires its new tenants to pay the rent for the first and last months of the annual lease and a $400 damage deposit, all at the time the lease is signed. In December 1998, a tenant paid $800 for January 1999 rent, $800 for December 1999 rent, and $400 for the damage deposit. In January 2000, Heron refunded the tenant's damage deposit. What are the effects of these payments on Heron's taxable income for 1998, 1999, and 2000?
    a. Assume Heron is a cash basis taxpayer.
    b. Assume Heron is an accrual basis taxpayer.

16. a. Gus is a cash basis taxpayer. On September 1, 1998, Gus gave a corporate bond to his son, Hans. The bond had a face amount of $10,000 and paid $900 of interest each January 31. On December 1, 1998, Gus gave common stocks to his daughter, Dena. Dividends totaling $720 had been declared on the stocks on November 30, 1998, and were payable on January 15, 1999. Dena became the shareholder of record in time to collect the dividends. What is Gus's 1999 gross income from the bond and stocks?
    b. Gus's mother was unable to pay her bills as they came due. Gus, his employer, and his mother's creditors entered into an arrangement whereby Gus's employer would withhold $500 per month from his salary and the employer would pay the $500 to the creditors. Gus's employer withheld $3,000 from his salary and paid that amount to the creditors. Is Gus required to pay tax on the $3,000?

17. Tracy, a cash basis taxpayer, is employed by Eagle Corporation, also a cash basis taxpayer. Tracy is a full-time employee of the corporation and receives a salary of $60,000 per year. He also receives a bonus equal to 10% of all collections from clients he serviced during the year. Determine the tax consequences of the following events to the corporation and to Tracy:
    a. On December 31, 1998, Tracy was visiting a customer. The customer gave Tracy a $3,000 check payable to the corporation for appraisal services Tracy performed during 1998. Tracy did not deliver the check to the corporation until January 1999.
    b. The facts are the same as in (a), except that the corporation is an accrual basis taxpayer and Tracy deposited the check on December 31, but the bank did not add the deposit to the corporation's account until January 1999.
    c. The facts are the same as in (a), except the customer told Tracy to hold the check until January when the customer could make a bank deposit that would cover the check.

18. Brad is the president of the Zinc Corporation. He and other members of his family control the corporation. Brad has a temporary need for $50,000, and the corporation has excess cash. He could borrow the money from a bank at 9%, and Zinc is earning 6% on its temporary investments. Zinc has made loans to other employees on several occasions. Therefore, Brad is considering borrowing $50,000 from the corporation. He will repay the loan principal in two years plus interest at 5%. Identify the relevant tax issues for Brad and Zinc Corporation.

19. On June 30, 1998, Ridge borrowed $52,000 from his employer. On July 1, 1998, Ridge used the money as follows:

Interest-free loan to Ridge's controlled corporation (operated by Ridge on a part-time basis)	$21,000
Interest-free loan to Tab (Ridge's son)	11,000
National Bank of Grundy 6% certificate of deposit ($14,840 due at maturity, June 30, 1999)	14,000
National Bank of Grundy 6.25% certificate of deposit ($6,773 due at maturity, June 30, 2000)	6,000
	$52,000

Ridge's employer did not charge him interest. The applicable Federal rate was 12% throughout the relevant period. Tab had investment income of $800 for the year, and he used the loan proceeds to pay medical school tuition. There were no other outstanding loans between Ridge and Tab. What are the effects of the preceding transactions on Ridge's taxable income for 1998?

20. Indicate whether the imputed interest rules should apply in the following situations:
    a. Mitch is a cash basis attorney who charges his clients based on the number of hours it takes to do the job. The bill is due upon completion of the work. However, for clients who make an initial payment when the work begins, Mitch grants a discount on the final bill. The discount is equal to 10% interest on the deposit.
    b. Local Telephone Company requires that customers make a security deposit. The deposit is refunded after the customer has established a good record for paying the telephone bill. The company pays 6% interest on the deposits.
    c. Lynn asked Kelly for a $125,000 loan to purchase a new home. Kelly made the loan and did not charge interest. Kelly never intended to collect the loan, and at the end of the year Kelly told Lynn that the debt was forgiven.

21. Vito is the sole shareholder of Vito, Inc. The corporation also employs him. On June 30, 1998, Vito borrowed $8,000 from Vito, Inc., and on July 1, 1999, he borrowed an additional $3,000. Both loans were due on demand. No interest was charged on the loans, and the Federal rate was 10% for all relevant dates. Vito used the money to purchase stock, and he had no investment income. Determine the tax consequences to Vito and Vito, Inc., in each of the following situations:
    a. The loans are considered employer-employee loans.
    b. The loans are considered corporation-shareholder loans.

22. Hawk Industries, Inc., has experienced financial difficulties as a result of its struggling business. The corporation has been behind on its mortgage payments for the last six months. The mortgage holder has offered to accept $80,000 in full payment of the $100,000 owed on the mortgage and payable over the next 10 years. The interest rate of the mortgage is 7%, and the market rate is now 8%. What tax issues are raised by the creditor's offer?

23. Determine the taxable life insurance proceeds in the following cases:
    a. When Monty died, his wife collected $50,000 on a group term insurance policy purchased by Monty's employer. Monty had never included the premiums in gross income.
    b. The Cardinal Software Company purchased an insurance policy on the life of a key employee. The company paid $50,000 in premiums and collected $500,000 of insurance proceeds.
    c. When Barbara died, she and her husband owed $15,000 on a loan. Under the terms of the loan, Barbara was required to purchase life insurance to pay the creditor the amount due at the date of Barbara's death. The creditor collected from the life insurance company the amount due at the time of Barbara's death. Is the creditor required to recognize income from the collection of the life insurance proceeds?

24. The Egret Company, which has a 40% (combined Federal and state) marginal tax rate, estimated that if its current president should die, the company would incur $200,000 in costs to find a suitable replacement. In addition, profits on various projects the president is responsible for would likely decrease by $300,000. The president has recommended that Egret purchase a $500,000 life insurance policy. How much insurance should the company carry on the life of its president to compensate for the after-tax loss that would result from the president's death, assuming the $200,000 costs of finding a president are deductible and the lost profits would have been taxable?

25. The Swan Partnership, a financial consulting company, has a cross-purchase agreement that requires the partnership to purchase a deceased partner's interest. The partner's interest is to be purchased from the deceased partner's estate with the price being 150% of the book value at the time of the partner's death. To finance the cross-purchase agreement, the partnership carries an insurance policy on the life of each of its partners.

During the year, a partner died. The partnership collected the $250,000 face amount of the life insurance policy on the deceased partner and purchased her interest for $225,000. Swan had paid $100,000 in premiums on the policy. What are the tax consequences of these transactions for the deceased partner and for the partnership?

26. White and Swan Modeling is a partnership. How does the tax benefit rule apply to White and Swan in the following transactions?
    a. In 1998, White and Swan paid Vera $5,000 for locating a potential client. The deal fell through, and in 1999, Vera refunded the $5,000 to the partnership.
    b. In 1998, White and Swan paid an attorney $300 for services in connection with a title search. Because the attorney was negligent, the partnership incurred some additional costs in acquiring the land. In 1999, the attorney refunded his $300 fee to White and Swan.

27. The exclusion of state and local bond interest from Federal income tax is often criticized as creating a tax haven for the wealthy. The critics, however, often fail to take into account the effect of market forces. In recent months, the long-term tax-exempt interest rate has been 5.45% while the long-term taxable rate for bonds of comparable risk was approximately 6.4%. On the other hand, state and local governments do enjoy a savings in interest costs because of the tax-favored status of their bonds. To date, Congress has concluded that the benefits gained by the states and municipalities and their residents outweigh any damages to our progressive income tax system. Do you agree with the proponents of the exclusion? Why or why not?

28. Robin Corporation is experiencing financial troubles and is considering negotiating the following with its creditors. Determine the tax consequences to Robin of the following plan:
    a. The Motor Finance Company will cancel $1,500 in accrued interest. Robin had deducted the interest in the prior year. Motor Finance Company will also reduce the principal on the note by $1,000. The note financed the purchase of equipment from a local dealer.
    b. The Trust Land Company, which sold Robin land and buildings, will reduce the mortgage on the building by $15,000.
    c. Ridge, Robin's sole shareholder, will cancel a $50,000 receivable from the corporation in exchange for additional stock.

RESEARCH PROBLEMS

Note: The **RIA OnPoint System 4 Student Version CD-ROM** *available with this text can be used in preparing solutions to the Research Problems. Alternatively, tax research materials contained in a standard tax library can be used.*

29. The Beige Real Estate Company borrowed $1,400,000 from the First National Bank to purchase a building. The loan was recourse; if Beige did not pay the mortgage, the bank could repossess the property. But if the fair market value of the property repossessed was less than or equal to the amount of the debt, Beige would not be responsible for the difference. When the fair market value of the property and the balance on the mortgage were $1,000,000, Beige was unable to make its monthly loan payment. After much negotiation, the bank reduced the principal to $800,000, which enabled Beige to make its payment in a timely manner. The IRS added $200,000 of income from discharge of indebtedness to Beige's taxable income for the year. Beige contends it has no gross income because the fair market value of the building is less than or equal to the reduced principal of the debt. Advise Beige on who is correct.

Partial list of research aids:
Rev.Rul. 91–31, 1991–1 C.B. 19.

30. The First Central Bank, an accrual basis taxpayer, has a credit card operation. Customers pay $30 per year for the right to use the card. If the customer decides to cancel the card during the year, the customer receives a refund of a prorated amount. The IRS position

is that the amounts received are interest and thus are not eligible for deferral under Revenue Procedure 71–21. The taxpayer argues that the prepaid income is for services that are to be rendered over 12 months and thus the prepaid income can be amortized over the 12-month period. Determine the appropriate tax treatment.

31. Edith Sanders gave common stock to her daughter, Joyce. The cost of the stock was $20,000, and its fair market value was $150,000. The uniform transfer tax on the gift was $30,000. Edith was liable for the transfer tax, but the gift was made on the condition that Joyce would pay the gift tax (i.e., a "net gift"). Joyce paid the $30,000 in accordance with the agreement.

    The IRS agent contends that Edith must treat the transactions as part sale and part gift. That is, 20% of the stock ($30,000/$150,000 = 0.20) was sold, and the balance was gifted to Joyce. According to the agent, Edith must recognize taxable gain of $26,000 [$30,000 − (0.20)($20,000)]. Edith is having difficulty understanding why she would be required to recognize any income since she made a gift of property and did not receive anything. Write a letter to the taxpayer that contains your advice and prepare a memo for the tax files. Edith's address is 400 Rock Street, Memphis, TN 38152.

32. Your client operates a well-known chain of retail stores. A shopping center developer has offered to rent space to your client at a very low price under a 10-year lease. Your client will be an "anchor tenant." While other tenants will lease a mere shell and be responsible for making the improvements necessary to operate their businesses, the developer has offered to make improvements with a maximum cost of $500,000 to meet specific needs of your client. These expenditures will be made as an inducement to your client to locate in the shopping center. Before deciding whether to accept the offer, your client asks your opinion about the tax consequences of receiving the $500,000 in improvements. What is your informed opinion?

CHAPTER 4

BUSINESS DEDUCTIONS

LEARNING OBJECTIVES

After completing Chapter 4, you should be able to:

1. Understand the meaning and application of the ordinary, necessary, and reasonableness requirements for the deduction of business expenses.

2. Describe the cash and accrual methods of accounting for business deductions.

3. Apply a variety of Internal Revenue Code deduction disallowance provisions.

4. Understand the limitations applicable to the charitable contribution deduction for corporations.

5. Recognize and apply the alternative tax treatments for research and experimental expenditures.

6. Determine the amount of cost recovery under MACRS, and apply the § 179 expensing election and the deduction limitations on listed property and automobiles when making the MACRS calculation.

7. Identify intangible assets that are eligible for amortization and calculate the amount of the deduction.

8. Determine the amount of depletion expense and recognize the alternative tax treatments for intangible drilling and development costs.

OUTLINE

Overview of Business Deductions, 4–2
Ordinary and Necessary Requirement, 4–2
Reasonableness Requirement, 4–3
Timing of Expense Recognition, 4–5
Cash Method Requirements, 4–5
Accrual Method Requirements, 4–6
Disallowance Possibilities, 4–7
Public Policy Limitations, 4–7
Political Contributions and Lobbying Activities, 4–9
Excessive Executive Compensation, 4–10
Disallowance of Deductions for Capital Expenditures, 4–10
Investigation of a Business, 4–11
Transactions between Related Parties, 4–12
Lack of Adequate Substantiation, 4–14
Expenses and Interest Related to Tax-Exempt Income, 4–14
Charitable Contributions, 4–15
Property Contributions, 4–16
Limitations Imposed on Charitable Contribution Deductions, 4–17
Research and Experimental Expenditures, 4–18
Expense Method, 4–18
Deferral and Amortization Method, 4–19
Other Expense Rules, 4–19
Interest Expense, 4–20
Taxes, 4–20
Cost Recovery Allowances, 4–21
Overview, 4–21
Modified Accelerated Cost Recovery System (MACRS), 4–22
Eligible Property under MACRS, 4–22
Cost Recovery for Personal Property, 4–24
Cost Recovery for Real Estate, 4–26
The MACRS Straight-Line Election, 4–27
Election to Expense Assets under § 179, 4–28
Business and Personal Use of Automobiles and Other Listed Property, 4–29
Alternative Depreciation System (ADS), 4–32
Amortization, 4–33
Depletion, 4–34
Intangible Drilling and Development Costs (IDC), 4–34
Depletion Methods, 4–35
Cost Recovery Tables, 4–38

OVERVIEW OF BUSINESS DEDUCTIONS

ORDINARY AND NECESSARY REQUIREMENT

1 LEARNING OBJECTIVE
Understand the meaning and application of the ordinary, necessary, and reasonableness requirements for the deduction of business expenses.

Section 162(a) permits a deduction for all **ordinary and necessary** expenses paid or incurred in carrying on a trade or business. To understand the scope of this provision, it is necessary to understand the meanings of the terms ordinary and necessary.

Neither ordinary nor necessary is defined in the Code or Regulations. However, the courts have had to deal with these terms on numerous occasions and have held that an expense is necessary if a prudent business person would incur the same expense and the expense is expected to be appropriate and helpful in the taxpayer's business.[1] Many expenses that are necessary are not ordinary.

EXAMPLE 1

Welch felt that it would be helpful for the development of his new business if he repaid the debts owed by a bankrupt corporation that he had worked for. Consequently, over a period of years, he took a portion of his income and repaid these debts, even though he was under no legal obligation to do so. Welch claimed these repayments as ordinary and necessary business expenses. The Supreme Court indicated that the payments were *necessary* for the development of Welch's business because they contributed toward Welch's reputation and built goodwill. However, the Court also indicated that the expenses were *not ordinary*,

---

[1] *Welch v. Helvering*, 3 USTC ¶1164, 12 AFTR 1456, 54 S.Ct. 8 (USSC, 1933).

CHAPTER 4 Business Deductions 4–3

> ### TAX IN THE NEWS
>
> #### PAYING RETAINERS TO KEEP LAWYERS FROM RIVALS
>
> In a recent Claims Court case, the IRS attempted to disallow a deduction for a taxpayer who paid a retainer to a law firm to ensure that the law firm would not do legal work for a hostile suitor. The taxpayer paid a retainer to the law firm for 16 years, even though the firm did little or no legal work for the taxpayer during that time.
>
> The IRS's position was that the payments were not deductible because they were capital expenditures rather than ordinary and necessary business expenses deductible under § 162. The Claims Court concluded that the taxpayer's long history of paying an annual retainer established the payments as an ordinary and necessary business expense and thus they were currently deductible.
>
> SOURCE: Adapted from Tom Herman, "Companies Can Deduct Retainers to Keep Lawyers from Rivals," *Wall Street Journal*, July 28, 1997, p. B8.

since the act of repaying the debts of a bankrupt company were unusual and not a normal method of doing business. Instead, the repayments were more appropriately classified as capital expenditures for goodwill.[2] ▼

An expense is ordinary if it is normal, usual, or customary in the type of business conducted by the taxpayer and is not capital in nature.[3] However, an expense need not be recurring to be deductible as ordinary.

EXAMPLE 2   Zebra Corporation engaged in a mail-order business. The post office judged that Zebra's advertisements were false and misleading. Under a fraud order, the post office stamped "fraudulent" on all letters addressed to Zebra's business and returned them to the senders. Zebra spent $30,000 on legal fees in an unsuccessful attempt to force the post office to stop. The legal fees (though not recurring) were ordinary business expenses because they were normal, usual, or customary in the circumstances.[4] ▼

REASONABLENESS REQUIREMENT

Although § 162 is intended to allow taxpayers to deduct a broad range of trade or business expenses, certain expenses are mentioned specifically:

- *Reasonable* salaries paid for services.
- Expenses for the use of business property.

The Code applies the **reasonableness requirement** solely to salaries and other compensation for services.[5] However, the courts have held that for *any* business expense to be ordinary and necessary, it must also be reasonable in amount.[6]

---

[2] *Welch v. Helvering*, 3 USTC ¶1164, 12 AFTR 1456, 54 S.Ct. 8 (USSC, 1933). For a contrasting decision, see *Dunn and McCarthy, Inc. v. Comm.*, 43–2 USTC ¶9688, 31 AFTR 1043, 139 F.2d 242 (CA–2, 1943), involving an *existing* business, where repayments to employees of a bankrupt corporation were held to be both ordinary and necessary.
[3] *Deputy v. DuPont*, 40–1 USTC ¶9161, 23 AFTR 808, 60 S.Ct. 363 (USSC, 1940).
[4] *Comm. v. Heininger*, 44–1 USTC ¶9109, 31 AFTR 783, 64 S.Ct. 249 (USSC, 1943).
[5] § 162(a)(1).
[6] *Comm. v. Lincoln Electric Co.*, 49–2 USTC ¶9388, 38 AFTR 411, 176 F.2d 815 (CA–6, 1949).

What constitutes reasonableness is a question of fact.[7] If an expense is unreasonable, the excess amount is not allowed as a deduction. The question of reasonableness usually arises with respect to closely held corporations with no separation of ownership and management.

Transactions between shareholders and a closely held company may result in the disallowance of deductions for excessive salaries, rent, and other expenses paid by the corporation to the shareholders. The courts will view an unusually large salary in light of all relevant circumstances and may find that the salary is reasonable despite its size. If excessive payments for salaries, rent, and other expenses are closely related to the percentage of stock owned by the recipients, the payments are generally treated as dividends.[8] Since dividends are not deductible by the corporation, the disallowance results in an increase in corporate taxable income. Deductions for reasonable salaries will not be disallowed solely because the corporation has paid insubstantial portions of its earnings as dividends to its shareholders.

EXAMPLE 3

Sparrow Corporation, a closely held corporation, is owned equally by Lupe, Carlos, and Ramon. The company has been highly profitable for several years and has not paid dividends. Lupe, Carlos, and Ramon are key officers of the company, and each receives a salary of $200,000. Salaries for similar positions in comparable companies average only $100,000. Amounts paid the owners in excess of $100,000 may be deemed unreasonable, and, if so, a total of $300,000 in salary deductions by Sparrow is disallowed. The disallowed amounts are treated as dividends rather than salary income to Lupe, Carlos, and Ramon because the payments are proportional to stock ownership. Salaries are deductible by the corporation, but dividends are not. ▼

PLANNING CONSIDERATIONS

Unreasonable Compensation

In substantiating the reasonableness of a shareholder-employee's compensation, an internal comparison test is sometimes useful. If it can be shown that nonshareholder-employees and shareholder-employees in comparable positions receive comparable compensation, it is indicative that compensation is not unreasonable.

Another possibility is to demonstrate that the shareholder-employee has been underpaid in prior years. For example, the shareholder-employee may have agreed to take a less-than-adequate salary during the unprofitable formative years of the business. He or she would expect the "postponed" compensation to be paid in later, more profitable years. The agreement should be documented, if possible, in the corporate minutes.

Keep in mind that in testing for reasonableness, the total pay package must be considered. Compensation includes all fringe benefits or perquisites, such as contributions by the corporation to a qualified pension plan, regardless of when the funds are available to the employee.

Common Business Deductions. The language of § 162 is broad enough to permit the deduction of many different types of ordinary and necessary business expenses. Some of the more common deductions are listed in Exhibit 4–1.

---

[7]*Kennedy, Jr. v. Comm.*, 82–1 USTC ¶9186, 49 AFTR2d 82–628, 671 F.2d 167 (CA–6, 1982), *rev'g* 72 T.C. 793 (1979).

[8]Reg. § 1.162–8.

EXHIBIT 4–1
Partial List of Business Deductions

Advertising	Pension and profit sharing plans
Bad debts	Rent or lease payments
Commissions and fees	Repairs and maintenance
Depletion	Salaries and wages
Depreciation	Supplies
Employee benefit programs	Taxes and licenses
Insurance	Travel and transportation
Interest	Utilities

TIMING OF EXPENSE RECOGNITION

LEARNING OBJECTIVE 2
Describe the cash and accrual methods of accounting for business deductions.

A taxpayer's accounting method is a major factor in determining taxable income. The method used determines *when* an item is includible in income and *when* an item is deductible on the tax return. Usually, the taxpayer's regular method of record keeping is used for income tax purposes.[9] The taxing authorities require that the method used clearly reflect income and that items be handled consistently.[10] The most common methods of accounting are the cash method and the accrual method.

Throughout the portions of the Code dealing with deductions, the phrase "paid or incurred" is used. A cash basis taxpayer is allowed a deduction only in the year an expense is *paid*. An accrual basis taxpayer is allowed a deduction in the year in which the liability for the expense is *incurred* (becomes certain).

CASH METHOD REQUIREMENTS

The expenses of cash basis taxpayers are deductible only when they are actually paid with cash or other property. Promising to pay or issuing a note does not satisfy the actually paid requirement.[11] However, the payment can be made with borrowed funds. Thus, taxpayers are allowed to claim the deduction at the time they charge expenses on credit cards. They are deemed to have simultaneously borrowed money from the credit card issuer and constructively paid the expenses.[12]

Although the cash basis taxpayer must have actually or constructively paid the expense, payment does not assure a current deduction. The Regulations require capitalization of any expenditure that creates an asset having a useful life that extends substantially beyond the end of the tax year.[13] Thus, cash basis and accrual basis taxpayers cannot take a current deduction for capital expenditures except through amortization, depletion, or depreciation over the tax life of the asset.

EXAMPLE 4
Redbird, Inc., a cash basis taxpayer, rents property from Bluejay, Inc. On July 1, 1998, Redbird paid $24,000 rent for the 24 months ending June 30, 2000. The prepaid rent extends 18 months after the close of the tax year—substantially beyond the year of payment. Therefore, Redbird must capitalize the prepaid rent and amortize the expense on a monthly basis. Redbird's deduction for 1998 is $6,000. ▼

---

[9] § 446(a).
[10] §§ 446(b) and (e); Reg. § 1.446–1(a)(2).
[11] *Page v. Rhode Island Trust Co., Exr.*, 37–1 USTC ¶9138, 19 AFTR 105, 88 F.2d 192 (CA–1, 1937).
[12] Rev.Rul. 78–39, 1978–1 C.B. 73. See also Rev.Rul. 80–335, 1980–2 C.B. 170, which applies to pay-by-phone arrangements.
[13] Reg. § 1.461–1(a).

The Tax Court and the IRS took the position that expenditures for assets expired or consumed by the end of the tax year following the year of payment must be prorated. The Ninth Circuit Court of Appeals held that such expenditures are currently deductible, however, and the Supreme Court apparently concurs with the Ninth Circuit's one-year rule.[14]

EXAMPLE 5

Assume the same facts as in Example 4, except that Redbird was required to pay only 12 months' rent in 1998, and paid $12,000 on July 1, 1998. The entire $12,000 is deductible in 1998. ▼

To obtain a current deduction under the one-year rule, the payment must be required, not a voluntary prepayment.[15] The taxpayer must also demonstrate that allowing the current deduction will not result in a material distortion of income. Generally, the deduction will be allowed if the item is recurring or was made for a business purpose rather than to manipulate income.[16]

PLANNING CONSIDERATIONS

Time Value of Tax Deductions

Cash basis taxpayers often have the ability to make early payments for their expenses at the end of the tax year. This permits the payments to be deducted in the year of payment instead of in the following tax year. In view of the time value of money, a tax deduction this year may be worth more than the same deduction next year. Before employing this strategy, the taxpayer must consider next year's expected income and tax rates and whether a cash-flow problem may develop from early payments. Thus, a variety of considerations must be taken into account when planning the timing of tax deductions.

ACCRUAL METHOD REQUIREMENTS

The period in which an accrual basis taxpayer can deduct an expense is determined by applying the *all events test* and the *economic performance test*. A deduction cannot be claimed until (1) all the events have occurred to create the taxpayer's liability and (2) the amount of the liability can be determined with reasonable accuracy. Once these requirements are satisfied, the deduction is permitted only if economic performance has occurred. The economic performance test is met only when the service, property, or use of property giving rise to the liability is actually performed for, provided to, or used by the taxpayer.[17]

EXAMPLE 6

On December 22, 1998, Robin, Inc., an entertainment business, sponsored a jazz festival in a rented auditorium at City College. Robin is responsible for cleaning up the auditorium after the festival and for reinstalling seats that were removed so more people could attend the festival. Since the college is closed over the Christmas holidays, the company hired by Robin to perform the work did not begin these activities until January 2, 1999. The cost to

---

[14]*Zaninovich v. Comm.*, 80–1 USTC ¶9342, 45 AFTR2d 80–1442, 616 F.2d 429 (CA–9, 1980), *rev'g* 69 T.C. 605 (1978). Cited by the Supreme Court in *Hillsboro National Bank v. Comm.*, 83–1 USTC ¶9229, 51 AFTR2d 83–874, 103 S.Ct. 1134 (USSC, 1983).
[15]*Bonaire Development Co. v. Comm.*, 82–2 USTC ¶9428, 50 AFTR2d 82–5167, 679 F.2d 159 (CA–9, 1982).

[16]*Keller v. Comm.*, 84–1 USTC ¶9194, 53 AFTR2d 84–663, 725 F.2d 1173 (CA–8, 1984), *aff'g* 79 T.C. 7 (1982).
[17]§ 461(h).

Robin is $1,200. Robin cannot deduct the $1,200 until 1999, when the services are performed. ▼

An exception to the economic performance requirement allows certain *recurring* items to be deducted if the following conditions are met:

- The item is recurring in nature and is treated consistently by the taxpayer.
- Either the accrued item is not material, or accruing it results in better matching of income and expenses.
- All the events have occurred that determine the existence of the liability, and the amount of the liability can be determined with reasonable accuracy.
- Economic performance occurs within a reasonable period (but not later than 8½ months after the close of the taxable year).[18]

▼ **EXAMPLE 7**   Towhee Company, an accrual basis, calendar year taxpayer, entered into a monthly maintenance contract during the year. Towhee makes a monthly accrual at the end of every month for this service and pays the fee sometime between the first and fifteenth of the following month when services are performed. The amount involved is immaterial, and all the other tests are met. The December 1998 accrual is deductible even though the service is performed on January 12, 1999. ▼

▼ **EXAMPLE 8**   Tanager, Inc., an accrual basis, calendar year taxpayer, shipped merchandise sold on December 30, 1998, via Greyhound Van Lines on January 2, 1999, and paid the freight charges at that time. Since Tanager reported the sale of the merchandise in 1998, the shipping charge should also be deductible in 1998. This procedure results in a better matching of income and expenses. ▼

Reserves for estimated expenses (frequently employed for financial accounting purposes) generally are not allowed for tax purposes because the economic performance test cannot be satisfied.

▼ **EXAMPLE 9**   Oriole Airlines is required by Federal law to test its engines after 3,000 flying hours. Aircraft cannot return to flight until the tests have been conducted. An unrelated aircraft maintenance company does all of the company's tests for $1,500 per engine. For financial reporting purposes, the company accrues an expense based upon $.50 per hour of flight and credits an allowance account. The actual amounts paid for maintenance are offset against the allowance account. For tax purposes, the economic performance test is not satisfied until the work has been done. Therefore, the reserve method cannot be used for tax purposes. ▼

DISALLOWANCE POSSIBILITIES

3 LEARNING OBJECTIVE
Apply a variety of Internal Revenue Code deduction disallowance provisions.

While most ordinary and necessary business expenses are deductible, the tax law contains provisions that disallow a deduction for certain expenditures. The most frequently encountered disallowance provisions are discussed below.

PUBLIC POLICY LIMITATIONS

Justification for Denying Deductions.
The courts developed the principle that a payment that is in violation of public policy is not a necessary expense and

---

[18] § 461(h)(3)(A).

is not deductible.[19] Although a bribe or fine may be appropriate, helpful, and even contribute to the profitability of an activity, allowing a deduction for such expenses would frustrate clearly defined public policy. A deduction would effectively represent an indirect governmental subsidy for taxpayer wrongdoing.

Accordingly, the IRS was free to restrict deductions if, in its view, the expenses were contrary to public policy. But since the law did not explain which actions violated public policy, taxpayers often had to go to court to determine whether an expense fell into this category.

Furthermore, the public policy doctrine was arbitrarily applied in cases where no clear definition had emerged. To resolve uncertainty, Congress enacted legislation that attempts to limit the use of the doctrine. Under the legislation, deductions are disallowed for specific types of expenditures that are considered contrary to public policy:

- Bribes and kickbacks, including those associated with Medicare or Medicaid.
- Two-thirds of the treble damage payments made to claimants resulting from violation of the antitrust law.[20]
- Fines and penalties paid to a government for violation of law.

EXAMPLE 10

Brown Corporation, a moving company, consistently loads its trucks with weights in excess of the limits allowed by state law. The additional revenue more than offsets the fines levied. The fines are for a violation of public policy and are not deductible. ▼

To be disallowed, a bribe or kickback must be illegal under either Federal or state law and must also subject the payer to a criminal penalty or the loss of license or privilege to engage in a trade or business. For a bribe or kickback that is illegal under state law, a deduction is denied only if the state law is generally enforced.

EXAMPLE 11

During the year, Otter Company, insurance brokers, paid $5,000 to Panther Company, real estate brokers. The payment represented 20% of the commissions Otter earned from customers referred by Panther. Under state law, the splitting of commissions by an insurance broker is an act of misconduct that could warrant a revocation of the broker's license. Otter's $5,000 payments to Panther are not deductible provided the state law is generally enforced. ▼

Legal Expenses Incurred in Defense of Civil or Criminal Penalties. To deduct legal expenses as trade or business expenses, the taxpayer must be able to show that the origin and character of the claim are directly related to a trade or business. Personal legal expenses are not deductible. Thus, legal fees incurred in connection with a criminal defense are deductible only if the crime is associated with the taxpayer's trade or business.[21]

EXAMPLE 12

Debra, a majority shareholder and chief financial officer of Blue Corporation, incurred legal expenses in connection with her defense in a criminal indictment for evasion of Blue's income taxes. Debra may deduct her legal expenses because she is deemed to be in the trade or business of being an executive. The legal action impairs her ability to conduct this business activity.[22] ▼

---

[19]*Tank Truck Rentals, Inc. v. Comm.*, 58–1 USTC ¶9366, 1 AFTR2d 1154, 78 S.Ct. 507 (USSC, 1958).
[20]§§ 162(c), (f), and (g).
[21]*Comm. v. Tellier*, 66–1 USTC ¶9319, 17 AFTR2d 633, 86 S.Ct. 1118 (USSC, 1966).
[22]Rev.Rul. 68–662, 1968–2 C.B. 69.

CHAPTER 4 Business Deductions

Expenses Related to an Illegal Business. The usual expenses of operating an illegal business (e.g., a numbers racket) are deductible.[23] However, § 162 disallows a deduction for fines, bribes to public officials, illegal kickbacks, and other illegal payments.

EXAMPLE 13

Grizzly, Inc., owns and operates a saloon. In addition, Grizzly operates an illegal gambling establishment out of the saloon's back room. In connection with the illegal gambling activity, Grizzly had the following expenses during the year:

Rent	$ 60,000
Payoffs to police	40,000
Depreciation on equipment	100,000
Wages	140,000
Interest	30,000
Criminal fines	50,000
Illegal kickbacks	10,000
Total	$430,000

All of the usual expenses (rent, depreciation, wages, and interest) are deductible; payoffs, fines, and kickbacks are not deductible. Of the $430,000 spent, $330,000 is deductible and $100,000 is not. ▼

An exception applies to expenses incurred in illegal trafficking in drugs.[24] Drug dealers are not allowed a deduction for ordinary and necessary business expenses incurred in their business. In arriving at gross income from the business, however, dealers may reduce total sales by the cost of goods sold.[25]

POLITICAL CONTRIBUTIONS AND LOBBYING ACTIVITIES

Political Contributions. Generally, no business deduction is permitted for direct or indirect payments for political purposes.[26] Historically, the government has been reluctant to extend favorable tax treatment to political expenditures by businesses. Allowing deductions might encourage abuses and enable businesses to have undue influence upon the political process.

Lobbying Expenditures. The Code places severe restrictions on the deductibility of expenses incurred in connection with lobbying activities.[27] These provisions deny deductions for expenditures incurred in connection with

- influencing state or Federal legislation,
- participating or intervening in any political campaign on behalf of, or in opposition to, any candidate for public office,
- attempting to influence voters with respect to elections, legislative matters, or referendums, and
- attempting to influence the actions of certain high-ranking public officials (including the President, Vice President, and cabinet-level officials).

---

[23]*Comm. v. Sullivan*, 58–1 USTC ¶9368, 1 AFTR2d 1158, 78 S.Ct. 512 (USSC, 1958).
[24]§ 280E.
[25]Reg. § 1.61–3(a). Gross income is defined as sales minus cost of goods sold. Thus, while § 280E prohibits any deductions for drug dealers, it does not modify the normal definition of gross income.
[26]§ 276.
[27]§ 162(e).

There are three exceptions to the disallowance provisions. First, an exception is provided for influencing *local* legislation (e.g., city and county governments). Second, the disallowance provision does not apply to activities devoted solely to *monitoring* legislation. Third, a *de minimis* exception allows the deduction of up to $2,000 of annual *in-house expenditures*, if the expenditures are not otherwise disallowed under the provisions discussed above. In-house lobbying expenditures do not include expenses paid to professional lobbyists or any portion of dues used by associations for lobbying. If in-house expenditures exceed $2,000, none of the in-house expenditures can be deducted.

Example 14

Egret Company pays a $10,000 annual membership fee to the Free Trade Group, a trade association for plumbing wholesalers. The trade association estimates that 70% of its dues are allocated to lobbying activities. Thus, Egret's deduction is limited to $3,000 ($10,000 × 30%), the amount that is not associated with lobbying activities. ▼

EXCESSIVE EXECUTIVE COMPENSATION

The Code contains a *millionaires provision* that applies to compensation paid by *publicly held* corporations.[28] The provision does not limit the amount of compensation that can be *paid* to an employee. Instead, it limits the amount the employer can *deduct* for the compensation of a covered executive to $1 million annually. Covered employees include the chief executive officer and the four other most highly compensated officers. Employee compensation *excludes* the following:

- Commissions based on individual performance.
- Certain performance-based compensation based on company performance according to a formula approved by a board of directors compensation committee (comprised solely of two or more outside directors) and by shareholder vote. The performance attainment must be certified by this compensation committee.
- Payments to tax-qualified retirement plans.
- Payments that are excludible from the employees' gross income (e.g., certain fringe benefits).

DISALLOWANCE OF DEDUCTIONS FOR CAPITAL EXPENDITURES

The Code specifically disallows a deduction for "any amount paid out for new buildings or for permanent improvements or betterments made to increase the value of any property or estate."[29] The Regulations further define capital expenditures to include expenditures that add to the value or prolong the life of property or adapt the property to a new or different use.[30] Incidental repairs and maintenance of the property are not capital expenditures and can be deducted as ordinary and necessary business expenses. Repairing a roof is a deductible expense, but replacing a roof is a capital expenditure subject to depreciation deductions over its useful life. The tune-up of a delivery truck is an expense; a complete overhaul probably is a capital expenditure.

Capitalization versus Expense. When an expenditure is capitalized rather than expensed, the deduction is at best deferred and at worst lost forever. Although

---

[28] § 162(m).
[29] § 263(a)(1).
[30] Reg. § 1.263(a)–1(b).

an immediate tax benefit for a large cash expenditure is lost, the cost may be deductible in increments over a longer period of time.

If the expenditure is for a tangible asset that has an ascertainable life, it is capitalized and may be deducted as depreciation over the life of the asset or as a cost recovery allowance over a specified statutory period under either ACRS or MACRS.[31] Land is not subject to depreciation (or cost recovery) since it does not have an ascertainable life.

EXAMPLE 15

Buffalo Corporation purchases a prime piece of land and an old but usable apartment building located in an apartment-zoned area. Buffalo pays $500,000 for the property and immediately has the building demolished at a cost of $100,000. The $500,000 purchase price and the $100,000 demolition costs must be capitalized, and the tax basis of the land is $600,000. Since land is a nondepreciable asset, no deduction is allowed. More favorable tax treatment might result if Buffalo rents the apartments in the old building for a period of time to attempt to establish that there is no intent to demolish the building. If Buffalo's attempt is successful, it might be possible to allocate a substantial portion of the original purchase price of the property to the building (a depreciable asset). When the building is later demolished, any remaining adjusted basis can be deducted as an ordinary (§ 1231) loss. ▼

INVESTIGATION OF A BUSINESS

Investigation expenses are paid or incurred to determine the feasibility of entering a new business or expanding an existing business. They include such costs as travel, engineering and architectural surveys, marketing reports, and various legal and accounting services. How such expenses are treated for tax purposes depends on a number of variables, including the following:

- The current business, if any, of the taxpayer.
- The nature of the business being investigated.
- Whether or not the acquisition actually takes place.

If the taxpayer is in a business the same as or similar to that being investigated, all investigation expenses are deductible in the year paid or incurred. The tax result is the same whether or not the taxpayer acquires the business being investigated.[32]

EXAMPLE 16

Terry, an accrual basis sole proprietor, owns and operates three motels in Georgia. In the current year, Terry incurs expenses of $8,500 in investigating the possibility of acquiring several additional motels located in South Carolina. The $8,500 is deductible in the current year whether or not Terry acquires the motels in South Carolina. ▼

When the taxpayer is not in a business that is the same as or similar to the one being investigated, the tax result depends on whether the new business is acquired. If the business is not acquired, all investigation expenses generally are nondeductible.[33]

EXAMPLE 17

Lynn, president and sole shareholder of Marmot Corporation, incurs expenses when traveling from Rochester, New York, to California to investigate the feasibility of acquiring several auto care centers. Marmot is in the residential siding business. If no acquisition takes place, Marmot may not deduct any of the expenses. ▼

---

[31] Depreciation and cost recovery allowances are discussed later in this chapter.

[32] *York v. Comm.*, 58–2 USTC ¶9952, 2 AFTR2d 6178, 261 F.2d 421 (CA–4, 1958).

[33] Rev.Rul. 57–418, 1957–2 C.B. 143; *Morton Frank*, 20 T.C. 511 (1953); and *Dwight A. Ward*, 20 T.C. 332 (1953).

If the taxpayer is not in a business that is the same as or similar to the one being investigated and actually acquires the new business, the expenses must be capitalized. At the election of the taxpayer, the expenses may be amortized over a period of 60 months or more, beginning with the month in which the business is acquired.[34]

EXAMPLE 18

Tina, a sole proprietor, owns and operates 10 restaurants located in various cities throughout the Southeast. She travels to Atlanta to discuss the acquisition of an auto dealership. In addition, she incurs legal and accounting costs associated with the potential acquisition. After incurring total investigation costs of $12,000, she acquires the auto dealership on October 1, 1998.

Tina must capitalize the $12,000 of investigation expenses for the auto dealership. If she elects to amortize the expenses over 60 months, she can deduct $600 ($12,000 × 3/60) in 1998. ▼

TRANSACTIONS BETWEEN RELATED PARTIES

The Code places restrictions on the recognition of gains and losses from **related-party transactions.** Without these restrictions, relationships created by birth, marriage, and business would provide endless possibilities for engaging in financial transactions that produce tax savings with no real economic substance or change. For example, to create an artificial loss, a corporation could sell investment property to its sole shareholder at a loss and deduct the loss on the corporate return. The shareholder could then hold the asset indefinitely. Although title to the property has changed, there has been no real economic loss if the shareholder and corporation are considered as an economic unit. A complex set of laws has been designed to eliminate such possibilities.

Losses. The Code provides for the disallowance of any losses from sales or exchanges of property directly or indirectly between related parties.[35] In addition to specified family relationships (e.g., brothers and sisters), certain business relationships are subject to this disallowance rule. For instance, a corporation and a shareholder are considered related parties if the shareholder owns more than 50 percent of the corporation.

When the property is subsequently sold to an unrelated party, any gain recognized is reduced by the loss previously disallowed. Any disallowed loss not used by the related-party buyer to offset his or her recognized gain on a subsequent sale or exchange to an unrelated party is permanently lost.

EXAMPLE 19

Anna, sole shareholder of Leopard Corporation, sells common stock with a basis of $1,000 to the corporation for $800. Leopard sells the stock several years later for $1,100. Anna's $200 loss is disallowed upon the sale to Leopard, and only $100 of gain ($1,100 selling price − $800 basis − $200 disallowed loss) is taxable to Leopard upon the subsequent sale. ▼

EXAMPLE 20

George sells common stock with a basis of $1,050 to his wholly owned corporation for $800. George's $250 loss is disallowed under the related-party rules. The corporation sells the stock eight months later to an unrelated party for $900. The corporation's gain of $100 ($900 selling price − $800 basis) is not recognized because of George's previously disallowed loss of $250. Note that the offset may result in only partial tax benefit upon the subsequent sale (as in this case). If George had not sold the property to the corporation, he could have

---

[34] § 195.   [35] § 267(a)(1).

recognized a $150 loss upon the sale to the unrelated party ($1,050 basis − $900 selling price). ▼

Unpaid Expenses and Interest. The law prevents related taxpayers from engaging in tax avoidance schemes where one related taxpayer uses the accrual method of accounting and the other uses the cash basis. The accrual basis allows the deduction of expenses when incurred, while the cash method requires that income be reported when received. In the absence of restrictions, an accrual basis, closely held corporation, for example, could borrow funds from a cash basis individual shareholder. At the end of the year, the corporation would accrue and deduct the interest expense, but the cash basis lender would not recognize interest income since no interest had been paid. Section 267 specifically defers the accrual of an interest deduction until the lender is required to include the interest in income; that is, when it is actually received by the cash basis taxpayer. This matching provision also applies to other expenses, such as salaries and bonuses.

The deduction deferral provision does not apply if both of the related taxpayers use the accrual method or both use the cash method. Likewise, it does not apply if the related party reporting income uses the accrual method and the related party taking the deduction uses the cash method.

Relationships and Constructive Ownership. Section 267 operates to disallow losses and defer deductions only between *related parties*. Losses or deductions generated by similar transactions with an unrelated party are allowed. Related parties include the following:

- Brothers and sisters (whether whole, half, or adopted), spouse, ancestors (parents, grandparents), and lineal descendants (children, grandchildren) of the taxpayer.
- A corporation owned more than 50 percent (directly or indirectly) by the taxpayer.
- Two corporations that are members of a controlled group.
- A series of other complex relationships between trusts, corporations, and individual taxpayers.

Constructive ownership provisions are applied to determine whether the taxpayers are related. Under these provisions, stock owned by certain relatives or related entities is deemed to be owned by the taxpayer for purposes of applying the loss and expense deduction disallowance provisions. A taxpayer is deemed to own not only his or her stock but the stock owned by his or her lineal descendants, ancestors, brothers and sisters or half-brothers and half-sisters, and spouse. The taxpayer is also deemed to own his or her proportionate share of stock owned by any partnership, corporation, estate, or trust of which he or she is a member. An individual is deemed to own any stock owned, directly or indirectly, by his or her partner. However, constructive ownership by an individual of the other partner's shares does not extend to the individual's spouse or other relatives (no double attribution).

EXAMPLE 21

The stock of Sparrow Corporation is owned 20% by Ted, 30% by Ted's father, 30% by Ted's mother, and 20% by Ted's sister. On July 1 of the current year, Ted loaned $10,000 to Sparrow Corporation at 8% annual interest, principal and interest payable on demand. For tax purposes, Sparrow uses the accrual basis, and Ted uses the cash basis. Both are on a calendar year. Since Ted is deemed to own the 80% owned by his parents and sister, he constructively owns 100% of Sparrow Corporation. If the corporation accrues the interest within the taxable year, no deduction can be taken until payment is made to Ted. ▼

LACK OF ADEQUATE SUBSTANTIATION

The tax law is built on a voluntary system. Taxpayers file their tax returns, report income and take deductions to which they are entitled, and pay their taxes through withholding or estimated tax payments during the year. The taxpayer has the burden of proof for substantiating expenses deducted on the returns and must retain adequate records. Upon audit, the IRS will disallow any undocumented or unsubstantiated deductions. These requirements have resulted in numerous conflicts between taxpayers and the IRS.

Some events throughout the year should be documented as they occur. For example, it is generally advisable to receive a pledge payment statement from a charity, in addition to a canceled check (if available), for proper documentation of a charitable contribution.[36] In addition, for a charitable contribution of $250 or more, a donor must obtain a *receipt* from the donee. Other types of deductible expenditures (such as travel and entertainment expenses, and depreciation on property used for both business and personal purposes) may require receipts or some other type of support.

EXPENSES AND INTEREST RELATED TO TAX-EXEMPT INCOME

Certain income, such as interest on municipal bonds, is tax-exempt.[37] The law also allows the taxpayer to deduct expenses incurred for the production of income.[38] Deduction disallowance provisions, however, make it impossible to make money at the expense of the government by excluding interest income and deducting interest expense.[39]

EXAMPLE 22

Oriole, Inc., a corporation in the 35% bracket, purchased $100,000 of 6% municipal bonds. At the same time, Oriole used the bonds as collateral on a bank loan of $100,000 at 8% interest. A positive cash flow would result from the tax benefit as follows:

Cash paid out on loan	($8,000)
Cash received from bonds	6,000
Tax savings from deducting interest expense	2,800
Net positive cash flow	$ 800

To eliminate the possibility illustrated in the preceding example, the Code specifically disallows a deduction for the expenses of producing tax-exempt income. Interest on any indebtedness incurred or continued to purchase or carry tax-exempt obligations also is disallowed.

Judicial Interpretations. It is often difficult to show a direct relationship between borrowings and investment in tax-exempt securities. Suppose, for example, that a taxpayer borrows money, adds it to existing funds, buys inventory and stocks, then later sells the inventory and buys municipal bonds. A series of transactions such as these can completely obscure any connection between the loan and the tax-exempt investment. One solution would be to disallow interest on any debt to the extent that the taxpayer holds any tax-exempt securities. The law was not intended to go to such extremes. As a result, judicial interpretations have tried to be reasonable in disallowing interest deductions.

---

[36] Rev.Proc. 92–71, 1992–2 C.B. 437, addresses circumstances where checks are not returned by a financial institution or where electronic transfers are made.

[37] § 103.
[38] § 212.
[39] § 265.

In one case, a company used municipal bonds as collateral on short-term loans to meet seasonal liquidity needs.[40] The Court disallowed the interest deduction on the grounds that the company could predict its seasonal liquidity needs. The company could anticipate the need to borrow the money to continue to carry the tax-exempt securities. The same company was allowed an interest deduction on a building mortgage, even though tax-exempt securities it owned could have been sold to pay off the mortgage. The Court reasoned that short-term liquidity needs would have been impaired if the tax-exempt securities were sold. Furthermore, the Court ruled that carrying the tax-exempt securities bore no relationship to the long-term financing of a construction project.

EXAMPLE 23

In January of the current year, Crane Corporation borrowed $100,000 at 8% interest. Crane used the loan proceeds to purchase 5,000 shares of stock in White Corporation. In July, Crane sold the stock for $120,000 and reinvested the proceeds in City of Denver bonds, the income from which is tax-exempt. Assuming the $100,000 loan remained outstanding throughout the entire year, Crane cannot deduct the interest attributable to the period when it held the bonds. ▼

CHARITABLE CONTRIBUTIONS

4 LEARNING OBJECTIVE
Understand the limitations applicable to the charitable contribution deduction for corporations.

Corporations and individuals are allowed to deduct contributions made to qualified domestic charitable organizations.[41] Qualified organizations include:[42]

- A state or possession of the United States or any subdivisions thereof.
- A corporation, trust, or community chest, fund, or foundation that is situated in the United States and is organized and operated exclusively for religious, charitable, scientific, literary, or educational purposes or for the prevention of cruelty to children or animals.
- A verterans' organization.
- A fraternal organization operating under the lodge system.
- A cemetery company.

The IRS publishes a list of organizations that have applied for and received tax-exempt status under § 501 of the Code.[43] This publication is updated frequently and may be helpful in determining if a gift has been made to a qualifying charitable organization.

Because gifts made to needy individuals are not deductible, a deduction will not be permitted if a gift is received by a donee in an individual capacity rather than as a representative of a qualified organization.

Generally, a deduction for a **charitable contribution** will be allowed only for the year in which the payment is made. However, an important exception is made for *accrual basis* corporations. They may claim the deduction in the year preceding payment if two requirements are met. First, the contribution must be *authorized* by the board of directors by the end of that year. Second, it must be *paid* on or before the fifteenth day of the third month of the following year.

---

[40]*The Wisconsin Cheeseman, Inc. v. U.S.*, 68–1 USTC ¶9145, 21 AFTR2d 383, 388 F.2d 420 (CA–7, 1968).
[41]§ 170.
[42]§ 170(c).
[43]Although the Cumulative List of Organizations, IRS Publication 78 (available by purchase from the Superintendent of Documents, U.S. Government Printing Office, Washington, DC 20402), may be helpful, not all organizations that qualify are listed in this publication. The list is also available on the Web at http://www.irs.ustreas.gov.

EXAMPLE 24

On December 28, 1998, Blue Company, a calendar year, accrual basis partnership, authorizes a $5,000 donation to the Atlanta Symphony Association (a qualified charitable organization). The donation is made on March 14, 1999. Because Blue Company is a partnership, the contribution can be deducted only in 1999.[44] However, if Blue Company is a corporation and the December 28, 1998 authorization was made by its board of directors, Blue may claim the $5,000 donation as a deduction for calendar year 1998. ▼

PROPERTY CONTRIBUTIONS

The amount that can be deducted for a noncash charitable contribution depends on the type of property contributed. Property must be identified as long-term **capital gain property** or ordinary income property. Long-term capital gain property is property that, if sold, would result in long-term capital gain for the taxpayer. Such property generally must be a capital asset and must be held for the long-term holding period (more than one year for charitable contribution purposes). **Ordinary income property** is property that, if sold, would result in ordinary income for the taxpayer. Examples of ordinary income property include inventory and short-term capital assets (held one year or less). Refer to Chapter 3 for a brief introduction to the distinction between capital and ordinary assets.

The deduction for a charitable contribution of long-term capital property is generally measured by its *fair market value*.

EXAMPLE 25

In 1998, Mallard Corporation donated a parcel of land (a capital asset) to Oakland Community College. Mallard acquired the land in 1988 for $60,000, and the fair market value on the date of the contribution was $100,000. The corporation's charitable contribution deduction (subject to a percentage limitation discussed later) is measured by the asset's fair market value of $100,000, even though the $40,000 appreciation on the land has never been included in Mallard's income. ▼

In two situations, a charitable contribution of long-term capital gain property is measured by the basis of the property, rather than fair market value. If a corporation contributes tangible personal property and the charitable organization puts the property to an *unrelated use*, the appreciation on the property is not deductible. Unrelated use is defined as use that is not related to the purpose or function that qualifies the organization for exempt status.

EXAMPLE 26

White Corporation donates a painting worth $200,000 to Western States Art Museum (a qualified charity), which exhibits the painting. White had acquired the painting in 1980 for $90,000. Because the museum put the painting to a related use, White is allowed to deduct $200,000, the fair market value of the painting. ▼

EXAMPLE 27

Assume the same facts as in the previous example, except that White Corporation donates the painting to the American Cancer Society, which sells the painting and deposits the $200,000 proceeds in the organization's general fund. White's deduction is limited to the $90,000 basis because it contributed tangible personal property that was put to an unrelated use by the charitable organization. ▼

---

[44]Each calendar year partner will report an allocable portion of the charitable contribution deduction as of December 31, 1999 (the end of the partnership's tax year). See Chapter 11.

The deduction for charitable contributions of long-term capital gain property to certain private nonoperating foundations (defined in §§ 4942 and 509) is also limited to the basis of the property.

As a general rule, the deduction for a contribution of ordinary income property is limited to the basis of the property. However, corporations enjoy two special exceptions where basis plus 50 percent of the appreciation on property is allowed on certain contributions. The first exception concerns inventory if the property is used in a manner related to the exempt purpose of the donee. Also, the charity must use the property solely for the care of the ill, the needy, or infants.

EXAMPLE 28

Lark Corporation, a grocery chain, donates canned goods to the Salvation Army to be used to feed the needy. Lark's basis in the canned goods is $2,000, and the fair market value (the sales price to customers) is $3,000. Lark's deduction is $2,500 [$2,000 basis + 50% ($3,000 − $2,000)]. ▼

The second exception involves gifts of scientific property to colleges and certain scientific research organizations for use in research, provided certain conditions are met.[45]

LIMITATIONS IMPOSED ON CHARITABLE CONTRIBUTION DEDUCTIONS

Both corporations and individuals are subject to percentage limits on the charitable contribution deduction.[46] The complex limitations for individual taxpayers are covered in Chapter 15.

For any one year, a corporate taxpayer's contribution deduction is limited to 10 percent of taxable income. For this purpose, taxable income is computed without regard to the charitable contribution deduction, any net operating loss carryback or capital loss carryback, and the dividends received deduction. Any contributions in excess of the 10 percent limitation may be carried forward to the five succeeding tax years. Any carryforward must be added to subsequent contributions and will be subject to the 10 percent limitation. In applying this limitation, the current year's contributions must be deducted first, with excess deductions from previous years deducted in order of time.[47]

EXAMPLE 29

During 1998, Orange Corporation (a calendar year taxpayer) had the following income and expenses:

Income from operations	$140,000
Expenses from operations	110,000
Dividends received	10,000
Charitable contributions made in May 1998	5,000

For purposes of the 10% limitation only, Orange Corporation's taxable income is $40,000 ($140,000 − $110,000 + $10,000). Consequently, the allowable charitable contribution deduction for 1998 is $4,000 (10% × $40,000). The $1,000 unused portion of the contribution can be carried forward to 1999, 2000, 2001, 2002, and 2003 (in that order) until exhausted. ▼

---

[45]These conditions are set forth in § 170(e)(4). For the inventory exception, see § 170(e)(3).

[46]The percentage limitations applicable to individuals and corporations are set forth in § 170(b).

[47]The carryover rules relating to all taxpayers are in § 170(d).

EXAMPLE 30

Assume the same facts as in the previous example. In 1999, Orange Corporation has taxable income (for purposes of the 10% limitation) of $50,000 and makes a charitable contribution of $4,500. The maximum deduction allowed for 1999 is $5,000 (10% × $50,000). The entire 1999 contribution of $4,500 and $500 of the 1998 charitable contribution carryforward are currently deductible. The remaining $500 of the 1998 carryforward may be carried over to 2000 (and later years, if necessary). ▼

RESEARCH AND EXPERIMENTAL EXPENDITURES

5 LEARNING OBJECTIVE
Recognize and apply the alternative tax treatments for research and experimental expenditures.

Section 174 covers the treatment of **research and experimental expenditures.** The Regulations define research and experimental expenditures as follows:

> . . . all such costs incident to the development of an experimental or pilot model, a plant process, a product, a formula, an invention, or similar property, and the improvement of already existing property of the type mentioned. The term does not include expenditures such as those for the ordinary testing or inspection of materials or products for quality control or those for efficiency surveys, management studies, consumer surveys, advertising, or promotions.[48]

Expenses in connection with the acquisition or improvement of land or depreciable property are not research and experimental expenditures. Rather, they increase the basis of the land or depreciable property. However, depreciation on a building used for research may be a research and experimental expense. Only the depreciation that is a research and experimental expense (not the cost of the asset) is subject to the three alternatives discussed below.

The law permits three alternatives for the handling of research and experimental expenditures:

- Expense in the year paid or incurred.
- Defer and amortize.
- Capitalize.

If the costs are capitalized, a deduction is not available until the research project is abandoned or is deemed worthless. Since many products resulting from research projects do not have a definite and limited useful life, a taxpayer should ordinarily elect to write off the expenditures immediately or to defer and amortize them. It is generally preferable to elect an immediate write-off of the research expenditures because of the time value of the tax deduction.

The law also provides for a research activities credit. The credit amounts to 20 percent of certain research and experimental expenditures.[49]

EXPENSE METHOD

A taxpayer can elect to expense all of the research and experimental expenditures incurred in the current year and all subsequent years. The consent of the IRS is not required if the method is adopted for the first taxable year in which such expenditures were paid or incurred. Once the election is made, the taxpayer must continue to expense all qualifying expenditures unless a request for a change is made to, and approved by, the IRS. In certain instances, a taxpayer may incur

---
[48] Reg. § 1.174–2(a)(1).
[49] § 41. See Chapter 13 for a detailed discussion of the research activities credit.

research and experimental expenditures before actually engaging in any trade or business activity. In such instances, the Supreme Court has applied a liberal standard of deductibility and permitted a deduction in the year of incurrence.[50]

DEFERRAL AND AMORTIZATION METHOD

Alternatively, research and experimental expenditures may be deferred and amortized if the taxpayer makes an election.[51] Under the election, research and experimental expenditures are amortized ratably over a period of not less than 60 months. A deduction is allowed beginning with the month in which the taxpayer first realizes benefits from the research and experimental expenditure. The election is binding, and a change requires permission from the IRS.

EXAMPLE 31

Gold Corporation decided to develop a new line of adhesives. The project was begun in 1998. Gold incurred the following expenses in 1998 and 1999 in connection with the project:

	1998	1999
Salaries	$25,000	$18,000
Materials	8,000	2,000
Depreciation and machinery	6,500	5,700

The benefits from the project will be realized starting in March 2000. If Gold Corporation elects a 60-month deferral and amortization period, there will be no deduction prior to March 2000, the month benefits from the project begin to be realized. The deduction for 2000 will be $10,867, computed as follows:

Salaries ($25,000 + $18,000)	$43,000
Materials ($8,000 + $2,000)	10,000
Depreciation ($6,500 + $5,700)	12,200
Total	$65,200
$65,200 × (10 months/60 months)	$10,867

The option to treat research and experimental expenditures as deferred expense is usually employed when a company does not have sufficient income to offset the research and experimental expenses. Rather than create net operating loss carryovers that might not be utilized because of the 20-year limitation on such carryovers, the deferral and amortization method may be used. The deferral of research and experimental expenditures should also be considered if the taxpayer expects higher tax rates in the future.

OTHER EXPENSE RULES

In addition to the provisions related to charitable contributions and research and experimental expenditures, a variety of other expenses are subject to special rules and limitations. Some of these rules are noted briefly in the paragraphs below.

---

[50] *Snow v. Comm.*, 74–1 USTC ¶9432, 33 AFTR2d 74–1251, 94 S.Ct. 1876 (USSC, 1974).

[51] § 174(b)(2).

INTEREST EXPENSE

Generally, corporations are not limited in the amount of interest expense they may deduct. However, the deductibility of expenses (including interest) from certain activities may be limited.[52] In contrast, individuals may not deduct interest expense on loans used for personal purposes, unless the loan is secured by a home. Furthermore, individuals may only deduct interest expense associated with investments to the extent of net investment income.[53]

Because the deductibility of interest expense associated with certain activities is limited, the IRS provides rules for allocating interest expense among activities. Under these rules, interest is allocated in the same manner as the debt with respect to which the interest is paid, and debt is allocated by tracing disbursements of the debt proceeds to specific expenditures. The interest tracing rules are complex and depend on whether loan proceeds are commingled with other cash and the length of time the loan proceeds are held before they are spent.

TAXES

As with interest expense, tax payments in a business or investment context are generally deductible. However, most Federal taxes are not deductible. Individuals may also deduct tax payments, subject to limitations (discussed in Chapter 15). One unique problem associated with determining the deductibility of taxes relates to real estate taxes paid during a year when the real estate is sold.

Real estate taxes for the entire year are apportioned between the buyer and seller based on the number of days the property was held by each during the real property tax year. This apportionment is required whether the tax is paid by the buyer or the seller or is prorated according to the purchase agreement. It is the apportionment that determines who is entitled to deduct the real estate taxes in the year of sale. In making the apportionment, the assessment date and the lien date are disregarded. The date of sale counts as a day the property is owned by the buyer.

EXAMPLE 32

A county's real property tax year runs from April 1 to March 31. Nuthatch Corporation, the owner on April 1, 1998, of real property located in the county, sells the real property to Crane, Inc., on June 30, 1998. Crane owns the real property from June 30, 1998, through March 31, 1999. The tax for the real property tax year April 1, 1998, through March 31, 1999, is $730. The portion of the real property tax treated as imposed upon Nuthatch, the seller, is $180 [(90/365) × $730, April 1 through June 29, 1998], and $550 [(275/365) × $730, June 30, 1998, through March 31, 1999] of the tax is treated as imposed upon Crane, the purchaser. ▼

If the actual real estate taxes are not prorated between the buyer and seller as part of the purchase agreement, adjustments are required. The adjustments are necessary to determine the amount realized by the seller and the adjusted basis of the property to the buyer. If the buyer pays the entire amount of the tax, it effectively has paid the seller's portion of the real estate tax and has therefore paid more for the property than the actual purchase price. Thus, the amount of real estate tax that is apportioned to the seller (for Federal income tax purposes) and paid by the buyer is added to the buyer's adjusted basis. The seller must increase the amount realized on the sale by the same amount.

---

[52] See, for example, the discussion of the passive activity limits in Chapter 5.

[53] See Chapter 15 for a more detailed discussion of the deductibility of interest by individuals.

CHAPTER 4 Business Deductions   4–21

▼ EXAMPLE 33

Seth sells real estate on October 3, 1998, for $50,000. The buyer, Wilma, pays the real estate taxes of $1,098 for the 1998 calendar year (a leap year), which is the real estate property tax year. Of the real estate taxes, $828 (for 276 days) is apportioned to and is deductible by the seller, Seth, and $270 (for 90 days) of the taxes is deductible by Wilma. The buyer has paid Seth's real estate taxes of $828 and has therefore paid $50,828 for the property. Wilma's basis is increased to $50,828, and the amount realized by Seth from the sale is increased to $50,828. ▼

The opposite result occurs if the seller (rather than the buyer) pays the real estate taxes. In this case, the seller reduces the amount realized from the sale by the amount that has been apportioned to the buyer. The buyer is required to reduce his or her adjusted basis by a corresponding amount.

▼ EXAMPLE 34

Silver Corporation sells real estate to Butch for $50,000 on October 3, 1998. While Silver held the property, it paid the real estate taxes of $1,098 for the calendar year, which is the real estate property tax year. Although Silver paid the entire $1,098 of real estate taxes, $270 of that amount is apportioned to Butch and is therefore deductible by him. The effect is that the buyer, Butch, has paid only $49,730 for the property. The amount realized by Silver, the seller, is reduced by $270, and Butch reduces his basis in the property to $49,730. ▼

COST RECOVERY ALLOWANCES

OVERVIEW

6 LEARNING OBJECTIVE
Determine the amount of cost recovery under MACRS, and apply the § 179 expensing election and the deduction limitations on listed property and automobiles when making the MACRS calculation.

Taxpayers may write off the cost of certain assets that are used in a trade or business or held for the production of income. A write-off may take the form of a *cost recovery allowance* (depreciation under prior law), depletion, or amortization. Tangible assets, other than natural resources, are written off through cost recovery allowances. Natural resources, such as oil, gas, coal, and timber, are *depleted*. Intangible assets, such as copyrights and patents, are *amortized*. Generally, no write-off is allowed for an asset that does not have a determinable useful life.

The tax rules for writing off the cost of business assets differ from the accounting rules. Several methods are available for determining depreciation for accounting purposes, including the straight-line, declining balance, and sum-of-the-years' digits methods. Historically, *depreciation* for tax purposes was computed using variations of these accounting methods. The **depreciation rules** continue to apply to assets that were placed in service before 1981 and to certain post-1980 assets that did not qualify for write-off under the **cost recovery system.**

In 1981, the depreciation system was replaced by the **accelerated cost recovery system (ACRS).** Under ACRS, write-offs for tax purposes were determined using cost recovery tables provided in the tax law. These cost recovery allowances generally were determined using shorter asset lives and more accelerated depreciation methods than were available under the depreciation system.

In 1986, ACRS was replaced by the **modified accelerated cost recovery system (MACRS),** which provided longer lives and less accelerated write-offs than ACRS. Cost recovery allowances for most property placed in service after 1980 and before 1987 continue to be determined using ACRS tables. Property placed in service after 1986 generally is subject to the MACRS rules. The MACRS rules for personal property and both ACRS and MACRS for real estate are covered in this text. Refer to IRS Publication 534 for coverage of the alternative depreciation system and ACRS for personal property.

MODIFIED ACCELERATED COST RECOVERY SYSTEM (MACRS)

MACRS provides separate cost recovery tables for realty (real property) and personalty (personal property). *Realty* generally includes land and buildings permanently affixed to the land. Write-offs are not available for land because it does not have a determinable useful life. Cost recovery allowances for real property, other than land, are based on recovery lives specified in the law. The IRS provides tables that specify cost recovery allowances for most types of realty.

Personalty is defined as any asset that is not realty. Personalty includes furniture, machinery, equipment, and many other types of assets. Do not confuse personalty (or personal property) with personal-use property. Personal-use property is any property (realty or personalty) that is held for personal use rather than for use in a trade or business or an income-producing activity. Cost recovery is not allowed for personal-use assets.

In summary, both realty and personalty can be either business-use/income-producing property or personal-use property. Examples include a residence (realty that is personal use), an office building (realty that is business use), a dump truck (personalty that is business use), and regular wearing apparel (personalty that is personal use). It is imperative that this distinction between the classification of an asset (realty or personalty) and the use to which the asset is put (business or personal) be understood.

ELIGIBLE PROPERTY UNDER MACRS

Assets used in a trade or business or for the production of income are eligible for cost recovery if they are subject to wear and tear, decay or decline from natural causes, or obsolescence. Assets that do not decline in value on a predictable basis or that do not have a determinable useful life (e.g., land, stock, antiques) are not eligible for cost recovery.

Cost Recovery Allowed or Allowable. The basis of cost recovery property must be reduced by the cost recovery *allowed* and by not less than the *allowable* amount. The allowed cost recovery is the cost recovery actually taken, whereas the allowable cost recovery is the amount that could have been taken under the applicable cost recovery method. If the taxpayer does not claim any cost recovery on property during a particular year, the basis of the property must still be reduced by the amount of cost recovery that should have been deducted (the *allowable* cost recovery).

EXAMPLE 35

On March 15, Heron Corporation paid $10,000 for a copier to be used in its business. The copier is five-year property. Heron elected to use the straight-line method of cost recovery, but did not take any cost recovery allowance in year 3 or 4. Therefore, the allowed cost recovery (cost recovery actually deducted) and the allowable cost recovery are as follows:[54]

---

[54]The cost recovery allowances are based on the half-year convention, which allows a half-year's cost recovery in the first and last years of the recovery period.

TAX IN THE NEWS

WHO GETS THE REFUND?

In October 1985, Ralston Purina Co. sold its subsidiary, Foodmaker, Inc., which owns and franchises Jack in the Box restaurants. At the time of the sale, several years of Foodmaker's tax returns were being audited by the IRS. The IRS was questioning accelerated depreciation deductions and investment tax credits that had been claimed on Jack in the Box restaurant buildings. Ralston and the buyers agreed that if the IRS decided Foodmaker was owed a refund, this money would be paid to Ralston. Likewise, if additional taxes were due, Ralston would reimburse the new owners.

In 1986, Foodmaker filed a return based on the assumption that the IRS's earlier tax claims would be proved wrong. In effect, this gave the $11.7 million refund to Foodmaker. Ralston claims that Foodmaker did not inform it of the refund claim associated with the 1986 tax return. In September 1996, Ralston learned that Foodmaker had claimed the refund 10 years earlier. Ralston now alleges that Foodmaker owes it at least $11 million plus interest from July 1986 and has filed a suit.

SOURCE: Adapted from Fred Faust, "Surprise! From Jack in the Box," *St. Louis Post-Dispatch*, June 2, 1997, Business Plus, p.5.

	Cost Recovery Allowed	Cost Recovery Allowable
Year 1	$1,000	$ 1,000
Year 2	2,000	2,000
Year 3	–0–	2,000
Year 4	–0–	2,000
Year 5	2,000	2,000
Year 6	1,000	1,000
Totals	$6,000	$10,000

The adjusted basis of the copier at the end of year 6 is $0 ($10,000 cost − $10,000 *allowable* cost recovery). If Heron sells the copier for $800 in year 7, it will recognize an $800 gain ($800 amount realized − $0 adjusted basis). ▼

Cost Recovery Basis for Personal-Use Assets Converted to Business or Income-Producing Use. If personal-use assets are converted to business or income-producing use, the basis for cost recovery and for loss is the lower of the adjusted basis or the fair market value at the time the property was converted. As a result of this basis rule, losses that occurred while the property was personal-use property will not be recognized for tax purposes through the cost recovery of the property.

EXAMPLE 36

Hans acquires a personal residence for $120,000. Four years later, when the fair market value is only $100,000, he establishes a consulting company and uses the residence solely for office space. The basis for cost recovery is $100,000, since the fair market value is less than the adjusted basis. The $20,000 decline in value is deemed to be personal (since it occurred while Hans held the property for personal use). Therefore, depreciation deductions will be based on $100,000 rather than $120,000. ▼

▼ **EXHIBIT 4–2**
Cost Recovery Periods: Personalty

Class	Examples
3-year	Tractor units for use over-the-road
	Any horse that is not a racehorse and is more than 12 years old at the time it is placed in service
	Any racehorse that is more than 2 years old at the time it is placed in service
	Breeding hogs
	Special tools used in the manufacturing of motor vehicles, such as dies, fixtures, molds, and patterns
5-year	Automobiles and taxis
	Light and heavy general-purpose trucks
	Buses
	Trailers and trailer-mounted containers
	Typewriters, calculators, and copiers
	Computers and peripheral equipment
	Breeding and dairy cattle
7-year	Office furniture, fixtures, and equipment
	Breeding and work horses
	Agricultural machinery and equipment
	Single-purpose agricultural or horticultural structures
	Railroad track
10-year	Vessels, barges, tugs, and similar water transportation equipment
	Assets used for petroleum refining or for the manufacture of grain and grain mill products, sugar and sugar products, or vegetable oils and vegetable oil products
15-year	Land improvements
	Assets used for industrial steam and electric generation and/or distribution systems
	Assets used in the manufacture of cement
	Assets used in pipeline transportation
	Electric utility nuclear production plant
	Municipal wastewater treatment plant
20-year	Farm buildings except single-purpose agricultural and horticultural structures
	Gas utility distribution facilities
	Water utilities
	Municipal sewer

COST RECOVERY FOR PERSONAL PROPERTY

The general effect of the MACRS legislation was to lengthen asset lives compared to those used under ACRS. MACRS provides that the cost recovery basis of eligible personalty (and certain realty) is recovered over 3, 5, 7, 10, 15, or 20 years. Property is classified by recovery period under MACRS based on asset depreciation range (ADR) midpoint lives provided by the IRS.[55] Examples of property in the different cost recovery categories are shown in Exhibit 4–2.[56]

Accelerated depreciation is allowed for these six MACRS classes of property. Two hundred percent declining-balance is used for the 3-, 5-, 7-, and 10-year classes, with a switchover to straight-line depreciation when it yields a larger amount. One hundred and fifty percent declining-balance is allowed for the 15- and 20-year

---

[55] Rev.Proc. 87–56, 1987–2 C.B. 674 is the source for the ADR midpoint lives.

[56] § 168(e).

classes, with an appropriate straight-line switchover. The appropriate computational methods and conventions are built into the tables, so it is not necessary to perform any calculations. To determine the amount of the cost recovery allowance, simply identify the asset by class and go to the appropriate table.[57]

The cost recovery allowance under MACRS is calculated by multiplying the cost recovery basis by the percentage that reflects the applicable cost recovery method and the applicable convention. The MACRS percentages for personalty are shown in Table 4–1 (MACRS tables begin on page 4–38).

EXAMPLE 37

Robin Corporation acquires a five-year class asset on April 10, 1998, for $30,000. Robin's cost recovery deduction for 1998 is $6,000 [$30,000 × .20 (Table 4–1)]. ▼

Taxpayers may elect the straight-line method to compute cost recovery allowances for each of these classes of property. Certain property is not eligible for accelerated cost recovery and must be depreciated under an alternative depreciation system (ADS). Both the straight-line election and ADS are discussed later in the chapter.

MACRS views property as placed in service in the middle of the first year and allows a half-year of cost recovery in the year of acquisition and in the final year of cost recovery.[58] Thus, for example, under this **half-year convention,** the statutory recovery period for three-year property begins in the middle of the year the asset is placed in service and ends three years later. In practical terms, this means the actual write-off periods cover 4, 6, 8, 11, 16, and 21 tax years. MACRS also allows for a half-year of cost recovery in the year of disposition or retirement.

EXAMPLE 38

Assume the same facts as in Example 37 and that Robin disposes of the asset on March 5, 2000. Robin's cost recovery deduction for 2000 is $2,880 [$30,000 × ½ × .192 (Table 4–1)]. ▼

Mid-Quarter Convention. Under the original ACRS rules for personal property, the half-year convention was used no matter when property was acquired during the year. Thus, if a substantial dollar amount of assets was acquired late in the tax year, the half-year convention still applied. MACRS contains a provision to curtail the benefits of such a tax strategy. If more than 40 percent of the value of property other than eligible real estate[59] is placed in service during the last quarter of the year, a **mid-quarter convention** applies.[60] Under the convention, property acquisitions are grouped by the quarter they were acquired for cost recovery purposes. Acquisitions during the first quarter are allowed 10.5 months of cost recovery; the second quarter, 7.5 months; the third quarter, 4.5 months; and the fourth quarter, 1.5 months. The percentages are shown in Table 4–2.

EXAMPLE 39

Silver Corporation acquires the following five-year class property in 1998:

Acquisition Dates	Cost
February 15	$ 200,000
July 10	400,000
December 5	600,000
Total	$1,200,000

---

[57] § 168(b).
[58] § 168(d)(4)(A).
[59] See Cost Recovery for Real Estate later in this chapter for a discussion of eligible real estate.
[60] § 168(d)(3).

If Silver Corporation uses the statutory percentage method, the cost recovery allowances for the first two years are computed as indicated below. Because more than 40% ($600,000/$1,200,000 = 50%) of the acquisitions are in the last quarter, the mid-quarter convention applies.

1998		
February 15	[$200,000 × .35 (Table 4–2)]	$ 70,000
July 10	($400,000 × .15)	60,000
December 5	($600,000 × .05)	30,000
Total		$160,000
1999		
February 15	[$200,000 × .26 (Table 4–2)]	$ 52,000
July 10	($400,000 × .34)	136,000
December 5	($600,000 × .38)	228,000
Total		$416,000

When property to which the mid-quarter convention applies is disposed of, the property is treated as though it were disposed of at the midpoint of the quarter. Hence, in the quarter of disposition, cost recovery is allowed for one-half of the quarter.

EXAMPLE 40

Assume the same facts as in Example 39, except that Silver Corporation sells the $400,000 asset on November 30, 1999. The cost recovery allowance for 1999 is computed as follows:

February 15	[$200,000 × .26 (Table 4–2)]	$ 52,000
July 10	[$400,000 × .34 × (3.5/4)]	119,000
December 5	($600,000 × .38)	228,000
Total		$399,000

COST RECOVERY FOR REAL ESTATE

Under the original ACRS rules, realty was assigned a 15-year recovery period. Real property other than low-income housing was depreciated using the 175 percent declining-balance method, with a switchover to straight-line when it yielded a larger amount. Low-income housing was depreciated using the 200 percent declining-balance method, with a straight-line switchover. In either case, zero salvage value was assumed. The Deficit Reduction Act of 1984 changed the recovery period for real property to 18 years. This applied generally to property placed in service after March 15, 1984. However, the 15-year recovery period was retained for low-income housing. ACRS recovery periods for real estate were changed again, from 18 years to 19 years, for property placed in service after May 8, 1985, and before January 1, 1987.

Under MACRS, the cost recovery period for residential rental real estate is 27.5 years, and the straight-line method is used for computing the cost recovery allowance. **Residential rental real estate** includes property where 80 percent or more of the gross rental revenues are from nontransient dwelling units (e.g., an apartment building). Hotels, motels, and similar establishments are not residential rental property. Low-income housing is classified as residential rental real estate. Nonresidential real estate has a recovery period of 39 years (27.5 or 31.5 years for such property placed in service before May 13, 1993) and is also depreciated using the straight-line method.[61]

---

[61] §§ 168(b), (c), and (e).

Concept Summary 4–1

MACRS Computational Rules: Statutory Percentage and Straight-Line Methods

	Personal Property	Real Property
Convention	Half-year or mid-quarter	Mid-month
Cost recovery deduction in the year of disposition	Half-year for year of disposition or half-quarter for quarter of disposition	Half-month for month of disposition

Some items of real property are not treated as real estate for purposes of MACRS. For example, single-purpose agricultural structures are in the 7-year MACRS class. Land improvements are in the 15-year MACRS class.

All eligible real estate placed in service after June 22, 1984 (under both ACRS and MACRS) is depreciated using the **mid-month convention**.[62] Regardless of when during the month the property is placed in service, it is deemed to have been placed in service at the middle of the month. In the year of disposition, a mid-month convention is also used.

Cost recovery is computed by multiplying the applicable rate (taken from a table) by the cost recovery basis. The MACRS real property rates are provided in Table 4–3.

Example 41

Badger Rentals, Inc., acquired a building on April 1, 1994, for $800,000. If the building is classified as residential rental real estate, the cost recovery allowance for 1998 is $29,088 (.03636 × $800,000). If the building is classified as nonresidential real estate, the 1998 cost recovery allowance is $25,400 (.03175 × $800,000). (See the middle section of Table 4–3 for percentages.) ▼

As part of the deficit reduction legislation of the Clinton administration,[63] nonresidential real estate placed in service after May 12, 1993, became subject to a 39-year recovery period. Percentages for 39-year real property are reflected in the bottom section of Table 4–3.

Example 42

Assume the same facts as in Example 41, except that Badger acquired the nonresidential building on November 19, 1998. The 1998 cost recovery allowance is $2,568 [$800,000 × .00321 (Table 4–3)]. ▼

An overview of MACRS rules is provided in Concept Summary 4–1.

THE MACRS STRAIGHT-LINE ELECTION

Although MACRS requires straight-line depreciation for all eligible real estate as previously discussed, the taxpayer may *elect* to use the straight-line method for personal property.[64] The property is depreciated using the class life (recovery period) of the asset with a half-year convention or a mid-quarter convention,

---

[62] For ACRS property placed in service prior to June 23, 1984, a full month convention was used.

[63] This legislation was part of the Revenue Reconciliation Act of 1993.
[64] § 168(b)(5).

whichever is applicable. The election is available on a class-by-class and year-by-year basis. The percentages for the straight-line election with a half-year convention appear in Table 4–4.

EXAMPLE 43

Terry acquires a 10-year class asset on August 4, 1998, for $100,000. He elects the straight-line method of cost recovery. Terry's cost recovery deduction for 1998 is $5,000 ($100,000 × .050). His cost recovery deduction for 1999 is $10,000 ($100,000 × .10). (See Table 4–4 for percentages.) ▼

ELECTION TO EXPENSE ASSETS UNDER § 179

For tax years beginning in 1998, § 179 permits a taxpayer to elect to write off up to $18,500 of the acquisition cost of tangible personal property used in a trade or business.[65] The maximum write-off under this provision increases to $25,000 on the following schedule:

Tax Year Beginning in	Maximum Expense Deduction
1998	$18,500
1999	19,000
2000	20,000
2001 or 2002	24,000
2003 and thereafter	25,000

Amounts that are expensed under § 179 may not be capitalized and depreciated. The **§ 179 expensing election** is an annual election and applies to the acquisition cost of property placed in service that year. The immediate expense election is not available for real property or for property used for the production of income.[66]

EXAMPLE 44

Kodiak Corporation acquires machinery (five-year class) on February 1, 1998, at a cost of $40,000 and elects to expense $18,500 under § 179. Kodiak's statutory percentage cost recovery deduction for 1998 is $4,300 [($40,000 cost − $18,500 expensed) × .200]. (See Table 4–1 for percentage.) Kodiak's total deduction for 1998 is $22,800 ($18,500 + $4,300). ▼

Annual Limitations. Two additional limitations apply to the amount deductible under § 179. First, the ceiling amount on the deduction is reduced dollar-for-dollar when property (other than ineligible real estate) placed in service during the taxable year exceeds $200,000. Second, the amount expensed under § 179 cannot exceed the aggregate amount of taxable income derived from the conduct of any trade or business by the taxpayer. Taxable income of a trade or business is computed without regard to the amount expensed under § 179. Any § 179 deduction in excess of taxable income is carried forward to future taxable years and added to other amounts eligible for expensing (and is subject to the ceiling rules for the carryforward years).

EXAMPLE 45

Jill owns a computer service and operates it as a sole proprietorship. In 1998, she will net $11,000 before considering any § 179 deduction. If Jill spends $204,000 on new equipment, her § 179 expense deduction is computed as follows:

---

[65] This amount was $10,000 for property placed in service in tax years beginning before January 1, 1993; $17,500 for property placed in service from January 1, 1993 to December 31, 1996; and $18,000 for property placed in service in tax years beginning in 1997.

[66] §§ 179(b) and (d).

TAX IN THE NEWS

A FERRARI AS MEDICAL EQUIPMENT

Babies do not always arrive during office hours. Obstetricians frequently need to get to the delivery room quickly. The question is whether "quickly" requires a red Ferrari sports car.

On August 26, 1995, the *Newport Daily Press* reported that a Chesapeake obstetrician purchased a red Ferrari and then wrote off the cost on his corporate tax return. On the return, the doctor claimed the purchase price was for an ultrasound machine and treated the amount as a business expense. From the *Daily Press* and other local media reports, it is unclear whether the $85,000 amount was expensed or whether it was capitalized and deducted as cost recovery.

§ 179 deduction before adjustment	$18,500
Less: Dollar limitation reduction ($204,000 − $200,000)	(4,000)
Remaining § 179 deduction	$14,500
Business income limitation	$11,000
§ 179 deduction allowed	$11,000
§ 179 deduction carryforward ($14,500 − $11,000)	$ 3,500

Effect on Basis. The basis of the property for cost recovery purposes is reduced by the § 179 amount after it is adjusted for property placed in service in excess of $200,000. This adjusted amount does not reflect any business income limitation.

EXAMPLE 46 Assume the same facts as in Example 45 and that the new equipment is five-year class property. Jill's statutory percentage cost recovery deduction for 1998 is $37,900 [($204,000 − $14,500) × .200]. (See Table 4–1 for percentage.) ▼

BUSINESS AND PERSONAL USE OF AUTOMOBILES AND OTHER LISTED PROPERTY

Limits exist on MACRS deductions for automobiles and other **listed property** used for both personal and business purposes.[67] These limits would apply, for example, to an automobile used by a sole proprietor partly for business purposes and partly for personal use.

If the listed property is *predominantly* used for business, the taxpayer is allowed to use the *statutory percentage method* to recover the cost. In cases where the property is *not predominantly* used for business, the cost is recovered using the *straight-line method*. The statutory percentage method results in a faster recovery of cost than the straight-line method. Listed property includes the following:

- Any passenger automobile.
- Any other property used as a means of transportation.
- Any property of a type generally used for purposes of entertainment, recreation, or amusement.

---

[67] § 280F.

- Any computer or peripheral equipment, with the exception of equipment used exclusively at a regular business establishment, including a qualifying home office.
- Any cellular telephone or other similar telecommunications equipment.
- Any other property specified in the Regulations.[68]

Automobiles and Other Listed Property Used Predominantly in Business.
For listed property to be considered as predominantly used in business, its business usage must exceed 50 percent.[69] The use of listed property for production of income does not qualify as business use for purposes of the more-than-50 percent test. However, both production of income and business use percentages are used to compute the cost recovery deduction.

EXAMPLE 47

On September 1, 1998, Emma places in service listed five-year recovery property. The property cost $10,000. If Emma uses the property 40% for business and 25% for the production of income, the property is not considered as predominantly used for business. The cost is recovered using straight-line cost recovery. Emma's cost recovery allowance for the year is $650 ($10,000 × 10% × 65%). If, however, Emma uses the property 60% for business and 25% for the production of income, the property is considered as used predominantly for business. Therefore, she may use the statutory percentage method. Emma's cost recovery allowance for the year is $1,700 ($10,000 × .200 × 85%). ▼

The method for determining the percentage of business usage for listed property is specified in the Regulations. The Regulations provide that for automobiles a mileage-based percentage is to be used. Other listed property is to use the most appropriate unit of time (e.g., hours) the property is actually used (rather than available for use).[70]

Limits on Cost Recovery for Automobiles.
The law places special limitations on the cost recovery deduction for passenger automobiles. These statutory dollar limits were imposed on passenger automobiles because of the belief that the tax system was being used to underwrite automobiles whose cost and luxury far exceeded what was needed for their business use.

A passenger automobile is any four-wheeled vehicle manufactured for use on public streets, roads, and highways with an unloaded gross vehicle weight rating of 6,000 pounds or less.[71] This definition specifically excludes vehicles used directly in the business of transporting people or property for compensation such as taxicabs, ambulances, hearses, and trucks and vans as prescribed by the Regulations.

The following limits apply to the cost recovery deductions for passenger automobiles for 1997:[72]

Year	Recovery Limitation*
1	$3,160
2	5,000
3	3,050
Succeeding years until all cost is recovered	1,775

*The indexed amounts for 1998 were not available at the time this text was written.

---

[68] § 280F(d)(4).
[69] § 280F(b)(4).
[70] Reg. § 1.280F–6T(e).
[71] § 280F(d)(5).
[72] § 280F(a)(2). The 1997 indexed amounts of $3,160, $5,000, $3,050, and $1,775 are used for the 1998 calculations that follow.

These limits are imposed before any percentage reduction for personal use. In addition, the limitation in the first year includes any amount the taxpayer elects to expense under § 179.[73] If the passenger automobile is used partly for personal use, the personal-use percentage is ignored for the purpose of determining the unrecovered cost available for deduction in later years.

EXAMPLE 48

On July 1, 1998, Dan places in service an automobile that cost $20,000. The car is always used 80% for business and 20% for personal use. The cost recovery for the automobile would be as follows:

1998	$2,528 [$20,000 × 20% (limited to $3,160) × 80%]
1999	$4,000 [$20,000 × 32% (limited to $5,000) × 80%]
2000	$2,440 [$20,000 × 19.2% (limited to $3,050) × 80%]
2001	$1,420 [$20,000 × 11.52% (limited to $1,775) × 80%]
2002	$1,420 [$20,000 × 11.52% (limited to $1,775) × 80%]
2003	$1,420 [$5,240 unrecovered cost ($20,000 − $14,760*) (limited to $1,775) × 80%]

*($3,160 + $5,000 + $3,050 + $1,775 + $1,775). Although the statutory percentage method appears to restrict the deduction to $922 [$20,000 × 5.76% (limited to $1,775) × 80%], the unrecovered cost of $5,240 (limited to $1,775) multiplied by the business usage percentage is deductible. At the start of 2001 (year 4), there is an automatic switch to the straight-line recovery method. Under this method, the unrecovered cost up to the maximum allowable limit ($1,775) is deductible in the last year of the recovery period (2003 or year 6). Because the limit may restrict the deduction, any remaining unrecovered cost is deductible in the next or succeeding year(s), subject to the maximum allowable yearly limit ($1,775), multiplied by the business usage percentage.

The total cost recovery for the years 1998–2003 is $13,228 ($2,528 + $4,000 + $2,440 + $1,420 + $1,420 + $1,420). The remaining cost will be recovered in future years. ▼

The cost recovery limitations are maximum amounts. If the regular calculation produces a lesser amount of cost recovery, the lesser amount is used.

EXAMPLE 49

On April 2, 1998, Gail places in service an automobile that cost $10,000. The car is always used 70% for business and 30% for personal use. The cost recovery allowance for 1998 is $1,400 ($10,000 × 20% × 70%), which is less than $2,212 ($3,160 × 70%). ▼

Note that the cost recovery limitations apply only to passenger automobiles and not to other listed property.

Automobiles and Other Listed Property Not Used Predominantly in Business.

The cost of listed property that does not pass the more-than-50 percent business usage test in the year the property is placed in service must be recovered using the straight-line method.[74] The straight-line method to be used is that required under the alternative depreciation system (introduced later in the chapter). This system requires a straight-line recovery period of five years for automobiles. However, even though the straight-line method is used, the cost recovery allowance for passenger automobiles cannot exceed the dollar limitations above.

If the listed property fails the more-than-50 percent business usage test, the straight-line method must be used for the remainder of the property's life. This applies even if at some later date the business usage of the property increases to more than 50 percent. Even though the straight-line method must continue to be used, however, the amount of cost recovery will reflect the increase in business usage.

---

[73] § 280F(d)(1).   [74] § 280F(b)(2).

Change from Predominantly Business Use. If the business-use percentage of listed property falls to 50 percent or lower after the year the property is placed in service, the property is subject to cost recovery *recapture*. The amount required to be recaptured and included in the taxpayer's return as ordinary income is the excess cost recovery. Excess cost recovery is the excess of the cost recovery deduction taken in prior years using the statutory percentage method over the amount that would have been allowed if the straight-line method had been used since the property was placed in service.[75]

After the business usage of the listed property drops below the more-than-50 percent level, the straight-line method must be used for the remaining life of the property.

Leased Automobiles. A taxpayer who leases a passenger automobile for business purposes must report an *inclusion amount* in gross income. The inclusion amount is computed from an IRS table for each taxable year for which the taxpayer leases the automobile. The purpose of this provision is to prevent taxpayers from circumventing the cost recovery dollar limitations by leasing, instead of purchasing, an automobile.

The dollar amount of the inclusion is based on the fair market value of the automobile and is prorated for the number of days the auto is used during the taxable year. The prorated dollar amount is then multiplied by the business and income-producing usage percentage to determine the amount to be included in gross income.[76] The taxpayer deducts the lease payments, multiplied by the business and income-producing usage percentage. The net effect is that the annual deduction for the lease payment is reduced by the inclusion amount.

EXAMPLE 50

On April 1, 1998, Jim leases and places in service a passenger automobile worth $40,000. The lease is to be for a period of five years. During the taxable years 1998 and 1999, Jim uses the automobile 70% for business and 30% for personal use. Assuming the dollar amounts from the IRS table for 1998 and 1999 are $188 and $412, Jim must include $99 in gross income for 1998 and $288 for 1999, computed as follows:

```
1998    $188 × (275/365) × 70% = $99
1999    $412 × (365/365) × 70% = $288
```

In addition, Jim can deduct 70% of the lease payments each year because this is the business-use percentage. ▼

Substantiation Requirements. Listed property is subject to the substantiation requirements of § 274. This means that the taxpayer must prove the business usage as to the amount of expense or use, the time and place of use, the business purpose for the use, and the business relationship to the taxpayer of persons using the property. Substantiation requires adequate records or sufficient evidence corroborating the taxpayer's statement. However, these substantiation requirements do not apply to vehicles that, by reason of their nature, are not likely to be used more than a *de minimis* amount for personal purposes.[77]

ALTERNATIVE DEPRECIATION SYSTEM (ADS)

The **alternative depreciation system (ADS)** must be used in lieu of MACRS for the following:[78]

---

[75] § 280F(b)(3).
[76] Reg. § 1.280F–7T(a).
[77] §§ 274(d) and (i).
[78] § 168(g).

- To calculate the portion of depreciation treated as an alternative minimum tax (AMT) adjustment for purposes of the corporate and individual AMT (see Chapter 13).
- To compute depreciation allowances for property for which any of the following is true:
  - Used predominately outside the United States.
  - Leased or otherwise used by a tax-exempt entity.
  - Financed with the proceeds of tax-exempt bonds.
  - Imported from foreign countries that maintain discriminatory trade practices or otherwise engage in discriminatory acts.
- To compute depreciation allowances for earnings and profits purposes (see Chapter 10).

Tables 4–5, 4–6, and 4–7 provide cost recovery rates under the ADS system. Additional details of the ADS system are beyond the scope of this chapter.

AMORTIZATION

LEARNING OBJECTIVE 7
Identify intangible assets that are eligible for amortization and calculate the amount of the deduction.

Taxpayers can claim an **amortization** deduction on certain intangible assets. The amount of the deduction is determined by amortizing the adjusted basis of such intangibles ratably over a 15-year period beginning in the month in which the intangible is acquired.[79]

An amortizable § 197 intangible is any § 197 intangible acquired after August 10, 1993, and held in connection with the conduct of a trade or business or for the production of income. Section 197 intangibles include goodwill and going-concern value, franchises (except sports franchises), trademarks, and trade names. Covenants not to compete, copyrights, and patents are also included if they are acquired in connection with the acquisition of a business. Generally, self-created intangibles are not § 197 intangibles. The 15-year amortization period applies regardless of the actual useful life of an amortizable § 197 intangible. No other depreciation or amortization deduction is permitted with respect to any amortizable § 197 intangible except those permitted under the 15-year amortization rules.

EXAMPLE 51
On June 1, 1998, Sally purchased and began operating the Falcon Cafe. Of the purchase price, $90,000 is correctly allocated to goodwill. The deduction for amortization for 1998 is $3,500 [($90,000/15) × (7/12)]. ▼

PLANNING CONSIDERATIONS

Structuring the Sale of a Business

On the sale of a sole proprietorship where the sales price exceeds the fair market value of the tangible assets and stated intangible assets, a planning opportunity may exist for both the seller and the buyer.

The seller's preference is for the excess amount to be allocated to *goodwill* because goodwill is a capital asset whose sale may result in favorably taxed long-term capital gain. Amounts received for a *covenant not to compete*, however, produce ordinary income, which is not subject to favorable long-term capital gain rates.

---
[79] § 197(a).

Because a covenant and goodwill both are amortized over a statutory 15-year period, the tax results of a covenant not to compete versus goodwill are the same for the *buyer*. However, the buyer should recognize that an allocation to goodwill rather than a covenant may provide a tax benefit to the seller. Therefore, the buyer, in negotiating the purchase price, should factor in the tax benefit to the seller of having the excess amount labeled goodwill rather than a covenant not to compete. Of course, if the noncompetition aspects of a covenant are important to the buyer, a portion of the excess amount can be assigned to a covenant.

Depletion

8 Learning Objective
Determine the amount of depletion expense and recognize the alternative tax treatments for intangible drilling and development costs.

Natural resources (e.g., oil, gas, coal, gravel, timber) are subject to **depletion,** which is simply a form of depreciation applicable to natural resources. Land generally cannot be depleted.

The owner of an interest in the natural resource is entitled to deduct depletion. An owner is one who has an economic interest in the property.[80] An economic interest requires the acquisition of an interest in the resource in place and the receipt of income from the extraction or severance of that resource.

Although all natural resources are subject to depletion, oil and gas wells are used as an example in the following paragraphs to illustrate the related costs and issues.

In developing an oil or gas well, the producer must make four types of expenditures.

- Natural resource costs.
- Intangible drilling and development costs.
- Tangible asset costs.
- Operating costs.

Natural resources are physically limited, and the costs to acquire them (e.g., oil under the ground) are, therefore, recovered through depletion. Costs incurred in making the property ready for drilling such as the cost of labor in clearing the property, erecting derricks, and drilling the hole are **intangible drilling and development costs (IDC).** These costs generally have no salvage value and are a lost cost if the well is not productive (dry). Costs for tangible assets such as tools, pipes, and engines are capital in nature. These costs must be capitalized and recovered through depreciation (cost recovery). Costs incurred after the well is producing are operating costs. These costs would include expenditures for such items as labor, fuel, and supplies. Operating costs are deductible when incurred (on the accrual basis) or when paid (on the cash basis).

The expenditures for depreciable assets and operating costs pose no unusual problems for producers of natural resources. The tax treatment of depletable costs and intangible drilling and development costs is quite a different matter.

INTANGIBLE DRILLING AND DEVELOPMENT COSTS (IDC)

Intangible drilling and development costs (IDC) can be handled in one of two ways at the option of the taxpayer. They can be either charged off as an expense in the

---
[80]Reg. § 1.611–1(b).

year in which they are incurred or capitalized and written off through depletion. The taxpayer makes the election in the first year such expenditures are incurred either by taking a deduction on the return or by adding them to the depletable basis. No formal statement of intent is required. Once made, the election is binding on both the taxpayer and the IRS for all such expenditures in the future. If the taxpayer fails to make the election to expense IDC on the original timely filed return the first year such expenditures are incurred, an automatic election to capitalize them has been made and is irrevocable.

As a general rule, it is more advantageous to expense IDC. The obvious benefit of an immediate write-off (as opposed to a deferred write-off through depletion) is not the only advantage. Since a taxpayer can use percentage depletion, which is calculated without reference to basis, the IDC may be completely lost as a deduction if they are capitalized.

DEPLETION METHODS

There are two methods of calculating depletion: cost and percentage. **Cost depletion** can be used on any wasting asset (and is the only method allowed for timber). **Percentage depletion** is subject to a number of limitations, particularly for oil and gas deposits. Depletion should be calculated both ways, and generally the method that results in the larger deduction is used. The choice between cost and percentage depletion is an annual election.

Cost Depletion. Cost depletion is determined by using the adjusted basis of the asset.[81] The basis is divided by the estimated recoverable units of the asset (e.g., barrels, tons) to arrive at the depletion per unit. The depletion per unit then is multiplied by the number of units sold (not the units produced) during the year to arrive at the cost depletion allowed. Cost depletion, therefore, resembles the units-of-production method of calculating depreciation.

EXAMPLE 52

On January 1, 1998, Pablo purchased the rights to a mineral interest for $1,000,000. At that time, the remaining recoverable units in the mineral interest were estimated to be 200,000. The depletion per unit is $5 [$1,000,000 (adjusted basis)/200,000 (estimated recoverable units)]. If during the year 60,000 units were mined and 25,000 were sold, the cost depletion would be $125,000 [$5 (depletion per unit) × 25,000 (units sold)]. ▼

If the taxpayer later discovers that the original estimate was incorrect, the depletion per unit for future calculations must be redetermined based on the revised estimate.[82]

EXAMPLE 53

Assume the same facts as in Example 52. In 1999, Pablo realizes that an incorrect estimate was made. The remaining recoverable units now are determined to be 400,000. Based on this new information, the revised depletion per unit is $2.1875 [$875,000 (adjusted basis)/400,000 (estimated recoverable units)]. Note that the adjusted basis is the original cost ($1,000,000) reduced by the depletion claimed in 1998 ($125,000). If 30,000 units are sold in 1999, the depletion for the year would be $65,625 [$2.1875 (depletion per unit) × 30,000 (units sold)]. ▼

---

[81] § 612.   [82] § 611(a).

> **TAX IN THE NEWS**
>
> **PERCENTAGE DEPLETION**
>
> On March 17, 1997, the U.S. Supreme Court declined to consider the IRS's appeal in a case against Exxon Corporation as to the proper way to calculate a depletion deduction. The disagreement involved the proper sales price of natural gas to be used in computing the percentage depletion deduction. The IRS argued that the depletion deduction for some natural gas sales should not be allowed to exceed the company's total income from those sales. Exxon argued that the law allows the use of a representative market price for natural gas in the field where it was produced, even if that price far exceeded the actual price received. At stake was about $1 billion of tax liability.
>
> SOURCE: Adapted from Bloomberg News, "Supreme Court Declines to Hear IRS Appeal in Exxon Tax Fight," *Fort Worth Star-Telegram*, March 18, 1997, Business, p.3.

Percentage Depletion. Percentage depletion (also referred to as statutory depletion) is a specified percentage provided for in the Code. The percentage varies according to the type of mineral interest involved. A sample of these percentages is shown in Exhibit 4–3. The rate is applied to the gross income from the property, but in no event may percentage depletion exceed 50 percent of the taxable income from the property before the allowance for depletion.[83]

EXAMPLE 54

Assuming gross income of $100,000, a depletion rate of 22%, and other expenses relating to the property of $60,000, the depletion allowance is determined as follows:

Gross income	$100,000
Less: Other expenses	(60,000)
Taxable income before depletion	$ 40,000
Depreciation allowance [the lesser of $22,000 (22% × $100,000) or $20,000 (50% × $40,000)]	20,000
Taxable income after depletion	$ 20,000

The adjusted basis of the property is reduced by $20,000, the depletion allowed. If the other expenses had been only $55,000, the full $22,000 could have been deducted, and the adjusted basis would have been reduced by $22,000. ▼

Note that percentage depletion is based on a percentage of the gross income from the property and makes no reference to cost. Thus, when percentage depletion is used, it is possible to deduct more than the original cost of the property. If percentage depletion is used, however, the adjusted basis of the property (for computing cost depletion) must be reduced by the amount of percentage depletion taken until the adjusted basis reaches zero.

---

[83] § 613(a). Special rules apply for certain oil and gas wells under § 613(a) (e.g., the 50% ceiling is replaced with a 100% ceiling, and the percentage depletion may not exceed 65% of the taxpayer's taxable income from all sources before the allowance for depletion).

▼ EXHIBIT 4–3
Sample of Percentage Depletion Rates

22% Depletion

Cobalt	Sulfur
Lead	Tin
Nickel	Uranium
Platinum	Zinc

15% Depletion

Copper	Oil and gas
Gold	Oil shale
Iron	Silver

14% Depletion

Borax	Magnesium carbonates
Calcium carbonates	Marble
Granite	Potash
Limestone	Slate

10% Depletion

Coal	Perlite
Lignite	Sodium chloride

5% Depletion

Gravel	Pumice
Peat	Sand

PLANNING CONSIDERATIONS

Switching Depletion Methods

Since the election to use the cost or percentage depletion method is an annual election, a taxpayer can use cost depletion (if higher) until the basis is exhausted and then switch to percentage depletion in the following years.

EXAMPLE 55

Assume the following facts for Warbler Company:

Remaining depletable basis	$ 11,000
Gross income (10,000 units)	100,000
Expenses (other than depletion)	30,000
Percentage depletion rate	22%

Since cost depletion is limited to the basis of $11,000 and the percentage depletion is $22,000, Warbler would choose the latter. The company's basis is then reduced to zero. In future years, however, Warbler can continue to take percentage depletion since percentage depletion is taken without reference to the remaining basis. ▼

Cost Recovery Tables

Summary of Cost Recovery Tables

Table 4–1   MACRS statutory percentage table for personalty.

Applicable depreciation methods: 200 or 150 percent declining-balance switching to straight-line.

Applicable recovery periods: 3, 5, 7, 10, 15, 20 years.

Applicable convention: half-year.

Table 4–2   MACRS statutory percentage table for personalty.

Applicable depreciation method: 200 percent declining-balance switching to straight-line.

Applicable recovery periods: 3, 5, 7 years.

Applicable convention: mid-quarter.

Table 4–3   MACRS straight-line table for realty.

Applicable depreciation method: straight-line.

Applicable recovery periods: 27.5, 31.5, 39 years.

Applicable convention: mid-month.

Table 4–4   MACRS optional straight-line table for personalty.

Applicable depreciation method: straight-line.

Applicable recovery periods: 3, 5, 7, 10, 15, 20 years.

Applicable convention: half-year.

Table 4–5   Alternative minimum tax declining-balance table for personalty.

Applicable depreciation method: 150 percent declining-balance switching to straight-line.

Applicable recovery periods: 3, 5, 7, 9.5, 10, 12 years.

Applicable convention: half-year.

Table 4–6   ADS straight-line table for personalty.

Applicable depreciation method: straight-line.

Applicable recovery periods: 5, 9.5, 12 years.

Applicable convention: half-year.

Table 4–7   ADS straight-line table for realty.

Applicable depreciation method: straight-line.

Applicable recovery period: 40 years.

Applicable convention: mid-month.

CHAPTER 4 Business Deductions

▼ **TABLE 4–1**
MACRS Accelerated Depreciation for Personal Property Assuming Half-Year Convention

For Property Placed in Service after December 31, 1986

Recovery Year	3-Year (200% DB)	5-Year (200% DB)	7-Year (200% DB)	10-Year (200% DB)	15-Year (150% DB)	20-Year (150% DB)
1	33.33	20.00	14.29	10.00	5.00	3.750
2	44.45	32.00	24.49	18.00	9.50	7.219
3	14.81*	19.20	17.49	14.40	8.55	6.677
4	7.41	11.52*	12.49	11.52	7.70	6.177
5		11.52	8.93*	9.22	6.93	5.713
6		5.76	8.92	7.37	6.23	5.285
7			8.93	6.55*	5.90*	4.888
8			4.46	6.55	5.90	4.522
9				6.56	5.91	4.462*
10				6.55	5.90	4.461
11				3.28	5.91	4.462
12					5.90	4.461
13					5.91	4.462
14					5.90	4.461
15					5.91	4.462
16					2.95	4.461
17						4.462
18						4.461
19						4.462
20						4.461
21						2.231

*Switchover to straight-line depreciation.

▼ **TABLE 4–2**
MACRS Accelerated Depreciation for Personal Property Assuming Mid-Quarter Convention

For Property Placed in Service after December 31, 1986 (Partial Table*)

3-Year

Recovery Year	First Quarter	Second Quarter	Third Quarter	Fourth Quarter
1	58.33	41.67	25.00	8.33
2	27.78	38.89	50.00	61.11

5-Year

Recovery Year	First Quarter	Second Quarter	Third Quarter	Fourth Quarter
1	35.00	25.00	15.00	5.00
2	26.00	30.00	34.00	38.00

7-Year

Recovery Year	First Quarter	Second Quarter	Third Quarter	Fourth Quarter
1	25.00	17.85	10.71	3.57
2	21.43	23.47	25.51	27.55

*The figures in this table are taken from the official tables that appear in Rev.Proc. 87–57, 1987–2 C.B. 687. Because of their length, the complete tables are not presented.

TABLE 4-3
MACRS Straight-Line Depreciation for Real Property Assuming Mid-Month Convention*

For Property Placed in Service after December 31, 1986: 27.5-Year Residential Real Property

The Applicable Percentage Is (Use the Column for the Month in the First Year the Property Is Placed in Service):

Recovery Year(s)	1	2	3	4	5	6	7	8	9	10	11	12
1	3.485	3.182	2.879	2.576	2.273	1.970	1.667	1.364	1.061	0.758	0.455	0.152
2–18	3.636	3.636	3.636	3.636	3.636	3.636	3.636	3.636	3.636	3.636	3.636	3.636
19–27	3.637	3.637	3.637	3.637	3.637	3.637	3.637	3.637	3.637	3.637	3.637	3.637
28	1.970	2.273	2.576	2.879	3.182	3.485	3.636	3.636	3.636	3.636	3.636	3.636
29	0.000	0.000	0.000	0.000	0.000	0.000	0.152	0.455	0.758	1.061	1.364	1.667

For Property Placed in Service after December 31, 1986, and before May 13, 1993: 31.5-Year Nonresidential Real Property

The Applicable Percentage Is (Use the Column for the Month in the First Year the Property Is Placed in Service):

Recovery Year(s)	1	2	3	4	5	6	7	8	9	10	11	12
1	3.042	2.778	2.513	2.249	1.984	1.720	1.455	1.190	0.926	0.661	0.397	0.132
2–19	3.175	3.175	3.175	3.175	3.175	3.175	3.175	3.175	3.175	3.175	3.175	3.175
20–31	3.174	3.174	3.174	3.174	3.174	3.174	3.174	3.174	3.174	3.174	3.174	3.174
32	1.720	1.984	2.249	2.513	2.778	3.042	3.175	3.175	3.175	3.175	3.175	3.175
33	0.000	0.000	0.000	0.000	0.000	0.000	0.132	0.397	0.661	0.926	1.190	1.455

For Property Placed in Service after May 12, 1993: 39-Year Nonresidential Real Property

The Applicable Percentage Is (Use the Column for the Month in the First Year the Property Is Placed in Service):

Recovery Year(s)	1	2	3	4	5	6	7	8	9	10	11	12
1	2.461	2.247	2.033	1.819	1.605	1.391	1.177	0.963	0.749	0.535	0.321	0.107
2–39	2.564	2.564	2.564	2.564	2.564	2.564	2.564	2.564	2.564	2.564	2.564	2.564
40	0.107	0.321	0.535	0.749	0.963	1.177	1.391	1.605	1.819	2.033	2.247	2.461

*The official tables contain a separate row for each year. For ease of presentation, certain years are grouped in these tables. In some instances, this will produce a difference of .001 for the last digit when compared with the official tables.

CHAPTER 4 Business Deductions

▼ **TABLE 4-4**
MACRS Straight-Line Depreciation for Personal Property Assuming Half-Year Convention*

For Property Placed in Service after December 31, 1986

MACRS Class	% First Recovery Year	Other Recovery Years — Years	Other Recovery Years — %	Last Recovery Year — Year	Last Recovery Year — %
3-year	16.67	2–3	33.33	4	16.67
5-year	10.00	2–5	20.00	6	10.00
7-year	7.14	2–7	14.29	8	7.14
10-year	5.00	2–10	10.00	11	5.00
15-year	3.33	2–15	6.67	16	3.33
20-year	2.50	2–20	5.00	21	2.50

*The official table contains a separate row for each year. For ease of presentation, certain years are grouped in this table. In some instances, this will produce a difference of .01 for the last digit when compared with the official table.

▼ **TABLE 4-5**
Alternative Minimum Tax: 150% Declining-Balance Assuming Half-Year Convention

For Property Placed in Service after December 31, 1986 (Partial Table*)

Recovery Year	3-Year 150%	5-Year 150%	7-Year 150%	9.5-Year 150%	10-Year 150%	12-Year 150%
1	25.00	15.00	10.71	7.89	7.50	6.25
2	37.50	25.50	19.13	14.54	13.88	11.72
3	25.00**	17.85	15.03	12.25	11.79	10.25
4	12.50	16.66**	12.25**	10.31	10.02	8.97
5		16.66	12.25	9.17**	8.74**	7.85
6		8.33	12.25	9.17	8.74	7.33**
7			12.25	9.17	8.74	7.33
8			6.13	9.17	8.74	7.33
9				9.17	8.74	7.33
10				9.16	8.74	7.33
11					4.37	7.32
12						7.33
13						3.66

*The figures in this table are taken from the official table that appears in Rev.Proc. 87–57, 1987–2 C.B. 687. Because of its length, the complete table is not presented.
**Switchover to straight-line depreciation.

TABLE 4–6
ADS Straight-Line for Personal Property Assuming Half-Year Convention

For Property Placed in Service after December 31, 1986 (Partial Table*)

Recovery Year	5-Year Class	9.5-Year Class	12-Year Class
1	10.00	5.26	4.17
2	20.00	10.53	8.33
3	20.00	10.53	8.33
4	20.00	10.53	8.33
5	20.00	10.52	8.33
6	10.00	10.53	8.33
7		10.52	8.34
8		10.53	8.33
9		10.52	8.34
10		10.53	8.33
11			8.34
12			8.33
13			4.17

*The figures in this table are taken from the official table that appears in Rev.Proc. 87–57, 1987–2 C.B. 687. Because of its length, the complete table is not presented. The tables for the mid-quarter convention also appear in Rev.Proc. 87–57.

TABLE 4–7
ADS Straight-Line for Real Property Assuming Mid-Month Convention

For Property Placed in Service after December 31, 1986

Recovery Year	\multicolumn{12}{c}{Month Placed in Service}											
	1	2	3	4	5	6	7	8	9	10	11	12
1	2.396	2.188	1.979	1.771	1.563	1.354	1.146	0.938	0.729	0.521	0.313	0.104
2–40	2.500	2.500	2.500	2.500	2.500	2.500	2.500	2.500	2.500	2.500	2.500	2.500
41	0.104	0.312	0.521	0.729	0.937	1.146	1.354	1.562	1.771	1.979	2.187	2.396

KEY TERMS

Accelerated cost recovery system (ACRS), 4–21

Alternative depreciation system (ADS), 4–32

Amortization, 4–33

Capital gain property, 4–16

Charitable contribution, 4–15

Cost depletion, 4–35

Cost recovery system, 4–21

Depletion, 4–34

Depreciation rules, 4–21

Half-year convention, 4–25

Intangible drilling and development costs (IDC), 4–34

Listed property, 4–29

Mid-month convention, 4–27

Mid-quarter convention, 4–25

Modified accelerated cost recovery system (MACRS), 4–21

Ordinary and necessary, 4–2

CHAPTER 4 Business Deductions   4–43

Ordinary income property, 4–16

Percentage depletion, 4–35

Reasonableness requirement, 4–3

Related-party transactions, 4–12

Research and experimental expenditures, 4–18

Residential rental real estate, 4–26

Section 179 expensing election, 4–28

Problem Materials

1. Ted is an agent for Waxwing Corporation, an airline manufacturer, and is negotiating a sale with a representative of the U.S. government and with a representative of a developing country. Waxwing has sufficient capacity to handle only one of the orders. Both orders will have the same contract price. Ted believes that if Waxwing will authorize a $500,000 payment to the representative of the foreign country, he can guarantee the sale. He is not sure that he can obtain the same result with the U.S. government. Identify the relevant tax issues for Waxwing.

2. Linda operates a drug-running operation. Which of the following expenses she incurs can reduce taxable income?
   a. Bribes paid to border guards.
   b. Salaries to employees.
   c. Price paid for drugs purchased for resale.
   d. Kickbacks to police.
   e. Rent on an office.

3. Cardinal Corporation is a trucking firm that operates in the Mid-Atlantic states. One of Cardinal's major customers frequently ships goods between Charlotte and Baltimore. Occasionally, the customer sends last-minute shipments that are outbound for Europe on a freighter sailing from Baltimore. To satisfy the delivery schedule in these cases, Cardinal's drivers must substantially exceed the speed limit. Cardinal pays for any related speeding tickets. During the past year, two drivers had their licenses suspended for thirty days each for driving at such excessive speeds. Cardinal continues to pay each driver's salary during the suspension periods.

   Cardinal believes that it is necessary to conduct its business in this manner if it is to be profitable, maintain the support of the drivers, and maintain the goodwill of customers. Evaluate Cardinal's business practices.

4. Quail Corporation anticipates that being positively perceived by the individual who is elected mayor will be beneficial for business. Therefore, Quail contributes to the campaigns of both the Democratic and the Republican candidates. The Republican candidate is elected mayor. Can Quail deduct any of the political contributions it made?

5. Carmine, Inc., a tobacco manufacturer, incurs certain expenditures associated with political contributions and lobbying activities. Which of these expenditures can be deducted?

Payments to Washington, D.C. law firm to lobby members of Congress	$800,000
Payments to Washington, D.C. law firm to lobby the Vice President	200,000
Payments to Washington, D.C. law firm to lobby the head of the FDA	25,000
Payments to Richmond law firm to lobby members of the state legislature	50,000
Payments to Williamsburg law firm to lobby members of the Williamsburg City Council	5,000
Political contribution to the Democratic National Committee	300,000
Political contribution to the Republican National Committee	350,000
Political contribution to Committee to Reelect the Mayor of Williamsburg	6,000

6. Ella owns 60% of the stock of Peach, Inc. The stock has declined in value since Ella purchased it five years ago. She is going to sell 5% of the stock to a relative to pay her 12-year-old daughter's private school tuition. Ella is also going to make a gift of 10% of her stock to another relative. Identify the relevant tax issues for Ella.

7. Which of the following are related parties under § 267?
   - Mother.
   - Sister.
   - Nephew.
   - Aunt.
   - Cousin.
   - Granddaughter.
   - Corporation in which the shareholder owns 45% of the stock.

8. Drew and his wife Cassie own all of the stock of Thrush, Inc. Cassie is the president and Drew is the vice president. Cassie and Drew are paid salaries of $400,000 and $300,000, respectively, each year. They consider the salaries to be reasonable based on a comparison with salaries paid for comparable positions in comparable companies. They project Thrush's taxable income for next year, before their salaries, to be $800,000. They decide to place their four teenage children on the payroll and to pay them total salaries of $100,000. The children will each work about five hours per week for Thrush.
   a. What are Drew and Cassie trying to achieve by hiring the children?
   b. Calculate the tax consequences of hiring the children on Thrush, Inc., and on Drew and Cassie's family.

9. Marcia, an attorney with a leading New York law firm, is convicted of failing to file Federal income tax returns for 1994–1996. Her justification for failing to do so was the pressures of her profession (80–90 hour workweeks). She is assessed taxes, interest, and penalties of $90,000 by the IRS. In addition, she incurs related legal fees of $60,000. Determine the amount that Marcia can deduct.

10. Jenny, the owner of a very successful restaurant chain, is exploring the possibility of expanding the chain into a city in the neighboring state. She incurs $20,000 of expenses associated with this investigation. Based on the regulatory environment for restaurants in the city, she decides not to do so. During the year, she also investigates opening a hotel that will be part of a national hotel chain. Her expenses for this are $15,000. The hotel begins operations on December 1. Determine the amount that Jenny can deduct in the current year for investigating these two businesses.

11. Janet Saxon sold stock (basis of $40,000) to her brother, Fred, for $32,000.
    a. What are the tax consequences to Janet?
    b. What are the tax consequences to Fred if he later sells the stock for $42,000? For $28,000? For $36,000?
    c. Write a letter to Janet in which you inform her of the tax consequences if she sells the stock to Fred for $32,000 and explain how a sales transaction could be structured that would produce better tax consequences for her. Janet's address is 32 Country Lane, Lawrence, KS 66045.

12. Lark Corporation (a calendar year corporation) had the following income and expenses in 1999:

Income from operations	$100,000
Expenses from operations	50,000
Charitable contribution	7,000
NOL carryover from prior year	10,000

    How much is Lark Corporation's charitable contribution deduction for 1999?

CHAPTER 4 Business Deductions

13. Dan Simms is the president and sole shareholder of Simms Corporation, 1121 Madison Street, Seattle, WA 98121. Dan plans for the corporation to make a charitable contribution to the University of Washington, a qualified public charity. He will have the corporation donate Jaybird Corporation stock with a basis of $8,000 and a fair market value of $20,000. Dan projects a $200,000 net profit for Simms Corporation in 1998 and a $100,000 net profit in 1999. Dan calls you on December 5, 1998, and asks whether he should make the contribution in 1998 or 1999. Write a letter advising Dan about the timing of the contribution.

14. Green Corporation, a manufacturing company, decided to develop a new line of fireworks. Because of the danger involved, Green purchased an isolated parcel of land for $300,000 and constructed a building for $1,220,000. The building was to be used for research and experimentation in creating the new fireworks. The project was begun in 1998. Green had the following expenses in connection with the project:

	1998	1999
Salaries	$160,000	$200,000
Utilities	20,000	30,000
Materials	40,000	40,000
Insurance	50,000	30,000
Cost of market survey to determine profit potential of new fireworks line	20,000	–0–
Depreciation on the building	30,000	31,000

    The benefits from the project will be realized starting in June 2000.
    a. If Green Corporation elects to expense research and experimental expenditures, determine the amount of the deduction for 1998, 1999, and 2000.
    b. If Green Corporation elects a 60-month deferral and amortization period, determine the amount of the deduction for 1998, 1999, and 2000.

15. On January 1, 1994, Black Company acquired an asset (three-year property) for $10,000 for use in its business. In the years 1994 and 1995, Black took $3,333 and $4,445 of cost recovery. The allowable cost recovery for the years 1996 and 1997 was $1,481 and $741, but Black did not take the deductions. In those years, Black had net operating losses, and the company wanted to "save" the deductions for later years. On January 1, 1998, the asset was sold for $2,000. Calculate the gain or loss on the sale of the asset in 1998.

16. Juan, a sole proprietor, acquires a five-year class asset on December 2, 1998, for $150,000. This is the only asset acquired by Juan during the year. He does not elect immediate expensing under § 179. On July 15, 1999, Juan sells the asset.
    a. Determine Juan's cost recovery for 1998.
    b. Determine Juan's cost recovery for 1999.

17. Pat, a sole proprietor, acquires a warehouse on November 1, 1998, at a cost of $4.5 million. On January 30, 2009, Pat sells the warehouse. Calculate Pat's cost recovery for 1998 and for 2009.

18. Janice acquired an apartment building on June 4, 1998, for $1.4 million. The value of the land is $200,000. Janice sold the apartment building on November 29, 2004.
    a. Determine Janice's cost recovery for 1998.
    b. Determine Janice's cost recovery for 2004.

19. Lori, who is single, is thinking about acquiring a new copier (five-year class property) for $30,000 in either December 1998 or January 1999. Lori expects the taxable income derived from her sole proprietorship (without regard to the amount expensed under § 179) to always be about $100,000. Lori will elect immediate expensing under § 179. Lori acquired three-year property for $140,000 in March 1998. Lori does not want to elect § 179 for this property.

a. Determine Lori's total deduction with respect to the copier if she acquires it in 1998.
b. Determine Lori's total deduction with respect to the copier if she acquires it in 1999.
c. What is your advice to Lori?

20. Jack owns a small business that he operates as a sole proprietor. In 1998, Jack will net $10,000 of business income before consideration of any § 179 deduction. Jack spends $207,000 on new equipment in 1998. If Jack also has $3,000 of § 179 deduction carryforwards from 1997, determine his § 179 expense deduction for 1998 and the amount of any carryforward.

21. Olga is the proprietor of a small business. In 1998, her business income, before consideration of any § 179 deduction, is $7,500. Olga spends $202,000 on new equipment and furniture for 1998. If Olga elects to take the § 179 deduction on a desk that cost $20,000 (included in the $202,000), determine her total cost recovery for 1998 with respect to the desk.

22. On March 10, 1998, Yoon purchased three-year class property for $20,000. On December 15, 1998, Yoon purchased five-year class property for $50,000. He has net business income of $19,000 before consideration of any § 179 deduction.
    a. Calculate Yoon's cost recovery for 1998, assuming he does not make the § 179 election or use straight-line cost recovery.
    b. Calculate Yoon's cost recovery for 1998, assuming he does elect to use § 179 and does not elect to use straight-line cost recovery.
    c. Assuming Yoon's marginal tax rate is 36%, determine his tax benefit from electing § 179.

23. John Johnson is considering acquiring an automobile at the beginning of 1998 that he will use 100% of the time as a taxi. The purchase price of the automobile is $25,000. John has heard of cost recovery limits on automobiles and wants to know how much of the $25,000 he can deduct in the first year. Write a letter to John in which you present your calculations. Also, prepare a memo for the tax files. John's address is 100 Morningside, Clinton, MS 39058.

24. On February 16, 1998, Ron purchased and placed into service a new car. The purchase price was $18,000. Ron drove the car 12,000 miles during the remainder of the year, 9,000 miles for business and 3,000 miles for personal use. Ron used the statutory percentage method of cost recovery. Calculate the total deduction Ron may take for 1998 with respect to the car.

25. On June 5, 1998, Leo purchased and placed in service a $19,000 car. The business-use percentage for the car is always 100%. Compute Leo's cost recovery deduction in 2004.

26. Midway through 1998, Abdel leases and places in service a passenger automobile. The lease will run for five years, and the payments are $430 per month. During 1998, Abdel uses the car 70% for business use and 30% for personal use. Assuming the inclusion dollar amount from the IRS table is $98, determine the tax consequences to Abdel from the lease for the year 1998.

27. Use the information given in Problem 26, but assume the inclusion dollar amount for 1999 is $180. Abdel uses the car 60% for business use and 40% for personal use in 1999. Determine Abdel's tax consequences from the lease in 1999.

28. Mike Saxon is negotiating the purchase of a business. The final purchase price has been agreed upon, but the allocation of the purchase price to the assets is still being discussed. Appraisals on a warehouse range from $1,200,000 to $1,500,000. If a value of $1,200,000 is used for the warehouse, the remainder of the purchase price, $800,000, will be allocated to goodwill. If $1,500,000 is allocated to the warehouse, goodwill will be $500,000. Mike wants to know what effect each alternative will have on cost recovery and amortization during the first year. Under the agreement, Mike will take over the business on January 1 of next year. Write a letter to Mike in which you present your calculations and recommendation. Also, prepare a memo for the tax files. Mike's address is 200 Rolling Hills Drive, Shavertown, PA 18708.

29. Marge and Stan are negotiating Stan's purchase of Marge's business. Both are in the 36% tax bracket. They have agreed that the tangible assets of the business are worth $100,000. Marge's adjusted basis for these assets is $70,000.

    The only other asset of the business is the going-concern value. Marge believes that this asset is worth about $50,000. Stan believes that it is worth somewhat less, probably about $40,000.

    Marge and Stan are handling their own negotiations since they do not believe in wasting money on attorneys or CPAs when such professional services are not required. Stan recalls from an MBA class he took five years ago that goodwill is not deductible, but that a covenant not to compete can be deducted over the covenant period.

    Stan believes that Marge, who is age 67 and in poor health, is going to retire. In order to maximize the tax benefits to himself, Stan increases his offer from $140,000 to $145,000 (i.e., "we'll split the difference") if Marge will agree to sign a five-year covenant with $45,000 of the $145,000 purchase price allocated to the covenant. Marge, who believes that the tax consequences of the sale ($145,000 amount realized − $70,000 adjusted basis = $75,000 recognized gain) will be the same regardless of whether the $45,000 is for goodwill or for a covenant, accepts the offer. Evaluate the decisions made by Marge and Stan.

30. Wes acquired a mineral interest during the year for $5 million. A geological survey estimated that 250,000 tons of the mineral remained in the deposit. During the year, 80,000 tons were mined, and 45,000 tons were sold for $6 million. Other expenses amounted to $4 million. Assuming the mineral depletion rate is 22%, calculate Wes's lowest taxable income.

RESEARCH PROBLEMS

*Note: The **RIA OnPoint System 4 Student Version CD-ROM** available with this text can be used in preparing solutions to the Research Problems. Alternatively, tax research materials contained in a standard tax library can be used.*

31. Falcon Corporation is the owner and operator of a large daily metropolitan newspaper. For at least 80 years, Falcon has collected and maintained a "clippings library." The library is a collection of past news items from Falcon's and other newspapers. The 7,800,000 items are well preserved, cataloged, and cross-listed under various categories. Falcon estimates that it has spent in excess of $10 million compiling and organizing the library. However, since this amount was deducted as incurred, the income tax basis of the library is zero. The fair market value of the library is $3 million. Falcon Corporation contributes the clippings library to the state historical society (a qualified organization) and claims a charitable contribution deduction of $3 million. Upon audit, the IRS disallows the entire amount of the deduction because the basis of the property is zero. Who is correct?

    Research aids:
    §§ 170(e)(1)(A) and 1221(3).

32. Sandra purchased the following personal property during 1998:

Date	Asset	Cost
June 1	Machine A	$20,000
July 10	Machine B	10,000
November 15	Machine C	25,000

    Sandra elects to take the § 179 expense on Machine C. Discuss what convention Sandra must use to determine her cost recovery deduction for 1998.

33. Juan owns a business that acquires exotic automobiles that are high-tech, state-of-the-art vehicles with unique design features or equipment. The exotic automobiles are not licensed nor are they set up to be used on the road. Rather, the cars are used exclusively

for car shows or related promotional photography. Juan would like to know whether he can take a cost recovery deduction with respect to the exotic automobiles on his Federal income tax return.

34. On March 5, 1998, Nell purchased equipment for $70,000. The equipment has an ADS midpoint of 9.5 years. Determine Nell's cost recovery deduction for computing 1998 taxable income using the straight-line method under ADS, assuming she does not make a § 179 election.

35. Bluejay and Cardinal, a partnership, opens a checking account on January 1 with an initial deposit of $10,000, consisting of $7,000 of borrowed funds (Debt A) and $3,000 of unborrowed funds. Subsequently, the following deposits and withdrawals were made from the account:

February 15	$6,000 invested in a passive activity (see Chapter 5)
June 10	$2,000 proceeds from Debt B deposited
July 23	$4,000 paid in business expenses

How much of the loan proceeds from Debt A is treated as being invested in the passive activity? How much of the loan proceeds from Debt B is treated as used in the business? How much of Debt B is treated as an investment?

CHAPTER 5

LOSSES AND LOSS LIMITATIONS

LEARNING OBJECTIVES

After completing Chapter 5, you should be able to:

1. Determine the amount, classification, and timing of the bad debt deduction.

2. Understand the tax treatment of worthless securities including § 1244 stock.

3. Identify a casualty and determine the amount, classification, and timing of casualty and theft losses.

4. Recognize the impact of the net operating loss carryback and carryover provisions.

5. Discuss tax shelters and the reasons for at-risk and passive loss limitations.

6. Describe how the at-risk limitation and the passive loss rules limit deductions for losses and identify taxpayers subject to these restrictions.

7. Discuss and be able to apply the definitions of activity, material participation, and rental activity under the passive loss rules.

8. Recognize the relationship between the at-risk and passive activity limitations.

9. Discuss the special treatment available to real estate activities.

OUTLINE

Bad Debts, 5–2
Specific Charge-Off Method, 5–3
Business versus Nonbusiness Bad Debts, 5–3
Loans between Related Parties, 5–4
Worthless Securities, 5–5
Small Business Stock, 5–6
Casualty and Theft Losses, 5–7
Definition of Casualty, 5–7
Definition of Theft, 5–8
When to Deduct Casualty Losses, 5–9

Measuring the Amount of Loss, 5–9
Casualty and Theft Losses of Individuals, 5–11
Net Operating Losses, 5–12
Introduction, 5–12
Carryback and Carryover Periods, 5–14
The Tax Shelter Problem, 5–15
At-Risk Limitations, 5–17
Passive Loss Limits, 5–18
Classification and Impact of Passive Income and Loss, 5–18

Taxpayers Subject to the Passive Loss Rules, 5–23
Activity Defined, 5–24
Material Participation, 5–25
Rental Activities, 5–30
Interaction of At-Risk and Passive Activity Limits, 5–33
Special Rules for Real Estate, 5–33
Disposition of Passive Activities, 5–36

Chapter 4 introduced rules governing the deductibility of trade and business expenses. This chapter extends the notion of deductibility to losses occurring in the course of business operations. In particular, special rules concerning the tax treatment of bad debts, casualty losses, and operating losses are reviewed. In addition, tax shelters and the rules that limit their usefulness as tax avoidance devices are discussed.

BAD DEBTS

1 LEARNING OBJECTIVE
Determine the amount, classification, and timing of the bad debt deduction.

If a taxpayer lends money or purchases a debt instrument and the debt is not repaid, a **bad debt** deduction is allowed. Similarly, if an accrual basis taxpayer sells goods or provides services on credit and the account receivable subsequently becomes worthless, a bad debt deduction is permitted.[1] No deduction is allowed, however, for a bad debt arising from the sale of a product or service when the taxpayer is on the cash basis because no income is reported until the cash has been collected. Permitting a bad debt deduction for a cash basis taxpayer would amount to a double deduction because the expenses of the product or service rendered are deducted when payments are made to suppliers and to employees or at the time of the sale.

EXAMPLE 1

Ella, a sole proprietor engaged in the practice of accounting, performed services for Pat for which she charged $8,000. Pat never paid the bill, and his whereabouts are unknown.

If Ella is an accrual basis taxpayer, the $8,000 is included in income when the services are performed. When it is determined that Pat's account will not be collected, the $8,000 is deducted as a bad debt.

If Ella is a cash basis taxpayer, the $8,000 is not included in income until payment is received. When it is determined that Pat's account will not be collected, the $8,000 is not deducted as a bad debt expense because it was never recognized as income. ▼

---
[1] Reg. § 1.166–1(e).

SPECIFIC CHARGE-OFF METHOD

Most taxpayers are required to use the **specific charge-off method** when accounting for bad debts. Some financial institutions are permitted to use an alternative **reserve method** for computing bad debt deductions.

A taxpayer using the specific charge-off method may claim a deduction when a specific *business* debt becomes either partially or wholly worthless or when a specific *nonbusiness* debt becomes wholly worthless.[2] For business debt, the taxpayer must satisfy the IRS that the debt is partially worthless and must demonstrate the amount of worthlessness. If a business debt previously deducted as partially worthless becomes totally worthless in a future year, only the remainder not previously deducted can be deducted in the future year.

In the case of total worthlessness, a deduction is allowed for the entire amount in the year that the debt becomes worthless. The amount of the deduction depends on the taxpayer's basis in the bad debt. If the debt arose from the sale of services or products and the face amount was previously included in income, that amount is deductible. If the taxpayer purchased the debt, the deduction equals the amount the taxpayer paid for the debt instrument.

Determining when a bad debt becomes worthless can be a difficult task. Legal proceedings need not be initiated against the debtor when the surrounding facts indicate that such action will not result in collection.

EXAMPLE 2

In 1997, Partridge Company lent $1,000 to Kay, who agreed to repay the loan in two years. In 1999, Kay disappeared after the note became delinquent. If a reasonable investigation by Partridge indicates that Kay cannot be found or that a suit against Kay would not result in collection, Partridge can deduct the $1,000 in 1999. ▼

Bankruptcy is generally an indication of at least partial worthlessness of a debt. Bankruptcy may create worthlessness before the settlement date. If this is the case, the deduction may be taken in the year of worthlessness.

EXAMPLE 3

In Example 2, assume Kay filed for personal bankruptcy in 1998 and that the debt is a business debt. At that time, Partridge learned that unsecured creditors (including Partridge) were ultimately expected to receive 20 cents on the dollar. In 1999, settlement is made and Partridge receives only $150. Partridge should deduct $800 ($1,000 loan – $200 expected settlement) in 1998 and $50 in 1999 ($200 balance – $150 proceeds). ▼

If a receivable is written off as uncollectible and is subsequently collected during the same tax year, the write-off entry is reversed. If a receivable has been written off as uncollectible, collection in a later tax year may result in income being recognized. Income will result if the deduction yielded a tax benefit in the year it was taken.

BUSINESS VERSUS NONBUSINESS BAD DEBTS

The nature of a debt depends upon whether the lender is engaged in the business of lending money or whether there is a proximate relationship between the creation of the debt and the *lender's* trade or business. Where either of these conditions is true, a bad debt is classified as a **business bad debt**. If these conditions are not met, a bad debt is classified as a **nonbusiness bad debt**. The use to which the

---

[2]§ 166(a) and Reg. § 1.166.

TAX IN THE NEWS

A BANK OR A SAVINGS AND LOAN? LOSS OF BAD DEBT RESERVE INFLUENCES DECISION

Robert McCarthy, Jr., chief executive of Parkvale Savings Bank, a savings and loan association, announced that Parkvale might convert to a commercial bank in 1997. One of the factors influencing this decision was a change in the Federal law that removed a tax advantage thrifts enjoyed over banks. Under the old law, which permitted use of the reserve method, thrifts were allowed to take a bad debt deduction of up to 8 percent of their taxable income. Under the new law, thrifts won't get that yearly tax break and must pay back the last nine years of liabilities. Parkvale would be required to pay back $1.4 million.

SOURCE: Adapted from Thomas Olson, "Thrift Mulls Switch to Bank," *Tribune Review—Greensburg, PA,* October 25, 1996, p. B3.

---

borrowed funds are put is of no consequence when making this classification decision.

EXAMPLE 4 Jamil lent his friend, Esther, $1,500. Esther used the money to start a business, which subsequently failed. Even though the proceeds of the loan were used in a business, the loan is a nonbusiness bad debt, because the business was Esther's, and not Jamil's. ▼

EXAMPLE 5 Horace operates a sole proprietorship that sells premium stereo equipment. Horace uses the accrual basis to account for sales of the stereo equipment. During the year, he sold a $4,000 stereo system to Herbie on credit. Later that year, the account receivable becomes worthless. The loan is a business bad debt, because the debt was related to Horace's business. ▼

Generally, nonbusiness bad debts are incurred only by individuals. It is assumed that any loans made by a corporation are related to its trade or business. Therefore, any bad debts resulting from loans made by a corporation are automatically business bad debts.

The distinction between a business bad debt and a nonbusiness bad debt is important. A business bad debt is deductible as an ordinary loss in the year incurred, whereas a nonbusiness bad debt is always treated as a short-term capital loss. Thus, regardless of the age of a nonbusiness bad debt, the deduction may be of limited benefit due to the $3,000 capital loss limitation for individuals (refer to the discussion in Chapter 3).

LOANS BETWEEN RELATED PARTIES

Loans between related parties raise the issue of whether the transaction was a *bona fide* loan or some other transfer, such as a gift, a disguised dividend payment, or a contribution to capital. The Regulations state that a bona fide debt arises from a debtor-creditor relationship based on a valid and enforceable obligation to pay a fixed or determinable sum of money. Thus, individual circumstances must be examined to determine whether advances between related parties are loans. Some considerations are these:

CONCEPT SUMMARY 5-1

The Tax Treatment of Bad Debts Using the Specific Charge-Off Method

	Business Bad Debts	Nonbusiness Bad Debts
Timing of deduction	A deduction is allowed when the debt becomes either partially or wholly worthless.	A deduction is allowed *only* when the debt becomes wholly worthless.
Character of deduction	The bad debt may be deducted as an ordinary loss.	The bad debt is taxed as a short-term capital loss, subject to the $3,000 capital loss limitation for individuals.
Recovery of amounts previously deducted	If the account recovered was written off during the current tax year, the write-off entry is reversed. If the account was written off in a previous tax year, income is created subject to the tax benefit rule.	If the account recovered was written off during the current tax year, the write-off entry is reversed. If the account was written off in a previous tax year, income is created subject to the tax benefit rule.

- Was a note properly executed?
- Was there a reasonable rate of interest?
- Was collateral provided?
- What collection efforts were made?
- What was the intent of the parties?

EXAMPLE 6

Ted, who is the sole shareholder of Penguin Corporation, lends the corporation $10,000 so that it can continue business operations. The note specifies a 2% interest rate and is payable on demand. Penguin has shown losses in each year of its five-year existence. The corporation also has liabilities greatly in excess of its assets. It is likely that Ted's transfer to the corporation would be treated as a contribution to capital rather than a liability. Consequently, no bad debt deduction would be allowed upon default by Penguin. ▼

WORTHLESS SECURITIES

2 LEARNING OBJECTIVE
Understand the tax treatment of worthless securities including § 1244 stock.

A loss is allowed for securities that become *completely* worthless during the year (**worthless securities**).[3] Such securities are shares of stock, bonds, notes, or other evidence of indebtedness issued by a corporation or government. The losses generated are treated as capital losses (refer to Chapter 3) deemed to have occurred on the *last day* of the tax year. By treating losses as having occurred on the last day of the tax year, a loss that would otherwise have been classified as short term (if the date of worthlessness were used) may be classified as mid-term or long term.

EXAMPLE 7

Falcon Company, a calendar year taxpayer, owns stock in Owl Corporation (a publicly held company). The stock was acquired as an investment on May 31, 1998, at a cost of $5,000. On April 1, 1999, the stock became worthless. Because the stock is deemed to have become

---
[3] § 165(g).

worthless as of December 31, 1999, Falcon has a capital loss from an asset held for 19 months (a long-term capital loss). ▼

SMALL BUSINESS STOCK

The general rule is that shareholders receive capital loss treatment for losses from sale or exchange of corporate stock. As noted in Chapter 3, the deductibility of capital losses is limited. However, it is possible to avoid capital loss limitations if the loss is sustained on **small business stock (§ 1244 stock).** Such a loss could arise from a sale of the stock or from the stock becoming worthless. Only *individuals*[4] who acquired the stock *from* the issuing corporation are eligible to receive ordinary loss treatment under § 1244. The ordinary loss treatment is limited to $50,000 ($100,000 for married individuals filing jointly) per year. Losses on § 1244 stock in excess of the statutory limits are treated as capital losses.

The issuing corporation must meet certain requirements for the loss on § 1244 stock to be treated as an *ordinary* loss. The principal requirement is that the total capitalization of the corporation is limited to a maximum of $1 million. This capital limit includes all money and other property received by the corporation for stock and all capital contributions made to the corporation. The $1 million test is made at the time the stock is issued. There are no requirements regarding the kind of stock issued. Section 1244 stock can be either common or preferred.

Section 1244 applies only to losses. If § 1244 stock is sold at a gain, the provision does not apply and the gain is capital gain (which, for individuals, may be subject to preferential tax treatment, as discussed in Chapter 3).

EXAMPLE 8

On July 1, 1997, Iris, a single individual, purchased 100 shares of Eagle Corporation common stock for $100,000. The Eagle stock qualified as § 1244 stock. On June 20, 1999, Iris sold all of the Eagle stock for $20,000, which resulted in a loss of $80,000. Because the Eagle stock is § 1244 stock, Iris would have $50,000 of ordinary loss and $30,000 of long-term capital loss. ▼

PLANNING CONSIDERATIONS

Maximizing the Benefits of § 1244

Because § 1244 limits the amount of loss classified as ordinary loss on a yearly basis, a taxpayer might maximize the benefits of § 1244 by selling the stock in more than one taxable year.

EXAMPLE 9

Mitch, a single individual, purchased small business stock in 1997 for $150,000 (150 shares at $1,000 per share). On December 20, 1999, the stock is worth $60,000 (150 shares at $400 per share). Mitch wants to sell the stock at this time. He earns a salary of $80,000 a year, has no other capital transactions, and does not expect any in the future. If Mitch sells all of the small business stock in 1999, his recognized loss will be $90,000 ($60,000 selling price − $150,000 cost). The loss will be characterized as a $50,000 ordinary loss and a $40,000 long-term capital loss. In computing taxable income for 1999, Mitch could deduct the $50,000 ordinary loss but could deduct only $3,000 of the capital loss (assuming he has no capital gains). The remainder of the capital loss could be carried over and used in future years subject to the capital loss limitations.

---

[4]The term *individuals* for this purpose includes a partnership but not a trust or an estate.

Alternatively, if Mitch sells 82 shares in 1999, he will recognize an ordinary loss of $49,200 [82 × ($1,000 − $400)]. If Mitch then sells the remainder of the shares in 2000, he will recognize an ordinary loss of $40,800 [68 × ($1,000 − $400)], successfully avoiding the capital loss limitation. Mitch could deduct the $49,200 ordinary loss in computing 1999 taxable income and the $40,800 ordinary loss in computing 2000 taxable income. ▼

CASUALTY AND THEFT LOSSES

3 LEARNING OBJECTIVE
Identify a casualty and determine the amount, classification, and timing of casualty and theft losses.

Losses on business property are deductible, whether attributable to casualty, theft, or some other cause (e.g., rust, termite damage, etc.). While all *business* property losses are generally deductible, the amount and timing of casualty and theft losses are determined using special rules. Furthermore, for individual taxpayers, who may deduct casualty losses on personal-use (nonbusiness) property as well as on business and investment property (held in partnerships and S corporations or in an individual capacity), a set of special limitations apply. Casualty gains are also afforded special consideration in the tax law.

DEFINITION OF CASUALTY

The term *casualty* generally includes *fire, storm, shipwreck,* and *theft.* In addition, losses from *other casualties* are deductible. Such losses generally include any loss resulting from an event that is (1) identifiable; (2) damaging to property; and (3) sudden, unexpected, and unusual in nature. The term also includes accidental loss of property provided the loss qualifies under the same rules as any other casualty.

A *sudden event* is one that is swift and precipitous and not gradual or progressive. An *unexpected event* is one that is ordinarily unanticipated and occurs without the intent of the taxpayer who suffers the loss. An *unusual event* is one that is extraordinary and nonrecurring and does not commonly occur during the activity in which the taxpayer was engaged when the destruction occurred.[5] Examples include hurricanes, tornadoes, floods, storms, shipwrecks, fires, sonic booms, vandalism, and mine cave-ins. A taxpayer also can take a deduction for a casualty loss from an automobile accident if the accident is not attributable to the taxpayer's willful act or willful negligence. Weather that causes damage (drought, for example) must be unusual and severe for the particular region to qualify as a casualty. Furthermore, damage must be to the *taxpayer's* property to be deductible.

Events That Are Not Casualties. Not all acts of God are treated as **casualty losses** for income tax purposes. Because a casualty must be sudden, unexpected, and unusual, progressive deterioration (such as erosion due to wind or rain) is not a casualty because it does not meet the suddenness test.

An example of an event that generally does not qualify as a casualty is insect damage. When termites caused damage over a period of several years, some courts have disallowed a casualty loss deduction.[6] On the other hand,

---
[5]Rev.Rul. 72–592, 1972–2 C.B. 101.
[6]*Fay v. Helvering,* 41–2 USTC ¶9494, 27 AFTR 432, 120 F.2d 253 (CA–2, 1941); *U.S. v. Rogers,* 41–1 USTC ¶9442, 27 AFTR 423, 120 F.2d 244 (CA–9, 1941).

some courts have held that termite damage over periods of up to 15 months after infestation constituted a sudden event and was, therefore, deductible as a casualty loss.[7] Despite the existence of some judicial support for the deductibility of termite damage as a casualty loss, the current position of the IRS is that termite damage is not deductible.[8]

Other examples of events that are not casualties are losses resulting from a decline in value rather than an actual loss of the property. For example, a taxpayer was allowed a loss for the actual flood damage to his property but not for the decline in market value due to the property's being flood-prone.[9] Similarly, a decline in value of an office building due to fire damage to nearby buildings is not deductible as a casualty.

DEFINITION OF THEFT

Theft includes, but is not necessarily limited to, larceny, embezzlement, and robbery.[10] Theft does not include misplaced items.[11]

Theft losses are treated like other casualty losses, but the *timing* of recognition of the loss differs. A theft loss is deducted in the year of discovery, not the year of the theft (unless, of course, the discovery occurs in the same year as the theft). If, in the year of the discovery, a claim exists (e.g., against an insurance company) and there is a reasonable expectation of recovering the adjusted basis of the asset from the insurance company, no deduction is permitted.[12] If, in the year of settlement, the recovery is less than the asset's adjusted basis, a partial deduction may be available. If the recovery is greater than the asset's adjusted basis, *casualty gain* may be recognized.

EXAMPLE 10

Sakura, Inc., owned a computer that was stolen from its offices in December 1997. The theft was discovered on June 3, 1998, and the corporation filed a claim with its insurance company that was settled on January 30, 1999. Assuming there is a reasonable expectation of full recovery, no deduction is allowed in 1998. A partial deduction may be available in 1999 if the actual insurance proceeds are less than the adjusted basis of the asset. (Loss measurement rules are discussed later in this chapter.) ▼

PLANNING CONSIDERATIONS

Documentation of Related-Taxpayer Loans, Casualty Losses, and Theft Losses

Since the validity of loans between related taxpayers might be questioned, adequate documentation is needed to substantiate a bad debt deduction if the loan subsequently becomes worthless. Documentation should include proper execution of the note (legal form) and the establishment of a bona fide purpose for the loan. In addition, it is desirable to stipulate a reasonable rate of interest and a fixed maturity date.

Because a theft loss deduction is not permitted for misplaced items, a police report and evidence of the value of the property (e.g., appraisals, pictures of the property, purchase receipts, etc.) are necessary to document a theft.

---

[7]*Rosenberg v. Comm.*, 52–2 USTC ¶9377, 42 AFTR 303, 198 F.2d 46 (CA–8, 1952); *Shopmaker v. U.S.*, 54–1 USTC ¶9195, 45 AFTR 758, 119 F.Supp. 705 (D.Ct. Mo., 1953).
[8]Rev.Rul. 63–232, 1963–2 C.B. 97.
[9]*S. L. Solomon*, 39 TCM 1282, T.C.Memo. 1980–87.
[10]Reg. § 1.165–8(d).
[11]*Mary Francis Allen*, 16 T.C. 163 (1951).
[12]Reg. §§ 1.165–1(d)(2) and 1.165–8(a)(2).

Similar documentation of the value of property should be provided to support a casualty loss deduction because the amount of loss is measured, in part, by the decline in fair market value of the property.

WHEN TO DEDUCT CASUALTY LOSSES

General Rule. Generally, a casualty loss is deducted in the year the loss occurs. However, no casualty loss is permitted if a reimbursement claim with a reasonable *prospect of full recovery* exists.[13] If the taxpayer has a partial claim, only part of the loss can be claimed in the year of the casualty, and the remainder is deducted in the year the claim is settled.

EXAMPLE 11

Fuchsia Corporation's new warehouse was completely destroyed by fire in 1998. Its cost and fair market value were $250,000. Fuchsia's only claim against the insurance company was on a $70,000 policy that was not settled by year-end. The following year, 1999, Fuchsia settled with the insurance company for $60,000. Fuchsia is entitled to a $180,000 deduction in 1998 and a $10,000 deduction in 1999. ▼

If a taxpayer receives reimbursement for a casualty loss sustained and deducted in a previous year, an amended return is not filed for that year. Instead, the taxpayer must include the reimbursement in gross income on the return for the year in which it is received to the extent that the previous deduction resulted in a tax benefit (refer to Chapter 3).

EXAMPLE 12

Golden Hawk, Inc., had a deductible casualty loss of $15,000 on its 1998 tax return. Golden Hawk's taxable income for 1998 was $60,000 after deducting the $15,000 loss. In June 1999, the corporation was reimbursed $13,000 for the prior year's casualty loss. Golden Hawk would include the entire $13,000 in gross income for 1999 because the deduction in 1998 produced a tax benefit. ▼

Disaster Area Losses. An exception to the general rule for the time of deduction is allowed for **disaster area losses,** which are casualties or disaster-related business losses sustained in an area designated as a disaster area by the President of the United States.[14] In such cases, the taxpayer may *elect* to treat the loss as having occurred in the taxable year immediately *preceding* the taxable year in which the disaster actually occurred. The rationale for this exception is to provide immediate relief to disaster victims in the form of accelerated tax benefits.

If the due date, plus extensions, for the prior year's return has not passed, a taxpayer makes the election to claim the disaster area loss on the prior year's tax return. If a disaster area is designated after the prior year's return has been filed, it is necessary to file either an amended return or a refund claim. In any case, the taxpayer must show clearly that such an election is being made.

MEASURING THE AMOUNT OF LOSS

Amount of Loss. The rules for determining the amount of a loss depend in part on whether business, investment, or personal-use (nonbusiness) property was involved. Another factor that must be considered is whether the property was partially or completely destroyed.

---

[13]Reg. § 1.165–1(d)(2)(i).   [14]§ 165(h).

> ### TAX IN THE NEWS
>
> **FILING RELIEF FOR DISASTER AREA VICTIMS**
>
> Federal revenue officials extended the deadline for filing tax returns from April 15 to May 30 for individuals and businesses in Minnesota counties that were declared a disaster area as a result of spring floods. The announcement informed taxpayers that they could claim uninsured flood casualty losses on either their 1996 or their 1997 returns. Those relying on this flood-related relief were to write "97 FLOODS" at the top of their returns.
>
> SOURCE: Adapted from Conrad deFiebre, "Tax Deadline Extended to May 30 for Flood Victims," *Minneapolis Star Tribune*, April 11, 1997, p. 19A.

If business property or investment property (e.g., rental property) is *completely destroyed*, the loss is equal to the adjusted basis[15] (typically cost less depreciation) of the property at the time of destruction.

EXAMPLE 13 Monty's Movers owned a truck, which was used only for business purposes. The truck was destroyed by fire. Monty, the proprietor, had unintentionally allowed his insurance coverage to expire. The fair market value of the truck was $39,000 at the time of the fire, and its adjusted basis was $40,000. Monty is allowed a loss deduction of $40,000 (the adjusted basis of the truck). ▼

A different measurement rule applies for *partial destruction* of business and investment property and for *partial* or *complete destruction* of personal-use property held by individuals. In these situations, the loss is the *lesser* of

- the adjusted basis of the property, or
- the difference between the fair market value of the property before the event and the fair market value immediately after the event.

EXAMPLE 14 Wynd and Rain, a law firm, owned an airplane that was used only for business purposes. The airplane was damaged in a crash. At the date of the crash, the fair market value of the plane was $52,000, and its adjusted basis was $32,000. After the crash, the plane was appraised at $24,000. The law firm's loss deduction is $28,000 (the lesser of the adjusted basis or the decrease in fair market value). ▼

Any insurance recovery reduces the loss for business, investment, and personal-use losses. In fact, a taxpayer may realize a gain if the insurance proceeds exceed the adjusted basis of the property. Chapter 8 discusses the treatment of net gains and losses on business property and income-producing property.

A special rule on insurance recovery applies to personal-use property. In particular, individuals are not permitted to deduct a casualty loss for damage to insured personal-use property unless an insurance claim is filed. This rule applies, whether the insurance provides partial or full reimbursement for the loss.[16]

Generally, an appraisal before and after the casualty is needed to measure the amount of loss. However, the *cost of repairs* to the damaged property is acceptable as a method of establishing the loss in value provided the following criteria are met:

---

[15] See Chapter 7 for a detailed discussion of basis rules.   [16] § 165(h)(4)(E).

- The repairs are necessary to restore the property to its condition immediately before the casualty.
- The amount spent for such repairs is not excessive.
- The repairs do not extend beyond the damage suffered.
- The value of the property after the repairs does not, as a result of the repairs, exceed the value of the property immediately before the casualty.[17]

Multiple Losses. When multiple casualty losses occur during the year, the amount of each loss is computed separately. The rules for computing loss deductions where multiple losses have occurred are illustrated in Example 15.

EXAMPLE 15

During the year, Swan Enterprises had the following business casualty losses:

| Asset | Adjusted Basis | Fair Market Value of the Asset | | Insurance Recovery |
		Before the Casualty	After the Casualty	
A	$900	$600	$-0-	$400
B	300	800	250	150

The following losses are allowed:

- Asset A: $500. The complete destruction of a business asset results in a deduction of the adjusted basis of the property (reduced by any insurance recovery) regardless of the asset's fair market value.
- Asset B: $150. The partial destruction of a business (or personal-use) asset results in a deduction equal to the lesser of the adjusted basis ($300) or the decline in value ($550), reduced by any insurance recovery ($150). ▼

CASUALTY AND THEFT LOSSES OF INDIVIDUALS

Recall from Chapter 3 that the individual income tax formula distinguishes between deductions *for* AGI and deductions *from* AGI. Casualty and theft losses incurred by an individual in connection with a business or with rental and royalty activities are deductible *for* AGI and are limited only by the rules previously discussed.[18] Losses from most other investment activities and personal-use losses are generally deducted *from* AGI. Investment casualty and theft losses (e.g., the theft of a security) are classified as miscellaneous itemized deductions (subject to a 2%-of-AGI floor). Casualty losses of personal-use property are subject to special limitations discussed below.

Personal-Use Property. In addition to the valuation rules discussed above, casualty loss deductions from personal-use property must be reduced by a $100 *per event* floor and a 10 percent-of-AGI *aggregate* floor.[19] The $100 floor applies separately to each casualty and applies to the entire loss from each casualty (e.g., if a storm damages both a taxpayer's residence and automobile, only $100 is subtracted from the total amount of the loss). All personal-use losses incurred during the year are then added together, and the total is reduced by 10 percent of the taxpayer's AGI. The resulting amount is the taxpayer's itemized deduction for personal-use casualty and theft losses.

---

[17] Reg. § 1.165–7(a)(2)(ii).
[18] § 62(a)(1).
[19] § 165(c)(3).

EXAMPLE 16

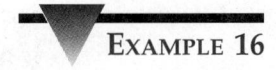

Rocky, who had AGI of $30,000, was involved in a motorcycle accident. His motorcycle, which was used only for personal use and had a fair market value of $12,000 and an adjusted basis of $9,000, was completely destroyed. He received $5,000 from his insurance company. Rocky's casualty loss deduction is $900 [$9,000 basis − $5,000 insurance − $100 floor − $3,000 (.10 × $30,000 AGI)]. The $900 casualty loss is an itemized deduction (*from* AGI). ▼

Where there are both casualty gains and losses from personal-use property, special netting rules apply. Generally, if casualty gains exceed losses during the year, the gains and losses are treated as capital gains and losses. Alternatively, if losses exceed gains, the casualty gains (and losses to the extent of gains) are treated as ordinary gains and losses. Any excess losses are deductible as personal-use casualty losses.

EXAMPLE 17

During the year, Hazel had AGI of $20,000 and the following personal casualty gain and loss (after deducting the $100-per-casualty floor):

Asset	Holding Period	Gain or (Loss)
A	Three years	($2,700)
B	Four months	200

Hazel computes the tax consequences as follows:

Personal casualty loss	($2,700)
Personal casualty gain	200
Net personal casualty loss	($2,500)

Since there is a net casualty loss, Hazel treats the gain and loss as ordinary items. The $200 gain and $200 of the loss are included in computing AGI. The excess casualty loss of $2,500 is subject to the 10%-of-AGI limitation, as follows:

Casualty loss in excess of gain ($2,700 − $200)	$ 2,500
Less: 10% of AGI (10% × $20,000)	(2,000)
Itemized deduction (*from* AGI)	$ 500

If Hazel had incurred a casualty gain of $2,700 on Asset A and a $200 casualty loss on Asset B (i.e., if the gain and loss had been reversed), then a net casualty gain of $2,500 would have resulted. In this circumstance, Hazel would have a long-term capital gain of $2,700 on Asset A and a short-term capital loss of $200 on Asset B. ▼

NET OPERATING LOSSES

INTRODUCTION

4 LEARNING OBJECTIVE
Recognize the impact of the net operating loss carryback and carryover provisions.

The requirement that every taxpayer file an annual income tax return (whether on a calendar year or a fiscal year) can lead to inequities for taxpayers who experience uneven income over a series of years. These inequities result from the application of progressive tax rates to taxable income determined on an annual basis.

EXAMPLE 18

Orange, Inc., realizes the following taxable income or loss over a five-year period: Year 1, $50,000; Year 2, ($30,000); Year 3, $100,000; Year 4, ($200,000); and Year 5, $380,000. Blue Corporation has taxable income of $60,000 every year. Note that both corporations have

Concept Summary 5–2

Casualty Gains and Losses

	Business-Use or Income-Producing Property	Personal-Use Property
Event creating the loss	Any event.	Casualty or theft.
Amount	The lesser of the decline in fair market value or the adjusted basis, but always the adjusted basis if the property is totally destroyed.	The lesser of the decline in fair market value or the adjusted basis.
Insurance	Insurance proceeds received reduce the amount of the loss.	Insurance proceeds received (or for which there is an unfiled claim) reduce the amount of the loss.
$100 floor	Not applicable.	Applicable per event.
Gains and losses	Gains and losses are netted (see detailed discussion in Chapter 8).	Personal casualty and theft gains and losses are netted.
Gains exceeding losses		The gains and losses are treated as gains and losses from the sale of capital assets.
Losses exceeding gains		The gains—and the losses to the extent of gains—are treated as ordinary items in computing AGI. The losses in excess of gains, to the extent they exceed 10% of AGI, are itemized deductions (*from* AGI).

total taxable income of $300,000 over the five-year period. Assume there is no provision for carryback or carryover of net operating losses. Orange and Blue would have the following five-year tax liabilities:

Year	Orange's Tax	Blue's Tax
1	$ 7,500	$10,000
2	–0–	10,000
3	22,250	10,000
4	–0–	10,000
5	129,200	10,000
	$158,950	$50,000

The computation of tax is made without regard to any NOL benefit. Rates applicable to 1998 are used to compute the tax.

Even though Orange and Blue realized the same total taxable income ($300,000) over the five-year period, Orange had to pay taxes of $158,950, while Blue paid taxes of only $50,000. ▼

To provide partial relief from this inequitable tax treatment, a deduction is allowed for **net operating losses (NOLs)**.[20] This provision permits an NOL for any

---
[20] § 172.

one year to be offset against taxable income in other years. The NOL provision provides relief only for losses from the operation of a trade or business or from casualty and theft.

Only C corporations and individuals are permitted an NOL deduction, since losses of partnerships and S corporations pass through to their owners. For C corporations, the NOL equals any negative taxable income for the year, with an adjustment for the dividend received deduction (see Chapter 9). In addition, deductions for prior-year NOLs are not allowed when determining a current-year NOL.

NOLs of individuals are computed by adding back to negative taxable income the excess of nonbusiness deductions (e.g., personal exemptions, the standard deduction, charitable contributions, alimony payments, etc.) over nonbusiness income. Business deductions that are allowed for determining the NOL include moving expenses, losses on rental property, loss on the sale of small business stock, one-half of the self-employment tax (refer to Chapter 1), and losses from a sole proprietorship, partnership, or S corporation.

CARRYBACK AND CARRYOVER PERIODS

General Rules. A current-year NOL is usually carried back and deducted against income over the two preceding tax years.[21] It is carried back first to the second year before the loss year and then to the year immediately preceding the loss year (until it fully offsets income). If the loss is not completely used against income in the carryback period, it is carried forward for 20 years following the loss year. NOLs that are not used within the 20-year carryforward period are lost. Thus, an NOL sustained in 1999 is used first in 1997 and 1998. Then, the loss is carried forward and offsets income in 2000 through 2019.

When an NOL is carried back, the taxpayer requests an immediate refund of prior years' taxes by filing an amended return for the previous two years. When an NOL is carried forward, the current return shows an NOL deduction for the prior year's loss. Thus, a struggling business with an NOL can receive rapid cash-flow assistance.

NOLs from Multiple Tax Years. Where there are NOLs in two or more years, the earliest year's loss is used first. Later years' losses can then be used until they are offset against income or lost. Thus, one year's return could show NOL carryovers from two or more years. Each loss is computed and applied separately.

Election to Forgo Carryback. A taxpayer can *irrevocably elect* not to carry back an NOL. The election is made on a corporate tax return (Form 1120) by checking the appropriate box. Individuals can make the election by attaching a statement to their tax return. If the election is made, the loss can *only* be carried forward for 20 years. This election may be desirable in circumstances where marginal tax rates in future years are expected to exceed rates in prior years.

---

[21] A three-year carryback period is available for any portion of an individual's NOL resulting from a casualty or theft loss. The three-year carryback rule also applies to NOLs that are attributable to presidentially declared disaster areas and are incurred by a small business or a taxpayer engaged in farming. For purposes of this provision, a small business is one whose average annual gross receipts for a three-year period are $5 million or less.

TAX IN THE NEWS

NOLs OF A BIOTECH COMPANY: THE VALUABLE ASSET

Aprogenex, a Houston biotech company, announced that it will reduce its operations to a minimal level. The company spent $29 million trying to develop new medical testing technology, but the business did not work out to the extent expected. The stock was delisted by the American Stock Exchange, and efforts to raise additional capital were unsuccessful.

Aprogenex does, however, possess substantial NOLs that could be valuable to other, more successful, biotech companies. In its press release, the company stated that one of its goals was to preserve the loss carryforwards and other items that could benefit shareholders.

SOURCE: Adapted from Bill Mintz, "Aprogenex to Cut Back Operations," *Houston Chronicle*, August 29, 1997, p. 2 of Business section.

THE TAX SHELTER PROBLEM

LEARNING OBJECTIVE 5
Discuss tax shelters and the reasons for at-risk and passive loss limitations.

Before Congress enacted legislation to reduce or eliminate their effectiveness, **tax shelters** were popular investments for tax avoidance purposes because they could generate losses and other benefits that could be used to offset income from other sources. Because of the tax avoidance potential of many tax shelters, they were attractive to wealthy taxpayers with high marginal tax rates. Many tax shelters merely provided an opportunity for "investors" to buy deductions and credits in ventures that were not expected to generate a profit, even in the long run.

Although it may seem odd that a taxpayer would intentionally invest in an activity that was designed to produce losses, there is a logical explanation. The typical tax shelter operated as a partnership and relied heavily on nonrecourse financing.[22] Accelerated depreciation and interest expense deductions generated large losses in the early years of the activity. At the very least, the tax shelter deductions deferred the recognition of any net income from the venture until the activity was sold. In the best of situations, the investor could realize additional tax savings by offsetting other income (e.g., salary, interest, and dividends) with losses flowing from the tax shelter. Ultimately, the sale of the investment would result in *tax-favored* capital gain. The following examples illustrate what was possible *before* Congress enacted legislation to curb tax shelter abuses.

EXAMPLE 19

Bob, who earned a salary of $300,000 as a business executive and dividend income of $15,000, invested $20,000 for a 10% interest in a cattle-breeding tax shelter. He did not participate in the operation of the business. Through the use of $800,000 of nonrecourse financing and available cash of $200,000, the partnership acquired a herd of an exotic breed of cattle costing $1 million. Depreciation, interest, and other deductions related to the activity resulted in a loss of $400,000, of which Bob's share was $40,000. Bob was allowed to deduct the $40,000 loss, even though he had invested and stood to lose only $20,000 if the investment turned sour. The net effect of the $40,000 deduction from the partnership was that a portion of Bob's salary and dividend income was "sheltered," and as a result, he was required to

---

[22]Nonrecourse debt is an obligation for which the borrower is not personally liable. An example of nonrecourse debt is a liability on real estate acquired by a partnership without the partnership or any of the partners assuming any liability for the mortgage. The acquired property generally is pledged as collateral for the loan.

calculate his tax liability on only $275,000 of income [$315,000 (salary and dividends) − $40,000 (deduction)] rather than $315,000. If this deduction were available under current law and if Bob was in the 39.6% income tax bracket, a tax savings of $15,840 ($40,000 × 39.6%) would be generated in the first year alone! ▼

A review of Example 19 shows that the taxpayer took a two-for-one write-off ($40,000 deduction, $20,000 investment). In the heyday of tax shelters, promoters often promised even larger write-offs for the investor.

The first major provision aimed at tax shelters is the **at-risk limitation.** Its objective is to limit a taxpayer's deductions to the amount that the taxpayer could actually lose from the investment (the amount at risk) if it turns out to be a financial disaster.

▼ **EXAMPLE 20**

Returning to the facts of the preceding example, under the current at-risk rules Bob would be allowed to deduct $20,000 (i.e., the amount that he could lose if the business failed). This deduction would reduce his other income and as a result, Bob would report $295,000 of income ($315,000 − $20,000). The remaining nondeductible $20,000 loss and any future losses flowing from the partnership would be suspended under the at-risk rules and would be deductible in the future only as Bob's at-risk amount increased. ▼

The second major attack on tax shelters came with the passage of the **passive loss** rules. These rules were intended to halt an investor's ability to benefit from the mismatching of an entity's expenses and income that often occurs in the early years of the business. Congress observed that despite the at-risk limitations, investors could still deduct losses flowing from an entity and thereby defer their tax liability on other income. These passive loss rules have, to a great degree, made the term *tax shelter* obsolete by suspending the deductibility of losses.

The passive loss rules require the taxpayer to segregate all income and losses into three categories: active, passive, and portfolio. In general, the passive loss limits disallow the deduction of passive losses against active or portfolio income, even when the taxpayer is at risk to the extent of the loss. Normally, passive losses can only offset passive income.

▼ **EXAMPLE 21**

Returning to the facts of Example 19, the passive activity loss rules further restrict Bob's ability to claim the $20,000 tax deduction shown in Example 20. Because Bob is a passive investor and does not materially participate in any meaningful way in the activities of the cattle-breeding operation, the $20,000 loss allowed under the at-risk rules is disallowed under the passive loss rules. The passive loss is disallowed because Bob does not generate any passive income that could absorb his passive loss. His salary (active income) and dividends (portfolio income) cannot be used to absorb any of the passive loss. Consequently, Bob's current-year taxable income is $315,000, and he receives no current benefit for his share of the partnership loss. However, all is not lost because Bob's share of the entity's loss is *suspended;* it is carried forward and can be deducted in the future when he has passive income or sells his interest in the activity. ▼

The following two sections explore the nature of the at-risk limits and passive activity loss rules and their impact on investors. Congress intentionally structured these rules so that investors evaluating potential investments must consider mainly the *economics* of the venture instead of the *tax benefits* or tax avoidance possibilities that an investment may generate.

TAX IN THE NEWS

THE IMPACT OF RECENT TAX LEGISLATION ON INVESTMENT CHOICES

With the recent reduction in the income tax rates on capital transactions, real estate investments are relatively more attractive than under earlier law. Gains on the sale of capital assets held for more than 18 months are taxed to individuals at no more than 20 percent. Persons contemplating investing in real estate, however, may be better off with stock and securities, which are subject to the same beneficial tax rates as real estate, but avoid the difficulties introduced by the at-risk and passive loss rules. Sorting out the tax differences between investments is not simple, as the tax rate is not the only or most important factor. In arriving at a decision, an investor needs to weigh other factors, including the following:

- The hassle of collecting rents and managing property.
- The desirability of owning physical assets that can be controlled (real estate can be directly controlled by the owner while owners of stock are at the mercy of those who manage the corporation).
- The additional leverage provided by real estate over stock and securities (real estate can be purchased with only a down payment, and the property appreciates while the rental receipts are used to pay off the loan).
- The steady stream of rent income available from real estate that can be offset for tax purposes by depreciation deductions versus dividends and interest from stock and securities.

SOURCE: Information from *USA Today*, August 15, 1997, p. 4B.

AT-RISK LIMITATIONS

LEARNING OBJECTIVE 6
Describe how the at-risk limitation and the passive loss rules limit deductions for losses and identify taxpayers subject to these restrictions.

The at-risk provisions limit the deductibility of losses from business and income-producing activities. These provisions, which apply to individuals and closely held corporations, are designed to prevent taxpayers from deducting losses in excess of their actual economic investment in an activity. In the case of an S corporation or a partnership, the at-risk limits apply at the owner level. Under the at-risk rules, a taxpayer's deductible loss from an activity for any taxable year is limited to the amount the taxpayer has at risk at the end of the taxable year (the amount the taxpayer could actually lose in the activity).

While the amount at risk generally vacillates over time, the initial amount considered at risk consists of the following:[23]

- The amount of cash and the adjusted basis of property contributed to the activity by the taxpayer.
- Amounts borrowed for use in the activity for which the taxpayer is personally liable.
- The adjusted basis of property pledged as security that is not used in the activity.

---
[23] § 465(b)(1).

This amount generally is increased each year by the taxpayer's share of income and is decreased by the taxpayer's share of losses and withdrawals from the activity. In addition, because *general partners* are jointly and severally liable for recourse debts of the partnership, their at-risk amounts are increased when the partnership increases its debt and are decreased when the partnership reduces its debt. However, a taxpayer generally is not considered at risk with respect to borrowed amounts if either of the following is true:

- The taxpayer is not personally liable for repayment of the debt (e.g., nonrecourse debt).
- The lender has an interest (other than as a creditor) in the activity.

An important exception provides that, in the case of an activity involving the holding of real property, a taxpayer is considered at risk for his or her share of any *qualified nonrecourse financing* that is secured by real property used in the activity.[24]

Subject to the passive activity rules discussed later in the chapter, a taxpayer may deduct a loss as long as the at-risk amount is positive. However, once the at-risk amount is exhausted, any remaining loss cannot be deducted until a later year. Any losses disallowed for any given taxable year by the at-risk rules may be deducted in the first succeeding year in which the rules do not prevent the deduction—that is, when and to the extent of a positive at-risk amount.

EXAMPLE 22

In 1998, Sue invests $40,000 in an oil partnership. The partnership, through the use of nonrecourse loans, spends $60,000 on deductible intangible drilling costs applicable to Sue's interest. Assume Sue's interest in the partnership is subject to the at-risk limits but is not subject to the passive loss limits. Since Sue has only $40,000 of capital at risk, she cannot deduct more than $40,000 against her other income and must reduce her at-risk amount to zero ($40,000 at-risk amount − $40,000 loss deducted). The nondeductible loss of $20,000 ($60,000 loss generated − $40,000 loss allowed) can be carried over to 1999.

In 1999, Sue has taxable income of $15,000 from the oil partnership and invests an additional $10,000 in the venture. Her at-risk amount is now $25,000 ($0 beginning balance + $15,000 taxable income + $10,000 additional investment). This enables Sue to deduct the $20,000 carryover loss and requires her to reduce her at-risk amount to $5,000 ($25,000 at-risk amount − $20,000 carryover loss allowed). ▼

An additional complicating factor is that previously allowed losses must be recaptured as income to the extent the at-risk amount is reduced below zero.[25] This rule applies in situations such as when the amount at risk is reduced below zero by distributions to the taxpayer or when the status of indebtedness changes from recourse to nonrecourse.

PASSIVE LOSS LIMITS

CLASSIFICATION AND IMPACT OF PASSIVE INCOME AND LOSS

Classification. The passive loss rules require income and loss to be classified into one of three categories: active, passive, or portfolio. **Active income** includes, but is not limited to, the following:

- Wages, salary, commissions, bonuses, and other payments for services rendered by the taxpayer.

---

[24] § 465(b)(6).   [25] § 465(e).

Concept Summary 5–3

Calculation of At-Risk Amount

Increases to a taxpayer's at-risk amount:

- Cash and the adjusted basis of property contributed to the activity.
- Amounts borrowed for use in the activity for which the taxpayer is personally liable.
- The adjusted basis of property pledged as security that is not used in the activity.
- Taxpayer's share of amounts borrowed for use in the activity that are qualified nonrecourse financing.
- Taxpayer's share of the activity's income.

Decreases to a taxpayer's at-risk amount:

- Withdrawals from the activity.
- Taxpayer's share of the activity's loss.
- Taxpayer's share of any reductions of debt for which recourse against the taxpayer exists or reductions of qualified nonrecourse debt.

- Profit from a trade or business in which the taxpayer is a material participant.
- Gain on the sale or other disposition of assets used in an active trade or business.
- Income from intangible property if the taxpayer's personal efforts significantly contributed to the creation of the property.

Portfolio income includes, but is not limited to, the following:

- Interest, dividends, annuities, and royalties not derived in the ordinary course of a trade or business.
- Gain or loss from the disposition of property that produces portfolio income or is held for investment purposes.

Section 469 provides that income or loss from the following activities is treated as *passive*:

- Any trade or business or income-producing activity in which the taxpayer does not materially participate.
- Subject to certain exceptions, all rental activities, whether the taxpayer materially participates or not.

Although the Code defines rental activities as passive activities, several exceptions allow losses from certain real estate rental activities to be offset against nonpassive (active or portfolio) income. The exceptions are discussed under Special Rules for Real Estate later in the chapter.

General Impact. Deductions or expenses generated by passive activities can only be deducted to the extent of income from passive activities. Any excess may not be used to offset income from active or portfolio income. Instead, any unused passive losses are suspended and carried forward to future years to offset passive income generated in those years. Otherwise, suspended losses may be used only when a taxpayer disposes of his or her entire interest in an activity. In that event, all current and suspended losses related to the activity may offset active and portfolio income.

TAX IN THE NEWS

KNOWLEDGE OF TAX LAWS IS A KEY TO REAL ESTATE SUCCESS

One often hears the sage investment advice to "buy low and sell high," or to "buy cheap, and, as much as possible, use other people's money." These tips, though often difficult to implement, can lead to rich rewards. To realize the full benefits of investing, however, whether in stocks and bonds or in real estate, an investor needs to know and be able to apply the tax law.

For example, due to the passive activity loss rules, a taxpayer that wishes to participate in a real estate investment should avoid being a passive investor. Becoming actively involved may be a better approach. Not only can actual participation by the owner lead to favorable tax results, but the fees and commissions of brokers and middlemen can be avoided.

People who buy real estate through partnerships often find the odds stacked against them. Not only is some of their money skimmed off the top in fees, but if the cost of the property is highly inflated or highly leveraged, many of the depreciation and interest deductions may be disallowed due to the operation of the passive activity loss rules. Thus, for some taxpayers, the answer to successful real estate investing is to participate actively in the operation of the real estate, avoid high fees, make a profit, and avoid the passive activity loss rules.

SOURCE: Information from John R. Hayes, "A Nice Little Sideline," *Forbes*, July 17, 1995, p. 306.

EXAMPLE 23

Kim, a physician, earns $150,000 from her full-time practice. She also receives $10,000 in dividends and interest from various portfolio investments, and her share of a passive loss from a tax shelter not limited by the at-risk rules is $60,000. Because the loss is a passive loss, it is not deductible against her other income. The loss is suspended and is carried over to the future. If Kim has passive income from this investment or from other passive investments in the future, she can offset the suspended loss against that passive income. If she does not have passive income to offset this suspended loss in the future, she will be allowed to offset the loss against other types of income when she eventually disposes of the passive activity. ▼

Impact of Suspended Losses. The actual economic gain or loss from a passive investment (including any suspended losses) can be determined when a taxpayer disposes of his or her entire interest in the investment. As a result, under the passive loss rules, upon a fully taxable disposition, any overall loss realized from the activity by the taxpayer is recognized and can be offset against passive, active, and portfolio income.

A fully taxable disposition generally involves a sale of the property to a third party at arm's length and thus, presumably, for a price equal to the property's fair market value. Gain recognized upon a transfer of an interest in a passive activity generally is treated as passive and is first offset by the suspended losses from that activity.

EXAMPLE 24

Rex sells an apartment building, a passive activity, with an adjusted basis of $100,000 for $180,000. In addition, he has suspended passive losses of $60,000 associated with the building. His total gain, $80,000, and his taxable gain, $20,000, are calculated as follows:

Net sales price	$ 180,000
Less: Adjusted basis	(100,000)
Total gain	$ 80,000
Less: Suspended losses	(60,000)
Taxable gain (passive)	$ 20,000

If current and suspended losses of the passive activity exceed the gain realized from the sale or if the sale results in a realized loss, the amount of

- any loss from the activity for the tax year (including losses suspended in the activity disposed of)

in excess of

- net income or gain for the tax year from all passive activities (without regard to the activity disposed of)

is treated as a loss that is not from a passive activity. In computing the loss from the activity for the year of disposition, any gain or loss recognized is included.

EXAMPLE 25

Dean sells an apartment building with an adjusted basis of $100,000 for $150,000. In addition, he has current and suspended passive losses of $60,000 associated with the building and has no other passive activities. His total gain, $50,000, and his deductible loss, $10,000, are calculated as follows:

Net sales price	$ 150,000
Less: Adjusted basis	(100,000)
Total gain	$ 50,000
Less: Suspended losses	(60,000)
Deductible loss	($ 10,000)

The $10,000 loss can be deducted against Dean's active income and portfolio income. ▼

Carryovers of Suspended Losses. In the above examples, it was assumed that the taxpayer had an interest in only one passive activity, and as a result, the suspended loss was related exclusively to the activity that was disposed of. When a taxpayer owns more than one passive activity, however, any suspended losses must be allocated among the activities. The allocation to an activity is made by multiplying the disallowed passive activity loss from all activities by the following fraction:

$$\frac{\text{Loss from activity}}{\text{Sum of losses for taxable year from all activities having losses}}$$

EXAMPLE 26

Diego has investments in three passive activities with the following income and losses for 1998:

Activity A	($ 30,000)
Activity B	(20,000)
Activity C	25,000
Net passive loss	($ 25,000)
Net passive loss allocated to:	
Activity A [$25,000 × ($30,000/$50,000)]	($ 15,000)
Activity B [$25,000 × ($20,000/$50,000)]	(10,000)
Total suspended losses	($ 25,000)

Suspended losses are carried over indefinitely and are offset in the future against any passive income from the activities to which they relate.[26]

EXAMPLE 27

Assume the same facts as in the preceding example and that Activity A produces $10,000 of income in 1999. Of the suspended loss of $15,000 from 1998 for Activity A, $10,000 is offset against the income from this activity. If Diego sells Activity A in early 2000, then the remaining $5,000 suspended loss is used in determining his final gain or loss. ▼

Passive Credits. Credits arising from passive activities are limited in much the same way as passive losses. Passive credits can be utilized only against regular tax attributable to passive income,[27] which is calculated by comparing the tax on all income (including passive income) with the tax on income excluding passive income.

EXAMPLE 28

Sam owes $50,000 of tax, disregarding net passive income, and $80,000 of tax, considering both net passive and other taxable income (disregarding the credits in both cases). The amount of tax attributable to the passive income is $30,000.

Tax due (before credits) including net passive income	$ 80,000
Less: Tax due (before credits) without including net passive income	(50,000)
Tax attributable to passive income	$ 30,000

▼

Sam in the preceding example can claim a maximum of $30,000 of passive activity credits; the excess credits are carried over. These passive activity credits (such as the low-income housing credit and rehabilitation credit) can only be used against the *regular* tax attributable to passive income. If a taxpayer has a net loss from passive activities during a given year, no credits can be used. Likewise, if a taxpayer has net passive income but the alternative minimum tax applies to that year, no passive activity credits can be used. (The alternative minimum tax and tax credits are addressed in detail in Chapter 13.)

Carryovers of Passive Credits. Tax credits attributable to passive activities can be carried forward indefinitely, much like suspended passive losses. Unlike passive losses, however, passive credits are lost forever when the activity is disposed of in a taxable transaction where loss is recognized. Credits are allowed on dispositions only when there is sufficient tax on passive income to absorb them.

EXAMPLE 29

Alicia sells a passive activity for a gain of $10,000. The activity had suspended losses of $40,000 and suspended credits of $15,000. The $10,000 gain is offset by $10,000 of the suspended losses, and the remaining $30,000 of suspended losses is deductible against Alicia's active and portfolio income. The suspended credits are lost forever because the sale of the activity did not generate any tax. This is true even if Alicia has positive taxable income or is subject to the alternative minimum tax. ▼

EXAMPLE 30

If Alicia in the preceding example had realized a $100,000 gain on the sale of the passive activity, the suspended credits could have been used to the extent of regular tax attributable to the net passive income.

Gain on sale	$ 100,000
Less: Suspended losses	(40,000)
Net gain	$ 60,000

---

[26] § 469(b).

[27] § 469(d)(2).

If the tax attributable to the net gain of $60,000 is $15,000 or more, the entire $15,000 of suspended credits can be used. If the tax attributable to the gain is less than $15,000, the excess of the suspended credit over the tax attributable to the gain is lost forever. ▼

When a taxpayer has adequate regular tax liability from passive activities to trigger the use of suspended credits, the credits lose their character as passive credits. They are reclassified as regular tax credits and made subject to the same limits as other credits (see Chapter 13).

Passive Activity Changes to Active. If a formerly passive activity becomes active, suspended losses are allowed to the extent of income from the now active business.[28] If any of the suspended loss remains, it continues to be treated as a loss from a passive activity. The excess suspended loss can be deducted against passive income or carried over to the next tax year and deducted to the extent of income from the now active business in the succeeding year(s).

TAXPAYERS SUBJECT TO THE PASSIVE LOSS RULES

The passive loss rules apply to individuals, estates, trusts, personal service corporations, and closely held C corporations.[29] Passive income or loss from investments in S corporations or partnerships (see Chapters 11 and 12) flows through to the owners, and the passive loss rules are applied at the owner level. Consequently, it is necessary to understand how the passive activity rules apply to both entities *and* their owners (including individual taxpayers).

Personal Service Corporations. Application of the passive loss limitations to **personal service corporations** is intended to prevent taxpayers from sheltering personal service income by creating personal service corporations and acquiring passive activities at the corporate level.

▼ **EXAMPLE 31**
Five tax accountants, who earn a total of $1 million a year in their individual practices, form a personal service corporation. Shortly after its formation, the corporation invests in a passive activity that produces a $200,000 loss during the year. Because the passive loss rules apply to personal service corporations, the corporation may not deduct the $200,000 loss against the $1 million of active income. ▼

Determination of whether a corporation is a *personal service corporation* is based on rather broad definitions. A personal service corporation is a corporation that meets both of the following conditions:

- The principal activity is the performance of personal services.
- Such services are substantially performed by owner-employees.

Generally, personal service corporations include those in the fields of health, law, engineering, architecture, accounting, actuarial science, performing arts, and consulting.[30] A corporation is treated as a personal service corporation if more than 10 percent of the stock (by value) is held by owner-employees.[31] A shareholder is treated as an owner-employee if he or she is an employee or shareholder on any day during the testing period.[32] For these purposes, shareholder and employee status do not have to occur on the same day.

---

[28] § 469(f).
[29] § 469(a).
[30] § 448(d)(2).
[31] § 469(j)(2).
[32] § 269A(b)(2).

Closely Held C Corporations. Application of the passive loss rules to closely held (non-personal service) corporations is also intended to prevent individuals from incorporating to avoid the passive loss limitations. A corporation is classified as a **closely held C corporation** if at any time during the taxable year, more than 50 percent of the value of its outstanding stock is owned, directly or indirectly, by or for not more than five individuals. Closely held corporations (other than personal service corporations) may offset passive losses against *active* income, but not against portfolio income.

EXAMPLE 32

Silver Corporation, a closely held (non-personal service) C corporation, has $500,000 of passive losses from a rental activity, $400,000 of active income, and $100,000 of portfolio income. The corporation may offset $400,000 of the $500,000 passive loss against the $400,000 of active business income, but may not offset the remainder against the $100,000 of portfolio income. Thus, $100,000 of the passive loss is suspended ($500,000 passive loss − $400,000 offset against active income). ▼

Application of the passive loss limitations to closely held corporations prevents shareholders from transferring their portfolio investments to such corporations in order to offset passive losses against portfolio income.

ACTIVITY DEFINED

7 LEARNING OBJECTIVE
Discuss and be able to apply the definitions of activity, material participation, and rental activity under the passive loss rules.

Identifying what constitutes an activity is a necessary first step in applying the passive loss limitation. The current rules used to delineate an activity state that, in general, a taxpayer can treat one or more trade or business activities or rental activities as a single activity if those activities form an *appropriate economic unit* for measuring gain or loss. The Regulations provide guidelines for identifying appropriate economic units.[33] These guidelines are designed to prevent taxpayers from arbitrarily combining different businesses in an attempt to circumvent the passive loss limitation. For example, combining a profitable active business and a passive business generating losses into one activity would allow the taxpayer to offset passive losses against active income.

To determine which ventures form an appropriate economic unit, all the relevant facts and circumstances must be considered. Taxpayers may use any reasonable method given the facts and circumstances, but five factors are given the greatest weight. It is not necessary to meet all of these conditions in order to treat multiple activities as a single activity.

- Similarities and differences in the type of business conducted in the various trades or businesses or rental activities.
- The extent of common control over the various activities.
- The extent of common ownership of the activities.
- The geographical location of the different units.
- Interdependencies among the activities (e.g., a retail activity and a warehouse business that stores the inventory used in the retail activity).

In addition to the above guidelines, special rules restrict the grouping of rental and nonrental activities.[34] The example below, adapted from the Regulations, illustrates the application of the activity grouping rules.[35]

---

[33] Reg. § 1.469–4.
[34] Reg. § 1.469–4(d).
[35] Reg. § 1.469–4(c)(3).

EXAMPLE 33

George owns a men's clothing store and a video game parlor in Chicago. He also owns a men's clothing store and a video game parlor in Milwaukee. Reasonable methods of applying the facts and circumstances test may result in any of the following groupings:

- All four businesses may be grouped into a single activity.
- The clothing stores may be grouped into an activity, and the video game parlors may be grouped into an activity.
- The Chicago businesses may be grouped into an activity, and the Milwaukee businesses may be grouped into an activity.
- Each of the four businesses may be treated as a separate activity. ▼

Once a set of activities has been grouped by the taxpayer using the above rules, the grouping cannot be changed unless a material change in the facts and circumstances occurs or the original grouping was clearly inappropriate. In addition, the Regulations also grant the IRS the right to regroup activities when one of the primary purposes of the taxpayer's grouping is to avoid the passive loss limitation and the grouping fails to reflect an appropriate economic unit.[36]

MATERIAL PARTICIPATION

If a taxpayer materially participates in a nonrental trade or business activity, any loss from that activity is treated as an active loss that can be offset against active income. If a taxpayer does not materially participate, however, the loss is treated as a passive loss, which can only be offset against passive income. Therefore, controlling whether a particular activity is treated as active or passive is an important part of the tax strategy of a taxpayer who owns an interest in one or more businesses. Consider the following examples.

EXAMPLE 34

Cameron, a corporate executive, earns a salary of $200,000 per year. In addition, he owns a separate business in which he participates. The business produces a loss of $100,000 during the year. If Cameron materially participates in the business, the $100,000 loss is an active loss that may be offset against his active income from his corporate employer. If he does not materially participate, the loss is passive and is suspended. Cameron may use the suspended loss in the future only when he has passive income or disposes of the activity. ▼

EXAMPLE 35

Connor, an attorney, earns $250,000 a year in his law practice. He owns interests in two activities, A and B, in which he participates. Activity A, in which he does not *materially* participate, produces a loss of $50,000. Connor has not yet met the material participation standard for Activity B, which produces income of $80,000. However, he can meet the material participation standard if he spends an additional 50 hours in Activity B during the year. Should Connor attempt to meet the material participation standard for Activity B? If he continues working in Activity B and becomes a material participant, the $80,000 of income from the activity is active, and the $50,000 passive loss from Activity A must be suspended. A more favorable tax strategy is for Connor to *not meet* the material participation standard for Activity B, thus making the income from that activity passive. This enables him to offset the $50,000 passive loss from Activity A against the passive income from Activity B. ▼

It is possible to devise numerous scenarios in which the taxpayer could control the tax outcome by increasing or decreasing participation in different activities. Examples 34 and 35 demonstrate two of the possibilities. The conclusion reached in most analyses of this type is that taxpayers will benefit by having profitable

---

[36]Reg. § 1.469–4(f).

activities classified as passive, so that any passive losses can be used to offset passive income. If the activity produces a loss, however, the taxpayer will benefit if it is classified as active so the loss is not subject to the passive loss limitations.

As discussed above, a nonrental trade or business in which a taxpayer owns an interest must be treated as a passive activity unless the taxpayer materially participates. As the Staff of the Joint Committee on Taxation explained, a participant is one who has "a significant nontax economic profit motive" for taking on activities and selects them for their economic value. In contrast, a passive investor mainly seeks a return from a capital investment (including a possible reduction in taxes) as a supplement to an ongoing source of livelihood.

Even if the concept or the implication of being a material participant is clear, the precise meaning of the term **material participation** can be vague. As enacted, § 469 required a taxpayer to participate on a *regular, continuous, and substantial basis* in order to be a material participant. In many situations, however, it was difficult or impossible to gain any assurance that this nebulous standard was met.

In response to this dilemma, Temporary Regulations[37] provide seven tests that are intended to help taxpayers cope with these issues. Material participation is achieved by meeting any one of the tests. These tests can be divided into three categories:

- Tests based on current participation.
- Tests based on prior participation.
- Test based on facts and circumstances.

Tests Based on Current Participation. The first four tests are quantitative tests that require measurement, in hours, of the individual's participation in the activity during the year.

1. *Does the individual participate in the activity for more than 500 hours during the year?*

The purpose of the 500-hour requirement is to restrict deductions from the types of trade or business activities that Congress intended to treat as passive activities. The 500-hour standard for material participation was adopted for the following reasons:[38]

- Few investors in traditional tax shelters devote more than 500 hours a year to such an investment.
- The IRS believes that income from an activity in which the taxpayer participates for more than 500 hours a year should not be treated as passive.

2. *Does the individual's participation in the activity for the taxable year constitute substantially all of the participation in the activity of all individuals (including nonowner employees) for the year?*

EXAMPLE 36 Ned, a physician, operates a separate business in which he participates for 80 hours during the year. He is the only participant and has no employees in the separate business. Ned meets the material participation standard of Test 2. If he had employees, it would be difficult to apply Test 2, because the Temporary Regulations do not define the term "substantially all." ▼

---

[37]Temp. and Prop.Reg. § 1.469–5T(a).   [38]T.D. 8175, 1988–1 C.B. 191.

3. *Does the individual participate in the activity for more than 100 hours during the year, and is the individual's participation in the activity for the year not less than the participation of any other individual (including nonowner employees) for the year?*

EXAMPLE 37

Adam, a college professor, owns a separate business in which he participates 110 hours during the year. He has an employee who works 90 hours during the year. Adam meets the material participation standard under Test 3, but probably does not meet it under Test 2 because his participation is only 55% of the total participation. It is unlikely that 55% would meet the substantially all requirement of Test 2. ▼

Tests 2 and 3 are included because the IRS recognizes that the operation of some activities does not require more than 500 hours of participation during the year.

4. *Is the activity a significant participation activity for the taxable year, and does the individual's aggregate participation in all significant participation activities during the year exceed 500 hours?*

A **significant participation activity** is a trade or business in which the individual's participation exceeds 100 hours during the year. This test treats taxpayers as material participants if their aggregate participation in several significant participation activities exceeds 500 hours. Test 4 thus accords the same treatment to an individual who devotes an aggregate of more than 500 hours to several significant participation activities as to an individual who devotes more than 500 hours to a single activity.

EXAMPLE 38

Mike owns five different businesses. He participated in each activity during the year as follows:

Activity	Hours of Participation
A	110
B	140
C	120
D	150
E	100

Activities A, B, C, and D are significant participation activities, and Mike's aggregate participation in those activities is 520 hours. Therefore, Activities A, B, C, and D are *not* treated as passive activities. Activity E is not a significant participation activity (not more than 100 hours), so it is not included in applying the 500-hour test. Activity E is treated as a passive activity, unless Mike meets one of the other material participation tests for that activity. ▼

EXAMPLE 39

Assume the same facts as in the preceding example, except that Activity A does not exist. All of the activities are now treated as passive. Activity E is not counted in applying the more-than-500-hour test, so Mike's aggregate participation in significant participation activities is 410 hours (140 in Activity B + 120 in Activity C + 150 in Activity D). He could meet the significant participation test for Activity E by participating for one more hour in the activity. This would cause Activities B, C, D, and E to be treated as nonpassive activities. However, before deciding whether to participate for at least one more hour in Activity E, Mike should assess how the participation would affect his overall tax liability. ▼

Tests Based on Prior Participation. Tests 5 and 6 are based on material participation in prior years. Under these tests, a taxpayer no longer participating in an activity can continue to be *classified* as a material participant. The IRS takes the position that material participation in a trade or business for a long period of time is likely to indicate that the activity represents the individual's principal livelihood, rather than a passive investment. Consequently, withdrawal from the activity or reduction of participation to the point where it is not material does not change the classification of the activity from active to passive.

5. *Did the individual materially participate in the activity for any 5 taxable years (whether consecutive or not) during the 10 taxable years that immediately precede the taxable year?*

EXAMPLE 40

Dawn, who owns a 50% interest in a restaurant, was a material participant in the operations of the restaurant from 1993 through 1997. She retired at the end of 1997 and is no longer involved in the restaurant except as an investor. Dawn will be treated as a material participant in the restaurant in 1998. Even if she does not become involved in the restaurant as a material participant again, she will continue to be treated as a material participant in 1999, 2000, 2001, and 2002. In 2003 and later years, Dawn's share of income or loss from the restaurant will be classified as passive unless she materially participates in those years. ▼

6. *Is the activity a personal service activity, and did the individual materially participate in the activity for any three preceding taxable years (whether consecutive or not)?*

As indicated above, the material participation standards for personal service activities differ from other businesses. An individual who was a material participant in a personal service activity for *any three years* prior to the taxable year continues to be treated as a material participant after withdrawal from the activity.

EXAMPLE 41

Evan, a CPA, retires from the EFG Partnership after working full-time in the partnership for 30 years. As a retired partner, he will continue to receive a share of the profits of the firm for the next 10 years, even though he will not participate in the firm's operations. Evan also owns an interest in a passive activity that produces a loss for the year. He continues to be treated as a material participant in the EFG Partnership, and his income from the partnership is active income. Therefore, he is not allowed to offset the loss from his passive investment against the income from the EFG Partnership. ▼

Facts and Circumstances Test. Test 7 is a facts and circumstances test to determine whether the taxpayer has materially participated.

7. *Based on all the facts and circumstances, did the individual participate in the activity on a regular, continuous, and substantial basis during the year?*

The Temporary Regulations do not define what constitutes regular, continuous, and substantial participation except to say that the taxpayer's activities will *not* be considered material participation under Test 7 in the following three circumstances:[39]

- The taxpayer satisfies the participation standards (whether or not a *material participant*) of any Code section other than § 469.

---

[39]Temp. and Prop.Reg. § 1.469–5T(b)(2).

- The taxpayer manages the activity, unless
  - no other person receives compensation for management services, and
  - no individual spends more hours during the tax year managing the activity than does the taxpayer.
- The taxpayer participates in the activity for 100 hours or less during the tax year.

A part of the Temporary Regulations has been reserved for further development of this test. Presumably, additional guidelines will be issued in the future. For the time being, taxpayers should rely on Tests 1 through 6 in determining whether the material participation standards have been met.

Participation Defined. Participation generally includes any work done by an individual in an activity that he or she owns. Participation does not include work if it is of a type not customarily done by owners *and* if one of its principal purposes is to avoid the disallowance of passive losses or credits. Also, work done in an individual's capacity as an investor (e.g., reviewing financial reports in a nonmanagerial capacity) is not counted in applying the material participation tests. However, participation by an owner's spouse counts as participation by the owner.[40]

EXAMPLE 42

Tom, who is a partner in a CPA firm, owns a computer store that has operated at a loss during the year. In order to offset this loss against the income from his CPA practice, Tom would like to avoid having the computer business classified as a passive activity. Through December 15, he has worked 400 hours in the business in management and selling activities. During the last two weeks of December, he works 80 hours in management and selling activities and 30 hours doing janitorial chores. Also during the last two weeks in December, Tom's wife participates 40 hours as a salesperson. She has worked as a salesperson in the computer store in prior years, but has not done so during the current year. If any of Tom's work is of a type not customarily done by owners and if one of its principal purposes is to avoid the disallowance of passive losses or credits, it is not counted in applying the material participation tests. It is likely that Tom's 480 hours of participation in management and selling activities will count as participation, but the 30 hours spent doing janitorial chores will not. However, the 40 hours of participation by his wife will count, and Tom will qualify as a material participant under the more-than-500-hour rule (480 + 40 = 520). ▼

Limited Partners. A *limited* partner is one whose liability to third-party creditors of the partnership is limited to the amount the partner has invested in the partnership. Such a partnership must have at least one *general* partner, who is fully liable in an individual capacity for the debts of the partnership to third parties. Generally, a *limited partner* is not considered a material participant unless he or she qualifies under Test 1, 5, or 6 in the above list. However, a *general partner* may qualify as a material participant by meeting any of the seven tests. If an unlimited, or general, partner also owns a limited interest in the same limited partnership, all interests are treated as a general interest.[41]

Corporations. Personal service corporations and closely held C corporations cannot directly participate in an activity. However, a corporation is deemed to materially participate if its owners materially participate in an activity of the corporation. Together, the participating owners must own directly or indirectly more than 50 percent of the value of the outstanding stock of the corporation.[42] Alternatively, a

---

[40]Temp. and Prop.Reg. § 1.469–5T(f)(3).
[41]Temp. and Prop.Reg. § 1.469–5T(e)(3)(ii).
[42]Reg. § 1.469–1T(g)(3)(i)(A).

closely held C corporation may be deemed to materially participate if, during the entire year, it has at least one full-time employee actively managing the business and at least three full-time nonowner employees working for the business. In addition, the corporation's trade or business expenses must exceed its gross income by 15 percent for the year.[43]

RENTAL ACTIVITIES

As discussed previously, § 469 specifies that, subject to certain exceptions, all rental activities are to be treated as passive activities.[44] A **rental activity** is defined as any activity where payments are received principally for the use of tangible (real or personal) property.[45] Importantly, an activity that is classified as a rental activity is subject to the passive activity loss rules, even if the taxpayer involved is a material participant.

EXAMPLE 43

Sarah owns an apartment building and spends an average of 60 hours a week in its operation. Assuming that the apartment building operation is classified as a rental activity, it is automatically subject to the passive activity rules, even though Sarah spends more than 500 hours a year in its operation. ▼

As suggested, Temporary Regulations provide that in certain situations activities involving rentals of real and personal property are *not* to be treated as rental activities.[46]

EXAMPLE 44

Dan owns a videocassette rental business. Because the average period of customer use is seven days or less, Dan's business is not treated as a rental activity. ▼

The fact that Dan's videocassette business in the previous example is not treated as a rental activity does not necessarily mean that it is classified as a nonpassive activity. Instead, the videocassette business is treated as a trade or business activity subject to the material participation standards. If Dan is a material participant, the business is treated as active. If he is not a material participant, it is treated as a passive activity.

Activities covered by any of the following six exceptions provided by the Temporary Regulations are not *automatically* treated as passive activities because they would not be classified as rental activities. Instead, the activities are only subject to the material participation tests.

1. *The average period of customer use is seven days or less.*

Under this exception, activities involving the short-term rental of tangible property such as automobiles, videocassettes, tuxedos, tools, and other such property are not treated as rental activities. The provision also applies to short-term rentals of hotel or motel rooms.

This exception is based on the presumption that a person who rents property for seven days or less is generally required to provide *significant services* to the customer. Providing such services supports a conclusion that the person is engaged in a service business rather than a rental business.

---

[43]Reg. § 1.469–1T(g)(3)(i)(B).
[44]§ 469(c)(2).
[45]§ 469(j)(8).
[46]Temp. and Prop.Reg. § 1.469–1T(e)(3)(ii).

2. *The average period of customer use is 30 days or less, and the owner of the property provides significant personal services.*

For longer-term rentals, the presumption that significant services are provided is not automatic, as it is in the case of the seven-day exception. Instead, the taxpayer must be able to prove that significant personal services are rendered in connection with the activity. Relevant facts and circumstances include the frequency with which such services are provided, the type and amount of labor required to perform such services, and the value of such services relative to the amount charged for the use of the property. Significant personal services include only services provided by individuals. This provision excludes such items as telephone and cable television services.

3. *The owner of the property provides extraordinary personal services. The average period of customer use is of no consequence in applying this test.*

Extraordinary personal services are services provided by individuals where the customers' use of the property is incidental to their receipt of the services. For example, a patient's use of a hospital bed is incidental to his or her receipt of medical services. Another example is the use of a boarding school's dormitory, which is incidental to the scholastic services received.

4. *The rental of the property is treated as incidental to a nonrental activity of the taxpayer.*

Rentals of real property incidental to a nonrental activity are not considered a passive activity. The Temporary Regulations provide that the following rentals are not passive activities.[47]

- *Property held primarily for investment.* This occurs where the principal purpose for holding the property is the expectation of gain from the appreciation of the property and the gross rent income is less than 2 percent of the lesser of (1) the unadjusted basis or (2) the fair market value of the property.

EXAMPLE 45

Ramon invests in vacant land for the purpose of realizing a profit on its appreciation. He leases the land during the period it is held. The land's unadjusted basis is $250,000, and the fair market value is $350,000. The lease payments are $4,000 per year. Because gross rent income is less than 2% of $250,000, the activity is not a rental activity. ▼

- *Property used in a trade or business.* This occurs where the property is owned by a taxpayer who is an owner of the trade or business using the rental property. The property must also have been used in the trade or business during the year or during at least two of the five preceding taxable years. The 2 percent test above also applies in this situation.

EXAMPLE 46

A farmer owns land with an unadjusted basis of $250,000 and a fair market value of $350,000. He used it for farming purposes in 1997 and 1998. In 1999, he leased the land to another farmer for $4,000. The activity is not a rental activity. ▼

- *Property held for sale to customers.* If property is held for sale to customers and rented during the year, the rental of the property is not a rental activity.

---

[47]Temp. and Prop.Reg. §§ 1.469–1T(e)(3)(vi)(B) through (E).

Concept Summary 5–4

Passive Activity Loss Rules: General Concepts

What is the fundamental passive activity rule?	Passive activity losses may be deducted only against passive activity income and gains. Losses not deducted are suspended and used in future years.
Who is subject to the passive activity rules?	Individuals. Estates. Trusts. Personal service corporations. Closely held C corporations.
What is a passive activity?	A trade or business or income-producing activity in which the taxpayer does not materially participate during the year, or rental activities, subject to certain exceptions, regardless of the taxpayer's level of participation.
What is an activity?	One or more trades or businesses or rental activities that comprise an appropriate economic unit.
How is an appropriate economic unit determined?	Based on a reasonable application of the relevant facts and circumstances.
What is material participation?	In general, the taxpayer participates on a regular, continuous, and substantial basis. More specifically, when the taxpayer meets the conditions of one of the seven tests provided in the Regulations.
What is a rental activity?	In general, an activity where payments are received for the use of tangible property. More specifically, a rental activity that does *not* meet one of the six exceptions provided in the Regulations. Special rules apply to rental real estate.

If, for instance, an automobile dealer rents automobiles held for sale to customers to persons who are having their own cars repaired, the activity is not a rental activity.

- *Lodging rented for the convenience of an employer.* If an employer provides lodging for an employee incidental to the employee's performance of services in the employer's trade or business, no rental activity exists.
- A partner who rents property to a partnership that is used in the partnership's trade or business does not have a rental activity.

These rules were written to prevent taxpayers from converting active or portfolio income into a passive activity for the purpose of offsetting other passive losses.

5. *The taxpayer customarily makes the property available during defined business hours for nonexclusive use by various customers.*

EXAMPLE 47 Pat is the owner-operator of a public golf course. Some customers pay daily greens fees each time they use the course, while others purchase weekly, monthly, or annual passes. The golf course is open every day from sunrise to sunset, except on certain holidays and on days when the course is closed due to inclement weather conditions. Pat is not engaged in a rental activity, regardless of the average period customers use the course. ▼

6. *The property is provided for use in an activity conducted by a partnership, S corporation, or joint venture in which the taxpayer owns an interest.*

CHAPTER 5 Losses and Loss Limitations

EXAMPLE 48

Joe, a partner in the Skyview Partnership, contributes the use of a building to the partnership. The partnership has net income of $30,000 during the year, of which Joe's share is $10,000. Unless the partnership is engaged in a rental activity, none of Joe's income from the partnership is income from a rental activity. ▼

INTERACTION OF AT-RISK AND PASSIVE ACTIVITY LIMITS

8 LEARNING OBJECTIVE
Recognize the relationship between the at-risk and passive activity limitations.

The determination of whether a loss is suspended under the passive loss rules is made *after* application of the at-risk rules, as well as other provisions relating to the measurement of taxable income. A loss that is not allowed for the year because the taxpayer is not at risk with respect to it is suspended under the at-risk provision and not under the passive loss rules. Further, a taxpayer's basis is reduced by deductions (e.g., depreciation) even if the deductions are not currently usable because of the passive loss rules.

EXAMPLE 49

Jack's adjusted basis in a passive activity is $10,000 at the beginning of 1998. His loss from the activity in 1998 is $4,000. Since Jack had no passive activity income, the $4,000 cannot be deducted. At year-end, Jack has an adjusted basis and an at-risk amount of $6,000 in the activity and a suspended passive loss of $4,000. ▼

EXAMPLE 50

Jack in the preceding example had a loss of $9,000 in the activity in 1999. Since the $9,000 exceeds his at-risk amount ($6,000) by $3,000, that $3,000 loss is disallowed by the at-risk rules. If Jack has no passive activity income, the remaining $6,000 is suspended under the passive activity rules. At year-end, he has a $3,000 loss suspended under the at-risk rules, $10,000 of suspended passive losses, and an adjusted basis and an at-risk amount in the activity of zero. ▼

EXAMPLE 51

Jack in Example 50 realized $1,000 of passive income in 2000. Because the $1,000 increases his at-risk amount, $1,000 of the $3,000 unused loss can be reclassified as a passive loss. If he has no other passive income, the $1,000 income is offset by $1,000 of suspended passive losses. At the end of 2000, Jack has

- no taxable passive income,
- $2,000 ($3,000 − $1,000) of unused losses under the at-risk rules,
- $10,000 of (reclassified) suspended passive losses ($10,000 + $1,000 of reclassified unused at-risk losses − $1,000 of passive losses offset against passive income), and
- an adjusted basis and an at-risk amount in the activity of zero. ▼

EXAMPLE 52

In 2001, Jack had no gain or loss from the activity in Example 51. He contributed $5,000 more to the passive activity. Because the $5,000 increases his at-risk amount, the $2,000 of losses suspended under the at-risk rules is reclassified as passive. Jack gets no passive loss deduction in 2001. At year-end, he has no suspended losses under the at-risk rules, $12,000 of suspended passive losses ($10,000 + $2,000 of reclassified suspended at-risk losses), and an adjusted basis and an at-risk amount of $3,000 ($5,000 additional investment − $2,000 of reclassified losses). ▼

SPECIAL RULES FOR REAL ESTATE

9 LEARNING OBJECTIVE
Discuss the special treatment available to real estate activities.

The passive loss limits contain two exceptions related to real estate activities. These exceptions allow all or part of real estate rental losses to be offset against active or portfolio income, even though the activity is a passive activity.

Real Estate Professionals. The first exception allows certain real estate professionals to avoid passive loss treatment for losses from real estate rental activities.[48] To qualify for nonpassive treatment, a taxpayer must satisfy both of the following requirements:

- More than half of the personal services that the taxpayer performs in trades or businesses are performed in real property trades or businesses in which the taxpayer materially participates.
- The taxpayer performs more than 750 hours of services in these real property trades or businesses as a material participant.

Taxpayers who do not satisfy the above requirements must continue to treat losses from real estate rental activities as passive losses.

EXAMPLE 53

During the current year, Della performed personal service activities as follows: 900 hours as a personal financial planner, 550 hours in a real estate development and leasing business, and 600 hours in real estate rental activities. Any loss Della incurred in either real estate activity will not be subject to the passive loss rules, since more than 50% of her personal services were devoted to real property trades or businesses and her material participation in those real estate activities exceeded 750 hours. Thus, any loss from the real estate rental activity could offset active and portfolio sources of income. ▼

As discussed earlier, a spouse's work is taken into consideration in satisfying the material participation requirement. However, the hours worked by a spouse are not taken into account when ascertaining whether a taxpayer has worked for more than 750 hours in real property trades or businesses during a year. Services performed by an employee are not treated as being related to a real estate trade or business unless the employee performing the services owns more than a 5 percent interest in the employer. Additionally, a closely held C corporation may also qualify for the passive loss relief if more than 50 percent of its gross receipts for the year are derived from real property trades or businesses in which it materially participates.[49]

Rental Real Estate Deduction. The second exception is more significant in that it is not restricted to real estate professionals. This exception allows individuals to deduct up to $25,000 of losses on real estate rental activities against active and portfolio income.[50] The potential annual $25,000 deduction is reduced by 50 percent of the taxpayer's AGI in excess of $100,000. Thus, the entire deduction is phased out at $150,000. If married individuals file separately, the $25,000 deduction is reduced to zero unless they lived apart for the entire year. If they lived apart for the entire year, the loss amount is $12,500 each, and the phase-out begins at $50,000. AGI for purposes of the phase-out is calculated without regard to IRA deductions, Social Security benefits, and net losses from passive activities.

To qualify for the $25,000 exception, a taxpayer must:[51]

- Actively participate in the real estate rental activity.
- Own 10 percent or more (in value) of all interests in the activity during the entire taxable year (or shorter period during which the taxpayer held an interest in the activity).

The difference between *active participation* and *material participation* is that the former can be satisfied without regular, continuous, and substantial involvement

---

[48] § 469(c)(7).
[49] § 469(c)(7)(B) and Reg. § 1.469–9.
[50] § 469(i).
[51] § 469(i)(6).

TAX IN THE NEWS

SHELTER FOR COLLEGE STUDENTS MAY BE TAX SHELTER FOR PARENTS

For some college students, living in a crowded and noisy dormitory is only a bad memory. Thanks to an increasingly popular investment option for parents, dorm rooms are being replaced by condominiums.

Typically, the parents purchase a condominium that will house their son or daughter, along with several other rent-paying students, while the child is in college. Meanwhile, any tax losses resulting from this passive investment may be deductible under the $25,000 rental real estate exception.

Parents across the country see these units as safe havens for their children as well as their money. Although such arrangements can lead to a savings in housing costs, buyers should be aware that the investment may ultimately prove to be a money loser if it is sold after only four years.

SOURCE: Information from *Wall Street Journal*, July 31, 1997, p. A1.

---

in operations as long as the taxpayer participates in making management decisions in a significant and bona fide sense. In this context, relevant management decisions include such decisions as approving new tenants, deciding on rental terms, and approving capital or repair expenditures.

The $25,000 allowance is available after all active participation rental losses and gains are netted and applied to other passive income. If a taxpayer has a real estate rental loss in excess of the amount that can be deducted under the real estate rental exception, that excess is treated as a passive loss.

EXAMPLE 54 Brad, who has $90,000 of AGI before considering rental activities, has $85,000 of losses from a real estate rental activity in which he actively participates. He also actively participates in another real estate rental activity from which he has $25,000 of income. He has other passive income of $36,000. The net rental loss of $60,000 is offset by the $36,000 of passive income, leaving $24,000 that can be deducted against other income. ▼

The $25,000 offset allowance is an aggregate of both deductions and credits in deduction equivalents. The deduction equivalent of a passive activity credit is the amount of deductions that reduces the tax liability for the taxable year by an amount equal to the credit.[52] A taxpayer with $5,000 of credits and a marginal tax rate of 28 percent would have a deduction equivalent of $17,857 ($5,000/28%).

If total deductions and deduction equivalents exceed $25,000, the taxpayer must allocate on a pro rata basis. First, the allowance must be allocated among the losses (including real estate rental activity losses suspended in prior years) and then to credits in the following order: (1) credits other than rehabilitation credits, (2) rehabilitation credits, and (3) low-income housing credits.

EXAMPLE 55 Kevin is an active participant in a real estate rental activity that produces $8,000 of income, $26,000 of deductions, and $1,500 of credits. Kevin, who has a 28% marginal tax rate, may deduct the net passive loss of $18,000 ($8,000 − $26,000). After deducting the loss, he has an available deduction equivalent of $7,000 ($25,000 − $18,000 passive loss). Therefore, the

---

[52] § 469(j)(5).

maximum amount of credits that he may claim is $1,960 ($7,000 × 28%). Since the actual credits are less than this amount, Kevin may claim the entire $1,500 credit. ▼

EXAMPLE 56

Kelly, who has a 28% marginal tax rate, is an active participant in three separate real estate rental activities. The relevant tax results for each activity are as follows:

- Activity A: $20,000 of losses.
- Activity B: $10,000 of losses.
- Activity C: $4,200 of credits.

Kelly's deduction equivalent from the credits is $15,000 ($4,200/28%). Therefore, the total passive deductions and deduction equivalents are $45,000 ($20,000 + $10,000 + $15,000), which exceeds the maximum allowable amount of $25,000. Consequently, Kelly must allocate pro rata first from among losses and then from among credits. Deductions from losses are limited as follows:

- Activity A: $25,000 × [$20,000/($20,000 + $10,000)] = $16,667.
- Activity B: $25,000 × [$10,000/($20,000 + $10,000)] = $8,333.

Since the amount of passive deductions exceeds the $25,000 maximum, the deduction balance of $5,000 and passive credits of $4,200 must be carried forward. Kelly's suspended losses and credits by activity are as follows:

	Total	Activity A	Activity B	Activity C
Allocated losses	$ 30,000	$ 20,000	$ 10,000	$ –0–
Allocated credits	4,200	–0–	–0–	4,200
Utilized losses	(25,000)	(16,667)	(8,333)	–0–
Suspended losses	5,000	3,333	1,667	–0–
Suspended credits	4,200	–0–	–0–	4,200

▼

DISPOSITION OF PASSIVE ACTIVITIES

Recall from an earlier discussion that if a taxpayer disposes of an entire interest in a passive activity, any suspended losses (and in certain cases, suspended credits) may be utilized when calculating the final economic gain or loss on the investment. In addition, if a loss ultimately results, that loss can be offset against other types of income. However, the consequences may differ if the activity is disposed of in a transaction that is not fully taxable. For example, if an interest in a passive activity is disposed of by gift, the suspended losses are added to the basis of the property.[53] Other rules apply if the activity is transferred in a nontaxable exchange, at death, or in an installment sale.

PLANNING CONSIDERATIONS

Utilizing Passive Losses

Taxpayers who have passive activity losses (PALs) should adopt a strategy of generating passive activity income that can be sheltered by existing passive losses. One approach is to buy an interest in a passive activity that is generating income (referred to as a passive income generator, or PIG). Then the PAL can offset

---
[53] § 469(j)(6).

income from the PIG. From a tax perspective, it would be foolish to buy a loss-generating passive activity (PAL) unless one has passive income to shelter or the activity is rental real estate that can qualify for the $25,000 exception or the exception available to real estate professionals.

A taxpayer with existing passive losses might consider buying rental property. If a large down payment is made and the straight-line method of MACRS (refer to Chapter 4) is elected, taxable income could be realized. The income would be sheltered by other passive losses, and depreciation expense would be spread out evenly and preserved for future years. Future gain realized upon the sale of the rental property could be sheltered by existing suspended passive losses.

Taxpayers with passive losses should consider all other trades or businesses in which they have an interest. If they show that they do not materially participate in the activity, the activity becomes a passive activity. Existing passive losses and suspended losses could shelter any income generated. Family partnerships in which certain members do not materially participate would qualify. The silent partner in any general partnership engaged in a trade or business would also qualify.

The passive loss rules can have a dramatic effect on a taxpayer's ability to claim passive losses currently. However, several steps can be taken to mitigate their impact:

- Replace passive activity debt with home equity indebtedness, which provides deductible interest to individuals (see Chapter 15).
- Carefully select the year in which a passive activity is to be disposed of at a gain, as it can be to the taxpayer's advantage to wait until sufficient passive losses have been generated to completely offset the gain recognized on the asset's disposition.
- Keep accurate records of all sources of income and losses, particularly any suspended passive losses and credits and the activities to which they relate, so that their potential tax benefit will not be lost.

KEY TERMS

Active income, 5–18

At-risk limitation, 5–16

Bad debt, 5–2

Business bad debt, 5–3

Casualty loss, 5–7

Closely held C corporation, 5–24

Disaster area losses, 5–9

Extraordinary personal services, 5–31

Material participation, 5–26

Net operating loss (NOL), 5–13

Nonbusiness bad debt, 5–3

Passive loss, 5–16

Personal service corporation, 5–23

Portfolio income, 5–19

Rental activity, 5–30

Reserve method, 5–3

Significant participation activity, 5–27

Small business stock (§ 1244 stock), 5–6

Specific charge-off method, 5–3

Tax shelters, 5–15

Theft loss, 5–8

Worthless securities, 5–5

Problem Materials

1. Several years ago Loon Finance Company lent Scott $20,000 to help him start a new business. In May of the current year, Scott filed for bankruptcy, and Loon was notified that it could expect to receive no more than 60 cents on the dollar. As of the end of the current year, Loon has not received any payments. Loon has contacted you about the possibility of taking a bad debt deduction of $8,000 for the current year. Assume that the company uses the specific charge-off method of accounting for bad debts.

    Write a letter to Loon Finance Company that contains your advice as to whether it can claim a bad debt deduction of $8,000 for the current year. Also, prepare a memo for the tax files. Loon's address is 100 Tyler Lane, Erie, PA 16563.

2. In 1996, Morgan lent the Peach Company $50,000. In 1997, Peach Company declared bankruptcy, and Morgan was told that he probably would receive $5,000 of the loan in settlement. In 1998, Morgan actually received $3,000 in final settlement on the loan. Determine Morgan's possible deductions with respect to the loan for 1996, 1997, and 1998.

3. Zenith, a single individual, had the following items for 1998:

    - Salary of $75,000.
    - Gain of $19,000 on the sale of § 1244 stock acquired three years ago.
    - Loss of $71,000 on the sale of § 1244 stock acquired two years ago.
    - Stock acquired on June 20, 1997, for $2,500 became worthless on April 3, 1998.

    Determine the impact of the above items on Zenith's income for 1998.

4. Mary, a single taxpayer, purchased 10,000 shares of § 1244 stock several years ago at a cost of $20 per share. In November of the current year, Mary receives an offer to sell the stock for $12 per share. She has the option of either selling all of the stock now or selling half of the stock now and half of the stock in January of next year. Mary's salary is $80,000 for the current year and will be $90,000 next year. Mary has long-term capital gains of $8,000 for the current year and will have $10,000 next year. If Mary's goal is to minimize her AGI for the two years, determine whether she should sell all of her stock this year or half of her stock this year and half next year.

5. When Helen returned from a vacation in Hawaii on November 8, 1998, she discovered that a burglar had stolen her silver, stereo, and color television. In the process of removing these items, the burglar damaged some furniture that originally cost $1,400. Helen's silver cost $12,000 and was valued at $16,500; the stereo system cost $8,400 and was valued at $6,200; the television cost $840 and was worth $560. Helen filed a claim with her insurance company and was reimbursed in the following amounts on December 20, 1998.

Silver	$2,800
Stereo	5,600
Television	490

    The insurance company disputed the reimbursement claimed by Helen for the damaged furniture, but she protested and was finally paid $280 on January 30, 1999. The repairs to the furniture totaled $1,550. Helen's AGI was $20,000 for 1998 and $500 for 1999. How much can Helen claim as a casualty and theft loss? In which year?

6. Upon returning home from a night out, John, an antique collector, found that a fire had damaged his home and destroyed some of his antiques. John's home was covered by an insurance policy that had a 20% deductible clause. The antiques were insured for their fair market value. Information with respect to the damaged and destroyed assets follows.

CHAPTER 5 Losses and Loss Limitations

Asset	Cost	FMV Before	FMV After	Insurance Recovery
Home	$250,000	$300,000	$175,000	$100,000
Antique clock	1,500	2,000	–0–	2,000
Antique table	4,000	3,000	–0–	3,000
Antique organ	15,000	20,000	–0–	20,000

If John's AGI is $80,000 before considering the effects of the fire, determine his deductible loss *from* AGI (i.e., his casualty loss itemized deduction).

7. Grackle Farming, Inc., owns a 500-acre farm in Minnesota. A tornado hit the area and destroyed a farm building and some farm equipment and damaged a barn. Fortunately for Grackle, the tornado occurred after the company had harvested its corn crop. Applicable information is as follows:

Asset	Cost	FMV Before	FMV After	Insurance Recovery
Building	$80,000	$100,000	$ –0–	$60,000
Equipment	40,000	50,000	–0–	25,000
Barn	90,000	120,000	90,000	25,000

Because of the extensive damage caused by the tornado, the President designated the area as a disaster area.

Grackle had $90,000 of taxable income last year. The company's taxable income for the current year, excluding the loss from the tornado, is $220,000.

Determine the amount of the corporation's loss and the year in which it should take the loss.

8. Toucan Corporation purchased an office building many years ago. The property included a large black oak tree approximately 80 feet in height and about 100 years old. The tree was the dominant feature in the front of the building, where it stood alone next to the street. Because of the age and stature of the tree, the corporation had it inspected regularly by a tree expert. In August of the current year, the corporation's CEO noticed that the entire top or crown of the tree had turned brown. Because none of the leaves on other trees in the area had turned brown, the tree expert was called in to inspect the tree. The inspection showed that the tree had been attacked by woodborers and was beyond saving and effectively dead. Identify the relevant tax issues for Toucan Corporation.

9. On January 7 of the current year, Sam dropped off to sleep while driving home from a business trip. Luckily, he was only slightly injured in the resulting accident, but the company car that he was driving was completely destroyed.

Sam is an employee of Snipe Industries. The corporation purchased the car new two years ago for $25,000. The automobile had a fair market value of $19,000 before the accident and $12,000 after the accident. The car was covered by an insurance policy that had a $1,000 deductible clause. The corporation is afraid that the policy will be canceled if it makes a claim for the damages. Therefore, Snipe is considering not filing a claim. The company believes that the casualty loss deduction will help mitigate the loss of the insurance reimbursement. The corporation's taxable income for the current year is $90,000.

Write a letter to Snipe Industries that contains your advice regarding the filing of an insurance claim for reimbursement for the damages to the company's car. Snipe Industries' address is 450 Colonel's Way, Warrensburg, MO 64093.

10. Assume the same facts as in Problem 9, except that Sam owns the car and it is a personal-use asset. Sam is considering not filing an insurance claim because his policy might be canceled. Would your advice regarding the insurance claim change? Why or why not?

11. In 1998, Fred invested $50,000 in a partnership. Fred's interest is not considered to be a passive activity. In 1998, his share of the partnership loss was $35,000, and in 1999, his share of the loss is $25,000. How much can Fred deduct in 1998 and 1999?

12. In the current year, Bill Parker (54 Oak Drive, St. Paul, MN 55162) is considering making an investment of $60,000 in Best Choice Partnership. The prospectus provided by Bill's broker indicates that the partnership investment is not a passive activity and that Bill's share of the entity's loss in the current year will likely be $40,000, while his share of the partnership loss next year will probably be $25,000. Write a letter to Bill in which you indicate how the losses would be treated for tax purposes in the current and next years.

13. In the current year, George and Susie White, both successful CPAs, paid cash for a limited partnership interest in a California avocado grove. In addition to the cash generated from the Whites, the grove's management borrowed a substantial sum to purchase assets necessary for its operation. The Whites' investment adviser told them that their share of the tax loss in the first year alone would be in excess of their initial cash investment, followed by several more years of losses. They feel confident that their interest in the avocado grove is a sound investment. Identify the tax issues facing the Whites.

14. Carmen wishes to invest $25,000 in a relatively safe venture and has discovered two alternatives that would produce the following income and loss over the next three years:

Year	Alternative 1 Income (Loss)	Alternative 2 Income (Loss)
1	($ 15,000)	($30,000)
2	(15,000)	20,000
3	45,000	25,000

She is interested in the after-tax effects of these alternatives over a three-year horizon. Assume that:

- Carmen's investment portfolio produces sufficient passive income to offset any potential passive loss that may arise from these alternatives.

- Carmen's marginal tax rate is 28%, and her cost of capital is 8% (the present value factors are 0.92593, 0.85734, and 0.79383).

- Each investment alternative possesses equal growth potential and comparable financial risk.

- In the loss years for each alternative, there is no cash flow from or to the investment (i.e., the loss is due to depreciation), while in those years when the income is positive, cash flows to Carmen equal the amount of the income.

Based on these facts, compute the present value of these two investment alternatives and determine which option Carmen should choose.

15. In 1994, Kay acquired an interest in a partnership in which she is not a material participant. The partnership was profitable until 1998. Kay's basis in her partnership interest at the beginning of 1998 was $40,000. In 1998, Kay's share of the partnership loss was $35,000. In 1999, her share of the partnership income was $15,000. How much can Kay deduct in 1998 and 1999?

16. Sarah has $100,000 that she wishes to invest, and she is considering the following two options:

- Option A—Investment in Bluebird Equity Mutual Fund, which would be expected to produce dividends of $8,000 per year.

- Option B—Investment in Redbird Limited Partnership (buys, sells, and operates avocado groves). Sarah's share of the partnership's income and loss over the next three years is expected to be:

CHAPTER 5 Losses and Loss Limitations

Year	Income (Loss)
1	($ 8,000)
2	(2,000)
3	34,000

Sarah is interested in the after-tax effects of these alternatives over a three-year horizon. Assume that:

- Sarah's investment portfolio produces no passive income.
- Sarah's cost of capital is 8% (the present value factors are 0.92593, 0.85734, and 0.79383), and her marginal tax rate is 31%.
- Each investment alternative possesses equal growth potential and equal financial risk.

Based on these facts, compute the present value of these two investment alternatives and determine which option Sarah should choose.

17. Leanne has investments in four passive activity partnerships purchased several years ago. Last year, the income and losses were as follows:

Activity	Income (Loss)
A	$ 60,000
B	(30,000)
C	(30,000)
D	(40,000)

In the current year, she sold her interest in Activity D for a $20,000 gain. Activity D, which had been profitable until last year, had a current loss of $1,000. How will the sale of Activity D affect Leanne's taxable income in the current year?

18. Leon sells his interest in a passive activity for $100,000 during the year. Determine the tax effect based on each of the following sets of independent facts:
    a. His adjusted basis in this investment is $35,000. Losses from prior years that were not deductible due to the passive loss restrictions total $40,000.
    b. His adjusted basis in this investment is $75,000. Losses from prior years that were not deductible due to the passive loss restrictions total $40,000.
    c. His adjusted basis in this investment is $75,000. Losses from prior years that were not deductible due to the passive loss restrictions total $40,000. In addition, suspended credits total $10,000.

19. Brown Corporation, a personal service corporation, earns active income of $500,000 in the current year. The corporation receives $60,000 in interest during the current year. In addition, Brown incurs a loss of $80,000 from an investment in a passive activity acquired three years ago. What is Brown's income for the current year after considering the passive investment?

20. White, Inc., earns $400,000 from operations in the current year. White also receives $36,000 in interest on various investments. During the year, White pays $150,000 to acquire a 20% interest in a passive activity that produces a $200,000 loss.
    a. How will these facts affect White's taxable income, assuming the corporation is a personal service corporation?
    b. How will these facts affect White's taxable income, assuming the corporation is a closely held, non-personal service corporation?

21. Green Corporation, a closely held C corporation, earns active income of $50,000 in the current year. Green receives $60,000 in interest during the year. In addition, Green

incurs a loss of $80,000 from an investment in a passive activity acquired last year. What is Green's net income for the current year after considering the passive investment?

22. Eleanor owns interests in a hardware store, bowling alley, and grocery store. Several full-time employees work at each enterprise. As of the end of November of the current year, Eleanor has worked 150 hours in the hardware store, 250 hours at the bowling alley, and 80 hours at the grocery store. In reviewing her financial records, you learn that she has no profitable passive investments; she expects these three ventures collectively to produce a loss. What recommendation would you offer Eleanor as she plans her activities for the remainder of the year?

23. Greg Reynolds (66 Hanover Street, Cincinnati, OH 45230), a syndicated radio talk show host, earns a $400,000 salary in the current year. He works approximately 30 hours per week in this job, which leaves him time to participate in several businesses he acquired in the current year. He owns a movie theater and a drugstore in Cincinnati. He also owns a movie theater and a drugstore in Indianapolis and a drugstore in Louisville. A preliminary analysis on December 1 of the current year shows projected income and losses for the various businesses as follows:

	Income (Loss)
Cincinnati movie theater (95 hours participation)	$ 56,000
Cincinnati drugstore (140 hours participation)	(89,000)
Indianapolis movie theater (90 hours participation)	34,000
Indianapolis drugstore (170 hours participation)	(41,000)
Louisville drugstore (180 hours participation)	(15,000)

Greg has full-time employees at each of the five businesses listed above. Consider all possible groupings for Greg's activities. Write a letter to him suggesting the grouping method and other strategies that will provide the greatest tax advantage. Greg does not know much about the tax law, so you should provide a concise, nontechnical explanation.

24. Rene retired from public accounting after a long and successful career of 45 years. As part of her retirement package, she continues to share in the profits and losses of the firm, albeit at a lower rate than when she was working full-time. Because Rene wants to stay busy during her retirement years, she has invested and works in a local hardware business, operated as a partnership. Unfortunately, the business has recently gone through a slump and has not been generating profits. Identify relevant tax issues for Rene.

25. Lee acquired a 20% interest in the ABC Partnership for $60,000 in 1993. The partnership was profitable until 1998, and Lee's amount at risk in the partnership interest was $120,000 at the end of 1997. ABC incurs a loss of $400,000 in 1998 and reports income of $200,000 in 1999. Assuming Lee is not a material participant in ABC, how much of his loss from ABC Partnership is deductible in 1998 and 1999, respectively?

26. Ken has a $40,000 loss from an investment in a partnership in which he does not participate. He paid $30,000 for his interest in the partnership. How much of the loss is disallowed by the at-risk rules? How much is disallowed by the passive loss rules?

27. Last year, Fran invested $40,000 for an interest in a partnership in which she is a material participant. Her share of the partnership's loss for the year was $50,000. In the current year, Fran's share of the partnership's income is $30,000. What is the effect on her taxable income for the current year?

28. Soong, a physician, earns $200,000 from his practice. He also receives $18,000 in dividends and interest on various portfolio investments. During the year, he pays $45,000 to acquire a 20% interest in a partnership that produces a $300,000 loss.
   a. What is the effect of the partnership loss on Soong's income assuming he was not a material participant during the year?

b. What is the effect of the partnership loss on Soong's income assuming he was a material participant during the year?

29. During the current year, Alan is determined to make better use of the tax losses that tend to flow from the various businesses that he owns. He is particularly sensitive to the limitations that the passive loss rules place on the deductibility of losses because of the disaster that occurred last year. His accountant informed him that he would not be able to claim any of the losses on his income tax return because of his lack of material participation. He has even suggested to his wife that she may have to put in some time at the businesses if his goals are to be accomplished. Identify the tax issues that Alan faces.

30. Sam invested $150,000 in a passive activity five years ago. On January 1, 1997, his amount at risk in the activity was $30,000. His share of income and loss in the activity for 1997 to 1999 was:

Year	Income (Loss)
1997	($ 40,000)
1998	(30,000)
1999	50,000

How much can Sam deduct in 1997 and 1998? What is his taxable income from the activity in 1999? Keep in mind the at-risk rules as well as the passive loss rules.

31. Joe Cook (125 Hill Street, Charleston, WV 25311) acquired an activity four years ago. The loss from the activity is $50,000 in the current year. He also earns a salary of $140,000 as a computer programmer in the current year. The activity is an apartment building in an exclusive part of the city, and Joe is an active participant. Joe has also informed you that he may not participate in the activity next year. Write a letter to Joe explaining the current tax impact of the loss and the consequences of not actively participating next year.

32. During the current year, Donald works 1,200 hours as a computer consultant, 600 hours in a real estate development business, and 500 hours in real estate rental activities. He earns $60,000 as a computer consultant, but loses $18,000 in the development business and $26,000 in the real estate rental business. How should Donald treat the losses on his current Federal income tax return?

33. You have just met with Scott Myers (603 Pittsfield Dr., Champaign, IL 61821), a successful full-time real estate developer and investor. During your meeting you discussed his tax situation, because you are starting to prepare his 1998 Federal income tax return. During your meeting, Scott mentioned that he and his wife, Susan, went to great lengths to maximize their participation in an apartment complex that they own and manage. In particular, Scott included the following activities in the 540 hours of participation for the current year:

- Time spent thinking about the rentals.

- Time spent by Susan on weekdays visiting the apartment complex to oversee operations of the buildings (i.e., in a management role).

- Time spent by both Scott and Susan on weekends visiting the apartment complex to assess operations. Scott and Susan always visited the complex together on weekends and both counted their hours (i.e., one hour at the complex was two hours of participation).

- Time spent on weekends driving around the community looking for other potential rental properties to purchase. Again, both Scott's hours and Susan's hours were counted, even when they drove together.

After reviewing Scott's records, you note that the apartment complex generated a significant loss this year. Prepare a letter to Scott describing your position on the deductibility of the loss.

34. During the current year, Roger performs the following personal services in three separate activities: 800 hours as a CPA, 400 hours in a real estate development business (he is not a material participant), and 600 hours in an apartment leasing operation. He expects that losses will be realized from the two real estate ventures while his CPA practice will show a profit. Roger files a joint return with his wife whose salary is $200,000. What is the character of the income and loss generated by these activities?

35. During the current year, Gene performs services as follows: 1,800 hours as a CPA in his tax practice and 50 hours in an apartment leasing operation in which he has a 15% interest. Because of his oversight duties, Gene is considered to be an active participant in the leasing operation. He expects that his share of the loss realized from the apartment leasing operation will be $30,000 while his tax practice will show a profit of approximately $80,000. Gene is single and has no other income besides that stated above. Discuss the character of income and losses generated by these activities.

36. Ted, a management consultant, owns an apartment complex that produces a profit of $60,000 in the current year. He earned $120,000 in his consulting business and had a $40,000 loss on a passive activity (not real estate). Ted worked for 800 hours at the apartment complex during the year, but characterizes the $60,000 profit as passive income so he can utilize the $40,000 passive loss. He claims that he is doing nothing wrong because the law is designed only to protect the passive loss deduction of real estate professionals and is not applicable to profits.

    Further, Ted thinks that he is justified in classifying the loss as passive because of the nature of the work he performed during the time devoted to managing the apartments. Ted feels certain that, of the 800 hours, between 300 and 400 hours were spent coaching and supporting about 20 underprivileged children living in the apartment complex as part of a year-round sports program. Ted says that his involvement not only benefits the children, but will make the apartment a more desirable place to live and thus could also benefit him economically in the long run. He sees the hours devoted to the sports program as an integral part of his job in managing the apartment complex, but feels that they should not count in determining whether the activity is passive. Ted asks you to prepare his return. What actions will you take?

37. Ida, who has AGI of $80,000 before considering rental activities, is active in three separate real estate rental activities. Ida has a marginal tax rate of 28%. She has $12,000 of losses from Activity A, $18,000 of losses from Activity B, and income of $10,000 from Activity C. She also has $2,100 of tax credits from Activity A. Calculate her deductions and credits allowed and the suspended losses and credits.

38. Ella has $105,000 of losses from a real estate rental activity in which she actively participates. She has other rent income of $25,000 and other passive income of $32,000. How much rental loss can Ella deduct against active and portfolio income (ignoring the at-risk rules)? Does she have any suspended losses to carry over?

RESEARCH PROBLEMS

*Note: The **RIA OnPoint System 4 Student Version CD-ROM** available with this text can be used in preparing solutions to the Research Problems. Alternatively, tax research materials contained in a standard tax library can be used.*

39. George Johnson, a Minnesota resident, parked his car on a lake while he was watching an iceboat race. During the race, the ice beneath his car unexpectedly gave way, and the car sank to the bottom of the lake. Write a letter to George advising him as to whether he can claim a casualty loss for the damage to the car. Also, prepare a memo for the tax files. George's address is 100 Apple Lane, St. Paul, MN 55123.

40. Bill owns an interest in a small engine repair shop in which he works 425 hours during the year. He has four full-time employees at the repair shop. Bill also owns an apartment building to which he devotes 1,300 hours during the year. He has no employees for the apartment activity. Are these activities active or passive? In your response, consider the impact of the significant participation rules.

41. Over the years, Bill Johnson (30 Brookfield Drive, Hampton, VA 23666) has taken great pride in his ability to spot exceptional rental real estate investments, particularly in terms of their appreciation potential. As a result, he has accumulated several properties. In the early years of his investment activities, he was able to devote only a limited amount of time to these ventures. In the current year, he retires from his full-time job and is able to devote most of his time to the management and operation of the rental activities. Bill summarizes the relevant tax attributes of each of the properties as follows:

Property	Suspended Passive Losses	Expected Current Year's Income (Loss)
A	None	$ 25,000
B	($ 20,000)	15,000
C	(40,000)	(15,000)

Bill is astute enough to know that he is a qualifying real estate professional for the current year. He materially participates in all three properties within the meaning of § 469(c)(7)(A). However, he is uncertain whether he should treat the properties as three separate activities or aggregate them and treat them as one activity.

Write a letter to Bill to assist him in making a decision. Because of Bill's expertise in the tax law, feel free to use technical language in your letter.

Partial list of research aids:
Reg. § 1.469–9(e).

CHAPTER 6

ACCOUNTING PERIODS AND METHODS

LEARNING OBJECTIVES

After completing Chapter 6, you should be able to:

1. Understand the relevance of the accounting period concept, the different types of accounting periods, and the limitations on their use.

2. Utilize the procedure for changing accounting methods.

3. Determine when the installment method of accounting can be used and apply the related calculation techniques.

4. Understand the alternative methods of accounting for long-term contracts (the completed contract method and the percentage of completion method) including the limitations on the use of the completed contract method.

5. Know when accounting for inventories is required, recognize the types of costs that must be included in inventories, and apply the LIFO method.

OUTLINE

Accounting Periods, 6–2
In General, 6–2
Specific Provisions for Partnerships, S Corporations, and Personal Service Corporations, 6–3
Making the Election, 6–6
Changes in the Accounting Period, 6–7
Taxable Periods of Less Than One Year, 6–7
Mitigation of the Annual Accounting Period Concept, 6–8

Change of Accounting Methods, 6–9
Correction of an Error, 6–10
Change from an Incorrect Method, 6–11
Net Adjustments Due to Change in Accounting Method, 6–11
Installment Method, 6–12
In General, 6–12
Contingent Sales Prices, 6–15
Imputed Interest, 6–16
Related-Party Sales, 6–17

Disposition of Installment Obligations, 6–19
Interest on Deferred Taxes, 6–20
Electing Out of the Installment Method, 6–20
Long-Term Contracts, 6–21
Completed Contract Method, 6–24
Percentage of Completion Method, 6–24
Inventories, 6–26
Determining Inventory Cost, 6–27
The LIFO Election, 6–30

Tax practitioners must deal with the issue of *when* particular items of income and expense are recognized as well as the basic issue of *whether* the items are includible in taxable income. Earlier chapters discussed the types of income subject to tax and allowable deductions (the *whether* issue) and explained the principal tax accounting methods available.[1] This chapter examines in more detail the issue of the periods in which income and deductions are reported (the *when* issue). Generally, a taxpayer's income and deductions must be assigned to particular 12-month periods—calendar years or fiscal years.

Income and deductions are placed within particular years through the use of tax accounting methods. As explained in Chapters 3 and 4, the basic accounting methods are the cash method, accrual method, and hybrid method. Other special purpose methods, such as the installment method and the methods used for long-term construction contracts, are available for specific circumstances or types of transactions.

Over the long run, the accounting period used by a taxpayer will not affect the aggregate amount of reported taxable income. However, taxable income for any particular year may vary significantly due to the use of a particular reporting period. Also, through the choice of accounting methods or accounting periods, it is possible to postpone the recognition of taxable income and to defer payment of the related tax. This chapter discusses the various alternatives for accounting periods and accounting methods.

ACCOUNTING PERIODS

IN GENERAL

1 LEARNING OBJECTIVE
Understand the relevance of the accounting period concept, the different types of accounting periods, and the limitations on their use.

A taxpayer who keeps adequate books and records may be allowed to elect a **fiscal year**, a 12-month period ending on the *last day* of a month other than December, for the **accounting period**. Otherwise, a *calendar year* must be used.[2] Frequently, corporations and other business entities can satisfy the record-keeping requirements

---
[1] Refer to Chapters 3 and 4.
[2] § 441(g).

and elect to use a fiscal year.[3] Often the fiscal year conforms to a natural business year (e.g., a summer resort's fiscal year may end on September 30, after the close of the season). Individuals seldom use a fiscal year because they do not maintain the necessary books and records, and because complications can arise as a result of changes in the tax law (e.g., often the transition rules and effective dates differ for fiscal year taxpayers).

Generally, a taxable year may not exceed 12 calendar months. However, if certain requirements are met, a taxpayer may elect to use an annual period that varies from 52 to 53 weeks.[4] In that case, the year-end must be on the same day of the week (e.g., the Tuesday falling closest to October 31 or the last Tuesday in October). The day of the week selected for ending the year will depend upon business considerations. For example, a retail business that is not open on Sundays may end its tax year on a Sunday so that it can take an inventory without interrupting business operations.

EXAMPLE 1

Wren Corporation is in the business of selling farm supplies. Its natural business year terminates at the end of October with the completion of harvesting. At the end of the fiscal year, Wren must take an inventory, which is most easily accomplished on a Tuesday. Therefore, Wren could adopt a 52–53 week tax year ending on the Tuesday closest to October 31. If Wren selects this method, the year-end date may fall in the following month if that Tuesday is closer to October 31. The tax year ending in 1998 will contain 53 weeks beginning on Wednesday, October 29, 1997, and ending on Tuesday, November 3, 1998. The tax year ending in 1999 will have 52 weeks beginning on Wednesday, November 4, 1998, and ending on Tuesday, November 2, 1999. ▼

SPECIFIC PROVISIONS FOR PARTNERSHIPS, S CORPORATIONS, AND PERSONAL SERVICE CORPORATIONS

Partnerships and S Corporations. When a partner's tax year and the partnership's tax year differ, the partner will enjoy a deferral of income. This results because the partner reports his or her share of the partnership's income and deductions for the partnership's tax year ending within or with the partner's tax year.[5] For example, if the tax year of the partnership ends on January 31, a calendar year partner will not report partnership profits for the first 11 months of the partnership tax year until the following year. Therefore, partnerships are subject to special tax year requirements.

In general, the partnership tax year must be the same as the tax year of the majority interest partner. A **majority interest partner** is a partner who owns a greater-than-50 percent interest in the partnership capital and profits. If there is no majority owner the partnership must adopt the same tax year as its principal partners. A **principal partner** is a partner with a 5 percent or more interest in the partnership capital or profits.[6]

EXAMPLE 2

The RST Partnership is owned equally by Rose Corporation, Silver Corporation, and Tom. The partners have the following tax years.

	Partner's Tax Year Ending
Rose	June 30
Silver	June 30
Tom	December 31

---

[3] Temp.Reg. § 1.441–1T(e)(2).
[4] § 441(f).
[5] Reg. § 1.706–1(a).
[6] §§ 706(b)(1)(B) and (b)(3).

The partnership's tax year must end on June 30. If Silver Corporation's as well as Tom's year ended on December 31, the partnership would be required to adopt a calendar year. ▼

If the principal partners do not all have the same tax year and no majority of partners have the same tax year, the partnership must use a year that results in the *least aggregate deferral* of income.[7] Under the **least aggregate deferral method**, the different tax years of the principal partners are tested to determine which produces the least aggregate deferral. This is calculated by first multiplying the combined percentages of the principal partners with the same tax year by the months of deferral for the test year. Once this is done for each set of principal partners with the same tax year, the resulting products are summed to produce the aggregate deferral. After calculating the aggregate deferral for each of the test years, the test year with the smallest summation (the least aggregate deferral) is the tax year for the partnership.

▼ **EXAMPLE 3**

The DE Partnership is owned equally by Dove Corporation and Egret, Inc. Dove's fiscal year ends on March 31, and Egret's fiscal year ends on August 31. The partnership must use the partner's fiscal year that will result in the least aggregate deferral of income. Therefore, the fiscal years ending March 31 and August 31 must both be tested.

Test for Fiscal Year Ending March 31

Partner	Year Ends	Profit %	Months of Deferral	Product
Dove	3–31	50	0	0
Egret	8–31	50	5	2.5
Aggregate deferral months				2.5

Thus, with a year ending March 31, Egret would be able to defer its half of the income for five months. That is, Egret's share of the partnership income for the fiscal year ending March 31, 1999, would not be included in its income until August 31, 1999.

Test for Fiscal Year Ending August 31

Partner	Year Ends	Profit %	Months of Deferral	Product
Dove	3–31	50	7	3.5
Egret	8–31	50	0	0
Aggregate deferral months				3.5

Thus, with a year ending August 31, Dove would be able to defer its half of the income for seven months. That is, Dove's share of the partnership income for the fiscal year ending August 31, 1999, would not be included in its income until March 31, 2000.

The year ending March 31 must be used because it results in the least aggregate deferral of income. ▼

Generally, S corporations must adopt a calendar year.[8] However, partnerships and S corporations may *elect* an otherwise *impermissible year* under any of the following conditions:

---

[7] Temp.Reg. § 1.706–1T(a)(2).

[8] §§ 1378(a) and (b).

- A business purpose for the year can be demonstrated.[9]
- The partnership's or S corporation's year results in a deferral of not more than three months' income, and the entity agrees to make required tax payments.[10]
- The entity retains the same year as was used for the fiscal year ending in 1987, provided the entity agrees to make required tax payments.

Business Purpose. The only business purpose for a fiscal year that the IRS has acknowledged is the need to conform the tax year to the *natural business year* of an entity.[11] An objective *gross receipts test* is applied to determine if the entity has a natural business year. At least 25 percent of the entity's gross receipts for the 12-month period must be realized in the final 2 months of the 12-month period for three consecutive years. Generally, only seasonal businesses qualify under this test.

EXAMPLE 4

A Virginia Beach motel had gross receipts as follows:

	1996	1997	1998
July–August receipts	$ 300,000	$250,000	$ 325,000
September 1–August 31 receipts	1,000,000	900,000	1,250,000
Receipts for 2 months divided by receipts for 12 months	30.0%	27.8%	26.0%

Since it satisfies the natural business year test, the motel will be allowed to use a fiscal year ending August 31. ▼

Required Tax Payments. For S corporations and partnerships that do not wish to use a required year or a business purpose year, another year-end may be elected, as long as the resulting deferral period does not exceed three months. This election is not free of costs. In particular, the electing entity must make a *required tax payment* for any year that the election is in effect.[12] The required tax payment is a refundable, non-interest-bearing deposit (not deductible for Federal tax purposes) made to the IRS. The deposit compensates the government for the interest lost on any deferred tax liability. The required tax payment is credited against future required tax payments or returned in the following year if the entity's partners or shareholders are required to pay tax on previously deferred income.

The amount due is computed by applying the highest individual tax rate plus 1 percent to an estimate of the deferral period income. The deferral period runs from the close of the fiscal year to the end of the calendar year. Estimated income for this period is based on the average monthly earnings for the previous fiscal year. The amount due is reduced by the balance of required tax payments on deposit for the previous year.[13]

EXAMPLE 5

Brown, Inc., an S corporation, elected a fiscal year ending September 30. Bob, a calendar year taxpayer, is the only shareholder. For the fiscal year ending September 30, 1998, Brown earned $100,000. Brown is permitted to have a September 30 fiscal year, since that year-end will result in only a three-month deferral of income for Bob. An annual tax payment is also

---

[9] §§ 706(b)(1)(C) and 1378(b)(2).
[10] §§ 444(b)(1) and (c)(1).
[11] Rev.Rul. 87–57, 1987–2 C.B. 117, and Rev.Proc. 87–32, 1987–1 C.B. 131.
[12] §§ 444(c) and 7519. No payment is required if the calculated amount is $500 or less.
[13] § 7519(b).

required. If required tax payments for the previous year were $5,000, the corporation must pay $5,150 by April 15, 1999, calculated as follows:

$$(\$100,000 \times \text{^{3}}/_{12} \times 40.6\%^*) - \$5,000 \text{ (credit from prior year)} = \$5,150.$$

*Maximum § 1 rate of 39.6% + 1%. ▼

Personal Service Corporations. A **personal service corporation (PSC)** is a corporation whose shareholder-employees provide personal services (e.g., medical, dental, legal, accounting, engineering, actuarial, consulting, or performing arts). Generally, a PSC must use a calendar year.[14] However, a PSC can *elect* a fiscal year under any of the following conditions:

- A business purpose for the year can be demonstrated.
- The PSC year results in a deferral of not more than three months' income, the corporation pays the shareholder-employee's salary during the portion of the calendar year after the close of the fiscal year, and the salary for that period is at least proportionate to the shareholder-employee's salary received for the preceding fiscal year.[15]
- The PSC retains the same year it used for the fiscal year ending in 1987, provided it satisfies the latter two requirements in the preceding option.

▼ **EXAMPLE 6**

Nancy's personal service corporation paid Nancy a salary of $120,000 during its fiscal year ending September 30, 1998. The corporation cannot satisfy the business purpose test for a fiscal year. The corporation can continue to use its fiscal year without any negative tax effects, provided Nancy receives at least $30,000 [(3 months/12 months) × $120,000] as salary during the period October 1 through December 31, 1998. ▼

If the salary test is not satisfied, the PSC can retain the fiscal year, but the corporation's deduction for salary for the subsequent fiscal year is limited to the following:

$$A + A(F/N),$$

where A = Amount paid after the close of the fiscal year,
F = Number of months in fiscal year minus number of months from the end of the fiscal year to the end of the ongoing calendar year, and
N = Number of months from the end of the fiscal year to the end of the ongoing calendar year.

▼ **EXAMPLE 7**

Assume the corporation in the previous example paid Nancy $10,000 of salary during the period October 1 through December 31, 1998. The deduction for Nancy's salary for the corporation's fiscal year ending September 30, 1999 is thus limited to $40,000 calculated as follows:

$$\$10,000 + \left[\$10,000 \left(\frac{12-3}{3}\right)\right] = \$10,000 + \$30,000 = \$40,000.$$

▼

MAKING THE ELECTION

A taxpayer elects to use a calendar or fiscal year by the timely filing of the initial tax return. For all subsequent years, the taxpayer must use this same period unless approval for change is obtained from the IRS.[16]

---

[14] § 441(i).
[15] §§ 444(b)(1), (c)(2), and 280H.
[16] Temp.Reg. §§ 1.441–1T(b)(3) and (4).

CHAPTER 6 Accounting Periods and Methods

CHANGES IN THE ACCOUNTING PERIOD

A taxpayer must obtain consent from the IRS before changing the tax year.[17] This consent requirement is significant in that it permits the IRS to issue authoritative administrative guidelines that must be met by taxpayers who wish to change their accounting period. An application for permission to change tax years must be made on Form 1128, Application for Change in Accounting Period. The application must be filed on or before the fifteenth day of the second calendar month following the close of the short period that results from the change in accounting period.[18]

EXAMPLE 8 Beginning in 1998, Gold Corporation, a calendar year taxpayer, would like to switch to a fiscal year ending March 31. The first period after the change in accounting period (January 1, 1998 through March 31, 1998) is less than a 12-month period and is referred to as a *short period*. Thus, the corporation must file Form 1128 by May 15, 1998. ▼

IRS Requirements. The IRS will not grant permission for the change unless the taxpayer can establish a substantial business purpose for the request. One substantial business purpose is to change to a tax year that coincides with the *natural business year* (discussed earlier).[19]

The IRS usually establishes certain conditions that a taxpayer must accept if approval for the change is to be granted. In particular, if a taxpayer has a net operating loss for the short period, the IRS may require that the loss be carried forward and allocated equally over the 6 following years.[20] Net operating losses (refer to Chapter 5) are ordinarily carried back for 2 years and forward for 20 years.

EXAMPLE 9 Parrot Corporation changed from a calendar year to a fiscal year ending September 30. The short-period return for the nine months ending September 30, 1998, reflected a $60,000 net operating loss. The corporation had taxable income for 1996 and 1997. As a condition for granting approval, the IRS requires Parrot to allocate the $60,000 loss over the next six years, rather than carrying the loss back to the two preceding years (the usual order for applying a net operating loss). Thus, Parrot Corporation will reduce its taxable income by $10,000 each year ending September 30, 1999, through September 30, 2004. ▼

TAXABLE PERIODS OF LESS THAN ONE YEAR

A **short taxable year** (or **short period**) is a period of less than 12 calendar months. A taxpayer may have a short year for (1) the first income tax return, (2) the final income tax return, or (3) a change in the tax year. If the short period results from a change in the taxpayer's annual accounting period, the taxable income for the period must be annualized. Due to the progressive tax rate structure, taxpayers could reap benefits from a short-period return if some adjustments were not required. Thus, the taxpayer is required to do the following:

1. Annualize the short-period income.

$$\text{Annualized income} = \text{Short-period income} \times \frac{12}{\text{Number of months in the short period}}$$

2. Compute the tax on the annualized income.
3. Convert the tax on the annualized income to a short-period tax, as follows:

---

[17] § 442. Under certain conditions, corporations are allowed to change tax years without obtaining IRS approval. See Reg. § 1.442–1(c)(1).
[18] Reg. § 1.442–1(b)(1).
[19] Rev.Proc. 87–32, 1987–1 C.B. 131, and Rev.Rul. 87–57, 1987–2 C.B. 117.
[20] Rev.Proc. 85–16, 1985–1 C.B. 517.

$$\text{Short-period tax} = \text{Tax on annualized income} \times \frac{\text{Number of months in the short period}}{12}.$$

EXAMPLE 10

Gray Corporation obtained permission to change from a calendar year to a fiscal year ending September 30, beginning in 1998. For the short period January 1 through September 30, 1998, the corporation's taxable income was $48,000. The relevant tax rates and the resultant short-period tax are as follows:

Amount of Taxable Income	Tax Rates
$0–$50,000	15% of taxable income
Over $50,000 but not over $75,000	$7,500 plus 25% of taxable income in excess of $50,000

Calculation of Short-Period Tax

Annualized income ($48,000 × 12/9) =	$64,000
Tax on annualized income [$7,500 + 0.25($64,000 − $50,000)] =	$11,000
Short-period tax = ($11,000 × 9/12) =	$ 8,250
Annualizing the income increases the tax by $1,050:	
Tax with annualizing	$ 8,250
Tax without annualizing ($48,000 × 0.15)	(7,200)
Increase in tax from annualizing	$ 1,050

Rather than annualize the short-period income, the taxpayer can (1) elect to calculate the tax for a 12-month period beginning on the first day of the short period and (2) convert the tax in (1) to a short-period tax as follows:[21]

$$\frac{\text{Taxable income for short period}}{\text{Taxable income for the 12-month period}} \times \text{Tax on the 12 months of income}.$$

EXAMPLE 11

Assume Gray Corporation's taxable income for the calendar year 1998 was $60,000. The tax on the full 12 months of income would have been $10,000 [$7,500 + .25($60,000 − $50,000)]. The short-period tax would be $8,000 [($48,000/$60,000) × $10,000]. Thus, if the corporation utilized this option, the tax for the short period would be $8,000 (rather than $8,250, as calculated in the preceding example). ▼

For individuals, annualizing requires some special adjustments,[22] but individuals rarely change tax years.

MITIGATION OF THE ANNUAL ACCOUNTING PERIOD CONCEPT

Several provisions in the Code are designed to give the taxpayer relief from the harsh results that can be produced by the combined effects of an arbitrary accounting period and a progressive rate structure. For example, under the net operating loss carryback and carryover rules, a loss in one year can be carried back and offset against taxable income for the preceding 2 years. Unused net

---

[21] § 443(b)(1).   [22] § 443(b)(2) and Reg. § 1.443–1(a)(2).

operating losses are then carried over for 20 years.[23] In addition, the Code provides special relief provisions for casualty losses pursuant to a natural disaster and for the reporting of insurance proceeds from destruction of crops.[24]

Restoration of Amounts Received under a Claim of Right. According to the **claim of right doctrine**, a taxpayer must report as income any receipts that are in dispute, as long as that taxpayer has received the funds in question without restriction.[25] If subsequent events require the taxpayer to return the disputed amount, the taxpayer is allowed a deduction in the year of repayment.

This deduction, however, may not make the taxpayer whole. If the deduction occurs when the taxpayer is in a *lower* tax bracket, the taxpayer will get a tax benefit from the deduction that is less than the tax paid when the income was first reported. To remedy this possibility, § 1341 allows a taxpayer to claim either a deduction in the year of repayment or a tax *credit* equal to the taxes that were originally paid on the disputed income. This option is available only if the amount in question exceeds $3,000 and the taxpayer appeared to have an *unrestricted right* to the income in question.[26]

EXAMPLE 12

Tanager Corporation received $200,000 from the sale of petroleum in 1998 when it was in the 34% tax bracket. In 1999, the owner of some adjoining land claimed that the petroleum deposit in question belonged to it and demanded that Tanager return the $200,000. After a lengthy trial, Tanager settled the claim by paying its neighbor $40,000 in 2000. In that year, however, Tanager's business operations had suffered a serious decline, and the corporation was in the 15% tax bracket. Accordingly, Tanager will choose a tax credit of $13,600 ($40,000 funds returned × 34%) rather than a current-year deduction, which would lower its taxes by only $6,000 ($40,000 × 15%). ▼

CHANGE OF ACCOUNTING METHODS

LEARNING OBJECTIVE 2
Utilize the procedure for changing accounting methods.

As explained more fully in Chapters 3 and 4, the Code allows taxpayers to use either the cash receipts and disbursements method, the accrual method, or some combination of the two. Taxpayers with more than one business may use a different method for each business,[27] but whichever method is used must *clearly reflect* the taxpayer's income.[28]

The two principal methods are themselves very different. The **cash method** focuses on when cash or its equivalent is received or paid. The **accrual method** reports income when it is earned as determined by legal and economic considerations. Deductions under this method are claimed when a taxpayer's liability has been established and *economic performance* has occurred. Chapter 3 explains when income is reported under these methods, and Chapter 4 explains when deductions may be taken.

But what happens if a taxpayer wants to change its accounting method? Some taxpayers may not change their method; for example, if inventories are a material factor in the business (see the final section of this chapter), the accrual method is *mandatory*.[29] Similarly, the cash method may not be used by corporations that have annual gross receipts in excess of $5 million or by partnerships that have a

---

[23]§ 172. Refer to Chapter 5.
[24]§§ 165(i) and 451(d). Refer to Chapter 5.
[25]*North American Consolidated Oil Co. v. Burnet*, 3 USTC ¶943, 11 AFTR 16, 52 S.Ct. 613 (USSC, 1932).
[26]§ 1341(a).
[27]§ 446(d).
[28]§ 446(b).
[29]Reg. § 1.446–1(a)(4)(i).

> ## TAX IN THE NEWS
>
> ### IRS FAILS TO IMPOSE ACCRUAL METHOD—AND PAYS FOR TRYING
>
> A nursing services corporation paid its employees before being paid by its customers for the nursing services it provided. As a result, at the end of the year, the company had nearly $250,000 in accounts receivable that had not been included in its cash basis income, even though the company had deducted the related employee expenses. The IRS claimed that this mismatching of revenues and expenses showed that the taxpayer was not entitled to use the cash method and was required to use the accrual method instead.
>
> The Tax Court, however, concluded that the taxpayer had not intentionally prepaid its expenses or deferred its income, that it had applied the cash method consistently, and that the resulting mismatch of income and expense was simply a product of that method. The court noted further that Congress was aware of the cash method's potential for such mismatching when it authorized the method's use. Therefore, the IRS's position was not substantially supported by the law, so the IRS had to pay the taxpayer's attorney fees!
>
> SOURCE: *Laura E. Austin*, T.C.Memo 1997–157: 73 TCM 2470.

corporation as a partner.[30] Within these limitations, however, a taxpayer can change accounting methods. This section considers the process of doing so and the adjustments that are required.

A taxpayer elects a particular accounting method when it files its initial tax return using that method. To change that method, the taxpayer must obtain the permission of the IRS. A request for change is made on Form 3115, Application for Change in Accounting Method. Generally, the form must be filed within the taxable year of the desired change.[31]

The term **accounting method** encompasses not only the overall accounting method used by the taxpayer (the cash or accrual method) but also the treatment of any material item of income or deduction.[32] Thus, a change in the method of deducting property taxes from a cash basis to an accrual basis that results in a deduction for taxes in a different year constitutes a change in an accounting method. Another example of accounting method change is a switch in the method or basis used in the valuation of inventories. However, a change in treatment resulting from a change in underlying facts does not constitute a change in the taxpayer's method of accounting.[33] For example, a change in employment contracts so that an employee accrues one day of vacation pay for each month of service rather than 12 days of vacation pay for a full year of service is a change in the underlying facts and is therefore not an accounting method change.

CORRECTION OF AN ERROR

A change in accounting method must be distinguished from the *correction of an error*. A taxpayer can correct an error (by filing amended returns) without permission, and the IRS can simply adjust the taxpayer's liability if an error is discovered on audit of the return. Some examples of errors are incorrect postings, errors in the

---

[30] §§ 448(a) and (b)(3).
[31] Rev.Proc. 97–21, 1997–1 C.B. 680.
[32] Reg. § 1.446–1(a)(1).
[33] Reg. § 1.446–1(e)(2)(ii).

calculation of tax liability or tax credits, deductions of business expense items that are actually personal, and omissions of income and deductions.[34] Unless the taxpayer or the IRS corrects the error within the statute of limitations, the taxpayer's total lifetime taxable income will be overstated or understated by the amount of the error.

CHANGE FROM AN INCORRECT METHOD

An *incorrect accounting method* is the consistent (year-after-year) use of an incorrect rule to report an item of income or expense. An incorrect accounting method generally will not affect a taxpayer's total lifetime income (unlike an error). That is, an incorrect method has a self-balancing mechanism. For example, deducting freight on inventory in the year the goods are purchased, rather than when the inventory is sold, is an incorrect accounting method. The total cost of goods sold over the life of the business is not affected, but the year-to-year income is incorrect.[35]

An incorrect method is not treated as a mechanical error that can be corrected by merely filing an amended tax return. Instead, permission must be obtained from the IRS to change to a correct method.

The tax return preparer and the taxpayer are subject to penalties if a tax return is prepared using an incorrect method of accounting and permission for a change to a correct method has not been requested.[36]

NET ADJUSTMENTS DUE TO CHANGE IN ACCOUNTING METHOD

In the year of a change in accounting method, some items of income and expense may have to be adjusted to prevent the change from distorting taxable income.

EXAMPLE 13

In 1998, White Corporation, with consent from the IRS, switched from the cash to the accrual basis for reporting sales and cost of goods sold. The corporation's accrual basis gross profit for the year was computed as follows:

Sales		$100,000
Beginning inventory	$15,000	
Plus: Purchases	60,000	
Less: Ending inventory	(10,000)	
Cost of goods sold		(65,000)
Gross profit		$ 35,000

At the end of the previous year, White Corporation had accounts receivable of $25,000 and accounts payable for merchandise of $34,000. The accounts receivable from the previous year in the amount of $25,000 were never included in gross income since White was on the cash basis and did not recognize the uncollected receivables. In the current year, the $25,000 was not included in the accrual basis sales since the sales were made in a prior year. Therefore, a $25,000 adjustment to income is required to prevent the receivables from being omitted from income.

The corollary of the failure to recognize a prior year's receivables is the failure to recognize a prior year's accounts payable. The beginning of the year's accounts payable was not included in the current or prior year's purchases. Thus, a deduction for the $34,000 was

---

[34]Reg. § 1.446–1(e)(2)(ii)(b).
[35]But see *Korn Industries v. U.S.*, 76–1 USTC ¶9354, 37 AFTR2d 76–1228, 532 F.2d 1352 (Ct.Cls., 1976).
[36]§ 446(f).

not taken in either year and is therefore included as an adjustment to income for the period of change.

An adjustment is also required to reflect the $15,000 beginning inventory that White deducted (due to the use of a cash method of accounting) in the previous year. In this instance, the cost of goods sold during the year of change was increased by the beginning inventory and resulted in a double deduction.

The net adjustment due to the change in accounting method is computed as follows:

Beginning inventory (deducted in prior and current year)	$15,000
Beginning accounts receivable (omitted from income)	25,000
Beginning accounts payable (omitted from deductions)	(34,000)
Net increase in taxable income	$ 6,000

Disposition of the Net Adjustment. Generally, if the IRS *requires* a taxpayer to change an accounting method, the net adjustment is added to or subtracted from the income for the year of the change. In cases of positive adjustments (increases in income) in excess of $3,000, a taxpayer is allowed to calculate the tax by spreading the adjustment over one or more previous years.[37]

To encourage taxpayers to *voluntarily* change from incorrect methods and to facilitate changes from one correct method to another, the IRS generally allows a taxpayer to spread the adjustment into future years. One-fourth of the adjustment is applied to the year of the change, and one-fourth is applied to each of the next three years.[38]

EXAMPLE 14

White Corporation in the preceding example voluntarily changed from an incorrect method (the cash basis was incorrect because inventories were material to the business) to a correct method. The company must add $1,500 (¼ × $6,000 positive adjustment) to its 1998, 1999, 2000, and 2001 income. ▼

INSTALLMENT METHOD

3 LEARNING OBJECTIVE
Determine when the installment method of accounting can be used and apply the related calculation techniques.

IN GENERAL

Under the general rule for computing gain or loss from the sale of property, a taxpayer recognizes the entire amount of gain or loss upon the sale or other disposition of the property.

EXAMPLE 15

Meadowlark, Inc., sells property to Pintail Corporation for $10,000 cash plus Pintail's note (fair market value and face amount of $90,000). Meadowlark's basis for the property was $15,000. Gain or loss is computed under either the cash or accrual basis as follows:

Amount realized:		
Cash down payment	$ 10,000	
Note receivable	90,000	
	$100,000	
Less: Basis in the property	(15,000)	
Realized gain	$ 85,000	

---

[37] § 481(b).   [38] Rev.Proc. 97–27, 1997–1 C.B. 680.

In this example, the general rule for recognizing gain or loss requires Meadowlark to pay tax on the *entire* gain in the year of sale even though it received only $10,000 cash. Congress enacted the installment sales provisions to prevent this sort of hardship by allowing the taxpayer to spread the gain from installment sales over the collection period.

Eligibility and Calculations. The **installment method** applies only to *gains* (not losses) from the sale of property where the seller will receive at least one payment *after* the year of sale. Even when this requirement is met, the installment method may not be used for sales of the following assets:

- Stocks or securities traded on an established market.[39]
- Property subject to *depreciation recapture*, as explained in Chapter 8.[40]
- Property held for sale in the ordinary course of business, other than residential lots if the seller "is not to make any improvements," time-share units of no more than six weeks per year, or property used or produced in the farming business.[41]

Thus, the installment method is most commonly employed in occasional sales of businesses and real estate, but not for items held as inventory. The tax treatment of inventories is discussed in the final section of this chapter.

The Nonelective Aspect. If a sale is eligible for the installment method, it *must* be reported on that basis.[42] A special election is required to report such a sale by any method other than the installment method. The election is discussed later in this section.

Computing the Gain for Each Year. The gain reported each year on an installment sale is computed by the following formula:

$$\frac{\text{Total gain}}{\text{Contract price}} \times \text{Payments received} = \text{Recognized gain.}$$

The taxpayer computes each variable as follows:

1. *Total gain* is the selling price reduced by selling expenses and the adjusted basis of the property, usually the taxpayer's cost.[43] The selling price is the total amount received by the seller, including notes receivable from the buyer and any seller's liabilities that are assumed by the buyer.
2. *Contract price* is the selling price less any seller's liabilities that are assumed by the buyer. Generally, the contract price is the amount, other than interest, that the seller will eventually receive from the buyer.
3. *Payments received* are the collections on the contract price received in the tax year. This generally is the cash received less any interest income collected for the period. If the buyer pays any of the seller's expenses, the seller regards such amounts as payments received.

---

[39] § 453(k)(2)(A).
[40] § 453(i).
[41] § 453(l).

[42] § 453(a).
[43] See Chapter 7 for the calculation of adjusted basis.

EXAMPLE 16

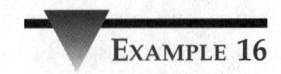

The seller is not a dealer, and the facts are as follows:

Sales price (amount realized):		
Cash down payment	$ 1,000	
Seller's mortgage assumed	3,000	
Notes payable to the seller	13,000	$17,000
Less: Selling expenses		(500)
Less: Seller's basis		(10,000)
Total gain		$ 6,500

The contract price is $14,000 ($17,000 sales price − $3,000 mortgage assumed). Assuming that $1,000 is the only payment received in the year of sale, the recognized gain in that year is computed as follows:

$$\frac{\$6{,}500 \text{ (total gain)}}{\$14{,}000 \text{ (contract price)}} \times \$1{,}000 = \$464.$$

If the sum of the seller's basis and selling expenses is less than the liabilities assumed by the buyer, the difference must be added to the contract price and to the payments (treated as *deemed payments*) received in the year of sale.[44] This adjustment to the contract price is required so that the ratio of total gain to contract price will not be greater than one. The adjustment also accelerates the reporting of income from the deemed payments.

EXAMPLE 17

Assume the same facts as in the preceding example, except that the seller's basis in the property is only $2,000. The total gain, therefore, is $14,500 [$17,000 − ($2,000 + $500)]. Payments in the year of sale are $1,500 and are calculated as follows:

Down payment	$1,000
Excess of mortgage assumed over seller's basis and expenses ($3,000 − $2,000 − $500)	500
	$1,500

The contract price is $14,500 [$17,000 (selling price) − $3,000 (seller's mortgage assumed) + $500 (excess of mortgage assumed over seller's basis and selling expenses)]. The gain recognized in the year of sale is computed as follows:

$$\frac{\$14{,}500 \text{ (total gain)}}{\$14{,}500 \text{ (contract price)}} \times \$1{,}500 = \$1{,}500.$$

In subsequent years, all amounts the seller collects on the note principal ($13,000) will be recognized gain ($13,000 × 100%) when received.

PLANNING CONSIDERATIONS

The Installment Method

The installment method enables a taxpayer to defer reporting taxable gain until subsequent years. Once the method is used for a particular sale, however, that method must be continued for the duration of that transaction. While the *time value of money* generally advises deferral of tax liability, deferral is not always beneficial. A taxpayer might be in a higher tax bracket in later years due to other transactions or the expansion of that

---

[44]Temp.Reg. § 15A.453–1(b)(2)(iii).

taxpayer's business. Similarly, Congress may raise tax rates in the future, and those higher rates usually apply to payments from an earlier year's installment sale, unless some special exception is created. In such circumstances, the taxpayer's increased tax liability might exceed any financial benefit obtained from deferring the tax on the original transaction, particularly if the deferral period was only a few years.

On the other hand, the installment method can be particularly useful if a taxpayer anticipates being in a *lower tax bracket* in later years. Whether due to a taxpayer's impending retirement or a significant reduction in a business's activities, this lower tax rate would mean less tax owed, in addition to the financial benefit gained by deferring taxes to a later year. Moreover, Congress also lowers tax rates from time to time, and a taxpayer might reap still further benefits from an installment sale that moves reported gain into a lower-tax rate year.

In either case, an installment sale necessarily entails the *nontax consideration* of credit risk. That is, an outright cash sale might be preferable to an installment sale if the buyer's creditworthiness is somewhat suspect. Even a creditworthy buyer, moreover, might find payment of its installment obligations difficult if general business conditions or specific industry factors cause a decline in its economic well-being. An installment sale, in other words, does not terminate a seller's exposure to the exigencies of the marketplace, and some sellers might prefer the certainty of an all-cash transaction despite its lack of deferral possibilities.

CONTINGENT SALES PRICES

Dispositions of business assets or even entire businesses sometimes employ open-ended or **contingent sales prices** to resolve disputes between the buyer and the seller about the value of the assets in question. Such transactions typically involve a portion of future receipts, profits in excess of some threshold, or some similar arrangement. Despite the absence of a specified sales price, the installment method can be used in these circumstances according to the following principles:

- If the sales contract sets forth a *maximum sales price*, that price is used.[45]
- If there is no maximum sales price but the payout is limited to a fixed number of years, divide the taxpayer's basis by that number and offset the result against the amount received each year.[46]
- If the sales agreement provides neither a maximum sales price nor a fixed payout period, use 15 years as the fixed payout term.[47]

The following examples illustrate how the installment method is applied when the sales price is contingent on future events.

EXAMPLE 18

Indigo, Inc., sells the rights to a newly patented blood analyzer to a major health products company for 10% of the earnings generated by this device, with a maximum sales price of $400,000. Indigo has a cost basis in this device of $100,000. In the first year after the sale, Indigo received $30,000. Since a maximum sales price is stipulated, it is used:

Maximum sales price	$ 400,000
Basis	(100,000)
Gain expected	$ 300,000

---

[45]Temp.Reg. § 15A.453–1(c)(2)(i).
[46]Temp.Reg. § 15A.453–1(c)(3)(i).
[47]Temp.Reg. § 15A.453–1(c)(4).

$$\frac{\text{Gain}}{\text{Contract price}} = \frac{\$300,000}{\$400,000} = 75\% \text{ (gross profit percentage)}.$$

Of the $30,000 received in the first year after the sale, $22,500 ($30,000 × 75%) is reported as gain. In each subsequent year, 75% of the amount received will be reported as gain. If the amount ultimately collected is less than the maximum sales price used, an appropriate adjustment will be made in the final year of the sales contract. ▼

EXAMPLE 19

Assume the same facts as in the preceding example, except that no maximum sales price is provided and the payout is limited to eight years. Accordingly, the taxpayer's basis of $100,000 is divided by 8, and the result ($12,500) is then offset against the amount received each year. In the first year:

Amount received	$ 30,000
Prorated basis	(12,500)
Gain reported	$ 17,500

▼

EXAMPLE 20

Assume the same facts as in the preceding example, except that there is no fixed payout term. In this case, the taxpayer's basis of $100,000 is divided by 15 years, and the result ($6,667) offsets the amount received:

Amount received	$ 30,000
Prorated basis	(6,667)
Gain reported	$ 23,333

▼

IMPUTED INTEREST

If a deferred payment contract for the sale of property with a selling price greater than $3,000 does not contain a reasonable interest rate, a reasonable rate is imputed.[48] The imputing of interest effectively restates the selling price of the property to the sum of the payments at the date of the sale and the discounted present value of the future payments. The difference between the present value of a future payment and the payment's face amount is taxed as interest income, as discussed in the following paragraphs. Thus, the **imputed interest** rules prevent sellers of capital assets from increasing the selling price to reflect the equivalent of unstated interest on deferred payments and thereby converting ordinary (interest) income into long-term capital gains.[49] In addition, the imputed interest rules affect the timing of income recognition.

Generally, if the contract does not charge at least the Federal rate, interest will be imputed at the Federal rate. The Federal rate is the interest rate the Federal government pays on new borrowing and is published monthly by the IRS.[50]

As a general rule, the buyer and seller must account for interest on the accrual basis with semiannual compounding.[51] Requiring the use of the accrual basis assures that the seller's interest income and the buyer's interest expense are reported in the same tax year. The following example illustrates the calculation and amortization of imputed interest.

---

[48]§§ 483 and 1274.
[49]Refer to Chapter 3 for classification of capital assets and the tax treatment of capital gains versus ordinary income.
[50]§ 1274(d)(1). There are three Federal rates: short-term (not over three years), mid-term (over three years but not over nine years), and long-term (over nine years).
[51]§§ 1274(a), 1273(a), and 1272(a).

EXAMPLE 21

Partridge & Associates, LLP, a cash basis taxpayer, sold land on January 1, 1998, for $200,000 cash and $6 million due on December 31, 1999, with 5% interest payable on December 31, 1998, and December 31, 1999. At the time of the sale, the Federal rate was 8% (compounded semiannually). Because Partridge did not charge at least the Federal rate, interest will be imputed at 8% (compounded semiannually).

Date	Payment	Present Value (at 8%) on 1/1/1998	Imputed Interest
12/31/1998	$ 300,000*	$ 277,500	$ 22,500
12/31/1999	6,300,000**	5,386,500	913,500
	$6,600,000	$5,664,000	$936,000

*$6 million × 5% = $300,000 interest.
**$6 million + $300,000 interest.

Thus, the selling price is restated to $5,864,000 ($200,000 cash + $5,664,000) rather than $6,200,000 ($200,000 + $6,000,000), and Partridge will recognize interest income in accordance with the following amortization schedule:

	Beginning Balance	Interest Income (at 8%)*	Received	Ending Balance
1998	$5,664,000	$462,182	($ 300,000)	$5,826,182
1999	5,826,182	473,818	(6,300,000)	–0–

*Compounded semiannually.

Congress has created several exceptions regarding the rate at which interest is imputed and the method of accounting for the interest income and expense. The general rules and exceptions are summarized in Concept Summary 6–1.

RELATED-PARTY SALES

Special limitations apply when an installment sale involves related parties. These limitations prevent undue deferral of tax liability under circumstances that the taxpayers involved can presumably control. Different limitations and different definitions of *related parties* apply to sales of nondepreciable and depreciable property.

Nondepreciable Property. When related parties sell nondepreciable property to one another on the installment method, § 453(e) treats the proceeds of any subsequent sale within two years as if they had been received by the first seller.

EXAMPLE 22

Joan sells some vacant land worth $100,000 to her son, Ed, with payment spread over 20 years in $5,000 annual payments. If Ed sells this property one year later for $100,000 in cash, this sum is treated as if Joan had received it, and she will report her gain accordingly. ▼

Had this rule not applied, the family unit (Joan and Ed) would have the entire proceeds of $100,000 in their possession, but could continue to report Joan's gain over the remaining 19 years of her original transaction with Ed. Note that the later sale by Ed does not produce any reportable gain, because the sales price that he received ($100,000) did not exceed the price he paid his mother for the property in the earlier transaction.

Concept Summary 6–1

Interest on Installment Sales

	Imputed Interest Rate
General rule	Federal rate
Exceptions:	
• Principal amount not over $2.8 million.[1]	Lesser of Federal rate or 9%
• Sale of land (with a calendar year ceiling of $500,000) between family members (the seller's spouse, brothers, sisters, ancestors, or lineal descendants).[2]	Lesser of Federal rate or 6%

	Method of Accounting for Interest	
	Seller's Interest Income	Buyer's Interest Expense
General rule[3]	Accrual	Accrual
Exceptions:		
• Total payments under the contract are $250,000 or less.[4]	Taxpayer's overall method	Taxpayer's overall method
• Sale of a farm (sales price of $1 million or less).[5]	Taxpayer's overall method	Taxpayer's overall method
• Sale of a principal residence.[6]	Taxpayer's overall method	Taxpayer's overall method
• Sale for a note with a principal amount of not over $2 million, the seller is on the cash basis, the property sold is not inventory, and the buyer agrees to report expenses by the cash method.[7]	Cash	Cash

[1] § 1274A. This amount is adjusted annually for inflation. For 1998, the amount is $3,823,100.
[2] §§ 1274(c)(3)(F) and 483(e).
[3] §§ 1274(a) and 1272(a)(3).
[4] §§ 1274(c)(3)(C) and 483.
[5] §§ 1274(c)(3)(A) and 483.
[6] §§ 1274(c)(3)(B) and 483.
[7] § 1274A(c). This amount is adjusted annually for inflation. For 1998, the amount is $2,730,800.

If Ed had waited two years before selling the property, the related-party sale rule would not have applied, and Joan could have reported her gain over the remaining term of her contract with Ed. During those two years, however, Ed would bear the economic risk that the property might *decline in value*. His obligation to make annual payments of $5,000 to Joan is not affected by the property's subsequent value. Moreover, the Code provides that the two-year period does not start running if the related-party reseller (Ed in this example) has *substantially diminished* the risk of loss by a sale option, put contract, or similar transaction.[52]

For this purpose, related parties include the first seller's brothers, sisters, ancestors (e.g., parents and grandparents), lineal descendants (e.g., children and grandchildren), controlled corporations, and partnerships, trusts, and estates in which the seller has an interest.[53]

---

[52] § 453(e)(2)(B).
[53] § 453(f)(1), cross-referencing §§ 267(b) and 318(a). Although spouses are related parties, the exemption of gain between spouses (§ 1041) makes the second-disposition rules inapplicable when the first sale was between spouses. See Chapter 7 for a discussion of interspousal transactions.

Depreciable Property. The installment method cannot be used to report a gain on the sale of depreciable property to a controlled entity. The purpose of this rule is to prevent the seller from deferring gain (until collections are received) while the related purchaser is enjoying a stepped-up basis for depreciation purposes.[54]

This prohibition on the use of the installment method applies to sales between the taxpayer and a partnership or corporation in which the taxpayer holds a more-than-50 percent interest. Constructive ownership rules are used in applying the ownership test (e.g., the taxpayer is considered to own stock owned by a spouse and certain other family members).[55] However, if the taxpayer can establish that tax avoidance was not a principal purpose of the transaction, the installment method can be used to report the gain.

EXAMPLE 23

Ali purchased an apartment building from his controlled corporation, Emerald Corporation. Ali was short of cash at the time of the purchase (December 1998), but was to collect a large cash payment in January 1999. The agreement required Ali to pay the entire arm's length price in January 1999. Ali had sound business reasons for acquiring the building. Emerald Corporation should be able to convince the IRS that tax avoidance was not a principal purpose for the installment sale because the tax benefits are not overwhelming. The corporation will report all of the gain in the year following the year of sale. ▼

DISPOSITION OF INSTALLMENT OBLIGATIONS

Generally, a taxpayer must recognize the deferred profit from an installment sale when the obligation is transferred to another party or is otherwise relinquished.[56] The rationale for accelerating the gain is that deferral is no longer appropriate when the taxpayer has sold the obligation and received the proceeds (under the wherewithal to pay concept).

Moreover, a gift or cancellation of an installment note is treated as a taxable disposition by the donor. The amount realized from the cancellation is the face amount of the note if the parties (obligor and obligee) are related to each other.[57]

EXAMPLE 24

Liz cancels a note issued by Tina (Liz's daughter) that arose in connection with the sale of property. At the time of the cancellation, the note had a basis to Liz of $10,000, a face amount of $25,000, and a fair market value of $20,000. Presuming the initial sale by Liz to Tina qualified as an installment sale, the cancellation results in gain of $15,000 ($25,000 − $10,000) to Liz. ▼

Certain exceptions to the recognition of gain provisions are provided for transfers of installment obligations pursuant to tax-free incorporations under § 351, contributions of capital to a partnership, certain corporate liquidations, transfers due to the taxpayer's death, and transfers between spouses or incident to divorce.[58] In such instances, the deferred profit is merely shifted to the transferee, who is responsible for the payment of tax on the subsequent collections of the installment obligations.

---

[54] § 453(g). Refer to Chapter 4 for the computation of depreciation deductions.
[55] §§ 1239(b) and (c).
[56] § 453B(a).
[57] § 453B(f)(2).
[58] §§ 453B(c), (d), and (g). See Chapters 7, 9, 10, and 12 for discussion of some of these subjects.

PLANNING CONSIDERATIONS

Terminating the Installment Method

As suggested earlier, an installment sale might look less appealing in retrospect if a taxpayer subsequently finds itself in a higher tax bracket. Whether this predicament is due to higher legislated rates or the expansion of the taxpayer's business, the taxpayer might be inclined to *terminate the installment sale methodology*. Disposing of the installment obligation often accomplishes this result, because any remaining deferred gain is thereby accelerated into the current year. To be sure, the taxpayer gives up the deferral benefit obtained when the transaction was set up as an installment sale, but saving taxes that would be paid in future years at higher rates may offset the loss of deferral benefits.

Disposing of an installment obligation, however, may not be easy. Financial obligations of most private businesses or other persons can often be difficult to sell at a price equal to their present value. Intermediaries may agree to purchase such obligations only at significant discounts to their face amount. If the maker of the note (i.e., the person obligated to pay the installment obligation) is experiencing any financial difficulty at the time, the note will be even harder to sell. Thus, *nontax considerations* may effectively preclude the acceleration of taxable gain by disposing of an installment obligation.

INTEREST ON DEFERRED TAXES

With the installment method, the seller earns interest on the receivable. The receivable includes the deferred gain. In effect, the seller is earning interest on the deferred taxes. Since the installment method provides interest-free loans to those taxpayers who use it, the Code requires the taxpayers to pay interest on the deferred taxes in some situations.[59]

The taxpayer is required to pay interest on the deferred taxes only if *both* of the following requirements are met:

- The installment obligation arises from the sale of property (other than farming property) for more than $150,000.
- Such installment obligations outstanding at the close of the tax year exceed $5 million.

Interest on the deferred taxes is payable only on the portion of the taxes that relates to the installment obligations in *excess* of $5 million. The interest is calculated using the underpayment rate in § 6621.

ELECTING OUT OF THE INSTALLMENT METHOD

A taxpayer can *elect not to use* the installment method. The election is made by reporting on a timely filed return the gain computed by the taxpayer's usual method of accounting (cash or accrual).[60] However, the Regulations provide that the amount realized by a cash basis taxpayer cannot be less than the value of the property sold. This rule differs from the usual cash basis accounting rules,[61] which measure the amount realized in terms of the fair market value of the property received. The net effect of the Regulations is that a cash basis taxpayer reports its gain as an

---

[59] § 453A.
[60] § 453(d) and Temp.Reg. § 15A.453–1(d). See also Rev.Rul. 82–227, 1982–2 C.B. 89.
[61] Refer to Chapter 3.

accrual basis taxpayer. The election is frequently applied to year-end sales by taxpayers who expect to be in a higher tax bracket in the following year.

EXAMPLE 25

On December 31, 1998, Blue Corporation sold land to Orange, Inc., for $20,000 (fair market value). The cash was to be paid on January 4, 1999. Blue is a cash basis taxpayer, and its basis in the land is $8,000. Blue has a large casualty loss and very little other income in 1998. Thus, its marginal tax rate in 1998 is 15%. Blue expects its rate to increase in 1999 to 34%.

The transaction constitutes an installment sale because a payment will be received in a tax year after the tax year of disposition. Orange's promise to pay Blue is an installment obligation, and under the Regulations, the value of the installment obligation is equal to the value of the property sold ($20,000). If Blue elects out of the installment method, it would shift $12,000 of gain ($20,000 − $8,000) from the expected higher rate in 1999 to the 15% rate in 1998. The expected tax savings based on the rate differentials may exceed the benefit of the tax deferral available with the installment method. ▼

Revocation of the Election. Permission of the IRS is required to revoke an election not to use the installment method.[62] The stickiness of the election is an added peril.

LONG–TERM CONTRACTS

4 LEARNING OBJECTIVE
Understand the alternative methods of accounting for long-term contracts (the completed contract method and the percentage of completion method) including the limitations on the use of the completed contract method.

A **long-term contract** is a building, installation, construction, or manufacturing contract that is entered into but not completed within the same tax year. However, a *manufacturing* contract is long term *only* if the contract is to manufacture (1) a unique item not normally carried in finished goods inventory or (2) items that normally require more than 12 calendar months to complete.[63] An item is *unique* if it is designed to meet a customer's particular needs and is not suitable for use by others. A contract to perform services (e.g., auditing or legal services) is not considered a contract for this purpose and thus cannot qualify as a long-term contract.

EXAMPLE 26

Raven & Co., Inc., a calendar year taxpayer, entered into two contracts during the year. One contract was to construct a building foundation. Work was to begin in October 1998 and be completed by June 1999. This contract is long term because it will not be entered into and completed in the same tax year. The fact that the contract requires less than 12 calendar months to complete is not relevant because the contract is not for manufacturing. The second contract was for architectural services to be performed over two years. These services will not qualify for long-term contract treatment because the taxpayer will not build, install, construct, or manufacture a product. ▼

Generally, the taxpayer must account for all direct and indirect costs incurred. Then, the production costs must be allocated to individual contracts. Furthermore, mixed services costs, costs that benefit contracts as well as the general administrative operations of the business, must be divided between administration and production. Exhibit 6–1 lists the types of costs that must be accounted for and allocated to contracts. The taxpayer must develop reasonable bases for cost allocations.[64]

---

[62] § 453(d)(3) and Temp.Reg. § 15A.453–1(d)(4).
[63] § 460(f) and Reg. § 1.451–3(b).
[64] Reg. § 1.451–3(d)(9).

▼ EXHIBIT 6–1
Contract Costs, Mixed Services Costs, and Current Expense Items for Contracts

	Contracts Eligible for the Completed Contract Method	Other Contracts
Contract costs:		
Direct materials (a part of the finished product).	Capital	Capital
Indirect materials (consumed in production but not in the finished product, e.g., grease and oil for equipment).	Capital	Capital
Storage, handling, and insurance on materials.	Expense	Capital
Direct labor (worked on the product).	Capital	Capital
Indirect labor (worked in the production process but not directly on the product, e.g., a construction supervisor).	Capital	Capital
Fringe benefits for direct and indirect labor (e.g., vacation, sick pay, unemployment, and other insurance).	Capital	Capital
Pension costs for direct and indirect labor:		
• Current cost.	Expense	Capital
• Past service costs.	Expense	Capital
Depreciation on production facilities:		
• For financial statements.	Capital	Capital
• Tax depreciation in excess of financial statements.	Expense	Capital
Depreciation on idle facilities.	Expense	Expense
Property taxes, insurance, rent, and maintenance on production facilities.	Capital	Capital
Bidding expenses—successful.	Expense	Capital
Bidding expenses—unsuccessful.	Expense	Expense
Interest to finance real estate construction.	Capital	Capital
Interest to finance personal property:		
• Production period of one year or less.	Expense	Expense
• Production period exceeds one year and costs exceed $1 million.	Capital	Capital
• Production period exceeds two years.	Capital	Capital
Mixed services costs:		
• Personnel operations.	Expense	Allocate
• Data processing.	Expense	Allocate
• Purchasing.	Expense	Allocate
Selling, general, and administrative expenses (including an allocated share of mixed services).	Expense	Expense
Losses.	Expense	Expense

EXAMPLE 27 Falcon, Inc., uses detailed cost accumulation records to assign labor and materials to its contracts in progress. The total cost of fringe benefits is allocated to a contract on the following basis:

$$\frac{\text{Labor on the contract}}{\text{Total salaries and labor}} \times \text{Total cost of fringe benefits.}$$

Similarly, storage and handling costs for materials are allocated to contracts on the following basis:

TAX IN THE NEWS

IRS SAYS THE CASH METHOD DOES NOT CLEARLY REFLECT THE INCOME OF SMALL CONTRACTORS

In a 1980 Tax Court decision, *Raymond Magnon*, 73 T.C. 980, the court ruled that a small contractor could use the cash method of accounting. More recently, the IRS was unsuccessful in attempting to require a contractor to change from the cash method to the percentage of completion method. The IRS argued that the cash method did not clearly reflect income, but the Tax Court disagreed [*Ansley-Sheppard-Burgess Company*, 104 T.C. 367 (1995)].

In other recent cases, however, the IRS has been successful in requiring small contractors to change from the cash method to the accrual method (*Thompson Electric Inc.*, T.C.Memo. 1995–292, and *J. P. Sheahan Associates*, T.C.Memo. 1995–239). The IRS has successfully argued that the accumulated costs for materials and labor, whether incurred by the contractor or its subcontractors, are subject to the inventory rules. Because inventories are a material income-producing factor, the cash method does not clearly reflect income, and the IRS can require the contractor to employ the accrual method.

SOURCE: "The IRS Insists General Contractor Use Inventories and Change to Accrual Method," *Journal of Taxation* (September 1995): 180.

$$\frac{\text{Contract materials}}{\text{Materials purchases}} \times \text{Storage and handling costs.}$$

The cost of the personnel operations, a mixed services cost, is allocated between production and general administration based on the number of employees in each function. The personnel cost allocated to production is allocated to individual contracts on the basis of the formula used to allocate fringe benefits. ▼

Contract costs are deducted when the revenue from the contract is recognized. Generally, two methods of accounting may be used to determine when the revenue from a contract is recognized:[65]

- The completed contract method.
- The percentage of completion method.

The *completed contract method may be used* for (1) home construction contracts (contracts in which at least 80 percent of the estimated costs are for dwelling units in buildings with four or fewer units) and (2) certain other real estate construction contracts. Other real estate contracts can qualify for the completed contract method if the following requirements are satisfied:

- The contract is expected to be completed within the two-year period beginning on the commencement date of the contract.
- The contract is performed by a taxpayer whose average annual gross receipts for the three taxable years preceding the taxable year in which the contract is entered into do not exceed $10 million.

All other contractors *must* use the percentage of completion method.

---

[65] § 460.

COMPLETED CONTRACT METHOD

Under the **completed contract method**, no revenue from the contract is recognized until the contract is completed and accepted. However, a taxpayer may not delay completion of a contract for the principal purpose of deferring tax.[66]

In some instances, the original contract price may be disputed, or the buyer may want additional work to be done on a long-term contract. If the disputed amount is substantial (i.e., it is not possible to determine whether a profit or loss will ultimately be realized on the contract), the Regulations provide that no amount of income or loss is recognized until the dispute is resolved. In all other cases, the profit or loss (reduced by the amount in dispute) is recognized in the current period upon completion of the contract. However, additional work may need to be performed with respect to the disputed contract. In this case, the difference between the amount in dispute and the actual cost of the additional work is recognized in the year the work is completed, rather than in the year in which the dispute is resolved.[67]

EXAMPLE 28

Magenta Corporation, a calendar year taxpayer utilizing the completed contract method of accounting, constructed a building for Kingfisher Enterprises, Inc., under a long-term contract. The gross contract price was $500,000. Magenta finished construction in 1998 at a cost of $475,000. When Kingfisher examined the building, it insisted that the building be repainted or the contract price be reduced. The estimated cost of repainting is $10,000. Since under the terms of the contract, Magenta is assured of a profit of at least $15,000 [($500,000 − $475,000) − $10,000] even if the dispute is ultimately resolved in Kingfisher's favor, Magenta must include $490,000 ($500,000 − $10,000) in gross income and is allowed deductions of $475,000 for 1998.

In 1999, Magenta and Kingfisher resolve their dispute, and Magenta repaints certain portions of the building at a cost of $6,000. Magenta must include $10,000 in 1999 gross income and may deduct the $6,000 expense in that year. ▼

EXAMPLE 29

Assume the same facts as in the previous example, except that the estimated cost of repainting the building is $50,000. Since the resolution of the dispute completely in Kingfisher's favor would mean a net loss on the contract for Magenta ($500,000 − $475,000 − $50,000 = $25,000 loss), Magenta does not recognize any income or loss until the year the dispute is resolved. ▼

Frequently, a contractor receives payment at various stages of completion. For example, when a contract is 50 percent complete, the contractor may receive 50 percent of the contract price less a retainage. The taxation of these payments is generally governed by Regulation § 1.451–5 "advance payments for goods and long-term contracts" (refer to Chapter 3). Generally, contractors are allowed to defer the advance payments until the payments are recognized as income under their method of accounting.

PERCENTAGE OF COMPLETION METHOD

The percentage of completion method must be used to account for long-term contracts unless the taxpayer qualifies for one of the two exceptions that allow the completed contract method to be used: home construction contracts and certain other real estate construction contracts.[68] Under the **percentage of completion**

---

[66] Reg. § 1.451–3(b)(2).
[67] Reg. §§ 1.451–3(d)(2)(ii)–(vii), Example (2).
[68] Certain residential construction contracts that do not qualify for the completed contract method may nevertheless use that method to account for 30% of the profit from the contract, with the remaining 70% reported by the percentage of completion method.

method, a portion of the gross contract price is included in income during each period as the work progresses. The revenue accrued each period (except for the final period) is computed as follows:[69]

$$\frac{C}{T} \times P,$$

where C = Contract costs incurred during the period,
T = Estimated total cost of the contract, and
P = Contract price.

All of the costs allocated to the contract during the period are deductible from the accrued revenue.[70] The revenue reported in the final period is simply the unreported revenue from the contract. Because T in this formula is an estimate that frequently differs from total actual costs, which are not known until the contract has been completed, the profit on a contract for a particular period may be overstated or understated.

EXAMPLE 30

Tan, Inc., entered into a contract that was to take two years to complete, with an estimated cost of $2,250,000. The contract price was $3,000,000. Costs of the contract for 1998, the first year, totaled $1,350,000. The gross profit reported by the percentage of completion method for 1998 was $450,000 {[($1,350,000/$2,250,000) × $3,000,000 = $1,800,000)] − $1,350,000}. The contract was completed at the end of 1999 at a total cost of $2,700,000. In retrospect, 1998 profit should have been $150,000 {[($1,350,000/$2,700,000) × $3,000,000 = $1,500,000] − $1,350,000}. Thus, taxes were overpaid for 1998. ▼

A *de minimis* rule enables a contractor to delay the recognition of income for a particular contract under the percentage of completion method. If less than 10 percent of the estimated contract costs have been incurred by the end of the taxable year, a taxpayer may defer the recognition of income and the related costs until the year in which cumulative contract costs are at least 10 percent of the estimated contract costs.[71]

Lookback Provisions. In the year a contract is completed, a *lookback* provision requires the recalculation of annual profits reported on the contract under the percentage of completion method. Interest is paid to the taxpayer if taxes were overpaid, and interest is payable by the taxpayer if there was an underpayment.[72] For a business taxpayer, the lookback interest paid by the taxpayer is deductible.

EXAMPLE 31

Assume Tan, Inc., in the preceding example, was in the 35% tax bracket in both years and the relevant interest rate was 10%. For 1998, the company paid excess taxes of $105,000 [($450,000 − $150,000) × .35]. When the contract is completed at the end of 1999, Tan, Inc., should receive interest of $10,500 for one year on its tax overpayment ($105,000 × .10). ▼

---

[69] § 460(b)(1)(A).
[70] Reg. § 1.451–3(c)(3).
[71] § 460(b)(5).

[72] §§ 460(b)(2) and (6). The taxpayer may elect not to apply the lookback method if the cumulative taxable income as of the close of each prior year is within 10% of the correct income for each prior year.

INVENTORIES

LEARNING OBJECTIVE 5
Know when accounting for inventories is required, recognize the types of costs that must be included in inventories, and apply the LIFO method.

Generally, tax accounting and financial accounting for inventories are much the same:

- The use of inventories is necessary to clearly reflect the income of any business engaged in the production and sale or purchase and sale of goods.[73]
- The inventories should include all finished goods, goods in process, and raw materials and supplies that will become part of the product (including containers).
- Inventory rules must give effect to the *best* accounting practice of a particular trade or business, and the taxpayer's method should be consistently followed from year to year.
- All items included in inventory should be valued at either (1) cost or (2) the lower of cost or market value.

The following are *not* acceptable methods or practices in valuing inventories:

- A reserve for anticipated price changes.
- Use of a constant price or nominal value for a so-called normal quantity of materials or goods in stock (e.g., the base stock method).
- Inclusion in inventory of stock in transit to which title is not vested in the taxpayer.
- The direct costing approach (excluding fixed indirect production costs from inventory).
- The prime costing approach (excluding all indirect production costs from inventory).

The reason for the similarities between tax and financial accounting for inventories is that § 471 sets forth what appears to be a two-prong test: "inventories shall be taken . . . on such basis . . . as conforming as nearly as may be to the *best accounting practice* in the trade or business and as most *clearly reflecting the income*." The best accounting practice is synonymous with generally accepted accounting principles (hereafter referred to as GAAP). However, the IRS determines whether an inventory method clearly reflects income.

In *Thor Power Tool Co. v. Comm.*,[74] there was a conflict between these two tests. The taxpayer's method of valuing obsolete parts was in conformity with GAAP. The IRS, however, successfully argued that the clear reflection of income test was not satisfied because the taxpayer's procedures for valuing its inventories were contrary to the Regulations. Under the taxpayer's method, inventories for parts in excess of estimated future sales were written off (expensed), although the parts were kept on hand and their asking prices were not reduced. [Under Regulation § 1.471–4(b), inventories cannot be written down unless the selling prices are also reduced.] The taxpayer contended that conformity to GAAP creates a presumption that the method clearly reflects income. The Supreme Court disagreed, concluding that the clear reflection of income test was *paramount*. Moreover, it is the opinion of the IRS that controls in determining whether a method of inventory clearly reflects income. Thus, the best accounting practice test was rendered practically meaningless. It follows that a taxpayer's method of inventory must strictly conform to the Regulations regardless of what GAAP may require.

---

[73] § 471(a) and Reg. §§ 1.471–1 and –2.

[74] 79–1 USTC ¶9139, 43 AFTR2d 79–362, 99 S.Ct. 773 (USSC, 1979).

DETERMINING INVENTORY COST

For merchandise purchased, cost is the invoice price less trade discounts plus freight and other handling charges.[75] Cash discounts approximating a fair interest rate can be deducted or capitalized at the taxpayer's option, as long as the method used is consistently applied.

Uniform Capitalization. Section 263A provides that, for inventory and property *produced* by a taxpayer, "... (A) the direct cost of such property, and (B) such property's share of those indirect costs (including taxes) part or all of which are allocable to such property" must be capitalized. The Committee Reports note that Congress wanted a set of capitalization rules that would apply to all types of businesses: contractors, manufacturers, farmers, wholesalers, and retailers.[76] Congress has labeled the resulting system the **uniform capitalization rules**, and practitioners refer to it as a *super-full absorption costing system*.

To value inventory under the uniform capitalization rules, a *producer* must apply the following steps:

- Classify all costs into three categories: (1) production, (2) general administrative expense, and (3) mixed services.
- Allocate mixed services costs to production and general administrative expenses.[77]
- Allocate the production costs between the cost of goods sold and the ending inventory.

In the Other Contracts column, Exhibit 6–1 (page 6–22) lists typical items that are included in the three categories of costs. The mixed services costs should be allocated to production on a rational basis. For example, the costs of operating the personnel department may be allocated between production and general administration based on the number of applications processed or the number of employees. In lieu of allocating each mixed services cost, a taxpayer may elect a *simplified method* that allocates the total of all mixed services costs to production as follows:[78]

$$\text{MSP} = \frac{\text{TP}}{\text{TC}} \times \text{TMS},$$

where MSP = Mixed services costs allocated to production,
TP = Total production costs, other than interest and mixed services,
TC = Total costs, other than interest, state, local or foreign income taxes, and mixed services costs, and
TMS = Total mixed services costs.

The usual cost accounting techniques (e.g., average cost per equivalent unit) can be used to allocate production costs between the cost of goods sold and the ending inventory.

Alternatively, a producer can elect to allocate mixed service costs to production on the basis of labor charges only (i.e., production labor as a percentage of total labor costs).

Costs included in the inventory of *wholesalers and retailers* are comparable to those of the producer. However, many of these costs are captured in the price these

---

[75] Reg. § 1.471–3(b).
[76] H. Rep. 99–841, 99th Cong., 2nd Sess., 1986, pp. 302–309. See also Reg. § 1.263A–1(a).
[77] Producers with mixed services costs of less than $200,000 for the year are not required to allocate mixed services costs if the simplified method is used to allocate their production costs. Reg. § 1.263A–1(b)(12).
[78] Reg. § 1.263A–1(h)(5).

taxpayers pay for the goods. The following additional costs must be capitalized by wholesalers and retailers:

- All storage costs for wholesalers.
- Offsite storage costs for retailers.
- Purchasing costs (e.g., buyers' wages or salaries).
- Handling, processing, assembly, and repackaging.
- The portion of mixed services costs allocable to these functions.

Mixed services costs must be allocated to offsite storage, purchasing, and packaging on the basis of direct labor costs of these departments as a percentage of total payroll. Thus, the storage, purchasing, and packaging costs allocated to ending inventory include some mixed services costs.

The uniform capitalization rules may cause some costs to be capitalized for tax purposes but not for financial accounting purposes. For example, a wholesaler's or a manufacturer's storage costs are generally expensed for financial reporting purposes, but must be capitalized for tax purposes. Also, a taxpayer may capitalize straight-line depreciation of production equipment for financial accounting purposes, but the actual tax depreciation must be capitalized under uniform capitalization.

Lower of Cost or Market. Except for those taxpayers who use the LIFO method (discussed below), inventories may be valued at the **lower of cost or market (replacement cost)**.[79] Taxpayers using LIFO *must value inventory at cost*. However, the write-down of damaged or shopworn merchandise and goods that are otherwise unsalable at normal prices is not considered an application of the lower of cost or market method. Such items should be valued at bona fide selling price less direct cost of disposal.[80]

In the case of excess inventories (as in *Thor Power Tool Co.*, discussed above), goods can be written down only to the taxpayer's offering price. If the offering price is not reduced, the goods must be valued at cost.

EXAMPLE 32

The Cardinal Publishing Company invested $50,000 to print 10,000 copies of a book ($5 each). Although only 7,000 copies were sold in the first 3 years and none in the next 5 years, management is convinced that the book will become a classic in 20 years. Cardinal leaves the price the same as it was when the book was first distributed ($15 per copy). The remaining 3,000 books, therefore, must be valued at cost ($15,000). ▼

In applying the lower of cost or market method, *each* item included in the inventory must be valued at the lower of its cost or market value.[81]

EXAMPLE 33

The taxpayer's ending inventory is valued as follows:

Item	Cost	Market	Lower of Cost or Market
A	$5,000	$ 4,000	$4,000
B	3,000	2,000	2,000
C	1,500	6,000	1,500
	$9,500	$12,000	$7,500

---

[79]Reg. § 1.472–4.
[80]Reg. § 1.471–2(c).
[81]Reg. § 1.471–4(c).

Under the lower of cost or market method, the taxpayer's inventory is valued at $7,500 rather than $9,500. ▼

Inventory Shrinkage. Because of accidents, thefts, and recording errors, a company's inventory per physical count and its inventory according to company records may differ. This difference is called *inventory shrinkage* and is typically recorded when a company completes its physical inventory. But many companies take their physical inventories at some time other than the last day of their taxable year. As a result, they need to adjust the ending inventory, per their accounting records, for the estimated shrinkage that has occurred since the last physical inventory. Section 471(b) allows a taxpayer to deduct this shrinkage based on its historical relationship with sales.

Determining Cost—Specific Identification, FIFO, and LIFO. In some cases, it is feasible to determine the cost of the particular item sold. For example, an automobile dealer can easily determine the specific cost of each automobile that has been sold. However, in most businesses it is necessary to resort to a flow of goods assumption such as *first in, first out* (FIFO), *last in, first out* (LIFO), or an *average cost* method. A taxpayer may use any of these methods, provided the method selected is consistently applied from year to year.

During a period of rising prices, LIFO generally produces a lower ending inventory valuation and results in a higher cost of goods sold than would be obtained under the FIFO method. The following example illustrates how LIFO and FIFO affect the computation of the cost of goods sold.

▼
EXAMPLE 34

On January 1, the taxpayer opened a retail store to sell refrigerators. At least 10 refrigerators must be carried in inventory to satisfy customer demands. The initial investment in the 10 refrigerators is $5,000 ($500 each). During the year, 10 refrigerators were sold at $750 each and were replaced at a cost of $6,000 ($600 each). Gross profit under the LIFO and FIFO methods is computed as follows:

		FIFO		LIFO
Sales (10 × $750)		$ 7,500		$ 7,500
Beginning inventory	$ 5,000		$ 5,000	
Purchases	6,000		6,000	
	$11,000		$11,000	
Ending inventory				
10 × $600	(6,000)			
10 × $500			(5,000)	
Cost of goods sold		(5,000)		(6,000)
Gross profit		$ 2,500		$ 1,500

▼

Dollar-Value LIFO. In the preceding example, the taxpayer was buying and selling a single product, a particular model of a refrigerator. The taxpayer employed the *specific goods LIFO* technique. Under the specific goods approach, if identical items are not on hand at the end of the period, the LIFO inventory is depleted, and all of the deferred profit is reported. Thus, taxpayers who frequently change the items carried in inventory would realize little benefit from LIFO. However, dollar-value LIFO avoids this LIFO depletion problem.

Under **dollar-value LIFO**, each inventory item is assigned to a pool. A *pool* is a collection of similar items and is treated as a separate inventory. Determining whether items are similar involves considerable judgment. In general, however, a taxpayer would prefer broad pools so that when a particular item is sold out, it can be replaced by increases in other items in the same pool. Typically, all products manufactured at a particular plant can be treated as a pool.[82] A department store may have a separate pool for each department. An automobile dealer may have separate pools for new cars, lightweight trucks, heavy-duty trucks, and car and truck parts.

At the end of the period, the ending inventory is valued at current-year prices and then at the LIFO base period (the year LIFO was adopted) prices. The ratio of the ending inventory at current prices to the ending inventory at base period prices is the *LIFO index*. If the total current inventory at base period prices is greater than the base period inventory at base period prices, a LIFO layer must be added. The LIFO index is applied to the LIFO layer to convert it to current prices.

EXAMPLE 35

Black Company adopted LIFO effective January 1, 1998. The base LIFO inventory (from December 31, 1997) was $1,000,000. On December 31, 1998, the inventory was $1,320,000 at end-of-1998 prices and $1,200,000 at end-of-1997 (the base period) prices. Thus, Black added a 1998 layer of $200,000 ($1,200,000 − $1,000,000) at base period prices. The layer must be converted to 1998 prices as follows:

$$\text{LIFO index} = \$1,320,000/\$1,200,000 = 1.10$$

$$\text{1998 layer} \times \text{LIFO index} = \$200,000 \times 1.10 = \$220,000$$

Therefore, the 1998 ending inventory is $1,000,000 + $220,000 = $1,220,000.

The inventory on December 31, 1999, is $1,325,000 using 1999 prices and $1,250,000 using base period prices. Thus, the LIFO index for 1999 is $1,325,000/$1,250,000 = 1.06. The LIFO inventory is $1,273,000, computed as follows:

	BLACK COMPANY LIFO Inventory December 31, 1999		
	Base Period Cost	LIFO Index	LIFO Layers
Base inventory	$1,000,000	1.00	$1,000,000
1998 layer	200,000	1.10	220,000
1999 layer	50,000	1.06	53,000
	$1,250,000		$1,273,000

THE LIFO ELECTION

A taxpayer may adopt LIFO by using the method in the tax return for the year of the change and by attaching Form 970 (Application to Use LIFO Inventory Method) to the tax return. Thus, a taxpayer need not request approval for the change. Once this election is made, it cannot be revoked. A prospective change from LIFO to any other inventory method can be made only if the consent of the IRS is obtained.[83]

The beginning inventory valuation for the first LIFO year is computed by the costing method employed in the preceding year. Thus, the beginning LIFO inventory is generally the same as the closing inventory for the preceding year. However,

---

[82]See Reg. § 1.472–8.
[83]Reg. §§ 1.472–3(a) and –5 and Rev.Proc. 84–74, 1984–2 C.B. 736 at 742.

since lower of cost or market cannot be used with LIFO, previous write-downs to market for items included in the beginning inventory must be *restored* to income. The amount the inventories are written up is an adjustment due to a change in accounting method.[84] However, the usual rules for disposition of adjustments are not applicable. Instead, the taxpayer spreads the adjustment ratably over the year of the change and the two succeeding years.[85]

EXAMPLE 36

In 1997, Chickadee, Inc., used the lower of cost or market FIFO inventory method. The FIFO cost of its ending inventory was $30,000, and the market value of the inventory was $24,000. Therefore, the ending inventory for 1997 was $24,000. Chickadee switched to LIFO in 1998 and was required to write up the beginning inventory to $30,000. Chickadee must add $2,000 ($6,000 ÷ 3) to its income for each of the years 1998, 1999, and 2000. ▼

Once a LIFO election is made for tax purposes, the taxpayer's financial reports to owners and creditors must also be prepared on the basis of LIFO. The *conformity* of financial reports to tax reporting is specifically required by § 472(c) and is strictly enforced by the IRS. However, the Regulations allow a taxpayer to make a footnote disclosure of the net income computed by another method of inventory valuation (e.g., FIFO).[86]

PLANNING CONSIDERATIONS

LIFO Inventory

During periods of anticipated cost increases, LIFO tends to reduce reported taxable income and thereby lowers current tax liabilities. This tendency reverses itself, however, if inventory *volumes* are not maintained. As older and therefore lower costs are matched against current income, a taxpayer's reported income will be *higher* under LIFO than under FIFO.

Taxpayers can usually avoid this phenomenon by ensuring that base inventory levels do not decrease. But *nontax considerations* often thwart this strategy. During periods of shortage, replacement goods may be unavailable. If interest rates are rising, a taxpayer may not want to increase its purchases and the corresponding cost of financing these purchases. If a recession is in progress, the taxpayer might be anticipating a slowdown in its sales and will resist acquiring additional inventory beyond its expected needs. As a result of these factors, inventory levels might go down, and taxable income will then increase.

In any case, the *financial statement conformity* requirement of LIFO can make this method unappealing to corporate management. While the permitted footnote disclosures can somewhat ameliorate the impact of LIFO on a company's reported earnings, such disclosures are often more effective with sophisticated creditors than with capital markets generally. Accordingly, management may wait until a general business slowdown has dampened earnings expectations before switching to LIFO and suffering from the typical drop in earnings that occurs with the switch.

---

[84]Reg. § 1.472–2(c).
[85]§ 472(d).
[86]Reg. § 1.472–2(e).

KEY TERMS

Accounting method, 6–10
Accounting period, 6–2
Accrual method, 6–9
Cash method, 6–9
Claim of right doctrine, 6–9
Completed contract method, 6–24
Contingent sales prices, 6–15
Dollar-value LIFO, 6–29
Fiscal year, 6–2
Imputed interest, 6–16
Installment method, 6–13
Least aggregate deferral method, 6–4
Long-term contract, 6–21
Lower of cost or market (replacement cost), 6–28
Majority interest partner, 6–3
Percentage of completion method, 6–24
Personal service corporation (PSC), 6–6
Principal partner, 6–3
Short taxable year (short period), 6–7
Uniform capitalization rules, 6–27

PROBLEM MATERIALS

1. Red, White, and Blue are unrelated corporations engaged in real estate development. The three corporations formed a joint venture (treated as a partnership) to develop a tract of land. Assuming the venture does not have a natural business year, what tax year must the joint venture adopt under the following circumstances?

		Tax Year Ending	Interest in Joint Venture
a.	Red	September 30	60%
	White	June 30	20%
	Blue	March 31	20%
b.	Red	September 30	30%
	White	June 30	40%
	Blue	January 31	30%

2. The Zinnia Wholesale Company is an S corporation that began business on March 1, 1998. William, a calendar year taxpayer, owns 100% of Zinnia. He has $300,000 taxable income from other sources each year. William will work approximately 30 hours a week for the corporation. Zinnia sells swimming pool supplies, and its natural business year ends in September. Approximately 80% of Zinnia's gross receipts occur in June through September.
   a. What tax year should Zinnia elect, assuming that William anticipates the company will produce a net profit for all years?
   b. What tax year should Zinnia elect, assuming it will lose $10,000 a month for the first 12 months and an average of $5,000 a month for the next 12 months? In the third year, the corporation will earn taxable income.

3. Andrew, a consultant, conducted his professional practice through Andrew, Inc. The corporation uses a fiscal year ending September 30 even though the business purpose test for a fiscal year cannot be satisfied. For the year ending September 30, 1998, the corporation paid Andrew a salary of $200,000, and during the period January through September 1998, the corporation paid him a salary of $160,000.
   a. How much salary should Andrew receive during the period October 1 through December 31, 1998?
   b. Assume that Andrew received only $40,000 salary during the period October 1 through December 31, 1998. What would be the consequences to Andrew, Inc.?

CHAPTER 6 Accounting Periods and Methods

4. Owl Corporation is in the business of sales and home deliveries of fuel oil and currently uses a calendar year for reporting its taxable income. However, Owl's natural business year ends May 31. For the short period, January 1 through May 31, 1998, the corporation earned $31,500. Assume the corporate tax rates are as follows: 15% on taxable income of $50,000 or less, 25% on taxable income over $50,000 but not over $75,000, and 34% on taxable income over $75,000.
   a. What must Owl Corporation do to change its taxable year?
   b. Compute Owl Corporation's tax for the short period.

5. This year, the taxpayer was required to switch from the cash to the accrual basis of accounting for sales and cost of goods sold. Taxable income for this year computed under the cash basis was $40,000. Relevant account balances were as follows:

	Beginning of the Year	End of the Year
Accounts receivable	$36,000	$30,000
Accounts payable	9,000	8,000
Inventory	7,000	10,000

   Compute the following:
   a. The adjustment due to the change in accounting method.
   b. The accrual basis taxable income for this year.

6. This year, the taxpayer changed from the cash to the accrual basis of accounting for sales, cost of goods sold, and accrued expenses. Taxable income for the year computed under the cash method was $45,000. Relevant account balances are as follows:

	Beginning of the Year	End of the Year
Accounts receivable	$ 5,000	$13,000
Accounts payable	–0–	–0–
Accrued expenses	5,000	6,000
Inventory	10,000	9,000

   a. Compute the accrual basis taxable income for this year and the adjustment due to the change in accounting method.
   b. Assuming the change was voluntary, how will the adjustment due to the change be treated?

7. Rochelle, a CPA, recently obtained a new client, the Hyacinth Engineering Corporation (annual gross receipts of $2 million). The company's previous accountant had filed all returns by the accrual method of accounting, the same method that was used to prepare financial statements submitted when the company applied for a loan in its first year of operation. Rochelle recognizes that under the accrual method of accounting the company is paying tax on its accounts receivable, whereas under the cash method of accounting the income could be deferred until the cash is collected. In many cases, it takes the company three months to collect a receivable. Rochelle also recognizes that the IRS will not allow the corporation to change to the cash method.
   Rochelle is considering the following plan. A new corporation would be formed. Each shareholder in Hyacinth would own the same percentage of stock in the new corporation. The key element of the plan is that the new corporation would elect the cash method. Hyacinth would complete its contracts in progress, collect its receivables, and gradually be liquidated. Meanwhile all new business would be channeled into the new corporation. Evaluate Rochelle's plan.

8. Jeffrey Robin, the president of Robin Furniture Corporation (average annual gross receipts of $4 million), has prepared the company's financial statements and income tax return for the past 25 years. However, in July 1999, after Jeffrey had filed the 1998 return, he hired you to prepare the 1999 corporate tax return because he has not studied taxes for over 20 years and suspects that the rules may have changed. Based upon an

initial examination of his trial balance and some account analyses, you have determined that the following items may require adjustments:

- The company uses the LIFO inventory method, as valued at cost. At the end of 1998, the company has written off $25,000 for inventory items that were still on hand but probably were not marketable (because the products are obsolete). No such write-off had been taken in prior years.

- The company expenses all freight on merchandise when the goods are received. The expensed freight allocable to the beginning inventory for 1999 was $12,000.

- The company accrues salaries and commissions, but expenses payroll taxes in the year paid. Because of large 1998 year-end bonuses that were not paid until the beginning of 1999, the company had $24,000 in accrued payroll taxes at the beginning of 1999.

- The company uses the accrual method and has a reserve for bad debts equal to 3% of accounts receivable, which is an accurate percentage. The balance in the account at the beginning of the year is $15,000.

Write a letter to Mr. Robin explaining the adjustments that will be required and how the changes will be implemented. The address of Robin Furniture Corporation is 1000 East Maryland, Evansville, IL 47722.

9. Your client, Hometown Motors Company, is an automobile dealer using the accrual method. The company also sells service contracts on automobiles. A customer who buys a contract can have the work performed by any authorized dealer. If someone other than Hometown does the work, the bill is nevertheless paid by Hometown. Contracts sell for $1,000 and provide protection for five years. When Hometown sells a service contract, the company also purchases an insurance contract (for $800) that reimburses Hometown for any cost it incurs under the service contract. In addition, if Hometown actually performs the service, the insurance company pays Hometown its normal charge.

   Hometown is caught between two tax accounting rules. Under the rule for prepaid income (refer to Chapter 3), the entire $1,000 revenue from a service contract must be included in gross income in the year the contract is sold. On the other hand, the cost of the insurance contract must be amortized over its five-year life ($800/5 years = $160 per year). Thus, in the year a contract is sold, Hometown must recognize $840 ($1,000 − $160) of income when the company has received a net amount of only $200 ($1,000 − $800).

   Should you suggest that the terms of the service and insurance contracts be changed so that (1) Hometown sells the insurance to the customer and receives a $200 commission, and (2) Hometown agrees to pay the customer if the insurance company goes out of existence or is otherwise unable to pay when the customer requires service? How do you respond if Hometown rejects this proposal but suggests that since the two forms of transactions produce the same economic results, you account for the service contracts as you suggest in the proposal?

10. Finch Corporation, a cash basis taxpayer, has agreed to sell land to Beige, Inc., a well-established and highly profitable company. Beige is willing to (1) pay $100,000 cash or (2) pay $25,000 cash and the balance ($75,000) plus interest at 10% (the Federal rate) in two years. Finch is in the 35% marginal tax bracket (combined Federal and state) for all years and believes it can reinvest the sales proceeds and earn a 14% before-tax rate of return.
    a. Should Finch accept the deferred payments option if its basis in the land is $10,000?
    b. Do you think your results would change if Finch's basis in the land were $90,000?

11. Purple & Company sold a cargo temperature detector to Hawk Manufacturing for 25% of gross sales in excess of $5 million annually, with a lifetime limit of $360,000. In the first year, Purple received $75,000. The cost basis of this device is $120,000. What is the profit that Purple must report for this year?

CHAPTER 6 Accounting Periods and Methods

12. Rose Brothers sold all the stock of a gas station company for 8% of gross receipts earned over the next 5 years. They paid $20,000 for their stock when the company was first incorporated. During the first year of the sales contract, Rose Brothers received $7,500. What is their reportable income for that year?

13. Grackle, Inc., sold an untested stereo enhancer to an electronics firm for 5% of the net profits from this machine, with no upper limit, no time limit, and no guarantees. Grackle paid $6,000 to develop the enhancer. In the first year, it received $500 from the electronics firm. Does Grackle have any reportable profit, and if so, how much?

14. On July 1, 1997, a cash basis taxpayer sold land for $800,000 due on the date of the sale and $6 million principal and $741,600 interest (6%) due on June 30, 1999. The seller's basis in the land was $1 million. The Federal short-term rate was 8%, compounded semiannually.
    a. Compute the seller's interest income and gain in 1997, 1998, and 1999.
    b. Same as (a), except that the amount due in two years was $2 million principal and $508,800 interest and the purchaser will use the cash method to account for interest.

15. Maroon, Inc., made an installment sale of land and a building to Nighthawk Corporation. There was no depreciation recapture on the building. At the time of the sale, the Federal rate was 8%, and the market rate on similar contracts was 10%. Under the contract, Nighthawk would make payments as follows:

Cash at closing, July 1, 1998	$ 50,000
Interest at 9%, due June 30, 1999*	27,607
Interest at 9%, due June 30, 2000*	27,607
Principal due June 30, 2000	300,000

    *Interest is compounded semiannually.

    a. Will interest be imputed on the contract?
    b. Assuming that Maroon is a cash basis taxpayer, what is its interest income for 1998 under the contract?
    c. Assuming that Nighthawk is an accrual basis taxpayer, what is its interest expense for 1998 under the contract?

16. On December 30, 1998, Father sold land to Son for $10,000 cash and a 7% installment note with a face amount of $190,000. In 1999, after paying $30,000 on the principal of the note, Son sold the land. In 2000, Son paid Father $25,000 on the note principal. Father's basis in the land was $50,000. Assuming Son sold the land for $250,000, compute Father's taxable gain in 1999.

17. George sold land to an unrelated party in 1997. His basis in the land was $40,000, and the selling price was $100,000—$25,000 payable at closing and $25,000 (plus 10% interest) due January 1, 1998, 1999, and 2000. What would be the tax consequences of the following? [Treat each part independently and assume (1) George did not elect out of the installment method and (2) the installment obligations have values equal to their face amounts.]
    a. In 1998, George gave to his daughter the right to collect all future payments on the installment obligations.
    b. In 1998, after collecting the payment due on January 1, George transferred the installment obligation to his 100%-controlled corporation in exchange for additional shares of stock.
    c. On December 31, 1998, George received the payment due on January 1, 1999. On December 15, 1999, George died, and the remaining installment obligation was transferred to his estate. The estate collected the amount due on January 1, 2000.

18. The Dove Construction Company reports its income by the completed contract method. At the end of 1998, the company completed a contract to construct a building at a total cost of $980,000. The contract price was $1,200,000. However, the customer refused to accept the work and would not pay anything on the contract because he claimed the

roof did not meet specifications. Dove's engineers estimated it would cost $140,000 to bring the roof up to the customer's standards. In 1999, the dispute was settled in the customer's favor; the roof was improved at a cost of $170,000, and the customer accepted the building and paid the $1,200,000.

   a. What would be the effects of the above on Dove's taxable income for 1998 and 1999?
   b. Same as (a), except that Dove had $1,100,000 accumulated cost under the contract at the end of 1998.

19. Daffodil Company is a real estate construction company with average annual gross receipts of $3 million. Daffodil uses the completed contract method, and the contracts require 18 months to complete.
   a. Which of the following costs would be allocated to construction in progress by Daffodil?
      1. The payroll taxes on direct labor.
      2. The current services pension costs for employees whose wages are included in direct labor.
      3. Accelerated depreciation on equipment used on contracts.
      4. Sales tax on materials assigned to contracts.
      5. The past service costs for employees whose wages are included in direct labor.
      6. Bidding expenses for contracts awarded.
   b. Assume that Daffodil generally builds commercial buildings under contracts with the owners and reports the income by the completed contract method. The company is considering building a series of similar stores for a retail chain. The gross profit margin would be a low percentage, but the company's gross receipts would triple. Write a letter to your client explaining the tax accounting implications of entering into these contracts. Daffodil's mailing address is P.O. Box 1000, Harrisonburg, VA 22807.

20. The Eagle Construction Company began business on April 1 this year. The company erects prefabricated steel buildings and operates as follows. After the customer selects a building model, Eagle orders the materials from the manufacturer. Eagle then erects the building on the customer's property. Eagle prices the contract at 150% of the cost of the prefabricated building. The customer pays 70% of the price at the time the materials are ordered and the balance of the original price when the building is completed. If Eagle buys more than $1 million in materials during the year, the manufacturer will give Eagle a 2% rebate the following February. Several buildings were under construction at the end of the year. Eagle had ordered more than $1 million in materials during the year, but had paid for only about $989,000 through December. What issues involving Eagle's accounting methods are raised by these facts?

21. Indicate the accounting method that should be used to compute the income from the following contracts:
   a. A contract to build six jet aircraft.
   b. A contract to build a new home. The contractor's average annual gross receipts are $15 million.
   c. A contract to manufacture 3,000 pairs of boots for a large retail chain. The manufacturer has several contracts to produce the same boot for other retailers.
   d. A contract to pave a parking lot. The contractor's average annual gross receipts are $2 million.

22. Ostrich Company makes gasoline storage tanks. Everything produced is under contract (that is, the company does not produce until it gets a contract for a product). Ostrich makes three basic models. However, the tanks must be adapted to each individual customer's location and needs (e.g., the location of the valves, the quality of the materials and insulation). Discuss the following issues relative to Ostrich's operations:
   a. An examining IRS agent contends that each of the company's contracts is to produce a "unique product." What difference does it make whether the product is unique or a "shelf item"?
   b. Producing one of the tanks takes over one year from start to completion, and the total cost is in excess of $1 million. What costs must be capitalized for this contract

CHAPTER 6 Accounting Periods and Methods 6–37

that are not subject to capitalization for a contract with a shorter duration and lower cost?
c. What must Ostrich do with the costs of bidding on contracts?
d. Ostrich frequently makes several cost estimates for a contract, using various estimates of materials costs. These costs fluctuate almost daily. Assuming Ostrich must use the percentage of completion method to report the income from the contract, what will be the consequence if the company uses the highest estimate of a contract's cost and the actual cost is closer to the lowest estimated cost?

23. Swallow Company is a large real estate construction company that reports its income by the percentage of completion method. In 1999, the company completed a contract at a total cost of $1,960,000. The contract price was $2,400,000. At the end of 1998, the year the contract was begun, Swallow estimated the total cost of the contract would be $2,100,000, and total accumulated costs on the contract at the end of 1998 were $1,400,000. The relevant tax rate is 34%, and the relevant Federal interest rate is 7%. Assume that all returns were filed and taxes were paid on March 15 following the close of the calendar tax year.
    a. Compute the gross profit on the contract for 1998 and 1999.
    b. Compute the lookback interest due with the 1999 return.
    c. Before bidding on a contract, Swallow generally makes three estimates of total contract costs: (1) optimistic, (2) pessimistic, and (3) most likely (based on a blending of optimistic and pessimistic assumptions). The company has asked you to write a letter explaining which of these estimates should be used for percentage of completion purposes. In writing your letter, you should consider the fact that Swallow is an S corporation; therefore, the income and deductions flow through to the shareholders who are all individuals in the 36% marginal tax bracket. The relevant Federal interest rate is 8%. Swallow's mailing address is 400 Front Avenue, Ashland, OR 97520.

24. Last year, Quail Construction Company began two contracts that were completed this year:

    • Contract #1. The company reported $300,000 cost and $150,000 profit on the contract. This year, the company completed the contract, incurring additional cost of $200,000 and reporting an additional $50,000 profit on the contract.

    • Contract #2. The company reported $500,000 cost and $100,000 profit on the contract. This year, the company incurred an additional $200,000 to complete the contract. The contract price was $650,000.

    Quail is a large real estate contractor and reports its profits by the percentage of completion method. The company's marginal tax rate in all relevant years was 34%, and the relevant Federal interest rate was 7%.
    a. Compute the lookback interest payable or receivable by Quail.
    b. Write a letter to Amos Brown, the president of Quail Construction Company, explaining to him the consequences of the company's errors in estimating contract costs. Quail's mailing address is 200 Country Road, Orono, ME 04469.

25. Bluebird Company, a furniture retailer, is adding a new line of merchandise. In the current year, the company purchased merchandise with an invoice price of $700,000, less a 2% discount for early payment. Freight and handling charges totaled $60,000. The company had to lease additional storage space in a warehouse three blocks from the store. The lease on the storage space was $30,000 for the year. A buyer was added to handle the new line of merchandise, and her salary was $35,000 for the year. Also, as a result of the increase in inventory of goods on hand, the company's insurance increased by $5,000. The invoice cost of the goods on hand at the end of the year was $105,000. Compute the company's ending inventory under the FIFO method.

26. Lavender Manufacturing Company began business in the current year. The company uses the simplified method to allocate mixed services costs to production. The company's costs and expenses for the year were as follows:

Direct labor	$1,250,000
Direct materials	2,000,000
Factory supervision	200,000
Personnel department	100,000
Computer operations	50,000
General administration	150,000
Marketing	100,000
Interest	25,000
	$3,875,000

a. Determine Lavender's total production costs for the year.
b. What suggestions can you offer regarding the allocation of the company's mixed services costs?

27. Flamingo Company produces small machinery. The company also produces parts used to repair the machinery. The parts may be sold for several years after the company has discontinued the product. Flamingo has on hand parts with an original cost of $600,000. The total offering price on these goods is $960,000. However, the company expects to sell only 80% of the parts on hand. The excess parts are kept in case the estimates are incorrect.
   a. Can Flamingo deduct the excess inventory under the lower of cost or market rule?
   b. Assume that Flamingo deducted the cost of the excess parts on hand. While the parts were still on hand, the company elected LIFO. What are the implications of the change in inventory method?

28. You recently told a client that some of his entertainment expenses were nondeductible personal items, and relations became a bit testy. In fact, he remarked at the time that he knew accountants who would accept those deductions "and they don't charge any more than you do." You have just discovered that this client rents a storage building with inventory items that were not included in his physical inventory, which you did not observe. Does this situation call for selective perception?

29. This year, Gallinule, Inc., changed from the use of the lower of cost or market FIFO method to the LIFO method. The ending inventory for last year was computed as follows:

Item	FIFO Cost	Replacement Cost	Lower of Cost or Market
A	$10,000	$ 9,000	$ 9,000
B	25,000	30,000	25,000
			$34,000

a. What is the correct beginning inventory for this year under the LIFO method?
b. What immediate tax consequences (if any) would result from the switch to LIFO?

30. Amber Company has used the dollar-value LIFO technique for the past three years. The company has only one inventory pool. Its beginning inventory for the current year was computed as follows:

	Base Period Cost	LIFO Index	LIFO Layer
Base inventory	$1,250,000	1.0	$1,250,000
Year 1 layer	450,000	1.15	517,500
Year 2 layer	100,000	1.05	105,000
	$1,800,000		$1,872,500

The ending inventory is $1,955,000 at current period prices and $1,700,000 at base period prices. Determine the company's LIFO inventory value as of the end of the current year.

31. Your client, Bluebell & Associates, is negotiating a sale of investment real estate for $24 million. Bluebell believes that the buyer would pay cash of $16 million and a note for $8 million, or $6 million cash and a note for $18 million. The notes will pay interest at slightly above the market rate. Bluebell realizes that the second option involves more risks of collection, but it is willing to accept that risk if the tax benefits of the installment sale are substantial. Write a letter advising Bluebell of the tax consequences of choosing the lower down payment and larger note option, assuming it has no other installment receivables. The company's address is 200 Jerdone, Gettysburg, PA 17325.

RESEARCH PROBLEMS

Note: *The RIA OnPoint System 4 Student Version CD-ROM available with this text can be used in preparing solutions to the Research Problems. Alternatively, tax research materials contained in a standard tax library can be used.*

32. White Electric Company generates electricity that it sells to residential, commercial, and industrial customers. The company uses coal to generate the electricity and accounts for the cost of the coal on a LIFO basis. That is, the coal on hand at the end of the year is deemed to be from the earliest purchases. This LIFO assumption is generally consistent with how the coal is actually used because newly purchased coal is placed on top of the coal on hand at the time of the delivery. The IRS agent contends that LIFO cannot be used to account for the coal because it is a supply rather than inventory. You concede that the coal is not inventory; however, you contend that because the LIFO assumption accurately depicts the cost of the coal used, the method used clearly reflects income, and therefore the IRS cannot change the method. Help your client resolve this issue with the IRS agent.

33. Violet Company discovered that certain equipment used in its repair operations had been accounted for as inventory rather than as fixed assets. This incorrect treatment applied to all years in which the equipment had been used, and all of those years are open under the statute of limitations. Violet filed amended returns for all years affected by the incorrect treatment to obtain a refund of overpayments of taxes for the years affected. The IRS refused to accept the amended returns. The IRS reasoned that Violet was actually changing accounting methods and this can only be accomplished through a request for change in methods. In addition, the IRS concluded that an adjustment due to a voluntary change in accounting method must be taken into income for the year of the change. Is the IRS correct? Write a letter to Agnes Boyd, the president of Violet Company, that contains your advice and prepare a memo for the tax files. Violet's address is 100 Whitaker's Mill, Fargo, ND 58105.

34. You recently contracted to perform tax services for a new funeral home. In preparing the initial tax return, you must decide whether the funeral home can use the cash method of accounting. When discussing this issue with the manager, the manager points out that the company is actually a service business and that the only materials involved are caskets, which average only 15% of the price of a funeral. Is the funeral home required to use the accrual method of accounting?

35. Ron receives appliances on consignment from the manufacturer and collects a 5% commission on any sales made during the year. Ron is an accrual basis taxpayer, and he made total sales of $750,000 during the year. Since the manufacturer is usually a few weeks behind in recording Ron's sales, at the end of the year only $600,000 of sales revenue was recorded. Ron argues that he should report income for the year of only $30,000 (5% × $600,000), since that was all he had a right to receive for the year. Ron had no right to the commissions on the other $150,000 sales until the manufacturer reported them in the following year. What is Ron's correct taxable income for the year? Explain.

CHAPTER 7

PROPERTY TRANSACTIONS: BASIS, GAIN AND LOSS, AND NONTAXABLE EXCHANGES

LEARNING OBJECTIVES

After completing Chapter 7, you should be able to:

1. Understand the computation of realized gain or loss on property dispositions.

2. Distinguish between realized and recognized gain or loss.

3. Explain how basis is determined for various methods of asset acquisition.

4. Describe various loss disallowance provisions.

5. Apply the nonrecognition provisions and basis determination rules for like-kind exchanges.

6. Explain the nonrecognition provisions available on the involuntary conversion of property.

7. Identify other nonrecognition provisions contained in the Code.

OUTLINE

Determination of Gain or Loss, 7–3
Realized Gain or Loss, 7–3
Recognized Gain or Loss, 7–6
Nonrecognition of Gain or Loss, 7–6
Recovery of Capital Doctrine, 7–7

Basis Considerations, 7–8
Determination of Cost Basis, 7–8
Gift Basis, 7–10
Property Acquired from a Decedent, 7–13
Disallowed Losses, 7–15
Conversion of Property from Personal Use to Business or Income-Producing Use, 7–16
Summary of Basis Adjustments, 7–18

General Concept of a Nontaxable Exchange, 7–18

Like-Kind Exchanges—§ 1031, 7–21
Like-Kind Property, 7–22
Exchange Requirement, 7–24
Boot, 7–24
Basis and Holding Period of Property Received, 7–25

Involuntary Conversions—§ 1033, 7–28
Involuntary Conversion Defined, 7–29
Replacement Property, 7–30
Time Limitation on Replacement, 7–31
Reporting Considerations, 7–32

Other Nonrecognition Provisions, 7–32

Transfer of Assets to Business Entity—§§ 351 and 721, 7–32
Exchange of Stock for Property—§ 1032, 7–32
Certain Exchanges of Insurance Policies—§ 1035, 7–33
Exchange of Stock for Stock of the Same Corporation—§ 1036, 7–33
Certain Reacquisitions of Real Property—§ 1038, 7–33
Rollovers into Specialized Small Business Investment Companies—§ 1044, 7–33
Sale of a Principal Residence—§ 121, 7–34
Transfers of Property between Spouses or Incident to Divorce—§ 1041, 7–34

This chapter and the following chapter are concerned with the income tax consequences of property transactions, including the sale or other disposition of property. The following questions are considered with respect to the sale or other disposition of property:

- Is there a realized gain or loss?
- If so, is that gain or loss recognized for tax purposes?
- If that gain or loss is recognized, is it ordinary or capital?
- What is the basis of any replacement property that is acquired?

This chapter discusses the determination of realized and recognized gain or loss and the basis of property. The following chapter covers the classification of recognized gain or loss as ordinary or capital.

For the most part, the rules discussed in Chapters 7 and 8 apply to all types of taxpayers. Individuals, partnerships, closely held corporations, limited liability companies, and publicly held corporations all own assets for use in business activities or as investments in entities that themselves conduct business activities. Individuals, however, are unique among taxpayers because they also own assets that are used in daily life and have no significant business or investment component. Because of that possibility, some property transaction concepts apply somewhat differently to individual taxpayers depending upon how a person uses the specific asset in question. Nevertheless, the material that follows pertains to taxpayers generally except where otherwise noted.

CHAPTER 7 Property Transactions: Basis, Gain and Loss, and Nontaxable Exchanges

DETERMINATION OF GAIN OR LOSS

REALIZED GAIN OR LOSS

LEARNING OBJECTIVE 1
Understand the computation of realized gain or loss on property dispositions.

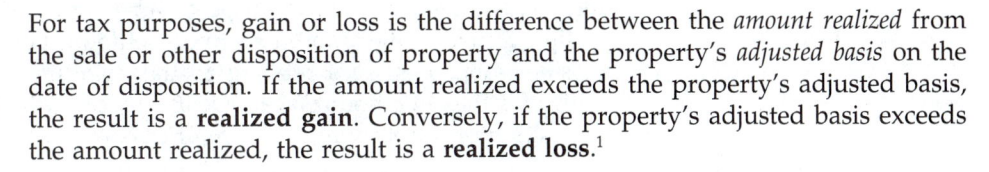

For tax purposes, gain or loss is the difference between the *amount realized* from the sale or other disposition of property and the property's *adjusted basis* on the date of disposition. If the amount realized exceeds the property's adjusted basis, the result is a **realized gain**. Conversely, if the property's adjusted basis exceeds the amount realized, the result is a **realized loss**.[1]

EXAMPLE 1
Lavender, Inc., sells Swan Corporation stock with an adjusted basis of $3,000 for $5,000. Lavender's realized gain is $2,000. If Lavender had sold the stock for $2,000, it would have had a $1,000 realized loss. ▼

Sale or Other Disposition. The term *sale or other disposition* is defined broadly to include virtually any disposition of property. Thus, trade-ins, casualties, condemnations, thefts, and bond retirements are all treated as dispositions of property. The most common disposition of property is a sale or exchange. Usually, the key factor in determining whether a disposition has taken place is whether an identifiable event has occurred[2] as opposed to a mere fluctuation in the value of the property.[3]

EXAMPLE 2
Heron & Associates owns Tan Corporation stock that cost $3,000. The stock has appreciated in value by $2,000 since Heron purchased it. Heron has no realized gain since mere fluctuation in value is not a disposition or identifiable event for tax purposes. Nor would Heron have a realized loss had the stock declined in value. ▼

Amount Realized. The **amount realized** from a sale or other disposition of property is the sum of any money received plus the fair market value of other property received. The amount realized also includes any real property taxes treated as imposed on the seller that are actually paid by the buyer.[4] The reason for including these taxes in the amount realized is that by paying the taxes, the purchaser is, in effect, paying an additional amount to the seller of the property.

The amount realized also includes any liability on the property disposed of, such as a mortgage debt, if the buyer assumes the mortgage or the property is sold subject to the mortgage.[5] The amount of the liability is included in the amount realized, even if the debt is nonrecourse and even if the amount of the debt is greater than the fair market value of the mortgaged property.[6]

EXAMPLE 3
Bunting & Co. sells property to Orange, Inc., for $50,000 cash. There is a $20,000 mortgage on the property. Bunting's amount realized from the sale is $70,000 if Orange assumes the mortgage or takes the property subject to the mortgage. ▼

The **fair market value** of property received in a sale or other disposition has been defined by the courts as the price at which the property will change hands

---

[1] § 1001(a) and Reg. § 1.1001–1(a).
[2] Reg. § 1.1001–1(c)(1).
[3] *Lynch v. Turrish*, 1 USTC ¶18, 3 AFTR 2986, 38 S.Ct. 537 (USSC, 1918).
[4] § 1001(b) and Reg. § 1.1001–1(b). Refer to Chapter 4 for a discussion of this subject.
[5] *Crane v. Comm.*, 47–1 USTC ¶9217, 35 AFTR 776, 67 S.Ct. 1047 (USSC, 1947). Although a legal distinction exists between the direct assumption of a mortgage and taking property subject to a mortgage, the tax consequences in calculating the amount realized are the same.
[6] *Comm. v. Tufts*, 83–1 USTC ¶9328, 51 AFTR2d 83–1132, 103 S.Ct. 1826 (USSC, 1983).

between a willing seller and a willing buyer when neither is compelled to sell or buy.[7] Fair market value is determined by considering the relevant factors in each case.[8] An expert appraiser is often required to evaluate these factors in arriving at fair market value. When the fair market value of the property received cannot be determined, the value of the property surrendered may be used.[9]

In calculating the amount realized, selling expenses such as advertising, commissions, and legal fees relating to the disposition are deducted. The amount realized is the net amount received directly or indirectly by the taxpayer from the disposition of property in the form of cash or anything else of value.

Adjusted Basis. The **adjusted basis** of property disposed of is the property's original basis adjusted to the date of disposition.[10] Original basis is the cost or other basis of the property on the date the property is acquired by the taxpayer. *Capital additions* increase and *recoveries of capital* decrease the original basis so that on the date of disposition the adjusted basis reflects the unrecovered cost or other basis of the property.[11] Adjusted basis is determined as follows:

Cost (or other adjusted basis) on date of acquisition
+ Capital additions
− Capital recoveries
= Adjusted basis on date of disposition

Capital Additions. Capital additions include the cost of capital improvements and betterments made to the property by the taxpayer. These expenditures are distinguishable from expenditures for the ordinary repair and maintenance of the property that are neither capitalized nor added to the original basis (refer to Chapter 4). The latter expenditures are deductible in the current taxable year if they are related to business or income-producing property. Amounts representing real property taxes treated as imposed on the seller but paid or assumed by the buyer are part of the cost of the property.[12] Any liability on property that is assumed by the buyer is also included in the buyer's original basis of the property. The same rule applies if property is acquired subject to a liability. In a similar fashion, amortization of the discount on bonds increases the adjusted basis of the bonds.[13]

EXAMPLE 4

Bluebird Corporation purchased some manufacturing equipment for $25,000. Whether Bluebird uses $25,000 from the business's cash account to pay for this equipment or uses $5,000 from that account and borrows the remaining $20,000, the basis of this equipment will be the same—namely, $25,000. Moreover, it does not matter whether Bluebird borrowed the $20,000 from the equipment's manufacturer, from a local bank, or from any other lender. ▼

Capital Recoveries. The following are examples of capital recoveries:

1. *Depreciation and cost recovery allowances.* The original basis of depreciable property is reduced by the annual depreciation charges (or cost recovery allowances) while the property is held by the taxpayer. The amount of depreciation that is subtracted from the original basis is the greater of the

---

[7]*Comm. v. Marshman,* 60–2 USTC ¶9484, 5 AFTR2d 1528, 279 F.2d 27 (CA–6, 1960).
[8]*O'Malley v. Ames,* 52–1 USTC ¶9361, 42 AFTR 19, 197 F.2d 256 (CA–8, 1952).
[9]*U.S. v. Davis,* 62–2 USTC ¶9509, 9 AFTR2d 1625, 82 S.Ct. 1190 (USSC, 1962).

[10]§ 1011(a) and Reg. § 1.1011–1.
[11]§ 1016(a) and Reg. § 1.1016–1.
[12]Reg. §§ 1.1001–1(b)(2) and 1.1012–1(b). Refer to Chapter 4 for a discussion of this subject.
[13]See Chapter 8 for a discussion of bond discount and the related amortization.

allowed or *allowable* depreciation on an annual basis.[14] In most circumstances, the allowed and allowable depreciation amounts are the same (refer to Chapter 4).

2. *Casualties and thefts.* A casualty or theft may result in the reduction of the adjusted basis of property.[15] The adjusted basis is reduced by the amount of the deductible loss. In addition, the adjusted basis is reduced by the amount of insurance proceeds received. However, the receipt of insurance proceeds may result in a recognized gain rather than a deductible loss. The gain increases the adjusted basis of the property.[16]

EXAMPLE 5

An insured truck owned by the Falcon Corporation is destroyed in an accident. The adjusted basis is $8,000, and the fair market value is $6,500. Falcon received insurance proceeds of $6,500. The amount of the casualty loss is $1,500 ($6,500 insurance proceeds − $8,000 adjusted basis). The adjusted basis becomes $0 ($8,000 pre-accident adjusted basis, reduced by the $1,500 casualty loss and the $6,500 of insurance proceeds received). ▼

EXAMPLE 6

Osprey, Inc., owned an insured truck that was destroyed in an accident. The adjusted basis and fair market value of the truck were $6,500 and $8,000, respectively. Osprey received insurance proceeds of $8,000. The amount of the casualty *gain* is $1,500 ($8,000 insurance proceeds − $6,500 adjusted basis). The adjusted basis is increased by the $1,500 casualty gain and is reduced by the $8,000 of insurance proceeds received ($6,500 basis before casualty + $1,500 casualty gain − $8,000 insurance proceeds = $0 basis). ▼

3. *Certain corporate distributions.* A corporate distribution to a shareholder that is not taxable is treated as a return of capital, and it reduces the basis of the shareholder's stock in the corporation.[17] Once the basis of the stock is reduced to zero, the amount of any subsequent distributions is a capital gain if the stock is a capital asset. See Chapter 10.

4. *Amortizable bond premium.* The basis in a bond purchased at a premium is reduced by the amortizable portion of the bond premium.[18] Investors in taxable bonds may *elect* to amortize the bond premium.[19] The amount of the amortized premium on taxable bonds is permitted as an interest deduction. Thus, the election produces the opportunity for an annual interest deduction to offset ordinary income in exchange for a larger capital gain or smaller capital loss on the disposition of the bond (due to the basis reduction). The amortization deduction is allowed for taxable bonds because the premium is viewed as a cost of earning the taxable interest from the bonds. The reason the basis of taxable bonds is reduced is that the amortization deduction is a recovery of the cost or basis of the bonds.

In contrast to the treatment of taxable bonds, the premium on tax-exempt bonds *must* be amortized, and no interest deduction is permitted. Furthermore, the basis of tax-exempt bonds is reduced even though the amortization is not allowed as a deduction. No amortization deduction is permitted on tax-exempt bonds because the interest income is exempt from tax, and the amortization of the bond premium merely represents an adjustment of the effective amount of such income.

---

[14] § 1016(a)(2) and Reg. § 1.1016–3(a)(1)(i).
[15] Refer to Chapter 5 for the discussion of casualties and thefts.
[16] Reg. § 1.1016–6(a).
[17] § 1016(a)(4) and Reg. § 1.1016–5(a).
[18] § 1016(a)(5) and Reg. § 1.1016–5(b). The accounting treatment of bond premium amortization is the same as for tax purposes. The amortization results in a decrease in the bond investment account.
[19] § 171(c).

Concept Summary 7–1

Recognized Gain or Loss

Amount Realized − Adjusted Basis

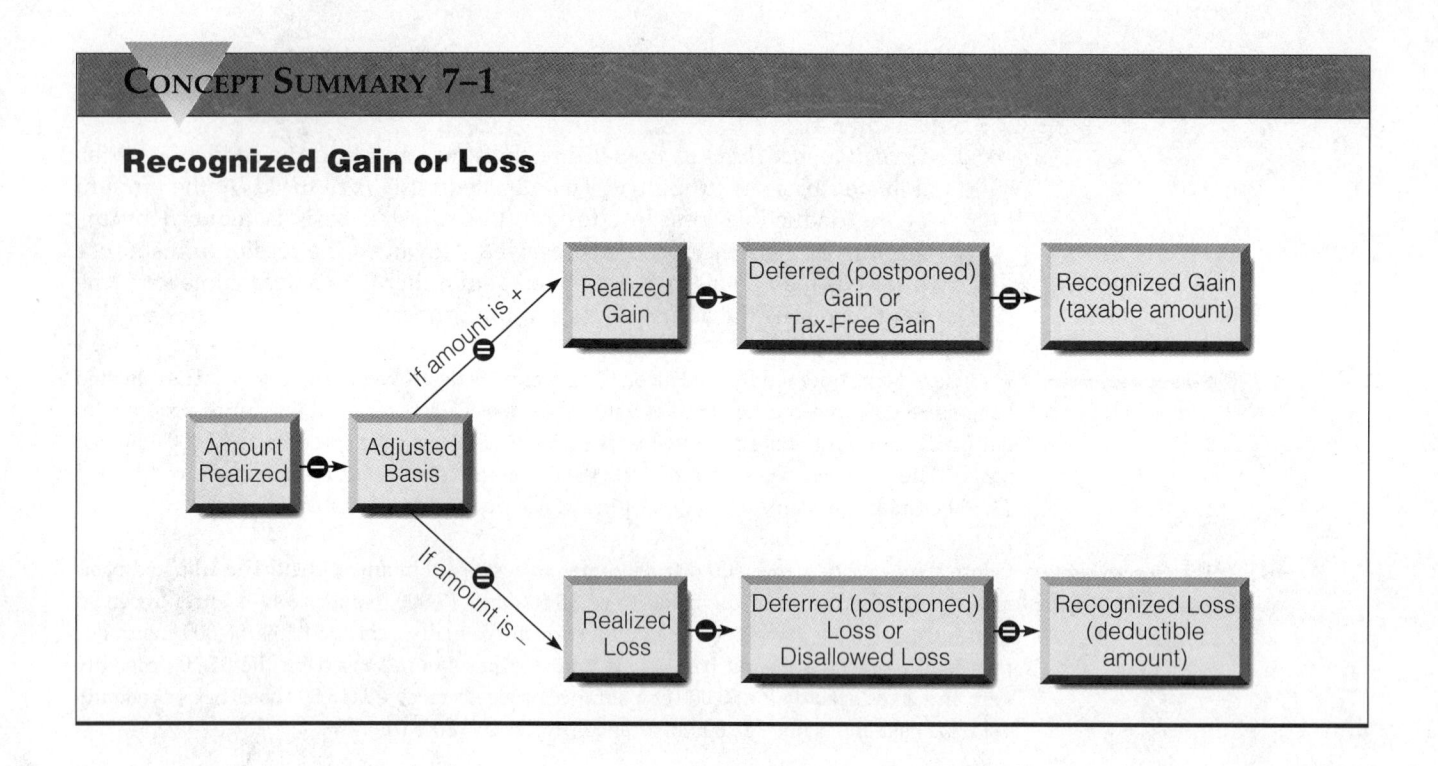

- If amount is +: Realized Gain − Deferred (postponed) Gain or Tax-Free Gain = Recognized Gain (taxable amount)
- If amount is −: Realized Loss − Deferred (postponed) Loss or Disallowed Loss = Recognized Loss (deductible amount)

EXAMPLE 7

Navy, Inc., purchases Eagle Corporation taxable bonds with a face value of $100,000 for $110,000, thus paying a premium of $10,000. The annual interest rate is 7%, and the bonds mature 10 years from the date of purchase. The annual interest income is $7,000 (7% × $100,000). If Navy elects to amortize the bond premium, the $10,000 premium is deducted over the 10-year period. Navy's basis for the bonds is reduced each year by the amount of the amortization deduction. If the bonds were tax-exempt, amortization of the bond premium and the basis adjustment would be mandatory, and no deduction would be allowed for the amortization. ▼

RECOGNIZED GAIN OR LOSS

2 LEARNING OBJECTIVE
Distinguish between realized and recognized gain or loss.

Recognized gain is the amount of the realized gain included in the taxpayer's gross income.[20] A **recognized loss**, on the other hand, is the amount of a realized loss that is deductible for tax purposes.[21] As a general rule, the entire amount of a realized gain or loss is recognized when it is realized.[22]

Concept Summary 7–1 summarizes the realized gain or loss and recognized gain or loss concepts.

NONRECOGNITION OF GAIN OR LOSS

In certain cases, a realized gain or loss is not recognized upon the sale or other disposition of property. One of the exceptions to the recognition of gain or loss involves nontaxable exchanges, which are covered later in this chapter. In addition, realized losses from the sale or exchange of property between certain related parties are not recognized.[23]

---

[20] § 61(a)(3) and Reg. § 1.61–6(a).
[21] § 165(a) and Reg. § 1.165–1(a).
[22] § 1001(c) and Reg. § 1.1002–1(a).
[23] § 267(a)(1).

Dispositions of Personal-Use Assets. For individual taxpayers, special rules apply to *personal-use* assets, that is, assets such as a residence or automobile that are not used in any business or investment activity. A loss from the sale, exchange, or condemnation of such assets is not recognized for tax purposes. An exception exists for casualty or theft losses from personal-use assets (refer to Chapter 5). In contrast, any gain realized from the disposition of personal-use assets is generally taxable.

EXAMPLE 8

Freda sells an automobile, which is held exclusively for personal use, for $6,000. The adjusted basis of the automobile is $5,000. Freda has a realized and recognized gain of $1,000. If she sold this automobile for $4,500, she would have a realized loss of $500, but the loss would not be recognized for tax purposes. ▼

RECOVERY OF CAPITAL DOCTRINE

Doctrine Defined. The **recovery of capital doctrine** is very significant and pervades all the tax rules relating to property transactions. The doctrine derives its roots from the very essence of the income tax—a tax on income or profit. Because the focus of the tax is on profit, a taxpayer is entitled to recover the cost or other original basis of property acquired without being taxed on that amount.

The cost or other original basis of depreciable property is recovered through annual depreciation deductions. The basis is reduced as the cost is recovered over the period the property is held. Therefore, when property is sold or otherwise disposed of, it is the adjusted basis (unrecovered cost or other basis) that is compared to the amount realized from the disposition to determine realized gain or loss.

EXAMPLE 9

Cardinal Corporation purchased a duplicating machine for $20,000 four years ago and has deducted depreciation totaling $13,000 during those years. Since Cardinal has recovered $13,000 through depreciation, the adjusted basis of this machine is $7,000 ($20,000 − $13,000). If Cardinal sells this machine, it deducts the $7,000 adjusted basis when determining whether it realized a gain or loss upon the disposition. ▼

Relationship of the Recovery of Capital Doctrine to the Concepts of Realization and Recognition. The general rules for the relationship between the recovery of capital doctrine and the realized and recognized gain and loss concepts are summarized as follows:

Rule 1. A realized gain that is *never recognized* results in the *permanent recovery* of more than the taxpayer's cost or other basis for tax purposes. For example, noncorporate taxpayers may exclude from gross income 50 percent of any gain realized on the sale of qualified small business stock held for more than five years under § 1202 (see Chapter 8).

Rule 2. A realized gain on which *recognition is postponed* results in the *temporary recovery* of more than the taxpayer's cost or other basis for tax purposes. For example, the recognition of gain from an exchange of like-kind property under § 1031 or an involuntary conversion under § 1033 may be deferred until a subsequent year, as discussed later in this chapter.

Rule 3. A realized loss that is *never recognized* results in the *permanent recovery* of less than the taxpayer's cost or other basis for tax purposes. For example, a loss on the sale of an automobile held for personal use is not deductible. Refer to Example 8.

Rule 4. A realized loss on which *recognition is postponed* results in the *temporary recovery* of less than the taxpayer's cost or other basis for tax purposes. For example, recognition of a loss on the exchange of like-kind property under § 1031 may be deferred until a subsequent year, as discussed later in this chapter.

BASIS CONSIDERATIONS

DETERMINATION OF COST BASIS

LEARNING OBJECTIVE 3
Explain how basis is determined for various methods of asset acquisition.

The basis of property is generally the property's cost. Cost is the amount paid for the property in cash or other property.[24] This general rule follows logically from the recovery of capital doctrine; that is, the cost or other basis of property is to be recovered tax-free by the taxpayer.

A *bargain purchase* of property is an exception to the general rule for determining basis. A bargain purchase may result when an employer transfers property to an employee at less than the property's fair market value (as compensation for services) or when a corporation transfers property to a shareholder at less than the property's fair market value (a dividend). These transfers create taxable income for the purchaser equal to the difference between fair market value and purchase price. The basis of property acquired in a bargain purchase is the property's fair market value.[25] If the basis of the property were not increased by the bargain amount, the taxpayer would be taxed on this amount again at disposition.

EXAMPLE 10
Wade buys a machine from his employer for $10,000. The fair market value of the machine is $15,000. Wade must include the $5,000 difference between cost and the fair market value of the machine in his gross income. The bargain element represents additional compensation to Wade. His basis for the machine is $15,000, the machine's fair market value. ▼

Identification Problems. Sometimes, it can be difficult to determine the cost of an asset being sold. This problem is frequently encountered in sales of corporate stock, because a taxpayer may purchase separate lots of a company's stock on different dates and at different prices. When the the stock is sold, if the taxpayer cannot identify the specific shares being sold, the stock sold is determined on a first-in, first-out (FIFO) basis. Thus, the holding period and cost of the stock sold are determined by referring to the purchase date and cost of the first lot of stock acquired.[26] But if the stock being sold can be adequately identified, then the basis and holding period of the specific stock sold is used in determining the nature and amount of gain or loss.[27] Thus, to avoid FIFO treatment when the sold securities are held by a broker, it is often necessary to provide specific instructions and receive written confirmation of the securities being sold.

EXAMPLE 11
Pelican, Inc., purchases 100 shares of Olive Corporation stock on July 1, 1996, for $5,000 ($50 a share) and another 100 shares of Olive stock on July 1, 1997, for $6,000 ($60 a share). Pelican sells 50 shares of the stock on January 2, 1998. The cost of the stock sold, assuming Pelican cannot adequately identify the shares, is $50 a share, or $2,500. This is the cost Pelican will compare to the amount realized in determining the gain or loss from the sale. ▼

---

[24] § 1012 and Reg. § 1.1012–1(a).
[25] Reg. §§ 1.61–2(d)(2)(i) and 1.301–1(j).
[26] *Kluger Associates, Inc.*, 69 T.C. 925 (1978).
[27] Reg. § 1.1012–1(c)(1).

CHAPTER 7 Property Transactions: Basis, Gain and Loss, and Nontaxable Exchanges

Allocation Problems. When a taxpayer acquires *several assets in a lump-sum purchase*, the total cost must be allocated among the individual assets.[28] Allocation is necessary because some of the assets acquired may be depreciable (e.g., buildings) and others not (e.g., land). In addition, only a portion of the assets acquired may be sold, or some of the assets may be capital or depreciable assets that receive special tax treatment upon subsequent sale or other disposition. The lump-sum cost is allocated on the basis of the fair market values of the individual assets acquired.

EXAMPLE 12

Magenta Corporation purchases a building and land for $800,000. Because of the depressed nature of the industry in which the seller was operating, Magenta was able to negotiate a very favorable purchase price. Appraisals of the individual assets indicate that the fair market value of the building is $600,000 and that of the land is $400,000. Magenta's basis for the building is $480,000 [($600,000/$1,000,000) × $800,000], and its basis for the land is $320,000 [($400,000/$1,000,000) × $800,000]. ▼

If a business is purchased and **goodwill** (or any other § 197 intangible asset) is involved, a special *residual allocation* rule applies. Initially, the purchase price of the business is allocated to four classes of assets in the following order:

- Class 1—cash, demand deposits, etc.
- Class 2—marketable securities, certificates of deposit, and foreign currency.
- Class 3—all other assets, except for § 197 intangible assets.
- Class 4—goodwill and other § 197 intangible assets.

Within each class of assets, the purchase price is allocated among the assets on the basis of their respective fair market values, and the amount allocated to any specific asset cannot exceed its fair market value. Therefore, any amount paid in excess of fair market value for tangible assets (classes 1 through 3) is allocated to goodwill and other intangible assets of the acquired business (class 4). This allocation of purchase price is applicable to both the buyer and the seller.[29]

EXAMPLE 13

Roadrunner, Inc., sells its business to Coyote Corporation. The two companies agree that the values of the specific assets are as follows:

Cash	$ 10,000
Marketable securities	5,000
Inventory	35,000
Building	500,000
Land	200,000

After negotiations, Roadrunner and Coyote agree on a sales price of $1 million. Applying the residual method, the purchase price is allocated first to cash, then to marketable securities up to their fair market value. Next, the purchase price is allocated to inventory, building, and land, all on the basis of their fair market values. The residual purchase price is allocated to goodwill, resulting in the following basis of assets to Coyote Corporation:

Cash	$ 10,000
Marketable securities	5,000
Inventory	35,000
Building	500,000
Land	200,000
Goodwill	250,000

▼

---

[28] Reg. § 1.61–6(a).

[29] § 1060 and Temp.Reg. § 1.338(b)–1T.

In the case of *nontaxable stock dividends*, the allocation depends upon whether the dividend is a common stock dividend on common stock or a preferred stock dividend on common stock. If the dividend is common on common, the cost of the original common shares is allocated to the total shares owned after the dividend.[30]

EXAMPLE 14

Yellow, Inc., owns 100 shares of Sparrow Corporation common stock for which it paid $1,100. Yellow receives a 10% common stock dividend, giving it a new total of 110 shares. Before the stock dividend, Yellow's basis was $11 per share ($1,100 ÷ 100 shares). The basis of each share after the stock dividend is $10 ($1,100 ÷ 110 shares). ▼

If the dividend is preferred stock on common, the cost of the original common shares is allocated between the common and preferred shares on the basis of their relative fair market values on the date of distribution.[31]

EXAMPLE 15

Brown Company owns 100 shares of Cardinal Corporation common stock for which it paid $1,000. Brown receives a stock dividend of 50 shares of preferred stock on the Cardinal common stock. The fair market values on the date of distribution of the preferred stock dividend are $30 a share for common stock and $40 a share for preferred stock. Thus, the total fair market value is $3,000 ($30 × 100) for common stock and $2,000 ($40 × 50) for preferred stock. The basis of Brown's common stock after the dividend is $600, or $6 a share [($3,000/$5,000) × $1,000], and the basis of the preferred stock is $400, or $8 a share [($2,000/$5,000) × $1,000]. ▼

GIFT BASIS

Although business entities can neither make nor receive gratuitous transfers, ownership interests in such entities are frequently the subject of lifetime and testamentary gifts. Partnership interests, stock in closely or publicly held corporations, and other assets are regularly passed from one generation of owners to another for a variety of family and business reasons. Special basis rules apply to such transfers.

When a taxpayer receives property as a gift, there is no cost to the recipient. Thus, under the cost basis provision, the donee's basis would be zero. With a zero basis, a sale by the donee would result in the entire amount realized being treated as taxable gain. Instead, the Code[32] assigns a basis to the property received that depends upon the following:

- The date of the gift.
- The basis of the property to the donor.
- The fair market value of the property.
- The amount of the gift tax paid, if any.

Gift Basis Rules if No Gift Tax Is Paid. If a property's fair market value on the date of gift exceeds the donor's basis in the property, the donor's basis carries over to the new owner.[33] This basis is called a *carryover basis* and is used in determining the donee's gain or loss.

---

[30] §§ 305(a) and 307(a). The holding period of the new shares includes the holding period of the old shares. § 1223(5) and Reg. § 1.1223–1(e). See Chapter 8 for a discussion of the importance of the holding period.
[31] Reg. § 1.307–1(a).
[32] § 1015(a).
[33] § 1015(a) and Reg. § 1.1015–1(a)(1). See Reg. § 1.1015–1(a)(3) for cases in which the facts necessary to determine the donor's adjusted basis are unknown. See Example 22 for the effect of depreciation deductions by the donee.

EXAMPLE 16 Melissa purchased stock two years ago for $10,000. She gave the stock to her son, Joe, this year, when the fair market value was $15,000. Joe subsequently sells the property for $15,000. Joe's basis is $10,000, and he has a realized gain of $5,000. ▼

If the property's fair market value on the date of gift is *lower* than the donor's basis in the property, the donee's basis cannot be determined until the donee disposes of the property. For the purpose of determining gain, the donor's basis will carry over, as in the preceding example. But for determining loss, the property's basis will be its market value when the gift was made.

EXAMPLE 17 Burt purchased stock three years ago for $10,000. He gave the stock to his son, Cliff, this year, when the fair market value was $7,000. Cliff later sells the stock for $6,000. For determining loss, Cliff's basis is $7,000, and the realized loss from the sale is $1,000 ($6,000 amount realized − $7,000 basis). ▼

Note that this last basis rule prevents the donee from receiving a tax benefit from the decline in value that occurred while the donor held the property. Therefore, in the preceding example, Cliff has a loss of only $1,000 rather than a loss of $4,000. The $3,000 difference represents the decline in value that occurred while Burt held the property. Ironically, however, a donee might be subject to income tax on the appreciation that occurred while the donor held the property, as illustrated in Example 16.

In any case, the operation of this differential basis rule produces a curious anomaly: if the sales proceeds fall *between* the donor's adjusted basis and the property's fair market value at the date of gift, no gain or loss is recognized.

EXAMPLE 18 Assume the same facts as in the preceding example, except that Cliff sold the stock for $8,000. To calculate gain, he would use a basis of $10,000, the donor's adjusted basis. But when a $10,000 basis is compared to $8,000 of sales proceeds, a *loss* is produced. Yet in determining loss, Cliff must use the property's market value at the date of gift—namely, $7,000. When a $7,000 basis is compared to sales proceeds of $8,000, a *gain* is produced. Accordingly, no gain or loss is recognized on this transaction. ▼

PLANNING CONSIDERATIONS

Gift Planning

Gifts of *appreciated property* can produce tax savings if the donee is in a lower tax bracket than the donor. The carryover basis rule effectively shifts the tax on the property's appreciation to the new owner, even if all of the appreciation arose while the property was owned by the donor.

On the other hand, donors should generally avoid making gifts of property that is worth less than the donor's adjusted basis (loss property). The operation of the basis rule for losses may result in either (1) a realized loss that is not deductible by either the donor or the donee or (2) reduced tax benefits when the loss is recognized by a donee facing lower marginal tax rates. Unless the property is expected to rebound in value before it is sold, a donor would be better advised to sell the depreciated property, deduct the resulting loss, and then transfer the proceeds to the prospective donee.

Adjustment for Gift Tax. If gift taxes are paid by the donor, the donee's basis may exceed the donor's basis. This occurs only if the fair market value of the property at the date of the gift exceeds the donor's adjusted basis (i.e., the property has appreciated in value). The portion of the gift tax paid that is related to the appreciation is added to the donor's basis in calculating the donee's basis for the property. In this circumstance, the following formula is used for calculating the donee's basis:[34]

$$\text{Donee's basis} = \text{Donor's adjusted basis} + \left(\frac{\text{Unrealized appreciation}}{\text{Fair market value at date of gift}} \times \text{Gift tax paid}\right)$$

EXAMPLE 19 Bonnie made a gift of stock to Peggy earlier this year, when the fair market value of the stock was $40,000. Bonnie had purchased the stock in 1982 for $10,000. Because the unrealized appreciation is $30,000 ($40,000 fair market value − $10,000 adjusted basis) and the fair market value is $40,000, three-fourths ($30,000/$40,000) of the gift tax paid is added to the basis of the property. If Bonnie paid gift tax of $4,000, Peggy's basis in the property (for determining both gain and loss) is $13,000 [$10,000 + $3,000 (¾ of the $4,000 gift tax)]. ▼

EXAMPLE 20 Don made a gift of stock to Matt earlier this year, when the fair market value of the stock was $40,000. Gift tax of $4,000 was paid by Don, who had purchased the stock in 1982 for $45,000. Because there is no unrealized appreciation at the date of the gift, none of the gift tax paid is added to Don's basis in calculating Matt's basis. ▼

For *gifts made before 1977*, the full amount of the gift tax paid is added to the donor's basis. However, the ceiling on this total is the fair market value of the property at the date of the gift. Thus, in Example 19, if the gift had been made before 1977, the basis of the property would be $14,000 ($10,000 + $4,000). In Example 20, the donee's basis would still be $45,000 ($45,000 + $0) for gains and $40,000 for losses.

Holding Period. The **holding period** for property acquired by gift begins on the date the donor acquired the property,[35] unless the special circumstance requiring use of the property's fair market value at the date of gift applies. If so, the holding period starts on the date of the gift.[36] The significance of the holding period for capital assets is discussed in Chapter 8.

The following example summarizes the basis and holding period rules for gift property.

EXAMPLE 21 Jill acquires 100 shares of Wren Corporation stock on December 30, 1992, for $40,000. On January 3 of this year, when the stock has a fair market value of $38,000, Jill gives it to Dennis and pays gift tax of $4,000. The basis is not increased by a portion of the gift tax paid because the property has not appreciated in value at the time of the gift. Therefore, Dennis's basis for determining gain is $40,000. Dennis's basis for determining loss is $38,000

---

[34] § 1015(d)(6).
[35] § 1223(2) and Reg. § 1.1223–1(b).
[36] Rev.Rul. 59–86, 1959–1 C.B. 209.

(fair market value), because the fair market value on the date of the gift is less than the donor's adjusted basis.

- If Dennis sells the stock for $45,000, he has a recognized gain of $5,000. The holding period for determining whether the capital gain is short term, mid-term, or long term begins on December 30, 1992, the date Jill acquired the property.
- If Dennis sells the stock for $36,000, he has a recognized loss of $2,000. The holding period for determining whether the capital loss is short term, mid-term, or long term begins on January 3 of this year, the date of the gift.
- If Dennis sells the property for $39,000, no gain or loss is recognized because the amount realized is between the property's fair market value when given ($38,000) and the donor's adjusted basis of $40,000. ▼

Basis for Depreciation. The basis for depreciation on depreciable gift property is the donee's basis for determining gain.[37] This rule is applicable even if the donee later sells the property at a loss and uses the property's fair market value at the date of gift in calculating the amount of the realized loss.

EXAMPLE 22

Vito gave a machine to Tina earlier this year, when the adjusted basis was $32,000 (cost of $40,000 − accumulated depreciation of $8,000) and the fair market value was $26,000. No gift tax was due. Tina's basis for determining gain is $32,000, and her loss basis is $26,000. During this year, Tina deducts depreciation (cost recovery) of $10,240 ($32,000 × 32%). Therefore, at the end of this year, Tina's basis determinations are calculated as follows:

	Gain Basis	Loss Basis
Donor's basis or fair market value	$ 32,000	$ 26,000
Depreciation	(10,240)	(10,240)
	$ 21,760	$ 15,760

▼

PROPERTY ACQUIRED FROM A DECEDENT

General Rules. The basis of property acquired from a decedent is generally the property's fair market value at the date of death (referred to as the *primary valuation amount*).[38] The property's basis is the fair market value six months after the date of death if the executor or administrator of the estate *elects* the alternate valuation date for estate tax purposes. This amount is referred to as the *alternate valuation amount*.

EXAMPLE 23

Linda and various other family members inherited stock in a closely held corporation from Linda's father, who died earlier this year. At the date of death, her father's adjusted basis for the stock Linda inherited was $35,000. The stock's fair market value at date of death was $50,000. The alternate valuation date was not elected. Linda's basis for income tax purposes is $50,000. This is commonly referred to as a *stepped-up basis*. ▼

EXAMPLE 24

Assume the same facts as in the preceding example, except that the stock's fair market value at date of death was $20,000. Linda's basis for income tax purposes is $20,000. This is commonly referred to as a *stepped-down basis*. ▼

If an estate tax return need not be filed because the estate is below the threshold amount for being subject to the estate tax (refer to Chapter 1), the alternate valuation

---

[37] § 1011 and Reg. §§ 1.1011–1 and 1.167(g)–1.   [38] § 1014(a).

date and amount are not available. Even if an estate tax return is filed and the executor elects the alternate valuation date, the six-months-after-death date is available only for property that the executor has not distributed before this date. Any property distributed or otherwise disposed of by the executor during this six-month period will have an adjusted basis to the beneficiary equal to the fair market value on the date of distribution or other disposition.[39]

The alternate valuation date can be elected *only if* the election results in both the value of the gross estate and the estate tax liability being reduced below the amounts they would have been if the primary valuation date had been used. This provision prevents the alternate valuation election from being used to increase the basis of the property to the beneficiary for income tax purposes without simultaneously increasing the estate tax liability (because of estate tax deductions or credits).[40]

EXAMPLE 25 Nancy inherited investment real estate from her father, who died earlier this year. Her father's adjusted basis for the property at date of death was $35,000. The property's fair market value was $750,000 at date of death and $760,000 six months after death. The alternate valuation date cannot be elected because the value of the gross estate has increased during the six-month period. Nancy's basis for income tax purposes is $750,000. ▼

EXAMPLE 26 Assume the same facts as in Example 25, except that the property's fair market value six months after death was $745,000. If the executor elects the alternate valuation date, Nancy's basis for income tax purposes is $745,000. ▼

EXAMPLE 27 Assume the same facts as in Example 26, except that the property is distributed four months after the date of the decedent's death. At the distribution date, the property's fair market value is $747,500. Since the executor elected the alternate valuation date, Nancy's basis for income tax purposes is $747,500. ▼

For inherited property, both unrealized appreciation and decline in value are taken into consideration in determining the basis of the property for income tax purposes. Contrast this with the carryover basis rules for property received by gift.

PLANNING CONSIDERATIONS

Property from a Decedent

If a taxpayer *retains appreciated property* until death, the property's basis will be "stepped up" to its market value at that time. Thus, no income tax will be paid on the property's appreciation by either the former owner (the decedent) or the new owner (the heir).

On the other hand, *depreciated property should be sold* prior to death. Otherwise, the property's basis in the heir's hands will be its declined fair market value, and neither the decedent nor the heir will be able to deduct the loss that occurred while the property was owned by the decedent.

Deathbed Gifts. The Code contains a provision designed to eliminate a tax avoidance technique occasionally described as *deathbed gifts*. If a person (or that person's spouse) receives from a decedent property that this person gave to the

---

[39] § 2032(a)(1) and Rev.Rul. 56–60, 1956–1 C.B. 443.   [40] § 2032(c).

decedent during the year before the decedent's death, the property does *not* get a stepped-up basis. Instead, the basis of that property is the donor's adjusted basis.[41]

EXAMPLE 28

Ned gives stock to his uncle, Vern, this year. Ned's basis for the stock is $1,000, and the fair market value is $9,000. No gift tax is due. Eight months later, Ned inherits the stock from Vern. At the date of Vern's death, the fair market value of the stock is $12,000. Ned's adjusted basis for the stock is $1,000. ▼

Holding Period of Property Acquired from a Decedent. The holding period of property acquired from a decedent is *deemed to be long term* (held for the required long-term holding period). This provision applies regardless of whether the property is disposed of at a gain or a loss.[42]

DISALLOWED LOSSES

LEARNING OBJECTIVE 4
Describe various loss disallowance provisions.

Related Taxpayers. Section 267 provides that realized losses from sales or exchanges of property between certain related parties are not recognized. This loss disallowance provision applies to several types of related-party transactions. The most common involve (1) members of a family and (2) transactions between an individual and a corporation in which the individual owns, directly or indirectly, more than 50 percent in value of the corporation's outstanding stock. Section 707 provides a similar loss disallowance provision if the related parties are a partner and a partnership in which the partner owns, directly or indirectly, more than 50 percent of the capital interests or profits interests in the partnership. Neither provision, however, prevents the recognition of *gains* between related parties. The rules governing the relationships covered by § 267 were discussed in Chapter 4.

Wash Sales. Section 1091 stipulates that in certain cases, a realized loss on the sale or exchange of stock or securities is not recognized. Specifically, if a taxpayer sells or exchanges stock or securities and within 30 days before *or* after the date of the sale or exchange acquires *substantially identical* stock or securities, any loss realized from the sale or exchange is not recognized because the transaction is a **wash sale**.[43] The term *acquire* means acquire by purchase or in a taxable exchange and includes an option to purchase substantially identical securities. *Substantially identical* means the same in all important particulars. Corporate bonds and preferred stock are normally not considered substantially identical to a corporation's common stock. However, if the bonds and preferred stock are convertible into common stock, they may be considered substantially identical under certain circumstances.[44] Attempts to avoid the application of the wash sale rules by having a related taxpayer repurchase the securities have been unsuccessful.[45] The wash sale provisions do *not* apply to gains.

Recognition of the loss is disallowed because the taxpayer is considered to be in substantially the same economic position after the sale and repurchase as before. This disallowance rule does not apply to taxpayers engaged in the business of buying and selling securities.[46] Investors, however, are not allowed to create losses through wash sales to offset income for tax purposes.

A realized loss that is not recognized is added to the *basis* of the substantially identical stock or securities whose acquisition resulted in the nonrecognition of

---

[41]§ 1014(e).
[42]§ 1223(11).
[43]§ 1091(a) and Reg. §§ 1.1091–1(a) and (f).
[44]Rev.Rul. 56–406, 1956–2 C.B. 523.
[45]*McWilliams v. Comm.*, 47–1 USTC ¶9289, 35 AFTR 1184, 67 S.Ct. 1477 (USSC, 1947).
[46]Reg. § 1.1091–1(a).

loss.[47] In other words, the basis of the replacement stock or securities is increased by the amount of the unrecognized loss. If the loss were not added to the basis of the newly acquired stock or securities, the taxpayer would never recover the entire basis of the old stock or securities. As a result, the wash sale rule operates to *defer* the recognition of the taxpayer's loss.

EXAMPLE 29

Oriole Manufacturing Co. sold 50 shares of Green Corporation stock (adjusted basis of $10,000) for $8,000. Ten days later, Oriole purchased 50 shares of the same stock for $7,000. Oriole's realized loss of $2,000 ($8,000 amount realized − $10,000 adjusted basis) is not recognized because it resulted from a wash sale. Oriole's basis in the newly acquired stock is $9,000 ($7,000 purchase price + $2,000 unrecognized loss from the wash sale). ▼

The basis of the new stock or securities includes the unrecovered portion of the basis of the formerly held stock or securities. Therefore, the *holding period* of the new stock or securities begins on the date of acquisition of the old stock or securities.[48]

The taxpayer may acquire less than the number of shares sold in a wash sale. In this case, the loss from the sale is prorated between recognized and unrecognized loss on the basis of the ratio of the number of shares acquired to the number of shares sold.[49]

PLANNING CONSIDERATIONS

Avoiding Wash Sales

The wash sale restriction can be avoided by replacing the sold security with a *similar* but not "substantially identical" security. For example, if IBM common stock is sold to claim an unrealized loss, the taxpayer could immediately acquire Intel common stock without triggering the wash sale rule.

Nontax considerations must also come into play, however, because IBM and Intel are two different companies with different investment prospects. Though both securities will be affected by many of the same factors, they will also be subject to different factors that may be even more significant than the ones they share.

CONVERSION OF PROPERTY FROM PERSONAL USE TO BUSINESS OR INCOME PRODUCING USE

As discussed previously, losses from the sale of personal-use assets are not recognized for tax purposes, but losses from the sale of business and income-producing assets are deductible. Can a taxpayer convert a personal-use asset that has declined in value to business (or income-producing) use and then sell the asset to recognize a business (or income-producing) loss? The tax law prevents this by specifying that the *basis for determining loss* on personal-use assets converted to business or income-producing use is the *lower* of the property's adjusted basis or its fair market value on the date of conversion.[50] The *gain basis* for converted property is the

---

[47]§ 1091(d) and Reg. § 1.1091–2(a).
[48]§ 1223(4) and Reg. § 1.1223–1(d).
[49]§ 1091(b) and Reg. § 1.1091–1(c).
[50]Reg. § 1.165–9(b)(2).

CHAPTER 7 Property Transactions: Basis, Gain and Loss, and Nontaxable Exchanges

property's adjusted basis on the date of conversion, regardless of whether property's use is business, income producing, or personal in nature.

EXAMPLE 30

Diane's personal residence has an adjusted basis of $75,000 and a fair market value of $60,000. When she converts the personal residence to rental property, her basis for determining loss is $60,000 (lower of $75,000 adjusted basis and fair market value of $60,000). The $15,000 decline in value is a personal loss and can never be recognized for tax purposes. Diane's basis for determining gain is $75,000.

The basis for determining loss is also the *basis for depreciating* the converted property.[51] This is an exception to the general rule that provides that the basis for depreciation is the basis for determining gain (e.g., property received by gift). This exception prevents the taxpayer from recovering a personal loss indirectly through depreciation of the higher original basis. Once property is converted, both its basis for loss and its basis for gain are adjusted for depreciation deductions from the date of conversion to the date of disposition.

EXAMPLE 31

At a time when his personal residence (adjusted basis of $40,000) is worth $50,000, Keith converts one-half of it to rental use. The property is not MACRS recovery property. At this point, the estimated useful life of the residence is 20 years and there is no estimated salvage value. After renting the converted portion for five years, Keith sells the property for $44,000. All amounts relate only to the building; the land has been accounted for separately. Keith has a $2,000 realized gain from the sale of the personal-use portion of the residence and a $7,000 realized gain from the sale of the rental portion. These gains are computed as follows:

	Personal Use	Rental
Original basis for gain and loss—adjusted basis on date of conversion (fair market value is higher than the adjusted basis)	$20,000	$20,000
Depreciation—five years	None	5,000
Adjusted basis—date of sale	$20,000	$15,000
Amount realized	22,000	22,000
Realized gain	$ 2,000	$ 7,000

As discussed later in this chapter, Keith can exclude the $2,000 gain from the sale of the personal-use portion of the residence under § 121. The $7,000 gain from the rental portion, however, is recognized currently.

EXAMPLE 32

Assume the same facts as in the preceding example, except that the fair market value on the date of conversion was $30,000 and the sales proceeds are $16,000. Keith has a $12,000 realized loss from the sale of the personal-use portion of the residence and a $3,250 realized loss from the sale of the rental portion. These losses are computed as follows:

---

[51] Reg. § 1.167(g)–1.

	Personal Use	Rental
Original basis for loss—fair market value on date of conversion (fair market value is lower than the adjusted basis)	*	$15,000
Depreciation—five years	None	3,750
Adjusted basis—date of sale	$20,000	$11,250
Amount realized	8,000	8,000
Realized loss	$12,000	$ 3,250

*Not applicable.

The $12,000 loss from the sale of the personal-use portion of the residence is not recognized. The $3,250 loss from the rental portion is recognized. ▼

SUMMARY OF BASIS ADJUSTMENTS

Some of the more common items that either increase or decrease the basis of an asset appear in Concept Summary 7–2.

In discussing the topic of basis, a number of specific techniques for determining basis have been presented. Although the various techniques are responsive to and mandated by transactions occurring in the marketplace, they possess enough common characteristics to be categorized as follows:

- The basis of the asset may be determined by its cost.
- The basis of the asset may be determined by the basis of another asset.
- The basis of the asset may be determined by its fair market value.
- The basis of the asset may be determined by the basis of the asset in the hands of another taxpayer.

GENERAL CONCEPT OF A NONTAXABLE EXCHANGE

A taxpayer who is going to replace a productive asset (e.g., machinery) used in a trade or business may structure the transaction as a sale of the old asset and the purchase of a new asset. Using this approach, any realized gain or loss on the sale of the old asset is recognized. The basis of the new asset is its cost. Conversely, the taxpayer may be able to trade the old asset for the new asset. This exchange of assets may produce beneficial tax consequences as a nontaxable exchange.

The tax law recognizes that nontaxable exchanges result in a change in the *form* but not the *substance* of a taxpayer's relative economic position. The replacement property received in the exchange is viewed as essentially a continuation of the old investment.[52] Additional justification for nontaxable treatment is that this type of transaction does not provide the taxpayer with the wherewithal to pay the tax on any realized gain.

The nonrecognition provisions for nontaxable exchanges do not apply to realized losses from the sale or exchange of personal-use assets. Such losses are never recognized (i.e., they are disallowed) because they are personal in nature.

---

[52] Reg. § 1.1002–1(c).

Concept Summary 7–2

Adjustments to Basis

Item	Effect	Refer to Chapter	Explanation
Amortization of bond discount.	Increase	7	Amortization is mandatory for certain taxable bonds and elective for tax-exempt bonds.
Amortization of bond premium.	Decrease	7	Amortization is mandatory for tax-exempt bonds and elective for taxable bonds.
Amortization of covenant not to compete.	Decrease	4	Covenant must be for a definite and limited time period. The amortization period is a statutory period of 15 years.
Amortization of intangibles.	Decrease	4	Goodwill is subject to amortization over a statutory period of 15 years.
Bad debts.	Decrease	5	Most taxpayers must use the specific charge-off method.
Capital additions.	Increase	7	Certain items, at the taxpayer's election, can be capitalized or deducted.
Casualty.	Decrease	7	For a casualty loss, the amount of the adjustment is the sum of the deductible loss and the insurance proceeds received. For a casualty gain, the amount of the adjustment is the insurance proceeds received reduced by the recognized gain.
Condemnation.	Decrease	7	See casualty explanation.
Cost recovery.	Decrease	4	§ 168 is applicable to tangible assets placed in service after 1980 whose useful life is expressed in terms of years.
Depletion.	Decrease	4	Use the greater of cost or percentage depletion. Percentage depletion can be deducted even when the basis is zero.
Depreciation.	Decrease	4	§ 167 is applicable to tangible assets placed in service before 1981 and to tangible assets not depreciated in terms of years.
Easement.	Decrease		If the taxpayer does not retain any use of the land, all of the basis is allocable to the easement transaction. However, if only part of the land is affected by the easement, only part of the basis is allocable to the easement transaction.
Improvements by lessee to lessor's property.	Increase	3	Adjustment occurs only if the lessor is required to include the fair market value of the improvements in gross income under § 109.
Imputed interest.	Decrease	6	Amount deducted is not part of the cost of the asset.
Inventory: lower of cost or market.	Decrease	6	Not available if the LIFO method is used.
Limited expensing under § 179.	Decrease	4	Occurs only if the taxpayer elects § 179 treatment.
Medical capital expenditure deducted as a medical expense.	Decrease	15	Adjustment is the amount of the deduction (the effect on basis is to increase it by the amount of the capital expenditure net of the deduction).

Item	Effect	Refer to Chapter	Explanation
Real estate taxes: apportionment between the buyer and seller.	Increase or decrease	4	To the extent the buyer pays the seller's pro rata share, the buyer's basis is increased. To the extent the seller pays the buyer's pro rata share, the buyer's basis is decreased.
Rebate from manufacturer.	Decrease		Since the rebate is treated as an adjustment to the purchase price, it is not included in the buyer's gross income.
Stock dividend.	Decrease	7	Adjustment occurs only if the stock dividend is nontaxable. While the basis per share decreases, the total stock basis does not change.
Stock rights.	Decrease	10	Adjustment to stock basis occurs only for nontaxable stock rights and only if the fair market value of the rights is at least 15% of the fair market value of the stock or, if less than 15%, the taxpayer elects to allocate the basis between the stock and the rights.
Theft.	Decrease	5	See casualty explanation.

In contrast, in a **nontaxable exchange**, recognition of gains or losses is *postponed* (i.e., deferred) until the new property received in the nontaxable exchange is subsequently disposed of in a taxable transaction. This is accomplished by assigning a carryover basis to the replacement property.

EXAMPLE 33

Starling Management Co. exchanges property with an adjusted basis of $10,000 and a fair market value of $12,000 for property with a fair market value of $12,000. The transaction qualifies for nontaxable exchange treatment. Starling has a realized gain of $2,000 ($12,000 amount realized − $10,000 adjusted basis). Its recognized gain is $0. Starling's basis in the replacement property is a carryover basis of $10,000. Assume the replacement property is nondepreciable. If Starling subsequently sells the replacement property for $12,000, the realized and recognized gain will be the $2,000 gain that was postponed (deferred) in the nontaxable transaction. If the replacement property is depreciable, the carryover basis of $10,000 is used in calculating depreciation. ▼

In some nontaxable exchanges, only some of the property involved in the transaction qualifies for nonrecognition treatment. If the taxpayer receives cash or other nonqualifying property, part or all of the realized gain from the exchange is recognized. In these instances, gain is recognized because the taxpayer has changed or improved its relative economic position and has the wherewithal to pay income tax to the extent of cash or other property received.

It is important to distinguish between a nontaxable disposition (or nonrecognition transaction, as the term is used in the statute) and a tax-free transaction. As previously mentioned, the term *nontaxable* refers to postponement of recognition via some version of carryover basis. In a *tax-free* transaction, the nonrecognition is permanent (e.g., see the discussion later in this chapter of the exclusion of gain from the sale of a principal residence).

Either way, nontaxable and tax-free transactions must be understood as exceptions to the Code's general rule that gains and losses are recognized when they are realized. These exceptions have their own sets of requirements, limitations, and restrictions, all of which must be satisfied for a transaction to be characterized as nontaxable or tax-free. Otherwise, the general rule of recognition applies to the gain or loss at hand.

LIKE-KIND EXCHANGES—§ 1031

5 LEARNING OBJECTIVE
Apply the nonrecognition provisions and basis determination rules for like-kind exchanges.

Section 1031 provides for nontaxable exchange treatment if the following requirements are satisfied:[53]

- The form of the transaction is an exchange.
- Both the property transferred and the property received are held either for productive use in a trade or business or for investment.
- The property is like-kind property.

Qualifying **like-kind exchanges** include exchanges of business for business, business for investment, investment for business, or investment for investment property. Property held for personal use does not qualify under the like-kind exchange provisions. Thus, the purpose for which the property is held by the taxpayer in question is critical. For example, if Janet uses a small truck in her trade or business, it may qualify for like-kind treatment, but if she uses this truck as her personal-use vehicle, it is ineligible for nonrecognition treatment under § 1031.

Some assets are excluded from like-kind treatment by statute. These excluded assets include a taxpayer's inventory or "stock in trade," as well as most forms of investment other than real estate. Thus, stocks, bonds, partnership interests (whether general or limited), and other securities, even though held for investment, do not qualify for like-kind exchange treatment.

The nonrecognition provision for like-kind exchanges is *mandatory* rather than elective. A taxpayer who wants to recognize a realized gain or loss will have to structure the transaction in a form that does not satisfy the statutory requirements for a like-kind exchange.

PLANNING CONSIDERATIONS

Like-Kind Exchanges

Because nonrecognition of gain or loss is mandatory in like-kind exchanges, a taxpayer must affirmatively *avoid such exchanges* if nonrecognition treatment is not desired. If an asset is worth less than its adjusted basis, a *loss would result* from its disposition. Accordingly, the taxpayer should sell this property outright to ensure the deductibility of the loss, assuming it would otherwise be deductible.

Even if *disposition would result in a gain*, a taxpayer might want to recognize this gain in the current taxable year. If so, a like-kind exchange should be avoided. Circumstances suggesting this strategy include:

- Unused capital loss carryovers, especially if the taxpayer is a corporation for which such carryovers are limited in duration (see Chapter 5).
- Unused net operating loss carryovers.

---
[53] § 1031(a) and Reg. § 1.1031(a)–1(a).

- Unused general business credit carryovers.
- Suspended or current passive activity losses.
- Expectations of higher tax rates in future years.

LIKE-KIND PROPERTY

The term *like-kind* is explained in the Regulations as follows: "The words 'like-kind' refer to the nature or character of the property and not to its grade or quality. One kind or class of property may not . . . be exchanged for property of a different kind or class."[54] The Regulations go on to explain that although real estate can be exchanged only for other real estate, the definition of real estate is quite broad. *Real estate* (or realty) includes principally rental buildings, office and store buildings, manufacturing plants, warehouses, and land. It is immaterial whether real estate is improved or unimproved. Thus, unimproved land can be exchanged for an apartment house. On the other hand, real property located in the United States exchanged for foreign real property (and vice versa) does not qualify as like-kind property. A similar provision applies to exchanges of foreign and domestic personalty.

In any case, real estate cannot be exchanged in a like-kind transaction for personalty. *Personalty* includes tangible assets other than real estate, such as machinery, equipment, trucks, automobiles, furniture, and fixtures. Thus, an exchange of a machine (personalty) for a small office building (realty) is not a like-kind exchange. Finally, the Code mandates that livestock of different sexes are not like-kind property.

EXAMPLE 34

Pheasant, Inc., made the following exchanges during the taxable year:

a. Inventory for a machine used in business.
b. Land held for investment for a building used in business.
c. Stock held for investment for equipment used in business.
d. A business truck for a business truck.
e. Livestock for livestock of a different sex.
f. Land held for investment in New York for land held for investment in London.

Exchanges (b), investment real property for business real property, and (d), business personalty for business personalty, qualify as exchanges of like-kind property. Exchanges (a), inventory; (c), stock; (e), livestock of different sexes; and (f), U.S. and foreign real estate do not qualify. ▼

The Regulations dealing with § 1031 like-kind exchanges provide greater specificity when determining whether depreciable tangible personalty is of a like kind. Such property held for productive use in a business is of like kind only if the exchanged property is within the same *general business asset class* (as specified by the IRS in Rev.Proc. 87–57) or the same *product class* (as specified by the Department of Commerce). Property included in a general business asset class is evaluated exclusively under the Revenue Procedure, rather than under the product class system.

The following are examples of general business asset classes:

- Office furniture, fixtures, and equipment.
- Information systems (computers and peripheral equipment).

---

[54] Reg. § 1.1031(a)–1(b).

TAX IN THE NEWS

MY LAND FOR YOUR JAIL

The Colonial Williamsburg Foundation (CW) has offered to swap 30 acres of undeveloped woodland for the Williamsburg Jail and Courthouse. A few years ago CW built a replica of the eighteenth-century Public Hospital (i.e., insane asylum). Now it is attempting to acquire the adjacent twentieth-century jail and courthouse in a § 1031 trade.

Why does CW want to own a twentieth-century jail and courthouse? It doesn't. CW wants the land for eventual expansion of its DeWitt Wallace Decorative Arts Gallery, which is located behind the Public Hospital. In addition, CW wants to preserve green space in Williamsburg, which would be threatened if a new courthouse and jail are built on land adjacent to the current courthouse and jail in Bicentennial Park.

Although the foundation is tax-exempt, the undeveloped 30 acres are owned by CW's for-profit subsidiary Williamsburg Developments, Inc. Therefore, to avoid recognizing the realized gain on the exchange, the subsidiary needs to avail itself of the § 1031 like-kind exchange provisions. Fortunately, the undeveloped land and the courthouse and jail are like-kind property.

SOURCE: Information from Bentley Boyd, "CW Presses for Moving Courthouse," *Newport News (Virginia) Daily Press*, September 15, 1993, pp. C1, C2; Bentley Boyd, "CW Boosts Proposal for Courthouse," *Newport News (Virginia) Daily Press*, September 29, 1993, pp. B1, B2.

- Airplanes.
- Automobiles and taxis.
- Buses.
- Light general-purpose trucks.
- Heavy general-purpose trucks.

These Regulations narrow the range of depreciable tangible personalty subject to § 1031 like-kind exchange treatment. For example, the exchange of office equipment for a computer does not qualify as an exchange of like-kind property. Even though both assets are depreciable tangible personalty, they are not like-kind property because they are in different general business asset classes. Accordingly, any realized gain or *loss* on the office equipment would be recognized currently.

The Regulations also provide that if the exchange transaction involves multiple assets of a business (e.g., a television station for another television station), the determination of whether the assets qualify as like-kind property will *not* be made at the business level.[55] Instead, the underlying assets must be evaluated.

Finally, a special provision applies if the taxpayers involved in the exchange are *related parties* under § 267(b). To qualify for like-kind exchange treatment, the taxpayer and the related party must not dispose of the like-kind property received in the exchange for two years after the date of the exchange. If such a disposition does occur, the postponed gain is recognized as of that disposition. Dispositions due to death, involuntary conversions, and certain non-tax avoidance transactions are excepted from this rule.

---

[55]Reg. § 1.1031(j)–1.

TAX IN THE NEWS

ARE THE CLEVELAND INDIANS STILL THE CLEVELAND INDIANS?

The Cleveland Indians were in the World Series in 1995 (losing to the Atlanta Braves) and made it to the American League playoffs (losing to the Baltimore Orioles) in 1996. Some fans were concerned, however, in March 1997, when the Indians traded one of their key players, Kenny Lofton, together with a relief pitcher to the Atlanta Braves for outfielders David Justice and Marquis Grissom. Many wondered whether the trade would help or hurt the Indians in their future bids for the championship.

General manager John Hart had an additional question when he made the deal: Did the trade qualify for § 1031 treatment? Since he made the trade, Hart must have believed that the answer to both questions was yes. Cleveland's performance in the 1997 postseason indicated that Hart knew what he was doing. The Indians came within two outs of winning game 7 of the World Series.

SOURCE: Adapted from *ESPN Sportszone*, March 26, 1997.

EXCHANGE REQUIREMENT

The transaction must generally involve a direct exchange of property to qualify as a like-kind exchange. The sale of old property and the purchase of new property, even though like kind, is not an exchange. However, the Code does provide a limited procedure for real estate to be exchanged for qualifying property that is acquired subsequent to the exchange.[56]

Of course, the taxpayer may want to avoid nontaxable exchange treatment. Recognition of gain gives the taxpayer a higher basis for depreciation. To the extent that such gains would, if recognized, either receive favorable capital gain treatment or be passive activity income that could offset passive activity losses, it might be preferable to avoid the nonrecognition provisions through an indirect exchange transaction. For example, a taxpayer may sell property to one company and subsequently purchase similar property from another company. The taxpayer may also want to avoid nontaxable exchange treatment so that a realized loss can be recognized.

BOOT

If the taxpayer in a like-kind exchange gives or receives some property that is not like-kind property, recognition may occur. Property that is not like-kind property, including cash, is often referred to as **boot**. Although the term *boot* does not appear in the Code, tax practitioners commonly use it rather than saying "property that does not qualify as like-kind property."

The *receipt* of boot will trigger recognition of gain if there is realized gain. The amount of the recognized gain is the *lesser* of the boot received or the realized gain (realized gain serves as the ceiling on recognition).

EXAMPLE 35

Blue, Inc., and White Corporation exchange machinery, and the exchange qualifies as like kind under § 1031. Since Blue's machinery (adjusted basis of $20,000) is worth $24,000 and White's machine has a fair market value of $19,000, White also gives Blue cash of $5,000.

---

[56] § 1031(a)(3).

Blue's recognized gain is $4,000, the lesser of the realized gain ($24,000 amount realized − $20,000 adjusted basis = $4,000) or the fair market value of the boot received ($5,000). ▼

EXAMPLE 36

Assume the same facts as in the preceding example, except that White's machine is worth $21,000 (not $19,000). Under these circumstances, White gives Blue cash of $3,000 to make up the difference. Blue's recognized gain is $3,000, the lesser of the realized gain ($24,000 amount realized − $20,000 adjusted basis = $4,000) or the fair market value of the boot received ($3,000). ▼

The receipt of boot does not result in recognition if there is realized loss.

EXAMPLE 37

Assume the same facts as in Example 35, except that the adjusted basis of Blue's machine is $30,000. Blue's realized loss is $6,000 ($24,000 amount realized − $30,000 adjusted basis = $6,000 realized loss). The receipt of the boot of $5,000 does not trigger recognition of Blue's loss. ▼

The *giving* of boot does not trigger recognition if the boot consists solely of cash.

EXAMPLE 38

Flicker, Inc., and Gadwall Corporation exchange equipment in a like-kind exchange. Flicker receives equipment with a fair market value of $25,000 and transfers equipment worth $21,000 (adjusted basis of $15,000) and cash of $4,000. Flicker's realized gain is $6,000 ($25,000 amount realized − $15,000 adjusted basis − $4,000 cash), none of which is recognized. ▼

If, however, the boot given is appreciated or depreciated property, gain or loss is recognized to the extent of the difference between the adjusted basis and the fair market value of the boot. For this purpose, *appreciated or depreciated property* is property with an adjusted basis that differs from fair market value.

EXAMPLE 39

Assume the same facts as in the preceding example, except that Flicker transfers equipment worth $10,000 (adjusted basis of $12,000) and boot worth $15,000 (adjusted basis of $9,000). Flicker's realized gain appears to be $4,000 ($25,000 amount realized − $21,000 adjusted basis). Since realization previously has served as a ceiling on recognition, it appears that the recognized gain is $4,000 (lower of realized gain of $4,000 or amount of appreciation on boot of $6,000). However, the recognized gain actually is $6,000 (full amount of the appreciation on the boot). In effect, Flicker must calculate the like-kind and boot parts of the transaction separately. That is, the realized loss of $2,000 on the like-kind property *is not* recognized ($10,000 fair market value − $12,000 adjusted basis), but the $6,000 realized gain on the boot *is* recognized ($15,000 fair market value − $9,000 adjusted basis). ▼

BASIS AND HOLDING PERIOD OF PROPERTY RECEIVED

If an exchange does not qualify as nontaxable under § 1031, gain or loss is recognized, and the basis of property received in the exchange is the property's fair market value. If the exchange qualifies for nonrecognition, the basis of property received must be adjusted to reflect any postponed (deferred) gain or loss. The *basis of like-kind property* received in the exchange is the property's fair market value less postponed gain or plus postponed loss. The *basis* of any *boot* received is the boot's fair market value.

EXAMPLE 40

Vireo Property Management Co. exchanges a building (used in its business) with an adjusted basis of $30,000 and fair market value of $38,000 for land with a fair market value of $38,000. The land is to be held as an investment. The exchange qualifies as like kind (an exchange of business real property for investment real property). Thus, the basis of the land is $30,000 (the land's fair market value of $38,000 less the $8,000 postponed gain on the building). If the land is later sold for its fair market value of $38,000, the $8,000 postponed gain is recognized. ▼

EXAMPLE 41

Assume the same facts as in the preceding example, except that the building has an adjusted basis of $48,000 and fair market value of only $38,000. The basis in the newly acquired land is $48,000 (fair market value of $38,000 plus the $10,000 postponed loss on the building). If the land is later sold for its fair market value of $38,000, the $10,000 postponed loss is recognized. ▼

The Code provides an alternative approach for determining the basis of like-kind property received:

Adjusted basis of like-kind property surrendered
+ Adjusted basis of boot given
+ Gain recognized
− Fair market value of boot received
− Loss recognized
= Basis of like-kind property received

This approach accords with the recovery of capital doctrine. That is, the unrecovered cost or other basis is increased by additional cost (boot given) or decreased by cost recovered (boot received). Any gain recognized is included in the basis of the new property. The taxpayer has been taxed on this amount and is now entitled to recover it tax-free. Any loss recognized is deducted from the basis of the new property since the taxpayer has already received a tax benefit on that amount.

The holding period of the property surrendered in the exchange carries over and *tacks on* to the holding period of the like-kind property received.[57] This rule derives from the basic concept of the new property as a continuation of the old investment. The boot received has a new holding period (from the date of exchange) rather than a carryover holding period.

Depreciation recapture potential carries over to the property received in a like-kind exchange.[58] See Chapter 8 for a discussion of this topic.

The following comprehensive example illustrates the like-kind exchange basis rules.

EXAMPLE 42

Stork & Company exchanged the following old machines for new machines in five independent like-kind exchanges:

Exchange	Adjusted Basis of Old Machine	Fair Market Value of New Machine	Adjusted Basis of Boot Given	Fair Market Value of Boot Received
1	$4,000	$9,000	$ –0–	$ –0–
2	4,000	9,000	3,000	–0–
3	4,000	9,000	6,000	–0–
4	4,000	9,000	–0–	3,000
5	4,000	3,500	–0–	300

---

[57]§ 1223(1) and Reg. § 1.1223–1(a). For like-kind exchanges after March 1, 1954, the tacked-on holding period applies only if the like-kind property surrendered was either a capital asset or § 1231 property. See Chapter 8 for the discussion of capital assets and § 1231 property.
[58]Reg. §§ 1.1245–2(a)(4) and 1.1250–2(d)(1).

CHAPTER 7 Property Transactions: Basis, Gain and Loss, and Nontaxable Exchanges

Stork's realized and recognized gains and losses and the basis of each of the like-kind properties received are as follows:

Exchange	Realized Gain (Loss)	Recognized Gain (Loss)	Old Adj. Basis	+	Boot Given	+	New Basis Calculation Gain Recognized	−	Boot Received	=	New Basis
1	$ 5,000	$ –0–	$4,000	+	$ –0–	+	$ –0–	−	$ –0–	=	$ 4,000*
2	2,000	–0–	4,000	+	3,000	+	–0–	−	–0–	=	7,000*
3	(1,000)	(–0–)	4,000	+	6,000	+	–0–	−	–0–	=	10,000**
4	8,000	3,000	4,000	+	–0–	+	3,000	−	3,000	=	4,000*
5	(200)	(–0–)	4,000	+	–0–	+	–0–	−	300	=	3,700**

*Basis may be determined in gain situations under the alternative method by subtracting the gain not recognized from the fair market value of the new property:
$9,000 − $5,000 = $4,000 for exchange 1.
$9,000 − $2,000 = $7,000 for exchange 2.
$9,000 − $5,000 = $4,000 for exchange 4.

**In loss situations, basis may be determined by adding the loss not recognized to the fair market value of the new property:
$9,000 + $1,000 = $10,000 for exchange 3.
$3,500 + $200 = $3,700 for exchange 5.

The basis of the boot received is the boot's fair market value.

If the taxpayer either assumes a liability or takes property subject to a liability, the amount of the liability is treated as boot given. For the taxpayer whose liability is assumed or whose property is taken subject to the liability, the amount of the liability is treated as boot received. The following example illustrates the effect of such a liability. In addition, the example illustrates the tax consequences for both parties involved in the like-kind exchange.

EXAMPLE 43

Jaeger & Company and Lark Enterprises, Inc., exchange real estate investments. Jaeger gives up property with an adjusted basis of $250,000 (fair market value $400,000) that is subject to a mortgage of $75,000 (assumed by Lark). In return for this property, Jaeger receives property with a fair market value of $300,000 (adjusted basis $200,000) and cash of $25,000.[59]

	Jaeger	Lark
Amount realized:		
Like-kind property received	$ 300,000	$ 400,000
Boot received:		
Cash	25,000	
Mortgage assumed	75,000	
	$ 400,000	$ 400,000
Adjusted basis:		
Like-kind property given	(250,000)	(200,000)
Boot given:		
Cash		(25,000)
Mortgage assumed		(75,000)
Realized gain	$ 150,000	$ 100,000
Recognized gain	$ 100,000*	None**
Deferred gain	$ 50,000	$ 100,000

---

[59] Example (2) of Reg. § 1.1031(d)–2 illustrates a special situation where both the buyer and the seller transfer liabilities that are assumed or property is acquired subject to a liability by the other party.

Basis of property transferred:		
Like-kind property	$ 250,000	$200,000
Cash		25,000
Mortgage assumed		75,000
	$ 250,000	$300,000
Plus: Gain recognized	100,000	
Less: Boot received	(100,000)	
Basis of new property	$ 250,000	$300,000

*Lesser of boot received ($25,000 cash + $75,000 mortgage assumed = $100,000) or gain realized ($150,000).
**No boot received.

INVOLUNTARY CONVERSIONS—§ 1033

6 LEARNING OBJECTIVE
Explain the nonrecognition provisions available on the involuntary conversion of property.

Section 1033 provides that a taxpayer who suffers an involuntary conversion of property may postpone recognition of *gain* realized from the conversion, if that taxpayer *reinvests* the amount realized from the conversion in replacement property. Thus, if the amount reinvested in replacement property is *less than* the amount realized, realized gain *is recognized* but only to the extent of the amount not reinvested. Any gain not recognized reduces the taxpayer's basis in the replacement property.[60] Thus, recognition of the gain is deferred until the replacement property is disposed of.

EXAMPLE 44

Sandpiper, Inc., receives insurance proceeds of $29,000 when some of its manufacturing equipment (adjusted basis of $25,000) is destroyed by fire. Sandpiper purchases new equipment costing $30,000, so none of its $4,000 gain ($29,000 amount realized − $25,000 adjusted basis) is recognized. Sandpiper's basis in the new equipment is $26,000 ($30,000 cost − $4,000 deferred gain). ▼

EXAMPLE 45

If Sandpiper, Inc., in the preceding example purchases new equipment that costs $28,000, it would recognize gain of $1,000, the difference between the $29,000 of insurance proceeds realized on the conversion and the $28,000 cost of the new equipment. The remaining $3,000 of gain would not be recognized; instead, it would reduce the company's basis in the new equipment to $25,000 ($28,000 cost − $3,000 deferred gain). ▼

By its terms, § 1033 is *elective*. A taxpayer need not postpone recognition of gain, even if replacement property is acquired. In essence, a taxpayer has three options:

- Reinvest the proceeds and elect § 1033's nonrecognition of gain.
- Reinvest the proceeds and not elect § 1033, thereby triggering recognition of gain under the customary rules applicable to property transactions.
- Not reinvest the proceeds and recognize the gain accordingly.

If a *loss* occurs on an involuntary conversion, § 1033 does not apply, and the general rules for loss recognition are effective. See Chapter 5 for deduction of losses.

---

[60] § 1033(b)(2).

PLANNING CONSIDERATIONS

Recognizing Involuntary Conversion Gains

Sometimes, a taxpayer may prefer to *recognize a gain from an involuntary conversion* and will choose not to elect § 1033, even though replacement property is acquired. Circumstances suggesting this strategy would include:

- The taxpayer realized the gain in a low-bracket tax year, quite possibly because of the events that caused the involuntary conversion, such as a flood and its aftermath that seriously disrupted the business.
- The taxpayer has an expiring net operating loss carryover that can offset most, if not all, of the gain from the involuntary conversion.
- The replacement property is depreciable, and the taxpayer would prefer an unreduced basis for this asset to maximize depreciation deductions in future years.

Nontax considerations might also come into play, perhaps suggesting that the property not be replaced at all. Even before the event that produced the involuntary conversion, the taxpayer might have been wanting to downsize the business or terminate it outright. In any case, the taxpayer might prefer to recognize the gain, pay the tax involved, and thereby free up the remaining proceeds for other uses—business, investment, or even personal—especially if the gain is small compared to the amount of proceeds received.

INVOLUNTARY CONVERSION DEFINED

An **involuntary conversion** results from the destruction (complete or partial), theft, seizure, requisition or condemnation, or the sale or exchange under threat or imminence of requisition or condemnation of the taxpayer's property.[61] This description includes fires (other than arson),[62] tornadoes, hurricanes, earthquakes, floods, and other natural disasters. In these circumstances, *gain* can result from insurance proceeds received in an amount that exceeds the taxpayer's historical cost of the property, especially if depreciation deductions have lowered the property's adjusted basis.

For requisitions and condemnations, the amount realized includes the compensation paid by the public authority acquiring the taxpayer's property. To prove the existence of a threat or imminence of condemnation, the taxpayer must obtain confirmation that there has been a decision to acquire the property for public use. In addition, the taxpayer must have reasonable grounds to believe the property will be taken.[63] The property does not have to be sold to the authority threatening to condemn it to qualify for § 1033 postponement. If the taxpayer satisfies the confirmation and reasonable grounds requirements, he or she can sell the property to another party.[64] Likewise, the sale of property to a condemning authority by a taxpayer who acquired the property from its former owner with the knowledge that the property was under threat of condemnation also qualifies as an involuntary conversion under § 1033.[65]

---

[61] § 1033(a) and Reg. §§ 1.1033(a)–1(a) and –2(a).
[62] Rev.Rul. 82–74, 1982–1 C.B. 110.
[63] Rev.Rul. 63–221, 1963–2 C.B. 332, and *Joseph P. Balistrieri*, 38 TCM 526, T.C.Memo. 1979–115.
[64] Rev.Rul. 81–180, 1981–2 C.B. 161.
[65] Rev.Rul. 81–181, 1981–2 C.B. 162.

> ## TAX IN THE NEWS
>
> ### A SOUND INVESTMENT—NOT
>
> A group of investors constructed a building and leased it to a city. This transaction is a normal event. The city later condemned the building so it would not have to make the lease payments. This is not a normal event.
>
> In 1988, the investors paid $3.5 million to construct the building, which was then leased to the city of Sheridan, Colorado (population of 5,300), for $200,000 per year for use as the city hall. When the city experienced financial difficulties and tried to get out of the lease, the investors rejected an offer by the city. Consequently, the city exercised its right of eminent domain and condemned its own city hall.
>
> Both the city and the trustee for the investors had the building appraised. As is frequently the case, the appraisers did not agree on the value. The city's appraiser valued the building at $600,000, while the investors' appraiser arrived at $2.8 million. Because the building was designed for governmental use, the city contended that it had a much lower value than a private structure.
>
> In final settlement, the city offered the investors $642,000. This amount results in a loss of $2.6 million for the investors. As the condemnation constitutes an involuntary conversion, the loss is deductible for Federal income tax purposes.
>
> SOURCE: Adapted from Marcy Lamm, "Colorado Town Condemns City Hall in Effort to Avoid Lease Payments," *Wall Street Journal*, July 1, 1996, p. B7A.

REPLACEMENT PROPERTY

The requirements for replacement property generally are more restrictive than those for like-kind property under § 1031. The basic requirement is that the replacement property be similar or related in service or use to the involuntarily converted property.[66]

Different interpretations of the phrase *similar or related in service or use* apply depending on whether the involuntarily converted property is held by an *owner-user* or by an *owner-investor* (e.g., lessor). For an owner-user, the *functional use test* applies, and for an owner-investor, the *taxpayer use test* applies.

Functional Use Test. Under this test, a taxpayer's use of the replacement property and of the involuntarily converted property must be the same. Replacing a manufacturing plant with a wholesale grocery warehouse does not meet this test. Instead, the plant must be replaced with another facility of similar functional use.

Taxpayer Use Test. The taxpayer use test for owner-investors provides the taxpayer with more flexibility in terms of what qualifies as replacement property than does the functional use test for owner-users. Essentially, the properties must be used by the taxpayer (the owner-investor) in similar endeavors. For example, rental property held by an owner-investor qualifies if replaced by other rental property, regardless of the type of rental property involved. The test is met when an investor replaces a manufacturing plant with a wholesale grocery warehouse

---

[66]§ 1033(a) and Reg. § 1.1033(a)–1.

CONCEPT SUMMARY 7-3

Replacement Property Tests

Type of Property and User	Like-Kind Test	Taxpayer Use Test	Functional Use Test
Land used by a manufacturing company is condemned by a local government authority.	X		
Apartment and land held by an investor are sold due to the threat or imminence of condemnation.	X		
An investor's rented shopping mall is destroyed by fire; the mall may be replaced by other rental properties (e.g., an apartment building).		X	
A manufacturing plant is destroyed by fire; replacement property must consist of another manufacturing plant that is functionally the same as the property converted.			X
Personal residence of taxpayer is condemned by a local government authority; replacement property must consist of another personal residence.			X

if both properties are held for the production of rental income.[67] The replacement of a rental residence with a personal residence does not meet the test.[68]

Special Real Property Test. In addition to the functional and taxpayer use tests, the Code provides a special rule for business or investment real property *that is condemned*. This rule applies the broad like-kind classification for real estate to such circumstances. Accordingly, improved real property can be replaced with unimproved real property.

The rules concerning the nature of replacement property are illustrated in Concept Summary 7–3.

TIME LIMITATION ON REPLACEMENT

The taxpayer normally has a two-year period after the close of the taxable year in which gain is realized from the involuntary conversion to replace the property (*the latest date*).[69] This rule affords as much as three years from the date of realization of gain to replace the property if the realization of gain took place on the first day of the taxable year.[70] If the involuntary conversion involved the condemnation of real property used in a trade or business or held for investment, the Code substitutes a three-year period for the normal two-year period. In this case, a taxpayer might have as much as four years from the date of realization of gain to replace the property.

EXAMPLE 46

Magpie, Inc.'s warehouse is destroyed by fire on December 16, 1997. The adjusted basis is $325,000. Magpie receives $400,000 from the insurance company on January 10, 1998. The company is a calendar year taxpayer. The latest date for replacement is December 31, 2000

---

[67] *Loco Realty Co. v. Comm.*, 62–2 USTC ¶9657, 10 AFTR2d 5359, 306 F.2d 207 (CA–8, 1962).
[68] Rev.Rul. 70–466, 1970–2 C.B. 165.
[69] §§ 1033(a)(2)(B) and (g)(4) and Reg. § 1.1033(a)–2(c)(3).
[70] A taxpayer can apply for an extension of this time period anytime before its expiration [Reg. § 1.1033(a)–2(c)(3)]. Also, the period for filing the application for extension can be extended if a taxpayer shows reasonable cause.

EXAMPLE 47

(the end of the taxable year in which realized gain occurred plus two years). The critical date is not the date the involuntary conversion occurred, but rather the date of gain realization (when the insurance proceeds are received). ▼

Assume the same facts as in the preceding example, except that Magpie's warehouse is condemned. The latest date for replacement is December 31, 2001 (the end of the taxable year in which realized gain occurred plus three years). ▼

The *earliest date* for replacement typically is the date the involuntary conversion occurs. However, if the property is condemned, it is possible to replace the condemned property before this date. In this case, the earliest date is the date of the threat or imminence of requisition or condemnation of the property. The purpose of this provision is to enable the taxpayer to make an orderly replacement of the condemned property.

REPORTING CONSIDERATIONS

Involuntary conversions from casualty and theft are reported first on Form 4684, Casualties and Thefts. Casualty and theft losses on personal-use property for an individual taxpayer are carried from Form 4684 to Schedule A of Form 1040. For other casualty and theft items, the Form 4684 amounts are generally reported on Form 4797, Sales of Business Property, unless Form 4797 is not required. In the latter case, the amounts are reported directly on the tax return involved.

Except for personal-use property, recognized gains and losses from involuntary conversions other than by casualty and theft are reported on Form 4797. As stated previously, if the property involved in the involuntary conversion (other than by casualty and theft) is personal-use property, any realized loss is not recognized. Any realized gain is treated as gain on a voluntary sale.

OTHER NONRECOGNITION PROVISIONS

7 LEARNING OBJECTIVE
Identify other nonrecognition provisions contained in the Code.

Several additional nonrecognition provisions are treated briefly in the remainder of this chapter.

TRANSFER OF ASSETS TO BUSINESS ENTITY—§§ 351 AND 721

Taxpayers can transfer assets to corporations in exchange for stock without recognizing gain or loss on the transfer per § 351. See Chapter 9 for the applicable restrictions and corresponding basis adjustments for the stock acquired. A similar provision (§ 721) allows the nontaxable transfer of assets to a partnership in exchange for an interest in that partnership. See Chapter 11 for a description of § 721.

EXCHANGE OF STOCK FOR PROPERTY—§ 1032

Under § 1032, a corporation does not recognize gain or loss on the receipt of money or other property in exchange for its stock (including treasury stock). In other words, a corporation does not recognize gain or loss when it deals in its own stock. This provision accords with the accounting treatment of such transactions.

CERTAIN EXCHANGES OF INSURANCE POLICIES—§ 1035

Under § 1035, no gain or loss is recognized from the exchange of certain insurance contracts or policies. The rules relating to exchanges not solely in kind (i.e., with boot) and the basis of the property acquired are the same as under § 1031. Exchanges qualifying for nonrecognition include the following:

- The exchange of life insurance contracts.
- The exchange of a life insurance contract for an endowment or annuity contract.
- The exchange of an endowment contract for another endowment contract that provides for regular payments beginning at a date not later than the date payments would have begun under the contract exchanged.
- The exchange of an endowment contract for an annuity contract.
- The exchange of annuity contracts.

EXCHANGE OF STOCK FOR STOCK OF THE SAME CORPORATION—§ 1036

A shareholder does not recognize gain or loss on the exchange of common stock solely for common stock in the same corporation or from the exchange of preferred stock for preferred stock in the same corporation. Exchanges between individual shareholders as well as between a shareholder and the corporation are included under this nonrecognition provision. The rules relating to exchanges not solely in kind and the basis of the property acquired are the same as under § 1031. For example, a nonrecognition exchange occurs when common stock with different rights, such as voting for nonvoting, is exchanged. A shareholder usually recognizes gain or loss from the exchange of common for preferred or preferred for common even though the stock exchanged is in the same corporation.

CERTAIN REACQUISITIONS OF REAL PROPERTY—§ 1038

Section 1038 provides that no loss is recognized from the repossession of real property sold on an installment basis. Gain, however, is recognized to a limited extent.

ROLLOVERS INTO SPECIALIZED SMALL BUSINESS INVESTMENT COMPANIES—§ 1044

Section 1044 provides a postponement opportunity associated with the sale of publicly traded securities. If the amount realized is reinvested in the common stock or partnership interest of a specialized small business investment company (SSBIC), the realized gain is not recognized. Gain will be recognized, however, to the extent of any amount not reinvested. To qualify, the taxpayer must reinvest the proceeds within 60 days of the date of sale. In calculating the basis of the SSBIC stock, the amount of the purchase price is reduced by the amount of the postponed gain.

Statutory ceilings are imposed on the amount of realized gain that can be postponed for any taxable year as follows:

- Individual taxpayer: Lesser of:
  - $50,000 ($25,000 for married filing separately).
  - $500,000 ($250,000 for married filing separately) reduced by the amount of such nonrecognized gain in all preceding taxable years.

- Corporate taxpayer: Lesser of:
  - $250,000.
  - $1,000,000 reduced by the amount of such nonrecognized gain in all preceding taxable years.

Investors ineligible for this postponement treatment include partnerships, S corporations, estates, and trusts.

SALE OF A PRINCIPAL RESIDENCE—§ 121

Section 121 allows individual taxpayers to exclude gain from the sale of a *principal residence*.[71] This provision applies to the first $250,000 of realized gain, or $500,000 on a joint return. For this purpose, the residence must have been owned and used by the taxpayer as the primary residence for two of the five years preceding the date of sale. This exclusion can be prorated, however, if a taxpayer failed to meet the two-year requirement due to a change in his or her employment or health. Moreover, a surviving spouse counts the ownership and usage periods of the decedent spouse in meeting the two-year test. This provision applies only to gains; losses on residences, like those of other personal-use assets, are not recognized for tax purposes.

TRANSFERS OF PROPERTY BETWEEN SPOUSES OR INCIDENT TO DIVORCE—§ 1041

Section 1041 provides for nontaxable exchange treatment on property transfers *between spouses during marriage*. The basis to the recipient spouse is a carryover basis.

Section 1041 also provides that transfers of property *between spouses or former spouses incident to divorce* are nontaxable transactions. Therefore, the basis to the recipient is a carryover basis. To be treated as incident to the divorce, the transfer must be related to the cessation of marriage or must occur within one year after the date on which the marriage ceases.

KEY TERMS

Adjusted basis, 7-4
Amount realized, 7-3
Boot, 7-24
Fair market value, 7-3
Goodwill, 7-9
Holding period, 7-12
Involuntary conversion, 7-29
Like-kind exchange, 7-21
Nontaxable exchange, 7-20
Realized gain, 7-3
Realized loss, 7-3
Recognized gain, 7-6
Recognized loss, 7-6
Recovery of capital doctrine, 7-7
Wash sale, 7-15

---

[71] For an extensive explanation of this provision, see Chapter 9 of *West's Federal Taxation: Advanced Taxation*.

CHAPTER 7 Property Transactions: Basis, Gain and Loss, and Nontaxable Exchanges

PROBLEM MATERIALS

1. Cormorant Properties, Inc., bought a rental house at the beginning of 1993 for $80,000, of which $10,000 is allocated to the land and $70,000 to the building. Early in 1995, Cormorant had a tennis court built in the backyard at a cost of $5,000. The company has deducted $32,200 for depreciation on the house and $1,300 for depreciation on the court. At the beginning of this year, Cormorant sells the house and tennis court for $125,000 cash.
    a. What is the company's realized gain or loss?
    b. If an original mortgage of $20,000 is still outstanding and the buyer assumes the mortgage in addition to the cash payment, what is Cormorant's realized gain or loss?
    c. If the buyer takes the property subject to the mortgage, what is Cormorant's realized gain or loss?

2. Black, Inc., owns a building (adjusted basis of $366,500 on January 1) that it rents to Lapwing & Longspur, which operates a restaurant in the building. The municipal health department closed the restaurant for two months this year because of health code violations. Under MACRS, the cost recovery deduction for this year would be $12,000. However, Black deducted cost recovery only for the 10 months the restaurant was open since it waived the rent income during the two-month period the restaurant was closed.
    a. What is the amount of the cost recovery deduction that Black should report on this year's income tax return?
    b. Calculate the adjusted basis of the building at the end of this year.

3. Nell owns a personal-use automobile that has an adjusted basis of $18,000. The fair market value of the automobile is $14,500.
    a. Calculate the realized and recognized loss if Nell sells the automobile for $14,500.
    b. Calculate the realized and recognized loss if Nell exchanges the automobile for another automobile worth $14,500.

4. Hubert's personal residence is condemned as part of an urban renewal project. His adjusted basis for the residence is $160,000. He receives condemnation proceeds of $150,000 and invests the proceeds in stock.
    a. Calculate Hubert's realized and recognized gain or loss.
    b. If the condemnation proceeds are $180,000, what are Hubert's realized and recognized gain or loss?
    c. What are Hubert's realized and recognized gain or loss in (a) if the house was rental property?

5. A warehouse owned by Marmot & Squirrel (a partnership) and used in its business (i.e., to store inventory) is being condemned by the city to provide a right of way for a highway. The warehouse has appreciated by $100,000 based on an estimate of fair market value. In the negotiations, the city is offering $40,000 less than what Marmot & Squirrel believes the property is worth. Alan, a real estate broker, has offered to purchase the property for $25,000 more than the city's offer. The partnership plans to invest the proceeds it will receive in an office building that it will lease to various tenants. Identify the relevant tax issues for Marmot & Squirrel.

6. Finch, Inc., purchases 100 shares of Bluebird Corporation stock on June 3, 1998, for $150,000. On August 25, 1998, Finch purchases an additional 50 shares of Bluebird stock for $60,000. According to market quotations, Bluebird stock is selling for $1,100 per share on December 31, 1998. Finch sells 60 shares of Bluebird stock on March 1, 1999, for $51,000.
    a. What is the adjusted basis of Finch's Bluebird stock on December 31, 1998?
    b. What is Finch's recognized gain or loss from the sale of Bluebird stock on March 1, 1999, assuming the shares sold are from the shares purchased on June 3, 1998?
    c. What is Finch's recognized gain or loss from the sale of Bluebird stock on March 1, 1999, assuming Finch cannot adequately identify the shares sold?

7. Randy Morgan purchases Agnes's sole proprietorship for $900,000. The assets of the business are as follows:

Asset	Agnes's Adjusted Basis	FMV
Accounts receivable	$ 70,000	$ 70,000
Inventory	90,000	100,000
Equipment	150,000	160,000
Furniture and fixtures	95,000	130,000
Building	190,000	250,000
Land	25,000	75,000

Randy and Agnes agree that $50,000 of the purchase price is for Agnes's five-year covenant not to compete.
   a. Calculate Agnes's realized and recognized gain.
   b. Determine Randy's basis for each of the assets.
   c. Write a letter to Randy informing him of the tax consequences of the purchase. Randy's address is 300 Riverside Drive, Cincinnati, OH 45207.

8. Rick has decided to dispose of the following assets that he received as gifts:
   a. In 1981, he received land worth $12,000. The donor's adjusted basis was $25,000. Rick sells the land for $8,000 this year.
   b. In 1993, he received stock worth $30,000. The donor's adjusted basis was $45,000. Rick sells the stock this year for $39,000.

What is the realized gain or loss from each of the preceding transactions? Assume in each transaction that no gift tax was paid.

9. Holly owns stock with an adjusted basis of $2,500 and a fair market value of $9,500. Holly expects the stock to continue to appreciate. Alice, Holly's best friend, has recently been operated on for cancer. Alice's physicians have told her that her life expectancy is between six months and one and a half years. One day at lunch, the two friends were discussing their tax situations (both feel they pay too much), when Alice mentioned that she had read a newspaper article about a tax planning opportunity that might be suitable for Holly. Holly would make a gift of the appreciated stock to Alice. In her will, Alice would bequeath the stock back to Holly. Since Alice is confident that she will live longer than a year, the basis of the stock to Holly would be the fair market value on the date of Alice's death. Alice would "feel good" because she had helped Holly "beat the tax system." You are Holly's tax adviser. How will you respond to Alice's proposal? Would your response change if the stock were a painting that Alice could enjoy for her remaining days?

10. Beth received a car from Sam as a gift. Sam paid $7,000 for the car. He had used it for business purposes and had deducted $2,000 for depreciation up to the time he gave the car to Beth. The fair market value of the car is $3,500.
   a. Assuming Beth uses the car for business purposes, what is her basis for depreciation?
   b. If the estimated useful life is two years (from the date of the gift), what is her depreciation deduction for each year? Use the straight-line method.
   c. If Beth sells the car for $800 one year after receiving it, what is her gain or loss?
   d. If Beth sells the car for $4,000 one year after receiving it, what is her gain or loss?

11. This year, Ron receives a gift of property that has a fair market value of $100,000 on the date of the gift. The donor's adjusted basis for the property was $32,000. Assume the donor paid gift tax of $20,000 on the gift.
   a. What is Ron's basis for gain and loss and for depreciation?
   b. If Ron had received the gift of property in 1975, what would be his basis for gain and loss and for depreciation?

12. Simon, who is retired, owns Teal, Inc., stock that has declined in value since he purchased it. He has decided either to give the stock to his nephew, Fred, who is a high school teacher, or to sell the stock and give the proceeds to Fred. Because nearly all of his wealth is invested in tax-exempt bonds, Simon faces a 15% marginal tax rate. Fred will use the cash or the proceeds from his sale of the stock to make the down payment on

the purchase of a house. Based on a recent conversation, Simon is aware that Fred has a 28% marginal tax rate. Identify the tax issues relevant to Simon in deciding whether to give the stock or the sale proceeds to Fred.

13. This year, Liz receives a gift of income-producing property that has an adjusted basis of $70,000 on the date of the gift. The fair market value of the property on the date of the gift is $50,000. The donor paid gift tax of $4,000. Liz later sells the property for $54,000. Determine her recognized gain or loss.

14. Dena inherits property from Mary, her mother. Mary's adjusted basis for the property is $100,000, and the fair market value is $725,000. Six months after Mary's death, the fair market value is $740,000. Dena is the sole beneficiary of Mary's estate.
    a. Can the executor of Mary's estate elect the alternate valuation date?
    b. What is Dena's basis for the property?

15. Earl's estate includes the following assets available for distribution to Robert, one of Earl's beneficiaries:

Asset	Earl's Adjusted Basis	FMV at Date of Death	FMV at Alternate Valuation Date
Cash	$10,000	$ 10,000	$ 10,000
Stock	40,000	125,000	60,000
Apartment building	60,000	300,000	325,000
Land	75,000	100,000	110,000

    The fair market value of the stock six months after Earl's death was $60,000. However, believing that the stock would continue to decline in value, the executor of the estate distributed the stock to Robert one month after Earl's death. Robert immediately sold the stock for $85,000.
    a. Determine Robert's basis for the assets if the primary valuation date and amount apply.
    b. Determine Robert's basis for the assets if the executor elects the alternate valuation date and amount.

16. Sheila sells land to Elane, her sister, for $40,000. Six months later Elane gives the land to Jacob, her son. No gift taxes are due. At the date of the gift, the land is worth $42,000. Jacob sells the land one month later for $43,000.
    a. Assuming Sheila's adjusted basis for the land is $25,000, what are Sheila and Jacob's recognized gain or loss on their respective sales?
    b. Assuming Sheila's adjusted basis for the land is $50,000, what are Sheila and Jacob's recognized gain or loss on their respective sales?

17. Peony Investors Co. sells 150 shares of Lavender, Inc., stock on December 28, 1998, for $75,000. On January 10, 1999, Peony purchases 100 shares of Lavender, Inc., stock for $80,000.
    a. Assuming Peony's adjusted basis for the stock sold is $60,000, what is its recognized gain or loss, and what is its basis for the new shares?
    b. Assuming Peony's adjusted basis for the stock sold is $90,000, what is its recognized gain or loss, and what is its basis for the new shares?
    c. Advise Peony on how it can avoid any negative tax consequences encountered in (b).

18. James retires from a public accounting firm to enter private practice. He had bought a home two years earlier for $40,000. Upon opening his business, he converts one-fourth of his home into an office. The fair market value of the home on the date of conversion (January 1, 1993) is $75,000. The adjusted basis is $56,000 (ignore land). James lives and works in the home for six years (after converting it to business use) and sells it at the end of the sixth year. He deducted $2,630 of cost recovery using the statutory percentage method.
    a. How much gain or loss is recognized if James sells the property for $44,000?
    b. How much gain or loss is recognized if he sells the property for $70,000?

19. Surendra's personal residence originally cost $180,000 (ignore land). After living in the house for five years, he converts it to rental property. At the date of conversion, the fair market value of the house is $150,000.
    a. Calculate Surendra's basis for loss for the rental property.
    b. Calculate Surendra's basis for depreciation for the rental property.
    c. Calculate Surendra's basis for gain for the rental property.

20. Ibis Co. owns undeveloped land with an adjusted basis of $110,000. Ibis exchanges this land for other undeveloped land worth $215,000.
    a. What are Ibis's realized and recognized gain or loss?
    b. What is Ibis's basis in the undeveloped land it receives?

21. Tex Wall owns undeveloped land that he is holding for investment. His adjusted basis is $175,000. On October 7, 1998, he exchanges the land with his 23-year-old daughter, Paige, for other undeveloped land that he will hold for investment. The appraised value of Paige's land is $250,000.
    a. Calculate Tex's realized and recognized gain or loss from the exchange with Paige and on a subsequent sale of the land by Tex to Baxter, a real estate broker, for $300,000 on February 15, 1999.
    b. Calculate Tex's realized and recognized gain or loss on the exchange with Paige if Tex does not sell the land received from Paige, but Paige sells the land received from Tex on February 15, 1999. Calculate Tex's basis for the land on October 7, 1998, and on February 15, 1999.
    c. Write a letter to Tex advising him on how he could avoid any recognition of gain associated with the October 7, 1998, exchange prior to his actual sale of the land. His address is The Corral, El Paso, TX 79968.

22. Snipe Corporation owns a computer with an adjusted basis of $5,000. Snipe exchanges the computer and cash of $7,000 for a laser printer worth $16,000.
    a. Calculate Snipe's recognized gain or loss on the exchange.
    b. Calculate Snipe's basis for the printer.

23. Raven Investments, Inc., owns land and a building with an adjusted basis of $125,000 and a fair market value of $275,000. Raven exchanges the land and building for land with a fair market value of $175,000 that it will use as a parking lot. In addition, Raven receives stock worth $100,000.
    a. What is the company's realized gain or loss?
    b. Its recognized gain or loss?
    c. The basis of the land and the stock received?

24. Ross Industries would like to dispose of some land that it acquired five years ago because the land will not continue to appreciate. Its value has increased by $50,000 during the five-year period. The company also intends to sell stock that has declined in value by $50,000 during the eight months since its purchase. Ross has four offers to acquire the stock and land:

    Buyer number 1: Exchange land.
    Buyer number 2: Purchase land for cash.
    Buyer number 3: Exchange stock.
    Buyer number 4: Purchase stock for cash.

    Identify the tax issues relevant to Ross in disposing of this land and stock.

25. What is the basis of the new property in each of the following exchanges?
    a. Apartment building held for investment (adjusted basis, $150,000) for office building to be held for investment (fair market value, $200,000).
    b. Land and building used as a barber shop (adjusted basis, $30,000) for land and building used as a grocery store (fair market value, $350,000).
    c. Office building (adjusted basis, $30,000) for bulldozer (fair market value, $42,000), both held for business use.

d. IBM common stock (adjusted basis, $14,000) for Exxon common stock (fair market value, $18,000).
e. Rental house (adjusted basis, $90,000) for mountain cabin to be held for personal use (fair market value, $115,000).

26. Hyacinth Realty Co. owns land in Iowa that was originally purchased for $130,000. Hyacinth has received an all-cash offer in the amount of $400,000 from a well-known shopping center developer. An international real estate broker has now offered some land located outside Florence, Italy, that is worth $400,000 in exchange for the Iowa property. Please write the company a letter analyzing these options from a tax standpoint. Hyacinth's address is 2501 Longview Lane, Des Moines, IA 50311.

27. Maroon Tool & Die Co. owns Machine A with an adjusted basis of $12,000, and a fair market value of $18,000. Maroon is considering two options for the disposal of Machine A. Under the first option, Maroon will transfer Machine A and $3,000 cash to Jabiru, Inc., a dealer, in exchange for Machine B, which has a fair market value of $21,000. Under the second option, Maroon will sell Machine A for $18,000 to Tern Company, a dealer. Maroon will then purchase Machine B from Jabiru for $21,000. Machine A and Machine B qualify as like-kind property.
    a. Calculate Maroon's recognized gain or loss and the basis for Machine B under the first option.
    b. Calculate Maroon's recognized gain or loss and the basis for Machine B under the second option.
    c. Advise Maroon on which option it should select.

28. Green Properties, Inc., exchanges real estate held for investment plus stock for real estate to be held for investment. The stock transferred has an adjusted basis of $15,000 and a fair market value of $10,000. The real estate transferred has an adjusted basis of $15,000 and a fair market value of $45,000. The real estate acquired has a fair market value of $55,000.
    a. What is Green's realized gain or loss?
    b. Its recognized gain or loss?
    c. The basis of the newly acquired real estate?

29. Avocet Management Co. exchanges a warehouse and the related land with Indigo, Inc., for an office building and the related land. Avocet's adjusted basis for the warehouse and land is $420,000. The fair market value of Indigo's office building and land is $410,000. Avocet's property has a $90,000 mortgage that Indigo assumes.
    a. Calculate Avocet's realized and recognized gain or loss.
    b. Calculate Avocet's adjusted basis for the office building and land received.
    c. As an alternative, Indigo has proposed that rather than assuming the mortgage, it will transfer cash of $90,000 to Avocet, which would use the cash to pay off the mortgage. Advise Avocet on whether this alternative would be beneficial to it from a tax perspective.

30. Determine the realized, recognized, and postponed gain or loss and the new basis for each of the following like-kind exchanges:

	Adjusted Basis of Old Asset	Boot Given	Fair Market Value of New Asset	Boot Received
a.	$ 7,000	$ –0–	$12,000	$4,000
b.	14,000	2,000	15,000	–0–
c.	3,000	7,000	8,000	500
d.	22,000	–0–	32,000	–0–
e.	10,000	–0–	11,000	1,000
f.	10,000	–0–	8,000	–0–

31. Turquoise Realty Co. owns an apartment house that has an adjusted basis of $1,100,000 but is subject to a mortgage of $250,000. Turquoise transfers the apartment house to

Dove, Inc., and receives from Dove $125,000 in cash and an office building with a fair market value of $1,125,000 at the time of the exchange. Dove assumes the $250,000 mortgage on the apartment house.
   a. What is Turquoise's realized gain or loss?
   b. What is its recognized gain or loss?
   c. What is the basis of the newly acquired office building?

32. Cardinal Computing's office building, which has an adjusted basis of $400,000, is destroyed by a tornado. Since Cardinal's business has excess office space, it decides not to replace the office building, but instead to contribute the proceeds to the working capital of its business.
   a. If the insurance proceeds are $525,000, what is Cardinal's recognized gain or loss?
   b. If the insurance proceeds are $380,000, what is Cardinal's recognized gain or loss?

33. For each of the following involuntary conversions, indicate whether the property acquired qualifies as replacement property:
   a. A shopping mall is destroyed by a tornado. The space in the mall was rented to various tenants. The owner of the mall uses the insurance proceeds to build a shopping mall in a neighboring community where no property has been damaged by tornadoes.
   b. A warehouse is destroyed by fire. Due to economic conditions in the area, the owner decides not to rebuild the warehouse. Instead, it uses the insurance proceeds to build a warehouse in another state.
   c. Swallow Fashions, Inc., owns a building that is destroyed by a hurricane. Due to an economic downturn in the area caused by the closing of a military base, Swallow decides to rent space for its retail outlet rather than to replace the building. It uses the insurance proceeds to buy a four-unit apartment building in another city. A realtor in that city will handle the rental of the apartments.
   d. Susan and Rick's personal residence is destroyed by a tornado. Since they would like to travel, they decide not to acquire a replacement residence. Instead, they invest the insurance proceeds in a duplex that they rent to tenants.

34. The city of Richmond is going to condemn some buildings in a run-down section of the city to build a park. Steve's principal residence is among those to be condemned. His adjusted basis for the house and land is $60,000. The appraised value of the house and land is $52,000. Steve is unaware of the future condemnation proceedings, but would like his family to move to a better neighborhood. Therefore, when Ross, a realtor, mentions that he may have a corporate client who would like to purchase the property for $65,000, Steve is ecstatic and indicates a willingness to sell.

Ross is having some "second thoughts" about his conversation with Steve. The potential corporate purchaser is a company owned by Ross and his wife. Ross is aware of the future condemnation proceedings. He considers himself a skilled negotiator and thinks he can negotiate a $130,000 price for the house. Ross is considering telling Steve that the corporate client has changed its mind. Ross would then indicate that he has learned the city will be condemning several buildings in order to create a park, but has not yet established the prices it will pay for the condemned property. He would also tell Steve that because he believes he can get more from the city than Steve would obtain, he is willing to gamble and purchase the property now from Steve for $65,000. Ross will point out several benefits available to Steve. These include (1) not having to deal with the city, (2) receiving an amount that exceeds both the appraised value and the original purchase cost of the home, and (3) receiving the money now. While admitting that he could reap a substantial profit, Ross would emphasize that he would also be taking on substantial risks. In addition, Ross would explain that when he sells the property to the city, he will defer the taxes by reinvesting the sales proceeds (due to involuntary conversion). Do you think Ross should make a new proposal to Steve based on his "second thoughts?" How do you think Steve will respond?

35. Lark Corporation's office building is destroyed by a hurricane in September. The adjusted basis is $210,000. Lark receives insurance proceeds of $390,000 in October.

CHAPTER 7   Property Transactions: Basis, Gain and Loss, and Nontaxable Exchanges

a. Calculate Lark's realized gain or loss, recognized gain or loss, and basis for the replacement property if it acquires an office building for $390,000 in October.
b. Calculate Lark's realized gain or loss, recognized gain or loss, and basis for the replacement property if it acquires a warehouse for $350,000 in October.
c. Calculate Lark's realized gain or loss and recognized gain or loss if it does not acquire replacement property.

36. Magenta, Inc.'s warehouse, which has an adjusted basis of $325,000 and a fair market value of $490,000, is condemned by an agency of the Federal government to make way for a highway interchange. The initial condemnation offer is $450,000. After substantial negotiations, the agency agrees to transfer to Magenta a surplus warehouse that it believes is worth $490,000.
    a. What are the recognized gain or loss and the basis of the replacement warehouse if Magenta's objective is to recognize as much gain as possible?
    b. Advise Magenta regarding what it needs to do by what date in order to achieve its objective.

37. What are the *maximum* postponed gain or loss and the basis for the replacement property for the following involuntary conversions?

	Property	Type of Conversion	Amount Realized	Adjusted Basis	Amount Reinvested
a.	Drugstore (business)	Condemned	$160,000	$120,000	$100,000
b.	Apartments (investment)	Casualty	100,000	120,000	200,000
c.	Grocery store (business)	Casualty	400,000	300,000	350,000
d.	Residence (personal)	Casualty	16,000	18,000	17,000
e.	Vacant lot (investment)	Condemned	240,000	160,000	240,000
f.	Residence (personal)	Casualty	20,000	18,000	19,000
g.	Residence (personal)	Condemned	18,000	20,000	26,000
h.	Apartments (investment)	Condemned	150,000	100,000	200,000

RESEARCH PROBLEMS

Note: The **RIA OnPoint System 4 Student Version CD-ROM** available with this text can be used in preparing solutions to the Research Problems. Alternatively, tax research materials contained in a standard tax library can be used.

38. As the result of a large inheritance from her grandmother, Beverly has a substantial investment portfolio. The securities are held in street name by her brokerage firm. Beverly's broker, Max, has standing oral instructions from her on sales transactions to sell the shares with the highest cost basis.

    In October 1994, Beverly phoned Max and instructed him to sell 6,000 shares of Color, Inc. Her portfolio has 15,000 shares of Color, Inc., which were purchased in several transactions over a three-year period. At the end of each month, the brokerage firm provides Beverly with a monthly statement that includes sales transactions. It does not identify the specific certificates transferred.

    In filing her 1994 income tax return, Beverly used the specific identification method to calculate the $90,000 gain on the sale of the Color shares. Now her 1994 return is being audited. The Revenue Agent has taken the position that under Reg. § 1.1012–1(c) Beverly should have used the FIFO method to report the sale of the Color shares. This would result in a recognized gain of $160,000. According to his interpretation of the Regulations, Beverly may not use the specific identification method and must use the FIFO method because the broker did not provide written confirmation of Beverly's sales instructions as required by the Regulations.

    Beverly has come to you for tax advice.

39. You are the new CPA for the Cleveland Indians, Inc. In a lunch conversation with the general manger you have learned that some player trades are likely. In particular, the general manager sees a need to improve the pitching staff. Discussions are in progress with the Seattle Mariners. They have offered to trade Randy Johnson (an all-star pitcher) and $5 million to the Indians in exchange for Marquis Grissom (an outfielder) and David Justice (an all-star outfielder). The Indians have countered by expressing interest in receiving Johnson and Edgar Martinez (an all-star third baseman) rather than cash. The general manager believes that if the Indians are going to give up the speed provided by Grissom and the power of Justice, they will need more than a starting pitcher in return. In addition, the general manager remembers from his MBA days that a player trade with no cash involved will provide better tax results. Before he finalizes a trade, he needs to be sure of the tax consequences. Provide a written opinion to the Indians on the way they should structure the trade. The mailing address is Jacobs Field, Cleveland, OH 44118.

40. Tex, a calendar year taxpayer, owns a dairy farm in Louisiana. He normally milks 100 cows per day and sells about 10% of his dairy cows per year. He replaces those sold with cows he has bred and raised. Due to a severe drought this year, he abandons his normal practice of sale and replacement and reduces the size of his herd by 25%. The sales proceeds associated with the herd reduction are $60,000, and the adjusted basis of the cows sold is $12,000. In the future, Tex plans to gradually increase the size of his herd back to 100. If Tex's objective is to minimize gain recognition, calculate his recognized gain on the sale.

CHAPTER 8

Property Transactions: Capital Gains and Losses, Section 1231, and Recapture Provisions

LEARNING OBJECTIVES

After completing Chapter 8, you should be able to:

1. Distinguish capital assets from ordinary assets.

2. Understand the relevance of a sale or exchange to classification as a capital gain or loss.

3. Determine the applicable holding period for a capital asset.

4. Describe the tax treatment of capital gains and losses for noncorporate taxpayers.

5. Describe the tax treatment of capital gains and losses for corporate taxpayers.

6. Distinguish § 1231 assets from ordinary assets and capital assets and calculate the § 1231 gain or loss.

7. Determine when recapture provisions apply and their effect.

OUTLINE

General Considerations, 8–2
Rationale for Separate Reporting of Capital Gains and Losses, 8–2
General Scheme of Taxation, 8–3
Capital Assets, 8–3
Definition of a Capital Asset, 8–3
Statutory Expansions, 8–6
Sale or Exchange, 8–7
Worthless Securities and § 1244 Stock, 8–7
Retirement of Corporate Obligations, 8–8
Options, 8–8
Patents, 8–10
Franchises, Trademarks, and Trade Names, 8–11
Lease Cancellation Payments, 8–12
Holding Period, 8–13
Special Holding Period Rules, 8–13
Short Sales, 8–15
Tax Treatment of Capital Gains and Losses of Noncorporate Taxpayers, 8–15
Capital Gains, 8–15
Capital Losses, 8–18
Small Business Stock, 8–23
Tax Treatment of Capital Gains and Losses of Corporate Taxpayers, 8–24
Section 1231 Assets, 8–24
Relationship to Capital Assets, 8–24
Rationale for Favorable Tax Treatment, 8–25
Property Included, 8–26
Property Excluded, 8–26
Nonpersonal-Use Capital Assets, 8–26
General Procedure for § 1231 Computation, 8–27
Section 1245 Recapture, 8–29
Section 1245 Property, 8–32
Observations on § 1245, 8–33
Section 1250 Recapture, 8–34
Computing Recapture on Nonresidential Real Property, 8–34
Computing Recapture on Residential Rental Housing, 8–35
Section 1250 Recapture Situations, 8–36
Additional Recapture for Corporations, 8–36
Unrecaptured § 1250 Gains, 8–39
Exceptions to §§ 1245 and 1250, 8–40
Gifts, 8–40
Death, 8–40
Charitable Transfers, 8–41
Certain Nontaxable Transactions, 8–41
Like-Kind Exchanges (§ 1031) and Involuntary Conversions (§ 1033), 8–41
Special Recapture Provisions, 8–42
Sale of Depreciable Property between Certain Related Parties, 8–42
Installment Sales, 8–42
Intangible Drilling Costs, 8–42
Reporting Procedures, 8–43

GENERAL CONSIDERATIONS

RATIONALE FOR SEPARATE REPORTING OF CAPITAL GAINS AND LOSSES

Since the earliest days of the Federal income tax, **capital assets** have received special treatment upon their disposition. Gains from these assets have historically received *preferential treatment* in the form of either partial exclusion of gain, lower rates, or a maximum tax rate. Losses from capital assets, however, have historically received less desirable treatment than losses from other assets. Further, because a taxpayer has complete control over the timing of dispositions, the Code imposes limitations on when capital losses can be deducted to prevent taxpayers from manipulating their tax liability excessively.

During World War II, capital asset treatment was extended to other assets. These assets are now called "§ 1231 assets" after the Code Section that prescribes their special treatment. Several years after World War II ended, Congress believed that this special treatment was no longer entirely warranted. Instead of repealing § 1231, however, Congress left that section in place but eroded many—but not all—of its benefits through *recapture provisions* in § 1245 and § 1250. Together, these

Code Sections constitute one of the most complicated areas of tax law affecting both individual taxpayers and business entities.

The treatment of capital assets and their hybrids in § 1231 remains among the most contentious tax policy issues and is frequently the focus of congressional debate and proposed amendments. This legislative turmoil reflects the various theories that purport to justify the separate treatment of these assets.

As already intimated, one concern is that taxpayers can time the realization of gains and losses by choosing when or even whether to sell the asset in question. If Lark Enterprises, Inc., owns stock with a basis of $20 per share and a current value of $80 per share, it does not pay tax on the $60 gain until it chooses to dispose of this stock in a taxable transaction. And for the most part, Lark has complete control over that decision. When it does dispose of the stock, however, its $60 gain is taxable in full, even though this gain may have accrued over many years. To mitigate the impact of this *bunching* of income in a single year and to offset the effect of inflation over the period of Lark's ownership of the stock, preferential treatment is prescribed for this **capital gain.**

The nature of this preferential treatment is discussed later in this chapter, but the essential point for now is that preferential treatment is confined to the excess of net long-term capital gains over net short-term **capital losses.** This cumbersome description requires taxpayers to separate their capital asset transactions from their transactions involving noncapital assets. It further requires taxpayers to separate their long-term (i.e., more than one year) transactions from their short-term (i.e., one year or less) transactions. Moreover, certain types of capital assets (principally real estate and "collectibles") receive specific treatment apart from the rates generally applicable to capital assets.

As a result of the need to distinguish and separately match capital gains and losses, the tax forms include very extensive reporting requirements for capital gains and losses. This chapter explains the principles underlying the forms. The forms are reproduced in Appendix B.

GENERAL SCHEME OF TAXATION

Recognized gains and losses must be properly classified. Proper classification depends upon three characteristics:

- The tax status of the property, including the specific type of asset.
- The manner of the property's disposition.
- The holding period of the property.

The three possible tax statuses are capital asset, § 1231 asset, and ordinary asset. Property disposition may be by sale, exchange, casualty, theft, or condemnation. The two relevant holding periods are one year or less (short term) and more than one year (long term).

CAPITAL ASSETS

DEFINITION OF A CAPITAL ASSET

1 LEARNING OBJECTIVE
Distinguish capital assets from ordinary assets.

Investments comprise the most typical category of capital assets and include corporate stocks and bonds, mutual funds, partnership interests, government securities, and vacant land. These assets can be held by any type of taxpayer—individuals, partnerships, limited liability companies, and corporations, whether closely held or publicly held. In addition, individuals own certain capital assets that are part of their daily life, such as residences, automobiles, furniture, and artwork. The classification of these *personal-use* assets as capital assets is relevant only when their disposition produces a recognized gain. Losses from the disposition of personal-use assets are not recognized for tax purposes, as explained in the preceding chapter.

Capital assets are not directly defined in the Code. Instead, § 1221 defines what is *not* a capital asset. A capital asset is property held by the taxpayer that is *not* any of the following:

- Inventory or property held primarily for sale to customers in the ordinary course of a business. The Supreme Court, in *Malat v. Riddell*,[1] defined *primarily* as meaning *of first importance* or *principally*.
- Accounts and notes receivable acquired from the sale of inventory or acquired for services rendered in the ordinary course of business.
- Depreciable property or real estate used in a business.
- Certain copyrights; literary, musical, or artistic compositions; or letters, memoranda, or similar property held by (1) a taxpayer whose efforts created the property; (2) in the case of a letter, memorandum, or similar property, a taxpayer for whom it was produced; or (3) a taxpayer who received the property as a lifetime gift from someone described in (1) or (2).
- U.S. government publications that are (1) received by a taxpayer from the U.S. government other than by purchase at the price at which they are offered for sale to the public or (2) held by a taxpayer who received the publication as a lifetime gift from someone described in (1).

Inventory. What constitutes inventory is determined by reference to the taxpayer's business.

EXAMPLE 1 Green Company buys and sells used cars. Its cars are inventory. Its gains from the sale of the cars are ordinary income. ▼

EXAMPLE 2 Soong sells her personal-use automobile at a $500 gain. The automobile is a personal-use asset and, therefore, a capital asset. The gain is a capital gain. ▼

Notice that no asset is inherently capital or ordinary. When Soong in Example 2 sells her capital asset automobile to Green Company in Example 1, that very same automobile loses its capital asset status, because it is inventory to Green Company. Similar transformations can occur if, for example, an art dealer sells a painting (inventory; *not* a capital asset) to a private collector (now a capital asset). Whether an asset is capital or ordinary, therefore, depends entirely on the relationship of *that asset* to the taxpayer who sold it. This classification dilemma is but one feature of capital asset treatment that makes this area so confused and perennially complicated.

Accounts and Notes Receivable. Collection of an accrual basis account receivable usually does not result in a gain or loss because the amount collected equals the receivable's basis. The *sale* of an account or note receivable may generate a gain or loss, however, because it will probably be sold for more or less than its basis. That gain or loss will be ordinary because the receivable is not a capital asset. A cash basis account receivable has no basis, so sale of such a receivable generates a gain, and that gain is ordinary income. Collection of a cash basis receivable also generates ordinary income.

---

[1] 66–1 USTC ¶9317, 17 AFTR2d 604, 86 S.Ct. 1030 (USSC, 1966).

CHAPTER 8 Property Transactions: Capital Gains and Losses, Section 1231, and Recapture Provisions

---

TAX IN THE NEWS

AN ARTIST'S DILEMMA

Artist Peter Max was the creator of valuable paintings that had no tax basis. If he sold the paintings, the entire proceeds from the sale would be ordinary income. Instead, Max *exchanged* the paintings for valuable real estate in the United States and in several other countries. The IRS contended that the exchange of the paintings was taxable and charged Max with failing to report more than $1 million of ordinary income.

EXAMPLE 3 Oriole Company, an accrual basis taxpayer, has accounts receivable of $100,000. Revenue of $100,000 was recorded and a $100,000 basis was established when the receivable was created. Because Oriole needs working capital, it sells the receivables for $83,000 to a financial institution. Accordingly, it has a $17,000 ordinary loss. If Oriole is a cash basis taxpayer, it has $83,000 of ordinary income because it would not have recorded any revenue earlier and the receivable would have no tax basis. ▼

Business Fixed Assets. Depreciable personal property and real estate (both depreciable and nondepreciable) used by a business are not capital assets. Thus, *business fixed assets* are not capital assets. Business fixed assets can sometimes be treated as capital assets pursuant to § 1231, however, as discussed later in this chapter.

Copyrights and Creative Works. Generally, the person whose efforts led to the copyright or creative work has an ordinary asset, not a capital asset. This rule makes the creator comparable to a taxpayer whose customary activity (salary, business profits) is taxed as ordinary income. *Creative works* include the works of authors, composers, and artists. Also, the person for whom a letter, memorandum, or other similar property was created has an ordinary asset. Finally, a person receiving a copyright, creative work, letter, memorandum, or similar property by lifetime gift from the creator or the person for whom the work was created also has an ordinary asset.

EXAMPLE 4 Wanda is a part-time music composer. A music publisher purchases one of her songs for $5,000. Wanda has a $5,000 ordinary gain from the sale of an ordinary asset. ▼

EXAMPLE 5 Ed received a letter from the President of the United States in 1962. In the current year, Ed sells the letter to a collector for $300. Ed has a $300 ordinary gain from the sale of an ordinary asset (because the letter was created for Ed). ▼

EXAMPLE 6 Isabella gives a song she composed to her son. Her son sells the song to a music publisher for $5,000. He has a $5,000 ordinary gain from the sale of an ordinary asset. If he inherits the song from Isabella, his basis for the song is its fair market value at Isabella's death. The song is a capital asset because the son's basis is not related to Isabella's basis for the song (i.e., the song was not a *lifetime* gift). ▼

U.S. Government Publications. U.S. government publications received from the U.S. government (or its agencies) for a reduced price are not capital assets. This prevents a taxpayer from later donating the publications to charity and claiming a charitable contribution equal to the fair market value of the publications. A charitable contribution of a capital asset generally yields a deduction equal to the asset's fair market value. Also, if such property is received by gift from the original purchaser, the property is not a capital asset to the donee. (For a more comprehensive explanation of charitable contributions of property, refer to Chapter 4.)

STATUTORY EXPANSIONS

Because of the uncertainty often associated with capital asset status, Congress has occasionally enacted Code Sections to clarify the definition in particular circumstances. These statutory expansions of the capital asset definition are discussed in this section.

Dealers in Securities. As a general rule, securities (stocks, bonds, and other financial instruments) held by a dealer are considered to be inventory and are not, therefore, subject to capital gain or loss treatment. A *dealer in securities* is a merchant (e.g., a brokerage firm) that regularly engages in the purchase and resale of securities to customers. The dealer must identify any securities being held for its own investment. Generally, if a dealer clearly identifies certain securities as held for investment purposes by the close of business on the acquisition date, gain from the securities' sale will be capital gain. However, the gain will be ordinary if the dealer ceases to hold the securities for investment prior to the sale. Losses are capital losses if at any time the securities have been clearly identified by the dealer as held for investment.[2]

Real Property Subdivided for Sale. Substantial real property development activities may result in the owner being considered a dealer for tax purposes. If so, income from the sale of real estate property lots will be treated as the sale of inventory and therefore will be taxed as ordinary income. However, § 1237 allows real estate investors to claim capital gain treatment if they engage *only* in *limited* development activities. To be eligible for § 1237 treatment, the following requirements must be met:

- The taxpayer is not a corporation.
- The taxpayer is not a real estate dealer.
- No substantial improvements have been made to the lots sold. *Substantial* generally means more than a 10 percent increase in the value of a lot. Shopping centers and other commercial or residential buildings are considered substantial, while filling, draining, leveling, and clearing operations are not.
- The taxpayer has held the lots sold for at least 5 years, except for inherited property. The substantial improvements test is less stringent if the property is held at least 10 years.

If the preceding requirements are met, all gain is capital gain until the taxable year in which the *sixth* lot is sold. Sales of contiguous lots to a single buyer in the same transaction count as the sale of one lot. Beginning with the taxable year in which the *sixth* lot is sold, five percent of the revenue from lot sales is potential ordinary income. That potential ordinary income is offset by any selling expenses from the lot sales. Practically, sales commissions often are at least 5 percent of the sales price, so usually none of the gain is treated as ordinary income.

---
[2] §§ 1236(a) and (b) and Reg. § 1.1236–1(a).

CHAPTER 8 Property Transactions: Capital Gains and Losses, Section 1231, and Recapture Provisions

Section 1237 does not apply to losses. A loss from the sale of subdivided real property is ordinary loss unless the property qualifies as a capital asset under § 1221. The following example illustrates the application of § 1237.

EXAMPLE 7

Ahmed owns a large tract of land and subdivides it for sale. Assume Ahmed meets all the requirements of § 1237 and during the tax year sells the first 10 lots to 10 different buyers for $10,000 each. Ahmed's basis in each lot sold is $3,000, and he incurs total selling expenses of $4,000 on the sales. Ahmed's gain is computed as follows:

Selling price (10 × $10,000)		$100,000
Basis (10 × $3,000)		(30,000)
Excess over basis		$ 70,000
Five percent of selling price	$ 5,000	
Selling expenses	(4,000)	
Amount of ordinary income		$ 1,000
Five percent of selling price	$ 5,000	
Excess of expenses over 5% of selling price	–0–	(5,000)
Capital gain		65,000
Total gain ($70,000 – $4,000 selling expenses)		$66,000

SALE OR EXCHANGE

LEARNING OBJECTIVE 2
Understand the relevance of a sale or exchange to classification as a capital gain or loss.

Recognition of capital gain or loss usually requires a **sale or exchange** of a capital asset. The Code uses the term *sale or exchange,* but does not define it. Generally, a property sale involves the receipt of money by the seller and/or the assumption by the purchaser of the seller's liabilities. An exchange involves the transfer of property for other property. Thus, an involuntary conversion (casualty, theft, or condemnation) is not a sale or exchange. In several situations, the determination of whether or when a sale or exchange has taken place has been clarified by the enactment of Code Sections that specifically provide for sale or exchange treatment. These situations are discussed below.

Recognized gains or losses from the cancellation, lapse, expiration, or any other termination of a right or obligation with respect to personal property (other than stock) that is or would be a capital asset in the hands of the taxpayer are capital gains or losses.[3] See the discussion under Options later in the chapter for more details.

WORTHLESS SECURITIES AND § 1244 STOCK

Occasionally, securities such as stock and bonds may become worthless due to the insolvency of their issuer. If the security is a capital asset, the loss is deemed to have occurred as the result of a sale or exchange on the *last day* of the tax year.[4] This last-day rule may have the effect of converting a short-term capital loss into a long-term capital loss. See Treatment of Capital Losses later in this chapter.

Section 1244 allows an *ordinary* deduction on disposition of stock at a loss. The stock must be that of a small business company, and the ordinary deduction is limited to $50,000 ($100,000 for married individuals filing jointly) per year.

---

[3] § 1234A. [4] § 165(g)(1).

RETIREMENT OF CORPORATE OBLIGATIONS

A debt obligation (e.g., a bond or note payable) may have a tax basis different from its redemption value because it may have been acquired at a premium or discount. Consequently, the collection of the redemption value may result in a loss or a gain. Generally, the collection of a debt obligation is *treated* as a sale or exchange.[5] Therefore, any loss or gain can be capital loss or gain because a sale or exchange has taken place. However, if the debt obligation was issued by an individual before June 9, 1997, or was purchased by the taxpayer before June 9, 1997, the collection of the debt obligation is not treated as a sale or exchange.

EXAMPLE 8

Osprey Co., Inc., purchases $1,000 of General Motors Corporation bonds for $980 in the open market. If the bonds are held to maturity, the $20 difference between Osprey's collection of the $1,000 redemption value and its cost of $980 is treated as capital gain. But if the obligation had been issued to Osprey by an individual before June 9, 1997, the $20 gain would be ordinary income because collection of the debt would not be a sale or exchange. ▼

OPTIONS

Frequently, a potential buyer of property wants to defer a final purchase decision, but wants to control the sale and/or the sale price in the meantime. **Options** are used to achieve such control. The potential purchaser (grantee) pays the property owner (grantor) for an option on the property. The grantee then becomes the option holder. An option usually sets the price at which a grantee can buy the property and expires after a specified period of time.

Sale of an Option. In addition to exercising an option or letting it expire, a grantee can often arrange for its sale or exchange. Such a sale or exchange generally results in capital gain or loss if the option property is (or would be) a capital asset to the grantee.[6]

EXAMPLE 9

Robin & Associates wants to buy some vacant land for investment purposes, but cannot afford the full purchase price. Instead, the firm convinces the landowner (grantor) to sell it the right to purchase the land for $100,000 anytime in the next two years. Robin & Associates (grantee) pays $3,000 for this option to buy the land. The option is a capital asset to Robin because if the firm actually purchased the land (the option property), the land would be a capital asset. Three months after purchasing the option, Robin sells it for $7,000. The firm has a $4,000 ($7,000 − $3,000) capital gain on this sale. ▼

Failure to Exercise Options. If an option holder (grantee) fails to exercise the option, the lapse of the option is considered a sale or exchange on the option expiration date. Thus, the resulting loss is a capital loss if the property subject to the option is (or would be) a capital asset in the hands of the grantee.

The grantor of an option on *stocks, securities, commodities, or commodity futures* receives short-term capital gain treatment upon the expiration of the option.[7] For example, an individual investor who owns stock (a capital asset) may sell a call option, entitling the buyer of the option to acquire the stock at a specified price higher than the stock's value at the date the option is granted. The writer of the call (the grantor) receives a premium for writing the option. If the price of the stock does not increase during the option period, the option will expire unexercised.

---

[5] § 1271.
[6] § 1234(a) and Reg. § 1.1234–1(a)(1).
[7] § 1234(b)(1).

Concept Summary 8–1

Options

	Effect on	
Event	**Grantor**	**Grantee**
Option is granted.	Receives value and has a contract obligation (a liability).	Pays value and has a contract right (an asset).
Option expires.	Has a short-term capital gain if the option property is stocks, securities, commodities, or commodity futures. Otherwise, gain is ordinary income.	Has a loss (capital loss if option property would have been a capital asset for the grantee). Otherwise, loss is ordinary.
Option is exercised.	Amount received for option increases proceeds from sale of the option property.	Amount paid for option becomes part of the basis of the option property purchased.
Option is sold or exchanged by grantee.	Result depends upon whether option later expires or is exercised (see above).	Could have gain or loss (capital gain or loss if option property would have been a capital asset for the grantee).

Upon the expiration of the option, the grantor must recognize a short-term capital gain equal to the premium received. These provisions do not apply to options held for sale to customers (the inventory of a securities dealer).

Options on property *other than* stocks, securities, commodities, or commodity futures result in ordinary income to the grantor when the option expires. For instance, the landowner in the preceding example would have ordinary income of $3,000 if Robin (the grantee) had allowed the option to expire.

Exercise of Options by Grantee. If an option is exercised, the amount paid for the option is added to the optioned property's selling price. This increases the gain (or reduces the loss) to the grantor resulting from the sale of the property. The grantor's gain or loss is capital or ordinary depending on the tax status of the property. The grantee adds the cost of the option to the basis of the property purchased.

EXAMPLE 10

Several years ago, Indigo, Inc., purchased 100 shares of Eagle Company stock for $5,000. On April 1 of this year, Indigo writes a call option on the stock, giving the grantee the right to buy the stock for $6,000 during the following six-month period. Indigo (the grantor) receives a call premium of $500 for writing the call.

- If the call is exercised by the grantee on August 1, Indigo has $1,500 ($6,000 + $500 − $5,000) of long-term capital gain from the sale of the stock. The grantee has a $6,500 ($500 option premium + $6,000 purchase price) basis for the stock.
- Assume that the option expired unexercised. Indigo has a $500 short-term capital gain equal to the call premium received for writing the option. This gain is not recognized until the option expires. The grantee has a loss from expiration of the option. The nature of that loss will depend upon whether the option was a capital asset or an ordinary asset in the hands of the grantee. ▼

Concept Summary 8–1 summarizes the rules for options.

PATENTS

Transfer of a **patent** is treated as the sale or exchange of a long-term capital asset when *all substantial rights* to the patent (or an undivided interest that includes all such rights) are transferred by a *holder*.[8] The transferor/holder may receive payment in virtually any form. Lump-sum or periodic payments are most common. The amount of the payments may also be contingent on the transferee/purchaser's productivity, use, or disposition of the patent. If the transfer meets these requirements, any gain or loss is *automatically a long-term* capital gain or loss. Whether the asset was a capital asset for the transferor, whether a sale or exchange occurred, and how long the transferor held the patent are all irrelevant.

EXAMPLE 11

Mei-Yen, a druggist, invents a pill-counting machine, which she patents. In consideration of a lump-sum payment of $200,000 plus $10 per machine sold, Mei-Yen assigns the patent to Drug Products, Inc. Assuming Mei-Yen has transferred all substantial rights, she automatically has a long-term capital gain from both the lump-sum payment and the $10 per machine royalty to the extent these proceeds exceed her basis for the patent. ▼

This special long-term capital gain or loss treatment for patents is intended to encourage technological development and scientific progress. In contrast, books, songs, and artists' works may be copyrighted, but copyrights and the assets they represent are not capital assets. Thus, the disposition of these assets by their creators usually results in ordinary gain or loss.

Substantial Rights. To receive favorable capital gain treatment, all *substantial rights* to the patent (or an undivided interest in it) must be transferred. All substantial rights to a patent means all rights (whether or not then held by the grantor) that are valuable at the time the patent rights (or an undivided interest in the patent) are transferred. All substantial rights have not been transferred when the transfer is limited geographically within the issuing country or when the transfer is for a period less than the remaining legal life of the patent. The circumstances of the entire transaction, rather than merely the language used in the transfer instrument, are to be considered in deciding whether all substantial rights have been transferred.[9]

EXAMPLE 12

Assume Mei-Yen, the druggist in the preceding example, only licensed Drug Products, Inc., to manufacture and sell the invention in Michigan. She retained the right to license the machine elsewhere in the United States. Mei-Yen has retained a substantial right and is not eligible for automatic long-term capital gain treatment. ▼

Holder Defined. The *holder* of a patent must be an *individual* and is usually the invention's creator. A holder may also be an individual who purchases the patent rights from the creator before the patented invention has been reduced to practice. However, the creator's employer and certain parties related to the creator do not qualify as holders. Thus, in the common situation where an employer has all rights to an employee's inventions, the employer is not eligible for long-term capital gain treatment. More than likely, the employer will have an ordinary asset because the patent was developed as part of its business.

---

[8] § 1235. [9] Reg. § 1.1235–2(b)(1).

FRANCHISES, TRADEMARKS, AND TRADE NAMES

A mode of operation, a widely recognized brand name (trade name), and a widely known business symbol (trademark) are all valuable assets. These assets may be licensed (commonly known as *franchising*) by their owner for use by other businesses. Many fast-food restaurants (such as McDonald's and Taco Bell) are franchises. The franchisee usually pays the owner (franchisor) an initial fee plus a contingent fee. The contingent fee is often based upon the franchisee's sales volume.

For Federal income tax purposes, a **franchise** is an agreement that gives the franchisee the right to distribute, sell, or provide goods, services, or facilities within a specified area.[10] A franchise transfer includes the grant of a franchise, a transfer by one franchisee to another person, or the renewal of a franchise.

Section 1253 provides that a transfer of a franchise, trademark, or trade name is *not* a sale or exchange of a capital asset when the transferor retains any significant power, right, or continuing interest in the property transferred.

Significant Power, Right, or Continuing Interest.

Significant powers, rights, or continuing interests include control over assignment, quality of products and services, sale or advertising of other products or services, and the right to require that substantially all supplies and equipment be purchased from the transferor. Also included are the right to terminate the franchise at will and the right to substantial contingent payments. Most modern franchising operations involve some or all of these powers, rights, or continuing interests.

In the unusual case where no significant power, right, or continuing interest is retained by the transferor, a sale or exchange may occur, and capital gain or loss treatment may be available. For capital gain or loss treatment to be available, the asset transferred must still qualify as a capital asset.

EXAMPLE 13

Orange, Inc., a franchisee, sells the franchise to a third party. Payments to Orange are not contingent, and all significant powers, rights, and continuing interests are transferred. The gain (payments − adjusted basis) on the sale is a capital gain to Orange. ▼

Noncontingent Payments.

When the transferor retains a significant power, right, or continuing interest, the transferee's noncontingent payments to the transferor are ordinary income to the transferor. The franchisee capitalizes the payments and amortizes them over 15 years. The amortization is subject to recapture under § 1245, discussed later in this chapter.

EXAMPLE 14

Grey Company signs a 10-year franchise agreement with DOH Donuts. Grey (the franchisee) makes payments of $3,000 per year for the first 8 years of the franchise agreement—a total of $24,000. Grey cannot deduct $3,000 per year as the payments are made. Instead, Grey must amortize the $24,000 total over 15 years. Thus, Grey may deduct $1,600 per year for each of the 15 years of the amortization period. The same result would occur if Grey had made a $24,000 lump-sum payment at the beginning of the franchise period. Assuming DOH Donuts (the franchisor) retains significant powers, rights, or a continuing interest, it will have ordinary income when it receives the payments from Grey. ▼

Contingent Payments.

Whether or not the transferor retains a significant power, right, or continuing interest, contingent franchise payments are ordinary income for the franchisor and an ordinary deduction for the franchisee. For this purpose, a payment qualifies as a contingent payment only if the following requirements are met:

---

[10] § 1253(b)(1).

Concept Summary 8–2

Franchises

	Effect on	
Event	Franchisor	Franchisee
Franchisor Retains Significant Powers and Rights		
Noncontingent payment	Ordinary income.	Capitalized and amortized over 15 years as an ordinary deduction; if franchise is sold, amortization is subject to recapture under § 1245.
Contingent payment	Ordinary income.	Ordinary deduction.
Franchisor Does *Not* Retain Significant Powers and Rights		
Noncontingent payment	Ordinary income if franchise rights are an ordinary asset; capital gain if franchise rights are a capital asset (unlikely).	Capitalized and amortized over 15 years as an ordinary deduction; if the franchise is sold, amortization is subject to recapture under § 1245.
Contingent payment	Ordinary income.	Ordinary deduction.

- The contingent amounts are part of a series of payments that are paid at least annually throughout the term of the transfer agreement.
- The payments are substantially equal in amount or are payable under a fixed formula.

EXAMPLE 15 TAK, a spicy chicken franchisor, transfers an eight-year franchise to Egret Corporation. TAK retains a significant power, right, or continuing interest. Egret, the franchisee, agrees to pay TAK 15% of sales. This contingent payment is ordinary income to TAK and a business deduction for Egret as the payments are made. ▼

Sports Franchises. Professional sports franchises (e.g., the Chicago Cubs) are not covered by § 1253.[11] However, § 1056 restricts the allocation of sports franchise acquisition costs to player contracts. Player contracts are usually one of the major assets acquired with a sports franchise. These contracts last only for the time stated in the contract. Therefore, owners of sports franchises would like to allocate franchise acquisition costs disproportionately to the contracts so that the acquisition costs will be amortizable more quickly, over the contracts' lives. Section 1056 prevents this by limiting the amount that can be allocated to player contracts to no more than 50 percent of the franchise acquisition cost. In addition, the seller of the sports franchise has ordinary income under § 1245 for the portion of the gain allocable to the disposition of player contracts.[12]

Concept Summary 8–2 summarizes the rules for franchises.

LEASE CANCELLATION PAYMENTS

The tax treatment of payments received for canceling a lease depends on whether the recipient of the payments is the **lessor** or the **lessee** and whether the lease is a capital asset or not.

---

[11] § 1253(e).

[12] See the discussion of § 1245 later in this chapter.

Lessee Treatment.
Lease cancellation payments received by a lessee (the tenant) are treated as an exchange.[13] Thus, these payments are capital gains if the lease is a capital asset. Generally, a lessee's lease is a capital asset if the property (either personalty or realty) is used for the lessee's personal use (e.g., his or her residence). A lessee's lease is an ordinary asset if the property is used in the lessee's trade or business.[14]

EXAMPLE 16

Merganser, Inc., owns an apartment building that it is going to convert into an office building. Vicki is one of the apartment tenants and receives $1,000 from Merganser to cancel the lease. Vicki has a capital gain of $1,000 (which is long term or short term depending upon how long she has held the lease). Merganser has an ordinary deduction of $1,000. ▼

Lessor Treatment.
Payments received by a lessor (the landlord) for a lease cancellation are always ordinary income because they are considered to be in lieu of rental payments.[15]

EXAMPLE 17

Finch & Company owns an apartment building near a university campus. Hui-Fen is one of the tenants. Hui-Fen is graduating early and offers Finch $800 to cancel the apartment lease. Finch accepts the offer. Finch has ordinary income of $800. Hui-Fen has a nondeductible payment since the apartment was personal-use property. ▼

HOLDING PERIOD

3 LEARNING OBJECTIVE
Determine the applicable holding period for a capital asset.

Property must be held more than one year to qualify for long-term capital gain or loss treatment.[16] Property not held for the required long-term period results in short-term capital gain or loss. To compute the **holding period,** start counting on the day after the property was acquired and include the day of disposition.

EXAMPLE 18

Mallard & Co. purchases a capital asset on January 15, 1997, and sells it on January 16, 1998. Mallard's holding period is more than one year. If Mallard had sold the asset on January 15, 1998, the holding period would have been exactly one year, and the gain or loss would have been short term. ▼

To be held for more than one year, a capital asset acquired on the last day of any month must not be disposed of until on or after the first day of the thirteenth succeeding month.[17]

EXAMPLE 19

Purple, Inc., purchases a capital asset on March 31, 1997. If Purple sells the asset on March 31, 1998, the holding period is one year, and Purple will have a short-term capital gain or loss. If Purple sells the asset on April 1, 1998, the holding period is more than one year, and it will have a long-term capital gain or loss. ▼

SPECIAL HOLDING PERIOD RULES

There are several special holding period rules.[18] The application of these rules depends on the type of asset and how it was acquired.

---

[13] § 1241 and Reg. § 1.1241–1(a).
[14] Reg. § 1.1221–1(b).
[15] *Hort v. Comm.*, 41–1 USTC ¶9354, 25 AFTR 1207, 61 S.Ct. 757 (USSC, 1941).
[16] § 1222.
[17] Rev.Rul. 66–7, 1966–1 C.B. 188.
[18] § 1223.

Nontaxable Exchanges. The holding period of property received in a like-kind exchange (and certain other qualified nontaxable exchanges) includes the holding period of the former asset if the property that was exchanged was either a capital asset or a § 1231 asset.

EXAMPLE 20 Red Manufacturing Corporation exchanges some vacant real estate it owns (a capital asset) for land closer to its factory. The transaction is a like-kind exchange, so the holding period of the new land includes the holding period of the old land. ▼

EXAMPLE 21 A lightning strike destroyed Vireo Company's generator (a § 1231 asset) in March. Vireo uses the entire insurance proceeds it received to acquire a comparable generator. The holding period of the new generator includes the holding period of the old generator. ▼

Nontaxable Transactions Involving Carryover of Another Taxpayer's Basis. If a transaction is nontaxable and the former owner's basis carries over to the present owner, the former owner's holding period is included in (tacked on to) the present owner's holding period.

EXAMPLE 22 Kareem acquired 100 shares of Robin Corporation stock for $1,000 on December 31, 1989. He transferred the shares by gift to Megan on December 31, 1997, when the stock was worth $2,000. Kareem's basis of $1,000 becomes the basis for determining gain or loss on a subsequent sale by Megan. Megan's holding period begins with the date the stock was acquired by Kareem. ▼

EXAMPLE 23 Assume the same facts as in the preceding example, except that the fair market value of the shares was only $800 on the date of the gift. If Megan sells the stock for a loss, its value at the date of the gift is her basis. Accordingly, the tacked-on holding period rule does not apply, and Megan's holding period begins with the date of the gift. So, if she sells the shares for $500 on April 1, 1998, Megan has a $300 recognized capital loss, and the holding period is from December 31, 1997, to April 1, 1998 (thus, the loss is short term). ▼

Disallowed Loss Transactions. Under several Code provisions, realized losses are disallowed. When a loss is disallowed, there is no carryover of holding period. Losses can be disallowed under § 267 (sale or exchange between related taxpayers) and § 262 (sale or exchange of personal-use assets) as well as other Code Sections. Taxpayers who acquire property in a disallowed loss transaction will begin a new holding period and will have a basis equal to the purchase price.

EXAMPLE 24 Janet sells her personal automobile at a loss. She may not deduct the loss because it arises from the sale of personal-use property. Janet purchases a replacement automobile for more than the selling price of her former automobile. Janet has a basis equal to the cost of the replacement automobile, and her holding period begins when she acquires the replacement automobile. ▼

Inherited Property. The holding period for inherited property is treated as long term no matter how long the property is actually held by the heir. The holding period of the decedent or the decedent's estate is not relevant to the heir's holding period.

EXAMPLE 25 Shonda inherits Blue Company stock from her father. She receives the stock on April 1, 1998, and sells it on November 1, 1998. Even though Shonda did not hold the stock more than one year, she receives long-term capital gain or loss treatment on the sale. ▼

SHORT SALES

A **short sale** occurs when a taxpayer sells borrowed property and repays the lender with substantially identical property either held on the date of the sale or purchased after the sale. Short sales typically involve corporate stock. The seller's objective is to make a profit in anticipation of a decline in the stock's price. If the price declines, the seller in a short sale recognizes a profit equal to the difference between the sales price of the borrowed stock and the price paid for its replacement.

Section 1233 provides that a short sale gain or loss is a capital gain or loss to the extent that the short sale property constitutes a capital asset of the taxpayer. This gain or loss is not recognized until the short sale is closed. Generally, the holding period of the short sale property is determined by how long the property used to close the short sale was held.

EXAMPLE 26
On January 4, Green & Associates sold short 100 shares of Osprey Corporation for $1,500. Green closed the transaction on July 28 of the same year by purchasing 100 shares of Osprey for $1,000. Because this stock was held less than one year (actually less than a day), Green's gain ($1,500 sale price − $1,000 cost) is short term.

EXAMPLE 27
Assume the same facts as in the preceding example, except that the January 4 short sale was not closed until July 28 of the *following* year. The result is the same, because the stock was acquired and used to close the transaction on the same day; that is, it was held less than a year.

If a taxpayer owns securities that are "substantially identical" to those sold short, § 1259 treats the short sale as a *constructive sale*, and the taxpayer recognizes gain (but not loss) as of that date. The holding period in such circumstances is determined by how long the securities in question were held.

EXAMPLE 28
Assume the same facts as in Example 26, except that Green & Associates owned 100 shares of Osprey Corporation when it sold short 100 shares on January 4. Green must recognize any gain on its 100 shares of Osprey as of January 4. If Green owned those shares more than one year as of that date, the gain is long term.

TAX TREATMENT OF CAPITAL GAINS AND LOSSES OF NONCORPORATE TAXPAYERS

LEARNING OBJECTIVE 4
Describe the tax treatment of capital gains and losses for noncorporate taxpayers.

This section discusses how capital gains and losses are taxed to noncorporate taxpayers, that is, individuals, noncorporate partners, trusts, and estates. The rules applicable to corporations are considered in the following section of this chapter.

CAPITAL GAINS

Gains from the sale or exchange of capital assets are taxed at various rates, depending upon the holding period (determined according to the rules explained in the preceding section), the taxpayer's general tax rate, and the type of asset involved.

Short-Term Gains. Gains on capital assets held one year or less are taxed as *ordinary income*. Accordingly, the applicable tax rates vary from 15 percent to 39.6 percent. Although short-term capital gains receive no preferential tax treatment compared to ordinary income, they do have one advantage: they can absorb capital losses without limit. As will be discussed later in this section, *capital losses* are deducted first against capital gains (without limits) and then against ordinary income, but only up to $3,000 per year.[19] Thus, someone with a large capital loss will find short-term capital gains attractive, even though such gains do not qualify for lower tax rates.

Planning Considerations

Timing Capital Gains

Taxpayers have considerable control over the timing of their capital gains through the mechanism of realization. Accordingly, a taxpayer might want to defer recognizing a large capital gain in a year with *substantial itemized deductions*, such as large personal casualty losses or the purchase of a new residence with large up-front interest expenses. In so doing, the taxpayer minimizes the loss of such deductions due to AGI limitations and deduction phase-outs applicable to some high-income individuals.

Nontax considerations, of course, often dictate when assets are sold. If a particular stock is peaking in popularity, selling it might be wise investment strategy, even if the taxpayer's current tax situation is not optimal. Similarly, if a taxpayer needs cash to start a business, purchase a home, or pay for a child's education or medical costs, the capital asset might need to be sold at a time when investment *and* tax considerations counsel otherwise. In these circumstances, however, a taxpayer might choose to *borrow* the money required and use the capital asset as collateral for the loan, rather than sell the asset. A loan does not trigger tax consequences, and the taxpayer can continue to hold the asset until a more opportune time—albeit at the cost of paying interest, which may be nondeductible.

Long-Term Gains. Gains on capital assets held more than one year are classified as *long-term* gains and are eligible for a special 20 percent tax rate, or 10 percent for taxpayers in the 15 percent tax bracket.[20] Long-term capital gain tax rates, therefore, are as follows:

Ordinary Income	Capital Gain	Differential
15%	10%	5
28	20	8
31	20	11
36	20	16
39.6	20	19.6

For persons in the 15 percent tax bracket, only the amount of the gain that would fall within that bracket is eligible for the 10 percent rate. Any remaining gain is taxed at 20 percent.

---

[19] § 1211(b).

[20] Starting in 2001, taxpayers in the 15% bracket will be eligible for an 8% tax rate on capital assets held more than *five years*. Taxpayers in the 28% and higher brackets will be eligible for an 18% tax rate on capital assets held more than five years if those assets were acquired *after* 2000 [§ 1(h)(2)]. Thus, this 18% rate will not apply until 2006—assuming that the law is not changed before then!

CHAPTER 8 Property Transactions: Capital Gains and Losses, Section 1231, and Recapture Provisions

EXAMPLE 29

Gene is an accounting student with taxable income from summer earnings and part-time work of $10,000 after applicable personal deductions. Gene sells stock that he purchased three years ago and realizes a capital gain of $18,000. His tax is determined as follows:

(a)	Regular tax (15%) on his earned income of $10,000	$1,500
(b)	10% on the portion of his capital gain that is within the 15% tax bracket ($25,350 in 1998 − $10,000 earnings taxed in [a] above = $15,350)	1,535
(c)	20% on the rest of his capital gain ($18,000 gain − $15,350 taxed in [b] above = $2,650)	530
	Tax due	$3,565

The tax on Gene's $18,000 capital gain is $2,065 ($1,535 + $530), an effective rate of 11.5%. ▼

In point of fact, relatively few capital gains are realized by persons in the 15 percent tax bracket. Thus, the tax rate that generally applies to long-term capital gains is 20 percent.

There are two major exceptions, however, to this general treatment. The first exception is so-called *28% property*, which consists of the following items:

- Assets held more than one year but not more than 18 months (*mid-term gain*) [§ 1(h)(8)(A)].
- **Collectibles** (works of art, rugs, antiques, gems, coins, stamps, and alcoholic beverages) held more than one year.
- The taxable half of the gain on sales of *qualified small business stock* (see the end of this section).

These assets are labeled *28% property*, because the gains that they produce are taxed at 28 percent rather than 20 percent. But this 28 percent rate is a *maximum* rate, so a taxpayer in the 15 percent bracket would pay only 15 percent. As a result, the applicable tax rates for gains on 28% property are as follows:

Ordinary Income	Applicable Rate	Differential
15%	15%	None
28	28	None
31	28	3
36	28	8
39.6	28	11.6

In other words, these gains receive preferential tax treatment only when realized by taxpayers in the top three tax brackets.

PLANNING CONSIDERATIONS

Gifts of Appreciated Securities

Persons with appreciated securities that have been held over one year may reduce the tax due on their sale by giving the securities to someone (often a child) who is in the *lowest tax bracket*. The donor's holding period carries over, along with his or her basis, and the donee's lower tax rate applies when the securities are sold. As a result, the gain is taxed at 15 percent or 10 percent, if the stock has been held more than 18 months, rather than 28 percent or 20 percent, respectively. The donee should be over age

> ### TAX IN THE NEWS
>
> #### SHOULD YOU INVEST IN STOCKS OR STOCK FUNDS?
>
> If you invest directly in stock, *you* decide how long the stock is held. But if you invest in a mutual fund, the fund manager makes that decision. On average, these managers hold their stocks just over 13 months. That satisfies the 12-month holding period but not the 18-month holding period. Moreover, 29 percent of capital gains distributed by diversified stock funds in 1996 were short-term gains.
>
> Ross Levin, a financial planner in Minneapolis, does not believe the mutual funds will change their investment strategies. He reckons that the 1997 tax changes "won't make a big difference in the way funds are managed. Mutual fund managers will still focus on getting the highest total return. Taxes are a secondary consideration."
>
> SOURCE: Adapted from Jonathan Clements, "Stock or Stock Funds? The Tax-Cut Plan Could Tip the Balance for Some Investors," *Wall Street Journal*, August 5, 1997, p. C1.

13 by year-end, however, or a *kiddie tax* will nullify most of the tax advantage being sought. The kiddie tax will subject the gain to the parent's tax rate. See Chapter 15.

Such gifts usually bear no gift tax due to the annual $10,000 exclusion. But the money received after payment of the tax belongs to the donee. It is not available to the donor, nor may it be used to pay a parent's essential support obligations. Moreover, these funds may affect a child's eligibility for need-based financial aid when applying to college.

The second major exception involves depreciable real estate that has been held more than 18 months. Some—but not all—of the gain attributable to depreciation deductions on apartments, office buildings, shopping centers, and warehouses is taxable at 25 percent rather than 20 percent. The amount that is taxed in this manner depends upon how much depreciation is "recaptured" as ordinary income under § 1250, as explained later in this chapter. Accordingly, these gains are called *unrecaptured § 1250 gain* [§ 1(h)(6)]. In any case, the 25 percent rate is a *maximum* rate, so the applicable tax rates for these gains from sale of depreciable real estate are as follows:

Ordinary Income	Applicable Rate	Differential
15%	15%	None
28	25	3
31	25	6
36	25	11
39.6	25	14.6

The capital gain tax rates for noncorporate taxpayers are summarized in Concept Summary 8–3.

CAPITAL LOSSES

As explained above, capital gains can be classified into four general categories:

- Short term—taxed as ordinary income.
- 28% property—taxed at 15 percent or 28 percent.

Concept Summary 8–3

Capital Gains of Noncorporate Taxpayers

Type of Asset	Applicable Rate
Held not more than one year.	15%–39.6%, same as ordinary income.
Held more than one year but not more than 18 months.	15% for lowest bracket taxpayers, 28% for all others.
Collectibles held more than one year.	15% for lowest bracket taxpayers, 28% for all others.
Taxable portion (50%) of gain on qualified small business stock held more than five years.	15% for lowest bracket taxpayers, 28% for all others.
Unrecaptured § 1250 gain on depreciable real estate held more than 18 months.	15% for lowest bracket taxpayers, 25% for all others.
Other assets held more than 18 months.	10% for lowest bracket taxpayers, 20% for all others.

- Unrecaptured § 1250 gain—taxed at 15 percent or 25 percent.
- Long term—taxed at 10 percent or 20 percent.

A taxpayer can also have losses from capital assets in *three* of these four categories. The *unrecaptured § 1250 gain* category contains only gain. When both gains and losses occur in the year, they must be netted against each other in the order specified below.

Step 1. Group all gains and losses into short-term, 28% property, unrecaptured § 1250, and long-term categories.

Step 2. Net the gains and losses within each category to obtain net short-term, 28% property, unrecaptured § 1250, and long-term gain or loss.

Step 3. Offset the net 28% property and unrecaptured § 1250 amounts if they are of opposite sign. Add them if they have the same sign. Then, offset the resulting amount against the net long-term amount, or add the amounts if they have the same sign.

Step 4. Offset the result of step 3 with the net short-term gain or loss from step 2 if they are of opposite sign. The netting rules offset net capital losses against the *highest taxed gain first*. Consequently, if there is a net short-term capital loss, it first offsets any net 28% property gain, any remaining loss offsets unrecaptured § 1250 gain, and then any remaining loss offsets long-term gain.

If the result of step 4 is *only* a short-term capital gain, the taxpayer is not eligible for a reduced tax rate. If the result of step 4 is a loss, a **net capital loss** exists, and the taxpayer may be eligible for a *capital loss deduction* (discussed later in this chapter). If there was no offsetting in step 4 because the short-term and step 3 results were both gains *or* if the result of the offsetting is either a 28% property and/or a long-term gain, a **net capital gain** exists, and the taxpayer may be eligible for a reduced tax rate. The net capital gain may consist of *long-term gain, unrecaptured § 1250 gain, and/or 28% property gain*. Each of these gains may be taxed at a different rate.

The four steps outlined above can have as many as 14 unique final results. See Concept Summary 8–4 later in the chapter for a partial list and the tax effect of each result. The following series of examples illustrates the capital gain and loss netting process for individuals.

Example 30

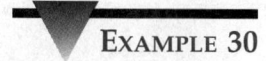

This example shows how a net short-term capital gain may result from the netting process.

Step	Short Term	28% Property	Unrecaptured § 1250	Long Term	Comment
1	$13,000	$12,000		$3,000	
	(2,000)	(20,000)			
2	$11,000	($8,000)		$3,000	
3		8,000	→	(8,000)	Netted because of opposite sign.
		$ –0–		($5,000)	
4	(5,000)	←	←	5,000	
	$ 6,000			$ –0–	The net short-term gain is taxed as ordinary income.

Example 31

This example shows how a net 28% property gain may result from the netting process.

Step	Short Term	28% Property	Unrecaptured § 1250	Long Term	Comment
1	$ 3,000	$ 15,000	$ 4,000	$ 3,000	
	(5,000)	(7,000)		(8,000)	
2	($ 2,000)	$ 8,000	$ 4,000	($ 5,000)	
3		(5,000)	←	5,000	Net long-term loss is netted against 28% gain first.
		$ 3,000		$ –0–	
4	2,000 →	(2,000)			Short term loss is netted against 28% gain first.
	$ –0–	$ 1,000	$ 4,000		
		Net 28% gain	Net 25% gain		

Example 32

This example shows how a net long-term capital loss may result from the netting process.

Step	Short Term	28% Property	Unrecaptured § 1250	Long Term	Comment
1	$ 3,000	$ 1,000		$ 3,000	
				(8,000)	
2	$ 3,000	$ 1,000		($ 5,000)	
3		(1,000)	→	1,000	Netted because of opposite sign.
		$ –0–		($ 4,000)	
4	(3,000)	→	→	3,000	The net short-term gain is netted against the net long-term loss, and the remaining loss is eligible for the capital loss deduction.
	$ –0–			($ 1,000)	

If a net loss remains after applying these rules for offsetting losses, a taxpayer may deduct up to $3,000 of that loss against ordinary income.[21] Losses in excess

---

[21] § 1211(b)(1). Married persons filing separate returns are limited to a $1,500 deduction per tax year.

CHAPTER 8 Property Transactions: Capital Gains and Losses, Section 1231, and Recapture Provisions 8–21

> ### CONCEPT SUMMARY 8–4
>
> ## Some Possible Final Results of the Capital Gain and Loss Netting Process
>
> | Result | Maximum Tax Rate | Comments |
> |---|---|---|
> | Net short-term loss | — | Eligible for capital loss deduction ($3,000 maximum per year). |
> | Net long-term loss (includes 28% property loss and/or long-term loss) | — | Eligible for capital loss deduction ($3,000 maximum per year). |
> | Net short-term loss *and* net long-term loss (includes 28% property loss and/or long-term loss) | — | Eligible for capital loss deduction ($3,000 maximum per year). Short-term capital losses are counted first toward the deduction. |
> | Net short-term gain | 15–39.6% | Taxed as ordinary income. |
> | Net long-term gain without unrecaptured § 1250 gain | 20% | Some or all of 20% gain may be taxed at 10% if other taxable income does not put taxpayer out of 15% rate bracket. |
> | Net long-term gain with unrecaptured § 1250 gain | 20% generally; but 25% on unrecaptured § 1250 gain | Some or all of 20% gain may be taxed at 10% if other taxable income (including 25% gain) does not put taxpayer out of the 15% rate bracket; unrecaptured § 1250 gain is taxed at 25%. |
> | Net 28% property gain | 28% | This gain is eligible for a 28% rate. |
> | Net long-term gain (without unrecaptured § 1250 gain) *and* net 28% property gain | 28% on net 28% property gain; 10%/20% on net long-term gain | The portion of taxable income taxed below 28% is absorbed first by ordinary taxable income and then by 28% property gain. |
> | Net long-term gain (with unrecaptured § 1250 gain) *and* net 28% property gain | 28% on net 28% property gain; 25% on unrecaptured § 1250 gain; 10%/20% on remainder of net long-term gain (if any) | The portion of taxable income taxed below 28% is absorbed first by ordinary taxable income and then by 28% property gain and 25% gain; then 10%/20% eligible gain is taxed. |
> | Net long-term gain (without unrecaptured § 1250 gain) *and* net 28% property gain *and* net short-term gain | Ordinary tax rate on net short-term gain; 28% on net 28% property gain; 10%/20% on net long-term gain | The portion of taxable income taxed below 28% is absorbed first by ordinary taxable income (including the net short-term gain), and then by 28% property gain. |
> | Net long-term gain (with unrecaptured § 1250 gain) *and* net 28% property gain *and* net short-term gain | Ordinary tax rate on net short-term gain; 28% on net 28% property gain; 25% on unrecaptured § 1250 gain; 10%/20% on remainder of net long-term gain | The portion of taxable income taxed below 28% is absorbed first by ordinary taxable income (including the net short-term gain) and then by 28% property gain and 25% gain; then 10%/20% gain is taxed. |

of $3,000 are carried over to future years where they are applied first against capital gains and then deducted up to $3,000 per year. Capital loss carryovers expire, however, when the taxpayer dies.

EXAMPLE 33

James incurred a $10,000 loss on his only capital asset transaction in 1998. If he has no other capital asset transactions from that point on, his $10,000 loss is deducted as follows:

Year	Deduction
1998	$3,000
1999	3,000
2000	3,000
2001	1,000

EXAMPLE 34 Assume the same facts as in the preceding example, except that James realizes a capital gain of $4,500 in 2000. At that time, his remaining capital loss carryover is $4,000 ($10,000 − $6,000 deducted previously). Since his capital gain in 2000 (i.e., $4,500) exceeds this loss carryforward, James can deduct the entire $4,000 against that year's capital gain. ▼

EXAMPLE 35 Assume the same facts as in Example 33, except that James died in late 1999. His remaining capital loss carryforward of $4,000 ($10,000 − $6,000 deducted previously) expires unused. ▼

When a taxpayer's capital loss exceeds $3,000 and derives from more than one category, it is used in the following order: first, short term; then, 28% property; and finally, long term. Unused losses are carried forward as follows: short-term losses carry forward as short-term losses, but 28% property losses and long-term losses *both* carry forward as 28% property losses.

EXAMPLE 36 Nancy incurs a long-term capital loss of $8,500 this year, of which $3,000 is deducted against her ordinary income. The remaining $5,500 ($8,500 loss − $3,000 deducted) carries forward as a loss on 28% property. ▼

PLANNING CONSIDERATIONS

Matching Gains with Losses

A taxpayer who has already realized a large capital gain may want to *match this gain with an offsetting capital loss*. Doing so will shelter the capital gain from taxation and will also free up an asset that has declined in value. Without the capital gain, after all, the taxpayer might hesitate to sell a loss asset, because the resulting capital loss may be deductible only in $3,000 annual increments.

Similarly, a taxpayer with a large realized capital loss might use the occasion to sell some appreciated assets. Doing so would enable the taxpayer to use the capital loss immediately and at the same time realize the benefit of the asset appreciation at little or no tax cost.

On the other hand, matching capital losses and long-term capital gains means that the taxpayer utilizes the capital loss against income that would otherwise qualify for a preferential tax rate of 10 to 28 percent. If the taxpayer's ordinary income is taxed at a higher rate, he or she might prefer to deduct the loss against that higher taxed income, even on a schedule of $3,000 per year. The *time value of money* must be considered; a current-year deduction at 10 to 28 percent might be worth more than a series of annual deductions at higher rates spread over several years.

Nontax considerations, such as investment prospects for the particular assets in question, are also important. But in the real world, future investment prospects are often unknowable or at least highly speculative, while tax impacts can be determined with relative certainty—which explains some of the late December selling activity in publicly traded securities and mutual funds.

SMALL BUSINESS STOCK

A special 50 percent *exclusion* is available to noncorporate taxpayers who derive capital gains from the sale or exchange of **qualified small business stock**.[22] Half of the gain is excluded from the taxpayer's gross income, and the other half is subjected to a maximum tax rate of 28 percent, as noted earlier in this section.

EXAMPLE 37

Yolanda realized a $100,000 gain on the sale of qualified small business stock. Assuming that Yolanda has a 36% marginal tax rate without considering this gain, $50,000 of this gain is excluded from her taxable income, and the other $50,000 is taxed at a maximum tax rate of 28%. Thus, Yolanda owes tax of $14,000 ($50,000 × 28%), an effective tax rate of 14% on the entire $100,000 capital gain. ▼

This treatment is more favorable than the capital gain tax treatment explained previously. Accordingly, Congress imposed additional restrictions to ensure that the gains receiving this treatment were derived in the circumstances that Congress intended to promote. These restrictions include the following:

- The stock must have been newly issued *after* August 10, 1993.
- The taxpayer must have held the stock *more than five years*.
- The issuing corporation must use at least 80 percent of its assets, determined by their value, in the *active conduct* of a trade or business.
- When the stock was issued, the issuing corporation's assets must not have exceeded $50 million, at adjusted basis, including the proceeds of the stock issuance.
- The corporation does not engage in banking, financing, insurance, investing, leasing, farming, mineral extraction, hotel or motel operation, restaurant operation, or any business whose principal asset is the *reputation or skill* of its employees (such as accounting, architecture, health, law, engineering, or financial services).

Even if each of these requirements is met, the amount of gain eligible for the exclusion is limited to the greater of 10 times the taxpayer's basis in the stock or $10 million per taxpayer per company,[23] computed on an aggregate basis.

EXAMPLE 38

Vanita purchased $100,000 of qualified small business stock when it was first issued in October 1993. In 1999, she sells the stock for $4 million. Her gain is $3.9 million ($4,000,000 − $100,000). Although this amount exceeds 10 times her basis ($100,000 × 10 = $1,000,000), it is *less* than $10 million, so the entire $3.9 million gain is eligible for the 50% exclusion. ▼

Transactions that fail to satisfy *any one* of the applicable requirements are taxed as capital gains (and losses) realized by noncorporate taxpayers generally. See Concept Summaries 8–3 and 8–4.

Gains are also eligible for *nonrecognition* treatment if the sale proceeds are invested in other qualified small business stock within 60 days.[24] To the extent that the sale proceeds are not so invested, gain is recognized, but the 50 percent exclusion still applies. To be eligible for this treatment, the stock sold must have been held more than six months.

EXAMPLE 39

Assume the same facts as in the preceding example, except that Vanita sold her stock in January 1998 and used $3.5 million of the sale proceeds to purchase other qualified small

---

[22] § 1202(a).
[23] For married persons filing separately, the limitation is $5 million.
[24] § 1045(a).

business stock one month later. Vanita's gain is recognized to the extent that the sale proceeds were not reinvested—namely, $500,000 ($4,000,000 sale proceeds − $3,500,000 reinvested). The 50% exclusion will apply, however, to this amount. ▼

TAX TREATMENT OF CAPITAL GAINS AND LOSSES OF CORPORATE TAXPAYERS

5 LEARNING OBJECTIVE
Describe the tax treatment of capital gains and losses for corporate taxpayers.

The treatment of a corporation's net capital gain or loss differs dramatically from the rules for noncorporate taxpayers discussed in the preceding section. Briefly, the differences are as follows:

- There is a capital gains alternative tax rate of 35 percent.[25] However, since the maximum corporate tax rate is 35 percent, the alternative tax is never beneficial. In other words, capital gains are taxed as ordinary income.
- Capital losses offset only capital gains. No deduction of capital losses is permitted against ordinary taxable income.
- There is a three-year carryback and a five-year carryover period for net capital losses.[26] Capital loss carryovers and carrybacks are always treated as short term, regardless of their original nature.

EXAMPLE 40

Sparrow Corporation has a $15,000 long-term capital loss for the current year and $57,000 of ordinary taxable income. Sparrow may not offset the $15,000 long-term capital loss against its ordinary income by taking a capital loss deduction. The $15,000 long-term capital loss becomes a $15,000 short-term capital loss for carryback and carryover purposes. This amount may offset capital gains in the three-year carryback period or, if not absorbed there, offset capital gains in the five-year carryover period. Any amount remaining after this carryover period expires is permanently lost. ▼

SECTION 1231 ASSETS

6 LEARNING OBJECTIVE
Distinguish § 1231 assets from ordinary assets and capital assets and calculate the § 1231 gain or loss.

Businesses own many assets that are used in the business rather than held for resale. In financial accounting, such assets are known as "fixed assets." For example, a foundry's 30,000-pound stamping machine is a fixed asset. It is also a depreciable asset. The building housing the foundry is another fixed asset. The remainder of this chapter largely deals with how to *classify* the gains and losses from the disposition of fixed assets. Chapter 4 discussed how to depreciate such assets. Chapter 7 discussed how to determine the adjusted basis and the amount of gain or loss from their disposition.

RELATIONSHIP TO CAPITAL ASSETS

At first glance, *classification of fixed assets* ought to be straightforward. Section 1221(2) specifically excludes from the capital asset definition any property that is depreciable or that is real estate "used in a trade or business." Accordingly, the foundry's stamping machine and the building housing the foundry described above are not capital assets. Therefore, one would expect gains to be taxed as ordinary income and losses to be deductible as ordinary losses. Since World War II, however, certain business assets have received more favorable treatment.

---

[25] § 1201.   [26] § 1212(a)(1).

Section 1231 provides that business assets held for more than one year can receive the best of both worlds: capital gain treatment on gains and ordinary loss treatment on losses. More specifically, this provision requires that gains and losses from **§ 1231 property** be compiled at the end of the taxable year; the *net result* is then classified as capital gain if a net gain is produced, or as ordinary loss if a net loss is produced. As a result, a particular disposition's character as capital or ordinary is not determined until the taxable year has concluded and all of the taxpayer's **§ 1231 gains and losses** are tabulated.

EXAMPLE 41 Brown & Co. sells business land and building at a $5,000 gain and equipment at a $3,000 loss. Both properties were held for more than one year. Brown's net gain is $2,000, and that net gain may be treated as a long-term capital gain under § 1231. ▼

EXAMPLE 42 Chickadee, Inc., sells equipment at a $10,000 loss and business land at a $2,000 gain. Both properties were held for more than one year. Chickadee's net loss is $8,000, and that net loss is an ordinary loss. ▼

RATIONALE FOR FAVORABLE TAX TREATMENT

This unusually generous tax treatment can be understood only in the unique historical context in which it arose. During World War II, certain companies, particularly shippers, were realizing enormous profits when their assets were destroyed by the enemy or requisitioned by the U.S. government for military use. Wartime shortages had inflated the value of these assets, and insurance proceeds or condemnation awards reflected these higher values. As a result, taxpayers often realized very large gains on business assets through no direct effort on their part. At the same time, the involuntary conversion relief provided by § 1033 (discussed in Chapter 7) was often unavailable because the very condition that precipitated these gains—namely, the war—also made *replacement* of the asset (which § 1033 requires) unlikely if not impossible. Accordingly, § 1033 could not prevent these gains from being recognized. With tax rates raised to finance the war, Congress believed that it was unfair to tax these essentially unsolicited gains at high ordinary income rates. The solution: *treat* gains from these *dispositions* as *capital gains*, which were subject to much lower tax rates at that time.

Section 1231 was *not limited to involuntary conversions* of business assets, however. When the government determined that it needed some factory for the war effort, it initiated condemnation proceedings. Such proceedings often were protracted, and some taxpayers chose to sell their business assets to others who were willing to work through that process. As a result, Congress felt that many sales and exchanges were similar to involuntary conversions in this context. Since such transactions could not easily be distinguished in practice from truly voluntary transactions, § 1231 extended its favorable capital gains treatment to include *all sales or exchanges of business assets*, not just involuntary conversions.

Meanwhile, other businesses had not reaped wartime profits and did not want the correlative impact of capital asset classification on their losses. Ordinary losses, after all, were fully deductible in the year incurred. As discussed in the preceding sections, capital losses could only offset capital gains and faced other timing restrictions depending on whether the business was conducted in corporate or noncorporate form. Accordingly, Congress saw fit to allow these businesses to retain their ability to claim business asset *losses as ordinary losses*.

Years after World War II, Congress decided that § 1231's highly favorable treatment was no longer entirely appropriate. Rather than repeal § 1231, however,

Congress chose to take back some—but not all—of its benefits through the *recapture provisions* of §§ 1245 and 1250, which are discussed later in this chapter.

PROPERTY INCLUDED

Section 1231 property includes the following:

- Depreciable or real property used in business (principally machinery and equipment, buildings, and land).
- Property held for the production of income if it has been involuntarily converted.
- Timber, coal, or domestic iron ore to which § 631 applies.
- Livestock held for draft, breeding, dairy, or sporting purposes.
- Unharvested crops on land used in business.
- Certain *purchased* intangible assets (such as patents and goodwill) that are eligible for amortization.

PROPERTY EXCLUDED

Section 1231 property does *not* include the following:

- Property not held for more than one year. Livestock must be held at least 12 months (24 months in some cases). Unharvested crops do not have to be held for more than one year, but the land must be so held.
- Property where casualty losses exceed casualty gains for the taxable year. If a taxpayer has a net casualty loss, the casualty gains and losses are treated as ordinary gains and losses.
- Inventory and property held primarily for sale to customers.
- Copyrights; literary, musical, or artistic compositions, etc.; and certain U.S. government publications.
- Accounts receivable and notes receivable arising in the ordinary course of the trade or business.

NONPERSONAL-USE CAPITAL ASSETS

When § 1231 assets are disposed of by casualty or theft, a special netting rule is applied. For simplicity, the term *casualty* is used to mean both casualty and theft dispositions. First, the casualty gains and losses from § 1231 assets *and* the casualty gains and losses from **long-term nonpersonal-use capital assets** are determined. For business entities, virtually any capital asset is a nonpersonal-use capital asset, because partnerships, limited liability companies, and corporations are incapable of using assets *personally*. This classification, therefore, is most significant to individual taxpayers who might use certain capital assets as part of their daily life. Thus, a painting held for investment would be a nonpersonal-use capital asset, while an antique bedroom suite would be a personal-use capital asset, as would be the taxpayer's home itself. In contrast, antique furniture on display in a corporation's main lobby is a nonpersonal (i.e., business) use capital asset.

Once the casualty gains and losses from § 1231 assets and nonpersonal-use capital assets are determined, they are netted together. If the result is a *net gain*, the net gain is treated as § 1231 gain, but if the result is a *net loss*, the net loss is deducted outside § 1231. Thus, whether these casualties get § 1231 treatment depends on the results of the casualty netting process.

Casualties and thefts are *involuntary conversions*, it should be recalled, and gains from such conversions need not be recognized if the proceeds are timely reinvested in similar property. Thus, the netting process described above would not consider any casualty and theft gains that are being deferred because insurance proceeds were reinvested according to the requirements of § 1033 (see Chapter 7). Section 1231, in other words, has no effect on whether a *realized* gain or loss is recognized. Instead, § 1231 merely dictates how a *recognized* gain will be classified.

This special netting process for casualties and thefts does not apply to *condemnation* gains and losses. As a result, if a § 1231 asset is disposed of by condemnation, any resulting gain or loss will get § 1231 treatment.

For individual taxpayers only, additional considerations apply. If the casualty gains and losses from § 1231 assets and nonpersonal-use capital assets result in a *net gain*, this net gain is § 1231 gain. But if the result is a *net loss*, the components are split up and treated as follows:

- The gains are ordinary income.
- Losses from § 1231 assets are deducted *for* adjusted gross income (AGI).
- Losses from nonpersonal-use capital assets are deducted *from* AGI, subject to a 2 percent-of-AGI limitation (see Chapter 15 for a discussion of the 2 percent-of-AGI limitation).

Finally, personal-use capital assets are not considered under § 1231, regardless of the manner of their disposition.

GENERAL PROCEDURE FOR § 1231 COMPUTATION

The tax treatment of § 1231 gains and losses depends on the results of a rather complex *netting* procedure. The steps in this netting procedure are as follows.

Step 1: Casualty Netting. Net all recognized long-term gains and losses from casualties of § 1231 assets and nonpersonal-use capital assets. This casualty netting is beneficial because if there is a net gain, the gain may receive long-term capital gain treatment. If there is a net loss, it receives ordinary loss treatment.

    a. If the casualty gains exceed the casualty losses, add the net gain to the other § 1231 gains for the taxable year.

    b. If the casualty losses exceed the casualty gains, exclude all casualty losses and gains from further § 1231 computation. The casualty gains are ordinary income and the casualty losses are deductible. For individual taxpayers, the casualty losses must be classified further. Section 1231 asset casualty losses are deductible *for* AGI, while other casualty losses are deductible *from* AGI.

Step 2: § 1231 Netting. After adding any net casualty gain from Step 1a to the other § 1231 gains and losses (including *recognized* § 1231 asset condemnation gains and losses), net all § 1231 gains and losses.

    a. If the gains exceed the losses, the net gain is offset by the "lookback" nonrecaptured § 1231 losses (see Step 3 below) from the prior five tax years. To the extent of this offset, the net § 1231 gain is classified as ordinary income. Any remaining gain is long-term capital gain.

    b. If the losses exceed the gains, the net loss is deducted against ordinary income. For individual taxpayers only, the gains are ordinary income, the § 1231 asset losses are deductible *for* AGI, and the other casualty losses are deductible *from* AGI.

Examples 43 and 44 illustrate the application of the § 1231 computation procedure.

EXAMPLE 43

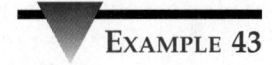

Falcon Management, Inc., had the following recognized gains and losses this year:

Capital Gains and Losses	
Long-term capital gain	$ 3,000
Long-term capital loss	(400)
Short-term capital gain	1,000
Short-term capital loss	(200)

Casualties	
Gain from insurance recovery on fire loss to building, owned five years	$ 1,200
Loss from theft of computer (uninsured), owned two years	(1,000)

§ 1231 Gains and Losses from Depreciable Business Assets Held Long Term	
Asset A	$ 300
Asset B	1,100
Asset C	(500)

Gains and Losses from Sale of Depreciable Business Assets Held Short Term	
Asset D	$ 200
Asset E	(300)

Falcon had no net § 1231 losses in prior tax years.

Disregarding the recapture of depreciation (discussed later in this chapter), Falcon's gains and losses receive the following tax treatment:

- The casualty netting of the § 1231 and nonpersonal-use capital assets contains two items—the $1,200 gain from the business building and the $1,000 loss from the computer. Consequently, there is a $200 net gain and that gain is treated as a § 1231 gain (added to the § 1231 gains).
- The gains from § 1231 transactions (Assets A, B, and C and the § 1231 asset casualty gain) exceed the losses by $1,100 ($1,600 − $500). This excess is a long-term capital gain and is added to Falcon's other long-term capital gains.
- Falcon's net long-term capital gain is $3,700 ($3,000 + $1,100 from § 1231 transactions − $400 long-term capital loss). Its net short-term capital gain is $800 ($1,000 − $200). The result is capital gain income of $4,500, which will be taxed at ordinary rates. If Falcon were an individual rather than a corporation, the $3,700 net long-term capital gain portion would be eligible for preferential capital gain treatment and the $800 net short-term capital gain would be taxed as ordinary income.
- Falcon treats the gain and loss from Assets D and E as ordinary gain and loss, because § 1231 does not apply unless the assets have been held more than one year.[27]

Results of the Gains and Losses on Falcon's Tax Computation	
Net long-term capital gain	$3,700
Net short-term capital gain	800
Ordinary gain from sale of Asset D	200
Ordinary loss from sale of Asset E	(300)
Gross income	$4,400

---

[27] § 1231(b)(1).

CHAPTER 8 Property Transactions: Capital Gains and Losses, Section 1231, and Recapture Provisions

EXAMPLE 44

Assume the same facts as in the preceding example, except that the loss from Asset C was $1,700 instead of $500.

- The treatment of the casualty gains and losses is the same.
- The losses from § 1231 transactions now exceed the gains by $100 ($1,700 − $1,600). As a result, the net loss is deducted in full as an ordinary loss.
- Capital gain income is $3,400 ($2,600 long-term + $800 short-term).

Results of the Gains and Losses on Falcon's Tax Computation	
Net long-term capital gain	$2,600
Net short-term capital gain	800
Net ordinary loss on Assets A, B, and C and § 1231 casualty gain	(100)
Ordinary gain from sale of Asset D	200
Ordinary loss from sale of Asset E	(300)
Gross income	$3,200

Step 3: § 1231 Lookback Provision. The net § 1231 gain from Step 2a is offset by the nonrecaptured net § 1231 losses for the five preceding taxable years.[28] For 1998, the lookback years are 1993, 1994, 1995, 1996, and 1997. To the extent of the nonrecaptured net § 1231 loss, the current-year net § 1231 gain is ordinary income. The *nonrecaptured* net § 1231 losses are those that have not already been used to offset net § 1231 gains. Only the net § 1231 gain exceeding this net § 1231 loss carryforward is given long-term capital gain treatment. The **§ 1231 lookback** provision and the other netting rules are included in Concept Summary 8–5. Examples 45 and 46 illustrate this provision.

EXAMPLE 45

Komodo Manufacturing Corporation sold various used machines and some business real estate during 1998 for a net § 1231 gain of $25,000. During 1997, Komodo had no § 1231 transactions, but in 1996, it had a net § 1231 loss of $17,000. This loss causes $17,000 of the 1998 gain to be treated as ordinary income, and the remaining 1998 gain of $8,000 ($25,000 of § 1231 gain − $17,000 nonrecaptured loss) is long-term capital gain. ▼

EXAMPLE 46

Assume the same facts as in the preceding example, except that Komodo had a net § 1231 loss of $37,000 in 1996 and a net § 1231 gain of $10,000 in 1997.

- The 1996 net § 1231 loss of $37,000 would cause the net § 1231 gain of $10,000 in 1997 to be treated as ordinary income, and $27,000 ($37,000 loss − $10,000 recaptured) would carry over to 1998.
- The remaining nonrecaptured § 1231 loss of $27,000 from 1996 completely offsets the § 1231 gain of $25,000 from 1998, making that entire gain ordinary income.
- The remaining nonrecaptured § 1231 loss from 1996 is $2,000 ($27,000 carried to 1998 − $25,000 recaptured). This recapture potential carries over to 1999. ▼

SECTION 1245 RECAPTURE

7 LEARNING OBJECTIVE
Determine when recapture provisions apply and their effect.

As the preceding section explained, when Congress determined that § 1231 was unduly generous, it chose to *recapture* some of § 1231's benefits rather than repeal that section altogether. This recapture phenomenon applies exclusively to the gain

---
[28] § 1231(c).

Concept Summary 8-5

Section 1231 Netting Procedure

```
§ 1231 asset and long-term nonpersonal-
use capital asset casualty* gains
            minus
§ 1231 asset and long-term nonpersonal-
use capital asset casualty* losses
```

- NET GAIN → Net gain (add to § 1231 gains)
- NET LOSS → Items are treated separately:
  - Gains are ordinary income
  - § 1231 asset losses are deductible *for* AGI
  - Other losses are deductible *from* AGI

↓ (and NET LOSS ↑)

§ 1231 gains minus § 1231 losses

↓ NET GAIN

Lookback Provision:
Net gain is offset against nonrecaptured net §1231 losses from prior 5 tax years

- Gain offset by lookback losses is ordinary gain
- Remaining gain is long-term capital gain

*Includes casualties and thefts.

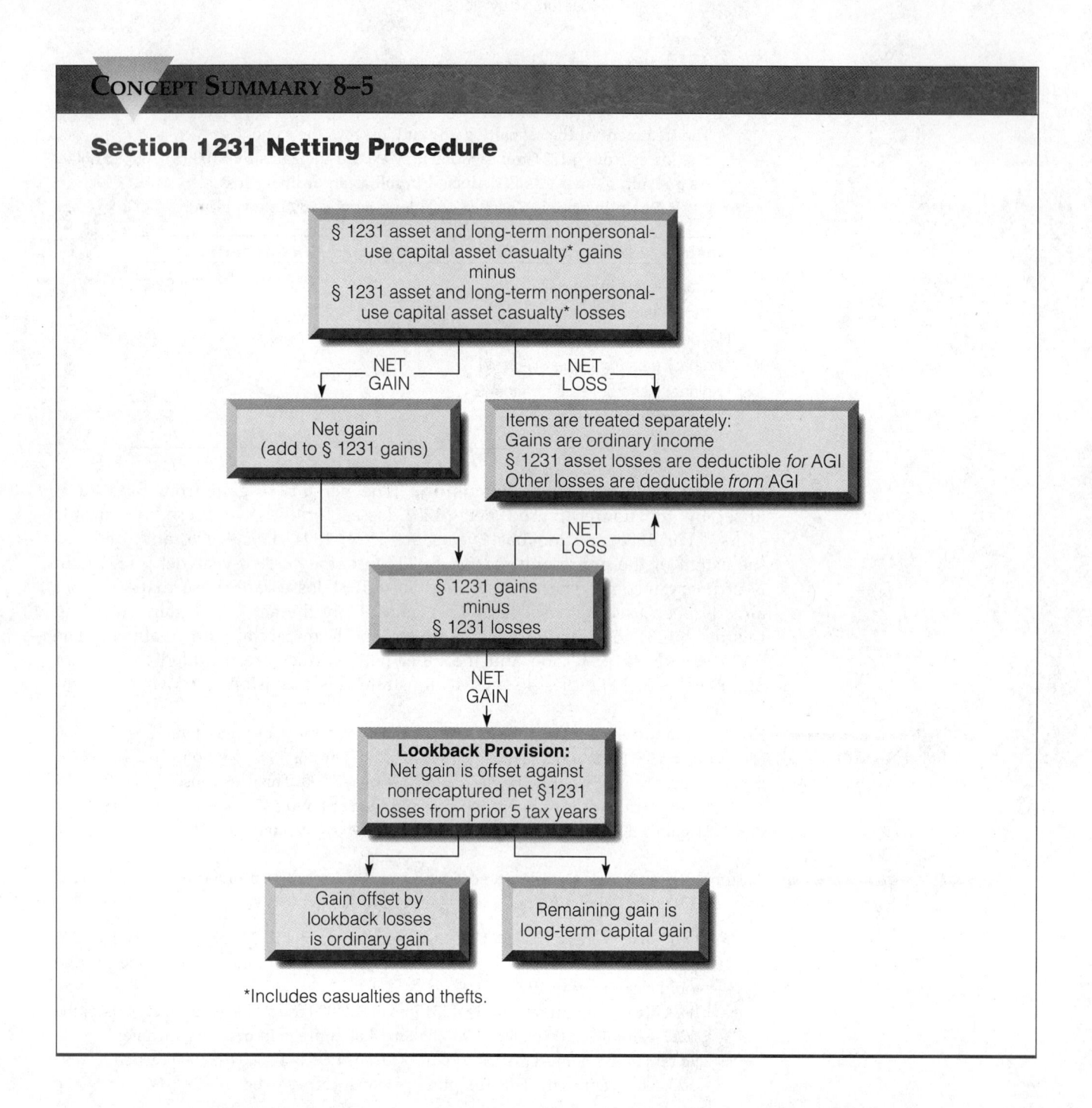

side of § 1231; the ordinary loss feature applicable to § 1231 property is not affected by the Code's recapture provisions. In essence, recapture takes part—often all—of the gain from the sale or exchange of a § 1231 asset and classifies it as *ordinary income* before the netting process of § 1231 begins. Accordingly, recaptured gain is computed *first*, without considering the other § 1231 transactions that occurred during the taxable year. This section discusses the § 1245 recapture rules, and the next section discusses the § 1250 recapture rules.

CHAPTER 8 Property Transactions: Capital Gains and Losses, Section 1231, and Recapture Provisions

Section 1245 requires taxpayers to treat all gain as ordinary gain unless the property is sold for more than its original cost. This result is accomplished by requiring that all gain be treated as ordinary gain to the extent of the depreciation taken on the property disposed of. Section 1231 gain results only if the property is disposed of for more than its original cost. The excess of the sales price over the original cost is § 1231 gain. Section 1245 applies primarily to personalty such as machinery, trucks, and office furniture.

EXAMPLE 47

Avocet, Inc., purchased a $100,000 machine and deducted $70,000 depreciation before selling it for $80,000. Avocet's gain is $50,000 [$80,000 amount realized − $30,000 adjusted basis ($100,000 cost − $70,000 depreciation taken)]. Section 1245 treats as ordinary income (not as § 1231 gain) any gain to the extent of depreciation taken. In this example, the entire $50,000 gain would be ordinary income. ▼

EXAMPLE 48

If Avocet, Inc., in the preceding example sold the machine for $120,000, it would have a gain of $90,000 ($120,000 amount realized − $30,000 adjusted basis). The § 1245 gain would be $70,000 (equal to the depreciation taken), and the remaining gain of $20,000 (equal to the excess of the sales price over the original cost) would be § 1231 gain. ▼

Section 1245 recapture applies to the portion of *recognized* gain from the sale or other disposition of § 1245 property that represents depreciation, including § 167 depreciation, § 168 cost recovery, § 179 immediate expensing, and § 197 amortization. Section 1245 merely *classifies* gain as ordinary income; it does not cause gain to be recognized. Thus, in Example 47, Avocet, Inc., recaptures as ordinary income only the $50,000 of actual gain, not the entire $70,000 of depreciation taken. In other words, § 1245 recaptures the lower of the depreciation taken or the gain recognized.

The method of depreciation (e.g., accelerated or straight-line) does not matter. All depreciation taken is potentially subject to recapture. Thus, § 1245 recapture is often referred to as *full recapture*. Any remaining gain after subtracting the amount recaptured as ordinary income will usually be § 1231 gain. However, the remaining gain is casualty gain if it is disposed of in a casualty event. For example, if the machine in Example 48 had been disposed of by casualty and the $120,000 received had been an insurance recovery, Avocet would still have a gain of $90,000, and $70,000 of that gain would still be recaptured by § 1245 as ordinary gain. The other $20,000 of gain, however, would be casualty gain.

The following examples illustrate the general application of § 1245.

EXAMPLE 49

On January 1, Cormorant Corporation sold for $13,000 a machine acquired several years ago for $12,000. The company had taken $10,000 of depreciation on the machine.

- The recognized gain from the sale is $11,000. This is the amount realized of $13,000 less the adjusted basis of $2,000 ($12,000 cost − $10,000 depreciation taken).
- Depreciation taken is $10,000. Therefore, since § 1245 recapture gain is the lower of depreciation taken or gain recognized, $10,000 of the $11,000 recognized gain is ordinary income, and the remaining $1,000 gain is § 1231 gain.
- The § 1231 gain of $1,000 is also equal to the excess of the sales price over the original cost of the property ($13,000 − $12,000 = $1,000 § 1231 gain). ▼

EXAMPLE 50

Assume the same facts as in the preceding example, except that the asset is sold for $9,000 instead of $13,000.

- The recognized gain from the sale is $7,000. This is the amount realized of $9,000 less the adjusted basis of $2,000.
- Depreciation taken is $10,000. Therefore, since the $10,000 depreciation taken exceeds the recognized gain of $7,000, the entire $7,000 recognized gain is ordinary income.
- The § 1231 gain is zero. There is no § 1231 gain because the selling price ($9,000) does not exceed the original purchase price ($12,000). ▼

EXAMPLE 51

Assume the same facts as in Example 49, except that the asset is sold for $1,500 instead of $13,000.

- The recognized loss from the sale is $500. This is the amount realized of $1,500 less the adjusted basis of $2,000.
- Since there is a loss, there is no depreciation recapture. All of the loss is § 1231 loss. ▼

If § 1245 property is disposed of in a transaction other than a sale, exchange, or involuntary conversion, the maximum amount recaptured is the excess of the property's fair market value over its adjusted basis. See the discussion under Exceptions to §§ 1245 and 1250 later in this chapter.

SECTION 1245 PROPERTY

Generally, **§ 1245 property** includes all depreciable personal property (e.g., machinery and equipment), including livestock. Buildings and their structural components usually are not § 1245 property. The following property is *also* subject to § 1245 treatment:

- Amortizable personal property such as goodwill, patents, copyrights, and leaseholds of § 1245 property. Professional baseball and football player contracts are § 1245 property.
- Amortization of reforestation expenditures.
- Expensing of costs to remove architectural and transportation barriers that restrict the handicapped and/or elderly.
- Elevators and escalators acquired before January 1, 1987.
- Certain depreciable tangible real property (other than buildings and their structural components) employed as an integral part of certain activities such as manufacturing and production. For example, a natural gas storage tank where the gas is used in the manufacturing process is § 1245 property.
- Pollution control facilities, railroad grading and tunnel bores, on-the-job training, and child care facilities on which amortization is taken.
- Single-purpose agricultural and horticultural structures and petroleum storage facilities (e.g., a greenhouse or silo).
- Although technically not § 1245 property, 15-year, 18-year, and 19-year *nonresidential real estate* for which accelerated cost recovery is used is subject to the § 1245 recapture rules. Such property would have been placed in service after 1980 and before 1987.

EXAMPLE 52

Heron & Co., Inc., acquired nonresidential rental property on January 1, 1986, for $100,000. The company used the statutory percentage method to compute the ACRS cost recovery. It sells the asset on January 15, 1998, for $120,000. The amount and nature of Heron's gain are computed as follows:

Amount realized			$120,000
Adjusted basis			
Cost		$100,000	
Less cost recovery:	1986–1997	(70,400)	
	1998	(175)	
January 15, 1998, adjusted basis			29,425
Gain realized and recognized			$ 90,575

The gain of $90,575 is treated as ordinary income to the extent of *all* depreciation taken because the property is 19-year nonresidential real estate for which accelerated depreciation was used. Thus, Heron reports ordinary income of $70,575 ($70,400 + $175) and § 1231 gain of $20,000 ($90,575 − $70,575). ▼

OBSERVATIONS ON § 1245

- In most instances, the total depreciation taken will exceed the recognized gain. Therefore, the disposition of § 1245 property usually results in ordinary income rather than § 1231 gain. Refer to Example 50.
- Recapture applies to the total amount of depreciation allowed or allowable regardless of the depreciation method used.
- Recapture applies regardless of the holding period of the property. Of course, the entire recognized gain would be ordinary income if the property was not held more than one year, because then § 1231 would not apply.
- Section 1245 does not apply to losses, which receive § 1231 treatment.
- Gains from the disposition of § 1245 assets may also be treated as passive activity gains (refer to Chapter 5).

PLANNING CONSIDERATIONS

Depreciation Recapture and § 179

Section 1245 recapture applies to all types of depreciation, including § 179 *immediate expensing*. Expensing under § 179, however, is elective and entirely within the discretion of the taxpayer. Choosing this option accelerates depreciation on the affected property but increases the potential recapture as well. Therefore, if a taxpayer anticipates that an asset will generate a gain when it is sold and that such sale will occur in the early years of the asset's life, the taxpayer might decide to forgo electing the additional depreciation under § 179.

On the other hand, electing § 179 remains attractive if little or no gain is anticipated upon an asset's disposition. After all, § 1245 recapture applies only to the extent that gain is actually realized. Moreover, even if a substantial gain is anticipated upon an asset's disposition, the *time value of money* might suggest that § 179 be elected if the disposition is expected to be many years away. In any case, the taxpayer can usually control when an asset is sold or exchanged and can thereby extend the time before the taxes saved by electing § 179 must be returned as § 1245 recapture.

SECTION 1250 RECAPTURE

Depreciable property that is not subject to § 1245 recapture faces a separate recapture computation mechanism in § 1250. For the most part, § 1250 applies to *depreciable real property* (principally buildings and their structural components), such as apartments, office buildings, factories, stores, and warehouses.[29] Intangible real property, such as leaseholds of **§ 1250 property,** is also included.

Section 1250 recapture is much less onerous than § 1245 recapture, but it is also much more complex. Section 1250 recaptures only a property's **additional depreciation,** which is the excess of the depreciation actually deducted over the amount that would have been allowed under the straight-line method of depreciation. For this reason, § 1250 recapture is often referred to as *partial recapture,* in contrast to § 1245's full recapture.

Since § 1250 recaptures only the excess over straight-line depreciation, the concept does not apply to properties that were depreciated using the straight-line method (unless they were held for one year or less). Real property placed in service *after 1986* can only be depreciated using the straight-line method, so there is *no § 1250 recapture* upon the disposition of such properties that are held for longer than one year.

But real estate is particularly long-lived, and many dispositions of such assets involve properties placed in service *before 1987,* when accelerated depreciation was often available for real estate. Accordingly, § 1250 will continue to play a major role in *classifying gain* from the disposition of real property for many years to come. Finally, § 1250 does not apply to losses.

If § 1250 property is disposed of in a transaction other than a sale, exchange, or involuntary conversion, the maximum amount recaptured is the excess of the property's fair market value over its adjusted basis. For example, if a corporation distributes property to its shareholders as a dividend, a gain results if the property's fair market value is greater than its adjusted basis. The maximum amount of § 1250 recapture will be the amount of that gain.

The following discussion describes the computational steps prescribed in § 1250 and reflected on Form 4797 (see Appendix B).

COMPUTING RECAPTURE ON NONRESIDENTIAL REAL PROPERTY

For § 1250 property other than residential rental property, the potential recapture is the amount of additional depreciation taken *since December 31, 1969.* If the property is held for one year or less (usually not the case), *all* depreciation taken, even under the straight-line method, is additional depreciation.

The following procedure is used to compute recapture on nonresidential real property under § 1250:

- Determine the recognized gain from the sale or other disposition of the property.
- Determine post-1969 additional depreciation.
- The *lower* of the recognized gain or the post-1969 additional depreciation is ordinary income.
- If any recognized gain remains (recognized gain less recapture), it is § 1231 gain. However, it would be casualty gain if the disposition was by casualty.

---

[29] As previously discussed, § 1245 applies to nonresidential real estate that was placed in service after 1980 and before 1987 and was depreciated using an accelerated method.

The following example illustrates the application of the § 1250 computation.

EXAMPLE 53

On January 3, 1980, Lark & Associates acquired a new building at a cost of $200,000 for use in the partnership's business. The building had an estimated useful life of 50 years and no estimated salvage value. Depreciation has been taken under the 150% declining-balance method through December 31, 1996. Pertinent information with respect to depreciation taken follows:

Year	Undepreciated Balance (Beginning of the Year)	Current Depreciation Provision	Straight-Line Depreciation	Additional Depreciation
1980	$200,000	$ 6,000	$ 4,000	$ 2,000
1981	194,000	5,820	4,000	1,820
1982	188,180	5,645	4,000	1,645
1983	182,535	5,476	4,000	1,476
1984	177,059	5,312	4,000	1,312
1985	171,747	5,152	4,000	1,152
1986	166,595	4,998	4,000	998
1987	161,597	4,848	4,000	848
1988	156,749	4,702	4,000	702
1989	152,047	4,561	4,000	561
1990	147,486	4,425	4,000	425
1991	143,061	4,292	4,000	292
1992	138,769	4,163	4,000	163
1993	134,606	4,038	4,000	38
1994	130,568	3,917	4,000	(83)
1995	126,651	3,800	4,000	(200)
1996	122,851	3,686	4,000	(314)
1997	119,165	3,575	4,000	(425)
Total 1980–1997		$84,410	$72,000	$12,410

On January 2, 1998, Lark sold the building for $180,000. Compute the amount of the partnership's § 1250 ordinary income and § 1231 gain.

- Lark's recognized gain from the sale is $64,410. This is the difference between the $180,000 amount realized and the $115,590 adjusted basis ($200,000 cost − $84,410 depreciation taken).
- Post-1969 additional depreciation is $12,410.
- The amount of post-1969 ordinary income is $12,410. Since the post-1969 additional depreciation of $12,410 is less than the recognized gain of $64,410, the entire gain is not recaptured.
- The remaining $52,000 ($64,410 − $12,410) gain is § 1231 gain. ▼

COMPUTING RECAPTURE ON RESIDENTIAL RENTAL HOUSING

Section 1250 recapture also applies to the sale or other disposition of residential rental housing. Property qualifies as *residential rental housing* only if at least 80 percent of gross rent income is derived from dwelling units.[30] The rules are the same as for

---

[30] § 168(e)(2)(A). Note that there may be residential, nonrental housing (e.g., a bunkhouse on a cattle ranch). Such property is commonly regarded as "nonresidential real estate." The rules for such property were discussed in the preceding section.

other § 1250 property, except that only the post-1975 additional depreciation need be recaptured.[31] Therefore, the additional depreciation for periods after 1975 is initially applied against the recognized gain, and such amounts may be recaptured in full as ordinary income. If any of the recognized gain is not absorbed by the recapture rules pertaining to the post-1975 period, the remaining gain is § 1231 gain.

EXAMPLE 54

Assume the same facts as in the preceding example, except that the building is residential rental housing.

- Post-1975 ordinary income is $12,410 (post-1975 additional depreciation of $12,410).
- The remaining $52,000 ($64,410 − $12,410) gain is § 1231 gain. ▼

Under § 1250, when straight-line depreciation is used, there is no § 1250 recapture potential unless the property is disposed of in the first year of use. For real property placed in service after 1986, only straight-line depreciation is allowed. Therefore, the application of § 1250 is limited to first-year dispositions.

EXAMPLE 55

Sanjay acquires a residential rental building on January 1, 1997, for $300,000. He receives an offer of $450,000 for the building and sells it on December 23, 1998.

- Sanjay takes $20,909 [($300,000 × .03485) + ($300,000 × .03636 × $11.5/12$) = $20,909] of total depreciation for 1997 and 1998, and the adjusted basis of the property is $279,091 ($300,000 − $20,909).
- Sanjay's recognized gain is $170,909 ($450,000 − $279,091).
- All of the gain is § 1231 gain. ▼

SECTION 1250 RECAPTURE SITUATIONS

The § 1250 recapture rules apply to the following property for which accelerated depreciation was used:

- Residential rental real estate acquired before 1987.
- Nonresidential real estate acquired before 1981.
- Real property used predominantly outside the United States.
- Certain government-financed or low-income housing.[32]

Concept Summary 8–6 compares and contrasts the § 1245 and § 1250 depreciation recapture rules. Concept Summary 8–7 integrates the depreciation recapture rules with the § 1231 netting process. It is an expanded version of Concept Summary 8–5.

ADDITIONAL RECAPTURE FOR CORPORATIONS

Although depreciation recapture is generally the same for all taxpayers, corporations that sell depreciable real estate face an additional amount of depreciation recapture. Section 291(a)(1) requires recapture of 20 percent of the excess of the amount that would be recaptured under § 1245 over the amount actually recaptured under § 1250. Buildings subject to recapture under § 1245 would have no such excess, so § 291 would not apply to these dispositions.

---

[31] §§ 1250(a)(1) and (2) and Reg. § 1.1250–1(d)(1)(i)(c). The post-1969 through 1975 recapture percentage is 100% less one percentage point for each full month the property is held over 100 months. This approach yields a zero percentage no matter when the property was acquired in the 1969–1975 period. For instance, if a building was acquired on January 3, 1975, and sold on January 3, 1998, it would have been held 276 months. The recapture percentage is zero because 100% − (276% − 100%) is less than zero.

[32] Described in § 1250(a)(1)(B).

CONCEPT SUMMARY 8-6

Comparison of § 1245 and § 1250 Depreciation Recapture

	§ 1245	§ 1250
Property affected	All depreciable personal property, but also nonresidential real property acquired after December 31, 1980, and before January 1, 1987, for which accelerated cost recovery was used. Also includes miscellaneous items such as § 179 expense and § 197 amortization of intangibles such as goodwill, patents, and copyrights.	Residential rental real property acquired after December 31, 1980, and before January 1, 1987, on which accelerated cost recovery was taken. Nonresidential real property acquired after December 31, 1969, and before January 1, 1976, on which accelerated depreciation was taken. Residential real and nonresidential real property acquired after December 31, 1975, and before January 1, 1981, on which accelerated depreciation was taken.
Depreciation recaptured	Potentially all depreciation taken. If the selling price is greater than or equal to the original cost, all depreciation is recaptured. If the selling price is between the adjusted basis and the original cost, only some depreciation is recaptured.	Additional depreciation (the excess of accelerated cost recovery over straight-line cost recovery or the excess of accelerated depreciation over straight-line depreciation). All depreciation taken if property disposed of in first year.
Limit on recapture	Lower of depreciation taken or gain recognized.	Lower of additional depreciation or gain recognized.
Treatment of gain exceeding recapture gain	Usually § 1231 gain.	Usually § 1231 gain.
Treatment of loss	No depreciation recapture; loss is usually § 1231 loss.	No depreciation recapture; loss is usually § 1231 loss.

EXAMPLE 56

Franklin Corporation purchased an office building on January 3, 1986, for $300,000. Accelerated depreciation was taken in the amount of $211,200 before the building was sold on January 5, 1998, for $250,000. Straight-line depreciation would have been $189,900 (using a 19-year recovery period under ACRS). The corporation's depreciation recapture and § 1231 gain are computed as follows:

Determine realized gain:	
Sales price	$250,000
Less: Adjusted basis [$300,000 (cost of building) − $211,200 (ACRS depreciation)]	(88,800)
Realized gain	$161,200

Because the building is 19-year real estate, it is treated as § 1245 recovery property. The gain of $161,200 is recaptured to the extent of all depreciation taken. Thus, all gain is ordinary income under § 1245, and there is no additional § 291 depreciation recapture. ▼

EXAMPLE 57

Assume the building in the preceding example is residential rental property, making it § 1250 property. Gain recaptured under § 1250 is $21,300 ($211,200 depreciation taken − $189,900 straight-line depreciation). However, for a corporate taxpayer, § 291(a)(1) causes additional § 1250 ordinary income of $27,980, computed as follows:

Concept Summary 8–7

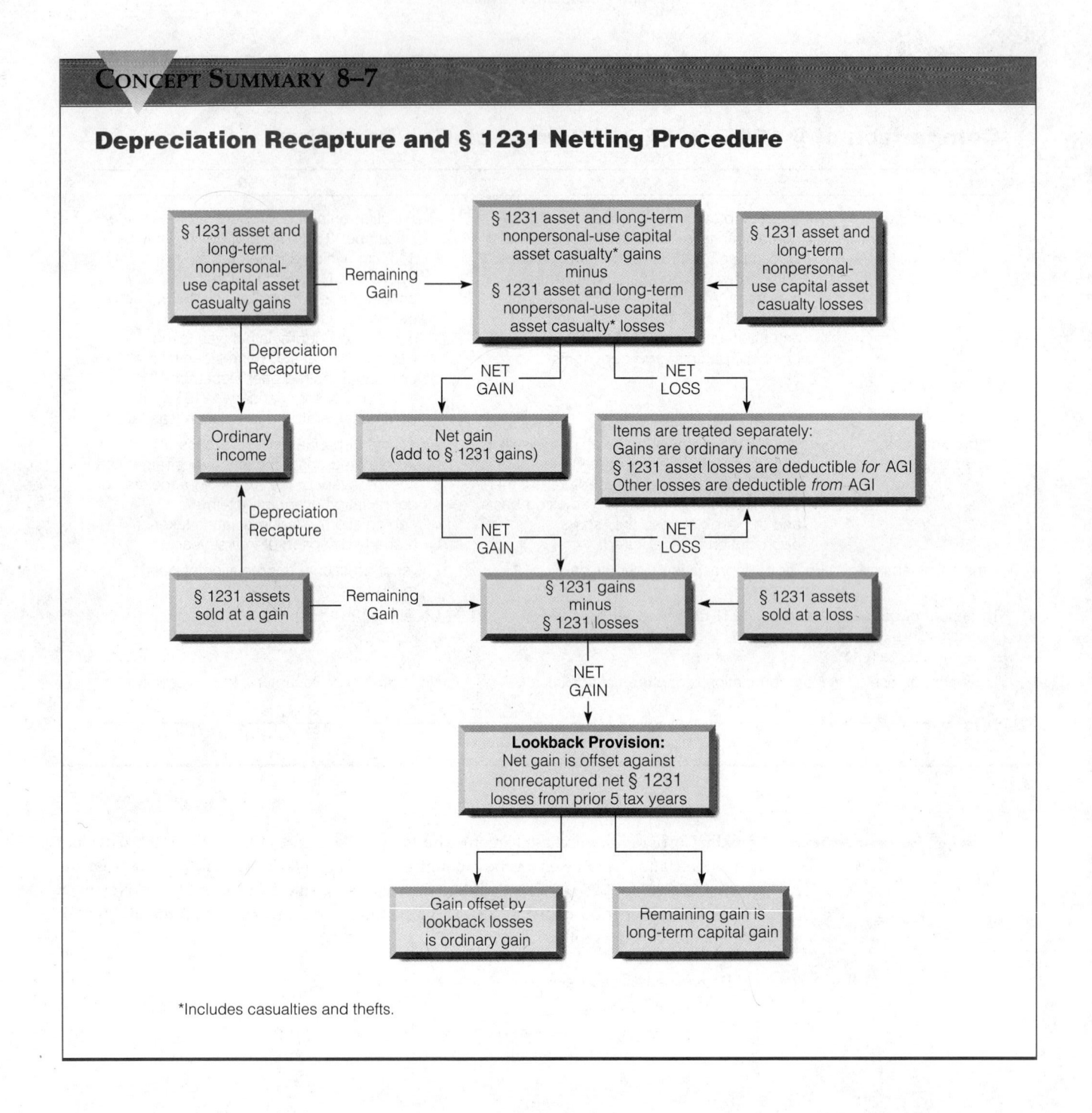

Depreciation Recapture and § 1231 Netting Procedure

```
§ 1231 asset and                    § 1231 asset and long-term              § 1231 asset and
long-term                           nonpersonal-use capital                 long-term
nonpersonal-     —Remaining Gain→   asset casualty* gains       ←           nonpersonal-
use capital asset                   minus                                   use capital asset
casualty gains                      § 1231 asset and long-term              casualty losses
                                    nonpersonal-use capital
       |                            asset casualty* losses
  Depreciation
  Recapture                          NET GAIN    /    NET LOSS
       ↓                                 ↓                ↓
   Ordinary                          Net gain         Items are treated separately:
   income                            (add to          Gains are ordinary income
                                     § 1231 gains)    § 1231 asset losses are deductible for AGI
       ↑                                              Other losses are deductible from AGI
  Depreciation
  Recapture                          NET GAIN    /    NET LOSS
                                         ↓                ↑
§ 1231 assets     —Remaining Gain→   § 1231 gains       ←         § 1231 assets
sold at a gain                       minus                        sold at a loss
                                     § 1231 losses
                                         ↓
                                       NET GAIN
                                         ↓
                                  Lookback Provision:
                                  Net gain is offset against
                                  nonrecaptured net § 1231
                                  losses from prior 5 tax years
                                     ↙                ↘
                            Gain offset by        Remaining gain is
                            lookback losses       long-term capital gain
                            is ordinary gain
```

*Includes casualties and thefts.

Ordinary income if property were § 1245 property	$161,200
Less: Gain recaptured under § 1250	(21,300)
Excess § 1245 gain	$139,900
Percentage that is ordinary gain	× 20%
Additional § 291 gain recaptured	$ 27,980
Ordinary income from depreciation recapture ($21,300 + $27,980)	$ 49,280
Section 1231 gain ($161,200 − $21,300 − $27,980)	111,920
Total gain	$161,200

EXAMPLE 58

Assume the building in the preceding example is commercial property and straight-line depreciation was used. An individual would report all of the gain as § 1231 gain. However, under § 291 a corporate taxpayer must still recapture as ordinary income 20% of the depreciation that would be ordinary income if the property were § 1245 property.

First, determine realized gain:	
Sales price	$ 250,000
Less: Adjusted basis [$300,000 (cost of building) − $189,900 (straight-line depreciation)]	(110,100)
Realized gain	$ 139,900
Second, determine § 291 gain:	
Ordinary income if property were § 1245 property	$ 139,900
Less: Ordinary income under § 1250	(−0−)
Excess ordinary income under § 1245	$ 139,900
Apply § 291 percentage	× 20%
Ordinary income under § 291	$ 27,980

For a corporate taxpayer, $27,980 of the $139,900 gain would be ordinary income, and $111,920 would be § 1231 gain. ▼

UNRECAPTURED § 1250 GAINS

As noted previously, *noncorporate taxpayers* pay tax at a maximum rate of 25 percent on their **unrecaptured § 1250 gains.** These gains represent that part of the gain on § 1250 property that is attributable to depreciation that was not recaptured by § 1250.

The procedure for computing this amount involves three distinct steps:

Step 1. Determine the part of the gain that is attributable to *depreciation deductions* claimed in prior years. The excess of the property's sale proceeds over its original basis is not affected. It remains § 1231 gain.

Step 2. Apply § 1250 to determine the portion of the gain calculated in Step 1 that is recaptured as ordinary income. This portion is taxable at rates of 15 percent to 39.6 percent, depending upon the seller's tax bracket, as explained previously.

Step 3. Subtract the gain recaptured under § 1250 (Step 2) from the gain derived in Step 1. This amount is the *unrecaptured § 1250 gain.*

EXAMPLE 59

Linda placed two apartment buildings in service during 1986 at a cost of $100,000 each. Assume that on each building, she claimed accelerated depreciation deductions of $78,000 and that straight-line depreciation would have been $64,000. Thus, her adjusted basis for each building is $22,000 ($100,000 cost − $78,000 depreciation deducted), and her potential § 1250 recapture is $14,000 ($78,000 accelerated depreciation − $64,000 straight-line). She now sells these buildings for $96,000 and $110,000, respectively, and computes her gain as follows:

	Building A	Building B
Amount realized	$ 96,000	$110,000
Adjusted basis	(22,000)	(22,000)
Gain realized	$ 74,000	$ 88,000
Depreciation recaptured per § 1250	(14,000)	(14,000)
Remaining gain	$ 60,000	$ 74,000
Unrecaptured § 1250 gain	(60,000)	(64,000)
§ 1231 gain	None	$ 10,000

▼

For property placed in service after 1986, § 1250 generally does not apply, because such property may use only straight-line depreciation. As a result, *all* of the gain attributable to depreciation on such assets is unrecaptured § 1250 gain.

EXAMPLE 60

Assume the same facts as in the preceding example, except that Linda placed the buildings in service in 1987, so straight-line depreciation was taken. Her adjusted basis for each building, therefore, is $36,000 ($100,000 cost − $64,000 depreciation deducted). Her gains are computed as follows:

	Building A	Building B
Amount realized	$ 96,000	$110,000
Adjusted basis	(36,000)	(36,000)
Gain realized	$ 60,000	$ 74,000
Unrecaptured § 1250 gain	(60,000)	(64,000)
§ 1231 gain	None	$ 10,000

If § 1245 applies, all of the depreciation taken is recaptured as ordinary income, and there is *no* unrecaptured § 1250 gain. So, if building B in Example 59 were an office building, $78,000 of the gain would be ordinary income per § 1245, and the remaining $10,000 would be § 1231 gain.

EXCEPTIONS TO §§ 1245 AND 1250

Recapture under §§ 1245 and 1250 does not apply to the following transactions.

GIFTS

The recapture potential carries over to the donee.[33]

EXAMPLE 61

Wade gives his daughter, Helen, § 1245 property with an adjusted basis of $1,000. The amount of recapture potential is $700. Helen uses the property in her business and claims further depreciation of $100 before selling it for $1,900. Helen's recognized gain is $1,000 [$1,900 amount realized − $900 adjusted basis ($1,000 carryover basis − $100 depreciation taken by Helen)], of which $800 is recaptured as ordinary income ($100 depreciation taken by Helen + $700 recapture potential carried over from Wade). The remaining gain of $200 is § 1231 gain. Even if Helen had used the property for personal purposes, the $700 recapture potential would have carried over. ▼

DEATH

Although not an attractive tax planning approach, death eliminates all recapture potential.[34] In other words, recapture potential does not carry over from a decedent to an estate or an heir.

EXAMPLE 62

Assume the same facts as in the preceding example, except that Helen receives the property as a result of Wade's death. The $700 recapture potential from Wade is extinguished at his

---

[33] §§ 1245(b)(1) and 1250(d)(1) and Reg. §§ 1.1245−4(a)(1) and 1.1250−3(a)(1).

[34] §§ 1245(b)(2) and 1250(d)(2).

death. Helen has a basis in the property equal to its fair market value (assume $1,700) at Wade's death. She will have a $300 gain when the property is sold because the selling price ($1,900) exceeds the property's adjusted basis of $1,600 ($1,700 basis to Helen − $100 depreciation) by $300. Because of § 1245, Helen has ordinary income of $100. The remaining gain of $200 is § 1231 gain. ▼

CHARITABLE TRANSFERS

The recapture potential reduces the amount of the charitable contribution deduction.[35]

▼ EXAMPLE 63

Bullfinch Corporation donates to a museum § 1245 property with a fair market value of $10,000 and an adjusted basis of $7,000. Assume that the amount of recapture potential is $2,000 (the amount of recapture that would occur if the property were sold). The company's charitable contribution deduction (subject to the limitations discussed in Chapter 4) is $8,000 ($10,000 fair market value − $2,000 recapture potential). ▼

CERTAIN NONTAXABLE TRANSACTIONS

In certain transactions, the transferor's adjusted basis for the property carries over to the transferee.[36] The recapture potential also carries over to the transferee.[37] Included in this category are transfers of property pursuant to the following:

- Nontaxable incorporations under § 351.
- Certain liquidations of subsidiary companies under § 332.
- Nontaxable contributions to a partnership under § 721.
- Nontaxable corporate reorganizations.

Gain may be recognized in these transactions if boot is received. If gain is recognized, it is treated as ordinary income to the extent of the recapture potential or the recognized gain, whichever is lower.[38]

LIKE-KIND EXCHANGES (§ 1031) AND INVOLUNTARY CONVERSIONS (§ 1033)

As explained in Chapter 7, realized gain is recognized to the extent of boot received under § 1031. Realized gain is also recognized to the extent the proceeds from an involuntary conversion are not reinvested in similar property under § 1033. Such recognized gain is subject to recapture as ordinary income under §§ 1245 and 1250. Any remaining recapture potential carries over to the property received in the exchange.

▼ EXAMPLE 64

Crane Corporation exchanges § 1245 property with an adjusted basis of $300 for § 1245 property with a fair market value of $6,000 plus $1,000 cash (boot). The exchange qualifies as a like-kind exchange under § 1031. Crane's realized gain is $6,700 ($7,000 amount realized − $300 adjusted basis of property). Since Crane received boot of $1,000, it recognizes gain to this extent. Assuming the recapture potential is $7,500, Crane recognizes § 1245 gain of $1,000. The remaining recapture potential of $6,500 carries over to the like-kind property received. ▼

---

[35] § 170(e)(1)(A) and Reg. § 1.170A–4(b)(1). In certain circumstances, § 1231 gain also reduces the amount of the charitable contribution. See § 170(e)(1)(B).

[36] §§ 1245(b)(3) and 1250(d)(3) and Reg. §§ 1.1245–4(c) and 1.1250–3(c).

[37] Reg. §§ 1.1245–2(a)(4) and (c)(2) and 1.1250–2(d)(1) and (3) and –3(c)(3).

[38] §§ 1245(b)(3) and 1250(d)(3) and Reg. §§ 1.1245–4(c) and 1.1250–3(c).

SPECIAL RECAPTURE PROVISIONS

SALE OF DEPRECIABLE PROPERTY BETWEEN CERTAIN RELATED PARTIES

Gain from related-party sales or exchanges of property that is depreciable by the new owner is recognized as ordinary income.[39] This provision applies to both direct and indirect sales or exchanges. A **related party** is defined as an individual and his or her controlled corporation or partnership or a taxpayer and any trust in which the taxpayer (or the taxpayer's spouse) is a beneficiary.

EXAMPLE 65

Isabella sells a personal-use automobile to her controlled corporation. The automobile, which was purchased two years ago, originally cost $5,000 and is sold for $7,000. The automobile is to be used in the corporation's business. If the related-party provision did not exist, Isabella would realize a $2,000 long-term capital gain, and her controlled corporation would be entitled to depreciate the automobile based upon its purchase price of $7,000. Under the related-party provision, Isabella's $2,000 gain is ordinary income. ▼

INSTALLMENT SALES

The recapture provisions effectively supersede the installment method of reporting gain discussed in Chapter 6. Section 453(i) provides that any § 1245 or § 1250 recapture *must* be recognized in the year of sale, and only the remaining gain is eligible for the installment method.

EXAMPLE 66

Olaf & Sons, a partnership, sold an apartment building for $50,000 cash and a $75,000 note due in two years. The adjusted basis of the property was $25,000, and the depreciation recapture under § 1250 is potentially $40,000. The partnership's gain is computed as follows:

Amount realized	$125,000
Adjusted basis	(25,000)
Total gain	$100,000
§ 1250 recapture	(40,000)
§ 1231 gain	$ 60,000

In the year of sale, Olaf & Sons must report the entire $40,000 of § 1250 ordinary income plus a portion of the $60,000 of § 1231 gain determined by applying the installment method to that gain:

$$\frac{\S\ 1231\ \text{gain}}{\text{Contract price}} \times \text{Payment received} = \frac{\$60,000}{\$125,000} \times \$50,000 = \$24,000.$$

Thus, the reported gain in the year of sale is $64,000 ($40,000 of § 1250 recapture + $24,000 of § 1231 gain), and the remaining $36,000 of § 1231 gain ($60,000 − $24,000) will be recognized as the $75,000 note is collected. ▼

INTANGIBLE DRILLING COSTS

Taxpayers may elect to either *expense or capitalize* intangible drilling and development costs for oil, gas, or geothermal properties.[40] **Intangible drilling and development costs (IDC)** include operator (one who holds a working or operating

---

[39] § 1239.

[40] § 263(c).

interest in any tract or parcel of land) expenditures for wages, fuel, repairs, hauling, and supplies. These expenditures must be incident to and necessary for the drilling of wells and preparation of wells for production. In most instances, taxpayers elect to expense IDC to maximize tax deductions during drilling.

Intangible drilling and development costs are subject to § 1254 recapture when the property is disposed of. The gain on the disposition of the property is subject to recapture as ordinary income.

REPORTING PROCEDURES

Noncapital gains and losses are reported on Form 4797, Sales of Business Property. Before filling out Form 4797, however, Form 4684, Casualties and Thefts, Part B, must be completed to determine whether any casualties will enter into the § 1231 computation procedure. Recall that gains from § 1231 asset casualties may be recaptured by § 1245 or § 1250. These gains will not appear on Form 4684. The § 1231 gains and nonpersonal-use long-term capital gains are netted against § 1231 and nonpersonal-use long-term capital losses on Form 4684 to determine if there is a net gain to transfer to Form 4797, Part I.

KEY TERMS

Additional depreciation, 8–34
Capital asset, 8–2
Capital gain, 8–3
Capital loss, 8–3
Collectibles, 8–17
Franchise, 8–11
Holding period, 8–13
Intangible drilling and development costs (IDC), 8–42
Lessee, 8–12
Lessor, 8–12

Long-term nonpersonal-use capital assets, 8–26
Net capital gain, 8–19
Net capital loss, 8–19
Options, 8–8
Patent, 8–10
Qualified small business stock, 8–23
Related party, 8–42
Sale or exchange, 8–7
Section 1231 gains and losses, 8–25

Section 1231 lookback, 8–30
Section 1231 property, 8–25
Section 1245 property, 8–32
Section 1245 recapture, 8–31
Section 1250 property, 8–34
Section 1250 recapture, 8–34
Short sale, 8–15
Unrecaptured § 1250 gain, 8–39

PROBLEM MATERIALS

1. Nancy had three property transactions during the year. She sold a vacation home used for personal purposes at a $21,000 loss. The home had been held for five years and had never been rented. Nancy also sold an antique clock for $3,500 that she had inherited from her grandmother. The clock was valued in Nancy's grandmother's estate at $2,000. Nancy owned the clock for only four months. Nancy sold these assets to finance her full-time occupation as a song writer. Near the end of the year, Nancy sold one of the songs she had written two years earlier. She received cash of $38,000 and a royalty interest in revenues derived from the merchandising of the song. Nancy had no tax basis for the song. What is Nancy's gross income?

2. Hyacinth, Inc., is a dealer in securities. The firm has spotted a fast-rising company and would like to buy and hold its stock for investment. The stock is currently selling for $15 per share, and Hyacinth thinks it will climb to $63 a share within two years. How can Hyacinth ensure that any gain it realizes will be taxed as long-term capital gain? Draft a letter responding to Hyacinth's inquiry. The firm's address is 200 Morningside Drive, Hattisburg, MS 39406.

3. Amaryllis Co. has owned a large tract of land for 15 years and subdivides it for sale. Assume Amaryllis meets all the requirements of § 1237. During the first year of sales, Amaryllis sells 20 lots for $30,000 each. Its selling expenses are 7% of the sale price of each lot. Amaryllis has a basis of $21,000 in each lot. Compute Amaryllis's total gain from the sale of these lots and indicate the nature of the gain.

4. Swan Songs, Inc., is in the business of buying song copyrights from struggling songwriters, holding those copyrights, and then reselling the songs to major record companies and singers. Swan has a four-month option to purchase a song copyright. The firm paid $2,000 for this option. A famous singer has heard the song and is willing to buy the option for $10,000. Swan thinks the song may be worth $35,000 in six months. If Swan exercises the option, it will have to pay $20,000 for the song. Assuming Swan is in the 34% tax bracket, which of these alternatives will give it a better after-tax cash flow?

5. Daniel purchased a one-year option on 20 acres of farmland for $45,000. Daniel's plans for the property did not work out, so he let the option expire unexercised. What tax issues does Daniel face in determining how to treat the $45,000?

6. An investment partnership is looking for vacant land to buy. For $10,000, it is granted an 11-month option to buy 10 acres of vacant land for $300,000. The owner (who is holding the land for investment) paid $12,000 for the land several years ago.
   a. Does the landowner have gross income when $10,000 is received for granting the option?
   b. Does the partnership have an asset when the option is granted?
   c. If the option lapses, does the landowner have a recognized gain? If so, what type of gain? Does the partnership have a recognized loss? If so, what type of loss?
   d. If the option is exercised and an additional $300,000 is paid for the land, how much recognized gain does the seller have? What type of gain? What is the partnership's tax basis for the property?

7. Vireo Corporation owns a patent on a part that Teal Corporation wishes to use as a component in a product it manufactures. Vireo had purchased the patent from the inventor before the inventor reduced the patent to practice. Vireo had intended to use the patented part in its business, but found that the part was not suitable. Teal is willing to pay Vireo $5,000 per month plus 1% of the manufactured cost of the part. How should Vireo construct the contract with Teal so that the $5,000 per month and 1% of manufactured cost are long-term capital gain?

8. Freys, Inc., sells a 12-year franchise to Red Company. The franchise contains many restrictions on how Red may operate its store. For instance, Red cannot use less than Grade 10 Idaho potatoes, must fry the potatoes at a constant 410 degrees, dress store personnel in Freys-approved uniforms, and have a Freys sign that meets detailed specifications on size, color, and construction. When the franchise contract is signed, Red makes a noncontingent $40,000 payment to Freys. During the same year, Red pays Freys $25,000—14% of Red's sales. How does Freys treat each of these payments? How does Red treat each of the payments?

9. Irene lives in an apartment near her college campus. Her lease runs out in July 1999, but her landlord could sell the building if he can convince all the tenants to cancel their leases and move out by the end of 1998. The landlord has offered Irene $1,000 to cancel her lease. Irene's lease began on August 1, 1998. What tax factors should Irene consider in deciding whether to take the landlord's offer?

10. Thrasher Corporation sells short 100 shares of ARC stock at $20 per share on January 15, 1998. It buys 200 shares of ARC stock on April 1, 1998, at $25 per share. On

May 2, 1998, Thrasher closes the short sale by delivering 100 of the shares purchased on April 1.

   a. What are the amount and nature of Thrasher's loss upon closing the short sale?
   b. When does the holding period for the remaining 100 shares begin?
   c. If Thrasher sells (at $27 per share) the remaining 100 shares on January 20, 1999, what will be the nature of its gain or loss?

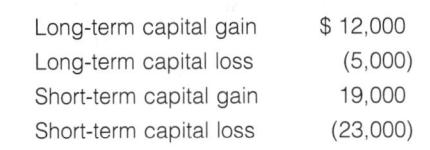

11. Elaine Case has the following transactions this year:

Long-term capital gain	$ 12,000
Long-term capital loss	(5,000)
Short-term capital gain	19,000
Short-term capital loss	(23,000)

    What is Elaine's net capital gain or loss? Draft a letter to Elaine describing how the net capital gain or loss will be treated on her tax return. Assume Elaine's income from other sources puts her in the 36% bracket. Elaine's address is 300 Ireland Avenue, Shepherdstown, WV 25443.

12. Suzanne has taxable income of $140,000 as of November 30 of this year. She wants to sell a Rodin sculpture that has appreciated $80,000 since she purchased it eight years ago, but she does not want to pay more than $10,000 of additional tax on the transaction. Suzanne also owns various stocks, some of which are currently worth less than their basis. How can she achieve her desired result?

13. Silver, Inc., has determined its taxable income as $115,000 before considering the results of its capital gain or loss transactions. Silver has a short-term capital loss of $14,000, a long-term capital loss of $28,000, and a short-term capital gain of $29,000. What is Silver's taxable income, and what (if any) are the amount and nature of its capital loss carryover?

14. June owns a sole proprietorship that Mallard, Inc., is going to purchase. They have agreed on a price for all the assets except goodwill and June's covenant not to compete against Mallard. June is willing to grant Mallard a two-year covenant not to compete for only $1 of compensation, but would like $25,000 for the business goodwill. Mallard would like to pay June $25,000 for the covenant not to compete and only $1 for the business goodwill. June is in the 36% tax bracket, and Mallard is in the 34% tax bracket. Which of these approaches is better for June? For Mallard?

15. Sally lives in an area that was hit hard by a hurricane. She has correctly determined that she has a $15,000 business property long-term casualty loss and a $11,000 business property long-term casualty gain. What tax issues must Sally deal with?

16. The taxpayer is an antiques collector and is going to sell an antique purchased many years ago for a large gain. The facts and circumstances indicate that the taxpayer might be classified as a dealer rather than an investor in antiques. The taxpayer will save $40,000 in taxes if the gain is treated as long-term capital gain rather than as ordinary income. The taxpayer is considering the following options as ways to assure the $40,000 tax savings:

    - Give the antique to his daughter, who is an investment banker, to sell.
    - Merely assume that he has held the antique as an investment.
    - Exchange the antique in a like-kind exchange for another antique he wants.

    One of the tax preparers the taxpayer has contacted has said he would be willing to prepare the return under the second option. Would you be willing to do so? Why? Evaluate the other options.

17. A painting that Tulip & Co. held for investment was destroyed in a flood. The painting was insured, and Tulip had a $30,000 gain from this casualty. It also had a $27,000 loss from an uninsured antique vase that was destroyed by the flood. The vase was also held for investment. Tulip had no other property transactions during the year and has

no nonrecaptured § 1231 losses from prior years. Compute Tulip's net gain or loss and identify how it would be treated. Also, write a letter to Tulip explaining the nature of the gain or loss. Tulip's address is 2000 Meridian Road, Hannibal Point, MO 34901.

18. Harold, a CPA, has a new client who recently moved to town. Harold prepares the client's current-year tax return, which shows a net § 1231 gain. Harold calls the client to request copies of the returns for the preceding five years to determine if there are any § 1231 lookback losses. The client says that the returns are "still buried in the moving mess somewhere" and cannot be found. The client also says that he does not remember any § 1231 net losses on the prior-year returns. What should Harold do? Justify your answer.

19. Yellow, Inc., has the following net § 1231 results for each of the years shown. What is the nature of the net gain in 1997 and 1998?

Tax Year	Net § 1231 Loss	Net § 1231 Gain
1993	$15,000	
1994	17,000	
1995	22,000	
1996		$10,000
1997		20,000
1998		29,000

20. Iris Co. owns two parcels of land (§ 1231 assets). One parcel can be sold at a loss of $50,000, and the other parcel can be sold at a gain of $60,000. The company has no nonrecaptured § 1231 losses from prior years. The parcels could be sold at any time because potential purchasers are abundant. The company has a $45,000 short-term capital loss carryover from a prior tax year and no capital assets that could be sold to generate long-term capital gains. What should Iris do based upon these facts? (Assume tax rates are constant and ignore the present value of future cash flow.)

21. Gray Industries (a sole proprietorship) sold three § 1231 assets during 1998. Data on these property dispositions are as follows:

Asset	Cost	Acquired	Depreciation	Sold for	Sold on
Rack	$100,000	10/10/93	$60,000	$55,000	10/10/98
Forklift	35,000	10/16/94	23,000	5,000	10/10/98
Bin	87,000	3/12/97	34,000	60,000	10/10/98

a. Determine the amount and the character of the recognized gain or loss from the disposition of each asset.
b. Assuming Gray has no nonrecaptured net § 1231 losses from prior years, how much of the 1998 recognized gains are treated as long-term capital gains?

22. Green Industries (a sole proprietorship) sold three § 1231 assets during 1998. Data on these property dispositions are as follows:

Asset	Cost	Acquired	Depreciation	Sold for	Sold on
Rack	$100,000	10/10/93	$60,000	$155,000	10/10/98
Forklift	35,000	10/16/94	23,000	5,000	10/10/98
Bin	87,000	3/12/97	34,000	60,000	10/10/98

a. Determine the amount and the character of the recognized gain or loss from the disposition of each asset.
b. Assuming Green has $5,000 nonrecaptured net § 1231 losses from the five prior years, how much of the 1998 recognized gains are treated as long-term capital gains?

CHAPTER 8 Property Transactions: Capital Gains and Losses, Section 1231, and Recapture Provisions   8–47

23. Gardenia Manufacturing purchases a $2,000,000 propane storage tank and places it on a permanent framework outside its plant. The propane is drawn from the tank through a hose and valve system into the burners underneath Gardenia's chemical vats. After $800,000 of cost recovery has been taken on the tank, it is sold for $1,300,000. What are the nature and amount of Gardenia's gain or loss from the disposition of the tank?

24. On December 1, 1996, Gray Manufacturing Company (a corporation) purchased another company's assets, including a patent. The patent was used in Gray's manufacturing operations; $40,500 was allocated to the patent, and it was amortized at the rate of $225 per month. On June 30, 1998, Gray sold the patent for $60,000. Nineteen months of amortization had been taken on the patent. What are the amount and nature of the gain Gray recognizes on the disposition of the patent? Write a letter to Gray discussing the treatment of the gain. Gray's address is 6734 Grover Street, Back Bay Harbor, ME 23890. The letter should be addressed to Siddim Sadatha, Controller.

25. Dave is the sole proprietor of a trampoline shop. During 1998, the following transactions occurred:

    - Unimproved land adjacent to the store was condemned by the city on February 1. The condemnation proceeds were $25,000. The land, acquired in 1982, had an allocable basis of $40,000. Dave has additional parking across the street and plans to use the condemnation proceeds to build his inventory.

    - A truck used to deliver trampolines was sold on January 2 for $3,500. The truck was purchased on January 2, 1994, for $6,000. On the date of sale, the adjusted basis was $2,509.

    - Dave sold an antique rowing machine at an auction. Net proceeds were $3,900. The rowing machine was purchased as used equipment 17 years ago for $5,200 and is fully depreciated.

    - Dave sold an apartment building for $200,000 on September 1. The rental property was purchased on September 1, 1995, for $150,000 and was being depreciated over a 27.5-year life using the straight-line method. At the date of sale, the adjusted basis was $124,783.

    - Dave sold a Buick on May 1 for $9,600. The vehicle had been used exclusively for personal purposes. It was purchased on September 1, 1994, for $20,800.

    - An adding machine used by Dave's bookkeeper was sold on June 1. Net proceeds of the sale were $135. The machine was purchased on June 2, 1994, for $350. It was being depreciated over a five-year life employing the straight-line method. The adjusted basis on the date of sale was $95.

    - Dave's trampoline stretching machine (owned two years) was stolen on May 5, but the business's insurance company will not pay any of the machine's value because Dave failed to pay the insurance premium. The machine had a fair market value of $8,000 and an adjusted basis of $6,000 at the time of theft.

    - Dave had AGI of $36,000 from sources other than those described above.

    - Dave has no nonrecaptured § 1231 lookback losses.

    a. For each transaction, what are the amount and nature of recognized gain or loss?
    b. What is Dave's 1998 AGI?

26. Macklin, a sole proprietor, used a drafting table in his business and completely depreciated its $3,700 cost. He now purchases a new drafting table for his business and takes the old drafting table home to use as a workbench. A similar workbench for home use would cost $450. Should Macklin report anything on his tax return regarding this conversion of his old drafting table?

27. On January 1, 1986, Cora Hassant acquired depreciable real property for $100,000. She used accelerated depreciation to compute the asset's cost recovery. The asset was sold

for $89,000 on January 3, 1998, when its adjusted basis was $29,600. Straight-line cost recovery for the period of time the asset was held would have been $63,300.
   a. What are the amount and nature of the gain if the real property was residential?
   b. What are the amount and nature of the gain if the real property was nonresidential?
   c. Cora is curious about how the recapture rules differ for residential rental real estate acquired in 1986 and for residential rental real estate acquired in 1987 and thereafter. Write a letter to Cora explaining the differences. Her address is 2345 Westridge Street #23, Homer, MT 67342.

28. Goshawk Corporation acquired residential rental property on January 3, 1986, for $400,000. The property was depreciated using the accelerated method and a 19-year recovery period under ACRS. Goshawk has claimed depreciation of $281,600. Straight-line depreciation during the period would have been $253,200. The corporation sold the property on January 1, 1998, for $440,000. What is the gain on the sale, and how is it taxed?

29. Assume that the property in the preceding problem was a commercial building, and that Goshawk Corporation used the straight-line method of depreciation with a 19-year recovery period under ACRS. What would be the gain, and how would it be taxed?

30. Joanne is in the 39.6% tax bracket and owns depreciable business equipment that she purchased several years ago for $135,000; she has taken $100,000 of depreciation on the equipment, and it is worth $85,000. Joanne's niece, Susan, is starting a new business and is short of cash. Susan has asked Joanne to gift the equipment to her so that Susan can use it in her business. Joanne no longer needs the equipment. Identify the alternatives available to Joanne if she wishes to help Susan and the tax effects of those alternatives. (Assume all alternatives involve the business equipment in one way or another, and ignore the gift tax.)

31. Gregor owns business equipment with a $55,000 adjusted basis; he paid $100,000 for the equipment, and it is currently worth $73,000. Gregor dies suddenly, and his son Adrian inherits the property. What is Adrian's basis for the property, and what happens to the § 1245 depreciation recapture potential?

32. Orange Corporation sells depreciable equipment for $59,000 to its sole shareholder, Jane. Orange had a $45,000 adjusted basis for the equipment and had originally paid $85,000 for it. Jane will use the equipment in her sole proprietorship business. The $59,000 sale price is the property's fair market value at the time of the sale. What are the consequences of this sale for Orange? For Jane?

33. Jay Company, Inc., sold three items of business equipment for a total of $300,000. None of the equipment was appraised to determine its value. Jay's cost and adjusted basis for the assets are as follows:

Asset	Cost	Adjusted Basis
Skidder	$230,000	$ 40,000
Driller	120,000	60,000
Platform	620,000	–0–
Total	$970,000	$100,000

Jay has been unable to establish the fair market values of the three assets. All it can determine is that combined they were worth $300,000 to the buyer in this arm's length transaction. How should Jay allocate the sales price and figure the gain or loss on the sale of the three assets?

34. Longspur Investments, Inc., sold property in 1998 for $250,000 cash and a note of $750,000 due in 1999. Longspur's basis in the property was $400,000, and $40,000 of the gain is subject to depreciation recapture under § 1245. Longspur is not a dealer in real estate. What is Longspur's gain in 1998, and how will it be taxed?

RESEARCH PROBLEMS

*Note: The **RIA OnPoint System 4 Student Version CD-ROM** available with this text can be used in preparing solutions to the Research Problems. Alternatively, tax research materials contained in a standard tax library can be used.*

35. The Banc Two Mortgage Company requires a fee of 1% of the remaining mortgage balance when a mortgage is paid off early. In the current year, Banc Two received $760,000 of such fees. What is the nature of the fee: ordinary income or capital gain?

36. Sidney owns a professional football franchise. He has received an offer of $80 million for the franchise, all the football equipment, the rights to concession receipts, the rights to a stadium lease, and the rights to all the player contracts he owns. Most of the players have been with the team for quite a long time and have contracts that were signed several years ago. The contracts have been substantially depreciated. Sidney is concerned about potential § 1245 recapture when the contracts are sold. He has heard about "previously unrecaptured depreciation with respect to initial contracts" and would like to know more about it. Find a definition for that phrase and write an explanation of it.

37. Gary makes a gift to Barbara of the copyright on his song, "I Love the Spartans." The song has a basis of $20,000 to Gary. Gary had owned the copyright for two years. The copyright has a fair market value of $25,000 at the date of the gift. Three years after receiving the copyright, Barbara sells it to Jim for $30,000.
    a. What is Barbara's recognized gain on the sale?
    b. What is the nature of Barbara's gain?

CHAPTER 9

Corporations: Organization, Capital Structure, and Operating Rules

LEARNING OBJECTIVES

After completing Chapter 9, you should be able to:

1. Identify the tax consequences of incorporating and transferring assets to controlled corporations.

2. Understand the special rules that apply when a corporation assumes a shareholder's liability.

3. Recognize the basis issues relevant to the shareholder and the corporation.

4. Understand the tax aspects of the capital structure of a corporation.

5. Recognize the tax differences between debt and equity investments.

6. Understand the tax rules unique to corporations.

7. Compute the corporate income tax.

8. Explain the tax rules unique to multiple corporations.

9. Describe the reporting process for corporations.

OUTLINE

An Introduction to Corporate Tax, 9–2
Comparison of Corporations and Other Forms of Doing Business, 9–3
Nontax Considerations, 9–4
Entity Classification prior to 1997, 9–5
Entity Classification after 1996, 9–6
Organization of and Transfers to Controlled Corporations, 9–8
In General, 9–8
Transfer of Property, 9–10
Stock, 9–11
Control of the Corporation, 9–11
Assumption of Liabilities—§ 357, 9–15
Basis Determination and Other Issues, 9–18
Recapture Considerations, 9–20
Capital Structure of a Corporation, 9–21
Capital Contributions, 9–21
Debt in the Capital Structure, 9–22
Corporate Operations, 9–24
Deductions Available Only to Corporations, 9–24
Determining the Corporate Income Tax Liability, 9–27
Tax Liability of Related Corporations, 9–28
Controlled Groups, 9–29
Procedural Matters, 9–32
Filing Requirements for Corporations, 9–32
Estimated Tax Payments, 9–33
Reconciliation of Taxable Income and Financial Net Income, 9–34
Form 1120 Illustrated, 9–35
Consolidated Returns, 9–38
Summary, 9–38

Business operations may be conducted in a number of different forms. As with many business decisions, consideration must be given to the tax consequences of choosing a particular business entity. This chapter deals with the unique tax consequences of operating an entity as a corporation, including:

- Classification of the entity as a corporation.
- The tax consequences to the shareholders and the corporation upon the formation of the corporation.
- The capital structure of the corporation.
- Determination of the corporate income tax liability.
- Corporate tax filing requirements.

AN INTRODUCTION TO CORPORATE TAX

Corporations are governed by Subchapter C or Subchapter S of the Internal Revenue Code. Those governed by Subchapter C are referred to as **C corporations** or **regular corporations**. Corporations governed by Subchapter S are referred to as **S corporations**.

S corporations, which do not pay Federal income tax, are similar to partnerships in that net profit or loss flows through to the shareholders to be reported on their separate returns. Also like partnerships, S corporations do not aggregate all income and expense items in computing net profit or loss. Certain items flow through to the shareholders and retain their separate character when reported on the shareholders' returns. See Chapter 12 for detailed coverage of S corporations.

Unlike proprietorships, partnerships, and S corporations, C corporations are taxpaying entities. This results in what is known as a *double tax* effect. A C corporation reports its income and expenses on Form 1120 (or Form 1120–A, the corporate short form). The corporation computes tax on the taxable income reported on the corporate tax return using the rate schedule applicable to corporations (refer to the rate schedule inside the front cover of this text). When a corporation distributes its income, the corporation's shareholders report dividend income on their own tax returns. Thus, income that has already been taxed at the corporate level is also taxed at the shareholder level.

EXAMPLE 1
Tan Corporation files Form 1120, which reports taxable income of $100,000. The corporation pays tax of $22,250. This leaves $77,750, all of which is distributed as a dividend to Carla, the sole shareholder of the corporation. Carla, who has income from other sources and has a 39.6% marginal tax rate, pays income tax of $30,789 on the distribution. The combined tax on the corporation's income is $53,039. ▼

EXAMPLE 2
Assume the same facts as in Example 1, except that the business is organized as a sole proprietorship. Carla reports the $100,000 net profit from the business on her tax return and pays tax of $39,600 ($100,000 net profit × 39.6% marginal rate). Therefore, operating the business as a sole proprietorship results in a tax saving of $13,439 ($53,039 tax from Example 1 − $39,600). ▼

Shareholders in closely held corporations frequently attempt to avoid double taxation by paying out all the profit of the corporation as salary to themselves.

EXAMPLE 3
Orange Corporation has net income of $180,000 during the year ($300,000 revenue − $120,000 operating expenses). Emilio is the sole shareholder of Orange Corporation. In an effort to avoid tax at the corporate level, Emilio has Orange pay him a salary of $180,000, which results in zero taxable income for the corporation. ▼

Will the strategy described in Example 3 effectively avoid double taxation? The answer depends on whether the compensation paid to the shareholder is *reasonable*. Section 162 provides that compensation is deductible only to the extent that it is reasonable in amount. The IRS is aware that many taxpayers use this strategy to bail out corporate profits and, in an audit, looks closely at compensation expense. If the IRS believes that compensation is too high based on the amount and quality of services performed by the shareholder, the compensation deduction of the corporation is reduced to a reasonable amount. Compensation that is determined to be unreasonable is usually treated as a constructive dividend to the shareholder and is not deductible by the corporation.

EXAMPLE 4
Assume the same facts as in Example 3, and that the IRS determines that $80,000 of the amount paid to Emilio is unreasonable compensation. As a result, $80,000 of the corporation's compensation deduction is disallowed and treated as a constructive dividend to Emilio. Orange has taxable income of $80,000. Emilio would report salary of $100,000 and a taxable dividend of $80,000. The net effect is that $80,000 is subject to double taxation. ▼

The unreasonable compensation issue is discussed in more detail in Chapter 10.

COMPARISON OF CORPORATIONS AND OTHER FORMS OF DOING BUSINESS

Comparison of the tax results in Examples 1 and 2 might lead to the conclusion that incorporation is not a wise tax strategy. In some cases that would be a correct conclusion, but in others it would not. In many situations, tax and nontax factors combine to make the corporate form of doing business the only reasonable choice.

Chapter 14 presents a detailed comparison of sole proprietorships, partnerships, S corporations, and C corporations as forms of doing business. However, it is appropriate at this point to consider some of the tax and nontax factors that favor corporations over other business entities.

Consideration of tax factors requires an examination of the corporate rate structure. As can be seen from the rate schedule inside the front cover of this textbook, corporate rates on taxable income up to $75,000 are lower than individual rates for persons in the 28 percent and higher brackets. Therefore, corporate tax will be lower than individual tax. Furthermore, there is no corporate marginal rate that is higher than the 39.6 percent top bracket for individuals. When dividends are paid, however, the double taxation problem occurs. This leads to an important question: Will incorporation ever result in Federal income tax savings? The following example illustrates a situation where this occurs.

EXAMPLE 5

Ned, an individual in the 39.6% tax bracket, owns a business that produces net profit of $50,000 each year. Ned has significant income from other sources, so he does not withdraw any of the profit from the business. If the business is operated as a proprietorship, Ned's Federal income tax on the net profit of the business is $19,800 ($50,000 × 39.6%). However, if the business is operated as a corporation and pays no dividends, the tax will be $7,500 ($50,000 × 15%). Operating as a corporation saves $12,300 of Federal income tax each year. If Ned invests his $12,300 tax savings each year for several years, it is possible that a positive cash flow will result, even though Ned will be required to pay tax on dividends distributed by the corporation some time in the future. ▼

Another tax consideration involves the nature of dividend income. All income and expense items of a proprietorship retain their character when reported on the proprietor's tax return. In the case of a partnership, several separately reported items (e.g., charitable contributions and long-term capital gains) retain their character when passed through to the partners. However, the tax attributes of income and expense items of a corporation are lost as they pass through the corporate entity to the shareholders.

EXAMPLE 6

During the current year, Waxwing Company receives tax-exempt interest, which is distributed to its owners. If Waxwing Company is a regular corporation, the distribution to the shareholders constitutes a taxable dividend. The fact that it originated from tax-exempt interest is of no consequence. On the other hand, if Waxwing is a partnership or an S corporation, the tax-exempt interest retains its identity and passes through tax-free to the individual owners. ▼

Losses of a C corporation are treated differently than losses of a proprietorship, partnership, or S corporation. A loss incurred by a proprietorship may be deductible by the owner, because all income and expense items are reported by the proprietor. Partnership and S corporation losses are passed through the entity and may be deductible by the partners or shareholders. C corporation losses, however, have no effect on the taxable income of the shareholders.

NONTAX CONSIDERATIONS

Nontax considerations will sometimes override tax considerations and lead to the conclusion that a business should be operated as a corporation. The following are some of the more important nontax considerations:

- Sole proprietors and *general* partners in partnerships face the danger of *unlimited liability*. That is, creditors of the business may file claims not only against the assets of the business but also against the *personal* assets of proprietors or general partners. Shareholders are protected from claims against their personal assets by state corporate law.

- The corporate form of business organization can provide a vehicle for raising large amounts of capital through widespread stock ownership. Most major businesses in the United States are operated as corporations.
- Shares of stock in a corporation are freely transferable, whereas a partner's sale of his or her partnership interest is subject to approval by the other partners.
- Shareholders may come and go, but a corporation can continue to exist. Death or withdrawal of a partner, on the other hand, may terminate the existing partnership and cause financial difficulties that result in dissolution of the entity. Thus, *continuity of life* is a distinct advantage of the corporate form of doing business.
- Corporations have *centralized management*. All management responsibility is assigned to a board of directors, who appoint officers to carry out the corporation's business. Partnerships, by contrast, may have decentralized management, in which every owner has a right to participate in the organization's business decisions; **limited partnerships**, though, may have centralized management. Centralized management is essential for the smooth operation of a widely held business.

ENTITY CLASSIFICATION PRIOR TO 1997

Prior to 1997 the definition of a corporation generally included "associations, joint stock companies, and insurance companies." What Congress originally intended by including **associations** in the definition has never been clear. To some extent, judicial decisions clarified the status of associations and the relationship between associations and corporations.

The designation given to the entity under state law was not controlling. In one case, an entity that was a business **trust** under state law was deemed to be an association (and therefore taxable as a corporation) for Federal income tax purposes.[1] In another case, a partnership of physicians was held to be an association even though state law applicable to the tax year in question prohibited the practice of medicine in the corporate form.[2] As an association, the partnership was taxed as a corporation.

Whether an entity was considered an association for Federal income tax purposes depended upon the number of corporate characteristics it possessed. Corporate characteristics included the following:[3]

1. Associates.
2. An objective to carry on a business and divide the gains.
3. Continuity of life.
4. Centralized management.
5. Limited liability.
6. Free transferability of interests.

An unincorporated organization was not classified as an association unless it possessed more corporate than noncorporate characteristics. In making the determination, the characteristics common to both corporate and noncorporate business organizations were disregarded.

---

[1] *Morrissey v. Comm.*, 36–1 USTC ¶9020, 16 AFTR 1274, 56 S.Ct. 289 (USSC, 1935).
[2] *U.S. v. Kinter*, 54–2 USTC ¶9626, 46 AFTR 995, 216 F.2d 418 (CA–9, 1954).
[3] Reg. § 301.7701.

Both corporations and partnerships generally have associates (shareholders and partners) and an objective to carry on a business and divide the gains. Thus, these two criteria were not considered when determining if a partnership was an association.

It then became a matter of determining whether the partnership possessed a majority of the remaining corporate characteristics (items 3 through 6). Did the partnership terminate upon the withdrawal or death of a partner (no continuity of life)? Was the management of the partnership centralized, or did all partners participate? Were all partners individually liable for the debts of the partnership, or was the liability of some limited to their actual investment in the partnership (limited partnership)? Could a partner freely transfer his or her interest without the consent of the other partners?

Courts had ruled that any partnership lacking two or more of these characteristics would not be classified as an association. Conversely, partnerships having three or more of these characteristics were classified as associations subject to the corporate income tax.[4]

For trusts, the first two characteristics were considered in testing for association status. The conventional type of trust often does not have associates and usually restricts its activities to investing rather than carrying on a trade or business. These characteristics, however, are possessed by corporations. Consequently, whether a trust qualified as an association depended upon the satisfaction of the first two corporate characteristics.

ENTITY CLASSIFICATION AFTER 1996

The determination of entity classification for Federal tax purposes was greatly simplified when the IRS issued its so-called *check-the-box* Regulations. These Regulations generally give taxpayers the ability to classify the tax status of a business entity, domestic or foreign, without analyzing the entity's nontax legal characteristics.[5] The new Regulations are effective January 1, 1997, regardless of an entity's tax accounting period.

The Regulations provide automatic classification rules for certain entities. Specifically, the following entities (referred to as *per se corporations*) are classified as corporations for tax purposes:[6]

- A business entity organized under a Federal, state, or Indian tribe statute that refers to the entity as incorporated or as a corporation, body corporate, or body politic.
- A business entity organized under a state statute that describes it as a joint-stock company or joint-stock association.
- An insurance company.
- A state-chartered business entity conducting banking activities if its deposits are insured by the FDIC or a similar program.
- A business entity wholly owned by a state or political subdivision.
- A business entity taxable as a corporation under other Sections of the Code (e.g., certain publicly traded partnerships).
- Certain foreign entities specifically identified in Regulation § 301.7701–2(b)(8).

---

[4] See *Zuckman v. U.S.*, 75–2 USTC ¶9778, 36 AFTR2d 6193, 524 F.2d 729 (Ct.Cls., 1975), and *P.G. Larson*, 66 T.C. 159 (1976).

[5] Reg. §§ 301.7701–1 through –4, and –6.
[6] Reg. § 301.7701–2(b).

Business Trusts. Pursuant to the Regulations, a trust is considered a business entity by reference to the real character of the organization. The fact that a business trust is technically cast in the trust form is not controlling.

Entities in Existence before January 1, 1997. For taxable periods *prior* to 1997, the tax classification of per se corporations is determined under the old entity classification rules (described above). Non-per se corporations may retain their pre-1997 classification for taxable periods *prior* to 1997 if certain conditions are met.[7] If these conditions are not met, non-per se corporations are classified under the old entity classification rules.

Per se corporations in existence before January 1, 1997, are automatically treated as corporations beginning in 1997, regardless of their prior classification. Non-per se entities in existence before January 1, 1997, generally can retain their previous (pre-1997) classification, if desired.

Entities Organized on or after January 1, 1997. All per se corporations, domestic or foreign, formed after January 1, 1997, are automatically treated as corporations for tax purposes. The regulations provide no exceptions to this rule. All other entities (*eligible entities*) are allowed to elect their classification for tax purposes as follows:

- Entities with more than one owner may elect to be classified as either a corporation or a partnership.
- Entities with only one owner may elect to be classified as a corporation or may disregard separate entity classification.

Default Classification for Domestic Eligible Entities. If a domestic eligible entity with more than one owner does not make an election, it is treated as a partnership for tax purposes. An eligible entity with only one owner is disregarded as an entity for tax purposes if entity classification is not elected.

Default Classification for Foreign Eligible Entities. Foreign eligible entities are given slightly different treatment if the entity's owner fails to make an election. In the case of entities with more than one owner, a foreign eligible entity will be treated as a partnership if any owner does not have limited liability. If all owners (regardless of the number of owners) have limited liability, the entity is treated as a corporation. Single-owner eligible entities are disregarded as entities if the owner does not have limited liability.

Elections. Eligible entities may elect their tax status by filing Form 8832, Entity Classification Election.[8] However, entities are not given the freedom to randomly change their status once an election has been made. Generally, an entity must wait 60 months before it is eligible to make a new election.

Related Issues. Taxpayers should carefully consider the tax consequences when determining entity classification. For example, if an eligible entity previously treated as a corporation elects to be treated as a partnership, the change in status is treated as a liquidation of the old corporation, followed by organization of a new partnership. Thus, the taxpayer must consider both the corporate liquidation provisions and the partnership organization rules.

---

[7] Reg. § 301.7701–3(f)(2).

[8] Reg. § 301.7701–3(c).

The inception of the **limited liability company (LLC)** in recent years led to many tax disputes prior to the issuing of the check-the-box Regulations. Due to the legal structure of LLCs, controversy arose over their tax classification. Like corporations, LLCs are allowed to operate with limited liability to the owners. In many states, however, LLCs do not possess the other corporate characteristics that would warrant their tax classification as a corporation. Thus, LLCs were frequently afforded partnership status for tax purposes. The *check-the-box* Regulations have clarified the previous tax uncertainties inherent in LLCs. Since LLCs are not technically "incorporated" under state law, they are not per se corporations (see list above). As mentioned, non-per se corporations are eligible entities and are given the freedom to make a classification election. As a result, LLC owners may now elect corporate or partnership status without the uncertainty that existed under prior law.

PLANNING CONSIDERATIONS

Consolidated Groups May Utilize New Regulations

The new check-the-box Regulations allow a single-owner eligible entity to be treated as a corporation or a division. Since LLCs are eligible entities, a C corporation that owns 100 percent of an LLC can treat the LLC as a division. At the same time, the parent corporation can enjoy the benefit of limited liability in the LLC operations. By electing division treatment, the income of the LLC flows directly to the parent corporation for tax purposes. Consequently, the parent corporation is able to avoid detailed and complex consolidated return Regulations and filing requirements.

ORGANIZATION OF AND TRANSFERS TO CONTROLLED CORPORATIONS

IN GENERAL

1 LEARNING OBJECTIVE
Identify the tax consequences of incorporating and transferring assets to controlled corporations.

Because gain or loss is usually realized, property transactions normally have tax consequences. Unless special provisions in the Code apply, a transfer of property to a corporation in exchange for stock is a taxable transaction. The amount of gain or loss is measured by the difference between the value of the stock received and the tax basis of the property transferred.

The Code, however, does permit nonrecognition of gain or loss in limited circumstances. For example, when a taxpayer exchanges some of his or her property for other property of a like kind, § 1031 provides that gain (or loss) on the exchange is postponed because there has not been a substantive change in the taxpayer's investment. The postponement of gain or loss is accomplished by a carryover of basis. Due to this carryover of basis, the potential gain or loss on the property given up is recognized when the property received in the exchange is sold.

In a similar fashion, § 351 provides for the nonrecognition of gain or loss upon the transfer of property to a corporation in exchange for stock. The nonrecognition of gain or loss under § 351 reflects the principle that gain should not be recognized when a taxpayer's investment has not substantively changed. Investment in a corporation's assets carries over to an investment in corporate stock. When only stock in the corporation is received, the shareholder is hardly in a position to pay a tax on any realized gain. As noted later, however, when the taxpayer receives property other than stock (i.e., *boot*) from the corporation, realized gain may be recognized.

The same principles govern the nonrecognition of gain or loss under § 1031 and § 351. The concept of nonrecognition of gain or loss, present in both provisions, causes gain or loss to be postponed until a substantive change in the taxpayer's investment occurs (such as a sale to or a taxable exchange with third parties). This approach is justified under the wherewithal to pay concept discussed in Chapter 1. A further justification for the nonrecognition of gain or loss provisions under § 351 is that tax rules should not impede the exercise of sound business judgment (e.g., choice of business entity).

EXAMPLE 7

Ron is considering incorporating his donut shop. He is concerned about his personal liability for the shop's obligations. Ron realizes that if he incorporates the shop, he will be liable only for the debts of the business that he has personally guaranteed. If Ron incorporates, the following assets will be transferred to the corporation:

	Tax Basis	Fair Market Value
Cash	$10,000	$ 10,000
Furniture and fixtures	20,000	60,000
Land and building	40,000	100,000
	$70,000	$170,000

In exchange, Ron will receive stock in the newly formed corporation worth $170,000. Without the nonrecognition provisions of § 351, Ron would recognize a taxable gain of $100,000 ($170,000 − $70,000) on the transfer. Under § 351, however, Ron does not recognize any gain because his economic status has not changed. Ron's investment in the assets of his unincorporated donut shop carries over to his investment in the incorporated donut shop. Thus, § 351 provides for tax neutrality on the initial incorporation of Ron's donut shop. ▼

When a taxpayer participates in a like-kind exchange, gain is deferred to the extent that the taxpayer receives like-kind property. The taxpayer must recognize gain on any "boot" (i.e., property of an unlike kind). For example, if a taxpayer exchanges a truck used in a business for another truck to be used in the business and also receives cash, the taxpayer has the wherewithal to pay an income tax on the cash involved. Further, the taxpayer's economic status has changed to the extent of the cash (not like-kind property) received. Thus, any "realized" gain on the exchange is recognized to the extent of the cash received. In like manner, if a taxpayer transfers property to a corporation and receives money or property other than stock, § 351(b) provides that gain is recognized to the extent of the lesser of the gain realized or the boot received (the amount of money and the fair market value of other property received). Gain is characterized according to the type of asset transferred.[9] Loss on a § 351 transaction is never recognized. The nonrecognition of gain or loss is accompanied by a carryover of basis.[10]

EXAMPLE 8

Abby and Bill form White Corporation. Abby transfers property with an adjusted basis of $30,000 and a fair market value of $60,000 for 50% of White's stock. Bill transfers property with an adjusted basis of $70,000 and a fair market value of $60,000 for the remaining 50%

---

[9] Rev.Rul. 68–55, 1968–1 C.B. 140.

[10] §§ 358(a) and 362(a). See the discussion preceding Example 26.

of the stock. The transfer qualifies under § 351. Abby has a deferred gain of $30,000, and Bill has a deferred loss of $10,000. Both have a carryover basis in the stock in White Corporation. Abby has a basis of $30,000 in her stock, and Bill has a basis of $70,000 in his stock. Assume instead that Abby receives stock and cash of $10,000. Abby would recognize a gain of $10,000. ▼

Section 351 is mandatory. If a transaction falls within its provisions, neither gain nor loss is recognized on the transfer (except that realized gain is recognized to the extent of boot received), and there is a carryover of basis.

There are three requirements for nonrecognition of gain or loss: (1) *property* is transferred (2) in exchange for *stock* and (3) the transferors must be in *control* of the transferee corporation immediately after the transfer. These three requirements are discussed below.

TRANSFER OF PROPERTY

Questions have arisen concerning what constitutes **property** for purposes of § 351. The Code specifically excludes services rendered from the definition of property. With this exception, the definition of property is comprehensive. Unrealized receivables for a cash basis taxpayer and installment obligations are considered property, for example.[11] The transfer of an installment obligation in a transaction qualifying under § 351 is not a disposition of the installment obligation. Thus, gain is not recognized to the transferor. Secret processes and formulas, as well as secret information in the general nature of a patentable invention, also qualify as property under § 351.[12]

Services are not considered to be property under § 351 for a critical reason. A taxpayer must report as income the fair market value of property received as compensation for services rendered.[13] Thus, if a taxpayer receives stock in a corporation as consideration for rendering services to the corporation, the taxpayer has taxable income. The amount of income is the fair market value of the stock received. The taxpayer's basis in the stock then is the fair market value of the stock.

▼ **EXAMPLE 9**

Ann and Bob form Brown Corporation and transfer the following property to it:

	Property Transferred		Number of Shares Issued
	Basis to Transferor	Fair Market Value	
From Ann:			
Personal services rendered to Brown Corporation	$ –0–	$20,000	200
From Bob:			
Installment obligation	5,000	40,000	
Inventory	10,000	30,000	800
Secret process	–0–	10,000	

The value of each share in Brown Corporation is $100.[14] Ann has taxable income of $20,000 on the transfer because services do not qualify as "property." She has a basis of $20,000 in her 200 shares of stock in Brown. Bob recognizes no gain on the transfer because all of the

---

[11] *Hempt Brothers, Inc. v. U.S.*, 74–1 USTC ¶9188, 33 AFTR2d 74–570, 490 F.2d 1172 (CA–3, 1974), and Reg. § 1.453–9(c)(2).
[12] Rev.Rul. 64–56, 1964–1 C.B. 133.
[13] §§ 61 and 83.
[14] The value of closely held stock normally is presumed to be equal to the value of the property transferred.

TAX IN THE NEWS

MAKING THE MOST OUT OF STOCK OPTIONS

In certain industries, businesses can enjoy spectacular success. Many high-tech ventures located in the Silicon Valley of California, for example, have achieved amazing growth.

When starting a business in this type of industry, stock options can be included as part of the compensation package to attract promising employees. The prospects of large profits from the exercise of these options can motivate the employees to forgo the larger cash salaries they could obtain elsewhere. Thus, the use of options saves the company much needed start-up capital and allows the recipient employees to share in its equity growth.

The classic example of this type of scenario is Microsoft, whose stock has risen an average 60 percent a year since its founding in 1986.

---

consideration he transferred to Brown qualifies as "property" under § 351 (and he has "control" of Brown). (See discussion below.) Bob has a basis of $15,000 in his stock in Brown. ▼

If property is transferred to a corporation in exchange for any property other than stock, the property constitutes boot. The boot is taxable to the transferor shareholder to the extent of any realized gain.[15]

STOCK

The Regulations state that the term "stock" does not include stock rights and stock warrants.[16] Generally, however, the term "stock" needs no clarification. It includes both common stock and preferred stock.

All debt constitutes boot. Included in debt are **securities** (e.g., long-term debt such as bonds). Thus, the receipt of debt in exchange for the transfer of appreciated property to a controlled corporation causes recognition of gain.

CONTROL OF THE CORPORATION

To qualify as a nontaxable transaction under § 351, the transferor(s) of the property must be in **control** of the corporation immediately after the exchange. Control means that the person or persons transferring *property* must have an 80 percent stock ownership in the transferee corporation. The transferor shareholders must own stock possessing at least 80 percent of the total combined voting power of all classes of stock entitled to vote and at least 80 percent of the total *number* of shares of all other classes of stock.[17]

Control Immediately after the Transfer.
Immediately after the exchange, the property transferors must control the corporation. Control can apply to a single person or to several taxpayers if they are all parties to an integrated transaction. The Regulations provide that when more than one person is involved, the exchange does not necessarily require simultaneous exchanges by two or more persons. The

---

[15] § 351(b).
[16] Reg. § 1.351–1(a)(1)(ii).
[17] § 368(c).

Regulations do, however, require that the rights of the parties (e.g., those transferring property to the corporation) be previously set out and determined. Also, the agreement to transfer property should be executed "... with an expedition consistent with orderly procedure."[18]

If two or more persons transfer property to a corporation for stock, the transfers should occur close together in time and should be made in accordance with an agreement among the parties.

EXAMPLE 10

Jack exchanges property with a basis of $60,000 and a fair market value of $100,000 for 70% of the stock of Gray Corporation. The other 30% is owned by Jane, who acquired it several years ago. The fair market value of Jack's stock is $100,000. Jack recognizes a taxable gain of $40,000 on the transfer because he does not have control immediately after the exchange. ▼

EXAMPLE 11

Lana, Leo, and Lori incorporate their respective businesses by forming Green Corporation. Lana exchanges her property for 300 shares in Green on January 5, 1998. Leo exchanges his property for 400 shares of Green Corporation stock on January 10, 1998, and Lori exchanges her property for 300 shares in Green on March 5, 1998. The three exchanges are part of a prearranged plan, so the control requirement is met. The nonrecognition provisions of § 351 apply to all of the exchanges. ▼

Control is not necessarily lost if stock received by shareholders in a § 351 exchange is sold or given to persons who are not parties to the exchange shortly after the transaction. However, failure to meet the control requirement might result if a *plan* for the ultimate disposition of the stock existed *before* the exchange.[19]

EXAMPLE 12

Lee and Pat form Black Corporation. They transfer appreciated property to the corporation with each receiving 50 shares of the stock. Shortly after the formation, Lee gives 25 shares to his son. Because Lee was not committed to make the gift, he is considered to own his original shares of the Black Corporation stock "immediately after the exchange." The requirements of § 351 are met, and neither Lee nor Pat is taxed on the exchange. ▼

PLANNING CONSIDERATIONS

Utilizing § 351

When using § 351(a), ensure that all parties transferring property (including cash) receive control of the corporation. Simultaneous transfers are not necessary, but a long period of time between transfers is vulnerable if the transfers are not properly documented as part of a single plan. To do this, the parties should document and preserve evidence of their intentions. Also, it is helpful to have some reasonable explanation for any delay in the transfers.

To meet the requirements of § 351, mere momentary control on the part of the transferor may not suffice if loss of control is compelled by a prearranged agreement.[20]

EXAMPLE 13

For many years, Zelda operated a business as a sole proprietor employing Zina as manager. To dissuade Zina from quitting and going out on her own, Zelda promised her a 30% interest in the business. To fulfill this promise, Zelda transferred the business to newly formed Green Corporation in return for all its stock. Immediately thereafter, Zelda transfers 30% of the stock to Zina. Section 351

---

[18]Reg. § 1.351–1.
[19]*Wilgard Realty Co. v. Comm.*, 42–1 USTC ¶9452, 29 AFTR 325, 127 F.2d 514 (CA–2, 1942).

[20]Rev.Rul. 54–96, 1954–1 C.B. 111.

probably does not apply to Zelda's transfer to Green Corporation. It appears that Zelda was under an obligation to relinquish control. If this is not the case and the loss of control was voluntary on Zelda's part, momentary control would suffice.[21] ▼

Be sure that later transfers of property to an existing corporation satisfy the control requirement if recognition of gain is to be avoided. Also with respect to later transfers, a transferor's interest cannot be counted if the value of stock received is relatively small compared with the value of stock already owned. Further, the primary purpose of the transfer may not be to qualify other transferors for § 351 treatment.[22]

Transfers for Property and Services.

Section 351 treatment is lost if stock is transferred to persons who did not contribute property, causing those who did to lack control immediately after the exchange.

EXAMPLE 14

Kate transfers property with a value of $60,000 and a basis of $5,000 for 600 shares of stock in newly formed Wren Corporation. Kevin receives 400 shares in Wren for services rendered to the corporation. Each share of stock is worth $100. Both Kate and Kevin have taxable gain on the transaction. Kevin is not part of the control group because he did not transfer property for stock. He has taxable income of $40,000 (400 shares × $100). Kate has a taxable gain of $55,000 [$60,000 (fair market value of the stock in Wren Corporation) − $5,000 (basis in the transferred property)]. Kate is taxed on the exchange because she received only 60% of the stock in Wren Corporation. ▼

A person who performs services for the corporation in exchange for stock and also transfers some property is treated as a member of the transferring group. That person is taxed on the value of the stock issued for services but not on the stock issued for property. In such a case, all the stock received by the person transferring both property and services is counted in determining whether the transferors acquired control of the corporation.[23]

EXAMPLE 15

Assume the same facts as in Example 14, except that Kevin transfers property worth $30,000 (basis of $3,000) in addition to services rendered to the corporation (valued at $10,000). Now Kevin becomes a part of the control group. Kate and Kevin together received 100% of the stock in Wren Corporation. Consequently, § 351 is applicable to the exchanges. Kate has no recognized gain. Kevin does not recognize gain on the transfer of the property but has taxable income to the extent of the value of the shares issued for services rendered. Thus, Kevin recognizes income of $10,000. ▼

Transfers for Services and Nominal Property.

To be a member of the group and aid in qualifying all transferors under the 80 percent control test, the person contributing services must transfer property having more than a small value relative to the value of services performed. Section 351 will not apply when a small amount of property is transferred and when the primary purpose of the transfer is to qualify the transaction under § 351 for concurrent transferors.[24]

EXAMPLE 16

Olga and Otis transfer property to Redbird Corporation, each in exchange for one-third of the stock. Olaf receives the other one-third of the stock for services rendered. The transaction

---

[21]Compare *Fahs v. Florida Machine and Foundry Co.*, 48–2 USTC ¶9329, 36 AFTR 1161, 168 F.2d 957 (CA–5, 1948), with *John C. O'Connor*, 16 TCM 213, T.C.Memo. 1957–50, aff'd. in 58–2 USTC ¶9913, 2 AFTR2d 6011, 260 F.2d 358 (CA–6, 1958).

[22]Reg. § 1.351–1(a)(1)(ii).
[23]Reg. § 1.351–1(a)(2), Ex. 3.
[24]Reg. § 1.351–1(a)(1)(ii).

will not qualify under § 351 because Olaf is not a member of the group transferring property and Olga and Otis together received only 66⅔% of the stock. The post-transfer control requirement is not met.

Assume instead that Olaf also transfers property. Then he is a member of the group, and the transaction qualifies under § 351. Olaf is taxed on the value of the stock issued for services, but the remainder of the transaction is tax-free. However, if the property transferred by Olaf is of a relatively small value in comparison to the stock he receives for his services, and the primary purpose for including the property is to cause the transaction to be tax-free for Olga and Otis, the exchange does not qualify under § 351. Gain or loss is recognized by all parties. ▼

The IRS generally requires that before a transferor who receives stock for both property and services can be included in the control group, the value of the property transferred must be at least 10 percent of the value of the services provided.[25] If the value of the property transferred is less than this amount, the IRS will not issue an advance ruling that the exchange meets the requirements of § 351.

EXAMPLE 17

Sara and Rick form White Corporation. Sara transfers land (worth $100,000, basis of $20,000) for 50% of the stock in White. Rick transfers equipment (worth $5,000, adjusted basis of $1,000) and provides services worth $95,000 for 50% of the stock. Rick's stock in White Corporation is unlikely to be counted in determining control for purposes of § 351; thus, the control requirement is not met. None of Rick's stock is counted in determining control because property he transferred has a nominal value in comparison to the value of the services rendered. Sara recognizes $80,000 of gain on the transfer of the land. She has a basis of $100,000 in her White stock. Rick must recognize income of $95,000 on the transfer for services rendered and a gain of $4,000 for property transferred. Rick also has a $100,000 basis in his White stock. ▼

Transfers to Existing Corporations. Once a corporation is in operation, § 351 also applies to any later transfers of property for stock by either new or existing shareholders.

EXAMPLE 18

Sam and Seth formed Blue Corporation three years ago. Both Sam and Seth transferred appreciated property to Blue in exchange for 500 shares each in the corporation. The original transfers qualified under § 351, and neither Sam nor Seth was taxed on the exchange. In the current year, Sam transfers property (worth $100,000, adjusted basis of $5,000) for 500 additional Blue shares. Sam has a taxable gain of $95,000 on the transfer. The exchange does not qualify under § 351 because Sam does not have 80% control of Blue Corporation. (Sam has 1,000 shares of the 1,500 shares outstanding, or a 66⅔% ownership.) ▼

If current shareholders transfer property with a small value relative to the value of stock already owned, a special rule applies (similar to the nominal property rule noted previously). In particular, if the purpose of the transfer is to qualify a transaction under § 351, the ownership of the current shareholders is not counted when determining control. Thus, in the preceding example, if Seth had contributed $200 for one share of stock at the time of Sam's contribution, Seth's ownership would not count toward the 80% control requirement and Sam would still have a taxable exchange.

---

[25]Rev.Proc. 77–37, 1977–2 C.B. 568; § 3.07.

ASSUMPTION OF LIABILITIES—§ 357

LEARNING OBJECTIVE 2
Understand the special rules that apply when a corporation assumes a shareholder's liability.

Without the special rules of § 357, the transfer of mortgaged property to a controlled corporation could require recognition of gain by the transferor to the extent of the mortgage whether the corporation assumed the mortgage or took property subject to it. This would be consistent with the rule in nontaxable like-kind exchanges under § 1031. Liabilities assumed by the other party are considered the equivalent of cash and treated as boot. Section 357(a) provides, however, that when the acquiring corporation **assumes a liability** or takes property subject to a liability in a § 351 transaction, the transfer does not result in boot to the transferor shareholder. Nevertheless, liabilities assumed by the transferee corporation are treated as boot in determining the basis of the stock received. The basis of the stock received is reduced by the amount of the liabilities assumed by the corporation.

EXAMPLE 19

Vera transfers property with an adjusted basis of $60,000, fair market value of $100,000, to Gray Corporation for 100% of the stock in Gray. The property is subject to a liability of $25,000 that Gray Corporation assumes. The exchange is tax-free under §§ 351 and 357. However, the basis to Vera of the Gray stock is $35,000 [$60,000 (basis of property transferred) − $25,000 (amount of liability)]. ▼

The general rule of § 357(a) has two exceptions. Section 357(b) provides that if the principal purpose of the assumption of the liabilities is to avoid tax *or* if there is no bona fide business purpose behind the exchange, the liabilities are treated as boot. Further, § 357(c) provides that if the sum of the liabilities exceeds the adjusted basis of the properties transferred, the excess is taxable gain.

Tax Avoidance or No Bona Fide Business Purpose. Satisfying the bona fide business purpose is not difficult if the liabilities were incurred in connection with the transferor's normal course of conducting a trade or business. But the bona fide business purpose requirement can cause difficulty if the liability is taken out shortly before the property is transferred and the proceeds are utilized for personal purposes.[26] This type of situation is analogous to a cash distribution by the corporation, which is taxed as boot.

EXAMPLE 20

Dan transfers real estate (basis of $40,000 and fair market value of $90,000) to a controlled corporation in return for stock in the corporation. Shortly before the transfer, Dan mortgages the real estate and uses the $20,000 proceeds to meet personal obligations. Along with the real estate, the mortgage is transferred to the corporation. In this case, the assumption of the mortgage appears to lack a bona fide business purpose. The amount of the liability is boot, and Dan has a taxable gain on the transfer of $20,000, computed as follows:

Stock	$ 70,000
Release of liability—treated as boot	20,000
Total amount realized	$ 90,000
Less: Basis of real estate	(40,000)
Realized gain	$ 50,000
Recognized gain	$ 20,000

▼

The effect of the application of § 357(b) is to taint *all* liabilities transferred even if some are supported by a bona fide business purpose.

---

[26]See, for example, *Campbell, Jr. v. Wheeler*, 65–1 USTC ¶9294, 15 AFTR2d 578, 342 F.2d 837 (CA–5, 1965).

EXAMPLE 21

Tim, an accrual basis taxpayer, incorporates his sole proprietorship. Among the liabilities transferred to the new corporation are trade accounts payable of $100,000 and a MasterCard bill of $5,000. Tim had used the MasterCard to purchase a wedding anniversary gift for his wife. Under these circumstances, the $105,000 of liabilities is boot that triggers recognition of gain to the extent gain is realized. ▼

Liabilities in Excess of Basis. Section 357(c) states that, if the sum of liabilities assumed and the liabilities to which transferred property is subject *exceeds* the total of the adjusted bases of the properties transferred, the excess is taxable gain. Without this provision, if liabilities exceed basis in property exchanged, a taxpayer would have a negative basis in the stock received in the controlled corporation.[27] Section 357(c) precludes the negative basis possibility by treating the excess over basis as gain to the transferor.

EXAMPLE 22

Andre transfers assets with an adjusted tax basis of $40,000 to a newly formed corporation in exchange for 100% of the stock. The corporation assumes $50,000 of liabilities on the transferred properties. Without § 357(c), Andre's basis in the stock of the new corporation would be a negative $10,000 [$40,000 (basis of property transferred) − $50,000 (liabilities assumed)]. Section 357(c) causes Andre to recognize a gain of $10,000. As a result, the stock has a zero basis in Andre's hands, determined as follows:

Basis in the property transferred	$40,000
Add: Gain recognized	10,000
Less: Liabilities assumed	50,000
Basis in the stock received	$ –0–

Thus, no negative basis results. ▼

The definition of liabilities under § 357(c) excludes obligations that would have been deductible to the transferor had those obligations been paid before the transfer. Thus, accounts payable of a cash basis taxpayer that give rise to a deduction are not considered to be liabilities for purposes of § 357(c).

EXAMPLE 23

Tina, a cash basis taxpayer, incorporates her sole proprietorship. In return for all of the stock of the new corporation, she transfers the following items:

	Adjusted Basis	Fair Market Value
Cash	$10,000	$10,000
Unrealized accounts receivable (amounts due to Tina but not yet paid to her)	–0–	40,000
Trade accounts payable	–0–	30,000
Note payable	5,000	5,000

Unrealized accounts receivable and trade accounts payable have a zero basis. Under the cash method of accounting, no income is recognized until the receivables are collected, and no deduction materializes until the payables are satisfied. The note payable has a basis because it was issued for consideration received.

---

[27] *Easson v. Comm.*, 33 T.C. 963 (1960), rev'd. in 61–2 USTC ¶9654, 8 AFTR2d 5448, 294 F.2d 653 (CA–9, 1961).

The accounts receivable and the trade accounts payable are disregarded for gain recognition purposes. Thus, Tina transfers only cash ($10,000) and a note payable ($5,000) and does not have liabilities in excess of basis for purposes of § 357(c). ▼

If §§ 357(b) and (c) both apply to the same transfer, § 357(b) dominates.[28] This could be significant because § 357(b) does not create gain on the transfer, as does § 357(c), but merely converts the liability to boot. Thus, the realized gain limitation continues to apply to § 357(b) transactions.

EXAMPLE 24

Chris owns land with a basis of $100,000 and a fair market value of $1,000,000. The land is subject to a mortgage of $300,000. One month prior to transferring the land to Robin Corporation, Chris borrows an additional $200,000 for personal purposes and gives the lender a second mortgage on the land. Robin Corporation issues stock worth $500,000 to Chris and assumes the mortgages on the land.

Both § 357(c) and § 357(b) apply to the transfer. The mortgages on the property ($500,000) exceed the basis of the property ($100,000). Thus, Chris has a gain of $400,000 under § 357(c). Chris borrowed $200,000 just prior to the transfer and used the $200,000 for personal purposes. Under § 357(b), Chris has boot of $500,000 in the amount of the liabilities (*all* of which is treated as boot). He has realized gain of $900,000 [$1,000,000 (fair market value of the land) – $100,000 (basis in the land)]. Gain is recognized to the extent of the boot of $500,000. Section 357(b) dominates over § 357(c). ▼

PLANNING CONSIDERATIONS

Avoiding § 351

Section 351(a) provides for the nonrecognition of gain on transfers to controlled corporations. As such, it is often regarded as a relief provision favoring taxpayers. In some situations, however, avoiding § 351(a) may produce a more advantageous tax result. The transferors might prefer to recognize gain on the transfer of property if the tax cost is low. For example, they may be in low tax brackets, or the gain may be a capital gain from which substantial capital losses can be offset. Also, recognition of gain will lead to a stepped-up basis in the transferred property in the corporation.

Another reason a particular transferor might wish to avoid § 351 concerns possible loss recognition. Recall that § 351 refers to the nonrecognition of both gains and losses. Section 351(b)(2) specifically states: "No loss to such recipient shall be recognized." A transferor who wishes to recognize loss has several alternatives:

- Sell the property to the corporation for its stock. The IRS could attempt to collapse the "sale," however, by taking the approach that the transfer really falls under § 351(a).[29]
- Sell the property to the corporation for other property or boot. Because the transferor receives no stock, § 351 is inapplicable.
- Transfer the property to the corporation in return for securities. Recall that § 351 does not apply to a transferor who receives securities. In both this and the previous alternatives, watch for the possible disallowance of the loss under the related-party rules.

---

[28]§ 357(c)(2)(A).
[29]*U.S. v. Hertwig*, 68–2 USTC ¶9495, 22 AFTR2d 5249, 398 F.2d 452 (CA–5, 1968).

Suppose loss property is to be transferred to the corporation and no loss is recognized by the transferor due to § 351(a). This could present an interesting problem in terms of assessing the economic realities involved.

EXAMPLE 25

Iris and Ivan form Wren Corporation with the following investment: property by Iris (basis of $40,000 and fair market value of $50,000) and property by Ivan (basis of $60,000 and fair market value of $50,000). Each receives 50% of the Wren stock. Has Ivan acted wisely in settling for only 50% of the stock? At first, it would appear so, since Iris and Ivan each invested property of the same value ($50,000). But what about tax considerations? Due to basis carryover, the corporation now has a basis of $40,000 in Iris's property and $60,000 in Ivan's property. In essence, Iris has shifted a possible $10,000 gain to the corporation while Ivan has transferred a $10,000 potential loss. With this in mind, an equitable allocation of the Wren stock would call for Ivan to receive a greater percentage interest than Iris. ▼

BASIS DETERMINATION AND OTHER ISSUES

3 LEARNING OBJECTIVE
Recognize the basis issues relevant to the shareholder and the corporation.

Recall that § 351(a) postpones gain or loss until the taxpayer's investment changes substantially. Postponement of the realized gain or loss is accomplished through a carryover of basis.

Basis of Stock to Shareholder. For a taxpayer transferring property to a corporation in a § 351 transaction, the basis of stock received in the transfer is the same as the basis the taxpayer had in the property transferred, increased by any gain recognized on the exchange and decreased by boot received. For basis purposes, boot received includes any liabilities transferred by the shareholder to the corporation.[30]

Basis of Property to Corporation. The basis of properties received by the corporation is the basis of the exchanged property in the hands of the transferor increased by the amount of any gain recognized to the transferor shareholder.[31]

The basis rules are summarized in Figures 9–1 and 9–2 and illustrated in Examples 26 and 27.

▼ **FIGURE 9–1**
Shareholder's Basis in Stock Received

Adjusted basis of property transferred	$xx,xxx
Plus: Gain recognized	x,xxx
Minus: Boot received (including any liabilities transferred)	(x,xxx)
Equals: Basis of stock received	$xx,xxx

▼ **FIGURE 9–2**
Corporation's Basis in Properties Received

Adjusted basis of property transferred	$xx,xxx
Plus: Gain recognized by transferor shareholder	xxx
Equals: Basis of property to corporation	$xx,xxx

---

[30] § 358(a). [31] § 362(a).

EXAMPLE 26

Maria and Ned form Brown Corporation. Maria transfers land (basis of $30,000 and fair market value of $70,000); Ned invests cash ($60,000). They each receive 50 shares in Brown Corporation, worth $1,200 per share, but Maria also receives $10,000 cash from Brown. The transfers of property, the realized and recognized gain on the transfers, and the basis of the stock in Brown Corporation to Maria and Ned are as follows:

	A	B	C	D	E	F
	Basis of Property Transferred	FMV of Stock Received	Boot Received	Realized Gain (B + C − A)	Recognized Gain (Lesser of C or D)	Basis of Stock in Brown (A − C + E)
From Maria: Land	$30,000	$60,000	$10,000	$40,000	$10,000	$30,000
From Ned: Cash	60,000	60,000	–0–	–0–	–0–	60,000

Brown Corporation has a basis of $40,000 in the land. The basis to Brown is Maria's basis of $30,000 plus her recognized gain of $10,000. ▼

EXAMPLE 27

Assume the same facts as in Example 26 except that Maria's basis in the land is $68,000 (instead of $30,000). Because recognized gain cannot exceed realized gain, the transfer generates only $2,000 of gain to Maria. The realized and recognized gain and the basis of the stock in Brown Corporation to Maria are as follows:

	A	B	C	D	E	F
	Basis of Property Transferred	FMV of Stock Received	Boot Received	Realized Gain (B + C − A)	Recognized Gain (Lesser of C or D)	Basis of Stock in Brown (A − C + E)
Land	$68,000	$60,000	$10,000	$2,000	$2,000	$60,000

Brown's basis in the land is $70,000 ($68,000 basis to Maria + $2,000 gain recognized by Maria). ▼

Stock Issued for Services Rendered. A corporation's disposition of stock for property is not a taxable exchange.[32] A transfer of shares for services is also not a taxable transaction to a corporation.[33] Can a corporation deduct the fair market value of the stock it issues in consideration of services as a business expense? Yes, unless the services are such that the payment is characterized as a capital expenditure.[34]

EXAMPLE 28

Carol and Carl form White Corporation. Carol transfers cash of $500,000 for 100 shares of White Corporation stock. Carl transfers property worth $480,000 (basis of $90,000) and agrees to serve as manager of the corporation for one year; in return, Carl receives 100 shares of stock in White. The value of Carl's services to White Corporation is $20,000. The transfers qualify under § 351. Carl is not taxed on the transfer of the appreciated property. However, Carl has income of $20,000, the value of the services he will render to White Corporation.

---

[32] § 1032.
[33] Reg. § 1.1032–1(a).
[34] Rev.Rul. 62–217, 1962–2 C.B. 59, modified by Rev.Rul. 74–503, 1974–2 C.B. 117.

White has a basis of $90,000 in the property it acquired from Carl. It has a business deduction under § 162 of $20,000 for the value of services Carl will render. ▼

EXAMPLE 29

Assume, in the preceding example, that Carl receives the 100 shares of White Corporation stock as consideration for the appreciated property and for providing legal services in organizing the corporation. The value of Carl's legal services is $20,000. Carl has no gain on the transfer of the property but has income of $20,000 for the value of the services rendered. White Corporation has a basis of $90,000 in the property it acquired from Carl and must capitalize the $20,000 as organizational expenses. ▼

Holding Period for Shareholder and Transferee Corporation. The shareholder's holding period for stock received for a capital asset or for § 1231 property includes the holding period of the property transferred to the corporation. The holding period of the property is *tacked on* to the holding period of the stock.[35] The holding period for stock received for any other property (e.g., inventory or property held primarily for sale) begins on the day after the exchange. The transferee corporation's holding period for property acquired in a § 351 transfer is the holding period of the transferor shareholder regardless of the character of the property to the transferor.

RECAPTURE CONSIDERATIONS

In a pure § 351(a) nontaxable transfer (no boot involved) to a controlled corporation, the recapture of accelerated cost recovery rules do not apply.[36] Moreover, any recapture potential of the property carries over to the corporation as it steps into the shoes of the transferor-shareholder for purposes of basis determination. However, to the extent that gain is recognized, the recapture rules are applied.

EXAMPLE 30

Paul transfers equipment (basis of $30,000 and fair market value of $100,000) to a controlled corporation in return for additional stock. If Paul had sold the equipment, it would have yielded a gain of $70,000, all of which would be recaptured as ordinary income under § 1245. If the transfer comes within § 351(a), Paul has no recognized gain and no accelerated cost recovery to recapture. If the corporation later disposes of the equipment in a taxable transaction, it must take into account the § 1245 recapture potential originating with Paul.

If Paul had received boot of $60,000, all of the recognized gain would be recaptured as ordinary income. The remaining $10,000 of recapture potential would carry over to the corporation. ▼

PLANNING CONSIDERATIONS

Other Considerations When Incorporating a Business

When a business is incorporated, the organizers must determine which assets and liabilities should be transferred to the corporation. A transfer of assets that produce passive income (rents, royalties, dividends, and interest) can cause the corporation to be a personal holding company in a tax year when operating income is low. Thus, the corporation could be subject to the personal holding company penalty tax (see the discussion in Chapter 10).

---

[35] §§ 1223(1) and (2).

[36] §§ 1245(b)(3) and 1250(d)(3).

A transfer of the accounts payable of a cash basis taxpayer may prevent the taxpayer from taking a tax deduction when the accounts are paid. These payables should generally be retained.

Leasing property to the corporation may be a more attractive alternative than transferring ownership. Leasing provides the taxpayer with the opportunity of withdrawing money from the corporation without the payment being characterized as a dividend. If the property is donated to a family member in a lower tax bracket, the lease income can be shifted as well. If the depreciation and other deductions available in connection with the property are larger than the lease income, a high tax rate taxpayer could retain the property until the income exceeds the deductions.

Shareholder debt in a corporation can be given to family members with low marginal tax rates. This technique also shifts income without a loss of control of the corporation.

CAPITAL STRUCTURE OF A CORPORATION

CAPITAL CONTRIBUTIONS

LEARNING OBJECTIVE 4
Understand the tax aspects of the capital structure of a corporation.

When a corporation receives money or property in exchange for capital stock (including treasury stock), neither gain nor loss is recognized by the recipient corporation. Nor does a corporation's gross income include shareholders' contributions of money or property to the capital of the corporation. Additional funds received from shareholders through voluntary pro-rata payments are not income to the corporation.[37] This is the case even though there is no increase in the outstanding shares of stock of the corporation. The payments represent an additional price paid for the shares held by the shareholders (increasing their basis) and are treated as additions to the operating capital of the corporation.

Contributions by nonshareholders, such as land contributed to a corporation by a civic group or a governmental group to induce the corporation to locate in a particular community, are also excluded from the gross income of a corporation.[38] However, property that is transferred to a corporation by a nonshareholder for services rendered or for merchandise sold by the corporation is taxable income to the corporation.[39]

EXAMPLE 31

A cable company charges its customers an initial fee to hook up to a new cable system installed in the area. These payments are used to finance the total cost of constructing the cable facilities. The customers will make monthly payments for the cable service. The initial payments are used for capital expenditures, but they represent payments for services to be rendered by the cable company. As such, they are taxable income and not contributions to capital by nonshareholders. ▼

The basis of property received by a corporation from a shareholder as a **capital contribution** is equal to the basis of the property in the hands of the shareholder increased by any gain recognized to the shareholder. The basis of property transferred to a corporation by a nonshareholder as a contribution to capital is zero.

---

[37]§ 118 and Reg. § 1.118–1.
[38]See *Edwards v. Cuba Railroad Co.*, 1 USTC ¶139, 5 AFTR 5398, 45 S.Ct. 614 (USSC, 1925).
[39]Reg. § 1.118–1. See also *Teleservice Co. of Wyoming Valley v. Comm.*, 27 T.C. 722 (1957), *aff'd.* in 58–1 USTC ¶9383, 1 AFTR2d 1249, 254 F.2d 105 (CA-3, 1958), *cert. den.* 78 S.Ct. 1360 (USSC, 1958).

If a corporation receives *money* as a contribution to capital from a nonshareholder, a special rule applies. The basis of any property acquired with the money during a 12-month period beginning on the day the contribution was received is reduced by the amount of the contribution. The excess of money received over the cost of new property is used to reduce the basis of other property held by the corporation and is applied in the following order:

- Depreciable property.
- Property subject to amortization.
- Property subject to depletion.
- All other remaining properties.

The basis of property within each category is reduced in proportion to the relative bases of the properties.[40]

EXAMPLE 32

A city donates land to Brown Corporation as an inducement for Brown to locate in the city. The receipt of the land does not produce taxable income to Brown, and the land's basis to the corporation is zero. In addition, the city pays the corporation $10,000 in cash. The money is not taxable income to the corporation. However, if the corporation purchases property with the $10,000 within the next 12 months, the basis of the property is reduced by $10,000. ▼

DEBT IN THE CAPITAL STRUCTURE

5 LEARNING OBJECTIVE
Recognize the tax differences between debt and equity investments.

Advantages of Debt. Shareholders must be aware of the tax differences between debt and equity in the capital structure. The advantages of issuing long-term debt are numerous. Interest on debt is deductible by the corporation, while dividend payments are not. Further, the shareholders are not taxed on loan repayments unless the repayments exceed basis. An investment in stock usually cannot be withdrawn tax-free. Withdrawals will be deemed to be taxable dividends from the distributing corporation.

EXAMPLE 33

Wade transfers cash of $100,000 to a newly formed corporation for 100% of the stock. In the first year of operations, the corporation has net income of $40,000. If the corporation distributes $9,500 to Wade, the distribution is a taxable dividend with no corresponding deduction to the corporation. Assume, instead, that Wade transfers cash of $50,000 for stock. In addition, he lends the corporation $50,000. The note is payable in equal annual installments of $5,000 and bears interest at the rate of 9%. At the end of the year, the corporation pays Wade $4,500 interest, which is taxable to Wade and tax deductible to the corporation. The $5,000 principal repayment on the loan is not taxed to Wade. ▼

Reclassification of Debt as Equity. If a debt instrument has too many features of stock, it may be treated as a form of stock by the IRS. As a result, the principal and interest payments are considered dividends. Under § 385, the IRS has the authority to characterize corporate debt wholly as equity or as part debt and part equity.

For the most part, the principles used to classify debt as equity developed in connection with closely held corporations where the holders of the debt are often shareholders. The rules have often proved inadequate for dealing with large, publicly traded corporations.

Section 385 lists several factors that *may* be used to determine whether a debtor-creditor relationship or a shareholder-corporation relationship exists. The thrust of § 385 is to authorize the Treasury to prescribe Regulations that provide more definite

---

[40] § 362(c). Reg. §§ 1.362–2(b) and 1.118–1.

guidelines for determining when debt should be reclassified as equity. To date, the Treasury has not drafted final Regulations. Consequently, taxpayers must rely on judicial decisions to determine whether a true debtor-creditor relationship exists.

The courts have identified the following factors to be considered when classifying a security as debt or equity:

- Whether the debt instrument is in proper form. An open account advance is more easily characterized as a contribution to capital than a loan evidenced by a properly written note executed by the shareholder.[41]
- Whether the debt instrument bears a reasonable rate of interest and has a definite maturity date. When a shareholder advance does not provide for interest, the return expected is that inherent in an equity interest (e.g., a share of the profits or an increase in the value of the shares).[42] Likewise, a lender unrelated to the corporation will usually be unwilling to commit funds to the corporation for an indefinite period of time (i.e., no definite due date).
- Whether the debt is paid on a timely basis. A lender's failure to insist upon timely repayment (or satisfactory renegotiation) indicates that the return sought does not depend upon interest income and the repayment of principal.
- Whether payment is contingent upon earnings. A lender ordinarily will not advance funds that are likely to be repaid only if the venture is successful.
- Whether the debt is subordinated to other liabilities. Subordination tends to eliminate a significant characteristic of the creditor-debtor relationship. Creditors should have the right to share with other general creditors in the event of the corporation's dissolution or liquidation. Subordination also destroys another basic attribute of creditor status—the power to demand payment at a fixed maturity date.[43]
- Whether holdings of debt and stock are proportionate. When debt and equity obligations are held in the same proportion, shareholders are, apart from tax considerations, indifferent as to whether corporate distributions are in the form of interest or dividends.
- Whether funds loaned to the corporation are used to finance initial operations or capital asset acquisitions. Funds used to finance initial operations or to acquire capital assets the corporation needs to operate are generally obtained through equity investments.
- Whether the corporation has a high ratio of shareholder debt to shareholder equity. **Thin capitalization** occurs when shareholder debt is high relative to shareholder equity. This indicates the corporation lacks reserves to pay interest and principal on debt when corporate income is insufficient to meet current needs.[44] In determining a corporation's debt-equity ratio, courts look at the relation of the debt both to the book value of the corporation's assets and to their actual fair market value.[45]

Section 385 also authorizes the Treasury to issue Regulations classifying an instrument either as *wholly* debt or equity or as *part* debt and *part* equity. This flexible

---

[41] *Estate of Mixon v. U.S.*, 72–2 USTC ¶9537, 30 AFTR2d 72–5094, 464 F.2d 394 (CA–5, 1972).

[42] *Slappey Drive Industrial Park v. U.S.*, 77–2 USTC ¶9696, 40 AFTR2d 77–5940, 561 F.2d 572 (CA–5, 1977).

[43] *Fin Hay Realty Co. v. U.S.*, 68–2 USTC ¶9438, 22 AFTR2d 5004, 398 F.2d 694 (CA–3, 1968).

[44] A court held that a debt-equity ratio of approximately 14.6:1 was not excessive. See *Tomlinson v. 1661 Corp.*, 67–1 USTC ¶9438, 19 AFTR2d 1413, 377 F.2d 291 (CA–5, 1967).

[45] In *Bauer v. Comm.*, 84–2 USTC ¶9996, 55 AFTR2d 84–433, 748 F.2d 1365 (CA–9, 1984), a debt-equity ratio of 92:1 resulted when book value was used. But the ratio ranged from 2:1 to 8:1 when equity included both paid-in capital and accumulated earnings.

approach is important because some instruments cannot readily be classified either wholly as stock or wholly as debt. It may also provide an avenue for the IRS to address problems in publicly traded corporations.

CORPORATE OPERATIONS

The rules related to gross income, deductions, and losses discussed in previous chapters of this text generally apply to corporations. In a few instances, it was noted that corporations face unique limitations such as the 10 percent of taxable income limitation for charitable contributions and the limitation allowing corporate capital losses to be deductible only against capital gains. Corporations also are permitted some deductions not generally available to other entities. These special deductions and other special rules regarding the determination of corporate income tax liability are discussed in the following paragraphs.

DEDUCTIONS AVAILABLE ONLY TO CORPORATIONS

Dividends Received Deduction.
The purpose of the **dividends received deduction** is to mitigate multiple taxation. Without the deduction, dividends paid between corporations could be subject to several levels of tax. For example, if Corporation A pays Corporation B a dividend, and B passes the dividend on to its shareholders, the dividend is taxed at three levels: Corporation A, Corporation B, and Corporation B's shareholders. The dividends received deduction alleviates this inequity by limiting or eliminating the amount of dividend income taxable to corporations.

As the following table illustrates, the amount of the dividends received deduction depends upon the percentage of ownership the recipient corporate shareholder holds in a domestic corporation making the dividend distribution.[46]

Percentage of Ownership by Corporate Shareholder	Deduction Percentage
Less than 20%	70%
20% or more (but less than 80%)	80%
80% or more*	100%

*The payor corporation must be a member of an affiliated group with the recipient corporation.

The dividends received deduction is limited to a percentage of the taxable income of the shareholder-corporation. For this purpose, taxable income is computed without regard to the net operating loss (NOL), the dividends received deduction, and any capital loss carryback to the current tax year. The percentage of taxable income limitation corresponds to the deduction percentage. Thus, if a corporate shareholder owns less than 20 percent of the stock in the distributing corporation, the dividends received deduction is limited to 70 percent of taxable income. However, the taxable income limitation does not apply if the corporation has an NOL for the current taxable year.[47]

The following steps summarize the computation of the deduction:

---

[46] § 243(a).

[47] § 246(b)(2).

1. Multiply the dividends received by the deduction percentage.
2. Multiply the taxable income by the deduction percentage.
3. The deduction is limited to the lesser of Step 1 or Step 2, unless subtracting the amount derived in Step 1 from taxable income is less than zero (i.e., it generates an NOL). If so, the amount derived in Step 1 should be used. This is referred to as the *NOL rule*.

EXAMPLE 34

Red, White, and Blue Corporations, three unrelated calendar year corporations, have the following transactions for the year:

	Red Corporation	White Corporation	Blue Corporation
Gross income from operations	$ 400,000	$ 320,000	$ 260,000
Expenses from operations	(340,000)	(340,000)	(340,000)
Dividends received from domestic corporations (less than 20% ownership)	200,000	200,000	200,000
Taxable income before the dividends received deduction	$ 260,000	$ 180,000	$ 120,000

In determining the dividends received deduction, use the three-step procedure described above:

Step 1 (70% × $200,000)	$140,000	$140,000	$140,000
Step 2			
70% × $260,000 (taxable income)	$182,000		
70% × $180,000 (taxable income)		$126,000	
70% × $120,000 (taxable income)			$ 84,000
Step 3			
Lesser of Step 1 or Step 2	$140,000	$126,000	
Deduction generates an NOL			$140,000

White Corporation is subject to the 70% of taxable income limitation. It does not qualify for NOL rule treatment since subtracting $140,000 (Step 1) from $180,000 (100% of taxable income) does not yield a negative figure. Blue Corporation qualifies under the NOL rule because subtracting $140,000 (Step 1) from $120,000 (100% of taxable income) yields a negative figure. In summary, each corporation has a dividends received deduction for the year as follows: $140,000 for Red Corporation, $126,000 for White Corporation, and $140,000 for Blue Corporation. ▼

Deduction of Organizational Expenditures.

Expenses incurred in connection with the organization of a corporation normally are chargeable to a capital account. That they benefit the corporation during its existence seems clear. But over what period should organizational expenses be amortized? The lack of a determinable and limited estimated useful life makes such a determination difficult. Section 248 was enacted to solve this problem.

Under § 248, a corporation may elect to amortize **organizational expenditures** over a period of 60 months or more. The period begins with the month in which the corporation begins business.[48] Organizational expenditures *subject to the election* include:

---

[48] The month in which a corporation begins business may not be immediately apparent. See Reg. § 1.248–1(a)(3). For a similar problem in the Subchapter S area, see Chapter 12.

- Legal services incident to organization (e.g., drafting the corporate charter, bylaws, minutes of organizational meetings, terms of original stock certificates).
- Necessary accounting services.
- Expenses of temporary directors and of organizational meetings of directors or shareholders.
- Fees paid to the state of incorporation.

Expenditures that *do not qualify* include those connected with issuing or selling shares of stock or other securities (e.g., commissions, professional fees, and printing costs) or with the transfer of assets to a corporation. Such expenditures reduce the amount of capital raised and are not deductible.

To qualify for the election, the expenditure must be *incurred* before the end of the taxable year in which the corporation begins business. In this regard, the corporation's method of accounting is of no consequence. Thus, an expense incurred by a cash basis corporation in its first tax year qualifies even though not paid until a subsequent year.

The election is made in a statement attached to the corporation's return for its first taxable year. The return and statement must be filed no later than the due date of the return (including any extensions).

If the election is not made on a timely basis, organizational expenditures cannot be deducted until the corporation ceases to do business and liquidates. These expenditures will be deductible if the corporate charter limits the life of the corporation.

EXAMPLE 35

Black Corporation, an accrual basis, calendar year taxpayer, was formed and began operations on May 1, 1998. The following expenses were incurred during its first year of operations (May 1–December 31, 1998):

Expenses of temporary directors and of organizational meetings	$500
Fee paid to the state of incorporation	100
Accounting services incident to organization	200
Legal services for drafting the corporate charter and bylaws	400
Expenses incident to the printing and sale of stock certificates	300

Assume Black Corporation makes a timely election under § 248 to amortize qualifying organizational expenses over a period of 60 months. The monthly amortization is $20 [($500 + $100 + $200 + $400) ÷ 60 months], and $160 ($20 × 8 months) is deductible in 1998. Note that the $300 of expenses incident to the printing and sale of stock certificates does not qualify for the election. These expenses cannot be deducted. Instead, they reduce the amount of the capital realized from the sale of stock. ▼

Organizational expenditures are distinguished from start-up expenditures covered by § 195. Start-up expenditures include various investigation expenses involved in entering a new business, whether incurred by a corporate or a noncorporate taxpayer. Start-up expenses also include operating expenses, such as rent and payroll, that are incurred by a corporation before it actually begins to produce any gross income. At the election of the taxpayer, such expenditures (e.g., travel, market surveys, financial audits, legal fees) can be amortized over a period of 60 months or longer rather than capitalized as part of the cost of the business.

PLANNING CONSIDERATIONS

Organizational Expenditures

To qualify for the 60-month amortization procedure of § 248, only organizational expenditures incurred in the first taxable year of the corporation can be considered. This rule could prove to be an unfortunate trap for corporations formed late in the year.

EXAMPLE 36

Thrush Corporation is formed in December 1998. Qualified organizational expenditures are incurred as follows: $2,000 in December 1998 and $3,000 in January 1999. If Thrush uses the calendar year for tax purposes, only $2,000 of the organizational expenditures qualify for amortization. ▼

The solution to the problem posed by Example 36 is for Thrush Corporation to adopt a fiscal year that ends on or beyond January 31. All organizational expenditures will then have been incurred before the close of the first taxable year.

DETERMINING THE CORPORATE INCOME TAX LIABILITY

LEARNING OBJECTIVE 7
Compute the corporate income tax.

Corporate Income Tax Rates. Corporate income tax rates have fluctuated widely over past years. Refer to the inside front cover of the text for a schedule of current corporate income tax rates.

EXAMPLE 37

Gold Corporation, a calendar year taxpayer, has taxable income of $90,000 for 1998. Its income tax liability is $18,850, determined as follows:

Tax on $75,000	$13,750
Tax on $15,000 × 34%	5,100
Tax liability	$18,850

▼

For a corporation that has taxable income in excess of $100,000 for any tax year, the amount of the tax is increased by the lesser of (1) 5 percent of the excess or (2) $11,750. In effect, the additional tax means a 39 percent rate for every dollar of taxable income from $100,000 to $335,000.[49]

EXAMPLE 38

Silver Corporation, a calendar year taxpayer, has taxable income of $335,000 for 1998. Its income tax liability is $113,900, determined as follows:

Tax on $100,000	$ 22,250
Tax on $235,000 × 39%	91,650
Tax liability	$113,900

Note that the tax liability of $113,900 is 34% of $335,000. Thus, due to the 39% rate (34% normal rate + 5% additional tax on taxable income between $100,000 and $335,000), the benefit of the lower rates on the first $75,000 of taxable income completely phases out at $335,000. Note that the normal rate drops back to 34% on taxable income between $335,000 and $10 million. ▼

Section 11(b) provides that qualified **personal service corporations (PSCs)** are taxed at a flat 35 percent rate on all taxable income. Thus, PSCs do not enjoy the

---

[49] § 11(b).

tax savings of being in the 15 percent to 34 percent brackets applicable to other corporations. For this purpose, a PSC is a corporation that is substantially employee owned. Also, it must engage in one of the following activities: health, law, engineering, architecture, accounting, actuarial science, performing arts, or consulting.

TAX LIABILITY OF RELATED CORPORATIONS

LEARNING OBJECTIVE 8
Explain the tax rules unique to multiple corporations.

Related corporations are subject to special rules for computing the income tax, the accumulated earnings credit, the AMT exemption, the § 179 election to expense certain depreciable assets, and the environmental tax exemption.[50] If these restrictions did not exist, the shareholders of a corporation could gain significant tax advantages by splitting a single corporation into *multiple* corporations. The next two examples illustrate the potential *income tax* advantage of multiple corporations.

EXAMPLE 39

Gray Corporation annually yields taxable income of $300,000. The corporate tax on $300,000 is $100,250, computed as follows:

Tax on $100,000	$ 22,250
Tax on $200,000 × 39%	78,000
Tax liability	$100,250

EXAMPLE 40

Assume that Gray Corporation in the previous example is divided equally into four corporations. Each corporation would have taxable income of $75,000, and the tax for each (absent the special provisions for related corporations) would be computed as follows:

Tax on $50,000	$ 7,500
Tax on $25,000 × 25%	6,250
Tax liability	$13,750

The total liability for the four corporations would be $55,000 ($13,750 × 4). The savings would be $45,250 ($100,250 − $55,000). ▼

To preclude the advantages that could be gained by using multiple corporations, the tax law requires special treatment for *controlled groups* of corporations. A comparison of Examples 39 and 40 reveals that the income tax savings that could be achieved by using multiple corporations result from having more of the total income taxed at lower rates. To close this potential loophole, the law limits a controlled group's taxable income in the tax brackets below 35 percent to the amount the corporations in the group would have if they were one corporation. Thus, in Example 40, under the controlled corporation rules, only $12,500 (one-fourth of the first $50,000 of taxable income) for each of the four related corporations would be taxed at the 15 percent rate. The 25 percent rate would apply to the next $6,250 (one-fourth of the next $25,000) of taxable income of each corporation. This equal allocation of the $50,000 and $25,000 amounts is required unless all members of the controlled group consent to an apportionment plan providing for an unequal allocation.

Similar limitations apply to the § 179 expense election and to the $40,000 exemption amount for purposes of computing the AMT (see Chapter 13).

---

[50]§ 1561(a). The AMT and the environmental tax are discussed in Chapter 13. Small corporations are not subject to the AMT for tax years beginning after 1997. See Chapter 13 for details.

CONTROLLED GROUPS

A **controlled group** of corporations includes parent-subsidiary groups, brother-sister groups, combined groups, and certain insurance companies. Groups of the first three types are discussed in the following sections. Insurance groups are not discussed in this text.

Parent-Subsidiary Controlled Group.
A **parent-subsidiary controlled group** consists of one or more *chains* of corporations connected through stock ownership with a common parent corporation. The ownership connection can be established through either a *voting power test* or a *value test*. The voting power test requires ownership of stock possessing at least 80 percent of the total voting power of all classes of stock entitled to vote.[51] The value test requires ownership of at least 80 percent of the total value of all shares of all classes of stock of each of the corporations, except the parent corporation, by one or more of the other corporations.

EXAMPLE 41 Aqua Corporation owns 80% of White Corporation. Aqua and White Corporations are members of a parent-subsidiary controlled group. Aqua is the parent corporation, and White is the subsidiary. ▼

The parent-subsidiary relationship illustrated in Example 41 is easy to recognize because Aqua Corporation is the direct owner of White Corporation. Real-world business organizations are often much more complex, sometimes including numerous corporations with chains of ownership connecting them. In these complex corporate structures, determining whether the controlled group classification is appropriate becomes more difficult. The ownership requirements can be met through direct ownership (refer to Example 41) or through indirect ownership, as illustrated in the two following examples.

EXAMPLE 42 Red Corporation owns 80% of the voting stock of White Corporation, and White Corporation owns 80% of the voting stock of Blue Corporation. Red, White, and Blue Corporations constitute a controlled group in which Red is the common parent and White and Blue are subsidiaries. This parent-subsidiary relationship is diagrammed in Figure 9–3. The same result would occur if Red Corporation, rather than White Corporation, owned the Blue Corporation stock. ▼

EXAMPLE 43 Brown Corporation owns 80% of the stock of Green Corporation, which owns 30% of Blue Corporation. Brown also owns 80% of White Corporation, which owns 50% of Blue Corporation. Brown, Green, Blue and White Corporations constitute a parent-subsidiary controlled group in which Brown is the common parent and Green, Blue and White are subsidiaries. This parent-subsidiary relationship is diagrammed in Figure 9–4. ▼

Brother-Sister Corporations.
A **brother-sister controlled group** *may* exist if two or more corporations are owned by five or fewer *persons* (individuals, estates, or trusts). Brother-sister status will apply if such a shareholder group meets an 80 percent total ownership test *and* a 50 percent common ownership test.[52]

- The *total* ownership test is met if the shareholder group possesses stock representing at least 80 percent of the total combined voting power of all classes of stock entitled to vote, *or* at least 80 percent of the total value of shares of all classes of stock of *each corporation*.

---
[51] § 1563(a)(1).
[52] § 1563(a)(2).

▼ **FIGURE 9–3**
Controlled Groups—Parent-Subsidiary Corporations

Red Corporation —80% Control→ White Corporation —80% Control→ Blue Corporation

Red is the common parent of a parent-subsidiary controlled group consisting of Red, White, and Blue Corporations.

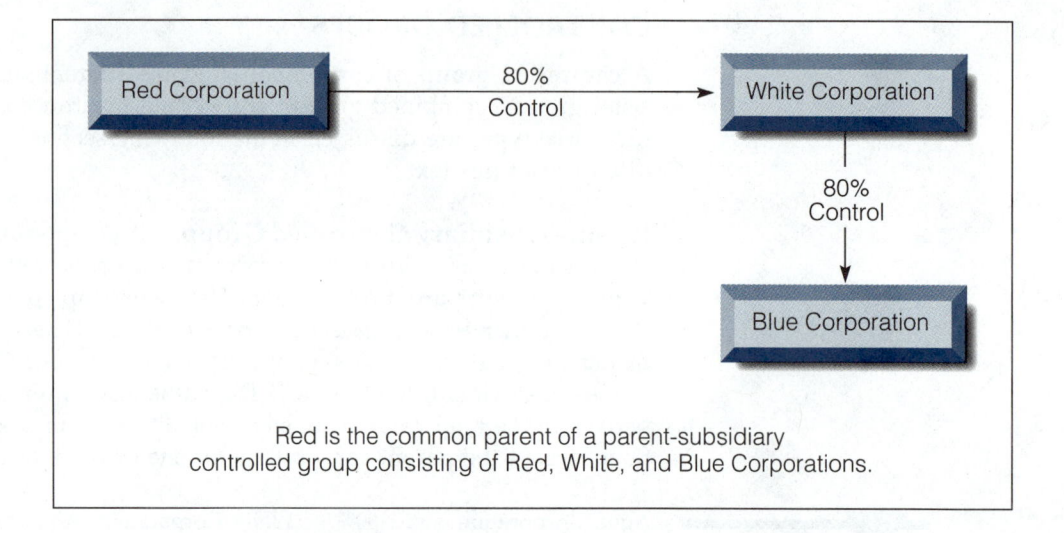

▼ **FIGURE 9–4**
Controlled Groups—Parent-Subsidiary Corporations

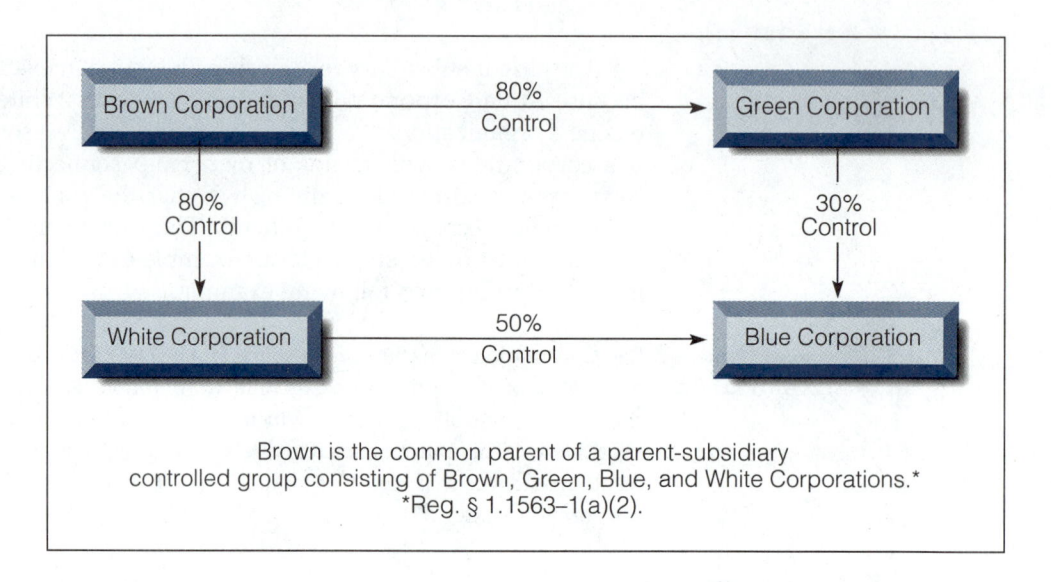

Brown Corporation —80% Control→ Green Corporation
Brown Corporation —80% Control→ White Corporation
Green Corporation —30% Control→ Blue Corporation
White Corporation —50% Control→ Blue Corporation

Brown is the common parent of a parent-subsidiary controlled group consisting of Brown, Green, Blue, and White Corporations.*
*Reg. § 1.1563–1(a)(2).

- The *common* ownership test is met if the shareholder group owns more than 50 percent of the total combined voting power of all classes of stock entitled to vote, *or* more than 50 percent of the total value of shares of all classes of stock of *each corporation*.

In applying the common ownership test, the stock held by each person is considered only to the extent that the stock ownership is equivalent for each corporation. That is, if a shareholder owns 30 percent of Silver Corporation and 20 percent of Gold Corporation, such shareholder has common ownership of 20 percent of each corporation.

EXAMPLE 44

Hawk, Eagle, Crane, and Dove Corporations each have only one class of stock outstanding. The stock is owned by the following unrelated individuals:

Individuals	Corporations				Common Ownership
	Hawk	Eagle	Crane	Dove	
Allen	40%	30%	60%	60%	30%
Barton	50%	20%	30%	20%	20%
Carter	10%	30%	10%	10%	10%
Dixon		20%		10%	
Total	100%	100%	100%	100%	60%

Five or fewer individuals (Allen, Barton, and Carter) with more than a 50% common ownership (60%) own at least 80% of all classes of stock in Hawk, Eagle, Crane, and Dove. They own 100% of Hawk, 80% of Eagle, 100% of Crane, and 90% of Dove. Consequently, Hawk, Eagle, Crane, and Dove are regarded as members of a brother-sister controlled group. ▼

EXAMPLE 45

Changing the facts in the preceding example, assume the ownership is as follows:

Individuals	Corporations				Common Ownership
	Hawk	Eagle	Crane	Dove	
Allen	20%	10%	5%	60%	5%
Barton	10%	20%	60%	5%	5%
Carter	10%	70%	35%	25%	10%
Dixon	60%			10%	
Total	100%	100%	100%	100%	20%

In this situation, the common ownership is only 20%. Consequently, the four corporations are not members of a brother-sister controlled group. However, Eagle and Crane would be brother-sister corporations because both the total ownership and the common ownership tests are met. Allen, Barton, and Carter own 100% of each corporation, and common ownership exceeds 50% (5% by Allen, 20% by Barton, and 35% by Carter). ▼

EXAMPLE 46

The outstanding stock of Black Corporation and Brown Corporation, each of which has only one class of stock outstanding, is owned as follows:

Individuals	Corporations		Identical Ownership
	Black	Brown	
Rossi	55%	100%	55%
Smith	45%		
Total	100%	100%	55%

Although the 50% common ownership test is met, the 80% test is not since there is no common ownership in Brown Corporation. Are Black and Brown brother-sister corporations? No, according to the U.S. Supreme Court.[53] ▼

Combined Groups. A combined controlled group exists if all of the following conditions are met:

---

[53]U.S. v. Vogel Fertilizer Co., 82–1 USTC ¶9134, 49 AFTR2d 82–491, 102 S.Ct. 821 (USSC, 1982). See also Reg. § 1.1563–1(a)(3), which was amended to comply with the conclusions reached in Vogel.

- Each corporation is a member of either a parent-subsidiary controlled group or a brother-sister controlled group.
- At least one of the corporations is a parent of a parent-subsidiary controlled group.
- The parent corporation is also a member of a brother-sister controlled group.

EXAMPLE 47

Robert owns 80% of all classes of stock of Red and Orange Corporations. Red Corporation, in turn, owns 80% of all classes of stock of Blue Corporation. Orange owns all the stock of Green Corporation. Red, Blue, Orange, and Green are members of the same combined group. As a result, Red, Blue, Orange, and Green are limited to taxable income in the tax brackets below 35% as though they were one corporation. This is also the case for the election to expense certain depreciable business assets under § 179 and the $40,000 exemption for purposes of computing the AMT. ▼

Application of § 482. Congress has recognized that a parent corporation has the power to shift income among its subsidiaries. Likewise, shareholders who control brother-sister groups can shift income and deductions among the related corporations.

When the true taxable income of a subsidiary or other related corporation has been understated or overstated, the IRS can reallocate the income and deductions of the related corporations under § 482. Section 482 permits the IRS to allocate gross income, deductions, and credits between any two or more organizations, trades, or businesses that are owned or controlled by the same interests. This is appropriate when the allocation is necessary to prevent avoidance of taxes or to reflect income correctly. Controlled groups of corporations, especially multinational corporations, are particularly vulnerable to § 482.

PROCEDURAL MATTERS

FILING REQUIREMENTS FOR CORPORATIONS

LEARNING OBJECTIVE 9
Describe the reporting process for corporations.

A corporation must file a Federal income tax return whether or not it has taxable income.[54] A corporation that was not in existence throughout an entire annual accounting period is required to file a return for the fraction of the year during which it was in existence. In addition, a corporation must file a return even though it has ceased to do business if it has valuable claims for which it will bring suit. A corporation is relieved of filing income tax returns only when it ceases to do business and retains no assets.

The corporate return is filed on Form 1120 unless the corporation is a small corporation entitled to file the shorter Form 1120–A. A corporation may file Form 1120–A if it meets *all* the following requirements:

- Gross receipts or sales are under $500,000.
- Total income (gross profit plus other income including gains on sales of property) is under $500,000.
- Total assets are under $500,000.
- The corporation is not involved in a dissolution or liquidation.
- The corporation is not a member of a controlled group under §§ 1561 and 1563.
- The corporation does not file a consolidated return.

---
[54] § 6012(a)(2).

- The corporation does not have ownership in a foreign corporation.
- The corporation does not have foreign shareholders who directly or indirectly own 50 percent or more of its stock.

Corporations electing under Subchapter S (see Chapter 12) file on Form 1120S. Forms 1120, 1120–A, and 1120S are reproduced in Appendix B.

The return must be filed on or before the fifteenth day of the third month following the close of a corporation's tax year. As noted in Chapter 6, a regular corporation, other than a PSC, can use either a calendar or a fiscal year to report its taxable income. The tax year of the shareholders has no effect on the corporation's tax year.

Corporations can receive an automatic extension of six months for filing the corporate return by filing Form 7004 by the due date for the return.[55] A Form 7004 must be accompanied by the corporation's estimated tax liability. However, the IRS may terminate the extension by mailing a 10-day notice to the taxpayer corporation. While this is a rare occurrence, the IRS has exercised this authority in cases where taxpayers file unnecessary extensions.

ESTIMATED TAX PAYMENTS

A corporation must make payments of estimated tax unless its tax liability can reasonably be expected to be less than $500. The required annual payment (which includes any estimated AMT liability) is the lesser of (1) 100 percent of the corporation's final tax or (2) 100 percent of the tax for the preceding year (if that was a 12-month tax year and the return filed showed a tax liability).[56] Estimated payments can be made in four installments due on or before the fifteenth day of the fourth month, the sixth month, the ninth month, and the twelfth month of the corporate taxable year. The full amount of the unpaid tax is due on the due date of the return without regard to extensions. For a calendar year corporation, the payment dates are as follows:

April 15

June 15

September 15

December 15

A corporation failing to pay its required estimated tax payments will be subjected to a nondeductible penalty on the amount by which the installments are less than the tax due. However, the underpayment penalty will not be imposed if the estimated payments are timely and are equal to the tax liability of the corporation for the prior year or equal to the tax due computed on an annualized basis. The annualization method allows corporate taxpayers to estimate their taxable income based on the corresponding portion of the tax year already passed.[57] If the annualized method is used for one installment and the corporation does not use this method for a subsequent installment, any shortfall from using the annualized method for a prior payment(s) must be made up in the subsequent installment payment. The penalty is imposed on each installment; that is, a corporation must pay one-fourth of its required annual payment by the due date of each installment.

---

[55]§ 6081.
[56]§§ 6655(d) and (e).
[57]§ 6655(e).

A *large* corporation cannot base its installment payments on its previous year's tax liability except for its first installment payment. A corporation is considered large if it had taxable income in excess of $1 million in any of its three preceding years.

RECONCILIATION OF TAXABLE INCOME AND FINANCIAL NET INCOME

Schedule M–1 on the last page of Form 1120 is used to reconcile net income as computed for financial accounting purposes with taxable income reported on the corporation's income tax return. The starting point on Schedule M–1 is net income per books (financial accounting net income). Additions and subtractions are entered for items that affect net income per books and taxable income differently. The following items are entered as additions (see lines 2 through 5 of Schedule M–1):

- Federal income tax liability (deducted in computing net income per books but not deductible in computing taxable income).
- The excess of capital losses over capital gains (deducted for financial accounting purposes but not deductible by corporations for income tax purposes).
- Income that is reported in the current year for tax purposes that is not reported in computing net income per books (e.g., prepaid income).
- Various expenses that are deducted in computing net income per books but are not deducted in computing taxable income (e.g., charitable contributions in excess of the 10 percent ceiling applicable to corporations).

The following subtractions are entered on lines 7 and 8 of Schedule M–1:

- Income reported for financial accounting purposes but not included in taxable income (e.g., tax-exempt interest).
- Expenses deducted on the tax return but not deducted in computing net income per books (e.g., a charitable contributions carryover deducted in a prior year for financial accounting purposes but deductible in the current year for tax purposes).

The result is taxable income (before the NOL deduction and the dividends received deduction).

EXAMPLE 48

During the current year, Tern Corporation had the following transactions:

Net income per books (after tax)	$92,400
Taxable income	50,000
Federal income tax liability (15% × $50,000)	7,500
Interest income from tax-exempt bonds	5,000
Interest paid on loan, the proceeds of which were used to purchase the tax-exempt bonds	500
Life insurance proceeds received as a result of the death of a key employee	50,000
Premiums paid on key employee life insurance policy	2,600
Excess of capital losses over capital gains	2,000

For book and tax purposes, Tern Corporation determines depreciation under the straight-line method. Tern's Schedule M–1 for the current year is as follows:

Schedule M-1 — Reconciliation of Income (Loss) per Books With Income per Return (See page 15 of instructions.)

1	Net income (loss) per books	92,400	7	Income recorded on books this year not included on this return (itemize):	
2	Federal income tax	7,500		Tax-exempt interest $ 5,000, Life	
3	Excess of capital losses over capital gains	2,000		insurance proceeds on key	
4	Income subject to tax not recorded on books this year (itemize):			employee $50,000	55,000
			8	Deductions on this return not charged against book income this year (itemize):	
5	Expenses recorded on books this year not deducted on this return (itemize):			a Depreciation . . . $	
a	Depreciation . . . $			b Contributions carryover $	
b	Contributions carryover $				
c	Travel and entertainment $ Int. on tax-exempt bonds $500, Prem. on key employee ins. $2,600	3,100	9	Add lines 7 and 8	55,000
6	Add lines 1 through 5	105,000	10	Income (line 28, page 1)—line 6 less line 9	50,000

Schedule M–2 reconciles unappropriated retained earnings at the beginning of the year with unappropriated retained earnings at year-end. Beginning balance plus net income per books, as entered on line 1 of Schedule M–1, less dividend distributions during the year equals ending retained earnings. Other sources of increases or decreases in retained earnings are also listed on Schedule M–2.

EXAMPLE 49

Assume the same facts as in the preceding example. Tern Corporation's beginning balance in unappropriated retained earnings is $125,000. During the year, Tern distributed a cash dividend of $30,000 to its shareholders. Based on these further assumptions, Tern's Schedule M–2 for the current year is as follows:

Schedule M-2 — Analysis of Unappropriated Retained Earnings per Books (Line 25, Schedule L)

1	Balance at beginning of year	125,000	5 Distributions:	a Cash	30,000
2	Net income (loss) per books	92,400		b Stock	
3	Other increases (itemize):			c Property	
			6	Other decreases (itemize):	
			7	Add lines 5 and 6	30,000
4	Add lines 1, 2, and 3	217,400	8	Balance at end of year (line 4 less line 7)	187,400

FORM 1120 ILLUSTRATED

Swift Corporation was formed on January 10, 1985, by James Brown and Martha Swift to sell men's clothing. Pertinent information regarding Swift is summarized as follows:

- The business address is 6210 Norman Street, Buffalo, TX 79330.
- The employer identification number is 75–3284680; the principal business activity code is 5600.
- James Brown and Martha Swift each own one-half of the outstanding common stock; no other class of stock is authorized. James Brown is president of the company and Martha Swift is secretary-treasurer. Both are full-time employees of the corporation and each receives a salary of $70,000. James's Social Security number is 299–50–2593; Martha's Social Security number is 400–40–6680.
- The corporation uses the accrual method of accounting and reports on a calendar year basis. The specific chargeoff method is used in handling bad debt losses, and inventories are determined using the lower of cost or market method. For book and tax purposes, the straight-line method of depreciation is used.
- During 1997, the corporation distributed a cash dividend of $35,000. Selected portions of Swift's profit and loss statement reflect the following debits and credits:

Account	Debit	Credit
Gross sales		$1,040,000
Sales returns and allowances	$ 50,000	
Purchases	506,000	
Dividends received from stock investments in less-than-20%-owned U.S. corporations		60,000
Interest income		
State bonds	$ 9,000	
Certificates of deposit	11,000	20,000
Premiums on term life insurance policies on the lives of James Brown and Martha Swift; Swift Corporation is the designated beneficiary		8,000
Salaries—officers		140,000
Salaries—clerical and sales		100,000
Taxes (state, local, and payroll)		35,000
Repairs		20,000
Interest expense		
Loan to purchase state bonds	$ 4,000	
Other business loans	10,000	14,000
Advertising		8,000
Rental expense		24,000
Depreciation		16,000
Other deductions		21,000

A comparative balance sheet for Swift Corporation reveals the following information:

Assets	January 1, 1997	December 31, 1997
Cash	$ 240,000	$ 163,850
Trade notes and accounts receivable	404,200	542,300
Inventories	300,000	356,000
Federal and state bonds	150,000	150,000
Prepaid Federal tax	—	1,700
Buildings and other depreciable assets	120,000	120,000
Accumulated depreciation	(44,400)	(60,400)
Land	10,000	10,000
Other assets	1,800	1,000
Total assets	$1,181,600	$1,284,450

Liabilities and Equity	January 1, 1997	December 31, 1997
Accounts payable	$ 150,000	$ 125,000
Other current liabilities	40,150	33,300
Mortgages	105,000	100,000
Capital stock	250,000	250,000
Retained earnings	636,450	776,150
Total liabilities and equity	$1,181,600	$1,284,450

CHAPTER 9   Corporations: Organization, Capital Structure, and Operating Rules   9–37

> ### TAX IN THE NEWS
>
> **SOFTWARE ISSUES AFFECT TAXPAYERS**
>
> Computer and software issues touch our lives in many ways. It should come as no surprise that such issues also affect taxpayers. Many businesses are currently struggling with the *year 2000 problem*. These businesses must convert their software programs so they will be *year 2000 compliant*; that is, the programs must be changed to recognize four digits in the year field, rather than two. The tax issue involves the treatment of costs incurred to make these changes. The IRS has announced that it will not challenge a taxpayer's treatment of conversion costs that are handled according to the rules of Revenue Procedure 69–21. These rules allow immediate expensing for conversion costs related to *developed* software. For *purchased* software, the costs are to be expensed over five years, or less if the established life of the software is less than five years.
>
> Another software-related issue concerns the right of the IRS to access a taxpayer's software. The Eight Circuit ruled that a bank holding company was required to produce a tax software preparation program licensed to the corporation by an accounting firm. The corporation argued that the program itself contained no explicit tax information related to the company and should not be subject to summons by the IRS. The court held that IRS summons power was used properly because the program "provided a critical link to the steps and processes that the corporation took in preparing its tax returns and was necessary to verify whether the information provided by the corporation was complete and accurate."
>
> SOURCES: IRS Announcement 97–50 (I.R.B. 1997-45) and *Norwest Corporation*, 97-2 USTC ¶50,510 (CA–9), *aff'g* unreported DC Minn. decision.

Net income per books (before any income tax accrual) is $234,000. During 1997, Swift Corporation made estimated tax payments to the IRS of $61,000. Swift Corporation's Form 1120 for 1997 is reproduced on the following pages.

Although most of the entries on Form 1120 for Swift Corporation are self-explanatory, the following comments may be helpful:

- In order to arrive at the cost of goods sold amount (line 2 on page 1), Schedule A (page 2) must be completed.
- Reporting of dividends requires the completion of Schedule C (page 2). Gross dividends are shown on line 4 (page 1), and the dividends received deduction appears on line 29b (page 1). Separating the dividend from the deduction facilitates the application of the 80 percent and 70 percent of taxable income exception (which did not apply in Swift's case).
- Income tax liability is $59,300, computed as follows:

Tax on $100,000	$22,250
Tax on $95,000 at 39%	37,050
	$59,300

The result is transferred to line 3 of Schedule J and ultimately is listed on line 31 (page 1). Because the estimated tax payment of $61,000 is more than the tax liability of $59,300, Swift will receive a tax refund of $1,700.

- In completing Schedule M–1 (page 4), the net income per books (line 1) is net of the Federal income tax ($234,000 − $59,300). The left-hand side of

Schedule M–1 (lines 2–5) represents positive adjustments to net income per books. After the negative adjustments are made (line 9), the result is taxable income before NOLs and special deductions (line 28, page 1).

- In completing Schedule M–2 (page 4) the beginning retained earnings figure of $636,450 is added to the net income per books as entered on Schedule M–1 (line 1). The dividends distributed in the amount of $35,000 are entered on line 5 and subtracted to arrive at the ending balance in unappropriated retained earnings of $776,150.
- Because this example lacks certain details, supporting schedules that would be attached to Form 1120 have not been included. For example, a Form 4562 would be included to verify the depreciation deduction (line 20, page 1), and other deductions (line 26, page 1) would be supported by a schedule.

CONSOLIDATED RETURNS

Corporations that are members of a parent-subsidiary affiliated group may be able to file a consolidated income tax return for a taxable year. Consolidated returns are beyond the scope of this text.

SUMMARY

The evolution of the check-the-box Regulations has provided taxpayers with a simplified method for determining an entity's tax classification. Nevertheless, taxpayers should not discount the importance of choosing the appropriate form of entity. As demonstrated in this chapter and Chapter 10, a variety of tax provisions applicable to corporations do not extend to other entities. Of particular importance are the different deductions available to corporations and the corporate income tax rate structure. Corporations must also be aware of their levels of debt to avoid equity reclassification. Such reclassification causes deductible interest paid on debt to become nondeductible dividend payments. Equally important are the timing and completeness requirements of the corporate filing provisions. Failure to comply with the appropriate filing provisions may result in heavy penalties and interest.

KEY TERMS

Association, 9–5

Assumption of liabilities, 9–15

Brother-sister controlled group, 9–29

C corporation, 9–2

Capital contribution, 9–21

Control, 9–11

Controlled group, 9–29

Dividends received deduction, 9–24

Limited liability company (LLC), 9–8

Limited partnership, 9–5

Organizational expenditures, 9–25

Parent–subsidiary controlled group, 9–29

Personal service corporation (PSC), 9–27

Property, 9–10

Regular corporation, 9–2

Related corporations, 9–28

S corporation, 9–2

Schedule M–1, 9–34

Securities, 9–11

Thin capitalization, 9–23

Trust, 9–5

CHAPTER 9 Corporations: Organization, Capital Structure, and Operating Rules   9–39

Form 1120
Department of the Treasury
Internal Revenue Service

U.S. Corporation Income Tax Return
For calendar year 1997 or tax year beginning .... , 1997, ending .... , 19 ....
► Instructions are separate. See page 1 for Paperwork Reduction Act Notice.

OMB No. 1545-0123

1997

A Check if a:
1 Consolidated return (attach Form 851) ☐
2 Personal holding co. (attach Sch. PH) ☐
3 Personal service corp. (as defined in Temporary Regs. sec. 1.441-4T—see instructions) ☐

Use IRS label. Otherwise, print or type.

Name: **Swift Corporation**
Number, street, and room or suite no. (If a P.O. box, see page 5 of instructions.)
6210 Norman Street
City or town, state, and ZIP code
Buffalo, TX 79330

B Employer identification number
75 : 3284680

C Date incorporated
1-10-85

D Total assets (see page 5 of instructions)
$ 1,284,450 | 00

E Check applicable boxes: (1) ☐ Initial return (2) ☐ Final return (3) ☐ Change of address

Income	1a Gross receipts or sales 1,040,000 00 b Less returns and allowances 50,000 00 c Bal ►	1c	990,000 00
	2 Cost of goods sold (Schedule A, line 8)	2	450,000 00
	3 Gross profit. Subtract line 2 from line 1c	3	540,000 00
	4 Dividends (Schedule C, line 19)	4	60,000 00
	5 Interest	5	11,000 00
	6 Gross rents	6	
	7 Gross royalties	7	
	8 Capital gain net income (attach Schedule D (Form 1120))	8	
	9 Net gain or (loss) from Form 4797, Part II, line 18 (attach Form 4797)	9	
	10 Other income (see page 6 of instructions—attach schedule)	10	
	11 **Total income.** Add lines 3 through 10 ►	11	611,000 00
Deductions (See instructions for limitations on deductions.)	12 Compensation of officers (Schedule E, line 4)	12	140,000 00
	13 Salaries and wages (less employment credits)	13	100,000 00
	14 Repairs and maintenance	14	20,000 00
	15 Bad debts	15	
	16 Rents	16	24,000 00
	17 Taxes and licenses	17	35,000 00
	18 Interest	18	10,000 00
	19 Charitable contributions (see page 8 of instructions for 10% limitation)	19	
	20 Depreciation (attach Form 4562) 20 16,000 00		
	21 Less depreciation claimed on Schedule A and elsewhere on return .. 21a	21b	16,000 00
	22 Depletion	22	
	23 Advertising	23	8,000 00
	24 Pension, profit-sharing, etc., plans	24	
	25 Employee benefit programs	25	
	26 Other deductions (attach schedule)	26	21,000 00
	27 **Total deductions.** Add lines 12 through 26 ►	27	374,000 00
	28 Taxable income before net operating loss deduction and special deductions. Subtract line 27 from line 11	28	237,000 00
	29 Less: **a** Net operating loss deduction (see page 9 of instructions) .. 29a		
	b Special deductions (Schedule C, line 20) 29b 42,000 00	29c	42,000 00
	30 **Taxable income.** Subtract line 29c from line 28	30	195,000 00
	31 **Total tax** (Schedule J, line 10)	31	59,300 00
Tax and Payments	32 Payments: **a** 1996 overpayment credited to 1997 32a		
	b 1997 estimated tax payments 32b 61,000 00		
	c Less 1997 refund applied for on Form 4466 32c ( ) d Bal ► 32d 61,000 00		
	e Tax deposited with Form 7004 .... 32e		
	f Credit for tax paid on undistributed capital gains (attach Form 2439) .. 32f		
	g Credit for Federal tax on fuels (attach Form 4136). See instructions .. 32g	32h	61,000 00
	33 Estimated tax penalty (see page 10 of instructions). Check if Form 2220 is attached ► ☐	33	
	34 **Tax due.** If line 32h is smaller than the total of lines 31 and 33, enter amount owed	34	
	35 **Overpayment.** If line 32h is larger than the total of lines 31 and 33, enter amount overpaid	35	1,700 00
	36 Enter amount of line 35 you want: **Credited to 1998 estimated tax** ► Refunded ►	36	1,700 00

Sign Here
Under penalties of perjury, I declare that I have examined this return, including accompanying schedules and statements, and to the best of my knowledge and belief, it is true, correct, and complete. Declaration of preparer (other than taxpayer) is based on all information of which preparer has any knowledge.

► Signature of officer   Date   Title

Paid Preparer's Use Only
Preparer's signature ►   Date   Check if self-employed ☐   Preparer's social security number
Firm's name (or yours if self-employed) and address ►   EIN ►   ZIP code ►

Cat. No. 11450Q

Form 1120 (1997) Page **2**

Schedule A — Cost of Goods Sold (See page 10 of instructions.)

1	Inventory at beginning of year	300,000 00
2	Purchases	506,000 00
3	Cost of labor	
4	Additional section 263A costs (attach schedule)	
5	Other costs (attach schedule)	
6	**Total.** Add lines 1 through 5	806,000 00
7	Inventory at end of year	356,000 00
8	**Cost of goods sold.** Subtract line 7 from line 6. Enter here and on page 1, line 2	450,000 00

9a Check all methods used for valuing closing inventory:
  (i) ☐ Cost as described in Regulations section 1.471-3
  (ii) ☒ Lower of cost or market as described in Regulations section 1.471-4
  (iii) ☐ Other (Specify method used and attach explanation.) ▶ _____

b Check if there was a writedown of subnormal goods as described in Regulations section 1.471-2(c) ▶ ☐
c Check if the LIFO inventory method was adopted this tax year for any goods (if checked, attach Form 970) ▶ ☐
d If the LIFO inventory method was used for this tax year, enter percentage (or amounts) of closing inventory computed under LIFO **9d**
e If property is produced or acquired for resale, do the rules of section 263A apply to the corporation? ☐ Yes ☒ No
f Was there any change in determining quantities, cost, or valuations between opening and closing inventory? If "Yes," attach explanation ☐ Yes ☒ No

Schedule C — Dividends and Special Deductions (See page 11 of instructions.)

		(a) Dividends received	(b) %	(c) Special deductions (a) × (b)
1	Dividends from less-than-20%-owned domestic corporations that are subject to the 70% deduction (other than debt-financed stock)	60,000	70	42,000
2	Dividends from 20%-or-more-owned domestic corporations that are subject to the 80% deduction (other than debt-financed stock)		80	
3	Dividends on debt-financed stock of domestic and foreign corporations (section 246A)		see instructions	
4	Dividends on certain preferred stock of less-than-20%-owned public utilities		42	
5	Dividends on certain preferred stock of 20%-or-more-owned public utilities		48	
6	Dividends from less-than-20%-owned foreign corporations and certain FSCs that are subject to the 70% deduction		70	
7	Dividends from 20%-or-more-owned foreign corporations and certain FSCs that are subject to the 80% deduction		80	
8	Dividends from wholly owned foreign subsidiaries subject to the 100% deduction (section 245(b))		100	
9	**Total.** Add lines 1 through 8. See page 12 of instructions for limitation			42,000
10	Dividends from domestic corporations received by a small business investment company operating under the Small Business Investment Act of 1958		100	
11	Dividends from certain FSCs that are subject to the 100% deduction (section 245(c)(1))		100	
12	Dividends from affiliated group members subject to the 100% deduction (section 243(a)(3))		100	
13	Other dividends from foreign corporations not included on lines 3, 6, 7, 8, or 11			
14	Income from controlled foreign corporations under subpart F (attach Form(s) 5471)			
15	Foreign dividend gross-up (section 78)			
16	IC-DISC and former DISC dividends not included on lines 1, 2, or 3 (section 246(d))			
17	Other dividends			
18	Deduction for dividends paid on certain preferred stock of public utilities			
19	**Total dividends.** Add lines 1 through 17. Enter here and on line 4, page 1 ▶	60,000		
20	**Total special deductions.** Add lines 9, 10, 11, 12, and 18. Enter here and on line 29b, page 1 ▶			42,000

Schedule E — Compensation of Officers (See instructions for line 12, page 1.)

Complete Schedule E only if total receipts (line 1a plus lines 4 through 10 on page 1, Form 1120) are $500,000 or more.

	(a) Name of officer	(b) Social security number	(c) Percent of time devoted to business	Percent of corporation stock owned		(f) Amount of compensation
				(d) Common	(e) Preferred	
1	James Brown	299-50-2593	100 %	50 %	%	70,000
	Martha Swift	400-40-6680	100 %	50 %	%	70,000
			%	%	%	
			%	%	%	
			%	%	%	
2	Total compensation of officers					140,000
3	Compensation of officers claimed on Schedule A and elsewhere on return					
4	Subtract line 3 from line 2. Enter the result here and on line 12, page 1					140,000

Form 1120 (1997) Page **3**

Schedule J — Tax Computation (See page 12 of instructions.)

1. Check if the corporation is a member of a controlled group (see sections 1561 and 1563) . . . . . ▶ ☐
   Important: Members of a controlled group, see instructions on page 12.
2a. If the box on line 1 is checked, enter the corporation's share of the $50,000, $25,000, and $9,925,000 taxable income brackets (in that order):
   (1) $ ____ (2) $ ____ (3) $ ____
 b. Enter the corporation's share of:
   (1) Additional 5% tax (not more than $11,750) $ ____
   (2) Additional 3% tax (not more than $100,000) $ ____
3. Income tax. Check this box if the corporation is a qualified personal service corporation as defined in section 448(d)(2) (see instructions on page 13) . . . . ▶ ☐ **3** 59,300 | 00
4a. Foreign tax credit (attach Form 1118) **4a**
 b. Possessions tax credit (attach Form 5735) **4b**
 c. Check: ☐ Nonconventional source fuel credit ☐ QEV credit (attach Form 8834) **4c**
 d. General business credit. Enter here and check which forms are attached: ☐ 3800
    ☐ 3468 ☐ 5884 ☐ 6478 ☐ 6765 ☐ 8586 ☐ 8830 ☐ 8826
    ☐ 8835 ☐ 8844 ☐ 8845 ☐ 8846 ☐ 8820 ☐ 8847 ☐ 8861 **4d**
 e. Credit for prior year minimum tax (attach Form 8827) **4e**
5. **Total credits.** Add lines 4a through 4e **5**
6. Subtract line 5 from line 3 . . . . **6** 59,300 | 00
7. Personal holding company tax (attach Schedule PH (Form 1120)) **7**
8. Recapture taxes. Check if from: ☐ Form 4255 ☐ Form 8611 . . . . **8**
9. Alternative minimum tax (attach Form 4626) **9**
10. **Total tax.** Add lines 6 through 9. Enter here and on line 31, page 1 . . . . **10** 59,300 | 00

Schedule K — Other Information (See page 14 of instructions.)

1. Check method of accounting: a ☐ Cash b ☐ Accrual c ☐ Other (specify) ▶ _____
2. See page 16 of the instructions and state the principal:
 a. Business activity code no. ▶ _5600_
 b. Business activity ▶ _Sales_
 c. Product or service ▶ _Men's Clothing_
3. At the end of the tax year, did the corporation own, directly or indirectly, 50% or more of the voting stock of a domestic corporation? (For rules of attribution, see section 267(c).) . . . . **No: X**
   If "Yes," attach a schedule showing: (a) name and identifying number, (b) percentage owned, and (c) taxable income or (loss) before NOL and special deductions of such corporation for the tax year ending with or within your tax year.
4. Is the corporation a subsidiary in an affiliated group or a parent-subsidiary controlled group? . . . . . . **No: X**
   If "Yes," enter employer identification number and name of the parent corporation ▶ _____
5. At the end of the tax year, did any individual, partnership, corporation, estate or trust own, directly or indirectly, 50% or more of the corporation's voting stock? (For rules of attribution, see section 267(c).) . . . . **Yes: X**
   If "Yes," attach a schedule showing name and identifying number. (Do not include any information already entered in 4 above.) Enter percentage owned ▶ _100_
6. During this tax year, did the corporation pay dividends (other than stock dividends and distributions in exchange for stock) in excess of the corporation's current and accumulated earnings and profits? (See secs. 301 and 316.) . . . **No: X**
   If "Yes," file Form 5452. If this is a consolidated return, answer here for the parent corporation and on **Form 851**, Affiliations Schedule, for each subsidiary.
7. Was the corporation a U.S. shareholder of any controlled foreign corporation? (See sections 951 and 957.) . . .
   If "Yes," attach Form 5471 for each such corporation. Enter number of Forms 5471 attached ▶ _____
8. At any time during the 1997 calendar year, did the corporation have an interest in or a signature or other authority over a financial account (such as a bank account, securities account, or other financial account) in a foreign country? **No: X**
   If "Yes," the corporation may have to file Form TD F 90-22.1. If "Yes," enter name of foreign country ▶ _____
9. During the tax year, did the corporation receive a distribution from, or was it the grantor of, or transferor to, a foreign trust? If "Yes," see page 15 of the instructions for other forms the corporation may have to file . . . . **No: X**
10. At any time during the tax year, did one foreign person own, directly or indirectly, at least 25% of: (a) the total voting power of all classes of stock of the corporation entitled to vote, or (b) the total value of all classes of stock of the corporation? If "Yes," **No: X**
 a. Enter percentage owned ▶ _____
 b. Enter owner's country ▶ _____
 c. The corporation may have to file Form 5472. Enter number of Forms 5472 attached ▶ _____
11. Check this box if the corporation issued publicly offered debt instruments with original issue discount . . ▶ ☐
    If so, the corporation may have to file Form 8281.
12. Enter the amount of tax-exempt interest received or accrued during the tax year ▶ $ _9,000_
13. If there were 35 or fewer shareholders at the end of the tax year, enter the number ▶ _2_
14. If the corporation has an NOL for the tax year and is electing to forego the carryback period, check here ▶ ☐
15. Enter the available NOL carryover from prior tax years (Do not reduce it by any deduction on line 29a.) ▶ $ _____

Form 1120 (1997) — Page 4

Schedule L — Balance Sheets per Books

	Assets	Beginning of tax year (a)	Beginning of tax year (b)	End of tax year (c)	End of tax year (d)
1	Cash		240,000		163,850
2a	Trade notes and accounts receivable	404,200		542,300	
b	Less allowance for bad debts	( )	404,200	( )	542,300
3	Inventories		300,000		356,000
4	U.S. government obligations		150,000		150,000
5	Tax-exempt securities (see instructions)				
6	Other current assets (attach schedule)				1,700
7	Loans to stockholders				
8	Mortgage and real estate loans				
9	Other investments (attach schedule)				
10a	Buildings and other depreciable assets	120,000		120,000	
b	Less accumulated depreciation	(44,400)	75,600	(60,400)	59,600
11a	Depletable assets				
b	Less accumulated depletion	( )		( )	
12	Land (net of any amortization)		10,000		10,000
13a	Intangible assets (amortizable only)				
b	Less accumulated amortization	( )		( )	
14	Other assets (attach schedule)		1,800		1,000
15	Total assets		1,181,600		1,284,450
	Liabilities and Stockholders' Equity				
16	Accounts payable		150,000		125,000
17	Mortgages, notes, bonds payable in less than 1 year				
18	Other current liabilities (attach schedule)		40,150		33,300
19	Loans from stockholders				
20	Mortgages, notes, bonds payable in 1 year or more		105,000		100,000
21	Other liabilities (attach schedule)				
22	Capital stock: a Preferred stock				
	b Common stock	250,000	250,000	250,000	250,000
23	Additional paid-in capital				
24	Retained earnings—Appropriated (attach schedule)				
25	Retained earnings—Unappropriated		636,450		776,150
26	Adjustments to shareholders' equity (attach schedule)				
27	Less cost of treasury stock		( )		( )
28	Total liabilities and stockholders' equity		1,181,600		1,284,450

Note: You are not required to complete Schedules M-1 and M-2 below if the total assets on line 15, column (d) of Schedule L are less than $25,000.

Schedule M-1 — Reconciliation of Income (Loss) per Books With Income per Return (See page 15 of instructions.)

1	Net income (loss) per books	174,700	7	Income recorded on books this year not included on this return (itemize):	
2	Federal income tax	59,300		Tax-exempt interest $ 9,000	
3	Excess of capital losses over capital gains				
4	Income subject to tax not recorded on books this year (itemize):				9,000
5	Expenses recorded on books this year not deducted on this return (itemize):		8	Deductions on this return not charged against book income this year (itemize):	
a	Depreciation $		a	Depreciation $	
b	Contributions carryover $		b	Contributions carryover $	
c	Travel and entertainment $				
	Prem. --- life ins. $8,000				
	Int. --- state bonds $4,000	12,000	9	Add lines 7 and 8	9,000
6	Add lines 1 through 5	246,000	10	Income (line 28, page 1)—line 6 less line 9	237,000

Schedule M-2 — Analysis of Unappropriated Retained Earnings per Books (Line 25, Schedule L)

1	Balance at beginning of year	636,450	5	Distributions: a Cash	35,000
2	Net income (loss) per books	174,700		b Stock	
3	Other increases (itemize):			c Property	
			6	Other decreases (itemize):	
			7	Add lines 5 and 6	35,000
4	Add lines 1, 2, and 3	811,150	8	Balance at end of year (line 4 less line 7)	776,150

CHAPTER 9 Corporations: Organization, Capital Structure, and Operating Rules

PROBLEM MATERIALS

1. Rosita, who owns a proprietorship, has scheduled an appointment to talk with you about the advisability of incorporating. At this time, you know nothing about Rosita's business or her existing tax situation. List the questions you will need to ask during the appointment so you can help her make an informed decision.

2. On June 17, 1998, Susan and Valerie started an investment firm called B&W Investments. During 1998, both Susan and Valerie lived and conducted their business in Illinois. B&W Investments is an unincorporated entity under Illinois state law. Neither Susan nor Valerie filed an election regarding the Federal tax classification of B&W Investments. Susan's husband, Bill, told Valerie and Susan that they must file a Form 1120 for the 1998 taxable year and will be taxed twice on B&W's earnings. Is Bill correct in his assessment?

3. DeRocco, Boals, and Loan, a North Carolina law firm formed on April 13, 1998, is an unincorporated entity under North Carolina state law. On April 13, 1998, Matt Loan, the law firm's majority and tax matters partner, filed Form 8832 to treat the firm as a corporation for tax purposes. Upon discovering Loan's action two days later, Craig Boals and Dan DeRocco informed Loan that it would be more beneficial to treat the entity as a partnership for Federal tax purposes. Loan would like to file another Form 8832 to change his election to a partnership. Can he accomplish this? Explain.

4. Indigo Company has approximately $200,000 in net income in 1998 before deducting any compensation or other payment to its sole owner, Kim. Kim is single. Her income aside from the company's profits is low. Discuss the tax aspects of each of the following arrangements:
   a. Kim operates Indigo Company as a proprietorship.
   b. Kim incorporates Indigo Company and pays herself a salary of $50,000 and no dividend.
   c. Kim incorporates the company and pays herself a $50,000 salary and a dividend of $108,250 ($150,000 − $41,750 corporate income tax).
   d. Kim incorporates the company and pays herself a salary of $200,000.

5. Mike owns 100% of White Company, which had net operating income of $60,000 in 1998 ($100,000 operating income − $40,000 operating expenses). In addition, White Company had a long-term capital gain of $10,000. Mike has sufficient income from other activities to place him in the 39.6% marginal tax bracket before considering results from White Company. Using this information, explain the tax treatment under the following circumstances:
   a. White Company is a corporation and pays no dividends during the year.
   b. White Company is a corporation and pays Mike $70,000 of dividends during the year.
   c. White Company is a corporation and pays Mike a $70,000 salary during the year.
   d. White Company is a proprietorship, and Mike withdraws $0 during the year.
   e. White Company is a proprietorship, and Mike withdraws $70,000 during the year.

6. Emily incorporates her sole proprietorship, but does not transfer a building used by the business to the corporation. Instead, the building is leased to the corporation for an annual rental. What tax reasons might Emily have for not transferring the building to the corporation when the business was incorporated?

7. Cecil and Edie form Heron Corporation with the following investment:

	Property Transferred		
	Basis to Transferor	Fair Market Value	Number of Shares Issued
From Cecil—			
Cash	$ 40,000	$ 40,000	
Installment obligation	140,000	360,000	40

	Property Transferred		
	Basis to Transferor	Fair Market Value	Number of Shares Issued
From Edie—			
Cash	140,000	140,000	
Equipment	120,000	180,000	60
Patent	4,000	280,000	

The installment obligation has a face amount of $360,000 and was acquired last year from the sale of land held for investment purposes (adjusted basis of $140,000).
 a. How much gain, if any, must Cecil recognize?
 b. What is Cecil's basis in the Heron Corporation stock?
 c. What is Heron Corporation's basis in the installment obligation?
 d. How much gain, if any, must Edie recognize?
 e. What is Edie's basis in the Heron Corporation stock?
 f. What is Heron Corporation's basis in the equipment and the patent?
 g. How would your answer change if Cecil received common stock and Edie received preferred stock?
 h. How would your answer change if Edie were a partnership?

8. Brad, Otis, Wade, and Andrea form Teal Corporation with the following investment:

	Property Transferred		
	Basis to Transferor	Fair Market Value	Number of Shares Issued
From Brad—			
Personal services rendered to Teal Corporation	$ –0–	$ 30,000	30
From Otis—			
Equipment	345,000	300,000	270*
From Wade—			
Cash	60,000	60,000	
Unrealized accounts receivable	–0–	90,000	150
From Andrea—			
Land & building	210,000	450,000	
Mortgage on land & building (liability)	300,000	300,000	150

*Otis receives $30,000 in cash in addition to the 270 shares.

The mortgage transferred by Andrea is assumed by Teal Corporation. The value of each share of Teal Corporation stock is $1,000.
 a. What, if any, is Brad's recognized gain or loss?
 b. What is Brad's basis in the Teal Corporation stock?
 c. How much gain or loss must Otis recognize?
 d. What is Otis's basis in the Teal Corporation stock?
 e. What is Teal Corporation's basis in the equipment?
 f. What, if any, is Wade's recognized gain or loss?
 g. What is Wade's basis in the Teal Corporation stock?
 h. What is Teal Corporation's basis in the unrealized accounts receivable?
 i. How much gain or loss must Andrea recognize?
 j. What is Andrea's basis in the Teal stock?
 k. What is Teal Corporation's basis in the land and building?

9. Sam, Seth, Pat, and Kelly form Lark Corporation with the following investment:

	Property Transferred		Number of Shares Issued
	Basis to Transferor	Fair Market Value	
From Sam—			
Inventory	$30,000	$96,000	30*
From Seth—			
Equipment ($30,000 of depreciation taken by Seth in prior years)	45,000	99,000	30**
From Pat—			
Secret process	15,000	90,000	30
From Kelly—			
Cash	30,000	30,000	10

*Sam receives $6,000 in cash in addition to the 30 shares.
**Seth receives $9,000 in cash in addition to the 30 shares.

Assume the value of each share of Lark Corporation stock is $3,000.
a. What, if any, is Sam's recognized gain or loss? How is any such gain or loss treated?
b. What is Sam's basis in the Lark Corporation stock?
c. What is Lark Corporation's basis in the inventory?
d. How much gain or loss must Seth recognize? How is the gain or loss treated?
e. What is Seth's basis in the Lark Corporation stock?
f. What is Lark Corporation's basis in the equipment?
g. What, if any, is Pat's recognized gain or loss?
h. What is Pat's basis in the Lark Corporation stock?
i. What is Lark Corporation's basis in the secret process?
j. How much income, if any, must Kelly recognize?
k. What is Kelly's basis in the Lark Corporation stock?

10. Jane, Jon, and Clyde incorporate their respective businesses and form Starling Corporation. Jane exchanges her property, basis of $50,000 and value of $200,000, for 200 shares in Starling Corporation on March 1 of the current year. Jon exchanges his property, basis of $70,000 and value of $300,000, for 300 shares in Starling a month and a half later on April 15. Clyde transfers his property, basis of $90,000 and value of $500,000, for 500 shares in Starling on May 10 of the current year.
    a. If the three exchanges are part of a prearranged plan, what gain will each of the parties recognize on the exchanges?
    b. Assume Jane and Jon exchanged their property for stock four years ago while Clyde transfers his property for 500 shares in the current year. The transfer is not part of a prearranged plan with Jane and Jon to incorporate their businesses. What gain will Clyde recognize on the transfer?
    c. If the property that Clyde contributes has a basis of $590,000 instead of $90,000, how would you advise the parties to structure the transaction?

11. Lee exchanges property, basis of $20,000 and fair market value of $500,000, for 65% of the stock of Pelican Corporation. The other 35% is owned by Abby, Lee's daughter, who acquired her stock last year. What are the tax issues?

12. Kate transfers property worth $400,000 (basis of $50,000) to Crow Corporation in exchange for 50% of Crow's stock. Kevin transfers a secret process worth $300,000 (zero basis) and services for 50% of Crow's stock. Kevin's services relate to his acquisition of the process and a letter of credit, which states that the newly formed Crow Corporation could obtain a loan to develop the process. The letter of credit is worth $100,000 according to Kevin. What are the tax issues?

13. Dan and Vera form Crane Corporation. Dan transfers land (worth $200,000, basis of $60,000) for 50% of the stock in Crane. Vera transfers machinery (worth $150,000, adjusted basis of $30,000) and provides services worth $50,000 for 50% of the stock.
    a. Will the transfers qualify under § 351?
    b. What are the tax consequences to Dan and Vera?
    c. What is Crane Corporation's basis in the land and the machinery?

14. Perry organized Cardinal Corporation 10 years ago by contributing property worth $1 million, basis of $200,000, for 2,000 shares of stock in Cardinal, representing 100% of the stock in the corporation. Perry later gave each of his children, Brittany and Julie, 500 shares of stock in Cardinal Corporation. In the current year, Perry transfers property worth $320,000, basis of $100,000, to Cardinal for 500 shares in the corporation. What gain, if any, will Perry recognize on this transfer?

15. Ann and Bob form Robin Corporation. Ann transfers property worth $420,000 (basis of $150,000) for 70 shares in Robin Corporation. Bob receives 30 shares for property worth $165,000 (basis of $30,000) and for legal services in organizing the corporation; the services are worth $15,000.
    a. What gain, if any, will the parties recognize on the transfer?
    b. What basis do Ann and Bob have in the stock in Robin Corporation?
    c. What is Robin Corporation's basis in the property and services it received from Ann and Bob?

16. Assume in Problem 15 that the property Bob transfers to Robin Corporation is worth $15,000 (basis of $3,000) and his services in organizing the corporation are worth $165,000. What are the tax consequences to Ann, Bob, and Robin Corporation?

17. Kim is an employee of Azure Corporation. In the current year, she receives a salary of $50,000 and is also given 20 shares of Azure stock for services she renders to the corporation. The shares in Azure Corporation are worth $1,000 each. How will the transfer of the 20 shares to Kim be handled for tax purposes by Kim and by Azure Corporation?

18. Brady transfers property with an adjusted basis of $150,000, fair market value of $1,200,000, to Swift Corporation for 100% of the stock. The property is subject to a liability of $180,000, which Swift assumes. What is the basis of the Swift stock to Brady? What is the basis of the property to Swift Corporation?

19. Three years ago, Chris exchanged an apartment worth $1,500,000 (basis of $300,000), which was subject to a mortgage of $200,000, for land worth $1,150,000, subject to a mortgage of $150,000, and cash of $300,000. In the current year, Chris transfers the land that he received in the exchange to newly formed Amber Corporation for all the stock in Amber. Amber Corporation assumes the original mortgage on the land, currently $100,000, and another $20,000 mortgage that Chris later placed on the land to secure a purchase of some business equipment. What are the tax issues?

20. Lori, a sole proprietor, was engaged in a service business and reported her income on a cash basis. On February 1, 1998, she incorporated her business and transferred the assets of the business to Green Corporation in return for all the stock in the corporation plus the corporation's assumption of the liabilities of her proprietorship. All the receivables and the unpaid trade payables were transferred to the newly formed corporation. The balance sheet of the corporation immediately following the incorporation appears on p. 9–47.
    Discuss the tax consequences of the incorporation of the business to Lori and to Green Corporation. Should Lori transfer the trade accounts payable to Green Corporation?

GREEN CORPORATION
BALANCE SHEET
February 1, 1998

Assets

	Basis to Green	Fair Market Value
Cash	$ 80,000	$ 80,000
Accounts receivable	–0–	240,000
Equipment (cost $180,000; depreciation $60,000)	120,000	320,000
Building (straight-line depreciation)	160,000	400,000
Land	40,000	160,000
	$400,000	$1,200,000

Liabilities and Stockholders' Equity

Liabilities:	
Accounts payable—trade	$ 120,000
Long-term notes payable—bank	360,000
Stockholders' equity:	
Common stock	720,000
	$1,200,000

21. Several entrepreneurs plan to form a corporation to construct a housing project. Travis, the party who will be contributing the land for the project, wants more security than shareholder status provides. He is contemplating two possibilities: receive corporate bonds for his land, or take out a mortgage on the land before transferring it to the corporation for stock. Comment on the tax effects of the choices Travis is considering. What other alternatives can you suggest?

22. Rita forms Pear Corporation by transferring land with a basis of $250,000, fair market value of $1,500,000. The land is subject to a mortgage of $750,000. Two weeks prior to incorporating Pear, Rita borrows $250,000 for personal purposes and gives the lender a second mortgage on the land. Pear Corporation issues stock worth $500,000 to Rita and assumes the mortgages on the land.
    a. What are the tax consequences to Rita and to Pear Corporation?
    b. Assume that Rita does not borrow the $250,000 prior to incorporating Pear. Rita transfers the land to Pear for all the stock in Pear. Pear Corporation then borrows $250,000 and gives the lenders a mortgage on the land. What are the tax consequences to Rita and to Pear Corporation?

23. Jean incorporates her sole proprietorship. Inadvertently, she transfers to the new corporation a credit charge for a family dinner she hosted. After the corporation pays the bill, she realizes her mistake and issues a note payable to the corporation for the charge. Has Jean avoided § 357(c)? Has she acted properly?

24. Sara and Jane form Wren Corporation. Sara transfers property, basis of $25,000 and value of $200,000, for 50 shares in Wren Corporation. Jane transfers property, basis of $10,000 and value of $185,000, and agrees to serve as manager of Wren for one year; in return Jane receives 50 shares in Wren. The value of Jane's services to Wren is $15,000.
    a. What gain will Sara and Jane recognize on the exchange?
    b. What basis will Wren Corporation have in the property transferred by Sara and Jane? How should Wren treat the value of the services Jane renders?

25. Assume in Problem 24, that Jane receives the 50 shares of Wren Corporation stock in consideration for the appreciated property and for providing legal services in organizing the corporation. The value of Jane's services is $15,000.

a. What gain does Jane recognize?
b. What is Wren Corporation's basis in the property transferred by Jane? How should Wren treat the value of the services Jane renders?

26. On January 10, 1998, Carol transferred machinery worth $100,000 (basis of $20,000) to a controlled corporation, Lark. The transfer qualified under § 351. Carol had deducted $85,000 of depreciation on the machinery while it was used in her proprietorship. On November 15, 1998, Lark Corporation sells the machinery for $95,000. What are the tax consequences to Carol and to Lark Corporation on the sale of the machinery?

27. The City of Tucson donates land to Rose Corporation as an inducement for Rose to locate there. The land is worth $100,000. The city also donates $50,000 in cash to Rose.
    a. What income, if any, must Rose recognize as a result of the transfer of land and cash to it by Tucson?
    b. What is Rose's basis in the land?
    c. If Rose uses $25,000 of its funds along with the $50,000 provided by the city to purchase property costing $75,000, what basis will it have in the property?

28. Emily Patrick (2624 Holkham Drive, Ivy, VA 22945) formed Teal Corporation a number of years ago with an investment of $200,000 cash, for which she received $20,000 in stock and $180,000 in bonds bearing interest of 8% and maturing in nine years. Several years later, Emily lent the corporation an additional $50,000 on open account. In the current year, Teal Corporation becomes insolvent and is declared bankrupt. During the corporation's existence, Emily was paid an annual salary of $60,000. Write a letter to Emily in which you explain how she should treat her losses for tax purposes.

29. In each of the following independent situations, determine the dividends received deduction. Assume that none of the corporate shareholders owns 20% or more of the stock in the corporations paying the dividends.

	Red Corporation	White Corporation	Blue Corporation
Income from operations	$ 700,000	$ 800,000	$ 700,000
Expenses from operations	(600,000)	(900,000)	(740,000)
Qualifying dividends	100,000	200,000	200,000

30. Snipe Corporation was formed on December 1, 1998. Qualifying organizational expenses were incurred and paid as follows:

Incurred and paid in December 1998	$12,000
Incurred in December 1998 but paid in January 1999	6,000
Incurred and paid in February 1999	3,600

Assume Snipe Corporation makes a timely election under § 248 to amortize organizational expenditures over a period of 60 months. What amount may be amortized in the corporation's first tax year under each of the following assumptions?
    a. Snipe Corporation adopts a calendar year and the cash basis of accounting for tax purposes.
    b. Same as (a), except that Snipe Corporation chooses a fiscal year of December 1–November 30.
    c. Snipe Corporation adopts a calendar year and the accrual basis of accounting for tax purposes.
    d. Same as (c), except that Snipe Corporation chooses a fiscal year of December 1–November 30.

31. Swallow Corporation, a cash basis and calendar year taxpayer, was formed and began operations on July 1, 1998. Swallow incurred the following expenses during its first year of operations (July 1–December 31, 1998):

Expenses of temporary directors and of organizational meetings	$2,400
Fee paid to the state of incorporation	1,200
Expenses in printing and sale of stock certificates	900
Legal services for drafting the corporate charter and bylaws (not paid until January of 1999)	3,600
Total	$8,100

If Swallow Corporation makes a timely election under § 248 to amortize qualifying organizational expenses, how much may the corporation deduct for tax year 1998?

32. In each of the following independent situations, determine the corporation's income tax liability. Assume that all corporations use a calendar year for tax purposes and that the tax year involved is 1998.

	Taxable Income
Moose Corporation	$ 44,000
Elk Corporation	246,000
Deer Corporation	1,420,000
Antelope Corporation	22,000,000

33. The outstanding stock in Black and White Corporations, each of which has only one class of stock, is owned by the following unrelated individuals:

	Corporations	
Shareholders	Black	White
Ahmad	20	16
Luis	5	54
Sara	75	30
Total	100	100

a. Determine if a brother-sister controlled group exists.
b. Assume that Luis owns no stock in Black Corporation and Sara owns 80 shares. Would a brother-sister controlled group exist? Why or why not?

34. The outstanding stock of Wren, Robin, Finch, and Jay is owned by the following unrelated individual and corporate shareholders as follows:

	Corporations			
Shareholders	Wren	Robin	Finch	Jay
Ann	30%	20%	30%	10%
Bob	50%		50%	5%
Carl	20%		20%	
Wren Corporation		80%		

Which corporations, if any, are members of a controlled group?

35. Eagle and Cardinal Corporations both have 100 shares of stock outstanding. Each shareholder paid $500 for his stock in each corporation, and the fair market value of the stock of each corporation is $800 per share. The stock is owned by the following unrelated individuals:

Shareholders	Eagle Shares	Cardinal Shares
George	30	15
Sam	5	50
Tom	65	35
Total	100	100

a. Does a brother-sister controlled group exist?
b. Will a brother-sister controlled group exist if Tom sells 10 of his shares in Cardinal Corporation to Sam?
c. Discuss any tax advantages that will result if Tom sells 10 of his Cardinal shares to Sam.
d. Sam has suggested to Tom that they complete the transaction in (c). Tom asks your advice and says that he has a 31% marginal tax rate. Write a letter to Tom Roland at 3435 Grand Avenue, South Point, OH 45680, explaining the tax advantages that will result if he sells 10 of his Cardinal shares to Sam. Also, identify any problems, both tax and nontax, that the sale could cause for Tom.

36. The outstanding stock in corporations Amber, Sand, Tan, Beige, and Purple, which have only one class of stock outstanding, is owned by the following unrelated individuals:

	Corporations				
Individuals	Amber	Sand	Tan	Beige	Purple
Anna	55%	51%	55%	55%	55%
Bill	45%	49%			
Carol			45%		
Don				45%	
Eve					45%
Total	100%	100%	100%	100%	100%

Determine if a brother-sister controlled group exists.

37. In each of the following independent situations, indicate whether the corporation may file Form 1120–A:

	Jay Corporation	Shrike Corporation	Martin Corporation
Sales of merchandise	$600,000	$400,000	$300,000
Total assets	200,000	360,000	400,000
Total income (gross profit plus other income, including gains)	480,000	490,000	380,000
Member of controlled group	no	yes	no
Ownership in foreign corporation	no	no	no

38. The following information for 1998 relates to Martin Corporation, a calendar year, accrual method taxpayer. You are to determine the amount of Martin's taxable income for the year using this information. You may use Schedule M–1 if provided by your instructor.

Net income per books (after tax)	$209,710
Federal income tax liability	30,050
Interest income from tax-exempt bonds	12,000

Interest paid on loan incurred to purchase tax-exempt bonds	1,200
Life insurance proceeds received as a result of the death of the president of the corporation	120,000
Premiums paid on policy on the life of the president of the corporation	6,240
Excess of capital losses over capital gains	4,800

39. For 1997, Rose Corporation, an accrual basis, calendar year taxpayer, had net income per books of $172,750 and the following special transactions:

Life insurance proceeds received on the death of the corporation president	$100,000
Premiums paid on the life insurance policy on the president	10,000
Prepaid rent received and properly taxed in 1996 but credited as rent income in 1997	15,000
Rent income received in 1997 ($10,000 is prepaid and relates to 1998)	25,000
Interest income on tax-exempt bonds	5,000
Interest on loan to carry tax-exempt bonds	3,000
MACRS depreciation in excess of straight-line (straight-line was used for book purposes)	4,000
Capital loss in excess of capital gains	6,000
Federal income tax liability and accrued tax provision for 1997	22,250

Using Schedule M–1 of Form 1120 (the most recent version available), compute Rose Corporation's taxable income for 1997.

40. In January, Don and Steve each invested $100,000 cash to form a corporation to conduct business as a retail golf equipment store. On January 5, they paid Bill, an attorney, to draft the corporate charter, file the necessary forms with the state, and write the bylaws. They leased a store building and began to acquire inventory, furniture, display equipment, and office equipment in February. They hired a sales staff and clerical personnel in March and conducted training sessions during the month. They had a successful opening on April 1, and sales increased steadily throughout the summer. The weather turned cold in October, and all local golf courses closed by October 15, which resulted in a drastic decline in sales. Don and Steve expect business to be very good during the Christmas season and then to taper off significantly from January 1 through February 28. The corporation accrued bonuses to Don and Steve on December 31, payable on April 15 of the following year. The corporation made timely estimated tax payments throughout the year. The corporation hired a bookkeeper in February, but he does not know much about taxation. Don and Steve have hired you as a tax consultant and have asked you to identify the tax issues that they should consider.

COMPREHENSIVE TAX RETURN PROBLEM

41. On September 9, 1992, Jennifer Jones and Jeff Shurts formed SnowPro Corporation to sell ski equipment. Pertinent information regarding SnowPro is summarized as follows:

- The business address is 2120 Adobe Drive, Las Cruces, NM 88011.

- The employer identification number is 75–3392543; the principal business activity code is 5600.

- Jennifer and Jeff each own one-half of the outstanding common stock; no other class of stock is authorized. Jennifer is president of the company, and Jeff is secretary-treasurer. Both are full-time employees of the corporation, and each receives a salary of $173,500. Jennifer's Social Security number is 399–50–2953; Jeff's Social Security number is 400–30–4495.

- The corporation uses the accrual method of accounting and reports on a calendar basis. Inventories are determined using the lower of cost or market method. For book and tax purposes, the straight-line method of depreciation is used.
- During 1997, the corporation distributed a cash dividend of $72,000.

Selected portions of SnowPro's profit and loss statement for 1997 reflect the following debits and credits:

Account	Debit	Credit
Gross sales		$2,570,000
Sales returns and allowances	$ 72,000	
Cost of goods sold	925,000	
Dividends received from stock investments in less-than-20%-owned U.S. corporations		108,000
Interest income		
State bonds	$12,600	
Certificates of deposit	9,000	21,600
Premiums on term life insurance policies on the lives of Jennifer and Jeff; SnowPro Corporation is the designated beneficiary	14,000	
Salaries—officers	347,000	
Salaries—clerical and sales	402,000	
Taxes (state, local, and payroll)	103,000	
Repairs	61,500	
Interest expense		
Loan to purchase state bonds	$ 7,200	
Other business loans	24,800	32,000
Advertising	75,400	
Rental expense	177,700	
Depreciation	36,000	

A comparative balance sheet for SnowPro Corporation reveals the following information:

Assets	January 1, 1997	December 31, 1997
Cash	$ 409,000	$ 281,194
Trade notes and accounts receivable	750,560	996,140
Inventories	540,000	640,800
Federal bonds	114,000	114,000
State bonds	156,000	156,000
Prepaid Federal tax	—	1,620
Buildings and other depreciable assets	216,000	216,000
Accumulated depreciation	(79,920)	(115,920)
Land	15,500	15,500
Other assets	5,740	4,300
Total assets	$2,126,880	$2,309,634

Liabilities and Equity	January 1, 1997	December 31, 1997
Accounts payable	$ 238,000	$ 220,004
Other current liabilities	104,270	63,600
Mortgages	234,000	225,000
Capital stock	405,000	405,000
Retained earnings	1,145,610	1,396,030
Total liabilities and equity	$2,126,880	$2,309,634

Net income per books (before any income tax accrual) is $454,000. During 1997, SnowPro Corporation made estimated tax payments of $133,200 to the IRS. Prepare a Form 1120 for SnowPro Corporation for tax year 1997.

RESEARCH PROBLEMS

Note: The RIA OnPoint System 4 Student Version CD-ROM available with this text can be used in preparing solutions to the Research Problems. Alternatively, tax research materials contained in a standard tax library can be used.

42. Herb is a shareholder-employee of Gander Corporation. The corporation owns a jet that it uses almost exclusively for legitimate business purposes. However, the corporation occasionally allows employees to use the jet for personal travel. In February, Herb and his wife were allowed to use the jet to fly from Minnesota to Arizona for a vacation. They were dropped off in Phoenix, and the jet returned to corporate headquarters in Minnesota. Two weeks later, the jet returned to Phoenix and transported Herb and his wife back to Minnesota. Herb has asked you to determine whether there are any tax consequences to his use of the corporate jet. He wants to know whether he will have to report income and whether the corporation will be allowed to deduct expenses related to the flights. Write a letter to Herbert Anson at 6455 West Barr Avenue, St Paul, MN 55164 to explain your conclusions.

43. Soon-Yi owns all the stock of White Corporation and 90% of the stock of Red Corporation. Red Corporation has had profitable years whereas White Corporation has suffered losses for several years. Red loaned White Corporation $90,000 in 1997 and did not charge White any interest on the loan. Upon audit of its 1997 return, the IRS determined that Red Corporation had interest income for 1997 in the amount of $9,900, causing Red to have a tax deficiency of $3,366 for 1997. Red is challenging the tax deficiency. It contends that White Corporation produced no taxable income from the use of the $90,000. Is the IRS correct in increasing the taxable income of Red Corporation?

Partial list of research aids:
Reg. §§ 1.482–2(a)(1) and 1.482–1(d)(4).
§ 7872.

44. For bona fide business purposes, Salisbury Group, Inc., decides to transfer its chemical manufacturing operation to a newly formed corporation, Concord Corporation, in a transaction that qualifies under § 351. Salisbury transfers all of the assets related to the chemical manufacturing operation in exchange for all of the Concord stock and Concord's assumption of all of the existing and contingent liabilities related to the chemical business. Both Salisbury Group and Concord are accrual basis corporations. Top management is aware that potential soil and groundwater environmental remediation costs may have to be incurred eventually to clean up the land of the chemical operation because of spillage over many years. Nevertheless, no attempts were made prior to the transfer to explore the scope of the potential cleanup or to initiate even a limited cleanup. In addition, Salisbury had not booked an entry reflecting the potential cleanup exposure. Two years later, however, Concord incurs $32 million to clean up the soil and water damages. Concord appropriately deducts a portion of the costs and capitalizes the remaining amount.

In reflecting back on these transactions, Salisbury's tax accountant, Fay Holmes, inquires whether the liability that was believed to exist at the time of Concord's incorporation could have triggered gain to Salisbury if, when aggregated with the other liabilities transferred, the liabilities exceeded the basis of the assets that Salisbury transferred to Concord. Prepare a letter that documents your response. Because Fay's background in tax matters is extensive, you should feel free to use technical language if appropriate. Ms. Holmes's address is Salisbury Group, Inc., P.O. Box 71, Concord, NC 28026.

CHAPTER 10

CORPORATIONS: EARNINGS & PROFITS AND DIVIDEND DISTRIBUTIONS

LEARNING OBJECTIVES

After completing Chapter 10, you should be able to:

1. Identify and understand the concept of earnings and profits.

2. Recognize the importance of earnings and profits in measuring the recipient shareholder's dividend income.

3. Understand the tax impact of property dividends on the recipient shareholder and the corporation making the distribution.

4. Understand the nature and treatment of constructive dividends.

5. Distinguish between taxable and nontaxable stock dividends and stock rights.

OUTLINE

Taxable Dividends—In General, 10–2

Earnings and Profits (E & P)— § 312, 10–3
Computation of E & P, 10–3
Summary of E & P Adjustments, 10–6
Current versus Accumulated E & P, 10–6
Allocating E & P to Distributions, 10–7

Property Dividends, 10–11
Property Dividends—Effect on the Shareholder, 10–11
Property Dividends—Effect on the Corporation, 10–12

Constructive Dividends, 10–14
Types of Constructive Dividends, 10–14

Tax Treatment of Constructive Dividends, 10–16

Stock Dividends and Stock Rights, 10–18
Stock Dividends—§ 305, 10–18
Stock Rights, 10–20

Restrictions on Corporate Accumulations, 10–21

This chapter shifts the focus from corporate formation and operations (addressed in Chapter 9) to the tax treatment of corporate distributions. As will become apparent in the subsequent discussion, the tax treatment of corporate distributions varies, depending upon a variety of considerations such as the following:

- The availability of earnings to be distributed.
- The basis of the stock in the hands of the shareholder.
- The character of the property being distributed.
- Whether the shareholder gives up ownership in return for the distribution.
- Whether the distribution is liquidating or nonliquidating in character.

Generally, the corporation cannot deduct distributions made to shareholders, but it may be required to recognize gain on distributions of appreciated property. In contrast, shareholders may be required to treat distributions as ordinary income, capital gain, or a nontaxable recovery of capital.

Since distributions provide no deduction to the paying corporation and often require income recognition by shareholders, a double tax results. Because of the possibility of a double tax, the tax treatment of distributions is often an issue of prime importance when dealing with corporations.

This chapter discusses the tax rules related to nonliquidating distributions (in the form of cash and property). Distributions of stock and stock rights are also addressed. The rules related to stock redemptions and corporate liquidations are beyond the scope of this text.

TAXABLE DIVIDENDS—IN GENERAL

To the extent that a distribution is made from corporate earnings and profits (E & P), the shareholder is deemed to receive a dividend, taxed as ordinary income. E & P (defined later in this chapter) is allocated to distributions on a pro rata basis, using both the accumulated E & P of the corporation since February 28, 1913, and the current-year E & P.[1] Generally, corporate distributions are presumed to be dividends, taxed as ordinary income, unless the parties to the transaction can show otherwise.

---

[1] § 316.

> ### TAX IN THE NEWS
>
> **CHRYSLER KEEPS PROMISE BY BOOSTING DIVIDEND AND STOCK BUYBACK PAYOUTS**
>
> In early 1996, Chrysler made a pledge to its shareholders to return any cash in excess of $7.5 billion. Soon after reporting a $2.7 billion profit through September 1996, Chrysler kept its promise and announced a 14 percent dividend increase on top of a $2 billion stock buyback for 1997. The dividend increase is Chrysler's seventh in the past three years. Since September 1993, Chrysler's total dividend payouts have increased by 433 percent. The $2 billion stock buyback represents a $1 billion increase from the initial 1997 buyback announcement.
>
> SOURCE: Information from Dave Phillips, "Chrysler Board Raises Dividend Again," *Bloomberg Business News—The Detroit News,* December 6, 1996.

The portion of a corporate distribution that is not taxed as a dividend (because of insufficient E & P) is nontaxable to the extent of the shareholder's basis in the stock. The stock basis is reduced accordingly. The excess of the distribution over the shareholder's basis is treated as a capital gain if the stock is a capital asset.[2]

EXAMPLE 1
At the beginning of the year, Amber Corporation (a calendar year taxpayer) has accumulated E & P of $30,000. The corporation has no current E & P. During the year, the corporation distributes $40,000 to its *equal* shareholders, Bob and Bonnie. Only $30,000 of the $40,000 distribution is a taxable dividend. Suppose Bob's basis in his stock is $8,000, while Bonnie's basis is $4,000. Under these conditions, Bob recognizes a taxable dividend of $15,000 and reduces the basis of his stock from $8,000 to $3,000. The $20,000 Bonnie receives from Amber Corporation is accounted for as follows: a taxable dividend of $15,000, a reduction in stock basis from $4,000 to zero, and a capital gain of $1,000. ▼

EARNINGS AND PROFITS (E & P)—§ 312

LEARNING OBJECTIVE 1
Identify and understand the concept of earnings and profits.

The Code does not define the term **earnings and profits.** Although E & P is similar in some respects to the accounting concept of retained earnings, E & P and retained earnings are often not the same.

E & P fixes the upper limit on the amount of dividend income that shareholders must recognize as a result of a distribution by the corporation. In this sense, E & P represents the corporation's economic ability to pay a dividend without impairing its capital. Thus, the effect of a specific transaction on the E & P account can be determined by considering whether or not the transaction increases or decreases the corporation's capacity to pay a dividend.

COMPUTATION OF E & P

To compute E & P in any year, certain adjustments are made to taxable income with the aim of making it conform more closely to the corporation's economic

---

[2]§ 301(c).

income. Both cash basis and accrual basis corporations use the same approach when determining E & P.[3]

Additions to Taxable Income. It is necessary to add all previously excluded income items back to taxable income to determine current E & P. Included among these positive adjustments are interest on municipal bonds, excluded life insurance proceeds (in excess of cash surrender value), Federal income tax refunds from tax paid in prior years, and the dividends received deduction.

EXAMPLE 2

A corporation collects $100,000 on a key employee life insurance policy (the corporation is the owner and beneficiary of the policy). At the time the policy matured on the death of the insured employee, it possessed a cash surrender value of $30,000. None of the $100,000 is included in the corporation's taxable income, but $70,000 is added to taxable income when computing current E & P. ▼

Subtractions from Taxable Income. Some of the corporation's nondeductible expenditures are subtracted from taxable income to arrive at E & P. These negative adjustments include related-party losses, excess capital losses, expenses incurred to produce tax-exempt income, Federal income taxes paid, nondeductible key employee life insurance premiums (net of increases in cash surrender value), and nondeductible fines and penalties.

EXAMPLE 3

A corporation sells property (basis of $10,000) to its sole shareholder for $8,000. Because of § 267 (disallowance of losses on sales between related parties), the $2,000 loss cannot be deducted in arriving at the corporation's taxable income. But since the overall economic effect of the transaction is a decrease in the corporation's assets by $2,000, the loss reduces the current E & P for the year of sale. ▼

EXAMPLE 4

A corporation pays a $10,000 premium on a key employee life insurance policy covering the life of its president. As a result of the payment, the cash surrender value of the policy is increased by $7,000. Although none of the $10,000 premium is deductible for tax purposes, current E & P is reduced by $3,000. ▼

Some E & P adjustments shift the effect of a transaction from the year of its inclusion in taxable income to the year in which it has an economic effect on the corporation. Charitable contribution carryovers, net operating loss carryovers and capital loss carryovers all serve as examples of this kind of adjustment.

EXAMPLE 5

During 1998, a corporation makes charitable contributions, $12,000 of which cannot be deducted in arriving at the taxable income for the year because of the 10% taxable income limitation. However, the $12,000 is carried forward to 1999 and fully deducted in that year. The excess charitable contribution reduces the corporation's current E & P for 1998 by $12,000 and increases its current E & P for 1999, when the deduction is allowed, by a like amount. The increase in E & P in 1999 is necessary because the charitable contribution carryover reduces the taxable income for that year (the starting point for computing E & P) and already has been taken into account in determining the E & P for 1998. ▼

Other Adjustments. In addition to the above adjustments, accounting methods used for determining E & P are generally more conservative than those allowed under the income tax. For example, the installment method is not permitted for

---

[3]Section 312 contains most of the adjustments necessary to determine E & P. It accomplishes this by setting out the effect of a number of transactions on E & P. Regulations relating to E & P begin at Reg. § 1.312–6.

CHAPTER 10 Corporations: Earnings & Profits and Dividend Distributions

E & P purposes. Thus, an adjustment is required for the deferred gain attributable to sales of property made during the year under the installment method. In particular, all principal payments are treated as having been received in the year of sale.[4]

EXAMPLE 6

In 1998, Cardinal Corporation, a calendar year taxpayer, sells unimproved real estate (basis of $20,000) for $100,000. Under the terms of the sale, beginning in 1999, Cardinal will receive two annual payments of $50,000 each with interest of 9%. Cardinal Corporation does not elect out of the installment method. Since Cardinal's taxable income for 1998 will not reflect any of the gain from the sale, the corporation must make an $80,000 positive adjustment for 1998 (the deferred profit component). Similarly, negative adjustments will be required in 1999 and 2000 (when the deferred profit is recognized under the installment method). ▼

The alternative depreciation system (ADS) must be used for purposes of computing E & P.[5] This method requires straight-line depreciation over a recovery period equal to the Asset Depreciation Range (ADR) midpoint life.[6] Thus, if MACRS cost recovery is used for income tax purposes, a positive or negative adjustment equal to the difference between MACRS and ADS must be made each year. Likewise, when assets are disposed of, an additional adjustment to taxable income is required to allow for the difference in gain or loss resulting from the difference in income tax basis and E & P basis.[7] The adjustments arising from depreciation are illustrated in the following example.

EXAMPLE 7

On January 2, 1996, White Corporation purchased equipment with an alternative recovery period of 10 years for $30,000. The equipment was then depreciated under MACRS. The asset was sold on July 2, 1998, for $27,000. For purposes of determining taxable income and E & P, cost recovery claimed on the equipment is summarized as follows:

Year	Cost Recovery Computation	MACRS	ADS	Adjustment Amount
1996	$30,000 × 14.29%	$ 4,287		
	$30,000 ÷ 10-year ADR recovery period × ½ (half-year for first year of service)		$1,500	$2,787
1997	$30,000 × 24.49%	7,347		
	$30,000 ÷ 10-year ADR recovery period		3,000	4,347
1998	$30,000 × 17.49% × ½ (half-year for year of disposal)	2,624		
	$30,000 ÷ 10-year ADR recovery period × ½ (half-year for year of disposal)		1,500	1,124
Total cost recovery		$14,258	$6,000	$8,258

Each year White Corporation will increase taxable income by the adjustment amount indicated above to determine E & P. In addition, when computing E & P for 1998, White will also reduce taxable income by $8,258 to account for the excess gain recognized for income tax purposes, as shown below.

---

[4] § 312(n)(5).
[5] § 312(k)(3)(A).
[6] See § 168(g)(2). The ADR midpoint life for most assets is set out in Rev.Proc. 87–56, 1987–2 C.B. 674. The recovery period is 5 years for automobiles and light-duty trucks and 40 years for real property. For assets with no class life, the recovery period is 12 years. Any amount expensed under § 179 is deducted over a period of 5 years in computing E & P. See § 312(k)(3)(B).
[7] § 312(f)(1).

	Income Tax	E & P
Amount realized	$ 27,000	$ 27,000
Adjusted basis for income tax ($30,000 cost − $14,258 MACRS)	(15,742)	
Adjusted basis for E & P ($30,000 cost − $6,000 ADS)		(24,000)
Gain on sale	$ 11,258	$ 3,000
Adjustment amount ($3,000 − $11,258)	($ 8,258)	

Gains and losses from property transactions generally affect the determination of E & P only to the extent that they are recognized for tax purposes. Thus, gains and losses deferred under the like-kind exchange provision and deferred involuntary conversion gains do not affect E & P until recognized. Accordingly, no adjustment is required for these items.

A variety of other adjustments are also required to determine current E & P. For example, cost depletion is required for E & P purposes, so an adjustment must be made to taxable income in cases where percentage depletion is used. Similarly, the percentage of completion method is required for E & P purposes when accounting for long-term contracts, so an adjustment is required when the completed contract method is employed. Intangible drilling costs and mine exploration and development costs may be deducted currently for income tax purposes, but must be capitalized for E & P. Once capitalized, these expenditures can be amortized under the E & P rules over 60 months for intangible drilling costs and over 120 months for mining exploration and development costs.[8]

SUMMARY OF E & P ADJUSTMENTS

E & P serves as a measure of the earnings of the corporation that are available for distribution as taxable dividends to the shareholders. Current E & P is determined by making a series of adjustments to the corporation's taxable income. These adjustments are reviewed in Concept Summary 10–1. Other items that affect E & P, such as property dividends, are covered later in the chapter and are not incorporated in the concept summary.

CURRENT VERSUS ACCUMULATED E & P

Accumulated E & P is the total of all previous years' current E & P (since February 28, 1913) as computed on the first day of each tax year, reduced by distributions made from E & P. It is important to distinguish between **current E & P** and **accumulated E & P**, since the taxability of corporate distributions depends on how these two accounts are allocated to each distribution made during the year. A complex set of rules governs the allocation process.[9] These rules are described in the following section and summarized in Concept Summary 10–2.

---

[8] § 312(n)(2).
[9] Regulations relating to the source of a distribution are at Reg. § 1.316–2.

CONCEPT SUMMARY 10–1

E & P Adjustments

Nature of the Transaction	Effect on Taxable Income in Arriving at Current E & P	
	Addition	Subtraction
Tax-exempt income	X	
Collection of proceeds from insurance policy on life of corporate officer	X	
Deferred gain on installment sale (all gain is added to E & P in year of sale)	X	
Future recognition of installment sale gross profit		X
Excess capital loss and excess charitable contribution (over 10% limitation) in year incurred		X
Deduction of charitable contribution, NOL, or capital loss carryovers in succeeding taxable year (increase E & P because deduction reduces taxable income while E & P was reduced in a prior year)	X	
Federal income taxes paid		X
Federal income tax refund	X	
Loss on sale between related parties		X
Nondeductible fines and penalties		X
Payment of premiums on insurance policy on life of corporate officer (in excess of increase in cash surrender value of policy)		X
Realized gain (not recognized) on an involuntary conversion	No effect	
Realized gain or loss (not recognized) on a like-kind exchange	No effect	
Percentage depletion (only cost depletion can reduce E & P)	X	
Accelerated depreciation (E & P is reduced only by straight-line, units-of-production, or machine hours depreciation)	X	
Intangible drilling costs deducted currently (reduce E & P in future years by amortizing costs over 60 months)	X	
Mine exploration and development costs (reduce in future years by amortizing costs over 120 months)	X	

ALLOCATING E & P TO DISTRIBUTIONS

2 LEARNING OBJECTIVE
Recognize the importance of earnings and profits in measuring the recipient shareholder's dividend income.

When a positive balance exists in both the current and the accumulated E & P accounts, corporate distributions are deemed to be made first from current E & P and then from accumulated E & P. When distributions exceed the amount of current E & P, it becomes necessary to allocate current and accumulated E & P to each distribution made during the year. Current E & P is allocated on a pro rata basis to each distribution. Accumulated E & P is applied in chronological order, beginning with the earliest distribution. As can be seen in the following example, this allocation is important if any shareholder sells stock during the year.

EXAMPLE 8

As of January 1 of the current year, Black Corporation has accumulated E & P of $10,000. Current E & P for the year amounts to $30,000. Megan and Matt are sole *equal* shareholders of Black from January 1 to July 31. On August 1, Megan sells all of her stock to Helen. Black makes two distributions to shareholders during the year: $40,000 to Megan and Matt ($20,000 to each) on July 1, and $40,000 to Matt and Helen ($20,000 to each) on December 1. Current and accumulated E & P are allocated to the two distributions as follows:

	Source of Distribution		
	Current E & P	Accumulated E & P	Return of Capital
July 1 distribution ($40,000)	$15,000	$10,000	$15,000
December 1 distribution ($40,000)	15,000	—	25,000

Thus, since 50% of the total distributions are made on July 1 and December 1, respectively, one-half of current E & P is allocated to each of the two distributions. Accumulated E & P is applied in chronological order, so the entire amount is attributed to the July 1 distribution. The tax consequences to the shareholders are presented below:

	Shareholder		
	Megan	Matt	Helen
July distribution ($40,000)			
Dividend income—			
From current E & P ($15,000)	$ 7,500	$ 7,500	$ –0–
From accumulated E & P ($10,000)	5,000	5,000	–0–
Return of capital ($15,000)	7,500	7,500	–0–
December distribution ($40,000)			
Dividend income—			
From current E & P ($15,000)	–0–	7,500	7,500
From accumulated E & P ($0)	–0–	–0–	–0–
Return of capital ($25,000)	–0–	12,500	12,500
Total dividend income	$12,500	$20,000	$ 7,500
Nontaxable return of capital (presuming sufficient basis in the stock investment)	$ 7,500	$20,000	$12,500

Because the balance in the accumulated E & P account is exhausted when it is applied to the July 1 distribution, Megan has more dividend income than Helen, even though both receive equal distributions during the year. In addition, each shareholder's basis is reduced by the nontaxable return of capital; any excess over basis results in capital gain. ▼

When the tax years of the corporation and its shareholders are not the same, it may be impossible to determine the amount of current E & P on a timely basis. For example, if shareholders use a calendar year and the corporation uses a fiscal year, then current E & P may not be ascertainable until after the shareholders' returns have been filed. To address this timing problem, the allocation rules presume that current E & P is sufficient to cover every distribution made during the year unless or until the parties can show otherwise.

EXAMPLE 9
Green Corporation uses the fiscal year of July 1 through June 30 for tax purposes. Carol, Green's only shareholder, uses a calendar year. As of July 1, 1998, Green Corporation has a zero balance in its accumulated E & P account. For fiscal year 1998–1999, the corporation suffers a $5,000 operating loss. On August 1, 1998, Green distributed $10,000 to Carol. The distribution is dividend income to Carol and is reported when she files her income tax return for the 1998 calendar year, on or before April 15, 1999. Because Carol cannot prove until June 30, 1999, that the corporation has a deficit for the 1998–1999 fiscal year, she must assume the $10,000 distribution is fully covered by current E & P. When Carol learns of the deficit, she can file an amended return for 1998 showing the $10,000 as a return of capital. ▼

Additional difficulties arise when either the current or the accumulated E & P account has a deficit balance. In particular, when current E & P is positive and accumulated E & P has a deficit balance, accumulated E & P is *not* netted against current E & P. Instead, the distribution is deemed to be a taxable dividend to the extent of the positive current E & P balance.

EXAMPLE 10

At the beginning of the current year, Brown Corporation has a deficit of $30,000 in accumulated E & P. For the year, it has current E & P of $10,000 and distributes $5,000 to its shareholders. The $5,000 distribution is treated as a taxable dividend since it is deemed to have been made from current E & P. This is the case even though Brown Corporation still has a deficit in accumulated E & P at the end of the year. ▼

In contrast to the above rule, when a deficit exists in current E & P and a positive balance exists in accumulated E & P, the accounts are netted at the date of distribution. If the resulting balance is zero or a deficit, the distribution is a return of capital. If a positive balance results, the distribution is a dividend to the extent of the balance. Any loss is allocated ratably during the year unless the parties can show otherwise.

EXAMPLE 11

At the beginning of the current year, Gray Corporation (a calendar year taxpayer) has accumulated E & P of $10,000. During the year, the corporation incurs a $15,000 net loss from operations that accrues ratably. On July 1, Gray Corporation distributes $6,000 in cash to Hal, its sole shareholder. To determine how much of the $6,000 cash distribution represents dividend income to Hal, the balance of both accumulated and current E & P as of July 1 is determined and netted. This is necessary because of the deficit in current E & P.

	Source of Distribution	
	Current E & P	**Accumulated E & P**
January 1		$10,000
July 1 (½ of $15,000 net loss)	($7,500)	2,500
July 1 distribution—($6,000):		
Dividend income: ($2,500)		
Return of capital: ($3,500)		

The balance in E & P on July 1 is $2,500. Thus, of the $6,000 distribution, $2,500 is taxed as a dividend, and $3,500 represents a return of capital. ▼

PLANNING CONSIDERATIONS

Corporate Distributions

In connection with the discussion of corporate distributions, the following points need reinforcement:

- Because E & P is the measure of dividend income, its periodic determination is essential to corporate planning. Thus, an E & P account should be established and maintained, particularly if the possibility exists that a corporate distribution might be a return of capital.
- Accumulated E & P is the sum of all past years' current E & P. There is no statute of limitations on the computation of E & P. The IRS can, for example, redetermine a corporation's current E & P for a tax year long since passed. Such a change affects

accumulated E & P and has a direct impact on the taxability of current distributions to shareholders.
- Distributions can be planned to avoid or minimize dividend exposure.

EXAMPLE 12 Flicker Corporation has accumulated E & P of $100,000 as of January 1 of the current year. During the year, it expects to have earnings from operations of $80,000 and to make a cash distribution of $60,000. Flicker Corporation also expects to sell an asset for a loss of $100,000. Thus, it anticipates a current E & P deficit of $20,000. The best approach is to recognize the loss as soon as possible and immediately thereafter make the cash distribution to the shareholders. Suppose these two steps take place on January 1. Because the current E & P has a deficit, the accumulated E & P account must be brought up to date (refer to Example 11 in this chapter). Thus, at the time of the distribution, the combined E & P balance is zero [$100,000 (beginning balance in accumulated E & P) − $100,000 (existing deficit in current E & P)], and the $60,000 distribution to the shareholders constitutes a return of capital. Current deficits are allocated pro rata throughout the year unless the parties can prove otherwise. Here they can. ▼

EXAMPLE 13 After several unprofitable years, Darter Corporation has a deficit in accumulated E & P of $100,000 as of January 1, 1998. Starting in 1998, Darter expects to generate annual E & P of $50,000 for the next four years and would like to distribute this amount to its shareholders. The corporation's cash position (for dividend purposes) will correspond to the current E & P generated. Compare the following possibilities:

1. On December 31 of 1998, 1999, 2000, and 2001, Darter Corporation distributes a cash dividend of $50,000.
2. On December 31 of 1999 and 2001, Darter Corporation distributes a cash dividend of $100,000.

The two alternatives are illustrated as follows:

Year	Accumulated E & P (First of Year)	Current E & P	Distribution	Amount of Dividend
Alternative 1				
1998	($100,000)	$50,000	$ 50,000	$50,000
1999	(100,000)	50,000	50,000	50,000
2000	(100,000)	50,000	50,000	50,000
2001	(100,000)	50,000	50,000	50,000
Alternative 2				
1998	($100,000)	$50,000	$ −0−	$ −0−
1999	(50,000)	50,000	100,000	50,000
2000	(50,000)	50,000	−0−	−0−
2001	−0−	50,000	100,000	50,000

Alternative 1 leads to an overall result of $200,000 in dividend income, since each $50,000 distribution is fully covered by current E & P. Alternative 2, however, results in only $100,000 of dividend income to the shareholders. The remaining $100,000 is a return of capital. Why? At the time Darter Corporation made its first distribution of $100,000 on December 31, 1999, it had a deficit of $50,000 in accumulated E & P (the original deficit of $100,000 is reduced by the $50,000 of current E & P from 1998). Consequently, the $100,000 distribution yields a $50,000 dividend (the current E & P for 1999) and $50,000 as a return of capital. As of January 1, 2000, Darter's accumulated E & P now has a deficit balance of $50,000, since a distribution cannot increase a deficit in E & P. Add in $50,000 of current E & P from 2000, and the balance as of January 1, 2001, is zero. Thus, the second distribution of $100,000 made on December 31, 2001, also yields $50,000 of dividends (the current E & P for 2001) and $50,000 as a return of capital. ▼

Concept Summary 10-2

Allocating E & P to Distributions

1. Current E & P is allocated first to distributions on a pro rata basis; then, accumulated E & P is applied (to the extent necessary) in chronological order beginning with the earliest distribution.
2. Unless and until the parties can show otherwise, it is presumed that current E & P covers all distributions.
3. When a deficit exists in accumulated E & P and a positive balance exists in current E & P, distributions are regarded as dividends to the extent of current E & P.
4. When a deficit exists in current E & P and a positive balance exists in accumulated E & P, the two accounts are netted at the date of distribution. If the resulting balance is zero or a deficit, the distribution is treated as a return of capital, first reducing the basis of the stock to zero, then generating capital gain. If a positive balance results, the distribution is a dividend to the extent of the balance. Any loss is allocated ratably during the year unless the parties can show otherwise.

PROPERTY DIVIDENDS

LEARNING OBJECTIVE 3
Understand the tax impact of property dividends on the recipient shareholder and the corporation making the distribution.

The previous discussion assumed that all distributions by a corporation to its shareholders are in the form of cash. Although most corporate distributions are cash, a corporation may distribute a **property dividend** for various reasons. The shareholders could want a particular property that is held by the corporation. Or a corporation that is strapped for cash may want to distribute a dividend to its shareholders.

Property distributions have the same impact as distributions of cash except for effects attributable to any difference between the basis and fair market value of the distributed property. In most situations, distributed property is appreciated, so its sale would result in a gain to the corporation. Distributions of property with a basis that differs from fair market value raise several tax questions.

- For the shareholder:
    1. What is the amount of the distribution?
    2. What is the new basis of the property in the shareholder's hands?

- For the corporation:
    1. Is a gain or loss recognized as a result of the distribution?
    2. What is the effect of the distribution on E & P?

PROPERTY DIVIDENDS—EFFECT ON THE SHAREHOLDER

When a corporation distributes property rather than cash to a shareholder, the amount distributed is measured by the fair market value of the property on the date of distribution.[10] As with a cash distribution, the portion of a property distribution covered by existing E & P is a dividend, and any excess is treated as a return of capital. If the fair market value of the property distributed exceeds the corporation's E & P and the shareholder's basis in the stock investment, a capital gain results.

---
[10] Section 301 describes the tax treatment of corporate distributions to shareholders.

TAX IN THE NEWS

STOCK BUYBACKS CONTINUE TO GROW

Publicly held companies are finding that buying back their own stock is a good way to reward their shareholders. According to the Securities Data Company of Newark, New Jersey, 1995 yielded a record 1,108 stock buyback announcements. Not only did the number of stock buybacks increase, but the dollar value of the buybacks exploded from $20 billion in 1991 to $99 billion in 1995. The recent increase in stock buybacks can be attributed to a number of factors, including the long-standing double tax on dividends.

Many think excess corporate cash earning the market rate of return is better off in shareholders' pockets. The return earned by shareholders is only taxed once, at the shareholder level. In many cases, shareholders receive the benefit of offsetting their basis in the purchased shares against the proceeds received, as opposed to a dividend, where the proceeds are fully taxable.

SOURCE: Information from "Corporate Stock Buybacks are Soaring," *Treasury Manager's Report*, February 16, 1996.

The amount distributed is reduced by any liabilities to which the distributed property is subject immediately before and immediately after the distribution and by any liabilities of the corporation assumed by the shareholder. The basis in the distributed property to the shareholder is the fair market value of the property on the date of the distribution.

EXAMPLE 14 Robin Corporation has E & P of $60,000. It distributes land with a fair market value of $50,000 (adjusted basis of $30,000) to its sole shareholder, Charles. The land is subject to a liability of $10,000, which Charles assumes. Charles has a taxable dividend of $40,000 [$50,000 (fair market value) − $10,000 (liability)]. The basis of the land to Charles is $50,000. ▼

EXAMPLE 15 Ten percent of Tan Corporation is owned by Red Corporation. Tan Corporation has ample E & P to cover any distributions made during the year. One distribution made to Red Corporation consists of a vacant lot with adjusted basis of $5,000 and a fair market value of $3,000. Red has a taxable dividend of $3,000, and its basis in the lot becomes $3,000. ▼

Distributing property that has depreciated in value as a property dividend may suggest poor planning. Note what happens in Example 15. The loss of $2,000 (adjusted basis $5,000, fair market value $3,000) disappears. As an alternative, if Tan Corporation sells the lot, it could use the loss to reduce its taxes. Then Tan could distribute the $3,000 of proceeds to shareholders.

PROPERTY DIVIDENDS—EFFECT ON THE CORPORATION

As noted earlier, the distribution of a property dividend raises two questions related to the corporation's tax position: Is a gain or loss recognized? What is the effect on E & P?

Recognition of Gain or Loss. All distributions of appreciated property generate gain to the distributing corporation.[11] In effect, a corporation that distributes

---

[11]Section 311 describes how corporations are taxed on distributions.

property is treated as if it had sold the property to the shareholder for its fair market value. However, the distributing corporation does not recognize loss on distributions of property.

EXAMPLE 16

A corporation distributes land (basis of $10,000 and fair market value of $30,000) to a shareholder. The corporation recognizes a gain of $20,000. ▼

EXAMPLE 17

Assume the property in Example 16 has a fair market value of $10,000 and a basis of $30,000. The corporation does not recognize a loss on the distribution. ▼

If the distributed property is subject to a liability in excess of basis or the shareholder assumes such a liability, a special rule applies. The fair market value of the property for purposes of determining gain on the distribution is treated as not being less than the amount of the liability.[12]

EXAMPLE 18

Assume the land in Example 16 is subject to a liability of $35,000. The corporation recognizes gain of $25,000 on the distribution. ▼

Effect of Corporate Distributions on E & P. Corporate distributions reduce E & P by the amount of money distributed or by the greater of the fair market value or the adjusted basis of property distributed, less the amount of any liability on the property.[13] E & P is increased by gain recognized on appreciated property distributed as a property dividend.

EXAMPLE 19

Crimson Corporation distributes property (basis of $10,000 and fair market value of $20,000) to Brenda, its shareholder. Crimson Corporation recognizes a gain of $10,000, which is added to its E & P. E & P is then reduced by $20,000, the fair market value of the property. Brenda has dividend income of $20,000. ▼

EXAMPLE 20

Assume the same facts as in Example 19, except that the adjusted basis in the hands of Crimson Corporation is $25,000. Because loss is not recognized and the adjusted basis is greater than fair market value, E & P is reduced by $25,000. Brenda reports dividend income of $20,000. ▼

EXAMPLE 21

Assume the same facts as in Example 20, except that the property is subject to a liability of $6,000. E & P is now reduced by $19,000 [$25,000 (adjusted basis) − $6,000 (liability)]. Brenda has a dividend of $14,000 [$20,000 (amount of the distribution) − $6,000 (liability)], and her basis in the property is $20,000. ▼

Under no circumstances can a distribution, whether cash or property, either generate a deficit in E & P or add to a deficit in E & P. Deficits can arise only through corporate losses.

EXAMPLE 22

Teal Corporation has accumulated E & P of $10,000 at the beginning of the current tax year. During the year, it has current E & P of $15,000. At the end of the year, it distributes cash of $30,000 to its sole shareholder, Walter. Teal's E & P at the end of the year is zero. The beginning E & P of $10,000 is increased by current E & P of $15,000 and reduced $25,000 by the dividend distribution. The remaining $5,000 of the distribution to Walter does not reduce E & P because a distribution cannot generate a deficit in E & P. ▼

---

[12] § 311(b)(2).   [13] §§ 312(a), (b), and (c).

CONSTRUCTIVE DIVIDENDS

LEARNING OBJECTIVE 4
Understand the nature and treatment of constructive dividends.

Any measurable economic benefit conveyed by a corporation to its shareholders can be treated as a dividend for Federal income tax purposes even though it is not formally declared or designated as a dividend. Also, it need not be issued pro rata to all shareholders.[14] Nor must the distribution satisfy the legal requirements of a dividend as set forth by applicable state law. This benefit, often described as a **constructive dividend,** is distinguishable from actual corporate distributions of cash and property in form only.

Constructive dividend situations usually arise in closely held corporations. Here, the dealings between the parties are less structured, and frequently, formalities are not preserved. The constructive dividend serves as a substitute for actual distributions. Usually, it is intended to accomplish some tax objective not available through the use of direct dividends. The shareholders may be attempting to bail out corporate profits in a form deductible to the corporation.[15] Alternatively, the shareholders may be seeking benefits for themselves while avoiding the recognition of income. Some constructive dividends are, in reality, disguised dividends. But not all constructive dividends are deliberate attempts to avoid actual and formal dividends; many are inadvertent. Thus, an awareness of the various constructive dividend situations is essential to protect the parties from unanticipated, undesirable tax consequences.

TYPES OF CONSTRUCTIVE DIVIDENDS

The most frequently encountered types of constructive dividends are summarized below.

Shareholder Use of Corporate-Owned Property. A constructive dividend can occur when a shareholder uses corporation property for personal purposes at no cost. Personal use of corporate-owned automobiles, airplanes, yachts, fishing camps, hunting lodges, and other entertainment facilities is commonplace in some closely held corporations. The shareholder has dividend income to the extent of the fair rental value of the property for the period of its personal use.

Bargain Sale of Corporate Property to a Shareholder. Shareholders often purchase property from a corporation at a cost below the fair market value of the property. These bargain sales produce dividend income to the extent of the difference between the property's fair market value on the date of sale and the amount the shareholder paid for the property.[16] These situations might be avoided by appraising the property on or about the date of the sale. The appraised value should become the price to be paid by the shareholder.

Bargain Rental of Corporate Property. A bargain rental of corporate property by a shareholder also produces dividend income. Here the measure of the constructive dividend is the excess of the property's fair rental value over the rent actually paid. Again, appraisal data should be used to avoid any questionable situations.

---

[14] See *Lengsfield v. Comm.*, 57–1 USTC ¶9437, 50 AFTR 1683, 241 F.2d 508 (CA–5, 1957).

[15] Recall that dividend distributions do not provide the distributing corporation with an income tax deduction, although they do reduce E & P.

[16] Reg. § 1.301–1(j).

Payments for the Benefit of a Shareholder. If a corporation pays an obligation of a shareholder, the payment is treated as a constructive dividend. The obligation involved need not be legally binding on the shareholder; it may, in fact, be a moral obligation.[17] Forgiveness of shareholder indebtedness by the corporation creates an identical problem.[18] Excessive rentals paid by a corporation for the use of shareholder property also are treated as constructive dividends.

Unreasonable Compensation. A salary payment to a shareholder-employee that is deemed to be **unreasonable compensation** is frequently treated as a constructive dividend. As a consequence, it is not deductible by the corporation. In determining the reasonableness of salary payments, the following factors are considered:

- The employee's qualifications.
- A comparison of salaries with dividend distributions.
- The prevailing rates of compensation for comparable positions in comparable business concerns.
- The nature and scope of the employee's work.
- The size and complexity of the business.
- A comparison of salaries paid with both gross and net income.
- The taxpayer's salary policy toward all employees.
- For small corporations with a limited number of officers, the amount of compensation paid the employee in question in previous years.[19]

Loans to Shareholders. Advances to shareholders that are not bona fide loans are constructive dividends. Whether an advance qualifies as a bona fide loan is a question of fact to be determined in light of the particular circumstances. Factors considered in determining whether the advance is a bona fide loan include the following:[20]

- Whether the advance is on open account or is evidenced by a written instrument.
- Whether the shareholder furnished collateral or other security for the advance.
- How long the advance has been outstanding.
- Whether any repayments have been made.
- The shareholder's ability to repay the advance.
- The shareholder's use of the funds (e.g., payment of routine bills versus nonrecurring, extraordinary expenses).
- The regularity of the advances.
- The dividend-paying history of the corporation.

If a corporation succeeds in proving that an advance to a shareholder is a bona fide loan, the advance is not a constructive dividend. But the shareholder may still have a constructive dividend equal to any imputed (forgone) interest.[21] Imputed interest is the difference between interest the Federal government pays on new borrowings, compounded semiannually, and the interest charged on the loan. When the imputed interest provision applies, the shareholder is deemed to have made

---

[17] *Montgomery Engineering Co. v. U.S.*, 64–2 USTC ¶9618, 13 AFTR2d 1747, 230 F.Supp. 838 (D.Ct.N.J., 1964); aff'd. in 65–1 USTC ¶9368, 15 AFTR2d 746, 344 F.2d 996 (CA–3, 1965).

[18] Reg. § 1.301–1(m).

[19] *Mayson Manufacturing Co. v. Comm.*, 49–2 USTC ¶9467, 38 AFTR 1028, 178 F.2d 115 (CA–6, 1949).

[20] *Fin Hay Realty Co. v. U.S.*, 68–2 USTC ¶9438, 22 AFTR2d 5004, 398 F.2d 694 (CA–3, 1968).

[21] See § 7872. Also, refer to the more detailed discussion of imputed interest in Chapter 3.

> ### TAX IN THE NEWS
>
> #### WHEN IS COMPENSATION UNREASONABLE?
>
> What is reasonable compensation for the head of the Chicago Stadium Corporation, which manages the arena where the Chicago Blackhawks hockey team and the Chicago Bulls basketball team play? For the fiscal year ending on July 31, 1977, the corporation paid its chairman and CEO, Arthur Wirtz, $335,750, but the IRS insisted reasonable compensation would be only $138,000 and disallowed the company's deduction for the remainder.
>
> A long legal battle ensued, but the Federal District Court in Chicago finally upheld the IRS [*Chicago Stadium Corporation v. U.S.*, 91–2 USTC ¶50,352 (D.Ct.Ill., 1991)]. Among other things, the court said that Wirtz was paid considerably more than the executives of similar arenas, yet he did not even work full-time for the corporation. Besides, much of his pay consisted of "commissions" for arranging to lease the arena to the Bulls, which he also controlled. Under the circumstances, said the court, the $138,000 allowed by the IRS was generous.

an interest payment to the corporation equal to the amount of imputed interest, and the corporation is deemed to have repaid the imputed interest to the shareholder through a constructive dividend. Consequently, the corporation receives interest income and makes a nondeductible dividend payment, and the shareholder has taxable dividend income that may be offset with an interest deduction.

EXAMPLE 23

Mallard Corporation lends its principal shareholder, Henry, $100,000 on January 2 of the current year. The loan is interest-free and payable on demand. On December 31, the imputed interest rules are applied. Assuming the Federal rate is 6%, compounded semiannually, the amount of imputed interest is $6,180. This amount is deemed paid by Henry to Mallard in the form of interest. Mallard is then deemed to return the amount to Henry as a constructive dividend. Thus, Henry has dividend income of $6,180, which may be offset with a deduction for the interest paid to Mallard. Mallard has interest income of $6,180 for the interest received, with no offsetting deduction for the dividend payment. ▼

Loans to a Corporation by Shareholders. Shareholder loans to a corporation may be reclassified as equity because the debt has too many features of stock. Any interest and principal payments made by the corporation to the shareholder are then treated as constructive dividends. This topic was covered more thoroughly in the discussion of "thin capitalization" in Chapter 9.

TAX TREATMENT OF CONSTRUCTIVE DIVIDENDS

Constructive distributions are treated the same for tax purposes as actual distributions.[22] Thus, a corporate shareholder is entitled to the dividends received deduction (refer to Chapter 9). The constructive distribution is taxable as a dividend only to the extent of the corporation's current and accumulated E & P. The burden of proving that the distribution constitutes a return of capital because of inadequate E & P rests with the taxpayer.[23]

---

[22]*Simon v. Comm.*, 57–2 USTC ¶9989, 52 AFTR 698, 248 F.2d 869 (CA–8, 1957).

[23]*DiZenzo v. Comm.*, 65–2 USTC ¶9518, 16 AFTR2d 5107, 348 F.2d 122 (CA–2, 1965).

Planning Considerations

Constructive Dividends

Tax planning can be particularly effective in avoiding constructive dividend situations. Shareholders should try to structure their dealings with the corporation on an arm's length basis. For example, reasonable rent should be paid for the use of corporate property, and a fair price should be paid for its purchase. The parties should make every effort to support the amount involved with appraisal data or market information obtained from reliable sources at or near the time of the transaction. Dealings between shareholders and a closely held corporation should be as formal as possible. In the case of loans to shareholders, for example, the parties should provide for an adequate rate of interest and written evidence of the debt. Shareholders also should establish and follow a realistic repayment schedule.

If shareholders wish to bail out corporate profits in a form deductible to the corporation, a balanced mix of the possible alternatives lessens the risk of constructive dividend treatment. Rent for the use of shareholder property, interest on amounts borrowed from shareholders, or salaries for services rendered by shareholders are all feasible substitutes for dividend distributions. But overdoing any one approach may attract the attention of the IRS. Too much interest, for example, may mean the corporation is thinly capitalized, and some of the debt may be reclassified as equity investment.

Much can be done to protect against the disallowance of unreasonable compensation. Example 24 is an illustration, all too common in a family corporation, of what *not* to do.

EXAMPLE 24

Bob Cole wholly owns Eagle Corporation. Corporate employees and annual salaries include Mrs. Cole ($30,000), Cole, Jr. ($20,000), Bob Cole ($160,000), and Ed ($80,000). The operation of Eagle Corporation is shared about equally between Bob Cole and Ed, who is an unrelated party. Mrs. Cole performed significant services for Eagle during its formative years but now merely attends the annual meeting of the board of directors. Cole, Jr., Bob Cole's son, is a full-time student and occasionally signs papers for the corporation in his capacity as treasurer. Eagle Corporation has not distributed a dividend for 10 years, although it has accumulated substantial E & P. Mrs. Cole, Cole, Jr., and Bob Cole run the risk of a finding of unreasonable compensation, based on the following factors:

- Mrs. Cole's salary is vulnerable unless proof is available that some or all of her $30,000 annual salary is payment for services rendered to the corporation in prior years, if she was underpaid for those years.[24]
- Cole, Jr.'s salary is also vulnerable; he does not appear to earn the $20,000 paid to him by the corporation. True, neither Cole, Jr., nor Mrs. Cole is a shareholder, but each one's relationship to Bob Cole is enough of a tie-in to raise the unreasonable compensation issue.
- Bob Cole's salary appears susceptible to challenge. Why is he receiving $80,000 more than Ed when it appears that they share equally in the operation of the corporation?
- The fact that Eagle Corporation has not distributed dividends over the past 10 years, even though it is capable of doing so, increases the likelihood of a constructive dividend. ▼

What could have been done to improve the tax position of the parties in Example 24? Mrs. Cole and Cole, Jr., are not entitled to a salary as neither seems to be performing any services for the corporation. Paying them a salary simply aggravates the problem. The IRS is more apt to consider *all* the salaries to members of the family as being excessive under the circumstances. Bob Cole should probably reduce his compensation to correspond to that paid Ed. He can then attempt to distribute corporate earnings to himself in some other form.

---

[24] See, for example, *R. J. Nicoll Co.*, 59 T.C. 37 (1972).

Paying some dividends to Bob Cole would also help alleviate the problem raised in Example 24. The IRS has been successful in denying a deduction for salary paid to a shareholder-employee, even when the payment was reasonable, in a situation where the corporation had not distributed any dividends.[25] Most courts, however, have not denied deductions for compensation solely because a dividend was not paid. A better approach is to compare an employee's compensation with the level of compensation prevalent in the particular industry.

The corporation can substitute *indirect* compensation for Bob Cole by paying expenses that benefit him personally but are nevertheless deductible to the corporation. For example, premiums paid by the corporation for sickness, accident, and hospitalization insurance for Bob Cole are deductible to the corporation and nontaxable to him.[26] Any payments under the policy are not taxable to Bob Cole unless they exceed his medical expenses.[27] The corporation can also pay for travel and entertainment expenses incurred by Cole on behalf of the corporation. Such expenditures must be primarily for the benefit of the corporation to be deductible. Bob Cole will not have taxable income in the amount of the expenditures.[28] The tax treatment of these benefits is discussed in more detail in Chapter 16.

When testing for reasonableness, the IRS looks at the total compensation package, including indirect compensation payments to a shareholder-employee. Thus, indirect payments must not be overlooked.

EXAMPLE 25

Cora, the president and sole shareholder of Willet Corporation, is paid an annual salary of $100,000 by the corporation. Cora would like to draw funds from the corporation but is concerned that additional salary payments might cause the IRS to contend her salary is unreasonable. Cora does not want Willet to pay any dividends. She also wishes to donate $50,000 to her alma mater to establish scholarships for needy students. Willet Corporation could make the contribution on Cora's behalf. The payment clearly benefits Cora, but the amount of the contribution will not be taxed to her.[29] Willet can take a charitable contribution deduction for the payment. ▼

EXAMPLE 26

Assume in Example 25 that Cora has made an individual pledge to the university to provide $50,000 for scholarships for needy students. Willet Corporation satisfies Cora's pledge by paying the $50,000 to the university. The $50,000 will be taxed to Cora.[30] In this context, the $50,000 payment to the university may be treated as *indirect* compensation to Cora. In determining whether Cora's salary is unreasonable, both the *direct* payment of $100,000 and the *indirect* $50,000 payment will be considered. Cora's total compensation package is $150,000. ▼

STOCK DIVIDENDS AND STOCK RIGHTS

STOCK DIVIDENDS—§ 305

5 LEARNING OBJECTIVE
Distinguish between taxable and nontaxable stock dividends and stock rights.

Historically, **stock dividends** were excluded from income on the theory that the ownership interest of the shareholder was unchanged as a result of the distribution.[31] The 1954 Code expanded upon this treatment by taxing stock dividends where (1) the stockholder could elect to receive either stock or property or (2) the stock

---

[25]*McCandless Tile Service v. U.S.*, 70–1 USTC ¶9284, 25 AFTR2d 70–870, 422 F.2d 1336 (Ct.Cls., 1970). The court in *McCandless* concluded that a return on equity of 15% of net profits was reasonable.
[26]Reg. § 1.162–10.
[27]The medical reimbursement plan must meet certain nondiscrimination requirements of § 105(h)(2).
[28]Reg. § 1.62–2(c)(4).
[29]*Henry J. Knott*, 67 T.C. 681 (1977).
[30]*Schalk Chemical Co. v. Comm.*, 62–1 USTC ¶9496, 9 AFTR2d 1579, 304 F.2d 48 (CA–9, 1962).
[31]See *Eisner v. Macomber*, 1 USTC ¶32, 3 AFTR 3020, 40 S.Ct. 189 (USSC, 1920).

dividends were in discharge of preference dividends. Because of the narrow scope of these provisions, corporations devised an assortment of methods to distribute stock dividends that qualified for tax-free treatment yet still affected shareholders' proportionate interests in the corporation.[32] Section 305 was amended to curtail the use of these methods.

The provisions of § 305 are based on the proportionate interest concept. As a general rule, stock dividends are excluded from income if they are pro rata distributions of stock or stock rights, paid on common stock. Five exceptions to this general rule exist. For each of these exceptions, listed below, stock distributions may be taxed.

1. Distributions payable in either stock or property, at the election of the shareholder.
2. Distributions of property to some shareholders, with a corresponding increase in the proportionate interest of other shareholders in either assets or E & P of the distributing corporation.
3. Distributions of preferred stock to some common shareholders and of common stock to other common shareholders.
4. Distributions of stock to preferred shareholders. Note, however, that changes in the conversion ratio of convertible preferred stock to account for a stock dividend or stock split are not taxable in some circumstances.
5. Distributions of convertible preferred stock, unless it can be shown that the distribution will not result in a disproportionate distribution.

Note that these exceptions to nontaxability of stock dividends deal with various disproportionate distribution situations.

Holders of convertible securities are considered shareholders. As a result, payment of interest on convertible debentures causes stock dividends paid on common stock to be taxable. This result is avoided if the conversion ratio or conversion price is adjusted to reflect the stock dividend.[33]

If stock dividends are not taxable, the corporation's E & P is not reduced.[34] If the stock dividends are taxable, the distributing corporation treats the distribution in the same manner as any other taxable property dividend.

If a stock dividend is taxable, basis of the newly received shares to the shareholder-distributee is fair market value, and the holding period starts on the date of receipt. If a stock dividend is not taxable, the basis of the stock on which the dividend is distributed is reallocated.[35] If the dividend shares are identical to these formerly held shares, basis in the old stock is reallocated by dividing the taxpayer's cost in the old stock by the total number of shares. If the dividend stock is not identical to the underlying shares (e.g., a stock dividend of preferred on common), basis is determined by allocating the basis of the formerly held shares between the old and new stock according to the fair market value of each. The holding period includes the holding period of the formerly held stock.[36]

EXAMPLE 27

Gail bought 1,000 shares of stock two years ago for $10,000. In the current tax year, Gail receives 10 shares of common stock as a nontaxable stock dividend. Gail's basis of $10,000 is divided by 1,010. Each share of stock has a basis of $9.90 instead of the pre-dividend $10 basis. ▼

EXAMPLE 28

Assume Gail received, instead, a nontaxable preferred stock dividend of 100 shares. The preferred stock has a fair market value of $1,000, and the common stock, on which the

---

[32]See "Stock Dividends," Senate Report 91–552, 1969–3 C.B. 519.
[33]See Reg. § 1.305–3(d) for illustrations on how to compute required adjustments on conversion ratios or prices.
[34]§ 312(d)(1).
[35]§ 307(a).
[36]§ 1223(5).

preferred is distributed, has a fair market value of $19,000. After the receipt of the stock dividend, the basis of the common stock is $9,500, and the basis of the preferred is $500, computed as follows:

Fair market value of common	$19,000
Fair market value of preferred	1,000
	$20,000
Basis of common: 19/20 × $10,000	$ 9,500
Basis of preferred: 1/20 × $10,000	$ 500

STOCK RIGHTS

The rules for determining taxability of **stock rights** are identical to those for determining taxability of stock dividends. If the rights are taxable, the recipient has income to the extent of the fair market value of the rights. The fair market value then becomes the shareholder-distributee's basis in the rights.[37] If the rights are exercised, the holding period for the new stock is the date the rights (whether taxable or nontaxable) are exercised. The basis of the new stock is the basis of the rights plus the amount of any other consideration given.

If stock rights are not taxable and the value of the rights is less than 15 percent of the value of the old stock, the basis of the rights is zero. However, the shareholder may elect to have some of the basis in the formerly held stock allocated to the rights.[38] The election is made by attaching a statement to the shareholder's return for the year in which the rights are received.[39] If the fair market value of the rights is 15 percent or more of the value of the old stock and the rights are exercised or sold, the shareholder must allocate some of the basis in the formerly held stock to the rights.

EXAMPLE 29

A corporation with common stock outstanding declares a nontaxable dividend payable in rights to subscribe to common stock. Each right entitles the holder to purchase one share of stock for $90. One right is issued for every two shares of stock owned. Fred owns 400 shares of stock purchased two years ago for $15,000. At the time of the distribution of the rights, the market value of the common stock is $100 per share, and the market value of the rights is $8 per right. Fred receives 200 rights. He exercises 100 rights and sells the remaining 100 rights three months later for $9 per right.

Fred need not allocate the cost of the original stock to the rights because the value of the rights is less than 15% of the value of the stock ($1,600 ÷ $40,000 = 4%). If Fred does not allocate his original stock basis to the rights, the tax consequences are as follows:

- Basis in the new stock is $9,000 ($90 × 100). The holding period of the new stock begins on the date the stock was purchased.
- Sale of the rights produces long-term capital gain of $900 ($9 × 100). The holding period of the rights starts with the date the original 400 shares of stock were acquired.

If Fred elects to allocate basis to the rights, the tax consequences are as follows:

- Basis in the stock is $14,423 [$40,000 ÷ $41,600 (value of rights and stock) × $15,000 (cost of stock)].
- Basis in the rights is $577 [$1,600 (value of rights) ÷ $41,600 (value of rights and stock) × $15,000 (cost of stock)].

---

[37] Reg. § 1.305–1(b).
[38] § 307(b)(1).
[39] Reg. § 1.307–2.

- When Fred exercises the rights, his basis in the new stock will be $9,288.50 [$9,000 (cost) + $288.50 (basis in 100 rights)].
- Sale of the rights would produce a long-term capital gain of $611.50 [$900 (selling price) − $288.50 (basis in the remaining 100 rights)]. ▼

RESTRICTIONS ON CORPORATE ACCUMULATIONS

Two provisions of the Code are designed to prevent corporations and their shareholders from avoiding the double tax on dividend distributions. Both provisions apply a penalty tax on undistributed income retained by the corporation. The rules underlying these provisions are complex and beyond the scope of this text. However, a brief description is provided as an introduction.

The *accumulated earnings tax* (in §§ 531–537) imposes a 39.6 percent tax on the current year's corporate earnings that have been accumulated without a reasonable business need. The burden of proving what constitutes a reasonable need is borne by the taxpayer. In determining accumulated income, most businesses are allowed a $250,000 minimum credit. Thus, most corporations can accumulate $250,000 in earnings over a series of years without fear of an accumulated earnings tax. Beyond the minimum credit, earnings can be accumulated for:

1. Working capital needs (to purchase inventory),
2. Retirement of debt incurred in connection with the business,
3. Investment or loans to suppliers or customers (if necessary to maintain the corporation's business), or
4. Realistic business contingencies, including lawsuits or self-insurance.

The *personal holding company (PHC) tax* (described in §§ 541–547) was enacted to discourage the sheltering of certain kinds of passive income in corporations owned by individuals with high marginal tax rates. Historically, the tax was aimed at "incorporated pocketbooks" that were frequently found in the entertainment and construction industries. For example, a taxpayer could shelter income from securities in a corporation, which would pay no dividends, and allow the corporation's stock to increase in value. Like the accumulated earnings tax, the PHC tax employs a 39.6 percent rate and is designed to force a corporation to distribute earnings to shareholders. However, in any single year, the IRS cannot impose both the PHC tax and the accumulated earnings tax. Generally, a company is considered a PHC and may be subject to the tax if:

1. More than 50 percent of the value of the outstanding stock was owned by five or fewer individuals at any time during the last half of the year, and
2. A substantial portion (60 percent or more) of the corporation's income is composed of passive types of income, including dividends, interest, rents, royalties, or certain personal service income.

KEY TERMS

Accumulated earnings and profits, 10–6

Constructive dividend, 10–14

Current earnings and profits, 10–6

Earnings and profits (E & P), 10–3
Property dividend, 10–11
Stock dividends, 10–18
Stock rights, 10–20
Unreasonable compensation, 10–15

PROBLEM MATERIALS

1. At the beginning of the year, Crane Corporation (a calendar year taxpayer) has accumulated E & P of $75,000. Its current E & P is $45,000. During the year, Crane Corporation distributes $135,000 ($67,500 each) to its equal shareholders, Pat and Chris. Pat has a basis of $12,000 in her stock, and Chris has a basis of $3,000 in his stock. How will the $135,000 distribution be treated for tax purposes?

2. In 1998, Gull Corporation received dividend income of $200,000 from a corporation in which it holds a 10% interest. Gull also received interest income of $40,000 from municipal bonds. The municipality used the proceeds from the sale of the bonds to construct a needed facility to house city documents and to provide office space for several city officials. Gull borrowed funds to purchase the municipal bonds and paid $20,000 in interest on the loan in 1998. Gull's taxable income exclusive of the items noted above was $150,000.
   a. What is Gull Corporation's taxable income for 1998 after considering the dividend income, the interest from the municipal bonds, and the interest paid on the indebtedness to purchase the municipals?
   b. What is Gull Corporation's E & P as of December 31, 1998, if its E & P account balance was $90,000 as of January 1, 1998?

3. In 1991, Beige Corporation made a cash distribution to its shareholders, one of whom was Steve Jordan. At that time, the parties involved believed that the distribution was a return of capital because Beige had no E & P. Accordingly, none of the shareholders reported dividend income. In Steve's case, he reduced the $200,000 original basis of his stock investment by $40,000, his share of the distribution. In 1998, it is discovered that E & P had been incorrectly computed. The 1991 distribution was fully covered by E & P and *should not have been treated as a return of capital*.
   In 1999, Steve sells his stock in Beige Corporation for $350,000. He plans to report a gain of $150,000 [$350,000 (selling price) – $200,000 (original basis)] on the sale. Although Steve realizes that he should have recognized dividend income of $40,000 for 1991, the statute of limitations has made this a closed year.
   Comment on Steve's situation.

4. Orange Corporation has a deficit in E & P of $90,000 on January 1, 1998. For 1998, Orange has a tax loss of $180,000 that increases the deficit in E & P by that amount.
   Orange's 1998 tax loss does not include any effect from a sale of land. The land, which had a basis of $450,000, was sold on November 15, 1998. In exchange, Orange received a $1,800,000 note. The note is to be paid in five installments, the first of which is payable on December 15, 1999. Because Orange did not elect out of the installment method, none of the $1,350,000 gain is taxable income for 1998.
   All of Orange's stock is owned by Nick, who has a basis of $150,000 in the stock. If Orange distributes $200,000 to Nick on December 31, 1998, how must Nick report the distribution for tax purposes?

5. Yellow Corporation distributes $50,000 to each of its three shareholders, Ted, Tiffany, and Maize Corporation. Discuss the issues involved in determining how the distribution is treated for tax purposes both to the shareholders and to Yellow Corporation.

6. Warbler Corporation is a calendar year taxpayer. At the beginning of the current year, Warbler has accumulated E & P of $200,000. The corporation incurs a current E & P deficit of $600,000 that accrues ratably throughout the year. On April 1, Warbler distributes $100,000 to its sole individual shareholder, Janice. If Janice has a basis in her stock of $25,000, how is the distribution taxed to her?

7. Complete the following schedule for each case. Assume the shareholder has ample basis in the stock investment.

	Accumulated E & P Beginning of Year	Current E & P	Cash Distributions (All on Last Day of Year)	Amount Taxable	Return of Capital
a.	$ 80,000	($ 20,000)	$100,000	$	$
b.	(100,000)	60,000	80,000		
c.	60,000	100,000	140,000		
d.	120,000	(40,000)	90,000		
e.	Same as (d), except the distribution of $90,000 is made on June 30 and the corporation uses the calendar year for tax purposes.				

8. Complete the following schedule. For each case, assume that there is one shareholder whose basis in the corporate stock is $20,000. Also assume that current losses accrue ratably throughout the year.

	Accumulated E & P Beginning of Year	Current E & P	Cash Distributions (All on Last Day of Year)	Amount Taxable	Capital Gain
a.	($140,000)	$ 160,000	$170,000	$	$
b.	80,000	20,000	110,000		
c.	(100,000)	70,000	50,000		
d.	200,000	(170,000)	90,000		
e.	Same as (d), except the distribution of $90,000 is made on June 30 and the corporation uses the calendar year for tax purposes.				

9. Dana, the sole shareholder of Tern Corporation, had a basis of $30,000 in Tern stock that he sold to Eli on July 30, 1998, for $180,000. Tern had accumulated E & P of $75,000 on January 1, 1998, and current E & P (for 1998) of $60,000. During 1998, Tern made the following distributions: $120,000 cash to Dana on July 1, and $120,000 cash to Eli on December 30. How will the distributions be taxed to Dana and to Eli? What gain will Dana recognize on the sale of his stock to Eli?

10. In determining Wren Corporation's current E & P for 1998, how should taxable income be adjusted by the following transactions?
    a. Collection of an installment note receivable resulting from a 1997 sale. (Wren Corporation did not elect out of the installment method.)
    b. An NOL carryover from 1997 fully used in 1998.
    c. An excess capital loss for 1998 that is not carried back.
    d. Collection on a key employee life insurance policy upon the death of the insured.
    e. Excess charitable contribution deduction on a donation made in 1998.

11. In each of the following *independent* situations, indicate the effect on taxable income and E & P, stating the amount of any increase (or decrease) as a result of the transaction. Assume E & P has already been increased by current taxable income.

	Transaction	Taxable Income Increase (Decrease)	E & P Increase (Decrease)
a.	Receipt of $15,000 tax-exempt income		
b.	Payment of $15,150 Federal income taxes		

	Transaction	Taxable Income Increase (Decrease)	E & P Increase (Decrease)
c.	Collection of $100,000 on life insurance policy on corporate president (assume no cash surrender value)		
d.	Charitable contribution, $30,000, $20,000 allowable as a deduction in the current tax year		
e.	Deduction of remaining $10,000 charitable contribution in succeeding year		
f.	Realized gain on involuntary conversion of $200,000 ($30,000 of gain is recognized)		

12. In each of the following *independent* situations, indicate the effect on taxable income and E & P, stating the amount of any increase (or decrease) as a result of the transaction. Assume E & P has already been increased by current taxable income.

	Transaction	Taxable Income Increase (Decrease)	E & P Increase (Decrease)
a.	Mine exploration and development costs incurred on July 1 of the current tax year and deductible from current taxable income in the amount of $60,000.		
b.	A $120,000 refund of Federal income taxes paid in previous year.		
c.	Payment of key employee life insurance premium. The premium paid was $18,000. As a result of the premium, the cash surrender value of the policy increased by $11,000.		
d.	MACRS depreciation of $150,000. ADS depreciation would have been $90,000.		
e.	Interest expense of $30,000 on loan used to purchase municipal bonds.		
f.	Capital losses incurred during the year of $30,000. Assume capital gains incurred during the year are $18,000.		
g.	Net operating loss carryforward of $11,000 deducted in the current year.		
h.	Sale of unimproved real estate, basis of $300,000, fair market value of $900,000 (no election out of installment method; payments in year of sale total $100,000).		

13. Sandpiper Corporation distributes property (basis of $80,000, fair market value of $110,000) to its sole shareholder, Ananda. The property is subject to a liability

of $135,000, which Ananda assumes. Sandpiper has E & P of $160,000 prior to the distribution.
   a. What gain, if any, does Sandpiper recognize on the distribution?
   b. What is the amount of Ananda's dividend income on the distribution?

14. Penguin Corporation, with E & P of $500,000, distributes land worth $110,000, adjusted basis of $150,000, to Orca, a corporate shareholder. The land is subject to a liability of $30,000, which Orca assumes.
   a. What is the amount of dividend income to Orca?
   b. What is Orca's basis in the land it received?
   c. How does the distribution affect Penguin Corporation's E & P account?

15. At the beginning of the current year, Dove Corporation (a calendar year taxpayer) has accumulated E & P of $40,000. During the year, Dove incurs a $30,000 loss from operations that accrued ratably. On July 1, Dove distributes $35,000 in cash to Marv, its sole shareholder. How will the $35,000 be taxed to Marv?

16. Snipe Corporation has E & P of $100,000. It distributes equipment with a fair market value of $90,000 (adjusted basis of $20,000) to its sole shareholder, Mary. The land is subject to a liability of $15,000, which Mary assumes. What are the tax consequences to Snipe Corporation and to Mary?

17. Gold Corporation distributes land with an adjusted basis of $100,000 and a fair market value of $60,000 to its shareholder, Homer. What are the tax consequences to Gold Corporation and to Homer?

18. Copper Corporation has two equal shareholders, Cybil and Sally. Cybil acquired her Copper stock three years ago by transferring property worth $600,000, basis of $200,000, for 60 shares of the stock. Sally acquired 60 shares in Copper Corporation two years ago by transferring property worth $620,000, basis of $70,000. Copper Corporation's accumulated E & P as of January 1 of the current year is $300,000. On March 1 of the current year, the corporation distributed to Cybil property worth $100,000, basis to Copper of $30,000. It distributed cash of $200,000 to Sally. On July 1 of the current year, Sally sold her stock to Dana for $800,000. On December 1 of the current year, Copper distributed cash of $80,000 each to Dana and to Cybil. What are the tax issues?

19. Whether compensation paid to a corporate employee is reasonable is a question of fact to be determined from the surrounding circumstances. How would the resolution of this problem be affected by each of the following factors?
   a. The employee is not a shareholder but is related to the sole owner of the corporate employer.
   b. The shareholder-employee never completed high school.
   c. The shareholder-employee is a full-time college student.
   d. The shareholder-employee was underpaid for her services during the formative period of the corporate employer.
   e. The corporate employer pays only a nominal dividend each year.
   f. Year-end bonuses are paid to all shareholder-employees, but not to nonshareholder employees.

20. Emu Corporation is a closely held company with accumulated E & P of $710,000 and current E & P of $175,000. Connor and Cameron equally own Emu. On a day-to-day basis, Connor and Cameron share management responsibilities equally, with Cameron focusing on operations and Connor focusing on sales. What are the tax consequences of the following transactions between Emu, Connor, and Cameron? How does each transaction affect Emu's E & P? Assume each transaction is independent.
   a. Emu sells a vacant lot (adjusted basis of $30,000, fair market value of $23,000) to Connor for $15,000.
   b. Emu lends Cameron $110,000 on January 1 of this year. The loan, evidenced by a note, is due on demand. No interest is charged on the loan. The current applicable Federal interest rate is 10%.
   c. Emu owns a cottage in Aspen, Colorado. It rents the cottage to tourists throughout the year. During the current year, Connor and Cameron each use the cottage for

two weeks and pay no rent to Emu. The rental value of the cottage is $3,500 per week. Cameron has indicated that the average maintenance cost per week for the rental is $600.

d. Cameron leases a truck to Emu for $12,000 for the year. If the corporation were to lease the same truck from a car dealer, the cost of the lease would be $7,000.

21. Shrike Corporation has beginning E & P of $300,000. Its current taxable income is $150,000. During the year, it distributed land worth $500,000, adjusted basis of $150,000, to Paul, its sole shareholder. Paul assumes a liability on the property in the amount of $50,000. The corporation had tax-exempt interest income of $10,000 and received $200,000 on a term life insurance policy on the death of a corporate officer. Premiums on the policy for the year were $5,000.
    a. What is the amount of taxable income to Paul?
    b. What is the E & P of Shrike Corporation after the property distribution?
    c. What is Paul's tax basis in the property received?

(Note: Disregard the effect of the corporate income tax.)

22. Verdigris Corporation owns 25% of the stock of Rust Corporation. Rust Corporation, with E & P of $150,000 on December 20, distributes land with a fair market value of $60,000 and a basis of $90,000 to Verdigris. The land is subject to a liability of $50,000, which Verdigris assumes.
    a. How is Verdigris Corporation taxed on the distribution?
    b. What is Rust Corporation's E & P after the distribution?

23. Stork Corporation, a cash basis, calendar year taxpayer, had the following income and expenses in the current year: income from services rendered, $200,000; salaries paid to employees, $70,000; tax-exempt interest, $20,000; dividends from a corporation in which Stork holds a 10% interest, $40,000; STCL on the sale of stock, $25,000; estimated Federal income taxes paid, $14,600. Stork Corporation purchased seven-year MACRS property in the current year for $90,000; no § 179 election was made. The property has a 10-year class life. Determine taxable income and E & P for Stork Corporation.

24. At the beginning of its taxable year, Green Corporation had E & P of $200,000. Green Corporation sold an asset at a loss of $200,000 on June 30. Green incurred a deficit in current E & P of $220,000, which includes the $200,000 loss on the sale of the asset, for the calendar year. Assume Green made a distribution of $60,000 to its sole individual shareholder on July 1. How will the shareholder be taxed on the $60,000?

25. Indigo Corporation, a calendar year taxpayer, had a deficit of $60,000 in accumulated E & P on January 1. Its net profits for the period January 1 through June 30 were $75,000, but its E & P for the entire taxable year was only $5,000. Indigo Corporation made a distribution of $15,000 to its sole individual shareholder on December 31. How will the shareholder be taxed on the distribution?

26. The stock in White Corporation is owned equally by Fred and Red Corporation. On January 1, White had a deficit in accumulated E & P of $150,000. Its current E & P was $105,000. During the year, White distributed cash of $45,000 to both Fred and Red Corporation. How will Fred and Red Corporation be taxed on the distribution? What is the accumulated E & P of White Corporation at the end of the year?

27. Cardinal Corporation is the sole shareholder of Quail Corporation. Plover Corporation is a prospective buyer of Quail Corporation but can pay only $300,000 of the $350,000 price Cardinal wants for its stock in Quail. Quail Corporation has $50,000 cash on hand that it distributes to Cardinal Corporation. Cardinal then sells its stock to Plover Corporation for $300,000. Your client, Cardinal Corporation, asks you the tax consequences to it on the sale if it has a basis of $100,000 in the Quail Corporation stock. (Assume Quail Corporation has sufficient E & P to cover the $50,000 distribution.) Prepare a letter to your client and a memo for the file. Cardinal's address is 1010 Keystone Street, Middleton, PA 17057.

28. Wren Corporation lends its principal shareholder, James, $200,000 on January 3 of the current year. The loan is interest-free. Assume the Federal rate is 10%. What are the tax consequences to Wren Corporation and to James with respect to the interest-free loan?

29. Crow Corporation declares a dividend permitting its shareholders to elect to receive $20 per share or 4 additional shares of Crow stock for every 10 shares currently held. Crow has only common stock outstanding. Crow stock has a fair market value of $50 per share. All shareholders elect to receive stock. Your client, Crow Corporation, asks whether the shareholders have any taxable income on the receipt of the stock. Prepare a letter to your client and a memo for the file. Crow's address is 1400 Boone Street, Baton Rouge, LA 70803.

30. Myrtle Adams paid $180,000 for 15 shares of stock in Petrel Corporation five years ago. In November 1997, she received a nontaxable stock dividend of 5 additional shares in Petrel Corporation. She sells the 5 shares in March 1998 for $60,000. What is her gain, and how is it taxed? Prepare a letter to your client and a memo for the file. Myrtle's address is 14009 Pine Street, Dover, DE 19901.

31. Lark Corporation declares a nontaxable dividend payable in rights to subscribe to common stock. One right and $60 entitle the holder to subscribe to one share of stock. One right is issued for each share of stock owned. At the date of distribution of the rights, the market value of the stock was $80 per share, and the market value of the rights was $20 per right. Karen, a shareholder, owns 100 shares of stock that she purchased two years ago for $3,000. Karen received 100 rights, of which she exercises 60 to purchase 60 additional shares. She sells the remaining 40 rights for $750. What are the tax consequences of these transactions to Karen?

32. Partridge Corporation has accumulated E & P of $300,000 as of January 1 of the current year. It expects to have earnings from operations of $240,000 and to make a cash distribution of $180,000 during the year. Partridge Corporation also expects to sell an asset for a loss of $300,000. Thus, it anticipates incurring a current E & P deficit of $60,000 for the year. What can Partridge do to cause its shareholders to have the least amount of dividend income?

33. Diver Corporation has a deficit in accumulated E & P of $200,000 as of January 1, 1998. Diver Corporation expects to generate annual E & P of $100,000 for the next four years, starting in 1998, and would like to distribute this amount to its shareholders. How should Diver Corporation distribute the $400,000 over the four-year period to provide the least amount of dividend income to its shareholders (all individuals)? Prepare a letter to your client, Diver Corporation, and a memo for the file. Diver Corporation's address is 1010 Oak Street, Oldtown, MD 20742.

RESEARCH PROBLEMS

*Note: The **RIA OnPoint System 4 Student Version CD-ROM** available with this text can be used in preparing solutions to the Research Problems. Alternatively, tax research materials contained in a standard tax library can be used.*

34. Wes and Edna were the sole shareholders of Bunting Corporation. They entered into a separation agreement providing that Wes would purchase Edna's stock in Bunting. In 1996, the court entered a judgment of divorce for Wes and Edna and incorporated their separation agreement, including the provision obligating Wes to purchase Edna's Bunting stock. On the same day, Edna and Bunting Corporation executed an agreement in which Bunting agreed to redeem Edna's stock. Bunting Corporation made one payment in redemption of Edna's stock in 1996 and a final payment in 1997. In 1997, the court that had entered the original judgment of divorce entered an order correcting the original judgment. The court changed the terms of the judgment requiring Wes to purchase Edna's Bunting stock and provided instead that Bunting Corporation agreed to redeem Edna's stock. In 1998, in auditing their returns, the IRS contended that the redemption of Edna's stock constituted a constructive dividend to Wes and increased his taxable income in 1996 and 1997 by the amount of the redemption payments paid

to Edna in those two years. Wes seeks your advice. Do the payments constitute taxable income to him?

35. Jaime Martinez is the president and majority shareholder of Black Corporation. During 1995, Jaime was paid a salary of $50,000 and received a year-end bonus of $200,000. Upon audit of Black Corporation in 1996, the IRS disallowed $150,000 of the amount paid to Jaime as being unreasonable. Under a repayment agreement, Jaime reimbursed Black Corporation for the $150,000 in 1997. On his 1995 return, Jaime had included the $150,000 in gross income. On his 1997 return, he deducted none of the repayment but elected the option set forth in § 1341(a)(5). Thus, Jaime claimed a credit for the amount of tax that was generated by the inclusion of the $150,000 on his 1995 return. Upon audit of his 1997 return in 1998, the IRS did not accept the credit approach but did permit a deduction of $150,000 for 1997. Because Jaime was in a higher tax bracket in 1995, a deficiency resulted for 1997. Jaime comes to you, a senior in a CPA firm, for advice. Should he challenge the tax deficiency for year 1997?
    a. Prepare a letter for Jaime as to his tax status. Jaime's address is 509 Maple Street, Camden, NJ 08102.
    b. Prepare a memo for your firm's client files.

36. Aqua Corporation wholly owns Egret Corporation. Aqua formed Egret four years ago with the transfer of several assets to the corporation, together with a substantial amount of cash. Aqua's basis in Egret stock is $5.5 million. Since it was formed, Egret has been a very profitable software company and currently has accumulated E & P of $4 million. The company's principal assets are software patents currently worth $5 million and cash and marketable securities of approximately $4.5 million (a total fair market value of $9.5 million).

    Aqua and Egret are members of an affiliated group and have made the election under § 243(b), so that Aqua is entitled to a 100% dividends received deduction. From a strategic perspective, Aqua is no longer interested in the software industry and so is considering a sale of Egret. In anticipation of a sale in the next year or two, the management of Aqua has contacted you for advice. If Egret is sold outright, then Aqua Corporation will have a capital gain of $4 million ($9.5 million fair market value less a basis of $5.5 million). As an alternative, it has been suggested that taxes on a future sale would be minimized if Egret pays Aqua a dividend (using existing cash and securities) equal to its E & P. With the 100% dividends received deduction, this payment would be a tax-free transfer from Egret to Aqua. Subsequent to the dividend payment, Egret could be sold for its remaining value of $5.5 million ($5 million in software patents plus $500,000 in cash), generating no additional loss or gain to Egret.
    a. Prepare a letter to the president of Aqua Corporation describing the results of your research on the proposed plan. The president's name and address is Bill Gateson, 601 Pittsfield Dr., Champaign, IL 61821.
    b. Prepare a memo for your firm's client files.

    Partial list of research aids:
    Waterman Steamship Corporation v. Comm., 70–2 USTC ¶9514, 26 AFTR2d 70–5185, 430 F.2d 1185 (CA–5, 1970).

37. Aaron Tuttle is the sole shareholder of Crimson Corporation, a profitable wholesaler of medical equipment and supplies. Aaron's daughter, Carol, majored in fashion design while in college and is currently unemployed. When the sole proprietor of a local fabric retail store is killed in an auto accident, the business is offered for sale by his estate. Carol is certain that she can operate the store successfully and convinces Aaron to this effect. To satisfy his daughter, Aaron proceeds as follows:

    - Forms Azure Corporation with a $10,000 cash investment. Aaron makes himself chairman of the board and appoints Carol as CEO.

    - Azure purchases the retail store from the estate of the owner for $100,000, using $10,000 cash as a down payment and issuing its notes for the balance.

    - Azure Corporation borrows $50,000 from Eagle Savings Association, pledging its assets as collateral for the loan. The funds are needed to meet operating expenses.

For the first year of its existence, Azure Corporation has an operating loss and ultimately is faced with the prospect of defaulting on its debt obligations. The creditors agree to refinance Azure's debt but only on condition that Aaron personally guarantee the loans. When losses continue and Azure still cannot service the debts, its creditors threaten action. Azure Corporation then borrows $300,000 from Crimson Corporation by issuing a note payable on demand and carrying an interest rate of 2% in excess of prime. Azure uses the loan funds to pay off all of its creditors and to satisfy the working capital needs of the business.

When Azure's financial situation further deteriorates, Crimson Corporation demands payment on its note. Unable to pay, Azure turns over its assets (realizable value of $35,000) to Crimson and ceases doing business. On its income tax return for the year, Crimson Corporation claims a bad debt deduction of $265,000.

Comment on the tax positions of Crimson Corporation and Aaron Tuttle.

CHAPTER 11

PARTNERSHIPS AND LIMITED LIABILITY ENTITIES

LEARNING OBJECTIVES

After completing Chapter 11, you should be able to:

1. Discuss governing principles and theories of partnership taxation.

2. Describe the tax effects of forming a partnership with cash and property contributions.

3. Examine the tax treatment of expenditures of a newly formed partnership and identify elections the partnership should make.

4. Calculate partnership taxable income and describe how partnership items affect a partner's income tax return.

5. Determine a partner's basis in the partnership interest.

6. Describe the limitations on deducting partnership losses.

7. Review the treatment of transactions between a partner and the partnership.

8. Describe the application of partnership tax law provisions to limited liability companies (LLCs) and limited liability partnerships (LLPs).

OUTLINE

Overview of Partnership Taxation, 11-2

Forms of Doing Business—Federal Tax Consequences, 11-3

What Is a Partnership? 11-3

Partnership Taxation and Reporting, 11-5

Partner's Ownership Interest in a Partnership, 11-7

Conceptual Basis for Partnership Taxation, 11-8

Anti-Abuse Provisions, 11-9

Formation of a Partnership: Tax Effects, 11-9

Gain or Loss on Contributions to the Partnership, 11-9

Exceptions to § 721, 11-10

Tax Issues Related to Contributed Property, 11-12

Inside and Outside Bases, 11-14

Tax Accounting Elections, 11-15

Initial Costs of a Partnership, 11-15

Operations of the Partnership, 11-17

Reporting Operating Results, 11-17

Partnership Allocations, 11-20

Basis of a Partnership Interest, 11-22

Loss Limitations, 11-28

Transactions between Partner and Partnership, 11-32

Guaranteed Payments, 11-32

Other Transactions between a Partner and a Partnership, 11-33

Partners as Employees, 11-34

Limited Liability Entities, 11-36

Limited Liability Companies, 11-36

Limited Liability Partnerships, 11-39

Summary, 11-39

OVERVIEW OF PARTNERSHIP TAXATION

Much of the new business in today's world of commerce is conducted in what the Internal Revenue Code would classify as *partnerships*. As evidence of their popularity, about 1.5 million tax returns are filed with the IRS annually.

Whether termed *joint ventures, working agreements, shared operating arrangements,* or some other designation, a partnership is formed when individuals or separate business entities get together for the specific purpose of earning profits by jointly operating a trade or business. For instance, a partnership likely exists when a U.S. business enters into a joint venture with a foreign distributor to gain access to an overseas consumer market. Or a number of businesses located in a blighted downtown area might work together to boost sales and customer traffic by forming a group that unifies and improves the appearance of the storefronts in the area, conducts joint advertising, and coordinates sales and coupon activities.

Partnerships allow a great degree of flexibility in the conduct of business: for example, a group can limit its goals to a specific list of agreed-to projects or to a given time period, or businesses can work together without altering any of their underlying capital structures. In many service professions, such as law, medicine, and accounting, state laws prohibit the owners from using a corporation to limit their liability to clients or patients, so the partnership form prevails.

The tax law addressing the transactions of partners and partnerships is found in Subchapter K of the Code. These provisions comprise only a few short pages in the Code, however. Most of the details of partnership tax law have evolved through extensive Regulations and a healthy number of court cases.

This chapter discusses the day-to-day tax consequences of operating as a partnership, as well as the general results of the owners forming the entity and conducting business with it. Matters such as partnership distributions and capital structure changes are discussed in *West's Federal Taxation: Advanced Taxation*.

FORMS OF DOING BUSINESS—FEDERAL TAX CONSEQUENCES

This chapter and the next chapter analyze two entities that offer certain advantages over C corporations. These entities are partnerships and S corporations, which are called *flow-through* or *pass-through* entities because the owners of the trade or business elect to avoid treating the enterprise as a separate taxable entity. Instead, the owners are taxed on a proportionate share of the firm's taxable income at the end of each of its taxable years, regardless of the amount of cash or property distributions the owners receive during the year. The entity serves as an information provider to the IRS and its owners with respect to the proportionate income shares, and the tax falls directly upon the owners of those shares.

A partnership may be especially advantageous in many cases. A partnership is subject to only a single level of taxation, whereas C corporation income is subject to *double taxation*. Corporate income is taxed at the entity level at rates up to 35 percent. Any after-tax income that is distributed to corporate owners is taxed again as a dividend at the owner level. Though partnership income may be subject to high individual rates (currently up to 39.6 percent), the resulting tax will likely be lower than a combined corporate-level tax and a second tax on dividends.

In addition, administrative and filing requirements are relatively simple for a partnership, and the entity offers certain planning opportunities not available to other entities. Both C and S corporations are subject to rigorous allocation and distribution requirements (generally, each allocation or distribution is proportionate to the ownership interest of the shareholder). A partnership, though, may adjust its allocations of income and cash flow among the partners each year according to their needs, as long as certain standards (discussed later in this chapter) are met. Any previously unrealized income (such as appreciation of corporate assets) of an S or C corporation is taxed at the entity level when the corporation liquidates, but a partnership generally may liquidate tax-free. Finally, many states impose reporting and licensing requirements on corporate entities, including S corporations. These include franchise or capital stock tax returns that may require annual assessments and costly professional preparation assistance. Partnerships, on the other hand, often have no reporting requirements beyond Federal and state informational tax returns.

Although partnerships may avoid many of the income tax and reporting burdens faced by other entities, they are subject to all other taxes in the same manner as any other business. Thus, the partnership files returns and pays the outstanding amount of pertinent sales taxes, property taxes, and payroll taxes.

In summary, partnerships offer advantages to both large and small businesses. For smaller business operations, a partnership enables several owners to combine their resources at low cost. It also offers simple filing requirements, the taxation of income only once, and the ability to discontinue operations relatively inexpensively. For larger business operations, a partnership offers a unique ability to raise capital with low filing and reporting costs (compared to corporate bond issuances, for example).

WHAT IS A PARTNERSHIP?

A partnership is an association of two or more persons to carry on a trade or business, with each contributing money, property, labor, or skill, and with all expecting to share in profits and losses.[1] For Federal income tax purposes, a

---
[1] § 7701(a)(2).

TAX IN THE NEWS

PARTNERSHIPS IN THE MOVIES

As movies have become more expensive to produce, many production studios have turned to limited partnerships as a lucrative source of investment capital. For example, the Walt Disney Company has sold limited partnership interests in Silver Screen Partnerships I, II, III, and IV and in Touchwood Pacific Partners I, L.P. Other studios have formed similar production partnerships.

In most cases the sponsoring studio injects capital for a small (1–5 percent) general partnership interest, and the limited partners contribute the remaining capital—hundreds of millions of dollars or more. The partnership agreement spells out the number and types of films the partnership intends to produce and provides a formula for allocating cash flows to the partners. Often the partnership agreement includes various benefits for the general partner (studio), such as a preferred allocation of cash flows (the first $1 million per year, for example), distribution fees for marketing the movies, and/or reimbursement of specified amounts of corporate overhead. Any cash remaining after these expenses is allocated under a fixed formula between the general and limited partners (for example, the limited partners may receive 90 percent of remaining cash flows).

Think about bank financing in comparison, and you will see why the studio finds partnerships so appealing: How many banks would allow the general partner to receive reimbursements and allocations before debt principal and interest are paid?

This capital-raising technique has proved so advantageous to the studios that some related industries, such as movie lighting contractors and special effects companies, have also used limited partnerships to raise capital. The next time you go to a movie, watch the credits at the end and think about the large number of people who invested cash in the movie hoping for a blockbuster!

---

partnership includes a syndicate, group, pool, joint venture, or other unincorporated organization, through which any business, financial operation, or venture is carried on. The entity must not be otherwise classified as a corporation, trust, or estate.

The IRS has issued Regulations that allow an eligible entity to "check the box" on the partnership tax return indicating that the entity wants to be taxed as a partnership.[2] The Regulations do not apply to publicly traded partnerships, which must be taxed as corporations under § 7704, but they do apply to most limited liability companies (discussed below). Thus, few barriers exist for those wishing to use the partnership rules. However, an entity that would otherwise be classified as a partnership may be excluded from partnership taxation rules if it is used for the following purposes.

- Investment (rather than the active conduct of a trade or business).
- Joint production, extraction, or use of property.
- Underwriting, selling, or distributing a specific security issue.[3]

A partnership must have at least two owners, so a sole proprietor or one-shareholder corporation cannot "check the box" and be taxed as a partnership.

---

[2] Reg. §§ 301.7701–1 to 301.7701–3, as discussed in Chapter 9 of this text.

[3] § 761(a).

Businesses operating in several forms are taxed as partnerships. Provisions controlling these legal forms of doing business typically are dictated by the laws of the states in which the businesses operate.

- In a **general partnership,** the partners share profits and losses in some specified manner, as dictated by the partnership agreement. Creditors can reach the assets of the business and the personal assets of the general partners to satisfy any outstanding debts. A general partner can be bankrupted by a judgment against the entity, even though the partner did not cause the violation triggering the damages.
- In a **limited partnership,** profits and losses are shared as the partners agree, but ownership interests are either general (creditors can reach the personal assets of the partner) or limited (a partner's exposure to entity liabilities is limited to the partner's own capital contributions). Usually, the general partners conduct most of the partnership business, and they have a greater say in making decisions that affect the entity operations.
- The **limited liability partnership (LLP)** is used chiefly in the service professions, such as accounting and consulting. The primary difference between an LLP and a general partnership is that an LLP partner is not liable for acts of negligence, fraud, or malpractice committed by the other partners.
- The **limited liability company (LLC)** is discussed in more detail later in this chapter. This entity is taxed as a partnership, but its capital structure resembles that of a corporation, with shares for sale and an owner's liability limited almost strictly to the extent of capital contributions. Some states allow LLCs to be owned solely by one person.

PARTNERSHIP TAXATION AND REPORTING

1 LEARNING OBJECTIVE
Discuss governing principles and theories of partnership taxation.

A partnership is not a taxable entity.[4] Rather, the taxable income or loss of the partnership flows through to the partners at the end of the entity's tax year.[5] Partners report their allocable share of the partnership's income or loss for the year on their tax returns. As a result, the partnership itself pays no Federal income tax on its income; instead, the partners' individual tax liabilities are affected by the activities of the entity.

EXAMPLE 1
Adam is a 40% partner in the ABC Partnership. Both Adam's and the partnership's tax years end on December 31. This year, the partnership generates $200,000 of ordinary taxable income. However, because the partnership needs capital for expansion and debt reduction, Adam makes no cash withdrawals during the year. He meets his living expenses by reducing his investment portfolio. Adam is taxed on his $80,000 allocable share of the partnership's income, even though he received no distributions from the entity during the year. This allocated income is included in Adam's gross income. ▼

EXAMPLE 2
Assume the same facts as in Example 1, except that the partnership realizes a taxable loss of $100,000. Adam's adjusted gross income is reduced by $40,000 because his proportionate share of the loss flows through to him from the partnership. He claims a $40,000 partnership loss for the year. (Note: Loss limitation rules discussed later in the chapter may result in some or all of this loss being deferred to a later year.) ▼

Many items of partnership income, expense, gain, or loss retain their tax identity as they flow through to the partners. These **separately stated items** may affect any

---
[4] § 701. [5] § 702.

two partners' tax liability computations differently.[6] For instance, the § 179 expense of a partnership is separately stated because one partner might be able to deduct his or her share of the expense completely, while another's deduction might be limited. Separately stated items include recognized gains and losses from property transactions, dividend income, preferences and adjustments for the alternative minimum tax (see Chapter 13), foreign tax payments, and expenditures that individual partners would treat as itemized deductions (e.g. charitable contributions).

Items that are not separately stated, because all partners will treat them the same on their individual tax returns, are aggregated and form the *ordinary income* of the partnership. Thus, profits from product sales, advertising expenses, and depreciation recapture amounts are combined to form the entity's ordinary income. This amount is then allocated among the partners and flows through to their tax returns. The ordinary income that flows through to a general partner, as well as any salary-like guaranteed payments (discussed in a later section) he or she receives, usually is subject to self-employment tax, as well as Federal income tax.[7]

EXAMPLE 3

Beth is a 25% partner in the BR Partnership. The cash basis entity collected sales income of $60,000 during 1999 and incurred $15,000 in business expenses. In addition, it sold a corporate bond for a $9,000 long-term capital gain. Finally, the partnership made a $1,000 contribution to the local Performing Arts Fund drive. The fund is a qualifying charity. BR and all of its partners use a calendar tax year.

For 1999, Beth is allocated ordinary taxable income of $11,250 [($60,000 − $15,000) × 25%] from the partnership. She also is allocated a flow-through of a $2,250 long-term capital gain and a $250 charitable contribution deduction. The ordinary income increases Beth's gross income, and the capital gain and charitable contribution are combined with her other similar activities for the year as though she had incurred them herself. These items could be treated differently on the tax returns of the various partners (e.g., because a partner may be subject to a percentage limitation on charitable contribution deductions for 1999), so they are not included in the computation of ordinary partnership income. Instead, the items flow through to the partners separately. ▼

Even though it is not a taxpaying entity, the partnership files an information tax return, Form 1065. Look at Form 1065 in Appendix B, and refer to it during the following discussion. The partnership reports the results of its trade or business activities (ordinary income or loss) on Form 1065, page 1. Schedule K (page 3 of Form 1065) accumulates all items that must be separately reported to the partners, including net trade or business income or loss (from page 1). The amounts on Schedule K are allocated to all the partners. Each partner receives a Schedule K–1, which shows that partner's share of partnership items.

EXAMPLE 4

The BR Partnership in Example 3 reports its $60,000 sales income on Form 1065, page 1, line 1. The $15,000 of business expenses are reported in the appropriate amounts on page 1, line 2 or lines 9–20. Partnership ordinary income of $45,000 is shown on page 1, line 22, and on Schedule K, line 1. The $9,000 capital gain and the $1,000 charitable contribution are reported only on Schedule K, on lines 4e and 8, respectively.

Beth receives a Schedule K–1 from the partnership that shows her shares of partnership ordinary income of $11,250, long-term capital gain of $2,250, and charitable contributions of $250 on lines 1, 4e, and 8, respectively.

She combines these amounts with similar items from other sources on her personal tax return. For example, if she has a $5,000 long-term capital loss from a stock transaction in

---

[6] § 703(a)(1). Certain large partnerships can elect to limit the number of separately stated items.

[7] § 1402(a).

1999, her overall net capital loss is $2,750. She then evaluates this net amount to determine the amount she may deduct on her Form 1040. ▼

As this example shows, one must look at both page 1 and Schedule K to get complete information regarding a partnership's operations for the year. Schedule K accumulates all partnership tax items and arrives at a total amount on line 25a. Schedule M–1, page 4, reconciles accounting income with this total of partnership tax items on Schedule K (line 25a). Schedule L generally shows an accounting-basis balance sheet, and Schedule M–2 reconciles beginning and ending partners' capital accounts.

PARTNER'S OWNERSHIP INTEREST IN A PARTNERSHIP

Each partner typically owns both a **capital interest** and a **profits (loss) interest** in the partnership. A capital interest is measured by a partner's **capital sharing ratio,** which is the partner's percentage ownership of the capital of the partnership. A partner's capital interest can be determined in several ways. The most widely accepted method measures the capital interest as the percentage of net assets (assets remaining after payment of all partnership liabilities) a partner would receive on immediate liquidation of the partnership.

A profits (loss) interest is simply the partner's percentage allocation of current partnership operating results. **Profit and loss sharing ratios** usually are specified in the partnership agreement. They are used to determine each partner's allocation of partnership ordinary taxable income and separately stated items.[8] The partnership can change its profit and loss allocations at any time by amending the partnership agreement.

Each partner's profit, loss, and capital sharing ratios may appear on the partner's Schedule K–1. In many cases, the three ratios are the same. A partner's capital sharing ratio generally equals the profit and loss sharing ratios if all profit and loss allocations, for each year of the partnership's existence, are in the same proportion as the partner's initial contributions to the partnership.

The partnership agreement may, in some cases, provide for a **special allocation** of certain items to specified partners, or it may allocate items in a different proportion from general profit and loss sharing ratios. These items are separately reported to the partner receiving the allocation. For a special allocation to be recognized for tax purposes, it must produce nontax economic consequences to the partners receiving the allocation.[9]

EXAMPLE 5

When the George-Helen Partnership was formed, George contributed cash and Helen contributed some City of Iuka bonds that she had held for investment purposes. The partnership agreement allocates all of the tax-exempt interest income from the bonds to Helen as an inducement for her to remain a partner. This is an acceptable special allocation for income tax purposes; it reflects the differing economic circumstances that underlie the partners' contributions to the capital of the entity. Since Helen would have received the exempt income if she had not joined the partnership, she can retain the tax-favored treatment via the special allocation. ▼

EXAMPLE 6

Assume the same facts as in Example 5. Three years after it was formed, the George-Helen Partnership purchased some City of Butte bonds. The municipal bond interest income of $15,000 flows through to the partners as a separately stated item, so it retains its tax-exempt status. The partnership agreement allocates all of this income to George because he is subject

---

[8] § 704(a).   [9] § 704(b).

to a higher marginal income tax bracket than is Helen. The partnership then allocates $15,000 more of the partnership's ordinary income to Helen than to George. These allocations are not effective for income tax purposes because they have no purpose other than reduction of the partners' combined income tax liability. ▼

A partner has a **basis in the partnership interest,** just as he or she would have a tax basis in any asset owned. When income flows through to a partner from the partnership, the partner's basis in the partnership interest increases accordingly. When a loss flows through to a partner, basis is reduced. A partner's basis is important when determining the treatment of distributions from the partnership to the partner, establishing the deductibility of partnership losses, and calculating gain or loss on the disposition of partnership interest.

EXAMPLE 7

Paul contributes $20,000 cash to acquire a 30% capital and profits interest in the Red Robin Partnership. In its first year of operations, the partnership earns ordinary income of $40,000 and makes no distributions to Paul. Paul's initial basis is the $20,000 he paid for the interest. He reports ordinary income of $12,000 (30% × $40,000 partnership income) on his individual return and increases his basis by the same amount, to $32,000. ▼

In allowing increases and decreases in a partner's basis in a partnership interest, the Code ensures that only one level of tax arises on the income or loss from partnership operations. In Example 7, if Paul sold his interest at the end of the first year for $32,000, he would have no gain or loss. If the Code did not provide for an adjustment of a partner's basis, Paul's basis would be $20,000, and he would be taxed on the gain of $12,000 in addition to being taxed on his $12,000 share of income. In other words, without the basis adjustment, partnership income would be subject to double taxation.

A partner's basis is not reflected anywhere on the Schedule K–1. Instead, each partner must maintain a personal record of adjustments to basis. Schedule K–1 does reconcile a partner's **capital account,** but the ending capital account balance is rarely the same amount as the partner's basis. Just as the tax and accounting bases of a specific asset may differ, a partner's capital account and basis in partnership interest may not be equal for a variety of reasons. For example, a partner's basis also includes the partner's share of partnership liabilities. These liabilities are not reported as part of the partner's capital account but are included in question F at the top of the partner's Schedule K–1.

CONCEPTUAL BASIS FOR PARTNERSHIP TAXATION

The unique tax treatment of partners and partnerships can be traced to two legal concepts that evolved long ago: the **aggregate** (or conduit) **concept** and the **entity concept.** These concepts have been used in both civil and common law and have influenced practically every partnership tax rule.

Aggregate (or Conduit) Concept. The aggregate (or conduit) concept treats the partnership as a channel through which income, credits, and deductions flow to the partners. Under this concept, the partnership is regarded as a collection of taxpayers joined in an agency relationship with one another. The imposition of the income tax on individual partners reflects the influence of this doctrine. The aggregate concept also has influenced the tax treatment of other pass-through entities, such as S corporations (Chapter 12) and trusts and estates.

CHAPTER 11 Partnerships and Limited Liability Entities

Entity Concept. The entity concept treats partners and partnerships as separate units and gives the partnership its own tax "personality" by (1) requiring a partnership to file an information tax return and (2) treating partners as separate and distinct from the partnership in certain transactions between a partner and the entity. A partner's recognition of capital gain or loss on the sale of the partnership interest illustrates this doctrine.

Combined Concepts. Some rules such as the provisions governing the formation, operation, and liquidation of a partnership contain a blend of both the entity and aggregate concepts.

ANTI-ABUSE PROVISIONS

Partnership operating income or losses can sometimes be shifted among partners, and partnership property gains and losses can sometimes be shifted from one partner to another. The Code contains many provisions designed to thwart unwarranted allocations, but the IRS believes opportunities still abound for tax avoidance. Regulations allow the IRS to recharacterize transactions that it considers to be "abusive."[10]

FORMATION OF A PARTNERSHIP: TAX EFFECTS

GAIN OR LOSS ON CONTRIBUTIONS TO THE PARTNERSHIP

2 LEARNING OBJECTIVE
Describe the tax effects of forming a partnership with cash and property contributions.

When a taxpayer transfers property to an entity in exchange for valuable consideration, a taxable exchange usually results. Typically, both the taxpayer and the entity realize and recognize gain or loss on the exchange.[11] The gain or loss recognized by the transferor is the difference between the fair market value of the consideration received and the adjusted basis of the property transferred.[12]

In most situations, however, neither the partner nor the partnership recognizes the gain or loss that is realized when a partner contributes property to a partnership in exchange for a partnership interest. Instead, recognition of any realized gain or loss is deferred.[13]

There are two reasons for this nonrecognition treatment. First, forming a partnership allows investors to combine their assets toward greater economic goals than could be achieved separately. Only the form of ownership, rather than the amount owned by each investor, has changed. Requiring that gain be recognized on such transfers would make the formation of some partnerships economically unfeasible. Congress does not want to hinder the creation of valid economic partnerships by requiring gain recognition when a partnership is created. Second, because the partnership interest received is typically not a liquid asset, the partner may not be able to generate the cash to pay the tax. Thus, deferral of the gain recognizes the economic realities of the business world and follows the wherewithal to pay principle.

EXAMPLE 8

Alicia transfers two assets to the Wren Partnership on the day the entity is created, in exchange for a 60% profit and loss interest (worth $60,000). She contributes cash of $40,000 and retail display equipment (basis to her as a sole proprietor, $8,000; fair market value,

---

[10] Reg. § 1.701–2.
[11] § 1001(c).
[12] § 1001(a).
[13] § 721.

$20,000). Since an exchange has occurred between two parties, Alicia *realizes* a $12,000 gain on this transaction. The gain realized is the fair market value of the partnership interest of $60,000 less the basis of the assets that Alicia surrendered to the partnership [$40,000 (cash) + $8,000 (equipment)].

Under § 721, Alicia *does not recognize* the $12,000 realized gain in the year of contribution. Alicia might not have had sufficient cash if she had been required to pay tax on the $12,000 gain. All that she received from the partnership was an illiquid partnership interest; she received no cash with which to pay any resulting tax liability. ▼

EXAMPLE 9

Assume the same facts as in Example 8, except that the equipment Alicia contributes to the partnership has an adjusted basis of $25,000. She has a $5,000 *realized* loss [$60,000 − ($40,000 + $25,000)], but she cannot deduct the loss. Realized losses, as well as realized gains, are deferred by § 721.

Unless it was essential that the partnership receive Alicia's display equipment rather than similar equipment purchased from an outside supplier, Alicia should have considered selling the equipment to a third party. This would have allowed her to deduct a $5,000 loss in the year of the sale. Alicia then could have contributed $60,000 cash (including the proceeds from the sale) for her interest in the partnership, and the partnership would have funds to purchase similar equipment. ▼

EXAMPLE 10

Five years after the Wren Partnership (Examples 8 and 9) was created, Alicia contributes another piece of equipment to the entity from her sole proprietorship. This property has a basis of $35,000 and a fair market value of $50,000. Alicia can defer the recognition of the $15,000 realized gain. Section 721 is effective *whenever* a partner makes a contribution to the capital of the partnership, not just when the partnership is formed. ▼

If a partner contributes only capital and § 1231 assets, the partner's holding period in the partnership interest is the same as that partner's holding period for the contributed assets. If cash and other assets that are not capital or § 1231 assets are contributed, the holding period in the partnership interest begins on the date the partnership interest is acquired. If multiple assets are contributed, the partnership interest is apportioned, and a separate holding period applies to each portion.

EXCEPTIONS TO § 721

The nonrecognition provisions of § 721 do not apply where:

- appreciated stocks are contributed to an investment partnership;
- the transaction is essentially a taxable exchange of properties;
- the transaction is a disguised sale of properties; or
- the partnership interest is received in exchange for services rendered to the partnership by the partner.

Investment Partnership. If the transfer consists of appreciated stocks and securities and the partnership is an investment partnership, it is likely that the realized gain on the stocks and securities will be recognized by the contributing partner at the time of contribution.[14] This provision prevents multiple investors from using the partnership form to diversify their investment portfolios on a tax-free basis.

Exchange. If a transaction is essentially a taxable exchange of properties, the tax is not deferred under the nonrecognition provisions of § 721.[15]

---

[14] § 721(b).

[15] Reg. § 1.731–1(c)(3).

EXAMPLE 11

Sara owns land, and Bob owns stock. Sara would like to have Bob's stock, and Bob wants Sara's land. If Sara and Bob both contribute their property to newly formed SB Partnership in exchange for interests in the partnership, the tax on the transaction appears to be deferred under § 721. The tax on a subsequent distribution by the partnership of the land to Bob and the stock to Sara also appears to be deferred under § 731. According to a literal interpretation of the statutes, no taxable exchange has occurred. Sara and Bob will find, however, that this type of tax subterfuge is not permitted. The IRS will disregard the passage of the properties through the partnership and will hold, instead, that Sara and Bob exchanged the land and stock directly. Thus, the transactions will be treated as any other taxable exchange. ▼

Disguised Sale. A similar result (i.e., recognition) occurs in a **disguised sale** of properties. A disguised sale is deemed to occur where a partner contributes property to a partnership and soon thereafter receives a distribution from the partnership. This distribution could be viewed as a payment by the partnership for purchase of the property.[16]

EXAMPLE 12

Kim transfers property to the KLM Partnership. The property has an adjusted basis of $10,000 and a fair market value of $30,000. Two weeks later, the partnership makes a distribution of $30,000 cash to Kim. Under the distribution rules of § 731, the distribution would not be taxable to Kim if the basis for her partnership interest prior to the distribution was greater than the $30,000 cash distributed. However, the transaction appears to be a disguised purchase-sale transaction, rather than a contribution and distribution. Therefore, Kim must recognize gain of $20,000 on transfer of the property, and the partnership is deemed to have purchased the property for $30,000. ▼

Extensive Regulations under § 707 outline situations in which the IRS will presume a disguised sale has occurred. For example, if both the following occur, a disguised sale is presumed to exist.

- A contractual agreement requires a contribution by one partner to be followed within two years by a specified distribution from the partnership.
- The distribution is to be made without regard to partnership profits. In other words, the forthcoming distribution is not subject to significant "entrepreneurial risk."

In some cases, assumption of the partner's liabilities by the partnership may be treated as a purchase price paid by the partnership. The IRS can also use a facts and circumstances test to treat a transaction as a disguised sale.

The Regulations also outline situations in which a distribution generally will *not* be deemed to be part of a disguised sale. They include a distribution that occurs more than two years after the property is contributed and a distribution that is deemed "reasonable" in relation to the capital invested by the partner and in relation to distributions made to other partners.

Services. A final exception to the nonrecognition provision of § 721 occurs when a partner receives an interest in the partnership as compensation for services rendered to the partnership. This is not a tax-deferred transaction because services are not treated as "property" that can be transferred to a partnership on a tax-free basis. Instead, the partner performing the services recognizes ordinary compensation income equal to the fair market value of the partnership interest received.[17]

The partnership may deduct the amount included in the *service partner's* income if the services are of a deductible nature. If the services are not deductible by the

---

[16] § 707(a)(2)(B).   [17] § 83(a).

partnership, they must be capitalized. For example, architectural plans created by a partner are capitalized to the structure built with those plans. Alternatively, day-to-day management services performed by a partner for the partnership usually are deductible by the partnership.

EXAMPLE 13

Bill, Carol, and Dave form the BCD Partnership, with each receiving a one-third interest in the entity. Dave receives his one-third interest as compensation for the accounting and tax planning services he rendered during the formation of the partnership. The value of a one-third interest in the partnership (for each of the parties) is $20,000. Dave recognizes $20,000 of compensation income, and he has a $20,000 basis in his partnership interest. The same result would occur if the partnership had paid Dave $20,000 for his services and he immediately contributed that amount to the entity for a one-third ownership interest. ▼

TAX ISSUES RELATED TO CONTRIBUTED PROPERTY

When a partner makes a tax-deferred contribution of an asset to the capital of a partnership, the entity assigns a *carryover basis* to the property.[18] The entity's basis in the asset is equal to the basis the partner held in the property prior to its transfer to the partnership. The partner's basis in the new partnership interest equals the prior basis in the contributed asset. The tax term for this basis concept is *substituted basis*. Thus, two assets are created out of one when a partnership is formed, namely, the property in the hands of the new entity and the new asset (the partnership interest) in the hands of the partner. Both assets are assigned a basis that is derived from the partner's basis in the contributed property.

To understand the logic of these rules, consider what Congress was attempting to accomplish in this deferral transaction. For both parties, realized gain is deferred, under the wherewithal to pay concept, until the asset or ownership interest is subsequently disposed of in a taxable transaction. The deferral is accomplished through the use of a substituted basis by the partner and a carryover basis by the partnership. This treatment is similar to the treatment of assets transferred to a controlled corporation and the treatment of like-kind exchanges.[19]

EXAMPLE 14

On June 1, José transfers property to the JKL Partnership in exchange for a one-third interest in the partnership. The property has an adjusted basis to José of $10,000 and a fair market value of $30,000 on June 1. José has a $20,000 realized gain on the exchange ($30,000 − $10,000), but under § 721, he does not recognize any of the gain. José's basis for his partnership interest is the amount necessary to recognize the $20,000 deferred gain if his partnership interest is subsequently sold for its $30,000 fair market value. This amount, $10,000, is the substituted basis. The basis of the property contributed to the partnership is the amount necessary to allow for the recognition of the $20,000 deferred gain if the property is subsequently sold for its $30,000 fair market value. This amount, also $10,000, is the carryover basis. ▼

The holding period for the contributed asset also carries over to the partnership. Thus, the partnership's holding period for the asset includes the period during which the partner owned the asset individually.

Depreciation Method and Period. If depreciable property is contributed to the partnership, the partnership usually is required to use the same cost recovery method and life used by the partner. The partnership merely "steps into the shoes" of the partner and continues the same cost recovery calculations. Thus,

---

[18] § 723.

[19] §§ 351 and 1031.

the partnership may not expense any part of the basis of depreciable property it receives from the transferor partner under § 179.

Receivables, Inventory, and Losses. To prevent ordinary income from being converted into capital gain, gain or loss is treated as ordinary when the partnership disposes of either of the following.[20]

- Contributed receivables that were unrealized in the contributing partner's hands at the contribution date. Such receivables include the right to receive payment for goods or services delivered (or to be delivered).
- Contributed property that was inventory in the contributor's hands on the contribution date, if the partnership disposes of the property within *five years of the contribution*. For this purpose, inventory includes all property except capital and real or depreciable business assets.

EXAMPLE 15

Tyrone operates a cash basis retail electronics and television store as a sole proprietor. Ramon is an enterprising individual who likes to invest in small businesses. On January 2 of the current year, Tyrone and Ramon form the TR Partnership. Their partnership contributions are listed below.

	Adjusted Basis	Fair Market Value
From Tyrone:		
Receivables	$ –0–	$ 2,000
Land used as parking lot*	1,200	5,000
Inventory	2,500	5,000
From Ramon:		
Cash	12,000	12,000

*The parking lot had been held for nine months at the contribution date.

Within 30 days of formation, TR collects the receivables and sells the inventory for $5,000 cash. It uses the land for the next 10 months as a parking lot, then sells it for $3,500 cash. TR realized the following income in the current year from these transactions.

- Ordinary income of $2,000 from collecting receivables.
- Ordinary income of $2,500 from sale of inventory.
- § 1231 gain of $2,300 from sale of land.

Since the land takes a carryover holding period, it is treated as having been held 19 months at the sale date. ▼

A similar rule is designed to prevent a capital loss from being converted into an ordinary loss. Under the rule, if contributed property is disposed of at a loss and the property had a "built-in" capital loss to the contributing partner at the contribution date, the loss is treated as a capital loss if the partnership disposes of the property *within five years of the contribution*. The capital loss is limited to the "built-in" loss on the date of contribution.[21]

---

[20]§ 724. For this purpose, § 724(d)(2) waives the holding period requirement in defining § 1231 property.

[21]§ 724(c).

Concept Summary 11-1

Partnership Formation and Basis Computation

1. Generally, partners or partnerships do not recognize gain or loss when property is contributed for capital interests.
2. Partners contributing property for partnership interests take the contributed property's adjusted basis for their *outside basis* in their partnership interest. The partners are said to take a substituted basis in their partnership interest.
3. The partnership will continue to use the contributing partner's basis for the *inside basis* in property it receives. The contributed property is said to take a carryover basis.
4. The holding period of a partner's interest includes that of contributed property when the property was a § 1231 asset or capital asset in the partner's hands. Otherwise, the holding period starts on the day the interest is acquired. The holding period of an interest acquired by a cash contribution starts at acquisition.
5. The partnership's holding period for contributed property includes the contributing partner's holding period.
6. Gain is recognized by a contributing partner when services are contributed, the capital contribution is a disguised sale or exchange, or the partnership is an investment company.
7. Special rules may apply when the partnership disposes of contributed receivables, inventory, or loss assets.

EXAMPLE 16

Assume the same facts as Example 15, except for the following.

- Tyrone held the land he contributed as an investment. It had a fair market value of $800 at the contribution date.
- TR used the land as a parking lot for 10 months and sold it for $650.

TR realizes the following income and loss from these transactions.

- Ordinary income of $2,000 from collecting receivables.
- Ordinary income of $2,500 from sale of inventory.
- Capital loss of $400 from sale of land ($1,200 − $800).
- § 1231 loss of $150 from sale of land ($800 − $650).

Since the land was sold within five years of the contribution date, the $400 built-in loss is a capital loss. The postcontribution loss of $150 is a § 1231 loss since TR used the property in its business. ▼

INSIDE AND OUTSIDE BASES

In this chapter, reference is made to the partnership's inside basis and the partners' outside basis. **Inside basis** refers to the adjusted basis of each partnership asset, as determined from the partnership's tax accounts. **Outside basis** represents each partner's basis in the partnership interest. Each partner "owns" a share of the partnership's inside basis for all its assets and should maintain a record of the outside basis.

In many cases—especially on formation of the partnership—the total of all the partners' outside bases equals the partnership's inside bases for all its assets. Differences between inside and outside basis arise when a partner's interest is sold to another person for more or less than the selling partner's share of the inside basis of partnership assets. The buying partner's outside basis equals the price paid for the interest, but the buyer's share of the partnership's inside basis is the same amount as the seller's share of the inside basis.

Concept Summary 11–1 reviews the rules that apply to partnership asset contribution and basis adjustments.

CHAPTER 11 Partnerships and Limited Liability Entities

LEARNING OBJECTIVE 3
Examine the tax treatment of expenditures of a newly formed partnership and identify elections the partnership should make.

TAX ACCOUNTING ELECTIONS

A newly formed partnership must make numerous tax accounting elections. These elections are formal decisions on how a particular transaction or tax attribute should be handled. Most of these elections must be made by the partnership rather than by the partners individually.[22] The *partnership* makes the elections involving the following items.

- Inventory method.
- Cost or percentage depletion method, excluding oil and gas wells.
- Accounting method (cash, accrual, or hybrid).
- Cost recovery methods and assumptions.
- Tax year.
- Amortization of organizational costs and amortization period.
- Amortization of start-up expenditures and amortization period.
- Optional basis adjustments for property (§ 754).
- Section 179 deductions for certain tangible personal property.
- Nonrecognition treatment for involuntary conversions gains.
- Election out of partnership rules.

Each partner is bound by the decisions made by the partnership relative to the elections. If the partnership fails to make an election, a partner cannot compensate for the error by making the election individually.

Though most elections are made by the partnership, each *partner* individually is required to make a specific election on the following relatively narrow tax issues:

- Whether to reduce the basis of depreciable property first when excluding income from discharge of indebtedness.
- Whether to claim cost or percentage depletion method for oil and gas wells.
- Whether to take a deduction or a credit for taxes paid to foreign countries.

INITIAL COSTS OF A PARTNERSHIP

In its initial stages, a partnership incurs expenses relating to some or all of the following: forming the partnership (organization costs), admitting partners to the partnership, marketing and selling partnership units to prospective partners (syndication costs), acquiring assets, starting business operations (start-up costs), negotiating contracts, and other items. Many of these expenditures are not currently deductible. However, the Code permits a ratable amortization of "organization" and "start-up" costs; acquisition costs for depreciable assets are included in the initial basis of the acquired assets; and costs related to some intangible assets may be amortized. "Syndication costs" may be neither amortized nor deducted.

Organization Costs. Organization costs are incident to the creation of the partnership and are capital in nature, such as accounting and legal fees associated with the partnership formation.[23] Costs incurred for the following purposes are *not* organization costs.

- Acquiring assets for the partnership.
- Transferring assets to the partnership.
- Admitting partners, other than at formation.
- Removing partners, other than at formation.

---

[22] § 703(b).
[23] § 709(b)(2).

- Negotiating operating contracts.
- Syndication costs.

A partnership can elect to amortize organization costs over a period of 60 months or more, starting with the month in which it begins business. The election must be made by the due date of the partnership's first tax return.[24] To qualify for amortization, organization costs must be incurred within a period that starts at a reasonable time before the partnership begins business and ends with the unextended due date of the partnership's first tax return. Cash method partnerships may not deduct amortization on organization costs in the year incurred if they are not paid by the end of the first year. However, the partnership can deduct the portion of expenditures that would have been deductible in a prior year, if they had been paid before that prior year's end.

EXAMPLE 17

The calendar year Bluejay Partnership is formed on May 1 of the current year and immediately starts business. Bluejay incurs $720 in legal fees for drafting the partnership agreement and $480 in accounting fees for tax advice of an organizational nature. The legal fees are paid in October of the current year. The accounting fees are paid in January of the following year. The partnership selects the cash method of accounting and elects to amortize its organization costs.

On its first tax return, Bluejay deducts $96 of organization costs [($720 legal fees/60 months) × 8 months]. No deduction is taken for the accounting fees since the partnership selected the cash method and the fees were paid the following year. On its tax return for next year, Bluejay deducts organization costs of $304 {[($720 legal fees/60 months) × 12 months] + [($480 accounting fees/60 months) × 20 months]}. This amount includes the $64 of accounting fees [($480/60) × 8] that could have been deducted on Bluejay's first tax return if they had been paid by the end of that year. ▼

Start-up Costs. Operating costs that are incurred after the entity is formed but before it begins business are known as start-up costs. Like organization costs, start-up costs are capitalized and may be amortized over a period of 60 months or more, starting with the month in which the partnership begins business.[25] Such costs include marketing surveys prior to conducting business, pre-operating advertising expenses, costs of establishing an accounting system, and salaries paid to executives and employees before the start of business.

Acquisition Costs of Depreciable Assets. Expenses may be incurred in changing the legal title in which certain assets are held from that of the contributing partner to the partnership name. These costs include legal fees incurred to transfer assets or transfer taxes imposed by some states. Such costs are depreciable assets in the hands of the partnership. However, since the partnership "steps into the shoes" of contributing partners for determining depreciation on preexisting contributed assets, acquisition costs are treated as a *new* asset, placed in service on the date the cost is incurred.

Syndication Costs. **Syndication costs** are capitalized, but no amortization election is available.[26] Syndication costs typically include the following expenditures incurred for promoting and marketing partnership interests.

- Brokerage fees.
- Registration fees.

---

[24] § 709(b)(1).
[25] § 195.
[26] § 709(a).

- Legal fees paid to the underwriter, placement agent, and issuer (general partner or the partnership) for security advice or advice on the adequacy of tax disclosures in the prospectus or placement memo for securities law purposes.
- Accounting fees related to offering materials.
- Printing costs of prospectus, placement memos, and other selling materials.

OPERATIONS OF THE PARTNERSHIP

4 LEARNING OBJECTIVE
Calculate partnership taxable income and describe how partnership items affect a partner's income tax return.

A key consideration in the taxation of partnerships is that a variety of entities can be partners and each may be affected differently by the partnership's operations. In particular, any combination of individuals, corporations, trusts, estates, or other partnerships may be partners. Furthermore, at the end of each year, every partner receives a share of the partnership's income, deductions, credits, and alternative minimum tax (AMT) preferences and adjustments. These flow-through items ultimately may be reported and taxed on a wide variety of income tax returns (e.g., Forms 1040 [Individuals], 1041 [Fiduciaries], 1120 [C corporations], and 1120S [S corporations]), each facing different limitations and rules. Thus, the ultimate tax treatment of partnership operations is directly affected by how the partnership reports its operating results. This topic is addressed in the following paragraphs.

REPORTING OPERATING RESULTS

The partnership's Form 1065 organizes and reports the transactions of the entity for the tax year, and each of the partnership's tax items is reported on Schedule K of that return. Each partner, and the IRS, receives a Schedule K–1 that reports the partner's allocable share of partnership income, credits, and preferences for the year. Form 1065 is due on the fifteenth day of the fourth month following the close of the partnership's tax year; for a calendar year partnership, this is April 15.

Classifying Income and Deductions. The measurement and reporting of partnership income require a two-step approach. Some items are not reported separately. These are netted at the partnership level and flow through to the partners as an aggregate number. Other items must be segregated and reported separately on the partnership return and each partner's Schedule K–1. Items passed through separately include the following.

- Short- and long-term capital gains and losses.
- Section 1231 gains and losses.
- Charitable contributions.
- Portfolio income items (dividends, interest, and royalties).
- Immediately expensed tangible personal property (§ 179).
- Items allocated differently from the general profit and loss ratio.
- Recovery of items previously deducted (tax benefit items).
- AMT preference and adjustment items.
- Passive activity items (rental real estate income or loss).
- Expenses related to portfolio income.
- Intangible drilling and development costs.
- Taxes paid to foreign countries and U.S. possessions.
- Nonbusiness and personal items (e.g., alimony, medical, and dental).[27]

---
[27]§ 702(a).

The reason for separately reporting the preceding items is rooted in the aggregate or conduit concept. These items may affect each partner differently. Thus, they must pass through without loss of identity so that the proper tax for each partner can be determined.[28]

A partnership is not allowed the following deductions.

- Net operating losses.
- Depletion of oil and gas interests.
- Dividends received deduction.

In addition, items that are only allowed by legislative grace to individuals, such as standard deductions or personal exemptions, are not allowed to the partnership. If a partnership makes a payment on behalf of a partner, such as for alimony, medical expenses, or other items that constitute itemized deductions to individuals, the partnership treats the payment as a distribution or guaranteed payment (discussed later) to the partner, and the partner determines whether he or she may claim the deduction.

EXAMPLE 18

Tiwanda is a one-third partner in the TUV Partnership. The partnership's transactions for the year are summarized below.

Fees received	$100,000
Salaries paid	30,000
Cost recovery deductions	10,000
Supplies, repairs	3,000
Payroll taxes paid	9,000
Contribution to art museum	6,000
Short-term capital gain	12,000
Passive income (rental operations)	7,500
Portfolio income (dividends received)	1,500
Exempt income (bond interest)	2,100
AMT adjustment (cost recovery)	3,600
Payment of partner Vern's alimony obligations	4,000

The partnership experienced a $20,000 net loss from operations last year, its first year of business.

The two-step computational process that is used to determine partnership income is applied in the following manner.

Nonseparately Stated Items (Ordinary Income)	
Fee income	$100,000
Salaries paid	–30,000
Cost recovery deductions	–10,000
Supplies, repairs	–3,000
Payroll taxes paid	–9,000
Ordinary income	$ 48,000

---

[28] § 702(b).

Separately Stated Items

Contribution to art museum	$ 6,000
Short-term capital gain	12,000
Passive income (rental operations)	7,500
Portfolio income (dividends received)	1,500
Exempt income (bond interest)	2,100
AMT adjustment (cost recovery)	3,600

Each of the separately stated items passes through proportionately to each partner and is included on the appropriate schedule or netted with similar items that the partner generated for the year. Thus, in determining what her tax liability will be on her Form 1040, Tiwanda includes a $2,000 charitable contribution, a $4,000 short-term capital gain, $2,500 of passive rent income, $500 of dividend income, and a $1,200 positive adjustment in computing alternative minimum taxable income. Tiwanda treats these items as if she had generated them herself. She must disclose her $700 share of exempt interest on the first page of her Form 1040. In addition, Tiwanda reports $16,000 as her share of the partnership's ordinary income, the net amount of the nonseparately stated items.

The partnership is not allowed a deduction for last year's $20,000 net operating loss—this item was passed through to the partners in the previous year. Moreover, the partnership is not allowed a deduction for personal expenditures (payment of Vern's alimony). ▼

Withdrawals. Capital withdrawals by partners during the year do not affect the partnership's income classification and reporting process. These items usually are treated as distributions made on the last day of the partnership's tax year. Thus, in Example 18, the payment of Vern's alimony by the partnership is probably treated as a distribution from the partnership to Vern.

PLANNING CONSIDERATIONS

Drafting the Partnership Agreement

Although a written partnership agreement is not required, many rules governing the tax consequences to partners and their partnerships refer to such an agreement. Remember that a partner's distributive share of income, gain, loss, deduction, or credit is determined in accordance with the partnership agreement. Consequently, if taxpayers operating a business in partnership form want a measure of certainty as to the tax consequences of their activities, a carefully drafted partnership agreement is crucial. An agreement that sets forth the obligations, rights, and powers of the partners should prove invaluable in settling controversies among them and provide some degree of certainty as to the tax consequences of the partners' actions.

Penalties. Each partner's share of partnership items should be reported on his or her individual tax return in the same manner as presented on the Form 1065. If a partner treats an item differently, the IRS must be notified of the inconsistent treatment.[29] If a partner fails to notify the IRS, a negligence penalty may be added to the tax due.

---

[29] § 6222.

CONCEPT SUMMARY 11-2

Tax Reporting of Partnership Activities

Event	Partnership Level	Partner Level
1. Compute partnership ordinary income.	Form 1065, line 22, page 1.	Schedule K–1 (Form 1065), line 1, page 1.
	Schedule K, Form 1065, line 1, page 3.	Each partner's share is passed through for separate reporting.
		Each partner's basis is increased.
2. Compute partnership ordinary loss.	Form 1065, line 22, page 1.	Schedule K–1 (Form 1065), line 1, page 1.
	Schedule K, Form 1065, line 1, page 3.	Each partner's share is passed through for separate reporting.
		Each partner's basis is decreased.
		The amount of a partner's loss deduction may be limited.
		Losses that may not be deducted are carried forward for use in future years.
3. Separately reported items like portfolio income, capital gain and loss, and § 179 deductions.	Schedule K, Form 1065, various lines, page 3.	Schedule K–1 (Form 1065), various lines, pages 1 and 2.
		Each partner's share of each item is passed through for separate reporting.
4. Net earnings from self-employment.	Schedule K, Form 1065, line 15, page 3.	Schedule K-1 (Form 1065), line 15, page 2.

To encourage the filing of a partnership return, a penalty of $50 per partner per month (or fraction thereof), but not to exceed five months, is imposed on the partnership for failure to file a complete and timely information return without reasonable cause.[30] A partnership with 10 or fewer individual and C corporation partners is automatically excluded from these penalties.[31] A husband and wife (or their estates) count as one partner in meeting this test.

PARTNERSHIP ALLOCATIONS

So far, all examples in this chapter have assumed that the partner has the same percentage interest in capital, profits, and losses. Thus, a partner who owns a 25 percent interest in partnership capital has been assumed to own 25 percent of partnership profits and 25 percent of partnership losses. Several special allocation rules can modify this result.

Economic Effect. The partnership agreement can provide that any partner may share capital, profits, and losses in different ratios. For example, a partner could have a 25 percent capital sharing ratio, yet be allocated 30 percent of the profits

---

[30] § 6698.
[31] § 6231(a)(1)(B). For this purpose, partners include individuals who are not nonresident aliens, as well as the estate of a decedent who was not a nonresident alien.

and 20 percent of the losses of the partnership, or, as in Examples 5 and 6, a partner could be allocated a specific amount or items of income, deduction, gain, or loss. Such special allocations are permissible if they follow certain rules contained in the Regulations under § 704(b).[32] Although these rules are too complex to discuss in detail, the general outline of one of these rules—the **economic effect test**—can be easily understood.

In general, the economic effect test requires the following.

- An allocation of income or gain to a partner must increase the partner's capital account, and allocation of a deduction or loss must decrease the partner's capital account.
- When the partner's interest is liquidated, the partner must receive assets that have a fair market value equal to the positive balance in the capital account.
- A partner with a negative capital account must restore that account upon liquidation of the interest. Restoration of a negative capital account can best be envisioned as a contribution of cash to the partnership equal to the negative balance.

These requirements are designed to ensure that a partner bears the economic burden of a loss or deduction allocation and receives the economic benefit of an income or gain allocation. Regulations outline specific allocation calculations that may be used and describe allowable methods of allocating depreciation deductions if the property is depreciable.[33]

EXAMPLE 19

Eli and Sanjay each contribute $20,000 cash to the newly formed ES Partnership. The partnership uses the cash to acquire a depreciable asset for $40,000. The partnership agreement provides that the depreciation is allocated 90% to Eli and 10% to Sanjay. Other items of partnership income, gain, loss, or deduction are allocated equally between the partners. Upon liquidation of the partnership, property will be distributed to the partners in accordance with their positive capital account balances. Any partner with a negative capital account must restore the capital account upon liquidation. First-year depreciation on the equipment is $4,000, and nothing else happens in the first year that affects the partners' capital accounts.

Eli's capital account is $16,400 ($20,000 − $3,600), and Sanjay's capital account has a balance of $19,600 ($20,000 − $400) after the first year of partnership operations. The Regulations require that a hypothetical sale of the asset for its $36,000 adjusted basis on the last day of the year and an immediate liquidation of the partnership should result in Eli and Sanjay receiving distributions equal to their capital accounts. According to the partnership agreement, Eli would receive $16,400, and Sanjay would receive $19,600 of the cash in a liquidating distribution. Eli, therefore, bears the economic burden of $3,600 depreciation since he contributed $20,000 to the partnership and would receive only $16,400 upon liquidation. Likewise, Sanjay's economic burden is $400 since he would receive only $19,600 of his original $20,000 investment. The agreement, therefore, has economic effect. ▼

EXAMPLE 20

Continue with the facts of Example 19. If the partnership agreement had provided that Eli and Sanjay each receive $18,000 of the liquidation proceeds, the "special" allocation of the depreciation would be defective. The IRS would require that the depreciation be allocated equally ($2,000 each) to the two partners to reflect the $2,000 economic burden borne by each partner. ▼

---

[32] Reg. § 1.704–1(b).
[33] Reg. § 1.704–3. The three allowable methods are the "traditional method," the "traditional method with curative allocations," and the "remedial allocation method." See also footnote 38.

Precontribution Gain or Loss. Income, gain, loss, and deductions relative to contributed property may not be allocated under the § 704(b) rules described above. Instead, **precontribution gain or loss** is allocated among the partners to take into account the variation between the basis of the property and its fair market value on the date of contribution.[34] For nondepreciable property, this means that *built-in gain or loss* on the date of contribution is allocated to the contributing partner when the property is eventually disposed of by the partnership in a taxable transaction.

EXAMPLE 21

Seth and Tim form the equal profit and loss sharing ST Partnership. Seth contributes cash of $10,000, and Tim contributes land purchased two years ago and held for investment. The land has an adjusted basis of $6,000 and fair market value of $10,000 at the contribution date. For accounting purposes, the partnership records the land at its fair market value of $10,000. For tax purposes, the partnership takes a carryover basis of $6,000 in the land. After using the land as a parking lot for five months, ST sells it for $10,600. No other transactions have taken place.

The accounting and tax gain from the land sale are computed as follows.

	Accounting	Tax
Amount realized	$10,600	$10,600
Less: Adjusted basis	10,000	6,000
Gain realized	$ 600	$ 4,600
Gain at contribution date to Tim	–0–	4,000
Remaining gain (split equally)	$ 600	$ 600

Seth recognizes $300 of the gain ($600 remaining gain ÷ 2), and Tim recognizes $4,300 [$4,000 built-in gain + ($600 ÷ 2)]. ▼

BASIS OF A PARTNERSHIP INTEREST

LEARNING OBJECTIVE 5
Determine a partner's basis in the partnership interest.

Previously, this chapter discussed how to compute a partner's adjusted basis when the partnership is formed. It was noted that the partner's adjusted basis in the newly formed partnership usually equals (1) the adjusted basis in any property contributed to the partnership plus (2) the fair market value of any services the partner performed for the partnership (i.e., the amount of ordinary income reported by the partner for services rendered to the partnership).

A partnership interest also can be acquired after the partnership has been formed. The method of acquisition controls how the partner's initial basis is computed. If the partnership interest is purchased from another partner, the purchasing partner's basis is the amount paid (cost basis) for the partnership interest. The basis of a partnership interest acquired by gift is the donor's basis for the interest plus, in certain cases, some or all of the transfer (gift) tax paid by the donor. The basis of a partnership interest acquired through inheritance is the fair market value of the interest on the date the partner dies (or alternate valuation date).

After the partnership begins its activities, or after a transferee partner is admitted to the partnership, the partner's basis is adjusted for numerous items. The following operating results *increase* a partner's adjusted basis.

- The partner's proportionate share of partnership income (including capital gains and tax-exempt income).
- The partner's proportionate share of any increase in partnership liabilities.

---
[34] § 704(c)(1)(A).

The following operating results *decrease* the partner's adjusted basis in the partnership.

- The partner's proportionate share of partnership deductions and losses (including capital losses).
- The partner's proportionate share of nondeductible expenses.
- The partner's proportionate share of any reduction in partnership liabilities.[35]

Under no circumstances can the partner's adjusted basis for the partnership interest be reduced below zero.

Increasing the adjusted basis for the partner's share of partnership taxable income is logical since the partner has already been taxed on the income. By increasing the partner's basis, the Code ensures that the partner is not taxed again on the income when he or she sells the interest or receives a distribution from the partnership.

It is also logical that the tax-exempt income should increase the partner's basis. If the income is exempt in the current period, it should not contribute to the recognition of gain when the partner either sells the interest or receives a distribution from the partnership.

EXAMPLE 22

Yuri is a one-third partner in the XYZ Partnership. His proportionate share of the partnership income during the current year consists of $20,000 of ordinary taxable income and $10,000 of tax-exempt income. None of the income is distributed to Yuri. The adjusted basis of Yuri's partnership interest before adjusting for his share of income is $35,000, and the fair market value of the interest before considering the income items is $50,000.

The unrealized gain inherent in Yuri's investment in the partnership is $15,000 ($50,000 − $35,000). Yuri's proportionate share of the income items should increase the fair market value of the interest to $80,000 ($50,000 + $20,000 + $10,000). By increasing the adjusted basis of Yuri's partnership interest to $65,000 ($35,000 + $20,000 + $10,000), the Code ensures that the unrealized gain inherent in Yuri's partnership investment remains at $15,000. This makes sense because the $20,000 of ordinary taxable income is taxed to Yuri this year and should not be taxed again when Yuri either sells his interest or receives a distribution. Similarly, the exempt income is exempt this year and should not increase Yuri's gain when he either sells his interest or receives a distribution from the partnership. ▼

Decreasing the adjusted basis for the partner's share of deductible losses, deductions, and noncapitalizable, nondeductible expenditures is logical for the same reasons. An item that is deductible currently should not contribute to creating a loss when a partner sells a partnership interest or receives a distribution from the partnership. Similarly, a noncapitalizable, nondeductible expenditure should never be deductible nor contribute to a loss when a subsequent sale or distribution transaction occurs.

Liability Sharing. A partner's adjusted basis is affected by the partner's share of partnership debt.[36] Partnership debt includes any partnership obligation that creates an asset, results in a deductible expense, or results in a nondeductible, noncapitalizable item at the partnership level. The definition of partnership debt includes most debt that is considered a liability under financial accounting rules except for accounts payable of a cash basis partnership and certain contingent liabilities.

Under § 752, an increase in a partner's share of partnership debt is treated as a cash contribution by the partner to the partnership. A partner's share of entity-

---

[35] §§ 705 and 752.   [36] § 752.

level debt increases as a result of increases in outstanding partnership debt. A decrease in a partner's share of partnership debt is treated as a cash distribution from the partnership to the partner. A partner's share of partnership debt decreases as a result of (1) decreases in total partnership debt and (2) assumption of a partner's debt by the entity.

EXAMPLE 23

Jim and Becky contribute property to form the JB Partnership. Jim contributes cash of $30,000. Becky contributes land with an adjusted basis and fair market value of $45,000, subject to a liability of $15,000. The partnership borrows $50,000 to finance construction of a building on the contributed land. At the end of the first year, the accrual basis partnership owes $3,500 in trade accounts payable to various vendors. No other operating activities occurred.

Partnership debt sharing rules are discussed later in this section, but assuming for simplicity that Jim and Becky share equally in liabilities, the partners' bases in their partnership interests are determined as follows.

Jim's Basis		Becky's Basis	
Contributed cash	$30,000	Basis in contributed land	$ 45,000
Share of debt on land (assumed by partnership)	7,500	Less: Debt assumed by partnership	(15,000)
Share of construction loans	25,000	Share of debt on land (assumed by partnership)	7,500
Share of trade accounts payable	1,750	Share of construction loan	25,000
		Share of trade accounts payable	1,750
	$64,250		$ 64,250

In this case, it is reasonable that the parties have an equal basis after contributing their respective properties, because each is a 50% owner and they contributed property with identical net bases and identical *net* fair market values. ▼

Decreases in a partner's share of partnership liabilities are treated as cash distributions and decrease the partner's interest basis. This limits the partner's ability to deduct current-year flow-through losses. If distributions continue after basis reaches zero, gain recognition occurs. Thus, liability balances should be reviewed carefully near the partnership's year-end to ensure the partners have no unanticipated tax results.

EXAMPLE 24

Assume the same facts as in Example 23, except the partnership reported an ordinary loss of $100,000 in its first year of operations. Ignoring possible loss deduction limitations, Jim and Becky each deduct a $50,000 ordinary loss, and their bases in their respective partnership interests are reduced to $14,250 (including a $34,250 share of liabilities).

In the second year, the partnership generated no taxable income or loss from operations, but repaid the $50,000 construction loan (assume from collection of accounts receivable reported as income in the prior year). The $25,000 reduction of each partner's share of partnership liabilities is treated as a cash distribution by the partnership to each partner. A cash distribution in excess of basis usually results in a capital gain (in this case $10,750) to each partner. The partners must pay tax on $10,750 of capital gain even though the partnership reported no taxable income. This gain can be thought of as a recapture of loss deductions the partners claimed during the first year. Such gains cause cash-flow difficulties to partners who are unaware that such a gain may occur. ▼

Two types of partnership debt exist. **Recourse debt** is partnership debt for which the partnership or at least one of the partners is personally liable. This liability can exist, for example, through the operation of state law or through personal guarantees that a partner makes to the creditor. Personal liability of a party related to a partner (under attribution rules) is treated as the personal liability of the partner. **Nonrecourse debt** is debt for which no partner (or party related to a partner) is personally liable. Lenders of nonrecourse debt generally require that collateral be pledged against the loan. Upon default, the lender can claim only the collateral, not the partners' personal assets. How liabilities are shared among the partners depends upon whether the debt is recourse or nonrecourse and when the liability was incurred.

Recourse Debt Rules. Recourse debt is shared among the partners and affects the basis of their partnership interests in accordance with a **constructive liquidation scenario.**[37]

Under this scenario, the following events are *deemed* to occur at the end of each taxable year of the partnership.

1. Most partnership assets (including cash) become worthless.
2. The worthless assets are sold at fair market value ($0), and losses on the deemed sales are determined.
3. These losses are allocated to the partners according to their loss sharing ratios. These losses reduce the partners' capital accounts.
4. Any partner with a (deemed) negative capital account balance is treated as contributing cash to the partnership to restore that negative balance to zero.
5. The cash deemed contributed by the partners with negative capital balances is used to pay the liabilities of the partnership.
6. The partnership is deemed to be liquidated immediately, and any remaining cash is distributed to partners with positive capital account balances.

The amount of a partner's cash contribution that would be used (in step 5 above) to pay partnership recourse liabilities is that partner's share of these partnership recourse liabilities.

EXAMPLE 25

On January 1 of the current year, Nina and Otis each contribute $20,000 cash to the newly created NO General Partnership. Each partner has a 50% interest in partnership capital, profits, and losses. The first year of partnership operations results in the following balance sheet as of December 31.

	Basis	Fair Market Value
Cash	$12,000	$12,000
Receivables	7,000	7,000
Land and buildings	50,000	50,000
	$69,000	$69,000
Recourse payables	$30,000	$30,000
Nina, capital	19,500	19,500
Otis, capital	19,500	19,500
	$69,000	$69,000

---

[37] Different rules apply to debt created before January 29, 1989.

The recourse debt is shared in accordance with the constructive liquidation scenario. All of the partnership assets (including cash) are deemed to be worthless and sold for $0. This creates a loss of $69,000 ($12,000 + $7,000 + $50,000), which is allocated equally between the two partners. The $34,500 loss allocated to each partner creates negative capital accounts of $15,000 each for Nina and Otis. If the partnership were actually liquidated, each partner would contribute $15,000 cash to the partnership; the cash would be used to pay the partnership recourse payables; and the partnership would be liquidated. Because each partner would be required to contribute $15,000 to pay the liabilities, each has a $15,000 share of the recourse payables. Accordingly, Nina and Otis each have an adjusted basis for their partnership interests of $34,500 ($19,500 + $15,000) on December 31. ▼

EXAMPLE 26

Assume the same facts as in Example 25, except that the partners allocate partnership losses 60% to Nina and 40% to Otis. The constructive liquidation scenario results in the $69,000 loss being allocated $41,400 to Nina and $27,600 to Otis. As a consequence, Nina's capital account has a negative balance of $21,900, and Otis's account has a negative balance of $8,100. Each partner is deemed to contribute cash equal to these negative capital accounts, and the cash would be used to pay the recourse liabilities under the liquidation scenario. Accordingly, Nina and Otis share $21,900 and $8,100, respectively, in the recourse debt. Note that the debt allocation percentages (73% to Nina and 27% to Otis) bear no relation to the partners' 60%/40% loss sharing ratios. ▼

Nonrecourse Debt Rules. Nonrecourse debt is allocated in three stages. First, an amount of debt equal to the amount of *minimum gain* is allocated to partners who share in minimum gain. In general, minimum gain approximates the amount of nonrecourse (mortgage) liability on a property in excess of the "book" basis of the property. The "book" basis for a property item usually is the same as its "tax" basis.

If a lender forecloses on partnership property, the result is treated as a deemed sale of the property for the mortgage balance. Gain is recognized for at least the amount of the liability in excess of the property's "book" basis—hence, minimum gain. Allocation of minimum gain among the partners should be addressed in the partnership agreement.

Second, the amount of nonrecourse debt equal to a *precontribution gain* under § 704(c) is allocated to the partner who contributed the property and debt to the partnership. For this purpose, the § 704(c) amount is the excess of the nonrecourse debt assumed by the partnership over the tax basis of the property.[38] Note that this calculation is only relevant when the "book" and "tax" bases of the contributed property are different.

Third, any remaining nonrecourse debt is allocated to the partners in accordance with either their profit sharing ratios or the manner in which they share in nonrecourse deductions. The partnership agreement should specify which allocation method is chosen. Most often, the profit sharing ratio is used.

EXAMPLE 27

Ted contributes a nondepreciable asset to the TK Partnership in exchange for a one-third interest in the capital, profits, and losses of the partnership. The asset has an adjusted tax basis to Ted and the partnership of $24,000 and a fair market value and "book" basis on the contribution date of $50,000. The asset is encumbered by a nonrecourse note of $35,000. Because the "book" basis exceeds the nonrecourse debt, there is no minimum gain. Under § 704(c) principles, the Regulations provide that the first $11,000 of the nonrecourse debt ($35,000 debt − $24,000 basis) is allocated to Ted. The remaining $24,000 nonrecourse debt

---

[38] A more complex calculation applies when the partnership allocates built-in gain under the "remedial allocation" method.

is shared according to the profit sharing ratio, so Ted's share is $8,000. Therefore, Ted shares in $19,000 ($11,000 + $8,000) of the nonrecourse debt.

Ted's basis in his partnership interest is determined as follows.

Substituted basis of contributed property	$ 24,000
Less: Liability assumed by partnership	(35,000)
Plus: Allocation of § 704(c) debt	11,000
Basis before remaining allocation	$ -0-
Plus: Allocation of remaining nonrecourse debt	8,000
Basis in partnership interest	$ 8,000

The § 704(c) allocation of nonrecourse debt prevents Ted from receiving a deemed distribution $35,000 in excess of his basis in property he contributed ($24,000). Without this required allocation of nonrecourse debt, in some cases, a contributing partner would be required to recognize gain on a contribution of property encumbered by nonrecourse debt. ▼

Other Factors Affecting Basis Calculations. The partner's basis is also affected by (1) postacquisition contributions of cash or property to the partnership; (2) postacquisition distributions of cash or property from the partnership; and (3) special calculations that are designed to allow the full deduction of percentage depletion for oil and gas wells. Postacquisition contributions of cash or property affect basis in the same manner as contributions made upon the creation of the partnership. Postacquisition distributions of cash or property reduce basis.

▼ **EXAMPLE 28**

Ed is a one-third partner in the ERM Partnership. On January 1, 1999, Ed's basis in his partnership interest was $50,000. During 1999, the calendar year, accrual basis partnership generated ordinary taxable income of $210,000. It also received $60,000 of interest income from City of Buffalo bonds. It paid $3,000 in nondeductible bribes to local law enforcement officials, so that the police would not notify the Federal government about the products that the entity had imported without paying the proper tariffs. On July 1, 1999, Ed contributed $20,000 cash and a computer (zero basis to him) to the partnership. Ed's monthly draw from the partnership is $3,000; this is not a guaranteed payment. The only liabilities that the partnership has incurred are trade accounts payable. On January 1, 1999, the trade accounts payable totaled $45,000; this account balance was $21,000 on January 1, 2000. Ed shares in one-third of the partnership liabilities for basis purposes.

Ed's basis in the partnership on December 31, 1999, is $115,000, computed as follows:

Beginning balance	$ 50,000
Share of ordinary partnership income	70,000
Share of exempt income	20,000
Share of nondeductible expenditures	(1,000)
Ed's basis in noncash capital contribution	-0-
Additional cash contributions	20,000
Capital withdrawal	(36,000)
Share of net decrease in partnership liabilities [⅓ × ($45,000 − $21,000)]	(8,000)
	$115,000

▼

▼ **EXAMPLE 29**

Assume the same facts as in Example 28. If Ed withdraws cash of $115,000 from the partnership on January 1, 2000, the withdrawal is tax-free to him and reduces his basis to zero. The distribution is tax-free because Ed has recognized his share of the partnership's net income throughout his association with the entity via the annual flow-through of his

FIGURE 11-1
Partner's Basis in Partnership Interest

> **Basis is generally adjusted in the following order:**
>
> Initial basis. Amount paid for interest, or gift or inherited basis (including share of partnership debt). Amount paid can be amount contributed to partnership or amount paid to another partner or former partner.
> + Partner's contributions
> + Since interest acquired, partner's share of partnership's
>
> - Debt increase
> - Income items
> - Exempt income items
> - Excess of depletion deductions over adjusted basis of property subject to depletion
>
> − Partner's distributions and withdrawals
> − Since interest acquired, partner's share of partnership's
>
> - Debt decrease
> - Nondeductible items not chargeable to a capital account
> - Special depletion deduction for oil and gas wells
> - Loss items
>
> **The basis of a partner's interest can never be negative.**

share of the partnership's income and expense items. Note that the $20,000 cash withdrawal of his share of the municipal bond interest retains its nontaxable character in this distribution. Ed receives the $20,000 tax-free because his basis was increased in 1999 when the partnership received the interest income. ▼

Entity-level liabilities, and thus a partner's interest basis, change from day to day, but interest basis generally needs to be computed only once or twice a year. When a partnership interest is sold, exchanged, or retired, however, the partner must compute the adjusted basis as of the date the transaction occurs. Computation of gain or loss requires an accurate calculation of the partner's adjusted basis on the transaction date.

Figure 11–1 summarizes the rules for computing a partner's basis in a partnership interest.

LOSS LIMITATIONS

LEARNING OBJECTIVE 6
Describe the limitations on deducting partnership losses.

Partnership losses flow through to the partners for use on their tax returns. However, the amount and nature of the losses that may be used in a partner's tax computations may be limited. When limitations apply, all or a portion of the losses are suspended until a triggering condition occurs. Only then can the losses be used to determine the partner's tax liability.

Three different limitations may apply to partnership losses that are passed through to a partner. The first is the overall limitation contained in § 704(d). This limitation allows the deduction of losses only to the extent the partner has adjusted basis for the partnership interest. Losses that are deductible under the overall limitation may then be subject to the at-risk limitation of § 465. Losses are deductible under this provision only to the extent the partner is at risk for the partnership interest. Any losses that survive this second limitation may be subject to a third limitation, the passive loss rules of § 469. Only losses that make it through all these applicable limitations are eligible to be deducted on the partner's tax return.

CHAPTER 11 Partnerships and Limited Liability Entities

EXAMPLE 30

Meg is a partner in a partnership that does not invest in real estate. On January 1, Meg's adjusted basis for her partnership interest is $50,000, and her at-risk amount is $35,000. Her share of losses from the partnership for the year is $60,000, all of which is passive. She has one other passive income-producing investment that produced $25,000 of passive income during the year.

Meg will be able to deduct $25,000 of partnership losses on her Form 1040. Her deductible loss is calculated as follows.

Applicable Provision	Deductible Loss	Suspended Loss
Overall limitation	$50,000	$10,000
At-risk limitation	35,000	15,000
Passive loss limitation	25,000	10,000

Meg can deduct only $50,000 under the overall limitation. Of this $50,000, only $35,000 is deductible under the at-risk limitation. Under the passive loss limitation, passive losses can only be deducted against passive income. Thus, Meg can deduct only $25,000 on her return. The remaining $35,000 of losses is suspended. ▼

Overall Limitation. A partner may only deduct losses flowing through from the partnership to the extent of the partner's adjusted basis in the partnership. A partner's adjusted basis in the partnership is determined at the end of the partnership's taxable year. It is adjusted for distributions and any partnership gains during the year, but it is determined *before considering any losses for the year*.

Losses that cannot be deducted because of this rule are suspended and carried forward (never back) for use against future increases in the partner's adjusted basis. Such increases might result from additional capital contributions or from sharing in additional partnership debts or future partnership income.

EXAMPLE 31

Carol and Dan do business as the CD Partnership, sharing profits and losses equally. All parties use the calendar year. At the start of the current year, the basis of Carol's partnership interest is $25,000. The partnership sustains an operating loss of $80,000 in the current year. Only $25,000 of Carol's $40,000 allocable share of the partnership loss (one-half of the $80,000 loss) can be deducted under the overall limitation. As a result, the basis of Carol's partnership interest is zero as of January 1 of the following year, and Carol must carry forward the remaining $15,000 of partnership losses. ▼

EXAMPLE 32

Assume the same facts as in Example 31, and that the partnership earns a profit of $70,000 for the next calendar year. Carol reports net partnership income of $20,000 ($35,000 distributive share of income – the $15,000 carryforward loss). The basis of Carol's partnership interest becomes $20,000. ▼

In Example 31, Carol's entire $40,000 share of the current-year partnership loss could have been deducted under the overall limitation in the current year if she had contributed an additional $15,000 or more in capital by December 31. Alternatively, if the partnership had incurred additional debt by the end of the current year, Carol's basis might have been increased to permit some or all of the loss to be deducted in that year. Thus, if partnership losses are projected for a given year, careful tax planning can ensure their deductibility under the overall limitation.

Notice that, in Figure 11–1, contributions to capital, distributions from the partnership, and partnership income items are taken into account before loss items. This ordering produces some unusual results in taxation of partnership distributions and deductibility of losses.

EXAMPLE 33

The Ellen-Glenn Partnership is owned equally by partners Glenn and Ellen. At the beginning of the year, Ellen's basis in her partnership interest is exactly $0. Her share of partnership income is $10,000 for the year, and she receives a $10,000 distribution from the partnership.

Under the basis adjustment ordering rules of Figure 11–1, Ellen's basis is first increased by the $10,000 of partnership income; then it is decreased by her $10,000 distribution. She reports her $10,000 share of partnership taxable income on her personal tax return. Her basis at the end of the year is again exactly $0 ($0 + $10,000 income − $10,000 distribution). ▼

EXAMPLE 34

Assume the same facts as in Example 33, except that Ellen's share of partnership operating results is a $10,000 loss instead of $10,000 income. She again receives a $10,000 distribution.

As mentioned earlier, a distribution of cash in excess of basis in the partnership interest results in a gain to the distributee partner. Under the basis adjustment ordering rules of Figure 11–1, Ellen's distribution is considered before the deductibility of the loss is evaluated under the overall limitation. This rule can be remembered as *losses last*.

Ellen recognizes gain on the $10,000 distribution because she has no basis in her partnership interest. The gain effectively ensures that she still has a $0 basis after the distribution. The loss cannot be deducted under the overall loss limitation rule because Ellen has no basis in her partnership interest. ▼

Given this $20,000 difference in partnership earnings in the two examples ($10,000 income versus $10,000 loss), does income taxed to Ellen differ in the same way? Actually, she reports $10,000 of income (gain) in each case: ordinary income in Example 33, and (probably) a capital gain from the distribution in Example 34. In Example 34, she also has a $10,000 suspended loss carryforward. These results are due solely to the basis adjustment ordering rules.

At-Risk Limitation. Under the at-risk rules, the partnership losses from business and income-producing activities that individual partners and closely held C corporation partners can deduct are limited to amounts that are economically invested in the partnership. Invested amounts include the adjusted basis of cash and property contributed by the partner and the partner's share of partnership earnings that has not been withdrawn.[39] A closely held C corporation exists when five or fewer individuals own more than 50 percent of the entity's stock under appropriate attribution and ownership rules.

When some or all of the partners are personally liable for partnership recourse debt, that debt is included in the adjusted basis of those partners. Usually, those partners also include the debt in their amount at risk.

No partner, however, carries any financial risk on nonrecourse debt. Therefore, as a general rule, partners cannot include nonrecourse debt in their amount at risk even though that debt is included in the adjusted basis of their partnership interest. This rule has an exception, however, that applies in many cases. Real estate nonrecourse financing provided by a bank, retirement plan, or similar party or by a Federal, state, or local government generally is deemed to be at risk.[40] Such debt is termed **qualified nonrecourse debt.** In summary, although the general rule provides that nonrecourse debt is not at risk, the overriding exception may provide that it is deemed to be at risk.

When determining a partner's loss deduction, the overall limitation rule is invoked first. That is, the deduction is limited to the partner's outside basis at the end of the partnership year. Then, the at-risk provisions are applied to see if the

---

[39]§ 465(a).   [40]§ 465(b)(6).

remaining loss is still deductible. Suspended losses are carried forward until a partner has a sufficient amount at risk in the activity to absorb them.[41]

EXAMPLE 35

Kelly invests $5,000 in the Kelly Green Limited Partnership as a 5% general partner. Shortly thereafter, the partnership acquires the master recording of a well-known vocalist for $250,000 ($50,000 from the partnership and $200,000 secured from a local bank via a *recourse* mortgage). Kelly's share of the recourse debt is $10,000, and her basis in her partnership interest is $15,000 ($5,000 cash investment + $10,000 debt share). Since the debt is recourse, Kelly's at-risk amount is also $15,000. Kelly's share of partnership losses in the first year of operations is $11,000. Kelly is entitled to deduct the full $11,000 of partnership losses under both the overall and the at-risk limitations because this amount is less than both her outside basis and at-risk amount. ▼

EXAMPLE 36

Assume the same facts as in Example 35, except the bank loan is nonrecourse (the partners have no direct liability under the terms of the loan in the case of a default). Kelly's basis in her partnership interest still is $15,000, but she can deduct only $5,000 of the flow-through loss. The amount she has at risk in the partnership does not include the nonrecourse debt. (The debt does not relate to real estate so it is not qualified nonrecourse debt.) ▼

Passive Activity Rules. A partnership loss share may also be disallowed under the passive activity rules. Recall from Chapter 5 that an activity is considered passive if the taxpayer (in this case, a partner) does not materially participate or if the activity is considered a rental activity. When this is the case, the losses from passive partnership activities are aggregated by each partner with his or her other passive income and losses. Any net loss is suspended and carried forward to future years. Thus, the limitation applies at the partner level and is computed after the basis and at-risk limitations discussed above.

PLANNING CONSIDERATIONS

Formation and Operation of a Partnership

In transferring assets to a partnership, potential partners should be cautious to ensure that they are not required to recognize any gain upon the creation of the entity. The nonrecognition provisions of § 721 are relatively straightforward and resemble the provisions under § 351. However, any partner can make a tax-deferred contribution of assets to the entity either at the inception of the partnership or later. This possibility is not available to less-than-controlling shareholders in a corporation.

The partners should anticipate the tax benefits and pitfalls that are presented in Subchapter K and should take appropriate actions to resolve any resulting problems. Typically, all that is needed is an appropriate provision in the partnership agreement (e.g., with respect to differing allocation percentages for gains and losses). Recall, however, that a special allocation of income, expense, or credit items in the partnership agreement must satisfy certain requirements before it is acceptable to the IRS.

---

[41]§ 465(a)(2).

Transactions between Partner and Partnership

LEARNING OBJECTIVE 7
Review the treatment of transactions between a partner and the partnership.

Many types of transactions occur between a partnership and one of its partners. The partner may contribute property to the partnership, perform services for the partnership, or receive distributions from the partnership. The partner may borrow money from or lend money to the partnership. Property may be bought and sold between the partner and the partnership. Several of these transactions were discussed earlier in the chapter. The remaining types of partner-partnership transactions are the focus of this section.

GUARANTEED PAYMENTS

If a partnership makes a payment to a partner in his or her capacity as a partner, the payment may be a draw against the partner's share of partnership income; a return of some or all of the partner's original capital contribution; or a guaranteed payment, among other treatments. A **guaranteed payment** is a payment for services performed by the partner or for the use of the partner's capital. The payment may not be determined by reference to partnership income. Guaranteed payments are usually expressed as a fixed-dollar amount or as a percentage of capital that the partner has invested in the partnership. Whether the partnership deducts or capitalizes the guaranteed payment depends on the nature of the payment.

EXAMPLE 37
David, Donald, and Dale formed the accrual basis DDD Partnership in 1999. According to the partnership agreement, David is to manage the partnership and receive a $21,000 distribution from the entity every year, payable in 12 monthly installments. Donald is to receive an amount that is equal to 18% of his capital account, as it is computed by the firm's accountant at the beginning of the year, payable in 12 monthly installments. Dale is the partnership's advertising specialist. He withdraws 3% of the partnership's net income every month for his personal use. David and Donald receive guaranteed payments from the partnership, but Dale does not. ▼

Guaranteed payments resemble the salary or interest payments of other businesses and receive somewhat similar treatment under partnership tax law.[42] In contrast to the provision that usually applies to withdrawals of assets by partners from their partnerships, guaranteed payments are deductible (or capitalized) by the entity. Deductible guaranteed payments, like any other deductible expenses of a partnership, can create an ordinary loss for the entity. Partners receiving a guaranteed payment report ordinary income, treated as paid on the last day of the entity's tax year.

EXAMPLE 38
Continue with the situation introduced in Example 37. For calendar year 1999, David receives the $21,000 as provided by the partnership agreement, Donald's guaranteed payment for 1999 is $17,000, and Dale withdraws $20,000 under his personal expenditures clause. Before considering these amounts, the partnership's ordinary income for 1999 is $650,000.

The partnership can deduct its payments to David and Donald, so the final amount of its 1999 ordinary income is $612,000 ($650,000 − $21,000 − $17,000). Thus, each of the equal partners is allocated $204,000 of ordinary partnership income for their 1999 individual income tax returns ($612,000 ÷ 3). In addition, David reports the $21,000 guaranteed payment as

---
[42] § 707(c).

income, and Donald includes the $17,000 guaranteed payment in his 1999 income. Dale's partnership draw is deemed to have come from his allocated $204,000 (or from the accumulated partnership income that was taxed to him in prior years) and is not taxed separately to him. ▼

EXAMPLE 39

Assume the same facts as in Example 37, except that the partnership's tax year ends on March 31, 2000. The total amount of the guaranteed payments is taxable to the partners on that date. Thus, even though David received 9 of his 12 payments for fiscal 2000 in the 1999 calendar year, all of his guaranteed payments are taxable to him in 2000. Similarly, all of Donald's guaranteed payments are taxable to him in 2000, rather than when they are received. The deduction for, and the gross income from, guaranteed payments is allowed on the same date that all of the other income and expense items relative to the partnership are allocated to the partners (on the last day of the entity's tax year). ▼

OTHER TRANSACTIONS BETWEEN A PARTNER AND A PARTNERSHIP

Certain transactions between a partner and the partnership are treated as if the partner were an outsider, dealing with the partnership at arm's length.[43] Loan transactions, rental payments, and sales of property between the partner and the partnership are generally treated in this manner. In addition, payments for services are treated this way when the services are short-term technical services that the partner also provides for parties other than the partnership.

EXAMPLE 40

Emilio, a one-third partner in the ABC Partnership, owns a tract of land that the partnership wishes to purchase. The land has a fair market value of $30,000 and an adjusted basis to Emilio of $17,000. If Emilio sells the land to the partnership, he recognizes a $13,000 gain on the sale, and the partnership takes a $30,000 cost basis in the land. If the land has a fair market value of $10,000 on the sale date, Emilio recognizes a $7,000 loss. ▼

The timing of the deduction by an accrual basis partnership for a payment for services rendered by a cash basis partner depends upon whether the payment is a guaranteed payment or a payment to a partner who is treated as an outsider. A guaranteed payment is includible in the partner's income on the last day of the partnership year when it is properly accrued by the partnership, even though the payment may not be made to the partner until the next taxable year. Conversely, the *partner's* method of accounting controls the timing of the deduction if the payment is treated as made to an outsider. This is because a deduction cannot be claimed for such amounts until the recipient partner is required to include the amount in income under the partner's method of accounting.[44] Thus, a partnership cannot claim a deduction until it actually makes the payment to the cash basis partner, but it could accrue and deduct a payment due to an accrual basis partner even if payment was not yet made.

EXAMPLE 41

Rachel, a cash basis taxpayer, is a partner in the accrual basis RTC Partnership. On December 31, 1999, the partnership accrues but does not pay $10,000 for deductible services that Rachel performed for the partnership during the year. Both Rachel and the partnership are calendar year taxpayers.

If the $10,000 accrual is a guaranteed payment, the partnership deducts the $10,000 in its calendar year ended December 31, 1999, and Rachel includes the $10,000 in her income

---

[43]§ 707(a).

[44]§ 267(a)(2).

for the 1999 calendar year. That Rachel is a cash basis taxpayer and does not actually receive the cash in 1999 is irrelevant.

If the payment is classified as a payment to an outsider, the partnership cannot deduct the payment until Rachel actually receives the cash. If, for example, Rachel performs janitorial services (i.e., not in her capacity as a partner) and receives the cash on March 25, 2000, the partnership deducts the payment and Rachel recognizes the income on that date. ▼

Sales of Property. Certain sales of property fall under special rules. No loss is recognized on a sale of property between a person and a partnership when the person owns, directly or indirectly, more than 50 percent of partnership capital or profits.[45] The disallowed loss may not vanish entirely, however. If the person eventually sells the property at a gain, the disallowed loss reduces the gain that would otherwise be recognized.

EXAMPLE 42

Barry sells land (adjusted basis to him, $30,000; fair market value, $45,000) to a partnership in which he controls a 60% capital interest. The partnership pays him $20,000 for the land. Barry cannot deduct his $10,000 realized loss. The sale apparently was not at arm's length, but the taxpayer's intentions are irrelevant. Barry and the partnership are related parties, and the loss is disallowed.

When the partnership sells the land to an outsider at a later date, it receives a sales price of $44,000. The partnership can offset the recognition of its $24,000 realized gain on the subsequent sale ($44,000 sales proceeds − $20,000 adjusted basis) by the amount of the $10,000 prior disallowed loss ($30,000 − $20,000). Thus, the partnership recognizes a $14,000 gain on its sale of the land. ▼

Using a similar rationale, any gain that is realized on a sale or exchange between a partner and a partnership in which the partner controls a capital or profit interest of more than 50 percent must be recognized as ordinary income, unless the asset is a capital asset to both the seller and the purchaser.[46]

EXAMPLE 43

Kristin purchases some land (adjusted basis, $30,000; fair market value, $45,000) for $45,000 from a partnership in which she controls a 90% profit interest. The land was a capital asset to the partnership. If Kristin holds the land as a capital asset, the partnership recognizes a $15,000 capital gain. However, if Kristin is a land developer and the property is not a capital asset to her, the partnership must recognize $15,000 ordinary income from the sale, even though the property was a capital asset to the partnership. ▼

PARTNERS AS EMPLOYEES

A partner usually does not qualify as an employee for tax purposes. For example, a partner receiving guaranteed payments is not regarded as an employee of the partnership for purposes of payroll taxes (e.g., FICA or FUTA). Moreover, since a partner is not an employee, the partnership cannot deduct its payments for the partner's fringe benefits. A general partner's distributive share of ordinary partnership income and guaranteed payments for services are generally subject to the Federal self-employment tax.[47]

---

[45] § 707(b).
[46] § 707(b)(2).
[47] § 1402(a).

Concept Summary 11-3

Partner-Partnership Transactions

1. Partners can transact business with their partnerships in a nonpartner capacity. These transactions include the sale and exchange of property, rentals, loans of funds, etc.
2. A payment to a partner may be classified as a guaranteed payment if it is for services or use of the partner's capital and is not based on partnership income. A guaranteed payment usually is deductible by the partnership and is included in the partner's income on the last day of the partnership's taxable year.
3. A payment to a partner may be treated as being to an outside (though related) party. Such a payment is deductible or capitalizable by the partnership at the time it must be included in income under the partner's method of accounting.
4. Guaranteed payments and payments to a partner that are treated as being to an outside party are deductible if the payment constitutes an ordinary and necessary (rather than capitalizable) business expense.
5. Losses are disallowed between a partner or related party and a partnership when the partner or related party owns more than a 50% interest in the partnership's capital or profits.
6. Income from a related-party sale is treated as ordinary income if the property is not a capital asset to both the transferor and the transferee.
7. Partners are not employees of their partnership, so the entity cannot deduct payments for partner fringe benefits, nor need it withhold or pay any payroll tax for payments to partners.

Concept Summary 11-3 reviews partner-partnership transactions, and Concept Summary 11-4 summarizes the advantages and disadvantages of the partnership form.

PLANNING CONSIDERATIONS

Transactions between Partners and Partnerships

Partners should be careful when engaging in transactions with the partnership to ensure that no negative tax results occur. A partner who owns a majority of the partnership generally should not sell property at a loss to the partnership because the loss is disallowed. Similarly, a majority partner should not sell a capital asset to the partnership at a gain, if the asset is to be used by the partnership as other than a capital asset. The gain on this transaction is taxed as ordinary income to the selling partner rather than as capital gain.

As an alternative to selling property to a partnership, the partner may lease it to the partnership. The partner recognizes rent income, and the partnership has a rent expense. A partner who needs more cash immediately can sell the property to an outside third party; then the third party can lease the property to the partnership for a fair rental.

The timing of the deduction for payments by accrual basis partnerships to cash basis partners varies depending on whether the payment is a guaranteed payment or is treated as a payment to an outsider. If the payment is a guaranteed payment, the deduction occurs when the partnership properly accrues the payment. If the payment is treated as a payment to an outsider, the actual date the payment is made controls the timing of the deduction.

Concept Summary 11–4

Advantages and Disadvantages of the Partnership Form

The partnership form may be attractive when one or more of the following factors is present:

- The entity is generating net taxable losses and/or valuable tax credits, which will be of use to the owners.
- Other means of reducing the effects of the double taxation of business income (e.g., compensation to owners, interest, and rental payments) have been exhausted.
- The entity does not generate material amounts of tax preference and adjustment items, which increase the alternative minimum tax liabilities of its owners.
- The entity is generating net passive income, which its owners can use to claim immediate deductions for net passive losses that they have generated from other sources.
- Given the asset holdings and distribution practices of the entity, the possibility of liability under the accumulated earnings and personal holding company taxes is significant.
- The owners wish to make special allocations of certain income or deduction items that are not possible under the C or S corporation forms.
- The owners anticipate liquidation of the entity within a short period of time. Liquidation of a C or S corporation would generate entity-level recognized gains on appreciated property distributed.
- The owners have adequate bases in their partnership interests to facilitate the deduction of flow-through losses and the assignment of an adequate basis to assets distributed in-kind to the partners.

The partnership form may be less attractive when one or more of the following factors is present:

- The maximum marginal tax rate applicable to individual owners is higher than the rate applicable to C corporations. Currently, marginal tax rates for individuals may exceed rates applicable to corporations.
- The entity is generating net taxable income, which is taxed directly to the owners who do not necessarily receive any funds from the entity with which to pay the tax.
- The type of income that the entity is generating (e.g., business and portfolio income) is not as attractive to its owners as net passive income would be because the owners could use net passive income to offset the net passive losses that they have generated on their own.
- The entity is in a high-exposure business, and the owners desire protection from personal liability. An LLC or LLP structure may be available, however, to limit personal liability.
- The owners want to avoid Federal self-employment tax.

LIMITED LIABILITY ENTITIES

LIMITED LIABILITY COMPANIES

LEARNING OBJECTIVE 8
Describe the application of partnership tax law provisions to limited liability (LLCs) and limited liability partnerships (LLPs).

The *limited liability company (LLC)* combines partnership taxation with limited personal liability for all owners of the entity. All states and the District of Columbia have passed legislation permitting the establishment of LLCs.

Taxation of LLCs. A properly structured LLC may be taxed as a partnership under the "check-the-box" Regulations discussed in Chapter 9. Because LLC members are not personally liable for the debts of the entity, the LLC is effectively treated as a limited partnership with no general partners. This may result in unusual application of partnership taxation rules. The IRS has not specifically ruled on most aspects of LLC taxation, so several of the following comments are based on speculation about how a partnership with no general partners would be taxed.

- Formation of a new LLC is treated in the same manner as formation of a partnership. Generally, no gain or loss is recognized by the LLC member or the LLC, the member takes a substituted basis in the LLC interest, and the LLC takes a carryover basis in the assets it receives.
- Contributed property with built-in gains is subject to the special allocation rules of § 704(c). Also, an LLC member contributing built-in gain property can be subject to tax on certain distributions within five years of the contribution.
- In allocating liabilities to the members for basis purposes, all liabilities are treated as if they are nonrecourse, even when they are nominally recourse in nature. This occurs because under the entity's legal structure, none of the members individually bears the economic risk of loss on a liability.
- An LLC's income and losses are allocated under § 704. Special allocations are permitted, as long as they meet the requirements outlined earlier in this chapter.
- Losses are subject to the three deductibility limitations outlined earlier. A loss must meet the basis, at-risk, and passive loss limitations to be currently deductible. Because the debt is considered nonrecourse to each of the members, it may not be included in the at-risk limitation unless it is "qualified nonrecourse financing." The IRS has not issued rulings as to whether a member is treated as a material or active participant of an LLC for passive loss purposes. Presumably, passive or active status will be based on the time the member spends in LLC activities.
- The initial accounting period and accounting method elections discussed earlier are applicable to an LLC.
- Transactions between an LLC and its members are treated as described earlier in the chapter. Under general partnership taxation rules, however, a limited partner's share of partnership income is *not* subject to self-employment taxes.
- The rules described in this chapter for distributions, sales of an interest, and retirement of a member's interest under § 736 all apply to an LLC. A distribution of appreciated property from a C or S corporation would result in taxable gain to the entity, whereas such property takes a carryover or substituted basis when distributed from an LLC.

Converting to an LLC. A partnership can convert to an LLC with few, if any, tax ramifications. The old elections of the partnership continue, and the partners retain their bases and ownership interests in the new entity. A C or S corporation that reorganizes as an LLC is treated as having liquidated prior to forming the new entity. The transaction is taxable to both the corporation and the shareholders.

Advantages of an LLC. An LLC offers certain advantages over a limited partnership.

- Generally, none of the members of an LLC is personally liable for the entity's debts. General partners in a limited partnership have personal liability for partnership recourse debts.
- Limited partners cannot participate in the management of a partnership. All owners of an LLC have the legal right to participate in the entity's management.

An LLC also offers certain advantages over an S corporation, including the following.

- An LLC can have an unlimited number of owners, while an S corporation is limited to 70 shareholders.

> ### TAX IN THE NEWS
>
> **PARTNERSHIPS AROUND THE WORLD—AND BEYOND**
>
> Technology continues to act as a catalyst—and incentive—for the creation of multinational joint ventures. AT&T, MCI, and Sprint are racing each other to align with partners in foreign telecommunications markets: each wants to have the widest service coverage area so it can offer efficient communications and computer networking to business clients with a global presence.
>
> Pharmaceutical companies find it advantageous to allow foreign partners to promote and distribute such products as imaging agents used in the detection of various cancers. Reciprocal agreements sometimes give each partner exclusive distribution rights for products created in the partners' separate research facilities.
>
> Finally, Primestar is a partnership of media giants, formed to develop a satellite-based cable TV system that may offer Internet access as well.
>
> At least one country, Bermuda, has recognized this trend and is trying to lure multinational joint ventures to its shores. In 1995, it passed the Overseas Partnerships Act and other legislation designed to encourage foreign investment.

- Any taxpayers, including corporations, nonresident aliens, other partnerships, and trusts, can be owners of an LLC. S corporation shareholders are limited (see Chapter 12).
- The transfer of property to an LLC in exchange for an ownership interest in the entity is governed by partnership tax provisions rather than corporate tax provisions. Thus, the transfers need not satisfy the 80 percent control requirement needed for tax-free treatment under the corporate tax statutes.
- The S corporation taxes on built-in gains and passive income do not apply to LLCs.
- An LLC can own 80 percent of the stock of another operating corporation. An S corporation cannot.
- An owner's basis in an LLC includes the owner's share of almost all LLC liabilities under § 752. Only certain S corporation liabilities are included in the S corporation shareholder's basis.
- An LLC may make special allocations under § 704(b), while S corporations must allocate income, loss, etc. on a per share/per day basis.
- The optional adjustments to basis election can be made for the benefit of the LLC and its owners. Such adjustments are not possible in an S corporation.

Disadvantages of an LLC. The disadvantages of an LLC stem primarily from the entity's relative newness. There is no established body of case law interpreting the various state statutes, so the application of specific provisions is uncertain. An additional uncertainty for LLCs that operate in more than one jurisdiction is which state's law will prevail and how it will be applied.

Among other factors, statutes differ from state to state as to the type of business an LLC can conduct—primarily the extent to which a service-providing firm can operate as an LLC. A service entity may find it cannot operate as an LLC in several jurisdictions where it conducts business. Despite these uncertainties and limitations, LLCs are being formed at increasing rates, and the ranks of multistate LLCs are rising quickly.

LIMITED LIABILITY PARTNERSHIPS

In 1991, Texas became the first state to allow professional practices to organize as registered *limited liability partnerships (LLPs)*. Since then, other states have adopted similar legislation. The difference between a general partnership and an LLP is small, but very significant. Recall that general partners are jointly and severally liable for all partnership debts. Partners in a registered LLP are jointly and severally liable for contractual liability (i.e., they are treated as general partners for commercial debt). They are also personally liable for their own malpractice or other torts. They are not, however, personally liable for the malpractice and torts of their partners. As a result, the exposure of their personal assets to lawsuits filed against other partners and the partnership is considerably reduced.

An LLP must have formal documents of organization and register with the state. Because the LLP is a general partnership in other respects, it does not have to pay any state franchise taxes on its operations—an important difference between LLPs and LLCs in states such as Texas and Florida. LLPs are taxed as partnerships under Federal tax statutes.

SUMMARY

Partnerships are popular among business owners because formation of the entity is relatively simple and tax-free. The Code places very few restrictions on who can be a partner. Partnerships are especially attractive when operating losses are anticipated, or when marginal rates that would apply to partnership income are less than those that would be paid by a C corporation. Partnerships do not offer the limited liability of a corporate entity, but the use of limited partnerships, LLCs, and LLPs can offer some protection to the owners.

Partnerships are tax-reporting, not taxpaying, entities. Distributive shares of ordinary income and separately stated items are taxed to the partners on the last day of the tax year. Special allocations and guaranteed payments are allowed and offer partners the ability to tailor the cash-flow and taxable amounts that are distributed by the entity to its owners. Deductions for flow-through losses may be limited by the passive activity, related-party, and at-risk rules, as well as by the partner's interest basis. The flexibility of the partnership rules of Subchapter K makes this form continually attractive to new businesses, especially in a global setting.

KEY TERMS

Aggregate concept, 11–8

Basis in partnership interest, 11–8

Capital account, 11–8

Capital interest, 11–7

Capital sharing ratio, 11–7

Constructive liquidation scenario, 11–25

Disguised sale, 11–11

Economic effect test, 11–21

Entity concept, 11–8

General partnership, 11–5

Guaranteed payment, 11–32

Inside basis, 11–14

Limited liability company (LLC), 11–5

Limited liability partnership (LLP), 11–5

Limited partnership, 11–5

Nonrecourse debt, 11–25

Outside basis, 11–14

Precontribution gain or loss, 11–22

Profit and loss sharing ratios, 11–7

Profits (loss) interest, 11–7
Qualified nonrecourse debt, 11–30
Recourse debt, 11–25
Separately stated item, 11–5
Special allocation, 11–7
Syndication costs, 11–16

Problem Materials

1. Dan is an attorney who is financially successful. Mary is a real estate developer who has little cash for investment. The two decide to buy some real estate. Dan will contribute the money to buy the properties and have veto power over which properties to purchase. Mary will make all other decisions. Profits and losses from the operation will be shared equally.
   a. Is this a partnership for tax purposes? Why or why not?
   b. Would your answer change if Dan had no veto power and was to receive a guaranteed 10% annual return on his money?

2. Larry and Ken form an equal partnership with a cash contribution of $50,000 from Larry and a property contribution (adjusted basis of $30,000 and a fair market value of $50,000) from Ken.
   a. How much gain, if any, must Larry recognize on the transfer? Must Ken recognize any gain?
   b. What is Larry's interest basis in the partnership?
   c. What is Ken's interest basis in the partnership?
   d. What basis does the partnership take in the property transferred by Ken?

3. James and Lynn form an equal partnership with a $40,000 cash contribution from James and a contribution of property (her basis $60,000, fair market value $40,000) from Lynn.
   a. Compute Lynn's realized and recognized gain or loss from the contribution.
   b. Compute James's basis in his partnership interest.
   c. Compute Lynn's basis in her partnership interest.
   d. What basis does the partnership take in Lynn's contributed asset?
   e. Are there more tax-effective ways to structure the transaction?

4. Three years after the S&P Partnership is formed, Sylvia, a 25% partner, contributes an additional $25,000 cash and land she has held for investment. Sylvia's basis in the land is $15,000, and its fair market value is $10,000. Her basis in the partnership interest was $50,000 before this contribution. The partnership uses the land as a parking lot for four years and then sells it for $8,000.
   a. How much gain or loss does Sylvia recognize on the contribution?
   b. What is Sylvia's basis in her partnership interest immediately following this contribution?
   c. How much gain or loss does S&P recognize on this contribution?
   d. What is S&P's basis in the property it receives from Sylvia?
   e. How much gain or loss does the partnership recognize on the later sale of the land, and what is the character of the gain or loss? How much is allocated to Sylvia?

5. Block, Inc., a calendar year general contractor, and Strauss, Inc., a development corporation with a July 31 year-end, formed the equal SB Partnership on January 1 of the current year. Both partners are C corporations. The partnership was formed to construct and lease shopping centers in Wilmington, Delaware. Block contributed equipment (basis of $650,000, fair market value of $650,000), building permits, and architectural designs that had been created by Block's employees (basis of $0, fair market value of $100,000).
   Strauss contributed land (basis of $50,000, fair market value of $250,000) and cash of $500,000. The cash was used as follows.

Legal fees for drafting partnership agreement	$ 10,000
Materials and labor costs for construction in progress on shopping center	400,000
Office expense (utilities, rent, overhead, etc.)	90,000

What issues must the partnership address in preparing its initial tax return?

6. Craig and Beth are equal members of the CB Partnership, formed on June 1 of the current year. Craig contributed land that he inherited from his father three years ago. Craig's father purchased the land in 1946 for $6,000. The land was worth $50,000 when the father died. The fair market value of the land was $75,000 at the date it was contributed to the partnership.

   Beth has significant experience developing real estate. After the partnership is formed, she will prepare a plan for developing the property and secure zoning approvals for the partnership. She would normally bill a third party $25,000 for these efforts. Beth will also contribute $50,000 cash in exchange for her 50% interest in the partnership. The value of her 50% interest is $75,000.
   a. How much gain or income will Craig recognize on his contribution of the land to the partnership? What is the character of any gain or income recognized?
   b. What basis will Craig take in his partnership interest?
   c. How much gain or income will Beth recognize on the formation of the partnership? What is the character of any gain or income recognized?
   d. What basis will Beth take in her partnership interest?
   e. Construct an opening balance sheet for the partnership reflecting the partnership's basis in assets and the fair market value of these assets.
   f. Outline any planning opportunities that may minimize current taxation to any of the parties.

7. Continue with the facts presented in Problem 6. At the end of the first year, the partnership distributes the $50,000 cash to Craig. No distribution is made to Beth.
   a. Under general tax rules, how would the payment to Craig be treated?
   b. How much income or gain would Craig recognize as a result of the payment?
   c. Under general tax rules, what basis would the partnership take in the land Craig contributed?
   d. What alternate treatment might the IRS try to impose?
   e. Under the alternate treatment, how much income or gain would Craig recognize?
   f. Under the alternate treatment, what basis would the partnership take in the land contributed by Craig?
   g. How can the transaction be restructured to minimize risk of IRS recharacterization?

8. The MDB Partnership was formed to acquire land and subdivide it as residential housing lots. On July 1, 1998, Maria contributed land valued at $100,000 to the partnership in exchange for a one-third interest. She had purchased the land in 1991 for $76,000 and held it for investment purposes (capital asset). The partnership holds the land as inventory.

   On the same date, Barry contributed land valued at $100,000 that he had purchased in 1989 for $120,000. He also became a one-third owner. Barry is a real estate developer, but he held this land personally for investment purposes. The partnership holds this land as inventory.

   In 1994, Deborah had sold a parcel of land held for development purposes on the installment basis. She, too, is a real estate developer. The note has a fair market value and remaining principal balance of $100,000. She contributed this note to the partnership on the same day in exchange for her one-third interest. Deborah's basis in the note was $60,000 on the contribution date; the deferred gain on the installment sale is $40,000.

   From 1998 to 2002, the partnership collects $20,000 per year on the installment obligation (plus adequate interest on the unpaid balance).

   In 1999, the partnership sells half of the land contributed by Maria for $124,000.

   In 2000, the partnership sells half of the subdivided real estate contributed by Barry for $44,000. The other half is finally sold in 2005 for $54,000.

a. What is each partner's initial basis in his or her partnership interest?
b. What is the amount of gross profit recognized each year on collection of the installment proceeds? What is the character of the gain or loss?
c. What is the amount of gain or loss recognized on the sale of the land contributed by Maria? What is the character of this gain or loss?
d. What is the amount of gain or loss recognized each year on the sale of the land contributed by Barry? What is the character of this gain or loss?

9. The partnership agreement for the MDB Partnership in Problem 8 provides that all gains and losses are allocated equally among the partners unless otherwise required under the tax law.
   a. How will the gains or losses determined in (b), (c), and (d) in Problem 8 be allocated to each of the partners?
   b. If the partnership earns $24,000 of interest income over the term of the installment note, how will this income be allocated to the partners? Assume no accrued interest existed on the day the note was contributed.
   c. Calculate each partner's basis in his or her partnership interest at December 31, 2005. Assume the partnership has no transactions through the end of the year 2005 other than the transactions described in Problem 8 and the collection of $24,000 of interest income in (b) above. Why are these balances the same or different?

10. The cash basis Thrush Partnership incurred the following organization and syndication costs in calendar 1998.

Attorney fees for preparing partnership agreement	$2,100
Printing costs for preparing documents that were used to help sell the partnership interests	4,000
Accounting fees for tax advice of an organizational nature	2,400

    The attorney fees and printing costs were incurred and paid in 1998. The accounting fees were incurred in December 1998 and paid in February 1999. If the partnership begins business in July 1998, how much of the organization costs can be amortized in 1998? In 1999?

11. Lisa and Lori are equal members of the Redbird Partnership. They are real estate investors who formed the partnership several years ago with equal cash contributions. Redbird then purchased a piece of land.

    On January 1 of the current year, to acquire a one-third interest in the entity, Lana contributed some land she had held for investment to the partnership. Lana purchased the land three years ago for $30,000; its fair market value at the contribution date was $40,000. No special allocation agreements were in effect before or after Lana was admitted to the partnership. The Redbird Partnership holds all land for investment.

    Immediately before Lana's property contribution, the balance sheet of the Redbird Partnership was as follows.

	Basis	FMV		Basis	FMV
Land	$5,000	$80,000	Lisa, capital	$2,500	$40,000
			Lori, capital	2,500	40,000
	$5,000	$80,000		$5,000	$80,000

    a. At the contribution date, what is Lana's basis in her interest in the Redbird Partnership?
    b. When does the partnership's holding period begin for the contributed land?
    c. On June 30 of the current year, the partnership sold the land contributed by Lana for $40,000. How much is the recognized gain or loss, and how is it allocated among the partners?
    d. Prepare a balance sheet reflecting basis and fair market value for the partnership immediately after the land sale.

12. Assume the same facts as in Problem 11, with the following exceptions.

    - Lana purchased the land three years ago for $50,000. Its fair market value was $40,000 when it was contributed to the partnership.
    - Redbird sold the land contributed by Lana for $34,000.

    a. How much is the recognized gain or loss, and how is it allocated among the partners?
    b. Prepare a balance sheet reflecting basis and fair market value for the partnership immediately after the land sale, along with schedules that support the amount in each partner's capital account.

13. Earl and Zelda are equal partners in the accrual basis EZ Partnership. At the beginning of the current year, Earl's capital account has a balance of $10,000, and the partnership has recourse debts of $30,000 payable to unrelated parties. All partnership recourse debt is shared equally between the partners. The following information about EZ's operations for the current year is obtained from the partnership's records.

Taxable income	$ 8,000
Tax-exempt interest income	2,000
§ 1231 gain	6,000
Long-term capital gain	2,000
Long-term capital loss	120
Short-term capital loss	600
IRS penalty	630
Charitable contribution to Girl Scouts	200
Cash distribution to Earl	14,000
Payment of Earl's medical expenses	6,000

    Assume that year-end partnership debt payable to unrelated parties is $40,000.
    a. If all transactions are reflected in his beginning capital and basis in the same manner, what is Earl's basis in the partnership interest at the beginning of the year?
    b. If all transactions are reflected in his beginning capital and basis in the same manner, what is Earl's basis in the partnership interest at the end of the current year?

14. Harlen will contribute $50,000 cash to the HJ Partnership. Jane currently operates a sole proprietorship with assets valued at $50,000. Jane's tax basis in these assets is $75,000. Jane will either contribute these assets to the partnership in exchange for a 50% interest, or she will sell the assets to Brady Salvage (a third party) for their $50,000 fair market value and contribute that cash to the partnership. The partnership needs assets similar to those Jane owns, but it can purchase new assets from a third party for $60,000. Describe the tax consequences of each alternative to both Jane and the partnership.

15. The RUB Partnership reported the following items during the current tax year.

Taxable income	$120,000
Municipal bond interest income	10,000
Gain on sale of real estate	60,000

    Taxable income includes $20,000 of income from collection of cash basis accounts receivable contributed by 25% partner Rolfe at the beginning of the year.

    The municipal bond income was earned on bonds contributed by 50% partner Una. None of the interest was accrued on the contribution date. The partnership agreement provides that all this income will be specially allocated to Una this year, and no offsetting allocation will be made now or later.

    The real estate gain resulted from the sale of a parcel of land contributed by 25% partner Bart. When the property was contributed, it was valued at $100,000 and Bart's basis was $80,000. The real estate is a capital asset to both Bart and the partnership.

    Prepare a schedule showing how each item is allocated to each of the three partners. The partnership will maintain capital account balances and perform all other record keeping required to meet the substantial economic effect requirements of § 704(b).

16. The KB Partnership is owned equally by Kay and Bob. Bob's basis is $15,000 at the beginning of the tax year. Kay's basis is $6,000 at the beginning of the year. KB reported the following income and expenses for the current tax year.

Sales revenue	$130,000 ord
Cost of sales	45,000 ord
Guaranteed payment to Kay	24,000 ord
Depreciation expense	12,500 ord
Utilities	15,000 ord
Rent	16,000 ord
Interest income	3,000 sep
Tax-exempt interest income	4,500 sep
Long-term capital loss	3,200 sep
Payment to Mount Vernon Hospital for Bob's medical expenses	10,000 cash distr

    a. Determine the ordinary partnership income and separately stated items for the partnership.
    b. Calculate Bob's basis in his partnership interest at the end of the tax year. What items should Bob report on his Federal income tax return?
    c. Calculate Kay's basis in her partnership interest at the end of the tax year. What items should Kay report on her Federal income tax return?

17. Assume the same facts as in Problem 16, except for the following.

    - Partnership revenues were $90,000 instead of $130,000.
    - Kay also received a distribution of $10,000 cash.

    a. Redetermine the ordinary income and separately stated items for the partnership.
    b. Calculate Bob's basis in his partnership interest at the end of the tax year. How much income or loss should Bob report on his Federal income tax return?
    c. Calculate Kay's basis in her partnership interest at the end of the tax year. How much income or loss should Kay report on her Federal income tax return?

18. At the beginning of the current year, Bill's basis in his 50% interest in the BP Partnership is $10,000, including an $85,000 share of partnership recourse debt. Near the beginning of the year, he contributed land valued at $180,000 to the partnership. Bill's basis in the land was $76,000, and a nonrecourse liability on the land (assumed by the partnership) was $90,000. The value of the land rose sharply when plans for a new freeway nearby were approved during the year, and the partnership sold the land near the end of the year for $260,000. The gain on the land sale is a capital gain since the land was held for investment purposes by both Bill and the partnership. BP used the proceeds from the land sale to pay the partnership's recourse and nonrecourse debts. Other than the gain on the land sale, the partnership reported an ordinary loss of $150,000 from operations. Bill is an active partner in the partnership.

    It is the last day of the current tax year. Bill has just called to ask you to help determine how his ownership interest in the partnership will affect his personal tax and financial situation this year.

    a. What issues related to each of the above transactions must be addressed to determine the tax consequences of owning the partnership interest for the current year?
    b. Make any necessary calculations and advise Bill regarding any year-end action you feel might be advisable.

19. Assume the same facts as in Problem 18, except as indicated below. Situations (a) and (b) are independent fact patterns.
    a. How would your advice to Bill change if he was not an active partner in the partnership and had no other passive activities? Identify the additional issues that arise in this situation.
    b. How would your advice to Bill change if his $10,000 basis included all $170,000 of partnership recourse debt (under a constructive liquidation calculation)? Identify

the additional issues that arise in this situation. (Assume the partnership repaid all debt before year-end and Bill is still an active partner.)

20. The MGP General Partnership was created this year on January 1 by having Miguel, George, and Pat each contribute $10,000 cash to the partnership in exchange for a one-third interest in partnership income, gains, losses, deductions, and credits. At the end of the year, the partnership balance sheet reads as follows.

	Basis	FMV
Assets	$40,000	$55,000
Recourse debt	$12,000	$12,000
Miguel, capital	11,000	16,000
George, capital	11,000	16,000
Pat, capital	6,000	11,000
	$40,000	$55,000

Pat's capital account is less than Miguel's and George's capital accounts because Pat has withdrawn more cash than the other partners.

Compute the basis of the partnership interest for each partner.

21. Your client, the Williams Institute of Technology (WIT), is a 60% partner in the Research Industries Partnership (RIP). WIT is located at 76 Bradford Lane, St. Paul, MN 55164. The controller, Jeanine West, has sent you the following note and a copy of WIT's 1999 Schedule K–1 from the partnership.

Excerpt from client's note
"RIP expects its 2000 operations to include the following.

Net loss from operations	$200,000
Capital gain from sale of land	100,000

The land was contributed by DASH, the other partner, when its value was $260,000. The partnership sold the land for $300,000. The partnership used this cash to repay all the partnership debt and pay for research and development expenditures, which a tax partner in your firm has said RIP can deduct this year.

We want to be sure we can deduct our full share of this loss, but we do not believe we will have enough basis. We are a material participant in this partnership's activities."

Items Reported on the 1999 Schedule K–1	
WIT's share of partnership recourse liabilities	$90,000
WIT's ending capital account balance	30,000

Draft a letter to the controller that describes the following.

- WIT's allocation of partnership items.
- WIT's basis in the partnership interest following the allocation.
- Any limitations on loss deductions.
- Any recommendations you have that would allow WIT to claim the full amount of losses in 2000.

WIT's 1999 K–1 accurately reflects the information needed to compute its basis in the partnership interest. The research expenditures are fully deductible this year, as the partner said.

Your client has experience researching issues in the Internal Revenue Code, so you may use some citations. However, be sure that the letter is written in layperson's terms and that legal citations are minimized.

22. Lee, Brad, and Rick form the LBR Partnership on January 1 of the current year. In return for a 25% interest, Lee transfers property (basis of $15,000, fair market value of $17,500) subject to a nonrecourse liability of $10,000. The liability is assumed by the partnership. Brad transfers property (basis of $16,000, fair market value of $7,500) for a 25% interest, and Rick transfers cash of $15,000 for the remaining 50% interest.
    a. How much gain must Lee recognize on the transfer?
    b. What is Lee's basis in his interest in the partnership?
    c. How much loss may Brad recognize on the transfer?
    d. What is Brad's basis in his interest in the partnership?
    e. What is Rick's basis in his interest in the partnership?
    f. What basis does the LBR Partnership take in the property transferred by Lee?
    g. What is the partnership's basis in the property transferred by Brad?

23. Assume the same facts as in Problem 22, except that the property contributed by Lee has a fair market value of $27,500 and is subject to a nonrecourse mortgage of $20,000.
    a. What is Lee's basis in his partnership interest?
    b. How much gain must Lee recognize on the transfer?
    c. What is Brad's basis in his partnership interest?
    d. What is Rick's basis in his partnership interest?
    e. What basis does the LBR Partnership take in the property transferred by Lee?

24. Sam has operated a microbrewery (sole proprietorship) in southern Oregon for the past 15 years. The business has been highly profitable lately, and demand for the product will soon exceed the amount Sam can produce with his present facilities. Marcie, a long-time fan of the brewery, has offered to invest $1,500,000 for equipment to expand production. The assets and goodwill of the brewery are currently worth $1,000,000 (tax basis is only $200,000). Sam will continue to manage the business. He is not willing to own less than 50% of whatever arrangement they arrive at. What issues should Sam and Marcie address and document before finalizing their venture?

25. Kim and Craig plan to form the KC General Partnership by the end of the current year. The partners will each contribute $30,000 cash to the venture. In addition, the partnership will borrow $140,000 from First State Bank. The partnership's land will serve as collateral, and both partners will be required to personally guarantee the debt.

    The tentative partnership agreement provides that 75% of operating income, gains, losses, deductions, and credits will be allocated to Kim for the first five years of the partnership's existence. The remaining 25% is allocated to Craig. Thereafter, all partnership items will be allocated equally. The agreement also provides that capital accounts will be properly maintained, and each partner must restore any deficit in the capital account upon the partnership's liquidation.

    The partners would like to know, before the end of the tax year, how the $140,000 liability will be allocated for basis purposes. Draft a memo to the tax planning file for the KC Partnership that describes how the debt will be shared between the partners for purposes of computing the adjusted basis of each partnership interest.

26. Chris Elton is a 15% partner in the Cardinal Partnership, which is a lessor of residential rental property. Her share of the partnership's losses for the current year is $70,000. Immediately before considering the deductibility of this loss, Chris's capital account (which, in this case, corresponds to her basis excluding liabilities) reflected a balance of $40,000. Her share of partnership recourse liabilities is $10,000, and her share of the nonrecourse liabilities is $6,000. The nonrecourse liability was obtained from an unrelated bank and is secured solely by the real estate.

    Chris is also a partner in the Bluebird Partnership, which has generated income from long-term (more than 30 days) equipment rental activities. Chris's share of Bluebird's income is $23,000.

    Chris performs substantial services for Bluebird and spends several hundred hours a year working for the Cardinal Partnership. Chris's modified adjusted gross income before considering partnership activities is $100,000. Your manager has asked you to determine how much of the $70,000 loss from Cardinal Chris can deduct on her current calendar year return. Draft a memo to the client's tax file describing the loss limitations. Be sure to identify any Code Sections under which losses are suspended.

27. Fred and Fran are equal partners in the calendar year F & F Partnership. Fred uses a fiscal year ending June 30, and Fran uses a calendar year. Fred receives an annual guaranteed payment of $50,000 from F & F. F & F's taxable income (after deducting Fred's guaranteed payment) was $40,000 for 1998 and $50,000 for 1999.
    a. What is the aggregate amount of income from the partnership that Fred must report for his tax year ending June 30, 1999?
    b. What is the aggregate amount of income from the partnership that Fran must report for her tax year ending December 31, 1999?
    c. If Fred's annual guaranteed payment is increased to $60,000 starting on January 1, 1999, and the partnership's taxable income for 1998 and 1999 is the same (i.e., $40,000 and $50,000, respectively), what is the aggregate amount of income from the partnership that Fred must report for his tax year ending June 30, 1999?

28. Ned, a 50% partner in the MN Partnership, is to receive a payment of $35,000 for services. He will also be allocated 50% of the partnership's profits or losses. After deducting the payment to Ned, the partnership has a loss of $25,000. Ned's basis in his partnership interest was $10,000 before these items.
    a. How much, if any, of the $25,000 partnership loss will be allocated to Ned?
    b. What is the net income from the partnership that Ned must report on his Federal income tax return?
    c. What is Ned's basis in his partnership interest following the guaranteed payment and loss allocation?

29. Four Lakes Partnership is owned by four sisters. Anne holds a 70% interest; each of the others owns 10%. Anne sells investment property to the partnership for its fair market value of $100,000. Her tax basis was $150,000.
    a. How much loss, if any, may Anne recognize?
    b. If the partnership later sells the property for $160,000, how much gain must it recognize?
    c. If Anne's basis in the investment property was $20,000 instead of $150,000, how much, if any, capital gain would she recognize on the sale?

30. Comment on the validity of the following statements:
    a. Since a partnership is not a taxable entity, it is not required to file any type of tax return.
    b. Each partner can choose a different method of accounting and depreciation computation in determining the gross income from the entity.
    c. Generally, a transfer of appreciated property to a partnership results in recognized gain to the contributing partner at the time of the transfer.
    d. A partner can carry forward, for an unlimited period of time, the partner's share of any partnership operating losses that exceed the partner's basis in the entity, provided the partner retains an ownership interest in the partnership.
    e. When a partner renders services to the entity in exchange for an unrestricted interest, that partner does not recognize any gross income.
    f. Losses on sales between a partner and the partnership always are nondeductible.
    g. A partnership may choose a year that results in the least aggregate deferral of tax to the partners, unless the IRS requires the use of a natural business year.
    h. A partner's basis in a partnership interest includes that partner's share of partnership recourse and nonrecourse liabilities.
    i. Built-in loss related to nondepreciable property contributed to a partnership must be allocated to the contributing partner to the extent the loss is eventually recognized by the partnership.
    j. Property that was held as inventory by a contributing partner, but is a capital asset in the hands of the partnership results in a capital gain if the partnership immediately sells the property.

31. A partnership's tax return preparer is responsible for accurately presenting information supplied by the partnership in that return. If a flow-through amount is significant to a certain partner, the preparer of the *partnership* return can be treated as the preparer of the *partner's* tax return with respect to that item.

    If a preparer misstates an item on a partnership return either by taking a position that is not supportable under current law or by willfully misreporting the item, "preparer penalties" can be assessed. Although these penalties are relatively small, their imposition may lead to the preparer's suspension from practice before the IRS or by a state accountancy board.

    As an example, assume Stan, a CPA, knowingly reported a $20,000 deduction for fines and penalties (nondeductible items) in determining the JB Partnership's $30,000 income from operations. This amount is allocated equally to partners Joe and Barb. Joe has other income of $35,000; Barb has other income of $1 million. Stan is treated as the preparer of Joe's tax return with respect to the improper $10,000 flow-through item since the fines and penalties are significant relative to Joe's income. Stan is not the preparer of Barb's return since the fines and penalties are not significant to her income.

    In a recent case, the preparer of a partnership return was considered to be the preparer of several partners' returns with respect to partnership items flowing through to the partners. The court reached this decision even though the return preparer never met the individual partners, received any direct fees from the partners, or otherwise performed services for them.

    Do you believe this is a reasonable approach for allocating responsibility for accurate preparation of a partner's tax return? Why or why not?

32. At one time, one partner could contribute cash and another partner could contribute appreciated property with no subsequent record-keeping requirements. Future depreciation deductions and gains on sale of the property could be allocated to both partners equally, thereby shifting income from one taxpayer to another. A partner in a lower tax bracket (or with expiring net operating losses and the like) could report his or her share of the gain on sale of the asset with a relatively low corresponding tax burden.

    Section 704(c)(1)(A) was added to the Code to ensure that the partner contributing the property pays tax on any built-in gain. This prevents income shifting among taxpayers and loss of revenue to the IRS.

    There is no corresponding provision for S corporations—gains and losses and depreciation expense are allocated among the shareholders without regard to any built-in appreciation on contributed property.

    What theory of partnership taxation supports this difference in treatment?

COMPREHENSIVE TAX RETURN PROBLEM

33. Sarah Henley (246–32–1958) and James Morgan (923–65–4326) are equal partners in the BBB Partnership—for "Bake-a-Better-Bagel"—a general partnership that operates a bakery in an exclusive retail area in Paradise Valley, Arizona. BBB's Federal I.D. number is 23–9676512. The partnership uses the accrual method of accounting and the calendar year for reporting purposes. It began business operations on June 6, 1992. Its current address is 5816 North Valley Boulevard, Paradise Valley, AZ 85023. The 1997 income statement for the partnership reflected net income of $112,010. The following information was taken from the partnership's financial statements for the current year.

Receipts	
Sales revenues	$429,900
Taxable interest from investments	3,200
Tax-exempt interest	1,000
Dividend income	1,800
Total receipts	$435,900

Cash payments
Purchases	$175,390
Rent	16,800
Utilities	18,250
Employee salaries	25,400
Contribution to United Fund	600
Meals and entertainment, subject to 50% disallowance	2,080
Guaranteed payment, James Morgan, managing partner	24,000
Office expense	995
Accounting fees	1,225
Payroll taxes	2,790
Sales tax	30,660
Business interest on mortgage on leasehold improvements	6,000
Repairs	1,200
Payment of beginning accounts payable	6,200
Commercial oven (§ 179 deduction)	8,600
Total cash disbursements	$320,190

Noncash expenses
Amortization	$ 600
Depreciation (excluding depreciation on commercial oven)	12,360
Accrual of ending utilities payable	3,000

The beginning and ending tax basis balance sheets for the partnership were as follows for 1997.

	Beginning	Ending
Cash	$15,505	$59,215
Inventory	36,875	42,935
U.S. Treasury notes	20,000	20,000
Short-term investments	26,000	26,000
Leasehold improvements	65,000	?
Equipment	30,000	?
Accumulated depreciation and § 179 write-off	(16,830)	?
Organization fees	3,000	3,000
Accumulated-amortization	(950)	(1,550)
Total assets	$178,600	$?
Accounts payable	$ 6,200	$ 3,000
Mortgage payable on leasehold improvements and equipment	75,000	75,000
Capital, Henley	48,700	?
Capital, Morgan	48,700	?
Total liabilities and capital	$178,600	$?

The partnership uses the lower of cost or market method for valuing inventory. It is not subject to the provisions of § 263A. The partnership will claim a § 179 deduction for the commercial oven acquired during the year. The partnership has a $2,600 tax preference item for depreciation on property placed in service after 1986.

No salaries were paid to partners other than James Morgan. Instead, both partners withdrew $3,000 per month as a distribution (draw) of operating profits. The partners have both guaranteed payment of the mortgage on the improvements and equipment.

The partners share equally in all partnership liabilities, since all initial contributions and all ongoing allocations and distributions are pro rata.

Neither of the partners sold any portion of their interests in the partnership during 1997. The partnership's operations are entirely restricted to the Phoenix metropolitan area (which includes Paradise Valley). Both partners are U.S. citizens. The partnership had no foreign operations, no foreign bank accounts, and no interest in any foreign trusts or other partnerships. The partnership is not publicly traded and is not a statutory tax shelter.

The IRS's business code for the partnership operations is 5460. The partnership is not subject to the consolidated audit procedures and does not have a tax matters partner. The partnership files its tax return in Ogden, Utah. Partner James Morgan lives at 297 E. Cactus Road, Tempe, AZ 85287.

a. Prepare Form 1065 and Schedule K for the BBB Partnership, leaving blank any items where insufficient information has been provided. Prepare any supporting schedules necessary. *Hint:* Prepare Schedule A first to determine cost of goods sold.
b. Prepare Schedule K–1 for James Morgan.

RESEARCH PROBLEMS

*Note: The **RIA OnPoint System 4 Student Version CD-ROM** available with this text can be used in preparing solutions to the Research Problems. Alternatively, tax research materials contained in a standard tax library can be used.*

34. Your clients, Mark Henderson and John Burton, each contributed $10,000 cash to form the Realty Management Partnership, a limited partnership. Mark is the general partner, and John is the limited partner. The partnership used the $20,000 cash to make a down payment on a building. The rest of the building's $200,000 purchase price was financed with an interest-only nonrecourse loan of $180,000, which was obtained from an independent third-party bank. The partnership allocates all partnership items equally between the partners except for the MACRS deductions and building maintenance, which are allocated 70% to John and 30% to Mark. The partnership definitely wishes to satisfy the "economic effect" requirements of Reg. § 1.704–1 and Reg. § 1.704–2 and will reallocate MACRS, if necessary, to satisfy the requirements of the Regulations. Under the partnership agreement, liquidation distributions will be paid in proportion to the partners' positive capital account balances. Capital accounts are maintained as required in the Regulations. Mark has an unlimited obligation to restore his capital account while John is subject to a qualified income offset provision. Assume all partnership items, except for MACRS, will net to zero throughout the first three years of the partnership operations. Also, assume that each year's MACRS deduction will be $10,000 (to simplify the calculations).

    Draft a letter to the partnership evaluating the allocation of MACRS in each of the three years under Reg. § 1.704–1 and Reg. § 1.704–2. The partnership's address is 53 East Marsh Ave., Smyrna, Georgia 30082. Do not address the "substantial" test.

35. Harrison has considerable experience as a leasing agent for residential rental properties. He is disappointed, though, that his salary with his present employer does not reflect the effort he puts forth.

    Alameda Properties has offered Harrison a position handling leasing activities for a new limited partnership that is being formed to construct and manage three apartment complexes in southern California. Alameda is willing to hire Harrison for two years to lease the properties, but is unable to pay the $60,000 salary Harrison requires without impairing its ability to pay necessary cash distributions to the limited partners.

    Alameda is willing to pay a $30,000 salary for two years, increasing to a market salary thereafter. Alameda is also willing to allow Harrison to purchase a 10% interest in the partnership, but Harrison cannot afford the required $20,000 capital contribution.

    The partnership expects to distribute cash flows from operations of approximately $150,000 per year, for an estimated seven-year holding period (taxable income will be much lower because depreciation and interest deductions will be greater than mortgage payments).

Harrison and Alameda Properties have approached you for assistance in structuring a mutually satisfactory arrangement. You are aware that a partner can be awarded an interest in the future profits of a partnership and have learned from a colleague that in 1993 the IRS issued a Revenue Procedure that outlines the types of profits interests that will not be subject to current taxation. Present a structure to Harrison and Alameda Properties that meets their respective goals, and outline the advantages and disadvantages to each party.

36. Fred and Grady have formed the FG Partnership to operate a retail establishment selling antique household furnishings. Fred is the general partner, and Grady is the limited partner. Both partners contribute $15,000 to form the partnership. The partnership uses the $30,000 contributed by the partners and a recourse loan of $100,000 obtained from an unrelated third-party lender to acquire $130,000 of initial inventory.

The partners believe they will have extensive losses in the first year due to advertising and initial cash-flow requirements. Fred and Grady have agreed to share losses equally. To make sure the losses can be allocated to both partners, they have included a provision in the partnership agreement requiring each partner to restore any deficit balance in his partnership capital account upon liquidation of the partnership.

Fred was also willing to include a provision that requires him to make up any deficit balance within 90 days of liquidation of the partnership. As a limited partner, Grady argued that he should not be subject to such a time requirement. The partners compromised and included a provision that requires Grady to restore a deficit balance in his capital account within two years of liquidation of the partnership. No interest will be owed on the deferred restoration payment.

Determine whether FG will be able to allocate the $100,000 recourse debt equally to the two partners to ensure they will be able to deduct their respective shares of partnership losses.

CHAPTER 12

S Corporations

LEARNING OBJECTIVES

After completing Chapter 12, you should be able to:

1. Explain the tax effects associated with S corporation status.
2. Identify corporations that qualify for the S election.
3. Understand how to make and terminate an S election.
4. Compute nonseparately stated income and allocate income, deductions, and credits to shareholders.
5. Understand how distributions to S corporation shareholders are taxed.
6. Calculate a shareholder's basis in S corporation stock.
7. Explain how losses in an S corporation are treated.
8. Compute the entity-level taxes on S corporations.

OUTLINE

Introduction, 12–2

An Overview of S Corporations, 12–2

When to Elect S Corporation Status, 12–4

Qualifying for S Corporation Status, 12–5

Definition of a Small Business Corporation, 12–5

Making the Election, 12–7

Shareholder Consents, 12–8

Loss of the Election, 12–9

Operational Rules, 12–12

Computation of Taxable Income, 12–12

Allocation of Income and Loss, 12–14

Tax Treatment of Distributions to Shareholders, 12–16

Tax Treatment of Property Distributions by the Corporation, 12–20

Shareholder's Basis, 12–21

Treatment of Losses, 12–24

Tax on Pre-election Built-in Gain, 12–28

Passive Investment Income Penalty Tax, 12–32

Other Operational Rules, 12–32

Summary, 12–33

LEARNING OBJECTIVE 1
Explain the tax effects associated with S corporation status.

INTRODUCTION

The **S corporation** rules were enacted to minimize the role of tax considerations in the entity choice that many small businesses face. S corporation status provides a compromise for small businesses: they can avoid the double taxation and loss limitations inherent in the regular corporate form while still enjoying many of the nontax benefits extended to C corporations.

S corporations are treated as corporations under state law. They are recognized as separate legal entities and generally provide shareholders with the same liability protection afforded by C corporations. Some states (such as Michigan) treat S corporations as C corporations for tax purposes, resulting in a state corporate income or franchise tax liability. For Federal income tax purposes, taxation of S corporations resembles that of partnerships. As with partnerships, the income, deductions, and tax credits of an S corporation flow through to shareholders annually, regardless of whether dividends are paid. Thus, income is taxed at the shareholder level and not at the corporate level. Dividends paid by the corporation are distributed tax-free to shareholders to the extent that the distributed earnings were previously taxed to the shareholders.

Although the tax treatment of S corporations and partnerships is similar, it is not identical. For instance, liabilities affect owners' basis differently and S corporations may incur a tax liability at the corporate level. In addition, a variety of C corporation provisions apply to S corporations. For example, the liquidation of C and S corporations is taxed in the same way. As a rule, where the S corporation provisions are silent, C corporation rules apply.

S corporation status must be elected by a *qualifying* corporation and consented to by its shareholders. Rules related to the S election and the tax treatment of S corporations are addressed in **Subchapter S** of the Internal Revenue Code (§§ 1361–1379). These rules are introduced in this chapter.

AN OVERVIEW OF S CORPORATIONS

Since the inception of S corporations in 1958, their popularity has waxed and waned with changes in the tax law. Before the Tax Reform Act of 1986, their ranks grew slowly. In contrast, in the two years following the 1986 law, the population of S corporations exploded; their numbers increased by 52 percent. By 1993, more than

1.9 million businesses were filing S corporation returns—48 percent of all corporate returns filed in that year. This rapid growth was driven by a change in the relationship of individual and corporate tax rates. Prior to 1986, maximum individual rates were higher than maximum corporate rates. Following the 1986 tax act, the relationship reversed. After 1993, maximum individual income tax rates were increased to 39.6 percent, again exceeding the maximum corporate rate (by 4.6 percentage points). Consequently, S corporations declined in popularity, although they remained the preferred business form of a wide range of enterprises. As the following examples illustrate, S corporations can be advantageous even when the top individual tax rate exceeds the top corporate tax rate.

EXAMPLE 1 An S corporation earns $300,000, and all after-tax income is distributed currently. The marginal individual tax rate applicable to shareholders is 39.6%, and the applicable marginal corporate tax rate is 34%. The entity's available after-tax earnings, compared with those of a similar C corporation, are computed below.

	C Corporation	S Corporation
Earnings	$ 300,000	$ 300,000
Less: Corporate tax	(102,000)	–0–
Available for distribution	$ 198,000	$ 300,000
Less: Tax at owner level	(78,408)	(118,800)
Available after-tax earnings	$ 119,592	$ 181,200

The S corporation generates an extra $61,608 of after-tax earnings ($181,200 − $119,592), when compared with a similar C corporation. The C corporation might be able to reduce this disadvantage, however, by paying out its earnings as compensation, rents, or interest expense. Tax at the owner level can also be deferred or avoided by not distributing after-tax earnings. ▼

EXAMPLE 2 A new corporation elects S status and incurs a net operating loss (NOL) of $300,000. The shareholders of the corporation may use their proportionate shares of the NOL to offset other taxable income in the current year, providing an immediate tax savings. In contrast, a newly formed C corporation is required to carry the NOL forward for up to 20 years and receives no tax benefit in the current year. Hence, an S corporation can accelerate NOL deductions and thereby provide greater present value for tax savings generated by the loss. ▼

Two recent developments have affected the popularity of S corporation status. As discussed in Chapter 11, a new form of business entity recently emerged that offers many of the advantages of S corporations. These new entities, limited liability companies (LLCs), avoid many of the restrictions that are imposed on S corporations. In addition, the Small Business Protection Act of 1996 liberalized a number of the S corporation rules. These changes, which provide greater flexibility in forming, operating, and restructuring S corporations, promise to reinvigorate their status as a viable alternative to LLCs.

WHEN TO ELECT S CORPORATION STATUS

Effective planning with S corporations begins with determining whether an S election is appropriate for the entity. The following factors should be considered.

- If shareholders are subject to high marginal rates relative to C corporation rates, it may be desirable to avoid S corporation status. Although a C corporation may be subject to double taxation, any double tax can be minimized with careful planning. For example, profits of the corporation may be taken out by the shareholders through compensation arrangements, as interest, or as rent income. Corporate profits can be transferred to shareholders as capital gain income through capital structure changes, such as stock redemptions, liquidations, or sales of stock to others. Alternatively, profits may be paid out as dividends in low tax years. Any distribution of profits or sale of stock can be deferred to a later year, thereby reducing the present value of shareholder taxes. Finally, shareholder-level tax on corporate profits can be eliminated by a step-up in basis of the stock upon the shareholder's death.
- S corporation status allows shareholders to realize tax benefits from corporate losses immediately—an important consideration in new business enterprises where operating losses are common. Thus, if corporate NOLs are anticipated and there is unlikely to be corporate income over the near term to offset with the NOLs, S corporation status is advisable. However, the deductibility of the losses to shareholders must also be considered. The at-risk and passive loss limitations (refer to Chapter 5) apply to losses generated by an S corporation. In addition, as discussed later in this chapter, shareholders may not deduct losses in excess of the basis in their stock. Together with the time value of money considerations of deferring any loss deduction, these limits may significantly reduce the benefits of an S election in a loss setting.
- If the entity electing S corporation status is currently a C corporation, any NOL carryovers from prior years (refer to Chapter 5) cannot be used in an S corporation year. Even worse, S corporation years use up the 20-year carryover period.
- The corporation may be subject to some corporate-level taxes if it elects S status. C corporations are not assessed these taxes. See the discussion of such taxes later in the chapter.
- Distributions of earnings from C corporations are usually taxed as ordinary income. In contrast, because S corporations are flow-through entities, all deduction and income items retain any special tax characteristics when they are reported on shareholders' returns. Whether this consideration favors S status depends upon the character of income and deductions of the S corporation.
- The S corporation rules impose significant requirements for qualifying as an S corporation. When electing S status, one should consider whether any of these requirements are likely to be violated at some point in the future.
- State and local tax laws should also be considered when making the S election. Although an S corporation usually escapes Federal income tax, it may not be immune from all state and local income taxes.
- The choice of S corporation status is affected by a variety of other factors. For example, the corporate alternative minimum tax (see Chapter 13) may be avoided in an S corporation. An in-depth discussion of entity choice is provided in Chapter 14.

CHAPTER 12 S Corporations

QUALIFYING FOR S CORPORATION STATUS

DEFINITION OF A SMALL BUSINESS CORPORATION

LEARNING OBJECTIVE 2
Identify corporations that qualify for the S election.

To achieve S corporation status, a corporation must *first* qualify as a **small business corporation**. A small business corporation:

- Is a domestic corporation (incorporated and organized in the United States).
- Is an eligible corporation (e.g., *not* an insurance company or a nonqualifying bank).
- Issues only one class of stock.
- Is limited to a maximum of 75 shareholders (35 shareholders before 1997).
- Has only individuals, estates, and certain trusts as shareholders.
- Has no nonresident alien shareholder.

Unlike other small business provisions in the tax law (e.g., § 1244), no maximum or minimum dollar sales or capitalization restrictions apply to S corporations.

If each of the above requirements is met, then the entity can elect S corporation status. The small business corporation definition is discussed in detail in the following paragraphs.

Ineligible Corporations. Foreign corporations, certain banks, insurance companies, and Puerto Rico or possessions corporations do not qualify as small business corporations. Prior to 1997, small business corporations were prohibited from being members of affiliated groups. Now, ownership of up to 100 percent of a C corporation is permitted. In addition, small business corporations are permitted (after 1996) to have wholly owned S corporation subsidiaries.[1]

One Class of Stock. A small business corporation may have only one class of stock issued and outstanding.[2] This restriction permits differences in voting rights, but not differences in distribution or liquidation rights.[3] Thus, two classes of common stock that are identical except that one class is voting and the other is nonvoting would be treated as a single class of stock for small business corporation purposes. In contrast, voting common stock and voting preferred stock (with a preference on dividends) would be treated as two classes of stock. Authorized and unissued stock or treasury stock of another class does not disqualify the corporation. Likewise, unexercised stock options, phantom stock, stock appreciation rights, warrants, and convertible debentures usually do not constitute a second class of stock.

The determination of whether stock provides identical rights to distributions and liquidation proceeds is made based on the provisions governing the operation of the corporation. These *governing provisions* include the corporate charter, articles of incorporation, bylaws, applicable state law, and binding agreements relating to distribution and liquidation proceeds. Employment contracts, loan agreements, and other commercial contracts are *not* considered governing provisions.[4] Such contracts violate the one-class-of-stock requirement only if their principal purpose is to circumvent the requirement.

---

[1] § 1361(b)(2).
[2] § 1361(b)(1)(D).
[3] § 1361(c)(4).
[4] Reg. § 1.1361–1(l)(2).

EXAMPLE 3

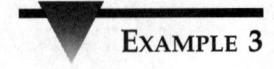

Blue, a small business corporation, has two equal shareholders, Smith and Jones. Both shareholders are employed by Blue and have binding employment contracts with the corporation. The compensation paid by Blue to Jones under her employment contract is reasonable in amount. The compensation paid to Smith under his employment contract, however, is excessive (a constructive dividend results). Smith's employment contract was not intended to circumvent the one-class-of-stock requirement. Because employment contracts are not considered governing provisions, Blue has only one class of stock. ▼

When constructive dividends are paid to shareholders under the imputed interest rules that apply to low-interest loans, the one-class-of-stock requirement generally is not violated. This is because debt instruments are not governing provisions.

Although the one-class-of-stock requirement seems straightforward, it is possible for debt to be reclassified as stock, resulting in unexpected loss of S corporation status.[5] To mitigate concern over possible reclassification of debt as a second class of stock, the law provides a set of *safe harbor* provisions.

First, *straight debt* issued in an S corporation year is not treated as a second class of stock and will not disqualify the S election.[6] The characteristics of straight debt are listed below.

- The debtor is subject to a written, unconditional promise to pay on demand or on a specified date a sum certain in money.
- The interest rate and payment date are not contingent on corporate profit, management discretion, or similar factors.
- The debt is not convertible into stock.
- The creditor is an individual (other than a nonresident alien), an estate, or qualified trust.
- Straight debt can be held by creditors actively and regularly engaged in the business of lending money.

In addition to the straight debt safe harbor, short-term unwritten advances from a shareholder that do not exceed $10,000 in the aggregate at any time during the corporation's taxable year generally are not treated as a second class of stock. Likewise, debt that is held by stockholders in the same proportion as their stock is not treated as a second class of stock, even if it would be reclassified as equity otherwise.[7]

Number of Shareholders. A small business corporation is limited to 75 shareholders (35 before 1997). If shares of stock are owned jointly by two individuals, they will generally be treated as separate shareholders. However, a husband and wife are considered one shareholder. Similarly, a widower or widow and his or her spouse's estate are treated as a single shareholder.[8] The treatment of a husband and wife as a single shareholder can have unexpected consequences in a divorce, as illustrated in the following example.

EXAMPLE 4

Fred and Wilma (husband and wife) jointly own 10 shares in Oriole, Inc., an S corporation, with the remaining 90 shares outstanding owned by 74 other shareholders. Fred and Wilma get divorced; pursuant to the property settlement approved by the court, the 10 shares held by Fred and Wilma are divided between them (5 to each). Before the divorce settlement, Oriole had 75 shareholders under the small business corporation rules. After the settlement, it has 76 shareholders and no longer qualifies as a small business corporation. ▼

---

[5] Refer to the discussion of debt-versus-equity classification in Chapter 9.
[6] § 1361(c)(5)(A).
[7] Reg. § 1.1361–1(l)(4).
[8] § 1361(c)(1).

Type of Shareholder Limitation.
Small business corporation shareholders may be individuals, estates, or certain trusts.[9] This limitation prevents partnerships and corporations from owning stock. Without this rule, partnership and corporate shareholders could easily circumvent the 75-shareholder limitation.

EXAMPLE 5 Paul and 80 other individuals wish to form an S corporation. Paul reasons that if the group forms a partnership, the partnership can then form an S corporation and act as a single shareholder, thereby avoiding the 75-shareholder rule. Paul's plan will not work, because partnerships cannot own stock in a small business corporation. ▼

Although partnerships and corporations cannot own small business corporation stock, small business corporations can be partners in a partnership or shareholders in a corporation. In this way, the 75-shareholder requirement can be bypassed in a limited sense. For example, if two small business corporations, each with 75 shareholders, form a partnership, then the shareholders of both corporations can enjoy the limited liability conferred by S corporation status and a single level of tax on partnership profits.

Nonresident Aliens.
Nonresident aliens cannot own stock in a small business corporation.[10] That is, individuals who are not U.S. citizens *must live in the United States* to own S corporation stock. Shareholders with nonresident alien spouses in community property states[11] therefore cannot own S corporation stock because the nonresident alien spouse would be treated as owning half of the community property.[12] Similarly, if a resident alien shareholder moves outside the United States, the S election will be terminated.

MAKING THE ELECTION

3 LEARNING OBJECTIVE
Understand how to make and terminate an S election.

To become an S corporation, a *small business corporation* (defined above) must file a valid election with the IRS. The election is made on Form 2553 (reproduced in Appendix B). For the election to be valid, it must be filed on a timely basis and all shareholders must consent. For S corporation status to apply in the current tax year, the election must be filed either in the previous year or on or before the fifteenth day of the third month of the current year.[13]

EXAMPLE 6 In 1999, a calendar year C corporation decides to become an S corporation beginning January 1, 2000. The S corporation election can be made at any time in 1999 or by March 15, 2000. An election after March 15, 2000, will not be effective until the 2001 tax year. ▼

Even if the 2½-month deadline is met, a current election is not valid unless the corporation qualifies as a small business corporation for the *entire* tax year. Otherwise, the election will be effective for the following tax year. Late current-year elections, after the 2½-month deadline, may be considered timely if there is reasonable cause for the late filing.

---

[9] § 1361(b)(1)(B).
[10] § 1362(b)(1)(C).
[11] Assets acquired by a married couple are generally considered community property in nine states: Arizona, California, Idaho, Louisiana, Nevada, New Mexico, Texas, Washington, and Wisconsin.
[12] See *Ward v. U.S.*, 81–2 USTC ¶9674, 48 AFTR2d 81–5942, 661 F.2d 226 (Ct.Cls., 1981), where the court found that the stock was owned as community property. Since the taxpayer-shareholder (a U.S. citizen) was married to a citizen and resident of Mexico, the nonresident alien prohibition was violated. If the taxpayer-shareholder had held the stock as separate property, the S election would have been valid.
[13] § 1362(b).

A corporation that does not yet exist cannot make an S corporation election.[14] Thus, for new corporations, a premature election may not be effective. A new corporation's 2½-month election period begins at the earliest occurrence of any of the following events.

- When the corporation has shareholders.
- When it acquires assets.
- When it begins doing business.[15]

EXAMPLE 7

Several individuals acquire assets on behalf of Rose Corporation on June 29 and begin doing business on July 3. They subscribe to shares of stock, file articles of incorporation for Rose, and become shareholders on July 7. The S election must be filed no later than 2½ months after June 29 (on or before September 12) to be effective for Rose's first tax year. ▼

SHAREHOLDER CONSENTS

A qualifying election requires the consent of all of the corporation's shareholders.[16] Consent must be in writing, and it must generally be filed by the election deadline. However, although no statutory authority exists for obtaining an extension of time for filing an S election (Form 2553), a shareholder may receive an extension of time to file a consent. A consent extension is available only if the Form 2553 is filed on a timely basis, reasonable cause is given, and the interests of the government are not jeopardized.[17]

EXAMPLE 8

Vern and Yvonne decide to convert their C corporation into a calendar year S corporation for 2000. At the end of February 2000 (before the election is filed), Yvonne travels to Ukraine and forgets to sign a consent to the election. Yvonne will not return to the United States until June and cannot be reached by fax. Vern files the S election on Form 2553 and also requests an extension of time to file Yvonne's consent to the election. Vern indicates that there is a reasonable cause for the extension: a shareholder is out of the country. Since the government's interest is not jeopardized, the IRS probably will grant Yvonne an extension of time to file the consent. Vern must file the election on Form 2553 on or before March 15, 2000, for the election to be effective for the 2000 calendar year. ▼

Both husband and wife must consent if they own their stock jointly (as joint tenants, tenants in common, tenants in the entirety, or community property). This requirement has led to considerable taxpayer grief—particularly in community property states where the spouses may not realize that their stock is jointly owned as a community asset.

EXAMPLE 9

Three shareholders, Monty, Dianne, and Amy, incorporate in January and file Form 2553. Amy is married and lives in California. Monty is single and Dianne is married; they live in North Carolina. Because Amy is married and lives in a community property state, her husband must also consent to the S election. Since North Carolina is not a community property state, Dianne's husband does not need to consent. ▼

---

[14]See, for example, *T.H. Campbell & Bros., Inc.*, 34 TCM 695, T.C.Memo. 1975–149, Ltr.Rul. 8807070.

[15]Reg. § 1.1372–2(b)(1). Also see, for example, *Nick A. Artukovich*, 61 T.C. 100 (1973).

[16]§ 1362(a)(2).

[17]Rev.Rul. 60–183, 1960–1 C.B. 625; *William Pestcoe*, 40 T.C. 195 (1963); Temp.Reg. § 18.1362–2(e).

Finally, for current-year S elections, persons who were shareholders during any part of the taxable year before the election date, but were not shareholders when the election was made, must also consent to the election.[18]

EXAMPLE 10

On January 15, 1999, the stock of Columbine Corporation (a calendar year C corporation) was held equally by three individual shareholders: Jim, Sally, and LuEllen. On that date, LuEllen sells her interest to Jim and Sally. On March 14, 1999, Columbine Corporation files Form 2553. Jim and Sally indicate their consent by signing the form. Columbine cannot become an S corporation until 2000, because LuEllen did not indicate consent. Had all three shareholders consented by signing Form 2553, S status would have taken effect as of January 1, 1999. ▼

PLANNING CONSIDERATIONS

Making a Proper Election

- Because S corporation status must be *elected*, strict compliance with the requirements is demanded by both the IRS and the courts. Any failure to meet a condition in the law may lead to loss of the S election and raise the specter of double tax.
- Make sure all shareholders consent. If any doubt exists concerning the shareholder status of an individual, it would be wise to request that he or she sign a consent anyway.[19] Missing consents are fatal to the election; the same cannot be said for too many consents.
- Be sure that the election is timely and properly filed. Either deliver the election to an IRS office in person, or send it by certified or registered mail, or via a major overnight delivery service. The date used to determine timeliness is the postmark date, not the date the IRS receives the election.
- Be careful to ascertain when the timely election period begins to run for a new corporation. An election made too soon (before the corporation is in existence) is worse than one made too late. If serious doubts exist as to when the election period begins, filing more than one election might be a practical means of guaranteeing the desired result.

LOSS OF THE ELECTION

An S election can be lost if any of the following occurs.

- Shareholders owning a majority of shares (voting and nonvoting) voluntarily revoke the election.
- A new shareholder owning more than one-half of the stock affirmatively refuses to consent to the election.
- The corporation no longer qualifies as a small business corporation.
- The corporation does not meet the passive investment income limitation.

Each of these conditions is discussed in detail in this section.

---

[18] § 1362(b)(2)(B)(ii).

[19] See *William B. Wilson*, 34 TCM 463, T.C.Memo. 1975–92.

Voluntary Revocation. A voluntary revocation of the S election requires the consent of shareholders owning a majority of shares on the day that the revocation is to be made.[20] A revocation filed up to and including the fifteenth day of the third month of the tax year is effective for the entire tax year, unless a later date is specified. Similarly, unless an effective date is specified, revocation made after the first 2½ months of the current tax year is effective for the following tax year.

EXAMPLE 11

The shareholders of Petunia Corporation, a calendar year S corporation, voluntarily revoke the S election on January 5, 1999. They do not specify a future effective date in the revocation. Assuming the revocation is properly executed and timely filed, Petunia will be a C corporation for the entire 1999 tax year. If the revocation is not made until June 1999, Petunia will remain an S corporation in 1999 and become a C corporation at the beginning of 2000. ▼

A corporation can revoke its S status *prospectively* by specifying a future date when the revocation is to be effective. A revocation that designates a future effective date splits the corporation's tax year into a short S corporation year and a short C corporation year. The day on which the revocation occurs is treated as the first day of the C corporation year. The corporation allocates income or loss for the entire year on a pro rata basis, based on the number of days in each short year.

EXAMPLE 12

Assume the same facts as in the preceding example, except that Petunia designates July 1, 1999, as the revocation date. Accordingly, June 30, 1999, is the last day of the S corporation's tax year. The C corporation's tax year runs from July 1, 1999 to December 31, 1999. Any income or loss for the 12-month period is allocated equally between the two short years, because the two short years lasted an equal number of days. ▼

Rather than using pro rata allocation, the corporation can elect to compute actual income or loss attributable to the two short years. This election requires the consent of everyone who was a shareholder at any time during the S corporation's short year and everyone who owns stock on the first day of the C corporation's year.[21]

Loss of Small Business Corporation Status. If an S corporation fails to qualify as a small business corporation at any time after the election has become effective, its status as an S corporation ends. The termination occurs on the day that the corporation ceases to be a small business corporation.[22] Thus, if the corporation ever has more than 75 shareholders, a second class of stock, or a nonqualifying shareholder, or otherwise fails to meet the definition of a small business corporation, the S election is terminated immediately.

EXAMPLE 13

Peony Corporation has been a calendar year S corporation for three years. On August 13, 1999, one of its 75 shareholders sells *some* of her stock to an outsider. Peony now has 76 shareholders, and it ceases to be a small business corporation. Peony is an S corporation through August 12, 1999, and a C corporation from August 13 to December 31, 1999. ▼

Passive Investment Income Limitation. The Code provides a **passive investment income (PII)** limitation for S corporations that were previously C corporations or for S corporations that have merged with C corporations. If an S corporation has C corporation E & P and passive income in excess of 25 percent of its gross

---

[20] § 1362(d)(1).
[21] § 1362(e)(3).
[22] § 1362(d)(2)(B).

receipts for three consecutive taxable years, the S election is terminated as of the beginning of the fourth year.[23]

EXAMPLE 14   For 1997, 1998, and 1999, Chrysanthemum Corporation, a calendar year S corporation, derived passive income in excess of 25% of its gross receipts. If Chrysanthemum holds accumulated E & P from years in which it was a C corporation, its S election is terminated as of January 1, 2000. ▼

PII includes dividends, interest, rents, gains and losses from sales of securities, and royalties net of investment deductions. Rents are not considered PII if the corporation renders significant personal services to the occupant.

EXAMPLE 15   Violet Corporation owns and operates an apartment building. The corporation provides utilities for the building, maintains the lobby, and furnishes trash collection for tenants. These activities are not considered significant personal services, so any rent income earned by the corporation will be considered PII.

Alternatively, if Violet also furnishes maid services to its tenants (personal services beyond what normally would be expected from a landlord in an apartment building), the rent income would no longer be PII. ▼

Reelection after Termination.   After an S election has been terminated, the corporation must wait five years before reelecting S corporation status. The five-year waiting period is waived if:

- there is a more-than-50-percent change in ownership of the corporation after the first year for which the termination is applicable, or
- the event causing the termination was not reasonably within the control of the S corporation or its majority shareholders.

PLANNING CONSIDERATIONS

Preserving the S Election

Unexpected loss of S corporation status can be costly to a corporation and its shareholders. Given the complexity of the rules facing these entities, constant vigilance is necessary to preserve the S election.

- As a starting point, the corporation's management and shareholders should be made aware of the various transactions that can lead to the loss of an election.
- Watch for possible violation of the PII limitation. Avoid a consecutive third year with excess passive income when the corporation has accumulated E & P from C corporation years. In this connection, assets that produce passive income (e.g., stocks and bonds, certain rental assets) might be retained by the shareholders in their individual capacities and kept out of the corporation.
- Prevent violations of the small business corporation limitations. Since most such violations result from transfers of stock, the corporation and its shareholders should consider adopting a set of stock transfer restrictions. A carefully designed set of restrictions could prevent sale of stock to nonqualifying entities or violation of the

---

[23] § 1362(d)(3)(A)(ii).

75-shareholder rule. Similarly, stock could be repurchased by the corporation under a buy-sell agreement upon the death of a shareholder, thereby preventing nonqualifying trusts from becoming shareholders.[24]

OPERATIONAL RULES

4 LEARNING OBJECTIVE
Compute nonseparately stated income and allocate income, deductions, and credits to shareholders.

S corporations are treated much like partnerships for tax purposes. With a few exceptions,[25] S corporations generally make tax accounting and other elections at the corporate level. Each year, the S corporation determines nonseparately stated income or loss and separately stated income, deductions, and credits. These items are taxed only once, as they pass through to shareholders. All items are allocated to each shareholder based on average ownership of stock throughout the year.[26] The flow-through of each item of income, deduction, and credit from the corporation to the shareholder is illustrated in Figure 12–1.

COMPUTATION OF TAXABLE INCOME

Subchapter S taxable income or loss is determined in a manner similar to the tax rules that apply to partnerships, except that S corporations recognize gains (but not losses) on distributions of appreciated property to shareholders.[27] Other special provisions affecting only the computation of C corporation income, such as the dividends received deduction, do not extend to S corporations.[28] Finally, as with partnerships, certain deductions of individuals are not permitted, including alimony payments, personal moving expenses, certain dependent care expenses, the personal exemption, and the standard deduction.

In general, S corporation items are divided into (1) nonseparately stated income or loss and (2) separately stated income, losses, deductions, and credits that could uniquely affect the tax liability of a shareholder. In essence, nonseparate items are aggregated into an undifferentiated amount that constitutes Subchapter S taxable income or loss. An S corporation's separately stated items are identical to those separately stated by partnerships. These items retain their tax attributes on the shareholder's return. Separately stated items include:

- Tax-exempt income.
- Capital gains and losses.
- Section 1231 gains and losses.
- Charitable contributions.
- Passive gains, losses, and credits.
- Certain portfolio income.
- Section 179 expense deduction.
- Tax preferences and adjustments for the alternative minimum tax (see Chapter 13).
- Depletion deductions.
- Foreign income or loss.

---

[24] Most such agreements do not create a second class of stock. Rev.Rul. 85–161, 1985–2 C.B. 191; *Portage Plastics Co. v. U.S.*, 72–2 USTC ¶9567, 30 AFTR2d 72–5229, 470 F.2d 308 (CA–7, 1973).

[25] Certain elections are made at the shareholder level (e.g., the choice between a foreign tax deduction or credit).

[26] § 1366(a), (b), and (c).

[27] § 1363(d).

[28] § 703(a)(2).

▼ FIGURE 12–1
Flow-Through of Separate Items of Income and Loss to S Corporation Shareholders

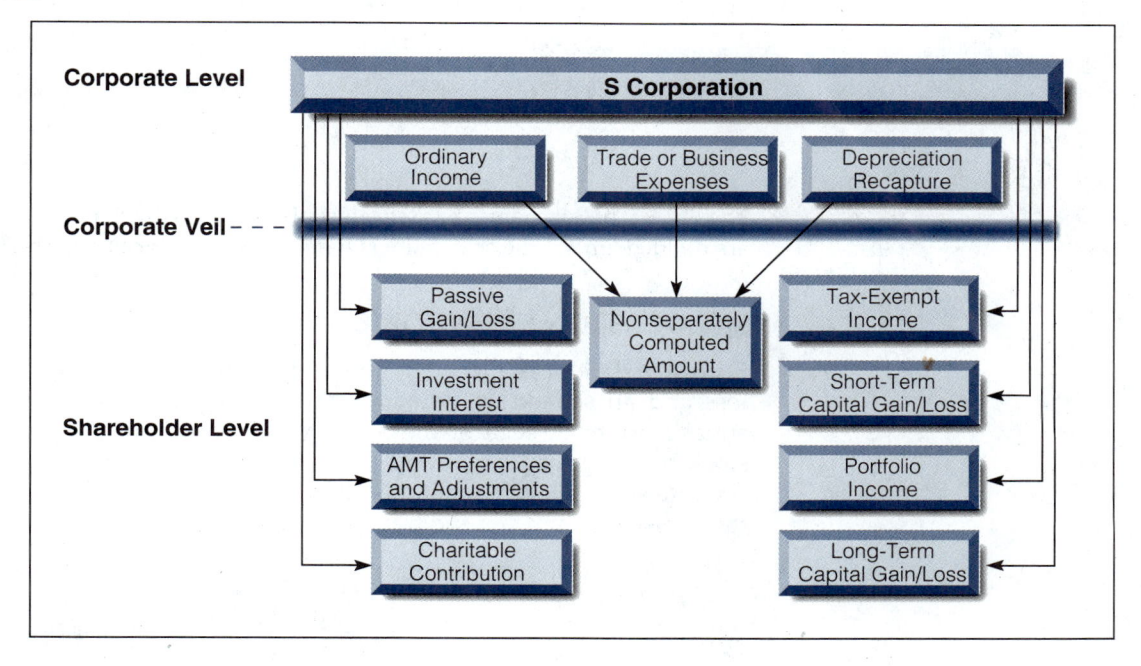

Corporate Level: S Corporation — Ordinary Income, Trade or Business Expenses, Depreciation Recapture

Corporate Veil

Shareholder Level: Passive Gain/Loss, Investment Interest, AMT Preferences and Adjustments, Charitable Contribution, Nonseparately Computed Amount, Tax-Exempt Income, Short-Term Capital Gain/Loss, Portfolio Income, Long-Term Capital Gain/Loss

- Wagering gains or losses.
- Recoveries of tax benefit items.
- Intangible drilling costs.
- Investment interest, income, and expenses.

EXAMPLE 16

The following is the income statement for Larkspur, Inc., an S corporation.

Sales		$ 40,000
Less cost of sales		(23,000)
Gross profit on sales		$ 17,000
Less: Interest expense	$1,200	
Charitable contributions	400	
Advertising expenses	1,500	
Other operating expenses	2,000	(5,100)
		$ 11,900
Add: Tax-exempt interest	$ 300	
Dividend income	200	
Long-term capital gain	500	1,000
Less: Short-term capital loss		(150)
Net income per books		$ 12,750

Subchapter S taxable income for Larkspur is calculated as follows, using net income for book purposes as a starting point.

Net income per books		$12,750
Separately stated items		
Deduct: Tax-exempt interest	$300	
Dividend income	200	
Long-term capital gain	500	(1,000)
Add: Charitable contributions	$400	
Short-term capital loss	150	550
Subchapter S taxable income		$12,300

The $12,300 of Subchapter S taxable income, as well as each of the separately stated items, are divided among the shareholders based upon their stock ownership. ▼

ALLOCATION OF INCOME AND LOSS

Each shareholder is allocated a pro rata portion of nonseparately stated income or loss and all separately stated items. The pro rata allocation method assigns an equal amount of each of the S items to each day of the year. If a shareholder's stock holding changes during the year, this allocation assigns the shareholder a pro rata share of each item for each day the stock is owned. On the date of transfer, the transferor (and not the transferee) is considered to own the stock.[29]

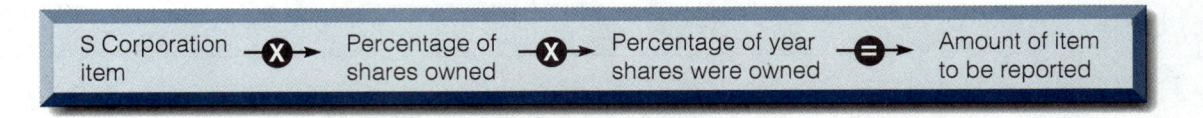

S Corporation item × Percentage of shares owned × Percentage of year shares were owned = Amount of item to be reported

The per-day allocation must be used, unless the shareholder disposes of his or her entire interest in the entity.[30] In case of a complete termination, a short year may result, as discussed below. If a shareholder dies during the year, his or her share of the pro rata items up to the date of death is reported on the final individual income tax return.

EXAMPLE 17

Assume in Example 16 that Pat, a shareholder, owned 10% of Larkspur's stock for 100 days and 12% for the remaining 265 days. Using the required per-day allocation method, Pat's share of the S corporation items is computed below.

	Schedule K Totals	Pat's Share 10%	Pat's Share 12%	Pat's Schedule K-1 Totals
Subchapter S taxable income	$12,300	$337	$1,072	$1,409
Tax-exempt interest	300	8	26	34
Dividend income	200	5	17	22
Long-term capital gain	500	14	44	58
Charitable contributions	400	11	35	46
Short-term capital loss	150	4	13	17

Pat's share of the Subchapter S taxable income is the total of $12,300 × [0.10 × (100/365)] plus $12,300 × [0.12 × (265/365)], or $1,409. Pat's Schedule K–1 totals flow through to his individual income tax return (Form 1040). ▼

---

[29] Reg. § 1.1377–1(a)(2)(ii).

[30] §§ 1366(a)(1) and 1377(a)(1).

EXAMPLE 18 If Pat in Example 17 dies after owning the stock 100 days, his share of the S corporation items is reported on his final individual income tax return (Form 1040). Thus, only the items in the column labeled 10% in Example 17 are reported on Pat's final tax return. S corporation items that occur after Pat's death most likely would flow through to the income tax return of Pat's estate (Form 1041). ▼

The Short-Year Election. If a shareholder's interest is completely terminated during the tax year (by disposition or death), all shareholders owning stock during the year and the corporation may elect to treat the S taxable year as two taxable years. The first year ends on the date of the termination. Under this election, an interim closing of the books is undertaken, and the shareholders report their shares of the S corporation items as they occurred during the short tax year.[31]

The short-year election provides an opportunity to shift income, losses, and credits between shareholders. The election is desirable in circumstances where more loss can be allocated to taxpayers with higher marginal rates.

EXAMPLE 19 Alicia, the owner of all of the shares of an S corporation, transfers her stock to Cindy halfway through the tax year. There is a $100,000 NOL for the entire tax year, but $30,000 of the loss occurs during the first half of the year. Without a short-year election, $50,000 of the loss would be allocated to Alicia and $50,000 would be allocated to Cindy. If the corporation makes the short-year election, Cindy is allocated $70,000 of the loss. The sales price of the stock probably would be increased to recognize the tax benefits being transferred from Alicia to Cindy. ▼

In the case of the death of a shareholder, a short-year election prevents the income and loss allocation to a deceased shareholder from being affected by post-death events.

EXAMPLE 20 Joey and Karl equally own Orchid, Inc., a calendar year S corporation. Joey dies on June 29 (not a leap year). Orchid has income of $250,000 for January 1 through June 29 and $750,000 for the remainder of the year. Without a short-year election, the income is allocated by assigning an equal portion of the annual income of $1 million to each day (or $2,739.73 per day) and allocating the daily portion between the shareholders. Joey is allocated 50% of the daily income for the 180 days from January 1 to June 29, or $246,575.70 [($2,739.73/2) × 180]. Joey's *estate* is allocated 50% of the income for the 185 days from June 30 to December 31, or $253,425.02 [($2,739.73/2) × 185].

If the short-year election is made, the income of $250,000 from January 1 to June 29 is divided equally between Joey and Karl, so that each is taxed on $125,000. The income of $750,000 from June 30 to December 31 is divided equally between Joey's estate and Karl, or $375,000 to each. ▼

PLANNING CONSIDERATIONS

Salary Structure

The amount of salary paid to a shareholder-employee of an S corporation can have varying tax consequences and should be considered carefully. Larger amounts might be advantageous if the maximum contribution allowed under the retirement plan has not been reached. Smaller amounts may be beneficial if the parties are trying to shift taxable

---

[31] § 1377(a)(2).

income to lower-bracket shareholders, reduce payroll taxes, curtail a reduction of Social Security benefits, or restrict losses that do not pass through because of the basis limitation.

A strategy of decreasing compensation and correspondingly increasing distributions to shareholder-employees often results in substantial savings in employment taxes. However, a shareholder of an S corporation cannot always perform substantial services and arrange to receive dividends rather than compensation so that the corporation may avoid paying employment taxes. The shareholder may be deemed an employee, and any dividends will be recharacterized as wages subject to FICA and FUTA taxes.[32] For planning purposes, some level of compensation should be paid to all shareholder-employees to avoid any recharacterization of distributions as deductible salaries—especially in personal service corporations.

Use of S corporations as an income-shifting device within a family (e.g., through a gift of stock from a high-marginal-rate taxpayer to a low-marginal-rate taxpayer) may be ineffective. The IRS can ignore such transfers unless the stock is purchased at fair market value.[33] Effectively, the IRS can require that reasonable compensation be paid to family members who render services or provide capital to the S corporation.

TAX TREATMENT OF DISTRIBUTIONS TO SHAREHOLDERS

5 LEARNING OBJECTIVE
Understand how distributions to S corporation shareholders are taxed.

S corporations do not generate earnings and profits (E & P) while the S election is in effect. Indeed, all profits are taxed in the year earned, as though they were distributed on a pro rata basis to the shareholders. Thus, distributions from S corporations do not constitute dividends in the traditional sense—there is no corporate E & P to distribute.

It is possible, however, for S corporations to have an accumulated E & P (AEP) account. This can occur when:

- the S corporation was previously a C corporation, or
- a C corporation with its own AEP merged into the S corporation.

Distributions from S corporations are measured as the cash received plus the fair market value of any other distributed property. The tax treatment of distributions differs, depending upon whether the S corporation has AEP.

S Corporation with No AEP. If the S corporation has no AEP, the distribution is a tax-free recovery of capital to the extent that it does not exceed the adjusted basis of the shareholder's stock. When the amount of the distribution exceeds the adjusted basis of the stock, the excess is treated as a gain from the sale or exchange of property (capital gain in most cases).

EXAMPLE 21

Hyacinth, Inc., a calendar year S corporation, has no AEP. During the year, Juan, an individual shareholder of the corporation, receives a cash dividend of $12,200 from Hyacinth. Juan's basis in his stock is $9,700. Juan recognizes a capital gain of $2,500, the excess of the distribution over the stock basis ($12,200 − $9,700). The remaining $9,700 is tax-free, but it reduces Juan's basis in his stock to zero. ▼

---

[32] Rev.Rul. 74–44, 1974–1 C.B. 287; *Spicer Accounting, Inc. v. U.S.*, 91–1 USTC ¶50,103, 66 AFTR2d 90–5806, 918 F.2d 90 (CA–9, 1990); *Radtke v. U.S.*, 90–1 USTC ¶50,113, 65 AFTR2d 90–1155, 895 F.2d 1196 (CA–7, 1990).

[33] § 1366(e) and Reg. § 1.1373–1(a).

S Corporation with AEP. For S corporations with AEP, a more complex set of rules applies. These rules blend the entity and conduit approaches to taxation, treating distributions of preelection (C corporation) and postelection (S corporation) earnings differently. Distributions of C corporation AEP are taxed as dividends, while distributions of previously taxed S corporation earnings are tax-free to the extent of the shareholder's adjusted basis in the stock.

The treatment of distributions is determined by their order. In particular, distributions are deemed to be first from previously taxed, undistributed earnings of the S corporation. Such distributions are tax-free and are determined by reference to a special account, the **accumulated adjustments account (AAA)**.[34] Next, AEP is distributed as taxable dividends. Any remaining distributions are tax-free to the extent of the shareholder's remaining stock basis,[35] with any excess being treated as capital gains.

EXAMPLE 22

Salvia, a calendar year S corporation, distributes $1,300 cash to its only shareholder, Otis, on December 31, 1999. Otis's basis in his stock is $1,400, his AAA is $500, and the corporation has AEP of $750 on December 31, 1999.

The first $500 of the distribution is a tax-free recovery of basis from the AAA. The next $750 is a taxable dividend distribution from AEP. Finally, the remaining $50 of cash is a tax-free recovery of basis. Immediately after the distribution, Salvia has no AAA or AEP. Otis's stock basis is $850.

	Corporate AAA	Corporate AEP	Otis's Stock Basis
Balance, 12/31/99	$ 500	$750	$1,400
Distribution ($1,300)	(500)	(750)	(550)*
Balance, 12/31/99	$ -0-	$ -0-	$ 850

*The reduction in basis includes the decrease in the AAA. It is the excess of the total distribution ($1,300) over the distribution of AEP ($750).

EXAMPLE 23

Assume the same facts as in the preceding example. During 2000, Salvia has no earnings and distributes $1,000 to Otis. Of the distribution, $850 is a tax-free recovery of basis, and $150 is taxed to Otis as a capital gain. ▼

With the consent of all of its shareholders, an S corporation can elect to have a distribution treated as if it were made from AEP rather than from the AAA. This mechanism is known as an *AAA bypass election*. This election may be desirable for distributions in years when S corporation shareholders have low marginal tax rates.

EXAMPLE 24

Rotor is a valid S corporation. It has $50 of AEP. An AAA bypass election for Rotor's next shareholder distribution would eliminate the need to track the AAA and would greatly simplify the accounting for future distributions. The cost for this simplification is the tax on $50 of dividend income. ▼

The Accumulated Adjustments Account. The AAA is the cumulative total of undistributed nonseparately and separately stated income and deduction items

---

[34]For S corporations in existence prior to 1983, an account similar to the AAA was used. This account, called *previously taxed income* (PTI), is distributed tax-free to shareholders after AAA has been distributed. See §§ 1368(c)(1) and (e)(1).

[35]§ 1368(c).

Concept Summary 12-1

Distributions from an S Corporation*

Where Earnings and Profits Exist	Where No Earnings and Profits Exist
1. Distributions are tax-free to the extent of the AAA.**	
2. Any PTI from pre-1983 tax years can be distributed tax-free.	
3. The remaining distribution constitutes ordinary dividend from AEP.†	
4. Any residual amount is applied as a tax-free reduction in basis of stock.	1. Distributions are nontaxable to the extent of adjusted basis in stock.
5. Excess is treated as gain from a sale or exchange of stock (capital gain in most cases).	2. Excess is treated as gain from a sale or exchange of stock (capital gain in most cases).

*A distribution of appreciated property by an electing corporation results in a gain at the corporate level that is allocated to and reported by the shareholders.
**Once stock basis reaches zero, any distribution from the AAA is treated as a gain from the sale or exchange of stock. Thus, basis is an upper limit on what a shareholder may receive tax-free.
†The AAA bypass election is available to pay out AEP before reducing the AAA [§ 1368(e)(3)].

---

for S corporation years beginning after 1982. As noted above, it provides a mechanism to ensure that earnings of an S corporation are taxed only once.

AAA is computed at the end of each tax year rather than at the time of a distribution. The account balance is determined by adding nonseparately computed income, positive separately stated items (except tax-exempt income), and depletion in excess of basis. Next, negative separately stated items and distributions are subtracted. If AAA becomes negative as a result of subtracting negative separately stated items, then the account is applied to distributions *prior* to subtracting the negative items. AAA is applied to the distributions made during the year on a pro rata basis (in a fashion similar to the application of current E & P, discussed in Chapter 9). The determination of AAA is summarized in Exhibit 12–1.

Although adjustments to AAA and stock basis adjustments are similar, there are some important differences between the two amounts. In particular,

- The AAA is not affected by tax-exempt income and related expenses.
- The AAA is not affected by Federal taxes attributable to a C corporation tax year.
- Unlike stock basis, the AAA can have a negative balance. All losses decrease the AAA balance, even those in excess of the shareholder's basis. However, distributions may not make the AAA negative or increase a negative balance in the account.
- Every shareholder has a proportionate interest in the AAA, regardless of his or her stock basis.[36] In fact, AAA is a corporate account, so there is no connection between the amount and any specific shareholder.[37] Thus, the benefits of AAA can be shifted from one shareholder to another. For example, when an S corporation shareholder sells stock to another party, any AAA balance on the purchase date can be distributed tax-free to the purchaser.

---

[36] § 1368(c).   [37] § 1368(e)(1)(A).

CHAPTER 12 S Corporations

▼ **EXHIBIT 12–1**
Adjustments to AAA

> *Increase by:*
> 1. Positive separately stated items other than tax-exempt income.
> 2. Nonseparately computed income.
> 3. Depletion in excess of basis in the property.
>
> *Decrease by:*
> 4. Negative separately stated items other than distributions (e.g., losses, deductions).
> 5. Distribution(s) from AAA (but not below zero).
>
> NOTE: When items 1 through 4 total to a negative number, subtract distributions (item 5) from AAA *before* negative separately stated items (item 4).

Schedule M–2. Schedule M–2 on page 4 of Form 1120S (reproduced below) contains a column labeled *Other adjustments account (OAA)*. This account includes items that affect basis but not the AAA, such as tax-exempt income and any related nondeductible expenses. Distributions are made from the OAA after AEP and the AAA are reduced to zero. Since the OAA represents adjustments to stock basis, distributions from this account are tax-free recoveries of capital.

▼ **EXAMPLE 25**

Poinsettia, an S corporation, records the following items.

AAA, beginning of the year	$ 8,500
Previously taxed income, beginning of the year	6,250
Ordinary income	25,000
Tax-exempt interest	4,000
Key employee life insurance proceeds received	5,000
Payroll penalty expense	2,000
Charitable contributions	3,000
Unreasonable compensation	5,000
Premiums on key employee life insurance	2,100
Distributions to shareholders	16,000

Poinsettia's Schedule M–2 appears as follows.

Schedule M-2 Analysis of Accumulated Adjustments Account, Other Adjustments Account, and Shareholders' Undistributed Taxable Income Previously Taxed (see page 21 of the instructions)

		(a) Accumulated adjustments account	(b) Other adjustments account	(c) Shareholders' undistributed taxable income previously taxed
1	Balance at beginning of tax year	8,500		6,250
2	Ordinary income from page 1, line 21	25,000		
3	Other additions		9,000**	
4	Loss from page 1, line 21	( )	( )	
5	Other reductions	(10,000*)	(2,100)	
6	Combine lines 1 through 5	23,500	6,900	
7	Distributions other than dividend distributions	16,000		
8	Balance at end of tax year. Subtract line 7 from line 6	7,500	6,900	6,250

*$2,000 (payroll penalty) + $3,000 (charitable contributions) + $5,000 (unreasonable compensation).
**$4,000 (tax-exempt interest) + $5,000 (life insurance proceeds).

▼

Effect of Terminating the S Election. Normally, distributions to shareholders from a C corporation are taxed as dividends to the extent of E & P. However, any distribution of *cash* by a C corporation to shareholders during a one-year period[38] following an S election termination receives special treatment. Such a distribution

---
[38] The period is *approximately* one year in length.

is treated as a tax-free recovery of stock basis to the extent that it does not exceed the AAA.[39] Since *only* cash distributions reduce the AAA during this *postelection termination period*, a corporation should not make property distributions during this time. Instead, the entity should sell property and distribute the proceeds to shareholders.

EXAMPLE 26

Quinn, the sole shareholder of Azalea, Inc., a calendar year S corporation, elects during 1999 to terminate the S election, effective January 1, 2000. As of the end of 1999, Azalea has an AAA of $1,300. Quinn can receive a nontaxable distribution of cash during a post-termination period of approximately one year to the extent of Azalea's AAA. Although a cash distribution of $1,300 during 2000 would be nontaxable to Quinn, it would reduce the adjusted basis of his stock. ▼

PLANNING CONSIDERATIONS

The Accumulated Adjustments Account

The AAA is needed to determine the tax treatment of distributions from S corporations with AEP *and* distributions made during the post-termination election period. Therefore, it is important for all S corporations (even those with no AEP) to maintain the AAA balance. Without an accurate AAA balance, distributions could needlessly be classified as taxable dividends. Alternatively, it will be costly to reconstruct the AAA after the S election terminates. Other observations about the AAA follow.

- Because tax-exempt income does not increase AAA, it may impose a tax cost on S corporations with AEP. In particular, distributions of tax-exempt income may hasten the use of any balance in the AAA, with no corresponding increase in the account. As a result, dividend distributions from AEP will be accelerated, resulting in more rapid recognition of tax liability.
- When AEP is present, a negative balance in the AAA may cause double taxation of S corporation income. With a negative AAA, a distribution of current income restores the negative AAA balance to zero, but is considered to be a distribution in excess of AAA and is taxable as a dividend to the extent of AEP.
- For distributions by an S corporation having AEP, any net negative adjustments (e.g., excess of losses and deductions over income) for the tax year are ignored. This increases shareholder exposure to AEP and taxable dividends.
- Distributions should be made when AAA is positive. If future years bring operating losses, AAA is reduced, and shareholder exposure to AEP and taxable dividends increases.

TAX TREATMENT OF PROPERTY DISTRIBUTIONS BY THE CORPORATION

An S corporation recognizes a gain on any distribution of appreciated property (other than in a reorganization) in the same manner as if the asset had been sold to the shareholder at its fair market value.[40] The corporate gain is passed through to the shareholders. There is an important reason for this rule. Without it, property might be distributed tax-free (other than for certain recapture items) and later sold

---

[39] §§ 1371(e) and 1377(b).

[40] § 311(b).

without income recognition to the shareholder because the shareholder's basis equals the asset's fair market value. The character of the gain—capital gain or ordinary income—depends upon the type of asset being distributed.

The S corporation does not recognize a loss for assets that are worth less than their basis. As with gain property, the shareholder's basis is equal to the asset's fair market value. Thus, the potential loss is postponed until the shareholder sells the stock of the S corporation. Since loss property receives a step-down in basis without any loss recognition by the S corporation, distributions of loss property should be avoided. See Concept Summary 12–2.

EXAMPLE 27

Yarrow, Inc., an S corporation for 10 years, distributes a tract of land held as an investment to its majority shareholder. The land was purchased for $22,000 many years ago and is currently worth $82,000. Yarrow recognizes a capital gain of $60,000, which increases the AAA by $60,000. Then the property dividend reduces AAA by $82,000 (the fair market value). The tax consequences are the same for appreciated property, whether it is distributed to the shareholders and they dispose of it, or the corporation sells the property and distributes the proceeds to the shareholders. ▼

EXAMPLE 28

Continue with the facts of Example 27. If the land had been purchased for $80,000 many years ago and was currently worth $30,000, the $50,000 realized loss would not be recognized at the corporate level, and the shareholder would take a $30,000 basis in the land. Since loss is not recognized on the distribution of property that has declined in value, the AAA is not reduced by the unrecognized loss. For the loss on the property to be recognized, the S corporation must sell the property. ▼

EXAMPLE 29

Assume the same facts as in Examples 27 and 28, except that Yarrow is a C corporation or a partnership. Assume the partner's basis in the partnership is $25,000 and ignore any corporate-level taxes. Compare the results.

	Appreciated Property		
	S Corporation	C Corporation	Partnership
Entity gain/loss	$60,000	$60,000	$ –0–
Owner's gain/loss/dividend	60,000	82,000*	–0–
Owner's basis	82,000	82,000	22,000
	Property That Has Declined in Value		
	S Corporation	C Corporation	Partnership
Entity gain/loss	$ –0–	$ –0–	$ –0–
Owner's gain/loss/dividend	–0–	30,000*	–0–
Owner's basis	30,000	30,000	25,000**

*Assume sufficient E & P.
**Basis in property cannot exceed basis in partnership interest. ▼

SHAREHOLDER'S BASIS

LEARNING OBJECTIVE 6
Calculate a shareholder's basis in S corporation stock.

The calculation of the initial tax basis of stock in an S corporation is similar to that for the basis of stock in a C corporation and depends upon the manner in which the shares are acquired (e.g., gift, inheritance, purchase, and exchange under § 351). Once the initial tax basis is determined, various transactions during the life of the corporation affect the shareholder's basis in the stock. Although each shareholder is required to compute his or her own basis in the S shares, neither Form 1120S nor Schedule K–1 provides a place for deriving this amount.

Concept Summary 12–2

Distribution of Property

	Appreciated Property	**Depreciated Property**
S corporation	Realized gain is recognized by the corporation, which passes it through to the shareholders. Such gain increases a shareholder's stock basis, generating a basis in the property equal to FMV. On the distribution, the shareholder's stock basis is reduced by the FMV of the property (but not below zero).	Realized loss is not recognized. The shareholder assumes a FMV basis in the property. Loss is postponed indefinitely.
C corporation	Realized gain is recognized under § 311(b) and increases E & P (net of tax). The shareholder assumes a FMV basis and has a FMV taxable dividend.	Realized loss is not recognized.
Partnership	No gain to the partnership or partner. Basis to the partner is limited to the partner's basis in the partnership.	Realized loss is not recognized.

A shareholder's basis is increased by stock purchases and capital contributions. Operations during the year cause the following additional upward adjustments to basis.[41]

- Nonseparately computed income.
- Separately stated income items (e.g., nontaxable income).
- Depletion in excess of basis in the property.

Basis then is reduced by distributions not reported as income by the shareholder (e.g., an AAA or PTI distribution). Next, the following items reduce basis (but not below zero).

- Nondeductible expenses of the corporation (e.g., fines, penalties, illegal kickbacks).
- Nonseparately computed loss.
- Separately stated loss and deduction items.

As under the partnership rules, basis first is increased by income items; then it is decreased by distributions and finally by losses. In most cases, this rule is advantageous.

EXAMPLE 30

In its first year of operations, Iris, Inc., a calendar year S corporation, earns income of $2,000. On February 2 in its second year of operations, Iris distributes $2,000 to Marty, its sole shareholder. During the remainder of the second year, the corporation incurs a $2,000 loss.

Under the S corporation ordering rules, the $2,000 distribution is tax-free AAA to Marty. The distribution is accounted for before the loss. The $2,000 loss is *not* passed through, though, because stock basis cannot be reduced below zero. ▼

A shareholder's basis in S corporation stock can never be reduced below zero. Once stock basis is zero, any additional basis reductions (losses or deductions, but

---
[41] § 1367(a).

not distributions) decrease (but not below zero) the shareholder's basis in loans made to the S corporation.[42] Any excess of losses or deductions over both stock and loan bases is not deductible in the current year. Losses can be deducted only to the extent that they offset stock or loan basis. Thus, until additional basis is created due to capital contributions or flow-through income, the loss deductions are suspended.

When there is a capital contribution or an item of flow-through income, then basis is first restored to the shareholder loans, up to the original principal amount.[43] Then, basis in the stock is restored.

EXAMPLE 31

Stacey, a sole shareholder, has a $7,000 stock basis and a $2,000 basis in a loan that she made to a calendar year S corporation at the beginning of the year. Subchapter S net income for the year is $8,200. The corporation also received $2,000 of tax-exempt interest income. Cash of $17,300 is distributed to Stacey on November 15. As a result, Stacey's basis in her stock is zero, and her loan basis is still $2,000 at the end of the year, because only losses and deductions (and not distributions) reduce the debt basis. Stacey recognizes a $100 capital gain ($17,300 − $17,200).

	Corporate AAA	Stacey's Stock Basis	Stacey's Loan Basis
Beginning balance	$ −0−	$ 7,000	$2,000
S net income	8,200	8,200	−0−
Tax-exempt income	−0−	2,000	−0−
Subtotal	$ 8,200	$ 17,200	$2,000
Distribution ($17,300)	(8,200)	(17,200)	−0−
Ending balance	$ −0−	$ −0−	$2,000

The basis rules for an S corporation are similar to the rules for determining a partner's interest basis in a partnership. However, a partner's basis in the partnership interest includes the partner's direct investment plus a *ratable share* of any partnership liabilities.[44] If a partnership borrows from a partner, the partner receives a basis increase as if the partnership had borrowed from an unrelated third party.[45] In contrast, except for loans from the shareholder to the corporation, corporate borrowing has no effect on S corporation shareholder basis. Loans from a shareholder to the S corporation have a tax basis only for the shareholder making the loan.

Except in the Eleventh Circuit, the fact that a shareholder has guaranteed a loan made to the corporation by a third party has no effect upon the shareholder's loan basis, unless payments actually have been made as a result of that guarantee.[46] If the corporation defaults on indebtedness and the shareholder makes a payment under the guarantee, the shareholder's debt basis is increased by the amount of the payment.[47]

If a loan's basis has been reduced and is not restored, income is recognized when the loan is repaid. If the corporation issued a note as evidence of the debt, repayment constitutes an amount received in exchange for a capital asset, and the amount that exceeds the shareholder's basis is entitled to capital gain treatment.[48]

---

[42] §§ 1366(d)(1)(A) and 1368(d)(1).
[43] § 1367(b)(2).
[44] § 752(a).
[45] Reg. § 1.752–1(e).
[46] See, for example, *Estate of Leavitt*, 90 T.C. 206 (1988), aff'd. 89–1 USTC ¶9332, 63 AFTR2d 89–1437, 875 F.2d 420 (CA–4, 1989); *Selfe v. U.S.*, 86–1 USTC ¶9115, 57 AFTR2d 86–464, 778 F.2d 769 (CA–11, 1985); *James K. Calcutt*, 91 T.C. 14 (1988).
[47] Rev.Rul. 70–50, 1970–1 C.B. 178.
[48] *Joe M. Smith*, 48 T.C. 872 (1967), aff'd. and rev'd. in 70–1 USTC ¶9327, 25 AFTR2d 70–936, 424 F.2d 219 (CA–9, 1970), and Rev.Rul. 64–162, 1964–1 C.B. 304.

However, if the loan is made on open account, the repayment constitutes ordinary income to the extent that it exceeds the shareholder's basis in the loan. Each repayment is prorated between the gain portion and the repayment of the debt.[49] Thus, a note should be given to ensure capital gain treatment for the income that results from a loan's repayment.

EXAMPLE 32

Phil is the sole shareholder of Falcon, a valid S corporation. At the beginning of 1999, Phil's basis in his stock was $10,000. During 1999, he made a loan to the corporation of $4,000 cash, using a written debt instrument and market interest rates. Falcon has no other outstanding debt.

Falcon generated a $13,000 taxable loss for 1999. Thus, at the beginning of the tax year 2000, Phil's stock basis was zero, and the basis in his loan to Falcon was $1,000.

Falcon repaid the loan in full on March 1, 2000. Phil recognized a $3,000 capital gain on the repayment. ▼

PLANNING CONSIDERATIONS

Working with Suspended Losses

Distributions made to shareholders with suspended losses usually create capital gain income, because there is no stock or debt basis to offset. Usually, distributions should be deferred until the shareholder creates stock basis in some form. In this way, no gross income is recognized until the suspended losses are fully used.

EXAMPLE 33

Continue with the facts of Example 32. Phil purchases $5,000 of additional stock in Falcon. Phil gets an immediate deduction for his investment, due to his $13,000 in suspended losses. Alternatively, if Falcon shows a $5,000 profit for the year, Phil pays no tax on the flow-through income, due to his $13,000 in suspended losses.

However, if Falcon distributes $5,000 to Phil in 2000 without earning any profit for the year, and prior to any capital contribution by him, Phil recognizes a $5,000 capital gain, because his stock basis is zero. ▼

TREATMENT OF LOSSES

LEARNING OBJECTIVE 7
Explain how losses in an S corporation are treated.

Net Operating Loss. One major advantage of an S election is the ability to pass through any net operating loss (NOL) of the corporation directly to the shareholders. A shareholder can deduct an NOL for the year in which the S corporation's tax year ends. The corporation is not entitled to any deduction for the NOL. A shareholder's basis in the stock is reduced to the extent of any pass-through of the NOL, and the shareholder's AAA is reduced by the same deductible amount.[50]

Deductions for an S corporation's NOL pass-through cannot exceed a shareholder's adjusted basis in the stock *plus* the basis of any loans made by the shareholder to the corporation. If a taxpayer is unable to prove the tax basis, the NOL pass-through can be denied.[51] As noted previously, once a shareholder's adjusted stock basis has been eliminated by an NOL, any excess NOL is used to reduce the shareholder's basis for any loans made to the corporation (but never below zero).

---

[49] Rev.Rul. 68–537, 1968–2 C.B. 372.
[50] §§ 1368(a)(1)(A) and (e)(1)(A).
[51] See *Donald J. Sauvigne*, 30 TCM 123, T.C.Memo. 1971–30.

The basis for loans is established by the actual advances made to the corporation, and not by indirect loans.[52] If the shareholder's basis is insufficient to allow a full flow-through and there is more than one type of loss (e.g., in the same year the taxpayer incurs both a passive loss and a net capital loss), the flow-through amounts are determined on a pro rata basis.

EXAMPLE 34

Ralph is a 50% owner of an S corporation for the entire year. His stock basis is $10,000, and his shares of the various corporate losses are as follows.

Ordinary loss from operations	$8,000
Capital loss	5,000
Section 1231 loss	3,000
Passive loss	2,000

The total $10,000 allocable flow-through loss produces the following deductions for losses.

$$\text{Ordinary loss} = \frac{\$8,000}{\$18,000} \times \$10,000 = \$\ 4,444.44$$

$$\text{Capital loss} = \frac{\$5,000}{\$18,000} \times \$10,000 = \$\ 2,777.78$$

$$\S\ 1231 \text{ loss} = \frac{\$3,000}{\$18,000} \times \$10,000 = \$\ 1,666.67$$

$$\text{Passive loss} = \frac{\$2,000}{\$18,000} \times \$10,000 = \$\ 1,111.11$$

Total allocated loss $10,000.00

When a shareholder has acquired stock at different times and for varying amounts, losses are applied against stock basis using a separate-share method.[53] Under the separate-share method, the basis of each share of stock is increased or decreased by an amount equal to the owner's pro rata portion of an income or loss item, determined on a per-share, per-day basis. Thus, an S corporation maintains a separate basis account for each block of stock.

Distributions made by an S corporation during a tax year are taken into account *before* applying loss limitations for the year. This is the same *losses last* ordering rule used for partnerships (refer to Chapter 11).

EXAMPLE 35

Dahlia, a calendar year S corporation is partly owned by Doris, who has a beginning stock basis of $10,000. During the year, Doris's share of a long-term capital gain is $2,000, and her share of an ordinary loss is $9,000. If Doris receives a $5,000 distribution, her deductible loss is only $7,000.

Beginning stock basis	$10,000
Add: LTCG	2,000
Subtotal	$12,000
Less: Distribution	(5,000)
Basis for loss limitation	$ 7,000
Deductible loss	($ 7,000)
Unused loss	($ 2,000)

---

[52] *Ruth M. Prashker*, 59 T.C. 172 (1972); *Frederick G. Brown v. U.S.*, 83-1 USTC ¶9364, 52 AFTR2d 82-5080, 706 F.2d 755 (CA-6, 1983).

[53] Reg. §§ 1.1367-1(b)(2) and (c)(3).

A shareholder's share of an NOL may be greater than both stock basis and loan basis. A shareholder is entitled to carry forward a loss to the extent that the loss for the year exceeds basis. Any loss carried forward may be deducted *only* by the *same* shareholder if and when the basis in the stock of or loans to the corporation is restored.[54]

EXAMPLE 36

Ginny owns ten percent of the stock of Pilot, a calendar-year S corporation. Her basis in the shares is $10,000 at the beginning of 1999. The indicated events are accounted for under the S rules as follows.

Tax Year	Event	Tax Consequences
1999	Ginny's share of Pilot's operating loss is $15,000.	Ginny deducts $10,000. Her stock basis is reduced to zero. She holds a $5,000 suspended loss.
2000	Ginny's share of Pilot's operating loss is $4,000.	No deduction for the loss, as Ginny has no stock basis to offset. Her suspended loss is now $9,000.
2001	Ginny's share of Pilot's operating loss is $7,000. She purchases an additional $10,000 stock from Pilot.	The purchase creates $10,000 stock basis. Ginny deducts $10,000—the current $7,000 loss and $3,000 of the suspended loss. Stock basis again is zero, and the new suspended loss is $6,000.
2002	Ginny sells all of her Pilot shares to Christina on January 1.	The $6,000 suspended loss disappears—it cannot be transferred to Christina.

Any suspended loss remaining at the end of an approximately one-year post-termination transition period is lost forever. Thus, if a shareholder has a suspended loss, he or she should increase the stock or loan basis and flow through the loss before disposing of the stock.

Net operating losses from C corporation years cannot be utilized at the corporate level (except with respect to built-in gain, discussed later in this chapter), nor can they be passed through to the shareholders. Further, the carryforward period continues to run during S status.[55] Consequently, the S election may not be appropriate for a corporation with NOL carryforwards. When a corporation is expecting losses in the future, an S election should be made *before* the loss years.

Passive Losses and Credits. Section 469 provides that net passive losses and credits are not deductible when incurred and must be carried over to a year when there is passive income. Thus, one must be aware of three major classes of income, losses, and credits—active, portfolio, and passive. S corporations are not directly subject to the limits of § 469, but corporate rental activities are inherently passive, and other activities of an S corporation may be passive unless the shareholder(s) materially participate(s) in operating the business. An S corporation may engage in more than one such activity.

If the corporate activity is rental or the shareholders do not materially participate, any passive losses or credits flow through. The shareholders are able to apply the losses or credits only against their income from other passive activities. A shareholder's stock basis is reduced by passive losses that flow through to the shareholder, even though the shareholder may not be entitled to a current deduction

---

[54]§ 1366(d).

[55]§ 1377(b).

due to the passive loss limitations. In general, elections involving the aggregation of amounts are made at the entity level, but they affect individual shareholders. The existence of material participation is determined at the shareholder level. There are seven tests for material participation, including a need to participate in the activity for more than 500 hours during the taxable year (refer to Chapter 5).[56]

EXAMPLE 37

Heather is a 50% owner of an S corporation engaged in a passive activity. A nonparticipating shareholder, she receives a salary of $6,000 for services as a result of the passive activity. This deduction creates a $6,000 passive loss at the corporate level. Heather has $6,000 of earned income as a result of the salary. The $6,000 salary creates a $6,000 deduction/passive loss, which flows through to the shareholders. Heather's $3,000 share of the loss may not be deducted against the $6,000 earned income. ▼

PLANNING CONSIDERATIONS

Loss Considerations

A loss in excess of tax basis may be carried forward and deducted only by the same shareholder in succeeding years. Thus, before disposing of the stock, a shareholder should increase stock/loan basis to flow through the loss. The next shareholder cannot acquire the carryover loss.

The NOL provisions create a need for sound tax planning during the last election year and the post-termination transition period. If it appears that the S corporation is going to sustain an NOL or use up any loss carryover, each shareholder's basis should be analyzed to determine if it can absorb the owner's share of the loss. If basis is insufficient to absorb the loss, further investments should be considered before the end of the post-termination transition year. Such investments can be accomplished through additional stock purchases from the corporation, or from other shareholders, to increase basis.

EXAMPLE 38

A calendar year C corporation has an NOL of $20,000 in 1998. The corporation makes a valid S election in 1999 and has another $20,000 NOL in that year. At all times during 1999, the stock of the corporation was owned by the same 10 shareholders, each of whom owned 10% of the stock. Tim, one of the shareholders, has an adjusted basis in his stock of $1,800 at the beginning of 1999. None of the 1998 NOL may be carried forward into the S year. Although Tim's share of the 1999 NOL is $2,000, his deduction for the loss is limited to $1,800 in 1999 with a $200 carryover to 2000. ▼

At-Risk Rules. The at-risk rules generally apply to S corporation shareholders. Essentially, an amount at risk is determined separately for each shareholder. The amount of the corporate losses that are passed through and deductible by the shareholders is not affected by the amount the corporation has at risk. A shareholder usually is considered at risk with respect to an activity to the extent of cash and the adjusted basis of other property contributed to the electing corporation, any amount borrowed for use in the activity for which the taxpayer has personal liability for payment from personal assets, and the net fair market value of personal assets that secure nonrecourse borrowing.[57] Any losses that are suspended under the at-risk rules are carried forward and are available during the post-termination

---

[56] Reg. § 1.469–5T(a).
[57] The at-risk rules and their significance for income tax purposes are discussed in Chapter 5.

CONCEPT SUMMARY 12–3

Treatment of S Corporation Losses

Step 1. Allocate total loss to the shareholder on a daily basis, based upon stock ownership.
Step 2. If the shareholder's loss exceeds his or her stock basis, apply any excess to the adjusted basis of indebtedness to the shareholder. Distributions do not reduce stock or debt basis.
Step 3. Where a flow-through loss exceeds the stock and debt basis, any excess is suspended and carried over to succeeding tax years.
Step 4. In succeeding tax years, any net increase in basis restores the debt basis first, up to its original amount.
Step 5. Once debt basis is restored, any remaining net increase restores stock basis.
Step 6. Any suspended loss from a previous year now reduces stock basis first and debt basis second.
Step 7. If the S election terminates, any suspended loss carryover may be deducted during the post-termination transition period to the extent of the stock basis at the end of this period. Any loss remaining at the end of the transition period is lost forever.

transition period. The S stock basis limitations and at-risk limitations are applied before the passive activity limitations.[58]

EXAMPLE 39 Shareholder Carl has a basis of $35,000 in his S corporation stock. He takes a $15,000 nonrecourse loan from a local bank and lends the proceeds to the S corporation. Carl now has a stock basis of $35,000 and a debt basis of $15,000. However, due to the at-risk limitation, he can deduct only $35,000 of losses from the S corporation. ▼

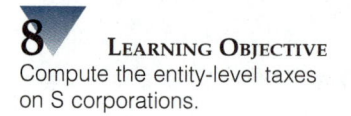

TAX ON PRE-ELECTION BUILT-IN GAIN

LEARNING OBJECTIVE 8
Compute the entity-level taxes on S corporations.

Without the **built-in gains tax**, it would be possible to avoid the corporate double tax on disposition of appreciated property by electing S corporation status.

EXAMPLE 40 Zinnia, Inc., a C corporation, owns a single asset with a basis of $100,000 and a fair market value of $500,000. If Zinnia sells this asset and distributes the cash to shareholders, there are two levels of tax, one at the corporate level and one at the shareholder level. Alternatively, if Zinnia distributes the asset to shareholders as a dividend, a double tax still results. In an attempt to avoid the double tax, Zinnia elects S corporation status. It then sells the asset and distributes the proceeds to shareholders. Without the § 1374 tax, the gain would be taxed only once, at the shareholder level. The distribution of sales proceeds would be a tax-free reduction of the AAA. ▼

The built-in gains tax of § 1374 generally applies to C corporations converting to S status after 1986. It is a *corporate-level* tax on any built-in gain recognized when the S corporation disposes of an asset in a taxable disposition within 10 calendar years after the date on which the S election took effect. The steps in computing the tax are summarized in Concept Summary 12–4.

General Rules. The base for the § 1374 tax includes any unrealized gain (appreciation) on assets (e.g., real estate, cash basis receivables, and goodwill) held by a corporation on the day it elects S status. The highest corporate tax rate (currently 35 percent) is applied to the unrealized gain when it is recognized by the corporation

---
[58] Reg. § 1.469–2T(d)(6).

Concept Summary 12–4

Calculation of the Built-in Gains Tax Liability

Step 1. Select the smaller of built-in gain or taxable income.*
Step 2. Deduct unexpired NOLs and capital losses from C corporation tax years.
Step 3. Multiply the tax base obtained in step 2 by the top corporate tax rate.
Step 4. Deduct any business credit carryforwards and AMT credit carryforwards arising in a C corporation tax year from the amount obtained in step 3.
Step 5. The corporation pays any tax resulting in step 4.

*Any net recognized built-in gain in excess of taxable income is carried forward to the next year within the 10-year recognition period.

(e.g., when the asset is sold). Any gain from the sale (net of the § 1374 tax)[59] also passes through as a taxable gain to shareholders.

EXAMPLE 41 Assume the same facts as in the preceding example. Section 1374 imposes a corporate-level tax that must be paid by Zinnia after it has elected S status. Upon sale of the asset, the corporation owes a tax of $140,000 (0.35 × $400,000). In addition, the shareholders report a $260,000 taxable gain ($400,000 − $140,000). Hence, the built-in gains tax effectively imposes a double tax on Zinnia and its shareholders. ▼

The maximum amount of gain that is recognized over the 10-year period is limited to the *aggregate net* built-in gain of the corporation at the time it converted to S status. Thus, at the time of the S election, unrealized gains of the corporation are reduced by unrealized losses. The net amount of gains and losses sets an upper limit on the tax base for the built-in gains tax. Any appreciation after the conversion to S status is subject to the regular S corporation pass-through rules.

EXAMPLE 42 Vinca is a former C corporation whose first S corporation year began on January 1, 1999. At that time, Vinca had two assets: X, with a value of $1,000 and a basis of $400, and Y, with a value of $400 and a basis of $600. The net unrealized built-in gain as of January 1, 1999, is $400. If asset X is sold for $1,200 during 1999, and asset Y is retained, the recognized built-in gain is limited to $400. The additional $200 of appreciation after electing S status is not part of the built-in gain. ▼

Loss assets on the date of conversion reduce the maximum built-in gain and any potential tax under § 1374.[60] In addition, built-in losses and built-in gains are netted each year to determine the annual § 1374 tax base. Thus, an incentive exists to contribute loss assets to a corporation before electing S status. However, the IRS indicates that contributions of loss property within two years before the earlier of the date of conversion or the date of filing an S election are presumed to have a tax avoidance motive and will not reduce the corporation's net unrealized built-in gain.

EXAMPLE 43 Connor owns all the stock of an S corporation, which in turn owns two assets on the S conversion date: asset 1 (basis of $5,000 and fair market value of $2,500) and asset 2 (basis of $1,000 and fair market value of $5,000). The S corporation has a potential net realized built-in gain of $1,500 (i.e., the built-in gain of $4,000 in asset 2 reduced by the built-in loss

---

[59] § 1366(f)(2).   [60] §§ 1374(c)(2) and (d)(1).

of $2,500 in asset 1). However, if Connor contributed the loss asset to the corporation within two years before the S election, built-in gain potential becomes $4,000 (the loss asset cannot be used to reduce built-in gain). ▼

The amount of built-in gain recognized in any year is limited to an *as if* taxable income for the year, computed as if the corporation were a C corporation. Any built-in gain that escapes taxation due to the taxable income limitation is carried forward and recognized in future tax years. Thus, a corporation can defer § 1374 tax liability whenever it has a low or negative taxable income.

EXAMPLE 44
Assume the same facts as in Example 42, except that if Vinca were a C corporation, its 1999 taxable income would be $300. The amount of built-in gain subject to tax in 1999 is $300. The excess built-in gain of $100 is carried forward and taxed in 2000 (assuming adequate C corporation taxable income). There is no statutory limit on the carryforward period, but the gain would effectively expire at the end of the 10-year recognition period applicable to all built-in gains.[61] ▼

Gains on sales or distributions of all assets by an S corporation are presumed to be built-in gains unless the taxpayer can establish that the appreciation accrued after the conversion to S status. Thus, it may be advisable to obtain an independent appraisal when converting a C corporation to an S corporation. Certainly, a memorandum should be prepared listing the fair market values of all assets, along with the methods used to arrive at the values.

Normally, tax attributes of a C corporation do not carry over to a converted S corporation. For purposes of the tax on built-in gain, however, certain carryovers are allowed. In particular, an S corporation can offset built-in gains with unexpired NOLs or capital losses from C corporation years.

EXAMPLE 45
Dogwood Corporation elects S status, effective for calendar year 1999. Dogwood has a $10,000 NOL carryover when it elects S status. As of January 1, 1999, one of Dogwood's capital assets has a basis of $50,000 and a fair market value of $110,000. Early in 2000, the asset is sold for $110,000. Dogwood recognizes a $60,000 built-in gain when the asset is sold. Dogwood's NOL reduces its built-in gain from $60,000 to $50,000. Thus, only $50,000 is subject to the built-in gains tax. ▼

EXAMPLE 46
An S corporation has a built-in gain of $100,000 and taxable income of $90,000. The built-in gains tax liability is calculated as follows.

Lesser of taxable income or built-in gain	$ 90,000
Less: NOL carryforward from C year	(12,000)
Capital loss carryforward from C year	(8,000)
Tax base	$ 70,000
Highest corporate tax rate	× 0.35
Tentative tax	$ 24,500
Less: Business credit carryforward from C year	(4,000)
Built-in gains tax liability	$ 20,500

The $10,000 realized (but not taxed) built-in gain in excess of taxable income may be carried forward to the next year, as long as the next year is within the 10-year recognition period. ▼

---

[61] § 1374(d)(7); Notice 90–27, 1990–1 C.B. 336.

PLANNING CONSIDERATIONS

Managing the Built-in Gains Tax

Although the two-year loss property contribution limitation introduces some potential problems, it still is possible for a corporation to minimize built-in gains and maximize built-in losses prior to the S election. A cash basis S corporation can accomplish this by reducing receivables, accelerating payables, and accruing compensation costs.

To further reduce or defer the tax, the corporation may take advantage of the taxable income limitation by shifting income and deductions to minimize taxable income in years when built-in gain is recognized. Although the postponed built-in gain is carried forward to future years, the time value of money makes the postponement beneficial. For example, paying compensation to shareholder-employees in place of a dividend distribution creates a deduction that reduces taxable income and postpones the built-in gains tax.

EXAMPLE 47

Tulip, Inc., an S corporation, has built-in gain of $110,000 and taxable income of $120,000 before payment of salaries to its shareholders. If Tulip pays at least $120,000 in salaries to the shareholders (rather than making a distribution), taxable income drops to zero, and the built-in gains tax is postponed. Thus, Tulip needs to keep the salaries as high as possible to postpone the built-in gains tax in future years and reap a benefit from the time value of money. Of course, paying the salaries may increase the payroll tax burden if the salaries are initially below FICA and FUTA limits. ▼

Giving built-in gain property to a charitable organization does not trigger the built-in gains tax. Built-in *loss* property may be sold in the same year that built-in gain property is sold to reduce or eliminate the built-in gains tax. Generally, the taxpayer should sell built-in loss property in a year when an equivalent amount of built-in gain property is sold. Otherwise, the built-in loss could be wasted.

LIFO Recapture Tax. When a corporation uses the FIFO method for its last year before making the S election, any built-in gain is recognized and taxed as the inventory is sold. A LIFO-basis corporation does not recognize this gain unless the corporation invades the LIFO layer during the 10-year recognition period. To preclude deferral of gain recognition under LIFO, any LIFO recapture amount at the time of the S election is subject to a corporate-level tax.

The taxable LIFO recapture amount equals the excess of the inventory's value under FIFO over the LIFO value. No negative adjustment is allowed if the LIFO value is higher than the FIFO value. The resulting tax is payable in four equal installments, with the first payment due on or before the due date for the corporate return for the last C corporation year (without regard to any extensions). The remaining three installments must be paid on or before the due dates of the succeeding corporate returns. No interest is due if payments are made by the due dates, and no estimated taxes are due on the four tax installments. The basis of the LIFO inventory is adjusted to account for this LIFO recapture amount, but the AAA is not decreased by payment of the tax.

EXAMPLE 48

Daffodil Corporation converts from a C corporation to an S corporation at the beginning of 1999. Daffodil used the LIFO inventory method in 1998 and had an ending LIFO inventory of $110,000 (FIFO value of $190,000). Daffodil must add $80,000 of LIFO recapture amount to its 1998 taxable income, resulting in an increased tax liability of $28,000 ($80,000 × 35%). Daffodil must pay one-fourth of the tax (or $7,000) with its 1998 corporate tax return. The three succeeding installments of $7,000 each are paid with Daffodil's next three tax returns. ▼

PASSIVE INVESTMENT INCOME PENALTY TAX

A tax is imposed on the excess passive income of S corporations that possess AEP from C corporation years. The tax rate is the highest corporate rate for the year. The rate is applied to excess net passive income (ENPI), which is determined using the following formula.

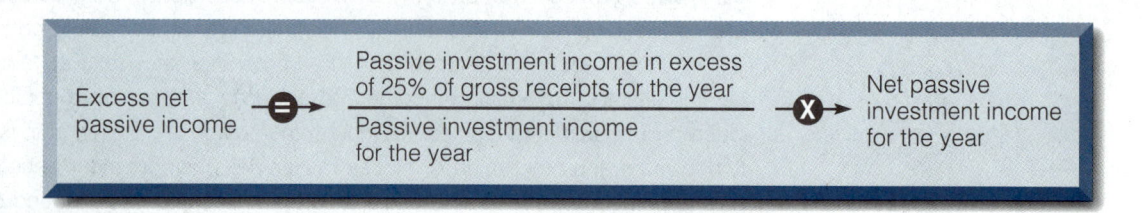

$$\text{Excess net passive income} = \frac{\text{Passive investment income in excess of 25\% of gross receipts for the year}}{\text{Passive investment income for the year}} \times \text{Net passive investment income for the year}$$

Passive investment income (PII) includes gross receipts derived from royalties, rents, dividends, interest, annuities, and sales and exchanges of stocks and securities.[62] Only the net gain from the disposition of capital assets (other than stocks and securities) is taken into account in computing gross receipts. Net passive income is passive income reduced by any deductions directly connected with the production of that income. Any passive income tax reduces the amount the shareholders must take into income.

The excess net passive income cannot exceed the corporate taxable income for the year before considering any NOL deduction or the special deductions allowed by §§ 241–250 (except the organizational expense deduction of § 248).[63]

EXAMPLE 49

At the end of 1999, Lilac Corporation, an electing S corporation, has gross receipts totaling $264,000 (of which $110,000 is PII). Expenditures directly connected to the production of the PII total $30,000. Therefore, Lilac has net PII of $80,000 ($110,000 − $30,000), and its PII for tax year 1999 exceeds 25% of its gross receipts by $44,000 ($110,000 PII − $66,000). Excess net passive income (ENPI) is $32,000, calculated as follows.

$$\text{ENPI} = \frac{\$44,000}{\$110,000} \times \$80,000 = \$32,000.$$

Lilac's PII tax for 1999 is $11,200 ($32,000 × 35%). ▼

OTHER OPERATIONAL RULES

Several other points may be made about the possible effects of various Code provisions on S corporations.

- An S corporation must make estimated tax payments with respect to any recognized built-in gain and excess passive investment income tax.
- An S corporation may own stock in another corporation, but an S corporation may not have a C corporation shareholder. An S corporation is *not* eligible for a dividends received deduction.
- An S corporation is *not* subject to the 10 percent of taxable income limitation applicable to charitable contributions made by a C corporation.
- Any family member who renders services or furnishes capital to an electing corporation must be paid reasonable compensation. Otherwise, the IRS can make adjustments to reflect the value of the services or capital.[64] This rule

---

[62] § 1362(d)(3)(D)(i).
[63] §§ 1374(d)(4), and 1375(a) and (b).
[64] § 1366(e). In addition, beware of an IRS search for the *real owner* of the stock under Reg. § 1.1373–1(a)(2).

may make it more difficult for related parties to shift Subchapter S taxable income to children or other family members.
- Although § 1366(a)(1) provides for a flow-through of S items to a shareholder, it does not apply to self-employment income.[65] Thus, a shareholder's portion of S income is not self-employment income and is not subject to the self-employment tax. Compensation for services rendered to an S corporation is, however, subject to FICA taxes.

EXAMPLE 50

Cody and Dana each own one-third of a fast-food restaurant, and their 14-year-old son owns the other shares. Both parents work full-time in the restaurant operations, but the son works infrequently. Neither parent receives a salary this year, when the taxable income of the S corporation is $160,000. The IRS can require that reasonable compensation be paid to the parents to prevent the full one-third of the $160,000 from being taxed to the son. Otherwise, this would be an effective technique to shift earned income to a family member to reduce the total family tax burden. Furthermore, low or zero salaries can reduce FICA taxes due to the Federal government. ▼

- An S corporation is placed on the cash method of accounting for purposes of deducting business expenses and interest owed to a cash basis related party.[66] Thus, the timing of the shareholder's income and the corporate deduction must match.
- The S election is not recognized by the District of Columbia and several states, including Connecticut, Michigan, New Hampshire, and Tennessee. Thus, some or all of the entity's income may be subject to a state-level income tax.
- An S corporation may issue § 1244 stock to its shareholders to obtain ordinary loss treatment.
- Losses may be disallowed due to a lack of a profit motive. If the activities at the corporate level are not profit motivated, the losses may be disallowed under the hobby loss rules of § 183 (see Chapter 16).[67]

SUMMARY

The S corporation rules are elective and can be used to benefit a number of small business owners.

- When the business is profitable, the S corporation election removes the threat of double taxation on corporate profits.
- When the business is generating losses, deductions for allocable losses are immediately available to the shareholders.

About one-half of all U.S. corporations operate under the S rules. Flow-through income is taxed to the shareholders, who increase basis in their corporate stock accordingly. In this manner, later shareholder (dividend) distributions can be made tax-free. Flow-through losses reduce stock and debt basis, but loss deductions are suspended when basis reaches zero. Flow-through items that could be treated differently by various shareholders are separately stated on Schedule K–1 of the Form 1120S.

---

[65]Rev.Rul. 59–221, 1959–1 C.B. 225.
[66]§ 267(b).

[67]*Michael J. Houston*, T.C.Memo. 1995–159; *Mario G. De Mendoza, III*, T.C.Memo. 1994–314.

Corporate-level taxes are seldom assessed on S corporations, but they guard against abuses of the S rules, such as shifting appreciated assets from higher C corporation rates to lower individual rates (the built-in gains tax) or doing the same with investment assets (the tax on excessive PII).

The S rules are designed for closely held businesses with simple capital structures. Eligibility rules are not oppressive, and they do not include any limitations on the corporation's capitalization value, sales, number or distribution of employees, or other operating measures. The S election process can be complex, though, and maintenance of S status must be monitored on an ongoing basis.

KEY TERMS

Accumulated adjustments account (AAA), 12–17

Built-in gains tax, 12–28

Passive investment income (PII), 12–10

S corporation, 12–2

Small business corporation, 12–5

Subchapter S, 12–2

PROBLEM MATERIALS

1. On March 2, 1999, the two 50% shareholders of a calendar year corporation decide to elect S status. One of the shareholders, Terry, had purchased her stock from a previous shareholder (a nonresident alien) on January 18, 1999. Identify any potential problems for Terry or the corporation.

2. Shelley asks your advice. Should she raise new funds for her existing S corporation by issuing stock or debt? Draft a memo for the file dated September 8, 1999, outlining what you will tell Shelley.

3. Collett's S corporation has a small amount of accumulated earnings and profits (AEP), requiring the use of the more complex distribution rules. His accountant tells him that this AEP forces the maintenance of the AAA figure each year. Identify relevant tax issues facing Collett.

4. Caleb Hudson owns 10% of an S corporation. He is confused with respect to his AAA and stock basis. Write a brief memo dated November 1, 1999, to Caleb identifying the key differences between AAA and his stock basis.

5. Burt is the custodian at Quaker Inn, an S corporation that has paid him bonuses over the years in the form of shares in the corporation. Burt now holds 276 shares in Quaker Inn.

    While listening to a television debate about a national health care plan, Burt decides that the company's health coverage is unfair. He is concerned about this because his wife, Dora, is seriously ill.

    During the second week in December, Burt informs Quaker's president that he would like a Christmas bonus of $75,000 cash, or else he will sell 10 shares of his stock to one of his relatives, a nonresident alien. The resulting loss of the S election would trigger about $135,000 in Federal corporate income taxes for the current year alone. Comment.

6. Ethel Corporation has filed a Federal Form 1120S for the last six years. The local IRS district has notified the firm that an audit of corporate tax returns will be conducted beginning next month. Carrie, Ethel's tax director, cannot find the original S election of the firm, stamped with the IRS's approval.

    The firm's shareholders and officers all agree that a local accountant filed the return, and that all appropriate parties signed the consent form. The local accountant passed away about two years ago, and there is no way to reconstruct his files. Several of the shareholders instruct Carrie to prepare a backdated Form 2553, which they will sign. The resulting loss of the S election would trigger about $535,000 in Federal corporate income taxes for the current year alone. Comment.

7. GoldCo has operated successfully as an S corporation for the last eight years, saving about $280,000 in Federal income taxes because of the election. The company currently has 75 shareholders, including Morrie and Kristy, a married couple who count as one shareholder for purposes of § 1361.

   Morrie and Kristy now announce that they are planning to be divorced. GoldCo's board of directors responds with the following list of suggestions. Comment.

   - Postpone the divorce for a year, during which the board will attempt to buy out the shares of one of the other shareholders.
   - Morrie and Kristy should remain married indefinitely for the good of the company.
   - The board will encourage two of the other shareholders to marry each other for the good of the company.
   - After Morrie and Kristy divorce, GoldCo should continue to file a Form 1120S, stating that they are still married and that the limitation on the number of shareholders is met.

8. Lynch's share of her S corporation's net operating loss is $41,000, but her stock basis is only $29,000. Point out any tax consequences to Lynch.

9. One of your clients is considering electing S status. Texas, Inc., is a six-year-old company with two equal shareholders, both of whom paid $30,000 for their stock. In 1999, Texas has a $110,000 NOL carryforward. Estimated income is $40,000 for 2000 and $25,000 for each of the next three years. Should Texas make an S election for 1999?

10. An S corporation's profit and loss statement shows net profits of $90,000 (book income). The corporation has three equal shareholders. From supplemental data, you obtain the following information about the corporation.

Administrative expenses	$21,200
Tax-exempt interest	2,000
Dividends received	9,000
Section 1231 gain	6,000
Section 1245 gain	10,000
Recovery of state income taxes	3,400
Short-term capital losses	6,000
Salary to owners (each)	10,000
Cost of goods sold	95,000

    a. Compute Subchapter S taxable income or loss.
    b. What would be the portion of taxable income or loss for Chang, one of the shareholders?

11. Noon, Inc., a calendar year S corporation in Ruston, Louisiana, is equally owned by Ralph and Thomas. Thomas dies on April 1 (not a leap year), and his estate selects a March 31 fiscal year. Noon has $400,000 of income for January 1 through March 31 and $600,000 for the remainder of the year.
    a. Determine how income is allocated to Ralph and Thomas under the pro rata approach.
    b. Determine how income is allocated to Ralph and Thomas under the per-books method.

12. Polly has been the sole shareholder of a calendar year S corporation since 1981. Polly's stock basis is $15,500, and she receives a distribution of $17,000. Corporate-level accounts are as follows.

AAA	$6,000
PTI*	9,000
AEP	500

*PTI = previously taxed income, under old-law provisions.

How is Polly taxed on the distribution?

13. On January 1, Kinney, Inc., an electing S corporation, has $4,000 AEP and a balance of $10,000 in the AAA. Kinney has two shareholders, Erin and Frank, each of whom owns 500 shares of Kinney's stock. Kinney's taxable income is $5,000. Kinney distributes $6,000 to each shareholder on February 1 and distributes another $3,000 to each shareholder on September 1. Assuming that Erin and Frank have sufficient stock basis, how are they taxed on the distributions?

14. Goblins, Inc., a calendar year S corporation, has $90,000 of AEP. Tobias, the sole shareholder, has an adjusted basis of $80,000 in his stock with a zero balance in the AAA. Determine the tax aspects if a $90,000 salary is paid to Tobias.

15. Assume the same facts as in Problem 14, except that Tobias receives a dividend of $90,000.

16. Using the categories in the following legend, classify each transaction as a plus (+) or minus (−) on Schedule M–2 of Form 1120S.

Legend

PTI	=	Shareholders' undistributed taxable income previously taxed
AAA	=	Accumulated adjustments account
OAA	=	Other adjustments account
NA	=	No direct effect on Schedule M

   a. Receipt of tax-exempt interest income.
   b. Unreasonable compensation determined.
   c. Section 1245 recapture income.
   d. Distribution of nontaxable income (PTI) from 1981.
   e. Nontaxable life insurance proceeds.
   f. Expenses related to tax-exempt securities.
   g. Charitable contributions.
   h. Business gifts in excess of $25.
   i. Nondeductible fines and penalties.
   j. Amortization of organization expenses.

17. Individuals Adam and Bonnie form an S corporation, with Adam contributing cash of $100,000 for a 50% interest and Bonnie contributing appreciated ordinary income property with an adjusted basis of $20,000 and a FMV of $100,000.
    a. Determine Bonnie's initial basis in her stock, assuming that she receives a 50% corporate ownership interest.
    b. The S corporation sells the property for $120,000. Determine Adam's and Bonnie's stock basis after the sale.

18. Bip Wallace is the only shareholder in Corso, a valid S corporation. Bip's stock basis at the beginning of the year is $100,000. Corso produces a $55,000 operating loss for the year. On November 1, it distributed $70,000 to Wallace. Show your computations as to the tax consequences in spreadsheet form and include them in a memo to your manager.

19. Compute the ending AAA and AEP balances for Faber, a valid S corporation.

Beginning AAA balance	$100,000
Beginning AEP balance	55,000
Operating loss	60,000
Shareholder distribution, May 1	70,000

20. Money, Inc., a calendar year S corporation, has two unrelated shareholders, each owning 50% of the stock. Both shareholders have a $400,000 stock basis as of January 1, and Money has AAA of $300,000 and AEP of $600,000. During the year, Money has operating income of $100,000. At the end of the year, Money distributes securities worth $1 million, with an adjusted basis of $800,000. Determine the tax effects of these transactions.

21. Assume the same facts as in Problem 20, except that the two shareholders consent under § 1368(e)(3) to distribute AEP first.

22. An S corporation's Form 1120S shows taxable income of $88,000 for the year. Matthew owns 40% of the stock throughout the year. The following information is obtained from the corporate records.

Salary paid to Matthew	$52,000
Tax-exempt interest income	3,000
Charitable contributions	6,000
Dividends received from a foreign corporation	5,000
Long-term capital loss	6,000
§ 1245 gain	11,000
Refund of prior state income taxes	5,000
Cost of goods sold	72,000
Short-term capital loss	7,000
Administrative expenses	18,000
Long-term capital gains	14,000
Selling expenses	11,000
Matthew's beginning stock basis	22,000
Matthew's additional stock purchases	9,000
Matthew's beginning AAA	21,000
Matthew's loan to corporation	20,000

a. Compute book income or loss.
b. Compute Matthew's ending stock basis.
c. Calculate ending corporate AAA.

23. At the beginning of the year, Malcolm, a 50% shareholder of a calendar year S corporation, has a stock basis of $22,000. During the year, the corporation has taxable income of $32,000. The following data are obtained from supplemental sources:

Dividends received	$12,000
Tax-exempt interest	18,000
Short-term capital gain	6,000
§ 1245 gain	10,000
§ 1231 gain	7,000
Charitable contributions	5,000
Political contributions	8,000
Short-term capital loss	12,000
Dividends to Malcolm	6,000
Selling expense	14,000
Beginning AAA	40,000

a. Compute Malcolm's ending stock basis.
b. Compute ending AAA.

24. For each of the following independent statements, indicate whether the transaction will increase (+), decrease (−), or have no effect (NE) on the adjusted basis of a shareholder's stock in an S corporation.

a. Expenses related to tax-exempt income.
b. Short-term capital gain.
c. Nonseparately computed loss.
d. Section 1231 gain.
e. Depletion *not* in excess of basis.
f. Separately computed income.
g. Nontaxable return-of-capital distribution by the corporation.
h. Administrative expenses.
i. Business gifts in excess of $25.
j. Section 1245 gain.
k. Dividends received by the S corporation.
l. LIFO recapture tax at S election.
m. Recovery of a bad debt.
n. Long-term capital loss.
o. Corporate dividends out of AAA.

25. Cloris owns 35% of the stock of an S corporation and lends the corporation $7,000 during the year. Her stock basis in the corporation at the end of the year is $25,000. If the corporation sustains a $110,000 operating loss during the year, what amount, if any, can Cloris deduct with respect to the operating loss?

26. Candy owns 40% of the stock of Park, a valid S corporation. Her stock basis is $25,000, and she loaned $8,000 to the corporation during the year. How much of Park's $110,000 operating loss can Candy deduct for this year? Show your computation of the tax consequences in spreadsheet form and include them in a memo to your manager.

27. Crew Corporation elects S status effective for tax year 1998. As of January 1, 1998, Crew's assets were appraised as follows.

	Adjusted Basis	Fair Market Value
Cash	$ 16,010	$ 16,010
Accounts receivable	–0–	55,400
Inventory (FIFO)	70,000	90,000
Investment in land	110,000	195,000
Building	220,000	275,000
Goodwill	–0–	93,000

In each of the following situations, calculate any § 1374 tax, assuming that the highest corporate rate is 35%.
a. During 1998, Crew collects $40,000 of the accounts receivable and sells 80% of the inventory for $99,000.
b. In 1999, Crew sells the land held for investment for $203,000.
c. In 2000, the building is sold for $270,000.

28. Bryan, a cash basis S corporation, has the following assets and liabilities on January 1, 1999, the date the S election is made.

	Adjusted Basis	Fair Market Value
Cash	$ 200,000	$ 200,000
Accounts receivable	–0–	105,000
Equipment	110,000	100,000
Land	1,800,000	2,500,000
Accounts payable	–0–	110,000

During 1999, Bryan collects the accounts receivable and pays the accounts payable. The land is sold for $3 million, and the taxable income for the year is $590,000. Calculate any § 1374 penalty tax.

29. Lejeune, Inc., an S corporation in Boone, North Carolina, has operating revenues of $400,000, taxable interest of $380,000, operating expenses of $250,000, and deductions attributable to the interest income of $140,000. Calculate any penalty tax payable by this S corporation or its shareholders.

30. At the end of 1998, Brew, an S corporation, has gross receipts of $190,000 and gross income of $170,000. Brew has $22,000 AEP and taxable income of $30,000. It reports passive investment income of $100,000, with $40,000 of expenses directly related to the production of passive investment income. Calculate Brew's excess net passive income and any penalty tax liability.

31. At the end of the year, a calendar year S corporation has rent income of $400,000 (significant services are rendered), interest income of $200,000, and royalty income of $150,000 (the trademark was purchased). It incurred operating expenses of $250,000 and deductions attributable to the interest income and trademark of $80,000. Calculate any passive income penalty tax.

32. During the year, Topp Corporation, an electing S corporation, has gross receipts totaling $320,000 ($160,000 of which is passive investment income). Expenditures directly connected to the production of the passive investment income total $30,000. Calculate any passive income penalty tax, assuming taxable income is $68,000.

33. Bonnie and Clyde each own one-third of a fast-food restaurant, and their 13-year-old daughter owns the other shares. Both parents work full-time in the restaurant, but the daughter works infrequently. Neither Bonnie nor Clyde receives a salary during the year, when the taxable income of the S corporation is $180,000. An IRS agent estimates that reasonable salaries for Bonnie, Clyde, and the daughter are $30,000, $35,000, and $10,000, respectively. What adjustments would you expect the IRS to impose upon these taxpayers?

34. An S corporation, C&C Properties, owns two rental real estate undertakings—Carrot and Cantalope. Each property generates an annual $10,000 loss for the year. The S corporation reports the aggregated results of the two ventures on Schedule K–1. The two equal shareholders, Dan and Marta, have a $7,000 stock basis before considering these losses. Marta actively participates in the management of Carrot, but does not actively participate in the Cantalope venture. Dan does not actively participate in either venture. What losses flow through?

35. One of your clients is considering electing S status. Dickens, Inc., is a seven-year-old company with two equal shareholders who are in the 39.6% tax bracket. In 1997, Dickens will have an NOL carryforward of approximately $310,000. The difference between LIFO and FIFO inventory is $200,000, and the company will distribute about 50% of taxable income (before any NOL). The company's estimated income, built-in gain recognition, and 8% present value of $1 are as follows.

	Taxable Income	Built-in Gain	Present Value of $1
1998	$210,000	$50,000	0.926
1999	250,000	40,000	0.857
2000	300,000	50,000	0.794
2001	400,000	40,000	0.735
2002	600,000	30,000	0.681

a. Should the corporation elect S corporation status?
b. Would your answer change if most of the taxable income is distributed?

36. Claude sells his shares in Ditta, a valid S corporation for $8,000. His basis in the shares is $122,000. The shares were issued under § 1244. Claude is single and the original owner of the shares. Determine his tax treatment for the sale.

COMPREHENSIVE TAX RETURN PROBLEM

37. Jay Mitchell (243–58–8695) and Stan Marshall (221–51–8695) are 70% and 30% owners of Dana, Inc. (73–8264911), a service company located in Dime Box, Texas. The company's S corporation election was on January 15, 1997. The following information was taken from the income statement for 1997.

Tax-exempt interest	$ 10,000	
Gross rents	50,000	
Gross royalties	100,000	
Service income	1,100,000	$1,260,000
Salaries and wages	$ 550,000	
Repairs	20,000	
Officers' compensation	150,000	
Bad debts	50,000	
Rent expense (operating)	50,000	
Taxes	50,000	
Expenses relating to tax-exempt income	5,000	
Charitable contributions	20,000	
Payroll penalties	15,000	
Advertising expenses	50,000	
Other deductions	100,000	1,060,000
Book income		$ 200,000

A partially completed comparative balance sheet appears as follows.

	Beginning of the Year	End of the Year
Cash	$60,000	$ 65,000
Accounts receivable	20,000	40,000
Loan to Jay Mitchell	–0–	20,000
Total	$80,000	$125,000
Accounts payable	$20,000	$ 18,000
Other current liabilities	–0–	12,000
Capital stock	60,000	60,000
Retained earnings	–0–	?
Previously taxed income	–0–	?
Accumulated adjustments account	–0–	?
Other adjustments account	–0–	?
Total liabilities/shareholders' equity	$80,000	$125,000

The corporation distributed $165,000 to the two shareholders during the year. From the available information, prepare Form 1120S and Schedule K–1 for Jay Mitchell. If any information is missing, make realistic assumptions.

CHAPTER 12 S Corporations

RESEARCH PROBLEMS

*Note: The **RIA OnPoint System 4 Student Version CD-ROM** available with this text can be used in preparing solutions to the Research Problems. Alternatively, tax research materials contained in a standard tax library can be used.*

38. Mel Bonilla contacts you with respect to the creation of two S corporations, each having approximately 40 shareholders. Most of the assets of the business will be held inside a limited liability company. Both S corporations will be 50% partners in the limited liability company. Draft a letter to Mel, indicating whether this business arrangement is appropriate. Mel's address is 10 Newton Avenue, Ocala, FL 34482.

39. Anita, the accountant for Rockhead, Inc., failed to file a Form 2553 for tax year 1997, even though the four shareholders of the corporation instructed her to qualify the corporation as an S corporation. For 1997 and 1998, Anita did file Forms 1120S, along with Schedule K–1s for all of the shareholders.

    When the IRS notified Anita that Rockhead was not a qualified S corporation, she argued that Form 2553 was "nonmandatory." She pointed out that Temp.Reg. § 18.1362–1(a) uses the word "should" rather than "shall" in reference to filing Form 2553.

    Anita provided the revenue agent with a copy of *Steve Brody*, 34 TCM 310, T.C.Memo. 1975–47, ¶75,047 P–H Memo T.C. Here, the IRS argued that the taxpayer had elected to be taxed under Subchapter S because the taxpayer filed Form 1120S. The IRS could not provide the court with the necessary Form 2553.

    As Rockhead's new tax adviser, prepare a memo for your file, analyzing Anita's argument.

40. Opal is a major shareholder of Nations, Inc., an electing S corporation. As an incentive to persuade Hugo to work for the corporation, Opal sells Hugo some of her stock at a 20% discount below fair market value. The reason for the discount was to compensate Hugo for accepting a salary from Nations below the market rate. Hugo paid the bargain price for the stock directly to Opal in the form of cash and a promissory note. Hugo is personally liable for the promissory note.

    In acquiring the Nations' stock from Opal, Hugo entered into an agreement restricting the transferability of the shares. Does this transaction create a second class of stock, thereby terminating the S election? Write a memo for the tax research file, analyzing the S election after the agreement is executed. *Solve this problem using just the Code and Income Tax Regulations.*

    Partial list of research aids:
    § 1361(b)(1)(D).
    Reg. § 1.1361–1(l)(2)(i).
    Ltr.Rul. 9525035.

41. Tom Lewitske owns an insolvent S corporation. A local bank discharged a debt of $32,500 that the S corporation owed to the bank. This amount was not in excess of the amount by which the S corporation was insolvent. Tom calls you and asks about the tax aspects of this discharge of indebtedness. Prepare a memo for the tax research file dated June 15, 1998, indicating what you told Tom over the phone.

CHAPTER 13

BUSINESS TAX CREDITS AND CORPORATE ALTERNATIVE MINIMUM TAX

LEARNING OBJECTIVES

After completing Chapter 13, you should be able to:

1. Explain how tax credits are used as a tool of Federal tax policy.
2. Work with various business-related tax credits.
3. Explain the reason for the alternative minimum tax.
4. Calculate the tax preferences that are included in calculating the AMT.
5. Identify and calculate AMT adjustments.
6. Understand the function of adjusted current earnings (ACE).
7. Compute the AMT liability for corporations.

OUTLINE

Tax Policy and Tax Credits, 13–2

Specific Business-Related Tax Credit Provisions, 13–3

General Business Credit, 13–3

Tax Credit for Rehabilitation Expenditures, 13–5

Business Energy Credits, 13–6

Work Opportunity Tax Credit, 13–7

Welfare-to-Work Credit, 13–8

Research Activities Credit, 13–8

Low-Income Housing Credit, 13–10

Disabled Access Credit, 13–11

Foreign Tax Credit, 13–11

Corporate Alternative Minimum Tax, 13–13

The AMT Formula, 13–14

Tax Preferences, 13–16

AMT Adjustments, 13–17

Adjusted Current Earnings (ACE), 13–23

Computing Alternative Minimum Taxable Income, 13–25

Exemption, 13–27

Minimum Tax Credit, 13–28

Other Aspects of the AMT, 13–28

The Individual Alternative Minimum Tax, 13–28

TAX POLICY AND TAX CREDITS

1 LEARNING OBJECTIVE
Explain how tax credits are used as a tool of Federal tax policy.

Federal tax law often serves other purposes besides merely raising revenue for the government. Evidence of equity, social, and economic considerations, among others, is found throughout the tax law. These considerations also have considerable import in the area of **tax credits.** Congress has generally used tax credits to promote social or economic objectives or to work toward greater tax equity among different types of taxpayers. For example, the disabled access credit was enacted to accomplish a social objective: to encourage taxpayers to renovate older buildings so they would be in compliance with the Americans with Disabilities Act. This Act requires businesses and institutions to make their facilities more accessible to persons with various types of disabilities. As another example, the foreign tax credit, which has been a part of the law for decades, has as its chief purpose the economic and equity objectives of mitigating the burden of multiple taxation on a single stream of income.

A tax credit should not be confused with an income tax deduction. Certain expenditures (e.g., business expenses) are permitted as deductions from gross income in arriving at taxable income. While the tax benefit received from a tax deduction depends on the tax rate, a tax credit is not affected by the tax rate of the taxpayer. All taxpayers can benefit equally when a tax credit is used.

EXAMPLE 1

Assume Congress wishes to encourage a certain type of expenditure. One way to accomplish this objective is to allow a tax credit of 25% for such expenditures. Another way is to allow a deduction for the expenditures. Assume Red Corporation's tax rate is 15%, while Blue Corporation's tax rate is 39%. The following tax benefits are available to each corporation for a $1,000 expenditure.

	Red	Blue
Tax benefit if a 25% credit is allowed	$250	$250
Tax benefit if a deduction is allowed	150	390

As these results indicate, tax credits can provide benefits on a more equitable basis than tax deductions often do. ▼

TAX IN THE NEWS

A CREDIT THAT WENT UP IN SMOKE

In 1997, Congress passed a special $50 billion tax credit for the tobacco industry to subsidize the cost of a proposed multibillion dollar national settlement between tobacco companies and the 50 states. Several state attorneys general had previously sued tobacco companies in an attempt to recover billions of state Medicaid dollars spent on tobacco-related health problems. Once tobacco industry foes became aware of the significant savings that would accrue to tobacco companies from the tobacco tax credit, Congress was under considerable pressure to cut out the tax break. Less than a month after the credit's passage, legislation was introduced to repeal the controversial credit. As a result, the tobacco credit goes on record as one of the shortest-lived credits in tax history.

As several news reports suggested, repeal of the tobacco tax credit may have signaled a change in congressional sentiment concerning special interest legislation for the tobacco industry. In fact, subsequent budget proposals included provisions that would increase the price of tobacco products.

SPECIFIC BUSINESS–RELATED TAX CREDIT PROVISIONS

GENERAL BUSINESS CREDIT

2 LEARNING OBJECTIVE
Work with various business-related tax credits.

As shown in Exhibit 13–1, the **general business credit** is comprised of a number of other credits, each of which is computed separately under its own set of rules. The general business credit combines these credits into one amount to limit the annual credit that can be used to offset a taxpayer's income tax liability. The idea behind combining the credits is to prevent a taxpayer from completely avoiding an income tax liability in any one year by offsetting it with several business credits that would otherwise be available.

Two special rules apply to the general business credit. First, any unused credit must be carried back 1 year, then forward 20 years. Second, for any tax year, the general business credit is limited to the taxpayer's *net income tax* reduced by the greater of:[1]

- The *tentative minimum tax* (see the discussion of AMT later in this chapter).
- 25 percent of *net regular tax liability* that exceeds $25,000.[2] This rule works to keep the general business credit from completely eliminating the tax liability for many taxpayers.

To understand these general business credit limitations, several terms need defining.

- *Net income tax* is the sum of the regular tax liability and the alternative minimum tax reduced by certain nonrefundable tax credits.

---

[1] § 38(c).
[2] § 38(c)(3)(B). This $25,000 amount is apportioned among the members of a controlled group.

▼ EXHIBIT 13-1
Principal Components of the General Business Credit

> The general business credit combines (but is not limited to) the following.
> - Tax credit for rehabilitation expenditures
> - Business energy credits
> - Work opportunity tax credit*
> - Research activities credit**
> - Welfare-to-work credit***
> - Low-income housing credit
> - Disabled access credit
>
> *Not available under current law for employees hired after June 30, 1998.
> **Scheduled to expire after June 30, 1998.
> ***Not available for employees hired after April 30, 1999.

- *Tentative minimum tax* (discussed later in this chapter) is reduced by any foreign tax credit allowed, as specified in Exhibit 13–2 (see page 13–15).
- *Regular tax liability* is determined from the appropriate tax table or tax rate schedule, based on taxable income. However, the regular tax liability does not include certain taxes (e.g., alternative minimum tax).
- *Net regular tax liability* is the regular tax liability reduced by certain nonrefundable credits (e.g., credit for child and dependent care expenses, foreign tax credit).

EXAMPLE 2

Tanager Company's general business credit for the current year is $70,000. Tanager's net income tax is $150,000, tentative minimum tax is $130,000, and net regular tax liability is $150,000. Tanager has no other tax credits. The general business credit allowed for the tax year is computed as follows.

Net income tax	$ 150,000
Less: The greater of—	
• $130,000 (tentative minimum tax)	
• $31,250 [25% × ($150,000 − $25,000)]	(130,000)
Amount of general business credit allowed for tax year	$ 20,000

Tanager then has $50,000 ($70,000 − $20,000) of unused general business credits that may be carried back or forward. ▼

Treatment of Unused General Business Credits. For tax years beginning after 1997, unused general business credits are initially carried back one year and reduce the tax liability of that year. Thus, the taxpayer may receive a tax refund as a result of the carryback. Any remaining unused credits are then carried forward 20 years.[3]

A FIFO method is applied to the carryovers and utilization of credits earned during a particular year. The oldest credits are used first in determining the amount of the general business credit. The FIFO method minimizes the potential for loss of a general business credit benefit due to the expiration of credit carryovers and generally works to the taxpayer's benefit.

---
[3]§ 39(a)(1). For prior tax years, unused general business credits were carried back 3 years and then forward 15 years.

CHAPTER 13 Business Tax Credits and Corporate Alternative Minimum Tax 13–5

EXAMPLE 3

This example illustrates the use of general business credit carryovers for the taxpayer's 1999 tax year.

General business credit carryovers (unused in prior tax years)		
1996	$ 4,000	
1997	6,000	
1998	2,000	
Total carryovers	$ 12,000	
1999 general business credit		$ 40,000
Total credit allowed in 1999		
Tax liability		$ 50,000
Less: Carryovers used		
1996	(4,000)	
1997	(6,000)	
1998	(2,000)	
Remaining tax		$ 38,000
1999 general business credit, fully offsets tax due		(38,000)
1999 unused amount carried forward to 2000		$ 2,000

The various credits that make up the general business credit are discussed in the paragraphs below.

TAX CREDIT FOR REHABILITATION EXPENDITURES

Taxpayers are allowed a tax credit for expenditures incurred to rehabilitate older industrial and commercial buildings and certified historic structures. The **rehabilitation expenditures credit** is intended to discourage businesses from moving from economically distressed areas (e.g., an inner city) to outlying locations and to encourage the preservation of historic structures. The current operating features of this credit follow.[4]

Rate of the Credit for Rehabilitation Expenses	Nature of the Property
10%	Nonresidential buildings and residential rental property, other than certified historic structures, originally placed in service before 1936
20%	Nonresidential and residential certified historic structures

Taxpayers who claim the rehabilitation credit must reduce the basis of the rehabilitated building by the credit allowed.[5]

EXAMPLE 4

Grosbeak, Inc., spent $60,000 to rehabilitate a building (adjusted basis of $40,000) that originally had been placed in service in 1932. Grosbeak is allowed a credit of $6,000 (10% × $60,000) for rehabilitation expenditures. It then increases the basis of the building by $54,000 [$60,000 (rehabilitation expenditures) − $6,000 (credit allowed)]. If the building were a historic structure, the credit allowed would be $12,000 (20% × $60,000), and the building's depreciable basis would increase by $48,000 [$60,000 (rehabilitation expenditures) − $12,000 (credit allowed)]. ▼

---

[4] § 47. [5] § 50(c).

▼ **TABLE 13–1**
Recapture Calculation for Rehabilitation Expenditures Credit

If the Property Is Held for	The Recapture Percentage Is
Less than 1 year	100
One year or more but less than 2 years	80
Two years or more but less than 3 years	60
Three years or more but less than 4 years	40
Four years or more but less than 5 years	20
Five years or more	0

To qualify for the credit, buildings must be substantially rehabilitated. A building has been *substantially rehabilitated* if qualified rehabilitation expenditures exceed the greater of:

- the adjusted basis of the property before the rehabilitation expenditures, or
- $5,000.

Qualified rehabilitation expenditures do not include the cost of acquiring a building, the cost of facilities related to a building (such as a parking lot), and the cost of enlarging an existing building. Stringent rules apply concerning the retention of the building's original internal and external walls.

Recapture of Tax Credit for Rehabilitation Expenditures. The rehabilitation credit taken is recaptured if the rehabilitated property is disposed of prematurely or if it ceases to be qualifying property. The **rehabilitation expenditures credit recapture** is added to the taxpayer's regular tax liability in the recapture year. The recapture amount also is *added* to the adjusted basis of the building.

The portion of the credit recaptured is a specified percentage of the credit that was taken by the taxpayer. This percentage is based on the period the property was held by the taxpayer, as shown in Table 13–1. If the property is held at least five years, no recapture can result.

EXAMPLE 5

On March 15, 1996, Chickadee Company rehabilitated a building qualifying for the 10% credit. The company spent $30,000 in qualifying rehabilitation expenditures and claimed a $3,000 credit ($30,000 × 10%). The basis of the building was increased by $27,000 ($30,000 − $3,000).

Chickadee sold the building on December 15, 1999. Chickadee recaptures a portion of the rehabilitation credit based on the schedule in Table 13–1. Because Chickadee held the rehabilitated property for more than three years but less than four, 40% of the credit, or $1,200, is added to the company's 1999 tax liability. The adjusted basis of the building is increased by the $1,200 recapture amount. ▼

BUSINESS ENERGY CREDITS

For many years, **business energy credits** have been allowed to encourage the conservation of natural resources and the development of alternative energy sources such as solar power to supplement oil and natural gas. Over the years, some of these credits have expired while new ones have been added. The most important business energy credits that remain are the 10 percent credits for solar energy property and geothermal property.

WORK OPPORTUNITY TAX CREDIT

The **work opportunity tax credit** was enacted to encourage employers to hire individuals from a variety of targeted and economically disadvantaged groups who started work before June 30, 1998. Examples of such targeted persons include qualified ex-felons, high-risk youths, food stamp recipients, veterans, summer youth employees, and persons receiving certain welfare benefits.[6]

Computation of the Work Opportunity Tax Credit: General. The credit generally is equal to 40 percent of the first $6,000 of wages (per eligible employee) for the first 12 months of employment. The credit is not available for wages paid to an employee after the first year of employment. If the employee's first year overlaps two of the employer's tax years, however, the employer may take the credit over two tax years. If the credit is claimed, the employer's tax deduction for wages is reduced by the amount of the credit.

To qualify an employer for the 40 percent credit, the employee must (1) be certified by a designated local agency as being a member of one of the targeted groups and (2) have completed at least 400 hours of service to the employer. If an employee meets the first condition but not the second, the credit is reduced to 25 percent, provided the employee has completed a minimum of 120 hours of service to the employer.

EXAMPLE 6

In January 1998, Green Company hires four individuals who are certified to be members of a qualifying targeted group. Each employee works 1,000 hours and is paid wages of $8,000 during the year. Green Company's work opportunity credit is $9,600 [($6,000 × 40%) × 4 employees]. If the tax credit is taken, Green reduces its deduction for wages paid by $9,600. No credit is available for wages paid to these employees after their first year of employment. ▼

EXAMPLE 7

On June 1, 1998, Maria, a calendar year taxpayer, hired Joe, a member of a targeted group, and obtained the required certification to qualify Maria for the work opportunity credit. During his seven months of work in 1998, Joe is paid $3,500 for 500 hours of work. Maria is allowed a credit of $1,400 ($3,500 × 40%) for 1998.

Joe continues to work for Maria in 1999 and is paid $7,000 through May 31, 1999. Because up to $6,000 of first-year wages are eligible for the credit, Maria is also allowed a 40% credit on $2,500 [$6,000 − $3,500 (wages paid in 1998)] of 1999 wages paid, or $1,000 ($2,500 × 40%). None of Joe's wages paid after May 31, the end of the first year of employment, is eligible for the credit. ▼

Computation of the Work Opportunity Tax Credit: Qualified Summer Youth Employees. The credit for qualified summer youth employees is allowed on wages for services during any 90-day period between May 1 and September 15. The maximum wages eligible for the credit are $3,000 per summer youth employee. The credit rate is the same as that under the general provision for the work opportunity tax credit. If the employee continues employment after the 90-day period as a member of another targeted group, the amount of the wages eligible for the general work opportunity tax credit as a member of the new target group is reduced by the wages paid to the employee as a qualified summer youth employee.

A *qualified summer youth employee* must be age 16 or 17 on the hiring date. An additional requirement for qualifying is that the individual's principal place of

[6] § 51.

abode must be within an economically disadvantaged area (specifically, an empowerment zone or an enterprise community).

WELFARE-TO-WORK CREDIT

Beginning in 1998, a **welfare-to-work credit**[7] is available to employers hiring individuals who have been long-term recipients of family assistance welfare benefits. In general, *long-term recipients* are those individuals who are certified by a designated local agency as being members of a family receiving assistance under a public aid program for the 18-month period ending on the hiring date. Unlike the work opportunity credit, which applies only to first-year wages paid to qualified individuals, the welfare-to-work credit is available for qualified wages paid in the first two years of employment. If an employee's first and second work years overlap two or more of the employer's tax years, the employer may take the credit during the applicable tax years. If the welfare-to-work credit is taken, the employer's tax deduction for wages is reduced by the amount of the credit.

An employer is prohibited from taking both the work opportunity credit and the welfare-to-work credit for wages paid to a qualified employee in a given tax year. The welfare-to-work credit is not available for employees hired after April 30, 1999.

Maximum Credit. The credit is equal to 35 percent of the first $10,000 of qualified wages paid to an employee in the first year of employment, plus 50 percent of the first $10,000 of qualified wages in the second year of employment, resulting in a maximum credit per qualified employee of $8,500 [$3,500 (year 1) + $5,000 (year 2)]. The credit rate is higher for second-year wages to encourage employers to retain qualified individuals, thereby promoting the overall welfare-to-work goal.

EXAMPLE 8

In April 1998, Blue Company hired three individuals who are certified as long-term family assistance recipients. Each employee is paid $12,000 during 1998. Two of the three individuals continue to work for Blue Company in 1999, earning $9,000 each during the year. No additional qualified employees are hired in 1999. Blue Company's welfare-to-work credit is $10,500 [(35% × $10,000) × 3 employees] for 1998 and $9,000 [(50% × $9,000) × 2 employees] for 1999. ▼

RESEARCH ACTIVITIES CREDIT

To encourage research and development (R & D) in the U.S. business community, a credit is allowed for certain qualifying expenditures paid or incurred from July 1, 1996 through June 30, 1998. The **research activities credit** is the *sum* of two components: an incremental research activities credit and a basic research credit.[8]

Incremental Research Activities Credit. The incremental research activities credit applies at a 20 percent rate to the *excess* of qualified research expenses for the taxable year (the credit year) over a base amount.

In general, *research expenditures* qualify if the research relates to discovering technological information that is intended for use in the development of a new or improved business component of the taxpayer. Such expenses qualify fully if the research is performed in-house (by the taxpayer or its employees). If the research

---

[7]§ 51A. [8]§ 41.

CHAPTER 13 Business Tax Credits and Corporate Alternative Minimum Tax

is conducted by persons outside the taxpayer's business (under contract), only 65 percent of the amount paid qualifies for the credit.[9]

EXAMPLE 9

Bobwhite Company incurs the following research expenditures for the tax year.

In-house wages, supplies, computer time	$50,000
Payment to Cutting Edge Scientific Foundation for research	30,000

Bobwhite's qualified research expenditures are $69,500 [$50,000 + ($30,000 × 65%)]. ▼

Beyond the general guidelines described above, the Code does not give specific examples of qualifying research. However, the credit is *not* allowed for research that falls into certain categories, including the following.[10]

- Research conducted after the beginning of commercial production of the business component.
- Surveys and studies such as market research, testing, and routine data collection.
- Research conducted *outside* the United States.
- Research in the social sciences, arts, or humanities.

Determining the *base amount* involves a relatively complex series of computations, meant to approximate recent historical levels of research activity by the taxpayer. Thus, the credit is allowed only for increases in research expenses.

EXAMPLE 10

Hawk, Inc., a calendar year taxpayer, incurs qualifying research expenditures of $200,000 during the tax year. If the base amount is $100,000, the incremental research activities credit is $20,000 [($200,000 − $100,000) × 20%]. ▼

Qualified research and experimentation expenditures are not only eligible for the 20 percent credit, but can also be *expensed* in the year incurred. In this regard, a taxpayer has two choices.[11]

- Use the full credit and reduce the expense deduction for research expenses by 100 percent of the credit.
- Retain the full expense deduction and reduce the credit by the product of 100 percent of the credit times the maximum corporate tax rate.

As an alternative to the expense deduction, the taxpayer may *capitalize* the research expenses and *amortize* them over 60 months or more. In this case, the amount capitalized and subject to amortization is reduced by the full amount of the credit *only* if the credit exceeds the amount allowable as a deduction.

EXAMPLE 11

This year, Thin Corporation's potential incremental research activities credit is $20,000. The amounts that Thin can deduct and the credit amount are computed as follows.

---

[9]§ 41(b)(3)(A). In the case of payments to a qualified research consortium, 75% of the amount paid qualifies for the credit.
[10]§ 41(d).
[11]§§ 174 and 280C(c). Recall the discussion of rules for deducting research and experimental expenditures in Chapter 4.

	Credit Amount	Deduction Amount
• Full credit and reduced deduction		
$20,000 − $0	$20,000	
$200,000 − $20,000		$180,000
• Reduced credit and full deduction		
$20,000 − [(1.00 × $20,000) × .35]	13,000	
$200,000 − $0		200,000
• Full credit and capitalize and elect to amortize costs over 60 months		
$20,000 − $0	20,000	
($200,000/60) × 12		40,000

Basic Research Credit. Corporations (other than S corporations or personal service corporations) are allowed an additional 20 percent credit for basic research expenditures incurred from July 1, 1996 through June 30, 1998, in *excess* of a base amount.[12] This credit is not available to individual taxpayers. *Basic research expenditures* are defined as amounts paid in cash to a qualified basic research organization, such as a college or university or a tax-exempt organization operated primarily to conduct scientific research.

Basic research is defined generally as any original investigation for the advancement of scientific knowledge not having a specific commercial objective. The definition excludes basic research conducted outside the United States and basic research in the social sciences, arts, or humanities.

LOW-INCOME HOUSING CREDIT

To encourage building owners and real estate developers to make affordable housing available for low-income individuals, Congress has made a credit available to owners of qualified low-income housing projects.[13]

More than any other, the **low-income housing credit** is influenced by nontax factors. For example, certification of the property by the appropriate state or local agency authorized to provide low-income housing credits is required. These credits are issued based on a nationwide allocation, dictated chiefly by nontax budgetary and housing policy concerns.

The amount of the credit is based on the qualified basis of the property. The qualified basis depends on the number of units rented to low-income tenants. Tenants are low-income tenants if their income does not exceed a specified percentage of the area median gross income. The amount of the credit is determined by multiplying the qualified basis by the credit rate. The credit is allowed over a 10-year period if the property continues to meet the required conditions. Generally, first-year credits are prorated based on the date the project is placed in service.

EXAMPLE 12

A partnership spends $100,000 to build a qualified low-income housing project completed January 1, 1998. The entire project is rented to low-income families. The credit rate for property placed in service during January 1998 is 8.41%.[14] The partners are allocated a credit of $8,410 ($100,000 × 8.41%) in 1998 and in each of the following nine years. ▼

---

[12] § 41(e).
[13] § 42.

[14] Rev.Rul. 98–4, I.R.B. No. 2, 18. The rate is subject to adjustment every month by the IRS.

Recapture of a portion of the credit may be required if the number of units set aside for low-income tenants falls below a minimum threshold, if the taxpayer disposes of the property or the interest in it, or if the taxpayer's *at-risk amount* decreases. See Chapter 11 to review the at-risk rules.

DISABLED ACCESS CREDIT

The **disabled access credit** is designed to encourage small businesses to make their businesses more accessible to disabled individuals. The credit is available for any eligible access expenditures paid or incurred by an eligible small business. The credit is calculated at the rate of 50 percent of the eligible expenditures that exceed $250 but do not exceed $10,250. Thus, the maximum amount for the credit is $5,000 ($10,000 × 50%).[15]

An *eligible small business* is one that during the previous year either had gross receipts of $1 million or less or had no more than 30 full-time employees. A sole proprietorship, partnership, regular corporation, or S corporation can qualify as such an entity.

Eligible access expenditures generally include any reasonable and necessary amounts that are paid or incurred to make certain changes to facilities. These changes must involve the removal of architectural, communication, physical, or transportation barriers that would otherwise make a business inaccessible to disabled and handicapped individuals. Examples of qualifying projects include installing ramps, widening doorways, and adding raised markings on elevator control buttons. However, the improved facility must have been placed into service prior to the enactment (November 5, 1990) of the credit.

To the extent a disabled access credit is available, no deduction or credit is allowed under any other provision of the tax law. The asset's adjusted basis is reduced by the amount of the credit.

EXAMPLE 13

This year Red, Inc., an eligible business, made $11,000 of capital improvements to business realty that had been placed in service in June 1990. The expenditures were intended to make Red's business more accessible to the disabled and were considered eligible expenditures for purposes of the disabled access credit. The amount of the credit is $5,000 [($10,250 maximum − $250 floor) × 50%]. The depreciable basis of the capital improvement is $6,000 [$11,000 (cost) − $5,000 (amount of the credit)]. ▼

FOREIGN TAX CREDIT

Both individual taxpayers and corporations may claim a credit for foreign income tax paid on income earned and subject to tax in another country or a U.S. possession.[16] The purpose of the **foreign tax credit (FTC)** is to reduce the possibility of double taxation of foreign income.

EXAMPLE 14

Ace Tools, Inc., a U.S. corporation, has a branch operation in Mexico, from which it earns taxable income of $750,000 for the current year. Ace pays income tax of $150,000 on these earnings to the Mexican tax authorities. Ace must also include the $750,000 in gross income for U.S. tax purposes. Assume that, before considering the FTC, Ace would owe $255,000 in U.S. income taxes on this foreign-source income. Thus, total taxes on the $750,000 could

---

[15] § 44.
[16] § 27 provides for the credit, but the qualifications and calculation procedure for the credit are contained in §§ 901–908. Alternatively, the taxpayer can *deduct* the foreign taxes paid.

equal $405,000 ($150,000 + $255,000)$, a 54% effective rate. But Ace takes the FTC of $150,000 against its U.S. tax liability on the foreign-source income. Ace Tools' total taxes on the $750,000 now are $255,000 ($150,000 + $105,000), a 34% effective rate. ▼

A ceiling limitation allows a foreign tax credit that is the *lesser* of the foreign taxes imposed or the *U.S. rate limitation* determined according to the following formula. Thus, where applicable foreign tax rates exceed those of the United States, the credit offsets no more than the marginal U.S. tax on the double-taxed income.

$$\frac{\text{Foreign-source taxable income}}{\text{Worldwide taxable income}} \times \frac{\text{U.S. tax}}{\text{before FTC}}$$

Foreign taxes paid but not allowed as a credit due to the U.S. rate limitation are carried back two tax years and then forward five years.

▼ **EXAMPLE 15** Oriole, Inc., a U.S. corporation, conducts business in a foreign country. Oriole's worldwide taxable income for the tax year is $120,000, consisting of $100,000 in income from U.S. operations and $20,000 of income from the foreign source. Foreign tax of $6,000 was paid to foreign tax authorities on the $20,000. Before the FTC, Oriole's U.S. tax on the $120,000 is $30,050. The corporation's FTC is $5,008 {lesser of $6,000 paid or $5,008 limitation [$30,050 × ($20,000/$120,000)]}. Oriole's net U.S. tax liability is $25,042 ($30,050 − $5,008). Thus, Oriole carries over $992 FTC ($6,000 − $5,008) because of the U.S. rate limitation. ▼

CONCEPT SUMMARY 13–1

Tax Credits

Credit	Computation	Comments
General business (§ 38)	May not exceed net income tax minus the greater of tentative minimum tax or 25% of net regular tax liability that exceeds $25,000.	Components include tax credit for rehabilitation expenditures, business energy credits, work opportunity tax credit, welfare-to-work credit, research activities credit, low-income housing credit, and disabled access credit. Unused credit may be carried back 1 year and forward 20 years. FIFO method applies to carryovers, carrybacks, and credits earned during current year.
Investment (§ 46)	Qualifying investment times energy percentage or rehabilitation percentage, depending on type of property. Part of general business credit and subject to its limitations.	Part of general business credit and therefore subject to same carryback, carryover, and FIFO rules. Energy percentage is 10%. Regular rehabilitation rate is 10%; rate for certified historic structures is 20%.
Work opportunity (§ 51)	Credit is limited to 35% of the first $6,000 of wages paid to each eligible employee. The employee must begin work before June 30, 1998.	Part of the general business credit and therefore subject to the same carryback, carryover, and FIFO rules. Purpose is to encourage employment of economically disadvantaged groups.
Welfare-to-work (§ 51A)	Credit is limited to 35% of first $10,000 of wages paid to eligible employee in first year of employment, plus 50% of first $10,000 of wages paid to same employee in second year of employment.	Part of general business credit and therefore subject to same carryback, carryover, and FIFO rules. Purpose is to encourage employment of long-term recipients of family assistance welfare benefits.

Credit	Computation	Comments
Research activities (§ 41)	Incremental credit is 20% of excess of computation-year expenditures minus a base amount. Basic research credit is allowed to certain corporations for 20% of cash payments to qualified organizations that exceed a specially calculated base amount. To qualify for the credit, research expenditures must be made between July 1, 1996 and June 30, 1998.	Part of general business credit and therefore subject to same carryback, carryover, and FIFO rules. Purpose is to encourage high-tech research in the United States.
Low-income housing (§ 42)	Appropriate rate times eligible basis (portion of project attributable to low-income units).	Part of general business credit and therefore subject to same carryback, carryover, and FIFO rules. Credit is available each year for 10 years. Recapture may apply. Purpose is to encourage construction of housing for low-income individuals.
Disabled access (§ 44)	Credit is 50% of eligible access expenditures that exceed $250, but do not exceed $10,250. Maximum credit is $5,000.	Part of general business credit and therefore subject to same carryback, carryover, and FIFO rules. Available only to eligible small businesses. Purpose is to encourage small businesses to become more accessible to disabled individuals.
Foreign tax (§ 27)	Foreign income/total worldwide taxable income × U.S. tax = overall limitation. Lesser of foreign taxes imposed or U.S. rate limitation.	Unused credits may be carried back two years and forward five years. Purpose is to prevent double taxation of foreign income.

Corporate Alternative Minimum Tax

LEARNING OBJECTIVE 3
Explain the reason for the alternative minimum tax.

A perception that many large corporations were not paying their fair share of Federal income tax was especially widespread in the early 1980s. A study released in 1986 reported that 130 of the 250 largest corporations in the United States (e.g., Reynolds Metals, General Dynamics, Georgia Pacific, and Texas Commerce Bankshares) paid no Federal tax, or received refunds, in at least one year between 1981 and 1985. Political pressure subsequently led to the adoption of an **alternative minimum tax (AMT)** to ensure that corporations with substantial economic income pay at least a minimum amount of Federal taxes.

The AMT limits the tax savings for some taxpayers who are seen as gaining "too much" from exclusions, deductions, and credits available under the law. A separate tax system with a proportional tax rate is applied each year to a corporation's economic income. If the tentative AMT is greater than the regular corporate income tax, then the corporation must pay the regular tax plus this excess, the AMT.

The corporate AMT is an important revenue raiser, accounting for 8 percent of corporate tax liabilities by 1991. Between 1987 and 1990, receipts from the corporate AMT increased from $2 billion to $8 billion, and the number of AMT taxpayers almost doubled from 17,000 to 32,000. But in 1991, AMT receipts dropped to $5.3 billion, paid by 30,400 corporations; of that amount, 78 percent was paid by a few hundred large corporations with assets greater than $500 million. More than 64 percent of this $5.3 billion was paid by the capital-intensive manufacturing, mining, construction, transportation, and utility sectors.

In general, a corporation is likely to pay AMT for one or more of three reasons.

- Cost recovery allowances resulting from a high level of investment in assets such as equipment and structures.
- Low taxable income or losses due to a cyclical downturn, strong international competition, or other factors.
- Investment at low real interest rates, which increases the company's deductions for depreciation relative to those for interest payments.

Since its inception, the AMT has been vulnerable to criticisms that it is too complex. Smaller corporations especially find that the imposition of a second tax structure unduly increases their compliance burdens. Thus, proposals to cut back or even repeal the AMT were considered by Congress throughout the 1990s. A special exemption from the AMT finally was adopted in 1997. For tax years beginning after 1997, most smaller corporations are not subject to the AMT at all. A corporation is exempted from the AMT if it meets the following tests.

- *Initial test.* The corporation must report average annual gross receipts of no more than $5 million for the three-year period ending with the first tax year after 1997.
- *Ongoing test.* If the initial test is passed, the corporation is exempt from the AMT as long as its average annual gross receipts do not exceed $7.5 million for the three years prior to the filing year.

A corporation that fails the initial test never can be exempt from the AMT. Furthermore, if the ongoing test is failed, the taxpayer is subject to the AMT provisions for that year and all subsequent tax years. Congress estimates that this provision will exempt up to 95 percent of all C corporations from the AMT in the future. Fewer than a dozen states have adopted provisions similar to the Federal AMT.

THE AMT FORMULA

The AMT is imposed in addition to the regular corporate tax, but is computed in a manner wholly separate and independent from it.[17] The AMT is a parallel income tax system that generally uses more conservative accounting methods than the regular income tax. Typically, more items are subject to tax under AMT rules, some gross income items are accelerated, and some deductions are deferred.

The formula for determining the AMT liability of corporate taxpayers appears in Exhibit 13–2 and follows the format of Form 4626 (Alternative Minimum Tax—Corporations).

The base for the AMT, **alternative minimum taxable income (AMTI),** begins with regular taxable income before any deductions for net operating losses (NOLs). A series of adjustments are then made. Most AMT adjustments relate to *timing differences* that arise because of separate income tax and AMT treatments. Adjustments that are caused by timing differences eventually reverse; that is, positive adjustments are offset by negative adjustments in the future, and vice versa.

The adjustments related to *circulation expenditures* illustrate this concept. Circulation expenditures include expenses incurred to establish, maintain, or increase the circulation of a newspaper, magazine, or other periodical.

In computing *taxable income*, individuals and corporations that are personal holding companies are allowed to deduct circulation expenditures in the year

---

[17]The AMT provisions are contained in §§ 55 through 59.

EXHIBIT 13–2
AMT Formula for Corporations

Regular taxable income before NOL deduction
Plus/minus: AMT adjustments (except ACE adjustment)
Plus: Tax preferences
Equals: AMTI before AMT NOL deduction and ACE adjustment
Plus/minus: ACE adjustment
Equals: AMTI before AMT NOL deduction
Minus: AMT NOL deduction (limited to 90%)
Equals: Alternative minimum taxable income (AMTI)
Minus: Exemption
Equals: Tentative minimum tax base
Times: 20% rate
Equals: Tentative minimum tax before AMT foreign tax credit
Minus: AMT foreign tax credit (limited to 90% or less)
Equals: Tentative minimum tax
Minus: Regular tax liability before credits minus regular foreign tax credit
Equals: Alternative minimum tax (AMT)

incurred. In computing AMTI, however, these expenditures must be capitalized and amortized ratably over the three-year period beginning with the year in which the expenditures were made.

EXAMPLE 16

Bobwhite, Inc., a personal holding company, incurred circulation expenditures of $30,000 in 1999. For income tax purposes, Bobwhite deducts $30,000 in 1999. For AMT purposes, the corporation is required to capitalize the expenditures and amortize them over a three-year period. Therefore, the deduction for AMT purposes is only $10,000. The AMT adjustment for 1999 is computed as follows.

Circulation expenditures deducted for income tax purposes	$30,000
Circulation expenditures deducted for AMT purposes	10,000
AMT adjustment (positive)	$20,000

EXAMPLE 17

Assume the same facts as in Example 16. The timing difference that gave rise to the positive adjustment in 1999 will reverse in the future. For AMT purposes, Bobwhite will deduct $10,000 in 2000 and $10,000 in 2001. The income tax deduction for circulation expenditures in each of those years will be $0, because the entire $30,000 expenditure was deducted in 1999. This results in a negative AMT adjustment of $10,000 each in 2000 and 2001. The AMT adjustments over the three-year period are summarized below.

Year	Income Tax Deduction	AMT Deduction	AMT Adjustment
1999	$30,000	$10,000	$ 20,000
2000	–0–	10,000	(10,000)
2001	–0–	10,000	(10,000)
Totals	$30,000	$30,000	$ –0–

Timing differences eventually reverse. Thus, positive AMT adjustments can be offset later by negative adjustments. ▼

TAX IN THE NEWS

THE AMT MAY HARM THE U.S. STEEL INDUSTRY

According to a recent release by the American Iron and Steel Institute, the AMT has had an adverse impact on steel and other marginally profitable capital-intensive industries. In one five-year period, a U.S. steel company reported $1.2 billion in losses to shareholders yet paid $200 million in AMT.

Most of the machinery and equipment used by a steel company is subject to 7-year capital cost recovery periods with 200 percent declining-balance depreciation under the regular corporate tax. For AMT purposes, however, taxpayers must use 15-year lives with 150 percent declining-balance depreciation.

Thus, the U.S. tax law may place U.S. businesses at a competitive disadvantage in world trade. Under the AMT, a U.S. steel company can recover only 37 percent of its investment in casting equipment in five years. This is to be contrasted with 58 percent in Japan, 81 percent in Germany, 90 percent in Korea, and 100 percent in Brazil. In the steel industry, advances in technology require a steady stream of investment in new equipment just to stay competitive. American companies have a more difficult time recovering the investment they must make to move to the next generation of technology.

Congress responded to this potential inequity with a change in the law that will benefit the steel industry. For tax years after 1998, the depreciation adjustment for real estate is eliminated, and the adjustment for depreciation of personal property is reduced. As a result, regular tax depreciation lives will be used for AMT purposes.

TAX PREFERENCES

LEARNING OBJECTIVE 4
Calculate the tax preferences that are included in calculating the AMT.

AMTI includes designated **tax preference items.** In many cases, this part of the AMT formula has the effect of subjecting otherwise nontaxable income to the AMT. Tax preferences always increase AMTI. Some of the principal tax preferences are discussed below.

Percentage Depletion. Congress originally enacted the percentage depletion rules to provide taxpayers with incentives to invest in the development of specified natural resources. Percentage depletion is computed by multiplying a rate specified in the Code times the gross income from the property (refer to Chapter 4). The percentage rate is based on the type of mineral involved. The basis of the property is reduced by the amount of depletion taken until the basis reaches zero. However, once the basis of the property reaches zero, taxpayers are allowed to continue taking percentage depletion deductions. Thus, over the life of the property, depletion deductions may greatly exceed the cost of the property.

The percentage depletion preference is equal to the excess of the regular income tax deduction for percentage depletion over the adjusted basis of the property at the end of the taxable year.[18] Basis is determined without regard to the depletion deduction for the taxable year. This preference item is figured separately for each piece of property for which the taxpayer is claiming depletion.

---

[18] § 57(a)(1). Percentage depletion on oil and gas wells taken by independent producers and royalty owners does not create an AMT preference. See § 613A(c).

CHAPTER 13 Business Tax Credits and Corporate Alternative Minimum Tax

EXAMPLE 18

Finch, Inc., owns a mineral property that qualifies for a 22% depletion rate. The basis of the property at the beginning of the year is $10,000. Gross income from the property for the year is $100,000. For regular income tax purposes, Finch's percentage depletion deduction (assume it is not limited by taxable income from the property) is $22,000. For AMT purposes, Finch has a tax preference of $12,000 ($22,000 − $10,000).

Intangible Drilling Costs. In computing the regular income tax, taxpayers are allowed to deduct certain intangible drilling and development costs in the year incurred, although such costs are normally capital in nature. The deduction is allowed for costs incurred in connection with oil and gas wells and geothermal wells.

For AMT purposes, excess intangible drilling costs (IDC) for the year are treated as a preference.[19] The preference for excess IDC is computed as follows.

> IDC expensed in the year incurred
> **Minus:** Deduction if IDC were capitalized and amortized over 10 years
> **Equals:** Excess of IDC expense over amortization
> **Minus:** 65% of net oil and gas and geothermal income
> **Equals:** Tax preference item

EXAMPLE 19

Nuthatch, Inc., incurred IDC of $50,000 during the year and elected to expense that amount. Net oil and gas income for the year was $60,000. Nuthatch's tax preference for IDC is $6,000 [($50,000 IDC − $5,000 10-year amortization) − (65% × $60,000 income)].

A taxpayer can avoid the preference for IDC by electing to amortize the expenditures over a 10-year period for regular income tax purposes.

Interest on Private Activity Bonds. Income from private activity bonds is not included in taxable income, and expenses related to carrying such bonds are not deductible for regular income tax purposes. However, interest on private activity bonds is included as a preference in computing AMTI. Expenses incurred in carrying the bonds are offset against the interest income in computing the tax preference.[20]

The Code contains a lengthy, complex definition of **private activity bonds**.[21] In general, such debt is issued by states or municipalities, but more than 10 percent of the proceeds are used to benefit private business. For example, a bond issued by a city whose proceeds are used to construct a factory that is leased to a private business at a favorable rate is a private activity bond.

AMT ADJUSTMENTS

5 LEARNING OBJECTIVE
Identify and calculate AMT adjustments.

As Exhibit 13–2 (page 13–15) indicates, the starting point for computing AMTI is the taxable income of the corporation before any NOL deduction. Certain *adjustments* must be made to this amount. Unlike tax preference items, which always increase AMTI, the adjustments may be either increases or decreases to taxable income.

---
[19] § 57(a)(2).
[20] § 57(a)(5).
[21] § 141.

> ### TAX IN THE NEWS
>
> #### MUNICIPAL BONDS AND THE AMT
>
> A number of investment and tax advisers are warning investors who have municipal bonds in their portfolios (either directly or through mutual funds) that the bonds may not be as tax-exempt as they think.
>
> More and more taxpayers are likely to become subject to the AMT in the future, with municipal bond investors being among the hardest hit. Private activity bond interest that is tax-exempt for regular income tax purposes is subject to taxation under the AMT. A prime reason investors are attracted to private activity bonds is that they offer a higher yield than other municipal bonds. But if the interest results in the taxpayer paying the AMT, this seemingly higher yield might actually be lower.

Although NOLs are separately stated in Exhibit 13–2, they are actually negative adjustments. They are separately stated in Exhibit 13–2 and on Form 4626 because they may not exceed more than 90 percent of AMTI. Thus, such adjustments cannot be determined until all other adjustments and tax preference items are considered.

Computing Adjustments. It is necessary to determine not only the amount of an adjustment, but also whether the adjustment is positive or negative. Careful study of Examples 16 and 17 reveals the following pattern with regard to *deductions*.

- If the deduction allowed for regular income tax purposes exceeds the deduction allowed for AMT purposes, the difference is a positive adjustment.
- If the deduction allowed for AMT purposes exceeds the deduction allowed for regular income tax purposes, the difference is a negative adjustment.

Conversely, the direction of an adjustment attributable to an *income* item can be determined as follows.

- If the income reported for regular income tax purposes exceeds the income reported for AMT purposes, the difference is a negative adjustment.
- If the income reported for AMT purposes exceeds the income reported for regular income tax purposes, the difference is a positive adjustment.

The principal AMT adjustments are discussed below.

Depreciation of Post-1986 Real Property. For real property placed in service after 1986 (MACRS property) and before 1999, AMT depreciation is computed under the alternative depreciation system (ADS), which uses the straight-line method over a 40-year life. The depreciation lives for regular tax purposes are 27.5 years for residential rental property and 39 years for all other real property.[22] The difference between AMT depreciation and regular income tax depreciation is treated as an adjustment in computing the AMT. The differences will be positive during the regular income tax life of the asset because the cost is written off over a shorter period for regular income tax purposes. For example, during the 27.5-year income tax life of residential real property, the regular income tax depreciation will exceed

---
[22]The 39-year life generally applies to nonresidential real property placed in service on or after May 13, 1993.

the AMT depreciation because AMT depreciation is computed over a 40-year period.

Table 4–3 is used to compute regular income tax depreciation on real property placed in service after 1986. For AMT purposes, depreciation on real property placed in service after 1986 is computed under the ADS (refer to Table 4–7).

EXAMPLE 20

In January 1998, Robin Rentals placed in service a residential building that cost $100,000. Depreciation for 1998 for regular income tax purposes is $3,485 ($100,000 cost × 3.485% from Table 4–3). For AMT purposes, depreciation is $2,396 ($100,000 cost × 2.396% from Table 4–7). In computing AMTI for 1998, Robin has a positive adjustment of $1,089 ($3,485 regular income tax depreciation − $2,396 AMT depreciation). ▼

After real property has been held for the entire depreciation period for regular income tax purposes, the asset will be fully depreciated. However, the depreciation period under the ADS is 41 years due to application of the half-year convention, so depreciation will continue for AMT purposes. This causes negative adjustments after the property has been fully depreciated for regular income tax purposes.

EXAMPLE 21

Assume the same facts as in the previous example. Regular income tax depreciation in the year 2026 (the twenty-ninth year of the asset's life) is zero (refer to Table 4–3). AMT depreciation is $2,500 ($100,000 cost × 2.500% from Table 4–7). Therefore, Robin has a negative AMT adjustment of $2,500 ($0 regular income tax depreciation − $2,500 AMT depreciation). ▼

After real property is fully depreciated for both regular income tax and AMT purposes, the positive and negative adjustments that have been made for AMT purposes will net to zero.

No AMT adjustment is computed for realty placed in service after 1998.[23]

Depreciation of Post-1986 Personal Property. For most personal property placed in service after 1986 (MACRS property), the MACRS deduction for regular income tax purposes is based on the 200 percent declining-balance method with a switch to straight-line when that method produces a larger depreciation deduction for the asset. Refer to Table 4–1 for computing regular income tax depreciation.

For AMT purposes, the taxpayer must use the ADS. This method is based on the 150 percent declining-balance method with a similar switch to straight-line for all personal property.[24] Refer to Table 4–5 for percentages to be used in computing AMT depreciation.

The MACRS deduction for personal property is larger than the ADS deduction in the early years of an asset's life. However, the ADS deduction is larger in the later years. This is so because ADS lives are sometimes longer than MACRS lives.[25] Over the ADS life of the asset, the same amount of depreciation is deducted for both regular income tax and AMT purposes. In the same manner as other timing adjustments, the AMT adjustments for depreciation will net to zero over the ADS life of the asset.

The taxpayer may elect to use the ADS for regular income tax purposes. If this election is made, no AMT adjustment is required because the depreciation deduction is the same for regular income tax and for the AMT. The election eliminates the burden of maintaining two sets of tax depreciation records at the cost of a higher regular tax liability.

---

[23] § 56(a)(1)(A)(i).
[24] § 56(a)(1).

[25] Class lives and recovery periods are established for all assets in Rev.Proc. 87–56, 1987–2 C.B. 674.

Pollution Control Facilities. For regular income tax purposes, the cost of certified pollution control facilities may be amortized over a period of 60 months. For AMT purposes, the cost of these facilities placed in service after 1986 and before 1999 is depreciated under the ADS over the appropriate class life, determined as explained above for depreciation of post-1986 property.[26] The required adjustment for AMTI is the difference between the amortization deduction allowed for regular income tax purposes and the depreciation deduction computed under the ADS. The adjustment may be positive or negative.

Mining Exploration and Development Expenditures. An income tax deduction is allowed for expenditures paid or incurred during the taxable year for *exploration* (ascertaining the existence, location, extent, or quality of a deposit or mineral) and for development of a mine or other natural deposit, other than an oil or gas well.[27] Mining *development* expenditures are expenses paid or incurred after the existence of ores and minerals in commercially marketable quantities has been determined.

For AMT purposes, however, mining exploration and development costs are capitalized and amortized ratably over a 10-year period.[28] The AMT adjustment for mining exploration and development costs is equal to the amount expensed minus the allowable expense if the costs had been capitalized and amortized ratably over a 10-year period. This provision does not apply to costs relating to an oil or gas well.

EXAMPLE 22

In 1999, Eagle Mining Company incurs $150,000 of mining exploration expenditures and deducts this amount for regular income tax purposes. For AMT purposes, these mining exploration expenditures must be amortized over a 10-year period. Eagle must make a positive adjustment for AMTI of $135,000 ($150,000 allowed for regular income tax − $15,000 for AMT) for 1999, the first year. In each of the next nine years for AMT purposes, Eagle is required to make a negative adjustment of $15,000 ($0 allowed for regular income tax − $15,000 for AMT). ▼

To avoid the AMT adjustments for mining exploration and development costs, a taxpayer may elect to amortize the expenditures over a 10-year period for regular income tax purposes.[29]

Use of Completed Contract Method of Accounting. For a long-term contract, taxpayers are required to use the percentage of completion method for AMT purposes.[30] However, in limited circumstances, taxpayers can use the completed contract method for regular income tax purposes.[31] The resulting AMT adjustment is equal to the difference between income reported under the percentage of completion method and the amount reported using the completed contract method.[32] The adjustment can be either positive or negative, depending on the amount of income recognized under the different methods.

A taxpayer can avoid an AMT adjustment on long-term contracts by using the percentage of completion method for regular income tax purposes rather than the completed contract method.

---

[26] § 56(a)(5).
[27] §§ 617(a) and 616(a).
[28] § 56(a)(2).
[29] §§ 59(e)(2)(D) and (E).
[30] § 56(a)(3).
[31] See Chapter 6 for a detailed discussion of the completed contract and percentage of completion methods of accounting.
[32] § 56(a)(3).

Adjusted Gain or Loss. When property is sold during the year or a casualty occurs to business or income-producing property, gain or loss reported for regular income tax may be different than gain or loss determined for the AMT. This difference occurs because the adjusted basis of the property for AMT purposes must reflect any current and prior AMT adjustments for the following.[33]

- Depreciation.
- Circulation expenditures.
- Mining exploration and development costs.
- Amortization of certified pollution control facilities.

A negative gain or loss adjustment is required if:

- the gain for AMT purposes is less than the gain for regular income tax purposes;
- the loss for AMT purposes is more than the loss for regular income tax purposes; or
- a loss is computed for AMT purposes and a gain is computed for regular income tax purposes.

Otherwise, the AMT gain or loss adjustment is positive.

EXAMPLE 23

In January 1998, Cardinal Corporation paid $100,000 for a duplex acquired for rental purposes. Regular income tax depreciation in 1998 was $3,485 ($100,000 cost × 3.485% from Table 4–3). AMT depreciation was $2,396 ($100,000 cost × 2.396% from Table 4–7). For AMT purposes, Cardinal made a positive adjustment of $1,089 ($3,485 regular income tax depreciation − $2,396 AMT depreciation).

Cardinal then sold the duplex on December 20, 1999, for $105,000. Regular income tax depreciation for 1999 is $3,485 [($100,000 cost × 3.636% from Table 4–3) × ($11.5/12$)]. AMT depreciation for 1999 is $2,396 [($100,000 cost × 2.500% from Table 4–7) × ($11.5/12$)]. Cardinal's positive AMT adjustment for 1999 is $1,089 ($3,485 regular income tax depreciation − $2,396 AMT depreciation).

Because depreciation on the duplex differs for regular income tax and AMT purposes, Cardinal's adjusted basis for the property is different for regular income tax and AMT purposes. Consequently, the gain or loss on disposition of the duplex is different for regular income tax and AMT purposes.

The adjusted basis of Cardinal's duplex for regular income tax purposes is $93,030 ($100,000 cost − $3,485 depreciation for 1998 − $3,485 depreciation for 1999). For AMT purposes, the adjusted basis is $95,208 ($100,000 cost − $2,396 depreciation for 1998 − $2,396 depreciation for 1999). The regular income tax gain is $11,970 ($105,000 amount realized − $93,030 regular income tax basis). The AMT gain is $9,792 ($105,000 amount realized − $95,208 AMT basis). Because the regular income tax and AMT gain on the sale of the duplex differ, Cardinal makes a negative AMT adjustment of $2,178 ($11,970 regular income tax gain − $9,792 AMT gain). The negative adjustment matches the $2,178 total of the two positive adjustments for depreciation ($1,089 in 1998 + $1,089 in 1999). ▼

Passive Activity Losses. Net losses on passive activities are not deductible in computing either the regular income tax or the AMT for individuals, closely held C corporations, and personal service corporations. This does not, however, eliminate the possibility of adjustments attributable to passive activities.

The rules for computing taxable income differ from the rules for computing AMTI. It follows, then, that the rules for computing a loss for regular income tax purposes differ from the AMT rules for computing a loss. Therefore, any *passive*

---

[33] § 56(a)(6).

loss computed for regular income tax purposes may differ from the passive loss computed for AMT purposes.

EXAMPLE 24

Robin, Inc., a personal service corporation, acquired two passive activities in 1999. Robin received net passive income of $10,000 from Activity A and had no AMT adjustments or preferences in connection with the activity. Activity B had gross income of $27,000 and operating expenses (not affected by AMT adjustments or preferences) of $19,000. Robin claimed MACRS depreciation of $20,000 for Activity B; depreciation under the ADS would have been $15,000. In addition, Robin deducted $10,000 of percentage depletion in excess of basis. The following comparison illustrates the differences in the computation of the passive loss for regular income tax and AMT purposes for Activity B.

	Regular Income Tax	AMT
Gross income	$ 27,000	$ 27,000
Deductions:		
Operating expenses	($ 19,000)	($ 19,000)
Depreciation	(20,000)	(15,000)
Depletion	(10,000)	–0–
Total deductions	($ 49,000)	($ 34,000)
Passive loss	($ 22,000)	($ 7,000)

Because the adjustment for depreciation ($5,000) applies and the preference for depletion ($10,000) is not taken into account in computing AMTI, the regular income tax passive activity loss of $22,000 for Activity B is reduced by these amounts, resulting in a passive activity loss of $7,000 for AMT purposes.

For regular income tax purposes, Robin would offset the $10,000 of net passive income from Activity A with $10,000 of the passive loss from Activity B. For AMT purposes, the corporation would offset the $10,000 of net passive income from Activity A with the $7,000 passive activity loss allowed from Activity B, resulting in passive activity income of $3,000. Thus, in computing AMTI, Robin makes a positive passive loss adjustment of $3,000 [$10,000 (passive activity loss allowed for regular income tax) – $7,000 (passive activity loss allowed for the AMT)].[34]

For regular income tax purposes, Robin, Inc., has a suspended passive loss of $12,000 [$22,000 (amount of loss) – $10,000 (used in 1999)]. This suspended passive loss can offset passive income in the future or can offset active or portfolio income when the corporation disposes of the loss activity (refer to Chapter 5). For AMT purposes, Robin's suspended passive loss is $0 [$7,000 (amount of loss) – $7,000 (amount used in 1999)]. ▼

PLANNING CONSIDERATIONS

Avoiding Preferences and Adjustments

Investments in state and local bonds are attractive for income tax purposes because the interest is not included in gross income. Some of these bonds are issued to generate funds that are not used for an essential function of the government (e.g., to provide infrastructure for shopping malls or industrial parks or to build sports facilities). The interest on such bonds is a tax preference item and could lead to the imposition of the AMT. When

---

[34] The depreciation adjustment and depletion preference are combined as part of the passive loss adjustment and are *not* reported separately.

the AMT applies, investors should take this factor into account. Perhaps an investment in regular tax-exempt bonds or even fully taxed private-sector bonds might yield a higher after-tax rate of return.

For a corporation anticipating AMT problems, capitalizing rather than expensing certain costs can avoid generating preferences and adjustments. The decision should be based on the present discounted value of after-tax cash flows under the available alternatives. Costs that may be capitalized and amortized, rather than expensed, include circulation expenditures, mining exploration and development costs, and research and experimentation expenditures.

ADJUSTED CURRENT EARNINGS (ACE)

LEARNING OBJECTIVE 6
Understand the function of adjusted current earnings (ACE).

The **adjusted current earnings (ACE)** rules make up a third, separate tax system, parallel to both AMT and taxable income. S corporations, real estate investment trusts, regulated investment companies, and real estate mortgage investment conduits are not subject to the ACE provisions.

The purpose of the ACE adjustment is to ensure that the mismatching of financial statement income and taxable income will not produce inequitable results. ACE represents another attempt by Congress to assure that large corporations with significant financial accounting income pay a fair share of Federal corporate income tax.

The ACE adjustment is tax-based and can be negative or positive. AMTI is increased by 75 percent of the excess of ACE over unadjusted AMTI, or AMTI is reduced by 75 percent of the excess of unadjusted AMTI over ACE. Any negative ACE adjustment is limited to the aggregate of the positive adjustments under ACE for prior years reduced by the previously claimed negative adjustments (see Figure 13–1).[35] Any unused negative adjustment is lost forever.

EXAMPLE 25

A calendar year corporation reports the following.

	1998	1999	2000
Unadjusted AMTI	$3,000,000	$3,000,000	$3,100,000
Adjusted current earnings	4,000,000	3,000,000	2,000,000

In 1998, since ACE exceeds unadjusted AMTI by $1 million, $750,000 (75% × $1,000,000) is the positive ACE adjustment. No adjustment is necessary for 1999. Unadjusted AMTI exceeds ACE by $1,100,000 in 2000, so there is a potential negative ACE adjustment of $825,000. Since the total increases to AMTI for prior years equal $750,000 (and there are no negative adjustments), only $750,000 of the potential negative ACE adjustment reduces AMTI for 2000. Further, $75,000 of negative ACE is lost forever. ▼

The starting point for computing ACE is AMTI, which is regular taxable income after AMT adjustments (other than the NOL and ACE adjustments) and tax preferences.[36] Pre-NOL AMTI is adjusted for the following items to determine ACE.

- *Exclusion items.* These are income items (net of related expenses) that are included in E & P, but never will be included in regular taxable income or AMTI (except on liquidation or disposal of a business). In essence, items

---

[35] §§ 56(g)(1) and (2). *Unadjusted AMTI* is AMTI before the ACE adjustment and the AMT NOL deduction.

[36] § 56(g)(3).

▼ FIGURE 13–1
Determining the ACE Adjustment*

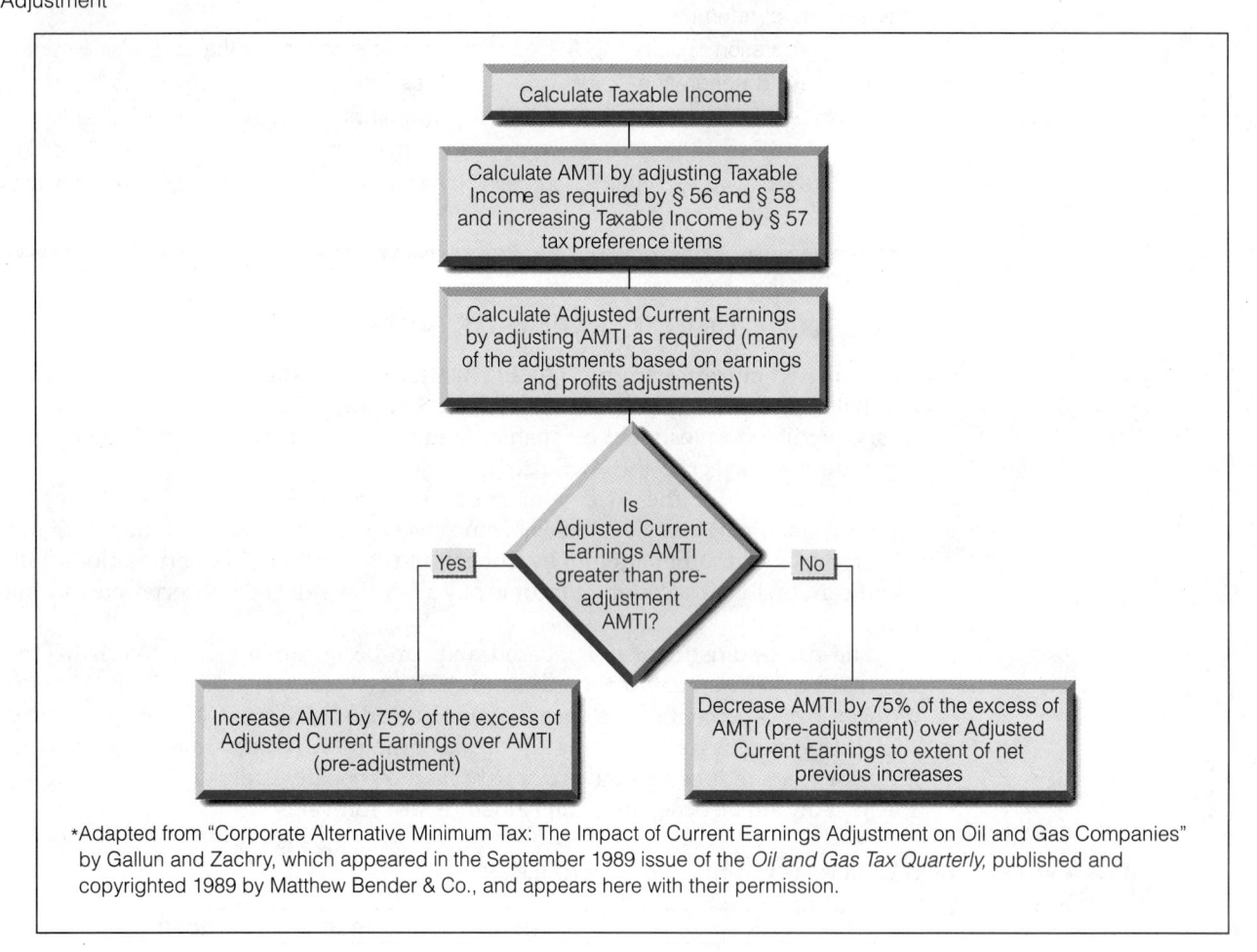

```
                    Calculate Taxable Income
                              │
                              ▼
              Calculate AMTI by adjusting Taxable
              Income as required by § 56 and § 58
              and increasing Taxable Income by § 57
                      tax preference items
                              │
                              ▼
              Calculate Adjusted Current Earnings
              by adjusting AMTI as required (many
              of the adjustments based on earnings
                    and profits adjustments)
                              │
                              ▼
                              Is
                      Adjusted Current
              Yes     Earnings AMTI      No
              ◄───    greater than pre-  ───►
                        adjustment
                          AMTI?

  Increase AMTI by 75% of the excess of    Decrease AMTI by 75% of the excess of
  Adjusted Current Earnings over AMTI      AMTI (pre-adjustment) over Adjusted
         (pre-adjustment)                  Current Earnings to extent of net
                                                    previous increases
```

*Adapted from "Corporate Alternative Minimum Tax: The Impact of Current Earnings Adjustment on Oil and Gas Companies" by Gallun and Zachry, which appeared in the September 1989 issue of the *Oil and Gas Tax Quarterly*, published and copyrighted 1989 by Matthew Bender & Co., and appears here with their permission.

that are permanently excluded from unadjusted AMTI but are included in E & P are therefore included in ACE (e.g., life insurance proceeds, interest on tax-exempt bonds, and tax benefit exclusions).

- *Depreciation.* For property placed in service before 1994, depreciation is calculated using the straight-line method over ADS useful lives. For property placed in service after 1993, the ACE depreciation adjustment is eliminated. This change will speed up the ACE depreciation allowance for capital-intensive industries, but computing the prior ACE depreciation adjustment for pre-1994 assets remains complex.
- *Disallowed items.* A deduction is not allowed in computing ACE if it is never deductible in computing E & P. A deduction *is not allowed* for the dividends received deduction of 70 percent (less than 20 percent ownership). A deduction *is allowed* for the dividends received deduction of 80 percent (20 percent but less than 80 percent ownership) and 100 percent (80 percent or more ownership).[37]
- *Other adjustments.* Additional adjustments, which are required for regular E & P purposes, are applied to arrive at ACE. These rules eliminate the tax

---

[37] §§ 56(g)(4)(C)(i) and (ii).

benefits of using intangible drilling costs, circulation expenditures, organization expense amortization, and installment sales.[38]
- *Both AMTI and ACE.* Items must be deductible for both AMTI *and* E & P purposes to be deductible for ACE. Thus, certain deductible items do not reduce ACE: excess charitable contributions, excess capital losses, disallowed travel and entertainment expenses, penalties, fines, bribes, and golden parachute payments.
- *Lessee improvements.* The value of improvements made by a lessee to a lessor's property that is excluded from the lessor's income is excluded from both unadjusted AMTI and ACE.
- *LIFO recapture adjustments.* An increase or decrease in the LIFO recapture amount will result in a corresponding increase or decrease in ACE.

EXAMPLE 26

Crimson Corporation makes the ACE adjustment calculation as follows.

AMTI		$5,780,000
Plus:		
Municipal bond interest	$210,000	
Installment gain	140,000	
70% dividends received deduction	300,000	
Income element in cash surrender life insurance	60,000	
Organization expense amortization	70,000	780,000
Subtotal		$6,560,000
Less:		
ACE depreciation in excess of amount allowed for AMTI (property placed in service before 1994)	$230,000	
Life insurance expense	10,000	240,000
Adjusted current earnings		$6,320,000
AMTI		−5,780,000
Base amount		$ 540,000
Times		.75
ACE adjustment (positive)		$ 405,000

ACE should not be confused with current earnings and profits (E & P). Many items are treated in the same manner, but certain items that are deductible in computing E & P (but are not deductible in calculating taxable income) generally are not deductible in computing ACE (e.g., Federal income taxes). Concept Summary 13–2 compares the impact various transactions will have on the determination of ACE and E & P.

COMPUTING ALTERNATIVE MINIMUM TAXABLE INCOME

LEARNING OBJECTIVE 7
Compute the AMT liability for corporations.

The following comprehensive example illustrates the effect of tax preferences and adjustments in arriving at AMTI.

---
[38]Reg. § 1.65(g)–1(f).

Concept Summary 13–2

Impact of Various Transactions on ACE and E & P

	Effect on Unadjusted AMTI in Arriving at ACE	Effect on Taxable Income in Arriving at E & P
Tax-exempt income (net of expenses)	Add	Add
Federal income tax	No effect	Subtract
Dividends received deduction (80% and 100% rules)	No effect	Add
Dividends received deduction (70% rule)	Add	Add
Exemption amount of $40,000	No effect	No effect
Key employee insurance proceeds	Add	Add
Excess charitable contribution	No effect	Subtract
Excess capital losses	No effect	Subtract
Disallowed travel and entertainment expenses	No effect	Subtract
Penalties and fines	No effect	Subtract
Intangible drilling costs deducted currently	Add	Add
Deferred gain on installment sales	Add	Add
Realized (not recognized) gain on an involuntary conversion	No effect	No effect
Loss on sale between related parties	Subtract	Subtract
Gift received	No effect	No effect
Net buildup on life insurance policy	Add	Add

EXAMPLE 27

For 1999, Tan Corporation (a calendar year, integrated oil company) had the following transactions.

Taxable income	$6,000,000
Mining exploration costs	500,000
Percentage depletion claimed (the property has a zero adjusted basis)	700,000
Donation of land held since 1980 as an investment (basis of $400,000 and fair market value of $500,000) to a qualified charity	500,000
Interest on City of Elmira (Michigan) bonds. The proceeds were used for nongovernmental purposes	300,000

Tan Corporation's AMTI for 1999 is determined as follows.

Taxable income		$6,000,000
Adjustments		
Excess mining exploration costs [$500,000 (amount expensed) − $50,000 (amount allowed over a 10-year amortization period)]		450,000
Tax preferences		
Excess depletion deduction	$700,000	
Interest on private activity municipal bonds	300,000	1,000,000
AMTI		$7,450,000

PLANNING CONSIDERATIONS

Optimum Use of the AMT and Regular Corporate Income Tax Rate Difference

A corporation that cannot avoid the AMT in a particular year often can save taxes by taking advantage of the difference between the AMT and the regular tax rates. In general, a corporation that expects to be subject to the AMT should consider accelerating income and deferring deductions for the remainder of the year. Since the difference between the regular tax and the AMT may be as much as 14 or 15 percentage points, this strategy may result in the income being taxed at less than it would be if reported in the next year. If the same corporation expects to be subject to the AMT for the next year (or years), this technique should be reversed.

EXAMPLE 28

Falcon Corporation expects to be in the 34% tax bracket in 2000 but is subject to the AMT in 1999. In late 1999, Falcon is contemplating selling a tract of unimproved land (basis of $200,000 and fair market value of $1 million). Under these circumstances, it may be preferable to sell the land in 1999. The gain of $800,000 ($1,000,000 – $200,000) generates a tax of $160,000 [$800,000 (recognized gain) × 20% (AMT rate)]. However, if the land is sold in 2000, the resulting tax is $272,000 [$800,000 (recognized gain) × 34% (regular corporate income tax rate)]. A nominal savings of $112,000 ($272,000 – $160,000) materializes by making the sale in 1999. ▼

Whenever one accelerates income or defers deductions, a present value analysis should be conducted. This technique is attractive only if it reduces the present value of tax liabilities.

EXEMPTION

The AMT is 20 percent of the excess of AMTI over an exemption amount. The exemption amount for a corporation is $40,000 reduced by 25 percent of the amount by which AMTI exceeds $150,000. The exemption phases out entirely when AMTI reaches $310,000.

EXAMPLE 29

Beige Corporation has AMTI of $180,000. Since the exemption amount is reduced by $7,500 [25% × ($180,000 – $150,000)], the amount remaining is $32,500 ($40,000 – $7,500). Thus, Beige Corporation's alternative minimum tax base (refer to Exhibit 13–2) is $147,500 ($180,000 – $32,500). ▼

PLANNING CONSIDERATIONS

Controlling the Timing of Preferences and Adjustments

In many situations, corporations with modest levels of income may be able to avoid the AMT by making use of the exemption. To maximize the exemption, taxpayers should attempt to avoid bunching positive adjustments and tax preferences in any one year. Rather, net these items against negative adjustments to keep AMTI low. When the expenditure is largely within the control of the taxpayer, timing to avoid bunching is more easily accomplished.

MINIMUM TAX CREDIT

The **minimum tax credit** acts to make the AMT merely a *prepayment of tax* for corporations. Essentially, the AMT paid in one tax year may be carried forward indefinitely and used as a credit against the corporation's future *regular* tax liability that exceeds its tentative minimum tax. The minimum tax credit may not be carried back and may not be offset against any future *minimum* tax liability.

EXAMPLE 30

Return to the facts of Example 27. AMTI exceeds $310,000, so there is no exemption amount. The tentative minimum tax is $1,490,000 (20% of $7,450,000). Assuming that Tan's regular tax liability for 1999 is $1,400,000, the AMT liability is $90,000 ($1,490,000 − $1,400,000). The minimum tax credit carried forward is $90,000, the current year's AMT. The credit can be used to reduce regular tax liability in future years (but not below the tentative alternative minimum tax). ▼

OTHER ASPECTS OF THE AMT

In addition to paying their regular tax liability, corporations must make estimated tax payments of the AMT liability. Even corporations that prepare quarterly financial statements may find this requirement adds to compliance costs.

The only credit that can be used to offset the AMT is the foreign tax credit (FTC). The general business credit and other credits discussed earlier in the chapter are unavailable in AMT years. The AMT FTC can reduce the tax by only 90 percent, reduced by the percent of AMTI that was offset by the AMT NOL.

EXAMPLE 31

An AMT taxpayer can use both the NOL and the FTC to reduce the year's AMT liability, but only to a maximum 90% reduction. Lake Corporation's AMTI before the AMT NOL deduction is $1 million. It applies a $400,000 AMT NOL to reduce its tax base. As a result, the maximum AMT FTC that Lake can claim is $100,000 [20% AMT rate × $500,000 AMTI remaining of the 90% possible reduction]. AMT taxpayers can use both the NOL deduction and the FTC to reduce the liability payable for a tax year, but the NOL is applied first, and the two provisions "share" the 90% tax reduction that they can create. ▼

The AMT is computed and reported by completing Form 4626.

PLANNING CONSIDERATIONS

The Subchapter S Option

Corporations that make the S election are not subject to the corporate AMT. As noted in Chapter 12, however, various AMT adjustments and preferences pass through to the individual shareholders. But one troublesome adjustment, the one involving the ACE adjustment, is eliminated since it does not apply to individual taxpayers.

THE INDIVIDUAL ALTERNATIVE MINIMUM TAX

The AMT applicable to individuals is similar to the corporate AMT. Most of the adjustments and preferences discussed above apply equally to individuals and corporations. However, there are several important differences.

TAX IN THE NEWS

THE AMT AND INFLATION

The AMT contains exemptions for the different taxpayer filing statuses. When the taxpayer's income reaches a certain amount, the exemption is subject to a phase-out.

Neither the AMT exemption nor the AMT rates are subject to indexing. Currently, only about 600,000 (0.5 percent) individual income tax returns must pay the AMT. Kenneth Kies, chief of staff of Congress's Joint Tax Committee, estimates that by 2006, the absence of indexing and the progressive AMT rates will cause about 6.2 million (4.5 percent) individual income tax returns to be subject to the AMT.

Several proposals were made to include an indexing provision for the AMT in the Taxpayer Relief Act of 1997, but none of them was included in the legislation that was enacted.

SOURCE: Adapted from Tom Herman, "Chances Improve for Important Changes in the Alternative Minimum Tax," *Wall Street Journal*, May 21, 1997, p. A1.

- The individual AMT rate is slightly progressive, with rates at 26 percent on the first $175,000 of AMTI and at 28 percent on any additional AMTI.
- The AMT exemption and phase-out amounts are tied to the individual's filing status for the year. The exemption phases out at a rate of $1 for every $4 of AMTI.

Filing Status	Initial Exemption Amount	Phase-Out Range Begins at	Phase-Out Range Ends at
Married, joint	$45,000	$150,000	$330,000
Married, separate	22,500	75,000	165,000
Single, head of household	33,750	112,500	247,500

- Individuals make no AMT adjustment for ACE.
- Some additional adjustments apply to individual taxpayers. In particular, taxes and miscellaneous itemized deductions subject to the 2 percent-of-AGI floor are not allowed as deductions for AMTI. Medical expenses are allowed only to the extent that they exceed 10 percent of AGI (instead of a 7.5 percent limitation for regular tax purposes). Interest expense deductions are limited to qualified residence interest, interest on certain student loans, and investment interest (subject to limitations). Finally, the standard deduction and personal and dependency exemptions are not allowed as deductions when computing AMTI. Other individual-specific adjustments also exist, including an adjustment accelerating the taxation of incentive stock options.
- Determination of the minimum tax credit is more complex for individual taxpayers. The credit applies only to AMT generated as a result of timing differences.

Although there are several computational differences, the individual AMT and the corporate AMT have the same objective: to force taxpayers who have more economic income than that reflected in taxable income to pay a fair share of Federal income tax.

KEY TERMS

Adjusted current earnings (ACE), 13–23

Alternative minimum tax (AMT), 13–13

Alternative minimum taxable income (AMTI), 13–14

Business energy credits, 13–6

Disabled access credit, 13–11

Foreign tax credit (FTC), 13–11

General business credit, 13–3

Low-income housing credit, 13–10

Minimum tax credit, 13–28

Private activity bonds, 13–17

Rehabilitation expenditures credit, 13–5

Rehabilitation expenditures credit recapture, 13–6

Research activities credit, 13–8

Tax credits, 13–2

Tax preference items, 13–16

Welfare-to-work credit, 13–8

Work opportunity tax credit, 13–7

PROBLEM MATERIALS

1. Canary, Inc., has a tentative general business credit of $110,000 for 1998. Canary's net regular tax liability before the general business credit is $125,000, and its tentative minimum tax is $100,000. Compute Canary's allowable general business credit for the year.

2. Burt Corporation has the following general business credit carryovers.

1995	$10,000
1996	30,000
1997	10,000
1998	40,000
Total carryovers	$90,000

   If the general business credit generated by activities during 1999 equals $90,000 and the total credit allowed during the current year is $160,000 (based on tax liability), what amounts of the current general business credit and carryovers can Burt use against its 1999 income tax liability? What is the amount of unused credit carried forward to 2000?

3. In January 1997, Iris Corporation purchased and placed into service a 1933 building that houses retail businesses. The cost was $200,000, of which $25,000 applied to the land. In modernizing the facility, Iris Corporation incurred $250,000 of renovation costs of the type that qualify for the rehabilitation credit. These improvements were placed into service in October 1999.
   a. Compute Iris Corporation's rehabilitation tax credit for 1999.
   b. Calculate the cost recovery deductions for the building and the renovation costs for 1999.

4. In the current year, Diane Lawson (123 Sunview Avenue, Jacksonville, FL 32231) acquires a qualifying historic structure for $250,000 (excluding the cost of land) with full intentions of substantially rehabilitating the building. Write a letter to Diane and a memo to the tax files explaining the computation that determines the rehabilitation tax credit available to her and the impact on the depreciable basis, assuming either $245,000 or $255,000 is incurred for the rehabilitation project. Because Diane must decide whether to pursue the renovation plan costing $245,000 or the one costing $255,000, you should indicate in the letter and the memo the differences in cash flow to Diane arising from the tax consequences associated with the two renovation projects.

5. The tax credit for rehabilitation expenditures is available to help offset the costs related to substantially rehabilitating certain buildings. The credit is calculated on the rehabilitation expenditures incurred and not on the acquisition cost of the building itself.

   You are a developer who buys, sells, and does construction work on real estate in the inner city of your metropolitan area. A potential customer approaches you about acquiring one of your buildings that easily could qualify for the 20% rehabilitation credit on historic structures. The stated sales price of the structure is $100,000 (based on appraisals ranging from $80,000 to $120,000), and the rehabilitation expenditures, if the job is done correctly, would be about $150,000.

   Your business has been slow recently due to the sluggish real estate market in your area, and the potential customer makes the following proposal: if you reduce the sales price of the building to $75,000, he will pay you $175,000 to perform the rehabilitation work. Although the buyer's total expenditures would be the same, he would benefit from this approach by obtaining a larger tax credit ($25,000 increased rehabilitation costs × 20% = $5,000).

   It has been a long time since you have sold any of your real estate. How will you respond?

6. Red Company hires six individuals on January 15, 1998, qualifying Red for the work opportunity tax credit. Three of these individuals receive wages of $7,000 each during 1998, for working 700 hours each. The other three receive wages of $4,000 each, for working 300 hours each.
   a. Calculate the amount of Red's work opportunity tax credit for 1998.
   b. Assume Red pays total wages of $120,000 to its employees during the year. How much of this amount is deductible in 1998 if the work opportunity tax credit is taken?

7. In March 1998, Wren Corporation hired three individuals, Trent, Bernice, and Benita, all of whom are certified as long-term family assistance recipients. Each employee is paid $11,000 during 1998. Only Bernice continued to work for Wren in 1999, earning $13,500. In February 1999, Wren hired Cassie, who was also certified as a long-term family assistance recipient. During 1999, Cassie earned $12,000. Wren does not claim the work opportunity credit with respect to any employees hired in 1998 or 1999.
   a. Compute Wren's welfare-to-work credit for 1998 and 1999.
   b. Wren pays total wages of $325,000 to its employees during 1998 and $342,000 during 1999. How much may Wren claim as a wage deduction for 1998 and 1999 if the welfare-to-work credit is claimed in both years?

8. Martin, Inc., a calendar year taxpayer, informs you that during the year it incurs expenditures of $30,000 that qualify for the incremental research activities credit. In addition, it is determined that the corporation's base amount for the year is $22,800.
   a. Determine Martin's incremental research activities credit for the year.
   b. Martin is in the 25% tax bracket. Determine which approach to the research expenditures and the research activities credit would provide the greatest tax benefit to Martin.

9. John and Susie rent a unit at an apartment complex owned by Mitch Brown, who has been Susie's friend since they attended business school together. One day Mitch told John and Susie about the thousands of tax dollars that he has saved by claiming the low-income housing credit for his investment in the apartment complex. Susie was pleased that Mitch had reduced his tax burden because she believes that the government rarely uses its resources wisely. Inadvertently, though, Mitch let slip that the complex "qualified" for the credit only because he overstated the percentage of low-income tenants living in the facility. Mitch admitted that by claiming that John and Susie were low-income tenants (even though they weren't), the percentage of low-income tenants was just enough for Mitch to "qualify" for the credit. Mitch said that because John and Susie were his friends, he was passing along some of his tax savings to them in the form of lower rent.

   John and Susie know that if they report Mitch, he will not only lose the economic benefit of the credit, but he will also have legal troubles. Further, if Mitch were to be sentenced to prison for the tax fraud, his children would necessarily become guardians of the state. In addition, John and Susie would have to pay higher rent. Evaluate the courses of action available to John and Susie.

10. Ahmed Zinna (16 Southside Drive, Charlotte, NC 28204), one of your clients, owns two retail establishments in downtown Charlotte, North Carolina, and has come to you seeking advice concerning the tax consequences of complying with the Americans with Disabilities Act. He understands that he needs to install various features at his stores (e.g., ramps, doorways, and restrooms that are handicapped accessible) to make them more accessible to disabled individuals. He inquires whether any tax credits are available to help offset the cost of the necessary changes. He estimates the cost of the planned changes to his facilities as follows.

Location	Projected Cost
Oak Street	$18,000
Maple Avenue	8,000

He reminds you that the Oak Street store was constructed in 1995 while the Maple Avenue store is in a building that was constructed in 1902. Ahmed operates his business as a sole proprietorship and has approximately eight employees at each location. Write a letter to Ahmed in which you summarize your conclusions concerning the tax consequences of his proposed capital improvements.

11. Purple Corporation is an international wholesaler headquartered in the United States. Of its worldwide taxable income of $3 billion, $1.25 billion is foreign-sourced. Before any credits, Purple's U.S. income tax liability is $1.05 billion. If income taxes paid to foreign countries totaled $600 million, what is Purple's U.S. income tax liability after benefiting from the foreign tax credit?

12. In each of the following independent situations, determine whether the corporation is exempted from the AMT provisions.
    a. Gold Corporation has average gross receipts of $5.5 million, $4.7 million, and $4.6 million in 1997, 1998, and 1999, respectively.
    b. Silver Corporation has average gross receipts of $4.6 million, $5.5 million and $4.95 million in 1998, 1999, and 2000, respectively.
    c. Copper Corporation has average gross receipts of $4.7 million, 4.9 million, and $5.12 million in 1997, 1998, and 1999 respectively.

13. In March 1998, Grackle, Inc., acquired equipment for its business at a cost of $250,000. The equipment is 5-year class property for regular income tax purposes and 9.5-year class property for AMT purposes.
    a. If Grackle depreciates the equipment using the method that will produce the greatest deduction for 1998, what is the amount of the AMT adjustment?
    b. How can Grackle reduce the AMT adjustment to $0? What circumstances would motivate Grackle to do so?
    c. Draft a letter to Helen Carlon, Grackle's controller, regarding the choice of depreciation methods. Helen's address is 500 Monticello Avenue, Glendale, AZ 85306.

14. In 1999, Grebe, Inc., incurred $180,000 of mining and exploration expenditures. Grebe elects to deduct the expenditures as quickly as the tax law allows for regular income tax purposes.
    a. How will Grebe's treatment of mining and exploration expenditures affect its regular income tax and AMT computations for 1999?
    b. How can Grebe avoid having AMT adjustments related to the mining and exploration expenditures?
    c. What factors should Grebe consider in deciding whether to deduct the expenditures in the year incurred?

15. Josepi's construction company builds personal residences that qualify for the use of the completed contract method. During the three-year period 1998–2000, Josepi recognized the following income on his two construction contracts.

Year	Contract 1	Contract 2
1998	$600,000*	$ -0-
1999	-0-	-0-
2000	-0-	700,000**

*Construction completed in 1998.
**Construction completed in 2000.

If Josepi had used the percentage of completion method, he would have recognized the following gross income from the contracts.

Year	Contract 1	Contract 2
1998	$40,000	$175,000
1999	-0-	225,000
2000	-0-	300,000

Calculate Josepi's AMT adjustments for 1998, 1999, and 2000.

16. Bobolink, Inc., sells an apartment building for $500,000. Its adjusted basis is $300,000 for regular income tax purposes and $330,000 for AMT purposes.
    a. Calculate Bobolink's gain for regular income tax purposes.
    b. Calculate Bobolink's gain for AMT purposes.
    c. Calculate Bobolink's AMT adjustment, if any.

17. Flicker, Inc., a closely held corporation, acquired a passive activity in 1999. Gross income from operations of the activity was $150,000. Operating expenses, not including depreciation, were $135,000. Regular income tax depreciation of $37,500 was computed under MACRS. AMT depreciation, computed under ADS, was $24,000. Compute Flicker's passive loss deduction and passive loss suspended for regular income tax purposes and for AMT purposes.

18. In each of the following independent situations, determine the tentative minimum tax.

	AMTI (Before the Exemption Amount)
Crane Corp.	$120,000
Rider Corp.	170,000
Mallard Corp.	340,000

19. For 1999, Peach Corporation (a calendar year integrated oil company) had the following transactions.

Taxable income	$5,000,000
Regular tax depreciation on realty in excess of ADS (placed in service in 1989)	1,700,000
Amortization of certified pollution control facilities	200,000
Tax-exempt interest on municipal bonds (funds were used for nongovernmental purposes)	300,000
Percentage depletion in excess of the property's adjusted basis	700,000

a. Determine Peach Corporation's AMTI.
b. Determine the tentative minimum tax base (refer to Exhibit 13–2).
c. Determine the tentative minimum tax.
d. What is the amount of the AMT?

20. Maize Corporation (a calendar year corporation) reports the following information for the years listed below.

	1998	1999	2000
Unadjusted AMTI	$5,000,000	$5,000,000	$7,000,000
Adjusted current earnings	7,000,000	5,000,000	3,000,000

Compute the ACE adjustment for each year.

21. Based upon the following facts, calculate adjusted current earnings (ACE).

Alternative minimum taxable income (AMTI)	$5,120,000
Municipal bond interest	630,000
Expenses related to municipal bonds	50,000
Key employee life insurance proceeds in excess of cash surrender value	2,000,000
Excess of FIFO over LIFO	160,000
Organization expense amortization	100,000
Cost of goods sold	6,220,000
Advertising expenses	760,000
Loss between related parties	260,000
Life insurance expense	300,000

22. Orange Corporation, a calendar year taxpayer, reported the following amounts. Calculate Orange's positive and negative ACE adjustments.

	Preadjusted AMTI	ACE
1998	$80,000	$70,000
1999	60,000	90,000
2000	50,000	40,000
2001	50,000	10,000

23. Determine whether each of the following transactions is a preference (P), an adjustment (A), or not applicable (NA) for purposes of the corporate AMT.
    a. Depletion in excess of basis taken by Giant Oil Company.
    b. Accelerated depreciation on property placed in service after 1986.
    c. Mining exploration and development costs.
    d. Adjusted current earnings.
    e. Tax-exempt interest on private activity bonds.
    f. Untaxed appreciation on property donated to charity.
    g. Dividends received deduction.

24. Allie, who was an accounting major in college, is the controller of a medium-size construction corporation. She prepares the corporate tax return each year. Due to reporting a home construction contract using the completed contract method, the corporation is subject to the AMT in 1999. Allie files the 1999 corporate return in early February 2000. The total tax liability is $58,000 ($53,000 regular income tax liability + $5,000 AMT).

In early March, Allie reads an article on minimizing income taxes. Based on this article, she decides that it would be beneficial for the corporation to report the home construction contract using the percentage of completion method on its 1999 return. Although this will increase the corporation's 1999 income tax liability, it will minimize the total income tax liability over the two-year construction period. Therefore, Allie files an amended return on March 14, 2000. Evaluate Allie's actions from both a tax avoidance and an ethical perspective.

RESEARCH PROBLEMS

*Note: The **RIA OnPoint System 4 Student Version CD-ROM** available with this text can be used in preparing solutions to the Research Problems. Alternatively, tax research materials contained in a standard tax library can be used.*

25. Isabella, a lover of early twentieth-century American history and architecture, discovers a 1920s house in a downtown district of Atlanta during a recent visit. She decides not only to purchase and renovate this particular home, but also to move the structure to her hometown of Little Rock, Arkansas, so her community can enjoy its architectural features. Being aware of the availability of the tax credit for rehabilitation expenditures incurred on old structures, she wants to maximize her use of the provision once the renovation work begins in Arkansas. Comment on whether the renovation expenditures incurred will qualify for the tax credit for rehabilitation expenditures.

26. Oriole Corporation is a large wholesaler of office products. To remain successful in a fiercely competitive industry, Oriole has automated and computerized many of its business operations. Specifically, the corporation has developed several new software programs to:

    - Maintain files of customer histories.
    - Create a paperless invoicing system.
    - Develop a computer-to-computer order entry system.
    - Monitor inventory levels more closely.

    Oriole estimates that it spent more than $1 million to develop and test the new software programs that are used throughout the business. To date, Oriole has not sold the software programs to the public, but it is contemplating doing so. Oriole has claimed a research and experimentation deduction for the costs associated with developing the software programs. The corporation also wants to claim the research activities credit relating to the software development. Can Oriole do so? Write a memo to the tax research file summarizing your conclusions.

27. Lynn is single and has no dependents. Based on the financial information presented below, compute Lynn's AMT for the year.

Income:	
Salary	$33,000
Taxable interest on corporate bonds	1,800
Dividend income	1,900
Business income	64,000
Expenditures:	
Medical expenses	$12,000
State income taxes	6,000
Real estate taxes	8,500
Mortgage (qualified housing) interest	9,200
Investment interest	5,500
Cash contributions to qualified charities	2,900

    Additional information:
    a. The $64,000 business income is from Acme Office Supplies Company, a sole proprietorship Lynn owns and operates. Acme claimed MACRS depreciation of $3,175 on real property used in the business. ADS depreciation on the property would have been $2,500.
    b. Lynn received interest of $30,000 on City of Columbus private activity bonds.

28. Pat, who is single and has no dependents, had a salary of $90,000 this year. She had interest and dividend income of $6,000, gambling income of $4,000, and $40,000 interest income from private activity bonds. Pat presents the following additional information.

Medical expenses (before 7.5%-of-AGI floor)	$12,000
State income taxes	4,100
Real estate taxes	2,800
Mortgage interest on residence	3,100
Investment interest expense	1,800
Gambling losses	5,100

Compute Pat's tentative minimum tax.

CHAPTER 14

COMPARATIVE FORMS OF DOING BUSINESS

LEARNING OBJECTIVES

After completing Chapter 14, you should be able to:

1. Identify the principal legal and tax forms for conducting a business.

2. Appreciate the relative importance of nontax factors in business decisions.

3. Distinguish between the forms for conducting a business according to whether they are subject to single taxation or double taxation.

4. Identify techniques for avoiding double taxation.

5. Understand and apply the conduit and entity concepts as they affect operations, capital changes, and distributions.

6. Analyze the effects of the disposition of a business on the owners and the entity for each of the forms for conducting a business.

OUTLINE

Forms of Doing Business, 14–3
Principal Forms, 14–3
Limited Liability Companies, 14–4
Nontax Factors, 14–5
Capital Formation, 14–5
Limited Liability, 14–6
Other Factors, 14–7
Single versus Double Taxation, 14–7
Overall Impact on Entity and Owners, 14–7
Alternative Minimum Tax, 14–8
State Taxation, 14–9
Minimizing Double Taxation, 14–10

Making Deductible Distributions, 14–10
Not Making Distributions, 14–11
Return of Capital Distributions, 14–12
Electing S Corporation Status, 14–12
Conduit versus Entity Treatment, 14–13
Effect on Recognition at Time of Contribution to the Entity, 14–14
Effect on Basis of Ownership Interest, 14–14
Effect on Results of Operations, 14–15

Effect on Recognition at Time of Distribution, 14–16
Effect on Passive Activity Losses, 14–17
Effect of At-Risk Rules, 14–17
Effect of Special Allocations, 14–18
Disposition of a Business or an Ownership Interest, 14–19
Sole Proprietorships, 14–19
Partnerships and Limited Liability Entities, 14–20
C Corporations, 14–21
S Corporations, 14–22
Overall Comparison of Forms of Doing Business, 14–22

A variety of factors, both tax and nontax, can affect the choice of the form of business entity. The form that is appropriate at one point in the life of an entity and its owners may not be appropriate at a different time.

EXAMPLE 1

Eva is a tax practitioner in Kentwood, the Dairy Center of the South. Many of her clients are dairy farmers. She recently had tax planning discussions with two of her clients, Jesse, a Line Creek dairy farmer, and Larry, a Spring Creek dairy farmer.

Jesse recently purchased his dairy farm. He is 52 years old and just retired after 30 years of service as a chemical engineer at an oil refinery in Baton Rouge. Eva recommended that he incorporate his dairy farm and elect S corporation status for Federal income tax purposes.

Larry has owned his dairy farm since 1988. He inherited it from his father. At that time, Larry retired after 20 years of service in the U.S. Air Force. He has a master's degree in Agricultural Economics from LSU. His farm is incorporated, and shortly after the date of incorporation, Eva had advised him to elect S corporation status. She now advises him to revoke the S election. ▼

Example 1 raises a number of interesting questions. Does Eva advise all of her dairy farmer clients to elect S corporation status initially? Why has she advised Larry to revoke his S election? Will she advise Jesse to revoke his S election at some time in the future? Will she advise Larry to make another S election at some time in the future? Why did she not advise Larry to dissolve his corporation outright? Could Larry and Jesse have achieved the same tax consequences for their dairy farms if they had operated the farms as limited liability entities or partnerships instead of incorporating? Does the way the farm is acquired (e.g., purchase versus inheritance) affect the choice of business entity for tax purposes?

This chapter provides the basis for comparing and analyzing the tax consequences of business decisions for various types of tax entities (sole proprietorship, partnership, corporation, limited liability entity, and S corporation). Understanding the comparative tax consequences for the different types of entities and being able to apply them effectively to specific fact patterns will result in effective tax planning,

TAX IN THE NEWS

SHOULD YOU CHECK THAT BOX?

The check-the-box rules have been evolving since their introduction into the Regulations in late 1996. They are designed to remove tax considerations from the owners' choice of the legal form in which to conduct business. These provisions act to reduce the owners' exposure to the double taxation of taxable business profits. But taxpayers considering the use of these rules have run into several complications.

- Changing tax entity classifications from year to year comes at a cost. Changing the business form from a corporation to a partnership might trigger taxes for both the entity and its owners, defeating the purpose of the entity change.
- State income tax laws do not always match those of the Code. Several states have been slow to adopt the check-the-box rules, and others have modified the rules in some way. For instance, in several states a one-member limited liability company does not receive the expected tax treatment as a partnership, but is reclassified as a corporation or sole proprietorship. Uncertainty as to the state income tax treatment of a check-the-box selection alone may keep the owners from excercising their supposed freedom of choice of tax entity.

which is exactly what Eva was doing with her two clients. As the following discussion illustrates, a variety of potential answers may exist for each of the questions raised by Eva's advice.

FORMS OF DOING BUSINESS

PRINCIPAL FORMS

LEARNING OBJECTIVE 1
Identify the principal legal and tax forms for conducting a business.

The principal *legal* forms for conducting a business entity are the sole proprietorship, partnership, limited liability entity, and corporation.[1] From a *Federal income tax* perspective, these same forms are available, but the corporate form can be taxed in either of two ways (S corporation and C or regular corporation). In most instances, the legal form and the tax form are the same.

The taxpayer generally is bound for tax purposes by the legal form that is selected. A major statutory exception to this is the ability of an S corporation to receive tax treatment similar to that of a partnership.[2] In addition, taxpayers sometimes can control which set of tax rules will apply to their business operations. Using the so-called check-the-box procedures,[3] a business entity (other than a sole proprietorship) can elect to be taxed using whichever set of rules it prefers. Thus, a corporation can choose to be taxed under the partnership rules for Federal tax purposes, while a limited liability company (LLC) can select the regular corporate tax rules. See Chapter 9 for a more detailed discussion of the check-the-box provisions.

---

[1] A business entity can also be conducted in the form of a trust or estate. These two forms are addressed in *West's Federal Taxation: Advanced Taxation*.

[2] §§ 1361 and 1362. See Chapter 12.
[3] Reg. §§ 301.7701–1 through –4, and –6.

An individual conducting a sole proprietorship files Schedule C of Form 1040. If more than one trade or business is conducted, a separate Schedule C is filed for each trade or business. A partnership files Form 1065. A corporation files Form 1120, and an S corporation files Form 1120S.

About 4.5 million corporations file U.S. income tax returns every year, and about 2 million of these use S corporation status. About 1.5 million partnership returns are filed every year, and more than 16 million individuals report sole proprietorship activities on Schedule C in a typical tax year.[4] The business entity forms that are growing in number the fastest are the sole proprietorship (twice as many as 15 years ago) and the partnership (perhaps due to the popularity of the new limited liability entities).

LIMITED LIABILITY COMPANIES

A **limited liability company (LLC)** is a hybrid business form that combines the corporate characteristic of limited liability for the owners with the tax characteristics of a partnership.[5] All of the states now permit this legal form for conducting a business.

The most frequently cited nontax benefit of an LLC is the limited liability of the owners. Compared to the other forms of ownership, LLCs offer additional benefits over other forms of business, including the following.

Advantages over S corporations

- Greater flexibility in terms of the number of owners, types of owners, special allocation opportunities, and capital structure.
- Inclusion of entity debt in the owner's basis for an ownership interest.
- More liberal deferral of gain recognition on contributions of appreciated property by an owner (determined under § 721 rather than § 351).
- For securities law purposes, an ownership interest in an LLC is not necessarily a security.

Advantages over C corporations

- Ability to pass tax attributes through to the owners.
- Absence of double taxation.

Advantages over limited partnerships

- Right of all owners to participate in the management of the business.
- Ability of all owners to have limited liability (no need for a general partner).
- For securities law purposes, an ownership interest in an LLC is not necessarily a security (the interest of a limited partner normally is classified as a security).

Advantages over general partnerships

- Limited liability for owners.
- Greater continuity of life.
- Limitation on an owner's ability to withdraw from the business.

Among the disadvantages associated with LLCs are the following.

- Absence of a developed body of case law on LLCs.

---

[4]*Statistics of Income Bulletin*, IR97–37, Summer 1997.
[5]Depending on state law, an LLC may be organized as a limited liability corporation or a limited liability partnership.

TAX IN THE NEWS

BIG 6 PARTNERSHIPS REORGANIZE AS LLPs

All of the Big 6 accounting firms have changed their organizational structure from general partnerships to limited liability partnerships (LLPs). These firms include Arthur Andersen, Coopers & Lybrand, Deloitte & Touche, Ernst & Young, KPMG Peat Marwick, and Price Waterhouse. Many other CPA firms are doing likewise.

An LLP helps to provide protection for the *personal* assets of the partners. Under the LLP organizational structure, the only partners whose personal assets are at risk are those actually involved in the negligence or wrongdoing in question. However, the accounting firm is still responsible for the full judgment. Thus, the capital of the firm is still at risk.

- Requirement in most states that there be at least two owners.
- Inability to qualify for § 1244 ordinary loss treatment.

NONTAX FACTORS

2 LEARNING OBJECTIVE
Appreciate the relative importance of nontax factors in business decisions.

Taxes are only one of many factors to consider when making a business decision. Above all, any business decision should make economic sense.

EXAMPLE 2
Larry is considering investing $10,000 in a limited partnership. He projects that he will be able to deduct the $10,000 capital contribution within the next two years (as his share of partnership losses). Since Larry's marginal tax rate is 36%, the deductions will produce a positive cash-flow effect of $3,600 ($10,000 × 36%). However, there is a substantial risk that he will not recover any of his original investment. If this occurs, his negative cash flow from the investment in the limited partnership is $6,400 ($10,000 − $3,600). Larry must decide if the investment makes economic sense. ▼

CAPITAL FORMATION

The ability of an entity to raise capital is a factor that must be considered. A sole proprietorship has the narrowest capital base. Compared to the sole proprietorship, the partnership has a greater opportunity to raise funds through the pooling of owner resources.

EXAMPLE 3
Adam and Beth decide to form a partnership, AB. Adam contributes cash of $200,000, and Beth contributes land with an adjusted basis of $60,000 and a fair market value of $200,000. The partnership is going to construct an apartment building at a cost of $800,000. AB pledges the land and the building to secure a loan of $700,000. ▼

The limited partnership offers even greater potential than the general partnership form because a limited partnership can secure funds from investors (i.e., future limited partners).

EXAMPLE 4 Carol and Dave form a limited partnership, CD. Carol contributes cash of $200,000, and Dave contributes land with an adjusted basis of $60,000 and a fair market value of $200,000. The partnership is going to construct a shopping center at a cost of $5 million. Included in this cost is the purchase price of $800,000 for land adjacent to that contributed by Dave. Thirty limited partnership interests are sold for $100,000 each to raise $3 million. CD then pledges the shopping center (including the land) and obtains nonrecourse creditor financing of another $2 million. ▼

Both the at-risk limitations and the passive activity loss provisions reduce the tax attractiveness of investments in real estate, particularly in the limited partnership form. In effect, the tax rules themselves place a severe curb on the economic consequences. Chapter 5 details these loss rules and their critical interaction.

Of the different business entities, the corporate form offers the greatest ease and potential for obtaining owner financing because it can issue additional shares of stock. The ultimate examples of this form are the large public companies that are listed on the stock exchanges.

LIMITED LIABILITY

A corporation offers its owners limited liability under state law. This absence of personal liability on the part of the owners is the most frequently cited advantage of the corporate form.

EXAMPLE 5 Ed, Fran, and Gabriella each invest $25,000 for all the shares of stock of Brown Corporation. Brown obtains creditor financing of $100,000. Brown is the defendant in a personal injury suit resulting from an accident involving one of its delivery trucks. The court awards a judgment of $2.5 million to the plaintiff. The award exceeds Brown's insurance coverage by $1.5 million. Even though the judgment probably will result in Brown's bankruptcy, the shareholders will have no personal liability for the unpaid corporate debts. ▼

Limited liability is not available to all corporations. For many years, state laws did not permit professional individuals (e.g., accountants, attorneys, architects, and physicians) to incorporate. Even though professionals now are allowed to incorporate, the statutes do not provide limited liability for the performance of professional services.

Even if state law provides for limited liability, the shareholders of small corporations may forgo this benefit. Quite often, a corporation may be unable to obtain external financing (e.g., a bank loan) at reasonable interest rates unless the shareholders guarantee the loan.

The limited partnership form provides limited liability to the limited partners. Their liability is limited to the amount invested. In contrast, a general partner has unlimited liability.

EXAMPLE 6 Hazel, the general partner, invests $250,000 in HIJ, a limited partnership. Iris and Jane, the limited partners, each invest $50,000. While the potential loss for Iris and Jane is limited to $50,000 each, Hazel's liability is unlimited. ▼

Indirectly, it may be possible to provide the general partner with limited liability by establishing a corporation as the general partner (see Figure 14–1). When a venture is structured this way, the general partner (the corporation) has limited its liability under the corporate statutes. In the figure, individual A is protected from personal liability by being merely the shareholder of Corporation A.

FIGURE 14–1
Limited Partnership with a Corporate General Partner

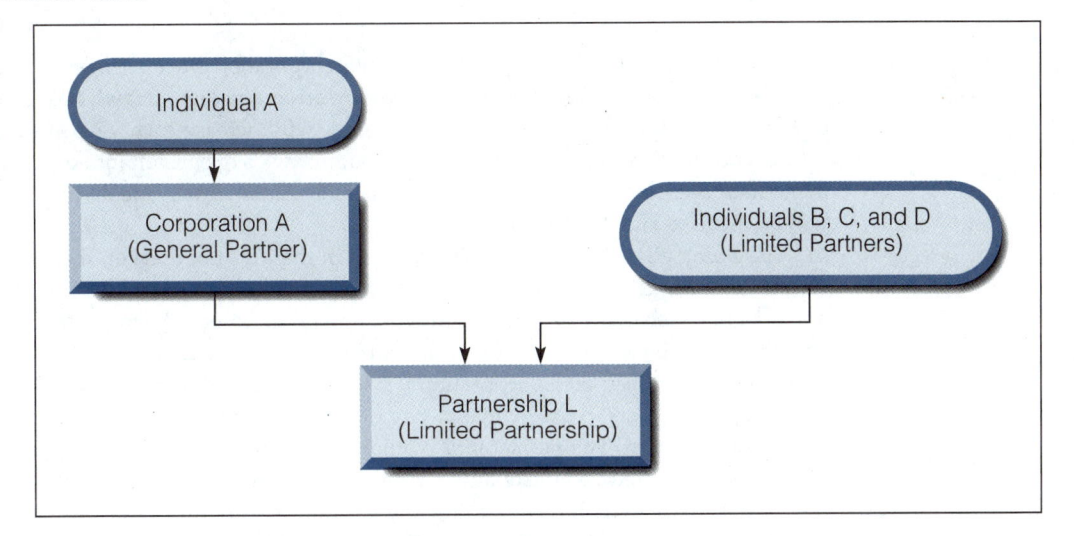

```
Individual A
    ↓
Corporation A              Individuals B, C, and D
(General Partner)          (Limited Partners)
         ↓         ↓
        Partnership L
      (Limited Partnership)
```

OTHER FACTORS

Other nontax factors may be significant in selecting an organization form, such as:

- Estimated life of the business.
- Number of owners and their roles in the management of the business.
- Freedom of choice in transferring ownership interests.
- Organizational formality, including the related cost and extent of government regulation.

SINGLE VERSUS DOUBLE TAXATION

OVERALL IMPACT ON ENTITY AND OWNERS

3 LEARNING OBJECTIVE
Distinguish between the forms for conducting a business according to whether they are subject to single taxation or double taxation.

The sole proprietorship, limited liability entity, and partnership are subject to *single* taxation. This result occurs because the owner(s) and the business generally are not considered separate entities for tax purposes. Therefore, the tax liability is levied at the owner level rather than at the entity level.

In contrast, a corporation and its owners can be subject to *double* taxation. This is frequently cited as the major tax disadvantage of the corporate form. The entity is taxed on the earnings of the corporation, and the owners are taxed on distributions to the extent they are made from corporate earnings.

The S corporation provides a way to avoid double taxation and possibly subject corporate earnings to a lower tax rate (the individual tax rate may be lower than the corporate tax rate). However, the ownership structure of an S corporation is restricted in both the number and type of shareholders. In addition, statutory exceptions subject the entity to taxation in certain circumstances.[6] To the extent

---
[6] Recall the Chapter 12 discussions of the taxes on an S corporation's built-in gains, LIFO recapture, and investment income.

these corporate-level taxes apply, double taxation results. Finally, the distribution policy of the S corporation may create difficulties under the *wherewithal to pay* concept.

EXAMPLE 7

Hawk Corporation has been operating as an S corporation since it began its business two years ago. For both of the prior years, Hawk incurred a tax loss. Hawk has taxable income of $75,000 this year and expects that its earnings will increase each year in the foreseeable future. Part of this earnings increase results from Hawk's expansion into other communities in the state. Since most of this expansion will be financed internally, no dividend distributions will be made to Hawk's shareholders.

Assuming all of Hawk's shareholders are in the 31% tax bracket, their tax liability on corporate earnings will be $23,250 ($75,000 × 31%). Even though Hawk will not distribute any cash to the shareholders, they still will be required to pay the tax liability. This creates a wherewithal to pay problem. In addition, the corporate tax liability would have been less if Hawk had not been an S corporation [(15% × $50,000) + (25% × $25,000) = $13,750].

The shareholders' wherewithal to pay problem could be resolved by terminating the S corporation election. The tax liability would then be imposed at the corporate level. Since Hawk does not intend to make any dividend distributions, double taxation at the present time would be avoided. Terminating the election also reduces the overall shareholder-corporation tax liability by $9,500 ($23,250 − $13,750).[7]

In making the decision about the form of business entity, Hawk's shareholders should consider more than the current taxable year. If the S election is terminated, another election might not be available for five years. Thus, the decision to revoke the election should be made using at least a five-year planning horizon. Perhaps a better solution would be to retain the election and distribute enough dividends to the S corporation shareholders to enable them to pay the shareholder tax liability. ▼

Two other variables that relate to the adverse effect of double taxation are the timing and form of corporate distributions. If no distributions are made, then only single taxation occurs in the short run.[8] To the extent that double taxation does occur in the future, the cash-flow effect should be discounted to its present value. Second, when the distribution is made, is it in the form of a dividend or a return of capital?[9] The owners likely would prefer to receive long-term capital gain (subject to lower tax rates) instead of ordinary income. Proper structuring of the distribution can accomplish this result.

ALTERNATIVE MINIMUM TAX

All of the forms of business are directly or indirectly subject to the alternative minimum tax (AMT).[10] For the sole proprietorship and the C corporation, the effect is direct (the AMT liability calculation is attached to the tax form that reports the entity's taxable income—Form 1040 or Form 1120). For the partnership, limited liability entity, and S corporation, the effect is indirect; the tax preferences and adjustments pass through from the entity to the owners, and the AMT liability

---

[7]The absence of distributions to shareholders could create an accumulated earnings tax (AET) problem under § 531. However, as long as earnings are used to finance expansion, the "reasonable needs" provision will be satisfied, and the corporation will avoid any AET. Refer to the discussion of the AET in Chapter 10.

[8]This assumes there is no accumulated earnings tax problem. See especially Example 10 in the subsequent discussion of distributions in Minimizing Double Taxation.

[9]Redemptions of stock and corporate liquidations may be taxed as a sale of stock to shareholders (i.e., as capital gain or loss). See § 302 and Chapter 1 of the *West's Federal Taxation: Advanced Taxation* text.

[10]§ 55.

calculation is *not* assessed on the tax form that reports the entity's taxable income—Form 1065 or Form 1120S.

When compared to other entities, the C corporation appears to have a slight advantage. The corporate AMT rate of 20 percent is less than the individual AMT rates of 26 and 28 percent. An even better perspective is provided by comparing the maximum AMT rate with the maximum regular rate for both the individual and the corporation. For the individual, the AMT rate is 71 percent (28%/39.6%) of the maximum regular rate. The AMT rate for the corporation is 57 percent (20%/35%) of the maximum regular rate. Therefore, on the basis of comparative rates, the C corporation appears to offer lower AMT tax burdens.

The apparent corporate AMT rate advantage may be more than offset by the ACE adjustment, which applies only to C corporations.[11] If the ACE adjustment continually causes the C corporation to be subject to the AMT, the owners should consider electing S corporation status (if eligibility requirements can be satisfied). Since the S corporation does not compute an ACE adjustment, it may be possible to reduce the tax liability.

The AMT does not apply to modest-sized C corporations after 1997. To be exempt from the tax, the corporation must meet both of the following tests.

- Average annual gross receipts of less than $5 million for the three tax years after 1994.
- Average annual gross receipts of less than $7.5 million for every subsequent three-tax-year period.

About 95 percent of all C corporations are likely to meet these tests and be exempt from the AMT in the future.

PLANNING CONSIDERATIONS

Planning for the AMT

If the AMT will apply in the current year, the entity should consider accelerating income and delaying deductions, so that current-year taxable income is taxed at the lower AMT rate. For a C corporation, the potential rate differential is 15 percentage points (20 percent AMT rate versus 35 percent regular tax rate). For an individual (i.e., either as a sole proprietor or as a partner), the potential tax rate differential is 11.6 percentage points (28 percent highest AMT rate versus 39.6 percent regular tax rate). A present value analysis should be used to assure that the income acceleration and deduction deferral do not increase actual tax liabilities.

STATE TAXATION

In selecting a form for doing business, the determination of the tax consequences should not be limited to Federal income taxes. Consideration also should be given to state income taxes and, if applicable, local income taxes.

The S corporation provides a good illustration of this point. Suppose that the forms of business being considered are a limited partnership or a corporation. An operating loss is projected for the next several years. The owners decide to operate the business in the corporate form. The principal nontax criterion for the decision

---

[11] §§ 56(c)(1) and (f). Refer to the discussion of the corporate AMT in Chapter 13.

TAX IN THE NEWS

WHO PAYS CORPORATE AMT?

One of the issues often raised in debates over tax legislation is whether the corporate AMT should be repealed. Among the topics discussed are the revenue generated, the related compliance costs, and the number of corporations subject to the AMT.

According to a General Accounting Office (GAO) report, only about 30,000 of the 2.1 million corporations potentially subject to the AMT paid any AMT (i.e., less than 1.5 percent) between 1987 and 1992. Approximately 2,000 corporations accounted for 85 percent of the corporate AMT paid during that period.

Proponents of the corporate AMT argue that these statistics show that the AMT is being paid by corporations targeted by the law (i.e., large corporations). Opponents argue that the same statistics show that the compliance costs borne by the mass of corporations do not justify the continuation of this tax system.

The post-1997 exemption from the AMT for small corporations may provide the needed solution. Large corporations must make minimal Federal income tax payments when the AMT applies. But most C corporations no longer need to compute the tax.

---

is the limited liability attribute of the corporation. The owners consent to an S corporation election, so the corporate losses can be passed through to the shareholders to deduct on their individual tax returns. However, assume that state law does not permit the S corporation election. Thus, the owners will not receive the tax benefits of the loss deductions that would have been available on their state income tax returns if they had chosen the limited partnership form. As a result of providing limited liability to the owner who would have been the general partner for the limited partnership, the loss deduction at the state level is forgone.

MINIMIZING DOUBLE TAXATION

4 LEARNING OBJECTIVE
Identify techniques for avoiding double taxation.

Only the corporate form is potentially subject to double taxation. Several techniques are available for eliminating or at least reducing the second layer of taxation.

- Making distributions to the shareholders that are deductible to the corporation.
- Not making distributions to the shareholders.
- Making distributions that qualify for return of capital treatment at the shareholder level.
- Making the S corporation election.

MAKING DEDUCTIBLE DISTRIBUTIONS

The following are typical distribution forms that will result in a deduction to the corporation.

- Salary payments to shareholder-employees.
- Lease or rental payments to shareholder-lessors.
- Interest payments to shareholder-creditors.

Recognizing the potential for abuse, the IRS scrutinizes these types of distributions carefully. All three forms are evaluated in terms of *reasonableness*.[12] In addition, interest payments to shareholders may lead to reclassification of some or all of the debt as equity.[13] IRS success with either approach raises the specter of double taxation.

EXAMPLE 8

Donna owns all the stock of Green Corporation and is also the chief executive officer. Green's taxable income before salary payments to Donna is as follows.

1997	1998	1999
$80,000	$50,000	$250,000

During the year, Donna receives a monthly salary of $3,000. In December of each year, Donna reviews the operations for the year and determines the year-end bonus she is to receive. Donna's yearly bonuses are as follows.

1997	1998	1999
$44,000	$14,000	$214,000

The apparent purpose of Green's bonus program is to reduce the corporate taxable income to zero and thereby avoid double taxation. An examination of Green's tax return by the IRS would likely result in a deduction disallowance for **unreasonable compensation.** ▼

EXAMPLE 9

Tom and Vicki each contribute $20,000 to TV Corporation for all of its stock. In addition, they each lend $80,000 to TV. The loan is documented by formal notes, the interest rate is 12%, and the maturity date is 10 years from the date of the loan.

The notes provide the opportunity for the corporation to make payments of $9,600 each year to both Tom and Vicki and for the payments not to be subject to double taxation. This happens because the interest payments are includible in the gross income of Tom and Vicki, but are deductible by TV in calculating its taxable income. At the time of repayment in 10 years, neither Tom nor Vicki recognizes gross income from the repayment; the $80,000 amount realized is equal to the basis for the note of $80,000.

If the IRS succeeded in reclassifying the notes as equity, Tom and Vicki still would have gross income of $9,600, but the interest would be reclassified as dividend income. Because dividend payments are not deductible by TV, the corporation's taxable income would increase by $19,200 ($9,600 × 2). To make matters worse, the repayment of the notes in 10 years would not qualify as a recovery of capital, resulting in additional dividend income for Tom and Vicki. ▼

NOT MAKING DISTRIBUTIONS

Double taxation will not occur unless the corporation makes (actual or deemed) distributions to the shareholders. A closely held corporation that does not make distributions may eventually encounter an accumulated earnings tax problem unless the reasonable needs requirement is satisfied. When making distribution decisions each year, the board of directors should be apprised of any potential accumulated earnings tax problem and take the appropriate steps to eliminate it.

---

[12]§ 162(a)(1). *Mayson Manufacturing Co. v. Comm.*, 49–2 USTC ¶9467, 38 AFTR 1028, 178 F.2d 115 (CA–6, 1949); *Harolds Club v. Comm.*, 65–1 USTC ¶9198, 15 AFTR2d 241, 340 F.2d 861 (CA–9, 1965).

[13]§ 385; Rev.Rul. 83–98, 1983–2 C.B. 40; *Bauer v. Comm.*, 84–2 USTC ¶9996, 55 AFTR2d 85–433, 748 F.2d 1365 (CA–9, 1984).

The accumulated earnings tax rate of 39.6 percent is the same as the maximum marginal tax rate for individual taxpayers.[14]

EXAMPLE 10

According to an internal calculation made by Dolphin Corporation, its accumulated taxable income is $400,000. The board of directors would prefer not to declare any dividends, but is considering a dividend declaration of $400,000 to avoid the accumulated earnings tax. All of the shareholders are in the 36% bracket.

If a dividend of $400,000 is declared, the tax cost to the shareholders is $144,000 ($400,000 × 36%). If a dividend is not declared and the IRS assesses the accumulated earnings tax, the tax cost to the corporation for the accumulated earnings tax would be $158,400 ($400,000 × 39.6%).

To make matters worse, Dolphin will have incurred the accumulated earnings tax cost without getting any funds out of the corporation to the shareholders. If the unwise decision were now made to distribute the remaining $241,600 ($400,000 − $158,400) to the shareholders, the additional tax cost at the shareholder level would be $86,976 ($241,600 × 36%). Therefore, the combined shareholder-corporation tax cost would be $245,376 ($158,400 + $86,976). This is 170% ($245,376/$144,000) of the tax cost that would have resulted from an initial dividend distribution of $400,000. ▼

Assuming that the accumulated earnings tax can be avoided (e.g., a growth company whose reasonable needs justify its failure to pay dividends), a policy of no distributions to shareholders can avoid the second layer of taxation on corporate earnings. The retained earnings will drive the value of the shares upward, equal to the accumulated after-tax cash. As a result of the step-up in basis rules for inherited property, the basis of the stock for the beneficiaries will be the fair market value at the date of the decedent's death rather than the decedent's basis.

RETURN OF CAPITAL DISTRIBUTIONS

The exposure to double taxation can be reduced if the corporate distributions to the shareholders can qualify for return of capital rather than dividend treatment. This can occur when the corporation's earnings and profits (E & P) are low or negative in amount. Review Example 1 in Chapter 10. In some cases, the stock redemption provisions offer an opportunity to avoid dividend treatment altogether. Under these rules, the distribution may be treated as a sale of the shareholder's stock, resulting in a tax-free recovery of basis and then recognition of low-tax long-term capital gain.

ELECTING S CORPORATION STATUS

Electing S corporation status generally eliminates double taxation. Several factors, listed below, should be considered when making this election.

- Are all the shareholders willing to consent to the election?
- Can the qualification requirements under § 1361 be satisfied at the time of the election?
- Can the S corporation requirements continue to be satisfied?
- For what period will the conditions that make the election beneficial continue to prevail?

---

[14] § 531. Refer to the discussion of the accumulated earnings tax in Chapter 10.

- Will the corporate distribution policy create wherewithal to pay problems at the shareholder level?

EXAMPLE 11

Emerald Corporation commenced business in January 1999. The two shareholders, Diego and Jaime, are both in the 31% tax bracket. The following operating results are projected for the first five years of operations.

1999	2000	2001	2002	2003
($50,000)	$400,000	$600,000	$800,000	$1,000,000

The corporation plans to expand rapidly. Therefore, no distributions will be made to shareholders. In addition, beginning in 2000, preferred stock will be offered to a substantial number of investors to help finance the expansion.

If the S corporation election is made for 1999, the $50,000 loss can be passed through to Diego and Jaime. The loss will generate a positive cash-flow effect of $15,500 ($50,000 × 31%). Assume that the election is either revoked or is involuntarily terminated at the beginning of 2000 as a result of the issuance of the preferred stock. The corporate tax liability for 2000 is $136,000 ($400,000 × 34%).

If the S corporation election is not made for 1999, the $50,000 loss is a net operating loss. The amount can be carried forward to reduce the 2000 corporate taxable income to $350,000 ($400,000 − $50,000). The resultant tax liability is $119,000 ($350,000 × 34%).

Should the S corporation election be made for just the one-year period? The answer is unclear. With an assumed after-tax rate of return to Diego and Jaime of 10%, the value of the $15,500 one year hence is $17,050 ($15,500 × 110%). Even considering the time value of money, the combined corporation-shareholder negative cash-flow effect of $118,950 ($136,000 − $17,050) in the case of an S election is about the same as the $119,000 corporate tax liability that would result for a regular corporation. ▼

CONDUIT VERSUS ENTITY TREATMENT

5 LEARNING OBJECTIVE
Understand and apply the conduit and entity concepts as they affect operations, capital changes, and distributions.

Under the **conduit concept,** the entity is viewed as merely an extension of the owners. Under the **entity concept,** the entity is regarded as being separate and distinct from its owners. The effects of the conduit and entity concepts extend to a variety of tax rules, including the following.

- Recognition at time of contribution to the entity.
- Basis of ownership interest.
- Results of operations.
- Recognition at time of distribution.
- Passive activity losses.
- At-risk rules.
- Special allocations.

The sole proprietorship is not analyzed separately because the owner and the business are the same tax entity. In one circumstance, however, a tax difference can result. Income recognition does not occur when an owner contributes an asset to a sole proprietorship. Thus, the business generally takes a carryover basis. However, if the asset is a personal-use asset, the sole proprietorship's basis is the *lower of* the adjusted basis or the fair market value at the date of contribution. If a personal-use asset is contributed to a partnership or corporation, this same *lower-of* rule applies.

EFFECT ON RECOGNITION AT TIME OF CONTRIBUTION TO THE ENTITY

Since the conduit approach applies to partnerships, § 721 provides for no recognition on the contribution of property to a partnership in exchange for a partnership interest. Section 721 protects both a contribution associated with the formation of the partnership and later contributions. The partnership takes a carryover basis in the contributed property, and the partners have a carryover basis in their partnership interests.[15]

Since the entity approach applies to corporations, the transfer of property to a corporation in exchange for its stock is a taxable event. However, if the § 351 control requirement is satisfied, no gain or loss is recognized. In this case, both the corporate property and the shareholders' stock have a carryover basis.[16] This control requirement makes it possible for shareholders who contribute appreciated property to the corporation *after* its formation to recognize gain.

To the extent that the fair market value of property contributed to the entity at the time of formation is not equal to the property's adjusted basis, a special allocation may be desirable. With a special allocation, the owner contributing the property receives the tax benefit or detriment for any recognized gain or loss that subsequently results because of the initial difference between the adjusted basis and the fair market value. For the partnership, this special allocation treatment is mandatory. No such allocation is available for a C corporation because the gain or loss is recognized at the corporation level rather than at the shareholder level. As with a C corporation, no such allocation is available for an S corporation. The recognized gain or loss is reported on the shareholders' tax returns according to their stock ownership.

EXAMPLE 12

Khalid contributes land with an adjusted basis of $10,000 and a fair market value of $50,000 for a 50% ownership interest. At the same time, Tracy contributes cash of $50,000 for the remaining 50% ownership interest. Because the entity is unable to obtain the desired zoning, it subsequently sells the land for $50,000.

If the entity is a C corporation, Khalid has a realized gain of $40,000 ($50,000 − $10,000) and a recognized gain of $0 resulting from the contribution. His basis in the stock is $10,000, and the corporation has a basis in the land of $10,000. The corporation realizes and recognizes a gain of $40,000 ($50,000 − $10,000) when it sells the land. Thus, what should have been Khalid's recognized gain is now the corporation's taxable gain. There is no way that the corporation can allocate the recognized gain directly to Khalid. The corporation could distribute the land to Khalid and let him sell it, but such a distribution is likely to be taxable to Khalid as a dividend, and gain on the distribution is also recognized at the corporate level.

If the entity is a partnership or limited liability entity, the tax consequences are the same as for the C corporation, except for the $40,000 recognized gain on the sale of the land. The partnership realizes and recognizes a gain of $40,000 ($50,000 − $10,000). However, even though Khalid's share of profits and losses is only 50%, all of the $40,000 recognized gain is allocated to him. If the entity is an S corporation, the tax consequences are the same as for the C corporation, except that Khalid reports $20,000 of the recognized gain on his tax return and Tracy reports $20,000. ▼

EFFECT ON BASIS OF OWNERSHIP INTEREST

In a partnership or limited liability entity, since the owner is the taxpayer, profits and losses of the partnership affect the owner's basis in the entity interest. Likewise,

---

[15]Refer to the pertinent discussion in Chapter 11.

[16]Refer to the pertinent discussion in Chapter 9.

the owner's basis is increased by the share of entity liability increases and is decreased by the share of liability decreases. Accordingly, ownership basis changes frequently.[17]

Because a C corporation is a taxpaying entity, the shareholder's basis for the stock is not affected by corporate profits and losses or corporate liability changes.

The treatment of an S corporation shareholder falls between that of the partner and the C corporation shareholder. The S corporation shareholder's stock basis is increased by the share of profits and decreased by the share of losses, but it usually is not affected by corporate liability increases or decreases.[18]

EXAMPLE 13

Peggy contributes cash of $100,000 to an entity for a 30% ownership interest. The entity borrows $50,000 and repays $20,000 of this amount by the end of the taxable year. The profits for the year are $90,000.

If the entity is a partnership, Peggy's basis at the end of the period is $136,000 ($100,000 investment + $9,000 share of net liability increase + $27,000 share of profits). If Peggy is a C corporation shareholder instead, her stock basis is $100,000 ($100,000 original investment). If the corporation is an S corporation, Peggy's stock basis is $127,000 ($100,000 + $27,000). ▼

EFFECT ON RESULTS OF OPERATIONS

The entity concept is responsible for producing potential double taxation for the C corporation if the corporation is taxed on its earnings, and the shareholders are taxed on the distribution of earnings. Thus, from the perspective of taxing the results of operations, the entity concept appears to provide a disadvantage to corporations. However, whether the entity concept actually produces disadvantageous results depends on the following.

- Whether the corporation generates positive taxable income.
- The tax rates that apply to the corporation and to the shareholders.
- The distribution policy of the corporation.

As discussed previously, techniques exist for getting cash out of the corporation to the shareholders without incurring double taxation (e.g., compensation payments to shareholder-employees, lease payments to shareholder-lessors, and interest payments to shareholder-creditors). Since these payments are deductible to the corporation, they reduce corporate taxable income. If the payments can be used to reduce corporate taxable income to zero, the corporation will have no tax liability.

The maximum individual tax rate (39.6 percent) currently exceeds the maximum corporate tax rate (35 percent). However, at some income levels, the corporate tax rate that applies is less than the applicable individual rate.

Double taxation occurs only if distributions are made to the shareholders. Thus, if no distributions are made and if the entity can avoid the accumulated earnings tax (e.g., based on the statutory credit or the reasonable needs adjustment) and the personal holding company tax (e.g., the corporation primarily generates active income), only one current level of taxation will occur. If the distribution can qualify for return of capital rather than dividend treatment, the shareholder tax liability is decreased. Finally, taxation of the earnings at the shareholder level can be avoided permanently if the stock passes through the decedent shareholder's estate.[19]

---

[17]§§ 705 and 752.
[18]Recall from Chapter 12 that pass-through S losses can reduce a *shareholder's* basis in loans to the entity.
[19]Recall Chapter 7's analysis of the basis step-up rules for property acquired from a decedent.

Application of the entity concept causes income and deductions to lose any unique tax characteristics when they are passed through to shareholders in the form of dividends. This may produce a negative result for net long-term capital gains, because potential beneficial treatment is lost. Since capital gains lose their identity when passed through in the form of dividends, they cannot be used to offset capital losses at the shareholder level. An even more negative result is produced when dividends are paid out of tax-exempt income. Tax-exempt income is excludible in calculating corporate taxable income, but is included in calculating current earnings and profits. Thus, exclusions from income may be taxed because of the entity concept.

Partnerships, limited liability entities, and S corporations use the conduit concept in reporting the results of operations. Any item that is subject to special treatment on the taxpayer-owner's tax return is reported separately to the owner. Other items are aggregated and reported as taxable income. Thus, taxable income merely represents the sum of income and deductions that are not subject to special treatment.[20]

Many of the problems that the entity concept may produce for the C corporation form are not present in pass-through entities. In particular, pass-through entities are not subjected to double taxation, problems with the reasonableness requirement, or loss of identity of the income or expense item at the owner level.

Only partnerships and limited liability entities completely apply the conduit concept when reporting the results of operations. In several circumstances, the S corporation is subject to taxation at the corporate level, including the tax on built-in gains. This limited application of the entity concept necessitates additional planning to attempt to avoid taxation at the corporate level.

EFFECT ON RECOGNITION AT TIME OF DISTRIBUTION

The application of the conduit concept results in distributions not being taxed to the owners. The application of the entity concept produces the opposite result. Therefore, tax-free distributions can be made to owners of flow-through entities, whereas distributions to C corporation shareholders may be taxable.

A combination entity/conduit concept applies to property distributions from S corporations. The conduit concept applies with respect to the shareholder. However, if the distributed property has appreciated in value, any realized gain is recognized at the corporate level.[21] This is the same treatment received by C corporations. Thus, corporate-level gain recognition is an application of the entity concept, whereas the pass-through of the gain to shareholders is an application of the conduit concept.

EXAMPLE 14

Tan, an S corporation, is equally owned by Leif and Matt. Tan distributes two parcels of land to Leif and Matt. Tan has a basis of $10,000 for each parcel. Each parcel has a fair market value of $15,000. The distribution results in a $10,000 ($30,000 − $20,000) recognized gain for Tan. Leif and Matt each report $5,000 of the gain on their individual income tax returns. ▼

Stock redemptions and complete liquidations receive identical treatment whether a C or an S corporation is involved.[22]

---

[20] §§ 701, 702, 1363, and 1366.
[21] § 311(b).
[22] §§ 302, 331, and 336.

EFFECT ON PASSIVE ACTIVITY LOSSES

The passive activity loss rules apply to flow-through entities, personal service corporations, and closely held C corporations. A *closely held C corporation* exists when more than 50 percent of the value of the outstanding stock at any time during the last half of the taxable year is owned by or for not more than five individuals. A corporation is classified as a *personal service corporation* if the following requirements are satisfied.[23]

- The principal activity of the corporation is the performance of personal services.
- The services are substantially performed by owner-employees.
- Owner-employees own more than 10 percent in value of the stock of the corporation.

The general passive activity loss rules apply to personal service corporations. Therefore, passive activity losses can be offset only against passive activity income. For closely held corporations, the application of the passive activity rules is less harsh. Passive activity losses can be offset against both active and passive income.

Since the conduit concept applies to partnerships, S corporations, and limited liability entities, the passive activity results are separately stated at the entity level and are passed through to the owners with their passive character maintained.

EFFECT OF AT-RISK RULES

The at-risk rules apply to all flow-through entities and to closely held C corporations. The rules produce a harsher result for partnerships and limited liability entities than for S corporations. This occurs because of the way liabilities affect partners' basis.

EXAMPLE 15

Walt is the general partner, and Ira and Vera are the limited partners in the WIV limited partnership. Walt contributes land with an adjusted basis of $40,000 and a fair market value of $50,000 for his partnership interest, and Ira and Vera each contribute cash of $100,000 for their partnership interests. They agree to share profits and losses equally. To finance construction of an apartment building, the partnership obtains $600,000 of nonrecourse financing [not qualified nonrecourse financing under § 465(b)(6)] using the land and the building as the pledged assets. Each partner's basis for the partnership interest is as follows.

	Walt	Ira	Vera
Contribution	$ 40,000	$100,000	$100,000
Share of nonrecourse debt	200,000	200,000	200,000
Basis	$240,000	$300,000	$300,000

Without the at-risk rules, Ira and Vera could pass through losses up to $300,000 each even though they invested only $100,000 and have no personal liability for the nonrecourse debt. However, the at-risk rules limit the loss pass-through to the at-risk basis, which is $100,000 for Ira and $100,000 for Vera.

The at-risk rules also affect the general partner. Since Walt is not at risk for the nonrecourse debt, his at-risk basis is $40,000. If the mortgage were recourse debt, his at-risk basis would be $640,000 ($40,000 + $600,000).

---

[23]§ 469, derived from the definition in § 269A.

TAX IN THE NEWS

IS GOLD AT RISK?

Over three thousand investors decided that a mining investment plan entitled "Gold for Tax Dollars" was too lucrative to let pass. The investment plan, advertised in a brochure printed to resemble a gold rush broadside, promised investors tax deductions up to four times the amount of their original investment. This promotional material emphasized that each investor's mine was to be operated as a sole proprietorship. There would be no limited partners. The purpose of this structure was ". . . to avoid the at-risk limitation rules applicable to partnerships." However, when the IRS explained to the Tax Court that each investor's mine consisted of several cubic yards of "auriferous gravel" —the exact amount depended on the dollar amount of the investment—the Court rejected the sole proprietorship spin (*Marion C. and Ruth Gray, et al.*, 88 T.C. 1306 [1987]). One of the investors in the scheme, who was a pilot, had managed "with substantial difficulty" to actually visit a purported mining site. He testified that he was unable to locate his own particular cubic yards of auriferous gravel and added, "I didn't even know if I was going to get out of there alive."

If, instead, the entity were an S corporation and Walt received 20% of the stock and Ira and Vera each received 40%, the basis for their stock would be as follows.

Walt	Ira	Vera
$40,000	$100,000	$100,000

In S corporations, nonrecourse debt does not affect the calculation of stock basis. The stock basis for each shareholder would remain the same even if the debt were recourse debt. Only direct loans by the shareholders increase the ceiling on loss pass-through. ▼

EFFECT OF SPECIAL ALLOCATIONS

An advantage of the conduit concept over the entity concept is the ability to make special allocations. Special allocations are not permitted in C corporations. Indirectly, however, the corporate form may be able to achieve results similar to those produced by special allocations through payments to owners (e.g., salary payments, lease rental payments, and interest payments) and through different classes of stock (e.g., preferred and common). However, even in these cases, the breadth of the treatment and the related flexibility are far less than that achievable under the conduit concept.

Although S corporations generally operate as conduits, they are treated more like C corporations than partnerships with respect to special allocations. This treatment results from the application of the per-share and per-day allocation rule in § 1377(a). Although S corporations are limited to one class of stock, they still can use salary, interest, and rental payments to owners to shift income to the desired recipient. However, the IRS has the authority to reallocate income among members of a family if fair returns are not provided for services rendered or capital invested.[24]

---

[24]§ 1366(e).

EXAMPLE 16

The stock of an S corporation is owned by Debra (50%), Helen (25%), and Joyce (25%). Helen and Joyce are Debra's adult children. Debra is subject to a 36% marginal tax rate, and Helen and Joyce have a 15% marginal tax rate. Only Debra is an employee of the corporation. She is paid an annual salary of $20,000, whereas employees with similar responsibilities in other corporations earn $100,000. The corporation generates earnings of approximately $200,000 each year.

It appears that the reason Debra is paid a low salary is to enable more of the earnings of the S corporation to be taxed to Helen and Joyce, who are in lower tax brackets. Thus, the IRS could use its statutory authority to allocate a larger salary to Debra. ▼

Partnerships and limited liability entities have many opportunities to use special allocations, including the following (refer to Chapter 11).

- The ability to share profits and losses differently from the share in capital.
- The ability to share profits and losses differently.
- A required special allocation for the difference between the adjusted basis and the fair market value of contributed property.
- The special allocation of some items if a substantial economic effect rule is satisfied.

DISPOSITION OF A BUSINESS OR AN OWNERSHIP INTEREST

6 LEARNING OBJECTIVE
Analyze the effects of the disposition of a business on the owners and the entity for each of the forms for conducting a business.

A key factor in evaluating the tax consequences of a business disposition is whether the disposition is viewed as the sale of an ownership interest or as a sale of assets. Generally, the tax consequences are more favorable to the seller if the transaction is treated as a sale of the ownership interest.

SOLE PROPRIETORSHIPS

Regardless of the form of the transaction, the sale of a sole proprietorship is treated as the sale of individual assets. Thus, gains and losses must be calculated separately for each asset. Classification as capital gain or ordinary income depends on the nature and holding period of the individual assets. Ordinary income property such as inventory will result in ordinary gains and losses. Section 1231 property such as land, buildings, and machinery used in the business will produce § 1231 gains and losses (subject to depreciation recapture under §§ 1245 and 1250). Capital assets such as investment land and stocks qualify for capital gain or loss treatment.

If the amount realized exceeds the fair market value of the identifiable assets, the excess is allocated to goodwill, which produces capital gain for the seller. If instead the excess payment were allocated to a covenant not to compete, the related gain would be classified as ordinary income rather than capital gain. Both goodwill and covenants are amortized over a 15-year statutory period.[25]

EXAMPLE 17

Seth, who is in the 36% tax bracket, sells his sole proprietorship to Wilma for $600,000. The identifiable assets are as follows.

---

[25]§ 197.

	Adjusted Basis	Fair Market Value
Inventory	$ 20,000	$ 25,000
Accounts receivable	40,000	40,000
Machinery and equipment*	125,000	150,000
Buildings**	175,000	250,000
Land	40,000	100,000
	$400,000	$565,000

*Potential § 1245 recapture of $50,000.
**Potential § 1250 recapture of $20,000.

The sale produces the following results for Seth.

	Gain (Loss)	Ordinary Income	§ 1231 Gain	Capital Gain
Inventory	$ 5,000	$ 5,000		
Accounts receivable	–0–			
Machinery and equipment	25,000	25,000		
Buildings	75,000	20,000	$ 55,000	
Land	60,000		60,000	
Goodwill	35,000			$35,000
	$200,000	$50,000	$115,000	$35,000

If the sale is structured this way, Wilma can deduct the $35,000 paid for goodwill over a 15-year period. If instead Wilma paid the $35,000 to Seth for a covenant not to compete for a period of seven years, she still would amortize the $35,000 over a 15-year period. However, Seth's $35,000 capital gain would now be taxed to him as ordinary income. If the covenant has no legal relevance to Wilma, in exchange for treating the payment as a goodwill payment, she should negotiate for a price reduction that reflects Seth's benefit from the lower capital gains tax. ▼

PARTNERSHIPS AND LIMITED LIABILITY ENTITIES

The sale of a partnership or limited liability entity can be structured as the sale of assets or as the sale of an ownership interest. If the transaction takes the form of an asset sale, it is treated the same as for a sole proprietorship. The sale of an ownership interest is treated as the sale of a capital asset, although ordinary income potential exists for unrealized receivables and substantially appreciated inventory. Thus, if capital gain treatment can produce beneficial results for the taxpayer (e.g., he or she has capital losses to offset or has beneficially treated net capital gain), the sale of an ownership interest is preferable.

From a buyer's perspective, tax consequences are not affected by the form of the transaction. If the transaction is an asset purchase, the basis for the assets equals the amount paid. If a buyer intends to continue to operate as an LLC or a partnership, the assets can be contributed to the entity under § 721. Therefore, the owner's basis in the entity interest is equal to the purchase price for the assets. Likewise, if ownership interests are purchased, the owner's basis is the purchase price paid.

The partnership's basis for the assets is the purchase price since the original partnership will have terminated.[26]

When the inside and outside basis of a partner's ownership interest differ (see Chapter 9), an election can be made to step up the partner's share of the entity's asset bases.[27] This tax-free basis step-up applies to all such exchanges by all of the partners as long as the election is in effect. The election allows asset basis to reflect the goodwill that a new partner has purchased.

EXAMPLE 18

Roz buys a one-third interest in the RST Partnership for $50,000 (outside basis). All of the entity's assets are depreciable, and their basis to the partnership (inside basis) is $90,000. If a § 754 election is in effect, the partnership can step up the basis of its depreciable assets by $20,000, the difference between Roz's outside and inside basis amounts [$50,000 − (⅓ × $90,000)]. All of the "new" asset basis is allocated to Roz. ▼

C CORPORATIONS

The sale of a business held by a C corporation can be structured as either an asset sale or a stock sale. The stock sale has the dual advantage to the seller of being less complex both as a legal transaction and as a tax transaction. It also has the advantage of providing a way to avoid double taxation. Finally, any gain or loss on the sale of the stock is treated as a capital gain or loss to the shareholder.

EXAMPLE 19

Jane and Zina each own 50% of the stock of Purple Corporation. They have owned the business for 10 years. Jane's basis in her stock is $40,000, and Zina's basis in her stock is $60,000. They agree to sell the stock to Rex for $300,000. Jane recognizes a long-term capital gain of $110,000 ($150,000 − $40,000), and Zina recognizes a long-term capital gain of $90,000 ($150,000 − $60,000). Rex has a basis in his stock of $300,000. Purple's basis in its assets does not change as a result of the stock sale. ▼

PLANNING CONSIDERATIONS

Selling Stock or Assets

Structuring the sale of the business as a stock sale may produce detrimental tax results for the purchaser. As Example 19 illustrates, the basis of the corporation's assets is not affected by the stock sale. If the fair market value of the stock exceeds the corporation's adjusted basis for its assets, the purchaser is denied the opportunity to step up the basis of the assets to reflect the amount in effect paid for them through the stock acquisition—no § 754 election is available to C corporations.

For an asset sale, the seller of the business can be either the corporation or its shareholders. If the seller is the corporation, the corporation sells the business (the assets), pays any debts not transferred, and makes a liquidating distribution to the shareholders. If the sellers are the shareholders, the corporation pays any debts that will not be transferred and makes a liquidating distribution to the shareholders; then the shareholders sell the business.

Regardless of the approach used for an asset sale, double taxation will occur. The corporation is taxed on the actual sale of the assets and is taxed as if it had sold the assets when it makes the liquidating distribution to the shareholders who then sell the distributed assets. The shareholders are taxed when they receive cash or assets distributed in-kind by the corporation.

---

[26]§ 708(b)(1)(B).   [27]§ 754.

The asset sale resolves the purchaser's problem of not being able to step up the basis of the assets to their fair market value. The basis for each asset is its purchase price. To operate in corporate form (assuming the purchaser is not a corporation), the purchaser needs to transfer the property to a corporation in a § 351 transaction.

From the perspective of the seller, the ideal form of the transaction is a stock sale. Conversely, from the purchaser's perspective, the ideal form is an asset price. Double taxation seldom can be avoided in either case. Therefore, the bargaining ability of the seller and the purchaser to structure the sale as a stock sale or an asset sale, respectively, is critical.

Rather than selling the entire business, an owner may sell only his or her ownership interest. Since the form of the transaction is a stock sale, the results for the selling shareholder will be the same as if all the shareholders had sold their stock (i.e., capital gain or loss).

S CORPORATIONS

Since the S corporation is a corporation, it is subject to the provisions for a C corporation discussed previously. Either an asset sale at the corporate level or a liquidating distribution of assets produces recognition at the corporate level. However, under the conduit concept applicable to the S corporation, the recognized amount is taxed at the shareholder level. Therefore, double taxation is avoided directly (only the shareholder is involved) for a stock sale and indirectly (the conduit concept ignores the involvement of the corporation) for an asset sale.

Double taxation might seem to be avoided by making an S corporation election prior to the liquidation of a C corporation, but the built-in gains tax closes this loophole; taxation occurs at the corporate level, and double taxation results.

Concept Summary 14–1 summarizes the tax consequences of business dispositions.

OVERALL COMPARISON OF FORMS OF DOING BUSINESS

Concept Summary 14–2 provides a detailed comparison of the tax consequences of the various forms of doing business.

PLANNING CONSIDERATIONS

Choosing a Business Form: Case Study

The chapter began with an example that illustrated the relationship between tax planning and the choice of business form; it also raised a variety of questions about the advice given by the tax practitioner. By this time, one should be able to develop various scenarios supporting the tax advice given. The actual fact situations that produced the tax adviser's recommendations were as follows.

- Jesse's experience in the dairy industry consists of raising a few heifers during the final five years of his employment. Eva anticipates that Jesse will generate tax losses for the indeterminate future. In addition, Jesse indicated that he and his wife must have limited liability associated with the dairy farm.
- Larry was born and raised on his father's dairy farm. Both his education and his Air Force managerial experience provide him with useful tools for managing his business. However, Larry inherited his farm when milk prices were at a low for the modern era. Since none of her dairy farm clients were profitable, Eva anticipated Larry would operate his dairy farm at a loss. Larry, like Jesse, felt that limited liability was imperative. Thus, he incorporated the dairy farm and made the S corporation election.

    For the first two years, Larry's dairy farm produced tax losses. Since then, the dairy farm has produced tax profits large enough to absorb the losses. Larry anticipates that his profits will remain relatively stable in the $50,000 to $75,000 range in the future. Since he is subject to a 31 percent marginal tax rate and anticipates that no dividend distributions will be made, his tax liability associated with the dairy farm will be reduced if he terminates the S corporation election.

As Jesse and Larry's example illustrates, selection of the proper business form can result in both nontax and tax advantages. Both of these factors should be considered in making the selection decision. Furthermore, this choice should be reviewed periodically, since a proper business form at one point in time may not be the proper form at a different time.

In looking at the tax attributes, consideration should be given to the tax consequences of the following.

- Contribution of assets to the entity by the owners at the time the entity is created and at later dates.
- Taxation of the results of operations.
- Distributions to owners.
- Disposition of an ownership interest.
- Termination of the entity.

Concept Summary 14–1

Tax Treatment of Disposition of a Business

Form of Entity	Form of Transaction	Tax Consequences — Seller	Tax Consequences — Buyer
Sole proprietorship	Sale of individual assets.	Gain or loss is calculated separately for the individual assets. Classification as capital or ordinary depends on the nature and holding period of the individual assets. If amount realized exceeds the fair market value of the identifiable assets, the excess is allocated to goodwill (except to the extent identified with a covenant not to compete), which is a capital asset.	Basis for individual assets is the allocated cost. Prefers that any excess of purchase price over the fair market value of identifiable assets be identified with a covenant not to compete if the covenant has legal utility. Otherwise, the buyer is neutral since both goodwill and covenants are amortized over a 15-year statutory period.
	Sale of the business.	Treated as a sale of the individual assets (as above).	Treated as a purchase of the individual assets (as above).
Partnership and limited liability entity	Sale of individual assets.	Treatment is the same as for the sole proprietorship.	Treatment is the same as for the sole proprietorship. If the intent is to operate in partnership form, the assets can be contributed to a partnership under § 721.
	Sale of ownership interest.	Entity interest is treated as the sale of a capital asset (subject to ordinary income potential for unrealized receivables and substantially appreciated inventory).	Basis for new owner's ownership interest is the cost. The new entity's basis for the assets is also the pertinent cost (i.e., contributed to the entity under § 721), since the original entity will have terminated.
C corporation	Sale of corporate assets by corporation (i.e., corporation sells assets, pays debts, and makes liquidating distribution to the shareholders).	Double taxation occurs. Corporation is taxed on the sale of the assets with the gain or loss determination and the classification as capital or ordinary treated the same as for the sole proprietorship. Shareholders calculate gain or loss as the difference between the stock basis and the amount received from the corporation in the liquidating distribution. Capital gain or loss usually results, since stock typically is a capital asset.	Basis for individual assets is the allocated cost. If the intent is to operate in corporate form, the assets can be contributed to a corporation under § 351.
	Sale of corporate assets by the shareholders (i.e., corporation pays debts and makes liquidating distribution to the shareholders).	Double taxation occurs. At the time of the liquidating distribution to the shareholders, the corporation is taxed as if it had sold the assets. Shareholders calculate gain or loss as the difference between the stock basis and the fair market value of the assets received from the corporation in the liquidating distribution. Capital gain or loss usually results, since stock typically is a capital asset.	Same as corporate asset sale.

Form of Entity	Form of Transaction	Tax Consequences	
		Seller	**Buyer**
	Sale of corporate stock.	Enables double taxation to be avoided. Since the corporation is not a party to the transaction, there are no tax consequences at the corporate level. Shareholders calculate gain or loss as the difference between the stock basis and the amount received for the stock. Capital gain or loss usually results, since stock typically is a capital asset.	Basis for the stock is its cost. The basis for the corporate assets is not affected by the stock purchase.
S corporation	Sale of corporate assets by corporation.	Recognition occurs at the corporate level on the sale of the assets, with the gain or loss determination and the classification as capital or ordinary treated the same as for the sole proprietorship. Conduit concept applicable to the S corporation results in the recognized amount being taxed at the shareholder level. Double taxation associated with the asset sale is avoided, because the shareholder's stock basis is increased by the amount of gain recognition and decreased by the amount of loss recognition. Shareholders calculate gain or loss as the difference between the stock basis and the amount received from the corporation in the liquidating distribution. Capital gain or loss usually results, since stock typically is a capital asset.	Basis for individual assets is the allocated cost. If the intent is to operate in corporate form (i.e., as an S corporation), the assets can be contributed to a corporation under § 351.
	Sale of corporate assets by the shareholders.	At the time of the liquidating distribution to the shareholders, recognition occurs at the corporation level as if the corporation had sold the assets. The resultant tax consequences for the shareholders and the corporation are the same as for the sale of corporate assets by the S corporation.	Same as corporate asset sale.
	Sale of corporate stock.	Same as the treatment for the sale of stock of a C corporation.	Same as the treatment for the purchase of stock of a C corporation.

Concept Summary 14–2

Tax Attributes of Different Forms of Business (Assume Partners and Shareholders Are All Individuals)

	Sole Proprietorship	Partnership/ Limited Liability Entity	S Corporation	C Corporation
Restrictions on type or number of owners	One owner. The owner must be an individual.	Must have at least 2 owners.	Only individuals, estates, and certain trusts can be owners. Maximum number of shareholders limited to 75.	None, except some states require a minimum of 2 shareholders.
Incidence of tax	Sole proprietorship's income and deductions are reported on Schedule C of the individual's Form 1040. A separate Schedule C is prepared for each business.	Entity not subject to tax. Owners in their separate capacity subject to tax on their distributive share of income. Entity files Form 1065.	Except for certain built-in gains and passive investment income when earnings and profits are present from C corporation tax years, entity not subject to Federal income tax. S corporation files Form 1120S. Shareholders are subject to tax on income attributable to their stock ownership.	Income subject to double taxation. Entity subject to tax, and shareholder subject to tax on any corporate dividends received. Corporation files Form 1120.
Highest tax rate	39.6% at individual level.	39.6% at owner level.	39.6% at shareholder level.	35% at corporate level plus 39.6% on any corporate dividends at shareholder level.
Choice of tax year	Same tax year as owner.	Selection generally restricted to coincide with tax year of majority owners or principal owners, or to tax year determined under the least aggregate deferral method.	Restricted to a calendar year unless IRS approves a different year for business purposes or other exceptions apply.	Unrestricted selection allowed at time of filing first tax return.
Timing of taxation	Based on owner's tax year.	Owners report their share of income in their tax year within which the entity's tax year ends. Owners in their separate capacities are subject to payment of estimated taxes.	Shareholders report their shares of income in their tax year within which the corporation's tax year ends. Generally, the corporation uses a calendar year, but see "Choice of tax year." Shareholders may be subject to payment of estimated taxes. Corporation may be subject to payment of estimated taxes for the taxes imposed at the corporate level.	Corporation subject to tax at close of its tax year. May be subject to payment of estimated taxes. Dividends are subject to tax at the shareholder level in the tax year received.

	Sole Proprietorship	Partnership/ Limited Liability Entity	S Corporation	C Corporation
Basis for allocating income to owners	Not applicable (only one owner).	Profit and loss sharing agreement. Cash basis items of cash basis entities are allocated on a daily basis. Other entity items are allocated after considering varying interests of owners.	Pro rata share based on stock ownership. Shareholder's pro rata share is determined on a daily basis, according to the number of shares of stock held on each day of the corporation's tax year.	Not applicable.
Contribution of property to the entity	Not a taxable transaction.	Generally not a taxable transaction.	Is a taxable transaction unless the § 351 requirements are satisfied.	Is a taxable transaction unless the § 351 requirements are satisfied.
Character of income taxed to owners	Retains source characteristics.	Conduit—retains source characteristics.	Conduit—retains source characteristics.	All source characteristics are lost when income is distributed to owners.
Basis for allocating a net operating loss to owners	Not applicable (only one owner).	Profit and loss sharing agreement. Cash basis items of cash basis entities are allocated on a daily basis. Other entity items are allocated after considering varying interests of owners.	Prorated among shareholders on a daily basis.	Not applicable.
Limitation on losses deductible by owners	Investment plus liabilities.	Owner's investment plus share of liabilities.	Shareholder's investment plus loans made by shareholder to corporation.	Not applicable.
Subject to at-risk rules?	Yes, at the owner level. Indefinite carryover of excess loss.	Yes, at the owner level. Indefinite carryover of excess loss.	Yes, at the shareholder level. Indefinite carryover of excess loss.	Yes, for closely held corporations. Indefinite carryover of excess loss.
Subject to passive activity loss rules?	Yes, at the owner level. Indefinite carryover of excess loss.	Yes, at the owner level. Indefinite carryover of excess loss.	Yes, at the shareholder level. Indefinite carryover of excess loss.	Yes, for closely held corporations and personal service corporations. Indefinite carryover of excess loss.
Tax consequences of earnings retained by entity	Taxed to owner when earned and increases his or her investment in the sole proprietorship.	Taxed to owners when earned and increases their respective interest bases in the entity.	Taxed to shareholders when earned and increases their respective interest bases in stock.	Taxed to corporation when earned and may be subject to penalty tax if accumulated unreasonably.

Overall Comparison of Forms of Doing Business

	Sole Proprietorship	Partnership/ Limited Liability Entity	S Corporation	C Corporation
Nonliquidating distributions to owners	Not taxable.	Not taxable unless money received exceeds recipient owner's basis in entity interest. Existence of § 751 assets may cause recognition of ordinary income.	Generally not taxable unless the distribution exceeds the shareholder's AAA or stock basis. Existence of accumulated earnings and profits could cause some distributions to be dividends.	Taxable in year of receipt to extent of earnings and profits or if exceeds basis in stock.
Capital gains	Taxed at owner level using maximum rate of 20%, 25%, or 28%.	Conduit—owners must account for their respective shares. Taxed at owner level.	Conduit, with certain exceptions (a possible penalty tax)—shareholders must account for their respective shares. Tax treatment determined at shareholder level.	Taxed at corporate level with a maximum 35% rate. No other benefits.
Capital losses	Only $3,000 of capital losses can be offset each tax year against ordinary income. Indefinite carryover.	Conduit—owners must account for their respective shares. Tax treatment determined at owner level.	Conduit—shareholders must account for their respective shares. Tax treatment determined at shareholder level.	Carried back three years and carried forward five years. Deductible only to the extent of capital gains.
§ 1231 gains and losses	Taxable or deductible at owner level. Five-year lookback rule for § 1231 losses.	Conduit—owners must account for their respective shares. Tax treatment determined at owner level.	Conduit—shareholders must account for their respective shares. Tax treatment determined at shareholder level.	Taxable or deductible at corporate level only. Five-year lookback rule for § 1231 losses.
Foreign tax credits	Available at owner level.	Conduit—tax payments passed through to owners.	Generally conduit—tax payments passed through to shareholders.	Available at corporate level only.
§ 1244 treatment of loss on sale of interest	Not applicable.	Not applicable.	Available.	Available.
Basis treatment of entity liabilities	Not applicable.	Includible in interest basis.	Not includible in stock basis.	Not includible in stock basis.
Built-in gains	Not applicable.	Not applicable.	Possible corporate tax.	Not applicable.
Special allocations to owners	Not applicable (only one owner).	Available if supported by substantial economic effect.	Not available.	Not applicable.
Availability of fringe benefits to owners	None.	None.	None unless a 2% or less shareholder.	Available within antidiscrimination rules.
Effect of liquidation/ redemption/ reorganization on basis of entity assets	Not applicable.	Usually carried over from entity to owner.	Taxable step-up to fair market value.	Taxable step-up to fair market value.

	Sole Proprietorship	Partnership/ Limited Liability Entity	S Corporation	C Corporation
Sale of ownership interest	Treated as the sale of individual assets. Classification of recognized gain or loss depends on the nature of the individual assets.	Treated as the sale of an entity interest. Recognized gain or loss is classified as capital, although appreciated inventory and receivables are subject to ordinary income treatment.	Treated as the sale of corporate stock. Recognized gain is classified as capital gain. Recognized loss is classified as capital loss, subject to ordinary loss treatment under § 1244.	Treated as the sale of corporate stock. Recognized gain is classified as capital gain. Recognized loss is classified as capital loss, subject to ordinary loss treatment under § 1244.
Distribution of appreciated property	Not taxable.	No recognition at the entity level.	Recognition at the corporate level to the extent of the appreciation. Conduit—amount of recognized gain is passed through to shareholders.	Taxable at the corporate level to the extent of the appreciation.
Splitting of income among family members	Not applicable (only one owner).	Difficult—IRS will not recognize a family member as an owner unless certain requirements are met.	Rather easy—gift of stock will transfer tax on a pro rata share of income to the donee. However, IRS can make adjustments to reflect adequate compensation for services.	Same as an S corporation, except that donees will be subject to tax only on earnings actually or constructively distributed to them. Other than unreasonable compensation, IRS generally cannot make adjustments to reflect adequate compensation for services and capital.
Organizational costs	Start-up expenditures are amortizable over 60 months.	Amortizable over 60 months.	Same as partnership.	Same as partnership.
Charitable contributions	Limitations apply at owner level.	Conduit—owners are subject to deduction limitations in their own capacities.	Conduit—shareholders are subject to deduction limitations in their own capacities.	Limited to 10% of taxable income before certain deductions.
Alternative minimum tax	Applies at owner level. AMT rates are 26% and 28%.	Applies at the owner level rather than at the entity level. AMT preferences and adjustments are passed through from the entity to the owners.	Applies at the shareholder level rather than at the corporate level. AMT preferences and adjustments are passed through from the S corporation to the shareholders.	Applies at the corporate level. AMT rate is 20%. Modest-sized C corporations are exempt.
ACE adjustment	Does not apply.	Does not apply.	Does not apply.	The adjustment is made in calculating AMTI. The adjustment is 75% of the excess of adjusted current earnings over unadjusted AMTI. If the unadjusted AMTI exceeds adjusted current earnings, the adjustment may be negative.

KEY TERMS

Conduit concept, 14–13

Entity concept, 14–13

Limited liability company (LLC), 14–4

Unreasonable compensation, 14–11

PROBLEM MATERIALS

1. Using the legend provided, indicate which form of business entity each of the following characteristics describes. Some of the characteristics may apply to more than one form of business entity.

   Legend
   SP = Applies to sole proprietorship
   P = Applies to partnership and limited liability entity
   S = Applies to S corporation
   C = Applies to C corporation

   a. Has limited liability.
   b. Greatest ability to raise capital.
   c. Subject to double taxation.
   d. Subject to accumulated earnings tax.
   e. Limit on types and number of shareholders.
   f. Has unlimited liability.
   g. Sale of the business can be subject to double taxation.

2. Using the legend provided, indicate which form of business entity each of the following characteristics describes. Some of the characteristics may apply to more than one form of business entity.

   Legend
   P = Applies to partnership and limited liability entity
   S = Applies to S corporation
   C = Applies to C corporation

   a. Basis for an ownership interest is increased by an investment by the owner.
   b. Basis for an ownership interest is decreased by a distribution to the owner.
   c. Basis for an ownership interest is increased by entity profits.
   d. Basis for an ownership interest is decreased by entity losses.
   e. Basis for an ownership interest is increased as the entity's liabilities increase.
   f. Basis for an ownership interest is decreased as the entity's liabilities decrease.

3. A business entity has the following assets and liabilities on its balance sheet.

	Net Book Value	Fair Market Value
Assets	$675,000	$950,000
Liabilities	100,000	100,000

   The business entity has just lost a product liability suit with damages of $5 million being awarded to the plaintiff. Although the business entity will appeal the judgment, legal counsel indicates the judgment is highly unlikely to be overturned by the appellate

court. The product liability insurance carried by the business has a policy ceiling of $3 million. What is the amount of liability of the entity and its owners if the form of the business entity is:
   a. A sole proprietorship?
   b. A partnership or LLC?
   c. A C corporation?
   d. An S corporation?

4. Ted is the managing partner of a regional accounting firm. Like many accounting firms, Ted's firm has expended considerable resources in defending itself against various liability claims, many of which are spurious.

   Ted is meeting with the firm's management committee this afternoon. On the agenda is a continuing discussion of ways to deal with liability issues. Ted has held private discussions with several members of the committee about changing the ownership form from a partnership to a Delaware limited liability company. All of the partners except Albert regard an LLC as a positive option. Albert, a founding partner of the firm who is approaching retirement, has vehemently argued that a professional accounting firm serves the public interest and that operation as an LLC is in conflict with that objective and the related public perception. As a member of the management committee, what position will you take? Why?

5. Red, White, Blue, and Orange generate taxable income as follows.

Corporation	Taxable Income
Red	$ 80,000
White	260,000
Blue	500,000
Orange	20,000,000

   a. Calculate the marginal and effective tax rates for each of the C corporations.
   b. Explain why the marginal tax rate for a C corporation can exceed 35%, but the effective tax rate cannot do so.

6. Amy and Jeff are going to operate their florist shop as a partnership or as an S corporation. After paying salaries of $40,000 to each of the owners, the shop's earnings are projected to be about $50,000. The earnings are to be invested in the growth of the business. Advise Amy and Jeff as to which of the two entity forms they should select. Summarize your thoughts in an outline, which you will distribute at the meeting.

7. Gary is an entrepreneur who likes to be actively involved in his business ventures. He is going to invest $400,000 in a business that he projects will produce a tax loss of approximately $75,000 per year in the short run. However, once consumers become aware of the new product being sold by the business and the quality of the service it provides, he is confident the business will generate a profit of at least $100,000 per year. Gary has substantial other income (from both business ventures and investment activities) each year. Advise Gary on the business form he should select for the short run. He will be the sole owner.

8. Jack, an unmarried taxpayer, is going to establish a manufacturing business. He anticipates that the business will be profitable immediately due to a patent that he holds. He anticipates that profits for the first year will be about $200,000 and will increase at a rate of about 20% per year for the foreseeable future. He will be the sole owner of the business. Advise Jack on the form of business entity he should select. Jack will be in the 36% tax bracket.

9. Silver Corporation will begin operations on January 1. Earnings for the next five years are projected to be relatively stable at about $100,000 per year. The shareholders of Silver are in the 31% tax bracket.

a. Silver will reinvest its after-tax earnings in the growth of the company. Should Silver operate as a C corporation or as an S corporation?
b. Silver will distribute its after-tax earnings each year to its shareholders. Should Silver operate as a C corporation or as an S corporation?

10. Mabel and Alan, who are in the 31% tax bracket, recently acquired a fast-food franchise. Both of them will work in the business and receive a salary of $80,000. They anticipate that the annual profits of the business, after deducting salaries, will be approximately $300,000. The entity will distribute enough cash each year to Mabel and Alan to cover their Federal income taxes associated with the franchise.
    a. What amount will the entity distribute if the franchise operates as a C corporation?
    b. What amount will the entity distribute if the franchise operates as an S corporation?
    c. What will be the amount of the combined entity/owner tax liability in (a) and (b)?

11. Parrott is a closely held corporation owned by 10 shareholders (each has 10% of the stock). Selected financial information provided by Parrott follows.

Taxable income	$8,000,000
Positive AMT adjustments (excluding ACE adjustment)	300,000
Negative AMT adjustments	(20,000)
Tax preferences	5,000,000
Retained earnings	500,000
Accumulated E & P	525,000
ACE adjustment	590,000

a. Calculate Parrott's tax liability as a C corporation.
b. Calculate Parrott's tax liability as an S corporation.
c. How would your answers in (a) and (b) change if Parrott is not closely held (e.g., 5,000 shareholders with no shareholder owning more than 2% of the stock)?

12. Pelican Corporation, an offshore drilling company, is going to sell land and a building that it no longer needs. The real estate is located at 200 Brando Row, Grand Isle, LA 70535. The adjusted basis for the real estate is $400,000 ($700,000 − $300,000 straight-line depreciation), and the fair market value is $500,000. ADS straight-line depreciation would have been $275,000. The buyer of the real estate would like to close the transaction prior to the end of the calendar year. Pelican is uncertain whether the tax consequences would be better if it sold the real estate this year or next year and is considering the following options.

- $500,000 in cash payable on December 31, 1999.

- The sale will be closed on December 31, 1999, with the consideration being a $500,000 note issued by the buyer. The maturity date of the note is January 2, 2000, with the real estate being pledged as security.

Pelican projects its taxable income for 1999 and 2000 to be $600,000 (gross receipts of $8.5 million) without the sale of the real estate. Pelican's accounting period is the calendar year. Determine the tax consequences to Pelican under either option and recommend which option Pelican should select. Send your recommendation to Corey Longwell, Pelican's tax director, whose office is at the equipment warehouse.

13. Heron Corporation has been in operation for 10 years. Since Heron's creation, all of the stock has been owned by Andy, who initially invested $200,000 in the corporation. Heron has been successful far beyond Andy's expectations, and the current fair market value of the stock is $10 million. While he has been paid a salary of $200,000 per year by the corporation, all of Heron's earnings have been reinvested in the growth of the corporation.

Heron is currently being audited by the IRS. One of the issues raised by the revenue agent is the possibility of the assessment of the accumulated earnings tax. Andy is not concerned about this issue because he believes Heron can easily justify the accumulations based on its past rapid expansion by opening new outlets. The expansion program is fully documented in the minutes of Heron's board of directors. Andy has provided this information to the revenue agent.

Two years ago, Andy decided that he would curtail any further expansion into new markets by Heron. In his opinion, further expansion would exceed his ability to manage the corporation effectively. Since the tax year under audit is three years ago, Andy sees no reason to provide the revenue agent with this information.

Heron will continue its policy of no dividend payments into the foreseeable future. Andy believes that if the accumulated earnings issue is satisfactorily resolved on this audit, it probably will not be raised again on any subsequent audits. Thus, double taxation in the form of the tax on dividends at the shareholder level or the accumulated earnings tax at the corporate level can be avoided.

What is Heron's responsibility to disclose to the revenue agent the expected change in its growth strategy? Are Andy's beliefs regarding future accumulated earnings tax issues realistic?

14. Fawn, a C corporation, has taxable income of $200,000 before paying salaries to the two shareholder-employees, Gus and Janet. Fawn follows a policy of distributing all after-tax earnings to the shareholders.
    a. Determine the tax consequences for Fawn, Gus, and Janet if the corporation pays salaries to Gus and Janet as follows.

Option 1		Option 2	
Gus	$120,000	Gus	$45,000
Janet	80,000	Janet	30,000

    b. Is Fawn likely to encounter any tax problems associated with either option?

15. Swallow, a C corporation, is owned by Sandra (50%) and Fran (50%). Sandra is the president, and Fran is the vice president for sales. Late in 1998, Swallow encounters working capital difficulties. Thus, Sandra and Fran each loan the corporation $100,000 on an 8% note that is due in five years with interest payable annually.
    a. Determine the tax consequences to Swallow, Sandra, and Fran for 1999 if the notes are classified as debt.
    b. Determine the tax consequences to Swallow, Sandra, and Fran for 1999 if the notes are classified as equity.

16. Liane owns land and a building that she has been using in her sole proprietorship. She is going to incorporate her sole proprietorship as a C corporation. Liane must decide whether to contribute the land and building to the corporation or to lease them to the corporation. The net income of the sole proprietorship for the past five years has averaged $200,000. Advise Liane on the tax consequences. Summarize your analysis in a memo to the tax file.

17. Marci and Jennifer each own 50% of the stock of Lavender, a C corporation. After paying each of them a "reasonable" salary of $125,000, the taxable income of Lavender is normally around $600,000. The corporation is about to purchase a $2,000,000 shopping mall ($1,500,000 allocated to the building and $500,000 allocated to the land). The mall will be rented to tenants at a net rental rate (including rental commissions, depreciation, etc.) of $500,000 annually. Marci and Jennifer will contribute $1 million each to the corporation to provide the cash required for the acquisition. Their CPA has suggested that Marci and Jennifer purchase the shopping mall as individuals and lease it to Lavender for a fair rental of $300,000. Both Marci and Jennifer are in the 39.6% tax bracket. The acquisition will occur on January 2, 1999. Determine whether the shopping mall should be acquired by Lavender or by Marci and Jennifer in accordance with their CPA's recommendation. Depreciation on the shopping mall in 1999 is $37,000.

18. Otto created Teal Corporation five years ago. The C corporation has paid Otto as president a salary of $100,000 each year. Annual earnings after taxes have been about

$500,000 each year. Teal has not paid any dividends nor does it intend to do so in the future. Instead, Otto wants his beneficiaries to receive the step-up in stock basis when he dies. Identify the relevant tax issues.

19. Tammy and Arnold own 40% of the stock of Roadrunner, an S corporation. The other 60% is owned by 74 other family members. Tammy and Arnold have agreed to a divorce and are in the process of negotiating a property settlement. Identify the relevant tax issues for Tammy and Arnold.

20. Eagle Corporation has been an electing S corporation since its incorporation 10 years ago. During the first three years of operations, it incurred total losses of $250,000. Since then Eagle has generated earnings of approximately $150,000 each year. None of the earnings have been distributed to the three equal shareholders, Claire, Lynn, and Todd, because the corporation has been in an expansion mode. At the beginning of 1999, Claire sells her stock to Nell for $400,000. Nell has reservations about the utility of the S election. Therefore, Lynn, Todd, and Nell are discussing whether the election should be continued. They expect the earnings to remain at approximately $150,000 each year. However, since they perceive that the company's expansion period is over and Eagle has adequate working capital, they may start distributing the earnings to the shareholders. All of the shareholders are in the 31% tax bracket. Advise the three shareholders on whether the S election should be maintained.

21. Bob and Carl each own 50% of the stock of Deer, a C corporation. When the corporation was organized, Bob contributed cash of $90,000, and Carl contributed land with an adjusted basis of $60,000 and a fair market value of $115,000. Deer assumed Carl's $25,000 mortgage on the land. In addition to the capital contributions, Bob and Carl each loaned the corporation $50,000. The maturity date of the loan is in 10 years, and the interest rate is 12%, the same as the Federal rate.
    a. Determine the tax consequences to Bob, Carl, and Deer of the initial contribution of assets, the shareholder loans, and the annual interest payments if the loans are classified as debt.
    b. Determine the tax consequences if the loans are reclassified as equity.

22. Agnes, Becky, and Carol form a business entity with each contributing the following.

	Adjusted Basis	Fair Market Value
Agnes: Cash	$100,000	$100,000
Becky: Land	60,000	120,000
Carol: Services		50,000

Their ownership percentages will be as follows.

Agnes	40%
Becky	40%
Carol	20%

Becky's land has a $20,000 mortgage that is assumed by the entity. Carol is an attorney who receives her ownership interest in exchange for legal services. Determine the recognized gain to the owners, the basis for their ownership interests, and the entity's basis for its assets if the entity is:
    a. A partnership.
    b. A C corporation.
    c. An S corporation.

23. Alicia contributes $25,000 to a business entity in exchange for a 20% ownership interest. During the first year of operations, the entity earns a profit of $150,000. At the end of that year, the entity has liabilities of $60,000.
    a. Calculate Alicia's basis for her stock if the entity is a C corporation.
    b. Calculate Alicia's basis for her stock if the entity is an S corporation.
    c. Calculate Alicia's basis for her partnership interest if the entity is a partnership.

24. An entity engages in the following transactions during the taxable year.
    - Sells stock held for three years as an investment for $30,000. The adjusted basis of the stock is $20,000.
    - Sells land used in the business for $65,000. The land had been used as a parking lot and originally cost $40,000.
    - Receives tax-exempt interest on municipal bonds of $5,000.
    - Receives dividends on IBM stock of $8,000.

    Describe the effect of these transactions on the entity and the owners of the entity if the entity is:
    a. A partnership.
    b. A C corporation.
    c. An S corporation.

25. Amber holds a 20% interest in a business to which she contributed $100,000 as part of the initial ownership group. During the life of the business, the following have occurred.
    - $300,000 cumulative losses, first three tax years.
    - $200,000 operating profit in the fourth tax year.
    - $75,000 distribution to owners at the end of the third tax year.
    - $50,000 payment to redeem 25% of Amber's ownership interest at the end of the fourth year. No other ownership redemptions have occurred.

    Determine the tax consequences to Amber if the entity is:
    a. A partnership.
    b. An S corporation.
    c. A C corporation.

26. An entity has the following income for the current year.

Operations	$80,000
Tax-exempt interest income	15,000
Long-term capital gain	45,000

    The entity has earnings and profits of $200,000 at the beginning of the year. A distribution of $90,000 is made to the owners.
    a. Calculate the taxable income if the entity is (1) a C corporation and (2) an S corporation.
    b. Determine the effect of the distribution on the shareholders if the entity is (1) a C corporation and (2) an S corporation.

27. Yellow, a personal service corporation, has the following types of income and losses.

Active income	$90,000
Portfolio income	20,000
Passive activity losses	50,000

    a. Calculate Yellow's taxable income.
    b. Assume that instead of being a personal service corporation, Yellow is a closely held corporation. Calculate Yellow's taxable income.

28. Rosa contributes $50,000 to a business entity in exchange for a 10% ownership interest. The business entity incurs a loss of $900,000 for 1999. The entity liabilities at the end of 1999 are $700,000. Of this amount, $150,000 is for recourse debt, and $550,000 is for nonrecourse debt.
    a. Assume the business entity is a partnership. How much of Rosa's share of the loss can be deducted on her 1999 individual tax return? What is Rosa's basis for her partnership interest at the end of 1999?

b. Assume the business entity is a C corporation. How much of Rosa's share of the loss can be deducted on her 1999 individual tax return? What is Rosa's basis for her stock at the end of 1999?

29. Megan owns 60% of a business entity, and Vern owns 40%. For 1999, the entity has a tax loss of $100,000. The owners would like to share profits with 60% for Megan and 40% for Vern and to share losses with 90% for Vern and 10% for Megan. Determine the tax consequences for 1999 if the entity is:
    a. A partnership.
    b. A C corporation.
    c. An S corporation.

30. Abby and Velma are equal owners of the AV Partnership. Abby invests $75,000 cash in the partnership. Velma contributes land and a building (basis to her of $50,000, fair market value of $75,000). The entity then borrows $200,000 cash using recourse financing and $100,000 using nonrecourse financing.
    a. Compute the outside basis in the partnership interest for Abby and Velma.
    b. Compute the at-risk amount for Abby and Velma.

31. Indicate which of the following special allocations are available for a partnership (P), a C corporation (C), and an S corporation (S).
    a. Share profits and losses differently from the share in capital.
    b. Share profits in a different percentage than losses.
    c. Special allocation of precontribution gain.
    d. Special allocation supported by substantial economic effect.
    e. Allocation to eliminate difference between inside and outside basis.

32. Sanjay contributes land to a business entity in January 1999 for a 30% ownership interest. Sanjay's basis for the land is $60,000, and the fair market value is $100,000. The business entity was formed three years ago by Polly and Rita, who have equal ownership. The entity is unsuccessful in getting the land rezoned from agricultural to residential. In October 1999, the land is sold for $110,000.

    Determine the tax consequences of the sale of the land for the entity and its owners if the entity is:
    a. A C corporation.
    b. An S corporation.
    c. A partnership.

33. Emily and Freda are negotiating with George to purchase the business that he operates in corporate form (George, Inc.). The assets of George, Inc., a C corporation, are as follows.

Asset	Basis	FMV
Cash	$ 20,000	$ 20,000
Accounts receivable	50,000	50,000
Inventory	100,000	110,000
Furniture and fixtures	150,000	170,000*
Building	200,000	250,000**
Land	40,000	150,000

*Potential depreciation recapture under § 1245 is $45,000.
**The straight-line method was used to depreciate the building. Accumulated depreciation is $340,000.

George's basis for the stock of George, Inc., is $560,000. George is subject to a 31% marginal tax rate, and George, Inc., faces a 34% marginal tax rate.
a. Emily and Freda purchase the *stock* of George, Inc., from George for $900,000. Determine the tax consequences to Emily and Freda, George, Inc., and George.
b. Emily and Freda purchase the *assets* from George, Inc., for $900,000. Determine the tax consequences to Emily and Freda, George, Inc., and George.

c. The purchase price is $550,000 because the fair market value of the building is $150,000, and the fair market value of the land is $50,000. No amount is assigned to goodwill. Emily and Freda purchase the *stock* of George, Inc., from George. Determine the tax consequences to Emily and Freda, George, Inc., and George.

34. Linda is the owner of a sole proprietorship. The entity has the following assets.

Asset	Basis	FMV
Cash	$10,000	$10,000
Accounts receivable	–0–	25,000
Office furniture and fixtures*	15,000	17,000
Building**	75,000	90,000
Land	60,000	80,000

*Potential depreciation recapture under § 1245 of $5,000.
**The straight-line method has been used to depreciate the building.

Linda sells the business for $260,000 to Juan.
  a. Determine the tax consequences to Linda, including the classification of any recognized gain or loss.
  b. Determine the tax consequences to Juan.
  c. Advise Juan on how the purchase agreement could be modified to produce more beneficial tax consequences for him.

35. Gail and Harry own the GH Partnership. They have conducted the business as a partnership for 10 years. The bases for their partnership interests are as follows.

Gail	Harry
$100,000	$150,000

GH Partnership holds the following assets.

Asset	Basis	FMV
Cash	$ 10,000	$ 10,000
Accounts receivable	30,000	28,000
Inventory	25,000	26,000
Building*	100,000	150,000
Land	250,000	400,000

*The straight-line method has been used to depreciate the building. Accumulated depreciation is $70,000.

Gail and Harry sell their partnership interests to Keith and Liz for $307,000 each.
  a. Determine the tax consequences of the sale to Gail, Harry, and GH Partnership.
  b. From a tax perspective, should it matter to Keith and Liz whether they purchase Gail and Harry's partnership interests or the partnership assets from GH Partnership?

36. Ted and Skip are going to purchase the Carp Partnership, as equal partners, from Jan and Gail for $400,000. Because of your negotiations on behalf of Ted and Skip, the transaction will be structured as a purchase of the partnership, not of its individual assets. Carp's inside basis in its assets is $350,000. Write a letter to Ted at 50 Lake Shore Drive, Erie, PA 16501, explaining the following.
  a. What outside basis do Ted and Skip take in the partnership?
  b. Can Carp change its inside asset basis as a result of the purchase of the entity?

37. Vladimir owns all the stock of Ruby Corporation. The fair market value of the stock (and Ruby's assets) is about four times his adjusted basis for the stock. Vladimir is negotiating with an investor group for the sale of the corporation. Identify the relevant tax issues for Vladimir.

38. Bill Evans will purchase either the stock or the assets of Dane Corporation. All of the Dane stock is owned by Chuck. Bill and Chuck agree that Dane is worth $500,000. The tax basis for Dane's assets is $350,000. Write a letter to Bill advising him on whether he should negotiate to purchase the stock or the assets. Bill's address is 100 Village Green, Chattanooga, TN 37403.

CHAPTER 15

INTRODUCTION TO THE TAXATION OF INDIVIDUALS

LEARNING OBJECTIVES

After completing Chapter 15, you should be able to:

1. Understand and apply the components of the Federal income tax formula for individuals.

2. Apply the rules for arriving at personal and dependency exemptions.

3. Use the proper method for determining the tax liability.

4. Identify and work with kiddie tax situations.

5. Recognize filing requirements and proper filing status.

6. Identify specific inclusions and exclusions applicable to individuals.

7. Determine an individual's allowable itemized deductions.

8. Understand the adoption expenses credit, child tax credit, education tax credits, child and dependent care credit, credit for the elderly, and earned income credit.

OUTLINE

The Individual Tax Formula, 15–2
Components of the Tax Formula, 15–3
Application of the Tax Formula, 15–7
Individuals Not Eligible for the Standard Deduction, 15–8
Special Limitations for Individuals Who Can Be Claimed as Dependents, 15–8

Personal and Dependency Exemptions, 15–9
Personal Exemptions, 15–9
Dependency Exemptions, 15–10
Phase-Out of Exemptions, 15–14

Tax Determination, 15–15
Tax Table Method, 15–15
Tax Rate Schedule Method, 15–16
Computation of Net Taxes Payable or Refund Due, 15–17
Unearned Income of Children under Age 14 Taxed at Parents' Rate, 15–18

Filing Considerations, 15–20
Filing Requirements, 15–21
Filing Status, 15–23

Overview of Income Provisions Applicable to Individuals, 15–26

Specific Inclusions Applicable to Individuals, 15–26
Alimony and Separate Maintenance Payments, 15–26
Prizes and Awards, 15–28
Unemployment Compensation, 15–29
Social Security Benefits, 15–29

Specific Exclusions Applicable to Individuals, 15–29
Gifts and Inheritances, 15–29
Scholarships, 15–30
Damages, 15–31
Workers' Compensation, 15–32
Accident and Health Insurance Benefits, 15–33
Educational Savings Bonds, 15–33

Itemized Deductions, 15–34
Medical Expenses, 15–35
Taxes, 15–38
Interest, 15–40
Charitable Contributions, 15–44
Miscellaneous Itemized Deductions Subject to Two Percent Floor, 15–49
Other Miscellaneous Deductions, 15–50
Overall Limitation on Certain Itemized Deductions, 15–50

Individual Tax Credits, 15–52
Adoption Expenses Credit, 15–52
Child Tax Credit, 15–53
Credit for Child and Dependent Care Expenses, 15–54
Education Tax Credits, 15–55
Tax Credit for Elderly or Disabled Taxpayers, 15–57
Earned Income Credit, 15–59

The individual income tax accounts for approximately 40 percent of Federal budget receipts, compared to approximately 10 percent for the corporate income tax. The tax laws affecting individuals have become increasingly more complex in recent years as the government adds new laws to protect or increase this important source of revenue. Taxpayers respond to each new tax act with techniques to exploit loopholes, and the government responds with loophole-closing provisions, making the individual income tax law even more complex.[1]

THE INDIVIDUAL TAX FORMULA

1 LEARNING OBJECTIVE
Understand and apply the components of the Federal income tax formula for individuals.

Individuals are subject to Federal income tax based on taxable income. This chapter explains how taxable income and the income tax of an individual taxpayer are determined. To compute taxable income, it is necessary to understand the tax formula in Figure 15–1 on the following page.

Although the tax formula is rather simple, determining an individual's taxable income can be quite complex because of the numerous provisions that govern the determination of gross income and allowable deductions.

---
[1] Refer to the discussion of tax complexity in Chapter 1.

▼ **FIGURE 15–1**
Individual Income Tax Formula

Income (broadly conceived)	$xx,xxx
Less: Exclusions	(x,xxx)
Gross income	$xx,xxx
Less: Deductions *for* adjusted gross income	(x,xxx)
Adjusted gross income (AGI)	$xx,xxx
Less: The greater of—	
Total itemized deductions *or* the standard deduction	(x,xxx)
Personal and dependency exemptions	(x,xxx)
Taxable income	$xx,xxx

After computing taxable income, the appropriate rates must be applied. This requires a determination of the individual's filing status, since different rates apply for single taxpayers, married taxpayers, and heads of household. The individual tax rate structure is progressive, with rates ranging from 15 percent to 39.6 percent.[2] For comparison, the lowest rate structure, which was in effect from 1913 to 1915, ranged from 1 to 7 percent, and the highest, in effect during 1944–1945, ranged from 23 to 94 percent.

Once the individual's tax has been computed, prepayments and credits are subtracted to determine whether the taxpayer owes additional tax or is entitled to a refund.

COMPONENTS OF THE TAX FORMULA

Before illustrating the application of the tax formula, a brief discussion of each of its components is helpful.

Income (Broadly Conceived). This includes all the taxpayer's income, both taxable and nontaxable. Although it is essentially equivalent to gross receipts, it does not include a return of capital or receipt of borrowed funds. Nor does gross income include unrealized appreciation in the value of a taxpayer's assets.

▼ **EXAMPLE 1** Dave needed money to purchase a house. He sold 5,000 shares of stock for $100,000. He had paid $40,000 for the stock. In addition, he borrowed $75,000 from a bank. Dave has taxable income of $60,000 from the sale of the stock ($100,000 selling price − $40,000 return of capital). He has no income from the $75,000 borrowed from the bank because he has an obligation to repay that amount. ▼

Exclusions. For various reasons, Congress has chosen to exclude certain types of income from the income tax base. The principal income exclusions are listed in Exhibit 15–1. The exclusions most commonly encountered by individual taxpayers (employee fringe benefits) are discussed in detail in Chapter 16.

---

[2] The Tax Table for 1997 and the Tax Rate Schedules for 1997 and 1998 are reproduced in Appendix A. The Tax Rate Schedules are also reproduced inside the front cover of this text.

▼ **EXHIBIT 15–1**
Partial List of Exclusions from Gross Income

Accident and health insurance proceeds
Annuity payments (to the extent proceeds represent a recovery of the taxpayer's investment)
Child support payments
Damages for personal injury or sickness
Fringe benefits of employees:
- Educational assistance payments provided by employer
- Employer-provided accident and health insurance
- Group term life insurance (for coverage up to $50,000)
- Meals and lodging (if furnished for convenience of employer)
- Tuition reductions for employees of educational institutions
- Miscellaneous benefits

Gains from sale of principal residence
Gifts and inheritances received
Interest from state and local bonds
Life insurance paid on death of insured
Scholarship grants (to a limited extent)
Social Security benefits (to a limited extent)
Workers' compensation benefits

▼ **EXHIBIT 15–2**
Partial List of Gross Income Items

Alimony	Interest
Bargain purchase from employer	Jury duty fees
Bonuses	Partnership income
Breach of contract damages	Pensions
Business income	Prizes (with some exceptions)
Commissions	Professional fees
Compensation for services	Punitive damages
Debts forgiven (with some exceptions)	Rents
Dividends	Rewards
Embezzled funds	Royalties
Farm income	Salaries
Fees	Severance pay
Gains from illegal activities	Strike and lockout benefits
Gains from sale of property	Supplemental unemployment benefits
Gambling winnings	Tips and gratuities
Hobby income	Wages

Gross Income. The Internal Revenue Code defines gross income broadly as "except as otherwise provided . . . , all income from whatever source derived."[3] The "except as otherwise provided" refers to exclusions. Gross income includes, but is not limited to, the items in Exhibit 15–2.

---
[3] § 61(a).

CHAPTER 15 Introduction to the Taxation of Individuals

EXAMPLE 2

Beth received the following amounts during the year:

Salary	$30,000
Interest on savings account	900
Gift from her aunt	10,000
Prize won in state lottery	1,000
Alimony from ex-husband	12,000
Child support from ex-husband	6,000
Damages for injury in auto accident	25,000
Increase in the value of stock held for investment	5,000

Review Exhibits 15–1 and 15–2 to determine the amount Beth must include in the computation of taxable income and the amount she may exclude. Then check your answer in footnote 4.[4] ▼

Deductions for Adjusted Gross Income. Individual taxpayers have two categories of deductions: (1) deductions *for* adjusted gross income (deductions to arrive at adjusted gross income) and (2) deductions *from* adjusted gross income. Deductions *for* adjusted gross income (AGI) include, but are not limited to, the following:[5]

- Ordinary and necessary expenses incurred in a trade or business.
- One-half of self-employment tax paid.
- Alimony paid.
- Certain payments to Individual Retirement Accounts and Medical Savings Accounts.
- Moving expenses.
- Forfeited interest penalty for premature withdrawal of time deposits.
- The capital loss deduction (limited to $3,000).

The principal deductions *for* AGI are discussed later in this chapter.

Adjusted Gross Income (AGI). AGI is an important subtotal that serves as the basis for computing percentage limitations on certain itemized deductions, such as medical expenses and charitable contributions. For example, medical expenses are deductible only to the extent they exceed 7.5 percent of AGI, and charitable contribution deductions may not exceed 50 percent of AGI. These limitations might be described as a 7.5 percent *floor* under the medical expense deduction and a 50 percent *ceiling* on the charitable contribution deduction.

EXAMPLE 3

Keith earned a salary of $23,000 in the current tax year. He contributed $2,000 to his Individual Retirement Account (IRA) and sustained a $1,000 capital loss on the sale of Wren Corporation stock. His AGI is computed as follows:

Gross income		
Salary		$23,000
Less deductions *for* AGI		
IRA contribution	$2,000	
Capital loss	1,000	(3,000)
AGI		$20,000

▼

---

[4]Beth must include $43,900 in computing taxable income ($30,000 salary + $900 interest + $1,000 lottery prize + $12,000 alimony). She can exclude $41,000 ($10,000 gift from aunt + $6,000 child support + $25,000 damages). The unrealized gain on the stock held for investment is not included in gross income. Such gain will be included in gross income only when it is realized upon disposition of the stock.

[5]See § 62 for a comprehensive list of items that are deductible *for* AGI.

EXAMPLE 4 Assume the same facts as in Example 3, and that Keith also had medical expenses of $1,800. Medical expenses may be included in itemized deductions to the extent they exceed 7.5% of AGI. In computing his itemized deductions, Keith may include medical expenses of $300 [$1,800 medical expenses − $1,500 (7.5% × $20,000 AGI)]. ▼

Itemized Deductions. As a general rule, personal expenditures are disallowed as deductions in arriving at taxable income. However, Congress has chosen to allow specific personal expenses as **itemized deductions.** Such expenditures include medical expenses, certain taxes and interest, and charitable contributions. Itemized deductions are discussed in detail later in this chapter.

EXAMPLE 5 Leo is the owner and operator of a video game arcade. All allowable expenses he incurs in connection with the arcade business are deductions *for* AGI. In addition, Leo paid medical expenses, mortgage interest, state income tax, and charitable contributions. These personal expenses are allowable as itemized deductions. ▼

Standard Deduction. The **standard deduction** is used by taxpayers who do not have itemized deductions in excess of the allowable standard deduction amount. The standard deduction is a specified amount that depends on the filing status of the taxpayer (e.g., single, married filing jointly, married filing separately). In the past, Congress has attempted to set the amount of the standard deduction at a level that would exempt poverty-level taxpayers from the income tax,[6] but it has not always been consistent in doing so.

The standard deduction is the sum of two components: a *basic* standard deduction and an *additional* standard deduction.[7] Taxpayers who are allowed a *basic* standard deduction are entitled to the applicable amount listed in Table 15–1. The standard deduction amounts are subject to adjustment for inflation each year. Currently, about 70 percent of all individual taxpayers choose to use the standard deduction in lieu of itemizing deductions.

Certain taxpayers are not allowed to claim *any* standard deduction, and the standard deduction is *limited* for others. These provisions are discussed later in the chapter.

A taxpayer who is age 65 or over *or* blind qualifies for an *additional standard deduction* of $850 or $1,050, depending on filing status (see amounts in Table 15–2). Two additional standard deductions are allowed for a taxpayer who is age 65 or over *and* blind. The additional standard deduction provisions also apply for a qualifying spouse who is age 65 or over or blind, but a taxpayer may not claim an additional standard deduction for a dependent.

▼ **TABLE 15–1**
Basic Standard Deduction Amounts

Filing Status	1997	1998
Single	$4,150	$4,250
Married, filing jointly	6,900	7,100
Surviving spouse	6,900	7,100
Head of household	6,050	6,250
Married, filing separately	3,450	3,550

---

[6] S.Rep. No. 92–437, 92nd Cong., 1st Sess., 1971, p. 54. Another purpose of the standard deduction was discussed in Chapter 1 under Influence of the Internal Revenue Service—Administrative Feasibility. The size of the standard deduction has a direct bearing on the number of taxpayers who are in a position to itemize deductions. Reducing the number of taxpayers who itemize also reduces the audit effort required from the IRS.

[7] § 63(c)(1).

▼ **TABLE 15–2**
Amount of Each Additional Standard Deduction

Filing Status	1997	1998
Single	$1,000	$1,050
Married, filing jointly	800	850
Surviving spouse	800	850
Head of household	1,000	1,050
Married, filing separately	800	850

To determine whether to itemize, the taxpayer compares the *total* standard deduction (the sum of the basic standard deduction and any additional standard deductions) to total itemized deductions. Taxpayers are allowed to deduct the *greater* of itemized deductions or the standard deduction. Taxpayers whose itemized deductions are less than the standard deduction compute their taxable income using the standard deduction rather than itemizing.

▼ **EXAMPLE 6**

Sara, who is single, is 66 years old. She had total itemized deductions of $5,100 during 1998. Her total standard deduction is $5,300 ($4,250 basic standard deduction plus $1,050 additional standard deduction). Sara should compute her taxable income for 1998 using the standard deduction ($5,300), since it exceeds her itemized deductions ($5,100). ▼

Personal and Dependency Exemptions. Exemptions are allowed for the taxpayer, for the taxpayer's spouse, and for each dependent of the taxpayer. The exemption amount is $2,650 in 1997 and $2,700 in 1998.

APPLICATION OF THE TAX FORMULA

The tax formula shown in Figure 15–1 is illustrated in Example 7.

▼ **EXAMPLE 7**

Grace, age 25, is single and has no dependents. She is a high school teacher and earned a $20,000 salary in 1998. Her other income consisted of a $1,000 prize won in a sweepstakes contest and $500 interest on municipal bonds received as a graduation gift in 1995. During 1998, she sustained a deductible capital loss of $1,000. Her itemized deductions are $4,400. Grace's taxable income for the year is computed as follows:

Income (broadly conceived)		
Salary		$20,000
Prize		1,000
Interest on municipal bonds		500
Total income		$21,500
Less: Exclusion—		
Interest on municipal bonds		(500)
Gross income		$21,000
Less: Deduction *for* adjusted gross income—		
Capital loss		(1,000)
Adjusted gross income		$20,000
Less: The greater of—		
Total itemized deductions	$4,400	
or the standard deduction	$4,250	(4,400)
Personal and dependency exemptions		
(1 × $2,700)		(2,700)
Taxable income		$12,900

▼

The structure of the individual income tax return (Form 1040, 1040A, or 1040EZ) differs somewhat from the tax formula in Figure 15–1. On the tax return, gross income generally is the starting point in computing taxable income. With few exceptions, exclusions are not reported on the tax return.

INDIVIDUALS NOT ELIGIBLE FOR THE STANDARD DEDUCTION

The following individual taxpayers are ineligible to use the standard deduction and therefore *must* itemize:[8]

- A married individual filing a separate return where either spouse itemizes deductions.
- A nonresident alien.
- An individual filing a return for a period of less than 12 months because of a change in annual accounting period.

SPECIAL LIMITATIONS FOR INDIVIDUALS WHO CAN BE CLAIMED AS DEPENDENTS

Special rules apply to the standard deduction and personal exemption of an individual who can be claimed as a dependent on another person's tax return.

When filing his or her own tax return, a *dependent's* basic standard deduction in 1998 is limited to the greater of $700 or the sum of the individual's earned income for the year plus $250.[9] However, if the sum of the individual's earned income plus $250 exceeds the normal standard deduction, the standard deduction is limited to the appropriate amount shown in Table 15–1. These limitations apply only to the basic standard deduction. A dependent who is 65 or over or blind or both is also allowed the additional standard deduction amount on his or her own return (refer to Table 15–2). These provisions are illustrated in Examples 8 through 11.

EXAMPLE 8 Susan, who is 17 years old and single, is claimed as a dependent on her parents' tax return. During 1998, she received $1,200 interest (unearned income) on a savings account. She also earned $500 from a part-time job. When Susan files her own tax return, her standard deduction is $750 (the greater of $700 or the sum of earned income of $500 plus $250). ▼

EXAMPLE 9 Assume the same facts as in Example 8, except that Susan is 67 years old and is claimed as a dependent on her son's tax return. In this case, when Susan files her own tax return, her standard deduction is $1,800 [$750 (the greater of $700 or the sum of earned income of $500 plus $250) + $1,050 (the additional standard deduction allowed because Susan is 65 or over)]. ▼

EXAMPLE 10 Peggy, who is 16 years old and single, earned $600 from a summer job and had no unearned income during 1998. She is claimed as a dependent on her parents' tax return. Her standard deduction is $850 (the greater of $700 or the sum of earned income of $600 plus $250). ▼

EXAMPLE 11 Jack, who is a 20-year-old, single, full-time college student, is claimed as a dependent on his parents' tax return. He worked as a musician during the summer of 1998, earning $4,300. Jack's standard deduction is $4,250 (the greater of $700 or the sum of earned income of $4,300 plus $250, but limited to the $4,250 standard deduction for a single taxpayer). ▼

---

[8] § 63(c)(6).
[9] § 63(c)(5). The $700 amount is *subject to* adjustment for inflation each year. The amount was $650 for 1997. The $250 amount is adjusted for inflation beginning in 1999. The $250 amount was created by the Taxpayer Relief Act of 1997.

A taxpayer who claims an individual as a dependent is allowed to claim an exemption for the dependent. The dependent cannot claim a personal exemption on his or her own return. Based on the tax formula, Jack in Example 11 would have taxable income of $50, determined as follows:

Gross income	$ 4,300
Less: Standard deduction	(4,250)
Personal exemption	(–0–)
Taxable income	$ 50

PERSONAL AND DEPENDENCY EXEMPTIONS

2 LEARNING OBJECTIVE
Apply the rules for arriving at personal and dependency exemptions.

The use of exemptions in the tax system is based in part on the idea that a taxpayer with a small amount of income should be exempt from income taxation. An exemption frees a specified amount of income from tax ($2,650 in 1997 and $2,700 in 1998). The exemption amount is indexed (adjusted) annually for inflation. An individual who is not claimed as a dependent by another taxpayer is allowed to claim his or her own personal exemption. In addition, a taxpayer may claim an exemption for each dependent.

EXAMPLE 12

Bonnie, who is single, supports her mother and father, who have no income of their own, and claims them as dependents on her tax return. Bonnie may claim a personal exemption for herself plus an exemption for each dependent. On her 1998 tax return, Bonnie may deduct $8,100 for exemptions ($2,700 per exemption × 3 exemptions). ▼

PERSONAL EXEMPTIONS

The Code provides a **personal exemption** for the taxpayer and an exemption for the spouse if a joint return is filed. However, when separate returns are filed, a married taxpayer cannot claim an exemption for his or her spouse *unless* the spouse has no gross income and is not claimed as the dependent of another taxpayer.

The determination of marital status generally is made at the end of the taxable year, except when a spouse dies during the year. Spouses who enter into a legal separation under a decree of divorce or separate maintenance before the end of the year are considered to be unmarried at the end of the taxable year. The following summary illustrates the effect of death or divorce upon marital status:

Description	Marital Status and Personal Exemptions
• Walt is the widower of Helen who died on January 3, 1998.	Walt and Helen are considered to be married for purposes of filing the 1998 return. Walt may claim two exemptions on his 1998 return.
• Bill and Jane entered into a divorce decree that is effective on December 31, 1998.	Bill and Jane are considered to be unmarried for purposes of filing the 1998 return. Bill and Jane each may claim a personal exemption on their separate returns.

DEPENDENCY EXEMPTIONS

As indicated in Example 12, the Code allows a taxpayer to claim a **dependency exemption** for each eligible individual. A dependency exemption may be claimed for each individual for whom the following five tests are met:[10]

- Support.
- Relationship or member of the household.
- Gross income.
- Joint return.
- Citizenship or residency.

A person who dies during the year can still be claimed as a dependent if all of the tests are met. In such a case, no proration is necessary, and the full amount of the exemption is allowed.

Support Test. Over one-half of the support of the individual must be furnished by the taxpayer. Support includes food, shelter, clothing, medical and dental care, education, etc. However, a scholarship received by a student is not included for purposes of determining whether the taxpayer furnished more than half of the child's support.[11]

EXAMPLE 13
Hal contributed $3,400 (consisting of food, clothing, and medical care) toward the support of his son, Sam, who earned $1,500 from a part-time job and received a $2,000 scholarship to attend a local university. Assuming that the other dependency tests are met, Hal can claim Sam as a dependent since he has contributed more than half of Sam's support. The $2,000 scholarship is not included as support for purposes of this test. ▼

If an individual does not spend funds that have been received from any source, the unspent amounts are not counted for purposes of the support test.

EXAMPLE 14
Emily contributed $3,000 to her father's support during the year. In addition, her father received $2,400 in Social Security benefits, $200 of interest, and wages of $600. Her father deposited the Social Security benefits, interest, and wages in his own savings account and did not use any of the funds for his support. Thus, the Social Security benefits, interest, and wages are not considered to be support provided by Emily's father. Emily may claim her father as a dependent if the other tests are met. ▼

Capital expenditures for items such as furniture, appliances, and automobiles are included in total support if the item does, in fact, constitute support.[12]

EXAMPLE 15
Norm purchased a television set costing $150 and gave it to his minor daughter. The television set was placed in the child's bedroom and was used exclusively by her. Norm should include the cost of the television set in determining the support of his daughter. ▼

EXAMPLE 16
Mark paid $6,000 for an automobile that was titled and registered in his name. Mark's minor son is permitted to use the automobile equally with Mark. Since Mark did not give the automobile to his son, the $6,000 cost is not includible as a support item. However, out-of-

---

[10] § 152.
[11] Reg. § 1.152–1(c).
[12] Rev.Rul. 57–344, 1957–2 C.B. 112; Rev.Rul. 58–419, 1958–2 C.B. 57.

pocket operating expenses incurred by Mark for the benefit of his son are includible as support. ▼

One exception to the support test involves a **multiple support agreement**. A multiple support agreement permits one of a group of taxpayers who furnish more than half of the support of an individual to claim a dependency exemption for that individual even if no one person provides more than 50 percent of the support.[13] Any person who contributed *more than 10 percent* of the support is entitled to claim the exemption if each person in the group who contributed more than 10 percent files a written consent. This provision frequently enables one of the children of aged dependent parents to claim an exemption when none of the children meets the 50 percent support test. Each person who is a party to the multiple support agreement must meet all other requirements (except the support requirement) for claiming the exemption. A person who does not meet the relationship or member-of-the-household test, for instance, cannot claim the dependency exemption under a multiple support agreement. It does not matter if he or she contributes more than 10 percent of the individual's support.

▼ **EXAMPLE 17**

Wanda, who resides with her son, Adam, received $6,000 from various sources during 1998. This constituted her entire support for the year. She received support from the following individuals:

	Amount	Percentage of Total
Adam, a son	$2,880	48
Bob, a son	600	10
Carol, a daughter	1,800	30
Diane, a friend	720	12
	$6,000	100

If Adam and Carol file a multiple support agreement, either may claim the dependency exemption for Wanda. Bob may not claim Wanda because he did not contribute more than 10% of her support. Bob's consent is not required in order for Adam and Carol to file a multiple support agreement. Diane does not meet the relationship or member-of-the-household test and cannot be a party to the agreement. The decision as to who claims Wanda rests with Adam and Carol. It is possible for Carol to claim Wanda, even though Adam furnished more of Wanda's support. ▼

Each person who qualifies under the more-than-10 percent rule (except for the person claiming the exemption) must complete Form 2120 (Multiple Support Declaration) waiving the exemption. The person claiming the exemption must attach all Forms 2120 to his or her own return.

Taxpayers should maintain adequate records of expenditures for support in the event a dependency exemption is questioned on audit by the IRS. The maintenance of adequate records is particularly important for exemptions arising from multiple support agreements.

---

[13] § 152(c).

PLANNING CONSIDERATIONS

Multiple Support Agreements and the Medical Expense Deduction

Generally, medical expenses are deductible only if they are paid on behalf of the taxpayer, his or her spouse, and their dependents.[14] Since deductibility may rest on dependency status, planning is important in arranging multiple support agreements.

EXAMPLE 18
During the year, Zelda will be supported by her two sons (Vern and Vito) and her daughter (Maria). Each will furnish approximately one-third of the required support. If the parties decide that the dependency exemption should be claimed by Maria under a multiple support agreement, any medical expenses incurred by Zelda should be paid by Maria. ▼

In planning a multiple support agreement, take into account which of the parties is most likely to exceed the 7.5 percent limitation. In Example 18, for instance, Maria might be a poor choice if she and her family do not expect to incur many medical and drug expenses of their own.

A second exception to the 50 percent support requirement can occur for a child of parents who are divorced or separated under a decree of separate maintenance. For decrees executed after 1984, the custodial parent is allowed to claim the exemption unless that parent agrees in writing not to claim a dependency exemption for the child.[15] Thus, claiming the exemption is dependent on whether a written agreement exists, *not* on meeting the support test.

EXAMPLE 19
Ira and Rita obtain a divorce decree in 1990. In 1998, their two children are in Rita's custody. Ira contributed over half of the support for each child. In the absence of a written agreement on the dependency exemptions, Rita (the custodial parent) is entitled to the exemptions in 1998. However, Ira may claim the exemptions if Rita agrees in writing. ▼

For the noncustodial parent to claim the exemption, the custodial parent must complete Form 8332 (Release of Claim to Exemption for Child of Divorced or Separated Parents). The release can apply to a single year, a number of specified years, or all future years. The noncustodial parent must attach a copy of Form 8332 to his or her return.

Relationship or Member-of-the-Household Test.
To be claimed as a dependent, an individual must be either a relative of the taxpayer or a member of the taxpayer's household. The Code contains a detailed listing of the various blood and marriage relationships that qualify. Note, however, that the relationship test is met if the individual is a qualifying relative of either spouse. Once established by marriage, a relationship continues regardless of subsequent changes in marital status.

---

[14] See the discussion of medical expenses later in this chapter.   [15] § 152(e).

The following individuals may be claimed as dependents of the taxpayer if the other tests for dependency are met:[16]

- A son or daughter of the taxpayer or a descendant of either, such as a grandchild.
- A stepson or stepdaughter of the taxpayer.
- A brother, sister, stepbrother, or stepsister of the taxpayer.
- The father or mother of the taxpayer or an ancestor of either, such as a grandparent.
- A stepfather or stepmother of the taxpayer.
- A nephew or niece of the taxpayer.
- An uncle or aunt of the taxpayer.
- A son-in-law, daughter-in-law, father-in-law, mother-in-law, brother-in-law, or sister-in-law of the taxpayer.
- An individual who, for the entire taxable year of the taxpayer, has as his or her principal place of abode the home of the taxpayer and is a member of the taxpayer's household. This does not include an individual who, at any time during the taxable year, was the spouse of the taxpayer.

The following rules are also prescribed in the Code:[17]

- A legally adopted child is treated as a natural child.
- A foster child qualifies if the child's principal place of abode is the taxpayer's household.

Gross Income Test. The dependent's gross income must be less than the exemption amount ($2,700 in 1998).[18] The gross income test is measured by income that is taxable. In the case of scholarships, for example, it excludes the nontaxable portion (e.g., amounts received for books and tuition) but includes the taxable portion (e.g., amounts received for room and board).

A parent may claim a dependency exemption for his or her child, even when the child's gross income exceeds $2,700, if the parent provided over half of the child's support and the child, at year-end, is under age 19 or is a full-time student under age 24. If the parent claims a dependency exemption, the dependent child may *not* claim a personal exemption on his or her own income tax return.

A child is defined as a son, stepson, daughter, stepdaughter, adopted son, or adopted daughter and may include a foster child.[19] For the child to qualify as a student for purposes of the dependency exemption, he or she must be a full-time student at an educational institution during some part of five calendar months of the year.[20] This exception to the gross income test for dependent children who are under age 19 or full-time students under age 24 permits a child or college student to earn money from part-time or summer jobs without penalizing the parent with the loss of the dependency exemption.

Joint Return Test. If a dependent is married, the supporting taxpayer (e.g., the parent of a married child) generally is not permitted a dependency exemption if

---

[16] § 152(a). However, under § 152(b)(5), a taxpayer may not claim someone who is a member of his or her household as a dependent if their relationship is in violation of local law. For example, the dependency exemption was denied because the taxpayer's relationship to the person claimed as a dependent constituted *cohabitation*, a crime under applicable state law. *Cassius L. Peacock, III*, 37 TCM 177, T.C.Memo. 1978–30.

[17] § 152(b)(2).
[18] § 151(c)(1).
[19] Reg. § 1.151–3(a).
[20] Reg. §§ 1.151–3(b) and (c).

the married individual files a joint return with his or her spouse.[21] The joint return rule does not apply, however, if the following conditions are met:

- The reason for filing is to claim a refund for tax withheld.
- No tax liability would exist for either spouse on separate returns.
- Neither spouse is required to file a return.

See Table 15–4 on page 15–21 and the related discussion concerning income level requirements for filing a return.

EXAMPLE 20

Paul provides over half of the support of his son, Quinn. He also provides over half of the support of Vera, who is Quinn's wife. During the year, both Quinn and Vera had part-time jobs. To recover the taxes withheld, they file a joint return. If Quinn and Vera have income low enough that they are not *required* to file a return, Paul is allowed to claim both as dependents. ▼

PLANNING CONSIDERATIONS

Problems with a Joint Return

A married person who files a joint return cannot be claimed as a dependent by another taxpayer. If a joint return has been filed, the damage may be undone if separate returns are substituted on a timely basis (on or before the due date of the return).

EXAMPLE 21

While preparing a client's 1997 income tax return on April 8, 1998, a tax practitioner discovered that the client's daughter had filed a joint return with her husband in late January of 1998. Presuming the daughter otherwise qualifies as the client's dependent, the exemption is not lost if she and her husband file separate returns on or before April 15, 1998. ▼

Citizenship or Residency Test. To be a dependent, the individual must be either a U.S. citizen, a U.S. resident, or a resident of Canada or Mexico for some part of the calendar year in which the taxpayer's tax year begins.

PHASE-OUT OF EXEMPTIONS

Several provisions of the tax law are intended to increase the tax liability of more affluent taxpayers who might otherwise enjoy some benefit from having some of their taxable income subject to the lower income tax brackets (e.g., 15 percent, 28 percent). One such provision phases out personal and dependency exemptions as AGI exceeds specified threshold amounts. For 1997 and 1998, the phase-out *begins* at the following threshold amounts (which are indexed annually for inflation):

	1997	1998
Joint return/surviving spouse	$181,800	$186,800
Head of household	151,500	155,650
Single	121,200	124,500
Married, filing separately	90,900	93,400

---

[21] § 151(c)(2).

Exemptions are phased out by 2 percent for each $2,500 (or fraction thereof) by which the taxpayer's AGI exceeds the threshold amounts. For a married taxpayer filing separately, the phase-out is 2 percent for each $1,250 or fraction thereof.

The allowable exemption amount can be determined with the following steps:

1. AGI − threshold amount = excess amount.
2. Excess amount/$2,500 = reduction factor [rounded up to the next whole increment (e.g., 18.1 = 19)] × 2 = phase-out percentage.
3. Phase-out percentage (from step 2) × exemption amount = amount of exemptions phased out.
4. Exemption amount − phase-out amount = allowable exemption deduction.

EXAMPLE 22

Frederico is married but files a separate return. His 1998 AGI is $113,400. He is entitled to one personal exemption.

1. $113,400 − $93,400 = $20,000 excess amount.
2. [($20,000/$1,250) × 2] = 32% (phase-out percentage).
3. 32% × $2,700 = $864 amount of exemption phased out.
4. $2,700 − $864 = $1,836 allowable exemption deduction.

Note that the exemption amount is completely phased out when the taxpayer's AGI exceeds the threshold amount by more than $122,500 ($61,250 for a married taxpayer filing a separate return), calculated as follows:

$122,501/$2,500 = 49.0004, rounded to 50 and multiplied by 2 = 100% (phase-out percentage). ▼

EXAMPLE 23

Bill and Isabella file a joint return claiming two personal exemptions and one dependency exemption for their child. Their 1998 AGI equals $310,800.

$310,800 − $186,800 = $124,000 excess amount

Since the excess amount exceeds $122,500, the exemptions are completely phased out. ▼

TAX DETERMINATION

TAX TABLE METHOD

3 LEARNING OBJECTIVE
Use the proper method for determining the tax liability.

Most taxpayers compute their tax using the Tax Table. Eligible taxpayers compute taxable income (as shown in Figure 15–1) and *must* determine their tax by reference to the Tax Table. The following taxpayers, however, may not use the Tax Table method:

- An individual who files a short period return (refer to Chapter 6).
- Individuals whose taxable income exceeds the maximum (ceiling) amount in the Tax Table. The 1997 Tax Table applies to taxable income below $100,000 for Form 1040.[22]
- An estate or trust.

The 1997 Tax Table is reproduced in Appendix A. This table will be used to illustrate the tax computation.

---

[22] Presumably, the 1998 Tax Table, which had not been issued at the date of publication of this text, will cover the same range of taxable income.

EXAMPLE 24

Pedro, a single taxpayer, is eligible to use the Tax Table. For 1997, he had taxable income of $25,025. To determine Pedro's tax using the Tax Table (see Appendix A), find the $25,000 to $25,050 income line. The first column to the right of the taxable income column is for single taxpayers. Pedro's tax for 1997 is $3,803. ▼

TAX RATE SCHEDULE METHOD

The Tax Rate Schedules contain rates of 15, 28, 31, 36, and 39.6 percent. Separate schedules are provided for the following filing statuses: single, married filing jointly, married filing separately, and head of household. The rate schedules for 1997 and 1998 are reproduced inside the front cover of this text and also in Appendix A.

The rate schedules are adjusted for inflation each year. Comparison of the 1997 and 1998 schedules for single taxpayers shows that the top amount to which the 15 percent bracket applies rose from $24,650 in 1997 to $25,350 in 1998. Thus, inflation allowed $700 ($25,350 − $24,650) more taxable income to be subject to the lowest 15 percent rate.

The 1998 rate schedule for single taxpayers is reproduced in Table 15–3. This schedule is used to illustrate the tax computations in Examples 25, 26, and 27.

▼ **TABLE 15–3**
1998 Tax Rate Schedule for Single Taxpayers

If Taxable Income Is . . .			Of the Amount
Over	But Not Over	The Tax Is:	Over
$ –0–	$ 25,350	15%	$ –0–
25,350	61,400	$ 3,802.50 + 28%	25,350
61,400	128,100	13,896.50 + 31%	61,400
128,100	278,450	34,573.50 + 36%	128,100
278,450		88,699.50 + 39.6%	278,450

EXAMPLE 25

Pat is single and had $18,000 of taxable income in 1998. His tax is $2,700 ($18,000 × 15%). ▼

EXAMPLE 26

Chris is single and had taxable income of $41,450 in 1998. Her tax is $8,310.50 [$3,802.50 + 28%($41,450 − $25,350)]. ▼

Note that $3,802.50, which is the starting point in the tax computation in Example 26, is 15 percent of the $25,350 taxable income in the first bracket. Income in excess of $25,350 is taxed at a 28 percent rate. This reflects the *progressive* (or graduated) rate structure on which the U.S. income tax system is based. A tax is progressive if a higher rate of tax applies as the tax base increases.

EXAMPLE 27

Carl is single and had taxable income of $81,900 in 1998. His tax is $20,251.50 [$13,896.50 + 31%($81,900 − $61,400)]. Note that the effect of this computation is to tax part of Carl's income at 15%, part at 28%, and part at 31%. An alternative computational method provides a clearer illustration of the progressive rate structure of the individual income tax:

Tax on $25,350 at 15%	$ 3,802.50
Tax on $61,400 − $25,350 at 28%	10,094.00
Tax on $81,900 − $61,400 at 31%	6,355.00
Total	$20,251.50

Carl's marginal rate (refer to Chapter 1) is 31%, and his average rate is 24.7% ($20,251.50 tax/$81,900 taxable income). ▼

A special computation limits the effective tax rate on long-term capital gain to a maximum rate of 28 percent. This beneficial tax treatment of long-term capital gain is discussed in detail in Chapter 8.

PLANNING CONSIDERATIONS

Shifting Income and Deductions across Time

It is natural for taxpayers to be concerned about the tax rates they are paying. How does a tax practitioner communicate information about rates to clients? There are several possibilities. For example, a taxpayer who is in the 15 percent bracket this year and expects to be in the 31 percent bracket next year should, if possible, defer payment of deductible expenses until next year to maximize the tax benefit of the deduction.

A note of caution is in order with respect to shifting income and expenses between years. Congress has recognized the tax planning possibilities of such shifting and has enacted many provisions to limit a taxpayer's ability to do so. Some of these limitations on the shifting of income and deductions are discussed in Chapters 3 through 6.

COMPUTATION OF NET TAXES PAYABLE OR REFUND DUE

The pay-as-you-go feature of the Federal income tax system requires payment of all or part of the taxpayer's income tax liability during the year. These payments take the form of Federal income tax withheld by employers or estimated tax paid by the taxpayer or both.[23] The payments are applied against the tax from the **Tax Table** or **Tax Rate Schedules** to determine whether the taxpayer will get a refund or pay additional tax.

Employers are required to withhold income tax on compensation paid to their employees and to pay this tax over to the government. The employer notifies the employee of the amount of income tax withheld on Form W–2 (Wage and Tax Statement). The employee should receive this form by January 31 after the year in which the income tax is withheld.

If taxpayers receive income that is not subject to withholding or income from which not enough tax is withheld, they must pay estimated tax. These individuals must file Form 1040–ES (Estimated Tax for Individuals) and pay in quarterly installments the income tax and self-employment tax estimated to be due.

The income tax from the Tax Table or the Tax Rate Schedules is reduced by the individual's tax credits. There is an important distinction between tax credits and tax deductions. Tax credits (including tax withheld) reduce the tax liability dollar-for-dollar. Tax deductions reduce taxable income on which the tax liability is based.

EXAMPLE 28

Gail is a taxpayer in the 28% tax bracket. As a result of incurring $1,000 in child care, she is entitled to a $200 child care credit ($1,000 child care expenses × 20% credit rate). She also contributed $1,000 to the American Cancer Society and included this amount in her itemized deductions. The child care credit results in a $200 reduction of Gail's tax liability for the year. The contribution to the American Cancer Society reduces taxable income by $1,000 and results in a $280 reduction in Gail's tax liability ($1,000 reduction in taxable income × 28% tax rate). ▼

---

[23] See § 3402 for withholding and § 6654 for estimated payments.

Selected tax credits for individuals are discussed later in this chapter. The following are some of the more common credits available for individuals:

- Child tax credit.
- Credit for child and dependent care expenses.
- Credit for the elderly.
- Earned income credit.

EXAMPLE 29

Kelly, age 30, is a head of household whose disabled dependent mother lives with him. During 1998, Kelly had the following: taxable income, $30,000; income tax withheld, $3,950; estimated tax payments, $600; and credit for dependent care expenses, $200. Kelly's net tax payable (refund due) is computed as follows:

Income tax (from 1998 Tax Rate Schedule)		$ 4,500
Less: Tax credits and prepayments—		
Credit for dependent care expenses	$ 200	
Income tax withheld	3,950	
Estimated tax payments	600	(4,750)
Net taxes payable (refund due if negative)		($ 250)

UNEARNED INCOME OF CHILDREN UNDER AGE 14 TAXED AT PARENTS' RATE

LEARNING OBJECTIVE 4
Identify and work with kiddie tax situations.

Most individuals compute taxable income using the tax formula shown in Figure 15–1. Special provisions govern the computation of taxable income and the tax liability for children under age 14 who have **unearned income** in excess of specified amounts.

Individuals who are claimed as dependents by other taxpayers cannot claim an exemption on their own return. This prevents parents from shifting the tax on investment income (such as interest and dividends) to a child by transferring ownership of the assets producing the income. Without this provision, the child would pay no tax on the income to the extent that it was sheltered by the child's exemption.

Current tax law also reduces or eliminates the possibility of saving taxes by shifting income from parents to children by taxing the net unearned of children under age 14 as if it were the parents' income.[24] Unearned income includes such income as taxable interest, dividends, capital gains, rents, royalties, pension and annuity income, and income (other than earned income) received as the beneficiary of a trust.

This provision, commonly referred to as the **kiddie tax**, applies to any child for any taxable year if the child has not reached age 14 by the close of the taxable year, has at least one living parent, and has unearned income of more than $1,400. The kiddie tax provision does not apply to a child age 14 or older. However, the limitation on the use of the standard deduction and the unavailability of the personal exemption do apply to such a child as long as he or she is eligible to be claimed as a dependent by a parent.

Net Unearned Income. Net unearned income of a dependent child is computed as follows:

---

[24] § 1(g).

Unearned income
Less: $700
Less: The greater of
   $700 of the standard deduction *or*
   The amount of allowable itemized deductions directly connected with the production of the unearned income
Equals: Net unearned income

If net unearned income is zero (or negative), the child's tax is computed without using the parent's rate. If the amount of net unearned income (regardless of source) is positive, the net unearned income will be taxed at the parent's rate. The $700 amounts in the preceding formula are subject to adjustment for inflation each year.

Tax Determination. If a child under age 14 has net unearned income, there are two options for computing the tax on the income. A separate return may be filed for the child, or the parents may elect to report the child's income on their own return. If a separate return is filed for the child, the tax on net unearned income (referred to as the *allocable parental tax*) is computed as though the income had been included on the parents' return. Form 8615 is used to compute the tax. The steps required in this computation are illustrated below.

EXAMPLE 30

Olaf and Olga have a child, Hans (age 10). In 1998, Hans received $2,900 of interest and dividend income and paid investment-related fees of $200. Olaf and Olga had $70,000 of taxable income, not including their child's investment income. Olaf and Olga do not make the parental election.

1. **Determine Hans's net unearned income**

Gross income (unearned)	$ 2,900
Less: $700	(700)
Less: The greater of	
• $700 or	
• Investment expense ($200)	(700)
Equals: Net unearned income	$ 1,500

2. **Determine allocable parental tax**

Parents' taxable income	$ 70,000
Plus: Hans's net unearned income	1,500
Equals: Revised taxable income	$ 71,500
Tax on revised taxable income	$ 14,515
Less: Tax on parents' taxable income	(14,095)
Allocable parental tax	$ 420

3. **Determine Hans's nonparental source tax**

Hans's AGI	$ 2,900
Less: Standard deduction	(700)
Less: Personal exemption	(–0–)
Equals: Taxable income	$ 2,200
Less: Net unearned income	(1,500)
Equals: Nonparental source taxable income	$ 700
Tax on nonparental source income at 15%	$ 105

4. Determine Hans's total tax liability

Nonparental source tax	$ 105
Allocable parental tax	420
Total tax	$ 525

Election to Report Certain Unearned Income on Parent's Return. If a child under age 14 is required to file a tax return and meets all of the following requirements, the parent may elect to report the child's unearned income that exceeds $1,400 on the parent's own tax return:

- Gross income is from interest and dividends only.
- Gross income is more than $700 but less than $7,000.
- No estimated tax has been paid in the name and Social Security number of the child, and the child is not subject to backup withholding.

If the parental election is made, the child is treated as having no gross income and then is not required to file a tax return.

The parent(s) must also pay an additional tax equal to the smaller of $105 or 15 percent of the child's gross income over $700. Parents who have substantial itemized deductions based on AGI may find that making the parental election increases total taxes for the family unit. Taxes should be calculated both with the parental election and without it to determine the appropriate choice.

PLANNING CONSIDERATIONS

Income of Minor Children

Taxpayers can use several strategies to avoid or minimize the effect of the rules that tax the unearned income of certain minor children at the parents' rate. The kiddie tax rules do not apply once a child reaches age 14. Parents should consider giving a younger child assets that defer taxable income until the child reaches age 14. For example, U.S. government Series EE savings bonds can be used to defer income until the bonds are cashed in.

Growth stocks typically pay little in the way of dividends. However, the unrealized appreciation on an astute investment may more than offset the lack of dividends. The child can hold the growth stock until he or she reaches age 14. If the stock is sold then at a profit, the profit is taxed at the child's low rates.

Taxpayers in a position to do so can employ their children in their business and pay them a reasonable wage for the work they actually perform (e.g., light office help, such as filing). The child's earned income is sheltered by the standard deduction, and the parents' business is allowed a deduction for the wages. The kiddie tax rules have no effect on earned income, even if it is earned from the parents' business.

FILING CONSIDERATIONS

5 LEARNING OBJECTIVE
Recognize filing requirements and proper filing status.

Under the category of filing considerations, the following questions need to be resolved:

- Is the taxpayer required to file an income tax return?
- If so, which form should be used?

TABLE 15-4
Filing Levels

Filing Status	1997 Gross Income	1998 Gross Income
Single		
Under 65 and not blind	$ 6,800	$ 6,950
Under 65 and blind	6,800	6,950
65 or older	7,800	8,000
Married, filing joint return		
Both spouses under 65 and neither blind	12,200	12,500
Both spouses under 65 and one or both spouses blind	12,200	12,500
One spouse 65 or older	13,000	13,350
Both spouses 65 or older	13,800	14,200
Married, filing separate return		
All—whether 65 or older or blind	2,650	2,700
Head of household		
Under 65 and not blind	8,700	8,950
Under 65 and blind	8,700	8,950
65 or older	9,700	10,000
Qualifying widow(er)		
Under 65 and not blind	9,550	9,800
Under 65 and blind	9,550	9,800
65 or older	10,350	10,650

- When and how should the return be filed?
- In computing the tax liability, which column of the Tax Table or which Tax Rate Schedule should be used?

The first three questions are discussed under Filing Requirements, and the last is treated under Filing Status.

FILING REQUIREMENTS

General Rules. An individual must file a tax return if certain minimum amounts of gross income have been received. The general rule is that a tax return is required for every individual who has gross income that equals or exceeds the sum of the exemption amount plus the applicable standard deduction.[25] For example, a single taxpayer under age 65 must file a tax return in 1998 if gross income equals or exceeds $6,950 ($2,700 exemption plus $4,250 standard deduction). Table 15–4 lists the income levels[26] that require tax returns under the general rule and under certain special rules.

The additional standard deduction for being age 65 or older is considered in determining the gross income filing requirements. For example, note in Table 15–4 that the 1998 filing requirement for a single taxpayer age 65 or older is $8,000 ($4,250 basic standard deduction + $1,050 additional standard deduction + $2,700 exemption). However, the additional standard deduction for blindness is not taken into account. The 1998 filing requirement for a single taxpayer under age 65 and blind is $6,950 ($4,250 basic standard deduction + $2,700 exemption).

---

[25] The exemption and standard deduction amounts for determining whether a tax return must be filed are adjusted for inflation each year.

[26] § 6012(a)(1).

A self-employed individual with net earnings of $400 or more from a business or profession must file a tax return regardless of the amount of gross income.

Even though an individual has gross income below the filing level amounts and therefore does not owe any tax, he or she must file a return to obtain a tax refund of amounts withheld by employers. A return is also necessary to obtain the benefits of the earned income credit allowed to taxpayers with little or no tax liability.

Filing Requirements for Dependents. Computation of the gross income filing requirement for an individual who can be claimed as a dependent on another person's tax return is subject to more complex rules. Such an individual must file a return if he or she has *either* of the following:

- Earned income only and gross income that is more than the total standard deduction (including any additional standard deduction) that the individual is allowed for the year.
- Unearned income only and gross income of more than $700 plus any additional standard deduction that the individual is allowed for the year.
- Both earned and unearned income and gross income of more than the larger of $700 or the sum of earned income plus $250 (but limited to the applicable basic standard deduction), plus any additional standard deduction that the individual is allowed for the year.

Thus, the filing requirement for a dependent who has *no unearned income* is the total of the *basic* standard deduction plus any *additional* standard deduction, which includes both the additional deduction for blindness and the deduction for being age 65 or older. For example, the 1998 filing requirement for a single dependent who is under 65 and not blind is $4,250, the amount of the basic standard deduction for 1998. The filing requirement for a single dependent who has no unearned income and is under 65 and blind is $5,300 ($4,250 basic standard deduction + $1,050 additional standard deduction).

Selecting the Proper Form. Individual taxpayers file a return on either Form 1040 (the long form), Form 1040A (the short form), or Form 1040EZ. Taxpayers who cannot use either Form 1040EZ or Form 1040A must use Form 1040. These forms are reproduced in Appendix B. Examine the forms to determine which form is appropriate for a particular taxpayer.

When and Where to File. Tax returns of individuals are due on or before the fifteenth day of the fourth month following the close of the tax year. For the calendar year taxpayer, the usual filing date is on or before April 15 of the following year.[27] When the due date falls on a Saturday, Sunday, or legal holiday, the last day for filing falls on the next business day. If the return is mailed to the proper address with sufficient postage and is postmarked on or before the due date, it is considered timely filed. The IRS may prescribe rules governing the filing of returns using various private parcel delivery services (e.g., Airborne Express, DHL, FedEx, UPS).

If a taxpayer is unable to file the return by the specified due date, an automatic four-month extension of time can be obtained by filing Form 4868 (Application for Automatic Extension of Time to File U.S. Individual Income Tax Return) by the return's due date.[28] Further extensions may be granted by the IRS upon a showing of good cause by the taxpayer. For this purpose, Form 2688 (Application for Extension

---

[27] § 6072(a).

[28] Reg. § 1.6081–4.

TAX IN THE NEWS

IS ALLOWING THE USE OF PLASTIC TO PAY TAXES A GOOD IDEA?

A provision in the Taxpayer Relief Act of 1997 permits the IRS to accept credit, debit, or charge cards for the payment of Federal income taxes. Although the provision is intended to benefit taxpayers, one can argue that it may cause more harm than good. Some feel that the easy accessibility of credit sources has resulted in many Americans becoming overburdened with credit card debt. Allowing the cards to be used for paying taxes will certainly further worsen the situation.

Other potential problems come to mind. What happens if the taxpayer charges the taxes and later refuses to pay the bill? Who gets stuck—the IRS or the credit card company? If the latter, is it desirable to have as a tax collector someone other than the IRS? A further problem is who absorbs the discount rate that merchants pay banks to process credit card transactions? Also, will credit card companies extend current incentives (e.g., cash rebates, frequent flyer miles) to holders who use the cards to pay Federal income taxes?

---

of Time to File U.S. Individual Income Tax Return) should be used. An extension of more than six months will not be granted if the taxpayer is in the United States.

Although obtaining an extension excuses a taxpayer from a penalty for failure to file, it does not insulate against the penalty for failure to pay. If more tax is owed, the filing of Form 4868 should be accompanied by an additional payment to cover the balance due. The return should be sent or delivered to the Regional Service Center of the IRS for the area where the taxpayer lives.[29]

If an individual taxpayer needs to file an amended return (e.g., because of a failure to report income or to claim a deduction or tax credit), Form 1040X is filed. The form generally must be filed within three years of the filing date of the original return or within two years from the time the tax was paid, whichever is later.

FILING STATUS

The amount of tax will vary considerably depending on which Tax Rate Schedule is used. This is illustrated in the following example.

EXAMPLE 31

The following amounts of tax (rounded to the nearest dollar) are computed using the 1998 Tax Rate Schedules (inside the front cover of this text). The taxpayer (or taxpayers in the case of a joint return) is assumed to have $40,000 of taxable income.

Filing Status	Amount of Tax
Single	$7,904.50
Married, filing joint return	6,000.00
Married, filing separate return	8,447.25
Head of household	6,786.50

---

[29]The Regional Service Centers and the geographical area each covers can be found in *Your Federal Income Tax*, IRS Publication 17 for 1997 or at http://www.ustreas.gov.

Rates for Single Taxpayers. A taxpayer who is unmarried or separated from his or her spouse by a decree of divorce or separate maintenance and does not qualify for another filing status must use the rates for single taxpayers. Marital status is determined as of the last day of the tax year, except when a spouse dies during the year. In that case, marital status is determined as of the date of death. State law governs whether a taxpayer is considered married, divorced, or legally separated.

Under a special relief provision, however, married persons who live apart may be able to qualify as single. Married taxpayers who are considered single under the *abandoned spouse rules* are allowed to use the head-of-household rates. See the discussion of this filing status under Abandoned Spouse Rules later in the chapter.

Rates for Married Individuals. The joint filing status was originally enacted in 1948 to establish equity between married taxpayers in common law states and those in community property states. Before the joint return rates were enacted, taxpayers in community property states were in an advantageous position relative to taxpayers in common law states because they could split their income. For instance, if one spouse earned $100,000 and the other spouse was not employed, each spouse could report $50,000 of income. Splitting the income in this manner caused the total income to be subject to lower marginal tax rates. Each spouse would start at the bottom of the rate structure.

Taxpayers in common law states did not have this income-splitting option, so their taxable income was subject to higher marginal rates. This inconsistency in treatment was remedied by the joint return provisions. The progressive rates in the joint return Tax Rate Schedule are constructed based on the assumption that income is earned equally by the two spouses.

If married individuals elect to file separate returns, each reports only his or her own income, exemptions, deductions, and credits, and each must use the Tax Rate Schedule applicable to married taxpayers filing separately. It is generally advantageous for married individuals to file a joint return, since the combined amount of tax is lower. However, special circumstances (e.g., significant medical expenses incurred by one spouse subject to the 7.5 percent limitation) may warrant the election to file separate returns. It may be necessary to compute the tax under both assumptions to determine the most advantageous filing status.

When Congress enacted the joint return filing status, the result was to favor married taxpayers. In certain situations, however, the parties would incur less tax if they were not married and filed separate returns. The additional tax that a joint return can cause, commonly called the **marriage penalty,** can develop when *both* spouses have significant taxable incomes.

EXAMPLE 32

John and Betty are employed, and each earns taxable income of $55,000 in 1998. If they *are not married* and file separate returns, each has a tax liability of $12,105, or a total of $24,210 ($12,105 × 2). If they are married to each other, the filing of a joint return produces a tax of $25,526 on taxable income of $110,000 ($55,000 + $55,000). Thus, being married results in $1,316 ($25,526 − $24,210) more tax! ▼

Although some have suggested changes to lessen the impact of the marriage penalty, any remedy is apt to make the tax law more complex.

The Code places some limitations on deductions, credits, etc., when married individuals file separately. If either spouse itemizes deductions, the other spouse must also itemize. Married taxpayers who file separately cannot claim either of the following credits:

- The credit for child and dependent care expenses (in most instances).
- The earned income credit.

The joint return rates also apply for two years following the death of one spouse, if the **surviving spouse** maintains a household for a dependent child.[30] This is referred to as surviving spouse status.

▼ **EXAMPLE 33** Fred dies in 1997 leaving Ethel with a dependent child. For the year of Fred's death (1997), Ethel files a joint return with Fred (presuming the consent of Fred's executor is obtained). For the next two years (1998 and 1999), Ethel, as a surviving spouse, may use the joint return rates. In subsequent years, Ethel may use the head-of-household rates if she continues to maintain a household as her home that is the domicile of the child. ▼

Rates for Heads of Household. Unmarried individuals who maintain a household for a dependent (or dependents) are entitled to use the **head-of-household** rates.[31] The tax liability resulting from the head-of-household rates falls between the liability using the joint return Tax Rate Schedule and the liability using the Tax Rate Schedule for single taxpayers.

To qualify for head-of-household rates, a taxpayer must pay more than half the cost of maintaining a household as his or her home. The household must also be the principal home of a dependent relative.[32] As a general rule, the dependent must live in the taxpayer's household for over half the year.

There are two exceptions to these requirements. One exception is that an *unmarried child* (child also means grandchild, stepchild, or adopted child) need not be a dependent in order for the taxpayer to qualify as a head of household.

▼ **EXAMPLE 34** Nancy maintains a household where she and Dan, her nondependent unmarried son, reside. Since Dan is not married, Nancy qualifies for the head-of-household rates. ▼

Another exception to the general rule is that head-of-household status may be claimed if the taxpayer maintains a *separate home* for his or her *parent or parents* if at least one parent qualifies as a dependent of the taxpayer.[33]

▼ **EXAMPLE 35** Rick, an unmarried individual, lives in New York City and maintains a household in Detroit for his dependent parents. Rick may use the head-of-household rates even though his parents do not reside in his New York home. ▼

Head-of-household status is not changed during the year by death of the dependent. As long as the taxpayer provided more than half of the cost of maintaining the household prior to the dependent's death, head-of-household status is preserved.

Abandoned Spouse Rules. When married persons file separate returns, several unfavorable tax consequences result. For example, the taxpayer must use the Tax Rate Schedule for married taxpayers filing separately. To mitigate such harsh treatment, Congress enacted provisions commonly referred to as the **abandoned spouse rules**. These rules allow a married taxpayer to file as a head of household if all of the following conditions are satisfied:

- The taxpayer does not file a joint return.
- The taxpayer paid more than one-half the cost of maintaining his or her home for the tax year.

---

[30] § 2(a).
[31] § 2(b).
[32] As defined in § 152(a). See § 2(b)(1)(A)(i).
[33] § 2(b)(1)(B).

- The taxpayer's spouse did not live in the home during the last six months of the tax year.
- The home was the principal residence of the taxpayer's child, stepchild, or adopted child for more than half the year.
- The taxpayer could claim the child, stepchild, or adopted child as a dependent.[34]

OVERVIEW OF INCOME PROVISIONS APPLICABLE TO INDIVIDUALS

6 LEARNING OBJECTIVE
Identify specific inclusions and exclusions applicable to individuals.

As indicated earlier in this chapter, the definition of gross income is broad enough to include almost all receipts of money, property, or services. However, the tax law provides for exclusion of many types of income. The following income provisions, which apply to all taxpayers (including individuals), were discussed in Chapter 3:

- Annuities.
- Interest from state and local bonds.
- Life insurance paid on death of insured.
- Imputed interest on below-market loans.
- Income from discharge of indebtedness.
- Income included under the tax benefit rule.

Most *exclusions* available only to individuals are for *fringe benefits* received by *employees* (refer to Exhibit 15–1). Fringe benefits are discussed in Chapter 16. Other specific inclusions and exclusions for individuals are discussed below.

SPECIFIC INCLUSIONS APPLICABLE TO INDIVIDUALS

The general principles of gross income determination as applied by the IRS and the courts have on occasion yielded results Congress found unacceptable. Consequently, Congress has provided more specific rules for determining the amount of gross income from certain sources. Some of these special rules appear in §§ 71–90 of the Code. The following provisions applicable to individuals are covered in this chapter:

- Alimony and separate maintenance payments.
- Prizes and awards.
- Unemployment compensation.
- Social Security benefits.

ALIMONY AND SEPARATE MAINTENANCE PAYMENTS

When a married couple divorce or become legally separated, state law generally requires a division of the property accumulated during the marriage. In addition,

---

[34]The dependency requirement does not apply, however, if the taxpayer could have claimed a dependency exemption except for the fact that the exemption was claimed by the noncustodial parent under a written agreement. Refer to Example 19 and the related discussion.

one spouse may have a legal obligation to support the other spouse. The Code distinguishes between the support payments (alimony or separate maintenance) and the property division in terms of the tax consequences.

Alimony and separate maintenance payments are deductible by the party making the payments and are includible in the gross income of the party receiving the payments.[35] Thus, taxation of the income is shifted from the income earner to the income beneficiary.

EXAMPLE 36

Pete and Tina were divorced, and Pete was required to pay Tina $15,000 of alimony each year. Pete earns $50,000 a year. Therefore, Tina must include the $15,000 in her gross income, and Pete is allowed to deduct $15,000 from his gross income. ▼

A transfer of property other than cash to a former spouse under a divorce decree or agreement is not a taxable event. The transferor is not entitled to a deduction and does not recognize gain or loss on the transfer. The transferee does not recognize income and has a cost basis equal to the transferor's basis.[36]

EXAMPLE 37

Paul transfers stock to Rosa as part of a 1998 divorce settlement. The cost of the stock to Paul is $12,000, and the stock's value at the time of the transfer is $15,000. Rosa later sells the stock for $16,000. Paul is not required to recognize gain from the transfer of the stock to Rosa, and Rosa has a realized *and* recognized gain of $4,000 ($16,000 − $12,000) when she sells the stock. ▼

In the case of cash payments, however, it is often difficult to distinguish between support payments (alimony) and property settlements. In 1984, Congress developed objective rules to classify these payments.[37]

Post-1984 Agreements and Decrees. Payments made under post-1984 agreements and decrees are classified as alimony only if the following conditions are satisfied:

1. The payments are in cash.
2. The agreement or decree does not specify that the payments are not alimony.
3. The payor and payee are not members of the same household at the time the payments are made.
4. There is no liability to make the payments for any period after the death of the payee.[38]

Requirement 1 simplifies the law by clearly distinguishing alimony from a property division; that is, if the payment is not in cash, it must be a property division. Requirement 2 allows the parties to determine by agreement whether or not the payments will be alimony. The prohibition on cohabitation—requirement 3—is aimed at assuring that the alimony payments are associated with duplicative living expenses (maintaining two households).[39] Requirement 4 is an attempt to prevent alimony treatment from being applied to what is, in fact, a payment for property rather than a support obligation. That is, a seller's estate generally will

---

[35] §§ 71 and 215.
[36] § 1041, added to the Code in 1984 to repeal the rule of *U.S. v. Davis*, 62–2 USTC ¶9509, 9 AFTR2d 1625, 82 S.Ct. 1190 (USSC, 1962). Under the *Davis* rule, which applied to pre-1985 divorces, a property transfer incident to divorce was a taxable event.
[37] More complex rules existed for determining the nature of payments under pre-1985 agreements.
[38] § 71(b)(1). This set of alimony rules can also apply to pre-1985 agreements and decrees if both parties agree in writing. The rules applicable to pre-1985 agreements and decrees are not discussed in this text.
[39] *Alexander Washington*, 77 T.C. 601 (1981) at 604.

receive payments for property due after the seller's death. Such payments after the death of the payee could not be for the payee's support.

Front-Loading. As a further safeguard against a property settlement being disguised as alimony, special rules apply to post-1986 agreements if payments in the first or second year exceed $15,000. If the change in the amount of the payments exceeds statutory limits, **alimony recapture** results to the extent of the excess alimony payments. In the third year, the payor must include the excess alimony payments for the first and second years in gross income, and the payee is allowed a deduction for these excess alimony payments. These complex alimony recapture provisions are covered in § 71(f) of the Code.

Child Support. While alimony is taxable, a taxpayer does *not* report income from the receipt of child support payments made by his or her former spouse. This result occurs because the money is received subject to the duty to use the money for the child's benefit. The payor is not allowed to deduct the child support payments because the payments are made to satisfy the payor's legal obligation to support the child.

In many cases, it is difficult to determine whether an amount received is alimony or child support. In the case of a post-1984 decree, if the amount of the payments would be reduced upon the happening of a contingency related to a child (e.g., the child attains age 21 or dies), the amount of the future reduction in the payment is deemed child support.[40]

EXAMPLE 38

A post-1984 divorce agreement provides that Matt is required to make periodic alimony payments of $500 per month to Grace. However, when Matt and Grace's child reaches age 21, marries, or dies (whichever occurs first), the payments will be reduced to $300 per month. Child support payments are $200 each month, and alimony is $300 each month. ▼

PRIZES AND AWARDS

The fair market value of prizes and awards must be included in gross income.[41] Therefore, TV giveaway prizes, magazine publisher prizes, door prizes, and awards from an employer to an employee in recognition of performance are fully taxable to the recipient.

An exception permits a prize or award to be excluded from gross income if all of the following requirements are satisfied:

- The prize or award is received in recognition of religious, charitable, scientific, educational, artistic, literary, or civic achievement (e.g., Nobel Prize, Pulitzer Prize).
- The recipient was selected without taking any action to enter the contest or proceeding.
- The recipient is not required to render substantial future services as a condition for receiving the prize or award.[42]
- The recipient arranges for the prize or award to be paid *directly* to a qualified governmental unit or nonprofit organization.

Another exception is provided to allow exclusion of certain employee achievement awards in the form of tangible personal property (e.g., a gold watch). The awards must be made in recognition of length of service or safety achievement.

---

[40] § 71(c)(2). Pre-1985 agreements can be amended so that the revision will apply.

[41] § 74.
[42] § 74(b).

Generally, the ceiling on the excludible amount for an employee is $400 per taxable year. However, if the award is a *qualified plan award*, the ceiling on the exclusion is $1,600 per taxable year.[43]

UNEMPLOYMENT COMPENSATION

The unemployment compensation program is sponsored and operated by the states and Federal government to provide a source of income for people who have been employed and are temporarily out of work. In a series of rulings over a period of 40 years, the IRS exempted unemployment benefits from tax. These payments were considered social benefit programs for the promotion of the general welfare. After experiencing dissatisfaction with the IRS's treatment of unemployment compensation, Congress amended the Code to provide that the benefits are taxable.[44]

SOCIAL SECURITY BENEFITS

If a taxpayer's income exceeds a specified base amount, as much as 50 or 85 percent of Social Security retirement benefits must be included in gross income. The taxable amount of benefits is determined through the application of one of two complex formulas described in § 86.

SPECIFIC EXCLUSIONS APPLICABLE TO INDIVIDUALS

GIFTS AND INHERITANCES

Beginning with the Income Tax Act of 1913 and continuing to the present, Congress has allowed the recipient of a **gift** to exclude the value of the property from gross income. The exclusion applies to gifts made during the life of the donor (*inter vivos* gifts) and transfers that take effect upon the death of the donor (bequests and inheritances).[45] However, the recipient of a gift of income-producing property is subject to tax on the income subsequently earned from the property. Also, as discussed in Chapter 1, the donor or the decedent's estate may be subject to gift or estate taxes on the transfer.

In numerous cases, gifts are made in a business setting. For example, a salesperson gives a purchasing agent free samples; an employee receives cash from his or her employer on retirement; a corporation makes payments to employees who were victims of a natural disaster; a corporation makes a cash payment to a deceased employee's spouse. In these and similar instances, it is frequently unclear whether the payment was a gift or whether it represents compensation for past, present, or future services.

The courts have defined a gift as "a voluntary transfer of property by one to another without adequate consideration or compensation therefrom."[46] If the payment is intended to be for services rendered, it is not a gift, even though the payment is made without legal or moral obligation and the payor receives no economic benefit from the transfer. To qualify as a gift, the payment must be made

---

[43] §§ 74(c) and 274(j).
[44] § 85.

[45] § 102.
[46] *Estate of D. R. Daly*, 3 B.T.A. 1042 (1926).

"out of affection, respect, admiration, charity or like impulses."[47] Thus, the cases on this issue have been decided on the basis of the donor's intent.

In a landmark case, *Comm. v. Duberstein*,[48] the taxpayer (Duberstein) received a Cadillac from a business acquaintance in appreciation for numerous customers Duberstein had referred to the acquaintance. Duberstein had supplied the businessman with the names of potential customers with no expectation of compensation. The Supreme Court concluded:

> ... despite the characterization of the transfer of the Cadillac by the parties [as a gift] and the absence of any obligation, even of a moral nature, to make it, it was at the bottom a recompense for Duberstein's past service, or an inducement for him to be of further service in the future.

Duberstein was therefore required to include the fair market value of the automobile in gross income.

In the case of cash or other property received by an employee from his or her employer, Congress has eliminated any ambiguity. Transfers from an employer to an employee cannot be excluded as a gift unless the transfer fits into a statutory exclusion provision other than the one for gifts.[49]

SCHOLARSHIPS

General Information. Payments or benefits received by a student at an educational institution may be (1) compensation for services, (2) a gift, or (3) a scholarship. If the payments or benefits are received as compensation for services (past or present), the fact that the recipient is a student generally does not render the amounts received nontaxable.[50]

EXAMPLE 39
State University waives tuition for all graduate teaching assistants. The tuition waived is intended as compensation for services and is therefore included in the graduate assistant's gross income. ▼

The **scholarship** rules are intended to provide exclusion treatment for education-related benefits that cannot qualify as gifts but are not compensation for services. According to the Regulations, "a scholarship is an amount paid or allowed to, or for the benefit of, an individual to aid such individual in the pursuit of study or research."[51] The recipient must be a candidate for a degree (either undergraduate or graduate) at an educational institution.[52]

EXAMPLE 40
Terry enters a contest sponsored by a local newspaper. Each contestant is required to submit an essay on local environmental issues. The prize is one year's tuition at State University. Terry wins the contest. The newspaper has a legal obligation to Terry (as contest winner). Thus, the benefits are not a gift. However, since the tuition payment aids Terry in pursuing her studies and is not compensation for services, the payment is a scholarship. ▼

A scholarship recipient may exclude from gross income the amount used for tuition and related expenses (fees, books, supplies, and equipment required for courses), provided the conditions of the grant do not require that the funds be

---

[47]*Robertson v. U.S.*, 52–1 USTC ¶9343, 41 AFTR 1053, 72 S.Ct. 994 (USSC, 1952).
[48]60–2 USTC ¶9515, 5 AFTR2d 1626, 80 S.Ct. 1190 (USSC, 1960).
[49]§ 102(c).
[50]Reg. § 1.117–2(a). See *C. P. Bhalla*, 35 T.C. 13 (1960), for a discussion of the distinction between a scholarship and compensation. See also *Bingler v. Johnson*, 69–1 USTC ¶9348, 23 AFTR2d 1212, 89 S.Ct. 1439 (USSC, 1969). For potential exclusion treatment, see the subsequent discussion of qualified tuition reductions.
[51]Prop.Reg. § 1.117–6(c)(3)(i).
[52]§ 117(a).

used for other purposes.[53] Amounts received for room and board are taxable and are treated as earned income for purposes of calculating the standard deduction for a taxpayer who is another taxpayer's dependent.[54]

EXAMPLE 41

Kelly received a scholarship of $9,500 from State University to be used to pursue a bachelor's degree. She spent $4,000 on tuition, $3,000 on books and supplies, and $2,500 for room and board. Kelly may exclude $7,000 ($4,000 + $3,000) from gross income. The $2,500 spent for room and board is includible in Kelly's gross income.

The scholarship was Kelly's only source of income. Her parents provided more than 50% of Kelly's support and claimed her as a dependent. Kelly's standard deduction will equal the taxable $2,500 portion of her scholarship, plus $250. Thus, she has no taxable income. ▼

Timing Issues. Frequently, the scholarship recipient is a cash basis taxpayer who receives the money in one tax year but pays the educational expenses in a subsequent year. The amount eligible for exclusion may not be known at the time the money is received. In that case, the transaction is held open until the educational expenses are paid.[55]

EXAMPLE 42

In August 1998, Sanjay received $10,000 as a scholarship for the academic year 1998–1999. Sanjay's expenditures for tuition, books, and supplies were as follows:

August–December 1998	$3,000
January–May 1999	4,500
	$7,500

Sanjay's gross income for 1999 includes $2,500 ($10,000 − $7,500) that is not excludible as a scholarship. None of the scholarship is included in his gross income in 1998. ▼

Disguised Compensation. Some employers make scholarships available solely to the children of key employees. The tax objective of these plans is to provide a nontaxable fringe benefit to the executives by making the payment to the child in the form of an excludible scholarship. However, the IRS has ruled that the payments are generally includible by the parent-employee as compensation for services.[56]

DAMAGES

A person who suffers harm caused by another is often entitled to **compensatory damages.** The tax consequences of the receipt of damages depend on the type of harm the taxpayer has experienced. The taxpayer may seek recovery for (1) a loss of income, (2) expenses incurred, (3) property destroyed, or (4) personal injury.

Generally, reimbursement for a loss of income is taxed in the same manner as the income replaced. Damages that are a recovery of expenses previously deducted by the taxpayer are generally taxable under the tax benefit rule (refer to Chapter 3).

A payment for damaged or destroyed property is treated as an amount received in a sale or exchange of the property. Thus, the taxpayer has a realized gain if the damage payments received exceed the property's basis. Damages for personal injuries receive special treatment under the Code.

---

[53]§ 117(b).
[54]Prop.Reg. § 1.117–6(h).
[55]Prop.Reg. § 1.117–6(b)(2).

[56]Rev.Rul. 75–448, 1975–2 C.B. 55. *Richard T. Armantrout,* 67 T.C. 996 (1977).

Personal Injury. The legal theory of personal injury damages is that the amount received is intended "to make the plaintiff [the injured party] whole as before the injury."[57] It follows that if the damage payments received were subject to tax, the after-tax amount received would be less than the actual damages incurred and the injured party would not be "whole as before the injury."

With regard to personal injury damages, a distinction is made between compensatory damages and **punitive damages.** Under specified circumstances, compensatory damages may be excluded from gross income. Under no circumstances may punitive damages be excluded from gross income.

Compensatory damages are intended to compensate the taxpayer for the damages incurred. Only those compensatory damages received on account of *physical personal injury or sickness* can be excluded from gross income.[58] Compensatory damages awarded on account of emotional distress are not received on account of physical injury or sickness and thus cannot be excluded from gross income (except to the extent of any amount received for medical care). Likewise, any amounts received for age discrimination or injury to one's reputation cannot be excluded.

Punitive damages are amounts the party that caused the harm must pay to the victim as punishment for outrageous conduct. Punitive damages are not intended to compensate the victim, but rather to punish the party that caused the harm. Thus, it follows that amounts received as punitive damages may actually place the victim in a better economic position than before the harm was experienced. Logically, punitive damages are thus included in gross income.

EXAMPLE 43

Tom, a television announcer, was dissatisfied with the manner in which Ron, an attorney, was defending the television station in a libel case. Tom stated on the air that Ron was botching the case. Ron sued Tom for slander, claiming damages for loss of income from clients and potential clients who heard Tom's statement. Ron's claim is for damages to his business reputation, and the amounts received are taxable.

Ron collected on the suit against Tom and was on his way to a party to celebrate his victory when a negligent driver, Norm, drove a truck into Ron's automobile, injuring Ron. Ron filed suit for the physical personal injuries and claimed as damages the loss of income for the period he was unable to work as a result of the injuries. Ron also collected punitive damages that were awarded because of Norm's extremely negligent behavior. Ron's wife also collected damages for the emotional distress she experienced as a result of the accident. Ron may exclude the amounts he received for damages, except the punitive damages. Ron's wife must include the amounts she received for damages in gross income because the amounts were not received because of physical personal injuries or sickness. ▼

WORKERS' COMPENSATION

State workers' compensation laws require the employer to pay fixed amounts for specific job-related injuries. The state laws were enacted so that the employee will not have to go through the ordeal of a lawsuit (and possibly not collect damages because of some defense available to the employer) to recover the damages. Although the payments are intended, in part, to compensate for a loss of future income, Congress has specifically exempted workers' compensation benefits from inclusion in gross income.[59]

---

[57] *C. A. Hawkins*, 6 B.T.A. 1023 (1928).
[58] § 104(a)(2).
[59] § 104(a)(1).

Concept Summary 15-1

Taxation of Damages

Type of Claim	Taxation of Award or Settlement
Breach of contract (generally loss of income)	Taxable.
Property damages	Recovery of cost, gain to the extent of the excess over basis. A loss is deductible for business property and investment property to the extent of basis over the amount realized. A loss may be deductible for personal-use property (see discussion of casualty losses in Chapter 5).
Personal injury	
Physical	All compensatory amounts are excluded unless previously deducted (e.g., medical expenses). Amounts received as punitive damages are included in gross income.
Nonphysical	Compensatory damages and punitive damages are included in gross income.

ACCIDENT AND HEALTH INSURANCE BENEFITS

The income tax treatment of **accident and health insurance benefits** depends on whether the policy providing the benefits was purchased by the taxpayer or the taxpayer's employer. Benefits collected under an accident and health insurance policy purchased by the taxpayer are excludible. In this case, benefits collected under the taxpayer's insurance policy are excluded even though the payments are a substitute for income.[60]

EXAMPLE 44
Bonnie purchased a medical and disability insurance policy. The insurance company paid Bonnie $200 per week to replace wages she lost while in the hospital. Although the payments serve as a substitute for income, the amounts received are tax-exempt benefits collected under Bonnie's insurance policy. ▼

EXAMPLE 45
Joe's injury results in a partial paralysis of his left foot. He receives $5,000 for the injury from his accident insurance company under a policy he had purchased. The $5,000 accident insurance proceeds are tax-exempt. ▼

A different set of rules applies if the accident and health insurance protection was purchased by the individual's employer, as discussed in Chapter 16.

EDUCATIONAL SAVINGS BONDS

The cost of a college education has risen dramatically during the past 10 years, increasing at a rate almost twice the change in the general price level. The U.S. Department of Education estimates that by the year 2007, the cost of attending a publicly supported university for four years will exceed $60,000. For a private university, the cost is expected to exceed $200,000.[61] Consequently, Congress has

---
[60]§ 104(a)(3).
[61]See generally, Knight and Knight, "New Ways to Manage Soaring Tuition Costs," *Journal of Accountancy* (March 1989): 207.

attempted to assist low- to middle-income parents in saving for their children's college education.

The assistance is in the form of an interest income exclusion on **educational savings bonds**.[62] The interest on U.S. government Series EE savings bonds may be excluded from gross income if the bond proceeds are used to pay qualified higher education expenses. The exclusion applies only if both of the following requirements are satisfied:

- The savings bonds are issued after December 31, 1989.
- The savings bonds are issued to an individual who is at least 24 years old at the time of issuance.

The redemption proceeds must be used to pay qualified higher education expenses. Qualified higher education expenses consist of tuition and fees paid to an eligible educational institution for the taxpayer, spouse, or dependent. In calculating qualified higher education expenses, the tuition and fees paid are reduced by excludible scholarships and veterans' benefits received. If the redemption proceeds (both principal and interest) exceed the qualified higher education expenses, only a pro rata portion of the interest will qualify for exclusion treatment.

EXAMPLE 46

Tracy's redemption proceeds from qualified savings bonds during the taxable year were $6,000 (principal of $4,000 and interest of $2,000). Tracy's qualified higher education expenses were $5,000. Since the redemption proceeds exceed the qualified higher education expenses, only $1,667 [($5,000/$6,000) × $2,000] of the interest is excludible. ▼

ITEMIZED DEDUCTIONS

7 LEARNING OBJECTIVE
Determine an individual's allowable itemized deductions.

Taxpayers are allowed to deduct specified expenditures as itemized deductions. Itemized deductions, which are reported on Schedule A, can be classified as follows:

- Expenses that are purely *personal* in nature.
- Expenses incurred by *employees* in connection with their employment activities.
- Expenses related to (1) the *production or collection of income* and (2) the *management of property* held for the production of income.[63]

Expenses in the third category, sometimes referred to as *nonbusiness expenses*, differ from trade or business expenses (discussed previously). Trade or business expenses, which are deductions *for* AGI, must be incurred in connection with a trade or business. Nonbusiness expenses, on the other hand, are expenses incurred in connection with an income-producing activity that does not qualify as a trade or business or a rental activity. Itemized deductions include, but are not limited to, the expenses listed in Exhibit 15–3 on the following page.

Allowable itemized deductions are deductible *from* AGI in arriving at taxable income if the taxpayer elects to itemize. The election to itemize is appropriate when total itemized deductions exceed the standard deduction based on the taxpayer's filing status. The more important itemized deductions are discussed below.

---

[62]§ 135.

[63]Section 212 allows itemized deductions for these types of activities. However, expenses related to the production of *rental or royalty income* are deductions *for* AGI, not itemized deductions, under § 62(a)(4).

EXHIBIT 15-3
Partial List of Itemized Deductions

Personal Expenditures
Medical expenses (in excess of 7.5% of AGI)
State and local income taxes
Real estate taxes
Personal property taxes
Interest on home mortgage
Charitable contributions (limited to a maximum of 50% of AGI)
Casualty and theft losses (in excess of 10% of AGI)
Tax return preparation fee (in excess of 2% of AGI)

Expenditures Related to Employment (in Excess of 2% of AGI)
Union dues
Professional dues and subscriptions
Certain educational expenses
Unreimbursed employee business expenses

Expenditures Related to Income-Producing Activities
Investment interest (to the extent of investment income)
Investment counsel fees (in excess of 2% of AGI)
Other investment expenses (in excess of 2% of AGI)

MEDICAL EXPENSES

Medical Expenses Defined. Medical expenses paid for the care of the taxpayer, spouse, and dependents are allowed as an itemized deduction to the extent the expenses are not reimbursed. The medical expense deduction is limited to the amount by which such expenses exceed 7.5 percent of the taxpayer's AGI.

EXAMPLE 47

During the year, Iris had medical expenses of $4,800, of which $1,000 was reimbursed by her insurance company. If her AGI for the year is $40,000, the itemized deduction for medical expenses is limited to $800 [$4,800 − $1,000 = $3,800 − (7.5% × $40,000)]. ▼

The term *medical care* includes expenditures incurred for the "diagnosis, cure, mitigation, treatment, or prevention of disease, or for the purpose of affecting any structure or function of the body."[64] Medical expense also includes premiums paid for health care insurance, prescribed drugs and insulin, and lodging while away from home for the purpose of obtaining medical care.

Cosmetic Surgery. Amounts paid for unnecessary cosmetic surgery are not deductible medical expenses. However, if cosmetic surgery is deemed necessary, it is deductible as a medical expense. Cosmetic surgery is necessary when it ameliorates (1) a deformity arising from a congenital abnormality, (2) a personal injury, or (3) a disfiguring disease.

Nursing Home Care. The cost of care in a nursing home or home for the aged, including meals and lodging, can be included in deductible medical expenses if the primary reason for being in the home is to get medical care. If the primary

---
[64] § 213(D).

reason for being there is personal, any costs for medical or nursing care can be included in deductible medical expenses, but the cost of meals and lodging must be excluded.

Capital Expenditures. The treatment of certain illnesses may require expenditures for equipment, special structures, or modification of the taxpayer's residence. Some examples of capital expenditures for medical purposes are swimming pools if the taxpayer does not have access to a neighborhood pool and air conditioners if they do not become permanent improvements (e.g., window units).[65] Other examples include dust elimination systems,[66] elevators,[67] and a room built to house an iron lung. These expenditures are medical in nature if they are incurred as a medical necessity upon the advice of a physician, the facility is used primarily by the patient alone, and the expense is reasonable.

Capital expenditures normally are adjustments to basis and are deductible only through depreciation. However, both a capital expenditure for a permanent improvement and expenditures made for the operation or maintenance of the improvement may qualify as medical expenses. If a capital expenditure qualifies as a medical expense, the allowable cost is deductible in the *year incurred*.

Medical Expenses for Spouse and Dependents. In computing the medical expense deduction, a taxpayer may include medical expenses for a spouse and for a person who was a dependent at the time the expenses were paid or incurred. Of the five requirements that normally apply in determining dependency status, neither the gross income nor the joint return test applies in determining dependency status for medical expense deduction purposes.

Transportation and Lodging. Payments for transportation to and from a hospital or other medical facility for medical care are deductible as medical expenses (subject to the 7.5 percent floor). Transportation expenses for medical care include bus, taxi, train, or plane fare, charges for ambulance service, and out-of-pocket expenses for the use of an automobile. A mileage allowance of 10 cents per mile[68] may be used instead of actual out-of-pocket automobile expenses. Whether the taxpayer chooses to claim out-of-pocket automobile expenses or the 10 cents per mile automatic mileage option, related parking fees and tolls can also be deducted. The cost of meals while en route to obtain medical care is not deductible.

A deduction is also allowed for the transportation expenses of a parent who must accompany a child who is receiving medical care or for a nurse or other person giving assistance to a person who is traveling to get medical care and cannot travel alone.

The deduction for lodging expenses included as medical expenses cannot exceed $50 per night for each person. The deduction is allowed not only for the patient but also for a person who must travel with the patient (e.g., a parent traveling with a child who is receiving medical care). Exhibit 15–4 presents examples of deductible and nondeductible medical expenses.

Medical Savings Accounts. Certain employees and self-employed taxpayers may deduct contributions to a Medical Savings Account (MSA). MSAs, which may be used in connection with *high-deductible* health insurance, can be used to

---

[65]Rev.Rul. 55–261, 1955–1 C.B. 307, modified by Rev.Rul. 68–212, 1968–1 C.B. 91.
[66]F. S. Delp, 30 T.C. 1230 (1958).
[67]Riach v. Frank, 62–1 USTC ¶9419, 9 AFTR2d 1263, 302 F.2d 374 (CA–9, 1962).
[68]Rev.Proc. 94–73, 1994–2 C.B. 816.

TAX IN THE NEWS

AVERAGE ITEMIZED DEDUCTIONS

Are your itemized deductions close to average for your income level? Actually, if you're a typical taxpayer, you take the standard deduction instead of itemizing. Approximately 70 percent of individual taxpayers take the standard deduction each year.

The IRS recently released statistics on the approximately 30 percent of individual taxpayers who did itemize in 1995—a year that saw itemized deductions rise nearly 10 percent over 1994. Statistics for the most popular deductions are listed in the following table. The table omits medical expenses because few taxpayers (approximately 5 percent) have medical expenses in excess of the 7.5 percent floor. Similarly, casualty losses (subject to a 10 percent floor) and miscellaneous itemized deductions (subject to a 2 percent floor) are omitted. For comparison, the standard deduction in 1995 was $3,900 for single taxpayers, $6,550 for married taxpayers filing jointly, and $5,750 for heads of household.

AGI	Taxes	Contributions	Interest	Total
$ 15,000–29,999	$ 2,270	$ 1,338	$ 5,442	$ 9,050
30,000–49,999	3,112	1,465	5,715	10,292
50,000–74,999	4,429	1,768	6,587	12,784
75,000–99,999	6,171	2,286	8,063	16,520
100,000–199,999	9,758	3,433	11,107	24,298
200,000+	36,076	16,882	25,046	78,004

These statistics reveal some interesting aspects of the U.S. lifestyle. For one thing, taxpayers at all income levels—even those with AGI of more than $200,000—owe money, as evidenced by the interest deduction. For another, as AGI increases, the percentage given to charity decreases. Those with AGI of $15,000 to $29,999 contribute 5.88 percent of their median income; least generous are taxpayers with AGI of $100,000 to $199,999, who contribute only 2.29 percent of their median income.

Finally, consider what taxpayers have left after meeting the expenses reflected in the table. A single taxpayer with AGI of $22,500, for example, would have only $13,450 left after paying typical itemized deductions for that income level ($22,500 − $9,050 itemized deductions). After paying $1,646 of this amount as Federal income taxes, the taxpayer would have $11,804 left for other expenses.

SOURCE: Information from "Tax Report: Itemized Deductions Surged on 1995 Returns," *Wall Street Journal*, July 16, 1997.

---

accumulate funds for the payment of health care expenses. Individuals who contribute to MSAs may deduct the contributions as deductions *for* AGI. An individual whose employer contributes to an MSA on behalf of the individual may exclude the contributions from gross income. Earnings from MSAs are not included in taxable income of the current year. MSA distributions that are used to pay for medical expenses not covered by a high-deductible plan are not subject to tax. However, distributions used for purposes other than the payment of medical expenses are taxable and are subject to an additional 15 percent penalty if made before age 65, death, or disability.

▼ EXHIBIT 15–4
Examples of Deductible and Nondeductible Medical Expenses

Deductible	Nondeductible
Medical (including dental, mental, and hospital) care	Funeral, burial, or cremation expenses
Prescription drugs	Nonprescription drugs (except insulin)
Special equipment	Bottled water
Wheelchairs	Diaper service, maternity clothes
Crutches	Programs for the general improvement of health
Artificial limbs	Weight reduction
Eyeglasses (including contact lenses)	Health spas
Hearing aids	Stop-smoking clinic
Transportation for medical care	Social activities (e.g., dancing and swimming lessons)
Medical and hospital insurance premiums	
Cost of alcohol and drug rehabilitation	Unnecessary cosmetic surgery

MSAs can be established by employers with 50 or fewer employees, self-employed individuals, and individuals without insurance coverage. High-deductible policies are those with deductibles between $1,500 and $2,250 for individuals (between $3,000 and $4,500 for families). The deduction is limited to 65 percent of the policy deductible for individuals (75 percent for families). MSAs are available on a four-year pilot basis, and eligibility is limited to 750,000 MSAs. After the four-year pilot period is over, Congress will decide whether to retain the MSA provisions and extend eligibility.

TAXES

A deduction is allowed for certain state and local taxes paid or accrued by a taxpayer.[69] The deduction was created to relieve the burden of multiple taxes upon the same source of revenue.

Deductible taxes must be distinguished from nondeductible fees. Fees for special privileges or services are not deductible as itemized deductions if personal in nature. Examples include fees for dog licenses, automobile inspection, automobile titles and registration, hunting and fishing licenses, bridge and highway tolls, drivers' licenses, parking meter deposits, postage, etc. These items, however, could be deductible if incurred as a business expense or for the production of income (refer to Chapter 4). Deductible and nondeductible taxes for purposes of computing itemized deductions are summarized in Exhibit 15–5.[70]

Personal Property Taxes. Deductible personal property taxes must be *ad valorem* (assessed in relation to the value of the property). Therefore, a motor vehicle tax based on weight, model, year, or horsepower is not an ad valorem tax. In contrast, a motor vehicle tax based on the value of the car is deductible.

---
[69] § 164.
[70] Most deductible taxes are listed in § 164, while the nondeductible items are included in § 275.

EXHIBIT 15–5
Deductible and Nondeductible Taxes

Deductible	Nondeductible
State, local, and foreign real property taxes	Federal income taxes
	FICA taxes imposed on employees
State and local personal property taxes	Employer FICA taxes paid on domestic household workers
State, local, and foreign income taxes	Estate, inheritance, and gift taxes
	General sales taxes
The environmental tax	Federal, state, and local excise taxes (e.g., gasoline, tobacco, spirits)
	Taxes on real property to the extent such taxes are to be apportioned and treated as imposed on another taxpayer
	Special assessments for streets, sidewalks, curbing, and other similar improvements

EXAMPLE 48

A state imposes a motor vehicle registration tax on 4% of the value of the vehicle plus 40 cents per hundredweight. Belle, a resident of the state, owns a car having a value of $4,000 and weighing 3,000 pounds. Belle pays an annual registration fee of $172. Of this amount, $160 (4% of $4,000) is deductible as a personal property tax. The remaining $12, based on the weight of the car, is not deductible. ▼

Real Estate Taxes. Real estate taxes of individuals are generally deductible. Taxes on personal-use property and investment property are deductible as itemized deductions. Taxes on business property are deductible as business expenses. Real property taxes on property that is sold during the year must be allocated between the buyer and the seller (refer to Chapter 4).

State and Local Income Taxes. The position of the IRS is that state and local *income* taxes imposed upon an individual are deductible only as itemized deductions, even if the taxpayer's sole source of income is from a business, rents, or royalties.

Cash basis taxpayers are entitled to deduct state income taxes withheld by the employer in the year the taxes are withheld. In addition, estimated state income tax payments are deductible in the year the payment is made by cash basis taxpayers even if the payments relate to a prior or subsequent year.[71] If the taxpayer overpays state income taxes because of excessive withholdings or estimated tax payments, the refund received is included in gross income of the following year to the extent that the deduction reduced the tax liability in the prior year.

EXAMPLE 49

Leona, a cash basis, unmarried taxpayer, had $800 of state income tax withheld during 1998. Additionally in 1998, Leona paid $100 that was due when she filed her 1997 state income tax return and made estimated payments of $300 on her 1998 state income tax. When Leona files her 1998 Federal income tax return in April 1999, she elects to itemize deductions, which amount to $5,500, including the $1,200 of state income tax payments and withholdings.

---

[71] Rev.Rul. 71–190, 1971–1 C.B. 70. See also Rev.Rul. 82–208, 1982–2 C.B. 58, where a deduction is not allowed when the taxpayer cannot, in good faith, reasonably determine that there is additional state income tax liability.

TAX IN THE NEWS

WORKING TO PAY TAXES

Although many exclusions, deductions, and other tax breaks are available, Americans still spend a significant part of each day working to pay Federal, state, and local taxes. According to a Tax Foundation study, the average American worked two hours and 49 minutes of each day to pay taxes in 1997. This is a new record, up one minute from 1996. The trend is disturbing. The comparable time in 1930 was 58 minutes.

SOURCE: "Tax Report: Americans Must Work Even Longer This Year to Pay Their Taxes," *Wall Street Journal*, April 4, 1997, p. A1.

As a result of overpaying her 1998 state income tax, Leona receives a refund of $200 early in 1999. She will include this amount in her 1999 gross income in computing her Federal income tax. It does not matter whether Leona received a check from the state for $200 or applied the $200 toward her 1999 state income tax. ▼

PLANNING CONSIDERATIONS

Timing the Payment of Deductible Taxes

It is sometimes possible to defer or accelerate the payment of certain deductible taxes, such as state income tax, real property tax, and personal property tax. For instance, the final installment of estimated state income tax is generally due after the end of a given tax year. Accelerating the payment of the final installment could result in larger itemized deductions for the current year.

INTEREST

For Federal income tax purposes, interest must be divided into four categories: business interest, personal interest, qualified residence interest, and investment interest. Business interest is fully deductible as an ordinary and necessary expense. Personal (consumer) interest is not deductible. This includes credit card interest, interest on car loans, and any other interest that is not business interest, qualified residence interest, or investment interest. Investment interest and qualified residence (home mortgage) interest are deductible, subject to limits discussed below.

Investment Interest. Taxpayers frequently borrow funds that they use to acquire investment assets. When the interest expense is large relative to the income from the investments, substantial tax benefits could result. Congress has therefore limited the deductibility of interest on funds borrowed for the purpose of purchasing or continuing to hold investment property. **Investment interest** expense is limited to **net investment income** for the year.[72]

Investment income is gross income from interest, dividends, annuities, and royalties not derived in the ordinary course of a trade or business. Income from a

---
[72] § 63(d).

passive activity and income from a real estate activity in which the taxpayer actively participates are not included in investment income (see Chapter 5).

Net capital gain attributable to the disposition of property producing the types of income just identified or from property held for investment purposes may be included as investment income at the taxpayer's election. To make this election, the taxpayer must agree to reduce capital gains qualifying for the alternative tax computation for net capital gain (see Chapter 8) by an equivalent amount.

EXAMPLE 50

Terry incurred $13,000 of interest expense related to her investments during the year. Her investment income included $4,000 of interest, $2,000 of dividends, and a $5,000 net capital gain on the sale of securities. Her investment income for purposes of computing the investment income limitation is $6,000 ($4,000 interest + $2,000 dividends). If she elects to treat the net capital gain as investment income, her investment income for purposes of computing the limitation is $11,000. ▼

Net investment income is the excess of investment income over investment expenses. Investment expenses are those deductible expenses directly connected with the production of investment income. Investment expenses do not include interest expense. When investment expenses fall into the category of miscellaneous itemized deductions that are subject to the 2 percent-of-AGI floor, some may not enter into the calculation of net investment income because of the floor.

EXAMPLE 51

Gina has AGI of $80,000, which includes dividends and interest income of $18,000. Besides investment interest expense, she paid $3,000 of city ad valorem property tax on stocks and bonds and had the following miscellaneous itemized expenses:

Safe deposit box rental	$ 120
Investment counsel fee	1,200
Unreimbursed business travel	850
Uniforms	600

Before Gina can determine her investment expenses for purposes of calculating net investment income, those miscellaneous expenses that are not investment expenses are disallowed before any investment expenses are disallowed under the 2%-of-AGI floor. This is accomplished by selecting the lesser of the following:

1. The amount of investment expenses included in the total of miscellaneous itemized deductions subject to the 2%-of-AGI floor.
2. The amount of miscellaneous expenses deductible after the 2%-of-AGI rule is applied.

The amount under item 1 is $1,320 [$120 (safe deposit box rental) + $1,200 (investment counsel fee)]. The item 2 amount is $1,170 [$2,770 (total of miscellaneous expenses) − $1,600 (2% of $80,000 AGI)].

Then, Gina's investment expenses are calculated as follows:

Deductible investment expenses treated as miscellaneous deductions (the lesser of item 1 or item 2)	$1,170
Plus: Ad valorem tax on investment property	3,000
Total investment expenses	$4,170

Gina's net investment income is $13,830 ($18,000 investment income − $4,170 investment expenses). ▼

After net investment income is determined, deductible investment interest expense can be calculated. Disallowed investment interest may be carried over to future years. No limit is placed on the length of the carryover period. The investment interest expense deduction is determined by completing Form 4952 (see Appendix B).

EXAMPLE 52

Adam is a single person employed by a law firm. His investment activities for the year are as follows:

Net investment income	$30,000
Investment interest expense	44,000

Adam's investment interest deduction is $30,000. The $14,000 of investment interest disallowed ($44,000 investment interest expense − $30,000 allowed) is carried over to future years. ▼

Qualified Residence Interest. **Qualified residence interest** is interest paid or accrued during the taxable year on indebtedness (subject to limitations) secured by any property that is a qualified residence of the taxpayer. Qualified residence interest falls into two categories: (1) interest on **acquisition indebtedness** and (2) interest on **home equity loans.** Before discussing each of these categories, however, the term *qualified residence* must be defined.

A qualified residence includes the taxpayer's principal residence and one other residence of the taxpayer or spouse. The principal residence is one that meets the requirement for nonrecognition of gain upon sale under § 121 (see Chapter 7). The one other residence, or second residence, refers to one that is used as a residence if not rented or, if rented, meets the requirements for a personal residence under the rental of vacation home rules. A taxpayer who has more than one second residence can make the selection each year of which one is the qualified second residence. A residence includes, in addition to a house in the ordinary sense, cooperative apartments, condominiums, and mobile homes and boats that have living quarters (sleeping accommodations and toilet and cooking facilities).

Although in most cases interest paid on a home mortgage is fully deductible, there are limitations.[73] Interest paid or accrued during the tax year on aggregate acquisition indebtedness of $1 million or less ($500,000 for married persons filing separate returns) is deductible as qualified residence interest. Acquisition indebtedness refers to amounts incurred in acquiring, constructing, or substantially improving a qualified residence of the taxpayer.

Qualified residence interest also includes interest on home equity loans. These loans utilize the personal residence of the taxpayer as security. Because the funds from home equity loans can be used for personal purposes (e.g., auto purchases, medical expenses), what would otherwise have been nondeductible consumer interest becomes deductible qualified residence interest. However, interest is deductible only on the portion of a home equity loan that does not exceed the lesser of:

- The fair market value of the residence, reduced by the acquisition indebtedness, or
- $100,000 ($50,000 for married persons filing separate returns).

EXAMPLE 53

Larry owns a personal residence with a fair market value of $150,000 and an outstanding first mortgage of $120,000. Therefore, his equity in his home is $30,000 ($150,000 − $120,000). Larry issues a lien on the residence and in return borrows $15,000 to purchase a new family automobile. All interest on the $135,000 of debt is treated as qualified residence interest. ▼

---

[73] § 163(h)(3).

EXAMPLE 54

Leon and Pearl, married taxpayers, took out a mortgage on their home for $200,000 in 1983. In March of the current year, when the home had a fair market value of $400,000 and they owed $195,000 on the mortgage, Leon and Pearl took out a home equity loan for $120,000. They used the funds to purchase an airplane to be used for recreational purposes. On a joint return, Leon and Pearl can deduct all of the interest on the first mortgage since it is acquisition indebtedness. Of the $120,000 home equity loan, only the interest on the first $100,000 is deductible. The interest on the remaining $20,000 is not deductible because it exceeds the statutory ceiling of $100,000. ▼

Interest Paid for Services. Mortgage loan companies commonly charge a fee for finding, placing, or processing a mortgage loan. Such fees are often called **points** and are expressed as a percentage of the loan amount. Borrowers often have to pay points to obtain the necessary financing. To qualify as deductible interest, the points must be considered compensation to a lender solely for the use or forbearance of money. The points cannot be a form of service charge or payment for specific services if they are to qualify as deductible interest.[74]

Points must be capitalized and are amortized and deductible ratably over the life of the loan. A special exception permits the purchaser of a personal residence to deduct qualifying points in the year of payment.[75] The exception also covers points paid to obtain funds for home improvements.

EXAMPLE 55

During 1998, Thelma purchased a new residence for $130,000 and paid points of $2,600 to obtain mortgage financing. At Thelma's election, the $2,600 can be claimed as an interest deduction for tax year 1998. ▼

Points paid to refinance an existing home mortgage cannot be immediately expensed, but must be capitalized and amortized as interest expense over the life of the new loan.[76]

EXAMPLE 56

Sandra purchased her residence four years ago, obtaining a 30-year mortgage at an annual interest rate of 12%. In the current year, Sandra refinances the mortgage in order to reduce the interest rate to 9%. To obtain the refinancing, she had to pay points of $2,600. The $2,600 paid comes under the usual rule applicable to points. The $2,600 must be capitalized and amortized over the life of the mortgage. ▼

Prepayment Penalty. When a mortgage or loan is paid off in full in a lump sum before its term, the lending institution may require an additional payment of a certain percentage applied to the unpaid amount at the time of prepayment. This is known as a prepayment penalty and is considered to be interest (e.g., personal, qualified residence, investment) in the year paid. The general rules for deductibility of interest also apply to prepayment penalties.

Interest Paid to Related Parties. Nothing prevents the deduction of interest paid to a related party as long as the payment actually took place and the interest meets the requirements for deductibility. Recall from Chapter 6 that a special rule for related taxpayers applies when the debtor uses the accrual basis and the related creditor is on the cash basis. If this rule is applicable, interest that has been accrued but not paid at the end of the debtor's tax year is not deductible until payment is made and the income is reportable by the cash basis recipient.

---

[74] Rev.Rul. 67–297, 1967–2 C.B. 87.
[75] § 461(g)(2).
[76] Rev.Rul. 87–22, 1987–1 C.B. 146.

Concept Summary 15–2

Deductibility of Personal, Investment, and Mortgage Interest

Type	Deductible	Comments
Personal (consumer) interest	No	Includes any interest that is not home mortgage interest, investment interest, or business interest. Examples include car loans, credit cards, etc.
Investment interest (*not* related to rental or royalty property)	Yes	Itemized deduction; limited to net investment income for the year; disallowed interest can be carried over to future years.
Investment interest (related to rental or royalty property)	Yes	Deduction *for* AGI; limited to net investment income for the year; disallowed interest can be carried over to future years.
Qualified residence interest on acquisition indebtedness	Yes	Deductible as an itemized deduction; limited to indebtedness of $1 million.
Qualified residence interest on home equity indebtedness	Yes	Deductible as an itemized deduction; limited to indebtedness equal to lesser of $100,000 or FMV of residence minus acquisition indebtedness.

Tax-Exempt Securities. The tax law provides that no deduction is allowed for interest on debt incurred to purchase or carry tax-exempt securities.[77] A major problem for the courts has been to determine what is meant by the words "to purchase or carry." Refer to Chapter 4 for a detailed discussion of these issues.

Prepaid Interest. Accrual method reporting is imposed on cash basis taxpayers for interest prepayments that extend beyond the end of the taxable year.[78] Such payments must be allocated to the tax years to which the interest payments relate. These provisions are intended to prevent cash basis taxpayers from *manufacturing* tax deductions before the end of the year by prepaying interest.

Classification of Interest Expense. Whether interest is deductible *for* AGI or as an itemized deduction depends on whether the indebtedness has a business, investment, or personal purpose. If the indebtedness is incurred in relation to a business (other than performing services as an employee) or for the production of rent or royalty income, the interest is deductible *for* AGI. If the indebtedness is incurred for personal use, such as qualified residence interest, any deduction allowed is reported on Schedule A of Form 1040 if the taxpayer elects to itemize. If the taxpayer is an employee who incurs debt in relation to his or her employment, the interest is considered to be personal, or consumer, interest. Business expenses appear on Schedule C of Form 1040, and expenses related to rents or royalties are reported on Schedule E.

CHARITABLE CONTRIBUTIONS

As noted in Chapter 4, individuals are allowed to deduct contributions made to qualified domestic organizations.[79] Contributions to qualified charitable organizations serve certain social welfare needs and thus relieve the government of the cost of providing these needed services to the community.

---

[77] § 265(a)(2).
[78] § 461(g)(1).
[79] § 170.

Criteria for a Gift. A **charitable contribution** is defined as a gift made to a qualified organization.[80] The major elements needed to qualify a contribution as a gift are a donative intent, the absence of consideration, and acceptance by the donee. Consequently, the taxpayer has the burden of establishing that the transfer was made from motives of disinterested generosity as established by the courts.[81] This test is quite subjective and has led to problems of interpretation (refer to the discussion of gifts in Chapter 3).

Benefit Received Rule. When a donor derives a tangible benefit from a contribution, he or she cannot deduct the value of the benefit.

EXAMPLE 57

Ralph purchases a ticket at $100 for a special performance of the local symphony (a qualified charity). If the price of a ticket to a symphony concert is normally $35, Ralph is allowed only $65 as a charitable contribution. ▼

An exception to this benefit rule provides for the deduction of an automatic percentage of the amount paid for the right to purchase athletic tickets from colleges and universities.[82] Under this exception, 80 percent of the amount paid to or for the benefit of the institution qualifies as a charitable contribution deduction.

Contribution of Services. No deduction is allowed for the value of one's services contributed to a qualified charitable organization. However, unreimbursed expenses related to the services rendered may be deductible. For example, the cost of a uniform (without general utility) that is required to be worn while performing services may be deductible, as are certain out-of-pocket transportation costs incurred for the benefit of the charity. In lieu of these out-of-pocket costs for an automobile, a standard mileage rate of 14 cents per mile is allowed for tax years beginning after December 31, 1997.[83] Deductions are permitted for transportation, reasonable expenses for lodging, and the cost of meals while away from home incurred in performing the donated services. The travel may not involve a significant element of personal pleasure, recreation, or vacation.[84]

Nondeductible Items. In addition to the benefit received rule and the restrictions placed on contribution of services, the following items may not be deducted as charitable contributions:

- Dues, fees, or bills paid to country clubs, lodges, fraternal orders, or similar groups.
- Cost of raffle, bingo, or lottery tickets.
- Cost of tuition.
- Value of blood given to a blood bank.
- Donations to homeowners associations.
- Gifts to individuals.
- Rental value of property used by a qualified charity.

Time of Deduction. A charitable contribution generally is deducted in the year the payment is made. This rule applies to both cash and accrual basis individuals. A contribution is ordinarily deemed to have been made on the date of delivery of the property to the donee. A contribution made by check is considered delivered on the date of mailing. Thus, a check mailed on December 31, 1998, is deductible

---

[80] § 170(c).
[81] *Comm. v. Duberstein*, 60–2 USTC ¶9515, 5 AFTR2d 1626, 80 S.Ct. 1190 (USSC, 1960).
[82] § 170(l).
[83] § 170(i). The rate was 12 cents per mile for tax year 1997.
[84] § 170(j).

on the taxpayer's 1998 tax return. If the contribution is charged on a bank credit card, the date the charge is made determines the year of deduction.

Record-Keeping Requirements. No deduction is allowed for contributions of $250 or more unless the taxpayer obtains written substantiation of the contribution from the charitable organization. The substantiation must specify the amount of cash and a description (but not value) of any property other than cash contributed. The substantiation must be obtained before the earlier of (1) the due date (including extensions) of the return for the year the contribution is claimed or (2) the date such return is filed.[85]

Additional information is required if the value of the donated property is over $500 but not over $5,000. Also, the taxpayer must file Section A of Form 8283 (Noncash Charitable Contributions) for such contributions.

For noncash contributions with a claimed value in excess of $5,000 ($10,000 in the case of nonpublicly traded stock), the taxpayer must obtain a qualified appraisal and must file Section B of Form 8283. This schedule must show a summary of the appraisal and must be attached to the taxpayer's return. Failure to comply with these reporting rules may result in disallowance of the charitable contribution deduction. Additionally, significant overvaluation exposes the taxpayer to rather stringent penalties.

Valuation Requirements. Property donated to a charity is generally valued at fair market value at the time the gift is made. The Code and Regulations give very little guidance on the measurement of the fair market value except to say, "The fair market value is the price at which the property would change hands between a willing buyer and a willing seller, neither being under any compulsion to buy or sell and both having reasonable knowledge of relevant facts."

Generally, charitable organizations do not attest to the fair market value of the donated property. Nevertheless, the taxpayer must maintain reliable written evidence of the following information concerning the donation:

- The fair market value of the property and how that value was determined.
- The amount of the reduction in the value of the property (if required) for certain appreciated property and how that reduction was determined.
- Terms of any agreement with the charitable organization dealing with the use of the property and potential sale or other disposition of the property by the organization.
- A signed copy of the appraisal if the value of the property was determined by appraisal. Only for a contribution of art with an aggregate value of $20,000 or more must the appraisal be attached to the taxpayer's return.

Limitations on Charitable Contribution Deduction. The potential charitable contribution deduction is the total of all donations, both money and property, that qualify for the deduction. After this determination is made, the actual amount of the charitable contribution deduction that is allowed for individuals for the tax year is limited as follows:

- If the qualifying contributions for the year total 20 percent or less of AGI, they are fully deductible.
- If the qualifying contributions are more than 20 percent of AGI, the deductible amount may be limited to either 20 percent, 30 percent, or 50 percent of

---
[85] § 170(f)(8).

Concept Summary 15–3

Determining the Deduction for Contributions of Property by Individuals

If the Type of Property Contributed Is:	And the Property Is Contributed to:	The Contribution Is Measured by:	But the Deduction Is Limited to:
Capital gain property	A 50% organization	Fair market value of the property	30% of AGI
Ordinary income property	A 50% organization	Lower of basis or FMV of the property	50% of AGI
Capital gain property (and the property is tangible personal property put to an unrelated use by the donee)	A 50% organization	Basis of the property	50% of AGI
Capital gain property (and the reduced deduction is elected)	A 50% organization	Basis of the property	50% of AGI
Capital gain property	A private nonoperating foundation that is not a 50% organization	Lower of basis or FMV of the property	The lesser of: 1. 20% of AGI 2. 50% of AGI minus other contributions to 50% organizations
Ordinary income property	A private nonoperating foundation that is not a 50% organization	Basis of the property	30% of AGI

AGI, depending on the type of property given and the type of organization to which the donation is made.

- In any case, the maximum charitable contribution deduction may not exceed 50 percent of AGI for the tax year.

To understand the complex rules for computing the amount of a charitable contribution, it is necessary to understand the distinction between **capital gain property**[86] and **ordinary income property**. These rules, which were discussed in Chapter 4, are summarized in Concept Summary 15–3.

In addition, it is necessary to understand when the 50 percent, 30 percent, and 20 percent limitations apply. If a taxpayer's contributions for the year exceed the applicable percentage limitations, the excess contributions may be carried forward and deducted during a five-year carryover period. These topics are discussed in the sections that follow.

Fifty Percent Ceiling. Contributions made to public charities may not exceed 50 percent of an individual's AGI for the year. Excess contributions may be carried over to the next five years.[87] The 50 percent ceiling on contributions applies to the following types of public charities:

---

[86]For charitable contribution purposes, the long-term holding period is more than one year.

[87]§ 170(d); Reg. § 170A–10.

- A church or a convention or association of churches.
- An educational organization that maintains a regular faculty and curriculum.
- A hospital or medical school.
- An organization supported by the government that holds property or investments for the benefit of a college or university.
- A Federal, state, or local governmental unit.
- An organization normally receiving a substantial part of its support from the public or a governmental unit.

In the remaining discussion of charitable contributions, public charities and private foundations (both operating and nonoperating) that qualify for the 50 percent ceiling will be referred to as 50 percent organizations.

The 50 percent ceiling also applies to contributions to the following organizations:

- All private operating foundations.
- Certain private nonoperating foundations that distribute the contributions they receive to public charities and private operating foundations within two and one-half months following the year they receive the contribution.
- Certain private nonoperating foundations in which the contributions are pooled in a common fund and the income and principal sum are paid to public charities.

Thirty Percent Ceiling. A 30 percent ceiling applies to contributions of cash and ordinary income property to private nonoperating foundations that are not 50 percent organizations. The 30 percent ceiling also applies to contributions of appreciated capital gain property to 50 percent organizations unless the taxpayer makes a special election (see Example 59 below).

In the event the contributions for any one tax year involve both 50 percent and 30 percent property, the allowable deduction comes first from the 50 percent property.

EXAMPLE 58

During the year, Lisa made the following donations to her church: cash of $2,000 and unimproved land worth $30,000. Lisa had purchased the land four years ago for $22,000 and held it as an investment. Therefore, it is long-term capital gain property. Lisa's AGI for the year is $50,000. Disregarding percentage limitations, Lisa's potential deduction is $32,000 [$2,000 (cash) + $30,000 (fair market value of land)].

In applying the percentage limitations, however, the current deduction for the land is limited to $15,000 [30% (limitation applicable to long-term capital gain property) × $50,000 (AGI)]. Thus, the total deduction is $17,000 ($2,000 cash + $15,000 land). Note that the total deduction does not exceed $25,000, which is 50% of Lisa's AGI. ▼

Under a special election, a taxpayer may choose to forgo a deduction of the appreciation on capital gain property. Referred to as the reduced deduction election, this enables the taxpayer to move from the 30 percent limitation to the 50 percent limitation.

EXAMPLE 59

Assume the same facts as in Example 58, except that Lisa makes the reduced deduction election. Now the deduction becomes $24,000 [$2,000 (cash) + $22,000 (basis in land)] because both donations fall under the 50% limitation. Thus, by making the election, Lisa has increased her charitable contribution deduction by $7,000 [$24,000 − $17,000 (Example 59)]. ▼

Although the reduced deduction election appears attractive, it should be considered carefully. The election sacrifices a deduction for the appreciation on long-term capital gain property that might eventually be allowed. Note that in Example 58, the potential deduction was $32,000, yet in Example 59 only $24,000 is allowed. The reason the potential deduction is decreased by $8,000 ($32,000 − $24,000) is that no carryover is allowed for the amount sacrificed by the election.

Twenty Percent Ceiling. A 20 percent ceiling applies to contributions of appreciated long-term capital gain property to private nonoperating foundations that are not 50 percent organizations. Also, recall from Chapter 4 that only the basis of the contributed property is allowed as a deduction.

Contribution Carryovers. Contributions that exceed the percentage limitations for the current year can be carried over for five years. In the carryover process, such contributions do not lose their identity for limitation purposes. Thus, if the contribution originally involved 30 percent property, the carryover will continue to be classified as 30 percent property in the carryover year.

EXAMPLE 60
Assume the same facts as in Example 58. Because only $15,000 of the $30,000 value of the land was deducted in the current year, the balance of $15,000 may be carried over to the following year. But the carryover will still be treated as long-term capital gain property and will be subject to the 30%-of-AGI limitation. ▼

In applying the percentage limitations, current charitable contributions must be claimed first before any carryovers can be considered. If carryovers involve more than one year, they are utilized in a first-in, first-out order.

MISCELLANEOUS ITEMIZED DEDUCTIONS SUBJECT TO TWO PERCENT FLOOR

No deduction is allowed for personal, living, or family expenses.[88] However, a taxpayer may incur a number of expenditures related to employment. If an employee or outside salesperson incurs unreimbursed business expenses or expenses that are reimbursed under a nonaccountable plan (see Chapter 16), including travel and transportation, the expenses are deductible as **miscellaneous itemized deductions**.[89] Certain other expenses also fall into the special category of miscellaneous itemized deductions. Some are deductible only to the extent they exceed 2 percent of the taxpayer's AGI. These miscellaneous itemized deductions include (but are not limited to) the following:

- Professional dues to membership organizations.
- Uniforms or other clothing that cannot be used for normal wear.
- Fees incurred for the preparation of one's tax return or fees incurred for tax litigation before the IRS or the courts.
- Job-hunting costs.
- Fee paid for a safe deposit box used to store papers and documents relating to taxable income-producing investments.
- Investment expenses that are deductible under § 212 as discussed previously in this chapter.
- Appraisal fees to determine the amount of a casualty loss or the fair market value of donated property.
- Hobby losses up to the amount of hobby income (see Chapter 16).

---

[88]§ 262.
[89]Actors and performing artists who meet certain requirements are not subject to this rule.

- Unreimbursed employee expenses (see Chapter 16).
- Certain employee business expenses that are reimbursed are not itemized deductions, but are deducted for AGI. Employee business expenses are discussed in depth in Chapter 16.

OTHER MISCELLANEOUS DEDUCTIONS

Certain expenses and losses do not fall into any category of itemized deductions already discussed but are nonetheless deductible. The following expenses and losses are deductible on Schedule A as Other Miscellaneous Deductions:

- Gambling losses up to the amount of gambling winnings.
- Impairment-related work expenses of a handicapped person.
- Federal estate tax on income in respect of a decedent.
- Deduction for repayment of amounts under a claim of right if more than $3,000.

Unlike the expenses and losses discussed previously under Miscellaneous Itemized Deductions, the above expenses and losses are not subject to the 2 percent-of-AGI floor.

OVERALL LIMITATION ON CERTAIN ITEMIZED DEDUCTIONS

Congress has enacted several provisions limiting tax benefits for high-income taxpayers. These limitations include the exemption phase-out (discussed earlier in this chapter) and a phase-out of itemized deductions. The phase-out of itemized deductions (also referred to as a *cutback* adjustment) applies to taxpayers whose AGI exceeds $124,500 ($62,250 for married taxpayers filing separately).[90] The limitation applies to the following frequently encountered itemized deductions:[91]

- Taxes.
- Home mortgage interest, including points.
- Charitable contributions.
- Unreimbursed employee expenses subject to the 2 percent-of-AGI floor.
- All other expenses subject to the 2 percent-of-AGI floor.

The following deductions are not subject to the limitation on itemized deductions:

- Medical and dental expenses.
- Investment interest expense.
- Nonbusiness casualty and theft losses.
- Gambling losses.

Taxpayers subject to the limitation must reduce itemized deductions by the lesser of:

- 3 percent of the amount by which AGI exceeds $124,500 ($62,250 if married filing separately).
- 80 percent of itemized deductions that are affected by the limit.

---

[90] For 1997, the limitation applied if AGI exceeded $121,200 ($60,600 for married taxpayers filing separately).

[91] Other deductions subject to the limitation include Federal estate tax on income in respect of a decedent, certain amortizable bond premiums, the deduction for repayment of certain amounts, certain unrecovered investments in an annuity, and impairment-related work expenses.

CHAPTER 15 Introduction to the Taxation of Individuals

The overall limitation is applied after applying all other limitations to itemized deductions that are affected by the overall limitation. Other limitations apply to charitable contributions, certain meals and entertainment expenses, and certain miscellaneous itemized deductions.

EXAMPLE 61

Herman, who is single, had AGI of $200,000 for 1998. He incurred the following expenses and losses during the year:

Medical expenses before the 7.5%-of-AGI limitation	$16,000
State and local income taxes	3,200
Real estate taxes	2,800
Home mortgage interest	7,200
Charitable contributions	2,000
Casualty loss (after $100 floor, before 10%-of-AGI limitation)	21,500
Unreimbursed employee expenses subject to 2%-of-AGI limitation	4,300
Gambling losses (Herman had $3,000 gambling income)	7,000

Herman's itemized deductions before the overall limitation are computed as follows:

Medical expenses [$16,000 − (7.5% × $200,000)]	$ 1,000
State and local income taxes	3,200
Real estate taxes	2,800
Home mortgage interest	7,200
Charitable contributions	2,000
Casualty loss [$21,500 − (10% × $200,000)]	1,500
Unreimbursed employee expenses [$4,300 − (2% × $200,000)]	300
Gambling losses (limited to $3,000 gambling income)	3,000
Total itemized deductions before overall limitation	$21,000

Herman's itemized deductions subject to the overall limitation are as follows:

State and local income taxes	$ 3,200
Real estate taxes	2,800
Home mortgage interest	7,200
Charitable contributions	2,000
Unreimbursed employee	300
Total itemized deductions before overall limitation	$15,500

Herman must reduce this amount by the smaller of the following:

• 3%($200,000 AGI − $124,500)	$ 2,265
• 80% of itemized deductions subject to limitation ($15,500 × 80%)	12,400

Therefore, the amount of the reduction is $2,265, and Herman has $18,735 of deductible itemized deductions, computed as follows:

Deductible itemized deductions subject to overall limitation ($15,500 − $2,265)	$13,235
Itemized deductions not subject to overall limitation:	
Medical expenses	1,000
Casualty loss	1,500
Gambling losses	3,000
Deductible itemized deductions	$18,735

TAX IN THE NEWS

FEW TAXPAYERS ARE AFFECTED BY THE THREE PERCENT FLOOR

The IRS *Statistics of Income Bulletin* for 1994 (the latest year available) shows that few taxpayers have to be concerned about the 3 percent floor for itemized deductions. In 1994, the AGI threshold for application of this limitation was $111,800 ($55,900 for married taxpayers filing separately). The IRS statistics for 1994 show that taxpayers with AGI of $91,226 or more ranked in the top 5 percent. Obviously, fewer than 5 percent of all taxpayers were subject to the 3 percent floor in 1994.

PLANNING CONSIDERATIONS

Effective Utilization of Itemized Deductions

An individual may use the standard deduction in one year and itemize deductions in another year. Therefore, it is frequently possible to obtain maximum benefit by shifting itemized deductions from one year to another. For example, if a taxpayer's itemized deductions and the standard deduction are approximately the same for each year of a two-year period, the taxpayer should use the standard deduction in one year and shift itemized deductions (to the extent permitted by law) to the other year. The individual could, for example, prepay a church pledge for a particular year or avoid paying end-of-the-year medical expenses to shift the deduction to the following year.

INDIVIDUAL TAX CREDITS

ADOPTION EXPENSES CREDIT

LEARNING OBJECTIVE 8
Understand the adoption expenses credit, child tax credit, education tax credits, child and dependent care credit, credit for the elderly, and earned income credit.

Qualifying adoption expenses paid or incurred by a taxpayer may give rise to the **adoption expenses credit**.[92] The provision is intended to assist taxpayers who incur nonrecurring costs directly associated with the adoption process, such as adoption fees, attorney fees, court costs, social service review costs, and transportation costs.

Up to $5,000 of costs incurred to adopt an eligible child qualify for the credit. An eligible child is one who is:

- under 18 years of age at the time of the adoption, or
- physically or mentally incapable of taking care of himself or herself.

A taxpayer may claim the credit in the year qualifying expenses were paid or incurred if the expenses were paid or incurred during or after the year in which the adoption was finalized. For qualifying expenses paid or incurred in a tax year prior to the year when the adoption was finalized, the credit must be claimed in the year the adoption was finalized. A married couple must file a joint return in order to claim the credit.

---
[92] § 23

EXAMPLE 62 In late 1998, Sam and Martha pay $2,500 in legal fees, adoption fees, and other expenses directly related to the adoption of an infant daughter, Susan. In 1999, they pay an additional $1,000, and in 2000, the year in which the adoption becomes final, they pay $3,000. Sam and Martha are eligible for a $5,000 credit in 2000. ▼

The amount of the credit that is otherwise available is subject to phase-out for taxpayers whose AGI (modified for this purpose) exceeds $75,000, and is phased out completely when AGI reaches $115,000. The resulting credit is calculated by reducing the allowable credit (determined without this reduction) by the amount determined using the following formula:

$$\text{Allowable credit} \times \frac{\text{AGI} - \$75,000}{\$40,000}.$$

EXAMPLE 63 Assume the same facts as in the previous example, except that Sam and Martha's AGI is $100,000 in each of the relevant years. As a result, their available credit in 2000 is reduced from $5,000 to $1,875 {$5,000 − [$5,000 × ($25,000/$40,000)]}. ▼

The credit is nonrefundable and is available to taxpayers only in a year in which this credit and the other nonrefundable credits do not exceed the taxpayer's liability. However, any unused adoption expenses credit may be carried over for up to five years, being utilized on a first-in, first-out basis.

CHILD TAX CREDIT

For the first time, beginning in 1998, individual taxpayers are permitted to take a tax credit based solely on the *number* of their dependent children under age 17. This **child tax credit**[93] is one of several "family-friendly" provisions enacted as part of the Taxpayer Relief Act of 1997 (TRA of 1997). To be eligible for the credit, the child must be under age 17, a U.S. citizen, and claimed as a dependent on the taxpayer's return.

Maximum Credit and Phase-Outs. The maximum credit available is $400 per child beginning in 1998, rising to $500 per child in 1999 and years thereafter. The available credit is phased out for higher-income taxpayers beginning when AGI reaches $110,000 for joint filers ($55,000 for married taxpayers filing separately) and $75,000 for single taxpayers. The credit is phased out by $50 for each $1,000 (or part thereof) of AGI above the threshold amounts. Since the maximum credit available to taxpayers depends on the number of qualifying children, the income level at which the credit is phased out completely also depends on the number of children qualifying for the credit.

EXAMPLE 64 Juanita and Alberto are married and file a joint tax return claiming their two children, ages six and eight as dependents. Their AGI for 1998 is $122,400. Juanita and Alberto's available child tax credit for 1998 is $150, computed as their maximum credit of $800 ($400 × 2 children) reduced by a $650 phase-out. Since Juanita and Alberto's AGI is in excess of the $110,000 threshold, the maximum credit must be reduced by $50 for every $1,000 (or part thereof) above the threshold amount {$50 × [($122,400 − $110,000)/$1,000]}. Thus, the credit reduction equals $650 [$50 × 13 (rounded up from 12.4)]. Therefore, Juanita and Alberto's child tax credit is $150 for 1998. ▼

---

[93] § 24.

CREDIT FOR CHILD AND DEPENDENT CARE EXPENSES

A credit is allowed to taxpayers who incur employment-related expenses for child or dependent care.[94] The **credit for child and dependent care expenses** is a specified percentage of expenses incurred to enable the taxpayer to work or to seek employment. Expenses on which the credit for child and dependent care expenses is based are subject to limitations.

Eligibility. To be eligible for the credit, an individual must maintain a household for either of the following:

- A dependent under age 13.
- A dependent or spouse who is physically or mentally incapacitated.

Generally, married taxpayers must file a joint return to obtain the credit. The credit may also be claimed by the custodial parent for a nondependent child under age 13 if the noncustodial parent is allowed to claim the child as a dependent under a pre-1985 divorce agreement or under a waiver in the case of a post-1984 agreement.

Eligible Employment-Related Expenses. Eligible expenses include amounts paid for household services and care of a qualifying individual that are incurred to enable the taxpayer to be employed. Child and dependent care expenses include expenses incurred in the home, such as payments for a housekeeper. Out-of-the-home expenses incurred for the care of a dependent under the age of 13 also qualify for the credit. In addition, out-of-the-home expenses incurred for an older dependent or spouse who is physically or mentally incapacitated qualify for the credit if that person regularly spends at least eight hours each day in the taxpayer's household. This makes the credit available to taxpayers who keep handicapped older children and elderly relatives in the home instead of institutionalizing them. Out-of-the-home expenses incurred for services provided by a dependent care center will qualify only if the center complies with all applicable laws and regulations of a state or unit of local government.

Child care payments to a relative are eligible for the credit unless the relative is a dependent of the taxpayer or the taxpayer's spouse or is a child (under age 19) of the taxpayer.

Earned Income Ceiling. The total for qualifying employment-related expenses is limited to an individual's earned income. For married taxpayers, this limitation applies to the spouse with the lesser amount of earned income. Special rules are provided for taxpayers with nonworking spouses who are disabled or are full-time students. If a nonworking spouse is physically or mentally disabled or is a full-time student, he or she is deemed to have earned income for purposes of this limitation. The deemed amount is $200 per month if there is one qualifying individual in the household or $400 per month if there are two or more qualifying individuals in the household. In the case of a student-spouse, the student's income is deemed to be earned only for the months that the student is enrolled on a full-time basis at an educational institution.

Calculation of the Credit. In general, the credit is equal to a percentage of unreimbursed employment-related expenses up to $2,400 for one qualifying individual and $4,800 for two or more individuals. The credit rate varies between 20

---

[94] § 21.

percent and 30 percent, depending on the taxpayer's AGI. The following chart shows the applicable percentage for taxpayers as AGI increases:

Adjusted Gross Income		Applicable Credit Rate
Over	But Not Over	
$ –0–	$10,000	30%
10,000	12,000	29%
12,000	14,000	28%
14,000	16,000	27%
16,000	18,000	26%
18,000	20,000	25%
20,000	22,000	24%
22,000	24,000	23%
24,000	26,000	22%
26,000	28,000	21%
28,000	No limit	20%

EXAMPLE 65

Nancy, who has two children under age 13, worked full-time while her spouse, Ron, attended college for 10 months during the year. Nancy earned $21,000 and incurred $5,000 of child care expenses. Ron is deemed to be fully employed and to have earned $400 for each of the 10 months (or a total of $4,000). Since Nancy and Ron have AGI of $21,000, they are allowed a credit rate of 24%. Nancy and Ron are limited to $4,000 in qualified child care expenses (the lesser of $4,800 or $4,000). Therefore, they are entitled to a tax credit of $960 (24% × $4,000) for the year. ▼

Reporting Requirements. The credit is claimed by completing and filing Form 2441, Credit for Child and Dependent Care Expenses (see Appendix B).

EDUCATION TAX CREDITS

Beginning in 1998, two new credits, the **HOPE scholarship credit** and **lifetime learning credit**,[95] are available to help qualifying low- and middle-income individuals defray the cost of higher education. The credits, both of which are nonrefundable, are available for qualifying tuition and related expenses incurred by students pursuing undergraduate or graduate degrees or vocational training. Room, board, and book costs are ineligible for the credits.

Maximum Credit. The HOPE scholarship credit permits a maximum credit of $1,500 per year (100 percent of first $1,000 of tuition expenses plus 50 percent of next $1,000 of tuition expenses) for the *first two years* of postsecondary education. The lifetime learning credit permits a maximum credit of 20 percent of tuition expenses (up to $5,000 per year) incurred after June 30, 1998, and in a year in which the HOPE scholarship credit is not claimed with respect to a given student's tuition and related expenses. The lifetime learning credit is intended for individuals who are beyond the first two years of postsecondary education. Beginning in 2003, the lifetime learning credit will be available for the first $10,000 of qualifying costs incurred per year.

---

[95] § 25A.

Eligible Individuals. Both education credits are available for qualified tuition and related expenses incurred by a taxpayer, taxpayer's spouse, or taxpayer's dependent. The HOPE scholarship credit is available per eligible student, while the lifetime learning credit is calculated per taxpayer. To be eligible for the HOPE credit, students must take at least one-half the full-time course load for at least one academic term at a qualifying educational institution. No comparable requirement exists for the lifetime learning credit. Therefore, taxpayers who are seeking new job skills or maintaining existing skills through graduate training or continuing education are eligible for the lifetime learning credit. Taxpayers who are married must file joint returns in order to claim either education credit.

Timing of Expenses. Qualifying tuition expenses must be *paid* during the tax year for education furnished by a qualifying institution during an academic year *beginning* during the tax year in question. If tuition expenses are paid during the tax year for an academic period beginning during the first three months of the following year, the expenses may be claimed during the payment year for purposes of the credit computation. This aspect of the credit computation permits taxpayers to prepay tuition expenses in order to maximize the available education credit. As a related item, qualifying tuition expenses paid with student loans are eligible for the education credits during the tax year when the costs are incurred and paid, not the tax year in which the loan is repaid.

Income Limitations. Both education credits are subject to income limitations and are combined for purposes of the limitation calculation. The allowable credit amount is phased out, beginning when the taxpayer's AGI reaches $40,000 ($80,000 for married taxpayers filing jointly). The credits are completely eliminated when AGI reaches $50,000 ($100,000 for married filing jointly). The calculated credit amount is reduced by the extent to which AGI exceeds $40,000 ($80,000 for married filing jointly) as a percentage of the $10,000 ($20,000 for married filing jointly) phase-out range.

Restrictions on Double Tax Benefit. Taxpayers are prohibited from receiving a double tax benefit associated with qualifying educational expenses. Therefore, taxpayers who claim an education credit may not deduct the expenses, nor may they claim the credit for amounts that are otherwise excluded from income (e.g., scholarships and employer-paid educational assistance).

EXAMPLE 66

Dean and Audry are married, file a joint tax return, have modified AGI under $80,000 and have two children. During fall 1998, Raymond is beginning his freshman year at State University, and Kelsey is beginning her senior year. Both Raymond and Kelsey are full-time students and may be claimed as dependents on their parents' tax return. Raymond's qualifying tuition expenses and fees total $4,600 for the academic year ($2,300 per semester) while Kelsey's qualifying tuition expenses total $5,200 for the academic year ($2,600 per semester). Dean and Audry pay the tuition and related expenses in full at the beginning of each semester. For 1998, Dean and Audry may claim a $1,500 HOPE scholarship credit [(100% × $1,000) + (50% × $1,000)] relating to Raymond's expenses and a $520 lifetime learning credit (20% × $2,600) relating to Kelsey's expenses. Kelsey's tuition expenses are ineligible for HOPE credit because she is beyond her first two years of postsecondary education. Finally, Dean and Audry could have increased their available lifetime learning credit for 1998 by prepaying some of Kelsey's tuition expenses. ▼

EXAMPLE 67

Assume the same facts as in Example 66, except that Dean and Audry's AGI for 1998 is $92,000. Dean and Audry are eligible to claim $808 in total education credits for 1998. Their available credits totaling $2,020 ($1,500 HOPE credit + $520 lifetime learning credit) must be reduced because their AGI exceeds the $80,000 limit for married taxpayers. The percentage reduction is computed as the amount by which AGI exceeds the limit, expressed as a percentage of the phase-out range, or [($92,000 − $80,000)/$20,000], resulting in a 60% reduction. Therefore, the maximum available credit for 1998 is $808 ($2,020 × 40% allowable portion). ▼

TAX CREDIT FOR ELDERLY OR DISABLED TAXPAYERS

The **credit for the elderly or disabled** was originally enacted in 1954 as the retirement income credit to provide tax relief on retirement income for individuals who were not receiving substantial benefits from tax-free Social Security payments.[96] Currently, the tax credit for the elderly or disabled applies to the following:

- Taxpayers age 65 or older.
- Taxpayers under age 65 who are retired with a permanent and total disability and who have disability income from a public or private employer on account of the disability.

The maximum allowable credit is $1,125 (15% × $7,500 of qualifying income), but the credit will be less for a taxpayer who receives Social Security benefits or has AGI exceeding specified amounts. Under these circumstances, the base used in the credit computation is reduced. Many taxpayers receive Social Security benefits or have AGI high enough to reduce the base for the credit to zero.

The eligibility requirements and the tax computation are somewhat complicated. Consequently, an individual may elect to have the IRS compute his or her tax and the amount of the tax credit.

The credit generally is based on an initial amount (referred to as the *base amount*) and the filing status of the taxpayer in accordance with Table 15–5. To qualify for the credit, married taxpayers who live together must file a joint return. For taxpayers under age 65 who are retired on permanent and total disability, the base amounts could be less than those shown in Table 15–5 because these amounts are limited to taxable disability income.

The initial base amount is reduced by (1) Social Security, Railroad Retirement, and certain excluded pension benefits and (2) one-half of the taxpayer's AGI in excess of the threshold amount (see Table 15–5), which is a function of the taxpayer's filing status. The credit may be calculated using the procedure presented in the following example.

EXAMPLE 68

Paul and Peggy, husband and wife, are both over age 65 and received Social Security benefits of $2,400 in the current year. On a joint return, they reported AGI of $14,000.

Base amount (from Table 15–5)		$ 7,500
Reduced by		
Qualifying nontaxable benefits	$2,400	
One-half of excess of AGI over threshold amount from Table 15–5 [($14,000 − $10,000) × ½]	2,000	(4,400)
Balance subject to credit		$ 3,100
Multiply by 15% credit rate		.15
Credit allowed		$ 465

▼

Schedule R of Form 1040 (see Appendix B) is used to calculate and report the credit.

---

[96] § 22.

TAX IN THE NEWS

PAYING FOR COLLEGE—UNDERSTANDING THE TAX LAW MAY BE HALF THE BATTLE

Taxpayers with college-bound children are the beneficiaries of several new tax breaks courtesy of the Taxpayer Relief Act of 1997. Although these new provisions will cut the cost of a college education, many people will likely need help from their friendly neighborhood tax adviser to understand the law and take advantage of these new provisions.

In particular, the 1997 tax bill created five new ways to help pay for college. Beginning in 1998, parents can contribute $500 per year to an education individual retirement account for any child under 18. No tax is due on the account earnings as long as the money is used for education expenses. Taxpayers will also be able to make penalty-free withdrawals from two other IRAs—a regular IRA or the new Roth IRA. The tax bill also expanded prepaid tuition plans to cover room and board costs in addition to tuition expenses and reinstated the deductibility of interest on student loans. Beginning in 1998, taxpayers can take an "above-the-line" deduction for up to $1,000 in student-loan interest, with the deduction rising to $2,500 in 2001.

Probably, the most significant tax break in the 1997 bill was the creation of two new education credits—the HOPE scholarship credit and the lifetime learning credit. The HOPE scholarship credit permits a maximum credit of $1,500 per year for the first two years of college tuition expenses. The lifetime learning credit can be used in subsequent years to save up to $1,000 per year in taxes if tuition expenses equal at least $5,000.

Although these tax law changes seem appealing, consider some of the intricacies involved in their use. To begin with, many of the benefits are phased out for higher-income taxpayers. For married taxpayers filing a joint return, the ability to contribute to an education IRA starts phasing out at $150,000, the student-loan interest deduction starts disappearing at $60,000, and the education credits begin phasing out at $80,000. Unfortunately, the complexity doesn't stop there.

Many of the new provisions are mutually exclusive to prevent taxpayers from receiving a double benefit. For example, taxpayers are prevented from contributing to both an education IRA and a state-sponsored prepaid tuition plan in the same year. Likewise, if money is withdrawn from an education IRA to pay for college, the taxpayer is prohibited from taking either education credit with respect to those expenditures. The new education credits can also create problems for taxpayers with Series EE savings bonds. If a taxpayer cashes in the bonds to pay for college and elects to exclude the bond interest from income, the credits are also unavailable.

Perhaps most subtle of all is the impact of the new education credits on the student's ability to receive financial aid. If the credits are used, the family's disposable income will rise, potentially reducing the amount of financial aid available in future years.

In sum, given the changes made by the 1997 bill, understanding the tax law may indeed be half the battle of paying for college.

SOURCE: Adapted from Jonathan Clements, "Tax Law Leads to Confusion about How to Pay for College," *Wall Street Journal*, August 26, 1997, p. C1.

▼ TABLE 15-5
Base Amounts for Tax Credit for Elderly or Disabled Taxpayers

Status	Base Amount	Threshold Amount
Single, head of household, or surviving spouse	$5,000	$ 7,500
Married, joint return, only one spouse qualified	5,000	10,000
Married, joint return, both spouses qualified	7,500	10,000
Married, separate returns, spouses live apart the entire year (amount for each spouse)	3,750	5,000

EARNED INCOME CREDIT

The **earned income credit,** which has been a part of the law for many years, has been justified as a means of providing tax equity to the working poor. More recently, the credit has also been designed to help offset regressive taxes that are a part of our tax system, such as the gasoline and Social Security taxes. In addition, the credit has been intended to encourage economically disadvantaged individuals to become contributing members of the workforce.[97]

Eligibility Requirements. Eligibility for the credit may depend not only on the taxpayer meeting the earned income and AGI thresholds, but also on whether he or she has a qualifying child. A qualifying child must meet the following tests:

- *Relationship test.* The individual must be a son, daughter, descendant of the taxpayer's son or daughter, stepson, stepdaughter, or an eligible foster child of the taxpayer. A legally adopted child of the taxpayer is considered the same as a child by blood.
- *Residency test.* The qualifying child must share the taxpayer's principal place of abode, which must be located within the United States, for more than one-half of the tax year of the taxpayer. Temporary absences (e.g., due to illness or education) are disregarded for purposes of this test. For foster children, however, the child must share the taxpayer's home for the entire year.
- *Age test.* The child must not have reached the age of 19 (24 in the case of a full-time student) as of the end of the tax year. In addition, a child who is permanently and totally disabled at any time during the year is considered to meet the age test.

In addition to being available for taxpayers with qualifying children, the earned income credit is also available to certain workers without children. However, this provision is available only to taxpayers aged 25 through 64 who cannot be claimed as a dependent on another taxpayer's return.

Amount of the Credit. In 1998, the earned income credit is determined by multiplying a maximum amount of earned income by the appropriate credit. Generally, earned income includes employee compensation and net earnings from self-employment but excludes items such as interest, dividends, pension benefits, and alimony. If a taxpayer has children, the credit percentage used in the calculation depends on the number of qualifying children. Thus, in 1998, the maximum earned income credit for a taxpayer with one qualifying child is $2,271 ($6,680 × 34%) and $3,756 ($9,390 × 40%) for a taxpayer with two or more qualifying children. However, the maximum earned income credit is phased out completely if the taxpayer's earned income or AGI exceeds certain thresholds. To the extent that the greater of

---

[97]§ 32. This credit is subject to indexation.

earned income or AGI exceeds $12,260 in 1998, the difference, multiplied by the appropriate phase-out percentage, is subtracted from the maximum earned income credit.

It is not necessary to actually compute the earned income credit. As part of the tax simplification process, the IRS issues an Earned Income Credit Table for the determination of the appropriate amount of the credit. This table and a worksheet are included in the instructions to both Form 1040 and Form 1040A.

Advance Payment. The earned income credit is a form of negative income tax (a refundable credit for taxpayers who do not have a tax liability). An eligible individual may elect to receive advance payments of the earned income credit from his or her employer (rather than receiving the credit from the IRS upon filing the tax return). The amount that can be received in advance is limited to 60 percent of the credit that is available to a taxpayer with only one qualifying child. If this election is made, the taxpayer must file a certificate of eligibility (Form W-5) with his or her employer and must file a tax return for the year the income is earned.

KEY TERMS

Abandoned spouse rules, 15-25

Accident and health insurance benefits, 15-33

Acquisition indebtedness, 15-42

Adoption expenses credits, 15-52

Alimony and separate maintenance payments, 15-27

Alimony recapture, 15-28

Capital gain property, 15-47

Charitable contribution, 15-45

Child tax credit, 15-53

Compensatory damages, 15-31

Credit for child and dependent care expenses, 15-54

Credit for the elderly or disabled, 15-57

Dependency exemption, 15-10

Earned income credit, 15-59

Educational savings bonds, 15-34

Gift, 15-29

Head of household, 15-25

Home equity loans, 15-42

HOPE scholarship credit, 15-55

Investment interest, 15-40

Itemized deductions, 15-6

Kiddie tax, 15-18

Lifetime learning credit, 15-55

Marriage penalty, 15-24

Medical expenses, 15-35

Miscellaneous itemized deductions, 15-49

Multiple support agreement, 15-11

Net investment income, 15-40

Ordinary income property, 15-47

Personal exemption, 15-9

Points, 15-43

Punitive damages, 15-32

Qualified residence interest, 15-42

Scholarships, 15-30

Standard deduction, 15-6

Surviving spouse, 15-25

Tax Rate Schedules, 15-17

Tax Table, 15-17

Unearned income, 15-18

PROBLEM MATERIALS

1. Compute the taxpayer's taxable income for 1998 in each of the following cases:
   a. Jack is married and files a joint return with his wife, Alice. Jack and Alice have two dependent children. They have AGI of $50,000 and $8,300 of itemized deductions.
   b. Pete is an unmarried head of household with two dependents. He has AGI of $45,000 and itemized deductions of $5,200.
   c. Iris, age 22, is a full-time college student who is claimed as a dependent by her parents. She earns $4,200 from a part-time job and has interest income of $1,500.
   d. Matt, age 20, is a full-time college student who is claimed as a dependent by his parents. He earns $2,500 from a part-time job and has interest income of $4,100. His itemized deductions related to the investment income are $800.

2. Compute taxable income for 1998 for Blake on the basis of the following information. His filing status is head of household.

Salary	$60,000
Alimony paid	1,200
Casualty loss (deductible portion)	7,500
Interest paid on home mortgage	4,200
Property taxes on home	2,200
State and local income taxes	1,500
Number of dependents (two children and both of Blake's parents)	4
Age	46

3. Compute taxable income for 1998 for Amber on the basis of the following information. Her filing status is single.

Inheritance received from mother	$29,000
Gift received from aunt	14,000
Cash dividend from stock investments	15,000
Interest income from savings accounts	11,000
Interest income on state and local bonds	11,000
Lottery winnings	3,600
Cash charitable contributions	4,000
Age	66

4. Determine the amount of the standard deduction allowed for 1998 in each of the following independent situations. In each case, assume the taxpayer is claimed as another person's dependent.
   a. Mona, age 16, has income as follows: $710 interest from a savings account and $800 from a part-time job.
   b. Aaron, age 18, earns $4,300 from a part-time job.
   c. Irving, age 71 and single, has income as follows: $3,100 nontaxable Social Security benefits and $1,050 from a part-time job.
   d. Maureen, age 67, is single and blind and has cash dividends of $1,300 from a stock investment.

5. Determine the number of personal and dependency exemptions in each of the following independent situations:
   a. Warren and Terri provide more than half of the support of their children, Demi and Paul. Demi, age 19, earns $3,200 from a part-time job. Paul, age 21, earns $2,800 from a part-time job.
   b. Hortense, age 64 and widowed, furnishes more than half of the support of her father, age 88 and blind. The father receives Social Security benefits of $4,300, interest on a savings account of $2,400, and interest on tax-exempt bonds of $10,000.
   c. Dennis and Ava provide more than half of the support of their son, Henry. Henry, age 25, is a full-time student in medical school. During the year, Henry receives $2,500 in dividends from stock investments.

d. Earl provides more than half of the support of his nephew, Brad, who lives with him. Brad, age 17 and a full-time student, earns $2,500 from a part-time job.

6. Martha, a widow, lives with her only son, Roland, and his family. Martha's only income consists of $70,000 in interest from tax-exempt bonds. She invests all of the income in stocks in her name. The stocks do not pay dividends. Martha's will provides that all of her property is to pass to Roland upon her death. Because of this expectation, Roland provides all of his mother's support, although she is in a position to provide her own support had she chosen to do so. On his tax return, Roland claims a dependency exemption for his mother. Is this proper procedure?

7. Melvin and Sarah Turner are married and file a joint return. Transactions for 1998 are as follows:

Salaries ($42,000 for Melvin and $39,000 for Sarah)	$81,000
Lottery winnings	1,200
Inheritance from Melvin's father	30,000
Gift from Sarah's mother	10,000
Short-term capital loss from sale of stock held as an investment	3,000

The Turners provided all of the support of their 20-year-old married daughter, Maryanne, and her husband, Boyd. Maryanne and Boyd live with the Turners, and neither has any gross income. The Turners also furnish over half of the support of Sarah's Aunt Edna, who lives in a nursing home. Edna, age 76, has interest of $2,700 from State of Alabama bonds. Melvin is age 65, and Sarah is 45. If the Turners have itemized deductions of $7,000, what is their taxable income for 1998?

8. Bob, age 13, is a full-time student supported by his parents who claim him on their tax return for 1998. Bob's parents present you with the following information and ask that you prepare Bob's Federal income tax return for the year:

Wages from a summer job	$2,100
Interest on savings account at First National Bank	950
Interest on City of Chicago bonds Bob received as a gift from his grandfather two years ago	750
Dividend from Owl Corporation	200

a. What is Bob's taxable income for 1998?
b. Bob's parents file a joint return for 1998 on which they report taxable income of $66,000. Compute Bob's 1998 tax liability.

9. Compute the 1998 tax liability for each of the following taxpayers:
a. Norm and Nancy, both age 46, are married, have two dependent children, and file a joint return. Their combined salaries totaled $66,000. They had deductions *for* AGI of $7,000 and total itemized deductions of $7,400.
b. Clark, age 45, is single and has no dependents. He had a salary of $42,000, deductions *for* AGI of $3,000, and total itemized deductions of $4,200.
c. David and Susan, both age 65, are married, have no dependents, and file a joint return. Their combined salaries were $92,000. They had deductions *for* AGI of $2,000 and itemized deductions of $8,500.

10. Peter, age 12, is claimed as a dependent on his parents' 1998 Federal income tax return, on which they reported taxable income of $95,000. During the summer, Peter earned $2,500 from a job as a model. His only other income consisted of $1,700 in interest on a savings account. Compute Peter's taxable income and tax liability.

11. Carmen, who is 12 years old, is claimed as a dependent on her parents' tax return. During 1998, she received $12,200 in dividends and interest and had no investment expenses related to this income. She also earned $2,000 wages from a part-time job. Compute the amount of income that is taxed at Carmen's parents' rate.

12. Bruce Smith and Wanda Brown are young professionals who are employed in well-paying jobs. They have been dating each other for several years and are considering

getting married in December 1998 or January 1999. For 1998, their respective AGIs are $65,000 and $68,000. They anticipate earning the same income in 1999. In both years, they will claim the standard deduction. Bruce and Wanda solicit your tax advice. Specifically, they wish to know what Federal income tax results from their getting married in 1998 or in 1999. Prepare a letter to Wanda (4339 Elm St., Apt. 39A, Cincinnati, OH 45221) setting forth the tax determination under each choice.

13. Which of the following taxpayers must file a tax return for 1998?
    a. Bob, age 19, is a full-time college student. He is claimed as a dependent by his parents. He earned $4,100 wages during the year.
    b. Anita, age 12, is claimed as a dependent by her parents. She earned interest income of $1,200 during the year.
    c. Earl, age 16, is claimed as a dependent by his parents. He earned wages of $2,700 and interest of $1,100 during the year.
    d. Karen, age 16 and blind, is claimed as a dependent by her parents. She earned wages of $2,600 and interest of $1,200 during the year.
    e. Pat, age 17, is claimed as a dependent by her parents. She earned interest income of $300 during the year. In addition, she earned $550 during the summer operating her own business at the beach, where she painted caricatures of her customers.

14. In each of the following independent situations, classify Darlene's filing status for tax year 1998:
    a. Darlene is a widow and maintains a household in which her two dependent children live. Darlene's husband died in 1996.
    b. Same as (a) except that Darlene's husband died in 1994 (not 1996).
    c. Darlene is single and lives alone. She maintains the household of her parents, only one of whom qualifies as her dependent.
    d. Darlene is married, but her husband disappeared for parts unknown in 1997. Darlene maintains the household in which she and her dependent children live.

15. Gina, a cash basis taxpayer, is single and has no dependents. She provides you with the following estimates for 1997 and 1998:

	1997	1998
Adjusted gross income	$56,000	$60,000
Charitable contributions	2,200	2,400
Interest on home mortgage	1,000	850
Property taxes	700	700

Can Gina decrease her taxable income over the two-year period by prepaying her 1998 charitable contributions in 1997?

16. Matt and Anita Huerta are married and live at 3486 International Blvd., El Paso, TX 79968; both have full-time jobs. Matt's Social Security number is 433-22-1111, and Anita's is 437-00-1112. The Huertas have four children, who live with them. Three of the children are their own, while the oldest is Anita's child from a prior marriage.

During 1998, the Huertas had the following receipts:

Salaries (Matt and Anita combined)	$71,000
Child support payments received by Anita from her former husband	3,600
Fees earned by Matt for jury duty service	90
Proceeds from a garage sale	1,180
Gift of cash received from Matt's mother	4,000
Cash prize won for being the ninth caller on a radio talk show	1,000

Matt's employer withheld Federal income taxes of $2,600, and Anita's employer withheld $3,400. The garage sale involved used clothing, toys, appliances, furniture and other personal effects, and household goods. The Huertas estimate that the cost of the items was in excess of $4,000.

Expenses for 1998 are summarized below:

Interest on home mortgage	$5,600
Property taxes on home	3,400
Charitable contributions	4,200

The Huertas furnish all of the support of Anita's widowed mother, who lives with them. The mother, although a U.S. resident, is still a citizen of Mexico. The mother helps with the household chores and takes care of the children while Anita and Matt are at work.

The Huertas also furnish all of the support of Anita's grandparents, who are over age 65. The grandparents live in Mexico and are citizens of Mexico.

Compute the Huertas' tax liability for 1998. Suggested software (if available): *TurboTax*.

17. Under the terms of their divorce agreement, Barry is to transfer common stock (cost of $25,000, market value of $60,000) to Sandra. Barry and Sandra have a 14-year-old child. Sandra will have custody of the child, and Barry is to pay $300 per month as child support. In addition, Sandra is to receive $1,000 per month for 10 years. However, the payments will be reduced to $750 per month when their child reaches age 21. In the first year under the agreement, Sandra receives the common stock and the correct cash payments for six months. How will the terms of the agreement affect Sandra's gross income?

18. For each of the following, determine the amount that should be included in gross income:
    a. Joe was selected as the most valuable player in the Super Bowl. In recognition of this, he was awarded a sports car worth $60,000 plus $50,000 in cash.
    b. Wanda won the Mrs. America beauty contest. She received various prizes valued at $75,000.
    c. George was awarded the Nobel Peace Prize. He directed the Nobel committee to pay the $950,000 prize to State University, his alma mater.

19. Alejandro was awarded an academic scholarship to State University. He received $5,000 in August and $6,000 in December 1998. Alejandro had enough personal savings to pay all expenses as they came due. Alejandro's expenditures for the relevant period were as follows:

Tuition, August 1998	$2,900
Tuition, December 1998	3,200
Room and board	
August–December 1998	3,000
January–May 1999	2,400
Books and educational supplies	
August–December 1998	800
January–May 1999	950

Determine the effect on Alejandro's gross income for 1998 and 1999.

20. Liz sued an overzealous bill collector and received the following settlement:

Damage to her automobile the collector attempted to repossess	$ 1,000
Physical damage to her arm caused by the collector	8,000
Loss of income while her arm was healing	6,000
Punitive damages	30,000

   a. What effect does the settlement have on Liz's gross income?
   b. Assume Liz also collected $40,000 of damages for slander to her personal reputation caused by the bill collector misrepresenting the facts to Liz's employer and other creditors. Is this $40,000 included in Liz's gross income?

21. Ed and Laura are married and together have AGI of $60,000 in 1998. They have no dependents and file a joint return. During the year, they paid $1,600 for medical insurance, $6,000 in doctor bills and hospital expenses and $900 for prescribed medicine and drugs.
    a. In December 1998, Ed and Laura received an insurance reimbursement of $1,200 for hospitalization expenses. Determine the deduction allowable for medical expenses paid during the year.
    b. Assume instead that Ed and Laura received the $1,200 insurance reimbursement in February 1999. Determine the deduction allowable for medical expenses incurred in 1998.
    c. Assume again that Ed and Laura received the $1,200 insurance reimbursement in February 1999. Discuss whether the reimbursement will be included in their gross income for 1999.

22. Steven, age 37, had his nose broken in a high school football game 20 years ago. As a result, his nose is slightly crooked. In addition, he thinks his nose is too long. In March, he scheduled an appointment with Dr. Keane to discuss surgery to improve his appearance, primarily to shorten his nose. Dr. Keane presented him with computer simulations showing several different possibilities for the size and shape of his nose. Steven selected a nose that was much shorter and completely straight.

    Steven called his CPA to ask if the cost of the surgery would be deductible. His CPA told him that unnecessary cosmetic surgery is not deductible, but hinted that most doctors can come up with a medical reason that would make such surgery deductible.

    Steven discussed the tax issue with Dr. Keane on his next visit, and the doctor indicated that the surgery would be necessary to repair Steven's deviated septum, which was caused by his football injury. Dr. Keane said that he would be willing to write a letter for Steven's files, stating that the surgery was medically necessary. Is Steven justified in taking a deduction for the cosmetic surgery?

23. A local opthalmologist's advertising campaign included a certificate for a free radial keratotomy for the lucky winner of a drawing. Ahmad held the winning ticket, which was drawn in December 1997. Ahmad had no vision problems and was uncertain what he should do with the prize. In February 1998, Ahmad's daughter, who lives with his former wife, was diagnosed with a vision problem that could be treated either with prescription glasses or a radial keratotomy. The divorce decree requires that Ahmad pay for all medical expenses incurred for his daughter. Identify the relevant tax issues for Ahmad.

24. Ibrahim developed a severe allergy condition, and his physician advised him to install a special air conditioning, heating, and filtration system in his home. The cost of installing the system was $7,200, and the increase in the value of the residence was determined to be $2,300. Ibrahim's AGI for the year was $40,000.
    a. How much of the expenditure can Ibrahim deduct as a medical expense?
    b. Assume the same facts as in (a), except that Ibrahim was paralyzed in a skiing accident and the expenditures were incurred to build entrance and exit ramps and widen the hallways in his home to accommodate his wheelchair. How much of the expenditure can Ibrahim deduct as a medical expense?

25. Andrea, who uses the cash method of accounting, lives in a state that imposes an income tax. In April 1998, she files her state return for 1997, and pays an additional $1,000 in state income taxes. During 1998, her withholdings for state income tax purposes amount to $7,400, and she pays estimated state income tax of $700. In April 1999, she files her state return for 1998, claiming a refund of $1,800. Andrea receives the refund in August 1999.
    a. Assuming Andrea itemizes deductions in 1998, how much may she claim as a deduction for state income taxes on her Federal return for calendar year 1998 (filed in April 1999)?
    b. Assuming Andrea itemized deductions in 1998, how will the refund of $1,800 that she received in 1999 be treated for Federal income tax purposes?

c. Assume Andrea itemizes deductions in 1998, and elects to have the $1,800 refund applied toward her 1999 state income tax liability. How will the $1,800 be treated for Federal income tax purposes?

d. Assuming Andrea did not itemize deductions in 1998, how will the refund of $1,800 received in 1999 be treated for Federal income tax purposes?

26. Irina incurred $39,000 of interest expense related to her investments in 1998. Her investment income included $10,000 of interest, $6,000 of dividends, and a $15,000 net capital gain on the sale of securities.

a. What is the maximum amount that Irina can treat as investment income for the year?

b. What other tax factors should Irina consider in deciding whether to elect to include net capital gain in her investment income?

27. In 1998, Myrna has $8,000 of investment income and the following miscellaneous itemized deductions:

Unreimbursed employee business expenses (meals included at 50%)	$1,400
Tax return preparation fee	440
Investment expenses	500

For purposes of the investment interest expense limitation, what is the total of Myrna's net investment income in each of the following independent situations:

a. AGI of $20,000.
b. AGI of $60,000.
c. AGI of $110,000.

28. Sid and Sara, married taxpayers, took out a mortgage on their home for $100,000 in 1987. In March of the current year, when the home had a fair market value of $200,000 and they owed $85,000 on the mortgage, Sid and Sara took out a home equity loan for $110,000. They used the funds to purchase a motor home to be used for recreational purposes. What is the maximum amount on which they can deduct home equity interest?

29. Darby contributed a painting to an art museum in 1998. She had owned the painting for 20 years, and it had a value of $120,000 at the time of the donation. The museum displayed the painting in its impressionist gallery.

a. Assume that Darby's AGI is $230,000 and her basis for the painting is $80,000. Would you recommend that she make the reduced deduction election?

b. Assume that Darby's AGI is $230,000 and her basis for the painting is $115,000. Would you recommend that she make the reduced deduction election?

30. In December each year, Alice Young contributes 10% of her gross income to the United Way (a 50% organization). Alice, who is in the 36% marginal tax bracket, is considering the following alternatives as charitable contributions in December 1998:

	Fair Market Value
(1) Cash donation	$21,000
(2) Unimproved land held for six years ($3,000 basis)	21,000
(3) Blue Corporation stock held for eight months ($3,000 basis)	21,000
(4) Gold Corporation stock held for two years ($26,000 basis)	21,000

Alice has asked you to help her decide which of the potential contributions listed above will be most advantageous taxwise. Evaluate the four alternatives, and write a letter to Alice to communicate your advice to her. Her address is 2622 Bayshore Drive, Berkeley, CA 94709.

31. The Skins Game, which involves four of the top golfers on the PGA Tour, is held each year on the weekend after Thanksgiving. Total prize money amounts to $510,000, and the leading money winner also receives an automobile as a prize. The announcers point out that 10% of the money won by each player goes to charity. In addition, on some

holes, the winner of the hole receives the keys to an automobile, which goes to the player's favorite charity. Identify the relevant tax issues for the players. Consider the following possibilities with respect to the car won by the leading money winner: (1) he might keep the car for his own use and sell his present car; (2) he might sell the new car; (3) he might give the car to a friend or relative; (4) he might donate the car to charity; or (5) he might give the car to his caddy.

32. Chris, who is single, had an AGI of $220,000 during 1998. He incurred the following expenses and losses during the year:

Medical expenses before 7.5%-of-AGI limitation	$19,000
State and local income taxes	4,100
Real estate taxes	2,200
Home mortgage interest	5,600
Charitable contributions	3,500
Casualty loss before 10% limitation (after $100 floor)	25,000
Unreimbursed employee expenses subject to 2%-of-AGI limitation	5,700
Gambling losses (Chris had $4,200 of gambling income)	8,000

Compute Chris's itemized deductions before and after the overall limitation.

33. Ann and Bill have been on the list of a local adoption agency for several years seeking to adopt a child. Finally, in 1998, good news came their way and an adoption seemed imminent. They paid qualified adoption expenses of $2,000 in 1998 and $4,000 in 1999. Assume the adoption becomes final in 1999. Ann and Bill always file a joint income tax return.
    a. Determine the amount of the adoption expenses credit available to Ann and Bill assuming their combined annual income is $50,000. In what year(s) will they benefit from the credit?
    b. Assuming Ann and Bill's modified AGI in 1998 and 1999 is $100,000, calculate the amount of the adoption expense credit.

34. Durell and Earline are married, file a joint return, and claim dependency exemptions for their two children, ages 5 years and 6 months. They also claim Earline's son from a previous marriage, age 18, as a dependent. Durell and Earline's combined AGI for 1998 is $56,000.
    a. Compute Durell and Earline's child tax credit for 1998.
    b. Assume the same facts, except that Durell and Earline's combined AGI for 1998 is $119,000. Compute their child tax credit for 1998.

35. Jim and Jill are husband and wife and have two dependent children under the age of 13. They both are gainfully employed and during the current year earned salaries as follows: $12,000 (Jim) and $4,500 (Jill). To care for their children while they work, they pay Megan (Jim's mother) $5,600. Megan does not qualify as a dependent of Jim and Jill. Assuming Jim and Jill file a joint return, what, if any, is their credit for child and dependent care expenses?

36. Colin has requested information concerning the availability of the HOPE scholarship credit and lifetime learning credit. Colin has two college-age children, Eliza, a freshman at State University, and Rhett, a senior at Out-of-State University. Both Eliza and Rhett are full-time students. Eliza's expenses for the 1998–1999 academic year are as follows: $4,500 tuition ($2,250 per semester), $800 for books and supplies, and $3,000 room and board. Rhett's expenses for the 1998–1999 academic year are as follows: $8,000 tuition ($4,000 per semester), $900 for books and supplies, and $3,500 room and board. Tuition and the applicable room and board costs are paid at the beginning of each semester. Colin is married, files a joint tax return, claims both children as dependents, and has a combined AGI with his wife of $95,000 for 1998.
    a. Determine Colin's education tax credit for 1998.
    b. What tax planning alternative would you suggest to Colin to increase his education tax credit for 1998?

37. Bernadette, a long-time client of yours, is an architect and president of the local Rotary chapter. To keep up-to-date with the latest developments in her profession, she attends continuing education seminars offered by the national association of architects. During 1998, Bernadette spent $2,000 on course tuition to attend such seminars. She also spent another $400 on architecture books during the year. Bernadette's son is a senior majoring in engineering at the University of the Midwest. During the 1998–1999 academic year, Bernadette's son incurred the following expenses: $4,200 tuition ($2,100 per semester) and $750 for books and supplies. Bernadette has the option of paying her son's tuition in advance or in installments throughout the academic year. Bernadette's son, whom she claims as a dependent, lives at home while attending school full-time. Bernadette is married, files a joint return, and has a combined AGI with her husband of $88,000.
    a. Calculate Bernadette's education tax credit for 1998 assuming her son's tuition expenses are paid in a manner to maximize the available credit in 1998.
    b. In her capacity as president of the local Rotary chapter, Bernadette has asked you to make a 30–45 minute speech outlining the different ways the tax law helps defray (1) the cost of higher education and (2) the cost of continuing education once someone is in the workforce. Prepare an outline of possible topics for presentation. A tentative title for your presentation is "How the Tax Law Can Help Pay for College and Continuing Professional Education."

38. Joe, age 68, and Emily, age 69, are married retirees who received the following income and retirement benefits during the current year:

Fully taxable pension from Joe's former employer	$ 5,000
Dividends and interest	8,000
Social Security benefits	1,750
	$14,750

    Assume Joe and Emily file a joint return, have no deductions for AGI, and do not itemize. Are they eligible for the tax credit for the elderly? If so, calculate the amount of the credit, assuming their tax liability before credits is $150.

39. Which of the following individuals qualify for the earned income credit for 1999?
    a. Eduardo is single, 19 years of age, and has no dependents. His income consists of $8,000 of wages.
    b. Kate maintains a household for a dependent 12-year-old son and is eligible for head-of-household tax rates. Her income consists of $10,500 of salary and $300 of taxable interest.
    c. Keith and Susan are married and file a joint return. Keith and Susan have no dependents. Their combined income consists of $18,500 of salary and $100 of taxable interest. Adjusted gross income is $18,600.
    d. George is a 26-year-old single taxpayer. He has no dependents and generates earnings of $9,000.

CUMULATIVE PROBLEMS

40. Alice and Bruce Byrd are married taxpayers, ages 47 and 45, who file a joint return. Their Social Security numbers are 034–48–4382 and 016–50–9556, respectively. They live at 473 Revere Avenue, Ames, MA 01850. Alice is the office manager for a dental clinic and earns an annual salary of $46,000. Bruce is the manager of a fast-food outlet owned and operated by Plymouth Corporation. His annual salary is $37,000.

    The Byrds have two children, Cynthia (age 23 and Social Security number 017–44–9126) and John (age 22 and Social Security number 017–27–4148), who live with them. Both children are full-time students at a nearby college. Alice's mother, Myrtle Jones (age 74 and Social Security number 016–15–8266), also lives with them. Her sole source of income is from Social Security benefits, which she deposits in a savings account.

During 1997, the Byrds furnished one-third of the total support of Bruce's widower father, Sam Byrd (age 70 and Social Security number 034–82–8583). Sam lives alone and receives the rest of his support from Bruce's sister and brother (one-third each). They have signed a multiple support agreement allowing Bruce to claim Sam as a dependent for 1997. Sam died in November, and Bruce received life insurance proceeds of $270,000 on December 28.

The Byrds had the following expenses relating to their personal residence during 1997:

Property taxes	$2,400
Interest on home mortgage	6,900
Repairs to roof	2,000
Utilities	3,200
Fire and theft insurance	1,300

Medical expenses for 1997 include:

Medical insurance premiums	$4,800
Doctor bill for Sam incurred in 1996 and not paid until 1997	2,600
Operation for Sam	4,900

The operation for Sam represents the one-third Bruce contributed toward his father's support.

Other relevant information follows:

- Alice and Bruce had $2,600 ($1,400 for Alice and $1,200 for Bruce) withheld from their salaries for state income taxes. When they filed their 1996 state return in 1997, they paid additional tax of $480.

- During 1997, Alice and Bruce attended a dinner dance sponsored by the Ames Police Disability Association (a qualified charitable organization). The Byrds paid $100 for the tickets. Cost of comparable entertainment would normally be $40. The Byrds contributed $1,700 to their church and gave used clothing (cost of $800 and fair market value of $300) to the Salvation Army. All donations are supported by receipts.

- In 1997, the Byrds received interest income of $1,950 from a savings account they maintained.

- Alice's employer requires that all employees wear uniforms to work. During 1997, Alice spent $440 on new uniforms and $112 on laundry charges. Bruce paid $120 for an annual subscription to the *Journal of Franchise Management*. Neither Alice's nor Bruce's employer reimburses for employee expenses.

- Alice and Bruce had $6,800 ($3,700 for Alice and $3,100 for Bruce) of Federal income tax withheld in 1997 and paid no estimated Federal income tax. Neither Alice nor Bruce wishes to designate $3 to the Presidential Election Campaign Fund.

Part 1—Tax Computation
Compute net tax payable or refund due for Alice and Bruce Byrd for 1997. If they have overpaid, the amount is to be refunded. If you use tax forms for your computations, you will need Form 1040 and Schedules A and B. Suggested software (if available): *TurboTax*.

Part 2—Tax Planning
Alice and Bruce are planning some significant changes for 1998. They have provided you with the following information and asked you to project their taxable income and tax liability for 1998.

- Myrtle became seriously ill in December 1997 and is no longer able to care for herself. As a result, Alice plans to take a one-year leave of absence from work during 1998 to care for her.

- The Byrds will use $70,000 of the life insurance proceeds they received as a result of Sam's death and pay off their mortgage in early January 1998. They will invest the remaining $200,000 in short-term certificates of deposit (CDs) and use the interest for living expenses during 1998.

- They expect to earn total interest of $13,500 on the CDs. Bruce has been awarded a 5% raise for 1998, and withholdings on his salary will increase accordingly.

- The Byrds will not incur any additional costs related to Sam's medical problem.

- Alice will not work at all during 1998, so none of her job-related expenses or withholdings will continue.

- The Byrds do not expect to owe additional state income tax when they file their 1997 return, but they do expect their charitable contributions and medical insurance premiums to continue at the 1997 level.

- Assume all other income and deduction items will continue at the same level in 1998 unless you have information that indicates otherwise.

41. Paul and Donna Decker are married taxpayers, ages 44 and 42, who file a joint return for 1997. The Deckers live at 1121 College Avenue, Carmel, IN 46032. Paul is an assistant manager at Carmel Motor Inn, and Donna is a teacher at Carmel Elementary School. They present you with W–2 Forms that reflect the following information:

	Paul	Donna
Salary	$37,000	$41,000
Federal tax withheld	6,992	5,900
State income tax withheld	700	760
FICA (Social Security tax) withheld	2,831	3,137
Social Security numbers	222-11-4567	333-11-9872

Donna is the custodial parent of two children from a previous marriage who reside with the Deckers through the school year. The children, Larry and Jane Parker, reside with their father, Bob, during the summer. Relevant information for the children follows:

	Larry	Jane
Age	11	9
Social Security numbers	305-11-4567	303-11-9872
Months spent with Deckers	9	9

Under the divorce decree, Bob pays child support of $150 per month per child during the nine months the children live with the Deckers. Bob says he spends $200 per month per child during the three summer months they reside with him. Donna and Paul can document that they provide $1,800 support per child per year. The divorce decree is silent as to which parent can claim the exemption for the children.

In August, Paul and Donna added a suite to their home to provide more comfortable accommodations for Hannah Snyder (263–33–4738), Donna's mother, who had moved in with them in February 1996 after the death of Donna's father. Not wanting to borrow money for this addition, Paul sold 300 shares of Acme Corporation stock for $50 per share on May 3, 1997, and used the proceeds of $15,000 to cover construction costs. The Deckers had purchased the stock on April 29, 1995, for $22 per share. They received dividends of $550 on the jointly owned stock a month before the sale.

Hannah, who is 66 years old, received $7,200 in Social Security benefits during the year, of which she gave the Deckers $1,700 to use toward household expenses and deposited the remainder in her personal savings account. The Deckers determine that they have spent $1,500 of their own money for food, clothing, medical expenses, and other items for Hannah. They do not know what the rental value of Hannah's suite would be, but they estimate it would be at least $300 per month.

Interest paid during the year included the following:

Home mortgage interest (paid to Carmel Federal Savings and Loan)	$4,890
Interest on an automobile loan (paid to Carmel National Bank)	920
Interest on Citibank Visa card	855

In July, Paul hit a submerged rock while boating. Fortunately, he was thrown from the boat, landed in deep water, and was uninjured. However, the boat, which was uninsured, was destroyed. Paul had paid $18,000 for the boat in June 1996, and its value was appraised at $14,500 on the date of the accident.

The Deckers paid doctor and hospital bills of $4,100 and were reimbursed $1,600 by their insurance company. They spent $780 for prescription drugs and medicines and $1,440 for premiums on their health insurance policy. They have filed additional claims of $700 with their insurance company and have been told they will receive payment for that amount in January 1998. Included in the amounts paid for doctor and hospital bills were payments of $360 for Hannah and $750 for the children.

Additional information of potential tax consequence follows:

Real estate taxes paid	$1,900
Cash contributions to church	800
Appraised value of books donated to public library	450
Paul's unreimbursed employee expenses to attend hotel management convention:	
Airfare	340
Hotel	130
Meals	95
Registration fee	100
Refund of state income tax for 1996 (the Deckers itemized on their 1996 return)	910

Compute net tax payable or refund due for the Deckers for 1997. If they have overpaid, the amount is to be credited toward their taxes for 1998. Suggested software (if available): *TurboTax*.

RESEARCH PROBLEMS

*Note: The **RIA OnPoint System 4 Student Version CD-ROM** available with this text can be used in preparing solutions to the Research Problems. Alternatively, tax research materials contained in a standard tax library can be used.*

42. Susan Carpenter, although married, lives alone. She maintains a household that includes her three-year-old son. Susan and her husband are not on good terms, but neither has ever bothered to file for legal separation or divorce. Susan is gainfully employed and provides all of the support for herself and her son. During the year, she utilizes the services of a day care center while she works.

    Susan has contacted you regarding her tax situation. She is particularly interested in ascertaining her filing status and whatever deductions and credits are available.

    a. Write a letter to Susan addressing her concerns. She lives at 3126 Kingsride Rd., Funston, UT 84602. Try to express yourself in nonlegal terms.
    b. Prepare a memo containing legal substantiation for your position. The memo is for inclusion in your firm's client files.

43. Judy and Greg married in 1989 and have since resided in California. In October 1995, Judy filed in state court to have her marriage to Greg annulled. The annulment was

granted in May 1996. Under California law, an annulment voids the marriage and, in effect, treats it as if it never occurred.

Judy filed her Federal income tax return for the calendar year 1995 using *single* filing status. Upon audit of the return, the IRS contends that Judy's correct filing status is *married filing separate*. Who is correct and why?

Partial list of research aids:
§ 7703(a)(1).
Reg. § 1.6013–4(a)(1).
Harold K. Lee, 64 T.C. 552 (1975).
Betty J. Shackelford, 70 TCM 945, T.C. Memo. 1995–484.

44. Jane suffers from a degenerative spinal disorder. Her physician recommended the installation of a swimming pool at her residence for her use to prevent the onset of permanent paralysis. Jane's residence had a market value of approximately $500,000 before the swimming pool was installed. The swimming pool was built, and an appraiser estimated that the value of Jane's home increased by $98,000 because of the addition.

The pool cost $194,000, and Jane claimed a medical deduction of $96,000 on her tax return. Upon audit of the return, the IRS determined that an adequate pool should have cost $70,000 and would increase the property value by only $31,000. Thus, the IRS claims that Jane should be entitled to a deduction of only $39,000.
   a. Is there any ceiling limitation on the amount deductible as a medical expense?
   b. Can capital expenditures be deducted as medical expenses?
   c. What is the significance of a "minimum adequate facility"? Should aesthetic or architectural qualities be considered in this determination?

45. Under the terms of a post-1986 divorce agreement, Al is to receive payments from Karen as follows: $60,000 in Year 1, $45,000 in Year 2, and $20,000 each year for Years 3 through 10. Al is also to receive custody of their minor son. The payments will decrease by $5,000 per year if the son dies or when he attains age 21 and will cease upon Al's death.
   a. What will be Al's taxable alimony in Year 1?
   b. What will be the effect of the Years 2 and 3 payments on Al's taxable income?

46. Vern, a widower, lives in an apartment with his three minor children (ages 3, 4, and 5) whom he supports. Vern earned $19,500 during 1997. He contributed $500 to an IRA and uses the standard deduction. Calculate the amount, if any, of Vern's earned income credit.

C·H·A·P·T·E·R

16

INDIVIDUALS AS EMPLOYEES AND PROPRIETORS

LEARNING OBJECTIVES

After completing Chapter 16, you should be able to:

1. Distinguish between employee and self-employed status.

2. Understand the exclusions from income available to employees who receive fringe benefits.

3. Apply the rules for computing deductible expenses of employees, including transportation, travel, moving, education, and entertainment expenses.

4. Appreciate the difference between accountable and nonaccountable employee plans.

5. Understand the tax provisions applicable to proprietors.

6. Distinguish between business and hobby activities and apply the rules limiting the deduction of hobby losses.

OUTLINE

Employee versus Self-Employed, 16-2
Factors Considered in Classification, 16-3
Exclusions Available to Employees, 16-5
Advantages of Qualified Fringe Benefits, 16-5
Employer-Sponsored Accident and Health Plans, 16-5
Medical Reimbursement Plans, 16-6
Long-Term Care Benefits, 16-7
Meals and Lodging Furnished for the Convenience of the Employer, 16-7
Group Term Life Insurance, 16-9
Qualified Tuition Reduction Plans, 16-10

Other Specific Employee Fringe Benefits, 16-11
Cafeteria Plans, 16-12
Flexible Spending Plans, 16-12
General Classes of Excluded Benefits, 16-13
Taxable Fringe Benefits, 16-17
Employee Expenses, 16-19
Transportation Expenses, 16-19
Travel Expenses, 16-21
Moving Expenses, 16-25
Education Expenses, 16-27
Entertainment Expenses, 16-30
Other Employee Expenses, 16-33
Classification of Employee Expenses, 16-35
Contributions to Individual Retirement Accounts, 16-39

Individuals as Proprietors, 16-41
The Proprietorship as a Business Entity, 16-41
Income of a Proprietorship, 16-42
Deductions Related to a Proprietorship, 16-42
Retirement Plans for Self-Employed Individuals, 16-44
Accounting Periods and Methods, 16-46
Estimated Payments, 16-46
Hobby Losses, 16-48
General Rules, 16-48
Presumptive Rule of § 183, 16-49
Determining the Amount of the Deduction, 16-49

An individual may be an employee or may be self-employed. The terms *proprietor* and *independent contractor* are both used to describe self-employed individuals. These terms are used interchangeably throughout this chapter.

In many cases, it is difficult to distinguish between employees and self-employed individuals. This chapter begins with a discussion of the factors that must be considered in determining whether an individual is an employee or is self-employed. This is followed by a discussion of tax rules applicable to employees and then by a discussion of provisions related to self-employed individuals.

EMPLOYEE VERSUS SELF-EMPLOYED

1 LEARNING OBJECTIVE
Distinguish between employee and self-employed status.

When one person performs services for another, the person performing the service is either an employee or self-employed (i.e., an **independent contractor**). Failure to recognize employee status can have serious consequences. Not only can interest and penalties result, but in several highly publicized cases, government careers have been squelched. This happened to three individuals that President Clinton nominated to his cabinet during his first term. Zoe Baird and Kimba Wood (both Attorney General nominees) and retired Admiral Bobby Inman (Secretary of Defense nominee) all had to withdraw from consideration when it was revealed that they had failed to report and pay payroll (Social Security) taxes on their household employees.

The determination of employment status is already controversial and can be expected to become an even greater problem in the future. As a means for achieving greater flexibility and cost control, businesses are increasingly relying on self-employed persons (i.e., independent contractors) rather than employees for many services.

The IRS is very much aware that businesses have a tendency to wrongly classify workers as self-employed rather than as employees. In some cases, misclassification is unintentional and results from difficulty in applying the complex set of rules related to employee versus independent contractor status. In other cases, misclassification may be an intentional strategy to avoid certain costs that are associated with employees. Unlike employees, self-employed persons do not have to be included in various fringe benefit programs and retirement plans. Furthermore, employers are not required to pay FICA and unemployment taxes (refer to Chapter 1) on compensation paid to independent contractors.

In terms of tax consequences, employment status also makes a great deal of difference to the worker. Allowable business expenses of self-employed taxpayers are classified as deductions *for* AGI and are reported on Schedule C (Profit or Loss from Business) of Form 1040.[1] On the other hand, unreimbursed business expenses incurred by employees are classified as itemized deductions and are deductible on Schedule A (as itemized deductions) only to the extent that the sum of certain miscellaneous itemized deductions exceeds 2 percent of the taxpayer's AGI. Unreimbursed employee expenses are reported on Form 2106 (Employee Business Expenses) and Schedule A (Itemized Deductions) of Form 1040.[2]

Employee expenses that are reimbursed under an **accountable plan** (covered later in this chapter) are also reported as deductions *for* AGI. Employee expenses that are not reimbursed under an accountable plan are treated in the same way as unreimbursed expenses—deductible *from* AGI and limited to the excess over 2 percent of AGI.

FACTORS CONSIDERED IN CLASSIFICATION

The pivotal issue in classifying an individual as an independent contractor or an employee is whether an employer-employee relationship exists. The IRS has created a complex *20-factor test* for determining whether a worker is an employee or an independent contractor. The courts, which have focused on a small number of these factors, generally hold that an individual is an employee if the individual or business acquiring the services[3]

- has the right to specify the end result and the ways and means by which that result is to be attained,
- can exert will and control over the person providing the services with respect not only to what shall be done but also to how it shall be done,
- has the right to discharge, without legal liability, the person performing the service,
- furnishes tools or a place to work, and
- bases payment on time spent rather than the task performed.

Each case is tested on its own merits, and the right to control the means and methods of accomplishment is the definitive test. Generally, physicians, lawyers, dentists, contractors, subcontractors, and others who offer services to the public are not classified as employees.

EXAMPLE 1

Arnold is a lawyer whose major client accounts for 60% of his billings. He does the routine legal work and income tax returns at the client's request. He is paid a monthly retainer in addition to amounts charged for extra work. Arnold is a self-employed individual. Even

---

[1] §§ 62(a)(1) and 162(a). See Appendix B for a reproduction of Schedule C.
[2] See Appendix B for reproductions of Form 2106 and Schedule A.
[3] Reg. § 31.3401(c)–(1)(b).

TAX IN THE NEWS

ARE GOLF CLUBS IN TROUBLE WITH THE IRS?

For many years, the IRS has not questioned the tax classification of caddies as independent contractors. See, for example, Revenue Ruling 69–26 (1969–1 C.B. 251). This classification is consistent with the manner in which the services are performed. Most caddies work when they want, receive minimum training at their golf courses, and are paid "by the bag" (not by the hour). Further, they are paid by the golfer (not the club).

Recent actions by the IRS, however, indicate that it now regards caddies as employees. If the IRS maintains this position and pursues its enforcement, serious tax consequences could result. Golf clubs could find themselves liable for past Social Security payments and even income tax withholding. Even worse could be the prospect of future record-keeping and reporting requirements. The added compliance costs could convince clubs to ditch the caddie system and replace it with less troublesome electric carts.

SOURCE: Adapted from M. C. Fondo, "IRS Bogey-Man Threatens Caddies," *Wall Street Journal*, June 3, 1997, p. A22.

---

though most of his income comes from one client, he still has the right to determine *how* the end result of his work is attained. ▼

EXAMPLE 2
Ellen is a lawyer hired by Arnold to assist him in the performance of services for the client mentioned in Example 1. Ellen is under Arnold's supervision; he reviews her work and pays her an hourly fee. Ellen is Arnold's employee. ▼

EXAMPLE 3
Frank is a licensed practical nurse who works as a private-duty nurse. He is under the supervision of the patient's doctor and is paid by the patient. Frank is not an employee of either the patient (who pays him) or the doctor (who supervises him). The ways and means of attaining the end result (care of the patient) are under his control. ▼

In addition to independent contractors, *employees* in a special category are allowed to file Schedule C and deduct expenses *for* AGI. These employees are called *statutory employees* because they are not common law employees under the rules explained above. The wages or commissions paid to statutory employees are not subject to Federal income tax withholding but are subject to Social Security tax.[4]

PLANNING CONSIDERATIONS

Self-Employed Individuals

Some taxpayers have the flexibility to be classified as either employees or self-employed individuals. Examples include real estate agents and direct sellers. These taxpayers should carefully consider all factors and not automatically assume that self-employed status is preferable.

---

[4] See Circular E, *Employer's Tax Guide* (IRS Publication 15), for further discussion of statutory employees.

It is advantageous to deduct one's business expenses for AGI and avoid the 2 percent floor for miscellaneous itemized deductions. However, a self-employed individual may incur additional expenses, such as local gross receipts taxes, license fees, franchise fees, personal property taxes, and occupation taxes. Record-keeping and filing requirements can also be quite burdensome.

One of the most expensive considerations is the **self-employment tax** imposed on independent contractors. For an employee in 1998, for example, the Social Security tax applies at a rate of 6.2 percent on a base amount of wages of $68,400, and the Medicare tax applies at a rate of 1.45 percent with no limit on the base amount. For self-employed persons, the rate, but not the base amount, for each tax doubles. Even though a deduction for AGI is allowed for one-half of the self-employment tax paid, an employee and a self-employed individual are not in the same tax position on equal amounts of earnings. For the applicability of these taxes to workers, see Chapter 1.

After analyzing all these factors, taxpayers in many cases may decide that employee status is preferable to self-employed status.

EXCLUSIONS AVAILABLE TO EMPLOYEES

2 LEARNING OBJECTIVE
Understand the exclusions from income available to employees who receive fringe benefits.

Several exclusions that are available to *all taxpayers* were discussed in Chapter 3; these include interest on obligations of state and local governments, life insurance proceeds, and income from discharge of indebtedness. Other exclusions, available only to *individuals*, were discussed in Chapter 15; these exclusions include gifts and inheritances, scholarships, and compensation for injuries and sickness. Exclusions available only to employees are discussed below.

ADVANTAGES OF QUALIFIED FRINGE BENEFITS

Exclusions available only to *employees* are generally referred to as *qualified fringe benefits*. The popularity of fringe benefits is attributable to the fact that the cost of such benefits is deductible by employers and excludible by employees.

EXAMPLE 4

Cardinal Corporation, which has a marginal tax rate of 35%, provides health insurance coverage to employees at a cost of $1,000 per employee. Because Cardinal can deduct the health insurance premiums paid to provide this coverage, the net cost to the corporation is $650 per employee ($1,000 cost − $350 tax savings). The employee is allowed to exclude the value of this fringe benefit, so there is no tax cost to the employee.

The average employee of Cardinal Corporation is in the 28% bracket. If Cardinal did not provide the health insurance coverage and the employee paid a $1,000 premium, the employee would have to use after-tax dollars to acquire the coverage. The employee would have to earn $1,389 to pay for the coverage [$1,389 wages − ($1,389 × 28% tax)]. The after-tax cost to the corporation of $1,389 in wages is $903 ($1,389 wages − $486 corporate tax savings). Thus, the cost of health insurance coverage is $253 less per employee ($903 − $650) because it is both deductible by the corporation and excludible by the employee. ▼

EMPLOYER-SPONSORED ACCIDENT AND HEALTH PLANS

Congress encourages employers to provide employees, retired former employees, and their dependents with accident and health benefits, disability insurance, and long-term care plans. The *premiums* are deductible by the employer and are excluded from the employee's income.[5] Although § 105(a) provides the general rule that the employee has includible income when he or she collects the insurance *benefits*, two exceptions are provided.

Section 105(b) generally excludes payments received for medical care of the employee, spouse, and dependents. However, if the payments are for expenses that do not meet the Code's definition of medical care,[6] the amount received must be included in gross income. In addition, the taxpayer must include in gross income any amounts received for medical expenses that were deducted by the taxpayer on a prior return.

EXAMPLE 5

In 1998, Tab's employer-sponsored health insurance plan paid $4,000 for hair transplants that did not meet the Code's definition of medical care. Tab must include the $4,000 in his gross income for 1998. ▼

Section 105(c) excludes payments for the permanent loss or the loss of the use of a member or function of the body or the permanent disfigurement of the employee, spouse, or a dependent. However, payments that are a substitute for salary (e.g., related to the period of time absent) are included in income.

EXAMPLE 6

Jill lost an eye in an automobile accident unrelated to her work. As a result of the accident, Jill incurred $2,000 of medical expenses, which she deducted on her return. She collected $10,000 from an accident insurance policy carried by her employer. The benefits were paid according to a schedule of amounts that varied with the part of the body injured (e.g., $10,000 for loss of an eye, $20,000 for loss of a hand). Because the payment was for loss of a member or function of the body, the $10,000 is excluded from income. Jill was absent from work for a week as a result of the accident. Her employer also provided her with insurance that reimbursed her for the loss of income due to illness or injury. Jill collected $500, which is includible in gross income. ▼

MEDICAL REIMBURSEMENT PLANS

As noted above, the amounts received through the insurance coverage (insured plan benefits) are excluded from income under § 105. Unfortunately, because of cost considerations, the insurance companies that issue this type of policy usually require a broad coverage of employees. An alternative is to have a plan that is not funded with insurance (a self-insured arrangement). Under a self-insured plan, the employer reimburses employees directly for any medical expenses. The benefits received under a self-insured plan can be excluded from the employee's income, if the plan does not discriminate in favor of highly compensated employees.[7]

Small employers (50 or fewer employees) have an alternative means of accomplishing a medical reimbursement plan. The employer can purchase a medical insurance plan with a high deductible (e.g., the employee is responsible for the first $2,000 of medical expenses) and then make contributions to the employee's **medical savings account (MSA)**. The employer can make contributions each year up to the maximum contribution of 65 percent of the deductible amount for an individual or 75 percent of the deductible amount in the case of family coverage. Withdrawals from the MSA must be used to reimburse the employee for the medical expenses paid by the employee that are not covered under the high-deductible plan. The employee is not taxed on the employer's contributions to the MSA, the earnings on the funds in the account, or the withdrawals made for medical expenses.

---

[5]§ 106, Reg. § 1.106–1, and Rev.Rul. 82–196, 1982–1 C.B. 106.
[6]See the discussion of medical care in Chapter 15.
[7]§ 105(h).

LONG-TERM CARE BENEFITS

Generally, long-term care insurance, which covers expenses such as the cost of care in a nursing home, is treated the same as accident and health insurance benefits. Thus, the employee does not recognize income when the employer pays the premiums. When benefits are received from the policy, whether the employer or the individual purchased the policy, the exclusion from gross income is limited to the greater of the following amounts:

- $175 (to be indexed) for each day the patient receives the long-term care.
- The actual cost of the care.

The excludible amount is reduced by any amounts received from other third parties (e.g., damages received).[8]

EXAMPLE 7

Hazel, who suffers from Alzheimer's disease, was a patient in a nursing home for the last 30 days of the year. While in the nursing home, she incurred total costs of $6,000. Medicare paid $3,200 of the costs. Hazel received $3,600 from her long-term care insurance policy (which paid $120 per day while she was in the facility). The amount Hazel may exclude is calculated as follows:

Greater of:		
Daily statutory amount of $175 ($175 × 30 days)	$5,250	
Actual cost of the care	6,000	$ 6,000
Less: Amount received from Medicare		(3,200)
Amount of exclusion		$ 2,800

Therefore, Hazel must include $800 ($3,600 − $2,800) of the long-term care benefits received in her gross income. ▼

The exclusion for long-term care insurance is not available if it is provided as part of a cafeteria plan or a flexible spending plan (discussed later in this chapter).

MEALS AND LODGING FURNISHED FOR THE CONVENIENCE OF THE EMPLOYER

Income can take any form, including meals and lodging. However, § 119 excludes from income the value of meals and lodging provided to the employee and the employee's spouse and dependents under the following conditions:[9]

- The meals and/or lodging are furnished by the employer, on the employer's business premises, for the convenience of the employer.
- In the case of lodging, the employee is required to accept the lodging as a condition of employment.

The courts have construed these requirements strictly, as discussed below.

Furnished by the Employer. The following two questions have been raised with regard to the *furnished by the employer* requirement:

- Who is considered an employee?
- What is meant by furnished?

---

[8]§ 7702B.
[9]§ 119(a). The meals and lodging are also excluded from FICA and FUTA tax. *Rowan Companies, Inc. v. U.S.*, 81–1 USTC ¶9479, 48 AFTR2d 81–5115, 101 S.Ct. 2288 (USSC, 1981).

As to the employee issue, the IRS and some courts have reasoned that because a partner is not an employee, the exclusion does not apply to a partner. However, the Tax Court and the Fifth Court of Appeals have ruled in favor of the taxpayer on this issue.[10]

On the issue of whether meals and lodging are *furnished* by the employer, the Supreme Court held that a *cash meal allowance* was ineligible for the exclusion because the employer did not actually furnish the meals.[11] Similarly, one court denied the exclusion where the employer paid for the food and supplied the cooking facilities but the employee prepared the meal.[12]

On the Employer's Business Premises. The *on the employer's business premises* requirement, applicable to both meals and lodging, has resulted in much litigation. The Regulations define business premises as simply "the place of employment of the employee."[13] Thus, the Sixth Court of Appeals held that a residence, owned by the employer and occupied by an employee, two blocks from the motel that the employee managed was not part of the business premises.[14] However, the Tax Court considered an employer-owned house across the street from the hotel that was managed by the taxpayer to be on the business premises of the employer.[15] Perhaps these two cases can be reconciled by comparing the distance from the lodging facilities to the place where the employer's business was conducted. The closer the lodging to the business operations, the more likely the convenience of the employer is served.

For the Convenience of the Employer. The *convenience of the employer* test is intended to focus on the employer's motivation for furnishing the meals and lodging rather than on the benefits received by the employee. If the employer furnishes the meals and lodging primarily to enable the employee to perform his or her duties properly, it does not matter that the employee considers these benefits to be a part of his or her compensation.

The Regulations give the following examples in which the tests for excluding meals are satisfied:[16]

- A waitress is required to eat her meals on the premises during the busy lunch and breakfast hours.
- A bank furnishes a teller meals on the premises to limit the time the employee is away from his or her booth during the busy hours.
- A worker is employed at a construction site in a remote part of Alaska. The employer must furnish meals and lodging due to the inaccessibility of other facilities.

Required as a Condition of Employment. The *required as a condition of employment* test applies only to lodging. If the employee's use of the housing would serve the convenience of the employer, but the employee is not required to use the housing, the exclusion is not available.

---

[10] Rev.Rul. 80, 1953–1 C.B. 62; *Comm. v. Doak*, 56–2 USTC ¶9708, 49 AFTR 1491, 234 F.2d 704 (CA–4, 1956); but see *G. A. Papineau*, 16 T.C. 130 (1951); *Armstrong v. Phinney*, 68–1 USTC ¶9355, 21 AFTR2d 1260, 394 F.2d 661 (CA–5, 1968).

[11] *Comm v. Kowalski*, 77–2 USTC ¶9748, 40 AFTR2d 6128, 98 S.Ct. 315 (USSC, 1977).

[12] *Tougher v. Comm.*, 71–1 USTC ¶9398, 27 AFTR2d 1301, 441 F.2d 1148 (CA–9, 1971).

[13] Reg. § 1.119–1(c)(1).

[14] *Comm. v. Anderson*, 67–1 USTC ¶9136, 19 AFTR2d 318, 371 F.2d 59 (CA–6, 1966).

[15] *J. B. Lindeman*, 60 T.C. 609 (1973).

[16] Reg. § 1.119–1(f).

TAX IN THE NEWS

THE IRS FINDS COMPENSATORY REASON FOR PROVIDING EMPLOYEE MEALS

A recent private letter ruling dealt with an employer that operated a cafeteria for its employees and provided meals at less than cost. The employer claimed it provided the meals because the employees did not have time to go to restaurants during the lunch period. The IRS reasoned that the employer could have solved the problem by lengthening the lunch period. The abbreviated lunch period shortened the workday, which the IRS concluded was a compensatory employee benefit. To justify the meal exclusion, the company would need to have a noncompensatory reason for providing the meals. Such a noncompensatory reason would serve as proof that the meals were provided "for the convenience of the employer." Because no such proof existed, the employees had to report gross income.

EXAMPLE 8

VEP, a utilities company, has all of its service personnel on 24-hour call for emergencies. The company encourages its employees to live near the plant so they can respond quickly to emergency calls. Company-owned housing is available rent-free. Only 10 of the employees live in the company housing because it is not suitable for families.

Although the company-provided housing serves the convenience of the employer, it is not required. Therefore, the employees who live in the company housing must include its value in gross income. ▼

In addition, if the employee has the option of cash or lodging, the employer-required test is not satisfied.

EXAMPLE 9

Khalid is the manager of a large apartment complex. The employer gives Khalid the option of rent-free housing (value of $6,000 per year) or an additional $5,000 per year. Khalid selects the housing option. Therefore, he must include $6,000 in gross income. ▼

Other housing exclusions are available for certain employees of educational institutions, ministers of the gospel, and military personnel.

GROUP TERM LIFE INSURANCE

For many years, the IRS did not attempt to tax the value of life insurance protection provided to an employee by the employer. Some companies took undue advantage of the exclusion by providing large amounts of insurance protection for executives. In response, Congress enacted § 79, which created a limited exclusion for group term life insurance. Current law allows an exclusion for premiums on the first $50,000 of group term life insurance protection.

The benefits of this exclusion are available only to employees. Proprietors and partners are not considered employees. Moreover, the Regulations generally require broad-scale coverage of employees to satisfy the group requirement (e.g., shareholder-employees would not constitute a qualified group). The exclusion applies only to term insurance (protection for a period of time but with no cash surrender value) and not to ordinary life insurance (lifetime protection plus a cash surrender value that can be drawn upon before death).

▼ **TABLE 16–1**
Uniform Premiums for $1,000 of Group Term Life Insurance Protection

Attained Age on Last Day of Employee's Tax Year	Cost of $1,000 of Protection for a One-Month Period
Under 30	$ .08
30–34	.09
35–39	.11
40–44	.17
45–49	.29
50–54	.48
55–59	.75
60–64	1.17
65–69	2.10
70 and over	3.76

As mentioned, the exclusion applies to the first $50,000 of group term life insurance protection. For each $1,000 of coverage in excess of $50,000, the employee must include the amounts indicated in Table 16–1 in gross income.[17]

EXAMPLE 10

Finch Corporation has a group term life insurance policy with coverage equal to the employee's annual salary. Keith, age 52, is president of the corporation and receives an annual salary of $75,000. Keith must include $144 in gross income from the insurance protection for the year.

[($75,000 − $50,000)/$1,000] × .48 × 12 months = $144. ▼

Generally, the amount that must be included in income, computed from Table 16–1, is much less than the price an individual would pay an insurance company for the same amount of protection. Thus, even the excess coverage provides some tax-favored income for employees when group term life insurance coverage in excess of $50,000 is desirable.

If the plan discriminates in favor of certain key employees (e.g., officers), the key employees are not eligible for the exclusion. In such a case, the key employees must include in gross income the greater of actual premiums paid by the employer or the amount calculated from the Uniform Premiums table in Table 16–1. The other employees are still eligible for the $50,000 exclusion and continue to use the Uniform Premiums table to compute the income from excess insurance protection.[18]

QUALIFIED TUITION REDUCTION PLANS

Employees (including retired and disabled former employees) of nonprofit educational institutions are allowed to exclude a tuition waiver from gross income, if the waiver is pursuant to a qualified tuition reduction plan.[19] The plan may not discriminate in favor of highly compensated employees. The exclusion applies to the employee, the employee's spouse, and the employee's dependent children. The exclusion also extends to tuition reductions granted by any nonprofit educational institution to employees of any other nonprofit educational institution (reciprocal agreements).

---

[17] Reg. § 1.79–3(d)(2).
[18] § 79(d).
[19] § 117(d).

EXAMPLE 11 ABC University allows the dependent children of XYZ University employees to attend ABC University with no tuition charge. XYZ University grants reciprocal benefits to the children of ABC University employees. The dependent children can also attend tuition-free the university where their parents are employed. Employees who take advantage of these benefits are not required to recognize gross income. ▼

Generally, the exclusion is limited to undergraduate tuition waivers. However, in the case of teaching or research assistants, graduate tuition waivers may also qualify for exclusion treatment. According to the Proposed Regulations, the exclusion is limited to the value of the benefit in excess of the employee's reasonable compensation.[20] Thus, a tuition reduction that is a substitute for cash compensation cannot be excluded.

EXAMPLE 12 Susan is a graduate research assistant. She receives a $5,000 salary for 500 hours of service over a nine-month period. This pay, $10 per hour, is reasonable compensation for Susan's services. In addition, Susan receives a waiver of $6,000 for tuition. Susan may exclude the tuition waiver from gross income. ▼

OTHER SPECIFIC EMPLOYEE FRINGE BENEFITS

Congress has enacted exclusions to encourage employers to (1) finance and make available child care facilities, (2) provide athletic facilities for employees, and (3) finance certain education expenses of employees. These provisions are summarized as follows:

- The employee can exclude from gross income the value of child and dependent care services paid for by the employer and incurred to enable the employee to work. The exclusion cannot exceed $5,000 per year ($2,500 if married and filing separately). For a married couple, the annual exclusion cannot exceed the earned income of the spouse who has the lesser amount of earned income. For an unmarried taxpayer, the exclusion cannot exceed the taxpayer's earned income.[21]
- The value of the use of a gymnasium or other athletic facilities by employees, their spouses, and their dependent children may be excluded from an employee's gross income. The facilities must be on the employer's premises, and substantially all of the use of the facilities must be by employees and their family members.[22]
- Qualified employer-provided educational assistance (tuition, fees, books, and supplies) at the undergraduate level is excludible from gross income. The exclusion is limited to a maximum of $5,250 annually.[23]
- The employee can exclude from gross income up to $5,000 of expenses incurred to adopt a child where the adoption expenses are paid or reimbursed by the employer under a qualified adoption assistance program.[24] The limit on the exclusion is increased to $6,000 if the child has special needs (is not physically or mentally capable of caring for himself or herself). The exclusion is phased out over the AGI range from $75,000 to $115,000.

---

[20] Prop.Reg. § 1.117–6(d).
[21] § 129. The exclusion applies to the same types of expenses that, if paid by the employee (and not reimbursed by the employer), would be eligible for the credit for child and dependent care expense discussed in Chapter 15.
[22] § 132(j)(4).
[23] § 127. Exclusion treatment applies for tax years beginning before June 1, 2000.
[24] § 137.

CAFETERIA PLANS

Generally, if an employee is offered a choice between cash and some other form of compensation, the employee is deemed to have constructively received the cash even when the noncash option is elected. Thus, the employee has gross income regardless of the option chosen.

An exception to this constructive receipt treatment is provided under the cafeteria plan rules. Under such a plan, the employee is permitted to choose between cash and nontaxable benefits (e.g., group term life insurance, health and accident protection, and child care). If the employee chooses the otherwise nontaxable benefits, the cafeteria plan rules allow the benefits to be excluded from the employee's income.[25] **Cafeteria plans** provide tremendous flexibility in tailoring the employee pay package to fit individual needs. Some employees (usually the younger group) prefer cash, while others (usually the older group) will opt for the fringe benefit program. However, long-term care insurance cannot be part of a cafeteria plan. Thus, an employer that wishes to provide long-term care benefits must provide such benefits separate from the cafeteria plan.[26]

EXAMPLE 13

Hawk Corporation offers its employees (on a nondiscriminatory basis) a choice of any one or all of the following benefits:

Benefit	Cost
Group term life insurance	$ 200
Hospitalization insurance for family members	2,400
Child care payments	1,800
	$4,400

If a benefit is not selected, the employee receives cash equal to the cost of the benefit.

Kay, an employee, has a spouse who works for another employer that provides hospitalization insurance but no child care payments. Kay elects to receive the group term life insurance, the child care payments, and $2,400 of cash. Only the $2,400 must be included in Kay's gross income. ▼

FLEXIBLE SPENDING PLANS

Flexible spending plans (often referred to as flexible benefit plans) operate much like cafeteria plans. Under these plans, the employee accepts lower cash compensation in return for the employer's agreement to pay certain costs that the employer can pay without the employee recognizing gross income. For example, assume the employer's health insurance policy does not cover dental expenses. The employee could estimate his or her dental expenses for the upcoming year and agree to a salary reduction equal to the estimated dental expenses. The employer then pays or reimburses the employee for the actual dental expenses incurred, up to the amount of the salary reduction. If the employee's actual dental expenses are less than the reduction in cash compensation, the employee cannot recover the difference. Hence, these plans are often referred to as *use or lose* plans. As is the case for cafeteria plans, flexible spending plans cannot be used to pay long-term care insurance premiums.

---

[25]§ 125.   [26]§ 125(f).

GENERAL CLASSES OF EXCLUDED BENEFITS

An employer can provide a variety of economic benefits to employees. Under the all-inclusive concept of income, the benefits are taxable unless one of the provisions previously discussed specifically excludes the item from gross income. The amount of the income is the fair market value of the benefit. This reasoning can lead to results that Congress considers unacceptable, as illustrated in the following example.

EXAMPLE 14

Vern is employed in New York as a ticket clerk for Trans National Airlines. Vern would like to visit his mother, who lives in Miami, Florida, but he has no money for plane tickets. Trans National has daily flights from New York to Miami that often leave with empty seats. The cost of a round-trip ticket is $400, and Vern is in the 28% tax bracket. If Trans National allows Vern to fly without charge to Miami, under the general gross income rules, Vern has income equal to the value of a ticket. Therefore, Vern must pay $112 tax (.28 × $400) on a trip to Miami. Because Vern does not have $112, he cannot visit his mother, and the airplane flies with another empty seat. ▼

If Trans National in Example 14 will allow employees to use resources that would otherwise be wasted, why should the tax laws interfere with the employee's decision to take advantage of the available benefit? Thus, to avoid the economic inefficiency that occurs in Example 14 and in similar situations, as well as to create uniform rules for fringe benefits, Congress established six broad classes of nontaxable employee benefits:[27]

- No-additional-cost services.
- Qualified employee discounts.
- Working condition fringes.
- *De minimis* fringes.
- Qualified transportation fringes.
- Qualified moving expense reimbursements.

No-Additional-Cost Services. Example 14 illustrates a no-additional-cost fringe benefit. **No-additional-cost services** are excluded from an employee's income if all of the following conditions are satisfied:

- The employee receives services, as opposed to property.
- The employer does not incur substantial additional cost, including forgone revenue, in providing the services to the employee.
- The services must be from the same line of business in which the employee works.
- The services are offered to customers in the ordinary course of the business in which the employee works.[28]

EXAMPLE 15

Assume that Vern in Example 14 can fly without charge only if the airline cannot fill the seats with paying customers. That is, Vern must fly on standby. Although the airplane may burn slightly more fuel because Vern is aboard and Vern may receive the same meal as paying customers, the additional costs would not be substantial. Thus, the trip could qualify as a no-additional-cost service. Note that the employer incurs no cost, so the employee reports no income.

On the other hand, assume that Vern is given a reserved seat on a flight that is frequently full. The employer would be forgoing revenue to allow Vern to fly. This forgone revenue would be a substantial additional cost, and thus the benefit would be taxable. ▼

---

[27]See, generally, § 132. [28]Reg. § 1.132–2.

Note that if Vern were employed in a hotel owned by Trans National, the receipt of the airline ticket would be taxable because Vern did not work in that line of business. However, the Code allows the exclusion for *reciprocal benefits* offered by employers in the same line of business.

EXAMPLE 16

Grace is employed as a desk clerk for Plush Hotels, Inc. The company and Chain Hotels, Inc., have an agreement that allows any of their employees to stay without charge in *either company's* resort hotels during the off-season. Grace would not be required to recognize income from taking advantage of the plan by staying in a Chain Hotel. ▼

The no-additional-cost exclusion extends to the employee's spouse and dependent children and to retired and disabled former employees. In the Regulations, the IRS has conceded that partners who perform services for the partnership are employees for purposes of the exclusion.[29] (As discussed earlier in the chapter, the IRS's position is that partners are not employees for purposes of the § 119 meals and lodging exclusion.) However, the exclusion is not extended to highly compensated employees unless the benefit is available on a nondiscriminatory basis.

Qualified Employee Discounts. When the employer sells goods or services (other than no-additional-cost benefits just discussed) to the employee for a price that is less than the price charged regular customers, the employee ordinarily recognizes income equal to the discount. However, **qualified employee discounts** can be excluded from the gross income of the employee, subject to the following conditions and limitations:

- The exclusion is not available for discounted sales of real property (e.g., a house) or for personal property of the type commonly held for investment (e.g., common stocks).
- The property or services must be from the same line of business in which the employee works.
- In the case of property, the exclusion cannot exceed the gross profit component of the price to customers.
- In the case of services, the exclusion is limited to 20 percent of the customer price.[30]

EXAMPLE 17

Silver Corporation, which operates a department store, sells a television set to a store employee for $300. The regular customer price is $500, and the gross profit rate is 25%. The corporation also sells the employee a service contract for $100. The regular customer price for the contract is $150. The employee must recognize income of $95, computed as follows:

Customer price for property	$ 500	
Less: Qualifying discount (25% gross profit × $500 price)	(125)	
	$ 375	
Employee price	(300)	
Excess discount recognized as income		$75
Customer price for service	$ 150	
Less: Qualifying discount (20%)	(30)	
	$ 120	
Employee price	100	
Excess discount recognized as income		20
Total income recognized		$95

▼

---

[29] Reg. § 1.132–1(b).

[30] § 132(c).

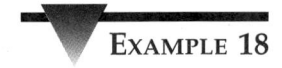

EXAMPLE 18 Assume the same facts as in Example 17, except that the employee is a clerk in a hotel operated by Silver Corporation. Because the line of business requirement is not met, the employee must recognize $200 of income ($500 − $300) from the discount on the television and $50 of income ($150 − $100) from the service contract. ▼

As in the case of no-additional-cost benefits, the exclusion applies to employees, their spouses and dependent children, and retired and disabled former employees. However, the exclusion does not extend to highly compensated individuals unless the discount is available on a nondiscriminatory basis.

Working Condition Fringes. Generally, an employee may exclude the cost of property or services provided by the employer if the employee could deduct the cost of those items if he or she had actually paid for them.[31] These benefits are called **working condition fringes**.

EXAMPLE 19 Mitch is a certified public accountant employed by an accounting firm. The employer pays Mitch's annual dues to professional organizations. Mitch is not required to include the payment of the dues in gross income because if he had paid the dues, he would have been allowed to deduct the amount as an employee business expense (as discussed later in this chapter). ▼

In many cases, this exclusion merely avoids reporting income and an offsetting deduction. However, in two specific situations, the working condition fringe benefit rules allow an exclusion where the expense would not be deductible if paid by the employee:

- Some automobile salespeople are allowed to exclude the value of certain personal use of company demonstrators (e.g., commuting to and from work).[32]
- The employee business expense would be eliminated by the 2 percent floor on miscellaneous deductions under § 67 (refer to Chapter 15).

Unlike the other fringe benefits discussed previously, working condition fringes can be made available on a discriminatory basis and still qualify for the exclusion.

***De Minimis* Fringes.** As the term suggests, *de minimis* **fringe benefits** are so small that accounting for them is impractical. The House Report contains the following examples of *de minimis* fringes:

- The typing of a personal letter by a company secretary, occasional personal use of a company copying machine, occasional company cocktail parties or picnics for employees, occasional supper money or taxi fare for employees because of overtime work, and certain holiday gifts of property with a low fair market value are excluded.
- The value of meals consumed in a subsidized eating facility (e.g., an employees' cafeteria) operated by the employer is excluded if the facility is located on or near the employer's business premises, if revenue equals or exceeds direct operating costs, and if nondiscrimination requirements are met.

When taxpayers venture beyond the specific examples contained in the House Report and the Regulations, there is obviously much room for disagreement as to what is *de minimis*. However, note that except in the case of subsidized eating

---

[31]§ 132(d).   [32]§ 132(j)(3).

facilities, *de minimis* fringe benefits can be granted in a manner that favors highly compensated employees.

Qualified Transportation Fringes. The intent of the exclusion for **qualified transportation fringes** is to encourage the use of mass transit for commuting to and from work. Qualified transportation fringes encompass the following transportation benefits provided by the employer to the employee:[33]

1. Transportation in a commuter highway vehicle between the employee's residence and the place of employment.
2. A transit pass.
3. Qualified parking.

Statutory dollar limits are placed on the amount of the exclusion. Categories (1) and (2) above are combined for purposes of applying the limit. In this case, the limit on the exclusion for 1998 is $65 per month. Category (3) has a separate limit. For qualified parking, the limit on the exclusion for 1998 is $175 per month. Both of these dollar limits are indexed annually for inflation.

A commuter highway vehicle is any highway vehicle with a seating capacity of at least six adults (excluding the driver). In addition, at least 80 percent of the vehicle's use must be for transporting employees between their residences and place of employment.

Qualified parking includes the following:

- Parking provided to an employee on or near the employer's business premises.
- Parking provided to an employee on or near a location from which the employee commutes to work via mass transit, in a commuter highway vehicle, or in a carpool.

Qualified transportation fringes may be provided directly by the employer or may be in the form of cash reimbursements.

EXAMPLE 20

Gray Corporation's offices are located in the center of a large city. The company pays for parking spaces to be used by the company officers. Steve, a vice president, receives $250 of such benefits each month. The parking space rental qualifies as a qualified transportation fringe. Of the $250 benefit received each month by Steve, $175 is excludible from gross income. The balance of $75 is included in his gross income. The same result would occur if Steve paid for the parking and was reimbursed by his employer. ▼

Qualified Moving Expense Reimbursements. Qualified moving expenses that are reimbursed or paid by the employer are excludible from gross income. A qualified moving expense is one that would be deductible under § 217. See the discussion of moving expenses later in this chapter.

Nondiscrimination Provisions. For no-additional-cost services and qualified employee discounts, if the plan is discriminatory in favor of *highly compensated employees*,[34] these key employees are denied exclusion treatment. However, any non-highly compensated employees who receive these benefits can still enjoy exclusion treatment.[35]

---

[33] § 132(f).
[34] See § 414(q) for the definition of highly compensated employee.
[35] § 132(j)(1).

EXAMPLE 21

Dove Company's officers are allowed to purchase goods from the company at a 25% discount. Other employees are allowed only a 15% discount. The company's gross profit margin on these goods is 30%.

Peggy, an officer in the company, purchased goods from the company for $750 when the price charged to customers was $1,000. Peggy must include $250 in gross income because the plan is discriminatory.

Leo, an employee of the company who is not an officer, purchased goods for $850 when the customer price was $1,000. Leo is not required to recognize income because he received a qualified employee discount. ▼

De minimis fringe benefits (except for subsidized eating facilities) and working condition fringe benefits can be provided on a discriminatory basis. The *de minimis* benefits are not subject to tax because the accounting problems that would be created are out of proportion to the amount of additional tax that would result. A nondiscrimination test would simply add to the compliance problems. In the case of working condition fringes, the types of services required vary with the job. Therefore, a nondiscrimination test probably could not be satisfied, although usually there is no deliberate plan to benefit a chosen few. Likewise, the qualified transportation fringe and the qualified moving expense reimbursement can be provided on a discriminatory basis.

TAXABLE FRINGE BENEFITS

If fringe benefits cannot qualify for any of the specific exclusions or do not fit into any of the general classes of excluded benefits, the employee must recognize gross income equal to the fair market value of the benefits received. Obviously, problems are frequently encountered in determining values. To help taxpayers cope with these problems, the IRS has issued extensive Regulations addressing the valuation of personal use of an employer's automobiles and meals provided at an employer-operated eating facility.[36]

If a fringe benefit plan discriminates in favor of highly compensated employees, generally those employees are not allowed to exclude the benefits they receive that other employees do not enjoy. However, the highly compensated employees, as well as the other employees, are generally allowed to exclude the nondiscriminatory benefits.[37]

EXAMPLE 22

MED Company has a medical reimbursement plan that reimburses officers for 100% of their medical expenses, but reimburses all other employees for only 80% of their medical expenses. Cliff, the president of the company, was reimbursed $1,000 during the year for medical expenses. Cliff must include $200 in gross income [(1 − .80) × $1,000 = $200]. Mike, an employee who is not an officer, received $800 (80% of his actual medical expenses) under the medical reimbursement plan. None of the $800 is includible in his gross income. ▼

---

[36]Reg. § 1.61–2T(j). Generally, the income from the personal use of the employer's automobile is based on the lease value of the automobile (what it would have cost the employee to lease the automobile). Meals are valued at 150% of the employer's direct costs (e.g., food and labor) of preparing the meals.

[37]§§ 79(d), 105(h), 127(b)(2), and 132(j)(1).

Concept Summary 16–1

General Classes of Fringe Benefits

Benefit	Description and Examples	Coverage Allowed	Effect of Discrimination
1. No-additional-cost services	The employee takes advantage of the employer's excess capacity (e.g., free passes for airline employees).	Current, retired, and disabled employees; their spouses and dependent children; spouses of deceased employees. Partners are treated as employees.	No exclusion for highly compensated employees.
2. Qualified discounts on goods	The employee is allowed a discount no greater than the gross profit margin on goods sold to customers.	Same as (1) above.	Same as (1) above.
3. Qualified discounts on services	The employee is allowed a discount (maximum of 20%) on services the employer offers to customers.	Same as (1) above.	Same as (1) above.
4. Working condition fringes	Expenses paid by the employer that would be deductible if paid by the employee (e.g., a mechanic's tools). Also, includes auto salesperson's use of a car held for sale.	Current employees, partners, directors, and independent contractors.	No effect.
5. *De minimis* items	Expenses so immaterial that accounting for them is not warranted (e.g., occasional supper money, personal use of the copy machine).	*Any recipient* of a fringe benefit.	No effect.
6. Qualified transportation fringes	Transportation benefits provided by the employer to employees, including commuting in a commuter highway vehicle, a transit pass, and qualified parking.	Current employees.	No effect.
7. Qualified moving expense reimbursements	Qualified moving expenses that are paid or reimbursed by the employer. A qualified moving expense is one that would be deductible under § 217.	Current employees.	No effect.

EMPLOYEE EXPENSES

3 LEARNING OBJECTIVE
Apply the rules for computing deductible expenses of employees, including transportation, travel, moving, education, and entertainment expenses.

Once the employment relationship is established, employee expenses fall into one of the following categories:

- Transportation.
- Travel.
- Moving.
- Education.
- Entertainment.
- Other.

These expenses are discussed below in the order presented. Keep in mind, however, that these expenses are not necessarily limited to employees. A deduction for business transportation, for example, is equally available to taxpayers who are self-employed.

TRANSPORTATION EXPENSES

Qualified Expenditures. An employee may deduct unreimbursed employment-related **transportation expenses** as an itemized deduction *from* AGI. Transportation expenses include only the cost of transporting the employee from one place to another when the employee is not away from home in travel status. Such costs include taxi fares, automobile expenses, tolls, and parking.

Commuting Expenses. Commuting between home and one's place of employment is a personal, nondeductible expense. The fact that one employee drives 30 miles to work and another employee walks six blocks is of no significance.[38]

EXAMPLE 23
Geraldo is employed by Sparrow Corporation. He drives 22 miles each way to work. The 44 miles he drives each workday are nondeductible commuting expenses. ▼

The rule that disallows a deduction for commuting expenses has several exceptions. An employee who uses an automobile to transport heavy tools to work and who otherwise would not drive to work is allowed a deduction, but only for the additional costs incurred to transport the work implements. Additional costs are those exceeding the cost of commuting by the same mode of transportation without the tools. For example, the rental of a trailer for transporting tools is deductible, but the expenses of operating the automobile generally are not deductible.[39] The Supreme Court has held that a deduction is permitted only when the taxpayer can show that the automobile would not have been used without the necessity to transport tools or equipment.[40]

Another exception is provided for an employee who has a second job. The expenses of getting from one job to another are deductible. If the employee goes home between jobs, the deduction is based on the distance between jobs.

EXAMPLE 24
In the current year, Cynthia holds two jobs, a full-time job with Blue Corporation and a part-time job with Wren Corporation. During the 250 days that she works (adjusted for weekends, vacation, and holidays), Cynthia customarily leaves home at 7:30 A.M. and drives

---

[38]*Tauferner v. U.S.*, 69–1 USTC ¶9241, 23 AFTR2d 69–1025, 407 F.2d 243 (CA–10, 1969).
[39]Rev.Rul. 75–380, 1975–2 C.B. 59.
[40]*Fausner v. Comm.*, 73–2 USTC ¶9515, 32 AFTR2d 73–5202, 93 S.Ct. 2820 (USSC, 1973).

30 miles to the Blue Corporation plant, where she works until 5:00 P.M. After dinner at a nearby café, Cynthia drives 20 miles to Wren Corporation and works from 7:00 to 11:00 P.M. The distance from the second job to Cynthia's home is 40 miles. Her deduction is based on 20 miles (the distance between jobs). ▼

If the taxpayer is required to incur a transportation expense to travel between work stations, that expense is deductible.

EXAMPLE 25
Thomas, a general contractor, drives from his home to his office, then drives to three building sites to perform his required inspections, and finally drives home. The costs of driving to his office and driving home from the last inspection site are nondeductible commuting expenses. The other transportation costs are deductible. ▼

Likewise, the commuting costs from home to a temporary work station and from the temporary work station to home are deductible.[41]

EXAMPLE 26
Vivian works for a firm in downtown Denver and commutes to work. She occasionally works in a customer's office. One day, Vivian drove directly to the customer's office, a round-trip distance from her home of 40 miles. She did not go into her office, which is a 52-mile round-trip. Her mileage for going to and from the customer's office is deductible. ▼

Also deductible are reasonable transportation costs between the general working area and a temporary work station outside that area.[42] What constitutes the general working area depends on the facts and circumstances of each situation. Furthermore, if an employee customarily works on several temporary assignments in a localized area, that localized area becomes the regular place of employment. Transportation from home to these locations becomes a personal, nondeductible commuting expense.

EXAMPLE 27
Sam, a building inspector in Minneapolis, regularly inspects buildings for building code violations for his employer, a general contractor. During one busy season, the St. Paul inspector became ill, and Sam was required to inspect several buildings in St. Paul. The expenses for transportation for the trips to St. Paul are deductible. ▼

Computation of Automobile Expenses. A taxpayer has two choices in computing automobile expenses. The actual operating cost, which includes depreciation (refer to Chapter 4), gas, oil, repairs, licenses, and insurance, may be used. Records must be kept that detail the automobile's personal and business use. Only the percentage allocable to business transportation and travel is allowed as a deduction.

Use of the **automatic mileage method** is the second alternative. For 1998 the deduction is based on 32.5 cents per mile for all business miles.[43] Parking fees and tolls are allowed in addition to expenses computed using the automatic mileage method.

Generally, a taxpayer may elect either method for any particular year. However, the following restrictions apply:

- The vehicle must be owned or leased by the taxpayer.
- If two or more vehicles are in use (for business purposes) at the same time (not alternately), a taxpayer may not use the automatic mileage method.

---

[41]Rev.Rul. 90–23, 1990–1 C.B. 28 as amplified by Rev.Rul. 94–47, 1994–2 C.B. 18.

[42]Rev.Rul. 190, 1953–2 C.B. 303 as amplified by Rev.Rul. 94–47, 1994–2 C.B. 18.

[43]Rev.Proc. 97–58, I.R.B. No. 52, 24. The rate was 31.5 cents a mile for 1997.

- A basis adjustment is required if the taxpayer changes from the automatic mileage method to the actual operating cost method. Depreciation is considered allowed for the business miles in accordance with the following schedule for the most recent five years:

Year	Rate per Mile
1998	12 cents
1997	12 cents
1996	12 cents
1995	12 cents
1994	12 cents

EXAMPLE 28

Tim purchased his automobile in 1995 for $15,000. Tim drove the automobile for 10,000 business miles in 1997; 8,500 miles in 1996; and 6,000 miles in 1995. The automobile is used for business 90% of the time. At the beginning of 1998, the basis of the business portion is $10,560.

Cost ($15,000 × 90%)	$13,500
Less depreciation:	
1997 (10,000 miles × 12 cents)	(1,200)
1996 (8,500 miles × 12 cents)	(1,020)
1995 (6,000 miles × 12 cents)	(720)
Adjusted basis 1/1/98	$10,560

- Use of the automatic mileage method in the first year the auto is placed in service is considered an election not to use the MACRS method of depreciation (refer to Chapter 4).
- A taxpayer may not switch to the automatic mileage method if the MACRS statutory percentage method or the election to expense under § 179 has been used.

TRAVEL EXPENSES

Definition of Travel Expenses. An itemized deduction is allowed for *unreimbursed* **travel expenses** related to a taxpayer's employment. Travel expenses are more broadly defined in the Code than are transportation expenses. Travel expenses include transportation expenses and meals and lodging while away from home in the pursuit of a trade or business. Meals cannot be lavish or extravagant. A deduction for meals and lodging is available only if the taxpayer is away from his or her tax home. Deductible travel expenses also include reasonable laundry and incidental expenses.

Away-from-Home Requirement. The crucial test for the deductibility of travel expenses is whether or not the employee is away from home overnight. "Overnight" need not be a 24-hour period, but it must be a period substantially longer than an ordinary day's work and must require rest, sleep, or a relief-from-work period.[44] A one-day business trip is not travel status, and meals and lodging for such a trip are not deductible.

---

[44] *U.S. v. Correll*, 68–1 USTC ¶9101, 20 AFTR2d 5845, 88 S.Ct 445 (USSC, 1967); Rev.Rul. 75–168, 1975–1 C.B. 58.

Temporary Assignments. The employee must be away from home for a temporary period. If the taxpayer-employee is reassigned to a new post for an indefinite period of time, that new post becomes his or her tax home. Temporary indicates that the assignment's termination is expected within a reasonably short period of time. The position of the IRS is that the tax home is the business location, post, or station of the taxpayer. Thus, travel expenses are not deductible if a taxpayer is reassigned for an indefinite period and does not move his or her place of residence to the new location.

EXAMPLE 29
Malcolm's employer opened a branch office in San Diego. Malcolm was assigned to the new office for three months to train a new manager and to assist in setting up the new office. He tried commuting from his home in Los Angeles for a week and decided that he could not continue driving several hours a day. He rented an apartment in San Diego, where he lived during the week. He spent weekends with his wife and children at their home in Los Angeles. Malcolm's rent, meals, laundry, incidentals, and automobile expenses in San Diego are deductible. To the extent that Malcolm's transportation expense related to his weekend trips home exceeds what his cost of meals and lodging would have been, the excess is personal and nondeductible. ▼

EXAMPLE 30
Assume that Malcolm in Example 29 was transferred to the new location to become the new manager permanently. His wife and children continued to live in Los Angeles until the end of the school year. Malcolm is no longer "away from home" because the assignment is not temporary. His travel expenses are not deductible. ▼

To curtail controversy in this area, the Code specifies that a taxpayer "shall not be treated as temporarily away from home during any period of employment if such period exceeds 1 year."[45]

Determining the Tax Home. Under ordinary circumstances, determining the location of a taxpayer's tax home does not present a problem. The tax home is the area in which the taxpayer derives his or her principal source of income; when the taxpayer has more than one place of employment, the tax home is based on the amount of time spent in each area.

It is possible for a taxpayer never to be away from his or her tax home. In other words, the tax home follows the taxpayer.[46] Under such circumstances, all meals and lodging remain personal and are not deductible.

EXAMPLE 31
Bill is employed as a long-haul truck driver. He is single, stores his clothes and other belongings at his parents' home, and stops there for periodic visits. Most of the time, Bill is on the road, sleeping in his truck and in motels. It is likely that Bill is never in travel status, as he is not away from home. Consequently, none of his meals and lodging is deductible. ▼

Restrictions on Travel Expenses. The possibility always exists that taxpayers will attempt to treat vacation or pleasure travel as deductible business travel. To prevent such practices, the law contains restrictions on certain travel expenses.

For convention travel expenses to be deductible, the convention must be directly related to the taxpayer's trade or business.[47]

---

[45] § 162(a).
[46] *Moses Mitnick*, 13 T.C. 1 (1949).
[47] § 274(h)(1).

EXAMPLE 32 Dr. Hill, a pathologist who works for a hospital in Ohio, travels to Las Vegas to attend a two-day session on recent developments in estate planning. No deduction is allowed for Dr. Hill's travel expenses. ▼

EXAMPLE 33 Assume the same facts as in Example 32, except that the convention deals entirely with recent developments in forensic medicine. Under these circumstances, a travel deduction is allowed. ▼

If the proceedings of the convention are videotaped, the taxpayer must attend convention sessions to view the videotaped materials along with other participants. This requirement does not disallow deductions for costs (other than travel, meals, and entertainment) of renting or using videotaped materials related to business.

EXAMPLE 34 A CPA is unable to attend a convention at which current developments in taxation are discussed. She pays $200 for videotapes of the lectures and views them at home later. The $200 is an itemized deduction if the CPA is an employee. If she is self-employed, the $200 is a deduction *for* AGI. ▼

The Code places stringent restrictions on the deductibility of travel expenses of the taxpayer's spouse or dependent.[48] Generally, the accompaniment by the spouse or dependent must serve a bona fide business purpose, and the expenses must be otherwise deductible.

EXAMPLE 35 Assume the same facts as in Example 33 with the additional fact that Dr. Hill is accompanied by Mrs. Hill. Mrs. Hill is not employed, but possesses secretarial skills and takes notes during the proceedings. No deduction is allowed for Mrs. Hill's travel expenses. ▼

EXAMPLE 36 Assume that Mrs. Hill in Example 35 is a nurse trained in pathology, who is employed by Dr. Hill as his assistant. Now, Mrs. Hill's travel expenses qualify as deductions. ▼

Travel as a form of education is not deductible.[49] If, however, the education qualifies as a deduction, the travel involved is deductible.

EXAMPLE 37 Greta, a German teacher, travels to Germany to maintain general familiarity with the language and culture. No travel expense deduction is deductible. ▼

EXAMPLE 38 Jean-Claude, a professor of French literature, travels to Paris to do specific library research that cannot be done elsewhere and to take courses that are offered only at the Sorbonne. The travel costs are deductible, assuming that the other requirements for deducting education expenses (discussed later in this chapter) are met. ▼

Combined Business and Pleasure Travel. To be deductible, travel expenses need not be incurred in the performance of specific job functions. Travel expenses incurred to attend a professional convention are deductible by an employee if attendance is connected with services as an employee. For example, an employee of a law firm can deduct travel expenses incurred to attend a meeting of the American Bar Association.

Travel deductions have been used in the past by persons who claimed a tax deduction for what was essentially a personal vacation. As a result, several provisions have been enacted to restrict deductions associated with combined business and pleasure trips. If the business/pleasure trip is from one point in the

---

[48] § 274(m)(3).   [49] § 274(m)(2).

United States to another point in the United States, the transportation expenses are deductible only if the trip is primarily for business.[50] If the trip is primarily for pleasure, no transportation expenses qualify as a deduction. Meals, lodging, and other expenses are allocated between business and personal days.

EXAMPLE 39

In the current year, Hana travels from Seattle to New York primarily for business. She spends five days conducting business and three days sightseeing and attending shows. Her plane and taxi fare amounts to $560. Her meals amount to $100 per day, and lodging and incidental expenses are $150 per day. She can deduct the transportation expenses of $560, since the trip is primarily for business (five days of business versus three days of sightseeing). Deductible meals are limited to five days and are subject to the 50% cutback (discussed later in the chapter) for a total of $250 [5 days × ($100 × 50%)], and other deductions are limited to $750 (5 days × $150). If Hana is an employee, the unreimbursed travel expenses are miscellaneous itemized deductions subject to the 2 percent-of-AGI floor. ▼

EXAMPLE 40

Assume Hana goes to New York for a two-week vacation. While there, she spends several hours renewing acquaintances with people in her company's New York office. Her transportation expenses are not deductible. ▼

When the trip is outside the United States, special rules apply.[51] Transportation expenses must be allocated between business and personal days unless (1) the taxpayer is away from home for seven days or less or (2) less than 25 percent of the time was for personal purposes. No allocation is required if the taxpayer has no substantial control over arrangements for the trip or the desire for a vacation is not a major factor in taking the trip. If the trip is primarily for pleasure, no transportation charges are deductible. Days devoted to travel are considered business days. Weekends, legal holidays, and intervening days are considered business days, provided that both the preceding and succeeding days were business days.

EXAMPLE 41

In the current year, Robert takes a trip from New York to Japan primarily for business purposes. He is away from home from June 10 through June 19. He spends three days vacationing and seven days conducting business (including two travel days). His airfare is $2,500, his meals amount to $100 per day, and lodging and incidental expenses are $160 per day. Since Robert is away from home for more than seven days and more than 25% of his time is devoted to personal purposes, only 70% (7 days business/10 days total) of the transportation is deductible. His deductions are as follows:

Transportation (70% × $2,500)		$1,750
Lodging ($160 × 7)		1,120
Meals ($100 × 7)	$ 700	
Less 50% cutback (discussed later in this chapter)	(350)	350
Total		$3,220

If Robert is gone the same period of time but spends only two days (less than 25% of the total) vacationing, no allocation of transportation is required. Since the pleasure portion of the trip is less than 25% of the total, all of the airfare qualifies for the travel deduction. ▼

Certain restrictions are imposed on the deductibility of expenses paid or incurred to attend conventions located outside North America. The expenses are

---

[50] Reg. § 1.162–2(b)(1).   [51] § 274(c) and Reg. § 1.274–4.

disallowed unless it is established that the meeting is directly related to a trade or business of the taxpayer. Disallowance also occurs unless the taxpayer shows that it is as reasonable for the meeting to be held in a foreign location as within the North American area.

The foreign convention rules do not operate to bar a deduction to an employer if the expense is compensatory in nature. For example, a trip to Rome won by a top salesperson is included in the gross income of the employee and is fully deductible by the employer.

PLANNING CONSIDERATIONS

Transportation and Travel Expenses

Adequate detailed records of all transportation and travel expenses should be kept. Since the regular mileage allowance is only 32.5 cents per mile, a new, expensive automobile used primarily for business may generate a higher expense based on actual cost. The election to expense part of the cost of the automobile under § 179, MACRS depreciation, insurance, repairs and maintenance, automobile club dues, and other related costs may result in automobile expenses greater than the automatic mileage allowance.

If a taxpayer wishes to sightsee or vacation on a business trip, it would be beneficial to schedule business on both a Friday and a Monday to turn the weekend into business days for allocation purposes. It is especially crucial to schedule appropriate business days when foreign travel is involved.

MOVING EXPENSES

Moving expenses are deductible for moves in connection with the commencement of work at a new principal place of work.[52] Both employees and self-employed individuals can deduct these expenses. To be eligible for a moving expense deduction, a taxpayer must meet two basic tests: distance and time.

Distance Test. To meet the distance test, the taxpayer's new job location must be at least 50 miles farther from the taxpayer's old residence than the old residence was from the former place of employment. In this regard, the location of the new residence is not relevant. This eliminates a moving expense deduction for (1) taxpayers who purchase a new home in the same general area without changing their place of employment and (2) taxpayers who accept a new job in the same area as their old job.

EXAMPLE 42 Harry is permanently transferred to a new job location. The distance from Harry's former home to his new job (80 miles) exceeds the distance from his former home to his old job (30 miles) by at least 50 miles. Harry has met the distance test for a moving expense deduction. (See the following diagram.)

---
[52]§ 217(a).

```
                    ┌──────────┐
                    │ Old Job  │
                    └──────────┘
                   ↗
              30 mi.
        ┌──────────────┐     80 mi.      ┌──────────┐
        │ Old Residence│ ──────────────→ │ New Job  │
        └──────────────┘                 └──────────┘
```

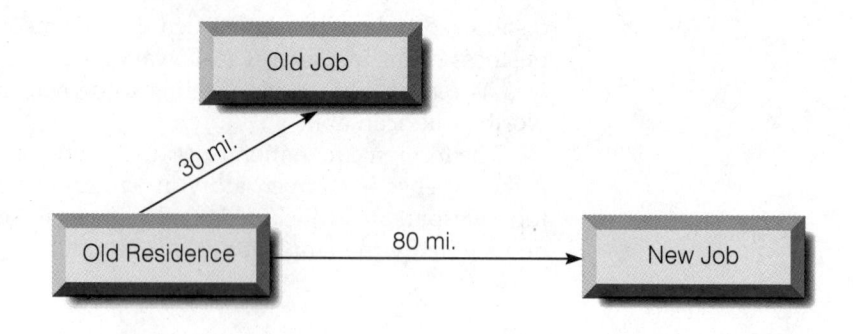

If Harry is not employed before the move, his new job must be at least 50 miles from his former residence. In this instance, Harry has also met the distance test if he was not previously employed. ▼

Time Test. To meet the time test, an employee must be employed on a full-time basis at the new location for 39 weeks in the 12-month period following the move. If the taxpayer is a self-employed individual, he or she must work in the new location for 78 weeks during the two years following the move. The first 39 weeks must be in the first 12 months. The time test is suspended if the taxpayer dies, becomes disabled, or is discharged or transferred by the new employer through no fault of the employee.

A taxpayer might not be able to meet the 39-week test by the due date of the tax return for the year of the move. For this reason, two alternatives are allowed. The taxpayer can take the deduction in the year the expenses are incurred, even though the 39-week test has not been met. If the taxpayer later fails to meet the test, either (1) the income of the following year is increased by an amount equal to the deduction previously claimed for moving expenses, or (2) an amended return is filed for the year of the move. The second alternative is to wait until the test is met and then file an amended tax return for the year of the move.

Treatment of Moving Expenses. *Qualified moving expenses* include reasonable expenses of:

- Moving household goods and personal effects.
- Traveling from the former residence to the new place of residence.

For this purpose, traveling includes lodging, but not meals, for the taxpayer and members of the household.[53] It does not include the cost of moving servants or others who are not members of the household. The taxpayer can elect to use actual auto expenses (no depreciation is allowed) or the automatic mileage method. In this case, moving expense mileage is limited in 1998 to 10 cents per mile (also 10 cents in 1997) for each car. These expenses are also limited by the reasonableness standard. For example, if one moves from Texas to Florida via Maine and takes six weeks to do so, the transportation and lodging must be allocated between personal and moving expenses.

▼ **EXAMPLE 43**   Jill is transferred by her employer from the Atlanta office to the San Francisco office. In this connection, she spends the following amounts:

---
[53] § 217(b).

Cost of moving furniture	$2,800
Transportation	700
Meals	200
Lodging	300

Jill's total qualified moving expense is $3,800 ($2,800 + $700 + $300). ▼

The moving expense deduction is allowed regardless of whether the employee is transferred by the existing employer or is employed by a new employer. It is allowed if the employee moves to a new area and obtains employment or switches from self-employed status to employee status (and vice versa). The moving expense deduction is also allowed if an individual is unemployed before obtaining employment in a new area.

Qualified moving expenses that are paid (or reimbursed) by the employer are not reported as part of the gross income of the employee.[54] Moving expenses that are paid (or reimbursed) by the employer and are not qualified moving expenses are included in the employee's gross income and are not deductible. The employer is responsible for allocating the reimbursement between the qualified and nonqualified moving expenses. Reimbursed qualified moving expenses are separately stated on Form W–2 given to the employee for the year involved. Qualified moving expenses that are not reimbursed and those of self-employed taxpayers are deductions *for* AGI.[55]

Form 3903 is used to report the details of the moving expense deduction if the employee is not reimbursed or if a self-employed person is involved.

PLANNING CONSIDERATIONS

Moving Expenses

Persons who retire and move to a new location incur personal nondeductible moving expenses. If the retired person accepts a full-time job in the new location before moving and meets the time and distance requirements, the moving expenses are deductible.

EXAMPLE 44

At the time of his retirement from the national office of a major accounting firm, Gordon had an annual salary of $220,000. He moves from New York City to Seattle to retire, and accepts a full-time teaching position at a Seattle junior college at an annual salary of $15,000. If Gordon satisfies the 39-week test, his moving expenses are deductible. The disparity between the two salaries (previous and current) is of no consequence. ▼

EDUCATION EXPENSES

General Requirements. Employees *and* self-employed individuals can deduct expenses incurred for education as ordinary and necessary business expenses, provided the expenses are incurred to maintain or improve existing skills required in the present job. An employee can also deduct expenses incurred to meet the express requirements of the employer or the requirements imposed by law to retain his or her employment status.

---

[54] §§ 132(a)(6) and (g).   [55] § 62(a)(15).

Education expenses are not deductible if the education is for either of the following purposes:

- To meet the minimum educational standards for qualification in the taxpayer's existing job.
- To qualify the taxpayer for a new trade or business.[56]

Thus, fees incurred for professional exams (the bar exam, for example) and fees for review courses (such as a CPA review course) are not deductible.[57] If the education incidentally results in a promotion or raise, the deduction still can be taken as long as the education maintained and improved existing skills and did not qualify the person for a new trade or business. A change in duties is not always fatal to the deduction if the new duties involve the same general work. For example, the IRS has ruled that a practicing dentist's education expenses incurred to become an orthodontist are deductible.[58]

Requirements Imposed by Law or by the Employer for Retention of Employment.
Taxpayers are permitted to deduct education expenses if additional courses are required by the employer or are imposed by law. Many states require a minimum of a bachelor's degree and a specified number of additional courses to retain a teaching job. In addition, some public school systems have imposed a master's degree requirement and require teachers to make satisfactory progress toward a master's degree in order to keep their positions. If the required education is the minimum degree required for the job, no deduction is allowed.

Professionals (such as physicians, attorneys, and CPAs) may deduct expenses incurred to meet continuing professional education requirements imposed by states as a condition for retaining a license to practice.

EXAMPLE 45

In order to meet continuing professional education requirements imposed by the State Board of Public Accountancy for maintaining her CPA license, Nancy takes an auditing course sponsored by a local college. The cost of the education is deductible. ▼

In contrast to the preceding example, a taxpayer classified as an Accountant I who went back to school to obtain a bachelor's degree was not allowed to deduct the expenses. Although some courses tended to maintain and improve his existing skills in his entry-level position, the degree was the minimum requirement for his job.[59]

Maintaining or Improving Existing Skills.
The *maintaining or improving existing skills* requirement in the Code has been difficult for both taxpayers and the courts to interpret. For example, a business executive is permitted to deduct the costs of obtaining an MBA on the grounds that the advanced management education is undertaken to maintain and improve existing management skills. The executive is eligible to deduct the costs of specialized, nondegree management courses that are taken for continuing education or to maintain or improve existing skills. Expenses incurred by the executive to obtain a law degree are not deductible, however, because the education constitutes training for a new trade or business. The Regulations deny a self-employed accountant a deduction for expenses relating to law school.[60]

---

[56] Reg. §§ 1.162–5(b)(2) and (3).
[57] Reg. § 1.212–1(f) and Rev.Rul. 69–292, 1969–1 C.B. 84.
[58] Rev.Rul. 74–78, 1974–1 C.B. 44.
[59] Reg. § 1.162–5(b)(2)(iii) Example (2); *Collin J. Davidson*, 43 TCM 743, T.C.Memo. 1982–119.
[60] Reg. § 1.162–5(b)(3)(ii) Example (1).

Planning Considerations

Education Expenses

Education expenses are treated as nondeductible personal items unless the individual is employed or is engaged in a trade or business. A temporary leave of absence for further education is one way to assure that the taxpayer is still treated as being engaged in a trade or business. An individual was permitted to deduct education expenses even though he resigned from his job, returned to school full-time for two years, and accepted another job in the same field upon graduation. The Court held that the student had merely suspended active participation in his field.[61]

If the time out of the field is too long, education expense deductions will be disallowed. For example, a teacher who left the field for four years to raise her child and curtailed her employment searches and writing activities was denied a deduction for education expenses. She was no longer actively engaged in the trade or business of being an educator.[62]

To secure the deduction, an individual should arrange his or her work situation to preserve employee or business status.

Classification of Specific Items. Education expenses include books, tuition, typing, transportation (e.g., from the office to night school), and travel (e.g., meals and lodging while away from home at summer school).

EXAMPLE 46

Bill, who holds a bachelor of education degree, is a secondary education teacher in the Los Angeles school system. The school board recently raised its minimum education requirement for new teachers from four years of college training to five. A grandfather clause allows teachers with only four years of college to continue to qualify if they show satisfactory progress toward a graduate degree. Bill enrolls at the University of Washington during the summer and takes three graduate courses. His unreimbursed expenses for this purpose are as follows:

Books and tuition	$2,600
Lodging while in travel status (June–August)	1,150
Meals while in travel status	800
Laundry while in travel status	220
Transportation	600

Bill has an itemized deduction as follows:

Books and tuition	$2,600
Lodging	1,150
Meals less 50% cutback (discussed later in this chapter)	400
Laundry	220
Transportation	600
	$4,970

---

[61]*Stephen G. Sherman*, 36 TCM 1191, T.C.Memo. 1977–301.
[62]*Brian C. Mulherin*, 42 TCM 834, T.C.Memo. 1981–454; *George A. Baist*, 56 TCM 778, T.C.Memo. 1988–554.

ENTERTAINMENT EXPENSES

Many taxpayers attempt to deduct personal **entertainment expenses** as business expenses. For this reason, the tax law restricts the deductibility of entertainment expenses. The Code contains strict record-keeping requirements and provides restrictive tests for the deduction of certain types of entertainment expenses.

The Fifty Percent Cutback. Only 50 percent of meal and entertainment expenses is deductible.[63] The limitation applies to employees, employers, and self-employed individuals. Although the 50 percent cutback can apply to either the employer or the employee, it will not apply twice. The cutback applies to the one who really pays (economically) for the meals or entertainment.

EXAMPLE 47

Jane, an employee of Pelican Corporation, entertains one of her clients. If Pelican Corporation does not reimburse Jane, she is subject to the cutback. If, however, Pelican Corporation reimburses Jane (or pays for the entertainment directly), Pelican suffers the cutback. ▼

In certain situations, however, a full 50 percent cutback seems unfair. If, for example, the hours of service are regulated (i.e., by the U.S. Department of Transportation) and away-from-home meals are frequent and necessary, the "three martini" business lunch type of abuse is unlikely. Consequently, the Taxpayer Relief Act of 1997 (TRA of 1997) eases the cutback rule for the following types of employees:

- Certain air transportation employees, such as flight crews, dispatchers, mechanics, and control tower operators.
- Interstate truck and bus drivers.
- Certain railroad employees, such as train crews and dispatchers.
- Certain merchant mariners.

Starting in 1998, the cutback is reduced by 5 percent at two-year intervals until it reaches 20 percent in year 2008 and thereafter. Thus, 80 percent of the cost of meals will eventually be allowed as a deduction.

Transportation expenses are not affected by the cutback rule—only meals and entertainment expenses are reduced. The cutback also applies to taxes and tips relating to meals and entertainment. Cover charges, parking fees at an entertainment location, and room rental fees for a meal or cocktail party are also subject to the 50 percent cutback.

EXAMPLE 48

Joe pays a $30 cab fare to meet his client for dinner. The meal costs $120, and Joe leaves a $20 tip. His deduction is $100 [($120 + $20) × 50% + $30 cab fare]. ▼

The cutback rule has a number of exceptions. One exception covers the case where the full value of the meals or entertainment is included in the compensation of the employee (or independent contractor).[64]

EXAMPLE 49

Myrtle wins an all-expense-paid trip to Europe for selling the most insurance for her company during the year. Her employer treats this trip as additional compensation to Myrtle. The cutback adjustment does not apply to the employer. ▼

A similar exception applies to meals and entertainment in a subsidized eating facility or where the *de minimis* fringe benefit rule is met.[65]

---

[63] § 274(n).
[64] §§ 274(e)(2) and (9).
[65] § 274(n)(2).

EXAMPLE 50 Canary Corporation gives a turkey, a fruitcake, and a bottle of wine to each employee at year-end. Since the *de minimis* fringe benefit exclusion applies to business gifts of packaged foods and beverages, their full cost is deductible by Canary. ▼

A similar exception applies to employer-paid recreational activities for employees (e.g., the annual golf outing or spring picnic).[66]

Classification of Expenses. Entertainment expenses are classified either as *directly related* to business or *associated with* business.[67] Directly related expenses are related to an actual business meeting or discussion. These expenses are distinguished from entertainment expenses that are incurred to promote goodwill, such as maintaining existing customer relations. To obtain a deduction for directly related entertainment, it is not necessary to show that actual benefit resulted from the expenditure as long as there was a reasonable expectation of benefit. To qualify as directly related, the expense should be incurred in a business setting. If there is little possibility of engaging in the active conduct of a trade or business due to the nature of the social facility, it is difficult to qualify the expenditure as directly related to business.

Expenses associated with, rather than directly related to, business entertainment must serve a specific business purpose, such as obtaining new business or continuing existing business. These expenditures qualify only if the expenses directly precede or follow a bona fide business discussion. Entertainment occurring on the same day as the business discussion is considered associated with business.

EXAMPLE 51 Jerry, a manufacturers' representative, took his client to play a round of golf during the afternoon. They had dinner the same evening, during which time business was discussed. After dinner, they went to a nightclub to have drinks and listen to a jazz band. The business dinner qualifies as directly related entertainment. The golf outing and the visit to the nightclub qualify as associated with entertainment. ▼

PLANNING CONSIDERATIONS

Entertainment Expenses

Taxpayers should maintain detailed records of amounts, time, place, business purpose, and business relationships. A credit card receipt details the place, date, and amount of the expense. A notation made on the receipt of the names of the person(s) attending, the business relationship, and the topic of discussion should constitute sufficient documentation.[68] Failure to provide sufficient documentation could lead to disallowance of entertainment expense deductions.

Associated with or goodwill entertainment requires a business discussion to be conducted immediately before or after the entertainment. Furthermore, a business purpose must exist for the entertainment. Taxpayers should arrange for a business discussion before or after such entertainment. They also must document the business purpose, such as obtaining new business from a prospective customer.

---

[66] § 274(e)(4).
[67] § 274(a)(1)(A).
[68] *Kenneth W. Guenther*, 54 TCM 382, T.C.Memo. 1987–440.

Restrictions upon Deductibility of Business Meals. Business meals are deductible only if[69]

- the meal is directly related to or associated with the active conduct of a trade or business,
- the expense is not lavish or extravagant under the circumstances, and
- the taxpayer (or an employee) is present at the meal.

A business meal with a business associate or customer is not deductible unless business is discussed before, during, or after the meal. This requirement does not apply to meals consumed while away from home in travel status.

EXAMPLE 52

Lacy travels to San Francisco for a business convention. She pays for dinner with three colleagues and is not reimbursed by her employer. They do not discuss business. She can deduct 50% of the cost of her meal. However, she cannot deduct the cost of her colleagues' meals. ▼

EXAMPLE 53

Lance, a party to a contract negotiation, buys dinner for other parties to the negotiation but does not attend the dinner. No deduction is allowed because Lance was not present. ▼

Restrictions upon Deductibility of Club Dues. The Code provides that: "No deduction shall be allowed . . . for amounts paid or incurred for membership in any club organized for business, pleasure, recreation, or other social purpose."[70] Although this prohibition seems quite broad, it does not apply to clubs whose primary purpose is public service and community volunteerism (e.g., Kiwanis, Lions, Rotary). Although *dues* are not deductible, actual entertainment at a club may qualify.

EXAMPLE 54

During the current year, Vincent spent $1,400 on business lunches at the Lakeside Country Club. The annual membership fee was $6,000, and Vincent used the facility 60% of the time for business. Presuming the lunches meet the business meal test, Vincent may claim $700 (50% cutback × $1,400) as a deduction. None of the club dues are deductible. ▼

Ticket Purchases for Entertainment. A deduction for the cost of a ticket for an entertainment activity is limited to the face value of the ticket.[71] This limitation is applied before the 50 percent cutback. The face value of a ticket includes any tax. Under this rule, the excess payment to a scalper for a ticket is not deductible. Similarly, the fee to a ticket agency for the purchase of a ticket is not deductible.

If a luxury skybox is used for entertainment that is directly related to or associated with business, the deduction is limited to the face value of nonluxury box seats. All seats in the luxury skybox are counted, even when some seats are unoccupied.

The taxpayer may also deduct stated charges for food and beverages under the general rules for business entertainment. The 50 percent cutback rule applies to deductions for skybox seats, food, and beverages.

EXAMPLE 55

In the current year, Pelican Company pays $6,000 to rent a 10-seat skybox at City Stadium for three football games. Nonluxury box seats at each event range in cost from $25 to $35 a seat. In March, a Pelican representative and five clients use the skybox for the first game. The entertainment follows a bona fide business discussion, and Pelican spends $86 for food and beverages during the game. The deduction for the first sports event is as follows:

---

[69] § 274(k).
[70] § 274(a)(3).
[71] § 274(l).

Food and beverages	$ 86
Deduction for seats ($35 × 10 seats)	350
Total entertainment expense	$436
50% limitation	× .50
Deduction	$218

Business Gifts. Business gifts are deductible to the extent of $25 per donee per year.[72] An exception is made for gifts costing $4 or less (e.g., pens with the employee's or company's name on them) or promotional materials. Such items are not treated as business gifts subject to the $25 limitation. In addition, incidental costs such as engraving of jewelry and nominal charges for gift-wrapping, mailing, and delivery are not included in the cost of the gift in applying the limitation. Gifts to superiors and employers are not deductible. Records must be maintained to substantiate business gifts.

OTHER EMPLOYEE EXPENSES

Office in the Home. Employees and self-employed individuals are not allowed a deduction for **office in the home expenses** unless a portion of the residence is used *exclusively and on a regular basis* as either:

- The principal place of business for any trade or business of the taxpayer.
- A place of business used by clients, patients, or customers.

Employees must meet an additional test: The use must be for the convenience of the employer rather than merely being "appropriate and helpful."[73]

The precise meaning of "principal place of business" was resolved by the U.S. Supreme Court. In a divided opinion, the Court established a very restrictive two-pronged test.[74] First, determine the relative importance of the activities performed at each business location (i.e., inside and outside the personal residence). Second, compare the time spent at each business location.

EXAMPLE 56

Dr. Smith is a self-employed anesthesiologist. During the year, he spends 30 to 35 hours per week administering anesthesia and postoperative care to patients in three hospitals, none of which provides him with an office. He also spends two to three hours per day in a room in his home that he uses exclusively as an office. He does not meet patients there, but he performs a variety of tasks related to his medical practice (e.g., contacting surgeons, bookkeeping, reading medical journals). None of Dr. Smith's expenses of the office in the home are deductible because the hospital procedures (i.e., administering to patients) are more important than those done at home. Also, more business time is spent outside the home than inside. ▼

EXAMPLE 57

Lori is a salesperson. Her only office is a room in her home that she uses regularly and exclusively to set up appointments, store product samples, and write up orders and other reports for the companies whose products she sells. Lori makes most of her sales to customers by telephone or mail from her home office. She spends an average of 30 hours a week working at home and 12 hours a week visiting prospective customers to deliver products

---

[72]§ 274(b)(1).
[73]§ 280A(c)(1).
[74]*Comm. v. Soliman*, 93–1 USTC ¶50,014, 71 AFTR2d 93–463, 113 S.Ct. 701 (USSC, 1993), *rev'g.* 91–1 USTC ¶50,291, 67 AFTR2d 91–1112, 935 F.2d 52 (CA–4, 1991) and 94 T.C. 20 (1990).

and occasionally take orders. Under these circumstances, Lori qualifies for the office in the home deduction. Visiting customers is less important to the business than the activities conducted in Lori's office.[75] ▼

Apparently, Congress was not satisfied with the U.S. Supreme Court's interpretation of the meaning of "principal place of business." In TRA of 1997, the Code was amended to provide that an office in the home qualifies as a principal place of business if both of the following are true:

- The office is used by the taxpayer to conduct administrative or management activities of a trade of business.
- There is no other fixed location of the trade or business where the taxpayer conducts these activities.

Unfortunately, the amendment is not effective until taxable years beginning after December 31, 1998. Once in place, however, the new rule will negate the result reached in Example 56 (see above).

The exclusive use requirement means that a specific part of the home must be used solely for business purposes. A deduction, if permitted, requires an allocation of total expenses of operating the home between business and personal use based on floor space or number of rooms.

Even if the taxpayer meets the above requirements, the allowable home office expenses cannot exceed the gross income from the business less all other business expenses attributable to the activity. That is, the home office deduction cannot create a loss. Furthermore, the home office expenses that are allowed as itemized deductions anyway (e.g., mortgage interest and real estate taxes) must be deducted first. All home office expenses of an employee are miscellaneous itemized deductions, except those (such as interest) that qualify as other personal itemized deductions. Home office expenses of a self-employed individual are trade or business expenses and are deductible *for* AGI. Any disallowed home office expenses are carried forward and used in future years subject to the same limitations.

▼ EXAMPLE 58

Rick is a certified public accountant employed by a regional CPA firm as a tax manager. He operates a separate business in which he refinishes furniture in his home. For this business, he uses two rooms in the basement of his home exclusively and regularly. The floor space of the two rooms constitutes 10% of the floor space of his residence. Gross income from the business totals $8,000. Expenses of the business (other than home office expenses) are $6,500. Rick incurs the following home office expenses:

Real property taxes on residence	$4,000
Interest expense on residence	7,500
Operating expenses of residence	2,000
Depreciation on residence (related to 10% business use)	250

Rick's deductions are determined as follows:

---

[75]Notice 93–12, 1993–1 C.B. 298 amplified by Rev.Rul. 94–24, 1994–1 C.B. 87.

Business income		$ 8,000
Less: Other business expenses		(6,500)
		$ 1,500
Less: Allocable taxes ($4,000 × 10%)	$400	
Allocable interest ($7,500 × 10%)	750	(1,150)
		$ 350
Less: Allocable operating expenses of the residence		(200)
		$ 150
Less: Allocable depreciation ($250, limited to remaining income)		150
		$ –0–

Rick has a carryover deduction of $100 (the unused excess depreciation). Because he is self-employed, the allocable taxes and interest ($1,150), the other deductible office expenses ($200 + $150), and $6,500 of other business expenses are deductible *for* AGI. ▼

The home office limitation cannot be circumvented by leasing part of one's home to an employer, using it as a home office, and deducting the expenses as a rental expense under § 212. Form 8829 (Expenses for Business Use of Your Home) may be used for computation of the office in the home deduction.

Miscellaneous Employee Expenses. Deductible miscellaneous employee expenses include special clothing and its upkeep, union dues, and professional expenses. Also deductible are professional dues, professional meetings, and employment agency fees for seeking new employment in the taxpayer's current trade or business, whether or not a new job is secured.

To be deductible, special clothing must be both specifically required as a condition of employment and not adaptable for regular wear. For example, a police officer's uniform is not suitable for off-duty activities. An exception is clothing used to the extent that it takes the place of regular clothing (e.g., some military uniforms).

EXAMPLE 59

Captain Roberts is on active duty in the U.S. Army. The cost of his regular uniforms is not deductible since such clothing is suitable for regular wear. Captain Roberts, however, spends over $1,100 to purchase "dress blues." Under military regulations, dress uniforms may be worn only during ceremonial functions (e.g., official events, parades). The $1,100 cost, to the extent it exceeds any clothing allowance, qualifies as a deduction. ▼

The current position of the IRS is that expenses incurred in seeking employment are deductible if the taxpayer is seeking employment in the same trade or business. The deduction is allowed whether or not the attempts to secure employment are successful. An unemployed taxpayer can take a deduction providing there has been no substantial lack of continuity between the last job and the search for a new one. No deduction is allowed for persons seeking their first job or seeking employment in a new trade or business.

CLASSIFICATION OF EMPLOYEE EXPENSES

4 LEARNING OBJECTIVE
Appreciate the difference between accountable and nonaccountable employee plans.

If employee expenses are reimbursed by the employer under an accountable plan, they are not reported by the employee at all. In effect, this result is equivalent to reporting the reimbursement as income and treating the expenses as deductions *for* AGI.[76] Alternatively, if the expenses are reimbursed under a nonaccountable

---

[76] § 62(a)(2).

> ## TAX IN THE NEWS
>
> ### NBA REFEREES MAY PAY A PRICE FOR NOT REPORTING INCOME
>
> Several NBA referees are the focus of an IRS investigation into a scheme involving reimbursement of millions of dollars in phony travel expenses. The NBA says it merely reimbursed the referees for travel based on their receipts. But some of the referees say the NBA knowingly paid higher travel reimbursements as a substitute for better pay.
>
> The scheme worked this way: Referees purchased first-class tickets and submitted photocopies of them to the NBA for reimbursement. They then exchanged the tickets for coach seats and pocketed the difference. The referees did not report the difference as income.
>
> As of fall 1997, at least four referees have been indicted by Federal grand juries for income tax fraud, with three pleading guilty. Further indictments are expected.

plan or are not reimbursed at all, then they are classified as deductions *from* AGI and can only be claimed if the taxpayer itemizes (subject to the 2 percent-of-AGI floor). Exceptions are made for moving expenses and the employment-related expenses of a qualified performing artist,[77] where a deduction *for* AGI is allowed. Thus, the tax treatment of reimbursements under accountable and nonaccountable plans differs significantly.

Accountable Plans. An accountable plan requires the employee to:

- Adequately account for (substantiate) the expenses. An employee renders an adequate accounting by submitting a record, with receipts and other substantiation, to the employer.[78]
- Return any excess reimbursement or allowance. An "excess reimbursement or allowance" is any amount that the employee does not adequately account for as an ordinary and necessary business expense.

The law provides that no deduction is allowed for any travel, entertainment, business gift, or listed property (automobiles, computers) expenditure unless properly substantiated by adequate records. The records should contain the following information:[79]

- The amount of the expense.
- The time and place of travel or entertainment (or date of gift).
- The business purpose of the expense.
- The business relationship of the taxpayer to the person entertained (or receiving the gift).

This means the taxpayer must maintain an account book or diary in which the above information is recorded at the time of the expenditure. Documentary evidence, such as itemized receipts, is required to support any expenditure for lodging while traveling away from home and for any other expenditure of $75 or more. If a taxpayer fails to keep adequate records, each expense must be established by a written or oral statement of the exact details of the expense and by other corroborating evidence.[80]

---

[77] As defined in § 62(b).
[78] Reg. § 1.162–17(b)(4).
[79] § 274(d).
[80] Reg. § 1.274–5T(c)(3).

CHAPTER 16 Individuals as Employees and Proprietors 16–37

EXAMPLE 60

Bertha has travel expenses substantiated only by canceled checks. The checks establish the date, place, and amount of the expenditure. Because neither the business relationship nor the business purpose is established, the deduction is disallowed.[81]

EXAMPLE 61

Dwight has travel and entertainment expenses substantiated by a diary showing the time, place, and amount of the expenditure. His oral testimony provides the business relationship and business purpose; however, since he has no receipts, any expenditures of $75 or more are disallowed.[82]

Deemed Substantiation. In lieu of reimbursing actual expenses for travel away from home, many employers reduce their paperwork by adopting a policy of reimbursing employees with a *per diem allowance*, a flat dollar amount per day of business travel. Of the substantiation requirements listed above, the amount of the expense is proved, or deemed substantiated, by using such a per diem allowance or reimbursement procedure. The amount of expenses that is deemed substantiated is equal to the lesser of the per diem allowance or the amount of the Federal per diem rate.

The regular Federal per diem rate is the highest amount that the Federal government will pay to its employees for lodging and meals[83] while in travel status away from home in a particular area. The rates are different for different locations.[84]

The use of the standard Federal per diem for meals constitutes an adequate accounting. Employees and self-employed persons can use the standard meal allowance instead of deducting the actual cost of daily meals, even if not reimbursed.

Only the amount of the expense is considered substantiated under the deemed substantiated method. The other substantiation requirements must be provided: place, date, business purpose of the expense, and the business relationship of the parties involved.

Nonaccountable Plans. A **nonaccountable plan** is one in which an adequate accounting or return of excess amounts, or both, is not required. All reimbursements of expenses are reported in full as wages on the employee's Form W–2. Any allowable expenses are deductible in the same manner as are unreimbursed expenses.

An employer may have an accountable plan and require employees to return excess reimbursements or allowances, but an employee may fail to follow the rules of the plan. In that case, the expenses and reimbursements are subject to nonaccountable plan treatment.

Unreimbursed Expenses. Unreimbursed employee expenses are treated in a straightforward manner. Meals and entertainment expenses are subject to the 50 percent limit. Total unreimbursed employee business expenses are usually reported as miscellaneous itemized deductions subject to the 2 percent-of-AGI floor (refer to Chapter 15). If the employee could have received, but did not seek, reimbursement for whatever reason, none of the employment-related expenses are deductible.

---

[81]*William T. Whitaker*, 56 TCM 47, T.C.Memo. 1988–418.
[82]*W. David Tyler*, 43 TCM 927, T.C.Memo. 1982–160.
[83]The meals per diem rate also covers incidental expenses, including laundry and cleaning of clothing and tips for waiters. Taxi fares and telephone calls are not included.
[84]Each current edition of *Your Federal Income Tax* (IRS Publication 17) contains the list and amounts for that year.

Planning Considerations

Unreimbursed Employee Business Expenses

The 2 percent floor for unreimbursed employee business expenses offers a tax planning opportunity for married couples. If one spouse has high miscellaneous expenses subject to the floor, it may be beneficial for the couple to file separate returns. If they file jointly, the 2 percent floor is based on the incomes of both. Filing separately lowers the reduction to 2 percent of only one spouse's income.

Other provisions of the law should be considered, however. For example, filing separately could cost a couple losses of up to $25,000 from self-managed rental units under the passive activity loss rules (discussed in Chapter 5).

Another possibility is to negotiate a salary reduction with one's employer in exchange for the 100 percent reimbursement of employee expenses. The employee is better off because the 2 percent floor does not apply. The employer is better off because certain expense reimbursements are not subject to Social Security and other payroll taxes.

Reporting Procedures. The reporting requirements range from no reporting at all (accountable plans when all requirements are met) to the use of some or all of the following forms: Form W–2 (Wage and Tax Statement), Form 2106 (Employee Business Expenses) or Form 2106–EZ (Unreimbursed Employee Business Expenses), and Schedule A (Itemized Deductions) for nonaccountable plans and unreimbursed employee expenses.

Reimbursed employee expenses that are adequately accounted for under an accountable plan are deductible *for* AGI on Form 2106. Allowed excess expenses, expenses reimbursed under a nonaccountable plan, and unreimbursed expenses are deductible *from* AGI on Schedule A, subject to the 2 percent-of-AGI floor.

When a reimbursement under an accountable plan is paid in separate amounts relating to designated expenses such as meals or entertainment, no problem arises. The reimbursements and expenses are reported as such on the appropriate forms. If the reimbursement is made in a single amount, an allocation must be made to determine the appropriate portion of the reimbursement that applies to meals and entertainment and to other employee expenses.

EXAMPLE 62

Elizabeth, who is employed by Green Company, had AGI of $42,000. During the year, she incurred $2,000 of transportation and lodging expense and $1,000 of meals and entertainment expense, all fully substantiated. Elizabeth received $1,800 reimbursement under an accountable plan. The reimbursement rate that applies to meals and entertainment is 33.33% ($1,000 meals and entertainment expense/$3,000 total expenses). Thus, $600 ($1,800 × 33.33%) of the reimbursement applies to meals and entertainment, and $1,200 ($1,800 − $600) applies to transportation and lodging. Elizabeth's itemized deduction consists of the $800 ($2,000 total − $1,200 reimbursement) of unreimbursed transportation and lodging expenses and $400 ($1,000 − $600) of unreimbursed meal and entertainment expenses as follows:

Transportation and lodging	$ 800
Meals and entertainment ($400 × 50%)	200
Total (reported on Form 2106)	$1,000
Less: 2% of $42,000 AGI (see limitation discussed below)	(840)
Deduction (reported on Schedule A)	$ 160

In summary, Elizabeth reports $3,000 of expenses and the $1,800 reimbursement on Form 2106 and $160 as a miscellaneous itemized deduction on Schedule A. ▼

▼ **TABLE 16–2**
Phase-Out of IRA Deduction of an Active Participant in 1998

AGI Filing Status	Phase-Out Begins*	Phase-Out Ends
Single and head of household	$30,000	$40,000
Married, filing joint return	50,000	60,000
Married, filing separate return	–0–	10,000

*The starting point for the phase-out is increased each year through 2007 for married filing jointly and through 2005 for other filing statuses.

CONTRIBUTIONS TO INDIVIDUAL RETIREMENT ACCOUNTS

Traditional IRAs. Employees not covered by another qualified plan can establish their own tax-deductible **Individual Retirement Accounts (IRAs)**. The contribution ceiling is the smaller of $2,000 (or $4,000 for spousal IRAs) or 100 percent of compensation. If the taxpayer is an active participant in another qualified plan, the traditional IRA deduction limitation is phased out *proportionately* between certain AGI ranges, as shown in Table 16–2.

AGI is calculated taking into account any § 469 passive losses and § 86 taxable Social Security benefits and ignoring any § 911 foreign income exclusion, § 135 savings bonds interest exclusion, and the IRA deduction. There is a $200 floor on the IRA deduction limitation for individuals whose AGI is not above the phase-out range.

▼ **EXAMPLE 63**

Daniel, who is single, has compensation income of $37,000 in 1998. He is an active participant in his employer's qualified retirement plan. Dan contributes $600 to an IRA. The deductible amount is reduced from $2,000 by $1,400 because of the phase-out mechanism:

$$\frac{\$7,000}{\$10,000} \times \$2,000 = \$1,400 \text{ reduction.}$$

▼

▼ **EXAMPLE 64**

Ben, an unmarried individual, is an active participant in his employer's qualified retirement plan. With AGI of $39,500, he would normally have an IRA deduction limit of $100 {$2,000 − [($39,500 − $30,000)/$10,000 × $2,000]}. However, because of the special floor provision, Ben is allowed a $200 IRA deduction. ▼

An individual is not considered an active participant in a qualified plan merely because the individual's spouse is an active participant in such a plan for any part of a plan year. Thus, most homemakers may take a full $2,000 deduction regardless of the participation status of their spouse, unless the couple has AGI above $150,000. If their AGI is above $150,000, the phase-out of the deduction begins at $150,000 and ends at $160,000 (phase-out over the $10,000 range.)

▼ **EXAMPLE 65**

Nell is covered by a qualified employer retirement plan at work. Her husband, Nick, is not an active participant in a qualified plan. If Nell and Nick's combined AGI is $135,000, Nell cannot make a deductible IRA contribution because she exceeds the income threshold for an active participant. However, since Nick is not an active participant, and their combined AGI does not exceed $150,000, he can make a deductible contribution of $2,000 to an IRA. ▼

To the extent that an individual is ineligible to make a deductible contribution to an IRA, *nondeductible contributions* can be made to separate accounts. The nondeductible contributions are subject to the same dollar limits as deductible contributions ($2,000 of earned income, $4,000 for a spousal IRA). Income in the account accumulates tax-free until distributed. Only the account earnings are taxed upon distribution because the account basis equals the contributions made by the taxpayer. A taxpayer may elect to treat deductible IRA contributions as nondeductible. If an individual has no taxable income for the year after taking into account other deductions, the election would be beneficial. The election is made on the individual's tax return for the taxable year to which the designation relates.

Roth IRAs. Beginning in 1998, TRA of 1997 authorizes a new type of IRA called a Roth IRA. Contributions to a Roth IRA are nondeductible. Qualified distributions from a Roth IRA are tax-free.

A taxpayer can make tax-free withdrawals from a Roth IRA after a five-year holding period if any of the following requirements is satisfied:

- The distribution is made on or after the date on which the participant attains age 59½.
- The distribution is made to a beneficiary (or the participant's estate) on or after the participant's death.
- The participant becomes disabled.
- The distribution is used to pay for qualified first-time homebuyer's expenses.

EXAMPLE 66
Edith establishes a Roth IRA at age 42 and contributes $2,000 per year for 20 years. The account is now worth $96,400, consisting of $40,000 of nondeductible contributions and $56,400 in accumulated earnings that have not been taxed. Edith may withdraw the $96,400 tax-free from the Roth IRA because she is over age 59½ and has met the five-year holding period requirement. ▼

If the taxpayer receives a distribution from a Roth IRA and does not satisfy the aforementioned requirements, the distribution may be taxable. If the distribution represents a return of capital, it is not taxable. Conversely, if the distribution represents a payout of earnings, it is taxable. Under the ordering rules for Roth IRA distributions, distributions are treated as first made from contributions (return of capital).

EXAMPLE 67
Assume the same facts as in Example 66, except that Edith is only age 50 and receives a distribution of $35,000. Since her adjusted basis for the Roth IRA is $40,000 (contributions made), the distribution is tax-free, and her adjusted basis is reduced to $5,000 ($40,000 − $35,000). ▼

Roth IRAs are subject to income limits. The maximum annual contribution is phased out beginning at AGI of $95,000 for single taxpayers and $150,000 for married couples who file a joint return. The phase-out range is $10,000 for married filing jointly and $15,000 for single taxpayers.

EXAMPLE 68
Bev would like to contribute $2,000 to her Roth IRA. However, her AGI is $105,000, so her contribution is limited to $667 ($2,000 − $1,333) calculated as follows:

$$\frac{\$10,000}{\$15,000} \times \$2,000 = \$1,333 \text{ reduction.}$$

▼

Education IRAs. Beginning in 1998, a distribution from an IRA to pay for qualified higher education expenses receives favorable tax treatment. Qualified higher education expenses include tuition, fees, books, supplies, and related equipment. Room and board qualify if the student's course load is at least one-half of the full-time course load. If the education IRA is used to pay the qualified higher education expenses of the designated beneficiary, the withdrawals are tax-free. To the extent the distributions during a tax year exceed qualified higher education expenses, part of the excess is treated as a return of capital (the contributions), and part is treated as a distribution of earnings. The distribution is presumed to be pro rata from each category. The exclusion for the distribution of earnings part is calculated as follows:

$$\frac{\text{Qualified higher education expenses}}{\text{Total distributions}} \times \text{Earnings} = \text{Exclusion}.$$

EXAMPLE 69

Meg receives a $2,500 distribution from her education IRA. She uses $2,000 to pay for qualified higher education expenses. On the date of the distribution, Meg's IRA account balance is $10,000, $6,000 of which represents her contributions. Since 60% ($6,000/$10,000) of her account balance represents her contributions, $1,500 ($2,500 × 60%) of the distribution is a return of capital, and $1,000 ($2,500 × 40%) is a distribution of earnings. The excludible amount of the earnings is calculated as follows:

$$\frac{\$2,000}{\$2,500} \times \$1,000 = \$800.$$

Meg's adjusted basis for her IRA is reduced to $10,500 ($12,000 − $1,500). ▼

The maximum amount that can be contributed annually to an education IRA for a beneficiary is $500. The contributions are not deductible. Education IRAs are subject to income limits. The maximum annual contribution is phased out beginning at $95,000 for single taxpayers and $150,000 for married couples who file a joint return. The phase-out range is $10,000 for married filing jointly and $15,000 for single taxpayers. Contributions cannot be made to an education IRA after the date on which the designated beneficiary attains age 18.

The education IRA exclusion is not available in any tax year in which the beneficiary claims the HOPE credit or the lifetime learning credit. Likewise, contributions cannot be made to a beneficiary's education IRA during any year in which contributions are made to a qualified state tuition program on behalf of the same beneficiary.

INDIVIDUALS AS PROPRIETORS

THE PROPRIETORSHIP AS A BUSINESS ENTITY

5 LEARNING OBJECTIVE
Understand the tax provisions applicable to proprietors.

A sole proprietorship is *not* a taxable entity separate from the individual who owns the proprietorship. A sole proprietor reports the results of business operations of the proprietorship on Schedule C of Form 1040. The net profit or loss from the proprietorship is then transferred from Schedule C to Form 1040, which is used by the taxpayer to determine tax liability. The proprietor reports all of the net profit from the business, regardless of the amount actually withdrawn from the proprietorship during the year.

Income and expenses of the proprietorship retain their character when reported by the proprietor. For example, ordinary income of the proprietorship is treated as ordinary income when reported by the proprietor, and capital gain of the proprietorship is treated as capital gain by the proprietor.

EXAMPLE 70

George is the sole proprietor of George's Record Shop. Gross income of the business in 1998 is $200,000, and operating expenses are $110,000. George also sells a capital asset held by the business for a $10,000 long-term capital gain. During 1998, he withdraws $60,000 from the business for living expenses. George reports the operating income and expenses of the business on Schedule C, resulting in net profit (ordinary income) of $90,000. Even though he withdrew only $60,000, George reports all of the $90,000 net profit from the business on Form 1040, where he computes taxable income for the year. He also reports a $10,000 long-term capital gain on his personal tax return (Schedule D). ▼

INCOME OF A PROPRIETORSHIP

The broad definition of gross income in § 61(a) applies equally to individuals and business entities, including proprietorships, corporations, and partnerships. Thus, it is assumed that asset inflows into a proprietorship are to be treated as income. Certain items may be excluded from income, but most of the exclusions available to an individual are related to the individual as an employee. Refer to Chapter 3 for a detailed discussion of gross income.

DEDUCTIONS RELATED TO A PROPRIETORSHIP

Ordinary and Necessary Business Expenses. The provisions that govern business deductions also are general, and not entity specific. The § 162 requirement that trade or business expenses be *ordinary and necessary* (refer to Chapter 4) applies to proprietorships as well as corporations, partnerships, and other business entities. However, certain specific deductions are available only to self-employed taxpayers. These deductions are covered in detail below.

Health Insurance Premiums. A self-employed taxpayer may deduct 45 percent of insurance premiums paid for medical coverage in 1998 as a deduction *for* AGI.[85] The deduction is allowed for premiums paid on behalf of the taxpayer, the taxpayer's spouse, and dependents of the taxpayer. The deduction is not allowed to any taxpayer who is eligible to participate in a subsidized health plan maintained by any employer of the taxpayer or of the taxpayer's spouse.

This deduction is reported in the Adjustments to Income section of Form 1040, not on Schedule C. Premiums paid for medical coverage of the employees of a self-employed taxpayer are deductible as business expenses on Schedule C, however.

▼ **EXAMPLE 71** Ellen, a sole proprietor of a restaurant, has two dependent children. During 1998, she paid health insurance premiums of $1,800 for her own coverage and $1,000 for coverage of her two children. Ellen can deduct $1,260 ($2,800 × 45%) as a deduction *for* AGI. She can include the remaining $1,540 ($2,800 − $1,260) as a medical expense (subject to the 7.5% floor) when computing itemized deductions. ▼

Self-Employment Tax. The tax on self-employment income is levied to provide Social Security and Medicare benefits (old age, survivors, and disability insurance and hospital insurance) for self-employed individuals. Individuals with net earnings of $400 or more from self-employment are subject to the self-employment tax.[86] For 1998, the self-employment tax is 12.4 percent of self-employment earnings up to a $68,400 *ceiling amount* (for the Social Security portion) plus 2.9 percent of the *total* amount of self-employment earnings (for the Medicare portion). Thus, the combined self-employment tax rate on earnings

---

[85] The rate will be 45% for tax years 1998 and 1999, 50% in 2000 and 2001, 60% in 2002, 80% in 2003 through 2005, 90% for 2006, and 100% after 2006. The rate was 40% in 1997.

[86] § 6017.

up to $68,400 is 15.3 percent. The ceiling amount is adjusted periodically for inflation.

For purposes of computing the *self-employment tax,* self-employed taxpayers are allowed a deduction from net earnings equal to one-half of the self-employment tax rate.[87] This deduction of 7.65 percent (one-half of the 15.3 percent rate) is reflected by multiplying net earnings from self-employment by 92.35 percent (100% − 7.65%), as shown in Example 72. For purposes of computing *taxable income,* an income tax deduction is allowed for one-half the amount of self-employment tax paid.[88]

Example 72 illustrates the computation of the self-employment tax, as well as the income tax deduction for one-half of self-employment tax paid. For income tax purposes, the amount to be reported on Schedule C is net earnings from self-employment *before* the deduction for one-half of the self-employment tax. The deduction of one-half of the self-employment tax paid is reported separately on Form 1040 as a deduction *for* AGI.

EXAMPLE 72

Computation of the self-employment tax is determined using the steps below. The self-employment tax is determined for two taxpayers with net earnings from self-employment for 1998 as follows: Ned, $55,000 and Terry, $80,000.

Computation of Self-Employment Tax for Ned

1. Net earnings	$55,000.00
2. Multiply line 1 by 92.35%.	$50,792.50
3. If the amount on line 2 is $68,400 or less, multiply the line 2 amount by 15.3%. This is the self-employment tax.	$ 7,771.25
4. If the amount on line 2 is more than $68,400, multiply the excess over $68,400 by 2.9% and add $10,465.20. This is the self-employment tax.	

Computation of Self-Employment Tax for Terry

1. Net earnings	$80,000.00
2. Multiply line 1 by 92.35%.	$73,880.00
3. If the amount on line 2 is $68,400 or less, multiply the line 2 amount by 15.3%. This is the self-employment tax.	
4. If the amount on line 2 is more than $68,400, multiply the excess over $68,400 by 2.9% and add $10,465.20. This is the self-employment tax.	$10,624.12

For income tax purposes, Ned has net earnings from self-employment of $55,000 and a deduction *for* AGI of $3,885.63 (one-half of $7,771.25). Terry has net earnings from self-employment of $80,000 and a deduction *for* AGI of $5,312.06 (one-half of $10,624.12). Both taxpayers benefit from the deduction for one-half of the self-employment tax paid. ▼

Wages of employees also are subject to Social Security and Medicare taxes. The total tax rate is also 15.3 percent, with 7.65 percent withheld from the employee's wages and the employer paying at a 7.65 percent rate. If an individual who is self-employed also receives wages from working as an employee of another organization, the ceiling amount of the Social Security portion on which the self-employment tax is computed is reduced.

---

[87] § 1402(a)(12).   [88] § 164(f).

Net earnings from self-employment include gross income from a trade or business less allowable trade or business deductions, the distributive share of any partnership income or loss derived from a trade or business activity, and net income from the rendering of personal services as an independent contractor. Gain or loss from the disposition of property (including involuntary conversions) is excluded from the computation of self-employment income unless the property involved is inventory.

RETIREMENT PLANS FOR SELF-EMPLOYED INDIVIDUALS

Self-employed individuals have several options for retirement funding. Individual Retirement Accounts (discussed earlier in this chapter) are available to both employees and self-employed individuals. Other options for self-employed individuals include, but are not limited to, H.R. 10 (Keogh) plans and SIMPLE plans, both of which are discussed below.

Keogh Plans. Self-employed individuals (e.g., partners and sole proprietors) are eligible to establish and receive qualified retirement benefits under **Keogh plans** (also known as H.R. 10 plans). Self-employed individuals who establish Keogh plans for themselves are also required to cover their *employees* under the plan.

Keogh investments can include a variety of funding vehicles, such as mutual funds, annuities, real estate shares, certificates of deposit, debt instruments, commodities, securities, and personal properties. When an individual decides to make all investment decisions, a *self-directed retirement plan* is established. Investment in most collectibles is not allowed in a self-directed plan.

A Keogh plan may be either a *defined contribution* plan or a *defined benefit* plan. In a defined contribution plan, the amount that can be contributed each year is subject to limitations. Retirement benefits depend on the amount contributed and the amount earned by the plan. In a defined benefit plan, the amount of retirement income is fixed and is determined on the basis of the employee's compensation while working, the number of years in the plan, and age on retirement.

A self-employed individual may annually contribute the smaller of $30,000 or 25 percent of earned income to a defined contribution Keogh plan.[89] If the defined contribution plan is a profit sharing plan, however, a 15 percent deduction limit applies. Under a defined benefit Keogh plan, the annual benefit is limited to the smaller of $130,000 (in 1998) or 100 percent of the average net earnings for the three highest years.[90]

Earned income refers to net earnings from self-employment.[91] Net earnings from self-employment means the gross income derived by an individual from any trade or business carried on by that individual, less appropriate deductions, plus the distributive share of income or loss from a partnership.[92] Earned income is reduced by contributions to a Keogh plan on the individual's behalf and by 50 percent of any self-employment tax.[93]

EXAMPLE 73

Pat, a partner, has earned income of $130,000 in 1998 (after the deduction for one-half of self-employment tax, but before any Keogh contribution). The maximum contribution to a defined contribution plan is $26,000, calculated from the following formula: $130,000 − .25X = X$, where X is earned income reduced by Pat's Keogh contribution. Solving this equation, $X = \$104,000$; thus, the contribution limit is $.25 \times \$104,000 = \$26,000$. To achieve the maximum

---

[89] § 415(c)(1).
[90] § 415(b)(1). The amount is indexed annually.
[91] § 401(c)(2).
[92] § 1402(a).
[93] §§ 401(c)(2)(A)(v) and 164(f).

contribution of $30,000, Pat would have to earn at least $150,000. In essence, a self-employed individual can contribute 20% of gross earned income. Pat could contribute only 13.043% of self-employment gross earned income if this were a profit sharing plan. ▼

Although a Keogh plan must be established before the end of the year in question, contributions may be made up to the normal filing date for that year.

PLANNING CONSIDERATIONS

Important Dates Related to IRAs and Keogh Plans

A Keogh or IRA participant may make a deductible contribution for a tax year up to the time prescribed for filing the individual's tax return. A Keogh plan must have been *established* by the end of the *prior* tax year (e.g., December 31) to obtain a deduction for the contribution made in the *current* year. An individual can establish an IRA during the *current* tax year (up to the normal filing date) and still receive a deduction for the contribution made in the *current* year.

SIMPLE Plans. Employers with 100 or fewer employees who do not maintain another qualified retirement plan may establish a *savings incentive match plan for employees* (SIMPLE plan).[94] The plan can be in the form of a § 401(k) plan or an IRA. The SIMPLE plan is not subject to the nondiscrimination and top-heavy rules that are normally applicable to § 401(k) plans.

All employees who received at least $5,000 in compensation from the employer during any two preceding years and who reasonably expect to receive at least $5,000 in compensation during the current year must be eligible to participate in the plan. The decision to participate is up to the employee. A *self-employed individual* may also participate in the plan.

The contributions made by the employee (a salary reduction approach) must be expressed as a percentage of compensation rather than as a fixed dollar amount. The plan must not permit the elective employee contribution for the year to exceed $6,000 (in 1998). Generally, the employer must either match elective employee contributions up to 3 percent of the employee's compensation or provide nonmatching contributions of 2 percent of compensation for each eligible employee. Thus, the maximum amount that may be contributed to the plan for 1998 is $10,800 [$6,000 employee contributions + $4,800 ($160,000 compensation ceiling × 3%) employer match].

No other contributions may be made to the plan other than the employee elective contribution and the required employer matching contribution (or nonmatching contribution under the 2 percent rule). All contributions are fully vested. An employer is required to make contributions to a SIMPLE § 401(k) plan once it is established, whereas an employer's contributions to a traditional § 401(k) plan are optional.

An employer's deduction for contributions to a SIMPLE § 401(k) plan is limited to the greater of 15 percent of the compensation paid or accrued or the amount that the employer is required to contribute to the plan. Thus, an employer may deduct contributions to a SIMPLE § 401(k) plan in excess of 15 percent of the $160,000 salary cap. A traditional § 401(k) plan is limited to 15 percent of the total compensation of plan participants for the year.

---

[94] § 408(p).

An employer is allowed a deduction for matching contributions only if the contributions are made by the due date (including extensions) for the employer's tax return. Contributions to a SIMPLE plan are excludible from the employee's gross income, and the SIMPLE plan is tax-exempt.

EXAMPLE 74 The Mauve Company has a SIMPLE plan for its employees under which it provides non-matching contributions of 2% of compensation for each eligible employee. The maximum amount that can be added to each participant's account in 1998 is $9,200, composed of the $6,000 employee salary reduction plus an employer contribution of $3,200 ($160,000 × 2%). ▼

Distributions from a SIMPLE plan are taxed under the IRA rules. Tax-free rollovers can be made from one SIMPLE account to another. A SIMPLE account can be rolled over to an IRA tax-free after a two-year period has expired since the individual first participated in the plan. Withdrawals of contributions during the two-year period beginning on the date an employee first participates in the SIMPLE plan are subject to a 25 percent early withdrawal tax rather than the 10 percent early withdrawal tax that otherwise would apply.

PLANNING CONSIDERATIONS

Factors Affecting Retirement Plan Choices

An IRA might not be the best retirement plan option for many self-employed taxpayers. The maximum amount that can be deducted is $2,000 per year ($4,000 for a spousal plan), which may be too low to provide funding for an adequate level of retirement income. Other options such as Keogh plans and SIMPLE plans allow larger contributions and larger deductions. However, a self-employed individual who establishes either a Keogh or a SIMPLE plan is required to cover employees under such plans. This can result in substantial expenditures, not only for the required contributions, but also for expenses of administering the plan. An advantage of an IRA is that coverage of employees is not required.

ACCOUNTING PERIODS AND METHODS

Proprietors may choose among accounting methods, just as other business entities do (refer to Chapter 6). The cash method is commonly used by proprietorships that provide services, while the accrual or hybrid method is required if inventory is a material income-producing factor.

The accounting period rules for proprietorships generally are much simpler than the rules for partnerships and S corporations. Because a proprietorship is not an entity separate from the proprietor, the proprietorship must use the same tax year-end as the proprietor. This does not preclude the use of a fiscal year for a proprietorship, but most proprietorships use the calendar year.

ESTIMATED PAYMENTS

Although the following discussion largely centers on self-employed taxpayers, some of the procedures may be applicable to employed persons. In many cases, for example, employed persons may be required to pay estimated tax if they have income that is not subject to withholding (e.g., income from rentals, dividends, or interest).

Estimated Tax for Individuals. Estimated tax is the amount of tax (including alternative minimum tax and self-employment tax) an individual expects to owe for the year after subtracting tax credits and income tax withheld. Any individual who has estimated tax for the year of $1,000 or more and whose withholding does not equal or exceed the required annual payment (discussed below) must make quarterly payments.[95] Otherwise, a penalty may be assessed. No quarterly payments are required, and no penalty will apply on an underpayment, if the taxpayer's estimated tax is under $1,000. No penalty will apply if the taxpayer had no tax liability for the preceding tax year, the preceding tax year was a taxable year of 12 months, and the taxpayer was a citizen or resident for the entire preceding tax year. In this regard, having no tax liability is not the same as having no additional tax to pay.

The required annual payment must first be computed. This is the smaller of the following amounts:

- Ninety percent of the tax shown on the current year's return.
- One hundred percent of the tax shown on the preceding year's return (the return must cover the full 12 months of the preceding year). For tax years beginning in 1999, the 100 percent requirement is increased to 105 percent if the AGI on the preceding year's return exceeds $150,000 ($75,000 if married filing separately).

In general, one-fourth of this required annual payment is due on April 15, June 15, and September 15 of the tax year and January 15 of the following year. Thus, the quarterly installment of the required annual payment reduced by the applicable withholding is the estimated tax to be paid. An equal part of withholding is deemed paid on each due date, even if a taxpayer's earnings fluctuate widely during the year. Payments are to be accompanied by the payment voucher from Form 1040–ES for the appropriate date.

Penalty on Underpayments. A nondeductible penalty is imposed on the amount of underpayment of estimated tax. The rate for this penalty is the same as the rate for underpayments of tax and is adjusted quarterly to reflect changes in the average prime rate.

An underpayment occurs when any quarterly payment (the sum of estimated tax paid and income tax withheld) is less than 25 percent of the required annual payment. The penalty is applied to the amount of the underpayment for the period of the underpayment.[96]

EXAMPLE 75

Marta made the following payments of estimated tax for 1998 and had no income tax withheld:

April 15, 1998	$1,400
June 15, 1998	2,300
September 15, 1998	1,500
January 15, 1999	1,800

Marta's actual tax for 1998 is $8,000, and her tax in 1997 was $10,000. Therefore, each installment should have been at least $1,800 [($8,000 × 90%) × 25%]. Of the payment on June 15, $400 will be credited to the unpaid balance of the first quarterly installment due on April 15,[97] thereby effectively stopping the underpayment penalty for the first quarterly period.

---

[95] § 6654(c)(1).
[96] § 6654(b)(2).

[97] Payments are credited to unpaid installments in the order in which the installments are required to be paid. § 6654(b)(3).

Of the remaining $1,900 payment on June 15, $100 is credited to the September 15 payment, resulting in this third quarterly payment being $200 short. Then $200 of the January 15 payment is credited to the September 15 shortfall, ending the period of underpayment for that portion due. The January 15, 1999, installment is now underpaid by $200, and a penalty will apply from January 15, 1999, to April 15, 1999 (unless paid sooner). Marta's underpayments for the periods of underpayment are as follows:

1st installment due:	$400 from April 15 to June 15
2nd installment due:	Paid in full
3rd installment due:	$200 from September 15, 1998 to January 15, 1999
4th installment due:	$200 from January 15, 1999 to April 15, 1999

If a possible underpayment of estimated tax is indicated, Form 2210 (see Appendix B) should be filed to compute the penalty due or to justify that no penalty applies.

HOBBY LOSSES

6 LEARNING OBJECTIVE
Distinguish between business and hobby activities and apply the rules limiting the deduction of hobby losses.

Employee deductions and deductions related to a proprietorship were discussed in previous sections of this chapter. Employees are allowed to deduct certain expenditures incurred in connection with their work activities. Expenses incurred by a self-employed taxpayer are deductible only if the taxpayer can show that the activity was entered into for the purpose of making a profit.

Certain activities may have either profit-seeking or personal attributes, depending upon individual circumstances. Examples include raising horses and operating a farm that is also used as a weekend residence. While personal losses are not deductible, losses attributable to profit-seeking activities may be deducted and used to offset a taxpayer's other income. For this reason, losses generated by hobbies are not deductible.

GENERAL RULES

If an individual can show that an activity has been conducted with the intent to earn a profit, losses from the activity are fully deductible. The hobby loss rules apply only if the activity is not engaged in for profit. Hobby expenses are deductible only to the extent of hobby income.[98]

The Regulations stipulate that the following nine factors should be considered in determining whether an activity is profit-seeking or a hobby:[99]

- Whether the activity is conducted in a businesslike manner.
- The expertise of the taxpayers or their advisers.
- The time and effort expended.
- The expectation that the assets of the activity will appreciate in value.
- The taxpayer's previous success in conducting similar activities.
- The history of income or losses from the activity.
- The relationship of profits earned to losses incurred.
- The financial status of the taxpayer (e.g., if the taxpayer does not have substantial amounts of other income, this may indicate that the activity is engaged in for profit).
- Elements of personal pleasure or recreation in the activity.

---

[98] § 183(b)(2).

[99] Reg. §§ 1.183–2(b)(1) through (9).

PRESUMPTIVE RULE OF § 183

The Code provides a rebuttable presumption that an activity is profit seeking if the activity shows a profit in at least three of any five prior consecutive years.[100] If the activity involves horses, a profit in at least two of seven consecutive years meets the presumptive rule. If these profitability tests are met, the activity is presumed to be a trade or business rather than a personal hobby. In this situation, the burden of proof shifts from the taxpayer to the IRS. That is, the IRS bears the burden of proving that the activity is personal rather than trade or business related.

EXAMPLE 76

Camille, an executive for a large corporation, is paid a salary of $200,000. Her husband is a collector of antiques. Several years ago, he opened an antique shop in a local shopping center and spends most of his time buying and selling antiques. He occasionally earns a small profit from this activity but more frequently incurs substantial losses. If the losses are business related, they are fully deductible against Camille's salary income on a joint return. The following approach should be considered in resolving this issue:

- Initially determine whether the antique activity has met the three-out-of-five-years profit test.
- If the presumption is not met, the activity may nevertheless qualify as a business if the taxpayer can show that the intent is to engage in a profit-seeking activity. It is not necessary to show actual profits.
- Attempt to fit the operation within the nine criteria prescribed in the Regulations and listed above. These criteria are the factors considered in trying to rebut the § 183 presumption. ▼

DETERMINING THE AMOUNT OF THE DEDUCTION

If an activity is deemed to be a hobby, the expenses are deductible only to the extent of the gross income from the hobby. These expenses must be deducted in the following order:

- Amounts deductible under other Code Sections without regard to the nature of the activity, such as property taxes and home mortgage interest.
- Amounts deductible under other Code Sections if the activity had been engaged in for profit, but only if those amounts do not affect adjusted basis. Examples include maintenance, utilities, and supplies.
- Amounts that affect adjusted basis and would be deductible under other Code Sections if the activity had been engaged in for profit.[101] Examples include depreciation, amortization, and depletion.

These deductions are deductible *from* AGI as itemized deductions to the extent they exceed 2 percent of AGI.[102] If the taxpayer uses the standard deduction rather than itemizing, all hobby loss deductions are wasted.

---

[100] § 183(d).
[101] Reg. § 1.183–1(b)(1).
[102] Reg. § 1.67–1T(a)(1)(iv) and Rev.Rul. 75–14, 1975–1 C.B. 90.

Hobby Losses

EXAMPLE 77

Jim, the vice president of an oil company, has AGI of $80,000. He decides to pursue painting in his spare time. He uses a home studio, comprising 10% of the home's square footage. During the current year, Jim incurs the following expenses:

Frames	$ 350
Art supplies	300
Fees paid to models	1,000
Expenses related to home:	
Total property taxes	900
Total home mortgage interest	10,000
Total home maintenance and utilities	3,600
Depreciation on 10% of home used as studio	500

During the year, Jim sold paintings for a total of $3,200. If the activity is held to be a hobby, Jim is allowed deductions as follows:

Gross income		$ 3,200
Deduct: Taxes and interest (10% of $10,900)		(1,090)
Remainder		$ 2,110
Deduct: Frames	$ 350	
Art supplies	300	
Models' fees	1,000	
Maintenance and utilities (10%)	360	2,010
Remainder		$ 100
Depreciation ($500, but limited to $100)		(100)
Net income		$ −0−

Jim includes the $3,200 of income in AGI, making his AGI $83,200. The taxes and interest are itemized deductions, deductible in full. Assuming Jim has no other miscellaneous itemized deductions, the remaining expenses of $2,110 are reduced by 2% of his AGI ($1,664); so the net deduction is $446. Since the property taxes and home mortgage interest are deductible anyway, the net effect is a $2,754 ($3,200 less $446) increase in taxable income. ▼

EXAMPLE 78

If Jim's activity in Example 77 were held to be a business, he could deduct expenses totaling $3,600 *for* AGI, as shown below. All these expenses would be trade or business expenses. His reduction in AGI would be as follows:

Gross income		$ 3,200
Deduct: Taxes and interest	$1,090	
Other business expenses	2,010	
Depreciation	500	(3,600)
Remainder		($ 400)

As in Example 77, Jim can deduct the remaining property taxes and home mortgage interest of $9,810 ($10,900 − $1,090) as itemized deductions. ▼

CHAPTER 16 Individuals as Employees and Proprietors

KEY TERMS

Accountable plan, 16–3
Automatic mileage method, 16–20
Cafeteria plan, 16–12
De minimis fringe benefits, 16–15
Education expenses, 16–28
Entertainment expenses, 16–30
Estimated tax, 16–47
Independent contractor, 16–2

Individual Retirement Account (IRA), 16–39
Keogh plan, 16–44
Medical savings account (MSA), 16–6
Moving expenses, 16–25
No-additional-cost services, 16–13
Nonaccountable plan, 16–37
Office in the home expenses, 16–33

Qualified employee discounts, 16–14
Qualified transportation fringes, 16–16
Self-employment tax, 16–5
Transportation expenses, 16–19
Travel expenses, 16–21
Working condition fringes, 16–15

PROBLEM MATERIALS

1. Rex, age 45, is an officer of Blue Company, which provided him with the following nondiscriminatory fringe benefits in 1998:
   a. Hospitalization insurance for Rex and his dependents. The cost of coverage for Rex was $450, and the additional cost for Rex's dependents was $400.
   b. Reimbursement of $700 from an uninsured medical reimbursement plan available to all employees.
   c. Group term life insurance protection of $120,000. (Each employee received coverage equal to twice his or her annual salary.)
   d. Salary continuation payments of $2,600 while Rex was hospitalized for an illness.

   While Rex was ill, he collected $1,600 on a salary continuation insurance policy he had purchased. Determine the amounts Rex must include in gross income.

2. The UVW Union and HON Corporation are negotiating contract terms. Assume the union members are in the 28% marginal tax bracket and all benefits are provided on a nondiscriminatory basis. Write a letter to the UVW Union members explaining the tax consequences of the options discussed below. The union's address is 905 Spruce Street, Washington, D.C. 20227.
   a. The company would impose a $100 deductible on medical insurance benefits. Most employees incur more than $100 each year in medical expenses.
   b. Employees would get an additional paid holiday with the same annual income (the same pay but less work).
   c. An employee who did not need health insurance (because the employee's spouse works and receives family coverage) would be allowed to receive the cash value of the coverage.

3. Sally and Bill are married and file joint returns. In 1998, Bill, an accountant, has a salary of $75,000, and Sally receives a salary of $25,000 as an apartment manager. What are the tax consequences of the following benefits that Bill and Sally's employers provide?
   a. Bill receives a reimbursement of $5,000 for child care expenses. Sally and Bill have three children who are not yet school age.
   b. Bill and Sally are provided a free membership at a local fitness and exercise club that allows them to attend three aerobic exercise sessions per week. The value of this type of membership is $1,600 per year.
   c. Bill is provided free parking at work. The value of the parking is $1,800 per year.

d. Sally is provided with a free apartment. Living in this apartment is a condition of her employment. Similar apartments rent for $1,200 per month.

4. Determine the taxpayer's gross income for each of the following:
   a. Alice is the manager of a plant. The company owns a house one mile from the plant (rental value of $6,000) that Alice is allowed to occupy.
   b. Pam works for an insurance company that allows employees to eat in the cafeteria for $.50 a meal. Generally, the cost to the insurance company of producing a meal is $5.00, and a comparable meal could be purchased for $4.00. Pam ate 150 meals in the cafeteria during the year.

5. Sparrow, Inc., has a wide variety of fringe benefits available to its employees. However, not all of the employees actually need the benefits. For example, some employees have working spouses whose employers provide health insurance benefits for the employee's families. In addition, Sparrow reimburses up to $5,000 for child care costs, but not all of the employees have children. Some employees have expressed a strong interest in long-term care insurance. Sparrow's management has asked you to write a memo explaining how the company can accommodate the varying needs of its employees at the lowest after-tax cost to the employee. Sparrow's address is 300 Harbor Drive, Vermilion, SD 57069.

6. Snowbird Corporation would like you to review its employee fringe benefits program with regard to the tax effects of the plan on the company's president (Polly), who is also the majority shareholder:
   a. All employees receive free tickets to State University football games. Polly is seldom able to attend the games and usually gives her tickets to her nephew. The cost of Polly's tickets for the year was $75.
   b. The company pays all parking fees for its officers but not for other employees. The company paid $1,200 for Polly's parking for the year.
   c. Employees are allowed to use the copy machine for personal purposes as long as the privilege is not abused. Polly is president of a trade association and made extensive use of the copy machine to prepare mailings to members of the association. The cost of the copies was $900.
   d. The company is in the household moving business. Employees are allowed to ship goods without charge whenever there is excess space on a truck. Polly purchased a dining room suite for her daughter. Company trucks delivered the furniture to the daughter. Normal freight charges would have been $600.
   e. The company has a storage facility for household goods. Officers are allowed a 20% discount on charges for storing their goods. All other employees are allowed a 10% discount. Polly's discounts for the year totaled $400.

7. Tom works for Roadrunner Motors, a company that manufactures automobiles. Tom purchased a new automobile from Roadrunner at the company's cost of $10,000. The retail selling price for the automobile is $15,000. Sue works for Coyote, Inc., an auto dealership, which sells the car manufactured by Roadrunner. Sue purchased an automobile identical to Tom's from Coyote. The price Sue pays is equal to Coyote's cost of the automobile ($13,500). Tom and Sue each receive a salary of $40,000 per year. Considering only the above information, do Tom and Sue have equal ability to pay income taxes for the year, and does equitable treatment occur? If not, how should the tax law be changed to produce equitable treatment?

8. Several of Egret Company's employees have asked the company to create a hiking trail that employees could use during their lunch hours. The company owns vacant land that is being held for future expansion, but would have to spend approximately $50,000 if it were to make a trail. Nonemployees would be allowed to use the facility as part of the company's effort to build strong community support. What are the relevant tax issues for the employees?

9. Thrush Corporation has 10 employees, three of whom are shareholders in the corporation. The company is considering adopting a group health insurance plan. Some of the employees have even expressed a willingness to take a cut in pay in order to obtain

health insurance. Three of the employees are interested in long-term care insurance. Fred Thrush, the majority shareholder, has asked your advice about structuring insurance benefits in a favorable tax manner. He is vaguely familiar with flexible benefit plans and has read some articles on medical savings accounts. Write a letter to Mr. Thrush, explaining the possible tax features of a plan to suit the company's and employees' needs. Thrush's address is 500 Fern Avenue, Scranton, PA 18509.

10. Alec has two jobs in 1998. He drives 40 miles to his first job. The distance from the first job to the second is 32 miles. During 1998, Alec worked 200 days at both jobs. On 150 days, he drove from the first job to the second job. On the remaining 50 days, he drove home (40 miles) and then to the second job (42 miles). Presuming the automatic mileage method is used, how much qualifies as a deduction?

11. In 1995, Heidi purchased a new automobile for $32,000. She used the car 80% for business purposes. *Total* miles driven were as follows: 11,000 in 1995, 18,000 in 1996, 12,000 in 1997, and 14,000 in 1998. If Heidi uses the automatic mileage method for all years, what is the adjusted basis of her automobile on January 1, 1999?

12. Louis took a business trip from Chicago to Seattle. He spent two days in travel, conducted business for eight days, and visited friends for five days. He incurred the following expenses:

Airfare	$ 950
Lodging	2,400
Meals	1,200
Entertainment of clients	800

Louis received no reimbursements. What amount can he deduct?

13. Chad is a self-employed computer consultant. During the year, he attended a two-day conference on the latest developments in computer technology. His expenses for the conference are as follows:

Airfare	$420
Hotel room	330
Meals	160
Registration fee and course materials	280

How much may Chad deduct for the conference? How is the deduction classified?

14. Monica travels from her office in Boston to Lisbon, Portugal, on business. Her absence of 13 days was spent as follows:

Thursday	Depart for and arrive at Lisbon
Friday	Business transacted
Saturday and Sunday	Vacationing
Monday through Friday	Business transacted
Saturday and Sunday	Vacationing
Monday	Business transacted
Tuesday	Depart Lisbon and return to office in Boston

a. For tax purposes, how many days has Monica spent on business?
b. What difference does it make?
c. Could Monica have spent more time than she did vacationing on the trip without loss of existing tax benefits? Explain.

15. Cole is both a CPA and an attorney. For several years, he has practiced law as an employee of a large law firm in Dallas. In 1998, Cole decides to quit his job and move

to El Paso, Texas. Four months after arriving in El Paso, Cole establishes a private practice as a CPA. Expenses in moving from Dallas to El Paso are as follows:

Cost of moving household effects	$5,100
Meals	120
Lodging	240

Mileage on two personal autos involved in the move is 1,400.
  a. How much, if any, can Cole deduct as a moving expense?
  b. How is the deduction, if any, classified (*for* or *from* AGI)?

16. After graduating from college with a degree in general business, Shari accepted employment with a bank. Currently, she works in the bank's loan department. During the year, Shari enrolled in an evening MBA program at a local university. In this connection, her expenses are as follows:

Books and tuition	$2,300
Transportation	180
Meals (before or after classes)	310

Shari also takes a correspondence course (cost of $190) entitled "How to Generate Customer Confidence." Presuming no reimbursement, which of these expenses may Shari deduct?

17. Dudley is a self-employed landscape architect. Since the business is quite competitive, Dudley is compelled to entertain extensively. During 1998, he incurred expenses for business meals as follows:

Taxi fares	$ 380
Meals	4,100
Tips	720
Cover charges	600

Presuming adequate substantiation, what is Dudley's deduction?

18. In 1998, Susan's sole proprietorship earns $220,000 of self-employment net income (after the deduction for one-half of self-employment tax).
  a. Calculate the maximum amount that Susan can deduct for contributions to a defined contribution Keogh plan.
  b. Suppose Susan contributes more than the allowable amount to the Keogh plan. What are the tax consequences to her?
  c. Can Susan retire and begin receiving Keogh payments at age 55?

19. Molly is unmarried and is an active participant in a qualified deductible (traditional) IRA plan. Her modified AGI is $34,000.
  a. Calculate the amount that Molly can contribute to the IRA and the amount she can deduct.
  b. Assume instead that Molly is a participant in a SIMPLE IRA and that she elects to contribute 4% of her compensation to the account, while her employer contributes 3%. What amount will be contributed for 1998? What amount will be vested?

20. Answer the following independent questions with respect to IRA contributions:
  a. Juan earns a salary of $25,000 and is not an active participant in any other qualified plan. His wife, Agnes, has no earned income. What is the maximum total deductible contribution to their IRAs? Juan wishes to contribute as much as possible to his own IRA.
  b. Abby has earned income of $23,000, and her husband has earned income of $1,900. They are not active participants in any other qualified plan. What is the maximum contribution to their IRAs?

c. Leo's employer makes a contribution of $3,500 to Leo's simplified employee pension plan. If Leo is single, has earned income of $32,000, and has AGI of $29,000, what amount, if any, can he contribute to an IRA?

21. Kay establishes a Roth IRA at age 43 and contributes $2,000 per year to the Roth IRA account for 22 years. The account is now worth $97,000, consisting of $44,000 in contributions plus $53,000 in accumulated earnings. How much of these funds may Kay withdraw tax-free?

22. Ruth is a professor who consults on the side. She uses one-fifth of her home exclusively for her consulting business, and clients regularly meet her there. Ruth is single and under 65. Her AGI (before considering consulting income) is $50,000. Other relevant data follow:

Income from consulting business	$5,000
Consulting expenses other than home office	2,400
Total costs relating to home	
Interest and taxes	6,000
Utilities	2,000
Maintenance and repairs	600
Depreciation (business part only)	1,500

Calculate Ruth's AGI for 1998.

23. Paige incurred the following expenses related to her employment as a chief executive officer:

Lodging while away from home	$2,800
Meals while away from home	1,200
Entertainment while away from home	2,000
Dues, subscriptions, and books	1,000
Transportation expenses	4,000

Her AGI was $100,000, and she received $6,600 in reimbursements under her employer's accountable plan. What are Paige's deductions *for* and *from* AGI?

24. Kenneth received $4,400 in reimbursements under an accountable plan after he had made an adequate accounting to his employer. His expenses were as follows:

Transportation expenses	$3,200
Meals	1,400
Lodging and incidentals	2,300
Dues, phone, and subscriptions	100
Entertainment	1,000

How much can Kenneth deduct *for* and *from* AGI? Assume he had AGI of $50,000 and no other miscellaneous itemized deductions.

25. During 1998, Helen, the owner of a store, had the following income and expenses:

Gross profit on sales	$63,000
Income from part-time job (subject to FICA)	24,000
Business expenses (related to store)	15,000
Fire loss on store building	1,200
Dividend income	200
Long-term capital gain on the sale of a stock investment	2,000

Compute Helen's self-employment tax and allowable income tax deduction for the self-employment tax paid.

26. In 1998, Fran has self-employed earnings of $150,000. Compute Fran's self-employment tax liability and the allowable income tax deduction for the self-employment tax paid.

27. Sandra, an orthodontist, is single and has net earnings of $90,000 from her orthodontic practice. In addition, she acquires antique books that she sells at antique shows. She participates in six to eight weekend antique shows per year. Her income and expenses for the current year are as follows:

Revenue from sale of antique books		$22,000
Expenses:		
Cost of goods sold	$12,000	
Show registration costs	3,000	
Advertising	1,000	
Dealer's license—annual fee	500	
Insurance	900	
Depreciation of display cases	1,200	

Sandra has no other items that would affect her AGI. Itemized deductions from taxes, interest, and charitable contributions are $19,000.
   a. Calculate Sandra's taxable income if the antique book activity is classified as a hobby.
   b. Calculate Sandra's taxable income if the antique book activity is classified as a business.

CUMULATIVE TAX RETURN PROBLEMS

28. Beth R. Jordan lives at 2322 Skyview Road, Mesa, AZ 85202. She is a tax accountant with Mesa Manufacturing Company. She also writes computer software programs for tax practitioners and has a part-time tax practice. Beth, age 35, is single and has no dependents. Her Social Security number is 111–35–2222. She wants to contribute $3 to the Presidential Election Campaign Fund.

During 1997, Beth earned a salary of $50,000 from her employer. She received interest of $290 from Home Federal Savings and Loan and $335 from Home State Bank. She received dividends of $500 from Gray Corporation, $400 from Blue Corporation, and $300 from Orange Corporation.

Beth received a $1,200 income tax refund from the state of Arizona on May 12, 1997. On her 1996 Federal income tax return, she reported total itemized deductions of $6,700, which included $2,000 of state income tax withheld by her employer.

Fees earned from her part-time tax practice in 1997 totaled $3,800. She paid $400 to have the tax returns processed by a computerized tax return service.

On February 1, 1997, Beth bought 500 shares of Gray Corporation common stock for $17.60 a share. On July 16, she sold the stock for $15 a share.

Beth bought a used utility vehicle for $3,000 on June 5, 1997. She purchased the vehicle from her brother-in-law, who was unemployed and was in need of cash. On November 2, 1997, she sold the vehicle to a friend for $3,400.

On January 2, 1986, Beth acquired 100 shares of Blue Corporation common stock for $30 a share. She sold the stock on December 19, 1997, for $75 a share.

During 1997, Beth received royalties of $14,000 on a software program she had written. Beth incurred the following expenditures in connection with her software-writing activities:

Cost of microcomputer (100% business use)	$7,000
Cost of printer (100% business use)	2,000
Office furniture	3,000
Supplies	650
Fee paid to computer consultant	3,500

Beth elected to expense the maximum portion of the cost of the microcomputer, printer, and furniture allowed under the provisions of § 179. This equipment and furniture were placed in service on January 15, 1997.

Although her employer suggested that Beth attend a convention on current developments in corporate taxation, Beth was not reimbursed for the travel expenses of $1,420 she incurred in attending the convention. The $1,420 included $200 for the cost of meals.

During 1997, Beth paid $300 for prescription medicines and $2,875 in doctor bills, hospital bills, and medical insurance premiums. Her employer withheld state income tax of $1,954. Beth paid real property taxes of $1,766 on her home. Interest on her home mortgage was $3,845, and interest to credit card companies was $320. Beth contributed $20 each week to her church and $10 each week to the United Way. Professional dues and subscriptions totaled $350.

Beth's employer withheld Federal income taxes of $9,500 during 1997. Beth paid estimated taxes of $1,600. What is the amount of Beth's net tax payable or refund due for 1997? If Beth has a tax refund due, she wants to have it credited toward her 1998 income tax. If you use tax forms for your solution, you will need Forms 1040, 2106, and 4562 and Schedules A, B, C, D, and SE. Suggested software (if available): *TurboTax*.

29. George M. and Martha J. Jordan have no dependents and are both under age 65. George is a statutory employee of Consolidated Jobbers (business code is 2634), and his Social Security number is 582–99–4444. Martha is an executive with General Corporation, and her Social Security number is 241–88–6642. The Jordans live at 321 Oak Street, Lincoln, NV 89553. They both want to contribute to the Presidential Election Campaign Fund.

   In 1997, George earned $49,000 in commissions. His employer withholds FICA but not Federal income taxes. George paid $10,000 in estimated taxes. Martha earned $62,000, from which $8,500 was withheld for Federal income taxes. Neither George nor Martha received any expense reimbursements.

   George uses his car (purchased on January 3, 1995) on sales calls and keeps a log of all miles driven. In 1997, he drove 36,000 miles, 24,554 of them for business. He made several out-of-state sales trips, incurring transportation costs of $1,600, meals of $800, and lodging costs of $750. During the year, he also spent $1,400 taking customers to lunch.

   Martha incurred the following expenses related to her work: taxi fares of $125, business lunches of $615, and a yearly commuter train ticket of $800. During the year, Martha received $1,200 in interest from the employees' credit union, $100,000 life insurance proceeds upon the death of her mother in December, and $500 in dividends from General Motors. She contributed $2,000 to her Individual Retirement Account. Neither George nor Martha is covered by an employee retirement plan. Martha gave a gift valued at $500 to the president of her firm upon his promotion to that position.

   The Jordans had additional expenditures as follows:

Charitable contributions (cash)	$1,200
Medical and dental expenses	1,400
Real property taxes	1,200
Home mortgage interest	9,381
Tax return preparation fee	150

   Part 1—Tax Computation
   Compute the Jordans' Federal income tax payable or refund due, assuming they file a joint income tax return for 1997. If they have overpaid, they want the amount refunded. You will need Form 1040 and Schedules A, B, and C. Suggested software (if available): *TurboTax*.

   Part 2—Tax Planning
   Martha and George ask your help in deciding what to do with the $100,000 Martha inherited in 1997. They are considering two conservative investment alternatives:

   - Invest in 8% long-term U.S. bonds.
   - Invest in 6.5% municipal bonds.

   a. Calculate the best alternative for next year. Assume that Martha and George will have the same income and deductions in 1998, except for the income from the investment they choose. In computing the tax, use the tax rate schedules for 1998.

b. What other factors should the Jordans take into account?
c. Write a memo to the Jordans, explaining their alternatives.

Suggested software (if available): *TurboTax*.

RESEARCH PROBLEMS

*Note: The **RIA OnPoint System 4 Student Version CD-ROM** available with this text can be used in preparing solutions to the Research Problems. Alternatively, tax research materials found in a standard tax library can be used.*

30. Tom Roberts, a chemical engineer, is a long-time employee of Teal Chemical Corporation. Tom's specialty is the design and construction of special-purpose chemical processing plants. Teal has decided to expand its presence in France and plans to transfer Tom to Paris on a three-year assignment. The planned foreign assignment will take Tom to age 65, Teal's normal retirement age.

    Tom has been advised regarding the major income tax ramifications of working abroad. He has not, however, been told about the treatment of moving expenses. Since Teal Corporation pays its employees a substantial foreign service salary increment, it reimburses for moving expenses. In connection with the move, Tom plans to sell his residence and place most of his furniture in storage. Probabilities are good that the sale of the residence will result in a loss.
    a. Write a letter to Tom regarding the income tax treatment of his moving expenses. Tom's address is 1389 Wilson Drive, Trent, NJ 08102. Be sure to include in the discussion the move from France back to the United States.
    b. Prepare a memo for your firm's client files.

31. Rick Beam has been an independent sales representative for various textile manufacturers for many years. His products consist of soft goods, such as tablecloths, curtains, and drapes. Rick's customers are clothing store chains, department stores, and smaller specialty stores. The employees of these companies who are responsible for purchasing merchandise are known as buyers. These companies generally prohibit their buyers from accepting gifts from manufacturers' sales representatives.

    Each year Rick gives cash gifts (never more than $25) to most of the buyers who are his customers. Generally, he cashes a large check in November and gives the money personally to the buyers around Christmas. Rick says, "This is one of the ways that I maintain my relationship with my buyers." He maintains adequate substantiation of all the gifts.

    Rick's deductions for these gifts have been disallowed by the IRS, based on Code § 162(c)(2). Rick is confused and comes to you, a CPA, for advice.
    a. Write a letter to Rick concerning his tax position on this issue. Rick's address is 948 Octavia Street, New Orleans, LA 70113.
    b. Prepare a memo for your files supporting the advice you have given.

32. Lyle has been a schoolteacher since he earned his bachelor of education degree 10 years ago. In 1997, the governing board of his school district passed a resolution requiring all teachers to begin pursuing an advanced degree in education. Because of this new requirement, Lyle spent the summer of 1998 taking graduate courses in education at a major university. For the summer activity, Lyle estimates his expenses as follows:

    | Books | $ 220 |
    | Tuition | 3,200 |
    | Room and board | 1,800 |
    | Transportation | 1,500 |

    Lyle kept no receipts and made no record of these expenses. When he files his income tax return for 1998, Lyle claims all of these expenses on Schedule C of Form 1040. In the event Lyle is audited by the IRS, comment on his vulnerability.

Partial list of research aids:
§§ 274(d), 6001, and 6662(b)(1).
Cohan v. Comm., 2 USTC ¶489, 8 AFTR 10552, 39 F.2d 540 (CA–2, 1930).
William F. Sanford, 50 T.C. 823 (1968).

33. Frank and Polly were married, but Frank died on February 25, 1998. During 1998, Frank earned $5,226 in wages, but Polly had no earned income. Neither had contributed any money to an IRA during 1998. What amount, if any, can be contributed to Frank's IRA and/or Polly's spousal IRA?

APPENDIX A

Tax Rate Schedules and Tables

1997 Income Tax Rates Schedules	A–2
1998 Income Tax Rates Schedules	A–2
1997 Tax Tables	A–3
Income Tax Rates—Estates and Trusts	A–15
Income Tax Rates—Corporations	A–15
Unified Transfer Tax Rates	A–16
Credit for State Death Taxes	A–17

1997 Tax Rate Schedules

Single—Schedule X

If taxable income is: Over—	But not over—	The tax is:		of the amount over—
$0	$ 24,650	.... 15%		$0
24,650	59,750	$3,697.50 +	28%	24,650
59,750	124,650	13,525.50 +	31%	59,750
124,650	271,050	33,644.50 +	36%	124,650
271,050	......	86,348.50 +	39.6%	271,050

Head of household—Schedule Z

If taxable income is: Over—	But not over—	The tax is:		of the amount over—
$0	$ 33,050	.... 15%		$0
33,050	85,350	$4,957.50 +	28%	33,050
85,350	138,200	19,601.50 +	31%	85,350
138,200	271,050	35,985.00 +	36%	138,200
271,050	......	83,811.00 +	39.6%	271,050

Married filing jointly or Qualifying widow(er)—Schedule Y–1

If taxable income is: Over—	But not over—	The tax is:		of the amount over—
$0	$ 41,200	.... 15%		$0
41,200	99,600	$6,180.00 +	28%	41,200
99,600	151,750	22,532.00 +	31%	99,600
151,750	271,050	38,698.50 +	36%	151,750
271,050	......	81,646.50 +	39.6%	271,050

Married filing separately—Schedule Y–2

If taxable income is: Over—	But not over—	The tax is:		of the amount over—
$0	$ 20,600	.... 15%		$0
20,600	49,800	$3,090.00 +	28%	20,600
49,800	75,875	11,266.00 +	31%	49,800
75,875	135,525	19,349.25 +	36%	75,875
135,525	......	40,823.25 +	39.6%	135,525

1998 Tax Rate Schedules

Single—Schedule X

If taxable income is: Over—	But not over—	The tax is:		of the amount over—
$0	$ 25,350	.... 15%		$0
25,350	61,400	$3,802.50 +	28%	25,350
61,400	128,100	13,896.50 +	31%	61,400
128,100	278,450	34,573.50 +	36%	128,100
278,450	......	88,699.50 +	39.6%	278,450

Head of household—Schedule Z

If taxable income is: Over—	But not over—	The tax is:		of the amount over—
$0	$ 33,950	.... 15%		$0
33,950	87,700	$5,092.50 +	28%	33,950
87,700	142,000	20,142.50 +	31%	87,700
142,000	278,450	36,975.50 +	36%	142,000
278,450	......	86,097.50 +	39.6%	278,450

Married filing jointly or Qualifying widow(er)—Schedule Y–1

If taxable income is: Over—	But not over—	The tax is:		of the amount over—
$0	$ 42,350	.... 15%		$0
42,350	102,300	$6,352.50 +	28%	42,350
102,300	155,950	23,138.50 +	31%	102,300
155,950	278,450	39,770.00 +	36%	155,950
278,450	......	83,870.00 +	39.6%	278,450

Married filing separately—Schedule Y–2

If taxable income is: Over—	But not over—	The tax is:		of the amount over—
$0	$ 21,175	.... 15%		$0
21,175	51,150	$3,176.25 +	28%	21,175
51,150	77,975	11,569.25 +	31%	51,150
77,975	139,225	19,885.00 +	36%	77,975
139,225	......	41,935.00 +	39.6%	139,225

1997 Tax Table

Use if your taxable income is less than $100,000. If $100,000 or more, use the Tax Rate Schedules.

Example. Mr. and Mrs. Brown are filing a joint return. Their taxable income on line 38 of Form 1040 is $25,300. First, they find the $25,300–25,350 income line. Next, they find the column for married filing jointly and read down the column. The amount shown where the income line and filing status column meet is $3,799. This is the tax amount they should enter on line 39 of their Form 1040.

Sample Table

At least	But less than	Single	Married filing jointly*	Married filing separately	Head of a household
			Your tax is—		
25,200	25,250	3,859	3,784	4,385	3,784
25,250	25,300	3,873	3,791	4,399	3,791
25,300	25,350	3,887	(3,799)	4,413	3,799
25,350	25,400	3,901	3,806	4,427	3,806

If line 38 (taxable income) is—		And you are—				If line 38 (taxable income) is—		And you are—				If line 38 (taxable income) is—		And you are—			
At least	But less than	Single	Married filing jointly*	Married filing separately	Head of a household	At least	But less than	Single	Married filing jointly*	Married filing separately	Head of a household	At least	But less than	Single	Married filing jointly*	Married filing separately	Head of a household
			Your tax is—						**Your tax is—**						**Your tax is—**		
$0	$5	$0	$0	$0	$0	1,300	1,325	197	197	197	197	2,700	2,725	407	407	407	407
5	15	2	2	2	2	1,325	1,350	201	201	201	201	2,725	2,750	411	411	411	411
15	25	3	3	3	3	1,350	1,375	204	204	204	204	2,750	2,775	414	414	414	414
25	50	6	6	6	6	1,375	1,400	208	208	208	208	2,775	2,800	418	418	418	418
50	75	9	9	9	9	1,400	1,425	212	212	212	212	2,800	2,825	422	422	422	422
75	100	13	13	13	13	1,425	1,450	216	216	216	216	2,825	2,850	426	426	426	426
100	125	17	17	17	17	1,450	1,475	219	219	219	219	2,850	2,875	429	429	429	429
125	150	21	21	21	21	1,475	1,500	223	223	223	223	2,875	2,900	433	433	433	433
150	175	24	24	24	24	1,500	1,525	227	227	227	227	2,900	2,925	437	437	437	437
175	200	28	28	28	28	1,525	1,550	231	231	231	231	2,925	2,950	441	441	441	441
200	225	32	32	32	32	1,550	1,575	234	234	234	234	2,950	2,975	444	444	444	444
225	250	36	36	36	36	1,575	1,600	238	238	238	238	2,975	3,000	448	448	448	448
250	275	39	39	39	39	1,600	1,625	242	242	242	242	**3,000**					
275	300	43	43	43	43	1,625	1,650	246	246	246	246						
300	325	47	47	47	47	1,650	1,675	249	249	249	249	3,000	3,050	454	454	454	454
325	350	51	51	51	51	1,675	1,700	253	253	253	253	3,050	3,100	461	461	461	461
350	375	54	54	54	54	1,700	1,725	257	257	257	257	3,100	3,150	469	469	469	469
375	400	58	58	58	58	1,725	1,750	261	261	261	261	3,150	3,200	476	476	476	476
400	425	62	62	62	62	1,750	1,775	264	264	264	264	3,200	3,250	484	484	484	484
425	450	66	66	66	66	1,775	1,800	268	268	268	268	3,250	3,300	491	491	491	491
450	475	69	69	69	69	1,800	1,825	272	272	272	272	3,300	3,350	499	499	499	499
475	500	73	73	73	73	1,825	1,850	276	276	276	276	3,350	3,400	506	506	506	506
500	525	77	77	77	77	1,850	1,875	279	279	279	279	3,400	3,450	514	514	514	514
525	550	81	81	81	81	1,875	1,900	283	283	283	283	3,450	3,500	521	521	521	521
550	575	84	84	84	84	1,900	1,925	287	287	287	287	3,500	3,550	529	529	529	529
575	600	88	88	88	88	1,925	1,950	291	291	291	291	3,550	3,600	536	536	536	536
600	625	92	92	92	92	1,950	1,975	294	294	294	294	3,600	3,650	544	544	544	544
625	650	96	96	96	96	1,975	2,000	298	298	298	298	3,650	3,700	551	551	551	551
650	675	99	99	99	99	**2,000**						3,700	3,750	559	559	559	559
675	700	103	103	103	103							3,750	3,800	566	566	566	566
700	725	107	107	107	107	2,000	2,025	302	302	302	302	3,800	3,850	574	574	574	574
725	750	111	111	111	111	2,025	2,050	306	306	306	306	3,850	3,900	581	581	581	581
750	775	114	114	114	114	2,050	2,075	309	309	309	309	3,900	3,950	589	589	589	589
775	800	118	118	118	118	2,075	2,100	313	313	313	313	3,950	4,000	596	596	596	596
800	825	122	122	122	122	2,100	2,125	317	317	317	317	**4,000**					
825	850	126	126	126	126	2,125	2,150	321	321	321	321						
850	875	129	129	129	129	2,150	2,175	324	324	324	324	4,000	4,050	604	604	604	604
875	900	133	133	133	133	2,175	2,200	328	328	328	328	4,050	4,100	611	611	611	611
900	925	137	137	137	137	2,200	2,225	332	332	332	332	4,100	4,150	619	619	619	619
925	950	141	141	141	141	2,225	2,250	336	336	336	336	4,150	4,200	626	626	626	626
950	975	144	144	144	144	2,250	2,275	339	339	339	339	4,200	4,250	634	634	634	634
975	1,000	148	148	148	148	2,275	2,300	343	343	343	343	4,250	4,300	641	641	641	641
1,000						2,300	2,325	347	347	347	347	4,300	4,350	649	649	649	649
						2,325	2,350	351	351	351	351	4,350	4,400	656	656	656	656
1,000	1,025	152	152	152	152	2,350	2,375	354	354	354	354	4,400	4,450	664	664	664	664
1,025	1,050	156	156	156	156	2,375	2,400	358	358	358	358	4,450	4,500	671	671	671	671
1,050	1,075	159	159	159	159	2,400	2,425	362	362	362	362	4,500	4,550	679	679	679	679
1,075	1,100	163	163	163	163	2,425	2,450	366	366	366	366	4,550	4,600	686	686	686	686
1,100	1,125	167	167	167	167	2,450	2,475	369	369	369	369	4,600	4,650	694	694	694	694
1,125	1,150	171	171	171	171	2,475	2,500	373	373	373	373	4,650	4,700	701	701	701	701
1,150	1,175	174	174	174	174	2,500	2,525	377	377	377	377	4,700	4,750	709	709	709	709
1,175	1,200	178	178	178	178	2,525	2,550	381	381	381	381	4,750	4,800	716	716	716	716
1,200	1,225	182	182	182	182	2,550	2,575	384	384	384	384	4,800	4,850	724	724	724	724
1,225	1,250	186	186	186	186	2,575	2,600	388	388	388	388	4,850	4,900	731	731	731	731
1,250	1,275	189	189	189	189	2,600	2,625	392	392	392	392	4,900	4,950	739	739	739	739
1,275	1,300	193	193	193	193	2,625	2,650	396	396	396	396	4,950	5,000	746	746	746	746
						2,650	2,675	399	399	399	399						
						2,675	2,700	403	403	403	403						

Continued on next page

* This column must also be used by a qualifying widow(er).

1997 Tax Table—Continued

If line 38 (taxable income) is—		And you are—				If line 38 (taxable income) is—		And you are—				If line 38 (taxable income) is—		And you are—			
At least	But less than	Single	Married filing jointly *	Married filing separately	Head of a household	At least	But less than	Single	Married filing jointly *	Married filing separately	Head of a household	At least	But less than	Single	Married filing jointly *	Married filing separately	Head of a household
		Your tax is—						Your tax is—						Your tax is—			
5,000						**8,000**						**11,000**					
5,000	5,050	754	754	754	754	8,000	8,050	1,204	1,204	1,204	1,204	11,000	11,050	1,654	1,654	1,654	1,654
5,050	5,100	761	761	761	761	8,050	8,100	1,211	1,211	1,211	1,211	11,050	11,100	1,661	1,661	1,661	1,661
5,100	5,150	769	769	769	769	8,100	8,150	1,219	1,219	1,219	1,219	11,100	11,150	1,669	1,669	1,669	1,669
5,150	5,200	776	776	776	776	8,150	8,200	1,226	1,226	1,226	1,226	11,150	11,200	1,676	1,676	1,676	1,676
5,200	5,250	784	784	784	784	8,200	8,250	1,234	1,234	1,234	1,234	11,200	11,250	1,684	1,684	1,684	1,684
5,250	5,300	791	791	791	791	8,250	8,300	1,241	1,241	1,241	1,241	11,250	11,300	1,691	1,691	1,691	1,691
5,300	5,350	799	799	799	799	8,300	8,350	1,249	1,249	1,249	1,249	11,300	11,350	1,699	1,699	1,699	1,699
5,350	5,400	806	806	806	806	8,350	8,400	1,256	1,256	1,256	1,256	11,350	11,400	1,706	1,706	1,706	1,706
5,400	5,450	814	814	814	814	8,400	8,450	1,264	1,264	1,264	1,264	11,400	11,450	1,714	1,714	1,714	1,714
5,450	5,500	821	821	821	821	8,450	8,500	1,271	1,271	1,271	1,271	11,450	11,500	1,721	1,721	1,721	1,721
5,500	5,550	829	829	829	829	8,500	8,550	1,279	1,279	1,279	1,279	11,500	11,550	1,729	1,729	1,729	1,729
5,550	5,600	836	836	836	836	8,550	8,600	1,286	1,286	1,286	1,286	11,550	11,600	1,736	1,736	1,736	1,736
5,600	5,650	844	844	844	844	8,600	8,650	1,294	1,294	1,294	1,294	11,600	11,650	1,744	1,744	1,744	1,744
5,650	5,700	851	851	851	851	8,650	8,700	1,301	1,301	1,301	1,301	11,650	11,700	1,751	1,751	1,751	1,751
5,700	5,750	859	859	859	859	8,700	8,750	1,309	1,309	1,309	1,309	11,700	11,750	1,759	1,759	1,759	1,759
5,750	5,800	866	866	866	866	8,750	8,800	1,316	1,316	1,316	1,316	11,750	11,800	1,766	1,766	1,766	1,766
5,800	5,850	874	874	874	874	8,800	8,850	1,324	1,324	1,324	1,324	11,800	11,850	1,774	1,774	1,774	1,774
5,850	5,900	881	881	881	881	8,850	8,900	1,331	1,331	1,331	1,331	11,850	11,900	1,781	1,781	1,781	1,781
5,900	5,950	889	889	889	889	8,900	8,950	1,339	1,339	1,339	1,339	11,900	11,950	1,789	1,789	1,789	1,789
5,950	6,000	896	896	896	896	8,950	9,000	1,346	1,346	1,346	1,346	11,950	12,000	1,796	1,796	1,796	1,796
6,000						**9,000**						**12,000**					
6,000	6,050	904	904	904	904	9,000	9,050	1,354	1,354	1,354	1,354	12,000	12,050	1,804	1,804	1,804	1,804
6,050	6,100	911	911	911	911	9,050	9,100	1,361	1,361	1,361	1,361	12,050	12,100	1,811	1,811	1,811	1,811
6,100	6,150	919	919	919	919	9,100	9,150	1,369	1,369	1,369	1,369	12,100	12,150	1,819	1,819	1,819	1,819
6,150	6,200	926	926	926	926	9,150	9,200	1,376	1,376	1,376	1,376	12,150	12,200	1,826	1,826	1,826	1,826
6,200	6,250	934	934	934	934	9,200	9,250	1,384	1,384	1,384	1,384	12,200	12,250	1,834	1,834	1,834	1,834
6,250	6,300	941	941	941	941	9,250	9,300	1,391	1,391	1,391	1,391	12,250	12,300	1,841	1,841	1,841	1,841
6,300	6,350	949	949	949	949	9,300	9,350	1,399	1,399	1,399	1,399	12,300	12,350	1,849	1,849	1,849	1,849
6,350	6,400	956	956	956	956	9,350	9,400	1,406	1,406	1,406	1,406	12,350	12,400	1,856	1,856	1,856	1,856
6,400	6,450	964	964	964	964	9,400	9,450	1,414	1,414	1,414	1,414	12,400	12,450	1,864	1,864	1,864	1,864
6,450	6,500	971	971	971	971	9,450	9,500	1,421	1,421	1,421	1,421	12,450	12,500	1,871	1,871	1,871	1,871
6,500	6,550	979	979	979	979	9,500	9,550	1,429	1,429	1,429	1,429	12,500	12,550	1,879	1,879	1,879	1,879
6,550	6,600	986	986	986	986	9,550	9,600	1,436	1,436	1,436	1,436	12,550	12,600	1,886	1,886	1,886	1,886
6,600	6,650	994	994	994	994	9,600	9,650	1,444	1,444	1,444	1,444	12,600	12,650	1,894	1,894	1,894	1,894
6,650	6,700	1,001	1,001	1,001	1,001	9,650	9,700	1,451	1,451	1,451	1,451	12,650	12,700	1,901	1,901	1,901	1,901
6,700	6,750	1,009	1,009	1,009	1,009	9,700	9,750	1,459	1,459	1,459	1,459	12,700	12,750	1,909	1,909	1,909	1,909
6,750	6,800	1,016	1,016	1,016	1,016	9,750	9,800	1,466	1,466	1,466	1,466	12,750	12,800	1,916	1,916	1,916	1,916
6,800	6,850	1,024	1,024	1,024	1,024	9,800	9,850	1,474	1,474	1,474	1,474	12,800	12,850	1,924	1,924	1,924	1,924
6,850	6,900	1,031	1,031	1,031	1,031	9,850	9,900	1,481	1,481	1,481	1,481	12,850	12,900	1,931	1,931	1,931	1,931
6,900	6,950	1,039	1,039	1,039	1,039	9,900	9,950	1,489	1,489	1,489	1,489	12,900	12,950	1,939	1,939	1,939	1,939
6,950	7,000	1,046	1,046	1,046	1,046	9,950	10,000	1,496	1,496	1,496	1,496	12,950	13,000	1,946	1,946	1,946	1,946
7,000						**10,000**						**13,000**					
7,000	7,050	1,054	1,054	1,054	1,054	10,000	10,050	1,504	1,504	1,504	1,504	13,000	13,050	1,954	1,954	1,954	1,954
7,050	7,100	1,061	1,061	1,061	1,061	10,050	10,100	1,511	1,511	1,511	1,511	13,050	13,100	1,961	1,961	1,961	1,961
7,100	7,150	1,069	1,069	1,069	1,069	10,100	10,150	1,519	1,519	1,519	1,519	13,100	13,150	1,969	1,969	1,969	1,969
7,150	7,200	1,076	1,076	1,076	1,076	10,150	10,200	1,526	1,526	1,526	1,526	13,150	13,200	1,976	1,976	1,976	1,976
7,200	7,250	1,084	1,084	1,084	1,084	10,200	10,250	1,534	1,534	1,534	1,534	13,200	13,250	1,984	1,984	1,984	1,984
7,250	7,300	1,091	1,091	1,091	1,091	10,250	10,300	1,541	1,541	1,541	1,541	13,250	13,300	1,991	1,991	1,991	1,991
7,300	7,350	1,099	1,099	1,099	1,099	10,300	10,350	1,549	1,549	1,549	1,549	13,300	13,350	1,999	1,999	1,999	1,999
7,350	7,400	1,106	1,106	1,106	1,106	10,350	10,400	1,556	1,556	1,556	1,556	13,350	13,400	2,006	2,006	2,006	2,006
7,400	7,450	1,114	1,114	1,114	1,114	10,400	10,450	1,564	1,564	1,564	1,564	13,400	13,450	2,014	2,014	2,014	2,014
7,450	7,500	1,121	1,121	1,121	1,121	10,450	10,500	1,571	1,571	1,571	1,571	13,450	13,500	2,021	2,021	2,021	2,021
7,500	7,550	1,129	1,129	1,129	1,129	10,500	10,550	1,579	1,579	1,579	1,579	13,500	13,550	2,029	2,029	2,029	2,029
7,550	7,600	1,136	1,136	1,136	1,136	10,550	10,600	1,586	1,586	1,586	1,586	13,550	13,600	2,036	2,036	2,036	2,036
7,600	7,650	1,144	1,144	1,144	1,144	10,600	10,650	1,594	1,594	1,594	1,594	13,600	13,650	2,044	2,044	2,044	2,044
7,650	7,700	1,151	1,151	1,151	1,151	10,650	10,700	1,601	1,601	1,601	1,601	13,650	13,700	2,051	2,051	2,051	2,051
7,700	7,750	1,159	1,159	1,159	1,159	10,700	10,750	1,609	1,609	1,609	1,609	13,700	13,750	2,059	2,059	2,059	2,059
7,750	7,800	1,166	1,166	1,166	1,166	10,750	10,800	1,616	1,616	1,616	1,616	13,750	13,800	2,066	2,066	2,066	2,066
7,800	7,850	1,174	1,174	1,174	1,174	10,800	10,850	1,624	1,624	1,624	1,624	13,800	13,850	2,074	2,074	2,074	2,074
7,850	7,900	1,181	1,181	1,181	1,181	10,850	10,900	1,631	1,631	1,631	1,631	13,850	13,900	2,081	2,081	2,081	2,081
7,900	7,950	1,189	1,189	1,189	1,189	10,900	10,950	1,639	1,639	1,639	1,639	13,900	13,950	2,089	2,089	2,089	2,089
7,950	8,000	1,196	1,196	1,196	1,196	10,950	11,000	1,646	1,646	1,646	1,646	13,950	14,000	2,096	2,096	2,096	2,096

* This column must also be used by a qualifying widow(er).

Continued on next page

1997 Tax Table—Continued

If line 38 (taxable income) is—		And you are—				If line 38 (taxable income) is—		And you are—				If line 38 (taxable income) is—		And you are—			
At least	But less than	Single	Married filing jointly *	Married filing separately	Head of a household	At least	But less than	Single	Married filing jointly *	Married filing separately	Head of a household	At least	But less than	Single	Married filing jointly *	Married filing separately	Head of a household
		Your tax is—						Your tax is—						Your tax is—			
14,000						**17,000**						**20,000**					
14,000	14,050	2,104	2,104	2,104	2,104	17,000	17,050	2,554	2,554	2,554	2,554	20,000	20,050	3,004	3,004	3,004	3,004
14,050	14,100	2,111	2,111	2,111	2,111	17,050	17,100	2,561	2,561	2,561	2,561	20,050	20,100	3,011	3,011	3,011	3,011
14,100	14,150	2,119	2,119	2,119	2,119	17,100	17,150	2,569	2,569	2,569	2,569	20,100	20,150	3,019	3,019	3,019	3,019
14,150	14,200	2,126	2,126	2,126	2,126	17,150	17,200	2,576	2,576	2,576	2,576	20,150	20,200	3,026	3,026	3,026	3,026
14,200	14,250	2,134	2,134	2,134	2,134	17,200	17,250	2,584	2,584	2,584	2,584	20,200	20,250	3,034	3,034	3,034	3,034
14,250	14,300	2,141	2,141	2,141	2,141	17,250	17,300	2,591	2,591	2,591	2,591	20,250	20,300	3,041	3,041	3,041	3,041
14,300	14,350	2,149	2,149	2,149	2,149	17,300	17,350	2,599	2,599	2,599	2,599	20,300	20,350	3,049	3,049	3,049	3,049
14,350	14,400	2,156	2,156	2,156	2,156	17,350	17,400	2,606	2,606	2,606	2,606	20,350	20,400	3,056	3,056	3,056	3,056
14,400	14,450	2,164	2,164	2,164	2,164	17,400	17,450	2,614	2,614	2,614	2,614	20,400	20,450	3,064	3,064	3,064	3,064
14,450	14,500	2,171	2,171	2,171	2,171	17,450	17,500	2,621	2,621	2,621	2,621	20,450	20,500	3,071	3,071	3,071	3,071
14,500	14,550	2,179	2,179	2,179	2,179	17,500	17,550	2,629	2,629	2,629	2,629	20,500	20,550	3,079	3,079	3,079	3,079
14,550	14,600	2,186	2,186	2,186	2,186	17,550	17,600	2,636	2,636	2,636	2,636	20,550	20,600	3,086	3,086	3,086	3,086
14,600	14,650	2,194	2,194	2,194	2,194	17,600	17,650	2,644	2,644	2,644	2,644	20,600	20,650	3,094	3,094	3,097	3,094
14,650	14,700	2,201	2,201	2,201	2,201	17,650	17,700	2,651	2,651	2,651	2,651	20,650	20,700	3,101	3,101	3,111	3,101
14,700	14,750	2,209	2,209	2,209	2,209	17,700	17,750	2,659	2,659	2,659	2,659	20,700	20,750	3,109	3,109	3,125	3,109
14,750	14,800	2,216	2,216	2,216	2,216	17,750	17,800	2,666	2,666	2,666	2,666	20,750	20,800	3,116	3,116	3,139	3,116
14,800	14,850	2,224	2,224	2,224	2,224	17,800	17,850	2,674	2,674	2,674	2,674	20,800	20,850	3,124	3,124	3,153	3,124
14,850	14,900	2,231	2,231	2,231	2,231	17,850	17,900	2,681	2,681	2,681	2,681	20,850	20,900	3,131	3,131	3,167	3,131
14,900	14,950	2,239	2,239	2,239	2,239	17,900	17,950	2,689	2,689	2,689	2,689	20,900	20,950	3,139	3,139	3,181	3,139
14,950	15,000	2,246	2,246	2,246	2,246	17,950	18,000	2,696	2,696	2,696	2,696	20,950	21,000	3,146	3,146	3,195	3,146
15,000						**18,000**						**21,000**					
15,000	15,050	2,254	2,254	2,254	2,254	18,000	18,050	2,704	2,704	2,704	2,704	21,000	21,050	3,154	3,154	3,209	3,154
15,050	15,100	2,261	2,261	2,261	2,261	18,050	18,100	2,711	2,711	2,711	2,711	21,050	21,100	3,161	3,161	3,223	3,161
15,100	15,150	2,269	2,269	2,269	2,269	18,100	18,150	2,719	2,719	2,719	2,719	21,100	21,150	3,169	3,169	3,237	3,169
15,150	15,200	2,276	2,276	2,276	2,276	18,150	18,200	2,726	2,726	2,726	2,726	21,150	21,200	3,176	3,176	3,251	3,176
15,200	15,250	2,284	2,284	2,284	2,284	18,200	18,250	2,734	2,734	2,734	2,734	21,200	21,250	3,184	3,184	3,265	3,184
15,250	15,300	2,291	2,291	2,291	2,291	18,250	18,300	2,741	2,741	2,741	2,741	21,250	21,300	3,191	3,191	3,279	3,191
15,300	15,350	2,299	2,299	2,299	2,299	18,300	18,350	2,749	2,749	2,749	2,749	21,300	21,350	3,199	3,199	3,293	3,199
15,350	15,400	2,306	2,306	2,306	2,306	18,350	18,400	2,756	2,756	2,756	2,756	21,350	21,400	3,206	3,206	3,307	3,206
15,400	15,450	2,314	2,314	2,314	2,314	18,400	18,450	2,764	2,764	2,764	2,764	21,400	21,450	3,214	3,214	3,321	3,214
15,450	15,500	2,321	2,321	2,321	2,321	18,450	18,500	2,771	2,771	2,771	2,771	21,450	21,500	3,221	3,221	3,335	3,221
15,500	15,550	2,329	2,329	2,329	2,329	18,500	18,550	2,779	2,779	2,779	2,779	21,500	21,550	3,229	3,229	3,349	3,229
15,550	15,600	2,336	2,336	2,336	2,336	18,550	18,600	2,786	2,786	2,786	2,786	21,550	21,600	3,236	3,236	3,363	3,236
15,600	15,650	2,344	2,344	2,344	2,344	18,600	18,650	2,794	2,794	2,794	2,794	21,600	21,650	3,244	3,244	3,377	3,244
15,650	15,700	2,351	2,351	2,351	2,351	18,650	18,700	2,801	2,801	2,801	2,801	21,650	21,700	3,251	3,251	3,391	3,251
15,700	15,750	2,359	2,359	2,359	2,359	18,700	18,750	2,809	2,809	2,809	2,809	21,700	21,750	3,259	3,259	3,405	3,259
15,750	15,800	2,366	2,366	2,366	2,366	18,750	18,800	2,816	2,816	2,816	2,816	21,750	21,800	3,266	3,266	3,419	3,266
15,800	15,850	2,374	2,374	2,374	2,374	18,800	18,850	2,824	2,824	2,824	2,824	21,800	21,850	3,274	3,274	3,433	3,274
15,850	15,900	2,381	2,381	2,381	2,381	18,850	18,900	2,831	2,831	2,831	2,831	21,850	21,900	3,281	3,281	3,447	3,281
15,900	15,950	2,389	2,389	2,389	2,389	18,900	18,950	2,839	2,839	2,839	2,839	21,900	21,950	3,289	3,289	3,461	3,289
15,950	16,000	2,396	2,396	2,396	2,396	18,950	19,000	2,846	2,846	2,846	2,846	21,950	22,000	3,296	3,296	3,475	3,296
16,000						**19,000**						**22,000**					
16,000	16,050	2,404	2,404	2,404	2,404	19,000	19,050	2,854	2,854	2,854	2,854	22,000	22,050	3,304	3,304	3,489	3,304
16,050	16,100	2,411	2,411	2,411	2,411	19,050	19,100	2,861	2,861	2,861	2,861	22,050	22,100	3,311	3,311	3,503	3,311
16,100	16,150	2,419	2,419	2,419	2,419	19,100	19,150	2,869	2,869	2,869	2,869	22,100	22,150	3,319	3,319	3,517	3,319
16,150	16,200	2,426	2,426	2,426	2,426	19,150	19,200	2,876	2,876	2,876	2,876	22,150	22,200	3,326	3,326	3,531	3,326
16,200	16,250	2,434	2,434	2,434	2,434	19,200	19,250	2,884	2,884	2,884	2,884	22,200	22,250	3,334	3,334	3,545	3,334
16,250	16,300	2,441	2,441	2,441	2,441	19,250	19,300	2,891	2,891	2,891	2,891	22,250	22,300	3,341	3,341	3,559	3,341
16,300	16,350	2,449	2,449	2,449	2,449	19,300	19,350	2,899	2,899	2,899	2,899	22,300	22,350	3,349	3,349	3,573	3,349
16,350	16,400	2,456	2,456	2,456	2,456	19,350	19,400	2,906	2,906	2,906	2,906	22,350	22,400	3,356	3,356	3,587	3,356
16,400	16,450	2,464	2,464	2,464	2,464	19,400	19,450	2,914	2,914	2,914	2,914	22,400	22,450	3,364	3,364	3,601	3,364
16,450	16,500	2,471	2,471	2,471	2,471	19,450	19,500	2,921	2,921	2,921	2,921	22,450	22,500	3,371	3,371	3,615	3,371
16,500	16,550	2,479	2,479	2,479	2,479	19,500	19,550	2,929	2,929	2,929	2,929	22,500	22,550	3,379	3,379	3,629	3,379
16,550	16,600	2,486	2,486	2,486	2,486	19,550	19,600	2,936	2,936	2,936	2,936	22,550	22,600	3,386	3,386	3,643	3,386
16,600	16,650	2,494	2,494	2,494	2,494	19,600	19,650	2,944	2,944	2,944	2,944	22,600	22,650	3,394	3,394	3,657	3,394
16,650	16,700	2,501	2,501	2,501	2,501	19,650	19,700	2,951	2,951	2,951	2,951	22,650	22,700	3,401	3,401	3,671	3,401
16,700	16,750	2,509	2,509	2,509	2,509	19,700	19,750	2,959	2,959	2,959	2,959	22,700	22,750	3,409	3,409	3,685	3,409
16,750	16,800	2,516	2,516	2,516	2,516	19,750	19,800	2,966	2,966	2,966	2,966	22,750	22,800	3,416	3,416	3,699	3,416
16,800	16,850	2,524	2,524	2,524	2,524	19,800	19,850	2,974	2,974	2,974	2,974	22,800	22,850	3,424	3,424	3,713	3,424
16,850	16,900	2,531	2,531	2,531	2,531	19,850	19,900	2,981	2,981	2,981	2,981	22,850	22,900	3,431	3,431	3,727	3,431
16,900	16,950	2,539	2,539	2,539	2,539	19,900	19,950	2,989	2,989	2,989	2,989	22,900	22,950	3,439	3,439	3,741	3,439
16,950	17,000	2,546	2,546	2,546	2,546	19,950	20,000	2,996	2,996	2,996	2,996	22,950	23,000	3,446	3,446	3,755	3,446

* This column must also be used by a qualifying widow(er).

Continued on next page

1997 Tax Table—Continued

If line 38 (taxable income) is—		And you are—				If line 38 (taxable income) is—		And you are—				If line 38 (taxable income) is—		And you are—			
At least	But less than	Single	Married filing jointly *	Married filing separately	Head of a household	At least	But less than	Single	Married filing jointly *	Married filing separately	Head of a household	At least	But less than	Single	Married filing jointly *	Married filing separately	Head of a household
		Your tax is—						Your tax is—						Your tax is—			
23,000						**26,000**						**29,000**					
23,000	23,050	3,454	3,454	3,769	3,454	26,000	26,050	4,083	3,904	4,609	3,904	29,000	29,050	4,923	4,354	5,449	4,354
23,050	23,100	3,461	3,461	3,783	3,461	26,050	26,100	4,097	3,911	4,623	3,911	29,050	29,100	4,937	4,361	5,463	4,361
23,100	23,150	3,469	3,469	3,797	3,469	26,100	26,150	4,111	3,919	4,637	3,919	29,100	29,150	4,951	4,369	5,477	4,369
23,150	23,200	3,476	3,476	3,811	3,476	26,150	26,200	4,125	3,926	4,651	3,926	29,150	29,200	4,965	4,376	5,491	4,376
23,200	23,250	3,484	3,484	3,825	3,484	26,200	26,250	4,139	3,934	4,665	3,934	29,200	29,250	4,979	4,384	5,505	4,384
23,250	23,300	3,491	3,491	3,839	3,491	26,250	26,300	4,153	3,941	4,679	3,941	29,250	29,300	4,993	4,391	5,519	4,391
23,300	23,350	3,499	3,499	3,853	3,499	26,300	26,350	4,167	3,949	4,693	3,949	29,300	29,350	5,007	4,399	5,533	4,399
23,350	23,400	3,506	3,506	3,867	3,506	26,350	26,400	4,181	3,956	4,707	3,956	29,350	29,400	5,021	4,406	5,547	4,406
23,400	23,450	3,514	3,514	3,881	3,514	26,400	26,450	4,195	3,964	4,721	3,964	29,400	29,450	5,035	4,414	5,561	4,414
23,450	23,500	3,521	3,521	3,895	3,521	26,450	26,500	4,209	3,971	4,735	3,971	29,450	29,500	5,049	4,421	5,575	4,421
23,500	23,550	3,529	3,529	3,909	3,529	26,500	26,550	4,223	3,979	4,749	3,979	29,500	29,550	5,063	4,429	5,589	4,429
23,550	23,600	3,536	3,536	3,923	3,536	26,550	26,600	4,237	3,986	4,763	3,986	29,550	29,600	5,077	4,436	5,603	4,436
23,600	23,650	3,544	3,544	3,937	3,544	26,600	26,650	4,251	3,994	4,777	3,994	29,600	29,650	5,091	4,444	5,617	4,444
23,650	23,700	3,551	3,551	3,951	3,551	26,650	26,700	4,265	4,001	4,791	4,001	29,650	29,700	5,105	4,451	5,631	4,451
23,700	23,750	3,559	3,559	3,965	3,559	26,700	26,750	4,279	4,009	4,805	4,009	29,700	29,750	5,119	4,459	5,645	4,459
23,750	23,800	3,566	3,566	3,979	3,566	26,750	26,800	4,293	4,016	4,819	4,016	29,750	29,800	5,133	4,466	5,659	4,466
23,800	23,850	3,574	3,574	3,993	3,574	26,800	26,850	4,307	4,024	4,833	4,024	29,800	29,850	5,147	4,474	5,673	4,474
23,850	23,900	3,581	3,581	4,007	3,581	26,850	26,900	4,321	4,031	4,847	4,031	29,850	29,900	5,161	4,481	5,687	4,481
23,900	23,950	3,589	3,589	4,021	3,589	26,900	26,950	4,335	4,039	4,861	4,039	29,900	29,950	5,175	4,489	5,701	4,489
23,950	24,000	3,596	3,596	4,035	3,596	26,950	27,000	4,349	4,046	4,875	4,046	29,950	30,000	5,189	4,496	5,715	4,496
24,000						**27,000**						**30,000**					
24,000	24,050	3,604	3,604	4,049	3,604	27,000	27,050	4,363	4,054	4,889	4,054	30,000	30,050	5,203	4,504	5,729	4,504
24,050	24,100	3,611	3,611	4,063	3,611	27,050	27,100	4,377	4,061	4,903	4,061	30,050	30,100	5,217	4,511	5,743	4,511
24,100	24,150	3,619	3,619	4,077	3,619	27,100	27,150	4,391	4,069	4,917	4,069	30,100	30,150	5,231	4,519	5,757	4,519
24,150	24,200	3,626	3,626	4,091	3,626	27,150	27,200	4,405	4,076	4,931	4,076	30,150	30,200	5,245	4,526	5,771	4,526
24,200	24,250	3,634	3,634	4,105	3,634	27,200	27,250	4,419	4,084	4,945	4,084	30,200	30,250	5,259	4,534	5,785	4,534
24,250	24,300	3,641	3,641	4,119	3,641	27,250	27,300	4,433	4,091	4,959	4,091	30,250	30,300	5,273	4,541	5,799	4,541
24,300	24,350	3,649	3,649	4,133	3,649	27,300	27,350	4,447	4,099	4,973	4,099	30,300	30,350	5,287	4,549	5,813	4,549
24,350	24,400	3,656	3,656	4,147	3,656	27,350	27,400	4,461	4,106	4,987	4,106	30,350	30,400	5,301	4,556	5,827	4,556
24,400	24,450	3,664	3,664	4,161	3,664	27,400	27,450	4,475	4,114	5,001	4,114	30,400	30,450	5,315	4,564	5,841	4,564
24,450	24,500	3,671	3,671	4,175	3,671	27,450	27,500	4,489	4,121	5,015	4,121	30,450	30,500	5,329	4,571	5,855	4,571
24,500	24,550	3,679	3,679	4,189	3,679	27,500	27,550	4,503	4,129	5,029	4,129	30,500	30,550	5,343	4,579	5,869	4,579
24,550	24,600	3,686	3,686	4,203	3,686	27,550	27,600	4,517	4,136	5,043	4,136	30,550	30,600	5,357	4,586	5,883	4,586
24,600	24,650	3,694	3,694	4,217	3,694	27,600	27,650	4,531	4,144	5,057	4,144	30,600	30,650	5,371	4,594	5,897	4,594
24,650	24,700	3,705	3,701	4,231	3,701	27,650	27,700	4,545	4,151	5,071	4,151	30,650	30,700	5,385	4,601	5,911	4,601
24,700	24,750	3,719	3,709	4,245	3,709	27,700	27,750	4,559	4,159	5,085	4,159	30,700	30,750	5,399	4,609	5,925	4,609
24,750	24,800	3,733	3,716	4,259	3,716	27,750	27,800	4,573	4,166	5,099	4,166	30,750	30,800	5,413	4,616	5,939	4,616
24,800	24,850	3,747	3,724	4,273	3,724	27,800	27,850	4,587	4,174	5,113	4,174	30,800	30,850	5,427	4,624	5,953	4,624
24,850	24,900	3,761	3,731	4,287	3,731	27,850	27,900	4,601	4,181	5,127	4,181	30,850	30,900	5,441	4,631	5,967	4,631
24,900	24,950	3,775	3,739	4,301	3,739	27,900	27,950	4,615	4,189	5,141	4,189	30,900	30,950	5,455	4,639	5,981	4,639
24,950	25,000	3,789	3,746	4,315	3,746	27,950	28,000	4,629	4,196	5,155	4,196	30,950	31,000	5,469	4,646	5,995	4,646
25,000						**28,000**						**31,000**					
25,000	25,050	3,803	3,754	4,329	3,754	28,000	28,050	4,643	4,204	5,169	4,204	31,000	31,050	5,483	4,654	6,009	4,654
25,050	25,100	3,817	3,761	4,343	3,761	28,050	28,100	4,657	4,211	5,183	4,211	31,050	31,100	5,497	4,661	6,023	4,661
25,100	25,150	3,831	3,769	4,357	3,769	28,100	28,150	4,671	4,219	5,197	4,219	31,100	31,150	5,511	4,669	6,037	4,669
25,150	25,200	3,845	3,776	4,371	3,776	28,150	28,200	4,685	4,226	5,211	4,226	31,150	31,200	5,525	4,676	6,051	4,676
25,200	25,250	3,859	3,784	4,385	3,784	28,200	28,250	4,699	4,234	5,225	4,234	31,200	31,250	5,539	4,684	6,065	4,684
25,250	25,300	3,873	3,791	4,399	3,791	28,250	28,300	4,713	4,241	5,239	4,241	31,250	31,300	5,553	4,691	6,079	4,691
25,300	25,350	3,887	3,799	4,413	3,799	28,300	28,350	4,727	4,249	5,253	4,249	31,300	31,350	5,567	4,699	6,093	4,699
25,350	25,400	3,901	3,806	4,427	3,806	28,350	28,400	4,741	4,256	5,267	4,256	31,350	31,400	5,581	4,706	6,107	4,706
25,400	25,450	3,915	3,814	4,441	3,814	28,400	28,450	4,755	4,264	5,281	4,264	31,400	31,450	5,595	4,714	6,121	4,714
25,450	25,500	3,929	3,821	4,455	3,821	28,450	28,500	4,769	4,271	5,295	4,271	31,450	31,500	5,609	4,721	6,135	4,721
25,500	25,550	3,943	3,829	4,469	3,829	28,500	28,550	4,783	4,279	5,309	4,279	31,500	31,550	5,623	4,729	6,149	4,729
25,550	25,600	3,957	3,836	4,483	3,836	28,550	28,600	4,797	4,286	5,323	4,286	31,550	31,600	5,637	4,736	6,163	4,736
25,600	25,650	3,971	3,844	4,497	3,844	28,600	28,650	4,811	4,294	5,337	4,294	31,600	31,650	5,651	4,744	6,177	4,744
25,650	25,700	3,985	3,851	4,511	3,851	28,650	28,700	4,825	4,301	5,351	4,301	31,650	31,700	5,665	4,751	6,191	4,751
25,700	25,750	3,999	3,859	4,525	3,859	28,700	28,750	4,839	4,309	5,365	4,309	31,700	31,750	5,679	4,759	6,205	4,759
25,750	25,800	4,013	3,866	4,539	3,866	28,750	28,800	4,853	4,316	5,379	4,316	31,750	31,800	5,693	4,766	6,219	4,766
25,800	25,850	4,027	3,874	4,553	3,874	28,800	28,850	4,867	4,324	5,393	4,324	31,800	31,850	5,707	4,774	6,233	4,774
25,850	25,900	4,041	3,881	4,567	3,881	28,850	28,900	4,881	4,331	5,407	4,331	31,850	31,900	5,721	4,781	6,247	4,781
25,900	25,950	4,055	3,889	4,581	3,889	28,900	28,950	4,895	4,339	5,421	4,339	31,900	31,950	5,735	4,789	6,261	4,789
25,950	26,000	4,069	3,896	4,595	3,896	28,950	29,000	4,909	4,346	5,435	4,346	31,950	32,000	5,749	4,796	6,275	4,796

* This column must also be used by a qualifying widow(er).

Continued on next page

1997 Tax Table—Continued

If line 38 (taxable income) is—		And you are—				If line 38 (taxable income) is—		And you are—				If line 38 (taxable income) is—		And you are—			
At least	But less than	Single	Married filing jointly *	Married filing separately	Head of a household	At least	But less than	Single	Married filing jointly *	Married filing separately	Head of a household	At least	But less than	Single	Married filing jointly *	Married filing separately	Head of a household
		Your tax is—						Your tax is—						Your tax is—			
32,000						**35,000**						**38,000**					
32,000	32,050	5,763	4,804	6,289	4,804	35,000	35,050	6,603	5,254	7,129	5,511	38,000	38,050	7,443	5,704	7,969	6,351
32,050	32,100	5,777	4,811	6,303	4,811	35,050	35,100	6,617	5,261	7,143	5,525	38,050	38,100	7,457	5,711	7,983	6,365
32,100	32,150	5,791	4,819	6,317	4,819	35,100	35,150	6,631	5,269	7,157	5,539	38,100	38,150	7,471	5,719	7,997	6,379
32,150	32,200	5,805	4,826	6,331	4,826	35,150	35,200	6,645	5,276	7,171	5,553	38,150	38,200	7,485	5,726	8,011	6,393
32,200	32,250	5,819	4,834	6,345	4,834	35,200	35,250	6,659	5,284	7,185	5,567	38,200	38,250	7,499	5,734	8,025	6,407
32,250	32,300	5,833	4,841	6,359	4,841	35,250	35,300	6,673	5,291	7,199	5,581	38,250	38,300	7,513	5,741	8,039	6,421
32,300	32,350	5,847	4,849	6,373	4,849	35,300	35,350	6,687	5,299	7,213	5,595	38,300	38,350	7,527	5,749	8,053	6,435
32,350	32,400	5,861	4,856	6,387	4,856	35,350	35,400	6,701	5,306	7,227	5,609	38,350	38,400	7,541	5,756	8,067	6,449
32,400	32,450	5,875	4,864	6,401	4,864	35,400	35,450	6,715	5,314	7,241	5,623	38,400	38,450	7,555	5,764	8,081	6,463
32,450	32,500	5,889	4,871	6,415	4,871	35,450	35,500	6,729	5,321	7,255	5,637	38,450	38,500	7,569	5,771	8,095	6,477
32,500	32,550	5,903	4,879	6,429	4,879	35,500	35,550	6,743	5,329	7,269	5,651	38,500	38,550	7,583	5,779	8,109	6,491
32,550	32,600	5,917	4,886	6,443	4,886	35,550	35,600	6,757	5,336	7,283	5,665	38,550	38,600	7,597	5,786	8,123	6,505
32,600	32,650	5,931	4,894	6,457	4,894	35,600	35,650	6,771	5,344	7,297	5,679	38,600	38,650	7,611	5,794	8,137	6,519
32,650	32,700	5,945	4,901	6,471	4,901	35,650	35,700	6,785	5,351	7,311	5,693	38,650	38,700	7,625	5,801	8,151	6,533
32,700	32,750	5,959	4,909	6,485	4,909	35,700	35,750	6,799	5,359	7,325	5,707	38,700	38,750	7,639	5,809	8,165	6,547
32,750	32,800	5,973	4,916	6,499	4,916	35,750	35,800	6,813	5,366	7,339	5,721	38,750	38,800	7,653	5,816	8,179	6,561
32,800	32,850	5,987	4,924	6,513	4,924	35,800	35,850	6,827	5,374	7,353	5,735	38,800	38,850	7,667	5,824	8,193	6,575
32,850	32,900	6,001	4,931	6,527	4,931	35,850	35,900	6,841	5,381	7,367	5,749	38,850	38,900	7,681	5,831	8,207	6,589
32,900	32,950	6,015	4,939	6,541	4,939	35,900	35,950	6,855	5,389	7,381	5,763	38,900	38,950	7,695	5,839	8,221	6,603
32,950	33,000	6,029	4,946	6,555	4,946	35,950	36,000	6,869	5,396	7,395	5,777	38,950	39,000	7,709	5,846	8,235	6,617
33,000						**36,000**						**39,000**					
33,000	33,050	6,043	4,954	6,569	4,954	36,000	36,050	6,883	5,404	7,409	5,791	39,000	39,050	7,723	5,854	8,249	6,631
33,050	33,100	6,057	4,961	6,583	4,965	36,050	36,100	6,897	5,411	7,423	5,805	39,050	39,100	7,737	5,861	8,263	6,645
33,100	33,150	6,071	4,969	6,597	4,979	36,100	36,150	6,911	5,419	7,437	5,819	39,100	39,150	7,751	5,869	8,277	6,659
33,150	33,200	6,085	4,976	6,611	4,993	36,150	36,200	6,925	5,426	7,451	5,833	39,150	39,200	7,765	5,876	8,291	6,673
33,200	33,250	6,099	4,984	6,625	5,007	36,200	36,250	6,939	5,434	7,465	5,847	39,200	39,250	7,779	5,884	8,305	6,687
33,250	33,300	6,113	4,991	6,639	5,021	36,250	36,300	6,953	5,441	7,479	5,861	39,250	39,300	7,793	5,891	8,319	6,701
33,300	33,350	6,127	4,999	6,653	5,035	36,300	36,350	6,967	5,449	7,493	5,875	39,300	39,350	7,807	5,899	8,333	6,715
33,350	33,400	6,141	5,006	6,667	5,049	36,350	36,400	6,981	5,456	7,507	5,889	39,350	39,400	7,821	5,906	8,347	6,729
33,400	33,450	6,155	5,014	6,681	5,063	36,400	36,450	6,995	5,464	7,521	5,903	39,400	39,450	7,835	5,914	8,361	6,743
33,450	33,500	6,169	5,021	6,695	5,077	36,450	36,500	7,009	5,471	7,535	5,917	39,450	39,500	7,849	5,921	8,375	6,757
33,500	33,550	6,183	5,029	6,709	5,091	36,500	36,550	7,023	5,479	7,549	5,931	39,500	39,550	7,863	5,929	8,389	6,771
33,550	33,600	6,197	5,036	6,723	5,105	36,550	36,600	7,037	5,486	7,563	5,945	39,550	39,600	7,877	5,936	8,403	6,785
33,600	33,650	6,211	5,044	6,737	5,119	36,600	36,650	7,051	5,494	7,577	5,959	39,600	39,650	7,891	5,944	8,417	6,799
33,650	33,700	6,225	5,051	6,751	5,133	36,650	36,700	7,065	5,501	7,591	5,973	39,650	39,700	7,905	5,951	8,431	6,813
33,700	33,750	6,239	5,059	6,765	5,147	36,700	36,750	7,079	5,509	7,605	5,987	39,700	39,750	7,919	5,959	8,445	6,827
33,750	33,800	6,253	5,066	6,779	5,161	36,750	36,800	7,093	5,516	7,619	6,001	39,750	39,800	7,933	5,966	8,459	6,841
33,800	33,850	6,267	5,074	6,793	5,175	36,800	36,850	7,107	5,524	7,633	6,015	39,800	39,850	7,947	5,974	8,473	6,855
33,850	33,900	6,281	5,081	6,807	5,189	36,850	36,900	7,121	5,531	7,647	6,029	39,850	39,900	7,961	5,981	8,487	6,869
33,900	33,950	6,295	5,089	6,821	5,203	36,900	36,950	7,135	5,539	7,661	6,043	39,900	39,950	7,975	5,989	8,501	6,883
33,950	34,000	6,309	5,096	6,835	5,217	36,950	37,000	7,149	5,546	7,675	6,057	39,950	40,000	7,989	5,996	8,515	6,897
34,000						**37,000**						**40,000**					
34,000	34,050	6,323	5,104	6,849	5,231	37,000	37,050	7,163	5,554	7,689	6,071	40,000	40,050	8,003	6,004	8,529	6,911
34,050	34,100	6,337	5,111	6,863	5,245	37,050	37,100	7,177	5,561	7,703	6,085	40,050	40,100	8,017	6,011	8,543	6,925
34,100	34,150	6,351	5,119	6,877	5,259	37,100	37,150	7,191	5,569	7,717	6,099	40,100	40,150	8,031	6,019	8,557	6,939
34,150	34,200	6,365	5,126	6,891	5,273	37,150	37,200	7,205	5,576	7,731	6,113	40,150	40,200	8,045	6,026	8,571	6,953
34,200	34,250	6,379	5,134	6,905	5,287	37,200	37,250	7,219	5,584	7,745	6,127	40,200	40,250	8,059	6,034	8,585	6,967
34,250	34,300	6,393	5,141	6,919	5,301	37,250	37,300	7,233	5,591	7,759	6,141	40,250	40,300	8,073	6,041	8,599	6,981
34,300	34,350	6,407	5,149	6,933	5,315	37,300	37,350	7,247	5,599	7,773	6,155	40,300	40,350	8,087	6,049	8,613	6,995
34,350	34,400	6,421	5,156	6,947	5,329	37,350	37,400	7,261	5,606	7,787	6,169	40,350	40,400	8,101	6,056	8,627	7,009
34,400	34,450	6,435	5,164	6,961	5,343	37,400	37,450	7,275	5,614	7,801	6,183	40,400	40,450	8,115	6,064	8,641	7,023
34,450	34,500	6,449	5,171	6,975	5,357	37,450	37,500	7,289	5,621	7,815	6,197	40,450	40,500	8,129	6,071	8,655	7,037
34,500	34,550	6,463	5,179	6,989	5,371	37,500	37,550	7,303	5,629	7,829	6,211	40,500	40,550	8,143	6,079	8,669	7,051
34,550	34,600	6,477	5,186	7,003	5,385	37,550	37,600	7,317	5,636	7,843	6,225	40,550	40,600	8,157	6,086	8,683	7,065
34,600	34,650	6,491	5,194	7,017	5,399	37,600	37,650	7,331	5,644	7,857	6,239	40,600	40,650	8,171	6,094	8,697	7,079
34,650	34,700	6,505	5,201	7,031	5,413	37,650	37,700	7,345	5,651	7,871	6,253	40,650	40,700	8,185	6,101	8,711	7,093
34,700	34,750	6,519	5,209	7,045	5,427	37,700	37,750	7,359	5,659	7,885	6,267	40,700	40,750	8,199	6,109	8,725	7,107
34,750	34,800	6,533	5,216	7,059	5,441	37,750	37,800	7,373	5,666	7,899	6,281	40,750	40,800	8,213	6,116	8,739	7,121
34,800	34,850	6,547	5,224	7,073	5,455	37,800	37,850	7,387	5,674	7,913	6,295	40,800	40,850	8,227	6,124	8,753	7,135
34,850	34,900	6,561	5,231	7,087	5,469	37,850	37,900	7,401	5,681	7,927	6,309	40,850	40,900	8,241	6,131	8,767	7,149
34,900	34,950	6,575	5,239	7,101	5,483	37,900	37,950	7,415	5,689	7,941	6,323	40,900	40,950	8,255	6,139	8,781	7,163
34,950	35,000	6,589	5,246	7,115	5,497	37,950	38,000	7,429	5,696	7,955	6,337	40,950	41,000	8,269	6,146	8,795	7,177

* This column must also be used by a qualifying widow(er).

Continued on next page

1997 Tax Table—Continued

If line 38 (taxable income) is—		And you are—				If line 38 (taxable income) is—		And you are—				If line 38 (taxable income) is—		And you are—			
At least	But less than	Single	Married filing jointly *	Married filing separately	Head of a household	At least	But less than	Single	Married filing jointly *	Married filing separately	Head of a household	At least	But less than	Single	Married filing jointly *	Married filing separately	Head of a household
		Your tax is—						Your tax is—						Your tax is—			
41,000						**44,000**						**47,000**					
41,000	41,050	8,283	6,154	8,809	7,191	44,000	44,050	9,123	6,971	9,649	8,031	47,000	47,050	9,963	7,811	10,489	8,871
41,050	41,100	8,297	6,161	8,823	7,205	44,050	44,100	9,137	6,985	9,663	8,045	47,050	47,100	9,977	7,825	10,503	8,885
41,100	41,150	8,311	6,169	8,837	7,219	44,100	44,150	9,151	6,999	9,677	8,059	47,100	47,150	9,991	7,839	10,517	8,899
41,150	41,200	8,325	6,176	8,851	7,233	44,150	44,200	9,165	7,013	9,691	8,073	47,150	47,200	10,005	7,853	10,531	8,913
41,200	41,250	8,339	6,187	8,865	7,247	44,200	44,250	9,179	7,027	9,705	8,087	47,200	47,250	10,019	7,867	10,545	8,927
41,250	41,300	8,353	6,201	8,879	7,261	44,250	44,300	9,193	7,041	9,719	8,101	47,250	47,300	10,033	7,881	10,559	8,941
41,300	41,350	8,367	6,215	8,893	7,275	44,300	44,350	9,207	7,055	9,733	8,115	47,300	47,350	10,047	7,895	10,573	8,955
41,350	41,400	8,381	6,229	8,907	7,289	44,350	44,400	9,221	7,069	9,747	8,129	47,350	47,400	10,061	7,909	10,587	8,969
41,400	41,450	8,395	6,243	8,921	7,303	44,400	44,450	9,235	7,083	9,761	8,143	47,400	47,450	10,075	7,923	10,601	8,983
41,450	41,500	8,409	6,257	8,935	7,317	44,450	44,500	9,249	7,097	9,775	8,157	47,450	47,500	10,089	7,937	10,615	8,997
41,500	41,550	8,423	6,271	8,949	7,331	44,500	44,550	9,263	7,111	9,789	8,171	47,500	47,550	10,103	7,951	10,629	9,011
41,550	41,600	8,437	6,285	8,963	7,345	44,550	44,600	9,277	7,125	9,803	8,185	47,550	47,600	10,117	7,965	10,643	9,025
41,600	41,650	8,451	6,299	8,977	7,359	44,600	44,650	9,291	7,139	9,817	8,199	47,600	47,650	10,131	7,979	10,657	9,039
41,650	41,700	8,465	6,313	8,991	7,373	44,650	44,700	9,305	7,153	9,831	8,213	47,650	47,700	10,145	7,993	10,671	9,053
41,700	41,750	8,479	6,327	9,005	7,387	44,700	44,750	9,319	7,167	9,845	8,227	47,700	47,750	10,159	8,007	10,685	9,067
41,750	41,800	8,493	6,341	9,019	7,401	44,750	44,800	9,333	7,181	9,859	8,241	47,750	47,800	10,173	8,021	10,699	9,081
41,800	41,850	8,507	6,355	9,033	7,415	44,800	44,850	9,347	7,195	9,873	8,255	47,800	47,850	10,187	8,035	10,713	9,095
41,850	41,900	8,521	6,369	9,047	7,429	44,850	44,900	9,361	7,209	9,887	8,269	47,850	47,900	10,201	8,049	10,727	9,109
41,900	41,950	8,535	6,383	9,061	7,443	44,900	44,950	9,375	7,223	9,901	8,283	47,900	47,950	10,215	8,063	10,741	9,123
41,950	42,000	8,549	6,397	9,075	7,457	44,950	45,000	9,389	7,237	9,915	8,297	47,950	48,000	10,229	8,077	10,755	9,137
42,000						**45,000**						**48,000**					
42,000	42,050	8,563	6,411	9,089	7,471	45,000	45,050	9,403	7,251	9,929	8,311	48,000	48,050	10,243	8,091	10,769	9,151
42,050	42,100	8,577	6,425	9,103	7,485	45,050	45,100	9,417	7,265	9,943	8,325	48,050	48,100	10,257	8,105	10,783	9,165
42,100	42,150	8,591	6,439	9,117	7,499	45,100	45,150	9,431	7,279	9,957	8,339	48,100	48,150	10,271	8,119	10,797	9,179
42,150	42,200	8,605	6,453	9,131	7,513	45,150	45,200	9,445	7,293	9,971	8,353	48,150	48,200	10,285	8,133	10,811	9,193
42,200	42,250	8,619	6,467	9,145	7,527	45,200	45,250	9,459	7,307	9,985	8,367	48,200	48,250	10,299	8,147	10,825	9,207
42,250	42,300	8,633	6,481	9,159	7,541	45,250	45,300	9,473	7,321	9,999	8,381	48,250	48,300	10,313	8,161	10,839	9,221
42,300	42,350	8,647	6,495	9,173	7,555	45,300	45,350	9,487	7,335	10,013	8,395	48,300	48,350	10,327	8,175	10,853	9,235
42,350	42,400	8,661	6,509	9,187	7,569	45,350	45,400	9,501	7,349	10,027	8,409	48,350	48,400	10,341	8,189	10,867	9,249
42,400	42,450	8,675	6,523	9,201	7,583	45,400	45,450	9,515	7,363	10,041	8,423	48,400	48,450	10,355	8,203	10,881	9,263
42,450	42,500	8,689	6,537	9,215	7,597	45,450	45,500	9,529	7,377	10,055	8,437	48,450	48,500	10,369	8,217	10,895	9,277
42,500	42,550	8,703	6,551	9,229	7,611	45,500	45,550	9,543	7,391	10,069	8,451	48,500	48,550	10,383	8,231	10,909	9,291
42,550	42,600	8,717	6,565	9,243	7,625	45,550	45,600	9,557	7,405	10,083	8,465	48,550	48,600	10,397	8,245	10,923	9,305
42,600	42,650	8,731	6,579	9,257	7,639	45,600	45,650	9,571	7,419	10,097	8,479	48,600	48,650	10,411	8,259	10,937	9,319
42,650	42,700	8,745	6,593	9,271	7,653	45,650	45,700	9,585	7,433	10,111	8,493	48,650	48,700	10,425	8,273	10,951	9,333
42,700	42,750	8,759	6,607	9,285	7,667	45,700	45,750	9,599	7,447	10,125	8,507	48,700	48,750	10,439	8,287	10,965	9,347
42,750	42,800	8,773	6,621	9,299	7,681	45,750	45,800	9,613	7,461	10,139	8,521	48,750	48,800	10,453	8,301	10,979	9,361
42,800	42,850	8,787	6,635	9,313	7,695	45,800	45,850	9,627	7,475	10,153	8,535	48,800	48,850	10,467	8,315	10,993	9,375
42,850	42,900	8,801	6,649	9,327	7,709	45,850	45,900	9,641	7,489	10,167	8,549	48,850	48,900	10,481	8,329	11,007	9,389
42,900	42,950	8,815	6,663	9,341	7,723	45,900	45,950	9,655	7,503	10,181	8,563	48,900	48,950	10,495	8,343	11,021	9,403
42,950	43,000	8,829	6,677	9,355	7,737	45,950	46,000	9,669	7,517	10,195	8,577	48,950	49,000	10,509	8,357	11,035	9,417
43,000						**46,000**						**49,000**					
43,000	43,050	8,843	6,691	9,369	7,751	46,000	46,050	9,683	7,531	10,209	8,591	49,000	49,050	10,523	8,371	11,049	9,431
43,050	43,100	8,857	6,705	9,383	7,765	46,050	46,100	9,697	7,545	10,223	8,605	49,050	49,100	10,537	8,385	11,063	9,445
43,100	43,150	8,871	6,719	9,397	7,779	46,100	46,150	9,711	7,559	10,237	8,619	49,100	49,150	10,551	8,399	11,077	9,459
43,150	43,200	8,885	6,733	9,411	7,793	46,150	46,200	9,725	7,573	10,251	8,633	49,150	49,200	10,565	8,413	11,091	9,473
43,200	43,250	8,899	6,747	9,425	7,807	46,200	46,250	9,739	7,587	10,265	8,647	49,200	49,250	10,579	8,427	11,105	9,487
43,250	43,300	8,913	6,761	9,439	7,821	46,250	46,300	9,753	7,601	10,279	8,661	49,250	49,300	10,593	8,441	11,119	9,501
43,300	43,350	8,927	6,775	9,453	7,835	46,300	46,350	9,767	7,615	10,293	8,675	49,300	49,350	10,607	8,455	11,133	9,515
43,350	43,400	8,941	6,789	9,467	7,849	46,350	46,400	9,781	7,629	10,307	8,689	49,350	49,400	10,621	8,469	11,147	9,529
43,400	43,450	8,955	6,803	9,481	7,863	46,400	46,450	9,795	7,643	10,321	8,703	49,400	49,450	10,635	8,483	11,161	9,543
43,450	43,500	8,969	6,817	9,495	7,877	46,450	46,500	9,809	7,657	10,335	8,717	49,450	49,500	10,649	8,497	11,175	9,557
43,500	43,550	8,983	6,831	9,509	7,891	46,500	46,550	9,823	7,671	10,349	8,731	49,500	49,550	10,663	8,511	11,189	9,571
43,550	43,600	8,997	6,845	9,523	7,905	46,550	46,600	9,837	7,685	10,363	8,745	49,550	49,600	10,677	8,525	11,203	9,585
43,600	43,650	9,011	6,859	9,537	7,919	46,600	46,650	9,851	7,699	10,377	8,759	49,600	49,650	10,691	8,539	11,217	9,599
43,650	43,700	9,025	6,873	9,551	7,933	46,650	46,700	9,865	7,713	10,391	8,773	49,650	49,700	10,705	8,553	11,231	9,613
43,700	43,750	9,039	6,887	9,565	7,947	46,700	46,750	9,879	7,727	10,405	8,787	49,700	49,750	10,719	8,567	11,245	9,627
43,750	43,800	9,053	6,901	9,579	7,961	46,750	46,800	9,893	7,741	10,419	8,801	49,750	49,800	10,733	8,581	11,259	9,641
43,800	43,850	9,067	6,915	9,593	7,975	46,800	46,850	9,907	7,755	10,433	8,815	49,800	49,850	10,747	8,595	11,274	9,655
43,850	43,900	9,081	6,929	9,607	7,989	46,850	46,900	9,921	7,769	10,447	8,829	49,850	49,900	10,761	8,609	11,289	9,669
43,900	43,950	9,095	6,943	9,621	8,003	46,900	46,950	9,935	7,783	10,461	8,843	49,900	49,950	10,775	8,623	11,305	9,683
43,950	44,000	9,109	6,957	9,635	8,017	46,950	47,000	9,949	7,797	10,475	8,857	49,950	50,000	10,789	8,637	11,320	9,697

* This column must also be used by a qualifying widow(er).

Continued on next page

1997 Tax Table—Continued

If line 38 (taxable income) is—		And you are—				If line 38 (taxable income) is—		And you are—				If line 38 (taxable income) is—		And you are—			
At least	But less than	Single	Married filing jointly *	Married filing separately	Head of a household	At least	But less than	Single	Married filing jointly *	Married filing separately	Head of a household	At least	But less than	Single	Married filing jointly *	Married filing separately	Head of a household
		Your tax is—						Your tax is—						Your tax is—			

50,000

At least	But less than	Single	MFJ	MFS	HoH
50,000	50,050	10,803	8,651	11,336	9,711
50,050	50,100	10,817	8,665	11,351	9,725
50,100	50,150	10,831	8,679	11,367	9,739
50,150	50,200	10,845	8,693	11,382	9,753
50,200	50,250	10,859	8,707	11,398	9,767
50,250	50,300	10,873	8,721	11,413	9,781
50,300	50,350	10,887	8,735	11,429	9,795
50,350	50,400	10,901	8,749	11,444	9,809
50,400	50,450	10,915	8,763	11,460	9,823
50,450	50,500	10,929	8,777	11,475	9,837
50,500	50,550	10,943	8,791	11,491	9,851
50,550	50,600	10,957	8,805	11,506	9,865
50,600	50,650	10,971	8,819	11,522	9,879
50,650	50,700	10,985	8,833	11,537	9,893
50,700	50,750	10,999	8,847	11,553	9,907
50,750	50,800	11,013	8,861	11,568	9,921
50,800	50,850	11,027	8,875	11,584	9,935
50,850	50,900	11,041	8,889	11,599	9,949
50,900	50,950	11,055	8,903	11,615	9,963
50,950	51,000	11,069	8,917	11,630	9,977

51,000

At least	But less than	Single	MFJ	MFS	HoH
51,000	51,050	11,083	8,931	11,646	9,991
51,050	51,100	11,097	8,945	11,661	10,005
51,100	51,150	11,111	8,959	11,677	10,019
51,150	51,200	11,125	8,973	11,692	10,033
51,200	51,250	11,139	8,987	11,708	10,047
51,250	51,300	11,153	9,001	11,723	10,061
51,300	51,350	11,167	9,015	11,739	10,075
51,350	51,400	11,181	9,029	11,754	10,089
51,400	51,450	11,195	9,043	11,770	10,103
51,450	51,500	11,209	9,057	11,785	10,117
51,500	51,550	11,223	9,071	11,801	10,131
51,550	51,600	11,237	9,085	11,816	10,145
51,600	51,650	11,251	9,099	11,832	10,159
51,650	51,700	11,265	9,113	11,847	10,173
51,700	51,750	11,279	9,127	11,863	10,187
51,750	51,800	11,293	9,141	11,878	10,201
51,800	51,850	11,307	9,155	11,894	10,215
51,850	51,900	11,321	9,169	11,909	10,229
51,900	51,950	11,335	9,183	11,925	10,243
51,950	52,000	11,349	9,197	11,940	10,257

52,000

At least	But less than	Single	MFJ	MFS	HoH
52,000	52,050	11,363	9,211	11,956	10,271
52,050	52,100	11,377	9,225	11,971	10,285
52,100	52,150	11,391	9,239	11,987	10,299
52,150	52,200	11,405	9,253	12,002	10,313
52,200	52,250	11,419	9,267	12,018	10,327
52,250	52,300	11,433	9,281	12,033	10,341
52,300	52,350	11,447	9,295	12,049	10,355
52,350	52,400	11,461	9,309	12,064	10,369
52,400	52,450	11,475	9,323	12,080	10,383
52,450	52,500	11,489	9,337	12,095	10,397
52,500	52,550	11,503	9,351	12,111	10,411
52,550	52,600	11,517	9,365	12,126	10,425
52,600	52,650	11,531	9,379	12,142	10,439
52,650	52,700	11,545	9,393	12,157	10,453
52,700	52,750	11,559	9,407	12,173	10,467
52,750	52,800	11,573	9,421	12,188	10,481
52,800	52,850	11,587	9,435	12,204	10,495
52,850	52,900	11,601	9,449	12,219	10,509
52,900	52,950	11,615	9,463	12,235	10,523
52,950	53,000	11,629	9,477	12,250	10,537

53,000

At least	But less than	Single	MFJ	MFS	HoH
53,000	53,050	11,643	9,491	12,266	10,551
53,050	53,100	11,657	9,505	12,281	10,565
53,100	53,150	11,671	9,519	12,297	10,579
53,150	53,200	11,685	9,533	12,312	10,593
53,200	53,250	11,699	9,547	12,328	10,607
53,250	53,300	11,713	9,561	12,343	10,621
53,300	53,350	11,727	9,575	12,359	10,635
53,350	53,400	11,741	9,589	12,374	10,649
53,400	53,450	11,755	9,603	12,390	10,663
53,450	53,500	11,769	9,617	12,405	10,677
53,500	53,550	11,783	9,631	12,421	10,691
53,550	53,600	11,797	9,645	12,436	10,705
53,600	53,650	11,811	9,659	12,452	10,719
53,650	53,700	11,825	9,673	12,467	10,733
53,700	53,750	11,839	9,687	12,483	10,747
53,750	53,800	11,853	9,701	12,498	10,761
53,800	53,850	11,867	9,715	12,514	10,775
53,850	53,900	11,881	9,729	12,529	10,789
53,900	53,950	11,895	9,743	12,545	10,803
53,950	54,000	11,909	9,757	12,560	10,817

54,000

At least	But less than	Single	MFJ	MFS	HoH
54,000	54,050	11,923	9,771	12,576	10,831
54,050	54,100	11,937	9,785	12,591	10,845
54,100	54,150	11,951	9,799	12,607	10,859
54,150	54,200	11,965	9,813	12,622	10,873
54,200	54,250	11,979	9,827	12,638	10,887
54,250	54,300	11,993	9,841	12,653	10,901
54,300	54,350	12,007	9,855	12,669	10,915
54,350	54,400	12,021	9,869	12,684	10,929
54,400	54,450	12,035	9,883	12,700	10,943
54,450	54,500	12,049	9,897	12,715	10,957
54,500	54,550	12,063	9,911	12,731	10,971
54,550	54,600	12,077	9,925	12,746	10,985
54,600	54,650	12,091	9,939	12,762	10,999
54,650	54,700	12,105	9,953	12,777	11,013
54,700	54,750	12,119	9,967	12,793	11,027
54,750	54,800	12,133	9,981	12,808	11,041
54,800	54,850	12,147	9,995	12,824	11,055
54,850	54,900	12,161	10,009	12,839	11,069
54,900	54,950	12,175	10,023	12,855	11,083
54,950	55,000	12,189	10,037	12,870	11,097

55,000

At least	But less than	Single	MFJ	MFS	HoH
55,000	55,050	12,203	10,051	12,886	11,111
55,050	55,100	12,217	10,065	12,901	11,125
55,100	55,150	12,231	10,079	12,917	11,139
55,150	55,200	12,245	10,093	12,932	11,153
55,200	55,250	12,259	10,107	12,948	11,167
55,250	55,300	12,273	10,121	12,963	11,181
55,300	55,350	12,287	10,135	12,979	11,195
55,350	55,400	12,301	10,149	12,994	11,209
55,400	55,450	12,315	10,163	13,010	11,223
55,450	55,500	12,329	10,177	13,025	11,237
55,500	55,550	12,343	10,191	13,041	11,251
55,550	55,600	12,357	10,205	13,056	11,265
55,600	55,650	12,371	10,219	13,072	11,279
55,650	55,700	12,385	10,233	13,087	11,293
55,700	55,750	12,399	10,247	13,103	11,307
55,750	55,800	12,413	10,261	13,118	11,321
55,800	55,850	12,427	10,275	13,134	11,335
55,850	55,900	12,441	10,289	13,149	11,349
55,900	55,950	12,455	10,303	13,165	11,363
55,950	56,000	12,469	10,317	13,180	11,377

56,000

At least	But less than	Single	MFJ	MFS	HoH
56,000	56,050	12,483	10,331	13,196	11,391
56,050	56,100	12,497	10,345	13,211	11,405
56,100	56,150	12,511	10,359	13,227	11,419
56,150	56,200	12,525	10,373	13,242	11,433
56,200	56,250	12,539	10,387	13,258	11,447
56,250	56,300	12,553	10,401	13,273	11,461
56,300	56,350	12,567	10,415	13,289	11,475
56,350	56,400	12,581	10,429	13,304	11,489
56,400	56,450	12,595	10,443	13,320	11,503
56,450	56,500	12,609	10,457	13,335	11,517
56,500	56,550	12,623	10,471	13,351	11,531
56,550	56,600	12,637	10,485	13,366	11,545
56,600	56,650	12,651	10,499	13,382	11,559
56,650	56,700	12,665	10,513	13,397	11,573
56,700	56,750	12,679	10,527	13,413	11,587
56,750	56,800	12,693	10,541	13,428	11,601
56,800	56,850	12,707	10,555	13,444	11,615
56,850	56,900	12,721	10,569	13,459	11,629
56,900	56,950	12,735	10,583	13,475	11,643
56,950	57,000	12,749	10,597	13,490	11,657

57,000

At least	But less than	Single	MFJ	MFS	HoH
57,000	57,050	12,763	10,611	13,506	11,671
57,050	57,100	12,777	10,625	13,521	11,685
57,100	57,150	12,791	10,639	13,537	11,699
57,150	57,200	12,805	10,653	13,552	11,713
57,200	57,250	12,819	10,667	13,568	11,727
57,250	57,300	12,833	10,681	13,583	11,741
57,300	57,350	12,847	10,695	13,599	11,755
57,350	57,400	12,861	10,709	13,614	11,769
57,400	57,450	12,875	10,723	13,630	11,783
57,450	57,500	12,889	10,737	13,645	11,797
57,500	57,550	12,903	10,751	13,661	11,811
57,550	57,600	12,917	10,765	13,676	11,825
57,600	57,650	12,931	10,779	13,692	11,839
57,650	57,700	12,945	10,793	13,707	11,853
57,700	57,750	12,959	10,807	13,723	11,867
57,750	57,800	12,973	10,821	13,738	11,881
57,800	57,850	12,987	10,835	13,754	11,895
57,850	57,900	13,001	10,849	13,769	11,909
57,900	57,950	13,015	10,863	13,785	11,923
57,950	58,000	13,029	10,877	13,800	11,937

58,000

At least	But less than	Single	MFJ	MFS	HoH
58,000	58,050	13,043	10,891	13,816	11,951
58,050	58,100	13,057	10,905	13,831	11,965
58,100	58,150	13,071	10,919	13,847	11,979
58,150	58,200	13,085	10,933	13,862	11,993
58,200	58,250	13,099	10,947	13,878	12,007
58,250	58,300	13,113	10,961	13,893	12,021
58,300	58,350	13,127	10,975	13,909	12,035
58,350	58,400	13,141	10,989	13,924	12,049
58,400	58,450	13,155	11,003	13,940	12,063
58,450	58,500	13,169	11,017	13,955	12,077
58,500	58,550	13,183	11,031	13,971	12,091
58,550	58,600	13,197	11,045	13,986	12,105
58,600	58,650	13,211	11,059	14,002	12,119
58,650	58,700	13,225	11,073	14,017	12,133
58,700	58,750	13,239	11,087	14,033	12,147
58,750	58,800	13,253	11,101	14,048	12,161
58,800	58,850	13,267	11,115	14,064	12,175
58,850	58,900	13,281	11,129	14,079	12,189
58,900	58,950	13,295	11,143	14,095	12,203
58,950	59,000	13,309	11,157	14,110	12,217

* This column must also be used by a qualifying widow(er).

Continued on next page

1997 Tax Table—Continued

If line 38 (taxable income) is—		And you are—				If line 38 (taxable income) is—		And you are—				If line 38 (taxable income) is—		And you are—			
At least	But less than	Single	Married filing jointly *	Married filing separately	Head of a household	At least	But less than	Single	Married filing jointly *	Married filing separately	Head of a household	At least	But less than	Single	Married filing jointly *	Married filing separately	Head of a household
		Your tax is—						Your tax is—						Your tax is—			
59,000						**62,000**						**65,000**					
59,000	59,050	13,323	11,171	14,126	12,231	62,000	62,050	14,231	12,011	15,056	13,071	65,000	65,050	15,161	12,851	15,986	13,911
59,050	59,100	13,337	11,185	14,141	12,245	62,050	62,100	14,246	12,025	15,071	13,085	65,050	65,100	15,176	12,865	16,001	13,925
59,100	59,150	13,351	11,199	14,157	12,259	62,100	62,150	14,262	12,039	15,087	13,099	65,100	65,150	15,192	12,879	16,017	13,939
59,150	59,200	13,365	11,213	14,172	12,273	62,150	62,200	14,277	12,053	15,102	13,113	65,150	65,200	15,207	12,893	16,032	13,953
59,200	59,250	13,379	11,227	14,188	12,287	62,200	62,250	14,293	12,067	15,118	13,127	65,200	65,250	15,223	12,907	16,048	13,967
59,250	59,300	13,393	11,241	14,203	12,301	62,250	62,300	14,308	12,081	15,133	13,141	65,250	65,300	15,238	12,921	16,063	13,981
59,300	59,350	13,407	11,255	14,219	12,315	62,300	62,350	14,324	12,095	15,149	13,155	65,300	65,350	15,254	12,935	16,079	13,995
59,350	59,400	13,421	11,269	14,234	12,329	62,350	62,400	14,339	12,109	15,164	13,169	65,350	65,400	15,269	12,949	16,094	14,009
59,400	59,450	13,435	11,283	14,250	12,343	62,400	62,450	14,355	12,123	15,180	13,183	65,400	65,450	15,285	12,963	16,110	14,023
59,450	59,500	13,449	11,297	14,265	12,357	62,450	62,500	14,370	12,137	15,195	13,197	65,450	65,500	15,300	12,977	16,125	14,037
59,500	59,550	13,463	11,311	14,281	12,371	62,500	62,550	14,386	12,151	15,211	13,211	65,500	65,550	15,316	12,991	16,141	14,051
59,550	59,600	13,477	11,325	14,296	12,385	62,550	62,600	14,401	12,165	15,226	13,225	65,550	65,600	15,331	13,005	16,156	14,065
59,600	59,650	13,491	11,339	14,312	12,399	62,600	62,650	14,417	12,179	15,242	13,239	65,600	65,650	15,347	13,019	16,172	14,079
59,650	59,700	13,505	11,353	14,327	12,413	62,650	62,700	14,432	12,193	15,257	13,253	65,650	65,700	15,362	13,033	16,187	14,093
59,700	59,750	13,519	11,367	14,343	12,427	62,700	62,750	14,448	12,207	15,273	13,267	65,700	65,750	15,378	13,047	16,203	14,107
59,750	59,800	13,533	11,381	14,358	12,441	62,750	62,800	14,463	12,221	15,288	13,281	65,750	65,800	15,393	13,061	16,218	14,121
59,800	59,850	13,549	11,395	14,374	12,455	62,800	62,850	14,479	12,235	15,304	13,295	65,800	65,850	15,409	13,075	16,234	14,135
59,850	59,900	13,564	11,409	14,389	12,469	62,850	62,900	14,494	12,249	15,319	13,309	65,850	65,900	15,424	13,089	16,249	14,149
59,900	59,950	13,580	11,423	14,405	12,483	62,900	62,950	14,510	12,263	15,335	13,323	65,900	65,950	15,440	13,103	16,265	14,163
59,950	60,000	13,595	11,437	14,420	12,497	62,950	63,000	14,525	12,277	15,350	13,337	65,950	66,000	15,455	13,117	16,280	14,177
60,000						**63,000**						**66,000**					
60,000	60,050	13,611	11,451	14,436	12,511	63,000	63,050	14,541	12,291	15,366	13,351	66,000	66,050	15,471	13,131	16,296	14,191
60,050	60,100	13,626	11,465	14,451	12,525	63,050	63,100	14,556	12,305	15,381	13,365	66,050	66,100	15,486	13,145	16,311	14,205
60,100	60,150	13,642	11,479	14,467	12,539	63,100	63,150	14,572	12,319	15,397	13,379	66,100	66,150	15,502	13,159	16,327	14,219
60,150	60,200	13,657	11,493	14,482	12,553	63,150	63,200	14,587	12,333	15,412	13,393	66,150	66,200	15,517	13,173	16,342	14,233
60,200	60,250	13,673	11,507	14,498	12,567	63,200	63,250	14,603	12,347	15,428	13,407	66,200	66,250	15,533	13,187	16,358	14,247
60,250	60,300	13,688	11,521	14,513	12,581	63,250	63,300	14,618	12,361	15,443	13,421	66,250	66,300	15,548	13,201	16,373	14,261
60,300	60,350	13,704	11,535	14,529	12,595	63,300	63,350	14,634	12,375	15,459	13,435	66,300	66,350	15,564	13,215	16,389	14,275
60,350	60,400	13,719	11,549	14,544	12,609	63,350	63,400	14,649	12,389	15,474	13,449	66,350	66,400	15,579	13,229	16,404	14,289
60,400	60,450	13,735	11,563	14,560	12,623	63,400	63,450	14,665	12,403	15,490	13,463	66,400	66,450	15,595	13,243	16,420	14,303
60,450	60,500	13,750	11,577	14,575	12,637	63,450	63,500	14,680	12,417	15,505	13,477	66,450	66,500	15,610	13,257	16,435	14,317
60,500	60,550	13,766	11,591	14,591	12,651	63,500	63,550	14,696	12,431	15,521	13,491	66,500	66,550	15,626	13,271	16,451	14,331
60,550	60,600	13,781	11,605	14,606	12,665	63,550	63,600	14,711	12,445	15,536	13,505	66,550	66,600	15,641	13,285	16,466	14,345
60,600	60,650	13,797	11,619	14,622	12,679	63,600	63,650	14,727	12,459	15,552	13,519	66,600	66,650	15,657	13,299	16,482	14,359
60,650	60,700	13,812	11,633	14,637	12,693	63,650	63,700	14,742	12,473	15,567	13,533	66,650	66,700	15,672	13,313	16,497	14,373
60,700	60,750	13,828	11,647	14,653	12,707	63,700	63,750	14,758	12,487	15,583	13,547	66,700	66,750	15,688	13,327	16,513	14,387
60,750	60,800	13,843	11,661	14,668	12,721	63,750	63,800	14,773	12,501	15,598	13,561	66,750	66,800	15,703	13,341	16,528	14,401
60,800	60,850	13,859	11,675	14,684	12,735	63,800	63,850	14,789	12,515	15,614	13,575	66,800	66,850	15,719	13,355	16,544	14,415
60,850	60,900	13,874	11,689	14,699	12,749	63,850	63,900	14,804	12,529	15,629	13,589	66,850	66,900	15,734	13,369	16,559	14,429
60,900	60,950	13,890	11,703	14,715	12,763	63,900	63,950	14,820	12,543	15,645	13,603	66,900	66,950	15,750	13,383	16,575	14,443
60,950	61,000	13,905	11,717	14,730	12,777	63,950	64,000	14,835	12,557	15,660	13,617	66,950	67,000	15,765	13,397	16,590	14,457
61,000						**64,000**						**67,000**					
61,000	61,050	13,921	11,731	14,746	12,791	64,000	64,050	14,851	12,571	15,676	13,631	67,000	67,050	15,781	13,411	16,606	14,471
61,050	61,100	13,936	11,745	14,761	12,805	64,050	64,100	14,866	12,585	15,691	13,645	67,050	67,100	15,796	13,425	16,621	14,485
61,100	61,150	13,952	11,759	14,777	12,819	64,100	64,150	14,882	12,599	15,707	13,659	67,100	67,150	15,812	13,439	16,637	14,499
61,150	61,200	13,967	11,773	14,792	12,833	64,150	64,200	14,897	12,613	15,722	13,673	67,150	67,200	15,827	13,453	16,652	14,513
61,200	61,250	13,983	11,787	14,808	12,847	64,200	64,250	14,913	12,627	15,738	13,687	67,200	67,250	15,843	13,467	16,668	14,527
61,250	61,300	13,998	11,801	14,823	12,861	64,250	64,300	14,928	12,641	15,753	13,701	67,250	67,300	15,858	13,481	16,683	14,541
61,300	61,350	14,014	11,815	14,839	12,875	64,300	64,350	14,944	12,655	15,769	13,715	67,300	67,350	15,874	13,495	16,699	14,555
61,350	61,400	14,029	11,829	14,854	12,889	64,350	64,400	14,959	12,669	15,784	13,729	67,350	67,400	15,889	13,509	16,714	14,569
61,400	61,450	14,045	11,843	14,870	12,903	64,400	64,450	14,975	12,683	15,800	13,743	67,400	67,450	15,905	13,523	16,730	14,583
61,450	61,500	14,060	11,857	14,885	12,917	64,450	64,500	14,990	12,697	15,815	13,757	67,450	67,500	15,920	13,537	16,745	14,597
61,500	61,550	14,076	11,871	14,901	12,931	64,500	64,550	15,006	12,711	15,831	13,771	67,500	67,550	15,936	13,551	16,761	14,611
61,550	61,600	14,091	11,885	14,916	12,945	64,550	64,600	15,021	12,725	15,846	13,785	67,550	67,600	15,951	13,565	16,776	14,625
61,600	61,650	14,107	11,899	14,932	12,959	64,600	64,650	15,037	12,739	15,862	13,799	67,600	67,650	15,967	13,579	16,792	14,639
61,650	61,700	14,122	11,913	14,947	12,973	64,650	64,700	15,052	12,753	15,877	13,813	67,650	67,700	15,982	13,593	16,807	14,653
61,700	61,750	14,138	11,927	14,963	12,987	64,700	64,750	15,068	12,767	15,893	13,827	67,700	67,750	15,998	13,607	16,823	14,667
61,750	61,800	14,153	11,941	14,978	13,001	64,750	64,800	15,083	12,781	15,908	13,841	67,750	67,800	16,013	13,621	16,838	14,681
61,800	61,850	14,169	11,955	14,994	13,015	64,800	64,850	15,099	12,795	15,924	13,855	67,800	67,850	16,029	13,635	16,854	14,695
61,850	61,900	14,184	11,969	15,009	13,029	64,850	64,900	15,114	12,809	15,939	13,869	67,850	67,900	16,044	13,649	16,869	14,709
61,900	61,950	14,200	11,983	15,025	13,043	64,900	64,950	15,130	12,823	15,955	13,883	67,900	67,950	16,060	13,663	16,885	14,723
61,950	62,000	14,215	11,997	15,040	13,057	64,950	65,000	15,145	12,837	15,970	13,897	67,950	68,000	16,075	13,677	16,900	14,737

* This column must also be used by a qualifying widow(er).

Continued on next page

1997 Tax Table — *Continued*

If line 38 (taxable income) is—		And you are—				If line 38 (taxable income) is—		And you are—				If line 38 (taxable income) is—		And you are—			
At least	But less than	Single	Married filing jointly *	Married filing separately	Head of a house-hold	At least	But less than	Single	Married filing jointly *	Married filing separately	Head of a house-hold	At least	But less than	Single	Married filing jointly *	Married filing separately	Head of a house-hold
		Your tax is—						Your tax is—						Your tax is—			
68,000						**71,000**						**74,000**					
68,000	68,050	16,091	13,691	16,916	14,751	71,000	71,050	17,021	14,531	17,846	15,591	74,000	74,050	17,951	15,371	18,776	16,431
68,050	68,100	16,106	13,705	16,931	14,765	71,050	71,100	17,036	14,545	17,861	15,605	74,050	74,100	17,966	15,385	18,791	16,445
68,100	68,150	16,122	13,719	16,947	14,779	71,100	71,150	17,052	14,559	17,877	15,619	74,100	74,150	17,982	15,399	18,807	16,459
68,150	68,200	16,137	13,733	16,962	14,793	71,150	71,200	17,067	14,573	17,892	15,633	74,150	74,200	17,997	15,413	18,822	16,473
68,200	68,250	16,153	13,747	16,978	14,807	71,200	71,250	17,083	14,587	17,908	15,647	74,200	74,250	18,013	15,427	18,838	16,487
68,250	68,300	16,168	13,761	16,993	14,821	71,250	71,300	17,098	14,601	17,923	15,661	74,250	74,300	18,028	15,441	18,853	16,501
68,300	68,350	16,184	13,775	17,009	14,835	71,300	71,350	17,114	14,615	17,939	15,675	74,300	74,350	18,044	15,455	18,869	16,515
68,350	68,400	16,199	13,789	17,024	14,849	71,350	71,400	17,129	14,629	17,954	15,689	74,350	74,400	18,059	15,469	18,884	16,529
68,400	68,450	16,215	13,803	17,040	14,863	71,400	71,450	17,145	14,643	17,970	15,703	74,400	74,450	18,075	15,483	18,900	16,543
68,450	68,500	16,230	13,817	17,055	14,877	71,450	71,500	17,160	14,657	17,985	15,717	74,450	74,500	18,090	15,497	18,915	16,557
68,500	68,550	16,246	13,831	17,071	14,891	71,500	71,550	17,176	14,671	18,001	15,731	74,500	74,550	18,106	15,511	18,931	16,571
68,550	68,600	16,261	13,845	17,086	14,905	71,550	71,600	17,191	14,685	18,016	15,745	74,550	74,600	18,121	15,525	18,946	16,585
68,600	68,650	16,277	13,859	17,102	14,919	71,600	71,650	17,207	14,699	18,032	15,759	74,600	74,650	18,137	15,539	18,962	16,599
68,650	68,700	16,292	13,873	17,117	14,933	71,650	71,700	17,222	14,713	18,047	15,773	74,650	74,700	18,152	15,553	18,977	16,613
68,700	68,750	16,308	13,887	17,133	14,947	71,700	71,750	17,238	14,727	18,063	15,787	74,700	74,750	18,168	15,567	18,993	16,627
68,750	68,800	16,323	13,901	17,148	14,961	71,750	71,800	17,253	14,741	18,078	15,801	74,750	74,800	18,183	15,581	19,008	16,641
68,800	68,850	16,339	13,915	17,164	14,975	71,800	71,850	17,269	14,755	18,094	15,815	74,800	74,850	18,199	15,595	19,024	16,655
68,850	68,900	16,354	13,929	17,179	14,989	71,850	71,900	17,284	14,769	18,109	15,829	74,850	74,900	18,214	15,609	19,039	16,669
68,900	68,950	16,370	13,943	17,195	15,003	71,900	71,950	17,300	14,783	18,125	15,843	74,900	74,950	18,230	15,623	19,055	16,683
68,950	69,000	16,385	13,957	17,210	15,017	71,950	72,000	17,315	14,797	18,140	15,857	74,950	75,000	18,245	15,637	19,070	16,697
69,000						**72,000**						**75,000**					
69,000	69,050	16,401	13,971	17,226	15,031	72,000	72,050	17,331	14,811	18,156	15,871	75,000	75,050	18,261	15,651	19,086	16,711
69,050	69,100	16,416	13,985	17,241	15,045	72,050	72,100	17,346	14,825	18,171	15,885	75,050	75,100	18,276	15,665	19,101	16,725
69,100	69,150	16,432	13,999	17,257	15,059	72,100	72,150	17,362	14,839	18,187	15,899	75,100	75,150	18,292	15,679	19,117	16,739
69,150	69,200	16,447	14,013	17,272	15,073	72,150	72,200	17,377	14,853	18,202	15,913	75,150	75,200	18,307	15,693	19,132	16,753
69,200	69,250	16,463	14,027	17,288	15,087	72,200	72,250	17,393	14,867	18,218	15,927	75,200	75,250	18,323	15,707	19,148	16,767
69,250	69,300	16,478	14,041	17,303	15,101	72,250	72,300	17,408	14,881	18,233	15,941	75,250	75,300	18,338	15,721	19,163	16,781
69,300	69,350	16,494	14,055	17,319	15,115	72,300	72,350	17,424	14,895	18,249	15,955	75,300	75,350	18,354	15,735	19,179	16,795
69,350	69,400	16,509	14,069	17,334	15,129	72,350	72,400	17,439	14,909	18,264	15,969	75,350	75,400	18,369	15,749	19,194	16,809
69,400	69,450	16,525	14,083	17,350	15,143	72,400	72,450	17,455	14,923	18,280	15,983	75,400	75,450	18,385	15,763	19,210	16,823
69,450	69,500	16,540	14,097	17,365	15,157	72,450	72,500	17,470	14,937	18,295	15,997	75,450	75,500	18,400	15,777	19,225	16,837
69,500	69,550	16,556	14,111	17,381	15,171	72,500	72,550	17,486	14,951	18,311	16,011	75,500	75,550	18,416	15,791	19,241	16,851
69,550	69,600	16,571	14,125	17,396	15,185	72,550	72,600	17,501	14,965	18,326	16,025	75,550	75,600	18,431	15,805	19,256	16,865
69,600	69,650	16,587	14,139	17,412	15,199	72,600	72,650	17,517	14,979	18,342	16,039	75,600	75,650	18,447	15,819	19,272	16,879
69,650	69,700	16,602	14,153	17,427	15,213	72,650	72,700	17,532	14,993	18,357	16,053	75,650	75,700	18,462	15,833	19,287	16,893
69,700	69,750	16,618	14,167	17,443	15,227	72,700	72,750	17,548	15,007	18,373	16,067	75,700	75,750	18,478	15,847	19,303	16,907
69,750	69,800	16,633	14,181	17,458	15,241	72,750	72,800	17,563	15,021	18,388	16,081	75,750	75,800	18,493	15,861	19,318	16,921
69,800	69,850	16,649	14,195	17,474	15,255	72,800	72,850	17,579	15,035	18,404	16,095	75,800	75,850	18,509	15,875	19,334	16,935
69,850	69,900	16,664	14,209	17,489	15,269	72,850	72,900	17,594	15,049	18,419	16,109	75,850	75,900	18,524	15,889	19,349	16,949
69,900	69,950	16,680	14,223	17,505	15,283	72,900	72,950	17,610	15,063	18,435	16,123	75,900	75,950	18,540	15,903	19,367	16,963
69,950	70,000	16,695	14,237	17,520	15,297	72,950	73,000	17,625	15,077	18,450	16,137	75,950	76,000	18,555	15,917	19,385	16,977
70,000						**73,000**						**76,000**					
70,000	70,050	16,711	14,251	17,536	15,311	73,000	73,050	17,641	15,091	18,466	16,151	76,000	76,050	18,571	15,931	19,403	16,991
70,050	70,100	16,726	14,265	17,551	15,325	73,050	73,100	17,656	15,105	18,481	16,165	76,050	76,100	18,586	15,945	19,421	17,005
70,100	70,150	16,742	14,279	17,567	15,339	73,100	73,150	17,672	15,119	18,497	16,179	76,100	76,150	18,602	15,959	19,439	17,019
70,150	70,200	16,757	14,293	17,582	15,353	73,150	73,200	17,687	15,133	18,512	16,193	76,150	76,200	18,617	15,973	19,457	17,033
70,200	70,250	16,773	14,307	17,598	15,367	73,200	73,250	17,703	15,147	18,528	16,207	76,200	76,250	18,633	15,987	19,475	17,047
70,250	70,300	16,788	14,321	17,613	15,381	73,250	73,300	17,718	15,161	18,543	16,221	76,250	76,300	18,648	16,001	19,493	17,061
70,300	70,350	16,804	14,335	17,629	15,395	73,300	73,350	17,734	15,175	18,559	16,235	76,300	76,350	18,664	16,015	19,511	17,075
70,350	70,400	16,819	14,349	17,644	15,409	73,350	73,400	17,749	15,189	18,574	16,249	76,350	76,400	18,679	16,029	19,529	17,089
70,400	70,450	16,835	14,363	17,660	15,423	73,400	73,450	17,765	15,203	18,590	16,263	76,400	76,450	18,695	16,043	19,547	17,103
70,450	70,500	16,850	14,377	17,675	15,437	73,450	73,500	17,780	15,217	18,605	16,277	76,450	76,500	18,710	16,057	19,565	17,117
70,500	70,550	16,866	14,391	17,691	15,451	73,500	73,550	17,796	15,231	18,621	16,291	76,500	76,550	18,726	16,071	19,583	17,131
70,550	70,600	16,881	14,405	17,706	15,465	73,550	73,600	17,811	15,245	18,636	16,305	76,550	76,600	18,741	16,085	19,601	17,145
70,600	70,650	16,897	14,419	17,722	15,479	73,600	73,650	17,827	15,259	18,652	16,319	76,600	76,650	18,757	16,099	19,619	17,159
70,650	70,700	16,912	14,433	17,737	15,493	73,650	73,700	17,842	15,273	18,667	16,333	76,650	76,700	18,772	16,113	19,637	17,173
70,700	70,750	16,928	14,447	17,753	15,507	73,700	73,750	17,858	15,287	18,683	16,347	76,700	76,750	18,788	16,127	19,655	17,187
70,750	70,800	16,943	14,461	17,768	15,521	73,750	73,800	17,873	15,301	18,698	16,361	76,750	76,800	18,803	16,141	19,673	17,201
70,800	70,850	16,959	14,475	17,784	15,535	73,800	73,850	17,889	15,315	18,714	16,375	76,800	76,850	18,819	16,155	19,691	17,215
70,850	70,900	16,974	14,489	17,799	15,549	73,850	73,900	17,904	15,329	18,729	16,389	76,850	76,900	18,834	16,169	19,709	17,229
70,900	70,950	16,990	14,503	17,815	15,563	73,900	73,950	17,920	15,343	18,745	16,403	76,900	76,950	18,850	16,183	19,727	17,243
70,950	71,000	17,005	14,517	17,830	15,577	73,950	74,000	17,935	15,357	18,760	16,417	76,950	77,000	18,865	16,197	19,745	17,257

* This column must also be used by a qualifying widow(er).

Continued on next page

1997 Tax Table—Continued

If line 38 (taxable income) is—		And you are—				If line 38 (taxable income) is—		And you are—				If line 38 (taxable income) is—		And you are—			
At least	But less than	Single	Married filing jointly *	Married filing separately	Head of a household	At least	But less than	Single	Married filing jointly *	Married filing separately	Head of a household	At least	But less than	Single	Married filing jointly *	Married filing separately	Head of a household
		Your tax is—						Your tax is—						Your tax is—			
77,000						**80,000**						**83,000**					
77,000	77,050	18,881	16,211	19,763	17,271	80,000	80,050	19,811	17,051	20,843	18,111	83,000	83,050	20,741	17,891	21,923	18,951
77,050	77,100	18,896	16,225	19,781	17,285	80,050	80,100	19,826	17,065	20,861	18,125	83,050	83,100	20,756	17,905	21,941	18,965
77,100	77,150	18,912	16,239	19,799	17,299	80,100	80,150	19,842	17,079	20,879	18,139	83,100	83,150	20,772	17,919	21,959	18,979
77,150	77,200	18,927	16,253	19,817	17,313	80,150	80,200	19,857	17,093	20,897	18,153	83,150	83,200	20,787	17,933	21,977	18,993
77,200	77,250	18,943	16,267	19,835	17,327	80,200	80,250	19,873	17,107	20,915	18,167	83,200	83,250	20,803	17,947	21,995	19,007
77,250	77,300	18,958	16,281	19,853	17,341	80,250	80,300	19,888	17,121	20,933	18,181	83,250	83,300	20,818	17,961	22,013	19,021
77,300	77,350	18,974	16,295	19,871	17,355	80,300	80,350	19,904	17,135	20,951	18,195	83,300	83,350	20,834	17,975	22,031	19,035
77,350	77,400	18,989	16,309	19,889	17,369	80,350	80,400	19,919	17,149	20,969	18,209	83,350	83,400	20,849	17,989	22,049	19,049
77,400	77,450	19,005	16,323	19,907	17,383	80,400	80,450	19,935	17,163	20,987	18,223	83,400	83,450	20,865	18,003	22,067	19,063
77,450	77,500	19,020	16,337	19,925	17,397	80,450	80,500	19,950	17,177	21,005	18,237	83,450	83,500	20,880	18,017	22,085	19,077
77,500	77,550	19,036	16,351	19,943	17,411	80,500	80,550	19,966	17,191	21,023	18,251	83,500	83,550	20,896	18,031	22,103	19,091
77,550	77,600	19,051	16,365	19,961	17,425	80,550	80,600	19,981	17,205	21,041	18,265	83,550	83,600	20,911	18,045	22,121	19,105
77,600	77,650	19,067	16,379	19,979	17,439	80,600	80,650	19,997	17,219	21,059	18,279	83,600	83,650	20,927	18,059	22,139	19,119
77,650	77,700	19,082	16,393	19,997	17,453	80,650	80,700	20,012	17,233	21,077	18,293	83,650	83,700	20,942	18,073	22,157	19,133
77,700	77,750	19,098	16,407	20,015	17,467	80,700	80,750	20,028	17,247	21,095	18,307	83,700	83,750	20,958	18,087	22,175	19,147
77,750	77,800	19,113	16,421	20,033	17,481	80,750	80,800	20,043	17,261	21,113	18,321	83,750	83,800	20,973	18,101	22,193	19,161
77,800	77,850	19,129	16,435	20,051	17,495	80,800	80,850	20,059	17,275	21,131	18,335	83,800	83,850	20,989	18,115	22,211	19,175
77,850	77,900	19,144	16,449	20,069	17,509	80,850	80,900	20,074	17,289	21,149	18,349	83,850	83,900	21,004	18,129	22,229	19,189
77,900	77,950	19,160	16,463	20,087	17,523	80,900	80,950	20,090	17,303	21,167	18,363	83,900	83,950	21,020	18,143	22,247	19,203
77,950	78,000	19,175	16,477	20,105	17,537	80,950	81,000	20,105	17,317	21,185	18,377	83,950	84,000	21,035	18,157	22,265	19,217
78,000						**81,000**						**84,000**					
78,000	78,050	19,191	16,491	20,123	17,551	81,000	81,050	20,121	17,331	21,203	18,391	84,000	84,050	21,051	18,171	22,283	19,231
78,050	78,100	19,206	16,505	20,141	17,565	81,050	81,100	20,136	17,345	21,221	18,405	84,050	84,100	21,066	18,185	22,301	19,245
78,100	78,150	19,222	16,519	20,159	17,579	81,100	81,150	20,152	17,359	21,239	18,419	84,100	84,150	21,082	18,199	22,319	19,259
78,150	78,200	19,237	16,533	20,177	17,593	81,150	81,200	20,167	17,373	21,257	18,433	84,150	84,200	21,097	18,213	22,337	19,273
78,200	78,250	19,253	16,547	20,195	17,607	81,200	81,250	20,183	17,387	21,275	18,447	84,200	84,250	21,113	18,227	22,355	19,287
78,250	78,300	19,268	16,561	20,213	17,621	81,250	81,300	20,198	17,401	21,293	18,461	84,250	84,300	21,128	18,241	22,373	19,301
78,300	78,350	19,284	16,575	20,231	17,635	81,300	81,350	20,214	17,415	21,311	18,475	84,300	84,350	21,144	18,255	22,391	19,315
78,350	78,400	19,299	16,589	20,249	17,649	81,350	81,400	20,229	17,429	21,329	18,489	84,350	84,400	21,159	18,269	22,409	19,329
78,400	78,450	19,315	16,603	20,267	17,663	81,400	81,450	20,245	17,443	21,347	18,503	84,400	84,450	21,175	18,283	22,427	19,343
78,450	78,500	19,330	16,617	20,285	17,677	81,450	81,500	20,260	17,457	21,365	18,517	84,450	84,500	21,190	18,297	22,445	19,357
78,500	78,550	19,346	16,631	20,303	17,691	81,500	81,550	20,276	17,471	21,383	18,531	84,500	84,550	21,206	18,311	22,463	19,371
78,550	78,600	19,361	16,645	20,321	17,705	81,550	81,600	20,291	17,485	21,401	18,545	84,550	84,600	21,221	18,325	22,481	19,385
78,600	78,650	19,377	16,659	20,339	17,719	81,600	81,650	20,307	17,499	21,419	18,559	84,600	84,650	21,237	18,339	22,499	19,399
78,650	78,700	19,392	16,673	20,357	17,733	81,650	81,700	20,322	17,513	21,437	18,573	84,650	84,700	21,252	18,353	22,517	19,413
78,700	78,750	19,408	16,687	20,375	17,747	81,700	81,750	20,338	17,527	21,455	18,587	84,700	84,750	21,268	18,367	22,535	19,427
78,750	78,800	19,423	16,701	20,393	17,761	81,750	81,800	20,353	17,541	21,473	18,601	84,750	84,800	21,283	18,381	22,553	19,441
78,800	78,850	19,439	16,715	20,411	17,775	81,800	81,850	20,369	17,555	21,491	18,615	84,800	84,850	21,299	18,395	22,571	19,455
78,850	78,900	19,454	16,729	20,429	17,789	81,850	81,900	20,384	17,569	21,509	18,629	84,850	84,900	21,314	18,409	22,589	19,469
78,900	78,950	19,470	16,743	20,447	17,803	81,900	81,950	20,400	17,583	21,527	18,643	84,900	84,950	21,330	18,423	22,607	19,483
78,950	79,000	19,485	16,757	20,465	17,817	81,950	82,000	20,415	17,597	21,545	18,657	84,950	85,000	21,345	18,437	22,625	19,497
79,000						**82,000**						**85,000**					
79,000	79,050	19,501	16,771	20,483	17,831	82,000	82,050	20,431	17,611	21,563	18,671	85,000	85,050	21,361	18,451	22,643	19,511
79,050	79,100	19,516	16,785	20,501	17,845	82,050	82,100	20,446	17,625	21,581	18,685	85,050	85,100	21,376	18,465	22,661	19,525
79,100	79,150	19,532	16,799	20,519	17,859	82,100	82,150	20,462	17,639	21,599	18,699	85,100	85,150	21,392	18,479	22,679	19,539
79,150	79,200	19,547	16,813	20,537	17,873	82,150	82,200	20,477	17,653	21,617	18,713	85,150	85,200	21,407	18,493	22,697	19,553
79,200	79,250	19,563	16,827	20,555	17,887	82,200	82,250	20,493	17,667	21,635	18,727	85,200	85,250	21,423	18,507	22,715	19,567
79,250	79,300	19,578	16,841	20,573	17,901	82,250	82,300	20,508	17,681	21,653	18,741	85,250	85,300	21,438	18,521	22,733	19,581
79,300	79,350	19,594	16,855	20,591	17,915	82,300	82,350	20,524	17,695	21,671	18,755	85,300	85,350	21,454	18,535	22,751	19,595
79,350	79,400	19,609	16,869	20,609	17,929	82,350	82,400	20,539	17,709	21,689	18,769	85,350	85,400	21,469	18,549	22,769	19,609
79,400	79,450	19,625	16,883	20,627	17,943	82,400	82,450	20,555	17,723	21,707	18,783	85,400	85,450	21,485	18,563	22,787	19,625
79,450	79,500	19,640	16,897	20,645	17,957	82,450	82,500	20,570	17,737	21,725	18,797	85,450	85,500	21,500	18,577	22,805	19,640
79,500	79,550	19,656	16,911	20,663	17,971	82,500	82,550	20,586	17,751	21,743	18,811	85,500	85,550	21,516	18,591	22,823	19,656
79,550	79,600	19,671	16,925	20,681	17,985	82,550	82,600	20,601	17,765	21,761	18,825	85,550	85,600	21,531	18,605	22,841	19,671
79,600	79,650	19,687	16,939	20,699	17,999	82,600	82,650	20,617	17,779	21,779	18,839	85,600	85,650	21,547	18,619	22,859	19,687
79,650	79,700	19,702	16,953	20,717	18,013	82,650	82,700	20,632	17,793	21,797	18,853	85,650	85,700	21,562	18,633	22,877	19,702
79,700	79,750	19,718	16,967	20,735	18,027	82,700	82,750	20,648	17,807	21,815	18,867	85,700	85,750	21,578	18,647	22,895	19,718
79,750	79,800	19,733	16,981	20,753	18,041	82,750	82,800	20,663	17,821	21,833	18,881	85,750	85,800	21,593	18,661	22,913	19,733
79,800	79,850	19,749	16,995	20,771	18,055	82,800	82,850	20,679	17,835	21,851	18,895	85,800	85,850	21,609	18,675	22,931	19,749
79,850	79,900	19,764	17,009	20,789	18,069	82,850	82,900	20,694	17,849	21,869	18,909	85,850	85,900	21,624	18,689	22,949	19,764
79,900	79,950	19,780	17,023	20,807	18,083	82,900	82,950	20,710	17,863	21,887	18,923	85,900	85,950	21,640	18,703	22,967	19,780
79,950	80,000	19,795	17,037	20,825	18,097	82,950	83,000	20,725	17,877	21,905	18,937	85,950	86,000	21,655	18,717	22,985	19,795

* This column must also be used by a qualifying widow(er).

Continued on next page

1997 Tax Table—Continued

If line 38 (taxable income) is—		And you are—				If line 38 (taxable income) is—		And you are—				If line 38 (taxable income) is—		And you are—			
At least	But less than	Single	Married filing jointly *	Married filing separately	Head of a house-hold	At least	But less than	Single	Married filing jointly *	Married filing separately	Head of a house-hold	At least	But less than	Single	Married filing jointly *	Married filing separately	Head of a house-hold
			Your tax is—						Your tax is—						Your tax is—		
86,000						**89,000**						**92,000**					
86,000	86,050	21,671	18,731	23,003	19,811	89,000	89,050	22,601	19,571	24,083	20,741	92,000	92,050	23,531	20,411	25,163	21,671
86,050	86,100	21,686	18,745	23,021	19,826	89,050	89,100	22,616	19,585	24,101	20,756	92,050	92,100	23,546	20,425	25,181	21,686
86,100	86,150	21,702	18,759	23,039	19,842	89,100	89,150	22,632	19,599	24,119	20,772	92,100	92,150	23,562	20,439	25,199	21,702
86,150	86,200	21,717	18,773	23,057	19,857	89,150	89,200	22,647	19,613	24,137	20,787	92,150	92,200	23,577	20,453	25,217	21,717
86,200	86,250	21,733	18,787	23,075	19,873	89,200	89,250	22,663	19,627	24,155	20,803	92,200	92,250	23,593	20,467	25,235	21,733
86,250	86,300	21,748	18,801	23,093	19,888	89,250	89,300	22,678	19,641	24,173	20,818	92,250	92,300	23,608	20,481	25,253	21,748
86,300	86,350	21,764	18,815	23,111	19,904	89,300	89,350	22,694	19,655	24,191	20,834	92,300	92,350	23,624	20,495	25,271	21,764
86,350	86,400	21,779	18,829	23,129	19,919	89,350	89,400	22,709	19,669	24,209	20,849	92,350	92,400	23,639	20,509	25,289	21,779
86,400	86,450	21,795	18,843	23,147	19,935	89,400	89,450	22,725	19,683	24,227	20,865	92,400	92,450	23,655	20,523	25,307	21,795
86,450	86,500	21,810	18,857	23,165	19,950	89,450	89,500	22,740	19,697	24,245	20,880	92,450	92,500	23,670	20,537	25,325	21,810
86,500	86,550	21,826	18,871	23,183	19,966	89,500	89,550	22,756	19,711	24,263	20,896	92,500	92,550	23,686	20,551	25,343	21,826
86,550	86,600	21,841	18,885	23,201	19,981	89,550	89,600	22,771	19,725	24,281	20,911	92,550	92,600	23,701	20,565	25,361	21,841
86,600	86,650	21,857	18,899	23,219	19,997	89,600	89,650	22,787	19,739	24,299	20,927	92,600	92,650	23,717	20,579	25,379	21,857
86,650	86,700	21,872	18,913	23,237	20,012	89,650	89,700	22,802	19,753	24,317	20,942	92,650	92,700	23,732	20,593	25,397	21,872
86,700	86,750	21,888	18,927	23,255	20,028	89,700	89,750	22,818	19,767	24,335	20,958	92,700	92,750	23,748	20,607	25,415	21,888
86,750	86,800	21,903	18,941	23,273	20,043	89,750	89,800	22,833	19,781	24,353	20,973	92,750	92,800	23,763	20,621	25,433	21,903
86,800	86,850	21,919	18,955	23,291	20,059	89,800	89,850	22,849	19,795	24,371	20,989	92,800	92,850	23,779	20,635	25,451	21,919
86,850	86,900	21,934	18,969	23,309	20,074	89,850	89,900	22,864	19,809	24,389	21,004	92,850	92,900	23,794	20,649	25,469	21,934
86,900	86,950	21,950	18,983	23,327	20,090	89,900	89,950	22,880	19,823	24,407	21,020	92,900	92,950	23,810	20,663	25,487	21,950
86,950	87,000	21,965	18,997	23,345	20,105	89,950	90,000	22,895	19,837	24,425	21,035	92,950	93,000	23,825	20,677	25,505	21,965
87,000						**90,000**						**93,000**					
87,000	87,050	21,981	19,011	23,363	20,121	90,000	90,050	22,911	19,851	24,443	21,051	93,000	93,050	23,841	20,691	25,523	21,981
87,050	87,100	21,996	19,025	23,381	20,136	90,050	90,100	22,926	19,865	24,461	21,066	93,050	93,100	23,856	20,705	25,541	21,996
87,100	87,150	22,012	19,039	23,399	20,152	90,100	90,150	22,942	19,879	24,479	21,082	93,100	93,150	23,872	20,719	25,559	22,012
87,150	87,200	22,027	19,053	23,417	20,167	90,150	90,200	22,957	19,893	24,497	21,097	93,150	93,200	23,887	20,733	25,577	22,027
87,200	87,250	22,043	19,067	23,435	20,183	90,200	90,250	22,973	19,907	24,515	21,113	93,200	93,250	23,903	20,747	25,595	22,043
87,250	87,300	22,058	19,081	23,453	20,198	90,250	90,300	22,988	19,921	24,533	21,128	93,250	93,300	23,918	20,761	25,613	22,058
87,300	87,350	22,074	19,095	23,471	20,214	90,300	90,350	23,004	19,935	24,551	21,144	93,300	93,350	23,934	20,775	25,631	22,074
87,350	87,400	22,089	19,109	23,489	20,229	90,350	90,400	23,019	19,949	24,569	21,159	93,350	93,400	23,949	20,789	25,649	22,089
87,400	87,450	22,105	19,123	23,507	20,245	90,400	90,450	23,035	19,963	24,587	21,175	93,400	93,450	23,965	20,803	25,667	22,105
87,450	87,500	22,120	19,137	23,525	20,260	90,450	90,500	23,050	19,977	24,605	21,190	93,450	93,500	23,980	20,817	25,685	22,120
87,500	87,550	22,136	19,151	23,543	20,276	90,500	90,550	23,066	19,991	24,623	21,206	93,500	93,550	23,996	20,831	25,703	22,136
87,550	87,600	22,151	19,165	23,561	20,291	90,550	90,600	23,081	20,005	24,641	21,221	93,550	93,600	24,011	20,845	25,721	22,151
87,600	87,650	22,167	19,179	23,579	20,307	90,600	90,650	23,097	20,019	24,659	21,237	93,600	93,650	24,027	20,859	25,739	22,167
87,650	87,700	22,182	19,193	23,597	20,322	90,650	90,700	23,112	20,033	24,677	21,252	93,650	93,700	24,042	20,873	25,757	22,182
87,700	87,750	22,198	19,207	23,615	20,338	90,700	90,750	23,128	20,047	24,695	21,268	93,700	93,750	24,058	20,887	25,775	22,198
87,750	87,800	22,213	19,221	23,633	20,353	90,750	90,800	23,143	20,061	24,713	21,283	93,750	93,800	24,073	20,901	25,793	22,213
87,800	87,850	22,229	19,235	23,651	20,369	90,800	90,850	23,159	20,075	24,731	21,299	93,800	93,850	24,089	20,915	25,811	22,229
87,850	87,900	22,244	19,249	23,669	20,384	90,850	90,900	23,174	20,089	24,749	21,314	93,850	93,900	24,104	20,929	25,829	22,244
87,900	87,950	22,260	19,263	23,687	20,400	90,900	90,950	23,190	20,103	24,767	21,330	93,900	93,950	24,120	20,943	25,847	22,260
87,950	88,000	22,275	19,277	23,705	20,415	90,950	91,000	23,205	20,117	24,785	21,345	93,950	94,000	24,135	20,957	25,865	22,275
88,000						**91,000**						**94,000**					
88,000	88,050	22,291	19,291	23,723	20,431	91,000	91,050	23,221	20,131	24,803	21,361	94,000	94,050	24,151	20,971	25,883	22,291
88,050	88,100	22,306	19,305	23,741	20,446	91,050	91,100	23,236	20,145	24,821	21,376	94,050	94,100	24,166	20,985	25,901	22,306
88,100	88,150	22,322	19,319	23,759	20,462	91,100	91,150	23,252	20,159	24,839	21,392	94,100	94,150	24,182	20,999	25,919	22,322
88,150	88,200	22,337	19,333	23,777	20,477	91,150	91,200	23,267	20,173	24,857	21,407	94,150	94,200	24,197	21,013	25,937	22,337
88,200	88,250	22,353	19,347	23,795	20,493	91,200	91,250	23,283	20,187	24,875	21,423	94,200	94,250	24,213	21,027	25,955	22,353
88,250	88,300	22,368	19,361	23,813	20,508	91,250	91,300	23,298	20,201	24,893	21,438	94,250	94,300	24,228	21,041	25,973	22,368
88,300	88,350	22,384	19,375	23,831	20,524	91,300	91,350	23,314	20,215	24,911	21,454	94,300	94,350	24,244	21,055	25,991	22,384
88,350	88,400	22,399	19,389	23,849	20,539	91,350	91,400	23,329	20,229	24,929	21,469	94,350	94,400	24,259	21,069	26,009	22,399
88,400	88,450	22,415	19,403	23,867	20,555	91,400	91,450	23,345	20,243	24,947	21,485	94,400	94,450	24,275	21,083	26,027	22,415
88,450	88,500	22,430	19,417	23,885	20,570	91,450	91,500	23,360	20,257	24,965	21,500	94,450	94,500	24,290	21,097	26,045	22,430
88,500	88,550	22,446	19,431	23,903	20,586	91,500	91,550	23,376	20,271	24,983	21,516	94,500	94,550	24,306	21,111	26,063	22,446
88,550	88,600	22,461	19,445	23,921	20,601	91,550	91,600	23,391	20,285	25,001	21,531	94,550	94,600	24,321	21,125	26,081	22,461
88,600	88,650	22,477	19,459	23,939	20,617	91,600	91,650	23,407	20,299	25,019	21,547	94,600	94,650	24,337	21,139	26,099	22,477
88,650	88,700	22,492	19,473	23,957	20,632	91,650	91,700	23,422	20,313	25,037	21,562	94,650	94,700	24,352	21,153	26,117	22,492
88,700	88,750	22,508	19,487	23,975	20,648	91,700	91,750	23,438	20,327	25,055	21,578	94,700	94,750	24,368	21,167	26,135	22,508
88,750	88,800	22,523	19,501	23,993	20,663	91,750	91,800	23,453	20,341	25,073	21,593	94,750	94,800	24,383	21,181	26,153	22,523
88,800	88,850	22,539	19,515	24,011	20,679	91,800	91,850	23,469	20,355	25,091	21,609	94,800	94,850	24,399	21,195	26,171	22,539
88,850	88,900	22,554	19,529	24,029	20,694	91,850	91,900	23,484	20,369	25,109	21,624	94,850	94,900	24,414	21,209	26,189	22,554
88,900	88,950	22,570	19,543	24,047	20,710	91,900	91,950	23,500	20,383	25,127	21,640	94,900	94,950	24,430	21,223	26,207	22,570
88,950	89,000	22,585	19,557	24,065	20,725	91,950	92,000	23,515	20,397	25,145	21,655	94,950	95,000	24,445	21,237	26,225	22,585

* This column must also be used by a qualifying widow(er).

Continued on next page

1997 Tax Table—Continued

If line 38 (taxable income) is—		And you are—				If line 38 (taxable income) is—		And you are—			
At least	But less than	Single	Married filing jointly *	Married filing separately	Head of a household	At least	But less than	Single	Married filing jointly *	Married filing separately	Head of a household
			Your tax is—						Your tax is—		

95,000

At least	But less than	Single	MFJ	MFS	HoH
95,000	95,050	24,461	21,251	26,243	22,601
95,050	95,100	24,476	21,265	26,261	22,616
95,100	95,150	24,492	21,279	26,279	22,632
95,150	95,200	24,507	21,293	26,297	22,647
95,200	95,250	24,523	21,307	26,315	22,663
95,250	95,300	24,538	21,321	26,333	22,678
95,300	95,350	24,554	21,335	26,351	22,694
95,350	95,400	24,569	21,349	26,369	22,709
95,400	95,450	24,585	21,363	26,387	22,725
95,450	95,500	24,600	21,377	26,405	22,740
95,500	95,550	24,616	21,391	26,423	22,756
95,550	95,600	24,631	21,405	26,441	22,771
95,600	95,650	24,647	21,419	26,459	22,787
95,650	95,700	24,662	21,433	26,477	22,802
95,700	95,750	24,678	21,447	26,495	22,818
95,750	95,800	24,693	21,461	26,513	22,833
95,800	95,850	24,709	21,475	26,531	22,849
95,850	95,900	24,724	21,489	26,549	22,864
95,900	95,950	24,740	21,503	26,567	22,880
95,950	96,000	24,755	21,517	26,585	22,895

96,000

At least	But less than	Single	MFJ	MFS	HoH
96,000	96,050	24,771	21,531	26,603	22,911
96,050	96,100	24,786	21,545	26,621	22,926
96,100	96,150	24,802	21,559	26,639	22,942
96,150	96,200	24,817	21,573	26,657	22,957
96,200	96,250	24,833	21,587	26,675	22,973
96,250	96,300	24,848	21,601	26,693	22,988
96,300	96,350	24,864	21,615	26,711	23,004
96,350	96,400	24,879	21,629	26,729	23,019
96,400	96,450	24,895	21,643	26,747	23,035
96,450	96,500	24,910	21,657	26,765	23,050
96,500	96,550	24,926	21,671	26,783	23,066
96,550	96,600	24,941	21,685	26,801	23,081
96,600	96,650	24,957	21,699	26,819	23,097
96,650	96,700	24,972	21,713	26,837	23,112
96,700	96,750	24,988	21,727	26,855	23,128
96,750	96,800	25,003	21,741	26,873	23,143
96,800	96,850	25,019	21,755	26,891	23,159
96,850	96,900	25,034	21,769	26,909	23,174
96,900	96,950	25,050	21,783	26,927	23,190
96,950	97,000	25,065	21,797	26,945	23,205

97,000

At least	But less than	Single	MFJ	MFS	HoH
97,000	97,050	25,081	21,811	26,963	23,221
97,050	97,100	25,096	21,825	26,981	23,236
97,100	97,150	25,112	21,839	26,999	23,252
97,150	97,200	25,127	21,853	27,017	23,267
97,200	97,250	25,143	21,867	27,035	23,283
97,250	97,300	25,158	21,881	27,053	23,298
97,300	97,350	25,174	21,895	27,071	23,314
97,350	97,400	25,189	21,909	27,089	23,329
97,400	97,450	25,205	21,923	27,107	23,345
97,450	97,500	25,220	21,937	27,125	23,360
97,500	97,550	25,236	21,951	27,143	23,376
97,550	97,600	25,251	21,965	27,161	23,391
97,600	97,650	25,267	21,979	27,179	23,407
97,650	97,700	25,282	21,993	27,197	23,422
97,700	97,750	25,298	22,007	27,215	23,438
97,750	97,800	25,313	22,021	27,233	23,453
97,800	97,850	25,329	22,035	27,251	23,469
97,850	97,900	25,344	22,049	27,269	23,484
97,900	97,950	25,360	22,063	27,287	23,500
97,950	98,000	25,375	22,077	27,305	23,515

98,000

At least	But less than	Single	MFJ	MFS	HoH
98,000	98,050	25,391	22,091	27,323	23,531
98,050	98,100	25,406	22,105	27,341	23,546
98,100	98,150	25,422	22,119	27,359	23,562
98,150	98,200	25,437	22,133	27,377	23,577
98,200	98,250	25,453	22,147	27,395	23,593
98,250	98,300	25,468	22,161	27,413	23,608
98,300	98,350	25,484	22,175	27,431	23,624
98,350	98,400	25,499	22,189	27,449	23,639
98,400	98,450	25,515	22,203	27,467	23,655
98,450	98,500	25,530	22,217	27,485	23,670
98,500	98,550	25,546	22,231	27,503	23,686
98,550	98,600	25,561	22,245	27,521	23,701
98,600	98,650	25,577	22,259	27,539	23,717
98,650	98,700	25,592	22,273	27,557	23,732
98,700	98,750	25,608	22,287	27,575	23,748
98,750	98,800	25,623	22,301	27,593	23,763
98,800	98,850	25,639	22,315	27,611	23,779
98,850	98,900	25,654	22,329	27,629	23,794
98,900	98,950	25,670	22,343	27,647	23,810
98,950	99,000	25,685	22,357	27,665	23,825

99,000

At least	But less than	Single	MFJ	MFS	HoH
99,000	99,050	25,701	22,371	27,683	23,841
99,050	99,100	25,716	22,385	27,701	23,856
99,100	99,150	25,732	22,399	27,719	23,872
99,150	99,200	25,747	22,413	27,737	23,887
99,200	99,250	25,763	22,427	27,755	23,903
99,250	99,300	25,778	22,441	27,773	23,918
99,300	99,350	25,794	22,455	27,791	23,934
99,350	99,400	25,809	22,469	27,809	23,949
99,400	99,450	25,825	22,483	27,827	23,965
99,450	99,500	25,840	22,497	27,845	23,980
99,500	99,550	25,856	22,511	27,863	23,996
99,550	99,600	25,871	22,525	27,881	24,011
99,600	99,650	25,887	22,540	27,899	24,027
99,650	99,700	25,902	22,555	27,917	24,042
99,700	99,750	25,918	22,571	27,935	24,058
99,750	99,800	25,933	22,586	27,953	24,073
99,800	99,850	25,949	22,602	27,971	24,089
99,850	99,900	25,964	22,617	27,989	24,104
99,900	99,950	25,980	22,633	28,007	24,120
99,950	100,000	25,995	22,648	28,025	24,135

$100,000 or over — use the Tax Rate Schedules on page A–2

* This column must also be used by a qualifying widow(er).

Income Tax Rates—Estates and Trusts

TAX YEAR 1998

Taxable Income			
Over—	But not Over—	The Tax Is:	Of the Amount Over—
$0	$1,700	15%	$0
1,700	4,000	$255 + 28%	1,700
4,000	6,100	899 + 31%	4,000
6,100	8,350	1,550 + 36%	6,100
8,350	—	2,360 + 39.6%	8,350

TAX YEAR 1997

Taxable Income			
Over—	But not Over—	The Tax Is:	Of the Amount Over—
$0	$1,650	15%	$0
1,650	3,900	$247.50 + 28%	1,650
3,900	5,950	877.50 + 31%	3,900
5,950	8,100	1,513.00 + 36%	5,950
8,100	—	2,287.00 + 39.6%	8,100

Income Tax Rates—Corporations

Taxable Income			
Over—	But not Over—	The Tax Is:	Of the Amount Over—
$0	$50,000	15%	$0
50,000	75,000	$7,500 + 25%	50,000
75,000	100,000	13,750 + 34%	75,000
100,000	335,000	22,250 + 39%	100,000
335,000	10,000,000	113,900 + 34%	335,000
10,000,000	15,000,000	3,400,000 + 35%	10,000,000
15,000,000	18,333,333	5,150,000 + 38%	15,000,000
18,333,333	—	35%	0

Unified Transfer Tax Rates

FOR GIFTS MADE AND FOR DEATHS AFTER 1983

If the Amount with Respect to Which the Tentative Tax to Be Computed Is:	The Tentative Tax Is:
Not over $10,000	18 percent of such amount.
Over $10,000 but not over $20,000	$1,800, plus 20 percent of the excess of such amount over $10,000.
Over $20,000 but not over $40,000	$3,800, plus 22 percent of the excess of such amount over $20,000.
Over $40,000 but not over $60,000	$8,200, plus 24 percent of the excess of such amount over $40,000.
Over $60,000 but not over $80,000	$13,000, plus 26 percent of the excess of such amount over $60,000.
Over $80,000 but not over $100,000	$18,200, plus 28 percent of the excess of such amount over $80,000.
Over $100,000 but not over $150,000	$23,800, plus 30 percent of the excess of such amount over $100,000.
Over $150,000 but not over $250,000	$38,800, plus 32 percent of the excess of such amount over $150,000.
Over $250,000 but not over $500,000	$70,800, plus 34 percent of the excess of such amount over $250,000.
Over $500,000 but not over $750,000	$155,800, plus 37 percent of the excess of such amount over $500,000.
Over $750,000 but not over $1,000,000	$248,300, plus 39 percent of the excess of such amount over $750,000.
Over $1,000,000 but not over $1,250,000	$345,800, plus 41 percent of the excess of such amount over $1,000,000.
Over $1,250,000 but not over $1,500,000	$448,300, plus 43 percent of the excess of such amount over $1,250,000.
Over $1,500,000 but not over $2,000,000	$555,800, plus 45 percent of the excess of such amount over $1,500,000.
Over $2,000,000 but not over $2,500,000	$780,800, plus 49 percent of the excess of such amount over $2,000,000.
Over $2,500,000 but not over $3,000,000	$1,025,800, plus 53 percent of the excess of such amount over $2,500,000.
Over $3,000,000*	$1,290,800, plus 55 percent of the excess of such amount over $3,000,000.

*For large taxable transfers (generally in excess of $10 million) there is a phase-out of the graduated rates and the unified tax credit.

TABLE FOR COMPUTATION OF MAXIMUM CREDIT FOR STATE DEATH TAXES

(A) Adjusted Taxable Estate* Equal to or More Than	(B) Adjusted Taxable Estate* Less Than	(C) Credit on Amount in Column (A)	(D) Rate of Credit on Excess Over Amount in Column (A) (Percentage)
0	$ 40,000	0	None
$ 40,000	90,000	0	0.8
90,000	140,000	$ 400	1.6
140,000	240,000	1,200	2.4
240,000	440,000	3,600	3.2
440,000	640,000	10,000	4.0
640,000	840,000	18,000	4.8
840,000	1,040,000	27,600	5.6
1,040,000	1,540,000	38,800	6.4
1,540,000	2,040,000	70,800	7.2
2,040,000	2,540,000	106,800	8.0
2,540,000	3,040,000	146,800	8.8
3,040,000	3,540,000	190,800	9.6
3,540,000	4,040,000	238,800	10.4
4,040,000	5,040,000	290,800	11.2
5,040,000	6,040,000	402,800	12.0
6,040,000	7,040,000	522,800	12.8
7,040,000	8,040,000	650,800	13.6
8,040,000	9,040,000	786,800	14.4
9,040,000	10,040,000	930,800	15.2
10,040,000		1,082,800	16.0

*Adjusted Taxable Estate = Taxable Estate − $60,000

APPENDIX B
Tax Forms

Form 1040EZ	Income Tax Return for Single and Joint Filers With No Dependents	B-3
Form 1040A	U.S. Individual Income Tax Return (Short Form)	B-5
Schedule 1	Interest and Dividend Income	B-7
Form 1040	U.S. Individual Income Tax Return	B-8
Schedules A & B	Itemized Deductions; Interest and Dividend Income	B-10
Schedule C	Profit or Loss from Business	B-12
Schedule D	Capital Gains and Losses	B-14
Schedule E	Supplemental Income and Loss	B-16
Schedule SE	Self-Employment Tax	B-18
Form 1065	U.S. Partnership Return of Income	B-20
Schedule K-1	Partner's Share of Income, Credits, Deductions, etc.	B-24
Form 1120-A	U.S. Corporation Short-Form Income Tax Return	B-26
Form 1120	U.S. Corporation Income Tax Return	B-28
Form 1120S	U.S. Income Tax Return for an S Corporation	B-32
Schedule K-1	Shareholder's Share of Income, Credits, Deductions, Etc.	B-36

Form 2106	Employee Business Expenses	B-38
Form 2106 EZ	Unreimbursed Employee Business Expenses	B-40
Form 2119	Sale of Your Home	B-42
Form 2210	Underpayment of Estimated Tax (individual)	B-44
Form 2220	Underpayment of Estimated Tax (corporation)	B-47
Form 2441	Child and Dependent Care Expenses	B-51
Form 2553	Election by a Small Business Corporation	B-53
Form 3903	Moving Expenses	B-55
Form 4562	Depreciation and Amortization	B-57
Form 4626	Alternative Minimum Tax— Corporations	B-59
Form 4684	Casualties and Thefts	B-61
Form 4797	Sales of Business Property	B-63
Form 6251	Alternative Minimum Tax— Individuals	B-65
Form 8582	Passive Activity Loss Limitations	B-67
Form 8615	Tax for Children Under Age 14 Who Have Investment Income of More Than $1,300	B-70
Form 8824	Like-Kind Exchanges	B-72
Form 8829	Expenses for Business Use of Your Home	B-74
Form 8832	Entity Classification Election	B-75

Tax Forms   B–3

Form 1040EZ   Department of the Treasury—Internal Revenue Service
Income Tax Return for Single and Joint Filers With No Dependents (99) **1997**   OMB No. 1545-0675

Use the IRS label here

Your first name and initial   Last name

If a joint return, spouse's first name and initial   Last name

Home address (number and street). If you have a P.O. box, see page 7.   Apt. no.

City, town or post office, state, and ZIP code. If you have a foreign address, see page 7.

Your social security number

Spouse's social security number

Presidential Election Campaign (See page 7.)

Note: *Checking "Yes" will not change your tax or reduce your refund.*
Do you want $3 to go to this fund? ▶   Yes ☐   No ☐
If a joint return, does your spouse want $3 to go to this fund? ▶   Yes ☐   No ☐

Dollars   Cents

Income

Attach Copy B of Form(s) W-2 here. Enclose but do not attach any payment with your return.

1. Total wages, salaries, and tips. This should be shown in box 1 of your W-2 form(s). Attach your W-2 form(s).   1

2. Taxable interest income. If the total is over $400, you cannot use Form 1040EZ.   2

3. Unemployment compensation (see page 9).   3

4. Add lines 1, 2, and 3. This is your **adjusted gross income.** If under $9,770, see page 9 to find out if you can claim the earned income credit on line 8a.   4

Note: *You must check Yes or No.*

5. Can your parents (or someone else) claim you on their return?
   Yes. Enter amount from worksheet on back. ☐
   No. If **single**, enter 6,800.00. If **married**, enter 12,200.00. See back for explanation. ☐   5

6. Subtract line 5 from line 4. If line 5 is larger than line 4, enter 0. This is your **taxable income.** ▶ 6

Payments and tax

7. Enter your Federal income tax withheld from box 2 of your W-2 form(s).   7

8a. **Earned income credit** (see page 9).
  b. Nontaxable earned income: enter type and amount below.
     Type _____ $ _____   8a

9. Add lines 7 and 8a. These are your **total payments.**   9

10. **Tax.** Use the amount on **line 6** to find your tax in the tax table on pages 20–24 of the booklet. Then, enter the tax from the table on this line.   10

Refund

Have it directly deposited! See page 13 and fill in 11b, 11c, and 11d.

11a. If line 9 is larger than line 10, subtract line 10 from line 9. This is your **refund.**   11a
▶ b. Routing number
▶ c. Type: ☐ Checking ☐ Savings   d. Account number

Amount you owe

12. If line 10 is larger than line 9, subtract line 9 from line 10. This is the **amount you owe.** See page 13 for details on how to pay.   12

I have read this return. Under penalties of perjury, I declare that to the best of my knowledge and belief, the return is true, correct, and accurately lists all amounts and sources of income I received during the tax year.

Sign here

Keep copy for your records.

Your signature   Spouse's signature if joint return

Date   Your occupation   Date   Spouse's occupation

For Official Use Only   1 2 3 4 5   6 7 8 9 10

For Privacy Act and Paperwork Reduction Act Notice, see page 18.   Cat. No. 11329W   1997 Form 1040EZ

1997 Form 1040EZ page 2

Use this form if	• Your filing status is single or married filing jointly.
	• You do not claim any dependents.
	• You had **only** wages, salaries, tips, taxable scholarship or fellowship grants, unemployment compensation, or Alaska Permanent Fund dividends, and your taxable interest income was not over $400. **But** if you earned tips, including allocated tips, that are not included in box 5 and box 7 of your W-2, you may not be able to use Form 1040EZ. See page 8.
	• You did not receive any advance earned income credit payments.
	• You (and your spouse if married) were under 65 on January 1, 1998, and not blind at the end of 1997.
	• Your taxable income (line 6) is less than $50,000.
	If you are not sure about your filing status, see page 6. If you have questions about dependents, use TeleTax topic 354 (see page 18). If you **cannot use this form,** use TeleTax topic 352 (see page 18).

Filling in your return

For tips on how to avoid common mistakes, see page 3.

Because this form is read by a machine, please print your numbers inside the boxes like this:

9 8 7 6 5 4 3 2 1 0   Do not type your numbers. Do not use dollar signs.

If you received a scholarship or fellowship grant or tax-exempt interest income, such as on municipal bonds, see the booklet before filling in the form. Also, see the booklet if you received a Form 1099-INT showing Federal income tax withheld or if Federal income tax was withheld from your unemployment compensation or Alaska Permanent Fund dividends.

Remember, you must report all wages, salaries, and tips even if you do not get a W-2 form from your employer. You must also report all your taxable interest income, including interest from banks, savings and loans, credit unions, etc., even if you do not get a Form 1099-INT.

Worksheet for dependents who checked "Yes" on line 5

Use this worksheet to figure the amount to enter on line 5 if someone can claim you (or your spouse if married) as a dependent, even if that person chooses not to do so. To find out if someone can claim you as a dependent, use TeleTax topic 354 (see page 18).

- **A.** Enter the amount from line 1 on the front.   **A.** _____
- **B.** Minimum standard deduction.   **B.** _____650.00
- **C.** Enter the LARGER of line A or line B here.   **C.** _____
- **D.** Maximum standard deduction. If single, enter 4,150.00; if married, enter 6,900.00.   **D.** _____
- **E.** Enter the SMALLER of line C or line D here. This is your standard deduction.   **E.** _____
- **F.** Exemption amount.
  - If single, enter 0.
  - If married and—
    —both you and your spouse can be claimed as dependents, enter 0.
    —only one of you can be claimed as a dependent, enter 2,650.00.   **F.** _____
- **G.** Add lines E and F. Enter the total here and on line 5 on the front.   **G.** _____

If you checked "No" on line 5 because no one can claim you (or your spouse if married) as a dependent, enter on line 5 the amount shown below that applies to you.

- Single, enter 6,800.00. This is the total of your standard deduction (4,150.00) and your exemption (2,650.00).
- Married, enter 12,200.00. This is the total of your standard deduction (6,900.00), your exemption (2,650.00), and your spouse's exemption (2,650.00).

Mailing your return

Mail your return by **April 15, 1998.** Use the envelope that came with your booklet. If you do not have that envelope, see page 28 for the address to use.

Paid preparer's use only

See page 14.

Under penalties of perjury, I declare that I have examined this return, and to the best of my knowledge and belief, it is true, correct, and accurately lists all amounts and sources of income received during the tax year. This declaration is based on all information of which I have any knowledge.

Preparer's signature ▶		Date	Check if self-employed ☐	Preparer's SSN
Firm's name (or yours if self-employed) and address ▶			EIN	
			ZIP code	

| Form **1040A** (99) | Department of the Treasury—Internal Revenue Service **U.S. Individual Income Tax Return** | **1997** | IRS Use Only—Do not write or staple in this space. |

OMB No. 1545-0085

Label (See page 14.) Use the IRS label. Otherwise, please print in **ALL CAPITAL LETTERS.**

LABEL HERE

Your first name | Init. | Last name
If a joint return, spouse's first name | Init. | Last name
Home address (number and street). If you have a P.O. box, see page 14. | Apt. no.
City, town or post office. If you have a foreign address, see page 14. | State | ZIP code

Your social security number

Spouse's social security number

For Privacy Act and Paperwork Reduction Act Notice, see page 42.

Presidential Election Campaign Fund (See page 14.)
Do you want $3 to go to this fund? . . . .
If a joint return, does your spouse want $3 to go to this fund? . . . .

Yes | No

Note: *Checking "Yes" will not change your tax or reduce your refund.*

1 ☐ Single

2 ☐ Married filing joint return (even if only one had income)

3 ☐ Married filing separate return. Enter spouse's social security number above and full name here. ▶ _____

4 ☐ Head of household (with qualifying person). (See page 15.) If the qualifying person is a child but not your dependent, enter this child's name here. ▶ _____

5 ☐ Qualifying widow(er) with dependent child (year spouse died ▶ 19___). (See page 16.)

6a ☐ **Yourself.** If your parent (or someone else) can claim you as a dependent on his or her tax return, **do not** check box 6a.

b ☐ **Spouse**

c **Dependents.** If more than six dependents, see page 16.

(1) First name	Last name	(2) Dependent's social security number	(3) Dependent's relationship to you	(4) No. of months lived in your home in 1997

No. of boxes checked on 6a and 6b ☐

No. of your children on 6c who:
• lived with you ☐
• did not live with you due to divorce or separation (see page 17) ☐

Dependents on 6c not entered above ☐

Add numbers entered in boxes above ☐

d Total number of exemptions claimed . . . . ▶

		Dollars	Cents
7	Wages, salaries, tips, etc. Attach Form(s) W-2.	**7**	
8a	**Taxable** interest income. Attach Schedule 1 if required.	**8a**	
b	**Tax-exempt** interest. DO NOT include on line 8a. **8b**		
9	Dividends. Attach Schedule 1 if required.	**9**	
10a	Total IRA distributions. **10a**	10b Taxable amount (see page 19). **10b**	
11a	Total pensions and annuities. **11a**	11b Taxable amount (see page 19). **11b**	
12	Unemployment compensation.	**12**	
13a	Social security benefits. **13a**	13b Taxable amount (see page 21). **13b**	
14	Add lines 7 through 13b (far right column). This is your **total income.** ▶	**14**	
15	IRA deduction (see page 21).	**15**	
16	Subtract line 15 from line 14. This is your **adjusted gross income.** If under $29,290 (under $9,770 if a child did not live with you), see the EIC instructions on page 27. ▶	**16**	

Attach Copy B of W-2 and 1099-R here.

Cat. No. 11327A

1997 Form **1040A**

1997 Form 1040A page 2

17	Enter the amount from line 16.	17
18a	Check if: ☐ **You** were 65 or older ☐ Blind / ☐ **Spouse** was 65 or older ☐ Blind — Enter number of boxes checked ▶ 18a	
b	If you are married filing separately and your spouse itemizes deductions, see page 23 and check here . . . . ▶ 18b ☐	
19	Enter the **standard deduction** for your filing status. **But** see page 24 if you checked any box on line 18a or 18b **OR** someone can claim you as a dependent. • Single—4,150 • Married filing jointly or Qualifying widow(er)—6,900 • Head of household—6,050 • Married filing separately—3,450	19
20	Subtract line 19 from line 17. If line 19 is more than line 17, enter 0.	20
21	Multiply $2,650 by the total number of exemptions claimed on line 6d.	21
22	Subtract line 21 from line 20. If line 21 is more than line 20, enter 0. This is your **taxable income**. **If you want the IRS to figure your tax, see page 24.** ▶	22
23	Find the tax on the amount on line 22 (see page 24).	23
24a	Credit for child and dependent care expenses. Attach Schedule 2. 24a	
b	Credit for the elderly or the disabled. Attach Schedule 3. 24b	
c	Adoption credit. Attach Form 8839. 24c	
d	Add lines 24a, 24b, and 24c. These are your **total credits**.	24d
25	Subtract line 24d from line 23. If line 24d is more than line 23, enter 0.	25
26	Advance earned income credit payments from Form(s) W-2.	26
27	Household employment taxes. Attach Schedule H.	27
28	Add lines 25, 26, and 27. This is your **total tax.** ▶	28
29a	Total Federal income tax withheld from Forms W-2 and 1099. 29a	
b	1997 estimated tax payments and amount applied from 1996 return. 29b	
c	**Earned income credit.** Attach Schedule EIC if you have a qualifying child. 29c	
d	Nontaxable earned income: amount ▶ [ ] and type ▶	
e	Add lines 29a, 29b, and 29c. These are your **total payments.** ▶	29e
30	If line 29e is more than line 28, subtract line 28 from line 29e. This is the amount you **overpaid.**	30
31a	Amount of line 30 you want **refunded to you.** If you want it directly deposited, see page 33 and fill in 31b, 31c, and 31d.	31a
b	Routing number [ ] c Type: ☐ Checking ☐ Savings	
d	Account number [ ]	
32	Amount of line 30 you want **applied to your 1998 estimated tax.** 32	
33	If line 28 is more than line 29e, subtract line 29e from line 28. This is the **amount you owe.** For details on how to pay, see page 34.	33
34	Estimated tax penalty (see page 34). 34	

Sign here

Under penalties of perjury, I declare that I have examined this return and accompanying schedules and statements, and to the best of my knowledge and belief, they are true, correct, and accurately list all amounts and sources of income I received during the tax year. Declaration of preparer (other than the taxpayer) is based on all information of which the preparer has any knowledge.

Your signature   Date   Your occupation

Keep a copy of this return for your records.

Spouse's signature. If joint return, BOTH must sign.   Date   Spouse's occupation

Paid preparer's use only

Preparer's signature ▶   Date   Check if self-employed ☐   Preparer's SSN

Firm's name (or yours if self-employed) and address ▶   EIN   ZIP code

Schedule 1 (Form 1040A)

Department of the Treasury—Internal Revenue Service

Interest and Dividend Income for Form 1040A Filers

(99)

1997

OMB No. 1545-0085

Name(s) shown on Form 1040A: First and initial(s) | Last

Your social security number

Part I — Interest Income (See pages 18 and 49.)

Note: *If you received a Form 1099–INT, Form 1099–OID, or substitute statement from a brokerage firm, enter the firm's name and the total interest shown on that form.*

1. List name of payer. If any interest is from a seller-financed mortgage and the buyer used the property as a personal residence, see page 49 and list this interest first. Also, show that buyer's social security number and address.

2. Add the amounts on line 1.

3. Excludable interest on series EE U.S. savings bonds issued after 1989 from Form 8815, line 14. You **must** attach Form 8815 to Form 1040A.

4. Subtract line 3 from line 2. Enter the result here and on Form 1040A, line 8a.

Part II — Dividend Income (See pages 19 and 49.)

Note: *If you received a Form 1099–DIV or substitute statement from a brokerage firm, enter the firm's name and the total dividends shown on that form.*

5. List name of payer

6. Add the amounts on line 5. Enter the total here and on Form 1040A, line 9.

For Paperwork Reduction Act Notice, see Form 1040A instructions.

Cat. No. 12075R

1997 Schedule 1 (Form 1040A)

Form **1040**	Department of the Treasury—Internal Revenue Service

U.S. Individual Income Tax Return **1997** (99) IRS Use Only—Do not write or staple in this space.

For the year Jan. 1–Dec. 31, 1997, or other tax year beginning , 1997, ending , 19   OMB No. 1545-0074

Label (See instructions on page 10.)

Use the IRS label. Otherwise, please print or type.

L A B E L   H E R E

Your first name and initial | Last name | Your social security number

If a joint return, spouse's first name and initial | Last name | Spouse's social security number

Home address (number and street). If you have a P.O. box, see page 10. | Apt. no.

For help in finding line instructions, see pages 2 and 3 in the booklet.

City, town or post office, state, and ZIP code. If you have a foreign address, see page 10.

Presidential Election Campaign (See page 10.)

Do you want $3 to go to this fund? . . . .
If a joint return, does your spouse want $3 to go to this fund? . . . .

Yes | No | Note: Checking "Yes" will not change your tax or reduce your refund.

Filing Status

Check only one box.

1 ☐ Single
2 ☐ Married filing joint return (even if only one had income)
3 ☐ Married filing separate return. Enter spouse's social security no. above and full name here. ▶
4 ☐ Head of household (with qualifying person). (See page 10.) If the qualifying person is a child but not your dependent, enter this child's name here. ▶
5 ☐ Qualifying widow(er) with dependent child (year spouse died ▶ 19   ). (See page 10.)

Exemptions

6a ☐ **Yourself.** If your parent (or someone else) can claim you as a dependent on his or her tax return, **do not** check box 6a. . . . .
b ☐ **Spouse** . . . .
c **Dependents:**

(1) First name Last name	(2) Dependent's social security number	(3) Dependent's relationship to you	(4) No. of months lived in your home in 1997

If more than six dependents, see page 10.

No. of boxes checked on 6a and 6b ____
No. of your children on 6c who:
• lived with you ____
• did not live with you due to divorce or separation (see page 11) ____
Dependents on 6c not entered above ____
Add numbers entered on lines above ▶ ☐

d Total number of exemptions claimed . . . .

Income

Attach Copy B of your Forms W-2, W-2G, and 1099-R here.

If you did not get a W-2, see page 12.

Enclose but do not attach any payment. Also, please use Form 1040-V.

7 Wages, salaries, tips, etc. Attach Form(s) W-2 7
8a Taxable interest. Attach Schedule B if required 8a
b Tax-exempt interest. DO NOT include on line 8a . . . 8b
9 Dividends. Attach Schedule B if required 9
10 Taxable refunds, credits, or offsets of state and local income taxes (see page 12) . . 10
11 Alimony received 11
12 Business income or (loss). Attach Schedule C or C-EZ 12
13 Capital gain or (loss). Attach Schedule D 13
14 Other gains or (losses). Attach Form 4797 14
15a Total IRA distributions . 15a   b Taxable amount (see page 13) 15b
16a Total pensions and annuities 16a   b Taxable amount (see page 13) 16b
17 Rental real estate, royalties, partnerships, S corporations, trusts, etc. Attach Schedule E 17
18 Farm income or (loss). Attach Schedule F 18
19 Unemployment compensation 19
20a Social security benefits . 20a   b Taxable amount (see page 14) 20b
21 Other income. List type and amount—see page 15 _____
21
22 Add the amounts in the far right column for lines 7 through 21. This is your **total income** ▶ 22

Adjusted Gross Income

If line 32 is under $29,290 (under $9,770 if a child did not live with you), see EIC inst. on page 21.

23 IRA deduction (see page 16) 23
24 Medical savings account deduction. Attach Form 8853 . 24
25 Moving expenses. Attach Form 3903 or 3903-F . . . 25
26 One-half of self-employment tax. Attach Schedule SE . 26
27 Self-employed health insurance deduction (see page 17) 27
28 Keogh and self-employed SEP and SIMPLE plans . . 28
29 Penalty on early withdrawal of savings 29
30a Alimony paid b Recipient's SSN ▶ _____ 30a
31 Add lines 23 through 30a . . . . ▶ 31
32 Subtract line 31 from line 22. This is your **adjusted gross income** . . . . . ▶ 32

For Privacy Act and Paperwork Reduction Act Notice, see page 38.   Cat. No. 11320B   Form **1040** (1997)

Form 1040 (1997) Page **2**

Tax Compu-tation	33	Amount from line 32 (adjusted gross income)	33	
	34a	Check if: ☐ **You** were 65 or older, ☐ Blind; ☐ **Spouse** was 65 or older, ☐ Blind. Add the number of boxes checked above and enter the total here . . . ▶ 34a		
	b	If you are married filing separately and your spouse itemizes deductions or you were a dual-status alien, see page 18 and check here . . . . ▶ 34b ☐		
	35	Enter the **larger** of your: { **Itemized deductions** from Schedule A, line 28, **OR** **Standard deduction** shown below for your filing status. **But** see page 18 if you checked any box on line 34a or 34b **or** someone can claim you as a dependent. • Single—$4,150 • Married filing jointly or Qualifying widow(er)—$6,900 • Head of household—$6,050 • Married filing separately—$3,450 }	35	
If you want the IRS to figure your tax, see page 18.	36	Subtract line 35 from line 33	36	
	37	If line 33 is $90,900 or less, multiply $2,650 by the total number of exemptions claimed on line 6d. If line 33 is over $90,900, see the worksheet on page 19 for the amount to enter .	37	
	38	**Taxable income.** Subtract line 37 from line 36. If line 37 is more than line 36, enter -0- .	38	
	39	**Tax.** See page 19. Check if any tax from **a** ☐ Form(s) 8814 **b** ☐ Form 4972 . . ▶	39	
Credits	40	Credit for child and dependent care expenses. Attach Form 2441	40	
	41	Credit for the elderly or the disabled. Attach Schedule R . .	41	
	42	Adoption credit. Attach Form 8839	42	
	43	Foreign tax credit. Attach Form 1116	43	
	44	Other. Check if from **a** ☐ Form 3800 **b** ☐ Form 8396 **c** ☐ Form 8801 **d** ☐ Form (specify) _____	44	
	45	Add lines 40 through 44	45	
	46	Subtract line 45 from line 39. If line 45 is more than line 39, enter -0- . . . . . ▶	46	
Other Taxes	47	Self-employment tax. Attach Schedule SE	47	
	48	Alternative minimum tax. Attach Form 6251	48	
	49	Social security and Medicare tax on tip income not reported to employer. Attach Form 4137	49	
	50	Tax on qualified retirement plans (including IRAs) and MSAs. Attach Form 5329 if required	50	
	51	Advance earned income credit payments from Form(s) W-2	51	
	52	Household employment taxes. Attach Schedule H	52	
	53	Add lines 46 through 52. This is your **total tax** . . . . ▶	53	
Payments	54	Federal income tax withheld from Forms W-2 and 1099 . .	54	
	55	1997 estimated tax payments and amount applied from 1996 return .	55	
	56a	**Earned income credit.** Attach Schedule EIC if you have a qualifying child **b** Nontaxable earned income: amount ▶ _____ and type ▶ _____	56a	
Attach Forms W-2, W-2G, and 1099-R on the front.	57	Amount paid with Form 4868 (request for extension) . .	57	
	58	Excess social security and RRTA tax withheld (see page 27)	58	
	59	Other payments. Check if from **a** ☐ Form 2439 **b** ☐ Form 4136	59	
	60	Add lines 54, 55, 56a, 57, 58, and 59. These are your **total payments** . . . . . ▶	60	
Refund	61	If line 60 is more than line 53, subtract line 53 from line 60. This is the amount you **OVERPAID**	61	
	62a	Amount of line 61 you want **REFUNDED TO YOU** . . . . ▶	62a	
Have it directly deposited! See page 27 and fill in 62b, 62c, and 62d.	▶ b	Routing number ☐☐☐☐☐☐☐☐☐ ▶ **c** Type: ☐ Checking ☐ Savings		
	▶ d	Account number ☐☐☐☐☐☐☐☐☐☐☐☐☐☐☐☐☐		
	63	Amount of line 61 you want **APPLIED TO YOUR 1998 ESTIMATED TAX** ▶	63	
Amount You Owe	64	If line 53 is more than line 60, subtract line 60 from line 53. This is the **AMOUNT YOU OWE.** For details on how to pay, see page 27 . . . . ▶	64	
	65	Estimated tax penalty. Also include on line 64	65	

Sign Here Keep a copy of this return for your records.	Under penalties of perjury, I declare that I have examined this return and accompanying schedules and statements, and to the best of my knowledge and belief, they are true, correct, and complete. Declaration of preparer (other than taxpayer) is based on all information of which preparer has any knowledge.		
	Your signature	Date	Your occupation
	Spouse's signature. If a joint return, BOTH must sign.	Date	Spouse's occupation
Paid Preparer's Use Only	Preparer's signature ▶	Date	Check if self-employed ☐	Preparer's social security no.
	Firm's name (or yours if self-employed) and address ▶		EIN
			ZIP code

Schedule A—Itemized Deductions

SCHEDULES A&B (Form 1040)
Department of the Treasury
Internal Revenue Service (99)

(Schedule B is on back)
▶ Attach to Form 1040. ▶ See Instructions for Schedules A and B (Form 1040).

OMB No. 1545-0074
1997
Attachment Sequence No. **07**

Name(s) shown on Form 1040 — Your social security number

Medical and Dental Expenses
Caution: Do not include expenses reimbursed or paid by others.
1. Medical and dental expenses (see page A-1) 1
2. Enter amount from Form 1040, line 33. 2
3. Multiply line 2 above by 7.5% (.075) 3
4. Subtract line 3 from line 1. If line 3 is more than line 1, enter -0- 4

Taxes You Paid
(See page A-2.)
5. State and local income taxes 5
6. Real estate taxes (see page A-2) 6
7. Personal property taxes 7
8. Other taxes. List type and amount ▶ 8
9. Add lines 5 through 8 9

Interest You Paid
(See page A-2.)

Note: Personal interest is not deductible.

10. Home mortgage interest and points reported to you on Form 1098 . 10
11. Home mortgage interest not reported to you on Form 1098. If paid to the person from whom you bought the home, see page A-3 and show that person's name, identifying no., and address ▶
. . . . 11
12. Points not reported to you on Form 1098. See page A-3 for special rules 12
13. Investment interest. Attach Form 4952 if required. (See page A-3.) 13
14. Add lines 10 through 13 14

Gifts to Charity
If you made a gift and got a benefit for it, see page A-3.

15. Gifts by cash or check. If you made any gift of $250 or more, see page A-3 15
16. Other than by cash or check. If any gift of $250 or more, see page A-3. You **MUST** attach Form 8283 if over $500 . 16
17. Carryover from prior year 17
18. Add lines 15 through 17 18

Casualty and Theft Losses
19. Casualty or theft loss(es). Attach Form 4684. (See page A-4.) 19

Job Expenses and Most Other Miscellaneous Deductions
(See page A-5 for expenses to deduct here.)

20. Unreimbursed employee expenses—job travel, union dues, job education, etc. You **MUST** attach Form 2106 or 2106-EZ if required. (See page A-4.) ▶ 20
21. Tax preparation fees 21
22. Other expenses—investment, safe deposit box, etc. List type and amount ▶ 22
23. Add lines 20 through 22 23
24. Enter amount from Form 1040, line 33. 24
25. Multiply line 24 above by 2% (.02) 25
26. Subtract line 25 from line 23. If line 25 is more than line 23, enter -0- 26

Other Miscellaneous Deductions
27. Other—from list on page A-5. List type and amount ▶ 27

Total Itemized Deductions
28. Is Form 1040, line 33, over $121,200 (over $60,600 if married filing separately)?
NO. Your deduction is not limited. Add the amounts in the far right column for lines 4 through 27. Also, enter on Form 1040, line 35, the **larger** of this amount or your standard deduction.
YES. Your deduction may be limited. See page A-5 for the amount to enter.
▶ 28

For Paperwork Reduction Act Notice, see Form 1040 instructions. Cat. No. 11330X Schedule A (Form 1040) 1997

Schedules A&B (Form 1040) 1997   OMB No. 1545-0074   Page **2**

Name(s) shown on Form 1040. Do not enter name and social security number if shown on other side.   **Your social security number**

Schedule B—Interest and Dividend Income

Attachment Sequence No. **08**

Part I
Interest Income

(See pages 12 and B-1.)

Note: If you received a Form 1099-INT, Form 1099-OID, or substitute statement from a brokerage firm, list the firm's name as the payer and enter the total interest shown on that form.

Note: *If you had over $400 in taxable interest income, you must also complete Part III.*

1   List name of payer. If any interest is from a seller-financed mortgage and the buyer used the property as a personal residence, see page B-1 and list this interest first. Also, show that buyer's social security number and address ▶

	Amount
1	

2   Add the amounts on line 1 . . . . | **2** |
3   Excludable interest on series EE U.S. savings bonds issued after 1989 from Form 8815, line 14. You MUST attach Form 8815 to Form 1040 . . . . | **3** |
4   Subtract line 3 from line 2. Enter the result here and on Form 1040, line 8a ▶ | **4** |

Part II
Dividend Income

(See pages 12 and B-1.)

Note: If you received a Form 1099-DIV or substitute statement from a brokerage firm, list the firm's name as the payer and enter the total dividends shown on that form.

Note: *If you had over $400 in gross dividends and/or other distributions on stock, you must also complete Part III.*

5   List name of payer. Include gross dividends and/or other distributions on stock here. Any capital gain distributions and nontaxable distributions will be deducted on lines 7 and 8 ▶

	Amount
5	

6   Add the amounts on line 5 . . . . | **6** |
7   Capital gain distributions. Enter here and on Schedule D | **7** |
8   Nontaxable distributions. (See the inst. for Form 1040, line 9.) | **8** |
9   Add lines 7 and 8 . . . . ▶ | **9** |
10   Subtract line 9 from line 6. Enter the result here and on Form 1040, line 9 ▶ | **10** |

Part III
Foreign Accounts and Trusts

(See page B-2.)

You must complete this part if you **(a)** had over $400 of interest or dividends; **(b)** had a foreign account; or **(c)** received a distribution from, or were a grantor of, or a transferor to, a foreign trust.   **Yes**   **No**

11a   At any time during 1997, did you have an interest in or a signature or other authority over a financial account in a foreign country, such as a bank account, securities account, or other financial account? See page B-2 for exceptions and filing requirements for Form TD F 90-22.1 . . . .

  b   If "Yes," enter the name of the foreign country ▶

12   During 1997, did you receive a distribution from, or were you the grantor of, or transferor to, a foreign trust? If "Yes," you may have to file Form 3520 or 926. See page B-2 . . . . .

For Paperwork Reduction Act Notice, see Form 1040 instructions.   Schedule B (Form 1040) 1997

SCHEDULE C
(Form 1040)

Department of the Treasury
Internal Revenue Service (99)

Profit or Loss From Business
(Sole Proprietorship)
▶ Partnerships, joint ventures, etc., must file Form 1065.
▶ Attach to Form 1040 or Form 1041. ▶ See Instructions for Schedule C (Form 1040).

OMB No. 1545-0074

1997

Attachment Sequence No. **09**

Name of proprietor

Social security number (SSN)

A	Principal business or profession, including product or service (see page C-1)	B Enter principal business code (see page C-6) ▶
C	Business name. If no separate business name, leave blank.	D Employer ID number (EIN), if any
E	Business address (including suite or room no.) ▶ .... City, town or post office, state, and ZIP code	
F	Accounting method: (1) ☐ Cash (2) ☐ Accrual (3) ☐ Other (specify) ▶	
G	Did you "materially participate" in the operation of this business during 1997? If "No," see page C-2 for limit on losses .	☐ Yes ☐ No
H	If you started or acquired this business during 1997, check here . . . . ▶ ☐	

Part I — Income

1	Gross receipts or sales. **Caution:** *If this income was reported to you on Form W-2 and the "Statutory employee" box on that form was checked, see page C-2 and check here* . . . . . . ▶ ☐	1	
2	Returns and allowances	2	
3	Subtract line 2 from line 1	3	
4	Cost of goods sold (from line 42 on page 2)	4	
5	**Gross profit.** Subtract line 4 from line 3	5	
6	Other income, including Federal and state gasoline or fuel tax credit or refund (see page C-2) . . .	6	
7	**Gross income.** Add lines 5 and 6 . . . . ▶	7	

Part II — Expenses. Enter expenses for business use of your home **only** on line 30.

8	Advertising	8	19	Pension and profit-sharing plans	19
9	Bad debts from sales or services (see page C-3) . .	9	20	Rent or lease (see page C-4):	
			a	Vehicles, machinery, and equipment .	20a
10	Car and truck expenses (see page C-3)	10	b	Other business property . .	20b
			21	Repairs and maintenance . .	21
11	Commissions and fees . .	11	22	Supplies (not included in Part III) .	22
12	Depletion	12	23	Taxes and licenses	23
13	Depreciation and section 179 expense deduction (not included in Part III) (see page C-3) . .	13	24	Travel, meals, and entertainment:	
			a	Travel	24a
			b	Meals and entertainment .	
14	Employee benefit programs (other than on line 19) . . .	14	c	Enter 50% of line 24b subject to limitations (see page C-4) .	
15	Insurance (other than health) .	15			
16	Interest:				
a	Mortgage (paid to banks, etc.) .	16a	d	Subtract line 24c from line 24b .	24d
b	Other	16b	25	Utilities	25
17	Legal and professional services	17	26	Wages (less employment credits) .	26
			27	Other expenses (from line 48 on page 2)	27
18	Office expense	18			

28	**Total expenses** before expenses for business use of home. Add lines 8 through 27 in columns ▶	28	
29	Tentative profit (loss). Subtract line 28 from line 7	29	
30	Expenses for business use of your home. Attach **Form 8829**	30	
31	**Net profit or (loss).** Subtract line 30 from line 29.		
	• If a profit, enter on **Form 1040, line 12,** and ALSO on **Schedule SE, line 2** (statutory employees, see page C-5). Estates and trusts, enter on Form 1041, line 3.	31	
	• If a loss, you MUST go on to line 32.		
32	If you have a loss, check the box that describes your investment in this activity (see page C-5).		
	• If you checked 32a, enter the loss on **Form 1040, line 12,** and ALSO on **Schedule SE, line 2** (statutory employees, see page C-5). Estates and trusts, enter on Form 1041, line 3.	32a ☐ All investment is at risk. 32b ☐ Some investment is not at risk.	
	• If you checked 32b, you MUST attach **Form 6198.**		

For Paperwork Reduction Act Notice, see Form 1040 instructions.   Cat. No. 11334P   Schedule C (Form 1040) 1997

Schedule C (Form 1040) 1997 Page **2**

Part III Cost of Goods Sold (see page C-5)

33 Method(s) used to
    value closing inventory: **a** ☐ Cost   **b** ☐ Lower of cost or market   **c** ☐ Other (attach explanation)

34 Was there any change in determining quantities, costs, or valuations between opening and closing inventory? If
    "Yes," attach explanation . . . . ☐ Yes   ☐ No

35	Inventory at beginning of year. If different from last year's closing inventory, attach explanation	
36	Purchases less cost of items withdrawn for personal use	
37	Cost of labor. Do not include salary paid to yourself	
38	Materials and supplies	
39	Other costs	
40	Add lines 35 through 39	
41	Inventory at end of year	
42	**Cost of goods sold.** Subtract line 41 from line 40. Enter the result here and on page 1, line 4	

Part IV Information on Your Vehicle. Complete this part **ONLY** if you are claiming car or truck expenses on line 10 and are not required to file Form 4562 for this business. See the instructions for line 13 on page C-3 to find out if you must file.

43 When did you place your vehicle in service for business purposes? (month, day, year) ▶ ...... / ...... / ......

44 Of the total number of miles you drove your vehicle during 1997, enter the number of miles you used your vehicle for:

  a Business ....   **b** Commuting ....   **c** Other ....

45 Do you (or your spouse) have another vehicle available for personal use? . . . . ☐ Yes   ☐ No

46 Was your vehicle available for use during off-duty hours? . . . . ☐ Yes   ☐ No

47a Do you have evidence to support your deduction? . . . . ☐ Yes   ☐ No

  b If "Yes," is the evidence written? . . . . ☐ Yes   ☐ No

Part V Other Expenses. List below business expenses not included on lines 8–26 or line 30.

Description	Amount

48 **Total other expenses.** Enter here and on page 1, line 27 . . . .

SCHEDULE D
(Form 1040)
Department of the Treasury
Internal Revenue Service (99)

Capital Gains and Losses

▶ Attach to Form 1040.　　▶ See Instructions for Schedule D (Form 1040).
▶ Use Schedule D-1 for more space to list transactions for lines 1 and 8.

OMB No. 1545-0074

1997

Attachment Sequence No. **12**

Name(s) shown on Form 1040　　　　　　　　　　　　　　　　　　　　　　Your social security number

Part I — Short-Term Capital Gains and Losses—Assets Held One Year or Less

(a) Description of property (Example: 100 sh. XYZ Co.)	(b) Date acquired (Mo., day, yr.)	(c) Date sold (Mo., day, yr.)	(d) Sales price (see page D-3)	(e) Cost or other basis (see page D-4)	(f) GAIN or (LOSS) FOR ENTIRE YEAR. Subtract (e) from (d)
1					

2 Enter your short-term totals, if any, from Schedule D-1, line 2 . . . . **2**

3 **Total short-term sales price amounts.** Add column (d) of lines 1 and 2 . . . **3**

4 Short-term gain from Forms 2119 and 6252, and short-term gain or (loss) from Forms 4684, 6781, and 8824 . . . . **4**

5 Net short-term gain or (loss) from partnerships, S corporations, estates, and trusts from Schedule(s) K-1 . . . . **5**

6 Short-term capital loss carryover. Enter the amount, if any, from line 9 of your 1996 Capital Loss Carryover Worksheet . . . . **6** (   )

7 **Net short-term capital gain or (loss).** Combine lines 1 through 6 in column (f) . . . . ▶ **7**

Part II — Long-Term Capital Gains and Losses—Assets Held More Than One Year

(a) Description of property (Example: 100 sh. XYZ Co.)	(b) Date acquired (Mo., day, yr.)	(c) Date sold (Mo., day, yr.)	(d) Sales price (see page D-3)	(e) Cost or other basis (see page D-4)	(f) GAIN or (LOSS) FOR ENTIRE YEAR. Subtract (e) from (d)	(g) 28% RATE GAIN or (LOSS) * (see instr. below)
8						

9 Enter your long-term totals, if any, from Schedule D-1, line 9 . . . . **9**

10 **Total long-term sales price amounts.** Add column (d) of lines 8 and 9 . . . **10**

11 Gain from Form 4797, Part I; long-term gain from Forms 2119, 2439, and 6252; and long-term gain or (loss) from Forms 4684, 6781, and 8824 . . **11**

12 Net long-term gain or (loss) from partnerships, S corporations, estates, and trusts from Schedule(s) K-1 . . . . **12**

13 Capital gain distributions **13**

14 Long-term capital loss carryover. Enter in both columns (f) and (g) the amount, if any, from line 14 of your 1996 Capital Loss Carryover Worksheet . . . **14** (   ) (   )

15 Combine lines 8 through 14 in column (g) **15**

16 **Net long-term capital gain or (loss).** Combine lines 8 through 14 in column (f) . . . . ▶ **16**

*****28% Rate Gain or Loss** includes all gains and losses in Part II, column (f) from sales, exchanges, or conversions (including installment payments received) **either:** • Before May 7, 1997, **or**
　　　　　　　　　　　　　　　　　　　　• After July 28, 1997, for assets held more than 1 year but **not** more than 18 months.
It also includes **ALL** "collectibles gains and losses" (as defined on page D-4).

For Paperwork Reduction Act Notice, see Form 1040 instructions.　　　Cat. No. 11338H　　　Schedule D (Form 1040) 1997

Schedule D (Form 1040) 1997 Page **2**

Part III — Summary of Parts I and II

17 Combine lines 7 and 16. If a loss, go to line 18. If a gain, enter the gain on Form 1040, line 13 — **17**
  Next: Complete Form 1040 through line 38. Then, go to **Part IV** to figure your tax if:
   • Both lines 16 and 17 are gains, **and**
   • Form 1040, line 38, is more than zero.

18 If line 17 is a loss, enter here and as a (loss) on Form 1040, line 13, the **smaller** of these losses:
   • The loss on line 17; **or**
   • ($3,000) or, if married filing separately, ($1,500) . . . . **18** ( )
  Next: Complete Form 1040 through line 36. Then, complete the **Capital Loss Carryover Worksheet** on page D-4 if:
   • The loss on line 17 exceeds the loss on line 18, **or**
   • Form 1040, line 36, is a loss.

Part IV — Tax Computation Using Maximum Capital Gains Rates

19 Enter your taxable income from Form 1040, line 38 . . . . **19**
20 Enter the **smaller** of line 16 or line 17 . . . . **20**
21 If you are filing Form 4952, enter the amount from Form 4952, line 4e **21**
22 Subtract line 21 from line 20. If zero or less, enter -0- **22**
23 Combine lines 7 and 15. If zero or less, enter -0- **23**
24 Enter the **smaller** of line 15 or line 23, but not less than zero . . . **24**
25 Enter your unrecaptured section 1250 gain, if any (see page D-4) . **25**
26 Add lines 24 and 25 . . . . **26**
27 Subtract line 26 from line 22. If zero or less, enter -0- **27**
28 Subtract line 27 from line 19. If zero or less, enter -0- **28**
29 Enter the **smaller** of line 19 or $41,200 ($24,650 if single; $20,600 if married filing separately; $33,050 if head of household) **29**
30 Enter the **smaller** of line 28 or line 29 . . . . **30**
31 Subtract line 22 from line 19. If zero or less, enter -0- **31**
32 Enter the **larger** of line 30 or line 31 . . . . **32**
33 Figure the tax on the amount on line 32. Use the Tax Table or Tax Rate Schedules, whichever applies . . . . ▶ **33**
34 Enter the amount from line 29 . . . . **34**
35 Enter the amount from line 28 . . . . **35**
36 Subtract line 35 from line 34. If zero or less, enter -0- **36**
37 Multiply line 36 by 10% (.10) . . . . ▶ **37**
38 Enter the **smaller** of line 19 or line 27 . . . . **38**
39 Enter the amount from line 36 . . . . **39**
40 Subtract line 39 from line 38. If zero or less, enter -0- **40**
41 Multiply line 40 by 20% (.20) . . . . ▶ **41**
42 Enter the **smaller** of line 22 or line 25 . . . . **42**
43 Add lines 22 and 32 . . . . **43**
44 Enter the amount from line 19 . . . . **44**
45 Subtract line 44 from line 43. If zero or less, enter -0- **45**
46 Subtract line 45 from line 42. If zero or less, enter -0- **46**
47 Multiply line 46 by 25% (.25) . . . . ▶ **47**
48 Enter the amount from line 19 . . . . **48**
49 Add lines 32, 36, 40, and 46 . . . . **49**
50 Subtract line 49 from line 48 . . . . **50**
51 Multiply line 50 by 28% (.28) . . . . ▶ **51**
52 Add lines 33, 37, 41, 47, and 51 . . . . **52**
53 Figure the tax on the amount on line 19. Use the Tax Table or Tax Rate Schedules, whichever applies **53**
54 **Tax.** Enter the **smaller** of line 52 or line 53 here and on Form 1040, line 39 . . . . . . ▶ **54**

SCHEDULE E (Form 1040) Department of the Treasury Internal Revenue Service (99)	**Supplemental Income and Loss** (From rental real estate, royalties, partnerships, S corporations, estates, trusts, REMICs, etc.) ▶ Attach to Form 1040 or Form 1041. ▶ See Instructions for Schedule E (Form 1040).	OMB No. 1545-0074 **1997** Attachment Sequence No. **13**

Name(s) shown on return   Your social security number

Part I — Income or Loss From Rental Real Estate and Royalties
Note: *Report income and expenses from your business of renting personal property on **Schedule C** or **C-EZ** (see page E-1). Report farm rental income or loss from **Form 4835** on page 2, line 39.*

1 Show the kind and location of each **rental real estate property:**
A ....
B ....
C ....

2 For each rental real estate property listed on line 1, did you or your family use it during the tax year for personal purposes for more than the greater of:
- 14 days, **or**
- 10% of the total days rented at fair rental value?
(See page E-1.)

	Yes	No
A		
B		
C		

		Properties			Totals
Income:		A	B	C	(Add columns A, B, and C.)
3 Rents received					3
4 Royalties received	4				4
Expenses:					
5 Advertising	5				
6 Auto and travel (see page E-2)	6				
7 Cleaning and maintenance	7				
8 Commissions	8				
9 Insurance	9				
10 Legal and other professional fees	10				
11 Management fees	11				
12 Mortgage interest paid to banks, etc. (see page E-2)	12				12
13 Other interest	13				
14 Repairs	14				
15 Supplies	15				
16 Taxes	16				
17 Utilities	17				
18 Other (list) ▶	18				
19 Add lines 5 through 18	19				19
20 Depreciation expense or depletion (see page E-2)	20				20
21 Total expenses. Add lines 19 and 20	21				
22 Income or (loss) from rental real estate or royalty properties. Subtract line 21 from line 3 (rents) or line 4 (royalties). If the result is a (loss), see page E-3 to find out if you must file **Form 6198**.	22				
23 Deductible rental real estate loss. **Caution:** *Your rental real estate loss on line 22 may be limited. See page E-3 to find out if you must file **Form 8582**. Real estate professionals must complete line 42 on page 2*	23	( )	( )	( )	
24 **Income.** Add positive amounts shown on line 22. **Do not** include any losses					24
25 **Losses.** Add royalty losses from line 22 and rental real estate losses from line 23. Enter total losses here					25 ( )
26 **Total rental real estate and royalty income or (loss).** Combine lines 24 and 25. Enter the result here. If Parts II, III, IV, and line 39 on page 2 do not apply to you, also enter this amount on Form 1040, line 17. Otherwise, include this amount in the total on line 40 on page 2					26

For Paperwork Reduction Act Notice, see Form 1040 instructions.   Cat. No. 11344L   Schedule E (Form 1040) 1997

Schedule E (Form 1040) 1997 — Attachment Sequence No. 13 — Page 2

Name(s) shown on return. Do not enter name and social security number if shown on other side. | Your social security number

Note: *If you report amounts from farming or fishing on Schedule E, you must enter your gross income from those activities on line 41 below. Real estate professionals must complete line 42 below.*

Part II — Income or Loss From Partnerships and S Corporations

Note: *If you report a loss from an at-risk activity, you MUST check either column (e) or (f) on line 27 to describe your investment in the activity. See page E-4. If you check column (f), you must attach Form 6198.*

27	(a) Name	(b) Enter P for partnership; S for S corporation	(c) Check if foreign partnership	(d) Employer identification number	Investment At Risk? (e) All is at risk	(f) Some is not at risk
A						
B						
C						
D						
E						

	Passive Income and Loss		Nonpassive Income and Loss		
	(g) Passive loss allowed (attach Form 8582 if required)	(h) Passive income from Schedule K–1	(i) Nonpassive loss from Schedule K–1	(j) Section 179 expense deduction from Form 4562	(k) Nonpassive income from Schedule K–1
A					
B					
C					
D					
E					
28a Totals					
b Totals					

29 Add columns (h) and (k) of line 28a **29**
30 Add columns (g), (i), and (j) of line 28b . . . . **30** ( )
31 Total partnership and S corporation income or (loss). Combine lines 29 and 30. Enter the result here and include in the total on line 40 below **31**

Part III — Income or Loss From Estates and Trusts

32	(a) Name	(b) Employer identification number
A		
B		

	Passive Income and Loss		Nonpassive Income and Loss	
	(c) Passive deduction or loss allowed (attach Form 8582 if required)	(d) Passive income from Schedule K–1	(e) Deduction or loss from Schedule K–1	(f) Other income from Schedule K–1
A				
B				
33a Totals				
b Totals				

34 Add columns (d) and (f) of line 33a **34**
35 Add columns (c) and (e) of line 33b . . . . **35** ( )
36 Total estate and trust income or (loss). Combine lines 34 and 35. Enter the result here and include in the total on line 40 below **36**

Part IV — Income or Loss From Real Estate Mortgage Investment Conduits (REMICs) — Residual Holder

37	(a) Name	(b) Employer identification number	(c) Excess inclusion from Schedules Q, line 2c (see page E-5)	(d) Taxable income (net loss) from Schedules Q, line 1b	(e) Income from Schedules Q, line 3b

38 Combine columns (d) and (e) only. Enter the result here and include in the total on line 40 below **38**

Part V — Summary

39 Net farm rental income or (loss) from **Form 4835**. Also, complete line 41 below **39**
40 TOTAL income or (loss). Combine lines 26, 31, 36, 38, and 39. Enter the result here and on Form 1040, line 17 ▶ **40**

41 **Reconciliation of Farming and Fishing Income.** Enter your **gross** farming and fishing income reported on Form 4835, line 7; Schedule K–1 (Form 1065), line 15b; Schedule K–1 (Form 1120S), line 23; and Schedule K–1 (Form 1041), line 14 (see page E-5) **41**

42 **Reconciliation for Real Estate Professionals.** If you were a real estate professional (see page E-4), enter the net income or (loss) you reported anywhere on Form 1040 from all rental real estate activities in which you materially participated under the passive activity loss rules . . . **42**

SCHEDULE SE	Self-Employment Tax	OMB No. 1545-0074
(Form 1040)	▶ See Instructions for Schedule SE (Form 1040).	1997
Department of the Treasury Internal Revenue Service (99)	▶ Attach to Form 1040.	Attachment Sequence No. 17

Name of person with **self-employment** income (as shown on Form 1040)	Social security number of person with **self-employment** income ▶	

Who Must File Schedule SE

You must file Schedule SE if:

- You had net earnings from self-employment from **other than** church employee income (line 4 of Short Schedule SE or line 4c of Long Schedule SE) of $400 or more, **OR**
- You had church employee income of $108.28 or more. Income from services you performed as a minister or a member of a religious order **is not** church employee income. See page SE-1.

Note: *Even if you had a loss or a small amount of income from self-employment, it may be to your benefit to file Schedule SE and use either "optional method" in Part II of Long Schedule SE. See page SE-3.*

Exception. If your only self-employment income was from earnings as a minister, member of a religious order, or Christian Science practitioner **and** you filed Form 4361 and received IRS approval not to be taxed on those earnings, **do not** file Schedule SE. Instead, write "Exempt–Form 4361" on Form 1040, line 47.

May I Use Short Schedule SE or MUST I Use Long Schedule SE?

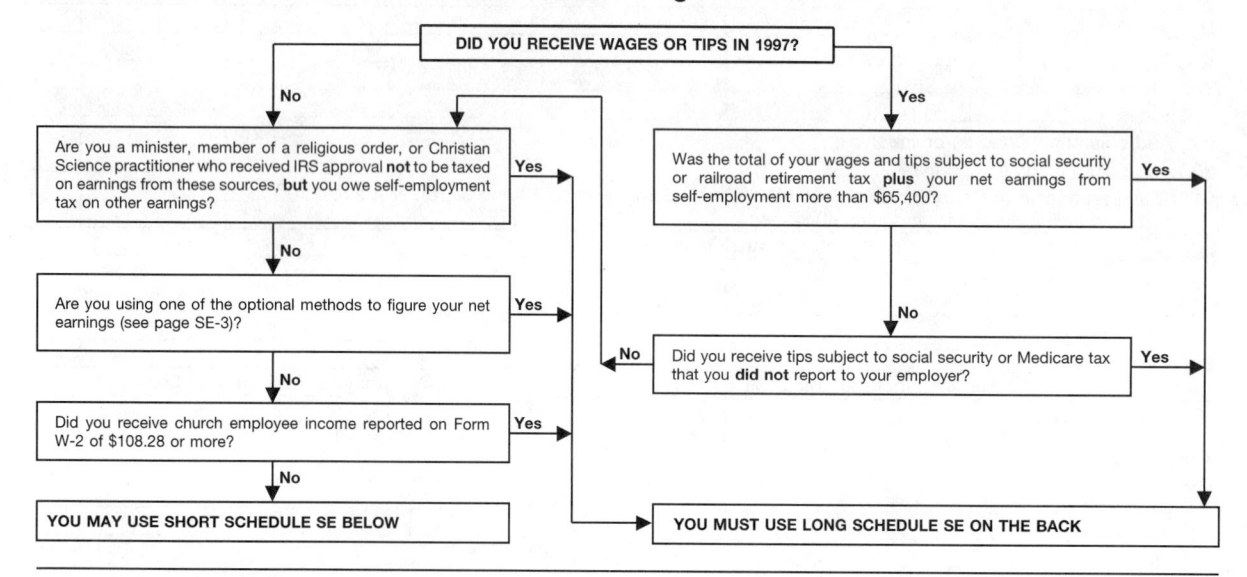

```
                        DID YOU RECEIVE WAGES OR TIPS IN 1997?
                          │                              │
                          No                             Yes
                          ▼                              ▼
  ┌────────────────────────────────────┐     ┌────────────────────────────────────┐
  │ Are you a minister, member of a    │     │ Was the total of your wages and    │
  │ religious order, or Christian      │ Yes │ tips subject to social security    │ Yes
  │ Science practitioner who received  │────▶│ or railroad retirement tax plus    │────▶
  │ IRS approval not to be taxed       │     │ your net earnings from             │
  │ on earnings from these sources,    │     │ self-employment more than $65,400? │
  │ but you owe self-employment        │     └────────────────────────────────────┘
  │ tax on other earnings?             │                      │
  └────────────────────────────────────┘                      No
                          │                                   ▼
                          No                   ┌────────────────────────────────────┐
                          ▼                    │ Did you receive tips subject to    │
  ┌────────────────────────────────────┐  No   │ social security or Medicare tax    │ Yes
  │ Are you using one of the optional  │◀──────│ that you did not report to your    │────▶
  │ methods to figure your net         │ Yes   │ employer?                          │
  │ earnings (see page SE-3)?          │────▶  └────────────────────────────────────┘
  └────────────────────────────────────┘
                          │
                          No
                          ▼
  ┌────────────────────────────────────┐
  │ Did you receive church employee    │ Yes
  │ income reported on Form            │────▶
  │ W-2 of $108.28 or more?            │
  └────────────────────────────────────┘
                          │
                          No
                          ▼
  ┌────────────────────────────────────┐     ┌────────────────────────────────────┐
  │ YOU MAY USE SHORT SCHEDULE SE BELOW│     │ YOU MUST USE LONG SCHEDULE SE ON THE BACK │
  └────────────────────────────────────┘     └────────────────────────────────────┘
```

Section A—Short Schedule SE. Caution: *Read above to see if you can use Short Schedule SE.*

1	Net farm profit or (loss) from Schedule F, line 36, and farm partnerships, Schedule K-1 (Form 1065), line 15a	1
2	Net profit or (loss) from Schedule C, line 31; Schedule C-EZ, line 3; and Schedule K-1 (Form 1065), line 15a (other than farming). Ministers and members of religious orders, see page SE-1 for amounts to report on this line. See page SE-2 for other income to report	2
3	Combine lines 1 and 2	3
4	**Net earnings from self-employment.** Multiply line 3 by 92.35% (.9235). If less than $400, **do not** file this schedule; you do not owe self-employment tax ▶	4
5	Self-employment tax. If the amount on line 4 is: • $65,400 or less, multiply line 4 by 15.3% (.153). Enter the result here and on **Form 1040, line 47.** • More than $65,400, multiply line 4 by 2.9% (.029). Then, add $8,109.60 to the result. Enter the total here and on **Form 1040, line 47.**	5
6	**Deduction for one-half of self-employment tax.** Multiply line 5 by 50% (.5). Enter the result here and on **Form 1040, line 26**	6

Schedule SE (Form 1040) 1997 — Attachment Sequence No. **17** — Page **2**

Name of person with **self-employment** income (as shown on Form 1040) | Social security number of person with **self-employment** income ▶

Section B—Long Schedule SE

Part I — Self-Employment Tax

Note: *If your only income subject to self-employment tax is church employee income, skip lines 1 through 4b. Enter -0- on line 4c and go to line 5a. Income from services you performed as a minister or a member of a religious order is not church employee income. See page SE-1.*

A If you are a minister, member of a religious order, or Christian Science practitioner **and** you filed Form 4361, but you had $400 or more of **other** net earnings from self-employment, check here and continue with Part I . . . . . . ▶ ☐

1 Net farm profit or (loss) from Schedule F, line 36, and farm partnerships, Schedule K-1 (Form 1065), line 15a. *Note: Skip this line if you use the farm optional method. See page SE-3* . . **1**

2 Net profit or (loss) from Schedule C, line 31; Schedule C-EZ, line 3; and Schedule K-1 (Form 1065), line 15a (other than farming). Ministers and members of religious orders, see page SE-1 for amounts to report on this line. See page SE-2 for other income to report. **Note:** *Skip this line if you use the nonfarm optional method. See page SE-3*. **2**

3 Combine lines 1 and 2 . . . . **3**

4a If line 3 is more than zero, multiply line 3 by 92.35% (.9235). Otherwise, enter amount from line 3 **4a**

  b If you elected one or both of the optional methods, enter the total of lines 15 and 17 here . . **4b**

  c Combine lines 4a and 4b. If less than $400, **do not** file this schedule; you do not owe self-employment tax. **Exception.** If less than $400 and you had **church employee income,** enter -0- and continue ▶ **4c**

5a Enter your **church employee income** from Form W-2. **Caution:** *See page SE-1 for definition of church employee income* **5a**

  b Multiply line 5a by 92.35% (.9235). If less than $100, enter -0- **5b**

6 **Net earnings from self-employment.** Add lines 4c and 5b **6**

7 Maximum amount of combined wages and self-employment earnings subject to social security tax or the 6.2% portion of the 7.65% railroad retirement (tier 1) tax for 1997 . . . . **7** 65,400 | 00

8a Total social security wages and tips (total of boxes 3 and 7 on Form(s) W-2) and railroad retirement (tier 1) compensation **8a**

  b Unreported tips subject to social security tax (from Form 4137, line 9) **8b**

  c Add lines 8a and 8b **8c**

9 Subtract line 8c from line 7. If zero or less, enter -0- here and on line 10 and go to line 11 . ▶ **9**

10 Multiply the **smaller** of line 6 or line 9 by 12.4% (.124) **10**

11 Multiply line 6 by 2.9% (.029). **11**

12 **Self-employment tax.** Add lines 10 and 11. Enter here and on **Form 1040, line 47** **12**

13 **Deduction for one-half of self-employment tax.** Multiply line 12 by 50% (.5). Enter the result here and on **Form 1040, line 26** **13**

Part II — Optional Methods To Figure Net Earnings (See page SE-3.)

Farm Optional Method. You may use this method **only** if:
- Your gross farm income[1] was not more than $2,400, **or**
- Your gross farm income[1] was more than $2,400 and your net farm profits[2] were less than $1,733.

14 Maximum income for optional methods . . . . **14** 1,600 | 00

15 Enter the **smaller** of: two-thirds (⅔) of gross farm income[1] (not less than zero) or $1,600. Also, include this amount on line 4b above **15**

Nonfarm Optional Method. You may use this method **only** if:
- Your net nonfarm profits[3] were less than $1,733 and also less than 72.189% of your gross nonfarm income,[4] **and**
- You had net earnings from self-employment of at least $400 in 2 of the prior 3 years.

Caution: *You may use this method no more than five times.*

16 Subtract line 15 from line 14 . . . . **16**

17 Enter the **smaller** of: two-thirds (⅔) of gross nonfarm income[4] (not less than zero) or the amount on line 16. Also, include this amount on line 4b above **17**

[1] From Schedule F, line 11, and Schedule K-1 (Form 1065), line 15b.
[2] From Schedule F, line 36, and Schedule K-1 (Form 1065), line 15a.
[3] From Schedule C, line 31; Schedule C-EZ, line 3; and Schedule K-1 (Form 1065), line 15a.
[4] From Schedule C, line 7; Schedule C-EZ, line 1; and Schedule K-1 (Form 1065), line 15c.

Appendix B

Form **1065**	**U.S. Partnership Return of Income**	OMB No. 1545-0099
Department of the Treasury Internal Revenue Service	For calendar year 1997, or tax year beginning ...., 1997, and ending ...., 19 .... ▶ See separate instructions.	**1997**

A Principal business activity	Use the IRS label. Otherwise, please print or type.	Name of partnership	**D** Employer identification number
B Principal product or service		Number, street, and room or suite no. If a P.O. box, see page 10 of the instructions.	**E** Date business started
C Business code number		City or town, state, and ZIP code	**F** Total assets (see page 10 of the instructions) $

G Check applicable boxes: (1) ☐ Initial return (2) ☐ Final return (3) ☐ Change in address (4) ☐ Amended return
H Check accounting method: (1) ☐ Cash (2) ☐ Accrual (3) ☐ Other (specify) ▶ ....
I Number of Schedules K-1. Attach one for each person who was a partner at any time during the tax year ▶ ....

Caution: *Include **only** trade or business income and expenses on lines 1a through 22 below. See the instructions for more information.*

Income

1a	Gross receipts or sales	1a	
b	Less returns and allowances	1b	1c
2	Cost of goods sold (Schedule A, line 8)		2
3	Gross profit. Subtract line 2 from line 1c		3
4	Ordinary income (loss) from other partnerships, estates, and trusts *(attach schedule)*		4
5	Net farm profit (loss) *(attach Schedule F (Form 1040))*		5
6	Net gain (loss) from Form 4797, Part II, line 18		6
7	Other income (loss) *(attach schedule)*		7
8	**Total income (loss).** Combine lines 3 through 7		8

Deductions (see page 11 of the instructions for limitations)

9	Salaries and wages (other than to partners) (less employment credits)		9
10	Guaranteed payments to partners		10
11	Repairs and maintenance		11
12	Bad debts		12
13	Rent		13
14	Taxes and licenses		14
15	Interest		15
16a	Depreciation (if required, attach Form 4562)	16a	
b	Less depreciation reported on Schedule A and elsewhere on return	16b	16c
17	Depletion **(Do not deduct oil and gas depletion.)**		17
18	Retirement plans, etc.		18
19	Employee benefit programs		19
20	Other deductions *(attach schedule)*		20
21	**Total deductions.** Add the amounts shown in the far right column for lines 9 through 20		21
22	**Ordinary income (loss)** from trade or business activities. Subtract line 21 from line 8		22

Please Sign Here

Under penalties of perjury, I declare that I have examined this return, including accompanying schedules and statements, and to the best of my knowledge and belief, it is true, correct, and complete. Declaration of preparer (other than general partner or limited liability company member) is based on all information of which preparer has any knowledge.

▶ Signature of general partner or limited liability company member ▶ Date

Paid Preparer's Use Only

Preparer's signature ▶	Date	Check if self-employed ▶ ☐	Preparer's social security no.
Firm's name (or yours if self-employed) and address ▶		EIN ▶ ZIP code ▶	

For Paperwork Reduction Act Notice, see separate instructions.   Cat. No. 11390Z   Form **1065** (1997)

Form 1065 (1997) Page **2**

Schedule A — Cost of Goods Sold (see page 13 of the instructions)

1	Inventory at beginning of year	1
2	Purchases less cost of items withdrawn for personal use	2
3	Cost of labor	3
4	Additional section 263A costs *(attach schedule)*	4
5	Other costs *(attach schedule)*	5
6	**Total.** Add lines 1 through 5	6
7	Inventory at end of year	7
8	**Cost of goods sold.** Subtract line 7 from line 6. Enter here and on page 1, line 2	8

9a Check all methods used for valuing closing inventory:
   (i) ☐ Cost as described in Regulations section 1.471-3
   (ii) ☐ Lower of cost or market as described in Regulations section 1.471-4
   (iii) ☐ Other (specify method used and attach explanation) ▶ _____

b Check this box if there was a writedown of "subnormal" goods as described in Regulations section 1.471-2(c) . . . ▶ ☐
c Check this box if the LIFO inventory method was adopted this tax year for any goods *(if checked, attach Form 970)* . ▶ ☐
d Do the rules of section 263A (for property produced or acquired for resale) apply to the partnership? . . ☐ Yes ☐ No
e Was there any change in determining quantities, cost, or valuations between opening and closing inventory? ☐ Yes ☐ No
   If "Yes," attach explanation.

Schedule B — Other Information

		Yes	No
1	What type of entity is filing this return? Check the applicable box:		
	a ☐ General partnership b ☐ Limited partnership c ☐ Limited liability company		
	d ☐ Other (see page 14 of the instructions) ▶ _____		
2	Are any partners in this partnership also partnerships?		
3	Is this partnership a partner in another partnership?		
4	Is this partnership subject to the consolidated audit procedures of sections 6221 through 6233? If "Yes," see **Designation of Tax Matters Partner** below		
5	Does this partnership meet **ALL THREE** of the following requirements?		
	a The partnership's total receipts for the tax year were less than $250,000;		
	b The partnership's total assets at the end of the tax year were less than $600,000; **AND**		
	c Schedules K-1 are filed with the return and furnished to the partners on or before the due date (including extensions) for the partnership return.		
	If "Yes," the partnership is not required to complete Schedules L, M-1, and M-2; Item F on page 1 of Form 1065; or Item J on Schedule K-1		
6	Does this partnership have any foreign partners?		
7	Is this partnership a publicly traded partnership as defined in section 469(k)(2)?		
8	Has this partnership filed, or is it required to file, **Form 8264,** Application for Registration of a Tax Shelter?		
9	At any time during calendar year 1997, did the partnership have an interest in or a signature or other authority over a financial account in a foreign country (such as a bank account, securities account, or other financial account)? See page 14 of the instructions for exceptions and filing requirements for Form TD F 90-22.1. If "Yes," enter the name of the foreign country. ▶ _____		
10	During the tax year, did the partnership receive a distribution from, or was it the grantor of, or transferor to, a foreign trust? If "Yes," the partnership may have to file Form 3520 or 926. See page 14 of the instructions		
11	Was there a distribution of property or a transfer (e.g., by sale or death) of a partnership interest during the tax year? If "Yes," you may elect to adjust the basis of the partnership's assets under section 754 by attaching the statement described under **Elections Made By the Partnership** on page 5 of the instructions		

Designation of Tax Matters Partner (see page 15 of the instructions)
Enter below the general partner designated as the tax matters partner (TMP) for the tax year of this return:

Name of designated TMP ▶ _____   Identifying number of TMP ▶ _____

Address of designated TMP ▶ _____

Form 1065 (1997) Page **3**

Schedule K — Partners' Shares of Income, Credits, Deductions, etc.

		(a) Distributive share items		(b) Total amount
Income (Loss)	1	Ordinary income (loss) from trade or business activities (page 1, line 22)	1	
	2	Net income (loss) from rental real estate activities *(attach Form 8825)*	2	
	3a	Gross income from other rental activities ... 3a		
	b	Expenses from other rental activities *(attach schedule)* ... 3b		
	c	Net income (loss) from other rental activities. Subtract line 3b from line 3a	3c	
	4	Portfolio income (loss):		
	a	Interest income	4a	
	b	Dividend income	4b	
	c	Royalty income	4c	
	d	Net short-term capital gain (loss) *(attach Schedule D (Form 1065))*	4d	
	e	Net long-term capital gain (loss) *(attach Schedule D (Form 1065))*:		
		(1) 28% rate gain (loss) ▶ .... **(2)** Total for year .... ▶	4e(2)	
	f	Other portfolio income (loss) *(attach schedule)*	4f	
	5	Guaranteed payments to partners	5	
	6	Net section 1231 gain (loss) (other than due to casualty or theft) *(attach Form 4797)*:		
	a	28% rate gain (loss) ▶.................... **b** Total for year .... ▶	6b	
	7	Other income (loss) *(attach schedule)*	7	
Deductions	8	Charitable contributions *(attach schedule)*	8	
	9	Section 179 expense deduction *(attach Form 4562)*	9	
	10	Deductions related to portfolio income (itemize)	10	
	11	Other deductions *(attach schedule)*	11	
Credits	12a	Low-income housing credit:		
		(1) From partnerships to which section 42(j)(5) applies for property placed in service before 1990	12a(1)	
		(2) Other than on line 12a(1) for property placed in service before 1990	12a(2)	
		(3) From partnerships to which section 42(j)(5) applies for property placed in service after 1989	12a(3)	
		(4) Other than on line 12a(3) for property placed in service after 1989	12a(4)	
	b	Qualified rehabilitation expenditures related to rental real estate activities *(attach Form 3468)*	12b	
	c	Credits (other than credits shown on lines 12a and 12b) related to rental real estate activities	12c	
	d	Credits related to other rental activities	12d	
	13	Other credits	13	
Investment Interest	14a	Interest expense on investment debts	14a	
	b	**(1)** Investment income included on lines 4a, 4b, 4c, and 4f above	14b(1)	
		(2) Investment expenses included on line 10 above	14b(2)	
Self-Employment	15a	Net earnings (loss) from self-employment	15a	
	b	Gross farming or fishing income	15b	
	c	Gross nonfarm income	15c	
Adjustments and Tax Preference Items	16a	Depreciation adjustment on property placed in service after 1986	16a	
	b	Adjusted gain or loss	16b	
	c	Depletion (other than oil and gas)	16c	
	d	**(1)** Gross income from oil, gas, and geothermal properties	16d(1)	
		(2) Deductions allocable to oil, gas, and geothermal properties	16d(2)	
	e	Other adjustments and tax preference items *(attach schedule)*	16e	
Foreign Taxes	17a	Type of income ▶		
	b	Name of foreign country or U.S. possession ▶		
	c	Total gross income from sources outside the United States *(attach schedule)*	17c	
	d	Total applicable deductions and losses *(attach schedule)*	17d	
	e	Total foreign taxes (check one): ▶ ☐ Paid ☐ Accrued	17e	
	f	Reduction in taxes available for credit *(attach schedule)*	17f	
	g	Other foreign tax information *(attach schedule)*	17g	
Other	18	Section 59(e)(2) expenditures: **a** Type ▶ .... **b** Amount ▶	18b	
	19	Tax-exempt interest income	19	
	20	Other tax-exempt income	20	
	21	Nondeductible expenses	21	
	22	Distributions of money (cash and marketable securities)	22	
	23	Distributions of property other than money	23	
	24	Other items and amounts required to be reported separately to partners *(attach schedule)*		

Form 1065 (1997) Page **4**

Analysis of Net Income (Loss)

1. Net income (loss). Combine Schedule K, lines 1 through 7 in column (b). From the result, subtract the sum of Schedule K, lines 8 through 11, 14a, 17e, and 18b 1

2. Analysis by partner type:

	(i) Corporate	(ii) Individual (active)	(iii) Individual (passive)	(iv) Partnership	(v) Exempt organization	(vi) Nominee/Other
a General partners						
b Limited partners						

Schedule L — Balance Sheets per Books (Not required if Question 5 on Schedule B is answered "Yes.")

Assets	Beginning of tax year		End of tax year	
	(a)	(b)	(c)	(d)
1 Cash				
2a Trade notes and accounts receivable				
b Less allowance for bad debts				
3 Inventories				
4 U.S. government obligations				
5 Tax-exempt securities				
6 Other current assets (attach schedule) . . .				
7 Mortgage and real estate loans				
8 Other investments (attach schedule)				
9a Buildings and other depreciable assets . . .				
b Less accumulated depreciation				
10a Depletable assets				
b Less accumulated depletion				
11 Land (net of any amortization)				
12a Intangible assets (amortizable only)				
b Less accumulated amortization				
13 Other assets (attach schedule)				
14 Total assets				
Liabilities and Capital				
15 Accounts payable				
16 Mortgages, notes, bonds payable in less than 1 year .				
17 Other current liabilities (attach schedule) . . .				
18 All nonrecourse loans				
19 Mortgages, notes, bonds payable in 1 year or more .				
20 Other liabilities (attach schedule)				
21 Partners' capital accounts				
22 Total liabilities and capital				

Schedule M-1 — Reconciliation of Income (Loss) per Books With Income (Loss) per Return
(Not required if Question 5 on Schedule B is answered "Yes." See page 23 of the instructions.)

1. Net income (loss) per books . . . . . .
2. Income included on Schedule K, lines 1 through 4, 6, and 7, not recorded on books this year (itemize): _____
3. Guaranteed payments (other than health insurance) . . . .
4. Expenses recorded on books this year not included on Schedule K, lines 1 through 11, 14a, 17e, and 18b (itemize):
   a Depreciation $ _____
   b Travel and entertainment $ _____
5. Add lines 1 through 4 . . . .
6. Income recorded on books this year not included on Schedule K, lines 1 through 7 (itemize):
   a Tax-exempt interest $ _____
7. Deductions included on Schedule K, lines 1 through 11, 14a, 17e, and 18b, not charged against book income this year (itemize):
   a Depreciation $ _____
8. Add lines 6 and 7 . . . .
9. Income (loss) (Analysis of Net Income (Loss), line 1). Subtract line 8 from line 5 . . . .

Schedule M-2 — Analysis of Partners' Capital Accounts (Not required if Question 5 on Schedule B is answered "Yes.")

1. Balance at beginning of year . . . . .
2. Capital contributed during year . . . . .
3. Net income (loss) per books . . . . . .
4. Other increases (itemize): _____
5. Add lines 1 through 4 . . . .
6. Distributions: **a** Cash . . . .
   b Property . . . .
7. Other decreases (itemize): _____
8. Add lines 6 and 7 . . . .
9. Balance at end of year. Subtract line 8 from line 5

SCHEDULE K-1 (Form 1065) Department of the Treasury Internal Revenue Service	**Partner's Share of Income, Credits, Deductions, etc.** ▶ See separate instructions. For calendar year 1997 or tax year beginning , 1997, and ending , 19	OMB No. 1545-0099 **1997**

Partner's identifying number ▶   **Partnership's identifying number** ▶

Partner's name, address, and ZIP code   **Partnership's name, address, and ZIP code**

- **A** This partner is a ☐ general partner ☐ limited partner
  ☐ limited liability company member
- **B** What type of entity is this partner? ▶ ....
- **C** Is this partner a ☐ domestic or a ☐ foreign partner?
- **D** Enter partner's percentage of: **(i)** Before change or termination **(ii)** End of year
  - Profit sharing . . . .% ......%
  - Loss sharing . . . .% ......%
  - Ownership of capital . . . .% ......%
- **E** IRS Center where partnership filed return:

- **F** Partner's share of liabilities (see instructions):
  - Nonrecourse . . . . $ ....
  - Qualified nonrecourse financing . $ ....
  - Other . . . . $ ....
- **G** Tax shelter registration number . ▶ ....
- **H** Check here if this partnership is a publicly traded partnership as defined in section 469(k)(2) . . . . ☐
- **I** Check applicable boxes: **(1)** ☐ Final K-1 **(2)** ☐ Amended K-1

J Analysis of partner's capital account:

(a) Capital account at beginning of year	(b) Capital contributed during year	(c) Partner's share of lines 3, 4, and 7, Form 1065, Schedule M-2	(d) Withdrawals and distributions	(e) Capital account at end of year (combine columns (a) through (d))
			( )	

		(a) Distributive share item		(b) Amount	(c) 1040 filers enter the amount in column (b) on:
Income (Loss)	1	Ordinary income (loss) from trade or business activities	1		See page 6 of Partner's Instructions for Schedule K-1 (Form 1065).
	2	Net income (loss) from rental real estate activities	2		
	3	Net income (loss) from other rental activities	3		
	4	Portfolio income (loss):			
	a	Interest	4a		Sch. B, Part I, line 1
	b	Dividends	4b		Sch. B, Part II, line 5
	c	Royalties	4c		Sch. E, Part I, line 4
	d	Net short-term capital gain (loss)	4d		Sch. D, line 5, col. (f)
	e	Net long-term capital gain (loss):			
		(1) 28% rate gain (loss)	e(1)		Sch. D, line 12, col. (g)
		(2) Total for year	e(2)		Sch. D, line 12, col. (f)
	f	Other portfolio income (loss) *(attach schedule)*	4f		Enter on applicable line of your return.
	5	Guaranteed payments to partner	5		See page 6 of Partner's Instructions for Schedule K-1 (Form 1065).
	6	Net section 1231 gain (loss) (other than due to casualty or theft):			
	a	28% rate gain (loss)	6a		
	b	Total for year	6b		
	7	Other income (loss) *(attach schedule)*	7		Enter on applicable line of your return.
Deductions	8	Charitable contributions (see instructions) *(attach schedule)*	8		Sch. A, line 15 or 16
	9	Section 179 expense deduction	9		See page 7 of Partner's Instructions for Schedule K-1 (Form 1065).
	10	Deductions related to portfolio income *(attach schedule)*	10		
	11	Other deductions *(attach schedule)*	11		
Credits	12a	Low-income housing credit:			
		(1) From section 42(j)(5) partnerships for property placed in service before 1990	a(1)		Form 8586, line 5
		(2) Other than on line 12a(1) for property placed in service before 1990	a(2)		
		(3) From section 42(j)(5) partnerships for property placed in service after 1989	a(3)		
		(4) Other than on line 12a(3) for property placed in service after 1989	a(4)		
	b	Qualified rehabilitation expenditures related to rental real estate activities	12b		See page 8 of Partner's Instructions for Schedule K-1 (Form 1065).
	c	Credits (other than credits shown on lines 12a and 12b) related to rental real estate activities	12c		
	d	Credits related to other rental activities	12d		
	13	Other credits	13		

For Paperwork Reduction Act Notice, see Instructions for Form 1065.   Cat. No. 11394R   Schedule K-1 (Form 1065) 1997

Schedule K-1 (Form 1065) 1997 Page **2**

		(a) Distributive share item		(b) Amount	(c) 1040 filers enter the amount in column (b) on:
Investment Interest	14a	Interest expense on investment debts	14a		Form 4952, line 1
	b	(1) Investment income included on lines 4a, 4b, 4c, and 4f	b(1)		See page 8 of Partner's Instructions for Schedule K-1 (Form 1065).
		(2) Investment expenses included on line 10	b(2)		
Self-employment	15a	Net earnings (loss) from self-employment	15a		Sch. SE, Section A or B
	b	Gross farming or fishing income	15b		See page 9 of Partner's Instructions for Schedule K-1 (Form 1065).
	c	Gross nonfarm income	15c		
Adjustments and Tax Preference Items	16a	Depreciation adjustment on property placed in service after 1986	16a		See page 9 of Partner's Instructions for Schedule K-1 (Form 1065) and Instructions for Form 6251.
	b	Adjusted gain or loss	16b		
	c	Depletion (other than oil and gas)	16c		
	d	(1) Gross income from oil, gas, and geothermal properties	d(1)		
		(2) Deductions allocable to oil, gas, and geothermal properties	d(2)		
	e	Other adjustments and tax preference items *(attach schedule)*	16e		
Foreign Taxes	17a	Type of income ▶			Form 1116, check boxes
	b	Name of foreign country or possession ▶			
	c	Total gross income from sources outside the United States *(attach schedule)*	17c		Form 1116, Part I
	d	Total applicable deductions and losses *(attach schedule)*	17d		
	e	Total foreign taxes (check one): ▶ ☐ Paid ☐ Accrued	17e		Form 1116, Part II
	f	Reduction in taxes available for credit *(attach schedule)*	17f		Form 1116, Part III
	g	Other foreign tax information *(attach schedule)*	17g		See Instructions for Form 1116.
Other	18	Section 59(e)(2) expenditures: **a** Type ▶			See page 9 of Partner's Instructions for Schedule K-1 (Form 1065).
	b	Amount	18b		
	19	Tax-exempt interest income	19		Form 1040, line 8b
	20	Other tax-exempt income	20		See page 9 of Partner's Instructions for Schedule K-1 (Form 1065).
	21	Nondeductible expenses	21		
	22	Distributions of money (cash and marketable securities)	22		
	23	Distributions of property other than money	23		
	24	Recapture of low-income housing credit:			
	a	From section 42(j)(5) partnerships	24a		Form 8611, line 8
	b	Other than on line 24a	24b		

Supplemental Information

25 Supplemental information required to be reported separately to each partner *(attach additional schedules if more space is needed)*:

_____

_____

_____

_____

_____

_____

_____

_____

_____

_____

Form 1120-A — U.S. Corporation Short-Form Income Tax Return

Form **1120-A**
Department of the Treasury
Internal Revenue Service

U.S. Corporation Short-Form Income Tax Return
See separate instructions to make sure the corporation qualifies to file Form 1120-A.
For calendar year 1997 or tax year beginning ...., 1997, ending ...., 19....

OMB No. 1545-0890

1997

A Check this box if the corp. is a personal service corp. (as defined in Temporary Regs. section 1.441-4T—see instructions) ▶ ☐

Use IRS label. Otherwise, print or type.

Name

Number, street, and room or suite no. (If a P.O. box, see page 5 of instructions.)

City or town, state, and ZIP code

B Employer identification number

C Date incorporated

D Total assets (see page 5 of instructions)
$

E Check applicable boxes: (1) ☐ Initial return (2) ☐ Change of address
F Check method of accounting: (1) ☐ Cash (2) ☐ Accrual (3) ☐ Other (specify) ▶

Income

1a	Gross receipts or sales _____ **b** Less returns and allowances _____ **c** Balance ▶	1c
2	Cost of goods sold (see page 10 of instructions)	2
3	Gross profit. Subtract line 2 from line 1c	3
4	Domestic corporation dividends subject to the 70% deduction	4
5	Interest	5
6	Gross rents	6
7	Gross royalties	7
8	Capital gain net income (attach Schedule D (Form 1120))	8
9	Net gain or (loss) from Form 4797, Part II, line 18 (attach Form 4797)	9
10	Other income (see page 6 of instructions)	10
11	**Total income.** Add lines 3 through 10 ▶	11

Deductions (See instructions for limitations on deductions)

12	Compensation of officers (see page 7 of instructions)	12
13	Salaries and wages (less employment credits)	13
14	Repairs and maintenance	14
15	Bad debts	15
16	Rents	16
17	Taxes and licenses	17
18	Interest	18
19	Charitable contributions (see page 8 of instructions for 10% limitation)	19
20	Depreciation (attach Form 4562) 20	
21	Less depreciation claimed elsewhere on return . . 21a	21b
22	Other deductions (attach schedule)	22
23	**Total deductions.** Add lines 12 through 22 ▶	23
24	Taxable income before net operating loss deduction and special deductions. Subtract line 23 from line 11	24
25	Less: **a** Net operating loss deduction (see page 9 of instructions) . 25a	
	b Special deductions (see page 10 of instructions) . . . 25b	25c
26	**Taxable income.** Subtract line 25c from line 24	26
27	**Total tax** (from page 2, Part I, line 7)	27

Tax and Payments

28	**Payments:**	
	a 1996 overpayment credited to 1997 . 28a	
	b 1997 estimated tax payments . 28b	
	c Less 1997 refund applied for on Form 4466 28c ( ) Bal ▶ 28d	
	e Tax deposited with Form 7004 . . . . . . 28e	
	f Credit for tax paid on undistributed capital gains (attach Form 2439) . 28f	
	g Credit for Federal tax on fuels (attach Form 4136). See instructions . 28g	
	h Total payments. Add lines 28d through 28g	28h
29	Estimated tax penalty (see page 10 of instructions). Check if Form 2220 is attached . ▶ ☐	29
30	**Tax due.** If line 28h is smaller than the total of lines 27 and 29, enter amount owed	30
31	**Overpayment.** If line 28h is larger than the total of lines 27 and 29, enter amount overpaid	31
32	Enter amount of line 31 you want: **Credited to 1998 estimated tax** ▶ _____ **Refunded** ▶	32

Sign Here

Under penalties of perjury, I declare that I have examined this return, including accompanying schedules and statements, and to the best of my knowledge and belief, it is true, correct, and complete. Declaration of preparer (other than taxpayer) is based on all information of which preparer has any knowledge.

▶ Signature of officer   Date   Title

Paid Preparer's Use Only

Preparer's signature ▶ _____ Date _____ Check if self-employed ▶ ☐ Preparer's social security number _____
Firm's name (or yours if self-employed) and address _____ EIN ▶ _____ ZIP code ▶ _____

For Paperwork Reduction Act Notice, see page 1 of the instructions.   Cat. No. 11456E   Form **1120-A** (1997)

Form 1120-A (1997) Page **2**

Part I — Tax Computation (See page 12 of instructions.)

1. Income tax. If the corporation is a qualified personal service corporation (see page 13), check here ▶ ☐ ... **1**
2a. General business credit. Check if from Form(s): ☐ 3800 ☐ 3468
   ☐ 5884 ☐ 6478 ☐ 6765 ☐ 8586 ☐ 8830 ☐ 8826
   ☐ 8835 ☐ 8844 ☐ 8845 ☐ 8846 ☐ 8820 ☐ 8847 ☐ 8861 **2a**
 b. Credit for prior year minimum tax (attach Form 8827) ... **2b**
3. **Total credits.** Add lines 2a and 2b ... **3**
4. Subtract line 3 from line 1 ... **4**
5. Recapture taxes. Check if from: ☐ Form 4255 ☐ Form 8611 ... **5**
6. Alternative minimum tax (attach Form 4626) ... **6**
7. **Total tax.** Add lines 4 through 6. Enter here and on line 27, page 1 ... **7**

Part II — Other Information (See page 14 of instructions.)

1. See page 16 and state the principal: **a.** Business activity code no. ▶ ....
   b. Business activity ▶ ....
   c. Product or service ▶ ....
2. At the end of the tax year, did any individual, partnership, estate, or trust own, directly or indirectly, 50% or more of the corporation's voting stock? (For rules of attribution, see section 267(c).) ... ☐ Yes ☐ No
   If "Yes," attach a schedule showing name and identifying number.
3. Enter the amount of tax-exempt interest received or accrued during the tax year ... ▶ $ _____
4. Enter amount of cash distributions and the book value of property (other than cash) distributions made in this tax year ... ▶ $ _____

5a. If an amount is entered on line 2, page 1, enter amounts from worksheet on page 10:
   (1) Purchases ...
   (2) Additional sec. 263A costs (attach schedule) ...
   (3) Other costs (attach schedule) .
 b. If property is produced or acquired for resale, do the rules of section 263A apply to the corporation? ... ☐ Yes ☐ No
6. At any time during the 1997 calendar year, did the corporation have an interest in or a signature or other authority over a financial account (such as a bank account, securities account, or other financial account) in a foreign country? ... ☐ Yes ☐ No
   If "Yes," the corporation may have to file Form TD F 90-22.1
   If "Yes," enter the name of the foreign country ▶ ....

Part III — Balance Sheets per Books

	Assets	(a) Beginning of tax year	(b) End of tax year
1	Cash		
2a	Trade notes and accounts receivable		
b	Less allowance for bad debts	( )	( )
3	Inventories		
4	U.S. government obligations		
5	Tax-exempt securities (see instructions)		
6	Other current assets (attach schedule)		
7	Loans to stockholders		
8	Mortgage and real estate loans		
9a	Depreciable, depletable, and intangible assets		
b	Less accumulated depreciation, depletion, and amortization	( )	( )
10	Land (net of any amortization)		
11	Other assets (attach schedule)		
12	Total assets		

Liabilities and Stockholders' Equity

13	Accounts payable		
14	Other current liabilities (attach schedule)		
15	Loans from stockholders		
16	Mortgages, notes, bonds payable		
17	Other liabilities (attach schedule)		
18	Capital stock (preferred and common stock)		
19	Additional paid-in capital		
20	Retained earnings		
21	Adjustments to shareholders' equity (attach schedule)		
22	Less cost of treasury stock	( )	( )
23	Total liabilities and stockholders' equity		

Part IV — Reconciliation of Income (Loss) per Books With Income per Return (You are not required to complete Part IV if the total assets on line 12, column (b), Part III are less than $25,000.)

1. Net income (loss) per books ...
2. Federal income tax ...
3. Excess of capital losses over capital gains ...
4. Income subject to tax not recorded on books this year (itemize) ....
5. Expenses recorded on books this year not deducted on this return (itemize)
6. Income recorded on books this year not included on this return (itemize) ....
7. Deductions on this return not charged against book income this year (itemize) ....
8. Income (line 24, page 1). Enter the sum of lines 1 through 5 less the sum of lines 6 and 7 ...

Appendix B

Form 1120
Department of the Treasury
Internal Revenue Service

U.S. Corporation Income Tax Return

For calendar year 1997 or tax year beginning _____ , 1997, ending _____ , 19 ___
▶ Instructions are separate. See page 1 for Paperwork Reduction Act Notice.

OMB No. 1545-0123

1997

A Check if a:
1 Consolidated return (attach Form 851) ☐
2 Personal holding co. (attach Sch. PH) ☐
3 Personal service corp. (as defined in Temporary Regs. sec. 1.441-4T— see instructions) ☐

Use IRS label. Otherwise, print or type.

Name

Number, street, and room or suite no. (If a P.O. box, see page 5 of instructions.)

City or town, state, and ZIP code

B Employer identification number

C Date incorporated

D Total assets (see page 5 of instructions)

E Check applicable boxes: (1) ☐ Initial return (2) ☐ Final return (3) ☐ Change of address $

Income

1a	Gross receipts or sales _____ **b** Less returns and allowances _____ **c** Bal ▶	1c
2	Cost of goods sold (Schedule A, line 8)	2
3	Gross profit. Subtract line 2 from line 1c	3
4	Dividends (Schedule C, line 19)	4
5	Interest	5
6	Gross rents	6
7	Gross royalties	7
8	Capital gain net income (attach Schedule D (Form 1120))	8
9	Net gain or (loss) from Form 4797, Part II, line 18 (attach Form 4797)	9
10	Other income (see page 6 of instructions—attach schedule)	10
11	**Total income.** Add lines 3 through 10 ▶	11

Deductions (See instructions for limitations on deductions.)

12	Compensation of officers (Schedule E, line 4)	12
13	Salaries and wages (less employment credits)	13
14	Repairs and maintenance	14
15	Bad debts	15
16	Rents	16
17	Taxes and licenses	17
18	Interest	18
19	Charitable contributions (see page 8 of instructions for 10% limitation)	19
20	Depreciation (attach Form 4562) 20	
21	Less depreciation claimed on Schedule A and elsewhere on return . . . 21a	21b
22	Depletion	22
23	Advertising	23
24	Pension, profit-sharing, etc., plans	24
25	Employee benefit programs	25
26	Other deductions (attach schedule)	26
27	**Total deductions.** Add lines 12 through 26 ▶	27
28	Taxable income before net operating loss deduction and special deductions. Subtract line 27 from line 11	28
29	**Less: a** Net operating loss deduction (see page 9 of instructions) . . . 29a	
	b Special deductions (Schedule C, line 20) 29b	29c
30	**Taxable income.** Subtract line 29c from line 28	30

Tax and Payments

31	**Total tax** (Schedule J, line 10)	31
32	**Payments: a** 1996 overpayment credited to 1997 32a	
	b 1997 estimated tax payments . . 32b	
	c Less 1997 refund applied for on Form 4466 32c ( ) **d** Bal ▶ 32d	
	e Tax deposited with Form 7004 . . . . 32e	
	f Credit for tax paid on undistributed capital gains (attach Form 2439) . . . 32f	
	g Credit for Federal tax on fuels (attach Form 4136). See instructions . . 32g	32h
33	Estimated tax penalty (see page 10 of instructions). Check if Form 2220 is attached . . . ▶ ☐	33
34	**Tax due.** If line 32h is smaller than the total of lines 31 and 33, enter amount owed	34
35	**Overpayment.** If line 32h is larger than the total of lines 31 and 33, enter amount overpaid	35
36	Enter amount of line 35 you want: **Credited to 1998 estimated tax** ▶ _____ **Refunded** ▶	36

Sign Here

Under penalties of perjury, I declare that I have examined this return, including accompanying schedules and statements, and to the best of my knowledge and belief, it is true, correct, and complete. Declaration of preparer (other than taxpayer) is based on all information of which preparer has any knowledge.

▶ _____ _____ ▶ _____
   Signature of officer   Date   Title

Paid Preparer's Use Only

Preparer's signature ▶ _____ Date _____ Check if self-employed ☐ Preparer's social security number _____

Firm's name (or yours if self-employed) and address ▶ _____ EIN ▶ _____ ZIP code ▶ _____

Cat. No. 11450Q

Form 1120 (1997) Page **2**

Schedule A — Cost of Goods Sold (See page 10 of instructions.)

1	Inventory at beginning of year	1
2	Purchases	2
3	Cost of labor	3
4	Additional section 263A costs (attach schedule)	4
5	Other costs (attach schedule)	5
6	**Total.** Add lines 1 through 5	6
7	Inventory at end of year	7
8	**Cost of goods sold.** Subtract line 7 from line 6. Enter here and on page 1, line 2	8

9a Check all methods used for valuing closing inventory:
 (i) ☐ Cost as described in Regulations section 1.471-3
 (ii) ☐ Lower of cost or market as described in Regulations section 1.471-4
 (iii) ☐ Other (Specify method used and attach explanation.) ▶ ....

 b Check if there was a writedown of subnormal goods as described in Regulations section 1.471-2(c) ▶ ☐
 c Check if the LIFO inventory method was adopted this tax year for any goods (if checked, attach Form 970) ▶ ☐
 d If the LIFO inventory method was used for this tax year, enter percentage (or amounts) of closing inventory computed under LIFO | 9d |
 e If property is produced or acquired for resale, do the rules of section 263A apply to the corporation? ☐ Yes ☐ No
 f Was there any change in determining quantities, cost, or valuations between opening and closing inventory? If "Yes," attach explanation ☐ Yes ☐ No

Schedule C — Dividends and Special Deductions (See page 11 of instructions.)

		(a) Dividends received	(b) %	(c) Special deductions (a) × (b)
1	Dividends from less-than-20%-owned domestic corporations that are subject to the 70% deduction (other than debt-financed stock)		70	
2	Dividends from 20%-or-more-owned domestic corporations that are subject to the 80% deduction (other than debt-financed stock)		80	
3	Dividends on debt-financed stock of domestic and foreign corporations (section 246A)		see instructions	
4	Dividends on certain preferred stock of less-than-20%-owned public utilities		42	
5	Dividends on certain preferred stock of 20%-or-more-owned public utilities		48	
6	Dividends from less-than-20%-owned foreign corporations and certain FSCs that are subject to the 70% deduction		70	
7	Dividends from 20%-or-more-owned foreign corporations and certain FSCs that are subject to the 80% deduction		80	
8	Dividends from wholly owned foreign subsidiaries subject to the 100% deduction (section 245(b))		100	
9	**Total.** Add lines 1 through 8. See page 12 of instructions for limitation			
10	Dividends from domestic corporations received by a small business investment company operating under the Small Business Investment Act of 1958		100	
11	Dividends from certain FSCs that are subject to the 100% deduction (section 245(c)(1))		100	
12	Dividends from affiliated group members subject to the 100% deduction (section 243(a)(3))		100	
13	Other dividends from foreign corporations not included on lines 3, 6, 7, 8, or 11			
14	Income from controlled foreign corporations under subpart F (attach Form(s) 5471)			
15	Foreign dividend gross-up (section 78)			
16	IC-DISC and former DISC dividends not included on lines 1, 2, or 3 (section 246(d))			
17	Other dividends			
18	Deduction for dividends paid on certain preferred stock of public utilities			
19	**Total dividends.** Add lines 1 through 17. Enter here and on line 4, page 1 ▶			
20	**Total special deductions.** Add lines 9, 10, 11, 12, and 18. Enter here and on line 29b, page 1 ▶			

Schedule E — Compensation of Officers (See instructions for line 12, page 1.)

Complete Schedule E only if total receipts (line 1a plus lines 4 through 10 on page 1, Form 1120) are $500,000 or more.

(a) Name of officer	(b) Social security number	(c) Percent of time devoted to business	Percent of corporation stock owned		(f) Amount of compensation
			(d) Common	(e) Preferred	
1		%	%	%	
		%	%	%	
		%	%	%	
		%	%	%	
		%	%	%	

2 Total compensation of officers
3 Compensation of officers claimed on Schedule A and elsewhere on return
4 Subtract line 3 from line 2. Enter the result here and on line 12, page 1

Form 1120 (1997)   Page **3**

Schedule J   Tax Computation (See page 12 of instructions.)

1. Check if the corporation is a member of a controlled group (see sections 1561 and 1563) . . . . ▶ ☐

   Important: Members of a controlled group, see instructions on page 12.

2a. If the box on line 1 is checked, enter the corporation's share of the $50,000, $25,000, and $9,925,000 taxable income brackets (in that order):

   (1) $ _____   (2) $ _____   (3) $ _____

   b. Enter the corporation's share of:

   (1) Additional 5% tax (not more than $11,750) $ _____

   (2) Additional 3% tax (not more than $100,000) $ _____

3. Income tax. Check this box if the corporation is a qualified personal service corporation as defined in section 448(d)(2) (see instructions on page 13) . . . . ▶ ☐   **3**

4a. Foreign tax credit (attach Form 1118) **4a**

   b. Possessions tax credit (attach Form 5735) **4b**

   c. Check: ☐ Nonconventional source fuel credit   ☐ QEV credit (attach Form 8834)   **4c**

   d. General business credit. Enter here and check which forms are attached: ☐ 3800

   ☐ 3468   ☐ 5884   ☐ 6478   ☐ 6765   ☐ 8586   ☐ 8830   ☐ 8826

   ☐ 8835   ☐ 8844   ☐ 8845   ☐ 8846   ☐ 8820   ☐ 8847   ☐ 8861   **4d**

   e. Credit for prior year minimum tax (attach Form 8827) **4e**

5. **Total credits.** Add lines 4a through 4e **5**

6. Subtract line 5 from line 3 . . . .   **6**

7. Personal holding company tax (attach Schedule PH (Form 1120)) **7**

8. Recapture taxes. Check if from: ☐ Form 4255   ☐ Form 8611 . . . .   **8**

9. Alternative minimum tax (attach Form 4626) **9**

10. **Total tax.** Add lines 6 through 9. Enter here and on line 31, page 1 . . . .   **10**

Schedule K   Other Information (See page 14 of instructions.)

1. Check method of accounting: a ☐ Cash

   b ☐ Accrual   c ☐ Other (specify) ▶ _____

2. See page 16 of the instructions and state the principal:

   a. Business activity code no. ▶ _____

   b. Business activity ▶ _____

   c. Product or service ▶ _____

3. At the end of the tax year, did the corporation own, directly or indirectly, 50% or more of the voting stock of a domestic corporation? (For rules of attribution, see section 267(c).) . . . .

   If "Yes," attach a schedule showing: **(a)** name and identifying number, **(b)** percentage owned, and **(c)** taxable income or (loss) before NOL and special deductions of such corporation for the tax year ending with or within your tax year.

4. Is the corporation a subsidiary in an affiliated group or a parent-subsidiary controlled group? . . . . . .

   If "Yes," enter employer identification number and name of the parent corporation ▶ _____
   _____

5. At the end of the tax year, did any individual, partnership, corporation, estate or trust own, directly or indirectly, 50% or more of the corporation's voting stock? (For rules of attribution, see section 267(c).) . . . .

   If "Yes," attach a schedule showing name and identifying number. (Do not include any information already entered in **4** above.) Enter percentage owned ▶ _____

6. During this tax year, did the corporation pay dividends (other than stock dividends and distributions in exchange for stock) in excess of the corporation's current and accumulated earnings and profits? (See secs. 301 and 316.) . . . . .

   If "Yes," file Form 5452. If this is a consolidated return, answer here for the parent corporation and on **Form 851,** Affiliations Schedule, for each subsidiary.

7. Was the corporation a U.S. shareholder of any controlled foreign corporation? (See sections 951 and 957.) . . .

   If "Yes," attach Form 5471 for each such corporation. Enter number of Forms 5471 attached ▶ _____

8. At any time during the 1997 calendar year, did the corporation have an interest in or a signature or other authority over a financial account (such as a bank account, securities account, or other financial account) in a foreign country?

   If "Yes," the corporation may have to file Form TD F 90-22.1.

   If "Yes," enter name of foreign country ▶ _____

9. During the tax year, did the corporation receive a distribution from, or was it the grantor of, or transferor to, a foreign trust? If "Yes," see page 15 of the instructions for other forms the corporation may have to file . . . .

10. At any time during the tax year, did one foreign person own, directly or indirectly, at least 25% of: **(a)** the total voting power of all classes of stock of the corporation entitled to vote, or **(b)** the total value of all classes of stock of the corporation? If "Yes,"

    a. Enter percentage owned ▶ _____

    b. Enter owner's country ▶ _____

    c. The corporation may have to file Form 5472. Enter number of Forms 5472 attached ▶ _____

11. Check this box if the corporation issued publicly offered debt instruments with original issue discount . . ▶ ☐

    If so, the corporation may have to file Form 8281.

12. Enter the amount of tax-exempt interest received or accrued during the tax year ▶ $ _____

13. If there were 35 or fewer shareholders at the end of the tax year, enter the number ▶ _____

14. If the corporation has an NOL for the tax year and is electing to forego the carryback period, check here ▶ ☐

15. Enter the available NOL carryover from prior tax years (Do not reduce it by any deduction on line 29a.) ▶ $ _____

Form 1120 (1997) Page **4**

Schedule L — Balance Sheets per Books

	Assets	Beginning of tax year (a)	Beginning of tax year (b)	End of tax year (c)	End of tax year (d)
1	Cash				
2a	Trade notes and accounts receivable				
b	Less allowance for bad debts	( )		( )	
3	Inventories				
4	U.S. government obligations				
5	Tax-exempt securities (see instructions)				
6	Other current assets (attach schedule)				
7	Loans to stockholders				
8	Mortgage and real estate loans				
9	Other investments (attach schedule)				
10a	Buildings and other depreciable assets				
b	Less accumulated depreciation	( )		( )	
11a	Depletable assets				
b	Less accumulated depletion	( )		( )	
12	Land (net of any amortization)				
13a	Intangible assets (amortizable only)				
b	Less accumulated amortization	( )		( )	
14	Other assets (attach schedule)				
15	Total assets				
	Liabilities and Stockholders' Equity				
16	Accounts payable				
17	Mortgages, notes, bonds payable in less than 1 year				
18	Other current liabilities (attach schedule)				
19	Loans from stockholders				
20	Mortgages, notes, bonds payable in 1 year or more				
21	Other liabilities (attach schedule)				
22	Capital stock: a Preferred stock				
	b Common stock				
23	Additional paid-in capital				
24	Retained earnings—Appropriated (attach schedule)				
25	Retained earnings—Unappropriated				
26	Adjustments to shareholders' equity (attach schedule)				
27	Less cost of treasury stock		( )		( )
28	Total liabilities and stockholders' equity				

Note: *You are not required to complete Schedules M-1 and M-2 below if the total assets on line 15, column (d) of Schedule L are less than $25,000.*

Schedule M-1 — Reconciliation of Income (Loss) per Books With Income per Return (See page 15 of instructions.)

1. Net income (loss) per books
2. Federal income tax
3. Excess of capital losses over capital gains
4. Income subject to tax not recorded on books this year (itemize): _____
5. Expenses recorded on books this year not deducted on this return (itemize):
   a. Depreciation $ _____
   b. Contributions carryover $ _____
   c. Travel and entertainment $ _____
6. Add lines 1 through 5
7. Income recorded on books this year not included on this return (itemize):
   Tax-exempt interest $ _____
8. Deductions on this return not charged against book income this year (itemize):
   a. Depreciation $ _____
   b. Contributions carryover $ _____
9. Add lines 7 and 8
10. Income (line 28, page 1)—line 6 less line 9

Schedule M-2 — Analysis of Unappropriated Retained Earnings per Books (Line 25, Schedule L)

1. Balance at beginning of year
2. Net income (loss) per books
3. Other increases (itemize): _____
4. Add lines 1, 2, and 3
5. Distributions: a Cash
   b Stock
   c Property
6. Other decreases (itemize): _____
7. Add lines 5 and 6
8. Balance at end of year (line 4 less line 7)

Form 1120S
U.S. Income Tax Return for an S Corporation

Department of the Treasury
Internal Revenue Service

▶ Do not file this form unless the corporation has timely filed Form 2553 to elect to be an S corporation.
▶ See separate instructions.

OMB No. 1545-0130

1997

For calendar year 1997, or tax year beginning _____ , 1997, and ending _____ , 19 ___

A Date of election as an S corporation

B Business code no. (see Specific Instructions)

Use IRS label. Otherwise, please print or type.

Name

Number, street, and room or suite no. (If a P.O. box, see page 9 of the instructions.)

City or town, state, and ZIP code

C Employer identification number

D Date incorporated

E Total assets (see Specific Instructions)
$

F Check applicable boxes: (1) ☐ Initial return (2) ☐ Final return (3) ☐ Change in address (4) ☐ Amended return
G Enter number of shareholders in the corporation at end of the tax year ▶

Caution: Include **only** trade or business income and expenses on lines 1a through 21. See the instructions for more information.

Income

1a	Gross receipts or sales _____ **b** Less returns and allowances _____ **c** Bal ▶	1c
2	Cost of goods sold (Schedule A, line 8)	2
3	Gross profit. Subtract line 2 from line 1c	3
4	Net gain (loss) from Form 4797, Part II, line 18 (attach Form 4797)	4
5	Other income (loss) (attach schedule)	5
6	**Total income (loss).** Combine lines 3 through 5 ▶	6

Deductions (see page 10 of the instructions for limitations)

7	Compensation of officers	7
8	Salaries and wages (less employment credits)	8
9	Repairs and maintenance	9
10	Bad debts	10
11	Rents	11
12	Taxes and licenses	12
13	Interest	13
14a	Depreciation (if required, attach Form 4562) . . . 14a _____	
b	Depreciation claimed on Schedule A and elsewhere on return . 14b _____	
c	Subtract line 14b from line 14a	14c
15	Depletion **(Do not deduct oil and gas depletion.)**	15
16	Advertising	16
17	Pension, profit-sharing, etc., plans	17
18	Employee benefit programs	18
19	Other deductions (attach schedule)	19
20	**Total deductions.** Add the amounts shown in the far right column for lines 7 through 19 ▶	20
21	**Ordinary income (loss) from trade or business activities.** Subtract line 20 from line 6	21

Tax and Payments

22	**Tax: a** Excess net passive income tax (attach schedule) . . . 22a _____	
b	Tax from Schedule D (Form 1120S) . . . 22b _____	
c	Add lines 22a and 22b (see pages 12 and 13 of the instructions for additional taxes)	22c
23	**Payments: a** 1997 estimated tax payments and amount applied from 1996 return 23a _____	
b	Tax deposited with Form 7004 . . . 23b _____	
c	Credit for Federal tax paid on fuels (attach Form 4136) . . . 23c _____	
d	Add lines 23a through 23c	23d
24	Estimated tax penalty. Check if Form 2220 is attached . . . . . ▶ ☐	24
25	**Tax due.** If the total of lines 22c and 24 is larger than line 23d, enter amount owed. See page 4 of the instructions for depository method of payment ▶	25
26	**Overpayment.** If line 23d is larger than the total of lines 22c and 24, enter amount overpaid ▶	26
27	Enter amount of line 26 you want: **Credited to 1998 estimated tax** ▶ _____ **Refunded** ▶	27

Please Sign Here

Under penalties of perjury, I declare that I have examined this return, including accompanying schedules and statements, and to the best of my knowledge and belief, it is true, correct, and complete. Declaration of preparer (other than taxpayer) is based on all information of which preparer has any knowledge.

▶ Signature of officer   Date   ▶ Title

Paid Preparer's Use Only

Preparer's signature ▶	Date	Check if self-employed ▶ ☐	Preparer's social security number
Firm's name (or yours if self-employed) and address ▶		EIN ▶	
		ZIP code ▶	

For Paperwork Reduction Act Notice, see the separate instructions.   Cat. No. 11510H   Form **1120S** (1997)

Form 1120S (1997) Page **2**

Schedule A — Cost of Goods Sold (see page 13 of the instructions)

1	Inventory at beginning of year	1
2	Purchases	2
3	Cost of labor	3
4	Additional section 263A costs *(attach schedule)*	4
5	Other costs *(attach schedule)*	5
6	**Total.** Add lines 1 through 5	6
7	Inventory at end of year	7
8	**Cost of goods sold.** Subtract line 7 from line 6. Enter here and on page 1, line 2	8

9a Check all methods used for valuing closing inventory:
  (i) ☐ Cost as described in Regulations section 1.471-3
  (ii) ☐ Lower of cost or market as described in Regulations section 1.471-4
  (iii) ☐ Other (specify method used and attach explanation) ▶ ....
 b Check if there was a writedown of "subnormal" goods as described in Regulations section 1.471-2(c) . . . . . . ▶ ☐
 c Check if the LIFO inventory method was adopted this tax year for any goods *(if checked, attach Form 970)*. . . . . ▶ ☐
 d If the LIFO inventory method was used for this tax year, enter percentage (or amounts) of closing inventory computed under LIFO . . . . | 9d |
 e Do the rules of section 263A (for property produced or acquired for resale) apply to the corporation? . . . . ☐ Yes ☐ No
 f Was there any change in determining quantities, cost, or valuations between opening and closing inventory? . . ☐ Yes ☐ No
  If "Yes," attach explanation.

Schedule B — Other Information

		Yes	No

1 Check method of accounting: **(a)** ☐ Cash **(b)** ☐ Accrual **(c)** ☐ Other (specify) ▶ ....
2 Refer to the list on page 23 of the instructions and state the corporation's principal:
  (a) Business activity ▶ .... **(b)** Product or service ▶ ....
3 Did the corporation at the end of the tax year own, directly or indirectly, 50% or more of the voting stock of a domestic corporation? (For rules of attribution, see section 267(c).) If "Yes," attach a schedule showing: **(a)** name, address, and employer identification number and **(b)** percentage owned.
4 Was the corporation a member of a controlled group subject to the provisions of section 1561?
5 At any time during calendar year 1997, did the corporation have an interest in or a signature or other authority over a financial account in a foreign country (such as a bank account, securities account, or other financial account)? (See page 14 of the instructions for exceptions and filing requirements for Form TD F 90-22.1.) . . . .
  If "Yes," enter the name of the foreign country ▶ ....
6 During the tax year, did the corporation receive a distribution from, or was it the grantor of, or transferor to, a foreign trust? If "Yes," the corporation may have to file Form 3520 or 926. See page 14 of the instructions
7 Check this box if the corporation has filed or is required to file **Form 8264,** Application for Registration of a Tax Shelter . . . . ▶ ☐
8 Check this box if the corporation issued publicly offered debt instruments with original issue discount . . ▶ ☐
  If so, the corporation may have to file **Form 8281,** Information Return for Publicly Offered Original Issue Discount Instruments.
9 If the corporation: **(a)** filed its election to be an S corporation after 1986, **(b)** was a C corporation before it elected to be an S corporation **or** the corporation acquired an asset with a basis determined by reference to its basis (or the basis of any other property) in the hands of a C corporation, and **(c)** has net unrealized built-in gain (defined in section 1374(d)(1)) in excess of the net recognized built-in gain from prior years, enter the net unrealized built-in gain reduced by net recognized built-in gain from prior years (see page 14 of the instructions) . . . . . ▶ $ ....
10 Check this box if the corporation had accumulated earnings and profits at the close of the tax year (see page 14 of the instructions) . . . . ▶ ☐

Form 1120S (1997) Page **3**

Schedule K   Shareholders' Shares of Income, Credits, Deductions, etc.

		(a) Pro rata share items	(b) Total amount	
Income (Loss)	1	Ordinary income (loss) from trade or business activities (page 1, line 21)	1	
	2	Net income (loss) from rental real estate activities *(attach Form 8825)*	2	
	3a	Gross income from other rental activities 3a		
	b	Expenses from other rental activities *(attach schedule)* . 3b		
	c	Net income (loss) from other rental activities. Subtract line 3b from line 3a	3c	
	4	Portfolio income (loss):		
	a	Interest income	4a	
	b	Dividend income	4b	
	c	Royalty income	4c	
	d	Net short-term capital gain (loss) *(attach Schedule D (Form 1120S))*	4d	
	e	Net long-term capital gain (loss) *(attach Schedule D (Form 1120S))*:		
		(1) 28% rate gain (loss) ▶ .... (2) Total for year ▶	4e(2)	
	f	Other portfolio income (loss) *(attach schedule)*	4f	
	5	Net section 1231 gain (loss) (other than due to casualty or theft) *(attach Form 4797)*:		
	a	28% rate gain (loss) ▶ .... b Total for year ▶	5b	
	6	Other income (loss) *(attach schedule)*	6	
Deductions	7	Charitable contributions *(attach schedule)*	7	
	8	Section 179 expense deduction *(attach Form 4562)*	8	
	9	Deductions related to portfolio income (loss) (itemize)	9	
	10	Other deductions *(attach schedule)*	10	
Investment Interest	11a	Interest expense on investment debts	11a	
	b (1)	Investment income included on lines 4a, 4b, 4c, and 4f above	11b(1)	
	(2)	Investment expenses included on line 9 above	11b(2)	
Credits	12a	Credit for alcohol used as a fuel *(attach Form 6478)*	12a	
	b	Low-income housing credit:		
		(1) From partnerships to which section 42(j)(5) applies for property placed in service before 1990	12b(1)	
		(2) Other than on line 12b(1) for property placed in service before 1990.	12b(2)	
		(3) From partnerships to which section 42(j)(5) applies for property placed in service after 1989	12b(3)	
		(4) Other than on line 12b(3) for property placed in service after 1989	12b(4)	
	c	Qualified rehabilitation expenditures related to rental real estate activities *(attach Form 3468)*	12c	
	d	Credits (other than credits shown on lines 12b and 12c) related to rental real estate activities	12d	
	e	Credits related to other rental activities	12e	
	13	Other credits	13	
Adjustments and Tax Preference Items	14a	Depreciation adjustment on property placed in service after 1986	14a	
	b	Adjusted gain or loss	14b	
	c	Depletion (other than oil and gas)	14c	
	d (1)	Gross income from oil, gas, or geothermal properties	14d(1)	
	(2)	Deductions allocable to oil, gas, or geothermal properties	14d(2)	
	e	Other adjustments and tax preference items *(attach schedule)*	14e	
Foreign Taxes	15a	Type of income ▶		
	b	Name of foreign country or U.S. possession ▶		
	c	Total gross income from sources outside the United States *(attach schedule)*	15c	
	d	Total applicable deductions and losses *(attach schedule)*	15d	
	e	Total foreign taxes (check one): ▶ ☐ Paid ☐ Accrued	15e	
	f	Reduction in taxes available for credit *(attach schedule)*	15f	
	g	Other foreign tax information *(attach schedule)*	15g	
Other	16	Section 59(e)(2) expenditures: **a** Type ▶ .... **b** Amount ▶	16b	
	17	Tax-exempt interest income	17	
	18	Other tax-exempt income	18	
	19	Nondeductible expenses	19	
	20	Total property distributions (including cash) other than dividends reported on line 22 below	20	
	21	Other items and amounts required to be reported separately to shareholders *(attach schedule)*		
	22	Total dividend distributions paid from accumulated earnings and profits	22	
	23	**Income (loss).** (Required only if Schedule M-1 must be completed.) Combine lines 1 through 6 in column (b). From the result, subtract the sum of lines 7 through 11a, 15e, and 16b	23	

Form 1120S (1997) Page **4**

Schedule L — Balance Sheets per Books

Assets	Beginning of tax year (a)	Beginning of tax year (b)	End of tax year (c)	End of tax year (d)
1 Cash				
2a Trade notes and accounts receivable				
b Less allowance for bad debts				
3 Inventories				
4 U.S. Government obligations				
5 Tax-exempt securities				
6 Other current assets (attach schedule)				
7 Loans to shareholders				
8 Mortgage and real estate loans				
9 Other investments (attach schedule)				
10a Buildings and other depreciable assets				
b Less accumulated depreciation				
11a Depletable assets				
b Less accumulated depletion				
12 Land (net of any amortization)				
13a Intangible assets (amortizable only)				
b Less accumulated amortization				
14 Other assets (attach schedule)				
15 Total assets				
Liabilities and Shareholders' Equity				
16 Accounts payable				
17 Mortgages, notes, bonds payable in less than 1 year				
18 Other current liabilities (attach schedule)				
19 Loans from shareholders				
20 Mortgages, notes, bonds payable in 1 year or more				
21 Other liabilities (attach schedule)				
22 Capital stock				
23 Additional paid-in capital				
24 Retained earnings				
25 Adjustments to shareholders' equity (attach schedule)				
26 Less cost of treasury stock		( )		( )
27 Total liabilities and shareholders' equity				

Schedule M-1 — Reconciliation of Income (Loss) per Books With Income (Loss) per Return
(You are not required to complete this schedule if the total assets on line 15, column (d), of Schedule L are less than $25,000.)

1 Net income (loss) per books		5 Income recorded on books this year not included on Schedule K, lines 1 through 6 (itemize):	
2 Income included on Schedule K, lines 1 through 6, not recorded on books this year (itemize):		a Tax-exempt interest $	
		6 Deductions included on Schedule K, lines 1 through 11a, 15e, and 16b, not charged against book income this year (itemize):	
3 Expenses recorded on books this year not included on Schedule K, lines 1 through 11a, 15e, and 16b (itemize):		a Depreciation $	
a Depreciation $			
b Travel and entertainment $		7 Add lines 5 and 6	
		8 Income (loss) (Schedule K, line 23). Line 4 less line 7	
4 Add lines 1 through 3			

Schedule M-2 — Analysis of Accumulated Adjustments Account, Other Adjustments Account, and Shareholders' Undistributed Taxable Income Previously Taxed (see page 21 of the instructions)

	(a) Accumulated adjustments account	(b) Other adjustments account	(c) Shareholders' undistributed taxable income previously taxed
1 Balance at beginning of tax year			
2 Ordinary income from page 1, line 21			
3 Other additions			
4 Loss from page 1, line 21	( )		
5 Other reductions	( )	( )	
6 Combine lines 1 through 5			
7 Distributions other than dividend distributions			
8 Balance at end of tax year. Subtract line 7 from line 6			

SCHEDULE K-1 (Form 1120S)
Shareholder's Share of Income, Credits, Deductions, etc.
▶ See separate instructions.

Department of the Treasury
Internal Revenue Service

For calendar year 1997 or tax year beginning _____, 1997, and ending _____, 19 ___

OMB No. 1545-0130

1997

Shareholder's identifying number ▶

Corporation's identifying number ▶

Shareholder's name, address, and ZIP code

Corporation's name, address, and ZIP code

A Shareholder's percentage of stock ownership for tax year (see instructions for Schedule K-1) . . . . ▶ _____ %
B Internal Revenue Service Center where corporation filed its return ▶ _____
C Tax shelter registration number (see instructions for Schedule K-1) . . . . ▶ _____
D Check applicable boxes: (1) ☐ Final K-1   (2) ☐ Amended K-1

		(a) Pro rata share items		(b) Amount	(c) Form 1040 filers enter the amount in column (b) on:
Income (Loss)	1	Ordinary income (loss) from trade or business activities	1		See pages 4 and 5 of the Shareholder's Instructions for Schedule K-1 (Form 1120S).
	2	Net income (loss) from rental real estate activities	2		
	3	Net income (loss) from other rental activities	3		
	4	Portfolio income (loss):			
	a	Interest	4a		Sch. B, Part I, line 1
	b	Dividends	4b		Sch. B, Part II, line 5
	c	Royalties	4c		Sch. E, Part I, line 4
	d	Net short-term capital gain (loss)	4d		Sch. D, line 5, col. (f)
	e	Net long-term capital gain (loss):			
		(1) 28% rate gain (loss)	e(1)		Sch. D, line 12, col. (g)
		(2) Total for year	e(2)		Sch. D, line 12, col. (f)
	f	Other portfolio income (loss) *(attach schedule)*	4f		(Enter on applicable line of your return.)
	5	Net section 1231 gain (loss) (other than due to casualty or theft):			
	a	28% rate gain (loss)	5a		See Shareholder's Instructions for Schedule K-1 (Form 1120S).
	b	Total for year	5b		
	6	Other income (loss) *(attach schedule)*	6		(Enter on applicable line of your return.)
Deductions	7	Charitable contributions *(attach schedule)*	7		Sch. A, line 15 or 16
	8	Section 179 expense deduction	8		See page 6 of the Shareholder's Instructions for Schedule K-1 (Form 1120S)
	9	Deductions related to portfolio income (loss) *(attach schedule)*	9		
	10	Other deductions *(attach schedule)*	10		
Investment Interest	11a	Interest expense on investment debts	11a		Form 4952, line 1
	b	(1) Investment income included on lines 4a, 4b, 4c, and 4f above	b(1)		See Shareholder's Instructions for Schedule K-1 (Form 1120S).
		(2) Investment expenses included on line 9 above	b(2)		
Credits	12a	Credit for alcohol used as fuel	12a		Form 6478, line 10
	b	Low-income housing credit:			
		(1) From section 42(j)(5) partnerships for property placed in service before 1990	b(1)		Form 8586, line 5
		(2) Other than on line 12b(1) for property placed in service before 1990	b(2)		
		(3) From section 42(j)(5) partnerships for property placed in service after 1989	b(3)		
		(4) Other than on line 12b(3) for property placed in service after 1989	b(4)		
	c	Qualified rehabilitation expenditures related to rental real estate activities	12c		See pages 6 and 7 of the Shareholder's Instructions for Schedule K-1 (Form 1120S).
	d	Credits (other than credits shown on lines 12b and 12c) related to rental real estate activities	12d		
	e	Credits related to other rental activities	12e		
	13	Other credits	13		

For Paperwork Reduction Act Notice, see the Instructions for Form 1120S.   Cat. No. 11520D   Schedule K-1 (Form 1120S) 1997

Schedule K-1 (Form 1120S) (1997) Page **2**

		(a) Pro rata share items		(b) Amount	(c) Form 1040 filers enter the amount in column (b) on:
Adjustments and Tax Preference Items	14a	Depreciation adjustment on property placed in service after 1986	14a		See page 7 of the Shareholder's Instructions for Schedule K-1 (Form 1120S) and Instructions for Form 6251
	b	Adjusted gain or loss	14b		
	c	Depletion (other than oil and gas)	14c		
	d	(1) Gross income from oil, gas, or geothermal properties	d(1)		
		(2) Deductions allocable to oil, gas, or geothermal properties	d(2)		
	e	Other adjustments and tax preference items *(attach schedule)*	14e		
Foreign Taxes	15a	Type of income ▶			Form 1116, Check boxes
	b	Name of foreign country or U.S. possession ▶			
	c	Total gross income from sources outside the United States *(attach schedule)*	15c		Form 1116, Part I
	d	Total applicable deductions and losses *(attach schedule)*	15d		
	e	Total foreign taxes (check one): ▶ ☐ Paid ☐ Accrued	15e		Form 1116, Part II
	f	Reduction in taxes available for credit *(attach schedule)*	15f		Form 1116, Part III
	g	Other foreign tax information *(attach schedule)*	15g		See Instructions for Form 1116
Other	16	Section 59(e)(2) expenditures: a Type ▶			See Shareholder's Instructions for Schedule K-1 (Form 1120S).
	b	Amount	16b		
	17	Tax-exempt interest income	17		Form 1040, line 8b
	18	Other tax-exempt income	18		See page 7 of the Shareholder's Instructions for Schedule K-1 (Form 1120S).
	19	Nondeductible expenses	19		
	20	Property distributions (including cash) other than dividend distributions reported to you on Form 1099-DIV	20		
	21	Amount of loan repayments for "Loans From Shareholders"	21		
	22	Recapture of low-income housing credit:			
	a	From section 42(j)(5) partnerships	22a		Form 8611, line 8
	b	Other than on line 22a	22b		

Supplemental Information

23 Supplemental information required to be reported separately to each shareholder *(attach additional schedules if more space is needed)*:

Appendix B

Form **2106**	**Employee Business Expenses**	OMB No. 1545-0139
Department of the Treasury Internal Revenue Service (99)	▶ See separate instructions. ▶ Attach to Form 1040.	**19**97 Attachment Sequence No. **54**

Your name	Social security number	Occupation in which you incurred expenses

Part I   Employee Business Expenses and Reimbursements

STEP 1   Enter Your Expenses

		Column A Other Than Meals and Entertainment	Column B Meals and Entertainment
1	Vehicle expense from line 22 or line 29		
2	Parking fees, tolls, and transportation, including train, bus, etc., that **did not** involve overnight travel or commuting to and from work		
3	Travel expense while away from home overnight, including lodging, airplane, car rental, etc. **Do not** include meals and entertainment		
4	Business expenses not included on lines 1 through 3. **Do not** include meals and entertainment		
5	Meals and entertainment expenses (see instructions)		
6	**Total expenses.** In Column A, add lines 1 through 4 and enter the result. In Column B, enter the amount from line 5		

Note: *If you were not reimbursed for any expenses in Step 1, skip line 7 and enter the amount from line 6 on line 8.*

STEP 2   Enter Reimbursements Received From Your Employer for Expenses Listed in STEP 1

7	Enter reimbursements received from your employer that were **not** reported to you in box 1 of Form W-2. Include any reimbursements reported under code "L" in box 13 of your Form W-2 (see instructions)		

STEP 3   Figure Expenses To Deduct on Schedule A (Form 1040)

8	Subtract line 7 from line 6		
	Note: *If **both columns** of line 8 are zero, **stop here**. If Column A is less than zero, report the amount as income on Form 1040, line 7.*		
9	In Column A, enter the amount from line 8. In Column B, multiply the amount on line 8 by 50% (.50). If either column is zero or less, enter -0- in that column		
10	Add the amounts on line 9 of both columns and enter the total here. **Also, enter the total on Schedule A (Form 1040), line 20.** (Fee-basis state or local government officials, qualified performing artists, and individuals with disabilities: See the instructions for special rules on where to enter the total.) ▶		

For Paperwork Reduction Act Notice, see instructions.   Cat. No. 11700N   Form **2106** (1997)

Form 2106 (1997) Page **2**

Part II Vehicle Expenses (See instructions to find out which sections to complete.)

Section A—General Information

		(a) Vehicle 1	(b) Vehicle 2
11	Enter the date vehicle was placed in service	/ /	/ /
12	Total miles vehicle was driven during 1997	miles	miles
13	Business miles included on line 12	miles	miles
14	Percent of business use. Divide line 13 by line 12	%	%
15	Average daily round trip commuting distance	miles	miles
16	Commuting miles included on line 12	miles	miles
17	Other miles. Add lines 13 and 16 and subtract the total from line 12	miles	miles

18 Do you (or your spouse) have another vehicle available for personal purposes? . . . . ☐ Yes ☐ No

19 If your employer provided you with a vehicle, is personal use during off-duty hours permitted? ☐ Yes ☐ No ☐ Not applicable

20 Do you have evidence to support your deduction? . . . . ☐ Yes ☐ No

21 If "Yes," is the evidence written? . . . . ☐ Yes ☐ No

Section B—Standard Mileage Rate (Use this section only if you own the vehicle.)

22 Multiply line 13 by 31½¢ (.315). Enter the result here and on line 1. (Rural mail carriers, see instructions.) **22**

Section C—Actual Expenses

		(a) Vehicle 1	(b) Vehicle 2
23	Gasoline, oil, repairs, vehicle insurance, etc.		
24a	Vehicle rentals		
b	Inclusion amount (see instructions)		
c	Subtract line 24b from line 24a		
25	Value of employer-provided vehicle (applies only if 100% of annual lease value was included on Form W-2—see instructions)		
26	Add lines 23, 24c, and 25		
27	Multiply line 26 by the percentage on line 14		
28	Depreciation. Enter amount from line 38 below		
29	Add lines 27 and 28. Enter total here and on line 1		

Section D—Depreciation of Vehicles (Use this section only if you own the vehicle.)

		(a) Vehicle 1	(b) Vehicle 2
30	Enter cost or other basis (see instructions)		
31	Enter amount of section 179 deduction (see instructions)		
32	Multiply line 30 by line 14 (see instructions if you elected the section 179 deduction)		
33	Enter depreciation method and percentage (see instructions)		
34	Multiply line 32 by the percentage on line 33 (see instructions)		
35	Add lines 31 and 34		
36	Enter the limit from the table in the line 36 instructions		
37	Multiply line 36 by the percentage on line 14		
38	Enter the **smaller** of line 35 or line 37. Also, enter this amount on line 28 above		

Form **2106-EZ**	**Unreimbursed Employee Business Expenses**	OMB No. 1545-1441
Department of the Treasury Internal Revenue Service (99)	▶ Attach to Form 1040.	**1997** Attachment Sequence No. **54A**

Your name	Social security number	Occupation in which you incurred expenses

Part I — General Information

You May Use This Form ONLY if All of the Following Apply:

- You are an employee deducting expenses attributable to your job.
- You **do not** get reimbursed by your employer for any expenses (amounts your employer included in box 1 of your Form W-2 are not considered reimbursements).
- If you are claiming vehicle expense,
  - **a** You own your vehicle, and
  - **b** You are using the standard mileage rate for 1997 **and** also used it for the year you first placed the vehicle in service.

Part II — Figure Your Expenses

1	Vehicle expense using the standard mileage rate. Complete Part III and multiply line 8a by 31½¢ (.315)	1
2	Parking fees, tolls, and transportation, including train, bus, etc., that **did not** involve overnight travel or commuting to and from work	2
3	Travel expense while away from home overnight, including lodging, airplane, car rental, etc. **Do not** include meals and entertainment	3
4	Business expenses not included on lines 1 through 3. **Do not** include meals and entertainment	4
5	Meals and entertainment expenses: $ _____ x 50% (.50)	5
6	**Total expenses.** Add lines 1 through 5. Enter here and **on line 20 of Schedule A (Form 1040).** (Fee-basis state or local government officials, qualified performing artists, and individuals with disabilities: See the instructions for special rules on where to enter this amount.)	6

Part III — Information on Your Vehicle. Complete this part ONLY if you are claiming vehicle expense on line 1.

7 When did you place your vehicle in service for business purposes? (month, day, year) ▶ _____ / _____ / _____

8 Of the total number of miles you drove your vehicle during 1997, enter the number of miles you used your vehicle for:

   a Business _____ **b** Commuting _____ **c** Other _____

9 Do you (or your spouse) have another vehicle available for personal use? ☐ Yes ☐ No

10 Was your vehicle available for use during off-duty hours? ☐ Yes ☐ No

11a Do you have evidence to support your deduction? ☐ Yes ☐ No

   b If "Yes," is the evidence written? ☐ Yes ☐ No

General Instructions

Section references are to the Internal Revenue Code.

Changes To Note

- The standard mileage rate has been increased to 31½ cents for each mile of business use in 1997.
- For tax years beginning after 1986, a fee-basis state or local government official can deduct the expenses incurred for services performed in that job in figuring adjusted gross income, rather than as a miscellaneous itemized deduction subject to the 2% limit. See the line 6 instructions for more details. You should file Form 1040X to amend any prior year income tax return affected by this retroactive change. However, you generally must file Form 1040X within 3 years after the date you filed your original return or within 2 years after the date you paid the tax, whichever is later.

Purpose of Form

You may use Form 2106-EZ instead of Form 2106 if you meet all the requirements listed in Part I of this form.

Recordkeeping

You cannot deduct expenses for travel (including meals unless you used the standard meal allowance), entertainment, gifts, or use of a car or other listed property, unless you keep records to prove the time, place, business purpose, business relationship (for entertainment and gifts), and amounts of these expenses. Generally, you must also have receipts for all lodging expenses (regardless of the amount) and any other expense of $75 or more.

For Paperwork Reduction Act Notice, see back of form.   Cat. No. 20604Q   Form **2106-EZ** (1997)

Form 2106-EZ (1997) Page **2**

Additional Information

If you need more information about employee business expenses, you will find the following publications helpful:

Pub. 463, Travel, Entertainment, Gift, and Car Expenses
Pub. 529, Miscellaneous Deductions
Pub. 587, Business Use of Your Home (Including Use by Day-Care Providers)
Pub. 946, How To Depreciate Property

Specific Instructions

Part II—Figure Your Expenses

Line 2. See the line 8b instructions on this page for the definition of commuting.

Line 3. Enter expenses for lodging and transportation connected with overnight travel away from your tax home (defined below). You cannot deduct any expenses for travel away from your tax home for any period of temporary employment of more than 1 year. **Do not** include expenses for meals and entertainment. For more details, including limits, see Pub. 463.

Generally, your **tax home** is your main place of business or post of duty regardless of where you maintain your family home. If you do not have a regular or main place of business because of the nature of your work, then your tax home is the place where you regularly live. If you do not fit in either of these categories, you are considered an itinerant and your tax home is wherever you work. As an itinerant, you are not away from home and cannot claim a travel expense deduction. For more details on your tax home, see Pub. 463.

Line 4. Enter other job-related expenses not listed on any other line of this form. Include expenses for business gifts, education (tuition and books), home office, trade publications, etc. For details, including limits, see Pub. 463 and Pub. 529. If you are deducting home office expenses, see Pub. 587 for special instructions on how to report these expenses. If you are deducting depreciation or claiming a section 179 deduction on a cellular telephone or other similar telecommunications equipment, a home computer, etc., see **Form 4562,** Depreciation and Amortization, to figure the depreciation and section 179 deduction to enter on line 4.

Do not include expenses for meals and entertainment, taxes, or interest on line 4. Deductible taxes are entered on lines 5 through 9 of Schedule A (Form 1040). Employees cannot deduct car loan interest.

Note: *If line 4 is your only entry, do not complete Form 2106-EZ unless you are:*

- *A fee-basis state or local government official claiming expenses in performing that job,*
- *A qualified performing artist claiming performing-arts-related business expenses, or*
- *An individual with a disability claiming impairment-related work expenses.*

See the line 6 instructions for definitions. If you are not required to file Form 2106-EZ, enter your expenses directly on Schedule A (Form 1040), line 20.

Line 5. Enter your allowable meals and entertainment expense and multiply the total by 50%. Include meals while away from your tax home overnight and other business meals and entertainment. Instead of actual cost, you may be able to claim the **standard meal allowance** for your daily meals and incidental expenses while away from your tax home overnight. Under this method, you deduct a specified amount, depending on where you travel, instead of keeping records of your actual meal expenses. However, you must still keep records to prove the time, place, and business purpose of your travel. See Pub. 463 to figure your deduction using the standard meal allowance.

Line 6. If you were a **fee-basis state or local government official** (defined below), include the expenses you incurred for services performed in that job in the total on Form 1040, line 31. Write "FBO" and the amount in the space to the left of line 31. Your employee business expenses are deductible whether or not you itemize deductions. A fee-basis state or local government official is an official who is an employee of a state or political subdivision of a state and is compensated, in whole or in part, on a fee basis.

If you were a **qualified performing artist** (defined below), include your performing-arts-related expenses in the total on Form 1040, line 31. Write "QPA" and the amount in the space to the left of line 31. Your performing-arts-related business expenses are deductible whether or not you itemize deductions. The expenses are not subject to the 2% limit that applies to most other employee business expenses.

A qualified performing artist is an individual who:

1. Performed services in the performing arts as an employee for at least two employers during the tax year,

2. Received from at least two of those employers wages of $200 or more per employer,

3. Had allowable business expenses attributable to the performing arts of more than 10% of gross income from the performing arts, and

4. Had adjusted gross income of $16,000 or less before deducting expenses as a performing artist.

To be treated as a qualified performing artist, a married individual must also file a joint return, unless the individual and his or her spouse lived apart for all of 1997. On a joint return, requirements **1**, **2**, and **3** must be figured separately for each spouse. However, requirement **4** applies to the combined adjusted gross income of both spouses.

If you were an **individual with a disability** and are claiming impairment-related work expenses (defined below), enter the part of the line 6 amount attributable to those expenses on Schedule A (Form 1040), line 27, instead of on Schedule A (Form 1040), line 20. Your impairment-related work expenses are not subject to the 2% limit that applies to most other employee business expenses.

Impairment-related work expenses are the allowable expenses of an individual with physical or mental disabilities for attendant care at his or her place of employment. They also include other expenses in connection with the place of employment that enable the employee to work. See Pub. 463 for more details.

Part III—Information on Your Vehicle

If you claim vehicle expense, you must provide certain information on the use of your vehicle by completing Part III. Include an attachment listing the information requested in Part III for any additional vehicles you used for business during the year.

Line 7. Date placed in service is generally the date you first start using your vehicle. However, if you first start using your vehicle for personal use and later convert it to business use, the vehicle is treated as placed in service on the date you started using it for business.

Line 8a. Do not include commuting miles on this line; commuting miles are not considered business miles. See the line 8b instructions for the definition of commuting.

Line 8b. If you do not know the total actual miles you used your vehicle for commuting during the year, figure the amount to enter on line 8b by multiplying the number of days during the year that you used your vehicle for commuting by the average daily round trip commuting distance in miles.

Generally, **commuting** is travel between your home and a work location. However, such travel is not commuting if you meet **any** of the following conditions:

1. You have at least one regular work location away from your home and you travel to a temporary work location in the same trade or business, regardless of the distance. A temporary work location is one where you perform services on an irregular or short-term basis (generally a matter of days or weeks).

2. You travel to a temporary work location outside the metropolitan area where you live and normally work.

3. Your home is your principal place of business under section 280A(c)(1)(A) (for purposes of deducting expenses for business use of your home) and you travel to another work location in the same trade or business, regardless of whether that location is regular or temporary and regardless of distance.

Paperwork Reduction Act Notice. We ask for the information on this form to carry out the Internal Revenue laws of the United States. You are required to give us the information. We need it to ensure that you are complying with these laws and to allow us to figure and collect the right amount of tax.

You are not required to provide the information requested on a form that is subject to the Paperwork Reduction Act unless the form displays a valid OMB control number. Books or records relating to a form or its instructions must be retained as long as their contents may become material in the administration of any Internal Revenue law. Generally, tax returns and return information are confidential, as required by section 6103.

The time needed to complete and file this form will vary depending on individual circumstances. The estimated average time is:

Recordkeeping	40 min.
Learning about the law or the form	5 min.
Preparing the form	28 min.
Copying, assembling, and sending the form to the IRS	20 min.

If you have comments concerning the accuracy of these time estimates or suggestions for making this form simpler, we would be happy to hear from you. See the Instructions for Form 1040.

Form **2119**	**Sale of Your Home**	OMB No. 1545-0072
Department of the Treasury Internal Revenue Service (99)	▶ Attach to Form 1040 for year of sale. ▶ See separate instructions. ▶ Please print or type.	**1997** Attachment Sequence No. **20**

Your first name and initial. If a joint return, also give spouse's name and initial.	Last name	Your social security number
If you are filing this form by itself and not with your tax return, see instructions on page 3.	Present address (no., street, and apt. no., rural route, or P.O. box no. if mail is not delivered to street address)	Spouse's social security number
	City, town or post office, state, and ZIP code	

Part I   Gain on Sale

1. Date your former main home was sold. If sold after May 6, 1997, see page 3 . . . . . ▶ **1**   __/__/__ mo. day yr.
2. Have you bought or built a new main home? . . . . ☐ Yes ☐ No
3. If any part of either main home was ever rented out or used for business, check here ▶ ☐ and see page 3.
4. Selling price of home. Do not include personal property items you sold with your home . . **4**
5. Expense of sale (see page 4) **5**
6. Subtract line 5 from line 4 . . . . **6**
7. Adjusted basis of home sold (see page 4) **7**
8. **Gain on sale.** Subtract line 7 from line 6. **If zero or less, stop** and attach this form to your return **8**
   - For sales **before May 7, 1997,** you must go to Part II or Part III, whichever applies. **But** if line 2 is "No," go to line 9.
   - For sales **after May 6, 1997,** you must go to Part IV on the back to figure any exclusion. **But** if you qualify and elect to use the rules for sales before May 7, 1997, go to Part II or Part III, whichever applies.
9. If you haven't replaced your home, do you plan to do so within the **replacement period** (see page 1)? . ☐ Yes ☐ No
   - If line 9 is "Yes," stop here, attach this form to your return, and see **Additional filing requirements** on page 1.
   - If line 9 is "No," you **must** go to Part II or Part III, whichever applies.

Part II   One-Time Exclusion of Gain for People Age 55 or Older—By completing this part, you are electing to take the one-time exclusion (see page 2). If you are not electing to take the exclusion, go to Part III now.

10. Who was age 55 or older on the date of sale? . . . . ☐ You ☐ Your spouse ☐ Both of you
11. Did the person who was 55 or older own and use the property as his or her main home for a total of at least 3 years of the 5-year period before the sale? See page 2 for exceptions. If "No," go to Part III now . . . ☐ Yes ☐ No
12. At the time of sale, who owned the home? . . . . ☐ You ☐ Your spouse ☐ Both of you
13. Social security number of spouse at the time of sale if you had a different spouse from the one above. If you were not married at the time of sale, enter "None" . . . . ▶ **13**
14. **Exclusion.** Enter the **smaller** of line 8 or $125,000 ($62,500 if married filing separate return). Then, go to line 15 . . . . **14**

Part III   Adjusted Sales Price, Taxable Gain, and Adjusted Basis of New Home

15. If line 14 is blank, enter the amount from line 8. Otherwise, subtract line 14 from line 8 . . **15**
    - If line 15 is zero, stop and attach this form to your return.
    - If line 15 is more than zero and line 2 is "Yes," go to line 16 now.
    - If you are reporting this sale on the installment method, stop and see page 4.
    - All others, stop and **enter the amount from line 15 on Schedule D, line 4 or line 11.**
16. Fixing-up expenses (see page 4 for time limits) **16**
17. If line 14 is blank, enter amount from line 16. Otherwise, add lines 14 and 16 . . . . . . **17**
18. **Adjusted sales price.** Subtract line 17 from line 6 . . . . **18**
19a. Date you moved into new home ▶ __/__/__ **b** Cost of new home (see page 5) . . **19b**
20. Subtract line 19b from line 18. If zero or less, enter -0- **20**
21. **Taxable gain.** Enter the **smaller** of line 15 or line 20 . . . . **21**
    - If line 21 is zero, go to line 22 and attach this form to your return.
    - If you are reporting this sale on the installment method, see the line 15 instructions and go to line 22.
    - All others, **enter the amount from line 21 on Schedule D, line 4 or line 11,** and go to line 22.
22. **Postponed gain.** Subtract line 21 from line 15 . . . . **22**
23. **Adjusted basis of new home.** Subtract line 22 from line 19b **23**

For Paperwork Reduction Act Notice, see page 6 of instructions.   Cat. No. 11710J   Form **2119** (1997)

Form 2119 (1997) Page **2**

Part IV — Exclusion and Taxable Gain for Sales After May 6, 1997

24 Did you (or your spouse if filing a joint return) own and use the property as your main home for a total of at least 2 years of the 5-year period before the sale? See page 3 for exceptions ☐ Yes ☐ No

25 Maximum exclusion. See page 5 for the amount to enter. **25**

26 Enter the amount from line 8 . . . .   **26**

27 **Exclusion.** Enter the **smaller** of line 25 or line 26. If line 26 is the smaller amount, stop and attach this form to your return. Otherwise, go to line 28 . . . .   **27**

28 **Taxable gain.** Subtract line 27 from line 26 . . . .   **28**

- If you are reporting this sale on the installment method, see the line 15 instructions.
- All others, enter the amount from line 28 on **Schedule D, line 4 or line 11.**

Sign here only if you are filing this form by itself and not with your tax return.

Under penalties of perjury, I declare that I have examined this form, including attachments, and to the best of my knowledge and belief, it is true, correct, and complete.

Your signature ▶ _____   Date _____

Spouse's signature ▶ _____   Date _____

If a joint return, both must sign.

Appendix B

Form **2210**	**Underpayment of**	OMB No. 1545-0140
Department of the Treasury Internal Revenue Service	**Estimated Tax by Individuals, Estates, and Trusts** ▶ See separate instructions. ▶ Attach to Form 1040, 1040A, 1040NR, 1040NR-EZ, or 1041.	**1997** Attachment Sequence No. **06**

Name(s) shown on tax return | Identifying number

Note: *In most cases, you **do not** need to file Form 2210. The IRS will figure any penalty you owe and send you a bill. File Form 2210 **only** if one or more boxes in Part I apply to you. If you do not need to file Form 2210, you still may use it to figure your penalty. Enter the amount from line 20 or line 32 on the penalty line of your return, but **do not** attach Form 2210.*

Part I — Reasons for Filing

If 1a, b, or c below applies to you, you may be able to lower or eliminate your penalty. But you MUST check the boxes that apply and file Form 2210 with your tax return. If 1d below applies to you, check that box and file Form 2210 with your tax return.

1   Check whichever boxes apply (if none apply, see the **Note** above):

a ☐ You request a **waiver.** In certain circumstances, the IRS will waive all or part of the penalty. See **Waiver of Penalty** on page 1 of the instructions.

b ☐ You use the **annualized income installment method.** If your income varied during the year, this method may reduce the amount of one or more required installments. See page 4 of the instructions.

c ☐ You had Federal income tax withheld from wages and, for estimated tax purposes, you treat the withheld tax as paid on the dates it was actually withheld, instead of in equal amounts on the payment due dates. See the instructions for line 22 on page 3.

d ☐ Your required annual payment (line 13 below) is based on your 1996 tax and you filed or are filing a joint return for either 1996 or 1997 but not for both years.

Part II — Required Annual Payment

2	Enter your 1997 tax after credits (see page 2 of the instructions). **Caution:** *Also see page 2 for a special rule if claiming the research credit*	2
3	Other taxes (see page 2 of the instructions)	3
4	Add lines 2 and 3	4
5	Earned income credit 5	
6	Credit for Federal tax paid on fuels 6	
7	Add lines 5 and 6	7
8	Current year tax. Subtract line 7 from line 4	8
9	Multiply line 8 by 90% (.90) 9	
10	Withholding taxes. **Do not** include any estimated tax payments on this line (see page 2 of the instructions)	10
11	Subtract line 10 from line 8. If less than $500, stop here; **do not** complete or file this form. You do not owe the penalty	11
12	Enter the tax shown on your 1996 tax return (110% of that amount if the adjusted gross income shown on that return is more than $150,000, or if married filing separately for 1997, more than $75,000). **Caution:** *See page 2 of the instructions*	12
13	**Required annual payment.** Enter the **smaller** of line 9 or line 12	13

Note: *If line 10 is equal to or more than line 13, stop here; you do not owe the penalty. Do not file Form 2210 unless you checked box 1d above.*

Part III — Short Method

(**Caution:** *See page 2 of the instructions to find out if you can use the short method. If you checked box **1b** or **c** in Part I, skip this part and go to Part IV.*)

14	Enter the amount, if any, from line 10 above 14	
15	Enter the total amount, if any, of estimated tax payments you made 15	
16	Add lines 14 and 15	16
17	**Total underpayment for year.** Subtract line 16 from line 13. If zero or less, stop here; you do not owe the penalty. Do not file Form 2210 unless you checked box 1d above	17
18	Multiply line 17 by .05986	18
19	• If the amount on line 17 was paid **on or after** 4/15/98, enter -0-. • If the amount on line 17 was paid **before** 4/15/98, make the following computation to find the amount to enter on line 19. Amount on × Number of days paid × .00025 line 17 before 4/15/98	19
20	**PENALTY.** Subtract line 19 from line 18. Enter the result here and on Form 1040, line 65; Form 1040A, line 34; Form 1040NR, line 65; Form 1040NR-EZ, line 26; or Form 1041, line 27 ▶	20

For Paperwork Reduction Act Notice, see page 1 of separate instructions.   Cat. No. 11744P   Form **2210** (1997)

Form 2210 (1997) Page 2

Part IV — Regular Method (See page 2 of the instructions if you are filing Form 1040NR or 1040NR-EZ.)

Section A—Figure Your Underpayment

		Payment Due Dates			
		(a) 4/15/97	(b) 6/15/97	(c) 9/15/97	(d) 1/15/98
21	**Required installments.** If box 1b applies, enter the amounts from Schedule AI, line 26. Otherwise, enter ¼ of line 13, Form 2210, in each column				
22	Estimated tax paid and tax withheld (see page 3 of the instructions). For column (a) only, also enter the amount from line 22 on line 26. If line 22 is equal to or more than line 21 for all payment periods, stop here; you do not owe the penalty. Do not file Form 2210 unless you checked a box in Part I *Complete lines 23 through 29 of one column before going to the next column.*				
23	Enter amount, if any, from line 29 of previous column				
24	Add lines 22 and 23				
25	Add amounts on lines 27 and 28 of the previous column				
26	Subtract line 25 from line 24. If zero or less, enter -0-. For column (a) only, enter the amount from line 22				
27	If the amount on line 26 is zero, subtract line 24 from line 25. Otherwise, enter -0-				
28	**Underpayment.** If line 21 is equal to or more than line 26, subtract line 26 from line 21. Then go to line 23 of next column. Otherwise, go to line 29 ▶				
29	Overpayment. If line 26 is more than line 21, subtract line 21 from line 26. Then go to line 23 of next column				

Section B—Figure the Penalty (Complete lines 30 and 31 of one column before going to the next column.)

		4/15/97	6/15/97	9/15/97	1/15/98
30	Number of days FROM the date shown above line 30 TO the date the amount on line 28 was paid or 4/15/98, whichever is earlier	Days:	Days:	Days:	Days:
31	Underpayment on line 28 (see page 3 of the instructions) × $\dfrac{\text{Number of days on line 30}}{365}$ × .09 ▶	$	$	$	$
32	**PENALTY.** Add the amounts in each column of line 31. Enter the total here and on Form 1040, line 65; Form 1040A, line 34; Form 1040NR, line 65; Form 1040NR-EZ, line 26; or Form 1041, line 27 ▶ 32				$

Form 2210 (1997) Page **3**

Schedule AI—Annualized Income Installment Method (see pages 4 and 5 of the instructions)

Estates and trusts, **do not** use the period ending dates shown to the right. Instead, use the following: 2/28/97, 4/30/97, 7/31/97, and 11/30/97.

		(a) 1/1/97–3/31/97	(b) 1/1/97–5/31/97	(c) 1/1/97–8/31/97	(d) 1/1/97–12/31/97

Part I   Annualized Income Installments   Caution: *Complete lines 20–26 of one column* **before** *going to the next column.*

			(a)	(b)	(c)	(d)
1	Enter your adjusted gross income for each period (see instructions). (Estates and trusts, enter your taxable income without your exemption for each period.)	1				
2	Annualization amounts. (Estates and trusts, see instructions.)	2	4	2.4	1.5	1
3	Annualized income. Multiply line 1 by line 2	3				
4	Enter your itemized deductions for the period shown in each column. If you do not itemize, enter -0- and skip to line 7. (Estates and trusts, enter -0-, skip to line 9, and enter the amount from line 3 on line 9.)	4				
5	Annualization amounts	5	4	2.4	1.5	1
6	Multiply line 4 by line 5 (see instructions if line 3 is more than $60,600)	6				
7	In each column, enter the full amount of your standard deduction from Form 1040, line 35, or Form 1040A, line 19 (Form 1040NR or 1040NR-EZ filers, enter -0-. **Exception:** Indian students and business apprentices, enter standard deduction from Form 1040NR, line 34 or Form 1040NR-EZ, line 10.)	7				
8	Enter the **larger** of line 6 or line 7	8				
9	Subtract line 8 from line 3	9				
10	In each column, multiply $2,650 by the total number of exemptions claimed (see instructions if line 3 is more than $90,900). (Estates and trusts and Form 1040NR or 1040NR-EZ filers, enter the exemption amount shown on your tax return.)	10				
11	Subtract line 10 from line 9	11				
12	Figure your tax on the amount on line 11 (see instructions)	12				
13	Form 1040 filers only, enter your self-employment tax from line 35 below	13				
14	Enter other taxes for each payment period (see instructions)	14				
15	Total tax. Add lines 12, 13, and 14	15				
16	For each period, enter the same type of credits as allowed on Form 2210, lines 2, 5, and 6 (see instructions)	16				
17	Subtract line 16 from line 15. If zero or less, enter -0-	17				
18	Applicable percentage	18	22.5%	45%	67.5%	90%
19	Multiply line 17 by line 18	19				
20	Add the amounts in all preceding columns of line 26	20				
21	Subtract line 20 from line 19. If zero or less, enter -0-	21				
22	Enter ¼ of line 13 on page 1 of Form 2210 in each column	22				
23	Enter amount from line 25 of the preceding column of this schedule	23				
24	Add lines 22 and 23 and enter the total	24				
25	Subtract line 21 from line 24. If zero or less, enter -0-	25				
26	Enter the **smaller** of line 21 or line 24 here and on Form 2210, line 21 ▶	26				

Part II   Annualized Self-Employment Tax

			(a)	(b)	(c)	(d)
27a	Net earnings from self-employment for the period (see instructions)	27a				
b	Annualization amounts	27b	4	2.4	1.5	1
c	Multiply line 27a by line 27b	27c				
28	Social security tax limit	28	$65,400	$65,400	$65,400	$65,400
29	Enter actual wages subject to social security tax or the 6.2% portion of the 7.65% railroad retirement (tier 1) tax	29				
30	Annualization amounts	30	4	2.4	1.5	1
31	Multiply line 29 by line 30	31				
32	Subtract line 31 from line 28. If zero or less, enter -0-	32				
33	Multiply the smaller of line 27c or line 32 by .124	33				
34	Multiply line 27c by .029	34				
35	Add lines 33 and 34. Enter the result here and on line 13 above ▶	35				

Tax Forms

Form **2220**
Department of the Treasury
Internal Revenue Service

Underpayment of Estimated Tax by Corporations

▶ See separate instructions.
▶ Attach to the corporation's tax return.

OMB No. 1545-0142

1997

Name | Employer identification number

Note: *In most cases, the corporation **does not** need to file Form 2220. (See Part I below for exceptions.) The IRS will figure any penalty owed and bill the corporation. If the corporation does not need to file Form 2220, it may still use it to figure the penalty. Enter the amount from line 32 on the estimated tax penalty line of the corporation's income tax return, but do not attach Form 2220.*

Part I Reasons for Filing—Check the boxes below that apply to the corporation. If any box is checked or the **Note** below applies, the corporation must file Form 2220 with the corporation's tax return, even if it does not owe the penalty. If the box on line 1 or line 2 applies, the corporation may be able to lower or eliminate the penalty. See page 1 of the instructions.

1 ☐ The corporation is using the annualized income installment method.
2 ☐ The corporation is using the adjusted seasonal installment method.
3 ☐ The corporation is a "large corporation" figuring its first required installment based on the prior year's tax.
   Note: *The corporation must also file Form 2220 if it is claiming a waiver of the penalty. See **Waiver of penalty** on page 2 of the instructions.*

Part II Figuring the Underpayment

4 Total tax. (**Caution:** *See page 2 of the instructions, which includes a special rule if claiming the research credit*) . | 4 |
5a Personal holding company tax included on line 4 (Schedule PH (Form 1120), line 26) . | 5a |
 b Interest due under the look-back method of section 460(b)(2) for completed long-term contracts included on line 4 . . . . | 5b |
 c Credit for Federal tax paid on fuels (see page 2 of the instructions) . . . . . | 5c |
 d **Total.** Add lines 5a through 5c . . . . | 5d |
6 Subtract line 5d from line 4. If the result is less than $500, **do not** complete or file this form. The corporation does not owe the penalty . . . . | 6 |
7 Enter the tax shown on the corporation's 1996 income tax return. (**CAUTION:** *See page 2 of the instructions before completing this line.*) . . . . | 7 |
8 Enter the **smaller** of line 6 or line 7. If the corporation must skip line 7, enter the amount from line 6 on line 8 . | 8 |

	(a)	(b)	(c)	(d)
9 **Installment due dates.** Enter in columns (a) through (d) the 15th day of the 4th (5th month of a private foundation's tax year that begins after August 5, 1997), 6th, 9th, and 12th months of the corporation's tax year . . . . . . ▶				
10 **Required installments.** If the box on line 1 and/or line 2 above is checked, enter the amounts from Schedule A, line 41. If the box on line 3 (but not 1 or 2) is checked, see page 2 of the instructions for the amounts to enter. If none of these boxes are checked, enter 25% of line 8 above in each column				
11 Estimated tax paid or credited for each period (see page 2 of the instructions). For column (a) only, enter the amount from line 11 on line 15				
Complete lines 12 through 18 of one column before going to the next column.				
12 Enter amount, if any, from line 18 of the preceding column				
13 Add lines 11 and 12				
14 Add amounts on lines 16 and 17 of the preceding column .				
15 Subtract line 14 from line 13. If zero or less, enter -0- .				
16 If the amount on line 15 is zero, subtract line 13 from line 14. Otherwise, enter -0-				
17 **Underpayment.** If line 15 is less than or equal to line 10, subtract line 15 from line 10. Then go to line 12 of the next column (see page 2 of the instructions). Otherwise, go to line 18. . . .				
18 **Overpayment.** If line 10 is less than line 15, subtract line 10 from line 15. Then go to line 12 of the next column . . .				

Complete Part III on page 2 to figure the penalty. If there are no entries on line 17, no penalty is owed.

For Paperwork Reduction Act Notice, see page 4 of the instructions. Cat. No. 11746L Form **2220** (1997)

Form 2220 (1997) Page **2**

Part III Figuring the Penalty

	(a)	(b)	(c)	(d)
19 Enter the date of payment or the 15th day of the 3rd month after the close of the tax year, whichever is earlier (see page 3 of the instructions). *(Form 990-PF and Form 990-T filers: Use 5th month instead of 3rd month.)*				
20 Number of days from due date of installment on line 9 to the date shown on line 19				
21 Number of days on line 20 after 4/15/97 and before 4/1/98				
22 Underpayment on line 17 × $\frac{\text{Number of days on line 21}}{365}$ × 9%	$	$	$	$
23 Number of days on line 20 after 3/31/98 and before 7/1/98				
24 Underpayment on line 17 × $\frac{\text{Number of days on line 23}}{365}$ × *%	$	$	$	$
25 Number of days on line 20 after 6/30/98 and before 10/1/98				
26 Underpayment on line 17 × $\frac{\text{Number of days on line 25}}{365}$ × *%	$	$	$	$
27 Number of days on line 20 after 9/30/98 and before 1/1/99				
28 Underpayment on line 17 × $\frac{\text{Number of days on line 27}}{365}$ × *%	$	$	$	$
29 Number of days on line 20 after 12/31/98 and before 2/16/99				
30 Underpayment on line 17 × $\frac{\text{Number of days on line 29}}{365}$ × *%	$	$	$	$
31 Add lines 22, 24, 26, 28, and 30	$	$	$	$

32 **Penalty.** Add columns (a) through (d), of line 31. Enter the total here and on Form 1120, line 33; Form 1120-A, line 29; or the comparable line for other income tax returns . . . . **32** $

*For underpayments paid after March 31, 1998, see **Lines 24, 26, 28,** and **30** on page 3 of the instructions.

Form 2220 (1997)   Page **3**

Schedule A   Annualized Income Installment Method and/or the Adjusted Seasonal Installment Method Under Section 6655(e) (see pages 3 and 4 of the instructions)

Form 1120S filers: *For lines 2, 14, 15, and 16, below, "taxable income" refers to excess net passive income or the amount on which tax is imposed under section 1374(a) (or the corresponding provisions of prior law), whichever applies.*

Part I—Annualized Income Installment Method		(a)	(b)	(c)	(d)
1 Annualization periods (see page 3 of the instructions).	1	First ____ months	First ____ months	First ____ months	First ____ months
2 Enter taxable income for each annualization period.	2				
3 Annualization amounts (see page 3 of the instructions).	3				
4 Annualized taxable income. Multiply line 2 by line 3.	4				
5 Figure the tax on the amount in each column on line 4 using the instructions for Form 1120, Schedule J, line 3 (or the comparable line of the tax return).	5				
6 Enter other taxes for each payment period (see page 3 of the instructions).	6				
7 Total tax. Add lines 5 and 6.	7				
8 For each period, enter the same type of credits as allowed on Form 2220, lines 4 and 5c (see page 3 of the instructions).	8				
9 Total tax after credits. Subtract line 8 from line 7. If zero or less, enter -0-.	9				
10 Applicable percentage.	10	25%	50%	75%	100%
11 Multiply line 9 by line 10.	11				
12 Add the amounts in all preceding columns of line 41 (see page 3 of the instructions).	12				
13 **Annualized income installments.** Subtract line 12 from line 11. If zero or less, enter -0-.	13				

Part II—Adjusted Seasonal Installment Method (**Caution:** *Use this method only if the base period percentage for any 6 consecutive months is at least 70%. See pages 3 and 4 of the instructions for more information.*)

		(a)	(b)	(c)	(d)
14 Enter taxable income for the following periods:		First 3 months	First 5 months	First 8 months	First 11 months
a Tax year beginning in 1994	14a				
b Tax year beginning in 1995	14b				
c Tax year beginning in 1996	14c				
15 Enter taxable income for each period for the tax year beginning in 1997.	15				
16 Enter taxable income for the following periods:		First 4 months	First 6 months	First 9 months	Entire year
a Tax year beginning in 1994	16a				
b Tax year beginning in 1995	16b				
c Tax year beginning in 1996	16c				
17 Divide the amount in each column on line 14a by the amount in column (d) on line 16a.	17				
18 Divide the amount in each column on line 14b by the amount in column (d) on line 16b.	18				
19 Divide the amount in each column on line 14c by the amount in column (d) on line 16c.	19				

Form 2220 (1997) Page 4

			(a) First 4 months	(b) First 6 months	(c) First 9 months	(d) Entire year
20	Add lines 17 through 19.	20				
21	Divide line 20 by 3.	21				
22	Divide line 15 by line 21.	22				
23	Figure the tax on the amount on line 22 using the instructions for Form 1120, Schedule J, line 3 (or the comparable line of the return).	23				
24	Divide the amount in columns (a) through (c) on line 16a by the amount in column (d) on line 16a.	24				
25	Divide the amount in columns (a) through (c) on line 16b by the amount in column (d) on line 16b.	25				
26	Divide the amount in columns (a) through (c) on line 16c by the amount in column (d) on line 16c.	26				
27	Add lines 24 through 26.	27				
28	Divide line 27 by 3.	28				
29	Multiply the amount in columns (a) through (c) of line 23 by columns (a) through (c) of line 28. In column (d), enter the amount from line 23, column (d).	29				
30	Enter other taxes for each payment period (see page 4 of the instructions).	30				
31	Total tax. Add lines 29 and 30.	31				
32	For each period, enter the same type of credits as allowed on Form 2220, lines 4 and 5c (see page 4 of the instructions).	32				
33	Total tax after credits. Subtract line 32 from line 31. If zero or less, enter -0-.	33				
34	Add the amounts in all preceding columns of line 41 (see page 4 of the instructions).	34				
35	**Adjusted seasonal installments.** Subtract line 34 from line 33. If zero or less, enter -0-.	35				

Part III—Required Installments

			1st installment	2nd installment	3rd installment	4th installment
36	If only one of the above parts is completed, enter the amount in each column from line 13 or line 35. If both parts are completed, enter the **smaller** of the amounts in each column from line 13 or line 35.	36				
37	Enter 25% of line 8 on page 1 of Form 2220 in each column. (**Note:** "Large corporations" see the instructions for line 10, on page 2, for the amounts to enter.)	37				
38	Enter the amount from line 40 of the preceding column.	38				
39	Add lines 37 and 38.	39				
40	If line 39 is more than line 36, subtract line 36 from line 39. Otherwise, enter -0-.	40				
41	**Required installments.** Enter the **smaller** of line 36 or line 39 here and on page 1 of Form 2220, line 10.	41				

Form **2441**	**Child and Dependent Care Expenses**	OMB No. 1545-0068
Department of the Treasury Internal Revenue Service (99)	▶ Attach to Form 1040. ▶ See separate instructions.	**1997** Attachment Sequence No. **21**

Name(s) shown on Form 1040 | Your social security number

Before you begin, you need to understand the following terms. See **Definitions** on page 1 of the instructions.

- Dependent Care Benefits
- Qualifying Person(s)
- Qualified Expenses
- Earned Income

Part I — Persons or Organizations Who Provided the Care—You **must** complete this part.
(If you need more space, use the bottom of page 2.)

1	(a) Care provider's name	(b) Address (number, street, apt. no., city, state, and ZIP code)	(c) Identifying number (SSN or EIN)	(d) Amount paid (see instructions)

Did you receive **dependent care benefits?**
— NO ▶ Complete only Part II below.
— YES ▶ Complete Part III on the back next.

Caution: *If the care was provided in your home, you may owe employment taxes. See the instructions for Form 1040, line 52.*

Part II Credit for Child and Dependent Care Expenses

2 Information about your **qualifying person(s).** If you have more than two qualifying persons, see the instructions.

(a) Qualifying person's name First Last	(b) Qualifying person's social security number	(c) Qualified expenses you incurred and paid in 1997 for the person listed in column (a)

3 Add the amounts in column (c) of line 2. DO NOT enter more than $2,400 for one qualifying person or $4,800 for two or more persons. If you completed Part III, enter the amount from line 24 . . . . **3**

4 Enter YOUR **earned income** **4**

5 If married filing a joint return, enter YOUR SPOUSE'S earned income (if student or disabled, see the instructions); **all others,** enter the amount from line 4 . . . . . . **5**

6 Enter the **smallest** of line 3, 4, or 5 . . . . **6**

7 Enter the amount from Form 1040, line 33 . . . . **7**

8 Enter on line 8 the decimal amount shown below that applies to the amount on line 7

If line 7 is—		Decimal amount is	If line 7 is—		Decimal amount is
Over	But not over		Over	But not over	
$0	10,000	.30	$20,000	22,000	.24
10,000	12,000	.29	22,000	24,000	.23
12,000	14,000	.28	24,000	26,000	.22
14,000	16,000	.27	26,000	28,000	.21
16,000	18,000	.26	28,000	No limit	.20
18,000	20,000	.25			

8   × .

9 Multiply **line 6** by the decimal amount on line 8. Enter the result. Then, see the instructions for the amount of credit to enter on Form 1040, line 40 . . . . **9**

For Paperwork Reduction Act Notice, see page 3 of the instructions.   Cat. No. 11862M   Form **2441** (1997)

Form 2441 (1997) Page **2**

Part III Dependent Care Benefits

10 Enter the total amount of **dependent care benefits** you received for 1997. This amount should be shown in box 10 of your W-2 form(s). DO NOT include amounts that were reported to you as wages in box 1 of Form(s) W-2 . . . . | 10 |

11 Enter the amount forfeited, if any. See the instructions . . . . | 11 |

12 Subtract line 11 from line 10 . . . . | 12 |

13 Enter the total amount of **qualified expenses** incurred in 1997 for the care of the **qualifying person(s)** . . . | 13 |

14 Enter the **smaller** of line 12 or 13 . . . . | 14 |

15 Enter YOUR **earned income** . . . . | 15 |

16 If married filing a joint return, enter YOUR SPOUSE'S earned income (if student or disabled, see the line 5 instructions); if married filing a separate return, see the instructions for the amount to enter; **all others,** enter the amount from line 15 . . . . | 16 |

17 Enter the **smallest** of line 14, 15, or 16 . . . . . . | 17 |

18 **Excluded benefits.** Enter here the **smaller** of the following:
  • The amount from line 17, or
  • $5,000 ($2,500 if married filing a separate return **and** you were required to enter your spouse's earned income on line 16). . . . . | 18 |

19 **Taxable benefits.** Subtract line 18 from line 12. Also, include this amount on Form 1040, line 7. On the dotted line next to line 7, write "DCB" . . . . | 19 |

To claim the child and dependent care credit, complete lines 20–24 below.

20 Enter $2,400 ($4,800 if two or more qualifying persons) . . . . | 20 |

21 Enter the amount from line 18 . . . . | 21 |

22 Subtract line 21 from line 20. If zero or less, **STOP.** You cannot take the credit. **Exception.** If you paid 1996 expenses in 1997, see the line 9 instructions . . . . . | 22 |

23 Complete line 2 on the front of this form. DO NOT include in column (c) any excluded benefits shown on line 18 above. Then, add the amounts in column (c) and enter the total here . . . . | 23 |

24 Enter the **smaller** of line 22 or 23. Also, enter this amount on line 3 on the front of this form and complete lines 4–9 . . . . | 24 |

Form 2553 (Rev. September 1997)
Election by a Small Business Corporation
(Under section 1362 of the Internal Revenue Code)

▶ For Paperwork Reduction Act Notice, see page 2 of instructions.
▶ See separate instructions.

Department of the Treasury
Internal Revenue Service

OMB No. 1545-0146

Notes:
1. This election to be an S corporation can be accepted only if all the tests are met under **Who May Elect** on page 1 of the instructions; all signatures in Parts I and III are originals (no photocopies); and the exact name and address of the corporation and other required form information are provided.
2. Do not file **Form 1120S,** U.S. Income Tax Return for an S Corporation, for any tax year before the year the election takes effect.
3. If the corporation was in existence before the effective date of this election, see **Taxes an S Corporation May Owe** on page 1 of the instructions.

Part I — Election Information

Please Type or Print

- Name of corporation (see instructions)
- Number, street, and room or suite no. (If a P.O. box, see instructions.)
- City or town, state, and ZIP code

A Employer identification number
B Date incorporated
C State of incorporation

D Election is to be effective for tax year beginning (month, day, year) ▶ __ / __ / __

E Name and title of officer or legal representative who the IRS may call for more information

F Telephone number of officer or legal representative
( )

G If the corporation changed its name or address after applying for the EIN shown in **A** above, check this box ▶ ☐

H If this election takes effect for the first tax year the corporation exists, enter month, day, and year of the **earliest** of the following: (1) date the corporation first had shareholders, (2) date the corporation first had assets, or (3) date the corporation began doing business ▶ __ / __ / __

I Selected tax year: Annual return will be filed for tax year ending (month and day) ▶ _____

If the tax year ends on any date other than December 31, except for an automatic 52-53-week tax year ending with reference to the month of December, you **must** complete Part II on the back. If the date you enter is the ending date of an automatic 52-53-week tax year, write "52-53-week year" to the right of the date. See Temporary Regulations section 1.441-2T(e)(3).

J Name and address of each shareholder; shareholder's spouse having a community property interest in the corporation's stock; and each tenant in common, joint tenant, and tenant by the entirety. (A husband and wife (and their estates) are counted as one shareholder in determining the number of shareholders without regard to the manner in which the stock is owned.)	**K** Shareholders' Consent Statement. Under penalties of perjury, we declare that we consent to the election of the above-named corporation to be an S corporation under section 1362(a) and that we have examined this consent statement, including accompanying schedules and statements, and to the best of our knowledge and belief, it is true, correct, and complete. We understand our consent is binding and may not be withdrawn after the corporation has made a valid election. (Shareholders sign and date below.)		**L** Stock owned		**M** Social security number or employer identification number (see instructions)	**N** Shareholder's tax year ends (month and day)
	Signature	Date	Number of shares	Dates acquired		

Under penalties of perjury, I declare that I have examined this election, including accompanying schedules and statements, and to the best of my knowledge and belief, it is true, correct, and complete.

Signature of officer ▶   Title ▶   Date ▶

See Parts II and III on back.

Cat. No. 18629R

Form **2553** (Rev. 9-97)

Form 2553 (Rev. 9-97) Page **2**

Part II — Selection of Fiscal Tax Year (All corporations using this part must complete item O and item P, Q, or R.)

O Check the applicable box to indicate whether the corporation is:
1. ☐ A new corporation adopting the tax year entered in item I, Part I.
2. ☐ An existing corporation retaining the tax year entered in item I, Part I.
3. ☐ An existing corporation changing to the tax year entered in item I, Part I.

P Complete item P if the corporation is using the expeditious approval provisions of Rev. Proc. 87-32, 1987-2 C.B. 396, to request **(1)** a natural business year (as defined in section 4.01(1) of Rev. Proc. 87-32) or **(2)** a year that satisfies the ownership tax year test in section 4.01(2) of Rev. Proc. 87-32. Check the applicable box below to indicate the representation statement the corporation is making as required under section 4 of Rev. Proc. 87-32.

1. Natural Business Year ▶ ☐ I represent that the corporation is retaining or changing to a tax year that coincides with its natural business year as defined in section 4.01(1) of Rev. Proc. 87-32 and as verified by its satisfaction of the requirements of section 4.02(1) of Rev. Proc. 87-32. In addition, if the corporation is changing to a natural business year as defined in section 4.01(1), I further represent that such tax year results in less deferral of income to the owners than the corporation's present tax year. I also represent that the corporation is not described in section 3.01(2) of Rev. Proc. 87-32. (See instructions for additional information that must be attached.)

2. Ownership Tax Year ▶ ☐ I represent that shareholders holding more than half of the shares of the stock (as of the first day of the tax year to which the request relates) of the corporation have the same tax year or are concurrently changing to the tax year that the corporation adopts, retains, or changes to per item I, Part I. I also represent that the corporation is not described in section 3.01(2) of Rev. Proc. 87-32.

Note: *If you do not use item P and the corporation wants a fiscal tax year, complete either item Q or R below. Item Q is used to request a fiscal tax year based on a business purpose and to make a back-up section 444 election. Item R is used to make a regular section 444 election.*

Q Business Purpose—To request a fiscal tax year based on a business purpose, you must check box Q1 and pay a user fee. See instructions for details. You may also check box Q2 and/or box Q3.

1. Check here ▶ ☐ if the fiscal year entered in item I, Part I, is requested under the provisions of section 6.03 of Rev. Proc. 87-32. Attach to Form 2553 a statement showing the business purpose for the requested fiscal year. See instructions for additional information that must be attached.

2. Check here ▶ ☐ to show that the corporation intends to make a back-up section 444 election in the event the corporation's business purpose request is not approved by the IRS. (See instructions for more information.)

3. Check here ▶ ☐ to show that the corporation agrees to adopt or change to a tax year ending December 31 if necessary for the IRS to accept this election for S corporation status in the event (1) the corporation's business purpose request is not approved and the corporation makes a back-up section 444 election, but is ultimately not qualified to make a section 444 election, or (2) the corporation's business purpose request is not approved and the corporation did not make a back-up section 444 election.

R Section 444 Election—To make a section 444 election, you must check box R1 and you may also check box R2.

1. Check here ▶ ☐ to show the corporation will make, if qualified, a section 444 election to have the fiscal tax year shown in item I, Part I. To make the election, you must complete **Form 8716**, Election To Have a Tax Year Other Than a Required Tax Year, and either attach it to Form 2553 or file it separately.

2. Check here ▶ ☐ to show that the corporation agrees to adopt or change to a tax year ending December 31 if necessary for the IRS to accept this election for S corporation status in the event the corporation is ultimately not qualified to make a section 444 election.

Part III — Qualified Subchapter S Trust (QSST) Election Under Section 1361(d)(2)*

Income beneficiary's name and address	Social security number
Trust's name and address	Employer identification number

Date on which stock of the corporation was transferred to the trust (month, day, year) . . . . ▶ __ / __ / __

In order for the trust named above to be a QSST and thus a qualifying shareholder of the S corporation for which this Form 2553 is filed, I hereby make the election under section 1361(d)(2). Under penalties of perjury, I certify that the trust meets the definitional requirements of section 1361(d)(3) and that all other information provided in Part III is true, correct, and complete.

_____   _____
Signature of income beneficiary or signature and title of legal representative or other qualified person making the election   Date

*Use Part III to make the QSST election only if stock of the corporation has been transferred to the trust on or before the date on which the corporation makes its election to be an S corporation. The QSST election must be made and filed separately if stock of the corporation is transferred to the trust after the date on which the corporation makes the S election.

Form 3903
Department of the Treasury
Internal Revenue Service

Moving Expenses
► Attach to Form 1040.

OMB No. 1545-0062

1997

Attachment Sequence No. **62**

Name(s) shown on Form 1040

Your social security number

Caution: *If you are a member of the armed forces, see the instructions before completing this form.*

1 Enter the number of miles from your **old home** to your **new workplace** . . | 1 | | miles

2 Enter the number of miles from your **old home** to your **old workplace** . . | 2 | | miles

3 Subtract line 2 from line 1. Enter the result but not less than zero . . . . | 3 | | miles

Is line 3 at least 50 miles?

Yes. Go to line 4. Also, see **Time Test** in the instructions.

No. You **cannot** deduct your moving expenses. Do not complete the rest of this form.

4 Transportation and storage of household goods and personal effects (see instructions) . . . | 4 |

5 Travel and lodging expenses of moving from your old home to your new home. **Do not** include meals (see instructions) . . . . | 5 |

6 Add lines 4 and 5 . . . . | 6 |

7 Enter the total amount your employer paid for your move (including the value of services furnished in kind) that is **not** included in the wages box (box 1) of your W-2 form. This amount should be identified with code **P** in box 13 of your W-2 form . . . . | 7 |

Is line 6 more than line 7?

Yes. Go to line 8.

No. You **cannot** deduct your moving expenses. If line 6 is less than line 7, subtract line 6 from line 7 and include the result in income on Form 1040, line 7.

8 Subtract line 7 from line 6. Enter the result here and on Form 1040, line 25. This is your **moving expense deduction** . . . . | 8 |

General Instructions

Purpose of Form

Use Form 3903 to figure your moving expense deduction if you moved to a new principal place of work (workplace) within the United States or its possessions. If you qualify to deduct expenses for more than one move, use a separate Form 3903 for each move.

For more details, see **Pub. 521,** Moving Expenses.

Note: *Use **Form 3903-F,** Foreign Moving Expenses, instead of this form if you are a U.S. citizen or resident alien who moved to a new principal workplace outside the United States or its possessions.*

Another Form You May Have To File

If you sold your main home in 1997, you must file **Form 2119,** Sale of Your Home, to report the sale.

Who May Deduct Moving Expenses

If you moved to a different home because of a change in job location, you may be able to deduct your moving expenses. You may be able to take the deduction whether you are self-employed or an employee. But you must meet certain tests explained next.

Distance Test

Your new principal workplace must be at least 50 miles farther from your old home than your old workplace was. For example, if your old workplace was 3 miles from your old home, your new workplace must be at least 53 miles from that home. If you did not have an old workplace, your new workplace must be at least 50 miles from your old home. The distance between the two points is the shortest of the more commonly traveled routes between them.

Time Test

If you are an employee, you must work full time in the general area of your new workplace for at least 39 weeks during the 12 months right after you move. If you are self-employed, you must work full time in the general area of your new workplace for at least 39 weeks during the first 12 months and a total of at least 78 weeks during the 24 months right after you move.

You may deduct your moving expenses even if you have not met the time test before your return is due. You may do this

For Paperwork Reduction Act Notice, see back of form.   Cat. No. 12490K   Form **3903** (1997)

if you expect to meet the 39-week test by the end of 1998 or the 78-week test by the end of 1999. If you deduct your moving expenses on your 1997 return but do not meet the time test, you will have to either:

• Amend your 1997 tax return by filing **Form 1040X,** Amended U.S. Individual Income Tax Return, or

• Report the amount of your 1997 moving expense deduction that reduced your 1997 income tax as income in the year you cannot meet the test. For more details, see **Time Test** in Pub. 521.

If you do not deduct your moving expenses on your 1997 return and you later meet the time test, you may take the deduction by filing an amended return for 1997. To do this, use Form 1040X.

Exceptions to the Time Test. The time test does not have to be met if any of the following apply:

• Your job ends because of disability.

• You are transferred for your employer's benefit.

• You are laid off or discharged for a reason other than willful misconduct.

• You meet the requirements (explained later) for retirees or survivors living outside the United States.

• You are filing this form for a decedent.

Members of the Armed Forces

If you are in the armed forces, you do not have to meet the **distance and time tests** if the move is due to a permanent change of station. A permanent change of station includes a move in connection with and within 1 year of retirement or other termination of active duty.

How To Complete the Form

First, complete lines 4 through 6 using your actual expenses. **Do not** reduce your expenses by any reimbursements or allowances you received from the government in connection with the move. Also, do not include any expenses for moving services that were provided by the government. If you and your spouse and dependents are moved to or from different locations, treat the moves as a single move.

Next, enter on line 7 the total reimbursements and allowances you received from the government in connection with the expenses you claimed on lines 4 and 5. **Do not** include the value of moving services provided by the government. Then, complete line 8 if applicable.

Retirees or Survivors Living Outside the United States

If you are a retiree or survivor who moved to a home in the United States or its possessions and you meet the following requirements, you are treated as if you moved to a new workplace located in the United States. You are subject to the distance test. Use this form instead of Form 3903-F to figure your moving expense deduction.

Retirees

You may deduct moving expenses for a move to a new home in the United States when you actually retire if both your old principal workplace and your old home were outside the United States.

Survivors

You may deduct moving expenses for a move to a home in the United States if you are the spouse or dependent of a person whose principal workplace at the time of death was outside the United States. In addition, the expenses must be for a move **(1)** that begins within 6 months after the decedent's death, and **(2)** from a former home outside the United States that you lived in with the decedent at the time of death.

Reimbursements

If your employer paid for any part of your move, your employer must give you a statement showing a detailed breakdown of reimbursements or payments for moving expenses. Employers may use **Form 4782,** Employee Moving Expense Information, or their own form.

You may choose to deduct moving expenses in the year you are reimbursed by your employer, even though you paid the expenses in a different year. However, special rules apply. See **How To Report** in Pub. 521.

Specific Instructions

You may deduct the following expenses you incurred in moving your family and dependent household members. Do not deduct expenses for employees such as a maid, nanny, or nurse.

Line 4

Enter the actual cost to pack, crate, and move your household goods and personal effects. You may also include the cost to store and insure household goods and personal effects within any period of 30 days in a row after the items were moved from your old home and before they were delivered to your new home.

Line 5

Enter the costs of travel from your old home to your new home. These include transportation and lodging on the way. Include costs for the day you arrive. Although not all the members of your household have to travel together or at the same time, you may only include expenses for one trip per person.

If you use your own car(s), you may figure the expenses by using either:

• Actual out-of-pocket expenses for gas and oil, or

• Mileage at the rate of 10 cents a mile.

You may add parking fees and tolls to the amount claimed under either method. Keep records to verify your expenses.

Paperwork Reduction Act Notice. We ask for the information on this form to carry out the Internal Revenue laws of the United States. You are required to give us the information. We need it to ensure that you are complying with these laws and to allow us to figure and collect the right amount of tax.

You are not required to provide the information requested on a form that is subject to the Paperwork Reduction Act unless the form displays a valid OMB control number. Books or records relating to a form or its instructions must be retained as long as their contents may become material in the administration of any Internal Revenue law. Generally, tax returns and return information are confidential, as required by Internal Revenue Code section 6103.

The time needed to complete and file this form will vary depending on individual circumstances. The estimated average time is:

Recordkeeping . . . . . . 33 min.
**Learning about the
law or the form** . . . . . . 7 min.
Preparing the form . . . . . 13 min.
**Copying, assembling, and
sending the form to the IRS** . 20 min.

If you have comments concerning the accuracy of these time estimates or suggestions for making this form simpler, we would be happy to hear from you. See the Instructions for Form 1040.

Tax Forms   B-57

Form **4562**	**Depreciation and Amortization**	OMB No. 1545-0172
Department of the Treasury Internal Revenue Service (99)	(Including Information on Listed Property) ▶ See separate instructions. ▶ Attach this form to your return.	**1997** Attachment Sequence No. **67**
Name(s) shown on return	Business or activity to which this form relates	Identifying number

Part I   Election To Expense Certain Tangible Property (Section 179) (Note: *If you have any "listed property," complete Part V before you complete Part I.*)

1	Maximum dollar limitation. If an enterprise zone business, see page 2 of the instructions	1	$18,000
2	Total cost of section 179 property placed in service. See page 2 of the instructions	2	
3	Threshold cost of section 179 property before reduction in limitation	3	$200,000
4	Reduction in limitation. Subtract line 3 from line 2. If zero or less, enter -0-	4	
5	Dollar limitation for tax year. Subtract line 4 from line 1. If zero or less, enter -0-. If married filing separately, see page 2 of the instructions	5	

(a) Description of property	(b) Cost (business use only)	(c) Elected cost
6		

7	Listed property. Enter amount from line 27	7	
8	Total elected cost of section 179 property. Add amounts in column (c), lines 6 and 7	8	
9	Tentative deduction. Enter the smaller of line 5 or line 8	9	
10	Carryover of disallowed deduction from 1996. See page 3 of the instructions	10	
11	Business income limitation. Enter the smaller of business income (not less than zero) or line 5 (see instructions)	11	
12	Section 179 expense deduction. Add lines 9 and 10, but do not enter more than line 11	12	
13	Carryover of disallowed deduction to 1998. Add lines 9 and 10, less line 12 ▶	13	

Note: *Do not use Part II or Part III below for listed property (automobiles, certain other vehicles, cellular telephones, certain computers, or property used for entertainment, recreation, or amusement). Instead, use Part V for listed property.*

Part II   MACRS Depreciation For Assets Placed in Service ONLY During Your 1997 Tax Year (Do Not Include Listed Property.)

Section A—General Asset Account Election

14   If you are making the election under section 168(i)(4) to group any assets placed in service during the tax year into one or more general asset accounts, check this box. See page 3 of the instructions ▶ ☐

Section B—General Depreciation System (GDS) (See page 3 of the instructions.)

(a) Classification of property	(b) Month and year placed in service	(c) Basis for depreciation (business/investment use only—see instructions)	(d) Recovery period	(e) Convention	(f) Method	(g) Depreciation deduction
15a 3-year property						
b 5-year property						
c 7-year property						
d 10-year property						
e 15-year property						
f 20-year property						
g 25-year property			25 yrs.		S/L	
h Residential rental property			27.5 yrs.	MM	S/L	
			27.5 yrs.	MM	S/L	
i Nonresidential real property			39 yrs.	MM	S/L	
				MM	S/L	

Section C—Alternative Depreciation System (ADS) (See page 6 of the instructions.)

16a Class life					S/L	
b 12-year			12 yrs.		S/L	
c 40-year			40 yrs.	MM	S/L	

Part III   Other Depreciation (Do Not Include Listed Property.) (See page 6 of the instructions.)

17	GDS and ADS deductions for assets placed in service in tax years beginning before 1997	17	
18	Property subject to section 168(f)(1) election	18	
19	ACRS and other depreciation	19	

Part IV   Summary (See page 7 of the instructions.)

20	Listed property. Enter amount from line 26	20	
21	**Total.** Add deductions on line 12, lines 15 and 16 in column (g), and lines 17 through 20. Enter here and on the appropriate lines of your return. Partnerships and S corporations—see instructions	21	
22	For assets shown above and placed in service during the current year, enter the portion of the basis attributable to section 263A costs	22	

For Paperwork Reduction Act Notice, see the separate instructions.   Cat. No. 12906N   Form **4562** (1997)

Form 4562 (1997) Page **2**

Part V — Listed Property—Automobiles, Certain Other Vehicles, Cellular Telephones, Certain Computers, and Property Used for Entertainment, Recreation, or Amusement

Note: *For any vehicle for which you are using the standard mileage rate or deducting lease expense, complete **only** 23a, 23b, columns (a) through (c) of Section A, all of Section B, and Section C if applicable.*

Section A—Depreciation and Other Information (Caution: *See page 8 of the instructions for limits for passenger automobiles.*)

23a Do you have evidence to support the business/investment use claimed? ☐ Yes ☐ No   23b If "Yes," is the evidence written? ☐ Yes ☐ No

(a) Type of property (list vehicles first)	(b) Date placed in service	(c) Business/ investment use percentage	(d) Cost or other basis	(e) Basis for depreciation (business/investment use only)	(f) Recovery period	(g) Method/ Convention	(h) Depreciation deduction	(i) Elected section 179 cost
24 Property used more than 50% in a qualified business use (See page 7 of the instructions.):								
		%						
		%						
		%						
25 Property used 50% or less in a qualified business use (See page 7 of the instructions.):								
		%			S/L –			
		%			S/L –			
		%			S/L –			
26 Add amounts in column (h). Enter the total here and on line 20, page 1.						26		
27 Add amounts in column (i). Enter the total here and on line 7, page 1							27	

Section B—Information on Use of Vehicles

Complete this section for vehicles used by a sole proprietor, partner, or other "more than 5% owner," or related person.
If you provided vehicles to your employees, first answer the questions in Section C to see if you meet an exception to completing this section for those vehicles.

	(a) Vehicle 1	(b) Vehicle 2	(c) Vehicle 3	(d) Vehicle 4	(e) Vehicle 5	(f) Vehicle 6
28 Total business/investment miles driven during the year (DO NOT include commuting miles)						
29 Total commuting miles driven during the year						
30 Total other personal (noncommuting) miles driven.						
31 Total miles driven during the year. Add lines 28 through 30.						
	Yes No	Yes No	Yes No	Yes No	Yes No	Yes No
32 Was the vehicle available for personal use during off-duty hours?						
33 Was the vehicle used primarily by a more than 5% owner or related person?						
34 Is another vehicle available for personal use?						

Section C—Questions for Employers Who Provide Vehicles for Use by Their Employees

*Answer these questions to determine if you meet an exception to completing Section B for vehicles used by employees who **are not** more than 5% owners or related persons.*

	Yes	No
35 Do you maintain a written policy statement that prohibits all personal use of vehicles, including commuting, by your employees?		
36 Do you maintain a written policy statement that prohibits personal use of vehicles, except commuting, by your employees? See page 9 of the instructions for vehicles used by corporate officers, directors, or 1% or more owners		
37 Do you treat all use of vehicles by employees as personal use?		
38 Do you provide more than five vehicles to your employees, obtain information from your employees about the use of the vehicles, and retain the information received?		
39 Do you meet the requirements concerning qualified automobile demonstration use? See page 9 of the instructions		

Note: *If your answer to 35, 36, 37, 38, or 39 is "Yes," you need not complete Section B for the covered vehicles.*

Part VI — Amortization

	(a) Description of costs	(b) Date amortization begins	(c) Amortizable amount	(d) Code section	(e) Amortization period or percentage	(f) Amortization for this year
40 Amortization of costs that begins during your 1997 tax year:						
41 Amortization of costs that began before 1997					41	
42 **Total.** Enter here and on "Other Deductions" or "Other Expenses" line of your return					42	

Form **4626**	**Alternative Minimum Tax—Corporations**	OMB No. 1545-0175
Department of the Treasury Internal Revenue Service	▶ See separate instructions. ▶ Attach to the corporation's tax return.	**1997**

Name | **Employer identification number**

1	Taxable income or (loss) before net operating loss deduction	**1**
2	**Adjustments and preferences:**	
a	Depreciation of post-1986 property **2a**	
b	Amortization of certified pollution control facilities **2b**	
c	Amortization of mining exploration and development costs **2c**	
d	Amortization of circulation expenditures (personal holding companies only) . . **2d**	
e	Adjusted gain or loss **2e**	
f	Long-term contracts **2f**	
g	Installment sales **2g**	
h	Merchant marine capital construction funds **2h**	
i	Section 833(b) deduction (Blue Cross, Blue Shield, and similar type organizations only) **2i**	
j	Tax shelter farm activities (personal service corporations only) **2j**	
k	Passive activities (closely held corporations and personal service corporations only) **2k**	
l	Loss limitations **2l**	
m	Depletion **2m**	
n	Tax-exempt interest from specified private activity bonds **2n**	
o	Charitable contributions **2o**	
p	Intangible drilling costs **2p**	
q	Accelerated depreciation of real property (pre-1987) **2q**	
r	Accelerated depreciation of leased personal property (pre-1987) (personal holding companies only) **2r**	
s	Other adjustments **2s**	
t	Combine lines 2a through 2s	**2t**
3	Preadjustment alternative minimum taxable income (AMTI). Combine lines 1 and 2t	**3**
4	**Adjusted current earnings (ACE) adjustment:**	
a	Enter the corporation's ACE from line 10 of the worksheet on page 8 of the instructions **4a**	
b	Subtract line 3 from line 4a. If line 3 exceeds line 4a, enter the difference as a negative amount (see examples beginning on page 4 of the instructions) . . **4b**	
c	Multiply line 4b by 75% (.75). Enter the result as a positive amount . . . **4c**	
d	Enter the excess, if any, of the corporation's total increases in AMTI from prior year ACE adjustments over its total reductions in AMTI from prior year ACE adjustments (see page 5 of the instructions). **Note:** You **must** enter an amount on line 4d (even if line 4b is positive) **4d**	
e	ACE adjustment: • If you entered a positive number or zero on line 4b, enter the amount from line 4c here as a positive amount. • If you entered a negative number on line 4b, enter the smaller of line 4c or line 4d here as a negative amount.	**4e**
5	Combine lines 3 and 4e. If zero or less, stop here; the corporation does not owe alternative minimum tax	**5**
6	Alternative tax net operating loss deduction (see page 5 of the instructions)	**6**
7	**Alternative minimum taxable income.** Subtract line 6 from line 5. If the corporation held a residual interest in a REMIC, see page 5 of the instructions	**7**

For Paperwork Reduction Act Notice, see separate instructions.   Cat. No. 12955I   Form **4626** (1997)

Form 4626 (1997) Page **2**

8	Enter the amount from line 7 (alternative minimum taxable income)	**8**
9	**Exemption phase-out computation** (if line 8 is $310,000 or more, skip lines 9a and 9b and enter -0- on line 9c):	
a	Subtract $150,000 from line 8 (if you are completing this line for a member of a controlled group, see page 5 of the instructions). If zero or less, enter -0- . .	**9a**
b	Multiply line 9a by 25% (.25).	**9b**
c	Exemption. Subtract line 9b from $40,000 (if you are completing this line for a member of a controlled group, see page 5 of the instructions). If zero or less, enter -0-	**9c**
10	Subtract line 9c from line 8. If zero or less, enter -0-	**10**
11	Multiply line 10 by 20% (.20).	**11**
12	Alternative minimum tax foreign tax credit. See page 5 of the instructions	**12**
13	Tentative minimum tax. Subtract line 12 from line 11.	**13**
14	Regular tax liability before all credits except the foreign tax credit and possessions tax credit . . .	**14**
15	**Alternative minimum tax.** Subtract line 14 from line 13. Enter the result on the appropriate line of the corporation's income tax return (e.g., Form 1120, Schedule J, line 9). If zero or less, enter -0- .	**15**

Tax Forms   B–61

Form **4684**

Department of the Treasury
Internal Revenue Service

Casualties and Thefts

▶ See separate instructions.
▶ Attach to your tax return.
▶ Use a separate Form 4684 for each different casualty or theft.

OMB No. 1545-0177

1997

Attachment Sequence No. **26**

Name(s) shown on tax return | Identifying number

SECTION A—Personal Use Property (Use this section to report casualties and thefts of property **not** used in a trade or business or for income-producing purposes.)

1 Description of properties (show type, location, and date acquired for each):
   Property **A** ....
   Property **B** ....
   Property **C** ....
   Property **D** ....

Properties (Use a separate column for each property lost or damaged from one casualty or theft.)

	A	B	C	D
2 Cost or other basis of each property				
3 Insurance or other reimbursement (whether or not you filed a claim). See instructions				
Note: *If line 2 is more than line 3, skip line 4.*				
4 Gain from casualty or theft. If line 3 is **more than** line 2, enter the difference here and skip lines 5 through 9 for that column. See instructions if line 3 includes insurance or other reimbursement you did not claim, or you received payment for your loss in a later tax year				
5 Fair market value **before** casualty or theft				
6 Fair market value **after** casualty or theft				
7 Subtract line 6 from line 5				
8 Enter the **smaller** of line 2 or line 7				
9 Subtract line 3 from line 8. If zero or less, enter -0-				

10 Casualty or theft loss. Add the amounts on line 9. Enter the total **10**

11 Enter the amount from line 10 or $100, whichever is **smaller** **11**

12 Subtract line 11 from line 10 .... **12**

Caution: *Use only one Form 4684 for lines 13 through 18.*

13 Add the amounts on line 12 of all Forms 4684 .... **13**

14 Combine the amounts from line 4 of all Forms 4684 .... **14**

15 • If line 14 is **more than** line 13, enter the difference here and on Schedule D. Do not complete the rest of this section (see instructions).
    • If line 14 is **less than** line 13, enter -0- here and continue with the form.
    • If line 14 is **equal to** line 13, enter -0- here. Do not complete the rest of this section. } **15**

16 If line 14 is **less than** line 13, enter the difference **16**

17 Enter 10% of your adjusted gross income (Form 1040, line 33). Estates and trusts, see instructions ... **17**

18 Subtract line 17 from line 16. If zero or less, enter -0-. Also enter result on Schedule A (Form 1040), line 19. Estates and trusts, enter on the "Other deductions" line of your tax return **18**

For Paperwork Reduction Act Notice, see page 4 of separate instructions.   Cat. No. 12997O   Form **4684** (1997)

Form 4684 (1997) Attachment Sequence No. **26** Page **2**

Name(s) shown on tax return. Do not enter name and identifying number if shown on other side. | Identifying number

SECTION B—Business and Income-Producing Property (Use this section to report casualties and thefts of property used in a trade or business or for income-producing purposes.)

Part I Casualty or Theft Gain or Loss (Use a separate Part I for each casualty or theft.)

19 Description of properties (show type, location, and date acquired for each):
Property **A** ....
Property **B** ....
Property **C** ....
Property **D** ....

Properties (Use a separate column for each property lost or damaged from one casualty or theft.)

	A	B	C	D
20 Cost or adjusted basis of each property				
21 Insurance or other reimbursement (whether or not you filed a claim). See the instructions for line 3. **Note:** If line 20 is **more than** line 21, skip line 22.				
22 Gain from casualty or theft. If line 21 is **more than** line 20, enter the difference here and on line 29 or line 34, column (c), except as provided in the instructions for line 33. Also, skip lines 23 through 27 for that column. See the instructions for line 4 if line 21 includes insurance or other reimbursement you did not claim, or you received payment for your loss in a later tax year				
23 Fair market value **before** casualty or theft				
24 Fair market value **after** casualty or theft				
25 Subtract line 24 from line 23				
26 Enter the **smaller** of line 20 or line 25				
Note: If the property was totally destroyed by casualty or lost from theft, enter on line 26 the amount from line 20.				
27 Subtract line 21 from line 26. If zero or less, enter -0-				

28 Casualty or theft loss. Add the amounts on line 27. Enter the total here and on line 29 **or** line 34 (see instructions). **28**

Part II Summary of Gains and Losses (from separate Parts I)

(a) Identify casualty or theft	(b) Losses from casualties or thefts		(c) Gains from casualties or thefts includible in income
	(i) Trade, business, rental or royalty property	(ii) Income-producing property	

Casualty or Theft of Property Held One Year or Less

29	( )	( )	
	( )	( )	
30 Totals. Add the amounts on line 29	( )	( )	

31 Combine line 30, columns (b)(i) and (c). Enter the net gain or (loss) here and on Form 4797, line 14. If Form 4797 is not otherwise required, see instructions . **31**

32 Enter the amount from line 30, column (b)(ii) here and on Schedule A (Form 1040), line 22. Partnerships, S corporations, estates and trusts, see instructions . **32**

Casualty or Theft of Property Held More Than One Year

33 Casualty or theft gains from Form 4797, line 32 . **33**

34		( )	( )	
		( )	( )	
35 Total losses. Add amounts on line 34, columns (b)(i) and (b)(ii)	( )	( )	

36 Total gains. Add lines 33 and 34, column (c) . **36**
37 Add amounts on line 35, columns (b)(i) and (b)(ii) . **37**
38 If the loss on line 37 is **more than** the gain on line 36:
   a Combine line 35, column (b)(i) and line 36, and enter the net gain or (loss) here. Partnerships and S corporations see the note below. All others enter this amount on Form 4797, line 14. If Form 4797 is not otherwise required, see instructions **38a**
   b Enter the amount from line 35, column (b)(ii) here. Partnerships and S corporations see the note below. Individuals enter this amount on Schedule A (Form 1040), line 22. Estates and trusts, enter on the "Other deductions" line of your tax return **38b**
39 If the loss on line 37 is **equal to** or **less than** the gain on line 36, combine these lines and enter here. Partnerships, see the note below. All others, enter this amount on Form 4797, line 3, column (g) and the net 28% rate gain or (loss), if applicable, in column (h) . **39**

Note: Partnerships, enter the amount from line 38a, 38b, or line 39 on Form 1065, Schedule K, line 7. S corporations, enter the amount from line 38a or 38b on Form 1120S, Schedule K, line 6.

Form 4797 — Sales of Business Property

(Also Involuntary Conversions and Recapture Amounts Under Sections 179 and 280F(b)(2))

► Attach to your tax return.   ► See separate instructions.

Department of the Treasury — Internal Revenue Service (99)

OMB No. 1545-0184
1997
Attachment Sequence No. 27

Name(s) shown on return

Identifying number

1 Enter here the gross proceeds from the sale or exchange of real estate reported to you for 1997 on Form(s) 1099-S (or a substitute statement) that you will be including on line 2, 10, or 20 . . . . **1**

Part I — Sales or Exchanges of Property Used in a Trade or Business and Involuntary Conversions From Other Than Casualty or Theft—Property Held More Than 1 Year

(a) Description of property	(b) Date acquired (mo., day, yr.)	(c) Date sold (mo., day, yr.)	(d) Gross sales price	(e) Depreciation allowed or allowable since acquisition	(f) Cost or other basis, plus improvements and expense of sale	(g) GAIN or (LOSS) for entire year. Subtract (f) from the sum of (d) and (e)	(h) 28% RATE GAIN or (LOSS) * (see instr. below)
2							

3 Gain, if any, from Form 4684, line 39 . . . . **3**

4 Section 1231 gain from installment sales from Form 6252, line 26 or 37 . . . . **4**

5 Section 1231 gain or (loss) from like-kind exchanges from Form 8824 . . . . **5**

6 Gain, if any, from line 32, from other than casualty or theft **6**

7 Combine lines 2 through 6 in columns (g) and (h). Enter gain or (loss) here, and on the appropriate line as follows: **7**

   Partnerships—Enter the gain or (loss) on Form 1065, Schedule K, lines 6a and 6b. Skip lines 8, 9, 11, and 12 below.

   S corporations—Report the gain or (loss) following the instructions for Form 1120S, Schedule K, lines 5 and 6. Skip lines 8, 9, 11, and 12 below, unless line 7, column (g) is a gain and the S corporation is subject to the capital gains tax.

   All others—If line 7, column (g) is zero or a loss, enter that amount on line 11 below and skip lines 8 and 9. If line 7, column (g) is a gain and you did not have any prior year section 1231 losses, or they were recaptured in an earlier year, enter the gain or (loss) in each column as a long-term capital gain or (loss) on Schedule D and skip lines 8, 9, and 12 below.

8 Nonrecaptured net section 1231 losses from prior years (see instructions) **8**

9 Subtract line 8 from line 7. If zero or less, enter -0-. Also enter on the appropriate line as follows (see instructions): **9**

   S corporations—Enter only the gain in column (g) on Schedule D (Form 1120S), line 14, and skip lines 11 and 12 below.

   All others—If line 9, column (g) is zero, enter the gain from line 7, column (g) on line 12 below. If line 9, column (g) is more than zero, enter the amount from line 8, column (g) on line 12 below, and enter the gain or (loss) in each column of line 9 as a long-term capital gain or (loss) on Schedule D.

* Corporations (other than S corporations) should not complete column (h). Partnerships and S corporations must complete column (h). All others must complete column (h) only if line 7, column (g), is a gain. 28% rate gain or loss includes all gains and losses in column (g) from sales, exchanges, or conversions (including installment payments received) **either (a)** before 5/7/97 **or (b)** after 7/28/97 for assets held more than 1 year but not more than 18 months.

Part II — Ordinary Gains and Losses

10 Ordinary gains and losses not included on lines 11 through 17 (include property held 1 year or less):

11 Loss, if any, from line 7, column (g) **11**

12 Gain, if any, from line 7, column (g) or amount from line 8, column (g) if applicable **12**

13 Gain, if any, from line 31 . . . . **13**

14 Net gain or (loss) from Form 4684, lines 31 and 38a **14**

15 Ordinary gain from installment sales from Form 6252, line 25 or 36 . . . . **15**

16 Ordinary gain or (loss) from like-kind exchanges from Form 8824 . . . . **16**

17 Recapture of section 179 expense deduction for partners and S corporation shareholders from property dispositions by partnerships and S corporations (see instructions) **17**

18 Combine lines 10 through 17 in column (g). Enter gain or (loss) here, and on the appropriate line as follows: **18**

   a For all except individual returns: Enter the gain or (loss) from line 18 on the return being filed.

   b For individual returns:

   (1) If the loss on line 11 includes a loss from Form 4684, line 35, column (b)(ii), enter that part of the loss here and on line 22 of Schedule A (Form 1040). Identify as from "Form 4797, line 18b(1)." See instructions . . . . **18b(1)**

   (2) Redetermine the gain or (loss) on line 18, excluding the loss, if any, on line 18b(1). Enter here and on Form 1040, line 14 . . . . **18b(2)**

For Paperwork Reduction Act Notice, see separate instructions.   Cat. No. 13086I   Form **4797** (1997)

Form 4797 (1997) Page **2**

Part III — Gain From Disposition of Property Under Sections 1245, 1250, 1252, 1254, and 1255

19	(a) Description of section 1245, 1250, 1252, 1254, or 1255 property:	(b) Date acquired (mo., day, yr.)	(c) Date sold (mo., day, yr.)
A			
B			
C			
D			

	These columns relate to the properties on lines 19A through 19D. ▶		Property A	Property B	Property C	Property D
20	Gross sales price (**Note:** *See line 1 before completing.*)	20				
21	Cost or other basis plus expense of sale	21				
22	Depreciation (or depletion) allowed or allowable	22				
23	Adjusted basis. Subtract line 22 from line 21	23				
24	Total gain. Subtract line 23 from line 20	24				
25	**If section 1245 property:**					
a	Depreciation allowed or allowable from line 22	25a				
b	Enter the **smaller** of line 24 or 25a	25b				
26	**If section 1250 property:** If straight line depreciation was used, enter -0- on line 26g, except for a corporation subject to section 291.					
a	Additional depreciation after 1975 (see instructions)	26a				
b	Applicable percentage multiplied by the **smaller** of line 24 or line 26a (see instructions)	26b				
c	Subtract line 26a from line 24. If residential rental property or line 24 is not more than line 26a, skip lines 26d and 26e	26c				
d	Additional depreciation after 1969 and before 1976	26d				
e	Enter the **smaller** of line 26c or 26d	26e				
f	Section 291 amount (corporations only)	26f				
g	Add lines 26b, 26e, and 26f	26g				
27	**If section 1252 property:** Skip this section if you did not dispose of farmland or if this form is being completed for a partnership.					
a	Soil, water, and land clearing expenses	27a				
b	Line 27a multiplied by applicable percentage (see instructions)	27b				
c	Enter the **smaller** of line 24 or 27b	27c				
28	**If section 1254 property:**					
a	Intangible drilling and development costs, expenditures for development of mines and other natural deposits, and mining exploration costs (see instructions)	28a				
b	Enter the **smaller** of line 24 or 28a	28b				
29	**If section 1255 property:**					
a	Applicable percentage of payments excluded from income under section 126 (see instructions)	29a				
b	Enter the **smaller** of line 24 or 29a (see instructions)	29b				

Summary of Part III Gains. Complete property columns A through D through line 29b before going to line 30.

30	Total gains for all properties. Add property columns A through D, line 24	30	
31	Add property columns A through D, lines 25b, 26g, 27c, 28b, and 29b. Enter here and on line 13	31	
32	Subtract line 31 from line 30. Enter the portion from casualty or theft on Form 4684, line 33. Enter the portion from other than casualty or theft on Form 4797, line 6, column (g), and if applicable, column (h)	32	

Part IV — Recapture Amounts Under Sections 179 and 280F(b)(2) When Business Use Drops to 50% or Less
See instructions.

			(a) Section 179	(b) Section 280F(b)(2)
33	Section 179 expense deduction or depreciation allowable in prior years	33		
34	Recomputed depreciation. See instructions	34		
35	Recapture amount. Subtract line 34 from line 33. See the instructions for where to report	35		

Form **6251**	**Alternative Minimum Tax—Individuals**	OMB No. 1545-0227
Department of the Treasury Internal Revenue Service (99)	▶ See separate instructions. ▶ Attach to Form 1040 or Form 1040NR.	**1997** Attachment Sequence No. **32**

Name(s) shown on Form 1040 | Your social security number

Part I — Adjustments and Preferences

1. If you itemized deductions on Schedule A (Form 1040), go to line 2. Otherwise, enter your standard deduction from Form 1040, line 35, here and go to line 6 . . . . **1**
2. Medical and dental. Enter the smaller of Schedule A (Form 1040), line 4 **or** 2½% of Form 1040, line 33 . . . **2**
3. Taxes. Enter the amount from Schedule A (Form 1040), line 9 . . . . **3**
4. Certain interest on a home mortgage not used to buy, build, or improve your home **4**
5. Miscellaneous itemized deductions. Enter the amount from Schedule A (Form 1040), line 26 . . . **5**
6. Refund of taxes. Enter any tax refund from Form 1040, line 10 or line 21 . . . . **6** ( )
7. Investment interest. Enter difference between regular tax and AMT deduction **7**
8. Post-1986 depreciation. Enter difference between regular tax and AMT depreciation **8**
9. Adjusted gain or loss. Enter difference between AMT and regular tax gain or loss **9**
10. Incentive stock options. Enter excess of AMT income over regular tax income **10**
11. Passive activities. Enter difference between AMT and regular tax income or loss **11**
12. Beneficiaries of estates and trusts. Enter the amount from Schedule K-1 (Form 1041), line 9 . . . **12**
13. Tax-exempt interest from private activity bonds issued after 8/7/86 . . . . **13**
14. Other. Enter the amount, if any, for each item below and enter the total on line 14.
    - **a** Charitable contributions
    - **b** Circulation expenditures
    - **c** Depletion
    - **d** Depreciation (pre-1987)
    - **e** Installment sales
    - **f** Intangible drilling costs
    - **g** Long-term contracts
    - **h** Loss limitations
    - **i** Mining costs
    - **j** Patron's adjustment
    - **k** Pollution control facilities
    - **l** Research and experimental
    - **m** Tax shelter farm activities
    - **n** Related adjustments **14**
15. **Total Adjustments and Preferences.** Combine lines 1 through 14 . . . . ▶ **15**

Part II — Alternative Minimum Taxable Income

16. Enter the amount from **Form 1040, line 36**. If less than zero, enter as a (loss) . . . . . . ▶ **16**
17. Net operating loss deduction, if any, from Form 1040, line 21. Enter as a positive amount . . . **17**
18. If Form 1040, line 33, is over $121,200 (over $60,600 if married filing separately), and you itemized deductions, enter the amount, if any, from line 9 of the worksheet for Schedule A (Form 1040), line 28 **18** ( )
19. Combine lines 15 through 18 . . . . ▶ **19**
20. Alternative tax net operating loss deduction. See page 5 of the instructions **20**
21. **Alternative Minimum Taxable Income.** Subtract line 20 from line 19. (If married filing separately and line 21 is more than $165,000, see page 5 of the instructions.) . . . . ▶ **21**

Part III — Exemption Amount and Alternative Minimum Tax

22. **Exemption Amount.** (If this form is for a child under age 14, see page 6 of the instructions.)

IF your filing status is . . .	AND line 21 is not over . . .	THEN enter on line 22 . . .
Single or head of household	$112,500	$33,750
Married filing jointly or qualifying widow(er)	150,000	45,000
Married filing separately	75,000	22,500

    22

    If line 21 is **over** the amount shown above for your filing status, see page 6 of the instructions.

23. Subtract line 22 from line 21. If zero or less, enter -0- here and on lines 26 and 28 . . . . ▶ **23**
24. If you completed Schedule D (Form 1040), and had an amount on line 25 or line 27 (as refigured for the AMT, if necessary), go to Part IV of Form 6251 to figure line 24. **All others:** If line 23 is $175,000 or less ($87,500 or less if married filing separately), multiply line 23 by 26% (.26). Otherwise, multiply line 23 by 28% (.28) and subtract $3,500 ($1,750 if married filing separately) from the result . . . . ▶ **24**
25. Alternative minimum tax foreign tax credit. See page 7 of the instructions **25**
26. Tentative minimum tax. Subtract line 25 from line 24 . . . . ▶ **26**
27. Enter your tax from Form 1040, line 39 (minus any tax from Form 4972 and any foreign tax credit from Form 1040, line 43) **27**
28. **Alternative Minimum Tax.** (If this form is for a child under age 14, see page 7 of the instructions.) Subtract line 27 from line 26. If zero or less, enter -0-. Enter here and on Form 1040, line 48 . . ▶ **28**

For Paperwork Reduction Act Notice, see separate instructions.   Cat. No. 13600G   Form **6251** (1997)

Form 6251 (1997) Page **2**

Part IV — Line 24 Computation Using Maximum Capital Gains Rates

29	Enter the amount from line 23	29
30	Enter the amount from Schedule D (Form 1040), line 27 (as refigured for the AMT, if necessary) 30	
31	Enter the amount from Schedule D (Form 1040), line 25 (as refigured for the AMT, if necessary) 31	
32	Add lines 30 and 31 32	
33	Enter the amount from Schedule D (Form 1040), line 22 (as refigured for the AMT, if necessary) 33	
34	Enter the **smaller** of line 32 or line 33	34
35	Subtract line 34 from line 29. If zero or less, enter -0-	35
36	If line 35 is $175,000 or less ($87,500 or less if married filing separately), multiply line 35 by 26% (.26). Otherwise, multiply line 35 by 28% (.28) and subtract $3,500 ($1,750 if married filing separately) from the result . . . . ▶	36
37	Enter the amount from Schedule D (Form 1040), line 36 (as figured for the regular tax)	37
38	Enter the **smallest** of line 29, line 30, or line 37	38
39	Multiply line 38 by 10% (.10) . . . . ▶	39
40	Enter the **smaller** of line 29 or line 30	40
41	Enter the amount from line 38	41
42	Subtract line 41 from line 40. If zero or less, enter -0-	42
43	Multiply line 42 by 20% (.20) . . . . ▶	43
44	Enter the amount from line 29	44
45	Add lines 35, 38, and 42	45
46	Subtract line 45 from line 44	46
47	Multiply line 46 by 25% (.25) . . . . ▶	47
48	Add lines 36, 39, 43, and 47	48
49	If line 29 is $175,000 or less ($87,500 or less if married filing separately), multiply line 29 by 26% (.26). Otherwise, multiply line 29 by 28% (.28) and subtract $3,500 ($1,750 if married filing separately) from the result	49
50	Enter the **smaller** of line 48 or line 49 here and on line 24 . . . . ▶	50

Form **8582**	**Passive Activity Loss Limitations**	OMB No. 1545-1008
Department of the Treasury Internal Revenue Service (99)	▶ See separate instructions. ▶ Attach to Form 1040 or Form 1041.	**19**97 Attachment Sequence No. **88**

Name(s) shown on return | Identifying number

Part I — 1997 Passive Activity Loss
Caution: *See the instructions for Worksheets 1 and 2 on page 7 before completing Part I.*

Rental Real Estate Activities With Active Participation (For the definition of active participation see **Active Participation in a Rental Real Estate Activity** on page 3 of the instructions.)

- **1a** Activities with net income (enter the amount from Worksheet 1, column (a)) **1a**
- **b** Activities with net loss (enter the amount from Worksheet 1, column (b)) . . . . **1b** ( )
- **c** Prior years unallowed losses (enter the amount from Worksheet 1, column (c)) . . . . **1c** ( )
- **d** Combine lines 1a, 1b, and 1c **1d**

All Other Passive Activities

- **2a** Activities with net income (enter the amount from Worksheet 2, column (a)) **2a**
- **b** Activities with net loss (enter the amount from Worksheet 2, column (b)) . . . . **2b** ( )
- **c** Prior years unallowed losses (enter the amount from Worksheet 2, column (c)) . . . . **2c** ( )
- **d** Combine lines 2a, 2b, and 2c **2d**

3 Combine lines 1d and 2d. If the result is net income or zero, all losses are allowed, including any prior year unallowed losses entered on line 1c or 2c. **Do not** complete Form 8582. Take the losses to the form or schedule you normally report them on.
If this line and line 1d are losses, go to line 4. Otherwise, enter -0- on line 9 and go to line 10 . **3**

Part II — Special Allowance for Rental Real Estate With Active Participation
Note: *Enter all numbers in Part II as positive amounts. See page 7 of the instructions for examples.*

4 Enter the **smaller** of the loss on line 1d or the loss on line 3 . . . . **4**

5 Enter $150,000. If married filing separately, see page 7 of the instructions **5**

6 Enter modified adjusted gross income, but not less than zero (see page 7 of the instructions) **6**

Note: *If line 6 is equal to or greater than line 5, skip lines 7 and 8, enter -0- on line 9, and then go to line 10. Otherwise, go to line 7.*

7 Subtract line 6 from line 5 . . . . **7**

8 Multiply line 7 by 50% (.5). **Do not** enter more than $25,000. If married filing separately, see page 9 of the instructions **8**

9 Enter the **smaller** of line 4 or line 8 . . . . **9**

Part III — Total Losses Allowed

10 Add the income, if any, on lines 1a and 2a and enter the total **10**

11 **Total losses allowed from all passive activities for 1997.** Add lines 9 and 10. See page 9 of the instructions to find out how to report the losses on your tax return **11**

For Paperwork Reduction Act Notice, see separate instructions. | Cat. No. 63704F | Form **8582** (1997)

Form 8582 (1997) Page **2**

Caution: *The worksheets are not required to be filed with your tax return and may be detached before filing Form 8582. Keep a copy of the worksheets for your records.*

Worksheet 1—For Form 8582, Lines 1a, 1b, and 1c (See page 6 of the instructions.)

Name of activity	Current year		Prior years	Overall gain or loss	
	(a) Net income (line 1a)	(b) Net loss (line 1b)	(c) Unallowed loss (line 1c)	(d) Gain	(e) Loss
Total. Enter on Form 8582, lines 1a, 1b, and 1c. ▶					

Worksheet 2—For Form 8582, Lines 2a, 2b, and 2c (See page 7 of the instructions.)

Name of activity	Current year		Prior years	Overall gain or loss	
	(a) Net income (line 2a)	(b) Net loss (line 2b)	(c) Unallowed loss (line 2c)	(d) Gain	(e) Loss
Total. Enter on Form 8582, lines 2a, 2b, and 2c. ▶					

Worksheet 3—Use this worksheet if an amount is shown on Form 8582, line 9 (See page 8 of the instructions.)

Name of activity	Form or schedule to be reported on	(a) Loss	(b) Ratio	(c) Special allowance	(d) Subtract column (c) from column (a)
Total ▶			1.00		

Worksheet 4—Allocation of Unallowed Losses (See page 8 of the instructions.)

Name of activity	Form or schedule to be reported on	(a) Loss	(b) Ratio	(c) Unallowed loss
Total ▶			1.00	

Worksheet 5—Allowed Losses (See page 8 of the instructions.)

Name of activity	Form or schedule to be reported on	(a) Loss	(b) Unallowed loss	(c) Allowed loss
Total ▶				

Form 8582 (1997) Page **3**

Worksheet 6—Activities With Losses Reported on Two or More Different Forms or Schedules (See page 8 of the instructions.)

Name of Activity:	(a)	(b)	(c) Ratio	(d) Unallowed loss	(e) Allowed loss
Form or Schedule To Be Reported on:					
1a Net loss plus prior year unallowed loss from form or schedule ▶					
b Net income from form or schedule ▶					
c Subtract line 1b from line 1a. If zero or less, enter -0- ▶					
Form or Schedule To Be Reported on:					
1a Net loss plus prior year unallowed loss from form or schedule ▶					
b Net income from form or schedule ▶					
c Subtract line 1b from line 1a. If zero or less, enter -0- ▶					
Form or Schedule To Be Reported on:					
1a Net loss plus prior year unallowed loss from form or schedule ▶					
b Net income from form or schedule ▶					
c Subtract line 1b from line 1a. If zero or less, enter -0- ▶					
Total .... ▶			1.00		

B-70 Appendix B

Form **8615**	**Tax for Children Under Age 14 Who Have Investment Income of More Than $1,300**	OMB No. 1545-0998 **1997**
Department of the Treasury Internal Revenue Service (99)	▶ Attach ONLY to the child's Form 1040, Form 1040A, or Form 1040NR.	Attachment Sequence No. **33**

Child's name shown on return | Child's social security number

A Parent's name (first, initial, and last). **Caution:** See instructions on back before completing. | **B** Parent's social security number

C Parent's filing status (check one):
☐ Single   ☐ Married filing jointly   ☐ Married filing separately   ☐ Head of household   ☐ Qualifying widow(er)

Part I Child's Net Investment Income

1 Enter the child's investment income, such as taxable interest and dividends. See instructions. If this amount is $1,300 or less, **stop;** do not file this form **1**

2 If the child **did not** itemize deductions on Schedule A (Form 1040 or Form 1040NR), enter $1,300. If the child **did** itemize deductions, see instructions **2**

3 Subtract line 2 from line 1. If the result is zero or less, **stop;** do not complete the rest of this form but **do** attach it to the child's return **3**

4 Enter the child's **taxable** income from Form 1040, line 38; Form 1040A, line 22; or Form 1040NR, line 37 . . . . ▶ **4**

5 Enter the **smaller** of line 3 or line 4 . . . . ▶ **5**

Part II Tentative Tax Based on the Tax Rate of the Parent Listed on Line A

6 Enter the parent's **taxable** income from Form 1040, line 38; Form 1040A, line 22; Form 1040EZ, line 6; TeleFile Tax Record, line J; Form 1040NR, line 37; or Form 1040NR-EZ, line 13. If the parent transferred property to a trust, see instructions **6**

7 Enter the total net investment income, if any, from Forms 8615, line 5, of **all other** children of the parent identified above. **Do not** include the amount from line 5 above **7**

8 Add lines 5, 6, and 7 . . . . **8**

9 Enter the tax on line 8 based on the **parent's** filing status. See instructions. If **Schedule D** (Form 1040) is used to figure the tax, check here . . . . ▶ ☐ **9**

10 Enter the parent's tax from Form 1040, line 39; Form 1040A, line 23; Form 1040EZ, line 10; TeleFile Tax Record, line J; Form 1040NR, line 38; or Form 1040NR-EZ, line 14. If **Schedule D** (Form 1040) was used to figure the tax, check here . . . . ▶ ☐ **10**

11 Subtract line 10 from line 9 and enter the result. If line 7 is blank, enter on line 13 the amount from line 11 and go to **Part III** **11**

12a Add lines 5 and 7 . . . . **12a**
  b Divide line 5 by line 12a. Enter the result as a decimal (rounded to three places) . . . . **12b**   × .
13 Multiply line 11 by line 12b . . . . ▶ **13**

Part III Child's Tax—If lines 4 and 5 above are the same, enter -0- on line 15 and go to line 16.

14 Subtract line 5 from line 4 . . . . **14**

15 Enter the tax on line 14 based on the **child's** filing status. See instructions. If **Schedule D** (Form 1040) is used to figure the tax, check here . . . . ▶ ☐ **15**

16 Add lines 13 and 15 . . . . **16**

17 Enter the tax on line 4 based on the **child's** filing status. See instructions. If **Schedule D** (Form 1040) is used to figure the tax, check here . . . . ▶ ☐ **17**

18 Enter the **larger** of line 16 or line 17 here and on Form 1040, line 39; Form 1040A, line 23; or Form 1040NR, line 38 . . . . ▶ **18**

General Instructions

Section references are to the Internal Revenue Code.

Purpose of form. For children under age 14, investment income over $1,300 is taxed at the parent's rate if the parent's rate is higher than the child's rate. If the child's investment income is more than $1,300, use this form to figure the child's tax.

Investment income. As used on this form, "investment income" includes all taxable income other than earned income as defined on page 2. It includes taxable interest, dividends, capital gains, rents, royalties, etc. It also includes pension and annuity income and income (other than earned income) received as the beneficiary of a trust.

Who must file. Generally, Form 8615 must be filed for any child who was under age 14 on January 1, 1998, had more than $1,300 of investment income, and is required to file a tax return. But if neither parent was alive on December 31, 1997, do not use Form 8615. Instead, figure the child's tax in the normal manner.

Note: *The parent may be able to elect to report the child's interest and dividends on his or her return. If the parent makes this election, the child will not have to file a return or Form 8615. For more details, see* **Form 8814,** *Parents' Election To Report Child's Interest and Dividends.*

Additional information. For more details, see **Pub. 929,** Tax Rules for Children and Dependents.

Incomplete information for parent. If the parent's taxable income or filing status or the net investment income of the parent's other children is not known by the due

For Paperwork Reduction Act Notice, see back of form.   Cat. No. 64113U   Form **8615** (1997)

date of the child's return, reasonable estimates may be used. Write "Estimated" on the appropriate line(s) of Form 8615. For more details, see Pub. 929.

Amended return. If after the child's return is filed the parent's taxable income changes or the net investment income of any of the parent's other children changes, the child's tax must be refigured using the adjusted amounts. If the child's tax changes, file **Form 1040X,** Amended U.S. Individual Income Tax Return, to correct the child's tax.

Alternative Minimum Tax. A child whose tax is figured on Form 8615 may owe the alternative minimum tax. For details, see **Form 6251,** Alternative Minimum Tax—Individuals, and its instructions.

Line Instructions

Lines A and B. If the child's parents were married to each other and filed a joint return, enter the name and social security number (SSN) of the parent who is listed first on the joint return.

If the parents were married but filed separate returns, enter the name and SSN of the parent who had the **higher** taxable income. If you do not know which parent had the higher taxable income, see Pub. 929.

If the parents were unmarried, treated as unmarried for Federal income tax purposes, or separated either by a divorce or separate maintenance decree, enter the name and SSN of the parent who had custody of the child for most of the year (the custodial parent).

Exception. If the custodial parent remarried and filed a joint return with his or her new spouse, enter the name and SSN of the person listed first on the joint return, even if that person is not the child's parent. If the custodial parent and his or her new spouse filed separate returns, enter the name and SSN of the person with the **higher** taxable income, even if that person is not the child's parent.

Note: *If the parents were unmarried but lived together during the year with the child, enter the name and SSN of the parent who had the **higher** taxable income.*

Line 1. If the child had no earned income (defined later), enter the child's adjusted gross income from Form 1040, line 33; Form 1040A, line 17; or Form 1040NR, line 33.

Child's Investment Income Worksheet—Line 1 (keep a copy for your records)

1. Enter the amount from the child's Form 1040, line 22; Form 1040A, line 14; or Form 1040NR, line 23, whichever applies ..... 1. _____
2. Enter the child's **earned income** (defined on this page) plus any deduction the child claims on Form 1040, line 29, or Form 1040NR, line 29, whichever applies .... 2. _____
3. Subtract line 2 from line 1. Enter the result here and on Form 8615, line 1 .... 3. _____

If the child had earned income, use the worksheet on this page to figure the amount to enter on line 1. But if the child files **Form 2555** or **2555-EZ** (relating to foreign earned income), has a net loss from self-employment, or claims a net operating loss deduction, you **must** use the worksheet in Pub. 929 instead.

Earned income includes wages, tips, and other payments received for personal services performed. Generally, it is the total of the amounts reported on Form 1040, lines 7, 12, and 18; Form 1040A, line 7; or Form 1040NR, lines 8, 13, and 19.

Line 2. If the child itemized deductions, enter the **greater** of:

- $1,300, **or**
- $650 plus the portion of the amount on **Schedule A** (Form 1040), line 28, or **Schedule A** (Form 1040NR), line 17, that is directly connected with the production of the investment income on Form 8615, line 1.

Line 6. If the parent's taxable income is less than zero, enter zero on line 6. If the parent filed a joint return, enter the taxable income shown on that return even if the parent's spouse is not the child's parent. If the parent transferred property to a trust that sold or exchanged the property in 1997 before August 6, 1997, include any gain that was taxed to the trust under section 644 in the amount entered on line 6. Enter "Sec. 644" and the amount on the dotted line next to line 6. Also, see the instructions for line 10.

Line 9. Figure the tax using the Tax Table, Tax Rate Schedules, or **Schedule D** (Form 1040), whichever applies. If any net capital gain is included on line 5, 6, or 7, Part IV of Schedule D must be used to figure the tax on the amount on line 8. See Pub. 929 for details on how to figure the net capital gain included on line 8.

Line 10. If the parent filed a joint return, enter the tax shown on that return even if the parent's spouse is not the child's parent. If the parent filed Form 8814, enter "Form 8814" and the total tax from line 8 of Form(s) 8814 on the dotted line next to line 10 of Form 8615.

If line 6 includes any gain taxed to a trust under section 644, add the tax imposed under section 644(a)(2)(A) to the tax shown on the parent's return and enter the total on line 10. Also, enter "Sec. 644" on the dotted line next to line 10.

Line 15. Figure the tax using the Tax Table, Tax Rate Schedule X, or Schedule D, whichever applies. If line 14 includes any net capital gain, use Schedule D to figure the tax. See Pub. 929 for details on how to figure the net capital gain included on line 14.

Line 17. Figure the tax as if these rules did not apply. For example, if the child has a net capital gain, use Schedule D to figure his or her tax.

Paperwork Reduction Act Notice. We ask for the information on this form to carry out the Internal Revenue laws of the United States. You are required to give us the information. We need it to ensure that you are complying with these laws and to allow us to figure and collect the right amount of tax.

You are not required to provide the information requested on a form that is subject to the Paperwork Reduction Act unless the form displays a valid OMB control number. Books or records relating to a form or its instructions must be retained as long as their contents may become material in the administration of any Internal Revenue law. Generally, tax returns and return information are confidential, as required by section 6103.

The time needed to complete and file this form will vary depending on individual circumstances. The estimated average time is: **Recordkeeping,** 13 min.; **Learning about the law or the form,** 13 min.; **Preparing the form,** 45 min.; and **Copying, assembling, and sending the form to the IRS,** 17 min.

If you have comments concerning the accuracy of these time estimates or suggestions for making this form simpler, we would be happy to hear from you. See the instructions for the tax return with which this form is filed.

Appendix B

Form 8824
Department of the Treasury
Internal Revenue Service

Like-Kind Exchanges
(and nonrecognition of gain from conflict-of-interest sales)
▶ See separate instructions.   ▶ Attach to your tax return.
▶ Use a separate form for each like-kind exchange.

OMB No. 1545-1190
1997
Attachment Sequence No. **49**

Name(s) shown on tax return | Identifying number

Part I — Information on the Like-Kind Exchange

Note: *If the property described on line 1 or line 2 is real or personal property located outside the United States, indicate the country.*

1 Description of like-kind property given up ▶ ....

2 Description of like-kind property received ▶ ....

3 Date like-kind property given up was originally acquired (month, day, year) . . . . **3** / /
4 Date you actually transferred your property to other party (month, day, year) . . . . . . **4** / /
5 Date the like-kind property you received was identified (month, day, year). See instructions . **5** / /
6 Date you actually received the like-kind property from other party (month, day, year) . . . **6** / /
7 Was the exchange made with a related party? If "Yes," complete Part II. If "No," go to Part III. See instructions.
   a ☐ Yes, in this tax year   b ☐ Yes, in a prior tax year   c ☐ No.

Part II — Related Party Exchange Information

8 Name of related party | Related party's identifying number

   Address (no., street, and apt., room, or suite no.)

   City or town, state, and ZIP code | Relationship to you

9 During this tax year (and before the date that is 2 years after the last transfer of property that was part of the exchange), did the related party sell or dispose of the like-kind property received from you in the exchange? ☐ Yes ☐ No

10 During this tax year (and before the date that is 2 years after the last transfer of property that was part of the exchange), did you sell or dispose of the like-kind property you received? . . . . ☐ Yes ☐ No

If both lines 9 and 10 are "No" and this is the year of the exchange, go to Part III. If either line 9 or line 10 is "Yes," the deferred gain or (loss) from line 24 **must** be reported on your return this tax year, **unless** one of the exceptions on line 11 applies. See **Related party exchanges** in the instructions.

11 If one of the exceptions below applies to the disposition, check the applicable box:
   a ☐ The disposition was after the death of either of the related parties.
   b ☐ The disposition was an involuntary conversion, and the threat of conversion occurred after the exchange.
   c ☐ You can establish to the satisfaction of the IRS that neither the exchange nor the disposition had tax avoidance as its principal purpose. If this box is checked, attach an explanation. See instructions.

Part III — Realized Gain or (Loss), Recognized Gain, and Basis of Like-Kind Property Received

Caution: *If you transferred **and** received (a) more than one group of like-kind properties, or (b) cash or other (not like-kind) property, see **Reporting of multi-asset exchanges** in the instructions.*

Note: *Complete lines 12 through 14 ONLY if you gave up property that was not like-kind. Otherwise, go to line 15.*

12 Fair market value (FMV) of other property given up . . . . . . | **12** |
13 Adjusted basis of other property given up . . . . | **13** |
14 Gain or (loss) recognized on other property given up. Subtract line 13 from line 12. Report the gain or (loss) in the same manner as if the exchange had been a sale **14**
15 Cash received, FMV of other property received, plus net liabilities assumed by other party, reduced (but not below zero) by any exchange expenses you incurred. See instructions **15**
16 FMV of like-kind property you received **16**
17 Add lines 15 and 16 . . . . **17**
18 Adjusted basis of like-kind property you gave up, net amounts paid to other party, plus any exchange expenses **not** used on line 15. See instructions **18**
19 **Realized gain or (loss).** Subtract line 18 from line 17 . . . . **19**
20 Enter the smaller of line 15 or line 19, but not less than zero **20**
21 Ordinary income under recapture rules. Enter here and on Form 4797, line 16. See instructions . **21**
22 Subtract line 21 from line 20. If zero or less, enter -0-. If more than zero, enter here and on Schedule D or Form 4797, unless the installment method applies. See instructions **22**
23 **Recognized gain.** Add lines 21 and 22 . . . . **23**
24 Deferred gain or (loss). Subtract line 23 from line 19. If a related party exchange, see instructions . **24**
25 **Basis of like-kind property received.** Subtract line 15 from the sum of lines 18 and 23 . . **25**

For Paperwork Reduction Act Notice, see back of form.   Cat. No. 12311A   Form **8824** (1997)

Form 8824 (1997) Page **2**

Name(s) shown on tax return. Do not enter name and social security number if shown on other side. | Your social security number

Part IV Section 1043 Conflict-of-Interest Sales. See instructions. Attach a copy of your certificate of divestiture.

Note: *This part is only to be used by officers or employees of the executive branch of the Federal Government for reporting nonrecognition of gain under section 1043 on the sale of property to comply with the conflict-of-inteest requirements. This part can be used only if the cost of the replacement property exceeds the basis of the divested property.*

26 Description of divested property ▶

27 Description of replacement property ▶

28 Date divested property was sold (month, day, year) . . . .   28 / /

29 Sales price of divested property. See instructions   29

30 Basis of divested property   30

31 **Realized gain.** Subtract line 30 from line 29   31

32 Cost of replacement property purchased within 60 days after date of sale   32

33 Subtract line 32 from line 29. If zero or less, enter -0-   33

34 Ordinary income under recapture rules. Enter here and on Form 4797, line 10. See instructions   34

35 Subtract line 34 from line 33. If zero or less, enter -0-. If more than zero, enter here and on Schedule D or Form 4797. See instructions   35

36 **Recognized gain.** Add lines 34 and 35   36

37 Deferred gain. Subtract line 36 from line 31   37

38 **Basis of replacement property.** Subtract line 37 from line 32   38

Paperwork Reduction Act Notice. We ask for the information on this form to carry out the Internal Revenue laws of the United States. You are required to give us the information. We need it to ensure that you are complying with these laws and to allow us to figure and collect the right amount of tax.

You are not required to provide the information requested on a form that is subject to the Paperwork Reduction Act unless the form displays a valid OMB control number. Books or records relating to a form or its instructions must be retained as long as their contents may become material in the administration of any Internal Revenue law. Generally, tax returns and return information are confidential, as required by Internal Revenue Code section 6103.

The time needed to complete and file this form will vary depending on individual circumstances. The estimated average time is: **Recordkeeping,** 26 min.; **Learning about the law or the fom,** 28 min.; **Preparing the form,** 1 hr., 2 min.; **Copying, assembling, and sending the form to the IRS,** 27 min.

If you have comments concerning the accuracy of these time estimates or suggestions for making this form simpler, we would be happy to hear from you. See the instructions for the tax return with which this form is filed.

Form **8829**	**Expenses for Business Use of Your Home**	OMB No. 1545-1266
Department of the Treasury Internal Revenue Service (99)	▶ File only with Schedule C (Form 1040). Use a separate Form 8829 for each home you used for business during the year. ▶ See separate instructions.	**1997** Attachment Sequence No. **66**

Name(s) of proprietor(s)   Your social security number

Part I   Part of Your Home Used for Business

1. Area used regularly and exclusively for business, regularly for day care, or for storage of inventory or product samples. See instructions **1**
2. Total area of home **2**
3. Divide line 1 by line 2. Enter the result as a percentage ..... **3** %
   - For day-care facilities not used exclusively for business, also complete lines 4–6.
   - All others, skip lines 4–6 and enter the amount from line 3 on line 7.
4. Multiply days used for day care during year by hours used per day . **4**   hr.
5. Total hours available for use during the year (365 days × 24 hours). See instructions   **5**   8,760 hr.
6. Divide line 4 by line 5. Enter the result as a decimal amount ... **6** .
7. Business percentage. For day-care facilities not used exclusively for business, multiply line 6 by line 3 (enter the result as a percentage). All others, enter the amount from line 3 ..... ▶ **7** %

Part II   Figure Your Allowable Deduction

8. Enter the amount from Schedule C, line 29, **plus** any net gain or (loss) derived from the business use of your home and shown on Schedule D or Form 4797. If more than one place of business, see instructions   **8**

See instructions for columns (a) and (b) before completing lines 9–20.   **(a) Direct expenses**   **(b) Indirect expenses**

9. Casualty losses. See instructions **9**
10. Deductible mortgage interest. See instructions . **10**
11. Real estate taxes. See instructions **11**
12. Add lines 9, 10, and 11 ..... **12**
13. Multiply line 12, column (b) by line 7 ..... **13**
14. Add line 12, column (a) and line 13 ..... **14**
15. Subtract line 14 from line 8. If zero or less, enter -0- . **15**
16. Excess mortgage interest. See instructions ... **16**
17. Insurance **17**
18. Repairs and maintenance **18**
19. Utilities **19**
20. Other expenses. See instructions **20**
21. Add lines 16 through 20 ..... **21**
22. Multiply line 21, column (b) by line 7 ..... **22**
23. Carryover of operating expenses from 1996 Form 8829, line 41 .. **23**
24. Add line 21 in column (a), line 22, and line 23 ..... **24**
25. Allowable operating expenses. Enter the **smaller** of line 15 or line 24 ..... **25**
26. Limit on excess casualty losses and depreciation. Subtract line 25 from line 15 . **26**
27. Excess casualty losses. See instructions **27**
28. Depreciation of your home from Part III below **28**
29. Carryover of excess casualty losses and depreciation from 1996 Form 8829, line 42 **29**
30. Add lines 27 through 29 ..... **30**
31. Allowable excess casualty losses and depreciation. Enter the **smaller** of line 26 or line 30 .. **31**
32. Add lines 14, 25, and 31 ..... **32**
33. Casualty loss portion, if any, from lines 14 and 31. Carry amount to **Form 4684**, Section B .. **33**
34. Allowable expenses for business use of your home. Subtract line 33 from line 32. Enter here and on Schedule C, line 30. If your home was used for more than one business, see instructions ▶ **34**

Part III   Depreciation of Your Home

35. Enter the **smaller** of your home's adjusted basis or its fair market value. See instructions .. **35**
36. Value of land included on line 35 ..... **36**
37. Basis of building. Subtract line 36 from line 35 ..... **37**
38. Business basis of building. Multiply line 37 by line 7 ..... **38**
39. Depreciation percentage. See instructions ..... **39** %
40. Depreciation allowable. Multiply line 38 by line 39. Enter here and on line 28 above. See instructions **40**

Part IV   Carryover of Unallowed Expenses to 1998

41. Operating expenses. Subtract line 25 from line 24. If less than zero, enter -0- **41**
42. Excess casualty losses and depreciation. Subtract line 31 from line 30. If less than zero, enter -0- .. **42**

For Paperwork Reduction Act Notice, see page 3 of separate instructions.   Cat. No. 13232M   Form **8829** (1997)

Tax Forms   B–75

Form **8832**
(December 1996)
Department of the Treasury
Internal Revenue Service

Entity Classification Election

OMB No. 1545-1516

Please Type or Print

Name of entity

Employer identification number (EIN)

Number, street, and room or suite no. If a P.O. box, see instructions.

City or town, state, and ZIP code. If a foreign address, enter city, province or state, postal code and country.

1 Type of election (see instructions):

a ☐ Initial classification by a newly-formed entity (or change in current classification of an existing entity to take effect on January 1, 1997)

b ☐ Change in current classification (to take effect later than January 1, 1997)

2 Form of entity (see instructions):

a ☐ A domestic eligible entity electing to be classified as an association taxable as a corporation.

b ☐ A domestic eligible entity electing to be classified as a partnership.

c ☐ A domestic eligible entity with a single owner electing to be disregarded as a separate entity.

d ☐ A foreign eligible entity electing to be classified as an association taxable as a corporation.

e ☐ A foreign eligible entity electing to be classified as a partnership.

f ☐ A foreign eligible entity with a single owner electing to be disregarded as a separate entity.

3 Election is to be effective beginning (month, day, year) (see instructions) . . . . ▶ ___/___/___

4 Name and title of person whom the IRS may call for more information

5 That person's telephone number

Consent Statement and Signature(s) (see instructions)

Under penalties of perjury, I (we) declare that I (we) consent to the election of the above-named entity to be classified as indicated above, and that I (we) have examined this consent statement, and to the best of my (our) knowledge and belief, it is true, correct, and complete. If I am an officer, manager, or member signing for all members of the entity, I further declare that I am authorized to execute this consent statement on their behalf.

Signature(s)	Date	Title

For Paperwork Reduction Act Notice, see page 2.   Cat. No. 22598R   Form **8832** (12-96)

General Instructions

Section references are to the Internal Revenue Code unless otherwise noted.

Paperwork Reduction Act Notice

We ask for the information on this form to carry out the Internal Revenue laws of the United States. You are required to give us the information. We need it to ensure that you are complying with these laws and to allow us to figure and collect the right amount of tax.

You are not required to provide the information requested on a form that is subject to the Paperwork Reduction Act unless the form displays a valid OMB control number. Books or records relating to a form or its instructions must be retained as long as their contents may become material in the administration of any Internal Revenue law. Generally, tax returns and return information are confidential, as required by section 6103.

The time needed to complete and file this form will vary depending on individual circumstances. The estimated average time is:

Recordkeeping . . .1 hr., 20 min.
Learning about the law or the form . . .1 hr., 41 min.
Preparing and sending the form to the IRS . . . .17 min.

If you have comments concerning the accuracy of these time estimates or suggestions for making this form simpler, we would be happy to hear from you. You can write to the Tax Forms Committee, Western Area Distribution Center, Rancho Cordova, CA 95743-0001. **DO NOT** send the form to this address. Instead, see **Where To File** on page 3.

Purpose of Form

For Federal tax purposes, certain business entities automatically are classified as corporations. See items **1** and **3** through **8** under the definition of corporation on this page. Other business entities may choose how they are classified for Federal tax purposes. Except for a business entity automatically classified as a corporation, a business entity with at least two members can choose to be classified as either an association taxable as a corporation or a partnership, and a business entity with a single member can choose to be classified as either an association taxable as a corporation or disregarded as an entity separate from its owner.

Generally, an eligible entity that does not file this form will be classified under the default rules described below. An eligible entity that chooses not to be classified under the default rules or that wishes to change its current classification must file Form 8832 to elect a classification. The IRS will use the information entered on this form to establish the entity's filing and reporting requirements for Federal tax purposes.

Default Rules

Existing entity default rule.— Certain domestic and foreign entities that are already in existence before January 1, 1997, and have an established Federal tax classification, generally do not need to make an election to continue that classification. However, for an eligible entity with a single owner that claimed to be a partnership under the law in effect before January 1, 1997, that entity will now be disregarded as an entity separate from its owner. If an existing entity decides to change its classification, it may do so subject to the rules in Regulations section 301.7701-3(c)(1)(iv). A foreign eligible entity is treated as being in existence prior to the effective date of this section only if the entity's classification is relevant at any time during the 60 months prior to January 1, 1997.

Domestic default rule.— Unless an election is made on Form 8832, a domestic eligible entity is:

1. A partnership if it has two or more members.

2. Disregarded as an entity separate from its owner if it has a single owner.

Foreign default rule.— Unless an election is made on Form 8832, a foreign eligible entity is:

1. A partnership if it has two or more members and at least one member does not have limited liability.

2. An association if all members have limited liability.

3. Disregarded as an entity separate from its owner if it has a single owner that does not have limited liability.

Definitions

Business entity.— A business entity is any entity recognized for Federal tax purposes that is not properly classified as a trust under Regulations section 301.7701-4 or otherwise subject to special treatment under the Code. See Regulations section 301.7701-2(a).

Corporation.— For Federal tax purposes, a corporation is any of the following:

1. A business entity organized under a Federal or state statute, or under a statute of a federally recognized Indian tribe, if the statute describes or refers to the entity as incorporated or as a corporation, body corporate, or body politic.

2. An association (as determined under Regulations section 301.7701-3).

3. A business entity organized under a state statute, if the statute describes or refers to the entity as a joint-stock company or joint-stock association.

4. An insurance company.

5. A state-chartered business entity conducting banking activities, if any of its deposits are insured under the Federal Deposit Insurance Act, as amended, 12 U.S.C. 1811 et seq., or a similar Federal statute.

6. A business entity wholly owned by a state or any political subdivision thereof.

7. A business entity that is taxable as a corporation under a provision of the Code other than section 7701(a)(3).

8. A foreign business entity listed in Regulations section 301.7701-2(b)(8). However, a foreign business entity listed in those regulations generally will not be treated as a corporation if all of the following apply:

a. The entity was in existence on May 8, 1996.

b. The entity's classification was relevant (as defined below) on May 8, 1996.

c. No person (including the entity) for whom the entity's classification was relevant on May 8, 1996, treats the entity as a corporation for purposes of filing that person's Federal income tax returns, information returns, and withholding documents for the tax year including May 8, 1996.

d. Any change in the entity's claimed classification within the 60 months prior to May 8, 1996, was a result of a change in the organizational documents of the entity, and the entity and all members of the entity recognized the Federal tax consequences of any change in the entity's classification within the 60 months prior to May 8, 1996.

e. The entity had a reasonable basis (within the meaning of section 6662) for treating the entity as other than a corporation on May 8, 1996.

f. Neither the entity nor any member was notified in writing on or before May 8, 1996, that the classification of the entity was under examination (in which case the entity's classification will be determined in the examination).

Binding contract rule.—If a foreign business entity described in Regulations section 301.7701-2(b)(8)(i) is formed after May 8, 1996, under a written binding contract (including an accepted bid to develop a project) in effect on May 8, 1996, and all times thereafter, in which the parties agreed to engage (directly or indirectly) in an active and substantial business operation in the jurisdiction in which the entity is formed, **8** on page 2 is applied by substituting the date of the entity's formation for May 8, 1996.

Eligible entity.—An eligible entity is a business entity that is not included in items **1** or **3** through **8** under the definition of corporation on page 2.

Limited liability.—A member of a foreign eligible entity has limited liability if the member has no personal liability for any debts of or claims against the entity by reason of being a member. This determination is based solely on the statute or law under which the entity is organized (and, if relevant, the entity's organizational documents). A member has personal liability if the creditors of the entity may seek satisfaction of all or any part of the debts or claims against the entity from the member as such. A member has personal liability even if the member makes an agreement under which another person (whether or not a member of the entity) assumes that liability or agrees to indemnify that member for that liability.

Partnership.—A partnership is a business entity that has **at least** two members and is not a corporation as defined on page 2.

Relevant.—A foreign eligible entity's classification is relevant when its classification affects the liability of any person for Federal tax or information purposes. The date the classification of a foreign eligible entity is relevant is the date an event occurs that creates an obligation to file a Federal tax return, information return, or statement for which the classification of the entity must be determined.

Effect of Election

The resulting tax consequences of a change in classification remain the same no matter how a change in entity classification is achieved. For example, if an organization classified as an association elects to be classified as a partnership, the organization and its owners must recognize gain, if any, under the rules applicable to liquidations of corporations.

Who Must File

File this form for an **eligible entity** that is one of the following:

- A domestic entity electing to be classified as an association taxable as a corporation.
- A domestic entity electing to change its current classification (even if it is currently classified under the default rule).
- A foreign entity that has more than one owner, all owners have limited liability, and it elects to be classified as a partnership.
- A foreign entity that has at least one owner without limited liability, and it elects to be classified as an association taxable as a corporation.
- A foreign entity with a single owner having limited liability, and it elects to have the entity disregarded as an entity separate from its owner.
- A foreign entity electing to change its current classification (even if it is currently classified under the default rule).

Do not file this form for an eligible entity that is:

- Tax-exempt under section 501(a), or
- A real estate investment trust (REIT), as defined in section 856.

When To File

See the instructions for line 3.

Where To File

File Form 8832 with the Internal Revenue Service Center, Philadelphia, PA 19255. Also attach a copy of Form 8832 to the entity's Federal income tax or information return for the tax year of the election. If the entity is not required to file a return for that year, a copy of its Form 8832 must be attached to the Federal income tax or information returns of all direct or indirect owners of the entity for the tax year of the owner that includes the date on which the election took effect. Although failure to attach a copy will not invalidate an otherwise valid election, each member of the entity is required to file returns that are consistent with the entity's election. In addition, penalties may be assessed against persons who are required to, but who do not, attach Form 8832 to their returns. Other penalties may apply for filing Federal income tax or information returns inconsistent with the entity's election.

Specific Instructions

Employer Identification Number (EIN)

Show the correct EIN on Form 8832. If the entity does not have an EIN, it generally must apply for one on **Form SS-4,** Application for Employer Identification Number. If the filing of Form 8832 is the only reason the entity is applying for an EIN, check the "Other" box on line 9 of Form SS-4 and write "Form 8832" to the right of that box. If the entity has not received an EIN by the time Form 8832 is due, write "Applied for" in the space for the EIN. **Do not** apply for a new EIN for an existing entity that is changing its classification. If you are electing to disregard an entity as separate from its owner, enter the owner's EIN.

Address

Include the suite, room, or other unit number after the street address. If the Post Office does not deliver mail to the street address and the entity has a P.O. box, show the box number instead of the street address.

Line 1

Check box 1a if the entity is choosing a classification for the first time **and** the entity does not want to be classified under the applicable default classification. **Do not** file this form if the entity wants to be classified under the default rules.

Check box 1b if the entity is changing its current classification to take effect later than January 1, 1997, whether or not the entity's current classification is the default classification. However, once an eligible entity makes an election to change its classification (other than an election made by an existing entity to change its classification as of January 1, 1997), the entity cannot change its classification by election again during the 60 months after the effective date of the election. However, the IRS may permit (by private letter ruling) the entity to change its classification by election within the 60-month period if more than 50% of the ownership interests in the entity as of the effective date of the election are owned by persons that did not own any interests in the entity on the effective date of the prior election.

Line 2

Check the appropriate box if you are changing a current classification (no matter how achieved), or are electing out of a default classification. **Do not** file this form if you fall within a default classification that is the desired classification for the new entity.

Line 3

Generally, the election will take effect on the date you enter on line 3 of this form or on the date filed if no date is entered on line 3. However, an election specifying an entity's classification for Federal tax purposes can take effect no more than 75 days prior to the date the election is filed, nor can it take effect later than 12 months after the date on which the election is filed. If line 3 shows a date more than 75 days prior to the date on which the election is filed, the election will take effect 75 days before the date it is filed. If line 3 shows an effective date more than 12 months from the filing date, the election will take effect 12 months after the date the election was filed.

Regardless of the date filed, an election will in no event take effect before January 1, 1997.

Consent Statement and Signatures

Form 8832 must be signed by:

1. Each member of the electing entity who is an owner at the time the election is filed; or

2. Any officer, manager, or member of the electing entity who is authorized (under local law or the organizational documents) to make the election and who represents to having such authorization under penalties of perjury.

If an election is to be effective for any period prior to the time it is filed, each person who was an owner between the date the election is to be effective and the date the election is filed, and who is not an owner at the time the election is filed, must also sign.

If you need a continuation sheet or use a separate consent statement, attach it to Form 8832. The separate consent statement must contain the same information as shown on Form 8832.

Appendix C
Glossary of Tax Terms

The words and phrases in this glossary have been defined to reflect their conventional use in the field of taxation. The definitions may therefore be incomplete for other purposes.

A

Abandoned spouse. The abandoned spouse provision enables a married taxpayer with a dependent child whose spouse did not live in the taxpayer's home during the last six months of the tax year to file as a head of household rather than as married filing separately.

Accelerated cost recovery system (ACRS). A method in which the cost of tangible property is recovered over a prescribed period of time. Enacted by the Economic Recovery Tax Act (ERTA) of 1981, the approach disregards salvage value, imposes a period of cost recovery that depends upon the classification of the asset into one of various recovery periods, and prescribes the applicable percentage of cost that can be deducted each year. § 168.

Accelerated depreciation. Various methods of depreciation that yield larger deductions in the earlier years of the life of an asset than the straight-line method. Examples include the double declining-balance and the sum-of-the-years' digits methods of depreciation.

Accident and health benefits. Employee fringe benefits provided by employers through the payment of health and accident insurance premiums or the establishment of employer-funded medical reimbursement plans. Employers generally are entitled to a deduction for such payments, whereas employees generally exclude the fringe benefits from gross income. §§ 105 and 106.

Accountable plan. An accountable plan is a type of expense reimbursement plan that requires an employee to render an adequate accounting to the employer and return any excess reimbursement or allowance. If the expense qualifies, it will be treated a deduction *for* AGI.

Accounting income. The accountant's concept of income is generally based upon the realization principle. Financial accounting income may differ from taxable income (e.g., accelerated depreciation might be used for Federal income tax and straight-line depreciation for financial accounting purposes). Differences are included in a reconciliation of taxable and accounting income on Schedule M–1 of Form 1120 for corporations. See *economic income*.

Accounting method. The method under which income and expenses are determined for tax purposes. Important accounting methods include the cash basis and the accrual basis. Special methods are available for the reporting of gain on installment sales, recognition of income on construction projects (the completed contract and percentage of completion methods), and the valuation of inventories (last-in, first-out and first-in, first-out). §§ 446–474. See also *accrual method, cash receipts method, completed contract method,* and *percentage of completion method*.

Accounting period. The period of time, usually a year, used by a taxpayer for the determination of tax liability. Unless a fiscal year is chosen, taxpayers must determine and pay their income tax liability by using the calendar year (January 1 through December 31) as the period of measurement. An example of a fiscal year is July 1 through June 30. A change in accounting period (e.g., from a calendar year to a fiscal year) generally requires the consent of the IRS. Some new taxpayers, such as a newly formed corporation, are free to select either an initial calendar or a fiscal year without the consent of the IRS. §§ 441–444. See also *annual accounting period concept*.

Accrual basis. See *accrual method*.

Accrual method. A method of accounting that reflects expenses incurred and income earned for any one tax year. In contrast to the cash basis of accounting, expenses do not have to be paid to be deductible, nor does income have to be received to be taxable. Unearned income (e.g., prepaid interest and rent) generally is taxed in the year of receipt regardless of the method of accounting used by the taxpayer. § 446(c)(2). See also *accounting method, cash receipts method,* and *unearned income*.

Accumulated adjustments account (AAA). An account that aggregates an S corporation's post-1982 income, loss, and deductions for the tax year (including nontaxable income and nondeductible losses and expenses). After the year-end income and expense adjustments are made, the account is reduced by distributions made during the tax year.

Accumulated earnings and profits. Net undistributed tax-basis earnings of the corporation aggregated from March 1, 1913, to the end of the prior tax year. Used to determine the amount of dividend income associated with a distribution to shareholders. See *current earnings and profits* and *earnings and profits*. § 316 and Reg. § 1.316–2.

Accumulated earnings tax (AET). A special tax imposed on corporations that accumulate (rather than distribute) their earnings beyond the reasonable needs of the business. The accumulated earnings tax and related interest are imposed on accumulated taxable income in addition to the corporate income tax. §§ 531–537.

Acquiescence. Agreement by the IRS on the results reached in certain judicial decisions; sometimes abbreviated *Acq.* or *A.* See also *nonacquiescence.*

Acquisition indebtedness. Debt incurred in acquiring, constructing, or substantially improving a qualified residence of the taxpayer. The interest on such loans is deductible as *qualified residence interest.* However, interest on such debt is deductible only on the portion of the indebtedness that does not exceed $1,000,000 ($500,000 for married persons filing separate returns). § 163(h)(3). See also *home equity loans.*

ACRS. See *accelerated cost recovery system.*

Active income. Active income includes wages, salary, commissions, bonuses, profits from a trade or business in which the taxpayer is a material participant, gain on the sale or other disposition of assets used in an active trade or business, and income from intangible property if the taxpayer's personal efforts significantly contributed to the creation of the property. The *passive activity loss* rules require classification of income and losses into three categories with active income being one of them.

Ad valorem tax. A tax imposed on the value of property. The most common ad valorem tax is that imposed by states, counties, and cities on real estate. Ad valorem taxes can be imposed on personal property as well. See also *personalty.*

Additional depreciation. The excess of the amount of depreciation actually deducted over the amount that would have been deducted had the straight-line method been used. § 1250(b). See also *Section 1250 recapture.*

Adjusted basis. The cost or other basis of property reduced by depreciation allowed or allowable and increased by capital improvements. Other special adjustments are provided in § 1016 and the related Regulations. See also *basis.*

Adjusted current earnings (ACE) adjustment. An adjustment in computing corporate alternative minimum taxable income (AMTI), computed at 75 percent of the excess of adjusted current earnings and profits over unadjusted AMTI. ACE computations reflect restrictions on the timing of certain recognition events. Exempt interest, life insurance proceeds, and other receipts that are included in earnings and profits but not in taxable income also increase the ACE adjustment. If unadjusted AMTI exceeds adjusted current earnings and profits, the ACE adjustment is negative. The negative adjustment is limited to the aggregate of the positive adjustments under ACE for prior years, reduced by any previously claimed negative adjustments. See also *alternative minimum tax* and *earnings and profits.*

Adjusted gross estate. The gross estate of a *decedent* reduced by § 2053 expense (e.g., administration, funeral) and §2054 losses (e.g., casualty). Necessary in testing for the extension of time for installment payment of estate taxes under § 6166. See also *gross estate.*

Adjusted gross income (AGI). A tax determination unique to individual taxpayers. Generally, it represents the gross income of an individual, less business expenses and less any appropriate capital loss adjustment. See also *gross income.*

AFTR. Published by Research Institute of America (formerly by Prentice-Hall), *American Federal Tax Reports* contain all of the Federal tax decisions issued by the U.S. District Courts, U.S. Court of Federal Claims, U.S. Courts of Appeals, and the U.S. Supreme Court.

AFTR2d. The second series of the *American Federal Tax Reports,* dealing with 1954 and 1986 Code case law.

Aggregate concept. The theory of partnership taxation under which, in certain cases, a partnership is treated as a mere extension of each partner.

Alimony and separate maintenance. Alimony deductions result from the payment of a legal obligation arising from the termination of a marital relationship. Payments designated as alimony generally are included in the gross income of the recipient and are deductible *for* AGI by the payer.

Allocable share of income. Certain entities receive conduit treatment under the Federal income tax law. This means the earned income or loss is not taxed to the entity, but is allocated to the owners or beneficiaries, regardless of the magnitude or timing of corresponding distributions. The portion of the entity's income that is taxed to the owner or beneficiary is the allocable share of the entity's income or loss for the period. The allocations are determined by (1) the partnership agreement for partners, (2) a weighted-average stock ownership computation for shareholders of an S corporation, and (3) the controlling will or trust instrument for the beneficiaries of an estate or trust.

Allocate. The assignment of income for various tax purposes. The income and expense items of an estate or trust are allocated between income and corpus components. Specific items of income, expense, gain, loss, and credit can be allocated to specific partners or shareholders in an S corporation, if a substantial economic nontax purpose for the allocation is established. See also *substantial economic effect.*

Alternate valuation date. Property passing from a decedent by death may be valued for estate tax purposes as of the date of death or the alternate valuation date. The alternate valuation date is six months from the date of death or the date the property is disposed of by the estate, whichever comes first. To use the alternate valuation date, the *executor* or *administrator* of the estate must make an affirmative election. Election of the alternate valuation date is not available unless it decreases the amount of the gross estate *and* reduces the estate tax liability.

Alternative depreciation system (ADS). A cost recovery system that produces a smaller deduction in early years than would be calculated under ACRS or MACRS. The alternative system must be used in certain instances and can be elected in other instances. § 168(g). See also *cost recovery allowance.*

Alternative minimum tax (AMT). The AMT is a fixed percentage of alternative minimum taxable income (AMTI). AMTI generally starts with the taxpayer's adjusted gross income (for individuals) or taxable income (for other taxpayers). To this amount, the taxpayer (1) adds designated preference items (e.g., tax-exempt interest income on private activity bonds), (2) makes other specified adjustments (e.g., to reflect a longer, straight-line cost recovery deduction), (3) subtracts certain AMT itemized deductions for individuals (e.g., interest incurred on housing but not taxes paid), and (4) subtracts an exemption amount (e.g., $40,000 on an individual joint return). The taxpayer must pay the greater of the resulting AMT (reduced by only the foreign tax credit) or the regular income tax (reduced by all allowable tax credits).

Alternative minimum taxable income (AMTI). A major component of the base for computing a taxpayer's *alternative minimum tax* (AMT). Generally, it is the taxable income for the year, modified for AMT adjustments and preferences.

Amortization. The tax deduction for the cost or other basis of an intangible asset over the asset's estimated useful life. Examples of amortizable intangibles include patents, copyrights, and leasehold interests. The intangible goodwill can be amortized for income tax purposes over a 15-year period. § 197. For tangible assets, see *depreciation*. For natural resources, see *depletion*. See also *estimated useful life* and *goodwill*.

Amount realized. The amount received by a taxpayer upon the sale or exchange of property. Amount realized is the sum of the cash and the fair market value of any property or services received by the taxpayer, plus any related debt assumed by the buyer. Determining the amount realized is the starting point for arriving at realized gain or loss. § 1001(b). See also *realized gain or loss* and *recognized gain or loss*.

AMT adjustments. In calculating AMTI, certain adjustments are added to or deducted from taxable income. These adjustments generally reflect timing differences. § 56.

Annual accounting period concept. In determining a taxpayer's income tax liability, only transactions taking place during a specified tax year are taken into consideration. For reporting and payment purposes, therefore, the tax life of taxpayers is divided into equal annual accounting periods. See also *accounting period* and *mitigation of the annual accounting period concept*.

Annual exclusion. In computing the taxable gifts for the year, each donor excludes the first $10,000 of a gift to each donee. Usually, the annual exclusion is not available for gifts of future interests. § 2503(b). See also *gift splitting*.

Annuity. A fixed sum of money payable to a person at specified times for a specified period of time or for life. If the party making the payment (i.e., the obligor) is regularly engaged in this type of business (e.g., an insurance company), the arrangement is classified as a commercial annuity. A private annuity involves an obligor that is not regularly engaged in selling annuities (e.g., a charity or family member).

Appellate court. For Federal tax purposes, appellate courts include the Courts of Appeals and the Supreme Court. If the party losing in the trial (or lower) court is dissatisfied with the result, the dispute may be carried to the appropriate appellate court. See also *Court of Appeals* and *trial court*.

Arm's length concept. The standard under which unrelated parties would carry out a transaction. Suppose Cardinal Corporation sells property to its sole shareholder for $10,000. In determining whether $10,000 is an arm's length price, one would ascertain the amount for which the corporation could have sold the property to a disinterested third party.

Articles of incorporation. The legal document specifying a corporation's name, period of existence, purpose and powers, authorized number of shares, classes of stock, and other conditions for operation. The organizers of the corporation file the articles with the state of incorporation. If the articles are satisfactory and other conditions of the law are satisfied, the state will issue a charter recognizing the organization's status as a corporation.

Assignment of income. A procedure whereby a taxpayer attempts to avoid the recognition of income by assigning to another the property that generates the income. Such a procedure will not avoid the recognition of income by the taxpayer making the assignment if it can be said that the income was earned at the point of the transfer. In this case, usually referred to as an anticipatory assignment of income, the income will be taxed to the person who earns it.

Association. An organization treated as a corporation for Federal tax purposes even though it may not qualify as such under applicable state law. An entity designated as a trust or a partnership, for example, may be classified as an association if it clearly possesses corporate attributes. Corporate attributes include centralized management, continuity of life, free transferability of interests, and limited liability. When the check-the-box Regulations were finalized, the association Regulations were withdrawn. Thus, for most entities, reclassification as an association is unlikely. § 7701(a)(3). See also *check-the-box Regulations*.

Assumption of liabilities. In a corporate takeover or asset purchase, the buyer often takes assets subject to preexisting debt. Such actions do not create *boot* received on the transaction for the new shareholder, unless there is no *bona fide* business purpose for the exchange, or the principal purpose of the debt assumption is the avoidance of tax liabilities. Gain is recognized to the extent that liabilities assumed exceed the bases of the transferred assets. § 357.

At-risk amount. A taxpayer has an amount at risk in a business or investment venture to the extent that personal assets have been subjected to the risks of the business. Typically, the taxpayer's at-risk amount includes (1) the amount of money or other property that the investor contributed to the venture for the investment, (2) the amount of any of the entity's liabilities for which the taxpayer personally is liable and that relate to the investment, and (3) an allocable share of nonrecourse debts incurred by the venture from third parties in arm's length transactions for real estate investments.

At-risk limitation. Generally, a taxpayer can deduct losses related to a trade or business, S corporation, partnership, or investment asset only to the extent of the at-risk amount. § 465. See *at-risk amount*.

Attribution. Under certain circumstances, the tax law applies attribution (constructive ownership) rules to assign to one taxpayer the ownership interest of another taxpayer. If, for example, the stock of Gold Corporation is held 60 percent by Marsha and 40 percent by Sidney, Marsha may be deemed to own 100 percent of Gold Corporation if Marsha and Sidney are mother and son. In that case, the stock owned by Sidney is attributed to Marsha. Stated differently, Marsha has a 60 percent direct and a 40 percent indirect interest in Gold Corporation. It can also be said that Marsha is the constructive owner of Sidney's interest.

Automatic mileage method. See *automobile expenses*.

Automobile expenses. Automobile expenses are generally deductible only to the extent the automobile is used in business or for the production of income. Personal commuting expenses are not deductible. The taxpayer may deduct actual expenses (including depreciation and insurance), or the standard (automatic) mileage rate may be used (30 cents per mile for 1995, 31 cents per mile for 1996, 31.5 cents per mile for 1997, and 32.5 cents per mile for 1998) during any one year. Automobile expenses incurred for medical purposes or in connection with job-related moving expenses are deductible to the extent of actual out-of-pocket expenses or at the rate of 10 cents per mile (14 cents for charitable activities).

B

Bad debt. A deduction is permitted if a business account receivable subsequently becomes partially or completely worthless, providing the income arising from the debt previously was included in income. Available methods are the specific charge-off method and the reserve method. However, except for certain financial institutions, the specific charge-off method must be used. A nonbusiness bad debt deduction is allowed as a short-term capital loss if the loan did not arise in connection with the creditor's trade or business activities. Loans between related parties (family members) generally are classified as nonbusiness. § 166. See also *nonbusiness bad debt*.

Bargain sale or purchase. A sale or purchase of property for less than fair market value. The difference between the sale or purchase price and the fair market value of the property may have tax consequences. If, for example, a corporation sells property worth $1,000 to one of its shareholders for $700, the $300 difference probably represents a constructive dividend to the shareholder. Suppose, instead, the shareholder sells the property (worth $1,000) to his or her corporation for $700. The $300 difference probably represents a contribution by the shareholder to the corporation's capital. Bargain sales and purchases among members of the same family may lead to gift tax consequences. See also *constructive dividend*.

Basis. The acquisition cost assigned to an asset for income tax purposes. For assets acquired by purchase, basis is cost (§ 1012). Special rules govern the basis of property received by virtue of another's death (§ 1014) or by gift (§ 1015), the basis of stock received on a transfer of property to a controlled corporation (§ 358), the basis of the property transferred to the corporation (§ 362), and the basis of property received upon the liquidation of a corporation (§ 334). See also *adjusted basis*.

Basis in partnership interest. The acquisition cost of the partner's ownership interest in the *partnership*. Includes purchase price and associated debt acquired from other partners and in the course of the entity's trade or business.

Bona fide. In good faith, or real. In tax law, this term is often used in connection with a business purpose for carrying out a transaction. Thus, was there a bona fide business purpose for a shareholder's transfer of a liability to a controlled corporation? § 357(b)(1)(B). See also *business purposes*.

Book value. The net amount of an asset after reduction by a related reserve. The book value of machinery, for example, is the amount of the machinery less the reserve for depreciation.

Boot. Cash or property of a type not included in the definition of a nontaxable exchange. The receipt of boot will cause an otherwise nontaxable transfer to become taxable to the extent of the lesser of the fair market value of the boot or the realized gain on the transfer. For example, see transfers to controlled corporations under § 351(b) and like-kind exchanges under § 1031(b). See also *like-kind exchange* and *realized gain or loss*.

Bribes and illegal payments. Section 162 denies a deduction for bribes or kickbacks, fines, and penalties paid to a government official or employee for violation of law, and two-thirds of the treble damage payments made to claimants for violation of the antitrust law. Denial of a deduction for bribes and illegal payments is based upon the judicially established principle that allowing such payments would be contrary to public policy.

Brother-sister controlled group. More than one corporation owned by the same shareholders. If, for example, Chris and Pat each own one-half of the stock in Wren Corporation and Redbird Corporation, Wren and Redbird form a brother-sister controlled group.

B.T.A. The Board of Tax Appeals was a trial court that considered Federal tax matters. This Court is now the U.S. Tax Court.

Built-in gains tax. A penalty tax designed to discourage a shift of the incidence of taxation on unrealized gains from a C corporation to its shareholders, via an S election. Under this provision, any recognized gain during the first 10 years of S status generates a corporate-level tax on a base not to exceed the aggregate untaxed built-in gains brought into the S corporation upon its election from C corporation taxable years.

Burden of proof. The requirement in a lawsuit to show the weight of evidence and thereby gain a favorable decision. Except in cases of tax fraud, the burden of proof in a tax case generally is on the taxpayer. See also *fraud*.

Business bad debt. A tax deduction allowed for obligations obtained in connection with a trade or business that have become either partially or completely worthless. In contrast to nonbusiness bad debts, business bad debts are deductible as business expenses. § 166. See also *nonbusiness bad debt*.

Business energy credits. See *energy tax credit*.

Business purpose. A justifiable business reason for carrying out a transaction. Mere tax avoidance is not an acceptable business purpose. The presence of a business purpose is crucial in the area of corporate reorganizations and certain liquidations. See also *bona fide*.

Buy-sell agreement. An arrangement, particularly appropriate in the case of a closely held corporation or a partnership, whereby the surviving owners (shareholders or partners) or the entity agrees to purchase the interest of a withdrawing owner. The buy-sell agreement provides for an orderly disposition of an interest in a business and may aid in setting the value of the interest for death tax purposes. See also *cross-purchase buy-sell agreement* and *entity buy-sell agreement*.

C

Cafeteria plan. An employee benefit plan under which an employee is allowed to select from among a variety of employer-provided fringe benefits. Some of the benefits may be taxable and some may be statutory nontaxable benefits (e.g. health and accident insurance and group term life insurance). The employee is taxed only on the taxable benefits selected. A cafeteria benefit plan is also referred to as a flexible benefit plan.

Capital account. The financial accounting analog of a partner's tax basis in the entity.

Capital asset. Broadly speaking, all assets are capital except those specifically excluded by the Code. Major categories of noncapital assets include property held for resale in the normal course of business (inventory), trade accounts and notes receivable, and depreciable property and real estate used in a trade or business (§ 1231 assets). § 1221. See also *capital gain* and *capital loss*.

Capital contribution. Various means by which a shareholder makes additional funds available to the corporation (placed at the risk of the business), sometimes without the receipt of additional stock. If no stock is received, the contributions are added to the basis of the shareholder's existing stock investment and do not generate gross income to the corporation. § 118.

Capital expenditure. An expenditure that should be added to the basis of the property improved. For income tax purposes, this generally precludes a full deduction for the expenditure in the year paid or incurred. Any cost recovery in the form of a tax deduction comes in the form of depreciation, depletion, or amortization. § 263.

Capital gain. The gain from the sale or exchange of a capital asset. See also *capital asset*.

Capital gain property. Property contributed to a charitable organization that, if sold rather than contributed, would have resulted in long-term capital gain to the donor. See also *ordinary income property*.

Capital interest. Usually, the percentage of the entity's net assets that a partner would receive on liquidation. Typically determined by the partner's capital sharing ratio.

Capital loss. The loss from the sale or exchange of a capital asset. See also *capital asset*.

Capital sharing ratio. A partner's percentage ownership of the entity's capital.

Carryover basis. When a taxpayer exchanges one asset for another, many provisions in the tax law allow the basis assigned to the received asset to be precisely that of the traded asset. Thus, no step-up or -down of basis occurs as a result of the exchange. For instance, when an investor contributes an asset to a corporation or partnership, the entity generally takes a carryover basis in the property.

Cash method. See *cash receipts method*.

Cash receipts method. A method of accounting that reflects deductions as paid and income as received in any one tax year. However, deductions for prepaid expenses that benefit more than one tax year (e.g., prepaid rent and prepaid interest) usually must be spread over the period benefited rather than deducted in the year paid. § 446(c)(1). See also *constructive receipt of income*.

Cash surrender value. The amount of money that an insurance policy would yield if cashed in with the insurance company that issued the policy.

Casualty loss. A casualty is defined as "the complete or partial destruction of property resulting from an identifiable event of a sudden, unexpected or unusual nature" (e.g., floods, storms, fires, auto accidents). Theft losses are also deductible. Generally, a casualty loss is deductible only if it is incurred in a trade or business or in a transaction entered into for profit. Individuals may also deduct personal casualty losses as itemized deductions subject to a $100 nondeductible floor per casualty and an annual floor of 10 percent of adjusted gross income that applies after the $100 floor has been applied. Special rules are provided for the netting of certain casualty gains and losses. § 165. See also *disaster area losses* and *Section 1231 gains and losses*.

CCH. Commerce Clearing House (CCH) is the publisher of a tax service and of Federal tax decisions (USTC series).

C corporation. A separate taxable entity, subject to the rules of Subchapter C of the Code. This business form may create a double taxation effect relative to its shareholders. The entity is subject to the regular corporate tax and a number of penalty taxes at the Federal level.

Cert. den. By denying the Writ of Certiorari, the U.S. Supreme Court refuses to accept an appeal from a U.S. Court of Appeals. The denial of certiorari does not, however, mean that the U.S. Supreme Court agrees with the result reached by the lower court. See also *certiorari*.

Certiorari. Appeal from a U.S. Court of Appeals to the U.S. Supreme Court is by Writ of Certiorari. The Supreme Court need not accept the appeal, and it usually does not (*cert. den.*) unless a conflict exists among the lower courts that must be resolved or a constitutional issue is involved. See also *cert. den.*

Cf. Compare.

Charitable contributions. Contributions are deductible (subject to various restrictions and ceiling limitations) if made to qualified nonprofit charitable organizations. A cash basis taxpayer is entitled to a deduction solely in the year of payment. Accrual basis corporations may accrue contributions at year-end if payment is properly authorized before the end of the year and payment is made within two and one-half months after the end of the year. § 170.

Check-the-box Regulations. These Regulations enable taxpayers to classify the tax status of a business entity without regard to its corporate or noncorporate characteristics. An entity with more than one owner can elect to be classified either as a partnership or as a corporation. An entity with only one owner can elect to be classified as a sole proprietorship or as a corporation. These Regulations should simplify tax administration and taxpayer compliance and reduce tax litigation.

Child and dependent care expenses credit. A tax credit ranging from 20 percent to 30 percent of employment-related expenses (child and dependent care expenses) for amounts of up to $4,800 is available to individuals who are employed (or deemed to be employed) and maintain a household for a dependent child under age 13, disabled spouse, or disabled dependent. § 21.

Child tax credit. A tax credit based solely on the number of qualifying children under age 17. The maximum credit available is $400 per child in 1998 ($500 per child in 1999 and after). A qualifying child must be claimed as a dependent on a parent's tax return in order to qualify for the credit. Taxpayers who qualify for the child tax credit also qualify for a supplemental credit. The supplemental credit is treated as a component of the earned income credit and is therefore refundable. The credit is phased out for higher-income taxpayers. § 24.

Circuit Court of Appeals. See *Court of Appeals*.

Claim of right doctrine. A judicially imposed doctrine applicable to both cash and accrual basis taxpayers holding that an amount is includible in income upon actual or constructive receipt if the taxpayer has an unrestricted claim to the payment. For the tax treatment of amounts repaid when previously included in income under the claim of right doctrine, see § 1341.

Claims Court. A trial court (court of original jurisdiction) that decides litigation involving Federal tax matters. Now known as the U.S. Court of Federal Claims, appeal from this court is to the Court of Appeals for the Federal Circuit.

Closely held corporation. A corporation where stock ownership is not widely dispersed. Rather, a few shareholders are in control of corporate policy and are in a position to benefit personally from that policy.

Collectibles. A special type of capital asset, the gain from which is taxed at a maximum rate of 28 percent if the holding period is more than 12 months. Examples include art, rugs, antiques, gems, metals, stamps, some coins and bullion, and alcoholic beverages held for investment.

Common law state. See *community property*.

Community property. Louisiana, Texas, New Mexico, Arizona, California, Washington, Idaho, Nevada, and Wisconsin have community property systems. The rest of the states are common law property jurisdictions. The difference between common law and community property systems centers around the property rights possessed by married persons. In a common law system, each spouse owns whatever he or she earns. Under a community property system, one-half of the earnings of each spouse is considered owned by the other spouse. Assume, for example, Jeff and Alice are husband and wife and their only income is the $50,000 annual salary Jeff receives. If they live in New York (a common law state), the $50,000 salary belongs to Jeff. If, however, they live in Texas (a community property state), the $50,000 salary is owned one-half each by Jeff and Alice. See also *separate property*.

Compensatory damages. Damages received or paid by the taxpayer can be classified as compensatory damages or as punitive damages. Compensatory damages are those paid to compensate one for harm caused by another. Compensatory damages are excludible from the recipient's gross income. See also *punitive damages*.

Complete termination redemption. See *redemption (complete termination)*.

Completed contract method. A method of reporting gain or loss on certain long-term contracts. Under this method of accounting, gross income and expenses are recognized in the tax year in which the contract is completed. Reg. § 1.451–3. See also *long-term contract* and *percentage of completion method*.

Concur. To agree with the result reached by another, but not necessarily with the reasoning or the logic used in reaching the result. For example, Judge Ricks agrees with Judges Stone and Talent (all being members of the same court) that the income is taxable but for a different reason. Judge Ricks would issue a concurring opinion to the majority opinion issued by Judges Stone and Talent.

Condemnation. The taking of property by a public authority. The taking is by legal action, and the owner of the property is compensated by the public authority.

Conduit concept. See *aggregate concept*.

Constructive dividend. A taxable benefit derived by a shareholder from his or her corporation that is not actually called a dividend. Examples include unreasonable compensation, excessive rent payments, bargain purchases of corporate property, and shareholder use of corporate property. Constructive dividends generally are found in closely held corporations. See also *bargain sale or purchase, closely held corporation,* and *unreasonable compensation.*

Constructive liquidation scenario. The means by which recourse debt is shared among partners in basis determination.

Constructive ownership. See *attribution.*

Constructive receipt of income. If income is unqualifiedly available although not physically in the taxpayer's possession, it is subject to the income tax. An example is accrued interest on a savings account. Under the constructive receipt of income concept, the interest is taxed to a depositor in the year available, rather than the year actually withdrawn. The fact that the depositor uses the cash basis of accounting for tax purposes is irrelevant. See Reg. § 1.451–2. See also *cash receipts method.*

Consumer interest. Interest expense of the taxpayer of a personal nature (not trade or business interest, investment interest, qualified residence interest, or passive activity interest). TRA of 1986 provided that no deduction is permitted for consumer interest. However, the provision was not fully effective until 1991. § 163(h). See also *interest on student loans* and *qualified residence interest.*

Continuity of life or existence. The death or other withdrawal of an owner of an entity does not terminate the existence of the entity. This is a characteristic of a corporation since the death or withdrawal of a shareholder does not affect the corporation's existence. Reg. § 301.7701–2(b). See also *association.*

Contributions to the capital of a corporation. See *capital contribution.*

Control. Holding a specified level of stock ownership in a corporation. For § 351, the new shareholder(s) must hold at least 80 percent of the total combined voting power of all voting classes of stock. Other tax provisions require different levels of control to bring about desired effects, such as 50 or 100 percent.

Controlled group. A controlled group of corporations is required to share the lower-level corporate tax rates and various other tax benefits among the members of the group. A controlled group may be either a brother-sister or a parent-subsidiary group.

Cost depletion. Depletion that is calculated based on the adjusted basis of the asset. The adjusted basis is divided by the expected recoverable units to determine the depletion per unit. The depletion per unit is multiplied by the units sold during the tax year to calculate cost depletion. See also *percentage depletion.*

Cost recovery allowance. The portion of the cost of an asset written off under ACRS (or MACRS), which replaced the depreciation system as a method for writing off the cost of an asset for most assets placed in service after 1980 (after 1986 for MACRS). § 168. See also *alternative depreciation system.*

Cost recovery system. See *cost recovery allowance.*

Court of Appeals. Any of 13 Federal courts that consider tax matters appealed from the U.S. Tax Court, a U.S. District Court, or the U.S. Court of Federal Claims. Appeal from a U.S. Court of Appeals is to the U.S. Supreme Court by Writ of Certiorari. See also *appellate court* and *trial court.*

Court of Federal Claims. See *Claims Court.*

Court of original jurisdiction. The Federal courts are divided into courts of original jurisdiction and appellate courts. A dispute between a taxpayer and the IRS is first considered by a court of original jurisdiction (i.e., a trial court). The four Federal courts of original jurisdiction are the U.S. Tax Court, U.S. District Court, the Court of Federal Claims, and the Small Cases Division of the U.S. Tax Court. See *Court of Appeals.*

Credit for child and dependent care expenses. See *child and dependent care expenses credit.*

Cross-purchase buy-sell agreement. Under this type of arrangement, the surviving owners of the business agree to buy out the withdrawing owner. Assume, for example, Ruth and Sam are equal shareholders in Eagle Corporation. Under a cross-purchase buy-sell agreement, Ruth and Sam would contract to purchase the other's interest should that person decide to withdraw from the business. See also *buy-sell agreement* and *entity buy-sell agreement.*

Current earnings and profits. Net tax-basis earnings of the corporation aggregated during the current tax year. A corporate distribution is deemed to be first from the entity's current earnings and profits and then from accumulated earnings and profits. Shareholders recognize dividend income to the extent of the earnings and profits of the corporation. A dividend results to the extent of current earnings and profits, even if there is a larger negative balance in accumulated earnings and profits.

D

Death tax. A tax imposed on property transferred by the death of the owner. See also *estate tax* and *inheritance tax.*

Decedent. An individual who has died.

Deduction. The Federal income tax is not imposed upon gross income. Rather, it is imposed upon taxable income. Congressionally identified deductions are subtracted from gross income to arrive at the tax base, taxable income.

Deferred compensation. Compensation that will be taxed when received and not when earned. An example is contributions by an employer to a qualified pension or profit sharing plan on behalf of an employee. The contributions will not be taxed to the employee until they are distributed (e.g., upon retirement). See also *qualified pension or profit sharing plan.*

Demand loan. A loan payable upon request by the creditor, rather than on a specific date.

De minimis fringe benefits. Benefits provided to employees that are too insignificant to warrant the time and effort required to account for the benefits received by each employee and the value of those benefits. Such amounts are excludible from the employee's gross income. § 132.

Dependency exemption. See *personal and dependency exemptions*.

Depletion. The process by which the cost or other basis of a natural resource (e.g., an oil or gas interest) is recovered upon extraction and sale of the resource. The two ways to determine the depletion allowance are the cost and percentage (or statutory) methods. Under cost depletion, each unit of production sold is assigned a portion of the cost or other basis of the interest. This is determined by dividing the cost or other basis by the total units expected to be recovered. Under percentage (or statutory) depletion, the tax law provides a special percentage factor for different types of minerals and other natural resources. This percentage is multiplied by the gross income from the interest to arrive at the depletion allowance. §§ 613 and 613A.

Depreciation. The deduction for the cost or other basis of a tangible asset over the asset's estimated useful life. For intangible assets, see *amortization*. For natural resources, see *depletion*. See also *estimated useful life*.

Depreciation recapture. Upon the disposition of depreciable property used in a trade or business, gain or loss is measured by the difference between the consideration received (the amount realized) and the adjusted basis of the property. The gain recognized could be § 1231 gain and qualify for long-term capital gain treatment. The recapture provisions of the Code (e.g., §§ 291, 1245, and 1250) may operate to convert some or all of the § 1231 gain into ordinary income. The justification for depreciation recapture is that it prevents a taxpayer from converting a dollar of ordinary deduction (in the form of depreciation) into deferred tax-favored income (§ 1231 or long-term capital gain). The depreciation recapture rules do not apply when the property is disposed of at a loss or via a gift. See also *Section 1231 gains and losses*.

Depreciation rules. See *cost recovery allowance*.

Determination letter. Upon the request of a taxpayer, an IRS District Director will comment on the tax status of a completed transaction. Determination letters frequently are used to clarify employee status, determine whether a retirement or profit sharing plan qualifies under the Code, and determine the tax-exempt status of certain nonprofit organizations.

Disabled access credit. A tax credit designed to encourage small businesses to make their facilities more accessible to disabled individuals. The credit is equal to 50 percent of the eligible expenditures that exceed $250 but do not exceed $10,250. Thus, the maximum amount for the credit is $5,000. The adjusted basis for depreciation is reduced by the amount of the credit. To qualify, the facility must have been placed in service before November 6, 1990. § 44. See also *general business credit*.

Disaster area losses. Losses from casualties sustained in an area designated as a disaster area by the President of the United States. In such an event, disaster losses may be treated as having occurred in the taxable year immediately preceding the year in which the disaster actually occurred. Thus, immediate tax benefits are provided to victims of a disaster. § 165(i). See also *casualty loss*.

Disguised sale. When a partner contributes property to the entity and soon thereafter receives a distribution from the partnership, the transactions are collapsed, and the distribution is seen as a purchase of the asset by the partnership. § 707(a)(2)(B).

Disproportionate. Not pro rata or ratable. Suppose, for example, Blue Corporation has two shareholders, Chris and Diane, each of whom owns 50 percent of its stock. If Blue Corporation distributes a cash dividend of $2,000 to Chris and only $1,000 to Diane, the distribution is disproportionate. The distribution would have been proportionate if Chris and Diane had received $1,500 each.

Disproportionate redemption. See *redemption (disproportionate)*.

Dissent. To disagree with the majority. If, for example, Judge Brown disagrees with the result reached by Judges Charles and Davis (all of whom are members of the same court), Judge Brown could issue a dissenting opinion.

Distributions in kind. A transfer of property *as is*. If, for example, a corporation distributes land to its shareholders, a distribution in kind has taken place. A sale of land followed by a distribution of the cash proceeds would not be a distribution in kind of the land.

District Court. A Federal District Court is a trial court for purposes of litigating Federal tax matters. It is the only trial court in which a jury trial can be obtained. See also *trial court*.

Dividend. A nondeductible distribution to the shareholders of a corporation. A dividend constitutes gross income to the recipient if it is from the current or accumulated earnings and profits of the corporation.

Dividends received deduction. A deduction allowed a shareholder that is a corporation for dividends received from a domestic corporation. The deduction usually is 70 percent of the dividends received, but it could be 80 or 100 percent depending upon the ownership percentage held by the recipient corporation. §§ 243–246.

Dollar-value LIFO. An inventory technique that focuses on the dollars invested in the inventory rather than on the particular items on hand each period. Each inventory item is assigned to a pool. A pool is a collection of similar items and is treated as a separate inventory. At the end of the period, each pool is valued in terms of prices at the time LIFO was adopted (base period prices). This valuation takes place regardless of whether a particular item was actually on hand in the year LIFO was adopted. The value is compared with current prices to determine if there has been an increase or decrease in inventories.

Donee. The recipient of a gift.

Donor. The maker of a gift.

E

Earned income. Income from personal services. Distinguished from passive, portfolio, and other unearned income (sometimes referred to as *active* income). See §§ 469, 911, and the related Regulations.

Earned income credit. A tax credit designed to provide assistance to certain low-income individuals who generally have a qualifying child. This is a refundable credit. To receive the most beneficial treatment, the taxpayer must have qualifying children. However, it is possible to qualify for the credit without having a child. To calculate the credit for a taxpayer with one or more children for 1998, a statutory rate of 34 percent for one child (40% for two or more children) is multiplied by the earned income (subject to a statutory maximum of $6,680 with one qualifying child or $9,390 with two or more qualifying children). Once the earned income exceeds $12,260, the credit is phased out using a 15.98 percent rate for one qualifying child and a 21.06 percent rate for two qualifying children. For the qualifying taxpayer without children, the credit is calculated on a maximum earned income of $4,460 applying a 7.65 percent rate with the phase-out beginning at $5,570 applying the same rate.

Earnings and profits (E&P). Measures the economic capacity of a corporation to make a distribution to shareholders that is not a return of capital. Such a distribution results in dividend income to the shareholders to the extent of the corporation's current and accumulated earnings and profits.

Economic effect test. Requirements that must be met before a special allocation may be used by a partnership. The premise behind the test is that each partner who receives an allocation of income or loss from a partnership bears the economic benefit or burden of the allocation.

Economic income. The change in the taxpayer's net worth, as measured in terms of market values, plus the value of the assets the taxpayer consumed during the year. Because of the impracticality of this income model, it is not used for tax purposes.

Economic performance test. One of the requirements that must be satisfied in order for an accrual basis taxpayer to deduct an expense. The accrual basis taxpayer first must satisfy the all events test. That test is not deemed satisfied until economic performance occurs. This occurs, when property or services are provided to the taxpayer, or in the case in which the taxpayer is required to provide property or services, whenever the property or services are actually provided by the taxpayer.

Education expenses. Employees may deduct education expenses that are incurred either (1) to maintain or improve existing job-related skills or (2) to meet the express requirements of the employer or the requirements imposed by law to retain employment status. The expenses are not deductible if the education is required to meet the minimum educational standards for the taxpayer's job or if the education qualifies the individual for a new trade or business. Reg. § 1.162–5. See also *HOPE scholarship credit* and *lifetime learning credit*.

Educational savings bonds. U.S. Series EE bonds whose proceeds are used for qualified higher educational expenses for the taxpayer, the taxpayer's spouse, or a dependent. The interest may be excluded from gross income, provided the taxpayer's adjusted gross income does not exceed certain amounts. § 135.

Employee stock ownership plan (ESOP). A type of qualified profit sharing plan that invests in securities of the employer. In a noncontributory ESOP, the employer usually contributes its shares to a trust and receives a deduction for the fair market value of the stock. Generally, the employee does not recognize income until the stock is sold after its distribution to him or her upon retirement or other separation from service. See also *qualified pension or profit sharing plan*.

Employment taxes. Employment taxes are those taxes that an employer must pay on account of its employees. Employment taxes include FICA (Federal Insurance Contributions Act) and FUTA (Federal Unemployment Tax Act) taxes. Employment taxes are paid to the IRS in addition to income tax withholdings at specified intervals. Such taxes can be levied on the employees, the employer, or both. See also *FICA tax* and *FUTA tax*.

En banc. The case was considered by the whole court. Typically, for example, only one of the judges of the U.S. Tax Court will hear and decide on a tax controversy. However, when the issues involved are unusually novel or of wide impact, the case will be heard and decided by the full Court sitting *en banc*.

Energy tax credit. A 10 percent tax credit is available to businesses that invest in certain energy property. The purpose of the credit is to create incentives for conservation and to develop alternative energy sources. The credit is available on the acquisition of solar and geothermal property. §§ 46 and 48.

Entertainment expenses. These expenses are deductible only if they are directly related to or associated with a trade or business. Various restrictions and documentation requirements have been imposed upon the deductibility of entertainment expenses to prevent abuses by taxpayers. See, for example, the provision contained in § 274(n) that disallows 50 percent (20 percent prior to 1994) of entertainment expenses. § 274.

Entity. An organization or being that possesses separate existence for tax purposes. Examples are corporations, partnerships, estates, and trusts.

Entity buy-sell agreement. The entity is to purchase a withdrawing owner's interest. When the entity is a corporation, the agreement generally involves a stock redemption on the part of the withdrawing shareholder. See also *buy-sell agreement* and *cross-purchase buy-sell agreement*.

Entity concept. The theory of partnership taxation under which a partnership is treated as a separate and distinct entity from the partners, and has its own tax attributes.

Equilibrium tax planning. Tax planning that takes into consideration the tax consequences to all parties in a transaction.

Estate tax. A tax imposed on the right to transfer property by death. Thus, an estate tax is levied on the decedent's estate and not on the heir receiving the property. See also *death tax* and *inheritance tax*.

Estimated tax. The amount of tax (including alternative minimum tax and self-employment tax, if applicable) an individual or corporation expects to owe for the year after subtracting tax credits and income tax withheld. The estimated tax must be paid in installments at designated intervals (usually quarterly).

Estimated useful life. The period over which an asset will be used by the taxpayer. Some assets do not have an estimated useful life. The estimated useful life of an asset is essential to measuring the annual tax deduction for depreciation and amortization.

Estoppel. The process of being stopped from proving something (even if true) in court due to a prior inconsistent action. It is usually invoked as a matter of fairness to prevent one party (either the taxpayer or the IRS) from taking advantage of a prior error.

Excise tax. A tax on the manufacture, sale, or use of goods; on the carrying on of an occupation or activity; or on the transfer of property. Thus, the Federal estate and gift taxes are, theoretically, excise taxes.

Exemption. An amount by which the tax base is reduced for all qualifying taxpayers. Individuals can receive personal and dependency exemptions, and taxpayers apply an exemption in computing their alternative minimum taxable income. Often, the exemption amount is phased out as the tax base becomes sizable.

Extraordinary personal services. Services provided where the customers' use of the property is incidental to their receipt of the services. For example, a patient's use of a hospital bed is incidental to his or her receipt of medical services. This is one of the six exceptions for determining whether an activity is a passive rental activity.

F

Fair market value. The amount at which property would change hands between a willing buyer and a willing seller, neither being under any compulsion to buy or to sell, and both having reasonable knowledge of the relevant facts. Reg. § 20.2031–1(b).

Federal District Court. See *District Court*.

Federal Register. The first place that the rules and regulations of U.S. administrative agencies (e.g., the U.S. Treasury Department) are published.

FICA tax. An abbreviation that stands for Federal Insurance Contributions Act, commonly referred to as the Social Security tax. The FICA tax is comprised of the Social Security tax (old age, survivors, and disability insurance) and the Medicare tax (hospital insurance) and is imposed on both employers and employees. The employer is responsible for withholding from the employee's wages the Social Security tax at a rate of 6.2 percent on a maximum wage base of $68,400 (for 1998) and the Medicare tax at a rate of 1.45 percent (no maximum wage base). The employer is required to match the employee's contribution. See also *employment taxes*.

Final Regulation. See *Regulations*.

First-in, first-out (FIFO). An accounting method for determining the cost of inventories. Under this method, the inventory on hand is deemed to be the sum of the cost of the most recently acquired units. See also *last-in, first-out (LIFO)*.

Fiscal year. A fiscal year is a 12-month period ending on the last day of a month other than December. In certain circumstances, a taxpayer is permitted to elect a fiscal year instead of being required to use a calendar year. See also *accounting period* and *taxable year*.

Flat tax. In its pure form, a flat tax would eliminate all exclusions, deductions, and credits and impose a one-rate tax on gross income.

Foreign tax credit or deduction. A U.S. citizen or resident who incurs or pays income taxes to a foreign country on income subject to U.S. tax may be able to claim some of these taxes as a deduction or a credit against the U.S. income tax. §§ 27, 164, and 901–905.

Form 706. The U.S. Estate Tax Return. In certain cases, this form must be filed for a decedent who was a resident or citizen of the United States.

Form 709. The U.S. Gift Tax Return.

Form 709–A. The U.S. Short Form Gift Tax Return.

Form 1065. The U.S. Partnership Return of Income. See Appendix B for a specimen form.

Form 1120. The U.S. Corporation Income Tax Return. See Appendix B for a specimen form.

Form 1120–A. The U.S. Short-Form Corporation Income Tax Return. See Appendix B for a specimen form.

Form 1120S. The U.S. Small Business Corporation Income Tax Return, required to be filed by S corporations. See Appendix B for a specimen form.

Franchise. An agreement that gives the transferee the right to distribute, sell, or provide goods, services, or facilities within a specified area. The cost of obtaining a franchise may be amortized over a statutory period of 15 years. In general, the franchisor's gain on the sale of franchise rights is an ordinary gain because the franchisor retains a significant power, right, or continuing interest in the subject of the franchise. §§ 197 and 1253.

Franchise tax. A tax levied on the right to do business in a state as a corporation. Although income considerations may come into play, the tax usually is based on the capitalization of the corporation.

Fraud. Tax fraud falls into two categories: civil and criminal. Under civil fraud, the IRS may impose as a penalty an amount equal to as much as 75 percent of the underpayment [§ 6651(f)]. Fines and/or imprisonment are prescribed for conviction of various types of criminal tax fraud (§§ 7201–7207). Both civil and criminal fraud require a specific intent on the part of the taxpayer to evade the tax; mere negligence is not enough. Criminal fraud requires the additional element of willfulness (i.e., done deliberately and with evil purpose). In practice, it becomes difficult to distinguish between the degree of intent necessary to support criminal, rather than civil, fraud. In either situation, the IRS has the burden of proving fraud. See also *burden of proof*.

Free transferability of interests. The capability of the owner of an entity to transfer his or her ownership interest to another without the consent of the other owners. It is a characteristic of a corporation since a shareholder usually can freely transfer the stock to others without the approval of the existing shareholders.

Fringe benefits. Compensation or other benefits received by an employee that are not in the form of cash. Some fringe benefits (e.g., accident and health plans, group term life insurance) may be excluded from the employee's gross income and thus are not subject to the Federal income tax.

Fruit and tree metaphor. The courts have held that an taxpayer that earns income from property or services cannot assign that income to another. For example, a father cannot assign his earnings from commissions to his child and escape tax on those amounts.

F.3d. An abbreviation for the third series of the *Federal Reporter*, the official series in which decisions of the U.S. Court of Federal Claims and the U.S. Court of Appeals are published. The second series is denoted F.2d.

F.Supp. The abbreviation for the *Federal Supplement*, the official series in which the reported decisions of the Federal District Courts are published.

FUTA tax. An employment tax levied on employers. Jointly administered by the Federal and state governments, the tax provides funding for unemployment benefits. FUTA applies at a rate of 6.2 percent in 1998 on the first $7,000 of covered wages paid during the year for each employee. The Federal government allows a credit for FUTA paid (or allowed under a merit rating system) to the state. The credit cannot exceed 5.4 percent of the covered wages. See also *employment taxes*.

G

General business credit. The summation of various nonrefundable business credits, including the welfare-to-work credit, work opportunity credit, tax credit for rehabilitation expenditures, research activities credit, low-income housing credit, and disabled access credit. The amount of general business credit that can be used to reduce the tax liability is limited to the taxpayer's net income tax reduced by the greater of (1) the tentative minimum tax or (2) 25 percent of the net regular tax liability that exceeds $25,000. Unused general business credits can be carried back 1 year and forward 20 years (back 3 years and forward 15 years for tax years beginning before January 1, 1998). §§ 38 and 39.

General partner. A partner who is fully liable in an individual capacity for the debts of the partnership to third parties. A general partner's liability is not limited to the investment in the partnership. See also *limited partner*.

General partnership. A partnership that is owned by one or more *general partners*. Creditors of a general partnership can collect amounts owned them from both the partnership assets and the assets of the partners individually.

Gift. A transfer of property for less than adequate consideration. Gifts usually occur in a personal setting (such as between members of the same family). They are excluded from the income tax base but may be subject to a transfer tax.

Gift splitting. A special election for Federal gift tax purposes under which husband and wife can treat a gift by one of them to a third party as being made one-half by each. If, for example, George (the husband) makes a gift of $20,000 to Shirley, Barbara (the wife) may elect to treat $10,000 of the gift as coming from her. The major advantage of the election is that it enables the parties to take advantage of the nonowner spouse's (Barbara in this case) annual exclusion and unified credit. § 2513. See also *annual exclusion*.

Gift tax. A tax imposed on the transfer of property by gift. The tax is imposed upon the donor of a gift and is based on the fair market value of the property on the date of the gift.

Goodwill. The reputation and built-up business of a company. For accounting purposes, goodwill has no basis unless it is purchased. In the purchase of a business, goodwill generally is the difference between the purchase price and the fair market value of the assets acquired. The intangible asset goodwill can be amortized for tax purposes over a 15-year period. Reg. § 1.167(a)–3. See also *amortization*.

Gross estate. The property owned or previously transferred by a *decedent* that is subject to the Federal estate tax. Distinguished from the *probate estate*, which is property actually subject to administration by the *administrator* or *executor* of an estate. §§ 2031–2046. See also *adjusted gross estate*.

Gross income. Income subject to the Federal income tax. Gross income does not include all economic income. That is, certain exclusions are allowed (e.g., interest on municipal bonds). For a manufacturing or merchandising business, gross income usually means gross profit (gross sales or gross receipts less cost of goods sold). § 61 and Reg. § 1.61–3(a). See also *adjusted gross income* and *taxable income*.

Group term life insurance. Life insurance coverage provided by an employer for a group of employees. Such insurance is renewable on a year-to-year basis, and typically no cash surrender value is built up. The premiums paid by the employer on the insurance are not taxed to the employees on coverage of up to $50,000 per person. § 79 and Reg. § 1.79–1(b).

Guaranteed payment. Payments made by a partnership to a partner for services rendered or for the use of capital to the extent that the payments are determined without regard to the income of the partnership. The payments are treated as though they were made to a nonpartner and thus are usually deductible by the entity.

H

Half-year convention. The half-year convention is a cost recovery convention that assumes all property is placed in service at mid-year and thus provides for a half-year's cost recovery for that year.

Head of household. An unmarried individual who maintains a household for another and satisfies certain conditions set forth in § 2(b). This status enables the taxpayer to use a set of income tax rates that are lower than those applicable to other unmarried individuals but higher than those applicable to surviving spouses and married persons filing a joint return.

Heir. A person who inherits property from a decedent.

Highly compensated employee. The employee group is generally divided into two categories for fringe benefit (including pension and profit sharing plans) purposes. These are (1) highly compensated employees and (2) non-highly compensated employees. For most fringe benefits, if the fringe benefit plan discriminates in favor of highly compensated employees, it will not be a qualified plan with respect, at a minimum, to the highly compensated employees.

Hobby. An activity not engaged in for profit. The Code restricts the amount of losses that an individual can deduct for hobby activities so that these transactions cannot be used to offset income from other sources. § 183.

Holding period. The period of time during which property has been held for income tax purposes. The holding period is significant in determining whether gain or loss from the sale or exchange of a capital asset is long term, mid-term, or short term. § 1223.

Home equity loans. Loans that utilize the personal residence of the taxpayer as security. The interest on such loans is deductible as *qualified residence interest*. However, interest is deductible only on the portion of the loan that does not exceed the lesser of: (1) the fair market value of the residence, reduced by the *acquisition indebtedness* or (2) $100,000 ($50,000 for married persons filing separate returns). A major benefit of a home equity loan is that there are no tracing rules regarding the use of the loan proceeds. § 163(h)(3).

HOPE scholarship credit. A tax credit for qualifying tuition expenses paid for the first two years of postsecondary education. Room, board, and book costs are ineligible for the credit. The maximum credit available is $1,500 per year per student, computed as 100 percent of the first $1,000 of tuition expenses, plus 50 percent of the second $1,000 of tuition expenses. Eligible students include the taxpayer, taxpayer's spouse, and taxpayer's dependents. To qualify for the credit, a student must take at least one-half the full-time course load for at least one academic term at a qualifying educational institution. The credit is phased out for higher-income taxpayers. § 25A.

Hot assets. Unrealized receivables and substantially appreciated inventory under § 751. When hot assets are present, the sale of a partnership interest or the disproportionate distribution of the assets can cause ordinary income to be recognized.

H.R. 10 plans. See *Keogh plans*.

Hybrid method. A combination of the accrual and cash methods of accounting. That is, the taxpayer may account for some items of income on the accrual method (e.g., sales and cost of goods sold) and other items (e.g., interest income) on the cash method.

I

Implicit tax. Implicit taxes arise because of differences in tax treatment among assets. Tax-favored investments in the market generally yield a lower return relative to other investments. This reduced return is the implicit tax paid by investors.

Imputed interest. For certain long-term sales of property, the IRS can convert some of the gain from the sale into interest income if the contract does not provide for a minimum rate of interest to be paid by the purchaser. The application of this procedure has the effect of forcing the seller to recognize less long-term capital gain and more ordinary income (interest income). § 483 and the related Regulations.

Income. For tax purposes, an increase in wealth that has been realized.

Income shifting. Occurs when an individual transfers some of his or her gross income to a taxpayer who is subject to a lower tax rate, thereby reducing the total income tax liability of the group. Income shifting produces a successful assignment of income. It can be accomplished by transferring income-producing property to the lower-bracket taxpayer or to an effective trust for his or her benefit, or by transferring ownership interests in a family partnership or in a closely held corporation.

Independent contractor. A self-employed person as distinguished from one who is employed as an employee.

Indexation. Various components of the tax formula are adjusted periodically for the effects of inflation, so that the effects of the formula are not eroded by price level changes. Tax rate schedules, personal and dependency exemption amounts, and the standard deduction, among other items, are indexed in this manner.

Individual retirement account (IRA). A type of retirement plan to which an individual with earned income can contribute a maximum of $2,000 ($2,000 each in the case of a married couple with a spousal IRA) per tax year. IRAs can be classified as traditional IRAs or Roth IRAs. With a traditional IRA, an individual can contribute and deduct a maximum of $2,000 per tax year. The deduction is a deduction *for* AGI. However, if the individual is an active participant in another qualified retirement plan, the deduction is phased out proportionally between certain AGI ranges (note that the phase-out limits the amount of the deduction and not the amount of the contribution). With a Roth IRA, an individual can contribute a maximum of $2,000 per tax year. No deduction is permitted. However, if a five-year holding period requirement is satisfied and if the distribution is a qualified distribution, the taxpayer can make tax-free withdrawals from a Roth IRA. The maximum annual contribution is phased out proportionally between certain AGI ranges. §§ 219 and 408A.

Inheritance tax. A tax imposed on the right to receive property from a *decedent*. Thus, theoretically, an inheritance tax is imposed on the heir. The Federal estate tax is imposed on the estate. See also *death tax* and *estate tax*.

In kind. See *distributions in kind*.

Inside basis. A partnership's basis in the assets it owns.

Installment method. A method of accounting enabling certain taxpayers to spread the recognition of gain on the sale of property over the collection period. Under this procedure, the seller arrives at the gain to be recognized by computing the gross profit percentage from the sale (the gain divided by the contract price) and applying it to each payment received. § 453.

Insured. A person whose life is the subject of an insurance policy. Upon the death of the insured, the life insurance policy matures, and the proceeds become payable to the designated beneficiary. See also *life insurance*.

Intangible asset. Property that is a "right" rather than a physical object. Examples are patents, stocks and bonds, goodwill, trademarks, franchises, and copyrights. See also *amortization* and *tangible property*.

Intangible drilling and development costs (IDC). Taxpayers may elect to expense or capitalize (subject to amortization) intangible drilling and development costs. However, ordinary income recapture provisions apply to oil and gas properties on a sale or other disposition if the expense method is elected. §§ 263(c) and 1254(a).

Interest-free loans. Bona fide loans that carry no interest (or a below-market rate). If made in a nonbusiness setting, the imputed interest element is treated as a gift from the lender to the borrower. If made by a corporation to a shareholder, a constructive dividend could result. In either event, the lender may recognize interest income, and the borrower may be able to deduct interest expense. § 7872.

Interest on student loans. The Taxpayer Relief Act of 1997 (TRA of 1997) provides for a limited ability to deduct interest on student loans to pay qualified higher education expenses (i.e., tuition, fees, books, supplies, room and board). For 1998, the ceiling on the deduction is $1,000. The deduction is allowed only with respect to interest paid on the loan during the first 60 months in which interest payments are required. The deduction is a deduction *for* AGI. § 221. See also *consumer interest*.

Internal Revenue Code. The collected statutes that govern the taxation of income, property transfers, and other transactions in the United States and the enforcement of those provisions. Enacted by Congress, the Code is amended frequently, but it has not been reorganized since 1954. However, because of the extensive revisions to the statutes that occurred with the Tax Reform Act of 1986, Title 26 of the U.S. Code is now known as the Internal Revenue Code of 1986.

Internal Revenue Service. The federal agency, a division of the Department of the Treasury, charged with implementing the U.S. revenue enforcement and collection provisions.

Interpretive Regulation. A Regulation issued by the Treasury Department that purports to explain the meaning of a particular Code Section. An interpretive Regulation is given less deference than a legislative Regulation. § 7805. See also *Legislative Regulation* and *Procedural Regulation*.

Investment income. Consisting of virtually the same elements as portfolio income, a measure by which to justify a deduction for interest on investment indebtedness. See also *investment indebtedness* and *portfolio income*.

Investment indebtedness. Debt incurred to carry or incur investments by the taxpayer in assets that will produce portfolio income. Limitations are placed upon interest deductions that are incurred in connection with the debt (generally to the corresponding amount of investment income).

Investment interest. Payment for the use of funds used to acquire assets that produce investment income. The deduction for investment interest is limited to *net investment income* for the tax year. See also *investment income*.

Investment tax credit (ITC). A tax credit that usually was equal to 10 percent (unless a reduced credit was elected) of the qualified investment in tangible personalty used in a trade or business. If the tangible personalty had a recovery period of five years or more, the full cost of the property qualified for the credit. Only 60 percent qualified for property with a recovery period of three years. However, the regular investment tax credit was repealed by TRA of 1986 for property placed in service after December 31, 1985. § 46. See also *general business credit*.

Involuntary conversion. The loss or destruction of property through theft, casualty, or condemnation. Any gain realized on an involuntary conversion can, at the taxpayer's election, be deferred for Federal income tax purposes if the owner reinvests the proceeds within a prescribed period of time in property that is similar or related in service or use. § 1033. See also *nontaxable exchange*.

IRA. See *individual retirement account*.

Itemized deductions. Personal and employee expenditures allowed by the Code as deductions from adjusted gross income. Examples include certain medical expenses, interest on home mortgages, state income taxes, and charitable contributions. Itemized deductions are reported on Schedule A of Form 1040. Certain miscellaneous itemized deductions are reduced by 2 percent of the taxpayer's adjusted gross income. In addition, a taxpayer whose adjusted gross income exceeds a certain level (indexed annually) must reduce the itemized deductions by 3 percent of the excess of adjusted gross income over that level. Medical, casualty and theft, and investment interest deductions are not subject to the 3 percent reduction. The 3 percent reduction may not reduce itemized deductions that are subject to the reduction to below 20 percent of their initial amount.

J

Joint tenants. Two or more persons having undivided ownership of property with the right of survivorship. Right of survivorship gives the surviving owner full ownership of the property. Suppose Bob and Tami are joint tenants of a tract of land. Upon Bob's death, Tami becomes the sole owner of the property. For the estate tax consequences upon the death of a joint tenant, see § 2040. See also *tenancy by the entirety* and *tenancy in common*.

Joint venture. A one-time grouping of two or more persons in a business undertaking. Unlike a partnership, a joint venture does not entail a continuing relationship among the parties. A joint venture is treated like a partnership for Federal income tax purposes. § 7701(a)(2).

K

Keogh plans. Retirement plans available to self-employed taxpayers. They are also referred to as H.R. 10 plans. Under such plans, a taxpayer may deduct each year up to either 20 percent of net earnings from self-employment or $30,000, whichever is less.

Kiddie tax. See *tax on unearned income of a child under age 14*.

L

Last-in, first-out (LIFO). An accounting method for valuing inventories for tax purposes. Under this method, it is assumed that the inventory on hand is valued at the cost of the earliest acquired units. § 472. See also *first-in, first-out (FIFO)*.

Leaseback. The transferor of property later leases it back. In a sale-leaseback situation, for example, Richard sells property to Sally and subsequently leases the property from Sally. Thus, Richard becomes the lessee and Sally the lessor.

Least aggregate deferral method. An algorithm set forth in the Regulations to determine the tax year for a partnership or S corporation with owners whose tax years differ. The entity selects the tax year that produces the least aggregate deferral of income for the owners.

Legislative Regulation. Some Code Sections give the Secretary of the Treasury or his delegate the authority to prescribe Regulations to carry out the details of administration or to otherwise complete the operating rules. Regulations issued pursuant to this type of authority truly possess the force and effect of law. In effect, Congress is almost delegating its legislative powers to the Treasury Department. See also *interpretive regulation* and *procedural regulation*.

Lessee. One who rents property from another. In the case of real estate, the lessee is also known as the tenant.

Lessor. One who rents property to another. In the case of real estate, the lessor is also known as the landlord.

Letter ruling. The written response of the IRS to a taxpayer's request for interpretation of the revenue laws, with respect to a proposed transaction (e.g., concerning the tax-free status of a reorganization). Not to be relied on as precedent by other than the party who requested the ruling.

Liabilities in excess of basis. On the contribution of capital to a corporation, an investor recognizes gain on the exchange to the extent that contributed assets carry liabilities with a face amount in excess of the tax basis of the contributed assets. This rule keeps the investor from holding the investment asset received with a negative basis. § 357(c).

Life insurance. A contract between the holder of a policy and an insurance company (the carrier) under which the company agrees, in return for premium payments, to pay a specified sum (the face value or maturity value of the policy) to the designated beneficiary upon the death of the insured. See also *insured*.

Life insurance proceeds. Generally, life insurance proceeds paid to a beneficiary upon the death of the insured are exempt from Federal income tax. An exception is provided when a life insurance contract has been transferred for valuable consideration to another individual who assumes ownership rights. In that case, the proceeds are income to the assignee to the extent that the proceeds exceed the amount paid for the policy plus any subsequent premiums paid. § 101.

Lifetime learning credit. A tax credit for qualifying tuition expenses for taxpayers pursuing education beyond the first two years of postsecondary education. Individuals who are completing their last two years of undergraduate studies, pursuing graduate or professional degrees, or otherwise seeking new job skills or maintaining existing job skills are all eligible for the credit. Eligible individuals include the taxpayer, taxpayer's spouse, and taxpayer's dependents. The maximum credit is 20 percent of the first $5,000 ($10,000 beginning in 2003) of qualifying tuition expenses and is computed per taxpayer. The credit is phased out for higher-income taxpayers. § 25A.

Like-kind exchange. An exchange of property held for productive use in a trade or business or for investment (except inventory and stocks and bonds) for other investment or trade or business property. Unless non-like-kind property (boot) is received, the exchange is nontaxable. § 1031. See also *boot* and *nontaxable exchange.*

Limited liability. The liability of an entity and its owners to third parties is limited to the investment in the entity. This is a characteristic of a corporation, as shareholders generally are not responsible for the debts of the corporation and, at most, may lose the amount paid in for the stock issued.

Limited liability company (LLC). A form of entity allowed by all of the states. The entity is taxed as a partnership in which all members or owners of the LLC are treated much like limited partners. There are no restrictions on ownership, all members may participate in management, and none has personal liability for the entity's debts.

Limited liability partnership (LLP). A form of entity allowed by many of the states, where a general partnership registers with the state as an LLP. Owners are general partners, but a partner is not liable for any malpractice committed by other partners. The personal assets of the partners are at risk for the entity's contractual liabilities, such as accounts payable. The personal assets of a specific partner are at risk for his or her own professional malpractice and tort liability, and for malpractice and torts committed by those whom he or she supervises.

Limited partner. A partner whose liability to third-party creditors of the partnership is limited to the amount he or she has invested in the partnership. See also *general partner* and *limited partnership.*

Limited partnership. A partnership in which some of the partners are limited partners. At least one of the partners in a limited partnership must be a general partner. See also *general partner* and *limited partner.*

Listed property. The term listed property includes (1) any passenger automobile, (2) any other property used as a means of transportation, (3) any property of a type generally used for purposes of entertainment, recreation, or amusement, (4) any computer or peripheral equipment (with an exception for exclusive business use), (5) any cellular telephone (or other similar telecommunications equipment), and (6) any other property of a type specified in the Regulations. If listed property is predominantly used for business, the taxpayer is allowed to use the statutory percentage method of cost recovery. Otherwise, the straight-line cost recovery method must be used. § 280F.

Lobbying expenditure. An expenditure made for the purpose of influencing legislation. Such payments can result in the loss of the exempt status and the imposition of Federal income tax on an exempt organization.

Long-term capital gain or loss. Results from the sale or other taxable exchange of a capital asset that had been held by the seller for more than one year or from other transactions involving statutorily designated assets, including § 1231 property and patents.

Long-term contract. A building, installation, construction, or manufacturing contract that is entered into but not completed within the same tax year. A manufacturing contract is a long-term contract only if the contract is to manufacture (1) a unique item not normally carried in finished goods inventory or (2) items that normally require more than 12 calendar months to complete. The two available methods to account for long-term contracts are the percentage of completion method and the completed contract method. The completed contract method can be used only in limited circumstances. § 460. See also *completed contract method* and *percentage of completion method.*

Long-term nonpersonal-use capital assets. Includes investment property with a long-term holding period. Such property disposed of by casualty or theft may receive § 1231 treatment. See also *Section 1231 gains and losses.*

Low-income housing credit. Beneficial treatment to owners of low-income housing is provided in the form of a tax credit. The calculated credit is claimed in the year the building is placed in service and in the following nine years. § 42. See also *general business credit.*

Lower of cost or market (replacement cost). An elective inventory method, whereby the taxpayer may value inventories at the lower of the taxpayer's actual cost or the current replacement cost of the goods. This method cannot be used in conjunction with the LIFO inventory method.

M

MACRS. See *accelerated cost recovery system (ACRS).*

Majority interest partner. A partner who has more than a 50 percent interest in partnership profits and capital. The term is of significance in determining the appropriate taxable year of a partnership. § 706(b). See also *accounting period* and *principal partner.*

Malpractice. Professional misconduct; an unreasonable lack of skill.

Marriage penalty. The additional tax liability that results for a married couple compared with what their tax liability would be if they were not married and filed separate returns.

Material participation. If a taxpayer materially participates in a nonrental trade or business activity, any loss from that activity is treated as an active loss that can be offset against active income. Material participation is achieved by meeting any one of seven tests provided in the Regulations.

Meaningful reduction test. A decrease in the shareholder's voting control. Used to determine whether a redemption qualifies for sale or exchange treatment.

Medical expenses. Medical expenses of an individual, spouse, and dependents are allowed as an itemized deduction to the extent that such amounts (less insurance reimbursements) exceed 7.5 percent of adjusted gross income. § 213.

Mid-month convention. The mid-month convention is a cost recovery convention that assumes property is placed in service in the middle of the month that it is actually placed in service.

Mid-quarter convention. The mid-quarter convention is a cost recovery convention that assumes property placed in service during the year is placed in service at the middle of the quarter in which it is actually placed in service. The mid-quarter convention applies if more than 40 percent of the value of property (other than eligible real estate) is placed in service during the last quarter of the year.

Mid-term capital gain or loss. Gain or loss from the disposition of a capital asset if the holding period is longer than 12 months but not longer than 18 months.

Minimum tax credit (AMT). When a corporation pays an alternative minimum tax, a minimum tax credit is created on a dollar-for-dollar basis, to be applied against regular tax liabilities incurred in future years. The credit is carried forward indefinitely, but it is not carried back. The effect of the credit for corporate taxpayers alternating between the AMT and regular tax models is to make the AMT liabilities a prepayment of regular taxes. Noncorporate AMT taxpayers are allowed the credit only with respect to the elements of the AMT that reflect timing differences between the two tax models.

Miscellaneous itemized deductions. A special category of itemized deductions that includes such expenses as professional dues, tax return preparation fees, job-hunting costs, unreimbursed employee business expenses, and certain investment expenses. Such expenses are deductible only to the extent they exceed 2 percent of adjusted gross income. § 67. See also *itemized deductions*.

Mitigation of the annual accounting period concept. Various tax provisions that provide relief from the effect of the finality of the annual accounting period concept. For example, the net operating loss carryover provisions allow the taxpayer to apply the negative taxable income of one year against a corresponding positive amount in another tax accounting period. See also *annual accounting period concept*.

Modified accelerated cost recovery system (MACRS). See *accelerated cost recovery system (ACRS)*.

Moving expenses. A deduction *for* AGI is permitted to employees and self-employed individuals provided certain tests are met. The taxpayer's new job must be at least 50 miles farther from the old residence than the old residence was form the former place of work. In addition, an employee must be employed on a full-time basis at the new location for 39 weeks in the 12-month period following the move. Deductible moving expenses include the cost of moving household and personal effects, transportation, and lodging expenses during the move. The cost of meals during the move is not deductible. Qualified moving expenses that are paid (or reimbursed) by the employer can be excluded from the employee's gross income. In this case, the related deduction by the employee is not permitted. §§ 62(a)(15), 132(a)(6), and 217.

Multiple support agreement. To qualify for a dependency exemption, the support test must be satisfied. This requires that over 50 percent of the support of the potential dependent be provided by the taxpayer. Where no one person provides more than 50 percent of the support, a multiple support agreement enables a taxpayer to still qualify for the dependency exemption. Any person who contributed more than 10 percent of the support is entitled to claim the exemption if each person in the group who contributed more than 10 percent files a written consent (Form 2120). Each person who is a party to the multiple support agreement must meet all the other requirements for claiming the dependency exemption. § 152(c). See also *personal and dependency exemptions*.

N

Necessary. Appropriate and helpful in furthering the taxpayer's business or income-producing activity. §§ 162(a) and 212. See also *ordinary*.

Net capital gain (NCG). The excess of the net long-term capital gain for the tax year over the net short-term capital loss. The net capital gain of an individual taxpayer is taxed at a maximum marginal rate of 28 percent. § 1221(11).

Net capital loss. The excess of the losses from sales or exchanges of capital assets over the gains from sales or exchanges of such assets. Up to $3,000 per year of the net capital loss may be deductible by noncorporate taxpayers against ordinary income. The excess net capital loss carries over to future tax years. For corporate taxpayers, the net capital loss cannot be offset against ordinary income, but it can be carried back 3 years and forward 5 years to offset net capital gains. §§ 1211, 1212 and 1221(10).

Net investment income. The excess of *investment income* over investment expenses. Investment expenses are those deductible expenses directly connected with the production of investment income. Investment expenses do not include investment interest. The deduction for *investment interest* for the tax year is limited to net investment income. § 163(d).

Net operating loss. To mitigate the effect of the annual accounting period concept, § 172 allows taxpayers to use an excess loss of one year as a deduction for certain past or future years. In this regard, a carryback period of 2 years and a carryforward period of 20 years currently are allowed. For NOLS in tax years beginning before August 6, 1997, the carryback period is 3 years and the carryforward period is 15 years. See also *mitigation of the annual accounting period concept*.

No-additional-cost services. Services that the employer may provide the employee at no additional cost to the employer. Generally, the benefit is the ability to utilize employer's excess capacity (vacant seats on an airliner). Such amounts are excludible from the recipient's gross income.

Nonaccountable plan. An expense reimbursement plan that does not have an accountability feature. The result is that employee expenses must be claimed as deductions *from AGI*. An exception is moving expenses, which are deductions *for AGI*. See also *accountable plan*.

Nonacquiescence. Disagreement by the IRS on the result reached in certain judicial decisions. *Nonacq.* or *NA*. See also *acquiescence*.

Nonbusiness bad debt. A bad debt loss that is not incurred in connection with a creditor's trade or business. The loss is classified as a short-term capital loss and is allowed only in the year the debt becomes entirely worthless. In addition to family loans, many investor losses are nonbusiness bad debts. § 166(d). See also *business bad debt*.

Nonrecourse debt. Debt secured by the property that it is used to purchase. The purchaser of the property is not personally liable for the debt upon default. Rather, the creditor's recourse is to repossess the related property. Nonrecourse debt generally does not increase the purchaser's at-risk amount.

Nonresident alien. An individual who is neither a citizen nor a resident of the United States. Citizenship is determined under the immigration and naturalization laws of the United States. Residency is determined under § 7701(b) of the Internal Revenue Code.

Nonseparately stated income. The net income of an S corporation that is combined and allocated to the shareholders. Other items, such as capital gains and charitable contributions, that could be treated differently on the individual tax returns of the shareholders are not included in this amount but are allocated to the shareholders separately.

Nontaxable exchange. A transaction in which realized gains or losses are not recognized. The recognition of gain or loss is postponed (deferred) until the property received in the nontaxable exchange is subsequently disposed of in a taxable transaction. Examples are § 1031 like-kind exchanges and § 1033 involuntary conversions. See also *involuntary conversion* and *like-kind exchange*.

Not essentially equivalent redemption. See *redemption (not equivalent to a dividend)*.

O

Occupational tax. A tax imposed on various trades or businesses. A license fee that enables a taxpayer to engage in a particular occupation.

Office in the home expenses. Employment and business-related expenses attributable to the use of a residence (e.g., den or office) are allowed only if the portion of the residence is exclusively used on a regular basis as a principal place of business of the taxpayer or as a place of business that is used by patients, clients, or customers. If the expenses are incurred by an employee, the use must be for the convenience of the employer as opposed to being merely appropriate and helpful. § 280A.

On all fours. A judicial decision exactly in point with another as to result, facts, or both.

Open transaction doctrine. A judicially imposed doctrine that allows the taxpayer to defer all gain until collecting an amount equal to the adjusted basis of assets transferred pursuant to an exchange transaction. This doctrine has been applied where the property received in an exchange has no ascertainable fair market value due to the existence of contingencies. See also *recovery of capital doctrine*.

Options. The sale or exchange of an option to buy or sell property results in capital gain or loss if the property is a capital asset. Generally, the closing of an option transaction results in short-term capital gain or loss to the writer of the call and the purchaser of the call option. § 1234.

Ordinary. Common and accepted in the general industry or type of activity in which the taxpayer is engaged. It comprises one of the tests for the deductibility of expenses incurred or paid in connection with a trade or business; for the production or collection of income; for the management, conservation, or maintenance of property held for the production of income; or in connection with the determination, collection, or refund of any tax. §§ 162(a) and 212. See also *necessary*.

Ordinary and necessary. See *necessary* and *ordinary*.

Ordinary income property. Property contributed to a charitable organization that, if sold rather than contributed, would have resulted in other than long-term capital gain to the donor (i.e., ordinary income property and short-term capital gain property). Examples are inventory and capital assets held for less than the long-term holding period.

Organizational expenditures. Items incurred early in the life of a corporate entity, qualifying for a 60-month amortization under Federal tax law. Amortizable expenditures exclude those incurred to obtain capital (underwriting fees) or assets (subject to cost recovery). Typically, amortizable expenditures include legal and accounting fees, and state incorporation payments. Such items must be incurred by the end of the entity's first tax year. § 248.

Original issue discount. The difference between the issue price of a debt obligation (e.g., a corporate bond) and the maturity value of the obligation when the issue price is *less than* the maturity value. OID represents interest and must be amortized over the life of the debt obligation using the effective interest method. The difference is not considered to be original issue discount for tax purposes when it is less than one-fourth of 1 percent of the redemption price at maturity multiplied by the number of years to maturity. §§ 1272 and 1273(a)(3).

Outside basis. A partner's basis in his or her partnership interest.

P

Parent-subsidiary controlled group. A *controlled* or *affiliated group* of corporations, where at least one corporation is at least 80 percent owned by one or more of the others. The affiliated group definition is more difficult to meet.

Partial liquidation. A stock redemption where noncorporate shareholders are permitted sale or exchange treatment, where an active business has existed for at least five years, and a portion of the outstanding stock in the entity is retired.

Partner. See *general partner* and *limited partner*.

Partnership. For income tax purposes, a partnership includes a syndicate, group, pool, or joint venture, as well as ordinary partnerships. In an ordinary partnership, two or more parties combine capital and/or services to carry on a business for profit as co-owners. § 7701(a)(2). See also *limited partnership*.

Passive investment income (PII). Gross receipts from royalties, certain rents, dividends, interest, annuities, and gains from the sale or exchange of stock and securities. With certain exceptions, if the passive investment income of an S corporation exceeds 25 percent of the corporation's gross receipts for three consecutive years, S status is lost.

Passive loss. Any loss from (1) activities in which the taxpayer does not materially participate or (2) rental activities (subject to certain exceptions). Net passive losses cannot be used to offset income from nonpassive sources. Rather, they are suspended until the taxpayer either generates net passive income (and a deduction of such losses is allowed) or disposes of the underlying property (at which time the loss deductions are allowed in full). One relief provision allows landlords who actively participate in the rental activities to deduct up to $25,000 of passive losses annually. However, a phase-out of the $25,000 amount commences when the landlord's AGI exceeds $100,000. See also *portfolio income*.

Patent. A patent is an intangible asset that may be amortized over a statutory 15-year period as a § 197 intangible. The sale of a patent usually results in favorable long-term capital gain treatment. §§ 197 and 1235.

Percentage depletion. Percentage depletion is depletion based on a statutory percentage applied to the gross income from the property. The taxpayer deducts the greater of cost depletion or percentage depletion. § 613. See also *cost depletion*.

Percentage of completion method. A method of reporting gain or loss on certain long-term contracts. Under this method of accounting, the gross contract price is included in income as the contract is completed. Reg. § 1.451–3. See also *completed contract method* and *long-term contract*.

Personal and dependency exemptions. The tax law provides an exemption for each individual taxpayer and an additional exemption for the taxpayer's spouse if a joint return is filed. An individual may also claim a dependency exemption for each dependent, provided certain tests are met. The amount of the personal and dependency exemptions is $2,650 in 1997 (and $2,700 in 1998). The exemption is subject to phase-out once adjusted gross income exceeds certain statutory threshold amounts.

Personal casualty gain. The recognized gain from any involuntary conversion of personal-use property arising from fire, storm, shipwreck, or other casualty, or from theft. See also *personal casualty loss*.

Personal casualty loss. The recognized loss from any involuntary conversion of personal-use property arising from fire, storm, shipwreck, or other casualty, or from theft. See also *personal casualty gain*.

Personal exemption. See *personal and dependency exemptions*.

Personal holding company (PHC). A corporation that satisfies the requirements of § 542. Qualification as a personal holding company means a penalty tax may be imposed on the corporation's undistributed personal holding company income for the year.

Personal holding company tax. A penalty tax imposed on certain closely held corporations with excessive investment income. The tax is assessed at the top individual tax rate on adjusted taxable income reduced by dividends paid. § 541.

Personal property. Generally, all property other than real estate. It is sometimes referred to as personalty when real estate is termed realty. Personal property can also refer to property not used in a taxpayer's trade or business or held for the production or collection of income. When used in this sense, personal property can include both realty (e.g., a personal residence) and personalty (e.g., personal effects such as clothing and furniture).

Personal service corporation (PSC). A corporation whose principal activity is the performance of personal services (e.g., health, law, engineering, architecture, accounting, actuarial science, performing arts, or consulting) and where such services are substantially performed by the employee-owners.

Personalty. Personalty is all property that is not attached to real estate (realty) and is movable. Examples of personalty are machinery, automobiles, clothing, household furnishings, inventory, and personal effects. See also *ad valorem tax*, *personal property*, and *realty*.

Points. Loan origination fees that may be deductible as interest by a buyer of property. A seller of property who pays points reduces the sellling price by the amount of the points paid for the buyer. While the seller is not permitted to deduct this amount as interest, the buyer may do so. See *prepaid interest* for the timing of the interest deduction.

Portfolio income. Income from interest, dividends, rentals, royalties, capital gains, or other investment sources. Net passive losses cannot be used to offset net portfolio income. See also *passive loss* and *investment income*.

Precedent. A previously decided court decision that is recognized as authority for the disposition of future decisions.

Precontribution gain or loss. Partnerships allow for a variety of *special allocations* of gain or loss among the partners, but gain or loss that is *built in* on an asset contributed to the partnership is assigned specifically to the contributing partner. § 704(c)(1)(A).

Preferences (AMT). See *alternative minimum tax (AMT)* and *tax preference items*.

Preferred stock bailout. A process where a shareholder used the issuance, sale, and later redemption of a preferred stock dividend to obtain long-term capital gains, without any loss of voting control over the corporation. In effect, the shareholder receives corporate profits without suffering the consequences of dividend income treatment. This procedure led Congress to enact § 306, which, if applicable, converts the prior long-term capital gain on the sale of the stock to ordinary income. Under these circumstances, the amount of ordinary income is limited to the shareholder's portion of the corporation's earnings and profits existing when the preferred stock was issued as a stock dividend.

Prepaid interest. In effect, the Code places cash basis taxpayers on an accrual basis for purposes of recognizing a deduction for prepaid interest. Thus, interest paid in advance is deductible as an interest expense only as it accrues. The one exception to this rule involves the interest element when a cash basis taxpayer pays points to obtain financing for the purchase of a principal residence (or to make improvements thereto) if the payment of points is an established business practice in the area in which the indebtedness is incurred and the amount is not excessive. § 461(g). See also *points*.

Presumption. An inference in favor of a particular fact. If, for example, the IRS issues a notice of deficiency against a taxpayer, a presumption of correctness attaches to the assessment. Thus, the taxpayer has the burden of proof of showing that he or she does not owe the tax listed in the deficiency notice. See also *rebuttable presumption*.

Previously taxed income (PTI). Before the Subchapter S Revision Act of 1982, the undistributed taxable income of an S corporation was taxed to the shareholders as of the last day of the corporation's tax year and usually could be withdrawn by the shareholders without tax consequences at some later point in time. The role of PTI has been taken over by the accumulated adjustments account. See also *accumulated adjustments account (AAA)*.

Principal partner. A partner with a 5 percent or greater interest in partnership capital or profits. This designation is relevant for determining the year-end of a partnership. § 706(b)(3). See also *majority interest partner*.

Private activity bonds. Interest on state and local bonds is excludible from gross income under § 103. Certain municipal bonds are labeled private activity bonds. Although the interest on such bonds in excludible for regular income tax purposes, it is treated as a tax preference under the AMT. See also *alternative minimum tax (AMT)*.

Private foundation. An *exempt organization* that is subject to additional statutory restrictions on its activities and on contributions made to it. Excise taxes may be levied on certain prohibited transactions, and the Code places more stringent restrictions on the deductibility of contributions to private foundations. § 509.

Procedural Regulation. A Regulation issued by the Treasury Department that is a housekeeping-type instruction indicating information that taxpayers should provide the IRS as well as information about the internal management and conduct of the IRS itself. See also *Interpretive Regulation* and *Legislative Regulation*.

Profit and loss sharing ratios. Specified in the partnership agreement and used to determine each partner's allocation of ordinary taxable income and separately stated items. Profits and losses can be shared in different ratios. The ratios can be changed by amending the partnership agreement. § 704(a).

Profits (loss) interest. A partner's percentage allocation of partnership operating results, determined by the *profit and loss sharing ratios*.

Property. Assets defined in the broadest legal sense. Property includes the *unrealized receivables* of a cash basis taxpayer, but not services rendered. § 351.

Property dividend. Generally treated in same manner as a cash distribution, measured by the FMV of the property on the date of distribution. The portion of the distribution representing E&P is a dividend; any excess is treated as a return of capital. Distribution of appreciated property causes the distributing corporation to recognize gain. The distributing corporation does not recognize loss on property that has depreciated in value.

Property tax. An *ad valorem* tax, usually levied by a city or county government, on the value of real or personal property that the taxpayer owns on a specified date. Most states exclude intangible property and assets owned by exempt organizations from the tax base, and some exclude inventory, pollution control or manufacturing equipment, and other items to provide relocation or retention incentives for the taxpayer.

Pro rata. Proportionately. Assume, for example, a corporation has 10 shareholders, each of whom owns 10 percent of the stock. A pro rata dividend distribution of $1,000 would mean that each shareholder would receive $100.

Pro se. The taxpayer represents himself or herself before the court without the benefit of counsel.

Proposed Regulation. A Regulation issued by the Treasury Department in proposed, rather than final, form. The interval between the proposal of a Regulation and its finalization permits taxpayers and other interested parties to comment on the propriety of the proposal. See also *Regulations* and *Temporary Regulation*.

Proprietorship. An unincorporated business owned by one individual. The taxable income from a proprietorship is determined on a Schedule C, and the results are reported on the owner's individual income tax return.

PTI. See *previously taxed income (PTI)*.

Public policy limitation. A concept developed by the courts precluding an income tax deduction for certain expenses related to activities deemed to be contrary to the public welfare. In this connection, Congress has incorporated into the Code specific disallowance provisions covering such items as illegal bribes, kickbacks, and fines and penalties. §§ 162(c) and (f).

Punitive damages. Damages received or paid by the taxpayer can be classified as compensatory damages or as punitive damages. Punitive damages are those awarded to punish the defendant for gross negligence or the intentional infliction of harm. Such damages are includible in gross income unless the claim arises out of physical injury or physical sickness. See also *compensatory damages*.

Q

Qualified employee discounts. Discounts offered employees on merchandise or services that the employer ordinarily sells or provides to customers. The discounts must be generally available to all employees. In the case of property, the discount cannot exceed the employer's gross profit (the sales price cannot be less than the employer's cost). In the case of services, the discounts cannot exceed 20 percent of the normal sales price. § 132.

Qualified nonrecourse debt. Issued on realty by a bank, retirement plan, or governmental agency. Included in the *at-risk amount* by the investor. § 465(b)(6).

Qualified pension or profit sharing plan. An employer-sponsored plan that meets the requirements of § 401. If these requirements are met, none of the employer's contributions to the plan will be taxed to the employee until distributed (§ 402). The employer is allowed a deduction in the year the contributions are made (§ 404).

Qualified real property business indebtedness. Indebtedness that was incurred or assumed by the taxpayer in connection with real property used in a trade or business and is secured by such real property. The taxpayer must not be a C corporation. For qualified real property business indebtedness, the taxpayer may elect to exclude some or all of the income realized from cancellation of debt on qualified real property. If the election is made, the basis of the property must be reduced by the amount excluded. The amount excluded cannot be greater than the excess of the principal amount of the outstanding debt over the fair market value (net of any other debt outstanding on the property) of the property securing the debt.

Qualified residence interest. A term relevant in determining the amount of interest expense the individual taxpayer may deduct as an itemized deduction for what otherwise would be disallowed as a component of personal interest (consumer interest). Qualified residence interest consists of interest paid on qualified residences (principal residence and one other residence) of the taxpayer. Debt that qualifies as qualified residence interest is limited to $1 million of debt to acquire, construct, or substantially improve qualified residences (acquisition indebtedness) plus $100,000 of other debt secured by qualified residences (home equity indebtedness). The home equity indebtedness may not exceed the fair market value of a qualified residence reduced by the acquisition indebtedness for that residence. § 163(h)(3). See also *consumer interest* and *home equity loans*.

Qualified small business corporation. A C corporation that has aggregate gross assets not exceeding $50 million and that is conducting an active trade or business. § 1202.

Qualified small business stock. Stock in a qualified small business corporation, purchased as part of an original issue after August 10, 1993. The shareholder may exclude from gross income 50 percent of the realized gain on the sale of the stock, if he or she held the stock for more than five years. § 1202.

Qualified transportation fringes. Transportation benefits provided by the employer to the employee. Such benefits include (1) transportation in a commuter highway vehicle between the employee's residence and the place of employment, (2) a transit pass, and (3) qualified parking. Qualified transportation fringes are excludible from the employee's gross income to the extent categories (1) and (2) above do not exceed $65 per month in 1998 and category (3) does not exceed $175 per month in 1998. These amounts are indexed annually for inflation. § 132.

Qualified tuition reduction plan. A type of fringe benefit plan that is available to employees of nonprofit educational institutions. Such employees (and the spouse and dependent children) are allowed to exclude a tuition waiver pursuant to a qualified tuition reduction plan from gross income. The exclusion applies to undergraduate tuition. In limited circumstances, the exclusion also applies to the graduate tuition of teaching and research assistants. § 117(d).

R

Realized gain or loss. The difference between the amount realized upon the sale or other disposition of property and the adjusted basis of the property. § 1001. See also *adjusted basis, amount realized, basis,* and *recognized gain or loss*.

Realty. Real estate. See also *personalty*.

Reasonableness. The Code includes a reasonableness requirement with respect to the deduction of salaries and other compensation for services. What constitutes reasonableness is a question of fact. If an expense is unreasonable, the amount that is classified as unreasonable is not allowed as a deduction. The question of reasonableness generally arises with respect to closely held corporations where there is no separation of ownership and management. § 162(a)(1).

Rebuttable presumption. A presumption that can be overturned upon the showing of sufficient proof. See also *presumption*.

Recapture. To recover the tax benefit of a deduction or a credit previously taken. See also *depreciation recapture*.

Recapture potential. A measure with respect to property that, if disposed of in a taxable transaction, would result in the recapture of depreciation (§ 1245 or § 1250), deferred LIFO gain, or deferred installment method gain.

Recognized gain or loss. The portion of realized gain or loss subject to income taxation. See also *realized gain or loss*.

Recourse debt. Debt for which the lender may both foreclose on the property and assess a guarantor for any payments due under the loan. A lender may also make a claim against the assets of any general partner in a partnership to which debt is issued, without regard to whether the partner has guaranteed the debt.

Recovery of capital doctrine. When a taxable sale or exchange occurs, the seller may be permitted to recover his or her investment (or other adjusted basis) in the property before gain or loss is recognized. See also *open transaction doctrine*.

Redemption. See *stock redemption*.

Redemption (complete termination). Sale or exchange treatment is available relative to this type of redemption. The shareholder must retire all of his or her outstanding shares in the corporation (ignoring family attribution rules), and cannot hold an interest, other than that of a creditor, for the 10 years following the redemption. § 302(b)(3).

Redemption (disproportionate). Sale or exchange treatment is available relative to this type of redemption. After the exchange, the shareholder owns less than 80 percent of his or her pre-redemption interest in the corporation, and only a minority interest in the entity. § 302(b)(2).

Redemption (not equivalent to a dividend). Sale or exchange treatment is available relative to this type of redemption. Although various safe harbor tests are failed, the nature of the redemption is such that dividend treatment is waived by the courts, because it represented a meaningful reduction in the shareholder's interest in the corporation. § 302(b)(1).

Redemption to pay death taxes. Sale or exchange treatment is available relative to this type of redemption, to the extent of the proceeds up to the total amount paid by the estate or heir for death taxes and administration expenses. The stock value must exceed 35 percent of the value of the decedent's adjusted gross estate. In meeting this test, one can combine shareholdings in corporations where the decedent held at least 20 percent of the outstanding shares.

Regular corporation. See *C corporation*.

Regulations. The U.S. Treasury Department Regulations (abbreviated Reg.) represent the position of the IRS as to how the Internal Revenue Code is to be interpreted. Their purpose is to provide taxpayers and IRS personnel with rules of general and specific application to the various provisions of the tax law. Regulations are published in the *Federal Register* and in all tax services. See also *Interpretive Regulation, Legislative Regulation, Procedural Regulation*, and *Proposed Regulation*.

Rehabilitation expenditures credit. A credit that is based on expenditures incurred to rehabilitate industrial and commercial buildings and certified historic structures. The credit is intended to discourage businesses from moving from older, economically distressed areas to newer locations and to encourage the preservation of historic structures. § 47. See *rehabilitation expenditures credit recapture*.

Rehabilitation expenditures credit recapture. When property that qualifies for the rehabilitation expenditures credit is disposed of or ceases to be used in the trade or business of the taxpayer, some or all of the tax credit claimed on the property may be recaptured as additional tax liability. The amount of the recapture is the difference between the amount of the credit claimed originally and what should have been claimed in light of the length of time the property was actually held or used for qualifying purposes. § 50. See *rehabilitation expenditures credit*.

Related corporation. See *controlled group*.

Related parties. Various Code sections define related parties and often include a variety of persons within this (usually detrimental) category. Generally, related parties are accorded different tax treatment from that applicable to other taxpayers who enter into similar transactions. For instance, realized losses that are generated between related parties are not recognized in the year of the loss. However, these deferred losses can be used to offset recognized gains that occur upon the subsequent sale of the asset to a nonrelated party. Other uses of a related-party definition include the conversion of gain upon the sale of a depreciable asset into all ordinary income (§ 1239) and the identification of constructive ownership of stock relative to corporate distributions, redemptions, liquidations, reorganizations, and compensation.

Related-party transactions. The tax law places restrictions upon the recognition of gains and losses between related parties because of the potential for abuse. For example, restrictions are placed on the deduction of losses from the sale or exchange of property between related parties. In addition, under certain circumstances, related-party gains that would otherwise be classified as capital gain are classified as ordinary income. §§ 267, 707(b), and 1239. See also *related parties*.

Remand. To send back. An appellate court may remand a case to a lower court, usually for additional fact finding. In other words, the appellate court is not in a position to decide the appeal based on the facts determined by the lower court. Remanding is abbreviated *rem'g*.

Rental activity. Any activity where payments are received principally for the use of tangible property is a rental activity. Temporary Regulations provide that in certain circumstances activities involving rental of real and personal property are not to be treated as rental activities. The Temporary Regulations list six exceptions.

Research activities credit. A tax credit whose purpose is to encourage research and development. It consists of two components: the incremental research activities credit and the basic research credit. The incremental research activities credit is equal to 20 percent of the excess qualified research expenditures over the base amount. The basic research credit is equal to 20 percent of the excess of basic research payments over the base amount. § 41. See also *general business credit*.

Research and experimental expenditures. The Code provides three alternatives for the tax treatment of research and experimentation expenditures. They may be expensed in the year paid or incurred, deferred subject to amortization, or capitalized. If the taxpayer does not elect to expense such costs or to defer them subject to amortization (over 60 months), the expenditures must be capitalized. § 174. Two types of research activities credits are available: the basic research credit and the incremental research activities credit. The rate for each type is 20 percent. § 41. See also *research activities credit*.

Reserve for bad debts. A method of accounting whereby an allowance is permitted for estimated uncollectible accounts. Actual write-offs are charged to the reserve, and recoveries of amounts previously written off are credited to the reserve. The Code permits only certain financial institutions to use the reserve method. § 166. See also *specific charge-off method*.

Reserve method. See *reserve for bad debts*.

Residential rental property. Buildings for which at least 80 percent of the gross rents are from dwelling units (e.g., an apartment building). This type of building is distinguished from nonresidential (commercial or industrial) buildings in applying the recapture of depreciation provisions. The term also is relevant in distinguishing between buildings that are eligible for a 27.5-year life versus a 39-year life for MACRS purposes. Generally, residential buildings receive preferential treatment.

Residential rental real estate. See *residential rental property*.

Return of capital. When a taxpayer reacquires financial resources that he or she previously had invested in an entity or venture, the return of his or her capital investment itself does not increase gross income for the recovery year. A return of capital may result from an annuity or insurance contract, the sale or exchange of any asset, or a distribution from a partnership or corporation.

Revenue neutrality. A description that characterizes tax legislation when it neither increases nor decreases the revenue result. Thus, any tax revenue losses are offset by tax revenue gains.

Revenue Procedure. A matter of procedural importance to both taxpayers and the IRS concerning the administration of the tax laws is issued as a Revenue Procedure (abbreviated Rev.Proc.). A Revenue Procedure is first published in an *Internal Revenue Bulletin* (I.R.B.) and later transferred to the appropriate *Cumulative Bulletin* (C.B.). Both the *Internal Revenue Bulletins* and the *Cumulative Bulletins* are published by the U.S. Government Printing Office.

Revenue Ruling. A Revenue Ruling (abbreviated Rev.Rul.) is issued by the National Office of the IRS to express an official interpretation of the tax law as applied to specific transactions. It is more limited in application than a Regulation. A Revenue Ruling is first published in an *Internal Revenue Bulletin* (I.R.B.) and later transferred to the appropriate *Cumulative Bulletin* (C.B.). Both the *Internal Revenue Bulletins* and the *Cumulative Bulletins* are published by the U.S. Government Printing Office.

Reversed (Rev'd.). An indication that a decision of one court has been reversed by a higher court in the same case.

Reversing (Rev'g.). An indication that the decision of a higher court is reversing the result reached by a lower court in the same case.

Rev.Proc. Abbreviation for an IRS Revenue Procedure. See *Revenue Procedure*.

Rev.Rul. Abbreviation for an IRS Revenue Ruling. See *Revenue Ruling*.

RIA. Research Institute of America is the publisher of two tax services and of Federal tax decisions (AFTR and AFTR2d series).

Right of survivorship. See *joint tenants*.

S

S corporation. The designation for a small business corporation. See also *Subchapter S*.

Sale or exchange. A requirement for the recognition of capital gain or loss. Generally, the seller of property must receive money or relief from debt in order to have sold the property. An exchange involves the transfer of property for other property. Thus *collection* of a debt is neither a sale nor an exchange. The term *sale or exchange* is not defined by the Code.

Sales tax. A state- or local-level tax on the retail sale of specified property. Generally, the purchaser pays the tax, but the seller collects it, as an agent for the government. Various taxing jurisdictions allow exemptions for purchases of specific items, including certain food, services, and manufacturing equipment. If the purchaser and seller are in different states, a *use tax* usually applies.

Schedule M–1. On the Form 1120, a reconciliation of book net income with Federal taxable income. Accounts for timing and permanent differences in the two computations, such as depreciation differences, exempt income, and nondeductible items.

Scholarships. Scholarships are generally excluded from the gross income of the recipient unless the payments are a disguised form of compensation for services rendered. However, the Code imposes restrictions on the exclusion. The recipient must be a degree candidate. The excluded amount is limited to amounts used for tuition, fees, books, supplies, and equipment required for courses of instruction. Amounts received for room and board are not eligible for the exclusion. § 117.

Section 179 expensing election. The election to expense a capital expenditure in the year an asset is placed in service rather than over the asset's useful life or cost recovery period. The annual ceiling on the deduction is $18,000 for 1997 and $18,500 for 1998. The ceiling amount is increased each year until it reaches $25,000 for 2003 and thereafter. However, the deduction is reduced dollar for dollar when § 179 property is placed in service during the taxable year exceeds $200,000. In addition, the amount expensed under § 179 cannot exceed the aggregate amount of taxable income derived from the conduct of any trade or business of the taxpayer.

Section 1231 property. Depreciable assets and real estate used in a trade or business and held for the appropriate holding period. Under certain circumstances, the classification also includes timber, coal, domestic iron ore, livestock (held for draft, breeding, dairy, or sporting purposes), and unharvested crops. § 1231(b). See also *Section 1231 gains and losses*.

Section 1231 gains and losses. If the combined gains and losses from the taxable dispositions of § 1231 assets plus the net gain from business involuntary conversions (of both § 1231 assets and long-term capital assets) is a gain, the gains and losses are treated as long-term capital gains and losses. In arriving at § 1231 gains, however, the depreciation recapture provisions (e.g., §§ 1245 and 1250) are first applied to produce ordinary income. If the net result of the combination is a loss, the gains and losses from § 1231 assets are treated as ordinary gains and losses. § 1231(a). See also *depreciation recapture* and *Section 1231 property*.

Section 1231 lookback. In order for gain to be classified as § 1231 gain, the gain must survive the § 1231 lookback. To the extent of nonrecaptured § 1231 losses for the five prior tax years, the gain is classified as ordinary income. § 1231(c).

Section 1244 stock. Stock issued under § 1244 by qualifying small business corporations. If § 1244 stock becomes worthless, the shareholders may claim an ordinary loss rather than the usual capital loss, within statutory limitations.

Section 1245 property. Property that is subject to the recapture of depreciation under § 1245. For a definition of § 1245 property, see § 1245(a)(3). See also *Section 1245 recapture*.

Section 1245 recapture. Upon a taxable disposition of § 1245 property, all depreciation claimed on the property is recaptured as ordinary income (but not to exceed recognized gain from the disposition).

Section 1250 property. Real estate that is subject to the recapture of depreciation under § 1250. For a definition of § 1250 property, see § 1250(c). See also *Section 1250 recapture*.

Section 1250 recapture. Upon a taxable disposition of § 1250 property, some of the depreciation or cost recovery claimed on the property may be recaptured as ordinary income.

Securities. Generally, stock, debt, and other financial assets. To the extent securities other than the stock of the transferee corporation are received in a § 351 exchange, the new shareholder realizes a gain.

Self-employment tax. A tax is levied on individuals with net earnings from self-employment to provide Social Security and Medicare benefits. If a self-employed individual also receives wages from an employer that are subject to FICA, the self-employment tax will be reduced. A partial deduction is allowed in calculating the self-employment tax. Individuals with net earnings of $400 or more from self-employment are subject to the tax.

Separate property. In a community property jurisdiction, property that belongs entirely to one of the spouses is separate property. Generally, it is property acquired before marriage or acquired after marriage by gift or inheritance. See also *community property*.

Separately stated item. Any item of a partnership or S corporation that might be taxed differently to any two owners of the entity. These amounts are not included in ordinary income of the entity, but are instead reported separately to the owners; tax consequences are determined at the owner level.

Severance tax. A tax imposed upon the extraction of natural resources.

Sham. A transaction without substance that will be disregarded for tax purposes.

Short sale. A short sale occurs when a taxpayer sells borrowed property (usually stock) and repays the lender with substantially identical property either held on the date of the short sale or purchased after the sale. No gain or loss is recognized until the short sale is closed, and such gain or loss is generally short-term. § 1223.

Short taxable year (short period). A tax year that is less than 12 months. A short taxable year may occur in the initial reporting period, in the final tax year, or when the taxpayer changes tax years.

Short-term capital gain or loss. Results from the sale or other taxable exchange of a capital asset that had been held by the seller for one year or less or from other transactions involving statutorily designated assets, including nonbusiness bad debts.

Significant participation activity. There are seven tests to determine whether an individual has achieved material participation in an activity, one of which is based on more than 500 hours of participation in significant participation activities. A significant participation activity is one in which the individual's participation exceeds 100 hours during the year.

Simplified employee pension (SEP) plan. An employer may make contributions to an employee's individual retirement account (IRA) in amounts not exceeding the lesser of 15 percent of compensation or $30,000 per individual. § 219(b)(2). See also *individual retirement account (IRA)*.

Small business corporation. A corporation that satisfies the definition of § 1361(b), § 1244(c), or both. Satisfaction of § 1361(b) permits an S election, and satisfaction of § 1244 enables the shareholders of the corporation to claim an ordinary loss on the worthlessness of stock.

Small business stock. See *Section 1244 stock, small business corporation*.

Small Cases Division of the U.S. Tax Court. Jurisdiction is limited to claims of $10,000 or less. There is no appeal from this court.

Special allocation. Any amount for which an agreement exists among the partners of a partnership outlining the method used for spreading the item among the partners.

Specific charge-off method. A method of accounting for bad debts in which a deduction is permitted only when an account becomes partially or completely worthless. See also *reserve for bad debts*.

Standard deduction. The individual taxpayer can either itemize deductions or take the standard deduction. The amount of the standard deduction depends on the taxpayer's filing status (single, head of household, married filing jointly, surviving spouse, or married filing separately). For 1998, the amount of the standard deduction ranges from $3,550 (for married, filing separately) to $7,100 (for married, filing jointly). Additional standard deductions of either $850 (for married taxpayers) or $1,050 (for single taxpayers) are available if the taxpayer is either blind or age 65 or over. Limitations exist on the amount of the standard deduction of a taxpayer who is another taxpayer's dependent. The standard deduction amounts are adjusted annually for inflation each year. § 63(c).

Step-down in basis. A reduction in the tax basis of property.

Step transaction. Disregarding one or more transactions to arrive at the final result. Assume, for example, that the shareholders of Black Corporation liquidate the corporation and receive cash and operating assets. Immediately after the liquidation, the shareholders transfer the operating assets to newly formed Brown Corporation. Under these circumstances, the IRS may contend that the liquidation of Black should be disregarded (thereby depriving the shareholders of capital gain treatment). What may really have happened is a *reorganization* of Black with a distribution of boot (ordinary income) to Black's shareholders. If so, there will be a carryover of basis in the assets transferred from Black to Brown.

Step-up in basis. An increase in the tax basis of property. The classic step-up in basis occurs when a decedent dies owning appreciated property. Since the estate or heir acquires a basis in the property equal to the property's fair market value on the date of death (or alternate valuation date if available and elected), any appreciation is not subject to the income tax. Thus, a step-up in basis is the result, with no income tax consequences.

Stock attribution. See *attribution*.

Stock dividend. Not taxable if pro rata distributions of stock or stock rights on common stock. Section 305 governs the taxability of stock dividends and sets out five exceptions to the general rule that stock dividends are nontaxable.

Stock redemption. A corporation buys back its own stock from a specified shareholder. Typically, the corporation recognizes any realized gain on the noncash assets that it uses to effect a redemption, and the shareholder obtains a capital gain or loss upon receipt of the purchase price.

Stock rights. An asset that conveys to the holder the power to purchase corporate stock at a specified price, often for a limited period of time. Stock rights received may be taxed as a distribution of earnings and profits. After the right is exercised, the basis of the acquired share includes the investor's purchase price or gross income, if any, to obtain the right. Disposition of the right also is a taxable event, with basis often assigned from the shares held prior to the issuance of the right.

Subchapter S. Sections 1361–1379 of the Internal Revenue Code. An elective provision permitting certain small business corporations (§ 1361) and their shareholders (§ 1362) to elect to be treated for income tax purposes in accordance with the operating rules of §§ 1363–1379. However, some S corporations usually avoid the corporate income tax, and corporate losses can be claimed by the shareholders.

Substance vs. form concept. A standard used when one must ascertain the true reality of what has occurred. Suppose, for example, that a father sells stock to his daughter for $1,000. If the stock is really worth $50,000 at the time of the transfer, the substance of the transaction is probably a gift to her of $49,000.

Substantial economic effect. Partnerships are allowed to *allocate* items of income, expense, gain, loss, and credit in any manner that is authorized in the partnership agreement, provided that the allocation has an economic effect aside from the corresponding tax results. The necessary substantial economic effect is present, for instance, if the post-contribution appreciation in the value of an asset that was contributed to the partnership by a partner was allocated to that partner for cost recovery purposes.

Substituted basis. When a taxpayer exchanges one asset for another, many provisions in the tax law allow an assignment of basis in the received asset to be that of the traded asset(s) in the hands of its former owner. Thus, no step-up or -down of basis occurs as a result of the exchange. For example, when an investor contributes an asset to a corporation or partnership, the partner generally takes a substituted basis in the partnership interest [i.e., the investment asset (partnership interest) has a basis equal to the aggregated bases of the assets contributed by that partner].

Surviving spouse. When a husband or wife predeceases the other spouse, the survivor is known as a surviving spouse. Under certain conditions, a surviving spouse may be entitled to use the income tax rates in § 1(a) (those applicable to married persons filing a joint return) for the two years after the year of death of his or her spouse. § 2.

Syndication costs. Incurred in promoting and marketing partnership interests for sale to investors. Examples include legal and accounting fees, printing costs for prospectus and placement documents, and state registration fees. These items are capitalized by the partnership as incurred, with no amortization thereof allowed.

T

Tangible property. All property that has form or substance and is not intangible. See also *intangible asset.*

Taxable income. The tax base with respect to the prevailing Federal income tax. Taxable income is defined by the Internal Revenue Code, Treasury Regulations, and pertinent court cases. Currently, taxable income includes gross income from all sources except those specifically excluded by statute. In addition, taxable income is reduced for certain allowable deductions. Deductions for business taxpayers must be related to a trade or business. Individuals can also deduct certain personal expenses in determining their taxable incomes. See also *gross income.*

Taxable year. The annual period over which income is measured for income tax purposes. Most individuals use a calendar year, but many businesses use a fiscal year based on the natural business year. See also *accounting period* and *fiscal year.*

Tax avoidance. Legal minimization of tax consequences through the evaluation and implementation of tax strategies.

Tax benefit rule. A provision that limits the recognition of income from the recovery of an expense or loss properly deducted in a prior tax year to the amount of the deduction that generated a tax saving. Assume that last year Gary had medical expenses of $3,000 and adjusted gross income of $30,000. Because of the 7.5 percent limitation, Gary could deduct only $750 of these expenses [$3,000 − (7.5% × $30,000)]. If, this year, Gary is reimbursed by his insurance company for $900 of these expenses, the tax benefit rule limits the amount of income from the reimbursement to $750 (the amount previously deducted with a tax saving).

Tax Court. The U.S. Tax Court is one of four trial courts of original jurisdiction that decide litigation involving Federal income, death, or gift taxes. It is the only trial court where the taxpayer must not first pay the deficiency assessed by the IRS. The Tax Court will not have jurisdiction over a case unless a statutory notice of deficiency (90-day letter) has been issued by the IRS and the taxpayer files the petition for hearing within the time prescribed.

Tax credits. Tax credits are amounts that directly reduce a taxpayer's tax liability. The tax benefit received from a tax credit is not dependent on the taxpayer's marginal tax rate, whereas the benefit of a tax deduction or exclusion is dependent on the taxpayer's tax bracket.

Tax evasion. Illegal efforts to reduce taxes through the use of fraud, deception, or other prohibited devices.

Tax-free exchange. Transfers of property specifically exempted from income tax consequences by the tax law. Examples are a transfer of property to a controlled corporation under § 351(a) and a like-kind exchange under § 1031(a). See also *nontaxable exchange.*

Tax on unearned income of a child under age 14. Passive income, such as interest and dividends, that is recognized by such a child is taxed *to him or her* at the rates that would have applied had the income been incurred by the child's parents, generally to the extent that the income exceeds $1,400. The additional tax is assessed regardless of the source of the income or the income's underlying property. If the child's parents are divorced, the custodial parent's rates are used. The parents' rates reflect any applicable alternative minimum tax and the phase-outs of lower tax brackets and other deductions. § 1(g).

Tax preference items. Various items that may result in the imposition of the alternative minimum tax. §§ 55–58. See also *alternative minimum tax (AMT).*

Tax rate schedules. Rate schedules appearing in Appendix A that are used by upper-income taxpayers and those not permitted to use the tax table. Separate rate schedules are provided for married individuals filing jointly, head of household, single taxpayers, estates and trusts, and married individuals filing separate returns. § 1.

Tax research. The method used to determine the best available solution to a situation that possesses tax consequences. Both tax and nontax factors are considered.

Tax shelters. The typical tax shelter generated large losses in the early years of the activity. Investors would offset these losses against other types of income and, therefore, avoid paying income taxes on this income. These tax shelter investments could then be sold after a few years and produce capital gain income, which was (and still is) taxed at a lower rate than ordinary income. The passive activity loss rules and the at-risk rules now limit tax shelter deductions.

Tax table. A tax table appearing in Appendix A that is provided for taxpayers with less than $100,000 of taxable income. Separate columns are provided for single taxpayers, married taxpayers filing jointly, head of household, and married taxpayers filing separately. § 3.

Tax treaty. An agreement between the U.S. Department of State and another country, designed to alleviate double taxation of income and asset transfers, and to share administrative information useful to tax agencies in both countries. The United States has income tax treaties with over 40 countries and transfer tax treaties with about 20.

Tax year. See *accounting period.*

T.C. An abbreviation for the U.S. Tax Court used in citing a Regular Decision of the U.S. Tax Court.

T.C.Memo. An abbreviation used to refer to a Memorandum Decision of the U.S. Tax Court.

Technical advice memoranda (TAMs). TAMs are issued by the National Office of the IRS in response to questions raised by IRS field personnel during audits. They deal with completed rather than proposed transactions and are often requested for questions related to exempt organizations and employee plans.

Temporary Regulation. A Regulation issued by the Treasury Department in temporary form. When speed is critical, the Treasury Department issues Temporary Regulations that take effect immediately. These Regulations have the same authoritative value as Final Regulations and may be cited as precedent for three years. Temporary Regulations are also issued as proposed Regulations. See also *Proposed Regulation* and *Regulations*.

Tenancy by the entirety. Essentially, a joint tenancy between husband and wife. See also joint tenants and *tenancy in common*.

Tenancy in common. A form of ownership where each tenant (owner) holds an undivided interest in property. Unlike a joint tenancy or a tenancy by the entirety, the interest of a tenant in common does not terminate upon that individual's death (there is no right of survivorship). Assume Tim and Cindy acquire real estate as equal tenants in common, each having furnished one-half of the purchase price. Upon Tim's death, his one-half interest in the property passes to his estate or heirs, not to Cindy. For a comparison of results, see also *joint tenants* and *tenancy by the entirety*.

Theft loss. A loss from larceny, embezzlement and robbery. It does not include misplacement of items. See also *casualty loss*.

Thin capitalization. When debt owed by a corporation to the shareholders becomes too large in relation to the corporation's capital structure (i.e., stock and shareholder equity), the IRS may contend that the corporation is thinly capitalized. In effect, this means that some or all of the debt is reclassified as equity. The immediate result is to disallow any interest deduction to the corporation on the reclassified debt. To the extent of the corporation's earnings and profits, interest payments and loan repayments on the reclassified debt are treated as dividends to the shareholders.

Trade or business. Any business or professional activity conducted by a taxpayer. The mere ownership of rental or other investment assets does not constitute a trade or business. Generally, a trade or business generates relatively little passive investment income.

Transportation expenses. Transportation expenses for an employee include only the cost of transportation (taxi fares, automobile expenses, etc.) in the course of employment when the employee is not away from home in travel status. Commuting expenses are not deductible. See also *automobile expenses*.

Travel expenses. Travel expenses include meals (generally subject to a 50 percent disallowance), lodging and transportation expenses while away from home in the pursuit of a trade or business (including that of an employee).

Treasury Regulations. See *Regulations*.

Trial court. The court of original jurisdiction; the first court to consider litigation. In Federal tax controversies, trial courts include U.S. District Courts, the U.S. Tax Court, the U.S. Court of Federal Claims, and the Small Cases Division of the U.S. Tax Court. See also *appellate court, Claims Court, District Court, Small Cases Division of the U.S. Tax Court,* and *Tax Court.*

Trust. A legal entity created by a grantor for the benefit of designated beneficiaries under the laws of the state and the valid trust instrument. The trustee holds a fiduciary responsibility to manage the trust's corpus assets and income for the economic benefit of all of the beneficiaries.

U

Unearned income. Income received but not yet earned. Normally, such income is taxed when received, even for accrual basis taxpayers.

Uniform capitalization rules. Under § 263A, the Regulations provide a set of rules that all taxpayers (regardless of the particular industry) can use to determine the items of cost (and means of allocating those costs) that must be capitalized with respect to the production of tangible property.

Unrealized receivables. Amounts earned by a cash basis taxpayer but not yet received. Because of the method of accounting used by the taxpayer, these amounts have no income tax basis. When unrealized receivables are distributed to a partner, they generally convert a transaction from nontaxable to taxable or convert otherwise capital gain to ordinary income.

Unreasonable compensation. A deduction is allowed for *reasonable* salaries or other compensation for personal services actually rendered. To the extent compensation is excessive (unreasonable), no deduction is allowed. The problem of unreasonable compensation usually is limited to closely held corporations, where the motivation is to pay out profits in some form that is deductible to the corporation. Deductible compensation therefore becomes an attractive substitute for nondeductible dividends when the shareholders also are employed by the corporation.

Unrecaptured § 1250 gain (25 percent gain). Gain from the sale of depreciable real estate held more than 18 months. The gain is equal to or less than the depreciation taken on such property and is reduced by § 1245 gain and § 1250 gain.

U.S. Court of Federal Claims. See *Claims Court*.

U.S. Supreme Court. The highest appellate court or the court of last resort in the Federal court system and in most states. Only a small number of tax decisions of the U.S. Courts of Appeal are reviewed by the U.S. Supreme Court under its certiorari procedure. The Supreme Court usually grants certiorari to resolve a conflict among the Courts of Appeal (e.g., two or more appellate courts have assumed opposing positions on a particular issue) or when the tax issue is extremely important (e.g., size of the revenue loss to the Federal government).

U.S. Tax Court. See *Tax Court*.

Use tax. A sales tax that is collectible by the seller where the purchaser is domiciled in a different state.

USSC. An abbreviation for the U.S. Supreme Court.

USTC. Published by Commerce Clearing House, *U.S. Tax Cases* contain all of the Federal tax decisions issued by the U.S. District Courts, U.S. Court of Federal Claims, U.S. Courts of Appeals, and the U.S. Supreme Court.

V

Value added tax (VAT). A national sales tax that taxes the increment in value as goods move through the production process. A VAT is much used in other countries but has not yet been incorporated as part of the U.S. Federal tax structure.

W

Wash sale. A loss from the sale of stock or securities that is disallowed because the taxpayer within 30 days before or after the sale, has acquired stock or securities substantially identical to those sold. § 1091.

Welfare-to-work credit. A tax credit available to employers hiring individuals who have been long-term recipients of family assistance welfare benefits. In general, long-term recipients are those individuals who are certified by a designated local agency as being members of a family receiving assistance under a public aid program for at least an 18-month period ending on the hiring date. The welfare-to-work credit is available for qualified wages paid in the first two years of employment. The maximum credit is equal to $8,500 per qualified employee, computed as 35 percent of the first $10,000 of qualified wages paid in the first year of employment, plus 50 percent of the first $10,000 of qualified wages paid in the second year of employment. § 51A. See also *general business credit*.

Wherewithal to pay. This concept recognizes the inequity of taxing a transaction when the taxpayer lacks the means with which to pay the tax. Under it, there is a correlation between the imposition of the tax and the ability to pay the tax. It is particularly suited to situations in which the taxpayer's economic position has not changed significantly as a result of the transaction.

Withholding allowances. The number of withholding allowances serves as the basis for determining the amount of income taxes withheld from an employee's salary or wages. The more withholding allowances claimed, the less income tax withheld by an employer. An employee may claim withholding allowances for personal exemptions for self and spouse (unless claimed as a dependent of another person), dependency exemptions, and special withholding allowances.

Work opportunity tax credit. Employers are allowed a tax credit equal to 40 percent of the first $6,000 of wages (per eligible employee) for the first year of employment. Eligible employees include certain hard-to-employ individuals (e.g., qualified ex-felons, high-risk youth, food stamp recipients, and veterans). For an employer to qualify for the 40 percent credit, the employees must (1) be certified by a designated local agency as being members of one of the targeted groups and (2) have completed at least 400 hours of service to the employer. For employees who meet the first condition but not the second, the credit rate is reduced to 25 percent provided the employees meet a minimum employment level of 120 hours of service to the employer. The employer's deduction for wages is reduced by the amount of the credit taken. For qualified summer youth employees, the 40 percent rate is applied to the first $3,000 of qualified wages. §§ 51 and 52.

Working condition fringe. A type of fringe benefit received by the employee that is excludible from the employee's gross income. It consists of property or services provided (paid or reimbursed) by the employer for which the employee could take a tax deduction if the employee had paid for them. § 132.

Worthless securities. A loss (usually capital) is allowed for a security that becomes worthless during the year. The loss is deemed to have occurred on the last day of the year. Special rules apply to securities of affiliated companies and small business stock.

Writ of Certiorari. See *certiorari*.

APPENDIX D-1
Table of Code Sections Cited

[See Title 26 U.S.C.A.]

I.R.C. Sec.	This Work Page
1	2–7, 6–6
1(g)	15–18
1(h)(2)	8–16
1(h)(6)	8–18
1(h)(8)(A)	8–17
2	2–7, 2–8
2(a)	2–4, 15–25
2(a)(1)(A)	2–6, 2–7
2(b)	15–25
2(b)(1)(A)(i)	15–25
2(b)(1)(B)	15–25
3.07	9–14
11(b)	9–27
12(d)	2–7
21	15–54
22	15–57
23	15–52
24	15–53
25A	15–55
27	13–11, 13–13
32	15–59
38	13–12
38(c)	13–3
38(c)(3)(B)	13–3
39(a)(1)	13–4
41	4–18, 13–8, 13–13
41(b)(3)(A)	13–9
41(d)	13–9
41(e)	13–10
42	13–10, 13–13
44	13–11, 13–13
46	13–12
47	13–5
50(c)	13–5
51	13–7, 13–12
51A	13–8, 13–12
55	14–8
55 through 59	13–14
56	13–24

I.R.C. Sec.	This Work Page
56(a)(1)	13–19
56(a)(1)(A)(i)	13–19
56(a)(2)	13–20
56(a)(3)	13–20
56(a)(5)	13–20
56(a)(6)	13–21
56(c)(1)	14–9
56(f)	14–9
56(g)(1)	13–23
56(g)(2)	13–23
56(g)(3)	13–23
56(g)(4)(C)	13–24
57	13–24
57(a)(1)	13–16
57(a)(2)	13–17
57(a)(5)	13–17
58	13–24
59(e)(2)(D)	13–20
59(e)(2)(E)	13–20
61	9–10
61(a)	15–4, 16–42
61(a)(3)	7–6
61(a)(12)	3–25
62	15–5
62(a)(1)	5–11, 16–3
62(a)(2)	16–35
62(a)(4)	15–34
62(a)(15)	16–27
62(b)	16–36
63(c)(1)	15–6
63(c)(5)	15–8
63(c)(6)	15–8
63(d)	15–40
67	16–15
71	15–27
71–90	3–17, 15–26
71(b)(1)	15–27
71(c)(2)	15–28
71(f)	15–28

Table of Code Sections Cited

I.R.C. Sec.	This Work Page
74	15–28
74(b)	15–28
74(c)	15–29
79	16–9
79(d)	16–10, 16–17
83	9–10
83(a)	11–11
85	15–29
86	15–29, 16–39
101	3–17
101–150	3–17
101(g)	3–24
102	3–17, 15–29
102(c)	15–30
103	3–17, 4–14
103(a)	3–22
103(b)	3–22
104(a)(1)	15–32
104(a)(2)	15–32
104(a)(3)	15–33
105	16–6
105(a)	16–6
105(b)	16–6
105(c)	16–6
105(h)	16–6, 16–17
105(h)(2)	10–18
106	16–6
108	3–17, 3–26
108(a)(1)(D)	3–27
108(b)	3–27
108(e)(5)	3–27
108(e)(6)	3–28
108(f)	3–28
109	3–17, 3–23, 7–19
111	3–21
111(a)	3–21
117	3–17
117(a)	15–30
117(b)	15–31
117(d)	16–10
118	9–21
119	16–7, 16–14
119(a)	16–7
121	7–17, 7–34, 15–42
125	16–12
125(f)	16–12
127	16–11
127(b)(2)	16–17
129	16–11
132	16–13
132(a)(6)	16–27
132(c)	16–14
132(d)	16–15
132(f)	16–16
132(g)	16–27
132(j)(1)	16–16, 16–17
132(j)(3)	16–15
132(j)(4)	16–11
135	15–34, 16–39
137	16–11
141	13–17
151(c)(1)	15–13
151(c)(2)	15–14
152	15–10
152(a)	15–13, 15–25
152(b)(2)	15–13
152(b)(5)	15–13
152(c)	15–11
152(e)	15–12
162	4–3, 4–4, 4–9, 9–3, 9–20, 16–42
162(a)	4–2, 16–3, 16–22
162(a)(1)	4–3, 14–11
162(c)	4–8
162(c)(2)	16–58
162(e)	4–9
162(f)	4–8
162(g)	4–8
162(m)	4–10
163(h)(3)	15–42
164	15–38
164(f)	16–43, 16–44
165(a)	7–6
165(c)(3)	5–11
165(g)	5–5
165(g)(1)	8–7
165(h)	5–9
165(h)(4)(E)	5–10
165(i)	6–9
166(a)	5–3
167	7–19, 8–31
168	7–19, 8–31
168(b)	4–25, 4–26
168(b)(5)	4–27
168(c)	4–26
168(d)(3)	4–25
168(d)(4)(A)	4–25
168(e)	4–24, 4–26
168(e)(2)(A)	8–35
168(g)	4–32
168(g)(2)	10–5
170	4–15, 15–44
170(b)	4–17
170(c)	4–15, 15–45
170(d)	4–17, 15–47
170(e)(1)(A)	4–47, 8–41
170(e)(1)(B)	8–41
170(e)(3)	4–17
170(e)(4)	4–17
170(f)(8)	15–46
170(i)	15–45

I.R.C. Sec.	This Work Page
170(j)	15–45
170(l)	15–45
171(c)	7–5
172	5–13, 6–9
174	13–9
174(b)(2)	4–19
179	4–1, 4–28, 4–29, 4–31, 4–45, 4–46, 4–47, 4–48, 7–19, 8–31, 8–33, 8–37, 9–28, 9–32, 10–5, 10–26, 11–6, 11–13, 11–15, 11–17, 11–20, 11–49, 12–12, 16–21, 16–25, 16–56
179(b)	4–28
179(d)	4–28
183	12–33, 16–49
183(b)(2)	16–48
183(d)	16–49
195	4–12, 9–26, 11–16
197	4–33, 7–9, 8–31, 8–37, 14–19
197(a)	4–33
211	2–6
212	4–14, 15–34, 15–49, 16–35
212(1)	2–6
213D	15–35
215	15–27
217	16–16, 16–18
217(a)	16–25
217(b)	16–26
241	2–6
241–250	12–32
243(a)	9–24
243(b)	10–28
246(b)(2)	9–24
248	9–25, 9–26, 9–27, 9–48, 9–49, 12–32
262	8–14, 15–49
263A	6–27, 11–49
263(a)(1)	4–10
263(c)	8–42
265	4–14
265(a)(2)	15–44
267	2–27, 4–13, 4–44, 7–15, 8–14, 10–4
267(a)	2–21, 2–27, 2–29
267(a)(1)	2–20, 4–12, 7–6
267(a)(2)	11–33
267(b)	2–20, 2–21, 6–18, 7–23, 12–33
267(b)(2)	2–20, 2–29
267(c)	2–21
267(c)(2)	2–27, 2–29
267(c)(4)	2–21, 2–29
269A	14–17
269A(b)(2)	5–23
274	4–32
274(a)(1)(A)	16–31
274(a)(3)	16–32
274(b)(1)	16–33
274(c)	16–24
274(d)	4–32, 16–36, 16–59
274(e)(2)	16–30
274(e)(4)	16–31
274(e)(9)	16–30
274(h)(1)	16–22
274(i)	4–32
274(j)	15–29
274(k)	16–32
274(l)	16–32
274(m)(2)	16–23
274(m)(3)	16–23
274(n)	16–30
274(n)(2)	16–30
275	15–38
276	4–9
280A through 280H	2–6
280A(c)(1)	16–33
280C(c)	13–9
280E	4–9
280F	4–29
280F(a)(2)	4–30
280F(b)(2)	4–31
280F(b)(3)	4–32
280F(b)(4)	4–30
280F(d)(1)	4–31
280F(d)(4)	4–30
280F(d)(5)	4–30
280H	6–6
291	8–36, 8–37, 8–38, 8–39
291(a)(1)	8–36, 8–37
301	10–11
301(c)	10–3
302	14–8, 14–16
305	10–18, 10–19
305(a)	7–10
307(a)	7–10, 10–19
307(b)(1)	10–20
311	10–12
311(b)	12–20, 12–22, 14–16
311(b)(2)	10–13
312	10–3, 10–4
312(a)	10–13
312(b)	10–13
312(c)	10–13
312(d)(1)	10–19
312(f)(1)	10–5
312(k)(3)(A)	10–5
312(k)(3)(B)	10–5
312(n)(2)	10–6
312(n)(5)	10–5
316	10–2
318(a)	6–18
331	14–16
332	8–41
336	14–16
341(e)	2–23

I.R.C. Sec.	This Work Page
351	2–8, 6–19, 7–32, 8–41, 9–8, 9–9, 9–10, 9–11, 9–12, 9–13, 9–14, 9–15, 9–17, 9–18, 9–19, 9–20, 9–46, 9–48, 9–53, 11–12, 11–31, 12–21, 14–4, 14–14, 14–22, 14–24, 14–25, 14–27
351(a)	9–12, 9–17, 9–18, 9–20
351(b)	9–9, 9–11
351(b)(2)	9–17
357	9–15
357(a)	9–15
357(b)	9–15, 9–17
357(c)	9–15, 9–16, 9–17, 9–47
357(c)(2)(A)	9–17
358(a)	9–9, 9–18
362(a)	9–9, 9–18
362(c)	9–22
368(a)(1)(E)	3–28
368(c)	9–11
385	9–22, 9–23, 14–11
385(a)	2–25
401(c)(2)	16–44
401(c)(2)(A)(v)	16–44
401(k)	16–45
408(p)	16–45
414(q)	16–16
415(b)(1)	16–44
415(c)(1)	16–44
441(f)	6–3
441(g)	6–2
441(i)	6–6
442	6–7
443(b)(1)	6–8
443(b)(2)	6–8
444(b)(1)	6–5, 6–6
444(c)	6–5
444(c)(1)	6–5
444(c)(2)	6–6
446(a)	4–5
446(b)	3–7, 3–13, 4–5, 6–9
446(d)	6–9
446(e)	3–8, 4–5
446(f)	6–11
448(a)	3–9, 6–10
448(b)	3–9
448(b)(3)	6–10
448(d)(2)	5–23
451(d)	6–9
453	3–7
453A	6–20
453(a)	6–13
453B(a)	6–19
453B(c)	6–19
453B(d)	6–19
453B(f)(2)	6–19
453B(g)	6–19

I.R.C. Sec.	This Work Page
453(d)	6–20
453(d)(3)	6–21
453(e)	6–17
453(e)(2)(B)	6–18
453(f)(1)	6–18
453(g)	6–19
453(i)	6–13, 8–42
453(k)(2)(A)	6–13
453(l)	6–13
460	3–7, 6–23
460(b)(1)(A)	6–25
460(b)(2)	6–25
460(b)(5)	6–25
460(b)(6)	6–25
460(f)	6–21
461(g)(1)	15–44
461(g)(2)	15–43
461(h)	4–6
461(h)(3)(A)	4–7
465	11–28
465(a)	11–30
465(a)(2)	11–31
465(b)(1)	5–17
465(b)(6)	5–18, 11–30, 14–17
465(e)	5–18
469	5–19, 5–26, 5–28, 5–30, 11–28, 12–26, 14–17, 16–39
469(a)	5–23
469(b)	5–22
469(c)(2)	5–30
469(c)(7)	5–34
469(c)(7)(A)	5–45
469(c)(7)(B)	5–34
469(d)(2)	5–22
469(f)	5–23
469(i)	5–34
469(i)(6)	5–34
469(j)(2)	5–23
469(j)(5)	5–35
469(j)(6)	5–36
469(j)(8)	5–30
471	6–26
471(a)	6–26
471(b)	6–29
472(c)	6–31
472(d)	6–31
481(b)	6–12
482	9–32
483	6–16, 6–18
483(e)	6–18
501	4–15
509	4–17
531	14–8, 14–12
531–537	10–21
541–547	10–21

I.R.C. Sec.	This Work Page
611(a)	4–35
612	4–35
613A(c)	13–16
613(a)	4–36
616(a)	13–20
617(a)	13–20
631	8–26
701	11–5, 14–16
702	11–5, 14–16
702(a)	11–17
702(b)	11–18
703	2–3
703(a)(1)	11–6
703(a)(2)	12–12
703(b)	11–15
704	11–37
704(a)	11–7
704(b)	11–7, 11–21, 11–22, 11–38, 11–43
704(c)	11–26, 11–27, 11–37
704(c)(1)(A)	11–22, 11–48
704(d)	11–28
705	11–23, 14–15
706(b)(1)(B)	6–3
706(b)(1)(C)	6–5
706(b)(3)	6–3
707	2–27, 7–15, 11–11
707(a)	11–33
707(a)(2)(B)	11–11
707(b)	11–34
707(b)(2)	11–34
707(c)	11–32
708(a)	2–38
708(b)(1)(B)	14–21
709(a)	11–16
709(b)(1)	11–16
709(b)(2)	11–15
721	7–32, 8–41, 11–9, 11–10, 11–11, 11–12, 11–31, 14–4, 14–14, 14–20, 14–24
721(b)	11–10
723	11–12
724	11–13
724(c)	11–13
724(d)(2)	11–13
731	11–11
736	11–37
751	14–28
752	11–23, 11–38, 14–15
752(a)	12–23
754	11–15, 14–21
761(a)	11–4
901–908	13–11
911	16–39
1001(a)	7–3, 11–9
1001(b)	7–3
1001(c)	7–6, 11–9

I.R.C. Sec.	This Work Page
1011	7–13
1011(a)	7–4
1012	7–8
1014(a)	7–13
1014(e)	7–15
1015(a)	7–10
1015(d)(6)	7–12
1016(a)	7–4
1016(a)(2)	7–5
1016(a)(4)	7–5
1016(a)(5)	7–5
1017	3–26
1031	7–7, 7–8, 7–21, 7–22, 7–23, 7–24, 7–25, 7–30, 7–33, 8–41, 9–8, 9–9, 9–15, 11–12
1031(a)	7–21
1031(a)(3)	7–24
1032	7–32, 9–19
1033	7–7, 7–28, 7–29, 8–25, 8–27, 8–41
1033(a)	7–29, 7–30
1033(a)(2)(B)	7–31
1033(b)(2)	7–28
1033(g)(4)	7–31
1035	7–33
1036	7–33
1038	7–33
1041	6–18, 7–34, 15–27
1044	7–33
1045(a)	8–23
1056	8–12
1060	7–9
1091	2–27, 7–15
1091(a)	2–29, 7–15
1091(b)	7–16
1091(d)	7–16
1201	8–24
1202	7–7
1202(a)	8–23
1211(b)	8–16
1211(b)(1)	8–20
1212(a)(1)	8–24
1221	3–29, 8–4, 8–7
1221(1)	2–6
1221(2)	8–24
1221(3)	4–47
1222	8–13
1223	8–13
1223(1)	7–26, 9–20
1223(2)	7–12, 9–20
1223(4)	7–16
1223(5)	7–10, 10–19
1223(11)	7–15
1231	4–11, 7–26, 8–1, 8–2, 8–3, 8–5, 8–14, 8–24, 8–25, 8–26, 8–27, 8–28, 8–29, 8–30, 8–31, 8–32, 8–33, 8–34, 8–35, 8–36, 8–37, 8–38, 8–39, 8–40, 8–41, 8–42, 8–43,

I.R.C. Sec.	This Work Page
1231 (continued)	8–46, 8–47, 9–20, 11–10, 11–13, 11–14, 11–17, 11–43, 12–12, 12–25, 12–35, 12–37, 12–38, 14–19, 14–20, 14–28
1231(b)(1)	8–28
1231(c)	8–29
1233	8–15
1234A	8–7
1234(a)	8–8
1234(b)(1)	8–8
1235	8–10
1236(a)	8–6
1236(b)	8–6
1237	8–6, 8–7, 8–44
1239	8–42
1239(b)	6–19
1239(c)	6–19
1241	8–13
1244	5–1, 5–5, 5–6, 5–38, 8–2, 8–7, 12–5, 12–33, 12–40, 14–5, 14–28, 14–29
1245	8–2, 8–11, 8–12, 8–26, 8–29, 8–30, 8–31, 8–32, 8–33, 8–34, 8–36, 8–37, 8–38, 8–39, 8–40, 8–41, 8–42, 8–43, 8–48, 8–49, 9–20, 12–35, 12–36, 12–37, 12–38, 14–19, 14–20, 14–36, 14–37
1245(b)(1)	8–40
1245(b)(2)	8–40
1245(b)(3)	8–41, 9–20
1250	8–2, 8–18, 8–19, 8–20, 8–21, 8–26, 8–30, 8–32, 8–33, 8–34, 8–35, 8–36, 8–37, 8–38, 8–39, 8–40, 8–41, 8–42, 8–43, 14–19, 14–20
1250(a)(1)	8–36
1250(a)(1)(B)	8–36
1250(a)(2)	8–36
1250(d)(1)	8–40
1250(d)(2)	8–40
1250(d)(3)	8–41, 9–20
1253	8–11, 8–12
1253(b)(1)	8–11
1253(e)	8–12
1254	8–43
1259	8–15
1271	8–8
1272(a)	6–16
1272(a)(2)	3–12
1272(a)(3)	3–12, 6–18
1273(a)	3–12, 6–16
1274	6–16
1274A	6–18
1274(a)	6–16, 6–18
1274A(c)	6–18
1274(c)(3)(A)	6–18
1274(c)(3)(B)	6–18
1274(c)(3)(C)	6–18
1274(c)(3)(F)	6–18
1274(d)(1)	6–16

I.R.C. Sec.	This Work Page
1341	6–9
1341(a)	6–9
1341(a)(5)	10–28
1361	12–35, 14–3, 14–12
1361–1379	2–6, 12–2
1361(b)(1)(B)	12–7
1361(b)(1)(D)	12–5, 12–41
1361(b)(2)	12–5
1361(c)(1)	12–6
1361(c)(4)	12–5
1361(c)(5)(A)	12–6
1362	14–3
1362(a)(2)	12–8
1362(b)	12–7
1362(b)(1)(C)	12–7
1362(b)(2)(B)(ii)	12–9
1362(d)(1)	12–10
1362(d)(2)(B)	12–10
1362(d)(3)(A)(ii)	12–11
1362(d)(3)(D)(i)	12–32
1362(e)(3)	12–10
1363	14–16
1363(d)	12–12
1366	14–16
1366(a)	12–12
1366(a)(1)	12–14, 12–33
1366(b)	12–12
1366(c)	12–12
1366(d)	12–26
1366(d)(1)(A)	12–23
1366(e)	12–16, 12–32, 14–18
1366(f)(2)	12–29
1367(a)	12–22
1367(b)(2)	12–23
1368(a)(1)(A)	12–24
1368(c)	12–17, 12–18
1368(c)(1)	12–17
1368(d)(1)	12–23
1368(e)(1)	12–17
1368(e)(1)(A)	12–18, 12–24
1368(e)(3)	12–18, 12–37
1371(a)(1)	2–38
1371(e)	12–20
1374	12–28, 12–29, 12–30, 12–38, 12–39
1374(c)(2)	12–29
1374(d)(1)	12–29
1374(d)(4)	12–32
1374(d)(7)	12–30
1375(a)	12–32
1375(b)	12–32
1377(a)	14–18
1377(a)(1)	12–14
1377(a)(2)	12–15
1377(b)	12–20, 12–26
1378(a)	6–4

I.R.C. Sec.	This Work Page	I.R.C. Sec.	This Work Page
1378(b)	6–4	6654(b)(3)	16–47
1378(b)(2)	6–5	6654(c)(1)	16–47
1402(a)	11–6, 11–34, 16–44	6655(d)	9–33
1402(a)(12)	16–43	6655(e)	9–33
1561	9–32	6662	2–8, 2–11, 2–27
1561(a)	9–28	6662(a)	2–25
1563	9–32	6662(b)(1)	2–25, 16–59
1563(a)(1)	9–29	6662(c)	2–25
1563(a)(2)	9–29	6698	11–20
2032(a)(1)	7–14	7519	6–5
2032(c)	7–14	7519(b)	6–5
2503(a)	2–38	7701(a)(2)	11–3
3402	15–17	7702B	16–7
4942	4–17	7703(a)(1)	15–72
6001	16–59	7704	11–4
6012(a)(1)	15–21	7805	2–7
6012(a)(2)	9–32	7805(a)	2–9
6017	16–42	7805(e)	2–9
6072(a)	15–22	7852(d)	2–7
6081	9–33	7872	9–53, 10–15
6110	2–10	7872(a)(1)	3–18
6222	11–19	7872(b)(2)	3–18
6231(a)(1)(B)	11–20	7872(c)	3–19
6621	6–20	7872(c)(2)	3–20
6654	15–17	7872(c)(3)	3–20
6654(b)(2)	16–47	7872(d)	3–20
		7872(f)(2)	3–18

APPENDIX D–2
Table of Regulations Cited

Temporary Treasury Regulations

Temp.Reg. Sec.	This Work Page
1.338(b)–1T	7–9
1.441–1T(b)(3)	6–6
1.441–1T(b)(4)	6–6
1.441–1T(e)(2)	6–3
1.469–1T(e)(3)(ii)	5–30
1.469–1T(e)(3)(vi)(B)–(E)	5–31
1.469–5T(a)	5–26, 12–27
1.469–5T(b)(2)	5–28
1.469–5T(e)(3)(ii)	5–29
1.469–5T(f)(3)	5–29
1.706–1T(a)(2)	6–4
1.1275–7T	3–12
15A.453–1(b)(2)(iii)	6–14
15A.453–1(c)(2)(i)	6–15
15A.453–1(c)(3)(i)	6–15
15A.453–1(c)(4)	6–15
15A.453–1(d)	6–20
15A.453–1(d)(4)	6–21
18.1362–1(a)	12–41
18.1362–2(e)	12–8

Treasury Regulations

Reg. Sec.	This Work Page
1.2	2–7, 2–8
1.61–1(a)	3–6
1.61–2(d)(2)(i)	7–8
1.61–2T(j)	16–17
1.61–3(a)	4–9
1.61–6(a)	7–6, 7–9
1.61–9(c)	3–16
1.61–12	3–6
1.62–2(c)(4)	10–18
1.65(g)–1(f)	13–25
1.67–1T(a)(1)(iv)	16–49
1.79–3(d)(2)	16–10
1.106–1	16–6
1.117–2(a)	15–30
1.117–6(b)(2)	15–31

Treasury Regulations

Reg. Sec.	This Work Page
1.117–6(c)(3)(i)	15–30
1.117–6(d)	16–11
1.117–6(h)	15–31
1.118–1	9–21, 9–22
1.119–1(c)(1)	16–8
1.119–1(f)	16–8
1.132–1(b)	16–14
1.132–2	16–13
1.151–3(a)	15–13
1.151–3(b)	15–13
1.151–3(c)	15–13
1.152–1(c)	15–10
1.162–2(b)(1)	16–24
1.162–5(b)(2)	16–28
1.162–5(b)(2)(iii)	16–28
1.162–5(b)(3)	16–28
1.162–5(b)(3)(ii)	16–28
1.162–8	4–4
1.162–10	10–18
1.162–17(b)(4)	16–36
1.165–1(a)	7–6
1.165–1(d)(2)	5–8, 5–9
1.165–7(a)(2)(ii)	5–11
1.165–8(a)(2)	5–8
1.165–8(d)	5–8
1.165–9(b)(2)	7–16
1.166	5–3
1.166–1(e)	5–2
1.167(g)–1	7–13, 7–17
1.170A–4(b)(1)	8–41
1.170A–4A(b)(2)(ii)(C)	2–38
1.174–2(a)(1)	4–18
1.183–1(b)(1)	16–49
1.183–2(b)(1) through (9)	16–48
1.212–1(f)	16–28
1.248–1(a)(3)	9–25
1.263A–1(a)	6–27
1.263A–1(b)(12)	6–27
1.263A–1(h)(5)	6–27
1.263(a)–1(b)	4–10
1.267(b)–1(b)(1)	2–27

Treasury Regulations

Reg. Sec.	This Work Page
1.274–4	16–24
1.274–5T(c)(3)	16–36
1.280F–6T(e)	4–30
1.280F–7T(a)	4–32
1.301–1(j)	7–8, 10–14
1.301–1(m)	10–15
1.305–1(b)	10–20
1.305–3(d)	10–19
1.307–1(a)	7–10
1.307–2	10–20
1.312–6	10–4
1.316–2	10–6
1.351–1	9–12
1.351–1(a)(1)(ii)	9–11, 9–13
1.351–1(a)(2)	2–7, 9–13
1.362–2(b)	9–22
1.442–1(b)(1)	6–7
1.442–1(c)(1)	6–7
1.443–1(a)(2)	6–8
1.446–1(a)(1)	6–10
1.446–1(a)(2)	4–5
1.446–1(a)(3)	3–8
1.446–1(a)(4)(i)	6–9
1.446–1(c)(1)(i)	3–8
1.446–1(c)(2)(i)	3–7
1.446–1(e)(2)(ii)	6–10
1.446–1(e)(2)(ii)(b)	6–11
1.451–1(a)	3–9
1.451–2	3–8
1.451–2(a)	3–11
1.451–2(b)	3–11
1.451–3(b)	6–21
1.451–3(b)(2)	6–24
1.451–3(c)(3)	6–25
1.451–3(d)(2)(ii)–(vii)	6–24
1.451–3(d)(9)	6–21
1.451–5	6–24
1.451–5(b)	3–13
1.451–5(c)	3–13
1.453–9(c)(2)	9–10
1.461–1(a)	4–5
1.469–1T(g)(3)	5–29, 5–30
1.469–2T(d)(6)	12–28
1.469–4	5–24
1.469–4(c)(3)	5–24
1.469–4(d)	5–24
1.469–4(f)	5–25
1.469–9	5–34
1.469–9(e)	5–45
1.471–1	6–26
1.471–2	6–26
1.471–2(c)	6–28
1.471–3(b)	6–27
1.471–4(b)	6–26

Reg. Sec.	This Work Page
1.471–4(c)	6–28
1.472–2(c)	6–31
1.472–2(e)	6–31
1.472–3(a)	6–30
1.472–4	6–28
1.472–5	6–30
1.472–8	6–30
1.482–1(d)(4)	9–53
1.482–2(a)(1)	9–53
1.611–1(b)	4–34
1.672(b)–1	2–38
1.701–2	11–9
1.704–1	11–50
1.704–1(b)	11–21
1.704–2	11–50
1.704–3	11–21
1.706–1(a)	6–3
1.731–1(c)(3)	11–10
1.752–1(e)	12–23
1.1001–1(a)	7–3
1.1001–1(b)	7–3
1.1001–1(b)(2)	7–4
1.1001–1(c)(1)	7–3
1.1001–2(a)	3–25
1.1002–1(a)	7–6
1.1002–1(c)	7–18
1.1011–1	7–4, 7–13
1.1012–1(a)	7–8
1.1012–1(b)	7–4
1.1012–1(c)	7–41
1.1012–1(c)(1)	7–8
1.1015–1(a)(1)	7–10
1.1015–1(a)(3)	7–10
1.1016–1	7–4
1.1016–3(a)(1)(i)	7–5
1.1016–5(a)	7–5
1.1016–5(b)	7–5
1.1016–6(a)	7–5
1.1031(a)–1(a)	7–21
1.1031(a)–1(b)	7–22
1.1031(d)–2	7–27
1.1031(j)–1	7–23
1.1032–1(a)	9–19
1.1033(a)–1	7–30
1.1033(a)–1(a)	7–29
1.1033(a)–2(a)	7–29
1.1033(a)–2(c)(3)	7–31
1.1091–1(a)	7–15
1.1091–1(c)	7–16
1.1091–1(f)	7–15
1.1091–2(a)	7–16
1.1221–1(b)	8–13
1.1223–1(a)	7–26
1.1223–1(b)	7–12

Table of Regulations Cited

Treasury Regulations

Reg. Sec.	This Work Page
1.1223–1(d)	7–16
1.1223–1(e)	7–10
1.1234–1(a)(1)	8–8
1.1235–2(b)(1)	8–10
1.1236–1(a)	8–6
1.1241–1(a)	8–13
1.1245–2(a)(4)	7–26, 8–41
1.1245–2(c)(2)	8–41
1.1245–4(a)(1)	8–40
1.1245–4(c)	8–41
1.1250–1(d)(1)(i)(c)	8–36
1.1250–2(d)(1)	7–26, 8–41
1.1250–2(d)(3)	8–41
1.1250–3(a)(1)	8–40
1.1250–3(c)	8–41
1.1361–1(l)(2)	12–5
1.1361–1(l)(2)(i)	12–41
1.1361–1(l)(4)	12–6
1.1367–1(b)(2)	12–25
1.1367–1(c)(3)	12–25
1.1372–2(b)(1)	12–8
1.1373–1(a)	12–16

Treasury Regulations

Reg. Sec.	This Work Page
1.1373–1(a)(2)	12–32
1.1377–1(a)(2)(ii)	12–14
1.1563–1(a)(2)	9–30
1.1563–1(a)(3)	9–31
1.6013–4(a)(1)	15–72
1.6081–4	15–22
1.6661–3(b)(2)	2–26
1.7872–2(b)(1)(i)	3–20
20.2031–7(f)	2–38
31.3401(c)–(1)(b)	16–3
170A–10	15–47
301.6114–1	2–7
301.6712–1	2–7
301.7701	9–5
301.7701–1	9–6, 11–4, 14–3
301.7701–2	9–6, 11–4, 14–3
301.7701–2(b)	9–6
301.7701–2(b)(8)	9–6
301.7701–3	9–6, 11–4, 14–3
301.7701–3(c)	9–7
301.7701–3(f)(2)	9–7
301.7701–4	9–6, 14–3
301.7701–6	9–6, 14–3

Appendix D-3
Table of Revenue Procedures and Revenue Rulings Cited

Revenue Procedure

Rev.Proc.	This Work Page
69–21	9–37
71–21	3–14, 3–37
77–37	2–37, 9–14
84–74	6–30
85–16	6–7
87–32	6–5, 6–7
87–56	2–34, 4–24, 10–5, 13–19
87–57	4–39, 4–41, 4–42, 7–22
92–71	4–14
92–89	2–39
94–73	15–36
96–31	2–38
97–21	6–10
97–27	6–12
97–58	16–20
98–3	2–10

Revenue Rulings

Rev.Rul.	This Work Page
48	2–10
54–96	9–12
55–261	15–36
56–60	7–14
56–406	7–15
57–344	15–10
57–418	4–11
58–419	15–10
59–44	2–27, 2–29
59–86	7–12
59–221	12–33
60–183	12–8
61	3–4
62–217	9–19
63–221	7–29
63–232	5–8
64–56	9–10
64–162	12–23
65–235	2–34
66–7	8–13
67–297	15–43
68–55	9–9

Revenue Rulings

Rev.Rul.	This Work Page
68–212	15–36
68–537	12–24
68–662	4–8
69–26	16–4
69–292	16–28
70–50	12–23
70–466	7–31
71–190	15–39
72–312	3–15
72–592	5–7
74–44	12–16
74–78	16–28
74–164	2–37
74–503	9–19
75–14	16–49
75–168	16–21
75–380	16–19
75–448	15–31
78–39	4–5
78–325	2–38
79–379	3–17
80	16–8
80–52	3–11
80–335	4–5
81–180	7–29
81–181	7–29
82–74	7–29
82–196	16–6
82–202	3–26
82–208	15–39
82–227	6–20
83–98	14–11
85–161	12–12
87–22	15–43
87–57	6–5, 6–7
90–23	16–20
91–31	3–36
94–24	16–34
94–47	16–20
96–48	2–10
98–4	13–10
190	16–20

Appendix E
Table of Cases Cited

A

Allen, Mary Francis, 5–8
American Automobile Association v. U.S., 3–13
Anderson v. Comm., 16–8
Ansley-Sheppard-Burgess Company, 6–23
Anton, M. G., 3–16
Armantrout, Richard T., 15–31
Armstrong v. Phinney, 16–8
Artnell Company v. Comm., 3–13
Artukovich, Nick A., 12–8
Augustus v. Comm., 2–24
Austin, Laura E., 6–10

B

Baist, George A., 16–29
Balistrieri, Joseph P., 7–29
Bauer v. Comm., 9–23, 14–11
Bedell v. Comm., 3–8
Bhalla, C. P., 15–30
Bingler v. Johnson, 15–30
Boise Cascade Corp. v. U.S., 3–13
Bonaire Development Co. v. Comm., 4–6
Brown v. Helvering, 3–9
Brown, Frederick G., v. U.S., 12–25
Burnet v. Sanford and Brooks, 3–9

C

Calcutt, James K., 12–23
Campbell, Jr. v. Wheeler, 9–15
Carr, Jack D., 2–17
Caruth Corporation v. U.S., 3–16
Catto v. U.S., 2–39
Cesarini v. U.S., 3–4
Chicago Stadium Corporation v. U.S., 10–16
Clark v. Comm., 2–39
Cohan v. Comm., 16–59
Comm. v. (see opposing party)
Commissioner v. Newman, 1–20
Consolidated-Hammer Dry Plate & Film Co. v. Comm., 3–13
Correll v. U.S., 16–21
Cowden v. Comm., 3–11
Crane v. Comm., 7–3

D

Daly, D. R., Estate of, 3–23, 15–29
Davidson, Collin J., 16–28
Davis v. U.S., 7–4, 15–27
De Mendoza, Mario G., III, 12–33
Delman, Estate of, v. Comm., 3–25
Delp, F. S., 15–36
Deputy v. DuPont, 4–3
DiZenzo v. Comm., 10–16
Doak v. Comm., 16–8
Duberstein v. Comm., 15–30, 15–45
Dunn and McCarthy, Inc. v. Comm., 4–3

E

Easson v. Comm., 9–16
Edwards v. Cuba Railroad Co., 9–21
Eisner v. Macomber, 3–5, 10–18
Estate of (see name of party)

F

F. W. Woolworth Co., 2–9
Fahs v. Florida Machine and Foundry Co., 9–13
Fausner v. Comm., 16–19
Fay v. Helvering, 5–7
Fin Hay Realty Co. v. U.S., 9–23, 10–15
Fischer, L. M., 3–11
Flint v. Stone Tracy Co., 1–14
Foxman v. Comm, 2–39
Frank, Morton, 4–11

G

Galt v. Comm., 3–15
Glenshaw Glass Co. v. Comm., 3–4
Golsen, Jack E., 2–14
Guenther, Kenneth W., 16–31

H

Harolds Club v. Comm., 14–11
Hawkins, C. A., 15–32
Heininger v. Comm., 4–3
Helvering v. Bruun, 3–23
Helvering v. Horst, 3–15

Hempt Brothers, Inc. v. U.S., 9–10
Hertwig v. U.S., 9–17
Hillsboro National Bank v. Comm., 4–6
Hort v. Comm., 8–13
Houston, Michael J., 12–33

I

Indianapolis Power & Light Co., v. Comm., 3–13

J

J. P. Sheahan Associates, 6–23
Jacobson v. Comm., 3–26
James v. U.S., 3–3

K

Kahler, Charles F., 3–8
Keller v. Comm., 4–6
Kennedy, Jr. v. Comm., 4–4
Kieselbach v. Comm., 3–22
Kinter v. U.S., 9–5
Kirby Lumber Co. v. U.S., 3–6, 3–25
Kluger Associates, Inc., 7–8
Knott, Henry J., 10–18
Korn Industries v. U.S., 2–39, 6–11
Kowalski v. Comm., 16–8

L

Landfield Finance Co. v. U.S., 3–24
Larson, P.G., 9–6
Leavitt, Estate of, 12–23
Lee, Harold K., 15–72
Lengsfield v. Comm., 10–14
Lincoln Electric Co. v. Comm., 4–3
Lindeman, J. B., 16–8
Loco Realty Co. v. Comm., 7–31
Lucas v. Earl, 3–14
Lucas v. North Texas Lumber Co., 3–9
Lynch v. Turrish, 7–3

M

Magnon, Raymond, 6–23
Malat v. Riddell, 8–4
Mantell, John, 3–12
Marshman v. Comm., 7–4
Mayson Manufacturing Co. v. Comm., 10–15, 14–11
McCandless Tile Service v. U.S., 10–18
McWilliams v. Comm., 7–15
Merchants Loan and Trust Co. v. Smietanka, 3–4
Miller v. Comm., 2–39
Miller, Harris M., 2–9
Mitnick, Moses, 16–22
Mixon, Estate of v. U.S., 9–23
Montgomery Engineering Co. v. U.S., 10–15
Morrissey v. Comm., 9–5
Mulherin, Brian C., 16–29

N

Nico, Severino R., Jr., 2–26
North American Consolidated Oil Co. v. Burnet, 6–9
North American Oil Consolidated Co. v. Burnet, 3–9
Norwest Corporation, 9–37

O

O'Connor, John C., 9–13
O'Malley v. Ames, 7–4

P

Page v. Rhode Island Trust Co., 4–5
Papineau, G. A., 16–8
Peacock, Cassius L., III, 15–13
Pestcoe, William, 12–8
Pollock v. Farmer's Loan & Trust Co., 1–13, 3–22
Portage Plastics Co. v. U.S., 12–12
Prashker, Ruth M., 12–25

R

R. J. Nicoll Co., 10–17
Radtke v. U.S., 12–16
Riach v. Frank, 15–36
Robertson v. U.S., 15–30
Rogers v. U.S., 5–7
Rosenberg v. Comm., 5–8
Rowan Companies, Inc. v. U.S., 16–7

S

Sanford, William F., 16–59
Sargent v. Comm., 3–15
Sauvigne, Donald J., 12–24
Schalk Chemical Co. v. Comm., 10–18
Schlude v. Comm., 3–13
Selfe v. U.S., 12–23
Shackelford, Betty J., 15–72
Sherman, Stephen G., 16–29
Shopmaker v. U.S., 5–8
Simon v. Comm., 10–16
Simons-Eastern Co. v. U.S., 2–18
Slappey Drive Industrial Park v. U.S., 9–23
Smith, Joe M., 12–23
Snow v. Comm., 4–19
Soliman v. Comm., 16–33
Solomon, S. L., 5–8
South Carolina v. Baker III, 3–22
Spicer Accounting, Inc. v. U.S., 12–16
Springer v. U.S., 1–14
Strauss, Julia A., 3–8
Sullivan v. Comm., 4–9

T

T.H. Campbell & Bros., Inc., 12–8
Tank Truck Rentals, Inc. v. Comm., 4–8

Tauferner v. U.S., 16–19
Teleservice Co. of Wyoming Valley v. Comm., 9–21
Tellier v. Comm., 4–8
Thompson Electric Inc., 6–23
Thor Power Tool Co. v. Comm., 3–6, 6–26
Tomerlin, James O., Trust, 2–9
Tomlinson v. 1661 Corp., 9–23
Tougher v. Comm., 16–8
Tufts v. Comm., 7–3
Tyler, W. David, 16–37

U

U.S. Trust Co. of New York v. Anderson, 3–22
United States v. (see opposing party)

V

Veenstra & DeHavaan Coal Co., 3–13
Vogel Fertilizer Co. v. U.S., 9–31

W

Ward v. U.S., 12–7
Ward, Dwight A., 4–11
Washington, Alexander, 15–27
Waterman Steamship Corporation v. Comm., 10–28
Welch v. Helvering, 4–2, 4–3
Whitaker, William T., 16–37
Wilgard Realty Co. v. Comm., 9–12
Wilson, William B., 12–9
Wisconsin Cheeseman, Inc. v. U.S., 4–15

Y

York v. Comm., 4–11

Z

Zaninovich v. Comm., 4–6
Zuckman v. U.S., 9–6

INDEX

A

Abandoned spouse rules, **15:**25–26
Accelerated cost recovery system (ACRS), **4:**21
See also Modified accelerated cost recovery system (MACRS)
ACCESS, **2:**29
Accident and health insurance benefits, **15:**33
Accident and health insurance plans, **16:**5-6
Accountable plan for employee expense reimbursement, **16:**3, **16:**36–37
Accounting
 financial, **6:**26
 tax, **6:**26
Accounting income, **3:**4–5
Accounting methods, **3:**7–10
 change of, **6:**9–10
  change from incorrect method, **6:**11
  correction of an error, **6:**10–11
  net adjustments due to change, **6:**11–12
 for proprietorships, **16:**46
 See also Accrual method of accounting; Cash receipts method of accounting; Hybrid method of accounting; Installment method of accounting; Long-term contracts
Accounting periods, **6:**2–3
 business purpose, **6:**5
 changes in, **6:**7
  IRS requirements, **6:**7
 making the election, **6:**6
 mitigation of annual accounting period concept, **6:**8–9
  restoration of amounts received under a claim of right, **6:**9
 partnerships and S corporations, **6:**3–5
 personal service corporations, **6:**6
 proprietorships, **16:**46
 required tax payments, **6:**5–6
 taxable periods of less than one year, **6:**7–8
Accounts and notes receivable, **8:**4–5
Accrual method of accounting, **3:**9–10, **6:**9–10
 deferral of advance payments for goods, **3:**13
 deferral of advance payments for services, **3:**14
 prepaid income, **3:**13
 timing of expense recognition, **4:**6–7

Accumulated adjustments account (AAA), **12:**17–19, **12:**20
Accumulated earnings and profits (AEP), **10:**6, **10:**7–11
 in S corporation, **12:**16–18, **12:**20
Accumulated earnings tax, **10:**21
Acquiescence, **2:**17
Act of God, **5:**7
Actions on Decisions, **2:**17, **2:**25
Active income, **5:**18–19
Active participation, **5:**34–35
Ad valorem taxes, **1:**10–12
Additional depreciation, **8:**34
Additional standard deduction, **15:**6, **15:**7
Adjusted basis, **7:**4
Adjusted current earnings (ACE), **13:**15, **13:**23–25, **13:**26
Adjusted gross income (AGI), **15:**5–6
 deductions for, **8:**27, **15:**5
 deductions from, **8:**27
 See also Gross income; Income
Adoption tax credit, **15:**52–53
Age test, for earned income credit, **15:**57
Agent, income received by, **3:**17
Aggregate (conduit) concept of partnership taxation, **11:**8
Alimony recapture, **15:**28
Alimony and separate maintenance payments, **15:**26–27
 child support, **15:**28
 front-loading, **15:**28
 post-1984 agreements and decrees, **15:**27–28
All events test, **4:**6
Allocable parent tax, **15:**19
Alternate valuation amount, **7:**13–14
Alternative depreciation system (ADS), **4:**32–33, **13:**19
Alternative minimum tax (AMT)
 AMT adjustments, computing, **13:**18
 corporate, **13:**13–15
  adjusted current earnings (ACE), **13:**23–25, **13:**26
  AMT adjustments, **13:**17–18
   adjusted gain or loss, **13:**21
   completed contract method of accounting, **13:**20
   computing, **13:**18
   depreciation of post-1986 personal property, **13:**19
   depreciation of post-1986 real property, **13:**18–19
   mining exploration and development expenditures, **13:**20
   passive activity losses, **13:**21–23
   pollution control facilities, **13:**20
  AMT formula, **13:**14–15
  exemption, **13:**27
  minimum tax credit, **13:**28
  other aspects, **13:**28
  tax preferences, **13:**16, **13:**23
   intangible drilling costs, **13:**17
   interest on private activity bonds, **13:**17
   percentage depletion, **13:**16–17
 individual, **13:**28–29
 single versus double taxation and, **14:**8–9
Alternative minimum taxable income (AMTI), **13:**14–15, **13:**23–25
 computation of, **13:**25–27
American Federal Tax Reports (AFTR), **2:**17–18
Amortizable bond premium, **7:**5–6
Amortizable Section 197 intangibles, **4:**33
Amortization, **4:**33
Amount realized, **7:**3
Annual accounting period concept, **1:**30–31
 mitigation of, **6:**8–9
Appellant, **2:**26
Appellate courts, **2:**12, **2:**13–16, **2:**17–18
Appellee, **2:**26
Asset depreciation range midpoint lives, **4:**24–25
Assets
 business fixed assets, **8:**5
 depreciable, **11:**16
 expensing of, **4:**28–29
 fixed, **8:**24
 intangible, **4:**33
 nonpersonal-use capital assets, **8:**26–27
 personal-use, **7:**7, **8:**4
  converted to business or income-producing use, **4:**21
 Section 1231 assets, **8:**2–3, **8:**24–30
 transfer of to business entity, **7:**32
 See also Capital assets
Assignment of income, **3:**14–15
Associations, **9:**5
At-risk limitation, **5:**17–18, **5:**19
 forms of doing business and, **14:**17–18
 interaction with passive activity limits, **5:**33
 in partnerships, **11:**30–31

I–1

in S corporations, **12:**27–28
Automatic mileage method of auto expense computation, **16:**20–21
Automobiles
  business and personal use of, **4:**29–30
    change from predominantly business use, **4:**32
    limits on cost recovery, **4:**30–31
    not used predominantly in business, **4:**31
    used predominantly in business, **4:**30
  computation of auto expenses, **16:**21–22
  leased, **4:**32
  passenger, **4:**29, **4:**30
  substantiation requirements, **4:**32
Awards, **15:**28–29
Away-from-home requirement for travel expenses, **16:**21

B

Bad debts, **5:**2
  business versus nonbusiness, **5:**3–4
  loans between related parties, **5:**4–5
  specific charge-off method, **5:**3, **5:**5
Bankruptcy, **3:**26–27
Bargain purchase of property, **7:**8
Basic research, **13:**10
Basic research credit, **13:**10
Basic standard deduction, **15:**6
Basis
  adjusted, **7:**4
  AMT and, **13:**21
  carryover, **7:**10, **9:**10, **11:**12
  conversion of property from personal use to business or income-producing use, **7:**16–18
  for cost recovery purposes, **4:**29
  determination of cost basis, **7:**8
    allocation problems, **7:**9–10
    identification problems, **7:**8
  for determining loss, **7:**17
  disallowed losses, **7:**15–16
  expensing of assets and, **4:**29
  gain basis, **7:**17
  gift basis, **7:**10–13
  inside and outside, **11:**14
  liabilities in excess of, **9:**16–18
  of like-kind property, **7:**25–28
  of ownership interest, **14:**14–15
  of partnership interest, **11:**8, **11:**22–24, **11:**28
  property acquired from a decedent, **7:**13–15
  of property to corporation, **9:**18–19
  shareholder's, in S corporation, **12:**21–24
  stepped-down, **7:**13
  stepped-up, **7:**13
  of stock to shareholder, **9:**18
  substituted, **11:**12
  summary of adjustments to, **7:**18, **7:**19–20
Below-market loans, **3:**19–20
Benefit received rule, **15:**45
Bluebook, **2:**27
Board of Tax Appeals, **2:**17
Boot, **7:**24–25
Bribes, **4:**8

Brother-sister controlled group, **9:**29–31
Built-in gain or loss, **11:**22
Built-in gains (Section 1374) tax, **12:**28–31
Business debt, **5:**3–4
Business deductions, **4:**4, **4:**5
  amortization, **4:**33
  charitable contributions, **4:**15–17
  cost recovery allowances, **4:**21–33, **4:**38–42
  depletion, **4:**34–37
  disallowance possibilities, **4:**7
    disallowance of deductions for capital expenditures, **4:**10–11
    excessive executive compensation, **4:**10
    expenses and interest related to tax-exempt income, **4:**14–15
    investigation of a business, **4:**11–12
    lack of adequate substantiation, **4:**14
    political contributions and lobbying activities, **4:**9–10
    public policy limitations, **4:**7–9
    transactions between related parties, **4:**12–13
  interest expense, **4:**20
  ordinary and necessary requirement, **4:**2–3
  reasonableness requirement, **4:**3–4
  research and experimental expenditures, **4:**18–19
  taxes, **4:**20–21
  timing of expense recognition, **4:**5
    accrual method requirements, **4:**6–7
    cash method requirements, **4:**5–6
Business energy credits, **13:**6–8
Business entertainment. *See* Entertainment expenses
Business entities
  flow-through, **1:**18, **1:**19
  losses in, **9:**4
  proprietorships as, **16:**41–42
  relationship of individuals to, **1:**19–20
  shifting tax liability between, **1:**25
  taxation of, **1:**16–18
  transfer of assets to, **7:**32
Business fixed assets, **8:**5
Business gifts, **16:**33
Business meals, deductibility of, **16:**32
Business trusts, **9:**5, **9:**6–7
Buy-sell agreements, **3:**24

C

C corporations
  closely held, **5:**24
  compared to limited liability companies, **14:**4
  compared to S corporations, **12:**2
  sale of, **14:**21–22
  taxation of, **1:**18
  See also Controlled corporations; Corporations
Cafeteria plans, **16:**12
Calendar year, **3:**7, **6:**2
Capital account, **11:**8
Capital additions, **7:**4
Capital assets, **8:**2, **8:**3–4
  accounts and notes receivable, **8:**4–5
  business fixed assets, **8:**5
  inventory, **8:**4

non-personal use, **8:**26–27
Section 1231 assets compared to, **8:**24–25
statutory expansions, **8:**6
  dealers in securities, **8:**6
  real property subdivided for sale, **8:**6–7
U.S. government publications, **8:**5–6
See also Sale or exchange; Section 1231 assets
Capital contributions, **9:**21–22
Capital expenditures
  disallowance of deductions for, **4:**10–11
  for medical purposes, **15:**36, **15:**38
Capital gain property, **4:**16, **15:**47
Capital gains and losses, **8:**4
  holding period rules for, **8:**13–15
  long-term, **8:**13, **8:**16–18, **8:**19
  mid-term, **8:**17, **8:**19
  netting process, **8:**18–22
  in property transactions, **3:**28–30
  sale or exchange, **8:**7–13
  short-term, **8:**15–16, **8:**18
  tax treatment of
    corporate taxpayers, **8:**24
    noncorporate taxpayers, **8:**15–22
Capital interest, in partnership, **11:**7
Capital recoveries, **7:**4–6
Capital withdrawals, **11:**19
Carryover basis, **7:**10, **9:**10, **11:**12
Cash receipts method of accounting, **3:**8–9, **6:**9–10
  amounts received under an obligation to repay, **3:**12
  constructive receipt, **3:**10–11
  original issue discount, **3:**11–12
  timing of expense recognition, **4:**5–6
Casualties, **7:**5
Casualty gains, **5:**13
Casualty losses, **1:**8–9, **5:**7, **5:**13
  definition of casualty, **5:**7
  events that are not casualties, **5:**7–8
  of individuals, **5:**11
    personal-use property, **5:**11–12
  measuring the amount of loss, **5:**9–10
  multiple losses, **5:**11
  when to deduct, **5:**9
    disaster area losses, **5:**9
  See also Theft losses
Casualty netting, **8:**27
CCH ACCESS tax service, **2:**30, **2:**31
CD-ROM services, **2:**30–31
Ceiling limitation formula, for foreign tax credit, **13:**12–13
Centralized management, **9:**5
Charitable contributions, **4:**15, **15:**44
  benefit received rule, **15:**45
  contribution carryovers, **15:**49
  criteria for a gift, **15:**45
  fifty percent ceiling, **15:**47–48
  limitation on deduction of, **15:**46–47
  limitations imposed on deduction of, **4:**17–18
  nondeductible items, **15:**45
  property contributions, **4:**16–17
  qualified organizations, **15:**45
  record-keeping requirements, **15:**46
  of services, **15:**45
  thirty percent ceiling, **15:**48–49
  time of deduction, **15:**45–46

twenty percent ceiling, **15**:49
valuation requirements, **15**:46
Charitable transfers, recapture rules for, **8**:41
Check-the-box Regulations, **9**:6, **9**:7, **14**:3
Child and dependent care expenses, tax credit for, **15**:54
    calculation of credit, **15**:54–55
    earned income ceiling, **15**:54
    eligibility, **15**:54
    eligible employment-related expenses, **15**:54
    reporting requirements, **15**:55
Child support, **15**:28
Child tax credit, **15**:53
Children
    unearned income of taxed at parents' rate, **15**:18
        election to report certain unearned income on parent's return, **15**:20
        net unearned income, **15**:18–19
        tax determination, **15**:19–20
Circuit Court of Appeals, **2**:13–16, **2**:26
Circulation expenditures, **13**:14, **13**:25
Citizenship or residency test, for dependency exemption, **15**:14
Civil penalties, legal expenses incurred in defense of, **4**:8
Claim of right doctrine, **3**:9–10, **6**:9
Clear reflection of income test, **6**:26
Client letter, **2**:30
Closely held C corporations, passive loss rules and, **5**:24
Closely held corporations, **9**:3
Club dues, deductibility of, **16**:32
Collectibles, **8**:17
Combined controlled group, **9**:31–32
Comm. v. Duberstein, **15**:30
Commerce Clearing House, **2**:17
Common ownership test, **9**:30
Community property states, **1**:32–33
Commuting expenses, **16**:19–20
Compensation-related loans, **3**:19, **3**:20
Compensatory damages, **15**:31–32
Completed contract method of accounting, **6**:22, **6**:23, **6**:24, **13**:20
Computer-assisted tax research, **2**:28
Condemnation gains and losses, **8**:27
Conduit concept, **14**:13–19
Conference Committee, **2**:4, **2**:5
Congress
    economic considerations of in making tax law, **1**:27–28
    history of involvement with income tax, **1**:14
Consolidated returns, **9**:38
Constructive dividends, **10**:14
    tax treatment of, **10**:16–18
    types of
        bargain rental of corporate property, **10**:14
        bargain sale of corporate property to shareholder, **10**:14
        loans to corporation by shareholders, **10**:16
        loans to shareholders, **10**:15–16
        payments for the benefit of shareholder, **10**:15
        shareholder use of corporate-owned property, **10**:14
        unreasonable compensation, **10**:15

Constructive liquidation scenario, **11**:25–26
Constructive ownership, **4**:13
Constructive receipt, **3**:10–11
Constructive sale, **8**:15
Contingent sales prices, **6**:15–16
Continuity of life, **9**:5
Controlled corporations, organization of and transfers to, **9**:8–10
    assumption of liabilities (Section 357), **9**:15
        liabilities in excess of basis exception, **9**:16–18
        tax avoidance or no bona fide business purpose exception, **9**:16
    basis determination, **9**:18
        basis of property to corporation, **9**:18–19
        basis of stock to shareholder, **9**:18
        holding period for shareholder and transferee corporation, **9**:20
        stock issued for services rendered, **9**:19–20
    control of transferee corporation, **9**:11
        control immediately after the transfer, **9**:11–12
        transfers for property and services, **9**:13–14
        transfers for services and nominal property, **9**:13–14
        transfers to existing corporations, **9**:14
    property transfers, **9**:10–11
    recapture considerations, **9**:20–21
    stock, **9**:11
Controlled groups, **9**:29–32
    application of Section 482, **9**:32
    brother-sister controlled group, **9**:29–31
    combined controlled group, **9**:31–32
    parent-subsidiary controlled group, **9**:29
Convenience of the employer requirement, **16**:8
Copyrights, **4**:33, **8**:5, **8**:32
Corporate accumulations, restrictions on, **10**:21
Corporate distributions, **7**:5, **10**:2
    constructive dividends, **10**:14–18
    double tax effect and, **14**:10–12
    earnings and profits, **10**:3–11
    effect of on E & P, **10**:13
    forms of doing business and, **14**:16–17
    property distributions in S corporations, **12**:20–21, **12**:22
    property dividends, **10**:11–13
    stock dividends and stock rights, **10**:18–22
    taxable dividends, **10**:2–3
Corporate obligations, retirement of, **8**:8
Corporation-shareholder loans, **3**:20
Corporations
    capital structure of
        capital contributions, **9**:21–22
        debt in
            advantages of, **9**:22
            reclassification of debt as equity (thin capitalization), **9**:22–24
    closely held, **9**:3
    loans to by shareholders, **10**:16
    material participation by, **5**:29–30

operations, **9**:24
    controlled groups, **9**:29–32
    deductions available only to corporations
        deduction of organizational expenditures, **9**:25–27
        dividends received deduction, **9**:24–25
    determining corporate tax liability, **9**:27–28
    tax liability of related corporations, **9**:28–29
    procedural matters
        estimated tax payments, **9**:33–34
        filing requirements, **9**:32–33
        Form 1120 illustrated, **9**:35–38
        reconciliation of taxable income and financial net income, **9**:34–38
    recapture for, **8**:36–37
    related, **9**:28–29
    taxation of, **9**:2–3
        comparison of corporations to other forms of doing business, **9**:3–4
        nontax considerations, **9**:4–5
    See also C corporations; Controlled corporations; S corporations
Cosmetic surgery, **15**:35
Cost basis, **7**:8–10
Cost depletion, **4**:35
Cost recovery allowances, **7**:4–5
Cost recovery system, **4**:21
    See also Accelerated cost recovery system (ACRS); Modified accelerated cost recovery system (MACRS)
Cot recovery tables, **4**:38–42
Court of Federal Claims, **2**:12–13, **2**:17–18
Court of original jurisdiction, **2**:12
Courts
    influence of on tax law, **1**:34
        judicial concepts relating to tax, **1**:34–35
        judicial influence on statutory provisions, **1**:35
Courts of Appeals, **2**:17–18
Covenants not to compete, **4**:33
Creative works, **8**:5
Creditors' gifts, **3**:26
Criminal penalties, legal expenses incurred in defense of, **4**:8
Cumulative Bulletin (C.B.), **2**:9–10, **2**:11, **2**:17
Current E & P, **10**:6, **10**:7–11
Current Tax Payment Act, **1**:14
Customs duties, **1**:12–13

D

Daily Tax Reports, **2**:10
Damages, **15**:31, **15**:33
    compensatory, **15**:32–33
    personal injury, **15**:32
    punitive, **15**:32
De minimis fringe benefits, **16**:15–16, **16**:17
Dealers in securities, **8**:6
Death, recapture and, **8**:40–41
Death taxes, **1**:8
    Federal estate tax, **1**:8–9
    state death taxes, **1**:9

Deathbed gifts, **7**:14–15
Debt
  bad, **5**:2–4, **5**:5
  cancellation of, **3**:27–28
  in capital structure, **9**:22–24
  nonrecourse, **11**:25, **11**:26–27
  recourse, **11**:25–26
  straight debt safe harbor, **12**:6
Deductions
  for adjusted gross income, **1**:15, **3**:3
  from adjusted gross income, **1**:15, **3**:3
  itemized, **1**:15, **15**:6, **15**:34–35, **15**:37
    averages, **15**:37
    charitable contributions, **15**:44–49
    interest, **15**:41–45
    medical expenses, **15**:35–38, **15**:38–39
    miscellaneous itemized deductions subject to two percent floor, **15**:49–50
    other miscellaneous deductions, **15**:50
    overall limitation on certain itemized deductions, **15**:50–52
    taxes, **15**:38–40
  standard, **1**:15, **15**:6–7, **15**:8
  tax credits compared to, **15**:17
Defendant, **2**:26
Deficit Reduction Act of 1984, **4**:26
Defined benefit plan, **16**:44
Defined contribution plan, **16**:44
Dependency exemption, **15**:7, **15**:10
  citizenship or residency test, **15**:14
  gross income test, **15**:13
  joint return test, **15**:13–14
  relationship or member-of-the-household test, **15**:12–13
  support test, **15**:10–12
Dependents
  credit for care expenses, **15**:54–55
  filing requirements for, **15**:22
  medical expenses of, **15**:36
  special limitations for individuals who can be claimed as, **15**:8–9
Depletion, **4**:34
  intangible drilling and development costs, **4**:34–35, **4**:35
  methods, **4**:35
    cost depletion, **4**:35
    percentage depletion, **4**:36–37
Depreciation
  additional, **8**:34
  AMT and, **13**:21, **13**:24
  basis for on gift property, **7**:13
  cost recovery allowances and, **7**:4–5
  method and period for contributions of property to partnership, **11**:12–13
  See also Recapture
Depreciation rules, **4**:21
Determination letters, **2**:11, **2**:26
Dicta, **2**:26
Disabled access credit, **13**:11
Disabled taxpayers, tax credit for, **15**:57, **15**:59
Disallowed loss transactions, holding period for, **8**:14
Disaster area losses, **5**:9
Discharge of indebtedness, income from, **3**:25–28
Disguised compensation, **15**:31
Disguised sale, **11**:11

Distance test for moving expenses, **16**:25–26
District Court, **2**:12, **2**:17–18
Dividends
  constructive, **10**:14–18
  income from, **3**:16–17, **9**:4
  nontaxable, **7**:11
  property, **10**:11–13
  stock, **10**:18–20
  taxable, **10**:2–3
Dividends received deduction, **9**:24–25, **13**:24
Divorce, transfers of property incident to, **7**:34
Dollar-value LIFO, **6**:29–30
Domestic eligible entities, default classification for, **9**:7
Double tax effect, **1**:18, **9**:2–3, **11**:3
  minimizing, **14**:10
    electing S corporation status, **14**:12–13
    making deductible distributions, **14**:10–11
    not making distributions, **14**:11–12
    return of capital distributions, **14**:12
  versus single taxation, **14**:7–8
    alternative minimum tax, **14**:8–9
    state taxation, **14**:10

E

Earned income credit, **15**:59–60
  advance payment, **15**:60
  amount of credit, **15**:59–60
  eligibility requirements, **15**:59
Earnings and profits (E & P), **10**:3
  ACE adjustment and, **13**:26
  allocating E & P to distributions, **10**:7–11
  computation of, **10**:3–4
    additions to taxable income, **10**:4
    other adjustments, **10**:4–6
    subtractions from taxable income, **10**:4
  effect of corporate distributions on, **10**:13
  summary of adjustments, **10**:6, **10**:7
Economic considerations in tax law, **1**:27–28
  encouragement of certain activities, **1**:27–28
  encouragement of certain industries, **1**:28
  encouragement of small business, **1**:28
Economic effect test, **11**:20–21
Economic income, **3**:4–5
Economic performance test, **4**:6, **4**:7, **6**:9
Education expenses, **16**:27–28
  classification of specific items, **16**:29
  maintaining or improving existing skills, **16**:28
  requirements imposed by law or by employer for retention of employment, **16**:28
Education IRAs, **16**:40–41
Education tax credits, **15**:55–57
Educational savings bonds, **15**:33–34
Effective tax rate, **1**:21–22
Eisner v. Macomber, **3**:5
Elderly or disabled taxpayers, credit for, **15**:57, **15**:59

Electronic tax services, **2**:29–30
Eligible access expenditures, **13**:11
Eligible small business, for disabled access credit, **13**:10
Employee
  accountable plans for reimbursement of expenses of, **16**:3
  expenses of, **16**:20
    classification of, **16**:35–36
      accountable plans, **16**:36–37
      nonaccountable plans, **16**:37
      reporting procedures, **16**:38
      unreimbursed, **16**:37–38
    education, **16**:27–29
    entertainment, **16**:30–33
    individual retirement accounts, **16**:39–41
    miscellaneous, **16**:35
    moving, **16**:25–27
    office in the home, **16**:33–35
    transportation, **16**:19–21
    travel, **16**:21–25
  highly compensated, **16**:16–17
  in-home office expenses of, **16**:33–35
  partner as, **11**:34
  self-employed person compared to, **16**:2–5
  services of, **3**:15
  statutory, **16**:4
  unreimbursed business expenses of, **16**:3, **16**:37–38
  See also Fringe benefits
Employee discounts, **16**:14–15
Employer-sponsored accident and health plans, **16**:5–6
Employment tax, **1**:3
Employment taxes, **1**:6
  FICA taxes, **1**:6, **1**:7
  self-employment tax, **1**:7
  unemployment taxes, **1**:8
Entertainment expenses, **16**:30
  business gifts, **16**:33
  business meals, **16**:32
  classification of expenses, **16**:31
  deductibility of club dues, **16**:32
  fifty percent cutback, **16**:30–31
  ticket purchases for entertainment, **16**:32–33
Entity classification, **14**:2–3
  after 1996, **9**:6
  business trusts, **9**:6–7
  domestic eligible entities, **9**:7
  elections, **9**:7
  entities in existence before January 1, 1997, **9**:7
  entities organized on or after January 1, 1997, **9**:7
  foreign eligible entities, **9**:7
  related issues, **9**:7–8
  prior to 1997, **9**:5–6
  See also Forms of doing business
Entity concept, **14**:13–19
  of partnership taxation, **11**:9
Equilibrium tax planning, **1**:20–21
Equity considerations in tax law, **1**:29
  alleviating the effect of multiple taxation, **1**:29–30
  coping with inflation, **1**:31
  mitigating the effect of the annual accounting period concept, **1**:30–31
  wherewithal to pay concept, **1**:30

Estimated tax payments
  for corporations, 9:33–34
  for individuals, 16:47
Excess net passive income (ENPI), 12:32
Excessive executive compensation, 4:10
Excise taxes, 1:4–5
Exemptions, 15:9
  dependency, 15:7, 15:10–15
  personal, 15:7, 15:9
  phase-out of, 15:14–15
Expensing of assets. *See* Section 179 expensing election
Extraordinary personal services, 5:31

F

Facts and circumstances test, 5:28–29
Fair market value, 4:16, 7:3–4
Federal Claims Reporter, 2:18
Federal District Court, 2:12, 2:13
Federal excise taxes, 1:4–5
Federal gift tax, 1:9–10
Federal Register, 2:9, 2:10
Federal Second Series (F.2d), 2:18
Federal Third Series (F.3d), 2:18
FICA tax, 1:6, 1:7, 1:8
FIFO, 6:29–30, 6:31, 7:8
  as method for utilizing tax credits, 13:4–5
Fifty percent ceiling for charitable contributions, 15:47–48
Filing status, 15:6–7
Final Regulations, 2:9
Financial net income, 9:34–38
Fiscal year, 3:7, 6:2–3, 6:5
Flexible spending plans, 16:12
Flint v. Stone Tracy Co., 1:14
Flow-through entities, 1:19, 11:3, 12:12
Foreign eligible entities, default classification for, 9:7
Foreign Sales Corporations (FSCs), 1:28
Foreign tax credit (FTC), 13:11–12
Form 1120, 9:35–38, 9:36–38
Forms of doing business
  comparison of, 9:3–5, 14:3–4
  conduit versus entity treatment, 14:13
    at-risk rules, 14:17–18
    basis of ownership interest, 14:14–15
    passive activity losses, 14:17
    recognition at time of contribution to the entity, 14:14
    recognition at time of distribution, 14:16–17
    results of operations, 14:15–16
    special allocations, 14:18–19
  disposition of business or ownership interest, 14:19, 14:24–25
    C corporations, 14:21–22
    partnerships and limited liability entities, 14:20–21
    S corporations, 14:22
    sole proprietorships, 14:19–20
  double taxation
    minimizing, 14:10–13
    single versus, 14:7–10
  federal tax consequences, 11:3
  limited liability company, 14:4–5
  nontax factors, 14:5
    capital formation, 14:5–6
    limited liability, 14:6–7
    other factors, 14:7

tax attributes, 14:26–29
Franchise taxes, 1:13
Franchises, 4:33, 8:11, 8:12
  contingent payments, 8:11–12
  noncontingent payments, 8:11
  significant power, right, or continuing interest, 8:11
  sports franchises, 8:12
Fringe benefits, 16:18
  cafeteria plans, 16:12
  employer-sponsored accident and health plans, 16:5–6
  excluded benefits, 16:12–14
    de minimis fringes, 16:16
    no-additional-cost services, 16:13
    nondiscrimination provisions, 16:16–17
    qualified employee discounts, 16:14–15
    qualified moving expense reimbursements, 16:16
    qualified transportation fringes, 16:16
    working condition fringes, 16:15–16
  flexible spending plans, 16:12
  group term life insurance, 16:9–10
  long-term care benefits, 16:7
  meals and lodging furnished for the convenience of the employer, 16:7
    for convenience of employer, 16:8
    on employer's business premises, 16:8
    furnished by employer, 16:7–8
    required as condition of employment, 16:8–9
  medical reimbursement plans, 16:6
  other specific fringes, 16:11
  qualified, 16:5
  qualified tuition reduction plans, 16:10–11
  taxable, 16:17
Fruit and tree metaphor, 3:14–15
Full recapture, 8:31
Functional use test, 7:30
Furnished by the employer requirement, 16:7–8
FUTA tax, 1:6, 1:8

G

GAAP (generally accepted accounting principles), 6:26
Gain
  built-in, 11:22
  computing on installment sale, 6:13–15
  condemnation, 8:27
  minimum, 11:26
  nonrecognition of, 7:6–7
    dispositions of personal-use assets, 7:7
    other provisions, 7:32–34
    Section 351, 9:8–14
  precontribution, 11:21–22, 11:26
  on property transactions, 3:28–30
  realized, 7:3
    adjusted basis, 7:4
    amount realized, 7:3–4
    capital additions, 7:4
    capital recoveries, 7:4–6
    sale or other disposition, 7:3

  recognition of, property dividends, 10:12–13
  recognized, 7:6, 8:27–30
  recovery of capital doctrine, 7:7–8
  Section 1231, 8:25
  See also Basis; Capital gains and losses
Gain basis, 7:17
General business credit, 13:3–4
  treatment of unused credits, 13:4–5
General Counsel Memoranda, 2:8, 2:11, 2:26
General Explanation of the Act, 2:27
General partners
  liability for recourse debt, 5:18
  unlimited liability of, 9:4
General partnership, 11:4
  compared to limited liability company, 14:4
General sales tax, 1:5
Generally accepted accounting principles (GAAP), 6:26
Gift basis, 7:10
  adjustment for gift tax, 7:12
  holding period, 7:12–13
  if no gift tax is paid, 7:10–11
Gift loans, 3:20
Gift splitting, 1:10
Gift taxes, 1:3, 1:9
  Federal gift tax, 1:9–10, 7:12
  state gift tax, 1:10
Gifts, 15:29–30
  criteria for, 15:45
  deathbed, 7:14–15
  recapture provisions for, 8:40
  See also Charitable contributions
Goods, deferral of advance payments for, 3:13
Goodwill, 4:33, 7:9, 8:32
Gross income, 3:2–3, 3:17, 15:4–5
  accounting and tax concepts of, 3:5–6
  economic and accounting concepts of, 3:3–4
  exclusions applicable to individuals
    damages, 15:31–32, 15:33
    educational savings bonds, 15:33–34
    gifts and inheritances, 15:29–30
    scholarships, 15:30–31
    workers' compensation, 15:32
  form of receipt, 3:6–7
  inclusions applicable to individuals, 15:26
    alimony and separate maintenance payments, 15:26–28
    prizes and awards, 15:28–29
    Social Security benefits, 15:29
    unemployment compensation, 15:29
  year of inclusion
    accounting methods, 3:7–10
    exceptions available to accrual basis taxpayers, 3:13–14
    exceptions available to cash basis taxpayers, 3:10–12
    taxable year, 3:7
  See also Adjusted gross income; income
Gross income test, for dependency exemption, 15:13
Gross receipts test, 6:5
Group term life insurance, 16:9–10
Guaranteed payments, 11:32–33

H

Half-year convention, 4:25
Heads of household, tax rates for, **15**:25
Health insurance benefits, **16**:5–6
Health Insurance and Portability Act of 1996, **15**:38–39
Highly compensated employees, **16**:16–17
Hobby losses, **12**:33, **16**:48–49
  determining the amount of the deduction, **16**:49–50
  presumptive rule of Section 183, **16**:49
Holding, **2**:26
Holding period, **8**:13
  in like-kind exchange, **7**:25–28
  for property acquired by gift, **7**:12–13
  of property acquired from a decedent, **7**:15
  for shareholder and transferee corporation, **9**:20
  short sales, **8**:15
  special rules, **8**:13
    disallowed loss transactions, **8**:14
    inherited property, **8**:14
    nontaxable exchanges, **8**:14
    nontaxable transactions involving carryover of another taxpayer's basis, **8**:14
Home equity loans, **15**:42–43
Home office expenses, **16**:33–35
HOPE scholarship credit, **15**:55–57
House of Representatives, **2**:4, **2**:5
House Ways and Means Committee, **2**:4, **2**:5, **2**:27
Hybrid method of accounting, **3**:10

I

Illegal business, expenses related to, **4**:9
Implicit tax, **1**:6, **1**:23
Imputed interest, **3**:18–21
Imputed interest rules, **6**:16–17
In-home office expenses, **16**:33–35
Income, **3**:17
  accounting and tax concepts of, **3**:5–6
  active, **5**:18–19
  assignment of, **3**:14–15
  broadly conceived, **15**:3
  economic and accounting concepts of, **3**:3–4
  exclusions from, **15**:3–4
  from discharge of indebtedness, **3**:25–28
  gains and losses from property transactions, **3**:28–30
  improvements on leased property, **3**:23
  imputed interest on loans for money, **3**:18–21
  interest on certain state and local government obligations, **3**:22–23
  life insurance proceeds, **3**:23–24
  net investment, **15**:40–41
  portfolio, **5**:19
  prepaid, **3**:13
  sources of
    income received by an agent, **3**:17
    personal services, **3**:14–15
    property, **3**:15–17
  tax benefit rule, **3**:21
  tax-exempt, **4**:14–15
  unearned, of children under 14, **15**:18–20
  windfall, **3**:4
  See also Adjusted gross income; gross income
Income tax, **1**:13
  history, **1**:13–15
  local, **1**:16
  state, **1**:15–16
  structure of, **1**:15–16
Income Tax Act of 1913, **15**:29
Income tax formula
  basic, **1**:15
  for individuals, **1**:16
Income tax formula for individuals, **1**:16
Incremental research activities credit, **13**:8–9
Independent contractor, **16**:2
  See also Self-employed persons
Individual Retirement Accounts (IRAs)
  educational, **16**:40–41
  Roth, **16**:40
  traditional, **16**:39–40
Inflation, **1**:31
Inheritances, **15**:29–30
Inherited property, **8**:14
Inside basis, **11**:14
Insolvency, **3**:26–27
Installment method of accounting, **6**:12–13
  computing gain for the period, **6**:13–14
  contingent sales price, **6**:15–16
  disposition of installment obligations, **6**:19
  electing out of, **6**:20–21
  eligibility and calculations, **6**:13
  imputed interest, **6**:16–17
  interest on deferred taxes, **6**:20
  nonelective aspect, **6**:13
  related-party sales, **6**:17
    depreciable property, **6**:19
    nondepreciable property, **6**:17–18
Installment sales, **13**:25
  interest on, **6**:18
  recapture provisions, **8**:42
Insurance policies, certain exchanges of, **7**:33
Intangible assets, **4**:33
Intangible drilling and development costs (IDC), **4**:34–35
  ACE adjustment and, **13**:25
  recapture provisions, **8**:42–43
  as tax preference item, **13**:17
Inter vivos gifts, **15**:29
Interest
  on certain state and local government obligations, **3**:22–23
  classification of interest expense, **15**:44
  deduction of
    as business expense, **4**:20
    for individuals, **15**:40–44, **15**:44
  on deferred taxes, **6**:20
  on home equity loans, **15**:42–43
  imputed, **3**:18–21, **6**:16–17
  income from, **3**:15–16
  on installment sales, **6**:18
  investment, **15**:40–42
  paid for services, **15**:43
  paid to related parties, **15**:43
  prepaid, **15**:44
  prepayment penalties, **15**:43
  on private activity bonds, **13**:17, **13**:22–23
  qualified residence interest, **15**:42–43
  on tax-exempt securities, **15**:44
  unpaid, **4**:13
Internal Revenue Bulletin (I.R.B.), **2**:9–10, **2**:10, **2**:11, **2**:17
Internal Revenue Code (IRC), **2**:2
  of 1939, **2**:3
  of 1954, **2**:3
  of 1986, **2**:3
  arrangement of, **2**:4, **2**:6
  citing, **2**:6–7
  interpreting, **2**:23–24
  origin of, **2**:3
Internal Revenue Service (IRS)
  influence of, **1**:33
    administrative feasibility, **1**:33–34
    as protector of the revenue, **1**:33
Internet, **2**:31–32
Interpretive Regulations, **2**:25
Inventories, **6**:26–27, **8**:4
  determining inventory cost, **6**:27
    dollar-value LIFO, **6**:29–30
    LIFO election, **6**:30–31
    lower of cost or market, **6**:28–29
    specific identification, FIFO, LIFO, **6**:29–30
    uniform capitalization, **6**:27–28
  treatment of when contributed to partnership, **11**:13–14
Investigation of a business, deduction of expenses for, **4**:11–12
Investment earnings, arising from reinvestment of life insurance proceeds, **3**:24
Investment interest, **15**:40–42
Investment partnership, **11**:10
Involuntary conversions (Section 1033), **7**:28, **8**:26–27
  defined, **7**:29
  recapture provisions, **8**:41
  replacement property, **7**:30
    functional use test, **7**:30
    special real property test, **7**:31
    taxpayer use test, **7**:30–31
  reporting considerations, **7**:32
  time limit on replacement, **7**:31–32
IRS Letter Ruling Reports, **2**:10
Itemized deductions. *See* Deductions

J

Joint Committee on Taxation, **2**:27
Joint Conference Committee, **2**:4, **2**:5
Joint return test, for dependency exemption, **15**:13–14

K

Keogh plans, **16**:44–45
Kickbacks, **4**:8
Kiddie tax, **8**:17–18, **15**:18–20
Kleinrock's tax service, **2**:31

L

Lease cancellation payments, **8**:12–13
Leased automobiles, **4**:32
Leased property, improvements on, **3**:22

Least aggregate deferral method, **6:**4
Legislative process for tax law, **2:**4, **2:**5
Legislative Regulations, **2:**25
Lessee, **8:**12–13
Lessee improvements, **13:**25
Lessor, **8:**12–13
Letter Ruling Review, **2:**10
Letter rulings, **2:**10–11, **2:**26
LEXIS/NEXIS, **2:**31
Liability
  assumption of (Section 357), **9:**15–18
  in excess of basis, **9:**16–18
  limited, **14:**4–5, **14:**6–7
  unlimited, **9:**4
Liability sharing, in partnership, **11:**23–27
Life insurance
  group term, **16:**9–10
  proceeds from, **3:**22–24
Lifetime learning tax credit, **15:**55–57
LIFO, **6:**29–30, **6:**30–31
  dollar-value, **6:**29–30
LIFO inventory adjustments, **13:**25
LIFO recapture adjustments, **13:**25
LIFO recapture tax, **12:**31
Like-kind exchanges (Section 1031), **7:**21, **9:**8–10
  basis and holding period of property received, **7:**25–28
  boot, **7:**24–25
  exchange requirement, **7:**24
  like-kind property, **7:**22–24
  recapture provisions, **8:**41
Limited liability company (LLC), **11:**5, **11:**36, **12:**3, **14:**4–5
  advantages of, **11:**37–38
  converting to, **11:**37
  disadvantages of, **11:**38
  taxation of, **1:**19, **9:**7–8, **11:**36
Limited liability partnership (LLP), **11:**5, **11:**39
  taxation of, **1:**19
Limited partners, material participation by, **5:**29
Limited partnership, **9:**5, **14:**7
  capital formation in, **14:**6
  compared to limited liability company, **14:**4
Listed property, limitations on MACRS deductions of, **4:**29–32
Loans
  below-market, **3:**19–20
  between related parties, **5:**4–5
  compensation-related, **3:**19, **3:**20
  corporation-shareholder, **3:**19, **3:**20
  gift, **3:**19, **3:**20
  imputed interest on, **3:**18–21
  original issue discount, **3:**10–11
  student loans, **3:**28
  tax avoidance, **3:**19–20
  to corporation by shareholders, **10:**16
  to shareholders, **10:**15–16
Lobbying expenses, **4:**9
Local income taxes, **1:**16, **15:**39–40
Long-term capital gains, **8:**16–18, **8:**19
Long-term care benefits, **16:**7
Long-term contracts, **6:**21–23
  completed contract method, **6:**22, **6:**23, **6:**24
  percentage of completion method, **6:**23, **6:**24–25
  lookback provisions, **6:**25
Long-term nonpersonal-use assets, **8:**25
Lookback provisions
  for long-term contracts, **6:**25
  Section 1231, **8:**30
Loss
  built-in, **11:**22
  in business entities, **9:**4
  condemnation, **8:**27
  disallowed
    holding period for transactions involving, **8:**14
    related taxpayers, **7:**15
    wash sales, **7:**15–16
  limitations on in partnerships, **11:**28–31
  nonrecognition of, **7:**6–7
    disposition of personal-use assets, **7:**7
    other provisions, **7:**32–34
    Section 351, **9:**8–14
  precontribution, **11:**26
  on property contributed to partnership, **11:**13
  on property transactions, **3:**28–30
  realized, **7:**3
    adjusted basis, **7:**4
    amount realized, **7:**3–4
    capital additions, **7:**4
    capital recoveries, **7:**4–6
    sale or other disposition, **7:**3
  recognition of, property dividends, **10:**12–13
  recognized, **7:**6
  recovery of capital doctrine, **7:**7–8
  in S corporations, **12:**28
  Section 1231, **8:**25
  suspended, **5:**20–21, **12:**22–23
  in transactions between related parties, **4:**12–13
  See also Capital gains and losses; Casualty losses; Net operating losses (NOLs); Theft losses
Low-income housing credit, **13:**10
Lower of cost or market (replacement cost), **6:**28–29
Lucas v. Earl, **3:**14–15
Lump-sum purchase, **7:**9

M

Majority interest partners, **6:**2–3
Malat v. Riddell, **8:**4
Marginal tax rate, **1:**21–22
Married individuals, tax rates for, **15:**24–25
Material participation, **5:**25–26
  corporations, **5:**29–30
  facts and circumstances test, **5:**28–29
  limited partners, **5:**29
  participation defined, **5:**29
  tests based on current participation, **5:**26–27
  tests based on prior participation, **5:**28
Meals and lodging furnished for the convenience of the employer, **16:**7–9
Medical expenses, **15:**35
  capital expenditures, **15:**36
  cosmetic surgery, **15:**35
  of dependents, **15:**36
  medical savings accounts, **15:**36–38
  nursing home care, **15:**35–36
  transportation and lodging, **15:**36
Medical reimbursement plans, **16:**6
Medical savings accounts (MSAs), **15:**36–38, **16:**6
Medicare tax, **1:**3, **1:**7, **16:**42–44
Member-of-the-household test, for dependency exemption, **15:**12–13
Memorandum decisions (U.S. Tax Court), **2:**16, **2:**17
Mid-month convention, **4:**27
Mid-quarter convention, **4:**25–26
Mid-term gain, **8:**17
Millionaire provision, **4:**10
Minimum gain, **11:**26
Minimum tax credit, **13:**28
Mining exploration and development expenditures, **13:**20
Modified accelerated cost recovery system (MACRS), **4:**21–22
  business and personal use of automobiles and other listed property, **4:**29–30
    autos and other listed property not used predominantly for business, **4:**31
    used predominantly for business, **4:**30
    change from predominantly business use, **4:**32
    cost recovery limits for autos, **4:**30–31
    leased autos, **4:**32
    substantiation requirements, **4:**32
  eligible property
    cost recovery allowed or allowable, **4:**22–23
    cost recovery basis for personal-use assets converted to business or income-producing use, **4:**23
  personal property, **4:**24–25
    depreciation of post-1986 personal property, **13:**19
    mid-quarter convention, **4:**25–26
  real estate, **4:**26–27, **13:**19
  straight-line election, **4:**29–30
  tables for, **4:**38–42
  See also Accelerated cost recovery system (ACRS)
Moving expenses, **16:**25
  distance test, **16:**25–26
  reimbursement of, **16:**16
  time test, **16:**27
Multiple support agreement, **15:**11–12
Multiple taxation, **1:**29–30
Municipal bonds. *See* Tax-exempt securities

N

Natural business year, **6:**5, **6:**6
Net capital gain (NCG), computation of, **8:**19–22
Net capital loss (NCL), computation of, **8:**19–22
Net income tax, **13:**4
Net investment income, **15:**40–42
Net operating losses (NOLs), **5:**12–14
  AMT and, **13:**18

carryback and carryover periods, **5:**14
    election to forgo carryback, **5:**14
    from multiple tax years, **5:**14
    in S corporations, **12:**24–26
Net regular tax liability, **13:**4
Newsgroups, **2:**32
No-additional-cost services, **16:**14
Nonaccountable plan for employee expense reimbursement, **16:**37
Nonacquiescence, **2:**17
Nonbusiness debt, **5:**3–4
Nonpersonal-use capital assets, **8:**26–27
Nonrecourse debt, **5:**18, **11:**25, **11:**26–27
    qualified, **5:**18, **11:**30–31
Nonresident aliens, as stockholders in S corporation, **12:**7
Nonresidential real property, computing recapture on, **8:**32–33, **8:**34–35
Nontaxable exchanges, **7:**18, **7:**20–21
    holding period for, **8:**14
    involuntary conversions, **7:**28–32
    like-kind exchanges (Section 1031), **7:**21–28
Nontaxable stock dividends, **7:**10
Nursing home care, **15:**35–36

O

Obligation to repay, amounts received under, **3:**12
Occupational taxes, **1:**13
Office in the home expenses, **16:**33–35
On the employer's business premises requirement, **16:**8
On-line services, **2:**31
OnPoint, **2:**31
Options, **8:**8, **8:**9
    exercise by grantee, **8:**9
    failure to exercise, **8:**8–9
    sale of, **8:**8
Ordinary income property, **4:**16, **15:**47
Ordinary and necessary requirement, **4:**2–3
Organization costs, **11:**15–16
Organizational expenditures, **13:**25
    deduction of, **9:**25–27
Original issue discount, **3:**11–12
Other adjustments account, **12:**19
Outside basis, **11:**14

P

Parent-subsidiary controlled group, **9:**29–30
Partial recapture, **8:**34
Participation, defined, **5:**29
Partnerships, **9:**2
    accounting period for, **6:**3–5
    advantages and disadvantages of partnership form, **11:**36
    anti-abuse provisions, **11:**9
    as associations, **9:**6
    conceptual basis for taxation, **11:**7
        aggregate (or conduit) concept, **11:**8
        entity concept, **11:**9
    definition of, **11:**3–5
    disposition of, **14:**20–21
    formation of, **11:**14
        exceptions to Section 721, **11:**10
            disguised sale, **11:**11
            exchange, **11:**10–11
            investment partnership, **11:**10
            services, **11:**11–12
        gain or loss on contributions to partnership, **11:**9–10
        initial costs, **11:**15
            acquisition costs of depreciable assets, **11:**16
            organization costs, **11:**15–16
            start-up costs, **11:**16
            syndication costs, **11:**16–17, **11:**17
        inside and outside bases, **11:**14
        tax accounting elections, **11:**14
        tax issues relative to contributed property, **11:**12
            depreciation method and period, **11:**12–13
            receivables, inventory, losses, **11:**13–14
    liability in, **9:**4
    operations, **11:**17
        basis of partnership interest, **11:**22–23, **11:**28, **12:**23
            current nonrecourse debt rules, **11:**25, **11:**26–27
            current recourse debt rules, **11:**25–26
            liability sharing, **11:**23–25
            other factors affecting basis calculations, **11:**27–28
        loss limitations, **11:**28–29
            at-risk limitation, **11:**31–32
            overall limitation, **11:**29–30
            passive activity rules, **11:**31
        partnership allocations, **11:**20
            economic effect, **11:**20–21
            precontribution gain or loss, **11:**22
        reporting operating results, **11:**17
            classifying income and deductions, **11:**17–19
            penalties, **11:**19–20
            withdrawals, **11:**19
    partner's ownership interest in, **11:**7–8
    taxation and reporting, **1:**18, **11:**5–7, **11:**20
    transactions between partner and partnership, **11:**32, **11:**33–34, **11:**35
        guaranteed payments, **11:**32–33
        partners as employees, **11:**34
        sales of property, **11:**34
Pass-through entities, **11:**3
Passenger automobile, **4:**30
Passive activity loss rules, **5:**32
    activities defined, **5:**24–25
    AMT and, **13:**21–23
    disposition of passive activities, **5:**36
    forms of doing business and, **14:**17
    interaction of at-risk and passive activity limits, **5:**33
    material participation, **5:**25–30
    for partnerships, **11:**31
    passive loss limits
        classification and impact of passive income and loss, **5:**18–19
        carryover of passive credits, **5:**22–23
        carryover of suspended losses, **5:**21–22
        general impact, **5:**19
        impact of suspended losses, **5:**20–21
        passive activity changes to active, **5:**23
        passive credits, **5:**22
    real estate special rules, **5:**33
        real estate professionals, **5:**34
        rental real estate deduction, **5:**34–36
    rental activities, **5:**30–33
    in S corporations, **12:**26–27
    taxpayers subject to, **5:**23
        closely held C corporations, **5:**24
        personal service corporations, **5:**23
Passive activity losses (PALs), utilizing, **5:**36–37
Passive credits, **5:**22
    carryovers of, **5:**22–23
Passive investment income penalty tax, **12:**32
Passive investment income (PII) limitation, in S corporation, **12:**10–11
Patents, **4:**33, **8:**10, **8:**32
    holder defined, **8:**10
    substantial rights, **8:**10
Per-day allocation, in S corporation, **12:**14–15
Percentage of completion method, **6:**23, **6:**24–25
Percentage depletion, **4:**36–37, **13:**16–17
Personal exemption, **15:**7, **15:**9
Personal holding company (PHC) tax, **10:**21
Personal injury damages, **15:**32
Personal property, depreciation of post-1986 personal property, **13:**19
Personal property taxes, deduction of, **15:**38–39
Personal service corporations (PSCs), **9:**28
    accounting period for, **6:**6
    passive loss rules and, **5:**23
Personal services, income from, **3:**14–15
Personal-use assets, **7:**7, **8:**4
    casualty loss deductions from, **5:**11–12
    converted to business or income-producing use, **4:**21, **7:**16–18
Personalty, **4:**22
    ad valorem taxes on, **1:**11–12
    cost recovery periods for, **4:**23–26
    as like-kind property, **7:**22
Petitioner, **2:**26
Plaintiff, **2:**26
Political considerations in tax law, **1:**31
    political expediency, **1:**32
    special interest legislation, **1:**32
    state and local government influences, **1:**32–33
Political contributions, **4:**9
Pollock v. Farmer's Loan and Trust Co., **1:**13–14
Pollution control facilities, **13:**20
Portfolio income, **5:**19
Postelection termination period, **12:**19–20
Precedents, **2:**14
Precontribution gain or loss, **11:**22, **11:**26
Prepaid income, **3:**13
Prepaid interest, **15:**44
Prepayment penalties, **15:**43
Primary valuation amount, **7:**13–14
Principal partner, **6:**2–3
Principal residence, sale of, **7:**34

Private activity bonds, interest on as tax preference item, **13**:17
Private Letter Rulings, **2**:10
Privileges and rights, taxes on, **1**:12–13
Prizes, **15**:28–29
Procedural Regulations, **2**:25
Profit and loss sharing ratios, **11**:7
Profits (loss) interest, in partnership, **11**:7
Progressive tax, **1**:3
Property
   bargain purchase of, **7**:8
   capital gain property, **4**:16, **15**:47
   charitable contributions of, **15**:47
   contributed to partnership, **11**:12–14
   conversion of from personal use to business or income-producing use, **4**:21, **7**:16–18
   depreciable, **6**:19
   distributions of in S corporations, **12**:20–21, **12**:22
   exchange of for stock, **7**:32
   income from, **3**:15
      dividends, **3**:16–17, **9**:4
      interest, **3**:15–16
   inherited, **8**:14
   like-kind, **7**:22–23
   listed, **4**:29–32
   nondepreciable, **6**:17–18
   ordinary income property, **4**:16, **15**:47
   personal
      casualty loss deductions from, **5**:11–12
      recovery periods and methods, **4**:21–22, **4**:23–26
   rental, **5**:30–33
   replacement (involuntary conversions), **7**:30–31
   sale of between person and partnership, **11**:34
   Section 1231, **8**:25, **8**:26
   Section 1245, **8**:32–33
   transfer of (Section 351), **9**:10–11
Property dividends, **10**:11
   effect on corporation, **10**:13
      effect of corporate distributions on E & P, **10**:13
      recognition of gain or loss, **10**:12–13
   effect on shareholder, **10**:11–12
Property transactions, gains and losses from, **3**:28–30
Proportional tax, **1**:3
Proposed Regulations, **2**:8–9
Proprietorships
   accounting periods and methods, **16**:46
   as business entity, **16**:40–41
   deductions related to, **16**:42
      health insurance premiums, **16**:42
      self-employment tax, **16**:42–44
   disposition of ownership interest in, **14**:19–20
   estimated payments, **16**:46
      estimated tax for individuals, **16**:47
      penalty for underpayments, **16**:47–48
   income of, **16**:41
   liability in, **9**:4
   retirement plans for self-employed persons, **16**:44–46
   taxation of, **1**:17–18

Public policy limitations on business deductions, **4**:7–9
   expenses related to illegal business, **4**:9
   legal expenses incurred in defense of civil or criminal penalties, **4**:8
Punitive damages, **15**:32

Q

Qualified employee discounts, **16**:14–15
Qualified fringe benefits, **16**:5
   See also Fringe benefits
Qualified moving expenses, **16**:26–27
   reimbursement of, **16**:16
Qualified nonrecourse debt, **11**:30–31
Qualified nonrecourse financing, **5**:18
Qualified real property indebtedness, **3**:26, **3**:27
Qualified residence interest, **15**:42–43
Qualified small business stock, **8**:17, **8**:23–24
Qualified transportation fringes, **16**:16
Qualified tuition reduction plans, **16**:10–11

R

Real estate
   as like-kind property, **7**:22
   nonresidential, recapture rules for, **8**:32–33, **8**:34–35
   residential rental, **4**:26–27
   special passive loss limits for, **5**:33–36
Real property
   certain reacquisitions of, **7**:33
   depreciation of post-1986 real property, **13**:18–19
   nonresidential, computing recapture on, **8**:32–33, **8**:34–35
   special test for involuntary conversion of, **7**:31
   subdivided for sale, **8**:6–7
Real property taxes, **1**:11
   deduction of for individuals, **15**:39
Realized gain, **7**:3
Realized gain or loss, **7**:7–8
Realized loss, **7**:3
Realty
   cost recovery allowances for, **4**:21–22, **4**:26–27
   taxes on, **1**:11
Reasonableness requirement, **4**:3–4
Recapture, **8**:2–3
   of alimony, **15**:28
   comparison of Sections 1245 and 1250, **8**:37
   for controlled corporations, **9**:20–21
   exceptions to Sections 1245 and 1250, **8**:40–41
      certain nontaxable transactions, **8**:41
      charitable transfers, **8**:41
      death, **8**:40–41
      gifts, **8**:40
      like-kind exchanges and involuntary conversions, **8**:41
   full, **8**:31
   partial, **8**:34
   of rehabilitation expenditures, **13**:6
   reporting procedures, **8**:43

Section 179 expensing election and, **8**:33
Section 1245, **8**:30–33
Section 1250, **8**:34–40
special provisions
   gain from sale of depreciable property between certain related parties, **8**:42
   installment sales, **8**:42
   intangible drilling costs, **8**:42–43
See also Section 1231 netting
Receivables, **11**:13
Recognized gain or loss, **7**:6, **7**:7–8, **8**:27–30
Recourse debt, **5**:18, **11**:25–26
Recovery of capital doctrine, **7**:7–8, **7**:26
Recurring items, **4**:7
Regressive tax, **1**:3
Regular decisions (U.S. Tax Court), **2**:16
Regular tax liability, **13**:4
Rehabilitation expenditures
   tax credit for, **13**:5–6
   recapture of tax credit, **13**:6
Related corporations, **9**:28–29
Related-party transactions, **4**:12–13
   constructive ownership, **4**:13
   definition of related party, **8**:42
   disallowed losses, **7**:15
   installment method of accounting and, **6**:17
      depreciable property, **6**:19
      nondepreciable property, **6**:18–19
   interest paid in, **15**:43
   like-kind exchanges, **7**:23
   loans, **5**:4–5
   losses, **4**:12–13
   recapture provisions, **8**:42
   unpaid interest and expenses, **4**:13
   wash sales, **7**:15–16
Relationship or member-of-the-household test, for dependency exemption, **15**:12–13
Relationship test for earned income credit, **15**:59
Rental activities, **5**:30–33
Rental real estate deduction, for passive losses, **5**:34–36
Required as a condition of employment test, **16**:8–9
Research activities credit, **13**:8–9
   basic research credit, **13**:10
   incremental research activities credit, **13**:8–9
Research and development expenses, **1**:27
Research expenditures, **13**:8
Research and experimental expenditures, **4**:18
   deferral and amortization method, **4**:19
   expense method, **4**:18–19
Research Institute of America (RIA), **2**:17
Reserve method for accounting for bad debts, **5**:3
Reserves for estimated expenses, **4**:7
Residency test
   for dependency exemption, **15**:14
   for earned income credit, **15**:59
Residential rental housing, computing recapture on, **8**:35–36

Residential rental real estate, MACRS for, **4**:26–27
Residual allocation rule, **7**:9
Respondent, **2**:26
Revenue Act
 of 1916, **1**:8
 of 1948, **1**:33
Revenue Procedures, **2**:9, **2**:9–10
Revenue Rulings, **2**:9, **2**:9–10, **2**:25
RIA OnPoint, **2**:31
Roth IRAs, **16**:40

S

S corporations
 accounting period for, **6**:3–5
 allocation of income and loss, **12**:14–15
  salary structure, **12**:15–16
  short-year election, **12**:15
 compared to limited liability companies, **14**:4
 computation of taxable income, **12**:12–14
 definition of small business corporation, **12**:5
  ineligible corporations, **12**:5
  nonresident aliens, **12**:7
  number of shareholders, **12**:6
  one class of stock, **12**:5–6
  shareholder consents, **12**:8–9
  type of shareholder limitation, **12**:7
 election
  loss of, **12**:9
   loss of small business corporation status, **12**:10
   passive investment income limitation, **12**:10–11
   reelection after termination, **12**:11
   voluntary revocation, **12**:10
  making, **12**:7–8
  when to elect, **12**:4
 income taxation of, **1**:18, **1**:19
 LIFO recapture tax, **12**:31
 losses, **12**:28
  at-risk rules, **12**:27–28
  net operating loss, **12**:24–26
  passive losses and credits, **12**:26–27
  suspended losses, **12**:22–23, **12**:24
 other operational rules, **12**:32–33
 overview of, **12**:2–3
 passive investment income penalty tax, **12**:32
 preelection built-in gain tax, **12**:28–31
 property distributions by corporation, **12**:20–21, **12**:22
 salary structure, **12**:15–16
 sale of, **14**:22
 shareholder's basis in, **12**:21–24
 tax treatment of distributions to shareholders, **12**:16, **12**:18
  accumulated adjustments account, **12**:17–19, **12**:20
  accumulated earnings and profits (AEP), **12**:16–17
  effect of terminating the S election, **12**:19–20
  Schedule M-2, **12**:19
 See also Controlled corporations; Corporations
Safe harbor provisions, **12**:6

Sale or exchange, **8**:7
 franchises, trademarks, and trade names, **8**:11–12
 lease cancellation payments, **8**:12–13
 options, **8**:8–9
 patents, **8**:10
 retirement of corporate obligations, **8**:8
 worthless securities and Section 1244 stock, **8**:7
 See also Capital assets
Sale or other disposition, **7**:3
Sales tax, **1**:3, **1**:5
Savings incentive match plan for employees (SIMPLE plan), **16**:45–46
Schedule M-1, **9**:34–35, **9**:37–38
Schedule M-2, **9**:35, **12**:19
Scholarships, **15**:30–31
 disguised compensation, **15**:31
 timing issues, **15**:31
Section 121 (sale of a principal residence), **7**:34
Section 179 expensing election, **4**:28, **8**:33
 annual limitations, **4**:28–29
 effect on basis, **4**:29
Section 183 (hobby losses), **12**:33, **16**:49
Section 197 intangibles, **4**:33
Section 351 (nonrecognition of gain or loss upon transfer of property to corporation), **9**:8–14, **9**:16–18
Section 351 (transfer of assets to business entity), **7**:32
Section 357 (assumption of liabilities), **9**:15–18
Section 465 (at-risk rules), **14**:17–18
Section 482 (allocation of gross income, deductions and credits), **9**:32
Section 721 (transfer of assets to business entity), **7**:32, **11**:9–12
Section 1031 (like-kind exchanges), **7**:21–28
Section 1032 (exchange of stock for property), **7**:32
Section 1033 (involuntary conversions), **7**:28–32
Section 1035 (certain exchanges of insurance policies), **7**:33
Section 1036 (exchange of stock for stock of the same corporation), **7**:33
Section 1038 (certain reacquisitions of real property), **7**:33
Section 1041 (transfers of property between spouses or incident to divorce), **7**:34
Section 1044 (rollovers into specialized small business investment companies), **7**:33–34
Section 1221 (what is not a capital asset), **8**:4
Section 1231 assets, **8**:2–3, **8**:24
 computation, **8**:27
  casualty netting, **8**:27
  lookback provision, **8**:29
  Section 1231 netting, **8**:27–30, **8**:38
  nonpersonal-use capital assets, **8**:26–27
  property included and excluded, **8**:26
  rationale for favorable tax treatment, **8**:25–26
 relationship to capital assets, **8**:24–25
 See also Capital assets
Section 1231 gains and losses, **8**:25

Section 1231 lookback, **8**:29
Section 1231 netting, **8**:27–30
Section 1231 property, **8**:25, **8**:26
Section 1237 (real property development activities), **8**:6–7
Section 1244 stock, **5**:6–7, **8**:7, **12**:33
Section 1245 property, **8**:32–33
Section 1245 recapture, **8**:29–33, **8**:37
 exceptions, **8**:40–41
Section 1250 recapture, **8**:34, **8**:36
 additional recapture for corporations, **8**:36–37
 compared to Section 1245 recapture, **8**:37
 exceptions, **8**:38
 nonresidential real property, **8**:34–35
 residential rental housing, **8**:35–36
 unrecaptured Section 1250 gains, **8**:18–22, **8**:39–40
Section 1374 (built-in gains tax), **12**:28–31
Securities
 appreciated, gifts of, **8**:17–18
 dealers in, **8**:6
 short sales of, **8**:15
 tax-exempt, **3**:22–23, **15**:44
 transfers of (Section 351), **9**:11–12
 worthless, **5**:4–6, **8**:7
Self-created intangibles, **4**:33
Self-directed retirement plan, **16**:44
Self-employed persons
 employees compared to, **16**:2–5
 in-home office expenses of, **16**:33–35
 retirement plans for, **16**:44
  Keogh plans, **16**:44–45
  SIMPLE plans, **16**:44–45
Self-employment tax, **1**:7, **16**:5, **16**:42–44
Seller cancellation, **3**:27
Senate, **2**:4, **2**:5
Senate Finance Committee, **2**:4, **2**:5, **2**:27
Separate maintenance agreements, **15**:27–28
Separately stated items, **11**:5–6
 for S corporation, **12**:12–14
Services
 charitable contribution of, **15**:45
 contributed to partnership, **11**:11–12
 deferral of advance payments for, **3**:14
 interest paid for, **15**:43
Severance taxes, **1**:13
Shareholder cancellation, **3**:28
Shareholders
 bargain sale or rental of corporate property to, **10**:14–15
 loans to, **10**:15–16
 loans to corporation by, **10**:16
 payments for benefit of, **10**:15
 in S corporation, **12**:7
 use of corporate property by, **10**:14
Short period, **6**:7–8
Short sales, **8**:15
Short taxable year, **6**:7–8
Short-term capital gains, **8**:15–16, **8**:19
Short-year election, **12**:15
Significant participation activity, **5**:27
Significant power, right, or continuing interest, **8**:11
SIMPLE plans, **16**:45–46
Single taxpayers, rates for, **15**:24
Sixteenth Amendment, **1**:14, **3**:4

Small business, encouragement of via tax laws, **1:**28
Small business corporation
  definition of, **12:**5–7
  loss of status as, **12:**10
  See also S corporations
Small Business Protection Act of 1996, **12:**3
Small business (Section 1244) stock, **5:**6–7, **8:**23–24
Small Cases Division (U.S. Tax Court), **2:**12
Social considerations in tax law, **1:**28–29
Social Security benefits, **15:**29
Social Security tax, **1:**7, **16:**42–44
Sole proprietorships. *See* Proprietorships
Special allocations, **14:**18–19
  of items to partners, **11:**7–8
Special interest legislation, **1:**32
Special real property test, **7:**31
Specialized small business investment company (SSBIC), **7:**33–34
Specific charge-off method of accounting for bad debts, **5:**3, **5:**4, **5:**5
Sports franchises, **8:**12
Spouses, transfer of property between or incident to divorce, **7:**34
Standard deduction, **1:**15, **15:**6–7
  individuals not eligible for, **15:**8
Start-up costs, **11:**16
State excise taxes, **1:**5
State gift taxes, **1:**10
State income taxes, **1:**16, **14:**9–10, **15:**39–40
State sales tax, **1:**3
Statutory employees, **16:**4
Statutory percentage method of cost recovery, **4:**29–30
Stepped-down basis, **7:**13
Stepped-up basis, **7:**13
Stock
  exchange of for property, **7:**32
  exchange of for stock of the same corporation, **7:**33
  issued for services rendered, **9:**19–20
  in S corporation, **12:**5–6
  transfer of (Section 351), **9:**11–12
Stock dividends, **10:**18–20
  nontaxable, **7:**10
Stock options, **9:**11
Stock rights, **10:**20–21
Straight debt safe harbor, **12:**6
Straight-line election, **4:**27–28, **4:**29–30
Student loans, **3:**28
Subchapter C, **9:**2
  See also C corporations
Subchapter S, **9:**2, **12:**2
  See also S corporations
Substantial rights, **8:**11
Substituted basis, **11:**12
Sudden event, **5:**7
Super-full absorption costing system, **6:**27–28
Support test, for dependency exemption, **15:**10–12
Supreme Court.
  accounting concept of income, **3:**5–6
  citations of, **2:**18–19
  clear reflection of income test, **6:**27
  definition of gross income, **3:**3
  legality of income tax, **1:**13–14

Supreme Court Reporter (S.Ct.), **2:**18–19
Suspended losses
  carryovers of, **5:**21–22
  in S corporations, **12:**22–23, **12:**24
Syndication costs, **11:**16–17

T

Tax avoidance, **1:**20
Tax avoidance loans, **3:**19–20
Tax bases, **1:**3–4
Tax benefit rule, **3:**21
Tax Court, **2:**12, **2:**26
  citing, **2:**16–17
  Small Cases Division, **2:**12
Tax Court of the United States Reports, **2:**16–17
Tax credits, **13:**2, **13:**12–13, **15:**17
  adoption expenses, **15:**52–53
  business-related
    business energy credits, **13:**6–8
    disabled access credit, **13:**10, **13:**11
    foreign tax credit, **13:**11–12
    general business credit, **13:**3–5
    low-income housing credit, **13:**10–11
    rehabilitation expenditures, **13:**5–6
    research activities credit, **13:**8–10
    welfare-to-work credit, **13:**8
  child tax credit, **15:**53
  education tax credits, **15:**55
    eligible individuals, **15:**56
    income limitations, **15:**56
    maximum credit, **15:**55
    restrictions and double tax benefits, **15:**56–57
    timing of expenses, **15:**56
  individual
    child and dependent care expenses, **15:**54–55
    earned income credit, **15:**59–60
    elderly or disabled taxpayers, **15:**57, **15:**59
  minimum tax credit, **13:**28
Tax determination
  computation of net taxes payable or refund due, **15:**17–18
  Tax Rate Schedule method, **15:**16–17
  tax table method, **15:**15–16
  unearned income of children under age 14 taxed at parents' rate, **15:**18–20
Tax evasion, **1:**20
Tax file memorandum, **2:**29
Tax filing, **15:**20–21
  filing requirements, **15:**21–22
    for dependents, **15:**22
    selecting the proper form, **15:**22
    when and where to file, **15:**22–23
  filing status, **15:**23
    abandoned spouse rules, **15:**25–26
    rates for heads of household, **15:**25
    rates for married individuals, **15:**24–25
    rates for single taxpayers, **15:**24
Tax formula
  determining the tax, **3:**3
  individual, **1:**15, **1:**16, **15:**2–3
    application, **15:**7–8
    components, **15:**3
      adjusted gross income, **15:**5–6

deductions for gross income, **3:**3, **15:**5
exclusions, **3:**2, **15:**3–4
gross income, **3:**2–3, **15:**4–5
income (broadly conceived), **3:**2, **15:**3
itemized deductions, **15:**6
personal and dependency exemptions, **15:**7
standard deduction, **15:**6–7
individuals not eligible for standard deduction, **15:**8
special limitations for individuals who can be claimed as dependents, **15:**8–9
Tax home, determining, **16:**22
Tax law, **1:**26, **2:**2
  administrative sources of, **2:**7
    letter rulings, **2:**10–11
    other administrative pronouncements, **2:**11
    revenue rulings and revenue procedures, **2:**9–10
    Treasury Department Regulations, **2:**7–9
  court influence, **1:**34–35
  economic considerations, **1:**27–28
  equity considerations, **1:**29–31
  IRS influence, **1:**33–34
  judicial sources of, **2:**12, **2:**19
    assessing significance of, **2:**25–26
    judicial citations (general), **2:**16
    judicial citations (U.S. District Court, Court of Federal Claims, Courts of Appeals), **2:**17–18
    judicial citations (U.S. Supreme Court), **2:**18–19
    judicial citations (U.S. Tax Court), **2:**16–17
    trial courts, **2:**12–13, **2:**15
    understanding judicial opinions, **2:**26
  policy considerations, **13:**2–3
  political considerations, **1:**31–33
  primary sources of, **2:**2, **2:**26–27
  revenue needs, **1:**27
  secondary sources of, **2:**26
  social considerations, **1:**28–29
  statutory sources of
    Internal Revenue Code, **2:**3, **2:**4, **2:**6–7
    legislative process, **2:**3–4, **2:**5
    tax treaties, **2:**7
Tax Notes, **2:**10
Tax periodicals, **2:**22–23
Tax planning
  AMT, **14:**9
  regular corporate income tax rate difference and, **13:**27
  built-in gains tax, **12:**31
  business entertainment expenses, **16:**31
  capital gains, **8:**22
  cash receipts method of accounting, **3:**9
  choosing form of business, **14:**22–23
  consolidated groups, **9:**8
  constructive dividends, **10:**17–18
  corporate distributions, **10:**9–10
  deductible tax payments, timing of, **15:**40

depletion methods, **4**:37
depreciation recapture and Section 179, **8**:33
documentation of related-taxpayer loans, casualty losses, and theft losses, **5**:8–9
educational expenses, **16**:29
equilibrium approach, **1**:20–21
  gift planning, **7**:11
  goal of, **1**:20–21
  income and deduction shifting across time, **15**:17
  incorporation, **9**:20–21
  installment method of accounting, **6**:14–15, **6**:20
  inventory, **6**:31
  involuntary conversion gains, **7**:29
  IRA contributions, **16**:45
  itemized deductions, **15**:52
  joint returns, **15**:14
  Keogh plans, **16**:45
  life insurance, **3**:25
  LIFO inventory, **6**:31
  like-kind exchanges, **7**:21–22
  minor children's income, **15**:20
  moving expenses, **16**:27
  multiple support agreements and medical expense deduction, **15**:12
  municipal bonds, **3**:22–23
  organizational expenditures, **9**:27
  overview of, **1**:20
  partnerships
    drafting partnership agreements, **11**:19
    formation and operation of, **11**:31
    transactions between partners and partnerships, **11**:35
  passive loss utilization, **5**:36–37
  preferences and adjustments
    avoiding, **13**:22–23
    controlling timing of, **13**:27
  prepaid income, **3**:14
  property from a decedent, **7**:14
  S corporations, **13**:28
    accumulated adjustments account, **12**:20
    election, **12**:9, **12**:11
    losses, **12**:27
    salary structure, **12**:15–16
  sale of business, **4**:33–34
  Section 351, **9**:12–13, **9**:17–18
  Section 1244 stock, **5**:6–7
  securities, appreciated, gifts of, **8**:17–18
  self-employed persons, **16**:4–5
  stock or asset sales, **14**:21
  suspended losses, **12**:24
tax burden determination, **1**:21–23
tax minimization strategies
  changing character of income and expenses, **1**:23–24
  shifting tax liability across jurisdictions, **1**:26
  shifting tax liability across time, **1**:24–25
  shifting tax liability between entities, **1**:25
tax-exempt securities, **3**:22–23
time value of deductions, **4**:6
transportation and travel expenses, **16**:26

unreasonable compensation, **4**:4
unreimbursed employee business expenses, **16**:38
wash sales, **7**:16
Tax preference items, **13**:20
  depreciation, **13**:21–23
  intangible drilling costs, **13**:17
  interest on private activity bonds, **13**:17
  percentage depletion, **13**:16–17
Tax Rate Schedules, **15**:16–17
Tax rates, **1**:3
  corporate, **9**:27–28
  for heads of household, **15**:25
  for married individuals, **15**:24–25
  for single taxpayers, **15**:24
Tax Reform Act of 1986, S corporations affected by, **12**:2–3
Tax research, **2**:20, **2**:21
  arriving at the solution or at alternative solutions, **2**:27
  assessing tax law sources, **2**:23
    Internal Revenue Code, **2**:23–24
    judicial sources, **2**:26
    other administrative sources, **2**:25
    other sources, **2**:26–27
    Treasury Regulations, **2**:24–25
    understanding judicial opinions, **2**:26
  communicating, **2**:28, **2**:28–29, **2**:29
  computer-assisted, **2**:28
    CD-ROM services, **2**:30
    electronic tax services, **2**:29–30
    Internet access, **2**:31–32
    on-line services, **2**:31
    tax-related Web sites, **2**:32
  follow-up procedures, **2**:28
  identifying the problem, **2**:20
  locating appropriate tax law sources, **2**:21–22
    tax periodicals, **2**:22–23
    tax services, **2**:22
  refining the problem, **2**:20–21
Tax services, **2**:22
Tax shelters, **5**:15–17
Tax tables, **15**:15–16, **15**:17
Tax treaties, **2**:7
Tax-exempt income, expenses and interest related to, **4**:14–15
Tax-exempt securities, **3**:22–23, **4**:14–15, **15**:44
Taxable dividends, **10**:2–3
Taxable income, **9**:34–38
  AMT and, **13**:14–15
  computation of for S corporation, **12**:12–14
  from discharge of indebtedness, **3**:25–26
Taxable year, **3**:7, **6**:3
  short, **6**:7–8
Taxes
  deduction of
    as business expense, **4**:20–21
    for individuals, **15**:38–40
  interest on deferred, **6**:20
  structure of, **1**:2
  types of
    ad valorem taxes, **1**:10–12, **15**:38–39
    death taxes, **1**:8–9
    employment tax, **1**:3, **1**:6–8
    Federal customs duties, **1**:12–13

FICA, **1**:6, **1**:7, **1**:8
franchise taxes, **1**:13
FUTA, **1**:6, **1**:8
gift, **1**:3
implicit tax, **1**:6, **1**:23
Medicare tax, **1**:3, **1**:7
occupational taxes, **1**:13
production and sales of goods, **1**:4–6
progressive, **1**:3
proportional, **1**:3
regressive, **1**:3
sales tax, **1**:3, **1**:5
severance taxes, **1**:13
transaction taxes, **1**:4
use tax, **1**:5–6
value added tax (VAT), **1**:6
Taxpayer Relief Act (TRA) of 1997, **16**:34
Taxpayer use test, **7**:30–31
Technical Advice Memoranda (TAMs), **2**:8, **2**:11
Temporary assignments, **16**:22
Temporary Regulations, **2**:9
Tentative minimum tax, **13**:3, **13**:5
Theft losses, **5**:7
  definition of theft, **5**:8
  of individuals, **5**:11–12
  measuring amount of, **5**:9–11
  when to deduct, **5**:9
  See also Casualty losses
Thefts, **7**:5
Thin capitalization problem, **9**:22–24
Thirty percent ceiling for charitable contributions, **15**:48–49
Thor Power Tool Co. v. Comm., **6**:26
Ticket purchases for entertainment, **16**:32–33
Time test for moving expenses, **16**:26
Total ownership test, **9**:30
Trade names, **4**:33, **8**:12
  See also Franchises
Trademarks, **4**:33, **8**:12
  See also Franchises
Transportation expenses, **16**:19
  commuting expenses, **16**:19–20
  computation of auto expenses, **16**:20–21
Travel expenses, **16**:21
  away-from-home requirement, **16**:21
  combined business and pleasure travel, **16**:23–25
  determining the tax home, **16**:22
  restrictions on, **16**:22–23
  temporary assignments, **16**:22
Treasury Decisions (TDs), **2**:11
Treasury Department Regulations, **2**:7–9
  interpretive, **2**:25
  legislative, **2**:25
  procedural, **2**:25
  proposed, **2**:9
  temporary, **2**:9
Trial courts, **2**:12–13, **2**:14
Trust
  as association, **9**:6
  business, **9**:6
Twenty percent ceiling for charitable contributions, **15**:49
Twenty-eight percent property, **8**:17, **8**:18–22

U

Unemployment compensation, **15**:29
Unemployment tax, **1**:8
Unexpected event, **5**:7
Uniform capitalization rules, **6**:27–28
United States Board of Tax Appeals Reports (B.T.A.), **2**:17
United States Reports, Lawyer's Edition (L.Ed.), **2**:19
United States Supreme Court Reports (U.S.), **2**:18–19
Unlimited liability, **9**:4
Unreasonable compensation, **9**:3, **10**:15, **10**:16
Unrecaptured Section 1250 gain, **8**:18–22
Unusual event, **5**:7

U.S. Court of Federal Claims. *See* Court of Federal Claims.
U.S. District Court. *See* District Court
U.S. government publications, **8**:5–6
U.S. Supreme Court. *See* Supreme Court
U.S. Tax Cases (USTC), **2**:17–18
U.S. Tax Court. *See* Tax Court
Use taxes, **1**:5–6

V

Value added tax (VAT), **1**:6
Value test, **9**:29
Voting power test, **9**:29

W

Wash sales, **7**:15–16
Web sites, tax-related, **2**:32
Welfare-to-work tax credit, **13**:8
Wherewithal to pay concept, **1**:30
Windfall income, **3**:4
Withholding of income taxes, **1**:14
Workers' compensation, **15**:32
Working condition fringes, **16**:15, **16**:17
World Wide Web, **2**:32
Worthless securities, **5**:5–6, **8**:7
  small business (Section 1244) stock, **5**:6–7
Writ of Certiorari, **2**:15, **2**:26

AMT Formula for Individuals

Regular Taxable Income

Plus or minus:	Adjustments
Plus:	Tax preferences
Equals:	Alternative minimum taxable income
Minus:	Exemption
Equals:	Alternative minimum tax base
Times:	26% and 28% graduated rates
Equals:	Tentative minimum tax before foreign tax credit
Minus:	Alternative minimum tax foreign tax credit
Equals:	Tentative minimum tax
Minus:	Regular income tax liability
Equals:	Alternative minimum tax (if amount is positive)

AMT Formula for Corporations

Regular Taxable Income before NOL Deduction

Plus or minus:	Adjustments (except ACE adjustment)
Plus:	Tax preferences
Equals:	AMTI before AMTNOL deduction and ACE adjustment
Plus or minus:	ACE adjustment
Equals:	Alternative minimum taxable income (AMTI) before AMTNOL deduction
Minus:	AMTNOL deduction (limited to 90% of AMTI before AMTNOL deduction)
Equals:	Alternative minimum taxable income (AMTI)
Minus:	Exemption
Equals:	Alternative minimum tax base
Times:	20% rate
Equals:	AMT before AMT foreign tax credit
Minus:	AMT foreign tax credit (possibly limited to 90% of AMT before AMT foreign tax credit)
Equals:	Tentative minimum tax
Minus:	Regular income tax liability before credits minus regular foreign tax credit
Equals:	Alternative minimum tax (AMT) if positive

Tax Formula for Corporate Taxpayers

Income (broadly conceived)	$xxx,xxx
Less: Exclusions (income that is not subject to tax)	(xx,xxx)
Gross Income	$xxx,xxx
Less: Certain business deductions	(xx,xxx)
Taxable Income	$xxx,xxx
Federal income tax (see Tax Rate Schedule inside front cover of text)	$ xx,xxx
Less: Tax credits (including Federal income withheld and other prepayments of Federal income taxes)	(x,xxx)
Tax Owed (or refund)	$ xx,xxx